Steps in Analyzing a Transaction

STEP 1. What accounts are involved?

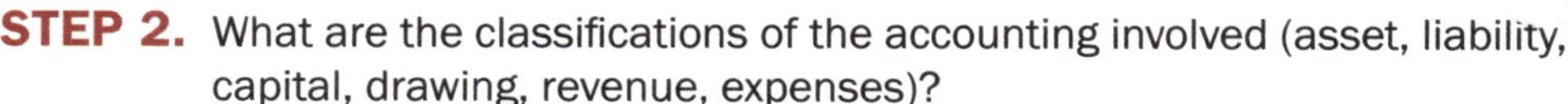

STEP 2. What are the classifications of the accounting involved (asset, liability, capital, drawing, revenue, expenses)?

STEP 3. Are the accounts increased or decreased?

STEP 4. Write the transaction as a debit to one account (or accounts) and a credit to another account (or accounts).

STEP 5. Is the equation in balance after the transaction has been recorded?

Journalizing and Posting

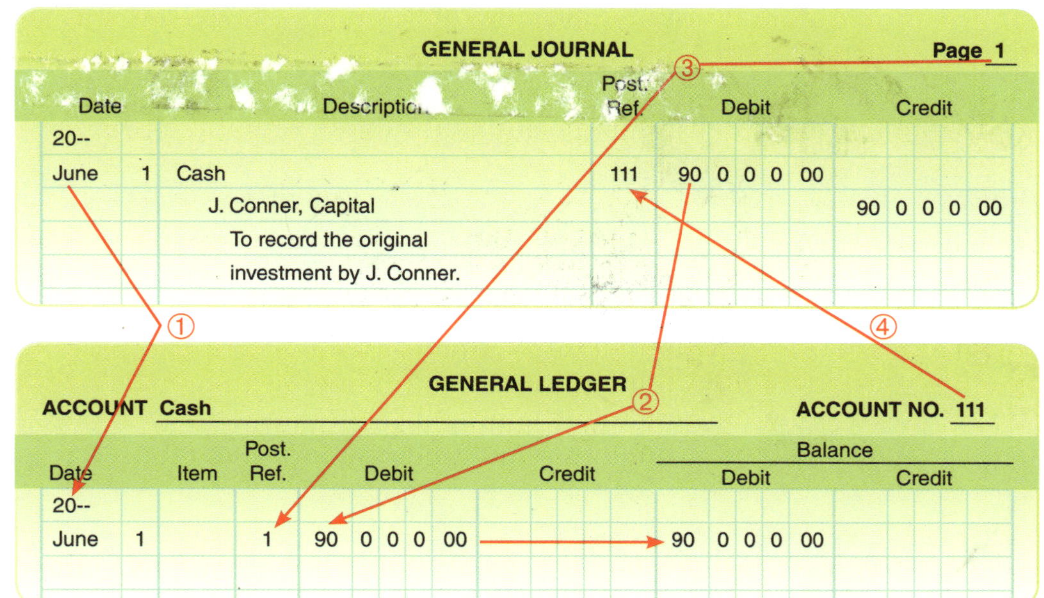

GENERAL JOURNAL — Page 1

Date		Description	Post. Ref.	Debit	Credit
20--					
June	1	Cash	111	90 0 0 0 00	
		J. Conner, Capital			90 0 0 0 00
		To record the original			
		investment by J. Conner.			

GENERAL LEDGER

ACCOUNT Cash — ACCOUNT NO. 111

Date		Item	Post. Ref.	Debit	Credit	Balance Debit	Balance Credit
20--							
June	1		1	90 0 0 0 00		90 0 0 0 00	

① Date of transaction
② Amount of transaction
③ Page number of the journal
④ Ledger account number

The Work Sheet

	A	B	C	D	E	F	G	H	I	J	K
1	Conner's Whitewater Adventures										
2	Work Sheet										
3	For Month Ended June 30, 20--										
4											
5		TRIAL BALANCE		ADJUSTMENTS		ADJUSTED TRIAL BALANCE		INCOME STATEMENT		BALANCE SHEET	
6	ACCOUNT NAME	DEBIT	CREDIT	DEBIT	CREDIT	DEBIT	CREDIT	DEBIT	CREDIT	DEBIT	CREDIT
7		Assets →				Assets →				Assets	
8			Liabilities →				Liabilities →				Liabilities
9			Capital →				Capital →				Capital
10		Drawing →				Drawing →				Drawing	
11			Revenue →				Revenue →		Revenue		
12		Expenses →				Expenses →		Expenses			
13											

College Accounting:

A Career Approach

12e

College Accounting: A Career Approach

12e

Cathy J. Scott
Navarro College

Australia • Brazil • Canada • Mexico • Singapore • Spain • United Kingdom • United States

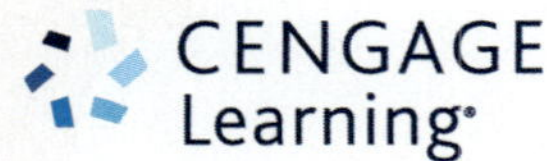

College Accounting: A Career Approach, Twelfth Edition

Cathy J. Scott

Chief Product Officer: Jim Donohue

Vice President, Development and Operations: Kris Tibbetts

Director of Development: Shelley Ryan

Product Development Manager: Laura Ansara

Product Director: Rob Dewey

Senior Product Manager: Sharon Oblinger

Content Developer: Julie Anderson

Product Assistant: A. J. Smiley

Associate Marketing Manager: Courtney Doyle Chambers

Marketing Manager: Heather Mooney

Marketing Coordinator: Eileen Corcoran

Content Project Manager: Darrell Frye

Media Developer: Lysa Kosins

Manufacturing Planner: Doug Wilke

Production Service: Cenveo Publisher Services

Rights Acquisition Specialist: Anne Sheroff

Permissions Research: PreMedia Global

Senior Art Director: Stacy Jenkins Shirley

Cover and Internal Designer: Lou Ann Thesing/ Laura Brown

Cover Image: © iStock Photo

Library of Congress Control Number: 2013954418

Student Edition:
ISBN-13: 978-1-285-73577-1
ISBN-10: 1-285-73577-3

Instructor Edition:
ISBN-13: 978-1-305-08409-4
ISBN-10: 1-305-08409-8

Cengage Learning
200 First Stamford Place, 4th Floor
Stamford, CT 06902
USA

Cengage Learning is a leading provider of customized learning solutions with office locations around the globe, including Singapore, the United Kingdom, Australia, Mexico, Brazil, and Japan. Locate your local office at: **www.cengage.com/global**

Cengage Learning products are represented in Canada by Nelson Education, Ltd.

To learn more about Cengage Learning Solutions, visit **www.cengage.com**

Purchase any of our products at your local college store or at our preferred online store **www.cengagebrain.com**

Printed in Canada
2 3 4 5 6 7 16 15 14

In memory of Douglas J. McQuaig (1923–2012)
We would especially like to dedicate this book in memory of Douglas J. McQuaig
not only for his foresight and years of contribution to this textbook, but also for the impact
he has made on accounting education.

About the Author

Cathy J. Scott

Cathy J. Scott is currently an Associate Professor of Accounting and the Accounting Program Coordinator at Navarro College. She is a proud recipient of the American Accounting Association's Two Year Outstanding Educator of the Year Award and of Navarro College's Teaching of Excellence Award. Professor Scott received her bachelor's degree from Nazareth College, an MBA from Amberton University, and a post-graduate Accounting degree from Keller Graduate School of Management. She is currently ABD in her PhD program at Capella University. Professor Scott made a career shift into academics after a 25-year accounting and consulting career within the automotive industry. She has been a popular seminar speaker in the area of accounting and financial management for automotive and recreational vehicle manufacturers, as well as dealer associations. She has also written numerous accounting-related articles for various automotive publications. Professor Scott is a member of the Institute of Management Accountants, Teachers of Accounting at Two-Year Colleges, The American Accounting Association, and the Texas Community College Association. She is a past co-chair for the American Accounting Association's Conference on Teaching and Learning Accounting and currently serves on the steering committee. Professor Scott is also the 2014 program co-chair for the Teaching, Learning and Curriculum section. In recent years, Professor Scott has become interested in improving online accounting education and student engagement in the classroom. She has spoken on numerous occasions about effective online learning techniques and innovative technology in the area of accounting education. In her free time, Professor Scott enjoys spending time with her family on her farm in North Texas, in addition to raising and showing her Arabian horses.

Preface

College Accounting is a course for the times. The practical concepts and skills students take away from the College Accounting course have the power to launch new careers and bright futures. Students of College Accounting have many different goals: to train for accounting careers; to develop skills that lend themselves to technical, managerial, and executive positions; or to go on and earn accounting or business degrees. *College Accounting: A Career Approach, 12e* maintains its dedicated emphasis on the significance of the fundamentals of accounting from a career development approach.

Accounting concepts and exercises are offered in a real-world context that encourages students to regard their coursework as true groundwork for launching their career. This edition gives students the opportunity to learn the fundamentals of accounting and then apply these concepts in QuickBooks. QuickBooks is the leading computerized accounting software for small to medium-sized companies, and many companies specifically hire college graduates with skills in QuickBooks. The QuickBooks material is introduced in a way that the instructor can use as little or as much of the QuickBooks material as he/she deems necessary.

This edition builds student skills in the areas of accounting knowledge, technology, ethics, communication, and critical thinking—providing students with skills needed to be successful in life and work.

LEARN IT

Proven Pedagogy

College Accounting: A Career Approach, 12e is built on the solid pedagogical foundation created by Douglas McQuaig and appreciated by instructors and students through 11 editions. Author Cathy J. Scott recognized the need for a new type of accounting text. Her understanding about the importance of QuickBooks to employers was the driving force behind this approach. The 12th edition incorporates engaging student-centered skills in the following areas: student success, real-world application, and teaching enhancements.

- **Learning Objectives** appear at the beginning of each chapter to help students focus on key learning outcomes. They are also highlighted in the margin alongside the related text discussion. A learning objective number serves as a reference to the objectives in the chapter review, exercises, and problems.
- **Key Terms** appear in blue and are defined in the text and repeated in the glossary at the end of each chapter. In addition, page numbers are included for each glossary term, making it easy for students to refer to a term in the chapter. This consistent emphasis on accounting terminology as the language of business is found throughout the text.
- **Remember** margin notes provide learning hints or summaries, often alerting students to common procedural pitfalls to help them complete their work successfully.
- **FYI** margin notes provide practical tips or information about accounting and business.
- **NEW! QuickBooks Tip** margin notes provide useful tips related to accounting that can be applied in QuickBooks.

QuickBooks Tip

Purchase orders can be printed or e-mailed immediately upon completion, or they can be marked to print or e-mail later. Figure Q9 shows the **Print Later** option selected.

- **Color-Coding of Documents and Reports** continues in the 12th edition. This tried and true visual system helps students recognize and remember key points. This use of color also helps students understand the flow of accounting data by clearly identifying the different documents and reports used in the accounting cycle. Students begin to visualize how accountants transform data into useful information.

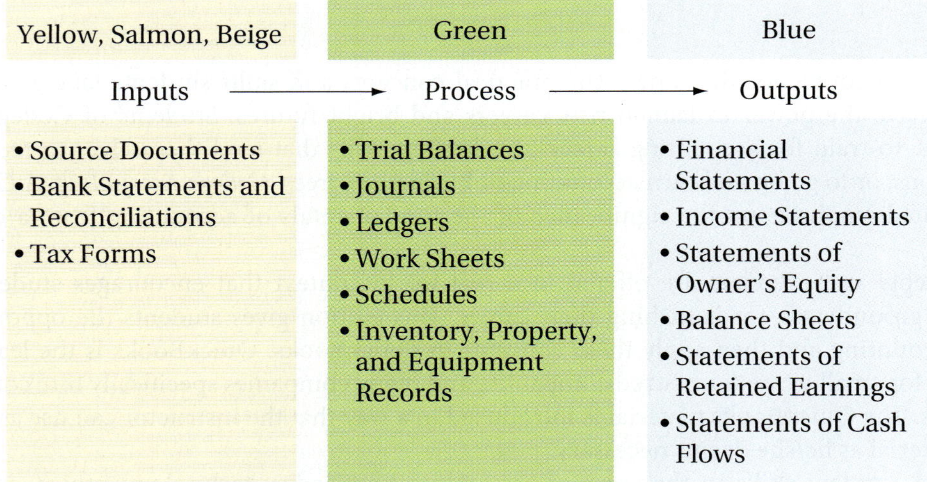

Yellow, Salmon, Beige
Green
Blue
Inputs
Process
Outputs
• Source Documents
• Bank Statements and Reconciliations
• Tax Forms
• Trial Balances
• Journals
• Ledgers
• Work Sheets
• Schedules
• Inventory, Property, and Equipment Records
• Financial Statements
• Income Statements
• Statements of Owner's Equity
• Balance Sheets
• Statements of Retained Earnings
• Statements of Cash Flows

Connecting the Classroom to the Real World

With a focus on small business, *College Accounting: A Career Approach, 12e* provides real-world context that keeps chapter and digital content relevant and vital. Many activities within the text, in QuickBooks, and in CengageNOW are designed to build student skills in areas of accounting knowledge, technology, ethics, communication, and critical thinking.

NEW! Accounting with QuickBooks

This new feature appears at the end of each chapter and explains how to apply the fundamentals of accounting processes directly within QuickBooks accounting software. Complete with clear screen captures, learning objectives, new accounting language, and QuickBooks Tips, this feature is a must for instructors who value the importance of teaching real-world technology skills in the classroom. This new, integrated approach of teaching the fundamentals of accounting with QuickBooks will help students understand how to utilize real-world accounting general ledger software, while developing marketable skills they can apply immediately in the workplace.

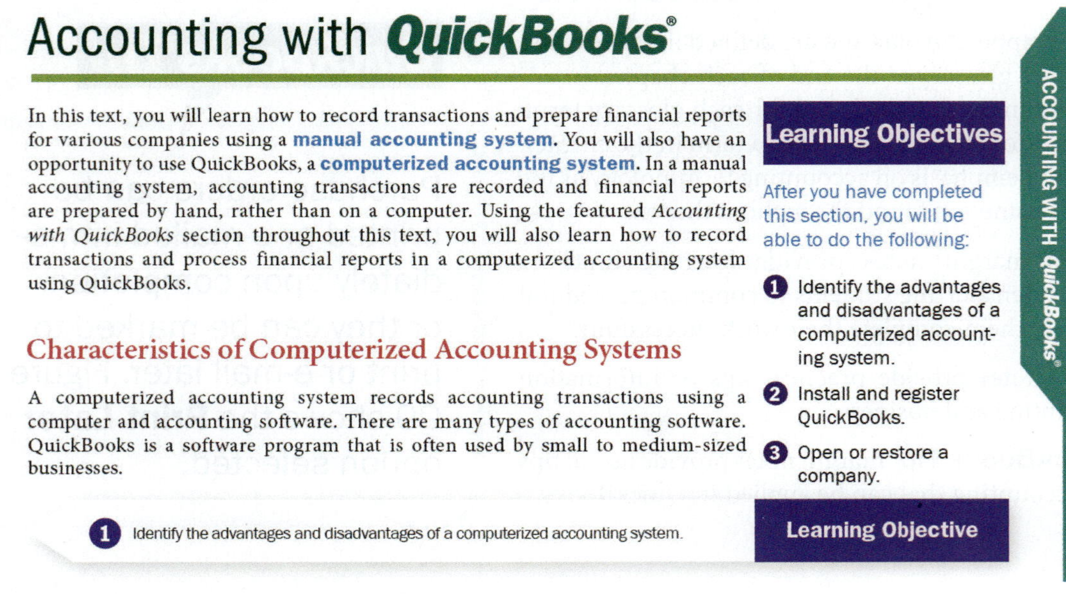

Accounting with QuickBooks®
In this text, you will learn how to record transactions and prepare financial reports for various companies using a manual accounting system. You will also have an opportunity to use QuickBooks, a computerized accounting system. In a manual accounting system, accounting transactions are recorded and financial reports are prepared by hand, rather than on a computer. Using the featured Accounting with QuickBooks section throughout this text, you will also learn how to record transactions and process financial reports in a computerized accounting system using QuickBooks.
Characteristics of Computerized Accounting Systems
A computerized accounting system records accounting transactions using a computer and accounting software. There are many types of accounting software. QuickBooks is a software program that is often used by small to medium-sized businesses.
1 Identify the advantages and disadvantages of a computerized accounting system.
Learning Objective
Learning Objectives
After you have completed this section, you will be able to do the following:
1 Identify the advantages and disadvantages of a computerized accounting system.
2 Install and register QuickBooks.
3 Open or restore a company.
ACCOUNTING WITH QuickBooks®

Chapter Email Openers

Every chapter begins with an email opener that simulates a mentor relationship between a student and her CPA friend. These emails set the stage for why the chapter content is important and provides a checklist of what students need to know to succeed.

Learning Objectives

After you have completed this chapter, you will be able to do the following:

1. Define and identify *asset*, *liability*, and *owner's equity* accounts.
2. Record, in column form, a group of business transactions involving changes in assets, liabilities, and owner's equity.
3. Define and identify *revenue* and *expense* accounts.
4. Record, in column form, a group of business transactions involving all five elements of the fundamental accounting equation.

To: **Amy Roberts, CPA**
Subject: **Starting My New Business**

Hi Amy,
Well, I've given it a lot of thought and have decided to take the "plunge"! I'm going to start my own business. I've been working for many years as a whitewater rafting guide and helping in the business office. I think I'm ready to go out on my own. I know a lot about rafting and operating tours, but I don't know much about accounting. Do you think you could help? Would you recommend I purchase accounting software like QuickBooks®?
Thanks,
Janie

To: **Janie Conner**
Subject: **RE: Starting My New Business**

Hi Janie,
Great! I'm so glad you've finally taken my advice and decided to open your own business. I will definitely help you learn accounting, and I would strongly recommend that you purchase an accounting software package like QuickBooks! There's a lot to learn—so let's take it step by step. I've made a list of some items for you to concentrate on first.

_____ 1. Understand what accounting is—what it does, what its purpose is.
_____ 2. Know the fundamental accounting equation. (This is important!)
_____ 3. Know examples of accounts that are included in each asset, liability, or owner's equity category.

Once you've learned these items, email me, and we'll move on! Good luck.
Amy

Accounting in Your Future

This feature provides insight into possible careers that use accounting knowledge. This feature is designed to encourage students to think about their futures in accounting.

ACCOUNTING IN YOUR FUTURE

PAYROLL DEPARTMENT

The payroll department is an important part of the accounting and finance functions at companies. Payroll personnel are responsible for ensuring that all company employees receive compensation and benefits critical to maintaining a productive and motivated workforce. Some payroll departments work closely with Information Technology, Human Resources, and other departments to ensure that the company's payroll is accurate, is up-to-date, and is serving the company's current business objectives. For these reasons, it is important to understand how payroll is determined, whether you are directly responsible for processing payroll or you are employed in another business department.

© iStockPhoto.com/klikk

You Make the Call

These features sharpen critical-thinking and problem-solving skills by placing the student in a realistic accounting dilemma. These exercises provide students with the opportunity to apply their knowledge of individual topics within the chapter. Each scenario is followed by a detailed, clearly explained solution.

YOU Make the Call

One of your fellow students is having trouble getting his accounting equation to balance after transaction (g). No matter how many times he computes the numbers, he can't get it to balance. When you look at his T accounts, you see that he has been crediting the expenses. He claims that expenses take away from owner's equity, so why should they be under the plus sign? How can you explain that he is partly correct?

SOLUTION

Your fellow student is correct in saying that expenses do take away from owner's equity, but the expense itself is increasing, which requires a debit, or increase, to the expense account. Expenses have the opposite signs of revenues—they are the costs of doing business and act in an opposite way to revenues. So the quick response to your classmate is to make sure the signs on expenses are the opposite of revenues and that expenses are debited when they happen.

Small Business Success

Appearing in select chapters, students will find this a motivating feature that emphasizes how accounting knowledge and best practices are critical to the success of a small business in a competitive environment.

SMALL BUSINESS **SUCCESS**

Do I Need an Accountant?

If you are not taking this class because you want to be an accountant or a bookkeeper, you might be taking the class because you plan on owning and operating a small business. Many new small business owners take on the responsibilities of being the accountant for their business. However, at some point, your business will begin to grow, and you may need to consider hiring someone to manage your accounting books so that your time is free to run the business.

An accountant can help you in many areas of your small business, such as:

- What should my business structure be—sole proprietorship, partnership, S corporation, or corporation?
- What software should I use for my accounting?
- How do I handle the payroll for employees?
- What are my requirements for filing taxes?
- What expenses are deductible for tax purposes?
- How do I prepare financial statements when applying for a loan?

So how do you find an accountant? The best way is by referrals. Ask other businesses in your industry for references or visit your local Certified Public Accounting Society website for more recommendations (www.aicpa.org/yellow/ypascpa.htm).

In the Real World

This feature appears in every chapter and provides real-world facts about companies with which students are familiar. These features are related to the chapter material and bring the real world into the classroom.

© iStockPhoto.com/ranplett

In the Real World

Publicly traded corporations such as Electronic Arts, Inc., a leading video game publisher, are required to file interim financial statements. These interim financial statements are filed using Form 10-Q and present the quarterly (every three months) financial position of the corporation. The interim financial statements are similar to the annual financial statements but are not as detailed and are typically not verified by an auditor.

NEW! Blueprint Problems

These new problems, available in CengageNOW, relate to the accounting cycle Practice Exercises for a Service and Merchandising Business. The Blueprint Problems are designed to help students see the big picture regarding fundamental accounting concepts by breaking concepts into smaller parts that build on each other through a systematic problem-solving process.

CENGAGENOW

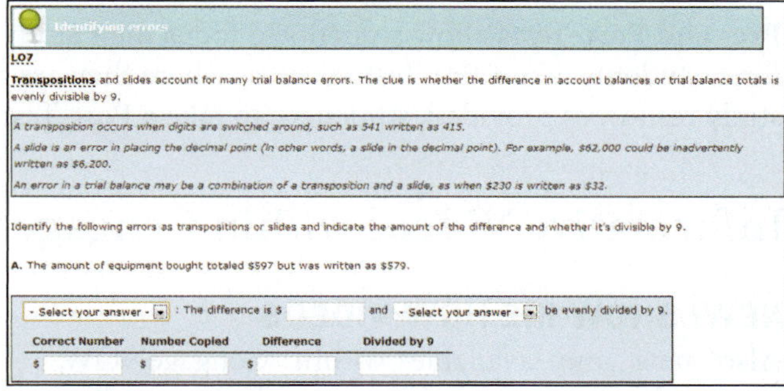

REVIEW IT

Chapter Review and Self Study

- **Practice Exercises** tied to learning objectives, with solutions provided, aid in student comprehension and study.
- **Glossary** terms are listed in alphabetical order in the chapter review section with page numbers for easy reference.
- **Quiz Yourself** provides a set of multiple-choice questions to be used as a self-quiz for students before they begin the chapter assignments. This is a great way for students to determine quickly if they "get it".

- **Before a Test Check** is a comprehensive chapter review feature that provides questions and brief application problems after every two to four chapters. The pre-test activities allow students to check their understanding of what they have read and practiced in the preceding chapters prior to taking a test.
- **NEW! Review It with QuickBooks** tests student knowledge about QuickBooks concepts introduced within each chapter.

Review It with *QuickBooks®*

_____ 1. The general journal report is located under ____________ in QuickBooks.
   a. Company & Financial
   b. Accountant & Taxes
   c. Custom Reports
   d. All of the above

_____ 2. Transactions can be recorded in QuickBooks by __________ or __________.
   a. journal entry method; general ledger method
   b. *Getting Around* screen; general ledger method
   c. journal entry method; *Getting Around* screen
   d. scanning method, journal entry method

_____ 3. The general ledger report is located under ____________ in QuickBooks.
   a. Company & Financial
   b. Accountant & Taxes
   c. Custom Reports
   d. All of the above

_____ 4. Which of the following transactions requires using a name when recording them in QuickBooks?
   a. Providing services for cash
   b. Purchasing equipment for cash
   c. Receiving and paying the utility bill
   d. Purchasing supplies on account

Answers:
1. b 2. c 3. b 4. d

CengageNOW Personalized Study Plan

Pre- and Post-Tests allow students to focus their study on the areas in which they are the weakest. First, students take a Pre-Test to assess where they are now. After students work through the study plan study resources provided, students can take a Post-Test to see how they have improved.

Informative Videos within CengageNOW

NEW! SHOW ME HOW VIDEOS

Also new and available within CengageNOW, these videos are narrated by the author, providing students with an illustrated example of how to work each practice exercise for every learning objective.

Larson Floral
Adjusted Trial Balance
June 30, 20—

Account Name	Debit	Credit
Cash	14,600	
Accounts Receivable	500	
Supplies	335	
Prepaid Insurance	320	
Delivery Van	28,275	
Accumulated Depreciation, Delivery Van		810
Accounts Payable		750
Wages Payable		300
E. Larson, Capital		37,435
E. Larson, Drawing	1,500	
Income from Services		12,170
Wages Expense	3,600	
Rent Expense	775	
Supplies Expense	710	
Advertising Expense	270	
Utilities Expense	250	
Insurance Expense	30	
Depreciation Expense, Delivery Van	300	
	51,465	51,465

Step 2

Wages Expense

3,600	3,600
0	

Income Summary

3,600	12,170

NEW! QuickBooks Demonstration Videos

QuickBooks Demonstration Videos, available in CengageNOW, provide students with step-by-step examples of how to use QuickBooks features covered in the new Accounting with QuickBooks section. Videos are available in various locations for easy access including the student companion site, within the Study Tools section in CengageNOW, as well as reminders within the QuickBooks data sets.

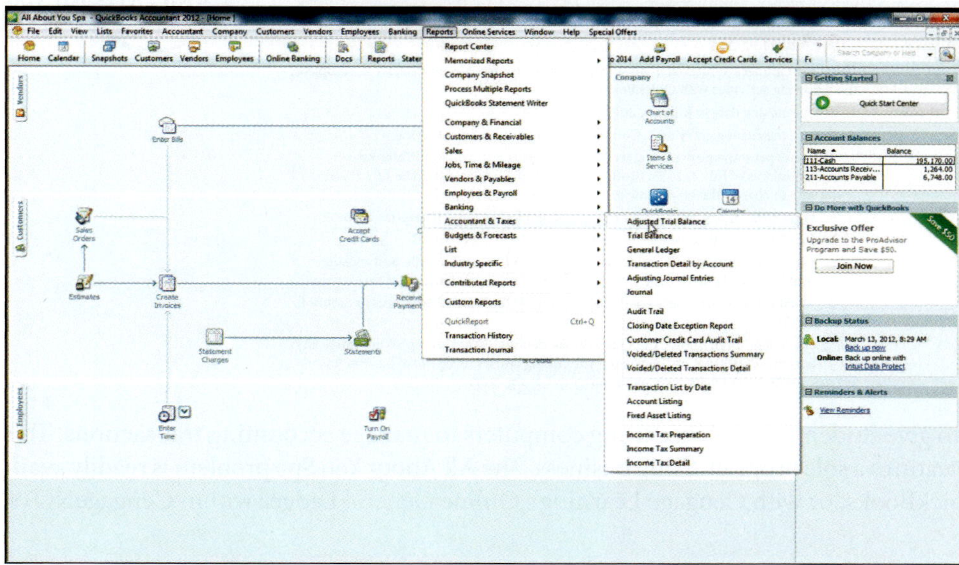

APPLY IT

Chapter Assignments

A variety of homework assignments are provided at the end of each chapter and in CengageNOW. Unique assignable content is also available within CengageNOW.

- **Discussion Questions** can be used for in-class discussion or for individual practice.
- **Exercises** are provided to help students learn and apply new concepts. Each exercise includes margin references to the appropriate learning objective and Chapter Review practice exercises.
- **Problems (A and B set)** are found in every chapter. For those problems that have an Excel icon in the margin, students have access to Excel templates found on the student website at CengageBrain.com. Some problems can be completed using Cengage Learning's Online General Ledger or QuickBooks. Each problem is designated with an icon to direct students to the correct application. Check figures appear alongside every A and B problem.
- **Accounting Cycle Review Problems A and B** (Chapters 1–5) and the **Comprehensive Review Problem** (Chapters 6–12) apply accounting procedures to help students understand the process they have just studied in a series of chapters. Accounting Cycle Review Problem A, "Blast Off" and B, "Wind in Your Sails" are both sole proprietorship service businesses that cover the full accounting cycle. The Comprehensive Review Problem covers the full accounting cycle for "Fabulous Furnishings," a sole proprietorship merchandising business. These problems can be completed manually, with QuickBooks or Cengage Learning's Online General Ledger within CengageNOW.
- **Activities** at the end of each chapter hone students' problem-solving and communication skills. Why Does It Matter?, What Would You Say?, What Do You Think?, What Would You Do?, What's on the Internet?, and What's Wrong With This Picture? are a series of brief exercises at the end of each chapter that help students keep the business perspective in mind.

- **NEW! Try It with QuickBooks** provides various accounting activities that can be completed using QuickBooks as well as suggested end-of-chapter problems that will enhance students' QuickBooks and critical-thinking skills. Some questions in this section can also be completed within CengageNOW.

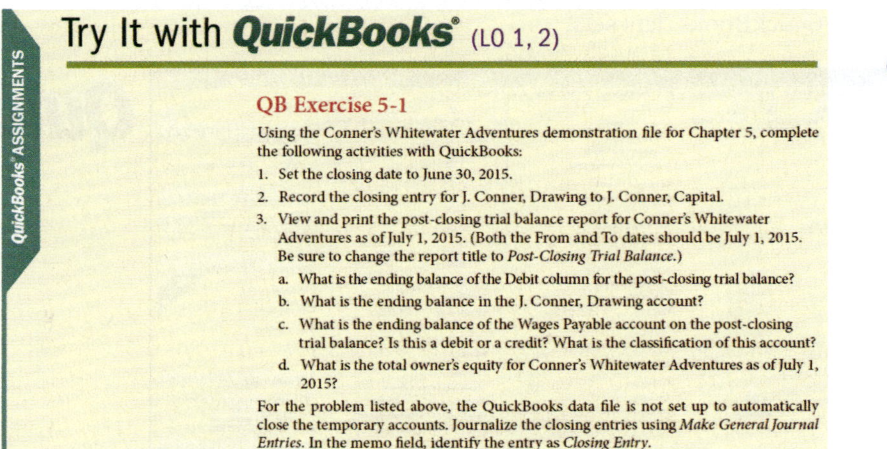

QuickBooks® ASSIGNMENTS

Try It with *QuickBooks*® (LO 1, 2)

QB Exercise 5-1

Using the Conner's Whitewater Adventures demonstration file for Chapter 5, complete the following activities with QuickBooks:

1. Set the closing date to June 30, 2015.
2. Record the closing entry for J. Conner, Drawing to J. Conner, Capital.
3. View and print the post-closing trial balance report for Conner's Whitewater Adventures as of July 1, 2015. (Both the From and To dates should be July 1, 2015. Be sure to change the report title to *Post-Closing Trial Balance*.)
   a. What is the ending balance of the Debit column for the post-closing trial balance?
   b. What is the ending balance in the J. Conner, Drawing account?
   c. What is the ending balance of the Wages Payable account on the post-closing trial balance? Is this a debit or a credit? What is the classification of this account?
   d. What is the total owner's equity for Conner's Whitewater Adventures as of July 1, 2015?

For the problem listed above, the QuickBooks data file is not set up to automatically close the temporary accounts. Journalize the closing entries using *Make General Journal Entries*. In the memo field, identify the entry as *Closing Entry*.

CENGAGENOW

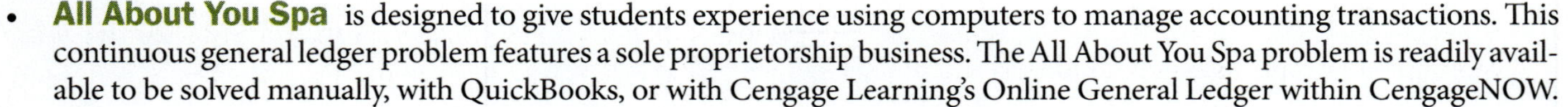

- **All About You Spa** is designed to give students experience using computers to manage accounting transactions. This continuous general ledger problem features a sole proprietorship business. The All About You Spa problem is readily available to be solved manually, with QuickBooks, or with Cengage Learning's Online General Ledger within CengageNOW.

DEMONSTRATE IT

Learning Outcomes

Learning Outcomes Reporting functionality within CengageNOW gives instructors the ability to analyze student end-of-chapter work from the gradebook. Each problem is tagged by topic, learning objective, level of difficulty, Bloom's Taxonomy, AICPA, ACBSP, and other business program standards to allow greater guidance in developing assessments and evaluating student progress.

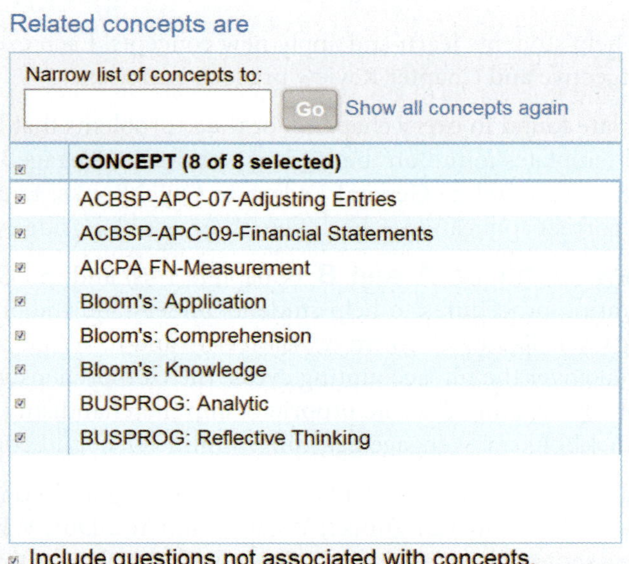

Test Bank provides questions clearly identified by all outcomes to allow greater guidance in developing assessments. The Test Bank also contains QuickBooks questions to analyze student understanding of the new QuickBooks content within the 12th edition.

INSTRUCTOR SUPPLEMENTS

CengageNOW for *College Accounting: A Career Approach, 12e* contains the following:

- **Auto-graded Homework** (static and algorithmic varieties), test bank, Personalized Study Plan, and eBook are all in one resource.
- **Enhanced Feedback** for additional guidance to help students complete an exercise or problem.
- **Assignment Options** are the most robust and flexible in the industry.
- **Smart Entry** helps eliminate common data entry errors and prevents students from guessing their way through homework.
- **Learning Outcomes Reporting** and the ability to analyze student work from the gradebook. Each problem is tagged by topic, learning objective, level of difficulty, Bloom's Taxonomy, AICPA, ACBSP, and other business programs standards to allow greater guidance in developing assessments and evaluating student progress.
- **NEW! SHOW ME HOW VIDEOS** narrated by the author, provide students with an illustrated example of how to work basic exercises for each learning objective.
- **NEW! QuickBooks Demonstration Videos** provide students with step-by-step instructions for applying accounting concepts using QuickBooks.
- **NEW! Blueprint Problems** present the fundamental accounting concepts and objectives for each chapter through a series of learning activities which reinforce concepts and enhance critical thinking.
- **Robust Study Tools** include a vast array of quizzing, puzzles, tutorials, and chapter videos.
- **IMPROVED! Cengage Learning Online General Ledger** is available within CengageNOW. Your students can solve selected end-of-chapter assignments in a format that emulates commercial general ledger software.

Instructor's Resource and Solutions Manual

This helpful guide provides suggested homework check questions, teaching and learning objectives, key points, lecture outlines, demonstration problem solutions, responses to discussion questions, and solutions to all text exercises, problems, and activities. Also included are transition guides from the 11th to 12th edition, reviews of T Account Placement and Representative Transactions, chart to gauge the difficulty levels of assignments, and estimate student completion time, and suggested abbreviations for account titles. Available in print and electronically on the password-protected section of the text's companion website at **http://login.cengage.com**.

Test Bank

Verified fully to ensure accuracy, the Test Bank includes questions clearly identified by topic, learning objectives, level of difficulty, Bloom's Taxonomy, AICPA, ACBSP, and other business program standards to allow greater guidance in developing assessments and evaluating student progress. The Test Bank also contains QuickBooks questions to analyze student understanding of the new QuickBooks content within the 12th edition. Available in print and electronically on the password-protected section of the text's companion website at **http://login.cengage.com**.

Instructor Companion Website

http://login.cengage.com

- Instructor's Resource and Solutions Manual in Microsoft Excel and PDF file format.
- Test Bank in Microsoft Word and PDF file format.

- PowerPoint® lecture slides—these slides enhance lectures and simplify class preparation. Each chapter contains the learning objectives along with figures directly from the text and practice exercises to help you create a powerful, customizable tool. The slides have an updated design, based on the interior of the textbook.
- Solutions to Excel template problems.
- NEW! Online testing system, **Cognero** is a full-featured online-assessment system that lets instructors manage content, create tests and have complete reporting functionality at the click of a button. Edit and manage test bank content from anywhere with Internet access. No special installs or downloads needed and compatible with any operating system or browser. Cognero is located within the Instructor Resource center at **http://login.cengage.com**.
- QuickBooks data file solutions are provided for completion of select end-of-chapter problems and all of the All About You Spa Problems as well as both Accounting Cycle Review Problems A and B, and the Comprehensive Review Problem.

STUDENT SUPPLEMENTS

Study Guide and Working Papers

The Study Guide and Working Papers are provided together in one convenient resource. The Study Guide portion reinforces learning with chapter outlines that are linked to chapter learning objectives. The Working Papers are tailored to the text's end-of-chapter assignments.

CengageNOW for *College Accounting: A Career Approach, 12e*

CENGAGENOW

CengageNOW is an online homework tool that not only provides students with the opportunity to complete homework assignments electronically, but also provides a vast array of study tools. CengageNOW allows students to test their mastery of new concepts through pre- and post-tests. Students engage with multimedia study tools via personalized study plans that target the areas on which they need to focus. Additional quizzes, tutorials, and videos are available as study tools.

Student Companion Website at CengageBrain.com

- Student PowerPoint slides—Modeled after the instructor slides and created in a way that allows students to print the slides and write notes as the instructor is lecturing.
- Flashcards
- Online quizzes
- Crossword puzzles
- Excel templates
- Glossary
- QuickBooks student files
- QuickBooks demonstration videos

Acknowledgments

During the revision of the twelfth edition, many instructors were consulted to review the text for thoughtful suggestions that helped guide the revision of *College Accounting: A Career Approach, 12e*. Those reviewers are as follows:

Kim Anderson
Elgin Community College

Johnnie Atkins
Rio Hondo College

Sara Barritt
Northeast Community College

Kathyrn Boeger
Barton Community College

Judy A. Boozer
Lane Community College

Anna M. Boulware
St. Charles Community College

Deanna R. Burnett
Howard College

Leonor M. Cabrera
Cañada College

Pat Celaya, CPA
The University of Texas at Brownsville

Edward F. Crosby
Lone Star College—Montgomery

Kerry Dolan
Great Falls College Montana State University

Theresa Gann
San Jacinto College

Michele Hill
Schoolcraft College

Carla Hogan
Shoreline Community College

Daniel J. Kerch
Pennsylvania Highlands Community College

Suzanne Laudadio
Durham Technical Community College

Jeannie Liu
Rio Hondo College

Mabel Machin
Valencia College

Michelle L. Masingill
North Idaho College

John J. Masserwick CPA,
Five Towns College

Karen S. Mozingo
Pitt Community College

Christopher O'Byrne
Cuyamaca College

Janet Pasterkamp
Arapahoe Community College

Barbara Rice
Gateway Community and Technical College

Morgan Rockett CPA,
Moberly Area Community College

Katrina Schultz
Valencia College

Stella Sorovigas Esq.,
Lansing Community College

Barbara Squires
Corning Community College

Ian R. Stapleton
Merced College

Timothy Szmanda
Mid-Plains Community College

Braj Tiwari
Los Angeles City College

Erol C. Tucker, Jr., CPA/CGMA
Victoria College

Mellissa Youngman
National Technical Institute for the Deaf/Rochester Institute of Technology

Sue Zimmerman
Lewis-Clark State College

We are happy to acknowledge **Erin Dischler** at *Milwaukee Area Technical College* for her hard work and creative ideas particularly for the new QuickBooks sections of the text as well as for her role in writing the Blueprint Problems. She also created the QuickBooks demonstration videos and has been a tremendous help with this revision.

We are especially thankful for the following instructors who truly recognize the importance of giving students the opportunity to understand the fundamentals of accounting and apply those concepts using QuickBooks. Those instructors who offered suggestions to the QuickBooks sections of this book are as follows:

Cindy L. Hinz
Jamestown Community College

Otto F. Rabe IV
Centralia College

A special thanks to the following verifiers for their detailed review of end-of-chapter materials, supplemental materials, as well as the test bank.

Jennifer Schneider, CPA
University of North Georgia

Tracey M. Lauterborn
Western International University

Cathy Scott would like to thank her family, Gale, Ryan, Tisha, Erica, Danny, Dasariea, Dustin, Adam, Amanda, Marie, Michael, Barry, and Ruth for their never-ending patience, love and support. She would also like to thank her friends and colleagues for their continuous encouragement and professional collaboration as well as the many students who have inspired her as an educator over the years. Cathy would like to thank *"Team College Accounting"* at Cengage Learning for their enthusiastic support of this edition's concept. It has been a pleasure working with each of you. She would also like to remember her late husband, Forrest, who saw her passion as an educator and encouraged her to follow her dreams.

Brief Contents

*This Appendix is available for download on the text website at CengageBrain.com

Contents

PART THREE THE ACCOUNTING CYCLE FOR A MERCHANDISING BUSINESS

*This Appendix is available for download on the text website at CengageBrain.com

College Accounting:

A Career Approach

12e

Introduction to Accounting

Learning Objectives

After you have completed this introduction to accounting, you will be able to do the following:

1. Define accounting.
2. Explain the importance of accounting information.
3. Describe the various career opportunities in accounting.
4. Define ethics.

To: **College Accounting Students**
Subject: **Welcome to the World of Accounting**

College Accounting Students,

Welcome to the *World of Accounting*. This book holds one of the keys to your future—knowledge of accounting and business! Throughout the pages of this text, you'll be introduced to individuals, just like yourself, who dreamed about working in, operating, or even owning a business. You will read about many real world companies and learn about the important role accounting plays in each.

I understand this may be a new experience for many of you, and thus, this book is designed to help you navigate the material and ultimately succeed. As you go through this book, you will find numerous tools and activities to help you understand accounting and how accounting impacts business success. I look forward to being your guide into the world of accounting. So let's get started on this great adventure!

Cathy Scott

© iStockPhoto.com/AVAVA

Accounting Language

Accountant (p. 4)
Accounting (p. 3)
Economic unit (p. 3)
Ethics (p. 8)
Financial Accounting Standards Board) (FASB) (p. 4)
Generally accepted accounting principles (GAAP) (p. 4)
International Accounting Standards Board (IASB) (p. 4)
International Financial Reporting Standards (IFRS) (p. 4)
Paraprofessional accountants (p. 7)
Sarbanes-Oxley Act (p. 9)
Securities and Exchange Commission (SEC) (p. 4)
Transaction (p. 3)

Accounting is often called the *language of business* because when confronted with events of a business nature, all people in society—owners, managers, creditors, employees, attorneys, engineers, and so on—must use accounting terms and concepts to describe these events. Examples of accounting terms are *net, gross, yield, valuation, accrued, deferred*—the list goes on and on. So it is logical that anyone entering the business world should know enough of its *language* to communicate with others and to understand their communications.

As you acquire knowledge of accounting, you will gain an understanding of the way businesses operate and the reasoning involved in making business decisions. Even if you are not involved directly in accounting activities, you will certainly need to be sufficiently acquainted with the *language* in order to understand the meaning of accounting information and how it is compiled, how it can be used, and what its limitations are.

You may be surprised to find that you are already familiar with many accounting terms. Recalling your personal business activities and relating them to your study of accounting will be very helpful to you. For example, when you purchased this textbook, you exchanged cash or a promise to pay cash for the book. As you will see, this exchange is an accounting event. You are going to recognize many activities and terms as you begin your study of accounting.

DEFINITION OF ACCOUNTING

Learning Objective

 1 Define accounting.

Accounting is the process of analyzing, classifying, recording, summarizing, and interpreting business transactions in financial or monetary terms. A business **transaction** is an event that has a direct effect on the operation of an economic unit, is expressed in terms of money, and is recorded. Examples of business transactions are buying or selling goods, renting a building, paying employees, and buying insurance.

The primary purpose of accounting is to provide the financial information needed for the efficient operation of an economic unit. The term **economic unit** includes not only business enterprises but also not-for-profit entities such as government bodies, churches and synagogues, clubs, and public charities. Business enterprises or organizations may be called firms or companies.

Another important purpose of accounting is to provide useful information for decision making in the business enterprise. Similar to decisions you must make in your daily life, accounting helps businesses make decisions. For example, knowing whether there is enough cash to purchase new equipment or whether the business is making a profit requires knowledge of accounting.

All business entities require some type of accounting records. Basically, an **accountant** is a person who keeps the financial history of the transactions of an economic unit in written or computerized form.

Accounting Standards

Because it is important that everyone who receives accounting reports be able to interpret them, a set of rules or guidelines for the accounting process has been developed. These guidelines or rules are known as **generally accepted accounting principles (GAAP)** and are developed by the **Financial Accounting Standards Board (FASB)**.

The FASB was created by the **Securities and Exchange Commission (SEC)** in 1973. The SEC is the agency responsible for regulating public companies that are traded on a U.S. stock exchange. The SEC relies on the FASB to create accounting standards. However, the ultimate responsibility for setting and enforcing accounting standards for public companies lies with the SEC.

With the globalization of the world economy, an international standard-setting board, the **International Accounting Standards Board (IASB)**, has been created to provide guidelines or rules on international accounting standards known as **International Financial Reporting Standards (IFRS)**. The IASB and FASB are currently working to combine GAAP and IFRS into one set of standards.

Bookkeeping and Accounting

While bookkeeping and accounting are closely related, there are differences between the two processes. Generally, bookkeeping involves the systematic recording of business transactions in financial terms. Accounting functions at a higher level. An accountant sets up the system that a bookkeeper uses to record business transactions. An accountant may supervise the work of the bookkeeper and prepare financial statements and tax reports. Although the bookkeeper's work is more routine, it is hard to draw a line where the bookkeeper's work ends and the accountant's begins.

IMPORTANCE OF ACCOUNTING INFORMATION

Learning Objective

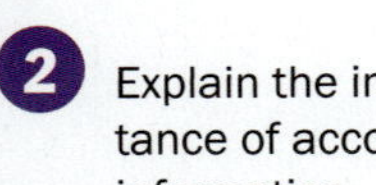

2 Explain the importance of accounting information.

Anyone who aspires to a position of leadership in business or government needs knowledge of accounting. A study of accounting gives a person the necessary background and gives him or her an understanding of the scope, functions, and policies of an organization. A person may not be doing the accounting work, but he or she will be dealing with accounting forms, language, and reports.

Users of Accounting Information

There are many users of accounting information, as outlined below.

OWNERS

Owners have invested their money or goods in a business organization. They want information regarding the company's earnings, its prospects for future earnings, and its ability to pay its debts.

MANAGERS

Managers and supervisors have to prepare financial reports, understand accounting data contained in reports and budgets, and express future plans in financial terms. People who have management jobs must know how accounting information is developed in order to evaluate performance in meeting goals.

CREDITORS

Creditors lend money or extend credit to the company for the purchase of goods and services. The company's creditors include suppliers, banks, and other lending institutions, such as loan companies. Creditors are interested in the firm's ability to pay its debts.

GOVERNMENT AGENCIES

Taxing authorities verify information submitted by companies concerning a variety of taxes, such as income taxes, sales taxes, and employment taxes. Public utilities, such as electric and gas companies, must provide financial information to regulatory agencies.

Accounting and Technology

Before the invention of computers, all business transactions were recorded by hand. Now computers perform routine recordkeeping operations and prepare financial reports. Computers are used today in all types of businesses, both large and small. All accounting positions now require workers to use computers, have knowledge of word processing and spreadsheet software, and possess an understanding of accounting software, such as QuickBooks and Peachtree®.

Even though virtually all businesses now use computers to do their accounting, the nature of accounting is the same. The computer is a powerful tool of the accountant. However, as a tool, the computer is only as useful as the operator's ability and understanding of accounting. The operator must be skilled to key the correct information into the computer program; otherwise, as the saying goes, "garbage in, garbage out."

CAREER OPPORTUNITIES IN ACCOUNTING

Learning Objective 3 Describe the various career opportunities in accounting.

There are a number of career opportunities in accounting in every industry. To find job opportunities in accounting, browse Internet job sites or read the newspapers' classified advertisements. Although the jobs listed in these ads require varying amounts of education and experience, many of them are for positions as accounting and auditing clerks, general bookkeepers, and accountants. The Bureau of Labor Statistics *Occupational Outlook Handbook* estimates that employment is expected to grow as fast as average for accountants, bookkeepers, clerks, and auditors. The number of accounting-related jobs is expected to grow by 14 percent between 2010 and 2020. The requirements and duties of these positions are discussed next. Figure 1, on page 6, provides a listing of the average salaries for some of these positions.

Accounting Clerk/Technician

An accounting clerk/technician performs routine recording of financial information. The duties of accounting clerks vary with the size of the company. In small businesses, accounting clerks handle most of the recordkeeping functions. In large companies, clerks specialize in one part of the accounting system, such as payroll, accounts receivable, accounts payable, cash, inventory, or purchases. The minimum requirement for most accounting clerk positions is usually one term or semester of accounting courses. Having experience in a related job and working in an office environment is also recommended. In addition, knowledge of word processing and

Figure 1
Salary ranges for various accounting positions

TITLE	SALARY RANGE
ACCOUNTING CLERK	$29,250–$39,500
– Accounts receivable/Accounts payable clerk	$32,000–$44,250[a]
	$31,250–$42,500[b]
	$29,000–$39,250[c]
– Inventory clerk	$31,000–$40,750[a]
	$29,000–$39,750[b]
– Payroll clerk	$32,750–$43,750[a]
	$31,750–$42,750[b]
	$29,250–$38,750[c]
BOOKKEEPER	$34,000–$45,500
PARAPROFESSIONAL ACCOUNTANT	$34,000–$45,500
ACCOUNTANT	
– Chief financial officer	$99,000–$430,250
– Controller	$71,500–$192,500
– Financial analyst (entry level)	$43,750–$119,750[a]
	$42,000–$103,500[b]
	$39,250–$87,250[c]
– Forensic accountant	$64,500–$106,000
– General accountant (entry level)	$41,000–$109,250[a]
	$38,500–$90,750[b]
	$36,250–$82,500[c]
– Internal auditor (entry level)	$47,500–$132,250[a]
	$45,500–$111,000[b]

[a]Large companies
[b]Midsize companies
[c]Small companies

Source: Robert Half International, 2013 *Salary Guide—Accounting & Finance*, © 2013 Robert Half International.

spreadsheet software is helpful. Accounting clerks/technicians should be detail-oriented and have good communication skills.

Auditing Clerk

Auditing clerks are an organization's financial recordkeepers. An auditing clerk's primary responsibility involves verifying transactions and records posted by other employees. Additional responsibilities include maintaining and updating individual or groups of accounting records, checking documents to ensure that they are mathematically correct,

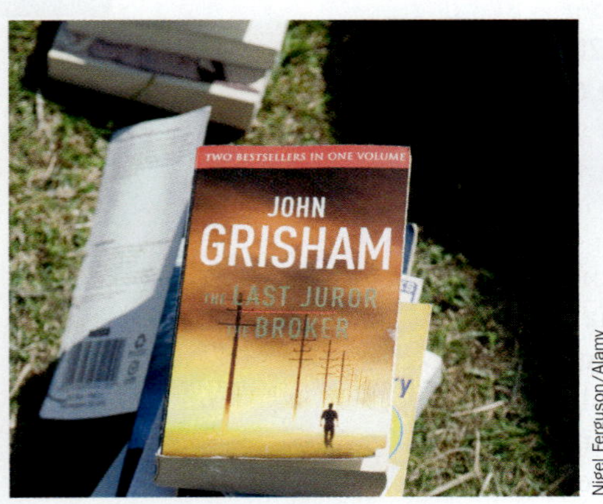

Nigel Ferguson/Alamy

In the Real World

Many famous people began their careers in accounting. For instance, author John Grisham received his undergraduate degree in accounting from Mississippi State University.

and correcting or noting errors for accountants or other workers to adjust. Most auditing clerks are required to have a high school degree at a minimum, while an associate degree in business or accounting is often preferred for some positions. Knowledge of word processing and spreadsheet software in addition to experience in a related job are also recommended.

General Bookkeeper

Many small- and medium-sized companies employ one person to oversee their bookkeeping operations. This person is called a general or full-charge bookkeeper. The general bookkeeper supervises the work of accounting clerks. Requirements for this job vary with the size of the company and the complexity of the accounting system. The minimum requirement for most general bookkeeper jobs is one or two years of accounting education as well as experience as an accounting clerk. Many companies require a certificate in business or accounting and experience working with computers and accounting software.

Paraprofessional Accountant

To bridge a gap between the general bookkeeper and the professional accountant, many firms are hiring **paraprofessional accountants**. They manage the duties of the general bookkeeper as well as many of the duties of a professional accountant. Paraprofessional accountants work under the direct supervision of a professional accountant. Qualifications generally include a two-year degree in accounting, knowledge of accounting software, and prior experience.

Certifications Available

Several organizations offer certification for accounting and auditing clerks, bookkeepers, and paraprofessional accountants. The Certified Bookkeeper (CB) designation is awarded by the American Institute of Professional Bookkeepers (www.aipb.org) and certifies that an individual has the knowledge needed to carry out bookkeeping functions. For certification, candidates must have at least two years of bookkeeping experience, pass an examination, and adhere to a code of ethics. The Accreditation Council for Accountancy and Taxation (www.acatcredentials.org) offers an Accredited Business Accountant® (ABA) certification designed for individuals who work with small- to medium-sized businesses in the areas of financial accounting, tax, and ethics. For accreditation, candidates must pass a one-day, seven-hour exam.

Accountant

The term *accountant* describes a fairly broad range of jobs. The accountant may design and manage the entire accounting system for a business. The accountant may also prepare financial statements and tax returns and perform audits. Many accountants enter the field with a four-year college degree in accounting; however, it is not unusual for accountants to start at entry-level positions and work their way up to management positions. Although accountants are employed in every kind of economic unit, they are classified into one of four categories: public accounting, managerial or private accounting, government and not-for-profit accounting, and internal auditing. We'll briefly look at these categories.

PUBLIC ACCOUNTING

Most public accountants are certified public accountants (CPAs). To become a CPA, a person must have a bachelor's degree, complete 150 hours of college course work (in most states), pass a rigorous examination, and complete a work experience requirement. CPAs design accounting systems, prepare tax returns, provide financial advice about business operations, and audit financial statements. Many CPAs work for a public accounting firm such as Deloitte LLP or own their own small business. CPAs can also be employed by corporations in the private sector in finance positions such as chief financial officers (CFOs), controllers, and financial analysts.

A relatively new and upcoming career opportunity in public accounting is forensic accounting. Forensic accountants specialize in investigating business crimes such as fraud, embezzlement, and money laundering. Accountants in this area of specialty require knowledge of accounting, law, and finance and work closely with law enforcement personnel. Individuals wanting to specialize in forensic accounting can apply for a Certified Fraud Examiner (CFE) certificate (www.acfe.com). Requirements for CFE certification include a minimum of a bachelor's degree and two years of professional experience in a field directly or indirectly related to the detection or deterrence of fraud.

If you are interested in learning more about becoming a CPA or other public accounting jobs, the American Institute of Certified Public Accountants (www.aicpa .org) has an excellent website called This Way to CPA (www.thiswaytocpa.com), that describes accounting degrees and job opportunities. This site includes study information, simulation games, scholarship and internship listings, profiles of successful CPAs, and career opportunities.

MANAGERIAL OR PRIVATE ACCOUNTING

Most people who are accountants are employed by private business organizations. These accountants (not necessarily CPAs) manage the accounting system, prepare budgets, determine costs of products, and provide financial information for managers and owners. Accountants have many opportunities to advance into top management positions. The Certified Management Accountant (CMA) has a solid understanding of financial planning and analysis, internal controls, decision making, and professional ethics. Requirements for CMA certification include having a bachelor's degree (in any area), passing the CMA exam, and having two years' experience in management accounting and/or financial management. You can find more information about the CMA exam at http://imanet.org.

GOVERNMENT AND NOT-FOR-PROFIT ACCOUNTING

Not-for-profit accounting is used for government agencies, hospitals, churches and synagogues, and schools. Accountants for these organizations prepare budgets and maintain records of revenues and expenses. Local, state, and federal government bodies employ vast numbers of people in accounting positions. For example, a top federal government employer in the area of accounting is the Internal Revenue Service (IRS).

INTERNAL AUDITING

Due to recent accounting regulations, the demand for internal auditors has increased. Internal auditors verify the effectiveness of an organization's accounting system and controls. They examine and ensure that the company's financial information is accurate and protected. Internal auditors also ensure that organizations are following government regulations and corporate policies. The Institute of Internal Auditors (http://theiia.org) sets international standards for internal auditors and offers a certification opportunity called the Certified Internal Auditor (CIA). Requirements for certification include having a bachelor's degree (in any area), having two years' experience in internal auditing, and passing the Certified Internal Auditor exam.

Learning Objective 4 Define ethics.

ETHICS

Ethics is a philosophy or code or system of morality—that is, how we conduct ourselves from day to day in a variety of situations requiring a decision, usually of a right or wrong nature. Ethics, as it relates to accounting, is the way accountants and other keepers of financial information conduct the business of accounting according to laws of the state and their own personal code or system of morality.

Many books, as well as classes, are available on the subject of ethics. All organizations provide a code of ethical conduct for their members. Your school may even have a Student Code of Conduct that discusses the ethical expectations and conduct of students. With mounting evidence of questionable business ethics reported in print and portrayed through visual media, understanding and learning about ethics is very important in the world of accounting.

Related to ethics, a recent change to the accounting profession is the **Sarbanes-Oxley Act**, commonly referred to as SOX. SOX was created as a response to various large-scale corporate accounting frauds, such as Enron and WorldCom. The Sarbanes-Oxley Act established a wide range of new rules related to the audit environment and internal controls.

Chapter Review

Study and Practice

1 Define accounting. — **Learning Objective**

Accounting is the process of analyzing, classifying, recording, summarizing, and interpreting business **transactions** in financial or monetary terms. It is also an information system and the language of business.

2 Explain the importance of accounting information. — **Learning Objective**

A study of accounting gives a person the necessary background to understand the scope, functions, and policies of an organization.

3 Describe the various career opportunities in accounting. — **Learning Objective**

Accounting and auditing clerks, bookkeepers, **paraprofessional accountants**, and **accountants** will find employment opportunities in several areas—in the public sector, the private sector, and not-for-profit organizations.

4 Define ethics. — **Learning Objective**

Ethics is a code of morality—that is, how we respond to a variety of situations on a daily basis that require a decision, usually of a right or wrong nature. Ethics, as it relates to accounting, is the way accountants and other keepers of financial information conduct themselves according to laws of the state and their own personal code or system of morality.

Glossary

Accountant A person who keeps the financial history of the transactions of an economic unit in written form. (*p. 4*)

Accounting The process of analyzing, classifying, recording, summarizing, and interpreting business transactions in financial or monetary terms. (*p. 3*)

Economic unit Includes both business enterprises and not-for-profit entities. (*p. 3*)

Ethics A philosophy or code or system of morality—that is, how we conduct ourselves from day to day in a variety of situations requiring a decision, usually of a right or wrong nature. (*p. 8*)

Financial Accounting Standards Board (FASB) The organization, created in 1973 by the SEC, that creates GAAP. (*p. 4*)

Generally accepted accounting principles (GAAP) The rules or guidelines used for carrying out the accounting process. (*p. 4*)

International Accounting Standards Board (IASB) The international organization that provides standards or rules for international financial reporting. (*p. 4*)

International Financial Reporting Standards (IFRS) The rules or guidelines that guide international financial reporting. (*p. 4*)

Paraprofessional accountants People who are qualified in accounting to assume the duties of a general bookkeeper as well as some of the duties of a professional accountant under that accountant's supervision. (*p. 7*)

Sarbanes-Oxley Act A U.S. federal law enacted as a response to a number of major corporate and accounting scandals that establishes a wide range of rules related to the audit environment and internal controls. (*p. 9*)

Securities and Exchange Commission (SEC) The agency responsible for regulating public companies traded on a U.S. stock exchange. (*p. 4*)

Transaction An event directly affecting an economic entity that can be expressed in terms of money and that must be recorded in the accounting records. (*p. 3*)

Activities

Why Does It Matter?

In this book, you hold one of the keys to your future—knowledge of accounting and business! Throughout the pages of this text, you'll be introduced to individuals just like yourself who dreamed about working in, operating, and even owning a business. You will read about businesses, such as a small cupcake business that has grown to international fame, an exotic catering business that brings food to far-reaching destinations, and an indoor rock-climbing business that caters to all ages. In all of these companies, one important skill stands out—knowing and understanding accounting!

So where do you see accounting in your future? Why is studying accounting so important?

chapter 1

Asset, Liability, Owner's Equity, Revenue, and Expense Accounts

Learning Objectives

After you have completed this chapter, you will be able to do the following:

1. Define and identify *asset*, *liability*, and *owner's equity* accounts.
2. Record, in column form, a group of business transactions involving changes in assets, liabilities, and owner's equity.
3. Define and identify *revenue* and *expense* accounts.
4. Record, in column form, a group of business transactions involving all five elements of the fundamental accounting equation.

To: Amy Roberts, CPA
Subject: Starting My New Business

Hi Amy,
Well, I've given it a lot of thought and have decided to take the "plunge"! I'm going to start my own business. I've been working for many years as a whitewater rafting guide and helping in the business office. I think I'm ready to go out on my own. I know a lot about rafting and operating tours, but I don't know much about accounting. Do you think you could help? Would you recommend I purchase accounting software like QuickBooks®?
Thanks,
Janie

To: Janie Conner
Subject: RE: Starting My New Business

Hi Janie,
Great! I'm so glad you've finally taken my advice and decided to open your own business. I will definitely help you learn accounting, and I would strongly recommend that you purchase an accounting software package like QuickBooks! There's a lot to learn—so let's take it step by step. I've made a list of some items for you to concentrate on first.

_____ 1. Understand what accounting is—what it does, what its purpose is.
_____ 2. Know the fundamental accounting equation. (This is important!)
_____ 3. Know examples of accounts that are included in each asset, liability, or owner's equity category.

Once you've learned these items, email me, and we'll move on! Good luck.
Amy

Ragnar Th Sigurdsson/Arctic Images/Alamy

As we stated in the Introduction, accounting is the process of analyzing, classifying, recording, summarizing, and interpreting business transactions. In this chapter, we will introduce the analyzing, classifying, and recording steps in the accounting process.

Accounting Language

ASSETS, LIABILITIES, AND OWNER'S EQUITY

The Fundamental Accounting Equation

Assets are properties or things of value, such as cash, equipment, copyrights, buildings, and land, owned and controlled by an economic unit or a business entity. By the term **business entity**, we mean that the business is an economic unit in itself and the assets or properties of the business are completely separate from the owner's personal assets. However, the owner has a claim on the assets of the business and generally has a responsibility for its debts. **The owner's right, claim, or financial interest is expressed by the word equity in the business.** Another term that can be used is **capital**. Whenever you see the term **owner's equity**, it means the owner's right to or investment in the business.

Assets	=	Owner's Equity
Properties or things of value owned by the business		Owner's *right* to or investment in the business

Suppose the total value of the assets is $80,000, and the business entity does not owe any amount against the assets. Then,

Assets	=	Owner's Equity
$80,000	=	$80,000

Learning Objective

1 Define and identify *asset, liability,* and *owner's equity* accounts.

Or suppose the assets consist of a truck that costs $35,000. The owner has invested $12,000 for the truck, and the business entity has borrowed the remainder from the bank, which is a **creditor** (one to whom money is owed). This business transaction or event can be shown as follows:

Assets	=	Liabilities	+	Owner's Equity
Items owned		*Amounts owed to creditors*		*Owner's investment*
$35,000	=	$23,000	+	$12,000

Even if the truck is not completely paid for (for example, a loan was taken out to pay for the truck), the truck is still considered an asset. The truck would be recorded at the total costs, and a liability would be recorded for the amount of the loan.

We have now introduced a new classification, **liabilities**, which represent debts. They are the amounts that the business entity owes its creditors. The debts may originate because the business bought goods or services on credit, borrowed money, or otherwise created an obligation to pay. The creditors' claims to the assets have priority over the claims of the owner.

An equation expressing the relationship of assets, liabilities, and owner's equity is called the **fundamental accounting equation**.

Assets = Liabilities + Owner's Equity

We'll deal with this equation constantly from now on. If we know two parts of this equation, we can determine the third. Let's look at some examples.

Determine Assets

Fundamental Accounting Equation Example 1: Millie Adair has $17,000 invested in her travel agency, and the agency owes creditors $5,000; that is, the agency has liabilities of $5,000. Then,

Assets	=	Liabilities	+	Owner's Equity
?	=	$5,000	+	$17,000

We can find the amount of the business's assets by adding the liabilities and the owner's equity.

$ 5,000 Liabilities
+17,000 Owner's Equity
$22,000 Assets

The completed equation now reads as follows:

Assets	=	Liabilities	+	Owner's Equity
$22,000	=	$5,000	+	$17,000

Determine Owner's Equity

Fundamental Accounting Equation Example 2: Larry Roland owns a car repair shop. His business has assets of $40,000, and it owes creditors $16,000; that is, it has liabilities of $16,000. Then,

Assets	=	Liabilities	+	Owner's Equity
$40,000	=	$16,000	+	?

We find the owner's equity by subtracting the liabilities from the assets.

$40,000 Assets
−16,000 Liabilities
$24,000 Owner's Equity

The completed equation now reads as follows:

Assets	=	Liabilities	+	Owner's Equity
$40,000	=	$16,000	+	$24,000

Like a balancing scale, the equation stays in balance by making equal or offsetting increases and decreases to one side or both sides.

Determine Liabilities

Fundamental Accounting Equation Example 3: Theo Viero's insurance agency has assets of $86,000; his investment (his equity) amounts to $46,000. Then,

Assets	=	Liabilities	+	Owner's Equity
$86,000	=	?	+	$46,000

To find the firm's total liabilities, we subtract the equity from the assets.

$ 86,000 Assets
−46,000 Owner's Equity
$ 40,000 Liabilities

The completed equation reads as follows:

Assets	=	Liabilities	+	Owner's Equity
$86,000	=	$40,000	+	$46,000

To: **Amy Roberts, CPA**
Subject: **Assets, Liabilities, and Owner's Equity**

Hi Amy,
Thanks for your help! I have purchased QuickBooks, and I am ready to install it on my computer. Do you have any tips for getting started? I am also doing really well with learning the fundamental accounting equation and identifying accounts. I can now identify most accounts as an asset, liability, or owner's equity. How does this knowledge apply to the transactions of my business?
Thanks,
Janie

To: **Janie Conner**
Subject: **RE: Asset, Liabilities, and Owner's Equity**

Hi Janie,
I'm glad to hear you have purchased QuickBooks. I'll provide you with some tips to get started and a demonstration file you can use to practice. Once you have learned a few more of the accounting basics, you will be ready to apply these in QuickBooks. Now that you know the fundamental accounting equation and also examples of accounts included in each asset, liability, or owners' equity category, you are ready to begin analyzing transactions. You will use your knowledge of accounts and apply this to the company's day-to-day transactions by recording these transactions in column form. This can be challenging, but I'll provide you with four easy steps to remember that will help you along the way. Let's get started!
Amy

Recording Business Transactions

Learning Objective 2 Record, in column form, a group of business transactions involving changes in assets, liabilities, and owner's equity.

As explained in the Introduction, business transactions are events that have a direct effect on the operations of an economic unit or enterprise and are expressed in terms of money. Each business transaction must be recorded in the accounting records. As business transactions are recorded, the amounts listed under the headings Assets, Liabilities, and Owner's Equity change. However, **the total of one side of the fundamental accounting equation must equal the total of the other side.** The categories under these three main headings are called **accounts**.

Let's look at a group of business transactions. These transactions are typical of those seen in a service or professional business. In these transactions, let's assume that J. Conner establishes her own business and calls it Conner's Whitewater Adventures. Conner's Whitewater Adventures is a **sole proprietorship**, or a one-owner business.

TRANSACTION (a). Owner deposited $90,000 in a bank account in the name of the business. Conner deposits $90,000 cash in a separate bank account in the name of Conner's Whitewater Adventures. This separate bank account will help Conner keep her business investment separate from her personal funds. This is an example of the **separate entity concept**, which says a business is treated as a separate economic or accounting entity. (See Figure 1.) The business is independent, or stands by itself; it is separate from its owners, creditors, and customers.

The Cash account consists of bank deposits and money on hand. The business now has $90,000 more in cash than before, and Conner's investment has increased by $90,000.

Figure 1
Separate entity concept

The account denoted by the owner's name followed by the word *Capital* indicates the amount of the owner's investment, or equity, in the business. The effect of this transaction on the fundamental accounting equation is as follows:

	Assets	=	**Liabilities**	+	**Owner's Equity**
	Items owned		*Amounts owed to creditors*		*Owner's investment*
	Cash	=			J. Conner, Capital
(a)	**+90,000**	=			**+90,000**

Besides cash, an investment may be in the form of goods, such as equipment. Therefore, the word *Capital* used under Owner's Equity does not always mean that cash was invested.

Accounting, as we said before, is the process of analyzing, classifying, recording, summarizing, and interpreting business transactions in terms of money. Look at transaction (a) above and see if you understand that we have gone through certain steps, which are stated below in question form.

STEP 1. **What accounts are involved?** Cash and J. Conner, Capital are involved.

STEP 2. **What are the classifications of the accounts involved?** Cash is an asset account, and J. Conner, Capital is an owner's equity account.

STEP 3. **Are the accounts increased or decreased?** Cash is increased because Conner's Whitewater Adventures has more cash now than it had before. J. Conner, Capital is increased because Conner has a greater investment now than she had before.

STEP 4. **Is the equation in balance after the transaction has been recorded?** Yes.

We will stress this step-by-step process throughout the text. This example serves as an introduction to **double-entry accounting**. The "double" entry method is demonstrated by the fact that each transaction must be recorded in at least two accounts, keeping the accounting equation in balance.

For example, transaction (a) resulted in a plus $90,000 and a plus $90,000 *on each side of the equation.* **The left side of the equation must always equal the right side of the equation.**

TRANSACTION (b). **Company bought equipment, paying cash, $38,000.** Conner's first task is to get her company ready for business; to do that, she needs the proper equipment. Accordingly, Conner buys equipment costing $38,000 and pays cash. **Note at this point that Conner does not invest any new money. She simply exchanges part of the business's cash for equipment.** Because equipment is a new type of property for the firm, a new account, Equipment, is created. Equipment is included under Assets because it is something of value owned by the business. As a result of this transaction, the accounting equation changes.

	Assets			=	**Liabilities**	+	**Owner's Equity**
	Items owned				*Amounts owed to creditors*		*Owner's investment*
	Cash	+	Equipment	=			J. Conner, Capital
Initial Investment	90,000			=			90,000
(b)	**−38,000**	**+**	**38,000**				
New balances	52,000	+	38,000	=			90,000
	90,000				90,000		

STEP 1. What accounts are involved? Cash and Equipment are involved.

STEP 2. What are the classifications of the accounts involved? Cash is an asset account, and Equipment is an asset account.

STEP 3. Are the accounts increased or decreased? Cash is decreased because Conner used cash to purchase the equipment. Equipment is increased because Conner's Whitewater Adventures has more equipment now than it had before.

STEP 4. Is the equation in balance after the transaction is recorded? Yes.

Remember that the recording of each transaction must yield an equation that is in balance. In this example, the transaction was recorded on *the same side*. Is that okay? Yes! For example, transaction (b) resulted in a minus $38,000 and a plus $38,000 on the *same side*, with nothing recorded on the other side. This results in an overall change of $0 ($38,000 – $38,000) for each side. It does not matter whether you change one side or both sides. **The important point is that whenever a transaction is properly recorded, the accounting equation remains in balance.**

TRANSACTION (c). Company bought equipment on account from a supplier, $4,320. Conner's Whitewater Adventures buys equipment costing $4,320 on credit from Signal Products.

The Equipment account shows an increase because the business now owns $4,320 more in equipment. The terms *on credit* or *on account* mean that Conner's Whitewater Adventures does not pay cash for the equipment but instead will owe Signal Products money to be paid in the future. This causes an increase in liabilities because the business now owes $4,320. The liability account **Accounts Payable** is used for short-term obligations or charge accounts, usually due within 30 days. Because Conner's Whitewater Adventures owes money to Signal Products, Signal Products is called a creditor of Conner's Whitewater Adventures. A total of $94,320 is now on each side of the equal sign.

	Assets			=	Liabilities	+	Owner's Equity
	Items owned				*Amounts owed to creditors*		*Owner's investment*
	Cash	+	Equipment	=	Accounts Payable	+	J. Conner, Capital
Previous balances	52,000	+	38,000	=			90,000
(c)			**+4,320**		**+4,320**		
New balances	52,000	+	42,320	=	4,320	+	90,000
	94,320				94,320		

STEP 1. What accounts are involved? Equipment and Accounts Payable are involved.

STEP 2. What are the classifications of the accounts involved? Equipment is an asset account, and Accounts Payable is a liability account.

STEP 3. Are the accounts increased or decreased? Equipment is increased because Conner's Whitewater Adventures has more equipment now than it had before. Accounts Payable is increased because Conner's owes more to creditors than it owed before.

STEP 4. Is the equation in balance after the transaction is recorded? Yes.

TRANSACTION (d). Company paid a creditor on account, $2,000. Conner's Whitewater Adventures pays $2,000 to Signal Products to be applied against the firm's liability of $4,320.

	Assets			=	Liabilities	+	Owner's Equity
	Items owned				*Amounts owed to creditors*		*Owner's investment*
	Cash	+	Equipment	=	Accounts Payable	+	J. Conner, Capital
Previous balances	52,000	+	42,320	=	4,320	+	90,000
(d)	**−2,000**				**−2,000**		
New balances	50,000	+	42,320	=	2,320	+	90,000
	92,320				92,320		

STEP 1. What accounts are involved? Cash and Accounts Payable are involved.

STEP 2. What are the classifications of the accounts involved? Cash is an asset account, and Accounts Payable is a liability account.

STEP 3. Are the accounts increased or decreased? Cash is decreased because Conner used cash to pay Signal Products. Accounts Payable is decreased because Conner's owes less now than it owed before.

STEP 4. Is the equation in balance after the transaction is recorded? Yes.

TRANSACTION (e). Owner invested equipment in the business. Conner invested her own computer equipment, having a **fair market value** of $5,200, in Conner's Whitewater Adventures. **Fair market value is the present worth of an asset.** It is the amount that would be received if the asset were sold on the open market. Examples of additional investments by owners may be in the form of equipment, cash, tools, or real estate.

	Assets			=	Liabilities	+	Owner's Equity
	Items owned				*Amounts owed to creditors*		*Owner's investment*
	Cash	+	Equipment	=	Accounts Payable	+	J. Conner, Capital
Previous balances	50,000	+	42,320	=	2,320	+	90,000
(e)			**+5,200**				**+5,200**
New balances	50,000	+	47,520	=	2,320	+	95,200
	97,520				97,520		

STEP 1. What accounts are involved? Equipment and J. Conner, Capital are involved.

STEP 2. What are the classifications of the accounts involved? Equipment is an asset account, and J. Conner, Capital is an owner's equity account.

STEP 3. Are the accounts increased or decreased? Equipment is increased because Conner's Whitewater Adventures now has more equipment than it had before. J. Conner, Capital is increased because Conner has a greater investment now than she had before.

STEP 4. Is the equation in balance after the transaction is recorded? Yes.

Summary of Transactions

Let's summarize the business transactions of Conner's Whitewater Adventures in column form. To test your understanding of the recording procedure, describe the nature of the transactions that have taken place.

	Assets		=	**Liabilities**	+	**Owner's Equity**
	Items owned			*Amounts owed to creditors*		*Owner's investment*
	Cash	+ Equipment	=	Accounts Payable	+	J. Conner, Capital
Transaction (a)	+90,000					+90,000
Transaction (b)	−38,000	+38,000				
Balance	52,000 +	38,000	=			90,000
Transaction (c)		+4,320		+4,320		
Balance	52,000 +	42,320	=	4,320	+	90,000
Transaction (d)	−2,000			−2,000		
Balance	50,000 +	42,320	=	2,320	+	90,000
Transaction (e)		+5,200				+5,200
Balance	50,000 +	47,520	=	2,320	+	95,200
	97,520			97,520		

The following observations apply to all types of business transactions:

1. Every transaction is recorded as an increase and/or decrease in two or more accounts.
2. One side of the equation is always equal to the other side of the equation.

In this chapter, we are using a column arrangement as a practical device to show how transactions are recorded. This arrangement is useful for showing increases and decreases in various accounts as a result of the transactions. We also show new balances after each transaction is recorded.

ACCOUNTING IN YOUR FUTURE

ACCOUNTING SKILLS

The future is yours
© iStockPhoto.com/klikk

You may wonder why taking an accounting class is important. One possible career for students who study accounting is as an entry-level accounting clerk for a company. As an accounting clerk, you would be the financial recordkeeper for the business. Your responsibilities would include maintaining accounting records, such as those you are learning about in this chapter. You might also be responsible for preparing financial statements, making bank deposits, and handling payroll.

Many businesses require that an accounting clerk have a high school diploma and some accounting course work. An associate degree in accounting is highly recommended. Minimum requirements are a knowledge of basic accounting terminology, concepts, and processes, and using a manual accounting system or an automated accounting system such as general ledger accounting software. Skills related to Microsoft® Word®, Excel®, and Outlook® also are helpful.* You need to be able to work with others in the accounting department and be attentive to detail and accuracy. Accounting clerks, sometimes called bookkeepers, can become certified bookkeepers by meeting the requirements of the American Institute of Professional Bookkeepers (www.aipb.org). The U.S. Department of Labor's Bureau of Labor Statistics (www.bls.gov) provides information about this field, including job locations and pay scales.

**Microsoft, Encarta, MSN, and Windows are either registered trademarks or trademarks of Microsoft Corporation in the United States and/or other countries.*

REVENUE AND EXPENSE ACCOUNTS

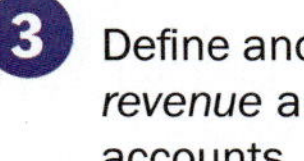

Learning Objective 3 Define and identify *revenue* and *expense* accounts.

Revenues are the amounts earned by a business. Examples of revenues are fees earned for performing services, income from selling merchandise, rent income from tenants for the use of property, and interest income for lending money. Revenues may be in the form of cash or credit card receipts. Revenues may also result from credit sales to charge customers, in which case cash will be received at a later time.

Expenses (or the costs of doing business) are the costs that relate to earning revenue. Examples of expenses are wages expense for labor performed, rent expense for the use of property, interest expense for the use of money, and advertising expense for the use of various media (for example, newspapers, radio, direct mail, and the Internet). Expenses may be paid in cash either when incurred or at a later time. Expenses to be paid at a later time involve Accounts Payable.

FYI *Incurred* is another word for *being responsible for* or *having taken place.*

Revenues and expenses directly affect owner's equity. **If a business earns revenue, an increase in owner's equity occurs. When a business incurs expenses, owner's equity decreases.** For the present, think of it this way: If the company makes money, the owner's equity is increased. If the company has to pay out money for the costs of doing business, the owner's equity is decreased. Revenues and expenses fall under the umbrella of owner's equity: Revenue increases owner's equity; expenses decrease owner's equity.

Figure 2
The umbrella of owner's equity

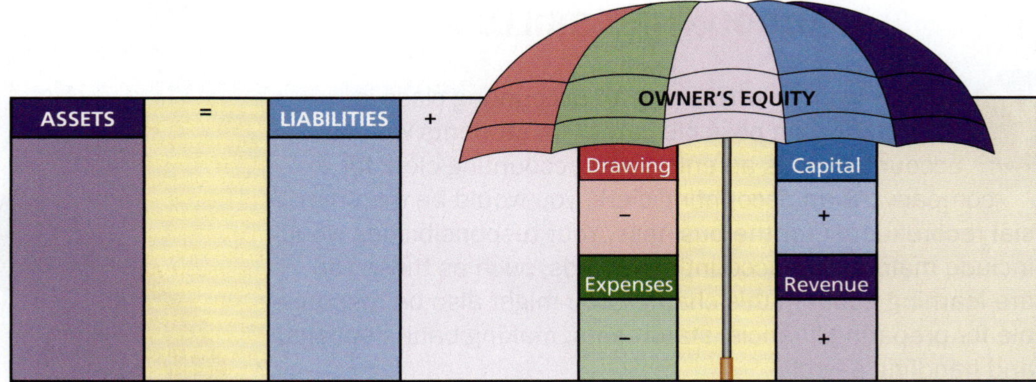

Chart of Accounts

The **chart of accounts** is the official list of accounts *tailor-made* for the business. All of the company's transactions must be recorded using the official account titles. The numbers preceding the account titles are the **account numbers**.

We now present the chart of accounts for Conner's Whitewater Adventures. Some of the accounts are new to you, but they will be explained as we move along. In the numbering of account titles, the 100s are used for assets, the 200s are used for liabilities, the 300s are used for owner's equity accounts, the 400s are used for revenue accounts, and the 500s are used for expense accounts.

CHART OF ACCOUNTS

Assets (100–199)
111 Cash
113 Accounts Receivable
115 Supplies
117 Prepaid Insurance
124 Equipment

Liabilities (200–299)
221 Accounts Payable

Owner's Equity (300–399)
311 J. Conner, Capital
312 J. Conner, Drawing

Revenue (400–499)
411 Income from Tours

Expenses (500–599)
511 Wages Expense
512 Rent Expense
514 Advertising Expense
515 Utilities Expense

While charts of accounts vary from business to business, the beginning numbers for assets, liabilities, owner's equity, revenues, and expenses are standard for a service business. Some account numbers are much longer than three digits. In any case, use the exact account titles listed in the company's chart of accounts.

For merchandising businesses selling goods (versus services), expenses will start with the 600s because accounts starting with the 500s are reserved for accounts related to the cost of the goods being sold.

Most accounting programs, such as QuickBooks, include a standard chart of accounts set up for many different types of businesses.

©Annette Shaff/Shutterstock.com

In the Real World

Every company must have a chart of accounts. For example, the popular Internet search provider Google has a chart of accounts similar to but much bigger than the example we're using. What might be some names of some accounts Google might have in its chart of accounts? Why is a listing of accounts so important?

Recording Business Transactions

Learning Objective 4 Record, in column form, a group of business transactions involving all five elements of the fundamental accounting equation.

Let's examine more transactions of Conner's Whitewater Adventures for the first month of operations. Soon after the opening of Conner's Whitewater Adventures, the first customers arrive, beginning a flow of revenue for the business.

TRANSACTION (f). Company sold services for cash, $8,000. Conner's Whitewater Adventures receives cash revenue of $8,000 in return for providing whitewater rafting tours for customers over a two-week period. In other words, the company earns $8,000 for services performed for cash customers. Revenue has the effect of increasing owner's equity, but because the company wants to know how much revenue is earned, we set up a special column for revenue. The revenue account for Conner's Whitewater Adventures is called Income from Tours. The accounting equation is affected as follows (PB stands for previous balance, and NB stands for new balance).

	Assets			=	**Liabilities**	+	**Owner's Equity**		
	Cash	+	Equipment	=	Accounts Payable	+	J. Conner, Capital	+	Revenue
PB	50,000	+	47,520	=	2,320	+	95,200		
(f)	**+8,000**								**+8,000** (Income from Tours)
NB	58,000	+	47,520	=	2,320	+	95,200	+	8,000
	105,520				105,520				

Let's review the mental process for formulating the entry.

STEP 1. What accounts are involved? In this transaction, they are Cash and Income from Tours.

STEP 2. What are the classifications of the accounts involved? Cash is an asset account, and Income from Tours is a revenue account and part of owner's equity.

STEP 3. Are the accounts increased or decreased? Cash is increased because Conner's Whitewater Adventures received cash. Income from Tours (revenue) is increased.

STEP 4. Is the equation in balance after the transaction has been recorded? Yes.

TRANSACTION (g). Company paid rent (an expense) for the month, $1,250. Shortly after opening the business, Conner's Whitewater Adventures pays the month's rent of $1,250. Rent is payment for the privilege of occupying property.

It seems logical that if revenue is added to owner's equity, expenses (the opposite of revenue) must be subtracted from owner's equity. To be consistent, a separate column is set up for expenses.

Because the time period represented by the rent payment is one month or less, we record the $1,250 as an expense. If the payment covered a period longer than one month, we would record the amount under an asset called Prepaid Rent.

	Assets			=	Liabilities	+	Owner's Equity				
	Cash	+	Equip.	=	Accounts Payable	+	J. Conner, Capital	+	Revenue	−	Expenses
PB	58,000	+	47,520	=	2,320	+	95,200	+	8,000		
(g)	**−1,250**										**+1,250** (Rent Expense)
NB	56,750	+	47,520	=	2,320	+	95,200	+	8,000	−	1,250
	104,270				104,270						

STEP 1. What accounts are involved? Cash and Rent Expense are involved.

STEP 2. What are the classifications of the accounts involved? Cash is an asset account, and Rent Expense is an owner's equity account.

STEP 3. Are the accounts increased or decreased? Cash is decreased because after the payment, Conner's Whitewater Adventures has less cash than before. Rent Expense is increased because now Conner's Whitewater Adventures has more rent expense than before.

STEP 4. Is **the equation in balance after the transaction is recorded?** Yes. Notice that in this equation, it looks as though the account doesn't balance—there is a negative entry on the left and a positive entry on the right. This is deceiving. The entry to Rent Expense is a positive entry in a negative column, thus creating an overall negative entry. It looks like this: − (+1,250) = −1,250.

TRANSACTION (h). Company bought supplies on credit, $675. Conner's Whitewater Adventures buys office supplies costing $675 on credit from Fineman Company. Computer paper, ink cartridges, invoice pads, pens and pencils, folders, filing cabinets, and calculators are considered supplies to be used by Conner's Whitewater Adventures for the business. Supplies are recorded as an asset until they are used. When supplies are used, they are taken from the asset account and placed in the expense account. We'll talk more about this later. For the time being, because Conner hasn't used the supplies yet, we will record them as an asset.

	Assets			=	Liabilities	+	Owner's Equity				
	Cash	+ Equip.	+ Supplies	=	Accounts Payable	+	J. Conner, Capital	+	Revenue	−	Expenses
PB	56,750	+ 47,520		=	2,320	+	95,200	+	8,000	−	1,250
(h)			**+675**		**+675**						
NB	56,750	+ 47,520	+ 675	=	2,995	+	95,200	+	8,000	−	1,250
	104,945				104,945						

STEP 1. What accounts are involved? Supplies and Accounts Payable are involved.

STEP 2. What are the classifications of the accounts involved? Supplies is an asset account, and Accounts Payable is a liability account.

STEP 3. Are the accounts increased or decreased? Supplies is increased as Conner's Whitewater Adventures now has more supplies than before. Accounts Payable is increased as Conner's Whitewater Adventures now owes money for the purchase of supplies.

STEP 4. Is the equation in balance after the transaction has been recorded? Yes.

TRANSACTION (i). Company paid cash for insurance, $1,875. Conner's Whitewater Adventures paid $1,875 for a three-month liability insurance policy. At the time of payment, the company has not used up the insurance; thus, it is not yet an expense. As the insurance expires (is used), it will become an expense. **However, because it is paid in advance for a period longer than one month, it has value over that longer period and is, therefore, recorded as Prepaid Insurance, an asset.**

At the end of the year or accounting period, an adjustment will have to be made to take out the expired portion (that is, coverage for the months that have been used up) and record it as an expense. We discuss this adjustment in a later chapter.

	Assets				=	Liabilities	+	Owner's Equity				
	Cash	+ Equip.	+ Supplies	+ Ppd. Ins.	=	Accounts Payable	+	J. Conner, Capital	+	Revenue	−	Expenses
PB	56,750	+ 47,520	+ 675		=	2,995	+	95,200	+	8,000	−	1,250
(i)	**−1,875**			**+1,875**								
NB	54,875	+ 47,520	+ 675	+ 1,875	=	2,995	+	95,200	+	8,000	−	1,250
	104,945					104,945						

STEP 1. What accounts are involved? Cash and Prepaid Insurance are involved.

STEP 2. What are the classifications of the accounts involved? Cash and Prepaid Insurance are both asset accounts.

STEP 3. Are the accounts increased or decreased? Cash is decreased because Conner's Whitewater Adventures is paying money, and Prepaid Insurance is increased because Conner's Whitewater Adventures has more insurance than before.

STEP 4. Is the equation in balance after the transaction is recorded? Yes.

Remember that each time a transaction is recorded, the total amount on one side of the equation **remains equal** to the total amount on the other side. As proof of this equality, look at the following computation:

Cash	$ 54,875	**Accounts Payable**	$ 2,995
Equipment	47,520	**J. Conner, Capital**	95,200
Supplies	675	**Revenue**	8,000
Prepaid Insurance	1,875	**Expenses**	−1,250
	$104,945		$104,945

Steps in Analyzing Transactions

Think through these steps each time you are presented with a transaction. We'll work through several more examples for Conner's Whitewater Adventures. However, we won't continue to show the steps. If you need extra help, write the steps in the margin.

Now that we have recorded transactions in all five classifications of accounts, let's review the steps we followed.

STEP 1. Read the transaction to understand what is happening and how it affects the business. For example, the business has more revenue or has more expenses or has more cash or owes less to creditors. Identify the accounts involved. Look for Cash first; you will quickly recognize whether cash is coming in or going out.

STEP 2. Decide on the classifications of the accounts involved. For example, Equipment is something the business owns, and it's an asset; Accounts Payable is an amount the business owes, and it's a liability.

STEP 3. Decide whether the accounts are increased or decreased.

STEP 4. After recording the transaction, make sure the accounting equation is in balance.

SMALL BUSINESS **SUCCESS**

Tools to Success—The U.S. Small Business Administration

Throughout the pages of this text, you will occasionally find a feature labeled Small Business Success. This feature is designed to provide insight into accounting issues surrounding small businesses. Some of you may own a small business when you graduate; maybe you are thinking of starting your own small bookkeeping firm. Many of you will work in small businesses such as a local or regional accounting firm. These features contain information that is useful to small and large businesses and will be helpful if you are thinking about owning your own business.

The U.S. Small Business Administration website (www.sba.gov) is a great place to find information about managing, accounting for, and running a small business. Take a moment to go to the website and review the tools that are available to small businesses. Click on the Starting & Managing link, and you will find information that deals with starting a new business, managing a business, and financing a business.

You can also find audio and video podcasts on the website that provide information about business success. If you are interested in hearing about successful small businesses, you can find a series on small business features. The series discusses various small businesses that have used the tools provided by the Small Business Administration and have grown to be successful and profitable entities.

Keep an eye out for the Small Business Success feature! It will give you insight into how businesses use the accounting information you are learning in this course.

TRANSACTION (j). Company received a bill for an expense, $620. Conner's Whitewater Adventures receives a bill from *The Times* for newspaper advertising, $620. **Conner's Whitewater Adventures has received the bill for advertising; it has not paid any cash.** Previously, we described an expense as cash paid or to be paid for the cost of doing business. An expense of $620 has now been incurred (or has taken place), and it should be recorded as an increase in expenses (Advertising Expense). Also, because the company owes $620 more than it did before and it intends to pay at a later time, this amount should be recorded as an increase in Accounts Payable. Notice that Cash is not used because the bill has not been paid.

	Assets								=	Liabilities	+	Owner's Equity				
	Cash	+	Equip.	+	Supplies	+	Ppd. Ins.		=	Accounts Payable	+	J. Conner, Capital	+	Revenue	−	Expenses
PB	54,875	+	47,520	+	675	+	1,875		=	2,995	+	95,200	+	8,000	−	1,250
(j)										**+620**						**+620** (Advertising Expense)
NB	54,875	+	47,520	+	675	+	1,875		=	3,615	+	95,200	+	8,000	−	1,870
	104,945									104,945						

TRANSACTION (k). Company sold services on account, $6,750. Conner's Whitewater Adventures signs a contract with Crystal River Lodge to provide rafting adventures for guests. Conner's Whitewater Adventures provides 27 one-day rafting tours and bills Crystal River Lodge for $6,750.

A company uses the **Accounts Receivable** account to record the amounts due from (legal claims against) charge customers. Because Conner's Whitewater Adventures' claim against Crystal River Lodge of $6,750 is promised to be paid, it is recorded in Accounts Receivable. Revenue is earned or recognized when the service is performed even though the $6,750 has not been received in cash. We count the $6,750 as an increase in revenue and an increase in Accounts Receivable. Keep in mind that Accounts Receivable is an asset, or something that is owned. Conner's Whitewater Adventures owns a claim of $6,750 against Crystal River Lodge.

	Assets									=	Liabilities	+	Owner's Equity				
	Cash	+	Equip.	+	Supplies	+	Ppd. Ins.	+	Accts. Rec.	=	Accounts Payable	+	J. Conner, Capital	+	Revenue	−	Expenses
PB	54,875	+	47,520	+	675	+	1,875			=	3,615	+	95,200	+	8,000	−	1,870
(k)									**+6,750**						**+6,750** (Income from Tours)		
NB	54,875	+	47,520	+	675	+	1,875	+	6,750	=	3,615	+	95,200	+	14,750	−	1,870
	111,695										111,695						

When Crystal River Lodge pays the $6,750 bill in cash, Conner's Whitewater Adventures records this transaction as an increase in Cash and a decrease in Accounts Receivable. At that time, Conner's Whitewater Adventures will *not* have to make an entry for the revenue because the **revenue was earned and recorded when the service was performed.**

TRANSACTION (l). Company paid creditor on account. Conner's Whitewater Adventures pays $1,500 to Signal Products, its creditor (the party to whom it owes money), as partial payment on account for the liability recorded in transaction (c).

	Assets									=	Liabilities	+	Owner's Equity				
	Cash	+	Equip.	+	Supplies	+	Ppd. Ins.	+	Accts. Rec.	=	Accounts Payable	+	J. Conner, Capital	+	Revenue	−	Expenses
PB	54,875	+	47,520	+	675	+	1,875	+	6,750	=	3,615	+	95,200	+	14,750	−	1,870
(l)	**−1,500**										**−1,500**						
NB	53,375	+	47,520	+	675	+	1,875	+	6,750	=	2,115	+	95,200	+	14,750	−	1,870
	110,195										110,195						

TRANSACTION (m). Company paid an expense in cash, $225. Conner's Whitewater Adventures receives a bill from Solar Power, Inc., for $225. Because the bill was not previously recorded as a liability and is to be paid immediately, we record the amount directly as an expense.

	Assets									=	Liabilities	+	Owner's Equity				
	Cash	+	Equip.	+	Supplies	+	Ppd. Ins.	+	Accts. Rec.	=	Accounts Payable	+	J. Conner, Capital	+	Revenue	−	Expenses
PB	53,375	+	47,520	+	675	+	1,875	+	6,750	=	2,115	+	95,200	+	14,750	−	1,870
(m)	**−225**																**+225** (Utilities Expense)
NB	53,150	+	47,520	+	675	+	1,875	+	6,750	=	2,115	+	95,200	+	14,750	−	2,095
	109,970										109,970						

TRANSACTION (n). Company paid creditor on account, $620. Conner's Whitewater Adventures pays $620 to *The Times* for advertising. Recall that this bill had previously been recorded as a liability in transaction (j).

	Assets									=	Liabilities	+	Owner's Equity				
	Cash	+	Equip.	+	Supplies	+	Ppd. Ins.	+	Accts. Rec.	=	Accounts Payable	+	J. Conner, Capital	+	Revenue	−	Expenses
PB	53,150	+	47,520	+	675	+	1,875	+	6,750	=	2,115	+	95,200	+	14,750	−	2,095
(n)	**−620**										**−620**						
NB	52,530	+	47,520	+	675	+	1,875	+	6,750	=	1,495	+	95,200	+	14,750	−	2,095
	109,350										109,350						

TRANSACTION (o). Company paid an expense in cash, $2,360. Conner's Whitewater Adventures pays wages of a part-time employee, $2,360.

	Assets					**= Liabilities +**	**Owner's Equity**		
	Cash	+ Equip.	+ Supplies	+ Ppd. Ins.	+ Accts. Rec.	= Accounts Payable	+ J. Conner, Capital	+ Revenue	− Expenses
PB	52,530	+ 47,520	+ 675	+ 1,875	+ 6,750	= 1,495	+ 95,200	+ 14,750	− 2,095
(o)	**−2,360**								**+2,360** (Wages Expense)
NB	50,170	+ 47,520	+ 675	+ 1,875	+ 6,750	= 1,495	+ 95,200	+ 14,750	− 4,455
	106,990					106,990			

TRANSACTION (p). Company buys equipment on account for $3,780, making a cash down payment of $1,850 and charging $1,930. Conner's Whitewater Adventures buys additional equipment from Signal Products for $3,780, paying $1,850 down with the remaining $1,930 on account. Because buying an item *on account* is the same as buying it *on credit,* both terms are used to describe such transactions and involve Accounts Payable.

	Assets					**= Liabilities +**	**Owner's Equity**		
	Cash	+ Equip.	+ Supplies	+ Ppd. Ins.	+ Accts. Rec.	= Accounts Payable	+ J. Conner, Capital	+ Revenue	− Expenses
PB	50,170	+ 47,520	+ 675	+ 1,875	+ 6,750	= 1,495	+ 95,200	+ 14,750	− 4,455
(p)	**−1,850**	**+3,780**				**+1,930**			
NB	48,320	+ 51,300	+ 675	+ 1,875	+ 6,750	= 3,425	+ 95,200	+ 14,750	− 4,455
	108,920					108,920			

Again, because the equipment is expected to last for years, Conner's Whitewater Adventures lists this $3,780 as an increase in the assets. Note that three accounts are involved in this transaction: Cash because cash was paid out, Equipment because the company has more equipment than it had before, and Accounts Payable because the company owes more now than it owed before.

TRANSACTION (q). Company receives cash on account from credit customer, $2,500. Conner's Whitewater Adventures receives $2,500 from Crystal River Lodge to apply against the amount billed in transaction (k). Because Crystal River Lodge now owes Conner's Whitewater Adventure less than it did before, Conner's Whitewater Adventures deducts the $2,500 from Accounts Receivable. An exchange of assets has no effect on the totals of the equation.

	Assets					**= Liabilities +**	**Owner's Equity**		
	Cash	+ Equip.	+ Supplies	+ Ppd. Ins.	+ Accts. Rec.	= Accounts Payable	+ J. Conner, Capital	+ Revenue	− Expenses
PB	48,320	+ 51,300	+ 675	+ 1,875	+ 6,750	= 3,425	+ 95,200	+ 14,750	− 4,455
(q)	**+2,500**				**−2,500**				
NB	50,820	+ 51,300	+ 675	+ 1,875	+ 4,250	= 3,425	+ 95,200	+ 14,750	− 4,455
	108,920					108,920			

Conner's Whitewater Adventures previously listed the amount as revenue [see transaction (k)], so it should *not* be recorded as revenue again.

TRANSACTION (r). Company sells services for cash, $8,570. Conner's Whitewater Adventures receives revenue from cash customers during the rest of the month, $8,570.

	Assets									=	Liabilities	+	Owner's Equity				
	Cash	+	Equip.	+	Supplies	+	Ppd. Ins.	+	Accts. Rec.	=	Accounts Payable	+	J. Conner, Capital	+	Revenue	−	Expenses
PB	50,820	+	51,300	+	675	+	1,875	+	4,250	=	3,425	+	95,200	+	14,750	−	4,455
(r)	**+8,570**														**+8,570** (Income from Tours)		
NB	59,390	+	51,300	+	675	+	1,875	+	4,250	=	3,425	+	95,200	+	23,320	−	4,455
	117,490										117,490						

TRANSACTION (s). Owner makes a cash withdrawal, $3,500. At the end of the month, Conner withdraws $3,500 in cash from the business for her personal living costs. A **withdrawal** (or drawing) may be considered the opposite of an investment in cash by the owner and is treated as a decrease in owner's equity. Withdrawals are different from expenses. Expenses are paid to someone else for the cost of goods or services used in the business. On the other hand, withdrawals are paid directly to the owner and do not involve the cost of goods or services used in the business. A withdrawal may consist of cash or other assets.

Because the owner takes cash out of the business, there is a decrease of $3,500 in Cash. This withdrawal of cash also decreases owner's equity and is denoted in the account labeled with the owner's name followed by the word *Drawing*. We record $3,500 under J. Conner, Drawing.

	Assets									=	Liabilities	+	Owner's Equity						
	Cash	+	Equip.	+	Supplies	+	Ppd. Ins.	+	Accts. Rec.	=	Accounts Payable	+	J. Conner, Capital	−	J. Conner, Drawing	+	Revenue	−	Expenses
PB	59,390	+	51,300	+	675	+	1,875	+	4,250	=	3,425	+	95,200			+	23,320	−	4,455
(s)	**−3,500**														**+3,500**				
NB	55,890	+	51,300	+	675	+	1,875	+	4,250	=	3,425	+	95,200	−	3,500	+	23,320	−	4,455
	113,990										113,990								

Summary of Transactions (f) through (s)

Figure 3 summarizes business transactions (f) through (s) of Conner's Whitewater Adventures with the transactions identified by letter. To test your understanding of the recording procedure, describe the nature of the transactions.

Figure 3
Summary of transactions (f) through (s)

	Assets					=	Liabilities +	Owner's Equity			
	Cash +	Equip. +	Supplies +	Ppd. Ins. +	Accts. Rec.	=	Accounts Payable +	J. Conner, Capital	− J. Conner, Drawing	+ Revenue	− Expenses
Bal.	50,000 +	47,520				=	2,320 +	95,200			
(f)	**+8,000**									**+8,000** (Income from Tours)	
Bal.	58,000 +	47,520				=	2,320 +	95,200		+ 8,000	
(g)	**−1,250**										**+1,250** (Rent Exp.)
Bal.	56,750 +	47,520				=	2,320 +	95,200		+ 8,000 −	1,250
(h)			**+675**				**+675**				
Bal.	56,750 +	47,520 +	675			=	2,995 +	95,200		+ 8,000 −	1,250
(i)	**−1,875**			**+1,875**							
Bal.	54,875 +	47,520 +	675 +	1,875		=	2,995 +	95,200		+ 8,000 −	1,250
(j)							**+620**				**+620** (Adv. Exp.)
Bal.	54,875 +	47,520 +	675 +	1,875		=	3,615 +	95,200		+ 8,000 −	1,870
(k)					**+6,750**					**+6,750** (Income from Tours)	
Bal.	54,875 +	47,520 +	675 +	1,875 +	6,750	=	3,615 +	95,200		+ 14,750 −	1,870
(l)	**−1,500**						**−1,500**				
Bal.	53,375 +	47,520 +	675 +	1,875 +	6,750	=	2,115 +	95,200		+ 14,750 −	1,870
(m)	**−225**										**+225** (Util. Exp.)
Bal.	53,150 +	47,520 +	675 +	1,875 +	6,750	=	2,115 +	95,200		+ 14,750 −	2,095
(n)	**−620**						**−620**				
Bal.	52,530 +	47,520 +	675 +	1,875 +	6,750	=	1,495 +	95,200		+ 14,750 −	2,095
(o)	**−2,360**										**+2,360** (Wages Exp.)
Bal.	50,170 +	47,520 +	675 +	1,875 +	6,750	=	1,495 +	95,200		+ 14,750 −	4,455
(p)	**−1,850**	**+3,780**					**+1,930**				
Bal.	48,320 +	51,300 +	675 +	1,875 +	6,750	=	3,425 +	95,200		+ 14,750 −	4,455
(q)	**+2,500**				**−2,500**						
Bal.	50,820 +	51,300 +	675 +	1,875 +	4,250	=	3,425 +	95,200		+ 14,750 −	4,455
(r)	**+8,570**									**+8,570** (Income from Tours)	
Bal.	59,390 +	51,300 +	675 +	1,875 +	4,250	=	3,425 +	95,200		+ 23,320 −	4,455
(s)	**−3,500**								**+3,500**		
Bal.	55,890 +	51,300 +	675 +	1,875 +	4,250	=	3,425 +	95,200	− 3,500	+ 23,320 −	4,455

Left Side of Equals Sign:		**Right Side of Equals Sign:**	
Cash	$ 55,890	**Accounts Payable**	$ 3,425
Equipment	51,300	**J. Conner, Capital**	95,200
Supplies	675	**J. Conner, Drawing**	−3,500
Prepaid Insurance	1,875	**Revenue**	23,320
Accounts Receivable	4,250	**Expenses**	−4,455
	$113,990		$113,990

YOU Make the Call

You've just been hired as an accounting clerk. The other accounting clerk, Sam, has asked you to check some transactions he analyzed. Use the transaction-analysis steps presented earlier in the chapter (see page 26) to determine the accuracy of the following transactions and write your own analysis.

SAM'S ANALYSES—FIND THE ERRORS

TRANSACTION 1. Received a bill for the month's rent, $1,000.

STEP 1. Cash and Rent Expense are the accounts involved.

STEP 2. Cash is an asset, and Rent Expense is an expense.

STEP 3. Cash is decreased, and Rent Expense is decreased.

TRANSACTION 2: Bought equipment on account for $1,800.

STEP 1. Equipment and Accounts Receivable are the accounts involved.

STEP 2. Equipment is an asset, and Accounts Receivable is an asset.

STEP 3. Equipment is decreased, and Accounts Receivable is increased.

SOLUTION

Sam's analyses for both transactions are incorrect.

TRANSACTION 1:

STEP 1. Accounts Payable and Rent Expense are the accounts involved.

STEP 2. The bill was received but not paid, therefore creating a liability. Cash is not involved because the business has not paid the monthly rent.

Accounts Payable is a liability, and Rent Expense is an expense.

STEP 3. Accounts Payable is increased, and Rent Expense is increased. Remember, the bill was only received, not paid; therefore, no cash is involved. Rent Expense increases, but its ultimate effect is a subtraction in the fundamental accounting equation.

TRANSACTION 2:

STEP 1. Equipment and Accounts Payable are the accounts involved.

STEP 2. Accounts Payable is involved because the business owes money to the seller. Accounts Payable is the account used to manage short-term liabilities. Accounts Receivable is the account used to keep track of what customers owe the business.

Equipment is an asset, and Accounts Payable is a liability.

STEP 3. Equipment is increased, and Accounts Payable is increased.

Accounting with ***QuickBooks®***

In this text, you will learn how to record transactions and prepare financial reports for various companies using a **manual accounting system**. You will also have an opportunity to use QuickBooks, a **computerized accounting system**. In a manual accounting system, accounting transactions are recorded and financial reports are prepared by hand, rather than on a computer. Using the featured *Accounting with QuickBooks* section throughout this text, you will also learn how to record transactions and process financial reports in a computerized accounting system using QuickBooks.

Learning Objectives

After you have completed this section, you will be able to do the following:

1. Identify the advantages and disadvantages of a computerized accounting system.
2. Install and register QuickBooks.
3. Open or restore a company.
4. Modify a company name.
5. View and use a chart of accounts.
6. Back up QuickBooks.
7. Close a company and exit QuickBooks.

Characteristics of Computerized Accounting Systems

A computerized accounting system records accounting transactions using a computer and accounting software. There are many types of accounting software. QuickBooks is a software program that is often used by small to medium-sized businesses.

Learning Objective

1 Identify the advantages and disadvantages of a computerized accounting system.

A majority of companies use some form of a computerized accounting system. They do so because the advantages of a computerized accounting system far outweigh the disadvantages. Some of the advantages of a computerized accounting system are as follows:

- **Automatic**—Computerized accounting systems automatically complete many parts of the accounting cycle. Once a user enters a transaction, the software posts the transaction to the ledger and updates the financial statements. In addition, computerized accounting systems perform financial calculations, such as totaling revenue and expenses and determining net income.
- **Timeliness**—Computerized accounting systems allow companies to prepare up-to-date financial reports quickly. Also, accountants can easily locate specific transactions they want to review or investigate.
- **Accuracy**—Errors, such as out-of-balance transactions, are eliminated using a computerized accounting system. The software alerts the user when a transaction is out of balance and will not let the user proceed until the transaction is balanced.
- **Ease of use**—Basic accounting systems, like QuickBooks, are easy to use and often require the user to have little previous accounting knowledge.
- **Security measures**—Computerized accounting systems provide a series of security measures that include passwords to restrict access and built-in error checks.
- **Analysis**—Companies can easily analyze their financial statements to identify performance measurements, including determining which services are and are not

profitable, the percentage of cash spent on expenses, and comparisons between the current and previous fiscal periods.

- **Inexpensive**—Basic accounting systems like QuickBooks are relatively inexpensive to purchase and use.

There are also disadvantages to using computerized accounting systems. These include:

- **Security risks**—Even with the security measures accounting software provides, computer systems can still be hacked, and data can be compromised. In addition, data can be lost through power and/or computer failures. Some risks can be lessened by using a virus protection program and by performing routine **backups**. Backups store company data files in a safe place, such as online, or on an external backup device such as a USB flash drive, CD, or external hard drive.
- **User error**—Although QuickBooks and other computerized accounting systems are designed to help reduce certain input errors, such as out-of-balance transactions, errors can still occur. Transactions can be recorded incorrectly, and valuable information can be lost or deleted.

Getting Started with QuickBooks

In the first few chapters of this text, we use Conner's Whitewater Adventures to demonstrate how to record transactions and process reports in a computerized accounting system. We will be using the accounting program QuickBooks Accountant; however, Intuit the company that provides QuickBooks, also offers various other versions, including QuickBooks online. The online version of QuickBooks is an example of **cloud computing**. This version is used via the Internet, rather than a local computer. With cloud computing, authorized users can access software and data anywhere they have an Internet connection. Data and software do not have to be stored on an actual computer. To compare the various QuickBooks financial software packages, you can visit www.intuit.com.

Learning Objective

Install and register QuickBooks.

QuickBooks Tip

Your instructor may want you to use a different version of QuickBooks. Don't worry. Most of the instructions are similar for all versions of QuickBooks, even if the look is a little different.

If your *College Accounting* textbook came with a trial version of QuickBooks software, you will need to install the software CD on your computer. To install QuickBooks, follow these steps:

STEP 1. Be sure to close all open programs on your computer. You may also have to adjust your computer's security settings and/or close your antivirus software prior to installation.

STEP 2. Insert the QuickBooks CD into your computer's CD drive.

STEP 3. The QuickBooks installation should automatically start once the CD is inserted. Follow the installation instructions as prompted on your computer screen. If you have a previous trial version of QuickBooks on your computer, you may need to uninstall the prior version before installing the current version from the CD.

STEP 4. Now enter the license and product numbers that came with your QuickBooks CD. Be sure to put the CD and the license/product numbers in a safe place until your trial version has expired. You may need these items later if you require technical support.

STEP 5. Be sure to register your QuickBooks trial version during installation. Your trial version of QuickBooks is valid for 140 days; however, the software must be registered within 30 days or a certain number of log-ins, for you to receive the entire trial period. It is recommended that you wait until your instructor tells you to install and register your QuickBooks trial software. This will ensure that you have the software available for the entire time period you need for your course.

QuickBooks Tip

If you forget to register your QuickBooks trial version when you install it, click on the Help menu, then click Register QuickBooks. You can also contact Intuit Support at www.intuit.com or 888-859-4056.

Setting up a Company

The first step in using QuickBooks is to set up a company. This involves entering company information, including the name of the company, address, and industry. In addition, the chart of accounts is created. Notice in Figure Q1 that the chart of accounts is similar to the one we have already discussed.

Figure Q1
Chart of accounts

Conner's Whitewater Adventures - Janie Conner - QuickBooks Accountant 20-- [Chart of Accounts]

File Edit View Lists Favorites Accountant Company Customers Vendors Employees Banking Reports Window Help

Name	⚡	Type
• 111 Cash		Bank
• 113 Accounts Receivable		Accounts Receivable
• 115 Supplies		Other Current Asset
• 117 Prepaid Insurance		Other Current Asset
• 124 Equipment		Fixed Asset
• 221 Accounts Payable		Accounts Payable
• 311 J. Conner, Capital		Equity
• 312 J. Conner, Drawing		Equity
• 411 Income from Tours		Income
• 511 Wages Expense		Expense
• 512 Rent Expense		Expense
• 514 Advertising Expense		Expense
• 515 Utilities Expense		Expense

This course will not discuss how to set up companies since that is typically covered in a stand-alone computerized accounting course. For all problems in this book, you will be provided with data files that already have the company information set up.

Learning Objective

3 Open or restore a company.

STEP 1. Save the .QBB data file to your computer.
The QuickBooks data files are located on the textbook website at CengageBrain.com. It is recommended that you set up a new folder for your QuickBooks files so they are easy to locate later. The QuickBooks problems for this text will use two types of QuickBooks files: the backup file (.QBB) and the working file (.QBW). Before you can start entering transactions into QuickBooks, you will need to convert the backup file (.QBB) to a working file (.QBW). This will be covered in Step 2.

QuickBooks Tip

You cannot click directly on a QuickBooks backup file (.QBB) to open it. QuickBooks backup files (.QBB) must be restored from the QuickBooks program first.

STEP 2. **Restore the file saved in Step 1.**

- From the **File** menu or the opening page, click **Open or Restore Company**. (See Figure Q2.)
- Select **Restore a Backup Copy** and click **Next**.
- Now select **Local Backup** and click **Next**.
- Locate the QuickBooks backup file you saved in **Step 1**. Click **Open**.
- When the window **Where do you want to restore the file?** appears, click **Next**.
- Select the location where you want to save your file.
- Name your file per your instructor's instructions. You will now see (.QBW) in the file type. Click **Save**.
- A message will appear that QuickBooks is being restored. Click **OK** when you see the following window: **Your data has been restored successfully**.

Figure Q2
Opening or restoring a company

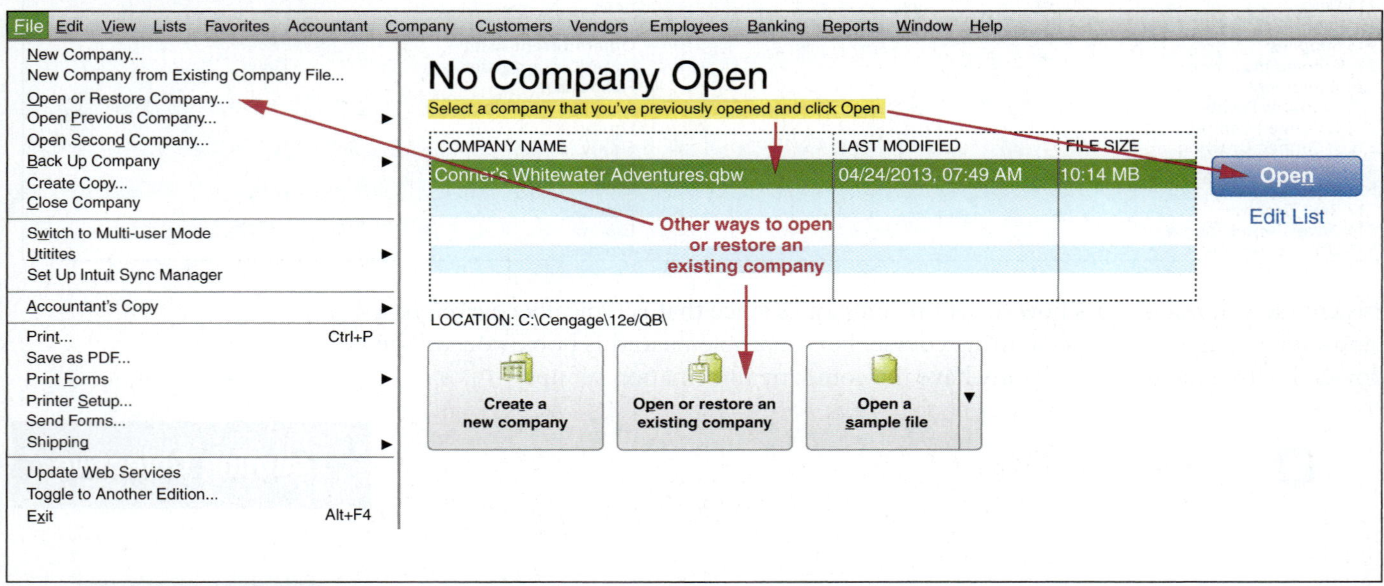

Learning Objective  4 Modify a company name.

Your instructor may want you to distinguish your company reports from others. To make this distinction, you can insert your name with the company name under **Company Information**.

STEP 1. Select **Company** from the menu bar.

STEP 2. Select **Company Information**. (See Figure Q3.)

Figure Q3
Accessing company information

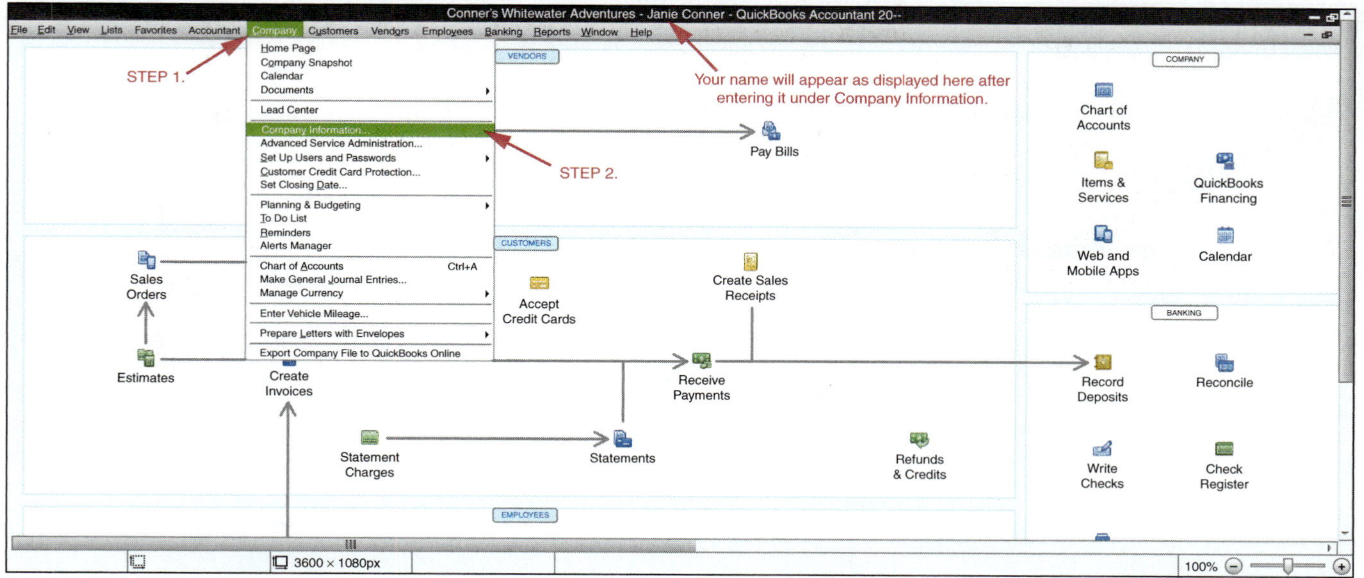

STEP 3. Enter your name as shown in Figure Q4 or according to your instructor's directions. Once you have added your name to the Company Name field, click **OK**.

Figure Q4
Company information screen

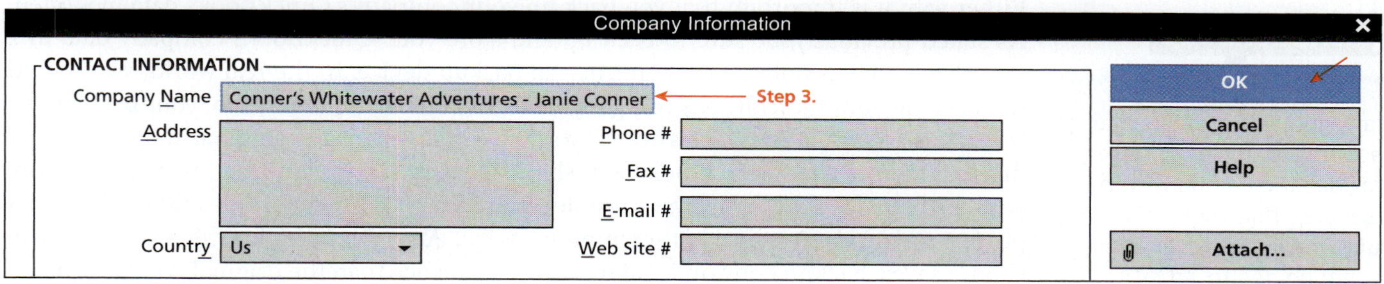

5 View and use a chart of accounts. **Learning Objective**

There are three ways to view a chart of accounts in QuickBooks. (See Figure Q5.)

1. Select **Lists** from the menu bar on the home page, and then select **Chart of Accounts** from the dropdown list.
2. Select **Company** from the menu bar on the home page, and then select **Chart of Accounts** from the dropdown list (as shown).
3. Select **Chart of Accounts** directly from the home page.

Figure Q5
Viewing chart of accounts

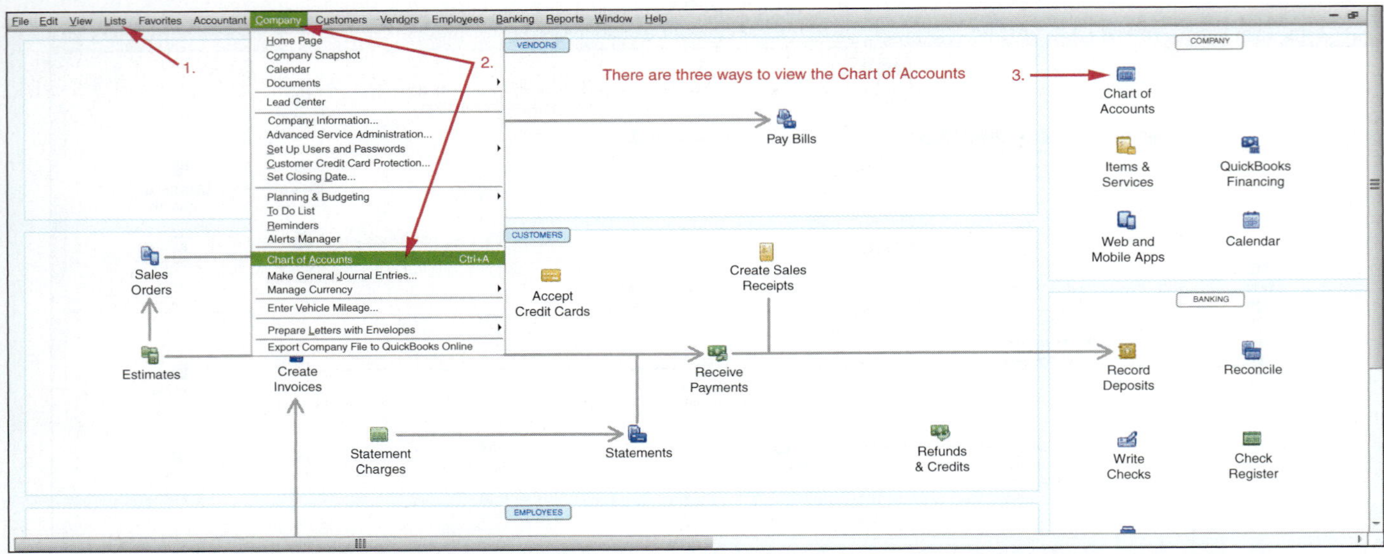

Learning Objective

6 Back up QuickBooks.

It is important to regularly back up your company's QuickBooks data files. You may decide to back up your company's data each time you close your QuickBooks company file, or you may decide to back up your company's data according to a predetermined schedule. Either way, it is important that you back up your company's QuickBooks data files often. As stated previously, be sure to back up and store your QuickBooks company data in a safe place, such as online or on an external backup device. In the real world, you should not back up your QuickBooks company data file to the computer where your original file is located. However, in the classroom, you will typically be storing your data on a flash drive. Be aware that QuickBooks will show a warning message when trying to restore your backup file (.QBB) to the same location as the company file (.QBW). For class purposes, you can ignore this warning message. As a reminder, in the real world you should save a backup copy on a different storage device than the original company file. It is also a good idea to store a backup copy offsite.

To start your backup, insert your external backup device, and then click on **Back Up Company**. A side menu item will appear. Select **Create Local Backup**. (See Figure Q6.)

QuickBooks Tip

Many companies choose to back up to the cloud. This provides the company with a secure offsite copy of its QuickBooks data, which cannot be destroyed by a disaster such as a fire or be intentionally deleted.

Figure Q6
Creating local backup

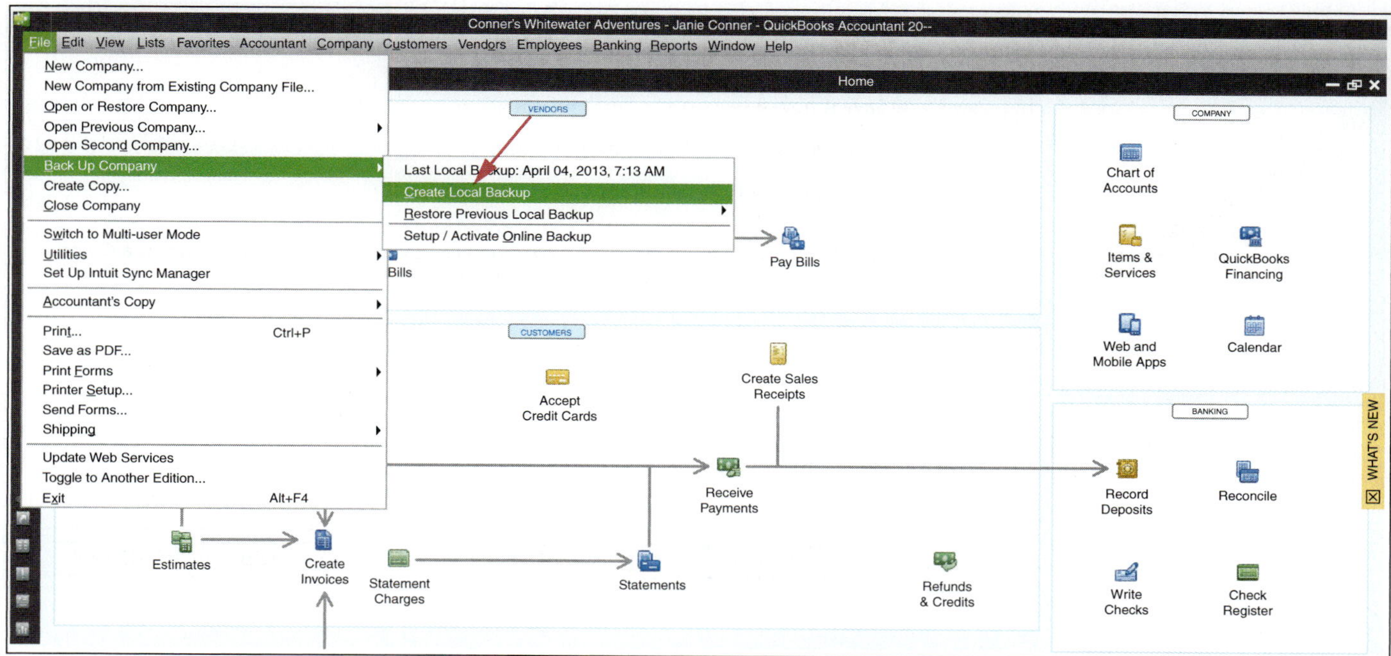

Now select **Local Backup**. Then select **Next** to proceed.

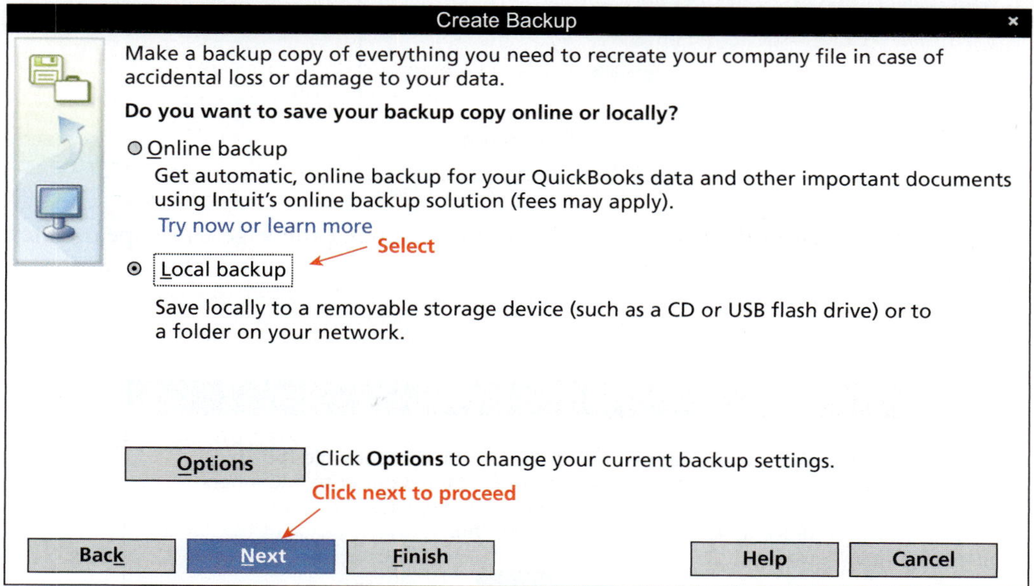

Figure Q7
Local backup

Select **Save It Now**, and then select **Next** to proceed.

Figure Q8
Saving backup copy

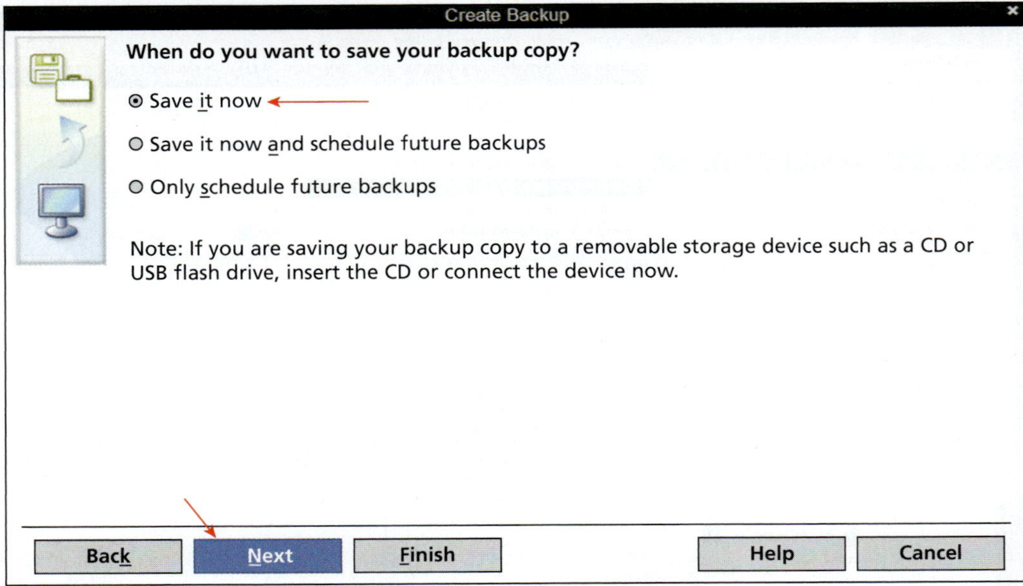

While your QuickBooks company file is backing up, the following message will appear:

Figure Q9
Verifying data integrity

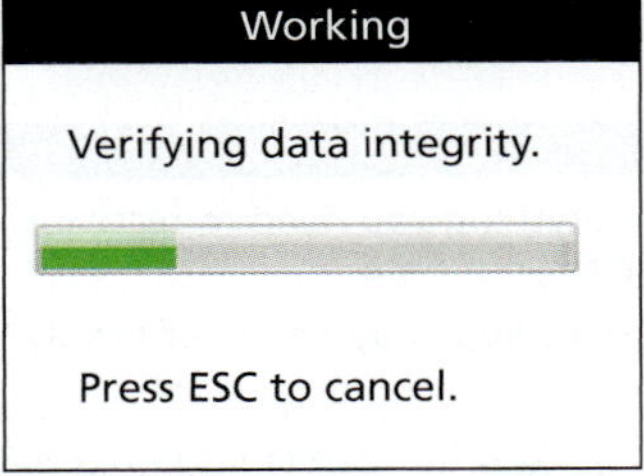

When your QuickBooks backup is complete, the following message will appear. Click **OK**.

Figure Q10
QuickBooks backup completion

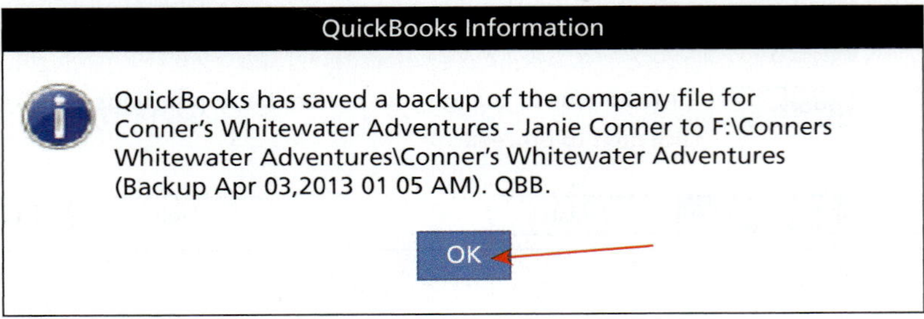

Learning Objective

7 Close a company and exit QuickBooks.

Complete the following steps to close a company and exit QuickBooks.

STEP 1. Select **File**.

STEP 2. Select **Close Company**.

STEP 3. Select **Exit**. You can also exit QuickBooks by clicking the ✕ in the top right-hand corner of your QuickBooks screen.

Figure Q11
Close and exit company

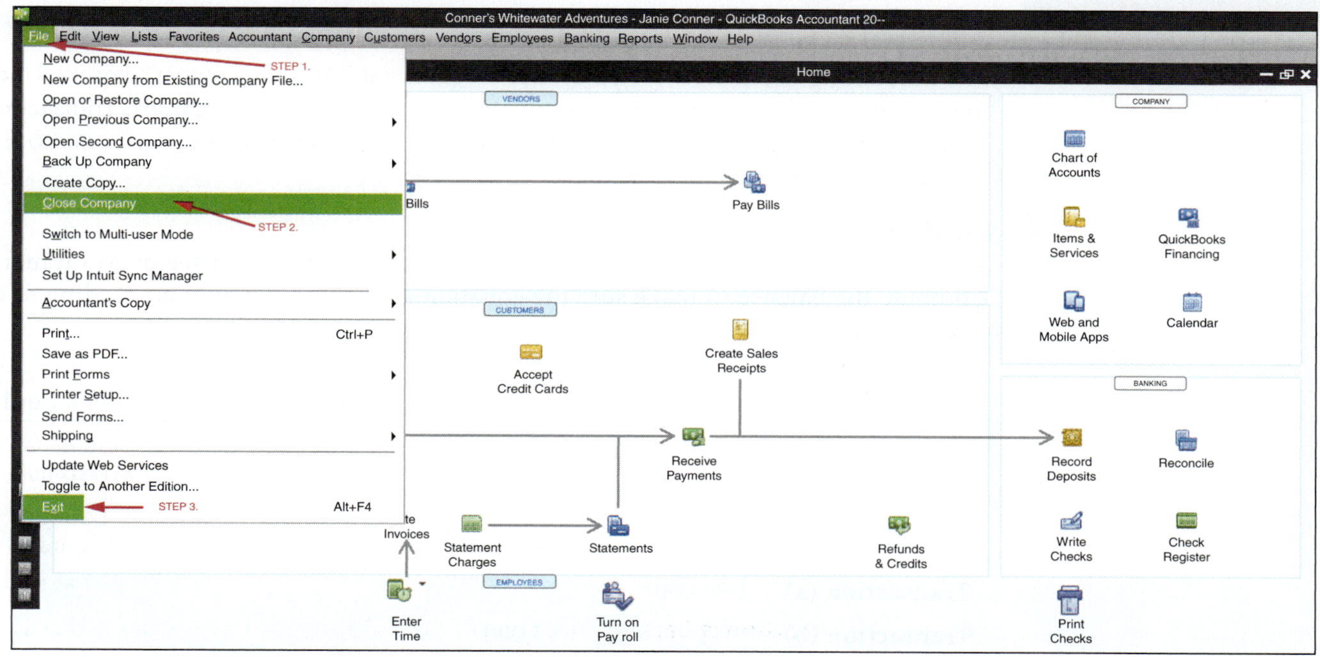

Chapter Review

Study and Practice

Learning Objective

1 Define and identify *asset*, *liability*, and *owner's equity* accounts.

Assets are cash, properties, or things of value owned by the business. **Liabilities** are amounts the business owes to creditors. **Owner's equity** is the owner's investment in or rights to the business. The **fundamental accounting equation** expresses the relationship of assets, liabilities, and owner's equity and is represented as:

Assets = Liabilities + Owner's Equity

CHAPTER REVIEW

PRACTICE EXERCISE 1

Complete the fundamental accounting equation:

Assets	=	**Liabilities**	+	**Owner's Equity**
Items owned		*Amounts owed to creditors*		*Owner's investment*
\$50,000	=	\$12,000	+	?

PRACTICE EXERCISE 1 • SOLUTION

\$50,000 Assets
−12,000 Liabilities
\$38,000 Owner's Equity

Learning Objective

Record, in column form, a group of business transactions involving changes in assets, liabilities, and owner's equity.

The accounting equation is stated as assets equals liabilities plus owner's equity. Under the appropriate classification, a separate column is set up for each **account**. Transactions are recorded by listing amounts as additions to or deductions from the various accounts. The equation must remain in balance.

PRACTICE EXERCISE 2

Write the corresponding amounts for each transaction where you see question marks. Compute the balance to make sure the equation is in balance before proceeding to the next transaction.

	Assets			=	**Liabilities**	+	**Owner's Equity**
	Items owned				*Amounts owed to creditors*		*Owner's investment*
	Cash	+	Equipment	=	Accounts Payable	+	J. Lawson, Capital
Transaction (a)	+90,000						?
Transaction (b)	?		+53,000				
Balance	?	+	?	=			?
Transaction (c)			?		+9,000		
Balance	?	+	?	=	?	+	?
Transaction (d)	?				−4,000		
Balance	?	+	?	=	?	+	?
Transaction (e)			?				+5,200
Balance	?	+	?	=	?	+	?
			?			?	

PRACTICE EXERCISE 2 • SOLUTION

	Assets			=	Liabilities	+	Owner's Equity
	Items owned				*Amounts owed to creditors*		*Owner's investment*
	Cash	+	Equipment	=	Accounts Payable	+	J. Lawson, Capital
Transaction (a)	+90,000						+90,000
Transaction (b)	−53,000		+53,000				
Balance	37,000	+	53,000	=			90,000
Transaction (c)			+9,000		+9,000		
Balance	37,000	+	62,000	=	9,000	+	90,000
Transaction (d)	−4,000				−4,000		
Balance	33,000	+	62,000	=	5,000	+	90,000
Transaction (e)			+5,200				+5,200
Balance	33,000	+	67,200	=	5,000	+	95,200
	100,200				100,200		

Learning Objective

3 Define and identify *revenue* and *expense* accounts.

Revenues consist of amounts earned by a business, such as fees earned for performing services, income from selling merchandise, rent income from tenants for the use of property, and interest earned for lending money. **Expenses** are the costs of earning revenue—that is, of doing business—such as wages expense, rent expense, interest expense, and advertising expense.

3 PRACTICE EXERCISE 3

Identify the revenue and expense accounts from the following list of accounts. If the account is a revenue account, write R. If the account is an expense account, write E. If it is neither, leave blank.

___	Accounts Payable	___	Service Income
___	Rent Expense	___	Utilities Expense
___	J. Martin, Drawing	___	Professional Fees Earned
___	Wages Expense	___	Accounts Receivable

PRACTICE EXERCISE 3 • SOLUTION

___	Accounts Payable	R	Service Income
E	Rent Expense	E	Utilities Expense
___	J. Martin, Drawing	R	Professional Fees Earned
E	Wages Expense	___	Accounts Receivable

Learning Objective  Record, in column form, a group of business transactions involving all five elements of the fundamental accounting equation.

The accounting equation has been expanded and should appear as follows:

Assets = Liabilities + Capital − Drawing + Revenue − Expenses

Accounts are classified and listed under each heading. Transactions are recorded by listing amounts as additions to or deductions from the various accounts. The equation must remain in balance.

PRACTICE EXERCISE 4

Record the following transactions in the grid provided below.

Transaction (a). Company bought equipment for $8,000 on account.
Transaction (b). Company sold services on account for $6,200.
Transaction (c). Customer paid $3,000 on account.
Transaction (d). Company owner invested personal computer system in the business, fair market value, $3,400 (Equipment).

	Assets			=	Liabilities	+	Owner's Equity						
	Cash	+ Equipment	+ Accounts Receivable	=	Accounts Payable	+	______, Capital	−	______, Drawing	+	Revenue	−	Expenses
(a)													
(b)													
Bal.													
(c)													
Bal.													
(d)													
Bal.													

PRACTICE EXERCISE 4 • SOLUTION

	Assets			=	Liabilities	+	Owner's Equity						
	Cash	+ Equipment	+ Accounts Receivable	=	Accounts Payable	+	______, Capital	−	______, Drawing	+	Revenue	−	Expenses
(a)		+8,000			+8,000								
(b)			+6,200								+6,200		
Bal.		+8,000	+6,200	=	+8,000						+6,200		
(c)	+3,000		−3,000										
Bal.	+3,000	+8,000	+3,200	=	+8,000						+6,200		
(d)		+3,400					+3,400						
Bal.	3,000	+ 11,400	+ 3,200	=	8,000	+	3,400			+	6,200		

17,600 = 17,600

Glossary

Account numbers The numbers assigned to accounts according to the chart of accounts. *(p. 22)*

Accounts The categories under the Assets, Liabilities, and Owner's Equity headings. *(p. 16)*

Accounts Payable A liability account used for short-term obligations or charge accounts, usually due within 30 days. *(p. 18)*

Accounts Receivable An account used to record the amounts due from (legal claims against) charge customers. *(p. 27)*

Assets Cash, properties, and other things of value owned by an economic unit or a business entity. *(p. 13)*

Backups Procedures that store company data files in a safe place, such as online or on a flash drive. *(p. 34)*

Business entity A business enterprise, separate and distinct from the persons who supply the assets it uses. *(p. 13)*

Capital The owner's investment, or equity, in an enterprise. *(p. 13)*

Chart of accounts The official list of account titles to be used to record the transactions of a business. *(p. 22)*

Cloud computing Software that is used via the Internet instead of from a local computer. Software and data can be accessed anywhere there is an Internet connection. *(p. 34)*

Computerized accounting An accounting system that records transactions using a computer and accounting software such as QuickBooks. *(p. 33)*

Creditor One to whom money is owed. *(p. 14)*

Double-entry accounting The system by which each business transaction is recorded in at least two accounts and the accounting equation is kept in balance. *(p. 17)*

Equity The value of a right or claim to or financial interest in an asset or group of assets. *(p. 13)*

Expenses The costs that relate to earning revenue (the costs of doing business); examples are wages, rent, interest, and advertising. They may be paid in cash immediately or at a future time (Accounts Payable). *(p. 21)*

Fair market value The present worth of an asset or the amount that would be received if the asset were sold to an outsider on the open market. *(p. 19)*

Fundamental accounting equation (Assets = Liabilities + Owner's Equity) An equation expressing the relationship of assets, liabilities, and owner's equity. *(p. 14)*

Liabilities Debts or amounts owed to creditors. *(p. 14)*

Manual accounting system An accounting system in which transactions are recorded by hand. *(p. 33)*

Owner's equity The owner's right to or investment in the business. *(p. 13)*

Revenues The amounts a business earns; examples are fees earned for performing services, sales of merchandise, rent income, and interest income. They may be in the form of cash, credit card receipts, or accounts receivable (charge accounts). *(p. 21)*

Separate entity concept The concept by which a business is treated as a separate economic or accounting entity. The business stands by itself, separate from its owners, creditors, and customers. *(p. 16)*

Sole proprietorship A one-owner business. *(p. 16)*

Withdrawal The taking of cash or other assets out of a business by the owner for his or her own use. (This is also referred to as drawing.) A withdrawal is treated as a decrease in owner's equity. *(p. 30)*

Quiz Yourself

_____ 1. _______ are properties or things of value owned and controlled by a business entity.
   a. Liabilities
   b. Owner's Equity
   c. Assets
   d. None of the above

_____ 2. Parish Tutoring Services has assets of $25,000 and liabilities of $10,000. What is the amount of owner's equity?
   a. $35,000
   b. $15,000
   c. $12,500
   d. $10,000

_____ 3. Which of the following accounts would increase owner's equity?
   a. Cash
   b. Accounts Payable
   c. Accounts Receivable
   d. Income from Tutoring

_____ 4. Which of the following statements is true?
   a. Every transaction is recorded as an increase and/or decrease in only one account.
   b. One side of the equation does not need to equal the other side of the equation.
   c. Double-entry accounting is demonstrated by the fact that each transaction must be recorded in at least two accounts.
   d. When a business earns revenue, owner's equity decreases.

_____ 5. M. Parish purchased supplies on credit. What is the impact on the accounting equation?
   a. Increase Supplies and decrease Cash.
   b. Increase Supplies Expense and increase Accounts Payable.
   c. Increase Supplies Expense and increase Accounts Receivable.
   d. Increase Supplies and increase Accounts Payable.

Answers:
1. c 2. b 3. d 4. c 5. d

Review It with QuickBooks®

_____ 1. Which of the following is *not* an advantage of a computerized accounting system?
   a. Security risks
   b. Timeliness
   c. Security measures
   d. Ease of use

_____ 2. The online version of QuickBooks is an example of cloud computing.
   a. True
   b. False

_____ 3. A QuickBooks file with the extension (.QBB) is
   a. a working file.
   b. a file stored in the cloud.
   c. a backup file.
   d. All of the above

_____ 4. Which file extension would indicate a QuickBooks working file?
   a. .QBB
   b. .QBX
   c. .QBW
   c. None of the above

Answers:
1. a 2. a 3. c 4. c

Chapter Assignments

Discussion Questions

1. Define *assets*, *liabilities*, *owner's equity*, *revenues*, and *expenses*.
2. Explain the separate entity concept.
3. How do Accounts Payable and Accounts Receivable differ?
4. Describe two ways to increase owner's equity and two ways to decrease owner's equity.
5. What is the effect on the fundamental accounting equation if supplies are purchased on account? How will the fundamental accounting equation change if supplies are purchased with cash? Explain how this purchase will or will not change the owner's equity.
6. When an owner withdraws cash or goods from the business, why is this considered an increase to the Drawing account and not an increase to the Wages Expense account?
7. Define *chart of accounts* and identify the categories of accounts.
8. What account titles would you suggest for the chart of accounts for a city touring company owned by W. Sanders? List the accounts by account category and include an appropriate account number for each.

Exercises

LO 1 — Practice Exercise 1

EXERCISE 1-1 Complete the following equations:

a. Assets of $40,000 = Liabilities of $17,200 + Owner's Equity of $_____
b. Assets of $_____ − Liabilities of $18,000 = Owner's Equity of $22,000
c. Assets of $27,000 − Owner's Equity of $15,000 = Liabilities of $_____

LO 1 — Practice Exercise 1

EXERCISE 1-2 Determine the following amounts:

a. The amount of the liabilities of a business that has $60,800 in assets and in which the owner has $34,500 equity.
b. The equity of the owner of a tour bus that cost $57,000 who owes $21,800 on an installment loan payable to the bank.
c. The amount of the assets of a business that has $11,780 in liabilities and in which the owner has $28,500 equity.

LO 1 — Practice Exercise 1

EXERCISE 1-3 Dr. L. M. Patton is an ophthalmologist. As of December 31, Dr. Patton owned the following property that related to his professional practice, Patton Eye Clinic:

Cash, $2,995 (A)
Professional Equipment, $63,000 (A)
Office Equipment, $8,450 (A)

On the same date, he owed the following business creditors:

Munez Supply Company, $3,816 (L)
Martin Equipment Sales, $3,728 (L)

Compute the following amounts in the accounting equation:

Assets $______ = Liabilities $______ + Owner's Equity $______

CHAPTER ASSIGNMENTS

LO 1, 3

Practice Exercises 1, 3

EXERCISE 1-4 Describe a business transaction that will do the following:

a. Increase an asset and increase a liability
b. Decrease an asset and decrease a liability
c. Decrease an asset and increase an expense
d. Increase an asset and increase owner's equity
e. Increase an asset and decrease an asset
f. Increase an asset and increase revenue

LO 2

Practice Exercise 2

EXERCISE 1-5 Describe a transaction that resulted in each of the following entries affecting the accounting equation.

	Assets					=	Liabilities	+	Owner's Equity
	Cash	+	Office Equipment	+	Professional Equipment	=	Accounts Payable	+	B. Lake, Capital
(a)	+18,200								+18,200
(b)	−1,375				+1,375				
Bal.	16,825			+	1,375	=			18,200
(c)			+640				+640		
Bal.	16,825	+	640	+	1,375	=	640	+	18,200
(d)	−2,200				+7,000		+4,800		
Bal.	14,625	+	640	+	8,375	=	5,440	+	18,200
(e)	−1,000						−1,000		
Bal.	13,625	+	640	+	8,375	=	4,440	+	18,200
			22,640					22,640	

LO 1, 3

Practice Exercises 1, 3

EXERCISE 1-6 Label each of the following accounts as asset (A), liability (L), owner's equity (OE), revenue (R), or expense (E).

a. Office Supplies
b. Professional Fees
c. Prepaid Insurance
d. R. Baker, Drawing
e. Accounts Payable
f. Service Income
g. R. Baker, Capital
h. Rent Expense
i. Accounts Receivable
j. Wages Expense

LO 2, 4

Practice Exercises 2, 4

EXERCISE 1-7 Describe a transaction that resulted in the following changes in accounts:

a. Rent Expense is increased by $1,050, and Cash is decreased by $1,050.
b. Advertising Expense is increased by $835, and Accounts Payable is increased by $835.
c. Accounts Receivable is increased by $372, and Service Income is increased by $372.

d. Cash is decreased by $410, and C. Tryon, Drawing, is increased by $410.
e. Equipment is increased by $1,850, Cash is decreased by $850, and Accounts Payable is increased by $1,000.
f. Cash is increased by $1,650, and Accounts Receivable is decreased by $1,650.

LO 2, 4

EXERCISE 1-8 Describe the transactions that are recorded in the following equation:

Practice Exercise 2, 4

	Assets					=	Liabilities	+	Owner's Equity						
	Cash	+	Accounts Receivable	+	Equipment	=	Accounts Payable	+	J. Onyx, Capital	−	J. Onyx, Drawing	+	Revenue	−	Expenses
(a)	+25,000				+4,500				+29,500						
(b)	−1,250														+1,250 (Rent Expense)
Bal.	23,750			+	4,500	=			29,500					−	1,250
(c)			+2,000										+2,000 (Income from Services)		
Bal.	23,750	+	2,000	+	4,500	=			29,500			+	2,000	−	1,250
(d)	−3,700				+16,000		+12,300								
Bal.	20,050	+	2,000	+	20,500	=	12,300	+	29,500			+	2,000	−	1,250
(e)	−2,500										+2,500				
Bal.	17,550	+	2,000	+	20,500	=	12,300	+	29,500	−	2,500	+	2,000	−	1,250
			40,050						40,050						

Problem Set A

PROBLEM 1-1A On June 1 of this year, J. Larkin, Optometrist, established the Larkin Eye Clinic. The clinic's account names are presented below. Transactions completed during the month follow.

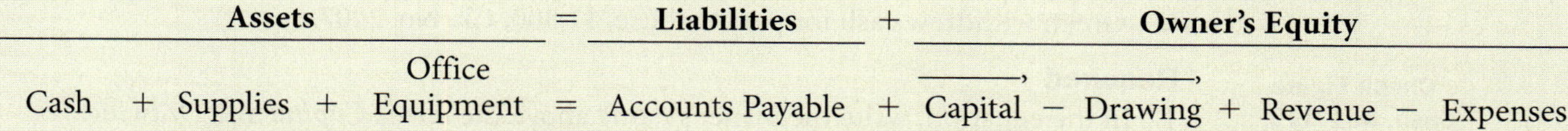

Assets					=	Liabilities	+	Owner's Equity						
Cash	+	Supplies	+	Office Equipment	=	Accounts Payable	+	______, Capital	−	______, Drawing	+	Revenue	−	Expenses

a. Larkin deposited $25,000 in a bank account in the name of the business.
b. Paid the office rent for the month, $950, Ck. No. 1001 (Rent Expense).
c. Bought supplies for cash, $357, Ck. No. 1002.

(Continued)

CHAPTER ASSIGNMENTS

d. Bought office equipment on account from NYC Office Equipment Store, $8,956.
e. Bought a computer from Warden's Office Outfitters, $1,636, paying $750 in cash and placing the balance on account, Ck. No. 1003.
f. Sold professional services for cash, $3,482 (Professional Fees).
g. Paid on account to Warden's Office Outfitters, $886, Ck. No. 1004.
h. Received and paid the bill for utilities, $382, Ck. No. 1005 (Utilities Expense).
i. Paid the salary of the assistant, $1,050, Ck. No. 1006 (Salary Expense).
j. Sold professional services for cash, $3,295 (Professional Fees).
k. Larkin withdrew cash for personal use, $1,250, Ck. No. 1007.

Check Figure
Left side of equals sign total, $37,101

Required

1. In the equation, write the owner's name above the terms *Capital* and *Drawing.*
2. Record the transactions and the balance after each transaction. Identify the account affected when the transaction involves revenues or expenses.
3. Write the account totals from the left side of the equals sign and add them. Write the account totals from the right side of the equals sign and add them. If the two totals are not equal, check the addition and subtraction. If you still cannot find the error, re-analyze each transaction.

PROBLEM 1-2A On July 1 of this year, R. Green established the Green Rehab Clinic. The organization's account headings are presented below. Transactions completed during the month of July follow.

Assets					=	Liabilities	+	Owner's Equity						
								______,		______,				
Cash	+ Supplies	+ Office Equipment	+	Professional Equipment	=	Accounts Payable	+	Capital	−	Drawing	+	Revenue	−	Expenses

a. Green deposited $30,000 in a bank account in the name of the business.
b. Paid the office rent for the month, $1,800, Ck. No. 2001 (Rent Expense).
c. Bought supplies for cash, $362, Ck. No. 2002.
d. Bought professional equipment on account from Rehab Equipment Company, $18,000.
e. Bought office equipment from Hi-Tech Computers, $2,890, paying $890 in cash and placing the balance on account, Ck. No. 2003.
f. Sold professional services for cash, $4,600 (Professional Fees).
g. Paid on account to Rehab Equipment Company, $700, Ck. No. 2004.
h. Received and paid the bill for utilities, $367, Ck. No. 2005 (Utilities Expense).
i. Paid the salary of the assistant, $1,150, Ck. No. 2006 (Salary Expense).
j. Sold professional services for cash, $3,868 (Professional Fees).
k. Green withdrew cash for personal use, $1,800, Ck. No. 2007.

Check Figure
Cash, $31,399

Required

1. In the equation, write the owner's name above the terms *Capital* and *Drawing.*
2. Record the transactions and the balance after each transaction. Identify the account affected when the transaction involves revenues or expenses.
3. Write the account totals from the left side of the equals sign and add them. Write the account totals from the right side of the equals sign and add them. If the two totals are not equal, check the addition and subtraction. If you still cannot find the error, re-analyze each transaction.

LO 1, 2, 3, 4

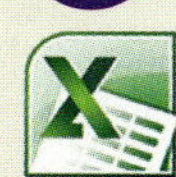

PROBLEM 1-3A S. Davis, a graphic artist, opened a studio for her professional practice on August 1. The account headings are presented below. Transactions completed during the month follow.

Assets					=	Liabilities	+	Owner's Equity			
Cash +	Supplies +	Prepaid Insurance +	Office Equipment +	Photo Equipment	=	Accounts Payable	+	______, Capital −	______, Drawing +	Revenue −	Expenses

a. Davis deposited $20,000 in a bank account in the name of the business.
b. Bought office equipment on account from Starkey Equipment Company, $4,120.
c. Davis invested her personal photographic equipment, $5,370. (Increase the account Photo Equipment and increase the account S. Davis, Capital.)
d. Paid the rent for the month, $1,500, Ck. No. 1000 (Rent Expense).
e. Bought supplies for cash, $215, Ck. No. 1001.
f. Bought insurance for two years, $1,840, Ck. No. 1002.
g. Sold graphic services for cash, $3,616 (Professional Fees).
h. Paid the salary of the part-time assistant, $982, Ck. No. 1003 (Salary Expense).
i. Received and paid the bill for telephone service, $134, Ck. No. 1004 (Telephone Expense).
j. Paid cash for minor repairs to graphics equipment, $185, Ck. No. 1005 (Repair Expense).
k. Sold graphic services for cash, $3,693 (Professional Fees).
l. Paid on account to Starkey Equipment Company, $650, Ck. No. 1006.
m. Davis withdrew cash for personal use, $1,800, Ck. No. 1007.

Required

1. In the equation, write the owner's name above the terms *Capital* and *Drawing*.
2. Record the transactions and the balance after each transaction. Identify the account affected when the transaction involves revenues or expenses.
3. Write the account totals from the left side of the equals sign and add them. Write the account totals from the right side of the equals sign and add them. If the two totals are not equal, check the addition and subtraction. If you still cannot find the error, re-analyze each transaction.

Check Figure
Right side of equals sign total, $31,548

LO 1, 2, 3, 4

PROBLEM 1-4A On March 1 of this year, B. Gervais established Gervais Catering Service. The account headings are presented below. Transactions completed during the month follow.

Assets						=	Liabilities	+	Owner's Equity			
Cash +	Accounts Receivable +	Supplies +	Prepaid Insurance +	Truck +	Catering Equipment	=	Accounts Payable	+	______, Capital −	______, Drawing +	Revenue −	Expenses

a. Gervais deposited $25,000 in a bank account in the name of the business.
b. Bought a truck from Kelly Motors for $26,329, paying $8,000 in cash and placing the balance on account, Ck. No. 500.
c. Bought catering equipment on account from Luigi's Equipment, $3,795.
d. Paid the rent for the month, $1,255, Ck. No. 501 (Rent Expense).
e. Bought insurance for the truck for one year, $400, Ck. No. 502.
f. Sold catering services for cash for the first half of the month, $3,012 (Catering Income).

(*Continued*)

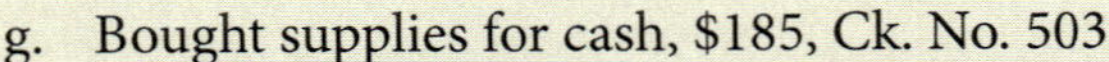

g. Bought supplies for cash, $185, Ck. No. 503.
h. Sold catering services on account, $4,307 (Catering Income).
i. Received and paid the heating bill, $248, Ck. No. 504 (Utilities Expense).
j. Received a bill from GC Gas and Lube for gas and oil for the truck, $128 (Gas and Oil Expense).
k. Sold catering services for cash for the remainder of the month, $2,649 (Catering Income).
l. Gervais withdrew cash for personal use, $1,550, Ck. No. 505.
m. Paid the salary of the assistant, $1,150, Ck. No. 506 (Salary Expense).

Check Figure
Cash, $17,873

Required

1. In the equation, write the owner's name above the terms *Capital* and *Drawing*.
2. Record the transactions and the balance after each transaction. Identify the account affected when the transaction involves revenues or expenses.
3. Write the account totals from the left side of the equals sign and add them. Write the account totals from the right side of the equals sign and add them. If the two totals are not equal, check the addition and subtraction. If you still cannot find the error, re-analyze each transaction.

 **LO 1, 2, 3, 4**

PROBLEM 1-5A In April, J. Rodriguez established an apartment rental service. The account headings are presented below. Transactions completed during the month of April follow.

Assets						=	Liabilities	+	Owner's Equity			
Cash +	Accounts Receivable +	Supplies +	Prepaid Insurance +	Truck +	Office Equipment	=	Accounts Payable	+	______, Capital −	______, Drawing +	Revenue −	Expenses

a. Rodriguez deposited $70,000 in a bank account in the name of the business.
b. Paid the rent for the month, $2,000, Ck. No. 101 (Rent Expense).
c. Bought supplies on account, $150.
d. Bought a truck for $23,500, paying $2,500 in cash and placing the remainder on account.
e. Bought insurance for the truck for the year, $2,400, Ck. No. 102.
f. Sold services on account, $4,700 (Service Income).
g. Bought office equipment on account from Stern Office Supply, $1,250.
h. Sold services for cash for the first half of the month, $8,250 (Service Income).
i. Received and paid the bill for utilities, $280, Ck. No. 103 (Utilities Expense).
j. Received a bill for gas and oil for the truck, $130 (Gas and Oil Expense).
k. Paid wages to the employees, $2,680, Ck. Nos. 104–106 (Wages Expense).
l. Sold services for cash for the remainder of the month, $3,500 (Service Income).
m. Rodriguez withdrew cash for personal use, $4,000, Ck. No. 107.

Check Figure
Cash, $67,890

Required

1. In the equation, write the owner's name above the terms *Capital* and *Drawing*.
2. Record the transactions and the balance after each transaction. Identify the account affected when the transaction involves revenues or expenses.
3. Write the account totals from the left side of the equals sign and add them. Write the account totals from the right side of the equals sign and add them. If the two totals are not equal, check the addition and subtraction. If you still cannot find the error, re-analyze each transaction.

Problem Set B

LO 1, 2, 3, 4

PROBLEM 1-1B In July of this year, M. Wallace established a business called Wallace Realty. The account headings are presented below. Transactions completed during the month follow.

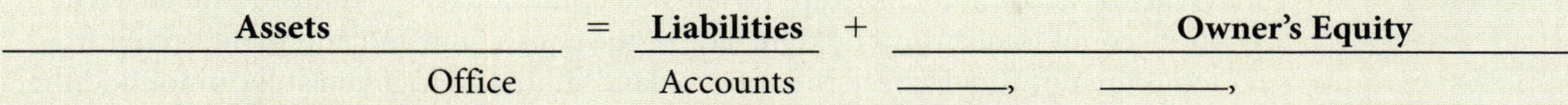

Assets			=	Liabilities	+	Owner's Equity						
		Office		Accounts		______,		______,				
Cash +	Supplies +	Equipment	=	Payable	+	Capital	−	Drawing	+	Revenue	−	Expenses

a. Wallace deposited $24,000 in a bank account in the name of the business.

b. Paid the office rent for the current month, $650, Ck. No. 1000 (Rent Expense).
c. Bought office supplies for cash, $375, Ck. No. 1001.
d. Bought office equipment on account from Dellos Computers, $6,300.
e. Received a bill from the *City Crier* for advertising, $455 (Advertising Expense).
f. Sold services for cash, $3,944 (Service Income).
g. Paid on account to Dellos Computers, $1,500, Ck. No. 1002.
h. Received and paid the bill for utilities, $340, Ck. No. 1003 (Utilities Expense).
i. Paid on account to the *City Crier*, $455, Ck. No. 1004.
j. Paid truck expenses, $435, Ck. No. 1005 (Truck Maintenance Expense).
k. Wallace withdrew cash for personal use, $1,500, Ck. No. 1006.

Required

1. In the equation, write the owner's name above the terms *Capital* and *Drawing*.
2. Record the transactions and the balance after each transaction. Identify the account affected when the transaction involves revenues or expenses.
3. Write the account totals from the left side of the equals sign and add them. Write the account totals from the right side of the equals sign and add them. If the two totals are not equal, check the addition and subtraction. If you still cannot find the error, re-analyze each transaction.

Check Figure
Left side of equals sign total, $29,364

LO 1, 2, 3, 4

PROBLEM 1-2B In March, K. Haas, M.D., established the Haas Sports Injury Clinic. The clinic's account headings are presented below. Transactions completed during the month of March follow.

Assets				=	Liabilities	+	Owner's Equity						
		Office	Professional		Accounts		______,		______,				
Cash +	Supplies +	Equipment +	Equipment	=	Payable	+	Capital	−	Drawing	+	Revenue	−	Expenses

a. Haas deposited $48,000 in a bank account in the name of the business.
b. Paid the rent for the month, $2,200, Ck. No. 1000 (Rent Expense).
c. Bought supplies for cash from Medco Co., $2,138.
d. Bought professional equipment on account from Med-Tech Company, $18,000.
e. Bought office equipment on account from Equipment Depot, $1,955.
f. Sold professional services for cash, $8,960 (Professional Fees).
g. Paid on account to Med-Tech Company, $3,000, Ck. No. 1001.
h. Received and paid the bill for utilities, $472, Ck. No. 1002 (Utilities Expense).
i. Paid the salary of the assistant, $1,738, Ck. No. 1003 (Salary Expense).

(*Continued*)

CHAPTER ASSIGNMENTS

j. Sold professional services for cash, $10,196 (Professional Fees).
k. Haas withdrew cash for personal use, $3,500, Ck. No. 1004.

Check Figure
Cash, $54,108

Required

1. In the equation, write the owner's name above the terms *Capital* and *Drawing*.
2. Record the transactions and the balance after each transaction. Identify the account affected when the transaction involves revenue, expenses, or a withdrawal.
3. Write the account totals from the left side of the equals sign and add them. Write the account totals from the right side of the equals sign and add them. If the two totals are not equal, check the addition and subtraction. If you still cannot find the error, re-analyze each transaction.

LO 1, 2, 3, 4

PROBLEM 1-3B P. Schwartz, Attorney at Law, opened his office on October 1. The account headings are presented below. Transactions completed during the month follow.

Assets					=	Liabilities	+	Owner's Equity			
		Prepaid	Office			Accounts		______,	______,		
Cash +	Supplies +	Insurance +	Equipment +	Library	=	Payable	+	Capital −	Drawing +	Revenue −	Expenses

a. Schwartz deposited $25,000 in a bank account in the name of the business.
b. Bought office equipment on account from QuipCo, $9,670.
c. Schwartz invested his personal law library, which cost $2,800.
d. Paid the office rent for the month, $1,700, Ck. No. 2000 (Rent Expense).
e. Bought office supplies for cash, $418, Ck. No. 2001.
f. Bought insurance for two years, $944, Ck. No. 2002.
g. Sold legal services for cash, $8,518 (Professional Fees).
h. Paid the salary of the part-time receptionist, $1,820, Ck. No. 2003 (Salary Expense).
i. Received and paid the telephone bill, $388, Ck. No. 2004 (Telephone Expense).
j. Received and paid the bill for utilities, $368, Ck. No. 2005 (Utilities Expense).
k. Sold legal services for cash, $9,260 (Professional Fees).
l. Paid on account to QuipCo, $2,670, Ck. No. 2006.
m. Schwartz withdrew cash for personal use, $2,500, Ck. No. 2007.

Check Figure
Right side of equals sign total, $45,802

Required

1. In the equation, write the owner's name above the terms *Capital* and *Drawing*.
2. Record the transactions and the balance after each transaction. Identify the account affected when the transaction involves revenues or expenses.
3. Write the account totals from the left side of the equals sign and add them. Write the account totals from the right side of the equals sign and add them. If the two totals are not equal, check the addition and subtraction. If you still cannot find the error, re-analyze each transaction.

LO 1, 2, 3, 4

PROBLEM 1-4B In March, T. Carter established Carter Delivery Service. The account headings are presented below. Transactions completed during the month of March follow.

Assets						=	Liabilities	+	Owner's Equity			
	Accounts		Prepaid				Accounts		______,	______,		
Cash +	Receivable +	Supplies +	Insurance +	Truck +	Equipment	=	Payable	+	Capital −	Drawing +	Revenue −	Expenses

a. Carter deposited $25,000 in a bank account in the name of the business.
b. Bought a used truck from Degroot Motors for $15,140, paying $5,140 in cash and placing the remainder on account.

c. Bought equipment on account from Flemming Company, $3,450.
d. Paid the rent for the month, $1,000, Ck. No. 3001 (Rent Expense).
e. Sold services for cash for the first half of the month, $6,927 (Service Income).
f. Bought supplies for cash, $301, Ck. No. 3002.
g. Bought insurance for the truck for the year, $1,200, Ck. No. 3003.
h. Received and paid the bill for utilities, $349, Ck. No. 3004 (Utilities Expense).
i. Received a bill for gas and oil for the truck, $218 (Gas and Oil Expense).
j. Sold services on account, $3,603 (Service Income).
k. Sold services for cash for the remainder of the month, $4,612 (Service Income).
l. Paid wages to the employees, $3,958, Ck. Nos. 3005–3007 (Wages Expense).
m. Carter withdrew cash for personal use, $1,250, Ck. No. 3008.

Required

Check Figure
Cash, $23,341

1. In the equation, write the owner's name above the terms *Capital* and *Drawing*.
2. Record the transactions and the balance after each transaction. Identify the account affected when the transaction involves revenues or expenses.
3. Write the account totals from the left side of the equals sign and add them. Write the account totals from the right side of the equals sign and add them. If the two totals are not equal, check the addition and subtraction. If you still cannot find the error, re-analyze each transaction.

LO 1, 2, 3, 4

PROBLEM 1-5B In October, A. Nguyen established an apartment rental service. The account headings are presented below. Transactions completed during the month of October follow.

Assets						=	Liabilities	+	Owner's Equity			
Cash	+ Accounts Receivable	+ Supplies	+ Prepaid Insurance	+ Truck	+ Office Equipment	=	Accounts Payable	+	______, Capital	− ______, Drawing	+ Revenue	− Expenses

a. Nguyen deposited $25,000 in a bank account in the name of the business.
b. Paid the rent for the month, $1,200, Ck. No. 2015 (Rent Expense).
c. Bought supplies on account, $225.
d. Bought a truck for $18,000, paying $1,000 in cash and placing the remainder on account.
e. Bought insurance for the truck for the year, $1,400, Ck. No. 2016.
f. Sold services on account, $5,000 (Service Income).
g. Bought office equipment on account from Henry Office Supply, $2,300.
h. Sold services for cash for the first half of the month, $6,050 (Service Income).
i. Received and paid the bill for utilities, $150, Ck. No. 2017 (Utilities Expense).
j. Received a bill for gas and oil for the truck, $80 (Gas and Oil Expense).
k. Paid wages to the employees, $1,400, Ck. Nos. 2018–2020 (Wages Expense).
l. Sold services for cash for the remainder of the month, $4,200 (Service Income).
m. Nguyen withdrew cash for personal use, $2,000, Ck. No. 2021.

Required

Check Figure
Cash, $28,100

1. In the equation, write the owner's name above the terms *Capital* and *Drawing*.
2. Record the transactions and the balance after each transaction. Identify the account affected when the transaction involves revenues or expenses.
3. Write the account totals from the left side of the equals sign and add them. Write the account totals from the right side of the equals sign and add them. If the two totals are not equal, check the addition and subtraction. If you still cannot find the error, re-analyze each transaction.

Try It with QuickBooks® (LO 2-7)

QB Exercise 1-1

Install and register the trial version of QuickBooks that came with your text following the steps on pages 34 and 35.
(If you are using a classroom computer with QuickBooks, skip this step.)

1. From the textbook website, CengageBrain.com, locate the QuickBooks data file for Conner's Whitewater Adventures labeled **Student_Data_CH1.QBB**.
2. Save **Student_Data_CH1.QBB** to your computer.
3. Restore the **Student_Data_CH1.QBB** file in QuickBooks.
4. Add your name to the company name (first name, last name) or as directed by your instructor.
5. Locate and open Conner's Whitewater Adventures' chart of accounts.
6. Answer the following questions from the chart of accounts:
   a. The revenue account 411—Income from Tours is identified as what type of account in QuickBooks?
   b. Account 111—Cash is an asset. What type of account is cash identified as in QuickBooks?
   c. What is the account number for J. Conner, Drawing?
   d. Accounts Receivable is an asset. What account type is assigned to this account in QuickBooks?
7. Back up the **Student_Data_CH1.QBW** file to your flash drive or backup device.
8. Close Conner's Whitewater Adventures.
9. Exit QuickBooks.

Activities

Why Does It Matter?

MAC'S CUSTOM CATERING, Eugene, Oregon

Mac's Custom Catering, an award-winning catering business located in Eugene, Oregon, specializes in providing "only the best for you and your guest." Mac's Custom Catering has been in business for over 30 years and is experienced in providing catering services at weddings, corporate events, and large sit-down events. It offers several signature buffet options, including "Northwest Bounty," "Hawaiian Luau," and "Italian Fest."

Imagine that you have been hired to set up the accounting system for a catering business such as Mac's. What accounts would be included in the chart of accounts? As you list the accounts, identify the type of account. Is the account an asset, a liability, or owner's equity?

What Would You Say?

A friend of yours wants to start her own pet-sitting business. She already has a business license that is required in her city. She has had a personal checking account for years. You have told her that she also needs to open a separate account for her business needs, but she does not understand why she needs to have two separate accounts. Explain to her why she should have a business account separate from her personal account. Use some of the language of business you have learned in your text's Introduction and in this chapter.

What Do You Think?

Read the following memorandum and provide the requested information.

MEMORANDUM

TO: Your Name
FROM: J. Perrault, Supervisor

DATE: July 31, 20--
SUBJECT: Calculations for Richter Co.

Please provide the following information ASAP (as soon as possible).

1. The balance of cash in Richter Company's checkbook shows $13,364. I need to know if this ties to or matches the Cash account balance. I do know that total assets amount to $43,560; Office Equipment amounts to $3,896; and other noncash assets are Professional Equipment, $24,375 and Prepaid Insurance, $1,925.
2. D. Richter, the owner, wants to know the amount of his owner's equity. I pulled the outstanding bills, which amount to $7,942.

Please put the information in a memo addressed to me. Thank you for your prompt response.

T Accounts, Debits and Credits, Trial Balance, and Financial Statements

Learning Objectives

After you have completed this chapter, you will be able to do the following:

1. Determine balances of T accounts.
2. Present the fundamental accounting equation using the T account form and label the plus and minus sides.
3. Present the fundamental accounting equation using the T account form and label the debit and credit sides.
4. Record directly in T accounts a group of business transactions involving changes in asset, liability, owner's equity, revenue, and expense accounts for a service business.
5. Prepare a trial balance.
6. Prepare (a) an income statement, (b) a statement of owner's equity, and (c) a balance sheet.
7. Recognize the effect of errors on account balances.

To: **Amy Roberts, CPA**
Subject: **What's Next?**

Hi Amy,
I feel as though I have a good understanding of what accounting is and what the different types of accounts are. I found some flashcards online and have been quizzing myself with the account names and types. I'm getting pretty good! I've also been practicing recording transactions in the column form.
I think I'm now ready to learn something new. After I record transactions in the column form, what happens next? Am I ready to start using QuickBooks?
Thanks,
Janie

To: **Janie Conner**
Subject: **RE: What's Next?**

Hi Janie,
Using the flashcards was a great idea! It's very important that you recognize the accounts and know whether each is an asset, a liability, or an owner's equity account. We're going to use that knowledge for this next challenge.
So here's your list of things to tackle:

_____ 1. Understand what debits and credits are and be able to apply each to the fundamental accounting equation.

_____ 2. Begin recording transactions in T accounts using debits and credits.

This is a lot to learn, but I know that with practice, you'll be successful!
You are not quite ready to record entries in QuickBooks yet, but you can review how to prepare financial reports with QuickBooks. You can use the demonstration file I previously sent you to practice.
Amy

Accounting Language

Balance sheet (p. 78)
Compound entry (p. 71)
Credit (p. 62)
Debit (p. 62)
Financial position (p. 78)
Financial statement (p. 76)
Footings (p. 60)
Income statement (p. 76)
Net income (p. 76)
Net loss (p. 76)
Normal balance (p. 60)
PDF (portable document format) (p. 85)
Profit and loss statement (p. 83)
Report form (p. 78)
Slide (p. 80)
Statement of owner's equity (p. 77)
T account form (p. 59)
Transposition (p. 80)
Trial balance (p. 75)

In the previous chapter, we introduced the fundamental accounting equation as *Assets = Liabilities + Owner's Equity*. We learned that the fundamental accounting equation includes five account classifications: Assets, Liabilities, Owner's Equity, Revenue, and Expenses. These are the only five classifications in accounting; so whether you are dealing with a small, one-owner business or a large corporation, you will encounter only these five major classifications of accounts. We also discussed the recording of transactions in the column form.

In this chapter, we will record the same transactions from Chapter 1 in T account form and prove the equality of both sides of the fundamental accounting equation using a trial balance. Before we begin, take a moment to review the transactions from Chapter 1 on pages 16–31.

THE T ACCOUNT FORM

In Chapter 1, we recorded business transactions in a column arrangement, which had the following advantages:

1. **In the process of analyzing the transaction, you**
   a. Recognized the need to determine which accounts were involved.
   b. Determined the classification of the accounts involved.
   c. Decided whether the transaction resulted in an increase or a decrease in each of these accounts.
2. **You further realized that after each transaction was recorded, the two sides of the fundamental accounting equation were in balance. In other words, the total of one side of the accounting equation equaled the total of the other side.**

Now instead of recording transactions in a column for each account, we will use a **T account form** for each account. *The T account form has the advantage of providing two sides for each account; one side is used to record increases in the account, and the other side is used to record decreases.* Notice that the Cash account column in the books of Conner's Whitewater Adventures (used in Chapter 1) and the new Cash T account have been presented on the next page. The results are identical. It's just a different way of presenting the same information.

Learning Objective

1 Determine balances of T accounts.

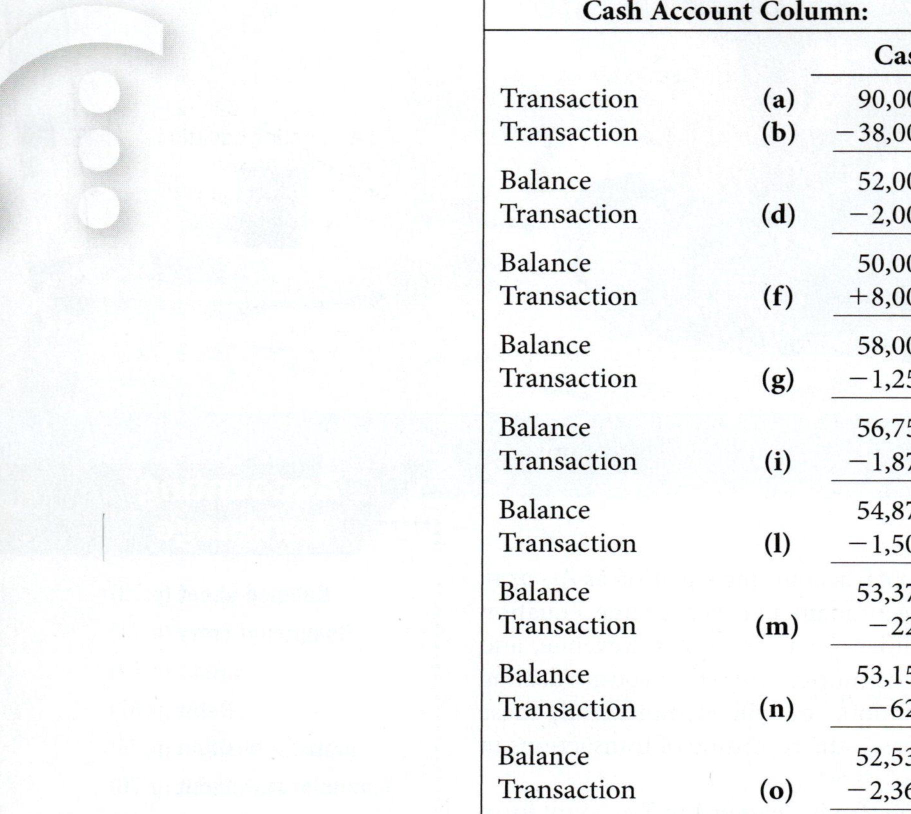

Cash Account Column:

		Cash
Transaction	(a)	90,000
Transaction	(b)	−38,000
Balance		52,000
Transaction	(d)	−2,000
Balance		50,000
Transaction	(f)	+8,000
Balance		58,000
Transaction	(g)	−1,250
Balance		56,750
Transaction	(i)	−1,875
Balance		54,875
Transaction	(l)	−1,500
Balance		53,375
Transaction	(m)	−225
Balance		53,150
Transaction	(n)	−620
Balance		52,530
Transaction	(o)	−2,360
Balance		50,170
Transaction	(p)	−1,850
Balance		48,320
Transaction	(q)	+2,500
Balance		50,820
Transaction	(r)	+8,570
Balance		59,390
Transaction	(s)	−3,500
		55,890

Cash T Account:

Cash	+		−
(a)	90,000	(b)	38,000
(f)	8,000	(d)	2,000
(q)	2,500	(g)	1,250
(r)	8,570	(i)	1,875
	109,070	(l)	1,500
		(m)	225
		(n)	620
		(o)	2,360
Footings		(p)	1,850
		(s)	3,500
			53,180
Bal.	**55,890**		

Steps to calculate balance in T Accounts:

STEP 1. Add each side separately and record the totals (called footings).

90,000 + 8,000 + 2,500 + 8,570 = 109,070
38,000 + 2,000 + 1,250 + 1,875 + 1,500 + 225 + 620 + 2,360 + 1,850 + 3,500 = 53,180

STEP 2. Large footing − Small footing = Balance

109,070 − 53,180 = 55,890

STEP 3. Place the balance (from Step 2) on the large footing side and double-underline it.

55,890 goes on the same side as 109,070.

After we record a group of transactions in a T account, we add both sides and record the totals, called **footings**. Next, we subtract one footing from the other to determine the balance of the account. For the Cash account, shown previously, the balance is $55,890 ($109,070 – $53,180).

We now record the balance on the side of the account having the larger footing, which, with a few minor exceptions, is the plus (+) side. The plus side of a T account is the side that represents the **normal balance** of that account. However, depending on the type of account, the normal balance may fall on either the left or right side of an account.

THE T ACCOUNT FORM WITH PLUS AND MINUS SIDES

To review, we presented the T account for Cash. Cash is classified as an asset account, and all asset accounts look like the following T account:

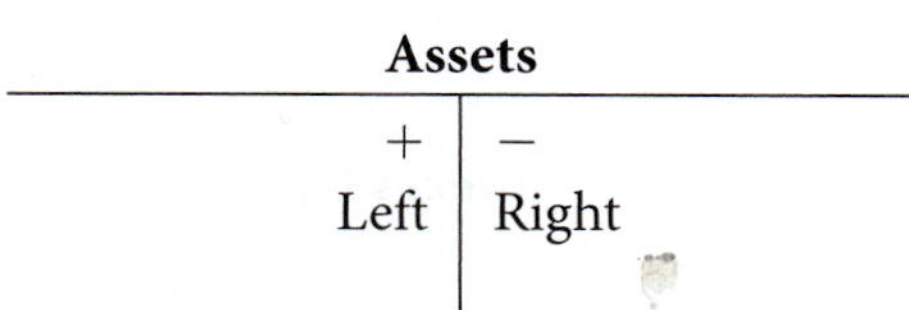

Learning Objective 2 Present the fundamental accounting equation using the T account form and label the plus and minus sides.

However, **not all classifications of accounts have the increase side on the left.** Liability accounts are on the other side of the fundamental accounting equation. So their increase and decrease are opposite those of assets. Liabilities are increased on the right side and decreased on the left side. All liabilities look like the following T account:

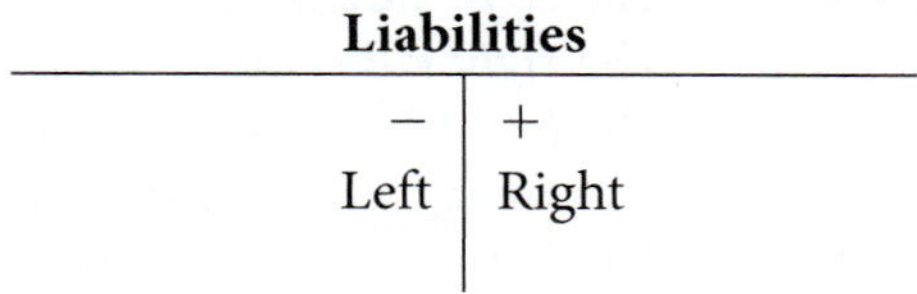

Owner's equity is similar to liabilities. Increases in owner's equity are recorded on the right side of the account. Decreases in owner's equity are recorded on the left side of the account.

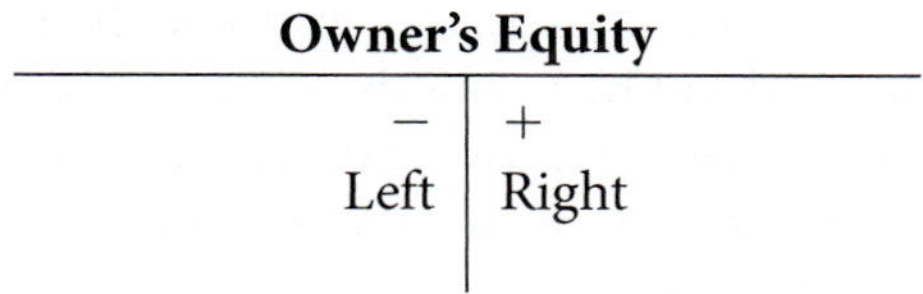

Recall that we placed capital, drawing, revenue, and expenses under the umbrella of owner's equity. Capital and revenue increase owner's equity, and drawing and expenses decrease owner's equity. The T accounts for this situation are as follows:

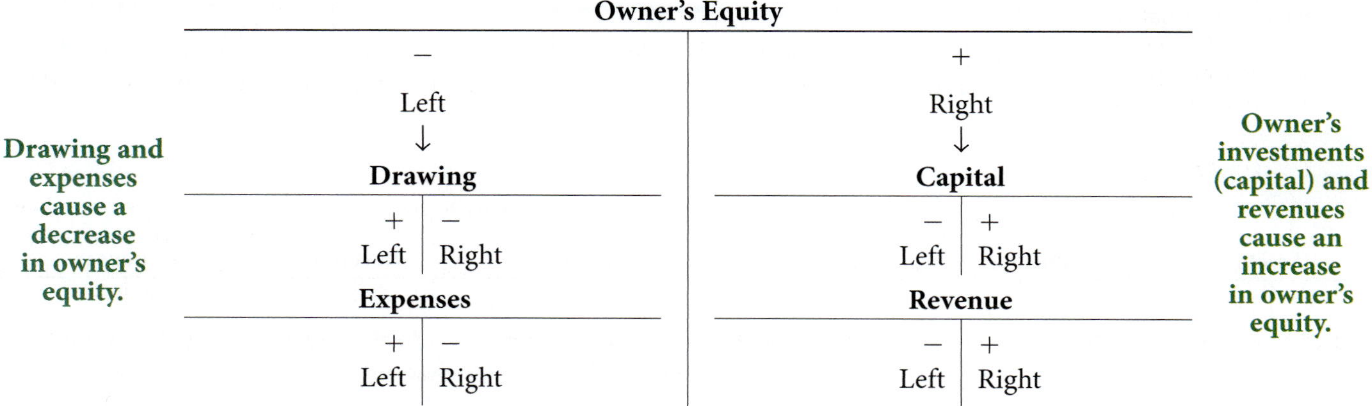

Increases in owner's equity are recorded on the right side of the account. Because capital and revenue increase owner's equity, additions are recorded on the right side.

Decreases in owner's equity are recorded on the left side of the account. Because drawing and expenses decrease owner's equity, additions to drawing and expenses are recorded on the left side.

We can now restate the equation with the T account forms and plus and minus signs for each account classification.

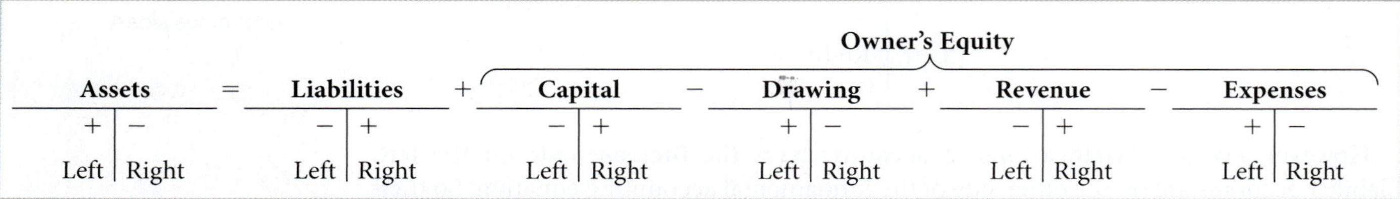

Assets	**The *left* side is the *increase* side.**
Liabilities	**The *right* side is the *increase* side.**
Capital	**The *right* side is the *increase* side.**
Drawing	**The *left* side is the *increase* side.**
Revenue	**The *right* side is the *increase* side.**
Expenses	**The *left* side is the *increase* side.**

Your accounting background up to this point has taught you to analyze business transactions to determine which accounts are involved and to recognize that each amount should be recorded as an increase or a decrease in these accounts. Now the recording process becomes a simple matter of knowing which side of the T accounts should be used to record increases and which should be used to record decreases. **Generally, you will not be using the minus side of the capital, drawing, revenue, and expense accounts because transactions involving these accounts usually result in increases in the accounts.** An exception to this statement is where errors have been made and require correction. Now let's add the last element to the T account before we record the familiar Conner's Whitewater Adventures transactions.

Learning Objective 3 Present the fundamental accounting equation using the T account form and label the debit and credit sides.

THE T ACCOUNT FORM WITH DEBITS AND CREDITS

The left side of a T account is called the **debit** side; the right side is called the **credit** side. The T accounts representing the accounting equation now contain both the signs and the words *Debit* and *Credit.*

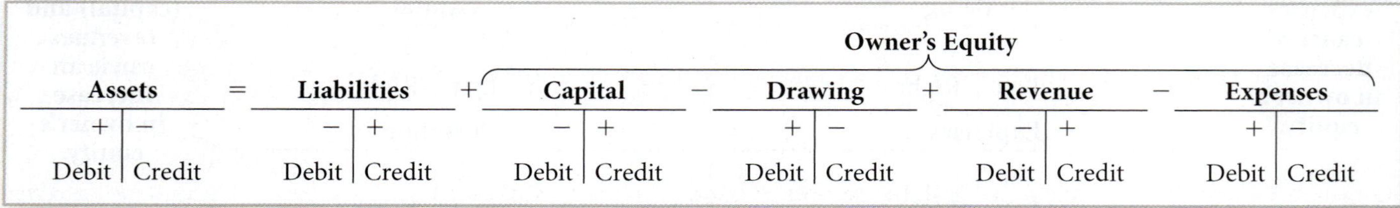

The following table summarizes debits and credits and the way they are affected by increases and decreases. **The critical rule to remember is that the amount placed on the debit side of one or more accounts *must* equal the amount placed on the credit side of another account or other accounts.**

Debits Signify		Credits Signify	
Increases in	Assets Drawing Expenses	Decreases in	Assets Drawing Expenses
Decreases in	Liabilities Capital Revenue	Increases in	Liabilities Capital Revenue

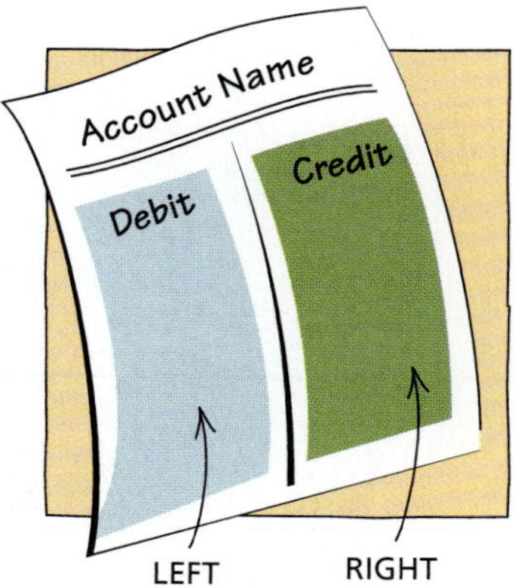

Debit is always the left side of the account, and credit is always the right side of the account. However, the + or − changes with the type of account.

RECORDING BUSINESS TRANSACTIONS IN T ACCOUNTS

Our task now is to learn how to record business transactions in the T account form. First, let's review the steps we've learned so far (Steps 1–3) in analyzing a business transaction. Then we will introduce a new step (Step 4).

Learning Objective 4 Record directly in T accounts a group of business transactions involving changes in asset, liability, owner's equity, revenue, and expense accounts for a service business.

STEP 1. What accounts are involved?

STEP 2. What are the classifications of the accounts involved (asset, liability, capital, drawing, revenue, expense)?

STEP 3. Are the accounts increased or decreased?

STEP 4. Write the transaction as a debit to one account (or accounts) and a credit to another account (or accounts).

STEP 5. Is the equation in balance after the transaction has been recorded?

For example, let's analyze the first transaction of the Conner's Whitewater Adventures transactions using this new five-step process. To formulate the entry, you must be able to visualize the fundamental accounting equation in the form of T accounts. With that in mind, the first transaction is as follows:

In transaction (a), Conner deposited $90,000 in a bank account in the name of the business. This transaction results in an increase to Cash with a debit and an increase in the Capital account with a credit.

Remember

A business is always treated as a separate economic entity—separate and independent from its owner(s). Notice that we only say "J. Conner" for transactions involving owner investments or drawing. For all other transactions, it is Conner's Whitewater Adventures that is involved in the transaction.

STEP 1. **What accounts are involved?** The two accounts involved are Cash and J. Conner, Capital.

STEP 2. **What are the classifications of the accounts involved?** Cash is an asset account, and J. Conner, Capital, is an owner's equity account.

STEP 3. **Are the accounts increased or decreased?** Cash is being deposited in the bank account, an increase to Cash. The owner has invested that cash in the business and has increased J. Conner, Capital.

STEP 4. **Write the transaction as a debit to one account (or accounts) and a credit to another account (or accounts).** Because Cash is an asset account and Cash is increased, Cash is debited. We now need an offsetting credit. J. Conner, Capital, is an owner's equity account and is increased. Thus, J. Conner, Capital, is credited.

STEP 5. Is the equation in balance after the transaction has been recorded? At least one account is debited, and at least one account is credited. And the total amount(s) debited equals the total amount(s) credited. You now have a debit equal to a credit, a $90,000 debit to Cash and a $90,000 credit to J. Conner, Capital.

The resulting transaction in T account form follows.

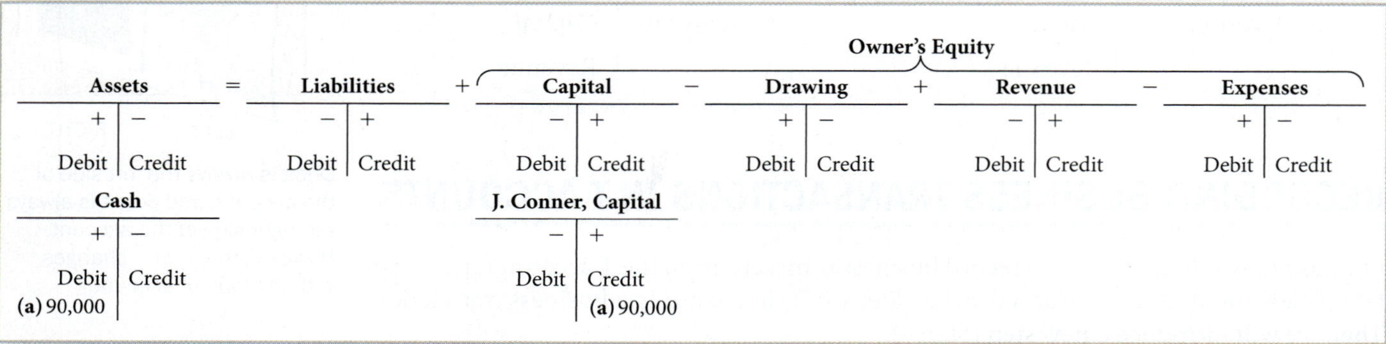

Let's go through the rest of the transactions for Conner's Whitewater Adventures. Because we already worked through Steps 1–3 in Chapter 1, we will discuss only Steps 4 and 5. In transaction (b), Conner's Whitewater Adventures bought equipment, paying cash, $38,000.

STEP 4. Write the transaction as a debit to one account (or accounts) and a credit to another account (or accounts).

This transaction results in an increase to Equipment with a debit and a decrease to Cash with a credit.

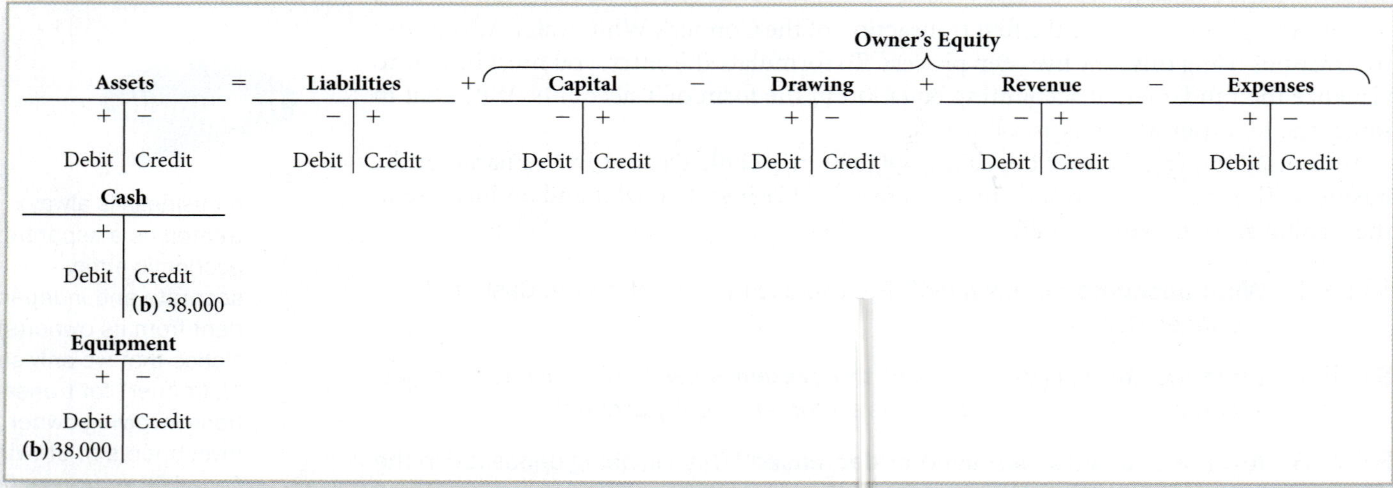

In transaction (c), Conner's Whitewater Adventures bought equipment on account from Signal Products, $4,320.

STEP 4. Write the transaction as a debit to one account (or accounts) and a credit to another account (or accounts).

This transaction results in an increase to Equipment with a debit and an increase to Accounts Payable with a credit.

				Owner's Equity						
Assets	=	**Liabilities**	+	**Capital**	−	**Drawing**	+	**Revenue**	−	**Expenses**
+ / −		− / +		− / +		+ / −		− / +		+ / −
Debit / Credit		Debit / Credit		Debit / Credit		Debit / Credit		Debit / Credit		Debit / Credit
Equipment		**Accounts Payable**								
+ / −		− / +								
Debit / Credit		Debit / Credit								
(c) 4,320 /		/ (c) 4,320								

In transaction (d), Conner's Whitewater Adventures paid Signal Products, a creditor, $2,000.

STEP 4. Write the transaction as a debit to one account (or accounts) and a credit to another account (or accounts).

This transaction results in a decrease to Cash with a credit and a decrease to Accounts Payable with a debit.

				Owner's Equity						
Assets	=	**Liabilities**	+	**Capital**	−	**Drawing**	+	**Revenue**	−	**Expenses**
+ / −		− / +		− / +		+ / −		− / +		+ / −
Debit / Credit		Debit / Credit		Debit / Credit		Debit / Credit		Debit / Credit		Debit / Credit
Cash		**Accounts Payable**								
+ / −		− / +								
Debit / Credit		Debit / Credit								
/ (d) 2,000		(d) 2,000 /								

In transaction (e), J. Conner invests her personal computer, with a fair market value of $5,200, in the business.

STEP 4. Write the transaction as a debit to one account (or accounts) and a credit to another account (or accounts).

Equipment, an asset account, increases and is recorded with a debit. J. Conner, Capital, owner's equity, increases and is recorded with a credit.

				Owner's Equity						
Assets	=	**Liabilities**	+	**Capital**	−	**Drawing**	+	**Revenue**	−	**Expenses**
+ / −		− / +		− / +		+ / −		− / +		+ / −
Debit / Credit		Debit / Credit		Debit / Credit		Debit / Credit		Debit / Credit		Debit / Credit
Equipment				**J. Conner, Capital**						
+ / −				− / +						
Debit / Credit				Debit / Credit						
(e) 5,200 /				/ (e) 5,200						

Here is a restatement of the accounts after recording transactions (a) through (e). To test your understanding of the process, look at each transaction and describe what happened.

Footings or subtotals are required to compute the balances of the accounts. The balances are written in the accounts on the side with the larger total.

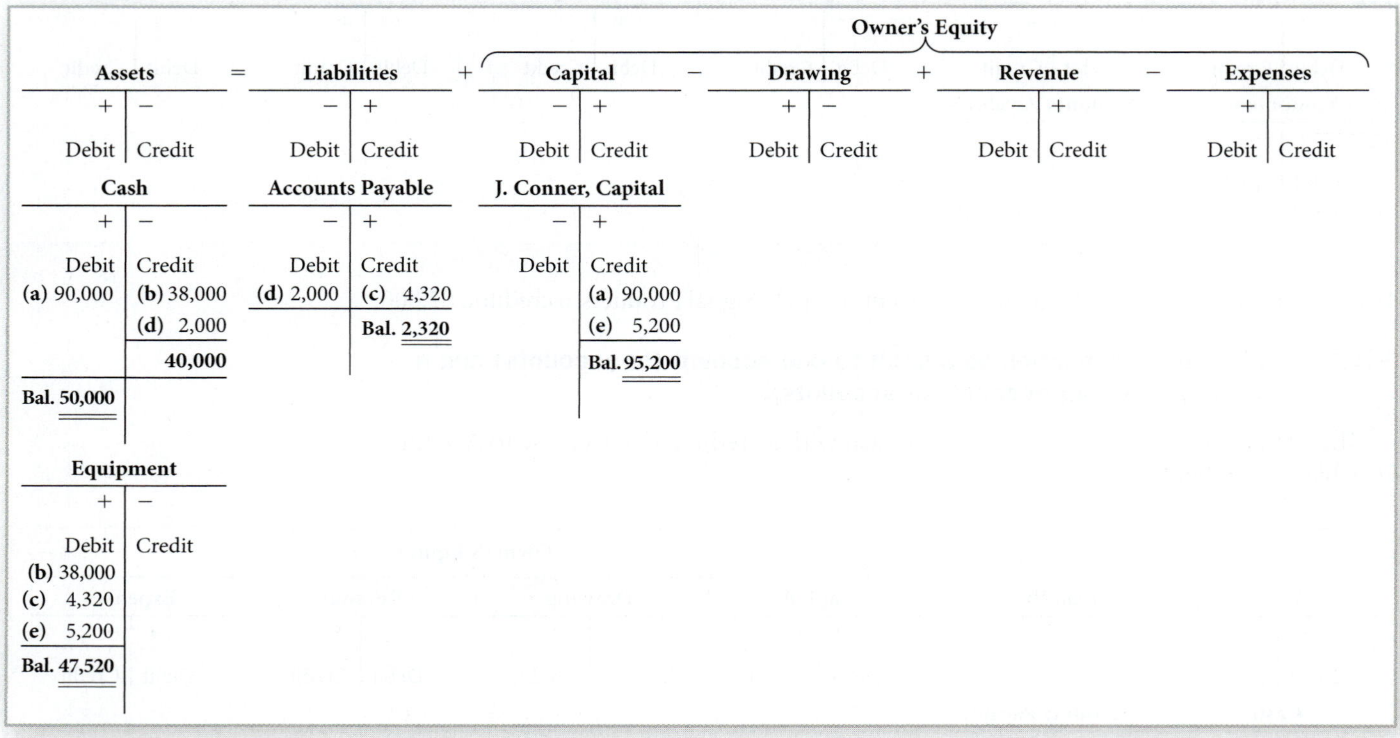

Let's pause to see if the debits are equal to the credits by listing the balances of the accounts.

STEP 5. Is the equation in balance after the transaction has been recorded?

Yes, the equation is in balance as shown below.

Account Name	Accounts with Normal Balances on the Left, or Debit, Side Assets Drawing Expenses	Accounts with Normal Balances on the Right, or Credit, Side Liabilities Capital Revenue
Cash	$50,000	
Equipment	47,520	
Accounts Payable		$ 2,320
J. Conner, Capital		95,200
	$97,520	$97,520

The normal balance of an account classification is on the plus side of the T account.

In transaction (f), Conner's Whitewater Adventures sold rafting tours for cash, $8,000.

STEP 4. Write the transaction as a debit to one account (or accounts) and a credit to another account (or accounts).

This transaction results in an increase to Cash with a debit and an increase to Income from Tours with a credit.

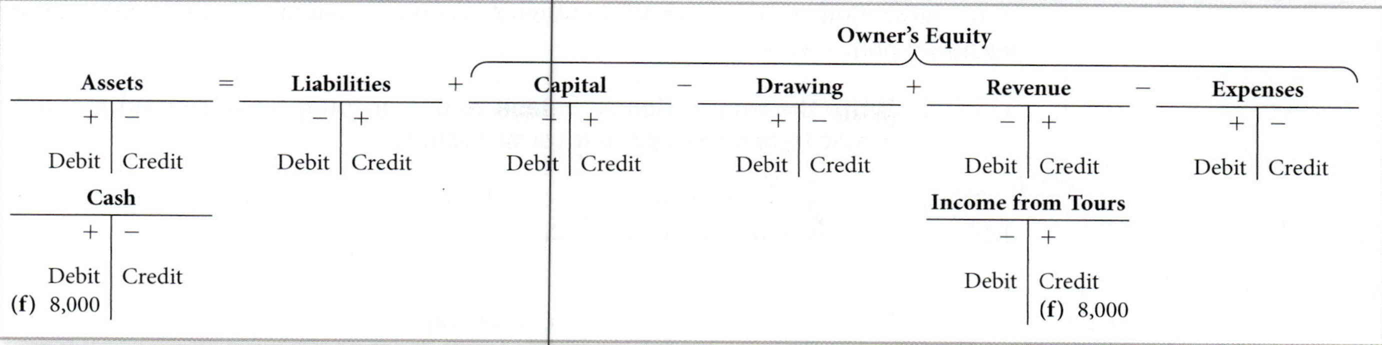

In transaction (g), Conner's Whitewater Adventures paid rent for the month, $1,250.

STEP 4. Write the transaction as a debit to one account (or accounts) and a credit to another account (or accounts).

This transaction results in an increase to Rent Expense with a debit and a decrease to Cash with a credit.

Owner's Equity

Assets	=	Liabilities	+	Capital	−	Drawing	+	Revenue	−	Expenses
+ | −		− | +		− | +		+ | −		− | +		+ | −
Debit | Credit		Debit | Credit		Debit | Credit		Debit | Credit		Debit | Credit		Debit | Credit

Cash		Rent Expense	
+	−	+	−
Debit	Credit	Debit	Credit
	(g) 1,250	(g) 1,250	

In transaction (h), Conner's Whitewater Adventures bought computer paper, ink cartridges, invoice pads, pens and pencils, folders, filing cabinets, and calculators on account from Fineman Company, $675.

STEP 4. Write the transaction as a debit to one account (or accounts) and a credit to another account (or accounts).

These items are considered supplies to be used by Conner's Whitewater Adventures and are recorded as an asset for $675 on account from Fineman Company. Remember, supplies are considered assets until they are used. When they are used, they are recorded as an expense. This transaction results in an increase to Supplies with a debit and an increase to Accounts Payable with a credit.

Owner's Equity

Assets	=	Liabilities	+	Capital	−	Drawing	+	Revenue	−	Expenses
+ | −		− | +		− | +		+ | −		− | +		+ | −
Debit | Credit		Debit | Credit		Debit | Credit		Debit | Credit		Debit | Credit		Debit | Credit

Supplies		Accounts Payable	
+	−	−	+
Debit	Credit	Debit	Credit
(h) 675			(h) 675

In transaction (i), Conner's Whitewater Adventures bought a three-month liability insurance policy, $1,875.

STEP 4. Write the transaction as a debit to one account (or accounts) and a credit to another account (or accounts).

This transaction results in an increase to the asset account Prepaid Insurance with a debit and a decrease to Cash with a credit.

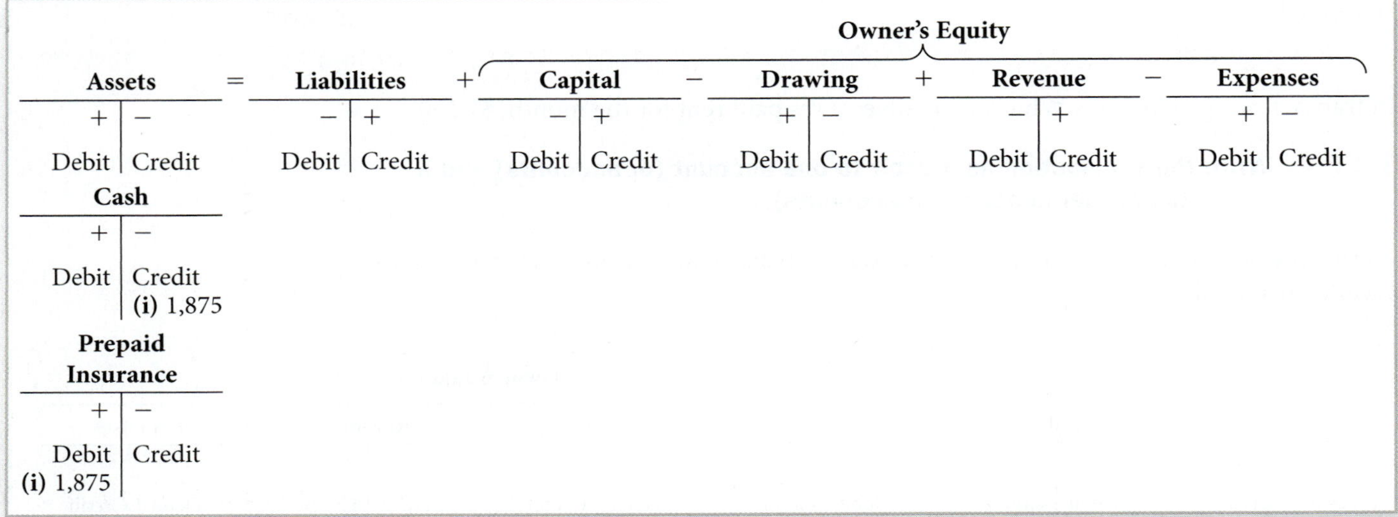

In transaction (j), Conner's Whitewater Adventures received a bill for newspaper advertising from *The Times*, $620.

STEP 4. Write the transaction as a debit to one account (or accounts) and a credit to another account (or accounts).

YOU Make the Call

One of your fellow students is having trouble getting his accounting equation to balance after transaction (g). No matter how many times he computes the numbers, he can't get it to balance. When you look at his T accounts, you see that he has been crediting the expenses. He claims that expenses take away from owner's equity, so why should they be under the plus sign? How can you explain that he is partly correct?

SOLUTION

Your fellow student is correct in saying that expenses do take away from owner's equity, but the expense itself is increasing, which requires a debit, or increase, to the expense account. Expenses have the opposite signs of revenues—they are the costs of doing business and act in an opposite way to revenues. So the quick response to your classmate is to make sure the signs on expenses are the opposite of revenues and that expenses are debited when they happen.

This results in an increase to Advertising Expense with a debit and an increase to Accounts Payable with a credit.

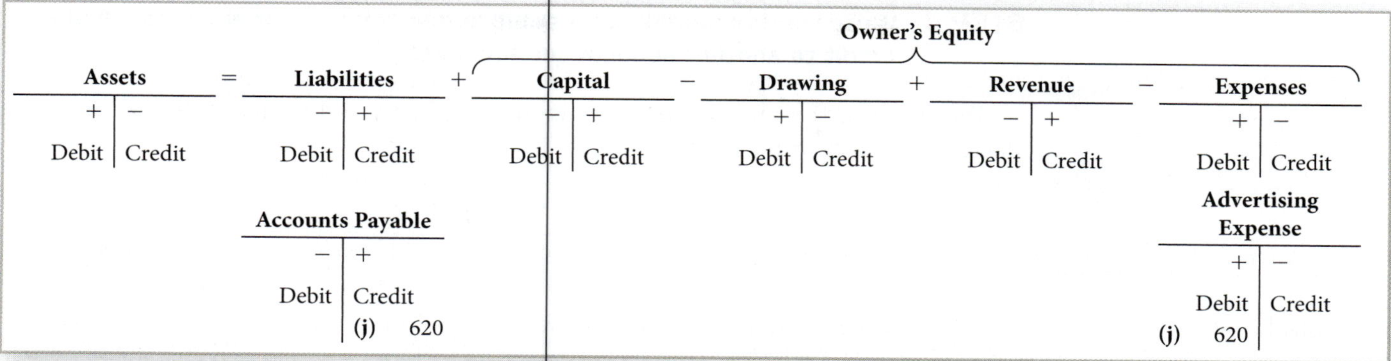

In transaction (k), Conner's Whitewater Adventures signs a contract with Crystal River Lodge to provide rafting adventures for guests. Conner's Whitewater Adventures provides 27 one-day rafting tours and bills Crystal River Lodge for $6,750.

STEP 4. Write the transaction as a debit to one account (or accounts) and a credit to another account (or accounts).

This results in an increase to Accounts Receivable with a debit and an increase to Income from Tours with a credit.

Owner's Equity

Assets = Liabilities + Capital − Drawing + Revenue − Expenses

Assets		Liabilities		Capital		Drawing		Revenue		Expenses	
+	−	−	+	−	+	+	−	−	+	+	−
Debit	Credit	Debit	Credit	Debit	Credit	Debit	Credit	Debit	Credit	Debit	Credit

Accounts Receivable	
+	−
Debit	Credit
(k) 6,750	

Income from Tours	
−	+
Debit	Credit
	(k) 6,750

In transaction (l), Conner's Whitewater Adventures pays on account to Signal Products, $1,500.

STEP 4. Write the transaction as a debit to one account (or accounts) and a credit to another account (or accounts).

This transaction results in a decrease to Accounts Payable with a debit and a decrease to Cash with a credit.

Owner's Equity

Assets = Liabilities + Capital − Drawing + Revenue − Expenses

Assets		Liabilities		Capital		Drawing		Revenue		Expenses	
+	−	−	+	−	+	+	−	−	+	+	−
Debit	Credit	Debit	Credit	Debit	Credit	Debit	Credit	Debit	Credit	Debit	Credit

Cash	
+	−
Debit	Credit
	(l) 1,500

Accounts Payable	
−	+
Debit	Credit
(l) 1,500	

In transaction (m), Conner's Whitewater Adventures received and paid Solar Power, Inc., for the electric bill, $225.

STEP 4. Write the transaction as a debit to one account (or accounts) and a credit to another account (or accounts).

The result of this transaction is an increase to Utilities Expense with a debit and a decrease to Cash with a credit.

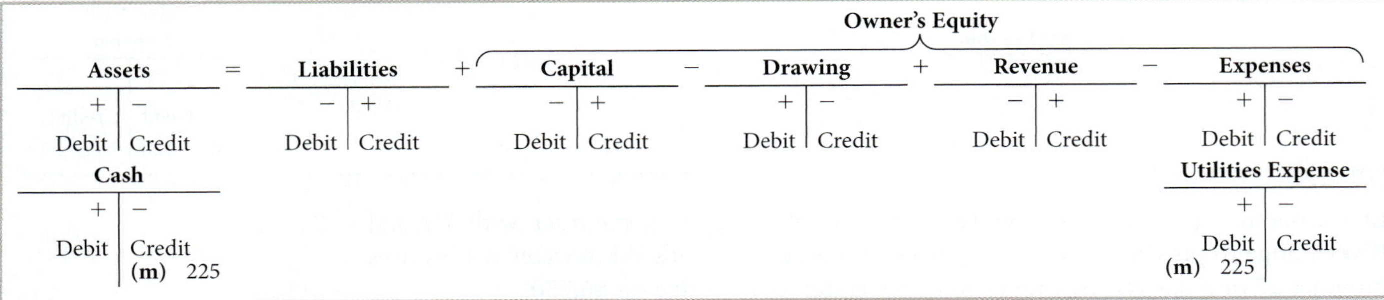

In transaction (n), Conner's Whitewater Adventures paid on account to *The Times*, $620.

STEP 4. Write the transaction as a debit to one account (or accounts) and a credit to another account (or accounts).

This transaction results in a decrease to Accounts Payable with a debit and a decrease to Cash with a credit. **Recall that this bill had previously been recorded as a liability in transaction (j).**

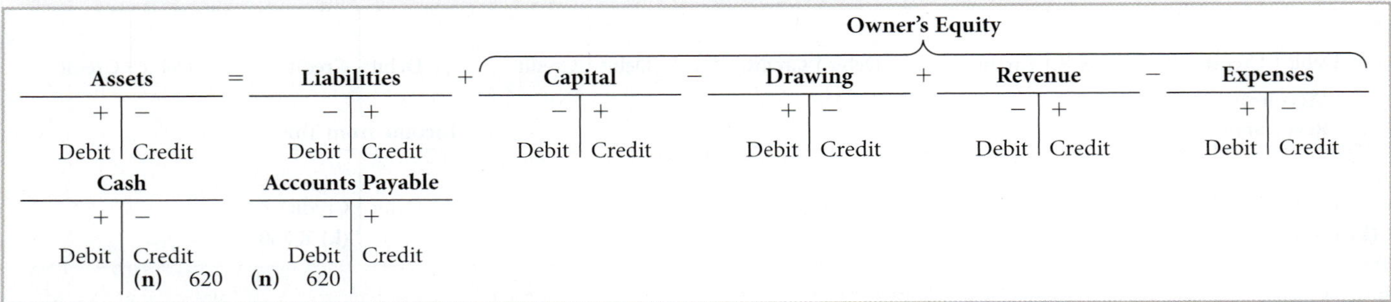

In transaction (o), Conner's Whitewater Adventures paid the wages of a part-time employee, $2,360.

STEP 4. Write the transaction as a debit to one account (or accounts) and a credit to another account (or accounts).

This transaction results in an increase to Wages Expense with a debit and a decrease to Cash with a credit.

Owner's Equity

Assets = Liabilities + Capital − Drawing + Revenue − Expenses

Assets	Liabilities	Capital	Drawing	Revenue	Expenses
+ | −	− | +	− | +	+ | −	− | +	+ | −
Debit | Credit	Debit | Credit	Debit | Credit	Debit | Credit	Debit | Credit	Debit | Credit
Cash					**Wages Expense**
+ | −					+ | −
Debit | Credit					Debit | Credit
(o) 2,360 (credit)					(o) 2,360 (debit)

In transaction (p), Conner's Whitewater Adventures bought additional equipment from Signal Products, $3,780, paying $1,850 in cash and placing the balance on account.

STEP 4. Write the transaction as a debit to one account (or accounts) and a credit to another account (or accounts).

This transaction results in an increase to Equipment with a debit, an increase to Accounts Payable with a credit, and a decrease to Cash with a credit. This is called a **compound entry**, which always involves more than one debit or more than one credit.

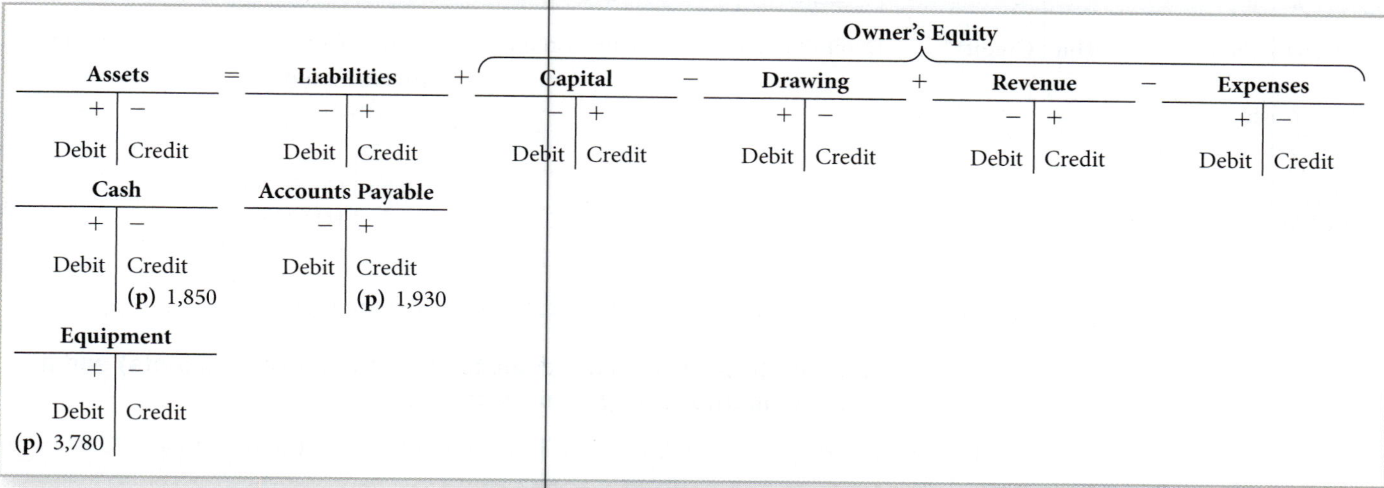

In transaction (q), Conner's Whitewater Adventures received $2,500 cash from Crystal River Lodge to apply against the amount billed in transaction (k).

STEP 4. Write the transaction as a debit to one account (or accounts) and a credit to another account (or accounts).

This transaction results in an increase to Cash with a debit and a decrease to Accounts Receivable with a credit.

Owner's Equity

Assets = Liabilities + Capital − Drawing + Revenue − Expenses

Assets: + | − Debit | Credit

Liabilities: − | + Debit | Credit

Capital: − | + Debit | Credit

Drawing: + | − Debit | Credit

Revenue: − | + Debit | Credit

Expenses: + | − Debit | Credit

Cash: + | − Debit (q) 2,500 | Credit

Accounts Receivable: + | − Debit | Credit (q) 2,500

In transaction (r), Conner's Whitewater Adventures sold tours for cash, $8,570.

STEP 4. Write the transaction as a debit to one account (or accounts) and a credit to another account (or accounts).

This transaction results in an increase to Cash with a debit and an increase to Income from Tours with a credit.

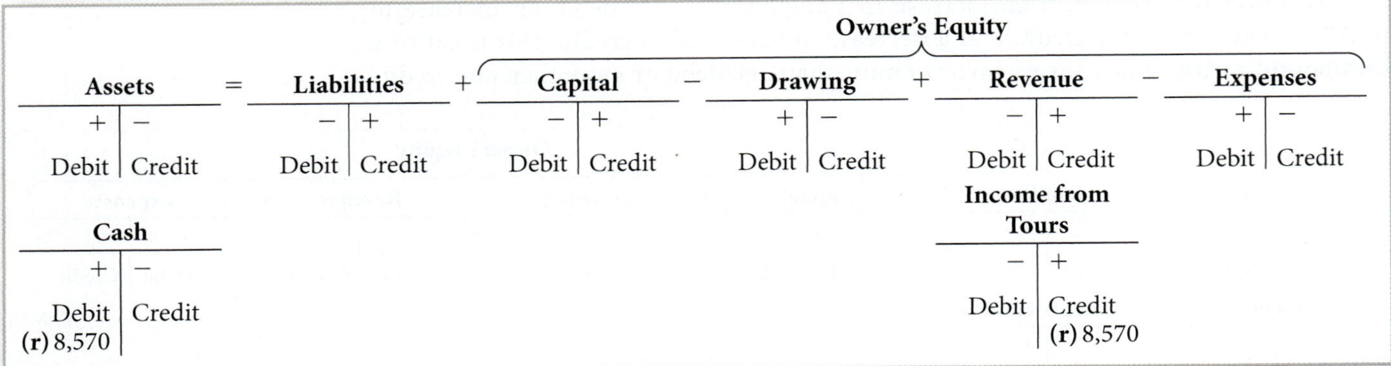

In transaction (s), J. Conner withdrew cash for her personal use, $3,500.

STEP 4. Write the transaction as a debit to one account (or accounts) and a credit to another account (or accounts).

This transaction increases J. Conner, Drawing with a debit and decreases Cash with a credit.

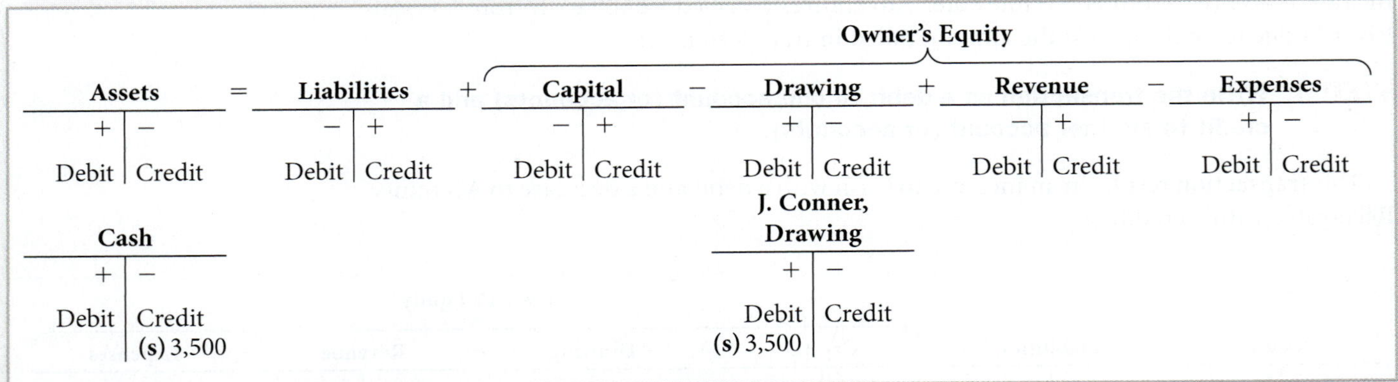

Remember that the Drawing account is used to record any withdrawals by the owner from the business. The Drawing account always decreases owner's equity.

Traditionally, accountants use the abbreviations Dr. for Debit and Cr. for Credit.

Summary of Transactions

The following T accounts provide a summary of all transactions for Conner's Whitewater Adventures. You will notice that the balance of each account is normally on the plus side. Note that in recording expenses, you normally place the entries only on the plus, or debit, side. Also, in recording revenue, you normally place the entries only on the plus, or credit, side.

Assets = Liabilities + Owner's Equity (Capital − Drawing + Revenue − Expenses)

	Assets	Liabilities	Capital	Drawing	Revenue	Expenses
Left side	+ Debit	− Debit	− Debit	+ Debit	− Debit	+ Debit
Right side	− Credit	+ Credit	+ Credit	− Credit	+ Credit	− Credit

Cash

+	−
(a) 90,000	(b) 38,000
(f) 8,000	(d) 2,000
(q) 2,500	(g) 1,250
(r) 8,570	(i) 1,875
109,070	(l) 1,500
	(m) 225
	(n) 620
	(o) 2,360
	(p) 1,850
	(s) 3,500
	53,180
Bal. 55,890	

Accounts Receivable

+	−
(k) 6,750	(q) 2,500
Bal. 4,250	

Supplies

+	−
(h) 675	
Bal. 675	

Prepaid Insurance

+	−
(i) 1,875	
Bal. 1,875	

Equipment

+	−
(b) 38,000	
(c) 4,320	
(e) 5,200	
(p) 3,780	
Bal. 51,300	

Accounts Payable

−	+
(d) 2,000	(c) 4,320
(l) 1,500	(h) 675
(n) 620	(j) 620
4,120	(p) 1,930
	7,545
	Bal. 3,425

J. Conner, Capital

−	+
	(a) 90,000
	(e) 5,200
	Bal. 95,200

J. Conner, Drawing

+	−
(s) 3,500	
Bal. 3,500	

Income from Tours

−	+
	(f) 8,000
	(k) 6,750
	(r) 8,570
	Bal. 23,320

Wages Expense

+	−
(o) 2,360	
Bal. 2,360	

Rent Expense

+	−
(g) 1,250	
Bal. 1,250	

Advertising Expense

+	−
(j) 620	
Bal. 620	

Utilities Expense

+	−
(m) 225	
Bal. 225	

Figure 1

Accounting memory tool

A memory tool that helps some students memorize debits and credits in T accounts is the equation A + D + E = L + C + R. All accounts on the left side of the equation have normal debit balances, and all accounts on the right side have normal credit balances. You can make up a memorable sentence or use this one—All Drippy Eels Love Curly Radishes. Picture an eel dripping with water devouring curly radishes.

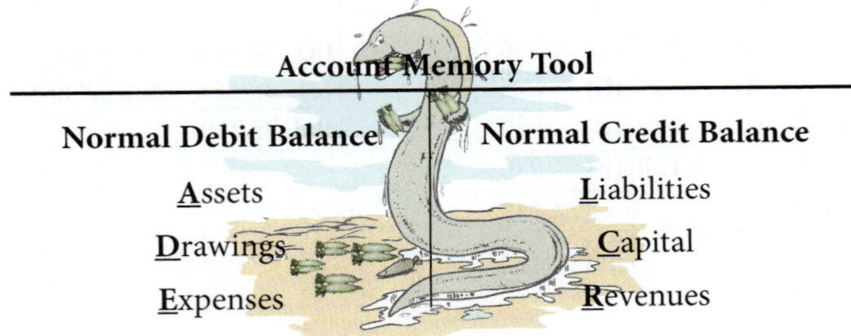

Account Memory Tool
Normal Debit Balance
Assets
Drawings
Expenses
Normal Credit Balance
Liabilities
Capital
Revenues

To: **Amy Roberts, CPA**
Subject: **Debits equal credits?**

Hi Amy,
I've recorded all of my transactions in T accounts using debits and credits. I know that my debits and credits need to equal. Is there an easy way to check this?
Thanks,
Janie

To: **Janie Conner**
Subject: **RE: Debits equal credits?**

Hi Janie,
You're correct! The total debits in the T accounts must always equal the total credits. One way to prove this is by preparing a trial balance. After the trial balance is prepared, you'll be able to prepare financial statements for your business. Financial statements will help you summarize the financial affairs of your business.
Let me know if you have any questions on these next two tasks:

_____ 1. Prepare a trial balance.
_____ 2. Prepare financial statements.

You can also practice preparing these same reports in QuickBooks using the demonstration file I previously sent you.
Thanks.
Amy

THE TRIAL BALANCE

5 Prepare a trial balance.

Learning Objective

After recording the transactions in the T accounts, you can prepare a trial balance by simply recording the balances of the T accounts in two columns. The **trial balance** is a listing of account balances in two columns—one labeled "Debit" and one labeled "Credit"—and is not considered a financial statement. It is, as the name implies, a trial run by the accountant to prove that the total of the debit balances equals the total of the credit balances. This is evidence of the equality of the two sides of the fundamental accounting equation. The accountant must prove that the accounts are in balance before preparing the company's financial statements.

In preparing a trial balance, shown in Figure 2, record the accounts with balances in the same order they are listed in the chart of accounts.

- Assets
- Liabilities
- Owner's Equity
- Revenue
- Expenses

Figure 2
Trial balance

Conner's Whitewater Adventures
Trial Balance
June 30, 20--

Account Name	Debit	Credit
Cash	55,890	
Accounts Receivable	4,250	
Supplies	675	
Prepaid Insurance	1,875	
Equipment	51,300	
Accounts Payable		3,425
J. Conner, Capital		95,200
J. Conner, Drawing	3,500	
Income from Tours		23,320
Wages Expense	2,360	
Rent Expense	1,250	
Advertising Expense	620	
Utilities Expense	225	
	121,945	121,945

Column headings identify information in each column

Accounts listed in order of the chart of accounts

Dollar signs not used on a trial balance

Single underline beneath figures to be added

Double underline beneath column totals

Remember, the normal balance of each account is on its plus side. The following table indicates where each of the account balances would normally be shown in a trial balance.

Account Titles	TRIAL BALANCE Left, or Debit, Balances	TRIAL BALANCE Right, or Credit, Balances
Assets	Assets	
Liabilities		Liabilities
Capital		Capital
Drawing	Drawing	
Revenue		Revenue
Expenses	Expenses	
Totals		

MAJOR FINANCIAL STATEMENTS

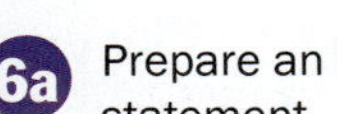

The three-line heading of a financial statement answers the questions Who? What? and When?

Earlier we listed summarizing as one of the five basic tasks of the accounting process. To accomplish this task, accountants use financial statements. A **financial statement** is a report prepared by accountants to summarize the financial affairs of a business for managers and others (both inside and outside the business).

Note that the headings of all financial statements require three lines:

1. Name of the company (or owner if there is no company name)
2. Title of the financial statement
3. Period of time covered by the financial statement, or its date

Also note that dollar signs are placed at the head of each column and with each total. Single lines are used to show that the figures above are being added or subtracted. Lines should be drawn across the entire column. A double line is drawn under the final total in a column.

The financial statements are all interconnected. The income statement must be prepared first, followed by the statement of owner's equity and then the balance sheet.

Learning Objective 6a Prepare an income statement.

The Income Statement

The **income statement** shows total revenue minus total expenses, which yields the net income or net loss. The income statement reports the results of business transactions involving revenue and expense accounts—in other words, how the business has performed—over a period of time, usually a month or a year. When total revenue exceeds total expenses over the period, the result is **net income**, or profit. When the total revenue is less than total expenses, the result is a **net loss**.

The income statement in Figure 3 shows the results of the first month of operations for Conner's Whitewater Adventures.

For convenience, the individual expense amounts are recorded in the first amount column. Thus, the total expenses ($4,455) may be subtracted directly from the total revenue ($23,320).

The income statement covers a period of time, whereas the balance sheet has only one date: the end of the financial period. On the income statement, the revenue for June less the expenses for June shows the results of operations—a net income of $18,865

QuickBooks Tip

The income statement is sometimes called the *statement of operations* or *earnings*. In QuickBooks, the income statement is called the *profit and loss statement*.

© iStockphoto.com/Yunus Arakon

In the Real World

Where to open a new location is an important business decision. For companies such as Apple, a manufacturer and seller of computers, iPads, iPods, and iPhones, the decision to expand to a new retail store location—as well as other operating decisions—is made from financial statements such as the income statement. You can find a copy of Apple's financial statements on the Internet at http://investor.apple.com. For fiscal year ended September 29, 2012, Apple reported net income of $41,733,000,000 on its income statement. Dell is a competitor of Apple. Would you expect the financial statements of Dell to look similar to Apple's? If so, why might this be beneficial to users of the financial statements?

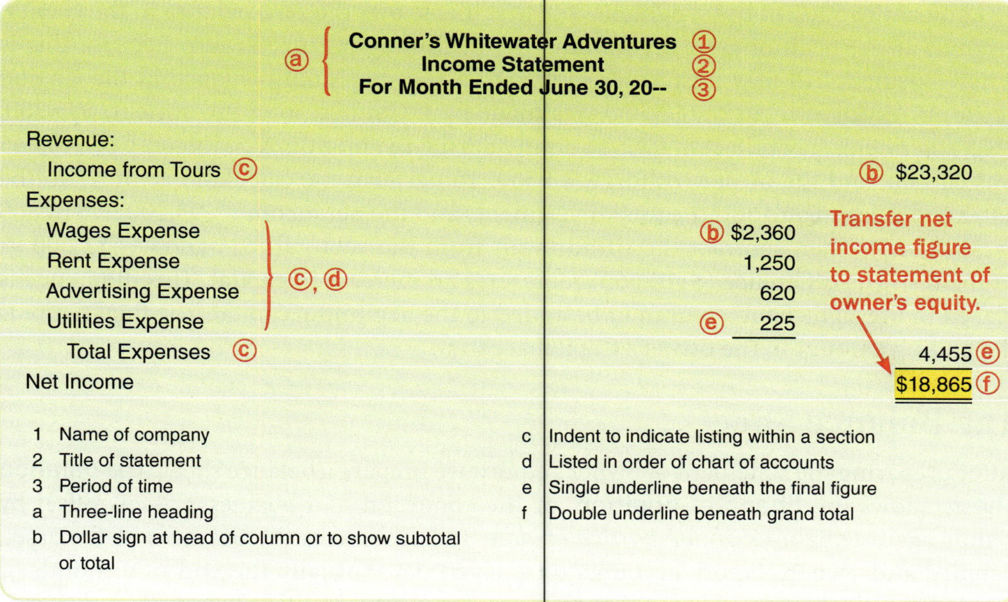

Conner's Whitewater Adventures
Income Statement
For Month Ended June 30, 20--

Revenue:		
Income from Tours		$23,320
Expenses:		
Wages Expense	$2,360	
Rent Expense	1,250	
Advertising Expense	620	
Utilities Expense	225	
Total Expenses		4,455
Net Income		$18,865

Figure 3
Income statement

FYI Compare the third line of the income statement heading with the third line of the balance sheet heading shown in Figure 5. Notice that the lines are different—the income statement covers a period of time, and the balance sheet has only one date: the end of the financial period.

To the accountant, the term *net income* means "clear" income, or profit after all expenses have been deducted. Expenses are usually listed in the same order as in the chart of accounts. Revenue and expense amounts are taken directly from the trial balance. If total expenses were greater than the revenue, then a net loss would be recorded.

Learning Objective 6b Prepare a statement of owner's equity.

The Statement of Owner's Equity

In the previous chapter, we said that revenue and expenses are connected with owner's equity through the financial statements. Now let's demonstrate this using a statement of owner's equity, shown in Figure 4, which the accountant prepares after he or she has determined the net income or net loss on the income statement.

The **statement of owner's equity** shows how—and why—the owner's equity, or Capital account, has changed over a stated period of time (in this case, the month of June). Notice the third line in the heading of Figure 4. It shows that the statement of owner's equity covers the same period of time as the income statement.

QuickBooks Tip The statement of owner's equity is not a standard report in QuickBooks. A customized report can be created if desired.

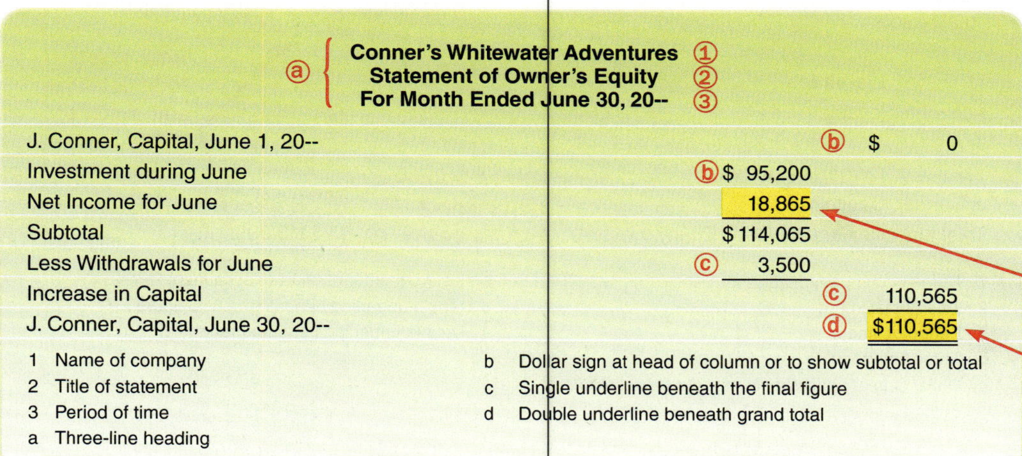

Conner's Whitewater Adventures
Statement of Owner's Equity
For Month Ended June 30, 20--

J. Conner, Capital, June 1, 20--		$ 0
Investment during June	$ 95,200	
Net Income for June	18,865	
Subtotal	$ 114,065	
Less Withdrawals for June	3,500	
Increase in Capital		110,565
J. Conner, Capital, June 30, 20--		$110,565

Figure 4
Statement of owner's equity

Remember

Here's another memory tool for recalling the order of statement preparation: Izzy Swung Off Every Branch (Income, Statement of Owner's Equity, Balance Sheet).

Look at the body of the statement. The first line shows the zero balance in the Capital account at the beginning of the month. The beginning balance is zero because this is a new business. All new businesses start with a zero beginning balance in the Capital account. An investment of $95,200 was made by J. Conner: total investment, $95,200. Two other items have affected owner's equity during the month: A net income of $18,865 was earned, and the owner withdrew $3,500. To perform the calculations, move to the left-hand column and add the total investments and the net income ($95,200 + $18,865 = $114,065). Then subtract the withdrawals from the subtotal ($114,065 − $3,500 = $110,565). The difference ($110,565) represents an increase in capital. This difference is placed in the right-hand column to be added to the beginning capital. The final figure is the ending amount in the owner's Capital account.

The Balance Sheet

Learning Objective

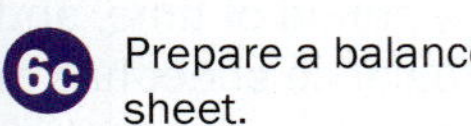

6c Prepare a balance sheet.

After preparing the statement of owner's equity, we prepare a balance sheet. The **balance sheet** shows the **financial position**, or the condition of a business's assets offset by claims against them *as of one particular date.* It summarizes the balances of the asset, liability, and owner's equity accounts on a given date (usually the end of a month or year). Thus, the balance sheet is like a snapshot—a picture of the financial condition of the business at that particular date.

The ending capital balance on the balance sheet is taken from the statement of owner's equity. Note that the accounts appear in the same order as in the chart of accounts.

In the **report form** of the balance sheet, the elements in the accounting equation are presented one on top of the other. A balance sheet prepared on June 30 for Conner's Whitewater Adventures in report form is shown in Figure 5.

Figure 5
Balance sheet

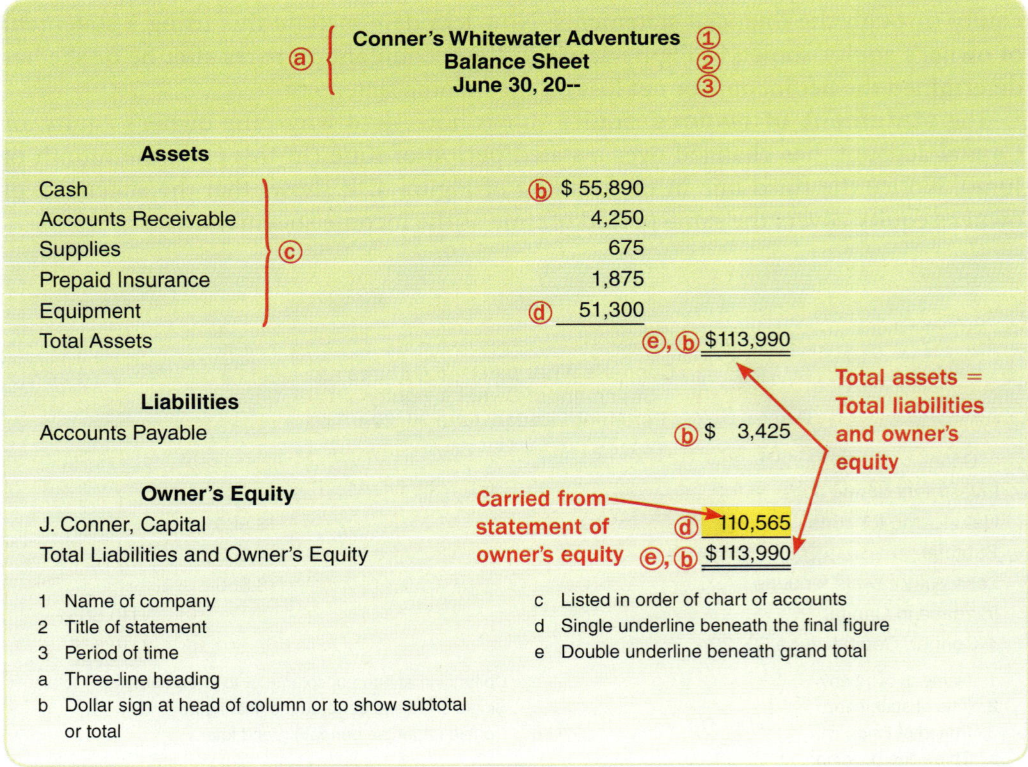

(a) Conner's Whitewater Adventures (1)
Balance Sheet (2)
June 30, 20-- (3)

Assets		
Cash (c)	(b) $ 55,890	
Accounts Receivable	4,250	
Supplies	675	
Prepaid Insurance	1,875	
Equipment	(d) 51,300	
Total Assets		(e), (b) $113,990
Liabilities		
Accounts Payable		(b) $ 3,425
Owner's Equity		
J. Conner, Capital		(d) 110,565
Total Liabilities and Owner's Equity		(e), (b) $113,990

1 Name of company
2 Title of statement
3 Period of time
a Three-line heading
b Dollar sign at head of column or to show subtotal or total
c Listed in order of chart of accounts
d Single underline beneath the final figure
e Double underline beneath grand total

ERRORS EXPOSED BY THE TRIAL BALANCE

If the debit and credit columns in a trial balance are not equal, it is evident that we have made an error. Possible mistakes include the following:

- Making errors in arithmetic, such as errors in adding the trial balance columns or in finding the balances of the accounts.
- Recording only half an entry, such as a debit without a corresponding credit or vice versa.
- Recording both halves of the entry on the same side, such as two debits rather than a debit and a credit.
- Recording one or more amounts incorrectly.

It's important to note that even when debits equal credits, this does not necessarily mean that no errors were made in recording the transactions. For example, a transaction may have been forgotten, it may have been included twice, or it may have been written for an incorrect amount. Although using a computer greatly reduces the occurrence of addition and subtraction errors, it does not prevent the occurrence of other kinds of errors, such as an incorrect amount being recorded.

Learning Objective 7 Recognize the effect of errors on account balances.

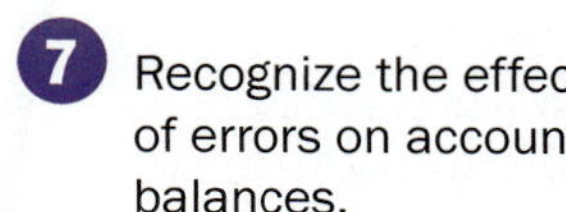

Computerized accounting software, like QuickBooks, prevents out-of-balance errors by requiring transactions to balance before updating.

ACCOUNTING IN YOUR FUTURE

ACCOUNTING CLERK

One of many variations in accounting jobs you might find is an accounting clerk. Responsibilities might include invoicing for customers' fees, collecting fees, and maintaining customer accounts. The job might also include some marketing and customer service activities; therefore, people skills would be vital.

As the accounting clerk, you would be required to provide the accountant with weekly reports so that the accountant could correctly report revenue. You would also need to manage financial information regarding collection expenses and marketing expenses, as well as any expenses related to customer service. Consider how knowing the accounting cycle would be beneficial in this position.

iStockPhoto.com/klikk

Procedure for Locating Errors

Suppose you are in a business situation where you have recorded transactions for a month in the account books and the accounts do not balance. To save yourself time, you need to have a definite procedure for tracking down the errors. The best method is to do everything in reverse, as follows:

STEP 1. Look at the pattern of balances to see if a normal balance was placed in the wrong column on the trial balance.

STEP 2. Re-add the trial balance columns.

STEP 3. Check the transferring of the figures from the accounts to the trial balance.

STEP 4. Verify the footings and balances of the accounts.

As an added precaution, form the habit of verifying all addition and subtraction as you go along. You can then correct many mistakes *before* the time comes to prepare a trial balance.

When the trial balance totals do not balance, the difference might indicate that you forgot to record half an entry in the accounts. For example, if the difference in the trial balance totals is $20, you may have recorded $20 on the debit side of one account without recording $20 on the credit side of another account.

Another possibility is to divide the difference by 2; this may provide a clue that you accidentally recorded half an entry twice. For example, if the difference in the trial balance is $600, you may have recorded $300 on the debit side of one account and an additional $300 on the debit side of another account. Look for a transaction that involved $300 and see if you recorded both a debit and a credit. By knowing which transactions to check, you can save a lot of time.

Transpositions and Slides

If the difference is evenly divisible by 9, the discrepancy may be either a transposition or a slide. A **transposition** means that the digits have been transposed, or switched around, when the numbers were copied from one place to another. For example, one transposition of digits in 916 can be written as 619.

Correct Number	Number Copied	Difference	Difference Divided by 9
$916	$619	$297	$297 ÷ 9 = $33

A **slide** is an error in placing the decimal point (in other words, a slide in the decimal point). For example, $27,000 could be inadvertently written as $2,700.

Correct Number	Number Copied	Difference	Difference Divided by 9
$27,000	$2,700	$24,300	$24,300 ÷ 9 = $2,700

Or the error may be a combination of a transposition and a slide, as when $450 is written as $54.

Correct Number	Number Copied	Difference	Difference Divided by 9
$450	$54	$396	$396 ÷ 9 = $44

Again, the difference is evenly divisible by 9 (with no remainder).

Accounting with QuickBooks®

Viewing and Printing Financial Reports with QuickBooks

QuickBooks allows users to print several types of financial reports. In this section, you will learn how to print standardized reports such as the trial balance, income statement (profit and loss statement in QuickBooks), and the balance sheet. The statement of owner's equity is not a standardized report in QuickBooks; however, a customized report can be created. In this text, we will use the **Reports** tab to access the reports in QuickBooks. Reports can also be accessed through the **Report Center**.

Learning Objectives

After you have completed this section, you will be able to do the following:

1. View and print a trial balance report.
2. View and print a profit and loss (income) statement.
3. View and print a balance sheet.
4. Save report as a PDF.
5. Export QuickBooks reports into Excel.

Learning Objective

1. View and print a trial balance report.

Similar to manual accounting, the trial balance is prepared after recording transactions. To view and print the trial balance, follow these steps. (See Figure Q1.)

STEP 1. Click the **Reports** tab.

STEP 2. Click **Accountant & Taxes**.

STEP 3. Click **Trial Balance**.

Figure Q1
Viewing a trial balance report

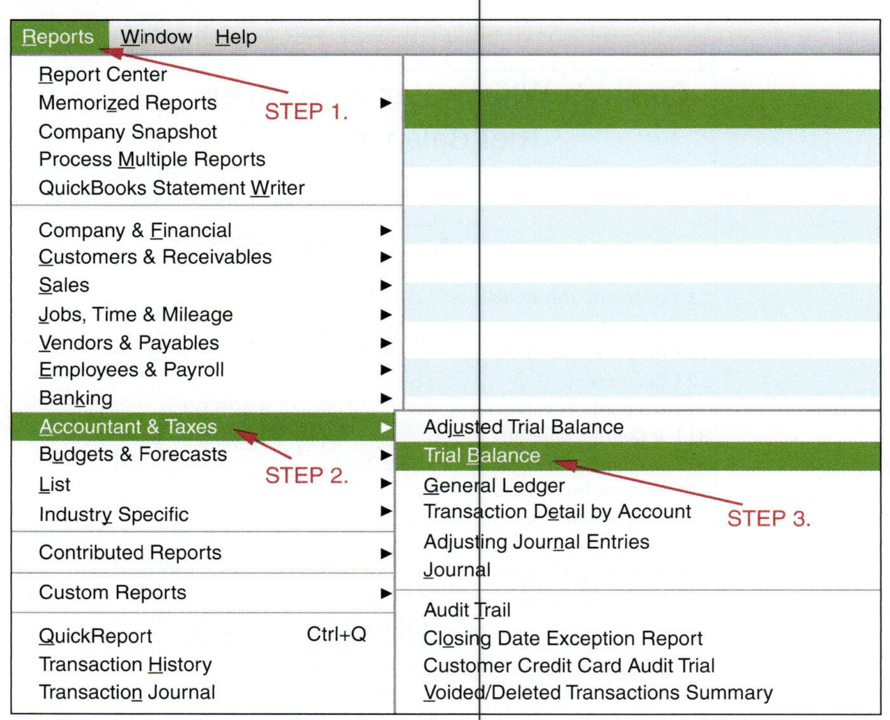

QuickBooks Tip

Remember to refresh reports after making changes to ensure report information has been updated.

STEP 4. Adjust the **From** and **To** dates and click **Refresh**.

Figure Q2
Adjusting report dates

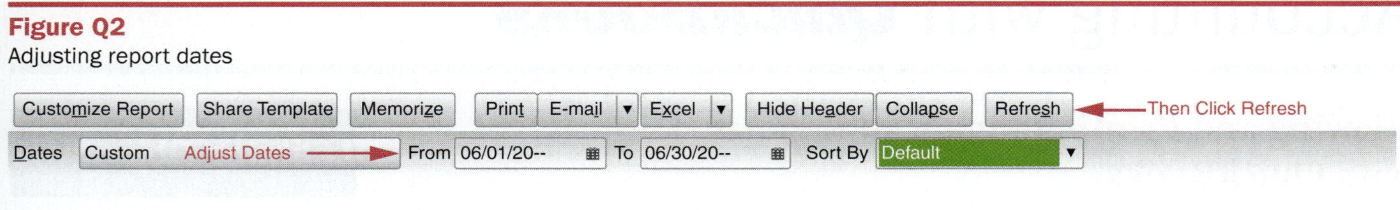

STEP 5. To print the report, click the **Print** button.

Figure Q3
Printing a report

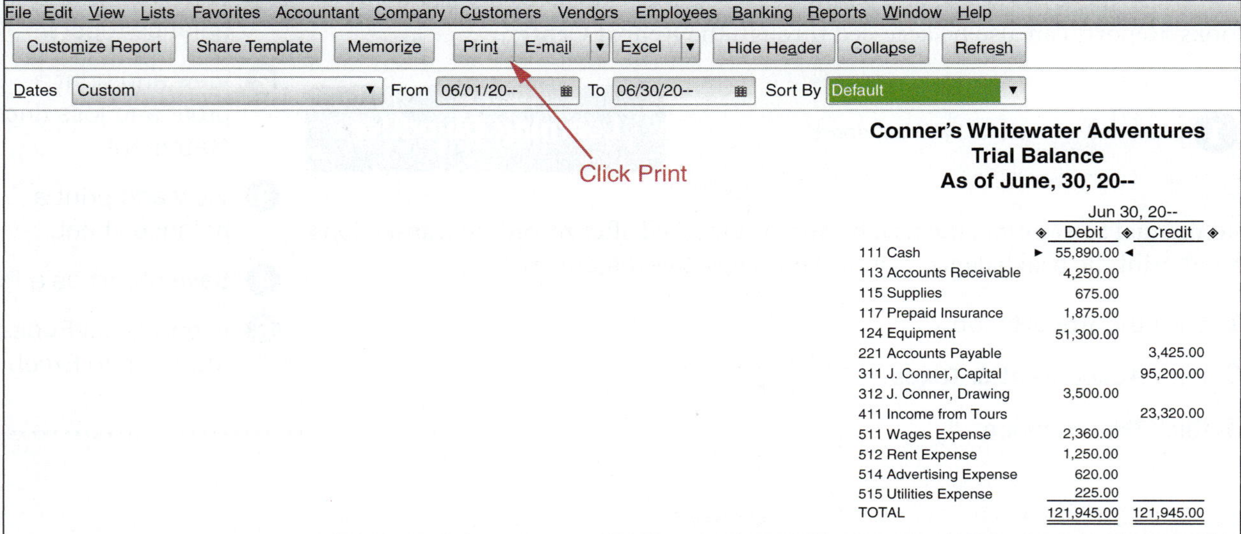

Figure Q4 shows the QuickBooks trial balance report for Conner's Whitewater Adventures.

Figure Q4
Trial balance report

Conner's Whitewater Adventures
Trial Balance
As of June 30, 20--

	Jun 30, 20--	
	Debit	**Credit**
111 Cash	55,890.00	
113 Accounts Receivable	4,250.00	
115 Supplies	675.00	
117 Prepaid Insurance	1,875.00	
124 Equipment	51,300.00	
221 Accounts Payable		3,425.00
311 J. Conner, Capital		95,200.00
312 J. Conner, Drawing	3,500.00	
411 Income from Tours		23,320.00
511 Wages Expense	2,360.00	
512 Rent Expense	1,250.00	
514 Advertising Expense	620.00	
515 Utilities Expense	225.00	
TOTAL	**121,945.00**	**121,945.00**

Learning Objective

2 View and print a profit and loss (income) statement.

QuickBooks refers to the income statement as the **profit and loss statement**. To view and print the profit and loss statement, follow these steps. (See Figure Q5.)

STEP 1. Click the **Reports** tab.

STEP 2. Click **Company & Financial**.

STEP 3. Click **Profit & Loss Standard**.

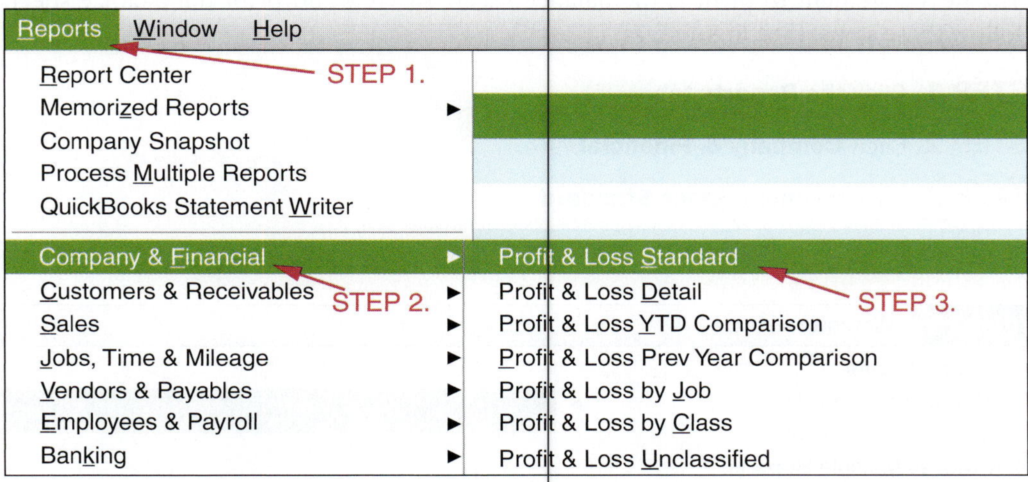

Figure Q5
Viewing a profit and loss statement

STEP 4. Adjust the **From** and **To** dates and click **Refresh**.

STEP 5. To print the report, click the **Print** button.

Figure Q6 shows the profit and loss statement for Conner's Whitewater Adventures.

Conner's Whitewater Adventures
Profit & Loss
June 20--

	Jun 20--
Income	
411 Income from Tours	23,320.00
Total Income	23,320.00
Expense	
511 Wages Expense	2,360.00
512 Rent Expense	1,250.00
514 Advertising Expense	620.00
515 Utilities Expense	225.00
Total Expense	4,455.00
Net Income	18,865.00

Figure Q6
Profit and loss statement

PREPARE THE STATEMENT OF OWNER'S EQUITY

The statement of owner's equity is not a standard option in QuickBooks. Your instructor may or may not want you to prepare a report that contains this information. If your instructor wants you to prepare a statement of owner's equity, a customized balance sheet report can be used to display this information. A statement of owner's equity is not a required QuickBooks report for this text.

Learning Objective

 View and print a balance sheet.

The next statement to print is the balance sheet. To view and print the balance sheet, follow these steps. (See Figure Q7.)

STEP 1. Click the **Reports** tab.

STEP 2. Click **Company & Financial**.

STEP 3. Click **Balance Sheet Standard**.

Figure Q7
Viewing a balance sheet

Reports Window Help

Report Center
Memorized Reports ▶
Company Snapshot
Process Multiple Reports
QuickBooks Statement Writer

Company & Financial ▶
Customers & Receivables ▶
Sales ▶
Jobs, Time & Mileage ▶
Vendors & Payables ▶
Employees & Payroll ▶
Banking ▶
Accountant & Taxes ▶
Budgets & Forecasts ▶
List ▶
Industry Specific ▶

Contributed Reports ▶

Custom Reports ▶

QuickReport Ctrl+Q
Transaction History
Transaction Journal

Profit & Loss Standard
Profit & Loss Detail
Profit & Loss YTD Comparison
Profit & Loss Prev Year Comparison
Profit & Loss by Job
Profit & Loss by Class
Profit & Loss Unclassified
Income by Customer Summary
Income by Customer Detail
Expenses by Vendor Summary
Expenses by Vendor Detail
Income & Expense Graph

Balance Sheet Standard
Balance Sheet Detail
Balance Sheet Summary
Balance Sheet Prev Year Comparison
Balance Sheet by Class
Net Worth Graph

STEP 1.
STEP 2.
STEP 3.

QuickBooks Tip

For the balance sheet, you will enter only the ending date of the report.

STEP 4. Adjust the **As of** date and click **Refresh**.

STEP 5. To print the report, click the **Print** button.

Figure Q8 shows the balance sheet for Conner's Whitewater Adventures.

Conner's Whitewater Adventures
Balance Sheet
As of June 30, 20--

	Jun 30, 20--
ASSETS	
Current Assets	
Checking/Savings	
111 Cash	55,890.00
Total Checking/Savings	55,890.00
Accounts Receivable	
113 Accounts Receivable	4,250.00
Total Accounts Receivable	4,250.00
Other Current Assets	
115 Supplies	675.00
117 Prepaid Insurance	1,875.00
Total Other Current Assets	2,550.00
Total Current Assets	62,690.00
Fixed Assets	
124 Equipment	51,300.00
Total Fixed Assets	51,300.00
TOTAL ASSETS	113,990.00
LIABILITIES & EQUITY	
Liabilites	
Current Liabilities	
Accounts Payable	
221 Accounts Payable	3,425.00
Total Accounts Payable	3,425.00
Total Current Liabilities	3,425.00
Total Liabilities	3,425.00
Equity	
311 J. Conner, Capital	95,200.00
312 J. Conner, Drawing	-3,500.00
Net Income	18,865.00
Total Equity	110,565.00
TOTAL LIABILITIES & EQUITY	113,990.00

Figure Q8
Balance sheet

Learning Objective

4 Save report as a PDF.

Many times, QuickBooks users will want to save a report electronically rather than printing the report in paper format. Using an electronic file format called **PDF (portable document format)** that converts a printed document into an electronic image is one way to do this. The easiest way to save any report as a PDF in QuickBooks is to click on **File** and then select **Save as PDF**. Next, you will be asked to name and save the PDF file to your computer. As an alternative, you may prefer to install a "virtual" printer using PDF software. Several types of PDF software can be downloaded to your computer, including free versions such as CutePDF™ Writer (www.cutepdf.com). To save a QuickBooks' report in PDF format, follow the previous steps to view and print a report. When you click the **Print** button, select the PDF software installed on your computer as your "virtual" printer. Then click **Print**. (See Figure Q9.)

QuickBooks Tip

Reports can also be saved to a PDF format through the email feature in QuickBooks.

Figure Q9
Printing reports as a PDF

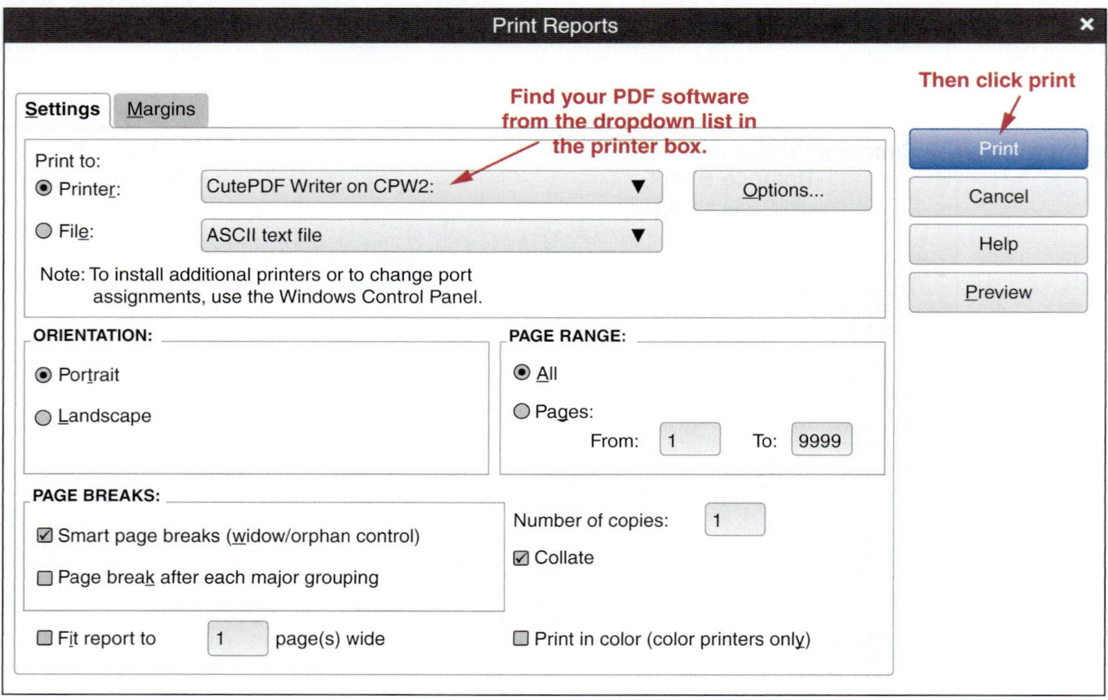

Learning Objective

5 Export QuickBooks reports into Excel.

QuickBooks Tip

Reports can also be saved in an Excel format through the email feature in QuickBooks.

QuickBooks users may also want to export financial report information into Excel. To export QuickBooks reports into Excel, follow the previous steps for viewing and printing a report. Then click **Excel** and **Create New Worksheet**. (See Figure Q10.)

Figure Q10
Creating an Excel worksheet

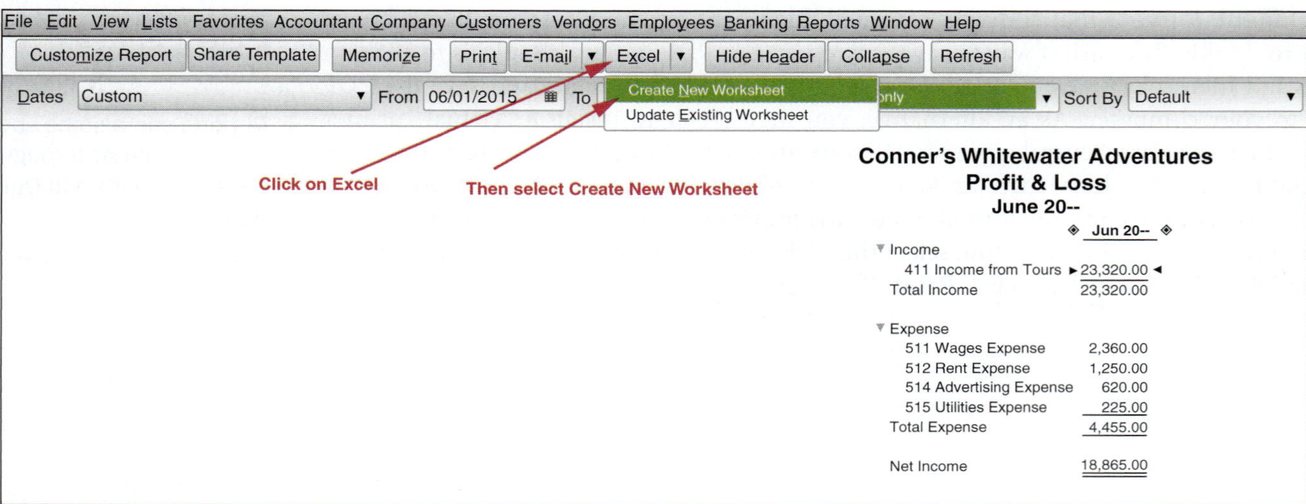

Chapter Review

Study and Practice

 Determine balances of T accounts. **Learning Objective**

To determine balances of T accounts, add the amounts listed on each side of the T account. The totals are called **footings**. To get the account balance, subtract the total of the smaller side from the total of the larger side. Record the account balance on the larger side.

PRACTICE EXERCISE 1

Using the T accounts presented below, determine the balances.

Cash

(a)	90,000	(b)	38,000
		(f)	1,200

Accounts Payable

(d)	1,500	(c)	4,500

J. Jay, Capital

		(a)	90,000
		(e)	5,000

J. Jay, Drawing

(f)	1,200		

Equipment

(b)	38,000	(d)	1,500
(c)	4,500		
(e)	5,000		

PRACTICE EXERCISE 1 • SOLUTION

Cash

(a)	90,000	(b)	38,000
		(f)	1,200
			39,200
Bal.	**50,800**		

Accounts Payable

(d)	1,500	(c)	4,500
		Bal.	**3,000**

J. Jay, Capital

		(a)	90,000
		(e)	5,000
		Bal.	**95,000**

J. Jay, Drawing

(f)	1,200		
Bal.	**1,200**		

Equipment

(b)	38,000	(d)	1,500
(c)	4,500		
(e)	5,000		
	47,500		
Bal.	**46,000**		

2 Present the fundamental accounting equation using the T account form and label the plus and minus sides. **Learning Objective**

The fundamental accounting equation can be restated in **T account form** using plus and minus sides. The following table summarizes the rules:

Assets	**The *left* side is the *increase* side.**
Liabilities	**The *right* side is the *increase* side.**

Capital	**The *right* side is the *increase* side.**
Drawing	**The *left* side is the *increase* side.**
Revenue	**The *right* side is the *increase* side.**
Expenses	**The *left* side is the *increase* side.**

PRACTICE EXERCISE 2

Using the fundamental accounting equation in T account form, label each side with plus and minus.

PRACTICE EXERCISE 2 • SOLUTION

Owner's Equity: Capital − Drawing + Revenue − Expenses

Assets		=	**Liabilities**		+	**Capital**		−	**Drawing**		+	**Revenue**		−	**Expenses**	
+	−		−	+		−	+		+	−		−	+		+	−

Learning Objective 3 Present the fundamental accounting equation using the T account form and label the debit and credit sides.

Each account category in the fundamental accounting equation has a debit and credit. The left side of a T account, regardless of the account category, is called the **debit** side. The right side is called the **credit** side. A debit or credit could signify either an increase or a decrease—it depends on the account category. The following table summarizes these rules:

Debits Signify		**Credits Signify**	
Increases in	Assets Drawing Expenses	Decreases in	Assets Drawing Expenses
Decreases in	Liabilities Capital Revenue	Increases in	Liabilities Capital Revenue

PRACTICE EXERCISE 3

Using the fundamental accounting equation in T account form label each side as debit and credit.

PRACTICE EXERCISE 3 • SOLUTION

Owner's Equity: Capital − Drawing + Revenue − Expenses

Assets		=	**Liabilities**		+	**Capital**		−	**Drawing**		+	**Revenue**		−	**Expenses**	
+	−		−	+		−	+		+	−		−	+		+	−
Debit	Credit		Debit	Credit		Debit	Credit		Debit	Credit		Debit	Credit		Debit	Credit

Record directly in T accounts a group of business transactions involving changes in asset, liability, owner's equity, revenue, and expense accounts for a service business.

Learning Objective

CHAPTER REVIEW

Transactions can be recorded directly into the T accounts. When analyzing a business transaction, follow these steps:

STEP 1. What accounts are involved?

STEP 2. What are the classifications of the accounts involved (asset, liability, capital, drawing, revenue, expense)?

STEP 3. Are the accounts increased or decreased?

STEP 4. Write the transaction as a debit to one account (or accounts) and a credit to another account (or accounts).

STEP 5. Is the equation in balance after the transaction has been recorded?

4 PRACTICE EXERCISE 4

Record the following transactions directly into the appropriate T accounts and determine the balance in each account.

a. J. Molson deposited $90,000 in the name of the business.

b. Bought equipment for cash, $38,000.

c. Bought advertising on account, $4,320.

d. Paid $2,000 on account.

e. J. Molson invested his personal equipment, valued at $5,200, in the business.

f. The business received cash from customers, $4,000.

g. J. Molson withdrew $1,200 from the business for personal use.

PRACTICE EXERCISE 4 • SOLUTION

Assets		=	Liabilities		+	Capital		−	Drawing		+	Revenue		−	Expenses	
+ Debit	− Credit		− Debit	+ Credit		− Debit	+ Credit		+ Debit	− Credit		− Debit	+ Credit		+ Debit	− Credit

Cash

+ Debit	− Credit
(a) 90,000	(b) 38,000
(f) 4,000	(d) 2,000
94,000	(g) 1,200
	41,200
Bal. 52,800	

Accounts Payable

− Debit	+ Credit
(d) 2,000	(c) 4,320
	Bal. 2,320

J. Molson, Capital

− Debit	+ Credit
	(a) 90,000
	(e) 5,200
	Bal. 95,200

J. Molson, Drawing

+ Debit	− Credit
(g) 1,200	
Bal. 1,200	

Fees Earned

− Debit	+ Credit
	(f) 4,000
	Bal. 4,000

Advertising Expense

+ Debit	− Credit
(c) 4,320	
Bal. 4,320	

Equipment

+ Debit	− Credit
(b) 38,000	
(e) 5,200	
Bal. 43,200	

Learning Objective  Prepare a trial balance.

A **trial balance** is a list of all account balances in two columns—one labeled "Debit" and one labeled "Credit." The trial balance shows that both sides of the accounting equation are equal. The heading consists of the company name, the title of the form (trial balance), and the date.

PRACTICE EXERCISE 5

Using the following account balances, prepare a trial balance for Collins's Backpack Adventures as of July 31, 20--.

Accounts Payable	$ 3,325	J. Collins, Drawing	$3,400
Accounts Receivable	4,150	Prepaid Insurance	1,675
Advertising Expense	680	Rent Expense	1,350
Cash	55,830	Supplies	575
Equipment	51,500	Utilities Expense	325
Income from Treks	23,220	Wages Expense	2,460
J. Collins, Capital	95,400		

PRACTICE EXERCISE 5 • SOLUTION

Collins's Backpack Adventures
Trial Balance
July 31, 20—

Account Name	Debit	Credit
Cash	55,830	
Accounts Receivable	4,150	
Supplies	575	
Prepaid Insurance	1,675	
Equipment	51,500	
Accounts Payable		3,325
J. Collins, Capital		95,400
J. Collins, Drawing	3,400	
Income from Treks		23,220
Wages Expense	2,460	
Rent Expense	1,350	
Advertising Expense	680	
Utilities Expense	325	
	121,945	121,945

Learning Objective  Present the fundamental accounting equation using the T account form and label the debit and credit sides.

(a) An **income statement** shows the results of operations of a business for a period of time. It includes revenue and expense accounts and reports either a **net income** or a **net loss**. (b) A **statement of owner's equity** shows the activity in the owner's equity, or Capital account, for a period of time. It includes the balance in the Capital account at the beginning of the period plus any additional investments and any increase or decrease in capital as the result of a net income (or a net loss) minus any withdrawals. (c) A **balance sheet** shows the financial condition of a business at a particular date in time. It summarizes the balances of the asset, liability, and owner's equity accounts on a given date.

PRACTICE EXERCISE 6

Use the trial balance in Practice Exercise 5 to prepare (a) an income statement, (b) a statement of owner's equity, and (c) a balance sheet. Assume that Collins's Backpack Adventures started business on July 1, 20--.

PRACTICE EXERCISE 6 • SOLUTION

(a)

Collins's Backpack Adventures
Income Statement
For Month Ended July 31, 20--

Revenue:		
Income from Treks		$23,220
Expenses:		
Wages Expense	$2,460	
Rent Expense	1,350	
Advertising Expense	680	
Utilities Expense	325	
Total Expenses		4,815
Net Income		$18,405

(b)

Collins's Backpack Adventures
Statement of Owner's Equity
For Month Ended July 31, 20--

J. Collins, Capital, July 1, 20--		$ 0
Investments during July	$ 95,400	
Net Income for July	18,405	
Subtotal	$113,805	
Less Withdrawals for July	3,400	
Increase in Capital		110,405
J. Collins, Capital, July 31, 20--		$ 110,405

(c)

Collins's Backpack Adventures
Balance Sheet
July 31, 20--

Assets		
Cash	$55,830	
Accounts Receivable	4,150	
Supplies	575	
Prepaid Insurance	1,675	
Equipment	51,500	
Total Assets		$ 113,730
Liabilities		
Accounts Payable		$ 3,325
Owner's Equity		
J. Collins, Capital		110,405
Total Liabilities and Owner's Equity		$ 113,730

CHAPTER REVIEW

Learning Objective  Recognize the effect of errors on account balances.

Transpositions and slides account for many trial balance errors. The clue is whether the difference in account balances or trial balance totals is evenly divisible by 9.

a. A **transposition** occurs when digits are switched around, such as 541 written as 415.

b. A **slide** is an error in placing the decimal point (in other words, a *slide* in the decimal point). For example, $62,000 could be inadvertently written as $6,200.

c. An error in a trial balance may be a combination of a transposition and a slide, as when $230 is written as $32.

7 PRACTICE EXERCISE 7

Identify the following errors as transpositions or slides and indicate the amount of the difference and whether it is divisible by 9.

a. The amount of supplies bought totaled $341, but it was written as $431.

b. Equipment was purchased for $3,500, but it was written as $35.

c. An error was made in the trial balance because $35 was written as $530.

PRACTICE EXERCISE 7 • SOLUTION

a. Transposition: The difference is $90 and can be evenly divided by 9.

Correct Number	Number Copied	Difference	Difference Divided by 9
$341	$431	$90	$90 ÷ 9 = $10

b. Slide: The difference is $3,465 and can be evenly divided by 9.

Correct Number	Number Copied	Difference	Difference Divided by 9
$3,500	$35	$3,465	$3,465 ÷ 9 = $385

c. Transposition and slide: The difference is $495 and can be evenly divided by 9.

Correct Number	Number Copied	Difference	Difference Divided by 9
$35	$530	$495	$495 ÷ 9 = $55

Glossary

Balance sheet A financial statement showing the financial position of an organization on a given date, such as June 30 or December 31. The balance sheet lists the balances in the asset, liability, and owner's equity accounts. *(p. 78)*

Compound entry A transaction that requires more than one debit or more than one credit to be recorded. *(p. 71)*

Credit The right side of a T account; to credit is to record an amount on the right side of a T account. Credits represent increases in liability, capital, or revenue accounts and decreases in asset, drawing, or expense accounts. *(p. 62)*

Debit The left side of a T account; to debit is to record an amount on the left side of a T account. Debits represent increases in asset, drawing, or expense accounts and decreases in liability, capital, or revenue accounts. *(p. 62)*

Financial position The resources or assets owned by an organization at a point in time, offset by the claims against those resources and owner's equity; shown on a balance sheet. *(p. 78)*

Financial statement A report prepared by accountants that summarizes the financial affairs of a business. *(p. 76)*

Footings The totals of each side of a T account. *(p. 60)*

Income statement A financial statement showing the results of business transactions involving revenue and expense accounts over a period of time. *(p. 76)*

Net income The result when total revenue exceeds total expenses over a period of time. *(p. 76)*

Net loss The result when total expenses exceed total revenue over a period of time. *(p. 76)*

Normal balance The plus side of a T account. *(p. 60)*

PDF (portable document format) An electronic file format that converts a printed document into an electronic image. *(p. 85)*

Profit and loss statement Another term for an income statement. *(p. 83)*

Report form The form of the balance sheet in which assets are placed at the top and liabilities and owner's equity are placed below. *(p. 78)*

Slide An error in placing the decimal point in a number. *(p. 80)*

Statement of owner's equity A financial statement showing the activity in the owner's equity, or Capital account, over the financial period. *(p. 77)*

T account form A form of account shaped like the letter *T* in which increases and decreases in the account may be recorded. One side of the *T* is for entries on the debit or left side. The other side of the *T* is for entries on the credit or right side. *(p. 59)*

Transposition An error that involves interchanging, or switching around, digits during the recording of a number. *(p. 80)*

Trial balance A list of all account balances to prove that the total of all debit balances equals the total of all credit balances. *(p. 75)*

Quiz Yourself

_____ 1. Determine the balance of the following T account:

Cash	
90,000	38,000
3,500	1,200
600	

a. 94,100 debit
b. 54,900 debit
c. 133,300 credit
d. 54,900 credit
e. 133,300 debit

_____ 2. Which of the following statements is correct?
a. Increases to cash are shown on the right side of the account.
b. Decreases to accounts payable are shown on the right side of the account.
c. Decreases to supplies are shown on the right side of the account.
d. Increases to rent expense are shown on the right side of the account.

_____ 3. Which of the following statements is false?
a. R. Flores, Capital is increased with a credit.
b. Prepaid Insurance is decreased with a credit.
c. Professional Fees is increased with a debit.
d. Rent Expense is increased with a debit.

_____ 4. R. Nelson invests his personal computer, with a fair market value of $2,500, in the business. How would this transaction be recorded?
a. A debit to R. Nelson, Capital, $2,500.
b. A credit to Cash, $2,500.
c. A credit to Professional Fees, $2,500
d. A debit to Computer, $2,500.

_____ 5. When preparing a trial balance, which of the following is correct?
a. The purpose of the trial balance is to prove that the total of all debit balances equals the total of all credit balances.
b. Advertising Expense would normally be recorded as a credit.
c. The trial balance is considered to be a financial statement.
d. Supplies would normally be recorded as a credit.

(Continued)

Use the following information for questions 6–8:

Flores's Catering
Trial Balance
February 28, 20—

Account Name	Debit	Credit
Cash	20,500	
Accounts Receivable	2,300	
Supplies	500	
Equipment	13,000	
Accounts Payable		3,500
R. Flores, Capital		22,000
R. Flores, Drawing	6,000	
Professional Fees		20,000
Rent Expense	2,400	
Advertising Expense	800	
	45,500	45,500

_____ 6. What would be the net income for Flores's Catering?
a. $45,500
b. $16,800
c. $19,800
d. $10,800

_____ 7. On which financial statement(s) would R. Flores, Drawing appear?
a. Income statement
b. Balance sheet
c. Statement of owner's equity
d. Income statement and statement of owner's equity

_____ 8. What is the amount of ending capital shown on the balance sheet for Flores's Catering?
a. $22,000
b. $20,000
c. $45,500
d. $32,800

_____ 9. Flores's Catering purchased equipment that cost $2,500 but it was recorded as $520. Which of the following statement(s) are correct?
a. This is a transposition error.
b. This is a slide error.
c. This is neither a transposition error nor a slide error.
d. Both a and b are correct.

Answers:
1.b 2.c 3.c 4.d 5.a 6.b 7.c 8.d 9.d

Review It with QuickBooks®

_____ 1. The trial balance report is located under _____________ in QuickBooks.
a. Company & Financial
b. Accountant & Taxes
c. Custom Reports
d. All of the above

_____ 2. The income statement is also known as the ___________ in QuickBooks.
a. Balance sheet
b. Trial balance
c. Profit and loss statement
d. Company & Financial

_____ 3. The balance sheet report is located under _____________ in QuickBooks.
   a. Company & Financial
   b. Accountant & Taxes
   c. Custom Reports
   d. All of the above

_____ 4. QuickBooks reports can be printed or saved as ________ files.
   a. PDF
   b. Excel
   c. Custom
   d. Both a and b are correct.

Answers:
1. b 2. c 3. a 4. d

Chapter Assignments

Discussion Questions

1. Explain how a trial balance and a balance sheet differ.
2. Explain why the term *debit* doesn't always mean "increase" and why the term *credit* doesn't always mean "decrease."
3. What are footings in accounting?
4. How are the three financial statements shown in this chapter connected?
5. What is a compound entry?
6. List two reasons why the debits and credits in the trial balance might not balance.
7. Give an example of a slide and an example of a transposition. Explain how you might decide whether an error is a slide or a transposition.
8. What do we mean when we say that capital, drawing, revenue, and expense accounts are under the umbrella of owner's equity?

Exercises

LO 2, 3

Practice Exercise 2, 3

EXERCISE 2-1 On a sheet of paper, draw the fundamental accounting equation with T accounts under each of the account classifications, with plus and minus signs and debit and credit on the appropriate side of each account. Under each of the classifications, draw T accounts, again with the correct plus and minus signs and debit and credit, for each of the following accounts of Barlow Engine Repair.

Cash
Accounts Receivable
Supplies
Equipment
Accounts Payable
D. Barlow, Capital
D. Barlow, Drawing
Income from Repairs
Wages Expense
Rent Expense
Utilities Expense
Miscellaneous Expense

2, 3

Practice Exercises 2, 3

EXERCISE 2-2 List the classification of each of the following accounts as A (asset), L (liability), OE (owner's equity), R (revenue), or E (expense). Write *Debit* or *Credit* to indicate the increase side, the decrease side, and the normal balance side.

Account	Classification	Increase Side	Normal Balance Side	Decrease Side
0. Cash	A	Debit	Debit	Credit
1. Wages Expense				
2. Equipment				
3. L. Cross, Capital				
4. Service Revenue				
5. L. Cross, Drawing				
6. Accounts Receivable				
7. Rent Expense				
8. Fees Earned				
9. Accounts Payable				

LO 2, 3, 4

Practice Exercise 4

EXERCISE 2-3 R. Dalberg operates Dalberg's Tours. The company has the following chart of accounts:

Assets	**Liabilities**	**Revenue**
Cash	Accounts Payable	Income from Tours
Accounts Receivable		
Supplies	**Owner's Equity**	**Expenses**
Prepaid Insurance	R. Dalberg, Capital	Wages Expense
Display Equipment	R. Dalberg, Drawing	Gas Expense
Van		Advertising Expense
Office Equipment		Utilities Expense

Using the chart of accounts, record the following transactions in pairs of T accounts. Give the T account to be debited first and the account to be credited to the right. Show debit and credit and plus and minus signs. (Example: Received and paid the bill for the month's rent, $480.)

Rent Expense		Cash	
+	−	+	−
Debit	Credit	Debit	Credit
480			480

a. Received and paid the electric bill, $175.
b. Bought supplies on account, $135.
c. Paid for insurance for one year, $580.
d. Made a payment on account to a creditor, $65.
e. Received and paid the telephone bill, $186.
f. Sold services on account, $1,375.
g. Received and paid the gasoline bill for the van, $130.
h. Received cash on account from customers, $1,458.
i. Dalberg withdrew cash for personal use, $700.

LO 4

Practice Exercise 4

EXERCISE 2-4 During the first month of operation, Graham Expeditions recorded the following transactions. Describe what has happened in each of the transactions (a) through (k).

Cash

Debit	Credit
(a) 4,500	(b) 525
(k) 1,125	(c) 98
	(e) 75
	(g) 500
	(i) 220
	(j) 1,500

Accounts Receivable

Debit	Credit
(h) 615	

Supplies

Debit	Credit
(d) 680	

Equipment

Debit	Credit
(f) 3,510	
(g) 2,000	

Accounts Payable

Debit	Credit
	(d) 680
	(g) 1,500

C. M. Graham, Capital

Debit	Credit
	(a) 4,500
	(f) 3,510

C. M. Graham, Drawing

Debit	Credit
(j) 1,500	

Income from Tours

Debit	Credit
	(h) 615
	(k) 1,125

Rent Expense

Debit	Credit
(b) 525	

Advertising Expense

Debit	Credit
(c) 98	

Utilities Expense

Debit	Credit
(i) 220	

Miscellaneous Expense

Debit	Credit
(e) 75	

LO 5

Practice Exercise 5

EXERCISE 2-5 Speedy Sewing Services, owned by T. Nguyen, hired a new bookkeeper who is not entirely familiar with the process of preparing a trial balance. All of the accounts have normal balances. Find the errors and prepare a corrected trial balance for December 31 of this year.

Speedy Sewing Services
Trial Balance
December 31, 20—

Account Name	Debit	Credit
Accounts Receivable		10,700
Cash	3,200	
Accounts Payable		9,500
Equipment	24,000	
T. Nguyen, Capital		22,800
T. Nguyen, Drawing		1,900
Prepaid Insurance		1,300
Income from Services		36,000
Wages Expense	17,500	
Rent Expense		4,500
Supplies	1,800	
Utilities Expense	3,400	
	49,900	86,700

 5, 6

Practice Exercises 5, 6

EXERCISE 2-6 During the first month of operations, Landish Modeling Agency recorded transactions in T account form. Foot and balance the accounts; then prepare a trial balance, an income statement, a statement of owner's equity, and a balance sheet dated March 31, 20--.

Cash

	Debit		Credit
(a)	8,200	(b)	350
(c)	8,400	(d)	1,600
(i)	7,580	(f)	175
		(g)	3,400
		(h)	2,200

Accounts Receivable

	Debit		Credit
(e)	2,600		

Supplies

	Debit		Credit
(j)	82		

Office Furniture

	Debit		Credit
(b)	350		

Office Equipment

	Debit		Credit
(k)	2,800		

Accounts Payable

	Debit		Credit
		(k)	2,800
		(j)	82

R. Landish, Capital

	Debit		Credit
		(a)	8,200

R. Landish, Drawing

	Debit		Credit
(h)	2,200		

Modeling Fees

	Debit		Credit
		(c)	8,400
		(e)	2,600
		(i)	7,580

Salary Expense

	Debit		Credit
(g)	3,400		

Rent Expense

	Debit		Credit
(d)	1,600		

Utilities Expense

	Debit		Credit
(f)	175		

LO 7

Practice Exercise 7

EXERCISE 2-7 The following errors were made in journalizing transactions. In each case, calculate the amount of the error and indicate whether the debit or the credit column of the trial balance will be understated or overstated.

	Amount of Difference	Debit or Credit Column of Trial Balance Understated or Overstated
0. Example: A $149 debit to Accounts Receivable was not recorded.	$149	Debit column understated
a. A $42 debit to Supplies was recorded as $420.		
b. A $155 debit to Accounts Receivable was recorded twice.		
c. A $179 debit to Prepaid Insurance was not recorded.		
d. A $65 credit to Cash was not recorded.		
e. A $190 debit to Equipment was recorded twice.		
f. A $57 debit to Utilities Expense was recorded as $75.		

LO 7

Practice Exercise 7

EXERCISE 2-8 Would the following errors cause the trial balance to have equal or unequal totals? As a result of the errors, which accounts are overstated (by how much) or understated (by how much)?

a. A purchase of office equipment for $380 was recorded as a debit to Office Equipment for $38 and a credit to Cash for $38.
b. A payment of $280 to a creditor was debited to Accounts Receivable and credited to Cash for $280 each.

c. A purchase of supplies for $245 was recorded as a debit to Equipment for $245 and a credit to Cash for $245.
d. A payment of $76 to a creditor was recorded as a debit to Accounts Payable for $76 and a credit to Cash for $67.

Problem Set A

LO 1, 2, 3, 4

PROBLEM 2-1A During December of this year, G. Elden established Ginny's Gym. The following asset, liability, and owner's equity accounts are included in the chart of accounts:

Cash
Exercise Equipment
Store Equipment
Office Equipment
Accounts Payable
G. Elden, Capital
Income from Services
Advertising Expense

During December, the following transactions occurred:

a. Elden deposited $35,000 in a bank account in the name of the business.
b. Bought exercise equipment for cash, $8,150, Ck. No. 1001.
c. Bought advertising on account from Hazel Company, $105.
d. Bought a display rack (Store Equipment) on account from Cyber Core, $790.
e. Bought office equipment on account from Office Aids, $185.
f. Elden invested her exercise equipment with a fair market value of $1,200 in the business.
g. Made a payment to Cyber Core, $200, Ck. No. 1002.
h. Sold services for the month of December for cash, $800.

Check Figure
Balance of Cash, $27,450

Required

1. Write the account classifications (Assets, Liabilities, Capital, Drawing, Revenue, Expense) in the fundamental accounting equation, as well as the plus and minus signs and *Debit* and *Credit*.
2. Write the account names on the T accounts under the classifications, place the plus and minus signs for each T account, and label the debit and credit sides of the T accounts.
3. Record the amounts in the proper positions in the T accounts. Write the letter next to each entry to identify the transaction.
4. Foot and balance the accounts.

LO 1, 2, 3, 4, 5

PROBLEM 2-2A B. Kelso established Computer Wizards during November of this year. The accountant prepared the following chart of accounts:

Assets
Cash
Supplies
Computer Software
Office Equipment
Neon Sign

Liabilities
Accounts Payable

Owner's Equity
B. Kelso, Capital
B. Kelso, Drawing

Revenue
Income from Services

Expenses
Wages Expense
Rent Expense
Advertising Expense
Utilities Expense
Miscellaneous Expense

(*Continued*)

The following transactions occurred during the month:

a. Kelso deposited $45,000 in a bank account in the name of the business.
b. Paid the rent for the current month, $1,800, Ck. No. 2001.
c. Bought office desks and filing cabinets for cash, $790, Ck. No. 2002.
d. Bought a computer and printer (Office Equipment) from Cyber Center for use in the business, $2,700, paying $1,700 in cash and placing the balance on account, Ck. No. 2003.
e. Bought a neon sign on account from Signage Co., $1,350.
f. Kelso invested her personal computer software with a fair market value of $600 in the business.
g. Received a bill from *Country News* for newspaper advertising, $365.
h. Sold services for cash, $1,245.
i. Received and paid the electric bill, $345, Ck. No. 2004.
j. Paid on account to *Country News,* a creditor, $285, Ck. No. 2005.
k. Sold services for cash, $1,450.
l. Paid wages to an employee, $925, Ck. No. 2006.
m. Received and paid the bill for the city business license, $75, Ck. No. 2007 (Miscellaneous Expense).
n. Kelso withdrew cash for personal use, $850, Ck. No. 2008.
o. Bought printer paper and letterhead stationery on account from Office Aids, $115.

Check Figure
Trial balance total, $50,840

Required

1. Record the owner's name in the Capital and Drawing T accounts.
2. Correctly place the plus and minus signs for each T account and label the debit and credit sides of the accounts.
3. Record the transactions in T accounts. Write the letter of each entry to identify the transaction.
4. Foot the T accounts and show the balances.
5. Prepare a trial balance, with a three-line heading, dated November 30, 20--.

LO 1, 2, 3, 4, 5, 6

PROBLEM 2-3A S. Myers, a speech therapist, opened a clinic in the name of Myers Clinic. Her accountant prepared the following chart of accounts:

Assets
Cash
Accounts Receivable
Office Equipment
Office Furniture

Liabilities
Accounts Payable

Owner's Equity
S. Myers, Capital
S. Myers, Drawing

Revenue
Professional Fees

Expenses
Salary Expense
Rent Expense
Utilities Expense
Miscellaneous Expense

The following transactions occurred during June of this year:

a. Myers deposited $40,000 in a bank account in the name of the business.
b. Bought waiting room chairs and tables (Office Furniture) on account, $1,330.
c. Bought a fax/copier/scanner combination (Office Equipment) from Max's Equipment for $595, paying $200 in cash and placing the balance on account, Ck. No. 1001.
d. Bought an intercom system (Office Equipment) on account from Regan Office Supply, $375.

e. Received and paid the telephone bill, $155, Ck. No. 1002.
f. Sold professional services on account, $1,484.
g. Received and paid the electric bill, $190, Ck. No. 1003.
h. Received and paid the bill for the state speech therapy convention, $450, Ck. No. 1004 (Miscellaneous Expense).
i. Sold professional services for cash, $2,575.
j. Paid on account to Regan Office Supply, $300, Ck. No. 1005.
k. Paid the rent for the current month, $940, Ck. No. 1006.
l. Paid salary of the receptionist, $880, Ck. No. 1007.
m. Myers withdrew cash for personal use, $800, Ck. No. 1008.
n. Received $885 on account from patients who were previously billed.

Required

1. Record the owner's name in the Capital and Drawing T accounts.
2. Correctly place the plus and minus signs for each T account and label the debit and credit sides of the accounts.
3. Record the transactions in the T accounts. Write the letter of each entry to identify the transaction.
4. Foot the T accounts and show the balances.
5. Prepare a trial balance as of June 30, 20--.
6. Prepare an income statement for June 30, 20--.
7. Prepare a statement of owner's equity for June 30, 20--.
8. Prepare a balance sheet as of June 30, 20--.

Check Figure
Net Income, $1,444

LO 1, 2, 3, 4, 5, 6

PROBLEM 2-4A On May 1, B. Bangle opened Self-Wash Laundry. His accountant listed the following chart of accounts:

Cash
Supplies
Prepaid Insurance
Equipment
Furniture and Fixtures
Accounts Payable
B. Bangle, Capital
B. Bangle, Drawing
Laundry Revenue
Wages Expense
Rent Expense
Utilities Expense
Miscellaneous Expense

The following transactions were completed during May:

a. Bangle deposited $35,000 in a bank account in the name of the business.
b. Bought chairs and tables (Furniture and Fixtures), paying cash, $1,870, Ck. No. 1000.
c. Bought supplies on account from Barnes Supply Company, $225.
d. Paid the rent for the current month, $875, Ck. No. 1001.
e. Bought washing machines and dryers (Equipment) from Lara Equipment Company, $12,500, paying $3,600 in cash and placing the balance on account, Ck. No. 1002.
f. Sold services for cash for the first half of the month, $1,925.
g. Bought insurance for one year, $1,560, Ck. No. 1003.
h. Paid on account to Lara Equipment Company, $1,800, Ck. No. 1004.
i. Received and paid electric bill, $285, Ck. No. 1005.
j. Sold services for cash for the second half of the month, $1,835.
k. Paid wages to an employee, $940, Ck. No. 1006.
l. Bangle withdrew cash for his personal use, $800, Ck. No. 1007.
m. Paid on account to Barnes Supply Company, $225, Ck. No. 1008.
n. Received and paid bill from the county for sidewalk repair assessment, $280, Ck. No. 1009 (Miscellaneous Expense).

(*Continued*)

CHAPTER ASSIGNMENTS

Check Figure
Trial balance total, $45,860

Required

1. Record the owner's name in the Capital and Drawing T accounts.
2. Correctly place the plus and minus signs for each T account and label the debit and credit sides of the accounts.
3. Record the transactions in the T accounts. Write the letter of each entry to identify the transaction.
4. Foot the T accounts and show the balances.
5. Prepare a trial balance as of May 31, 20--.
6. Prepare an income statement for May 31, 20--.
7. Prepare a statement of owner's equity for May 31, 20--.
8. Prepare a balance sheet as of May 31, 20--.

LO 6

PROBLEM 2-5A The financial statements for Daniels' Custom Haircuts for the month of October follow.

Daniels' Custom Haircuts
Income Statement
(a)

Revenue:		
Professional Fees		$25,000
Expenses:		
Salary Expense	$1,200	
Rent Expense	3,000	
Utilities Expense	600	
Miscellaneous Expense	450	
Total Expenses		(b)
Net Income		$19,750

(c)
Statement of Owner's Equity
(d)

Q. Daniels, Capital, October 1, 20--		$ 0
Investments during October	$ (e)	
Net Income for October	(f)	
Subtotal	$29,750	
Less Withdrawals for October	4,000	
Increase in Capital		(g)
Q. Daniels, Capital, October 31, 20--		$25,750

Daniels' Custom Haircuts
Balance Sheet
(h)

Assets		
Cash	$16,000	
Accounts Receivable	2,400	
Office Equipment	10,000	
Office Furniture	8,000	
Total Assets		$ (i)
Liabilities		
Accounts Payable		$ 10,650
Owner's Equity		
Q. Daniels, Capital		(j)
Total Liabilities and Owner's Equity		$ (k)

Required
Solve for the missing information.

Problem Set B

LO 1, 2, 3, 4

PROBLEM 2-1B During February of this year, H. Rose established Rose Shoe Hospital. The following asset, liability, and owner's equity accounts are included in the chart of accounts:

Cash	Accounts Payable
Shop Equipment	H. Rose, Capital
Store Equipment	Income from Services
Office Equipment	Advertising Expense

The following transactions occurred during the month of February:

a. Rose deposited $25,000 cash in a bank account in the name of the business.
b. Bought shop equipment for cash, $1,525, Ck. No. 1000.
c. Bought advertising on account from Milland Company, $325.
d. Bought store shelving on account from Inger Hardware, $750.
e. Bought office equipment from Shara's Office Supply, $625, paying $225 in cash and placing the balance on account, Ck. No. 1001.
f. Paid on account to Inger Hardware, $750, Ck. No. 1002.
g. Rose invested his personal leather working tools with a fair market value of $800 in the business.
h. Sold services for the month of February for cash, $250.

(*Continued*)

CHAPTER ASSIGNMENTS

Check Figure
Cash balance, $22,750

Required

1. Write the account classifications (Assets, Liabilities, Capital, Drawing, Revenue, Expense) in the fundamental accounting equation, as well as the plus and minus signs and *Debit* and *Credit*.
2. Write the account names on the T accounts under the classifications, place the plus and minus signs for each T account, and label the debit and credit sides of the T accounts.
3. Record the amounts in the proper positions in the T accounts. Write the letter next to each entry to identify the transaction.
4. Foot and balance the accounts.

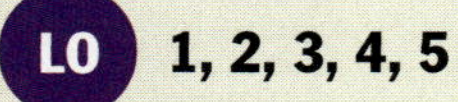
LO 1, 2, 3, 4, 5
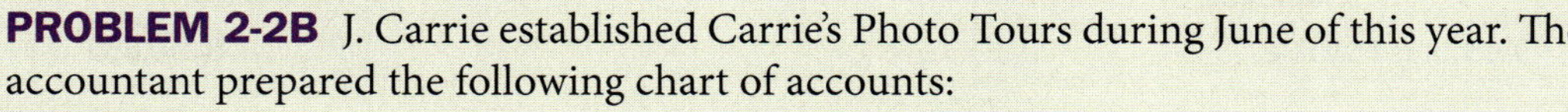

PROBLEM 2-2B J. Carrie established Carrie's Photo Tours during June of this year. The accountant prepared the following chart of accounts:

Assets
Cash
Supplies
Computer Software
Office Equipment
Neon Sign

Liabilities
Accounts Payable

Owner's Equity
J. Carrie, Capital
J. Carrie, Drawing

Revenue
Income from Services

Expenses
Wages Expense
Rent Expense
Advertising Expense
Utilities Expense
Miscellaneous Expense

The following transactions occurred during the month of June:

a. Carrie deposited $30,000 cash in a bank account in the name of the business.
b. Bought office equipment for cash, $1,850, Ck. No. 1001.
c. Bought computer software from Morey's Computer Center, $640, paying $350 in cash and placing the balance on account, Ck. No. 1002.
d. Paid current month's rent, $950, Ck. No. 1003.
e. Sold services for cash, $1,575.
f. Bought a neon sign from The Sign Company, $1,335, paying $435 in cash and placing the balance on account, Ck. No. 1004.
g. Received bill from *The Gossiper* for advertising, $445.
h. Bought supplies on account from City Supply, $460.
i. Received and paid the electric bill, $380, Ck. No. 1005.
j. Paid on account to *The Gossiper*, $245, Ck. No. 1006.
k. Sold services for cash, $3,474.
l. Paid wages to an employee, $930, Ck. No. 1007.
m. Carrie invested his personal computer (Office Equipment) with a fair market value of $1,000 in the business.
n. Carrie withdrew cash for personal use, $800, Ck. No. 1008.
o. Received and paid the bill for city business license, $75, Ck. No. 1009 (Miscellaneous Expense).

Check Figure
Trial balance total, $37,899

Required

1. Record the owner's name in the Capital and Drawing T accounts.
2. Correctly place the plus and minus signs for each T account and label the debit and credit sides of the accounts.

3. Record the transactions in the T accounts. Write the letter of each entry to identify the transaction.
4. Foot the T accounts and show the balances.
5. Prepare a trial balance, with a three-line heading, dated June 30, 20--.

 1, 2, 3, 4, 5, 6

PROBLEM 2-3B D. Johnston, a physical therapist, opened Johnston's Clinic. His accountant provided the following chart of accounts:

Assets	Owner's Equity	Expenses
Cash	D. Johnston, Capital	Salary Expense
Accounts Receivable	D. Johnston, Drawing	Rent Expense
Office Equipment	**Revenue**	Utilities Expense
Office Furniture	Professional Fees	Miscellaneous Expense
Liabilities		
Accounts Payable		

The following transactions occurred during July of this year:

a. Johnston deposited $35,000 in a bank account in the name of the business.
b. Bought filing cabinets (Office Equipment) on account from Muller Office Supply, $560.
c. Paid cash for chairs and carpeting (Office Furniture) for the waiting room, $835, Ck. No. 1000.
d. Bought a photocopier from Rob's Office Equipment, $650, paying $250 in cash and placing the balance on account, Ck. No. 1001.
e. Received and paid the telephone bill, which included installation charges, $185, Ck. No. 1002.
f. Sold professional services on account, $2,255.
g. Received and paid the bill for the state physical therapy convention, $445, Ck. No. 1003 (Miscellaneous Expense).
h. Received and paid the electric bill, $335, Ck. No. 1004.
i. Received cash on account from credit customers, $1,940.
j. Paid on account to Muller Office Supply, $250, Ck. No. 1005.
k. Paid the office rent for the current month, $1,245, Ck. No. 1006.
l. Sold professional services for cash, $1,950.
m. Paid the salary of the receptionist, $960, Ck. No. 1007.
n. Johnston withdrew cash for personal use, $1,200, Ck. No. 1008.

Required

1. Record the owner's name in the Capital and Drawing T accounts.
2. Correctly place the plus and minus signs for each T account and label the debit and credit sides of the accounts.
3. Record the transactions in the T accounts. Write the letter of each entry to identify the transaction.
4. Foot the T accounts and show the balances.
5. Prepare a trial balance as of July 31, 20--.
6. Prepare an income statement for July 31, 20--.
7. Prepare a statement of owner's equity for July 31, 20--.
8. Prepare a balance sheet as of July 31, 20--.

Check Figure
Net Income, $1,035

1, 2, 4, 5, 6

PROBLEM 2-4B On July 1, K. Resser opened Resser's Business Services. Resser's accountant listed the following chart of accounts:

Cash	K. Resser, Drawing
Supplies	Business Services Revenue
Prepaid Insurance	Wages Expense
Equipment	Rent Expense
Furniture and Fixtures	Utilities Expense
Accounts Payable	Miscellaneous Expense
K. Resser, Capital	

The following transactions were completed during July:

a. Resser deposited $25,000 in a bank account in the name of the business.
b. Bought tables and chairs (Furniture and Fixtures) for cash, $725, Ck. No. 1200.
c. Paid the rent for the current month, $1,750, Ck. No. 1201.
d. Bought computers and copy machines (Equipment) from Ferber Equipment, $15,700, paying $4,000 in cash and placing the balance on account, Ck. No. 1202.
e. Bought supplies on account from Wiggins's Distributors, $535.
f. Sold services for cash, $1,742.
g. Bought insurance for one year, $1,375, Ck. No. 1203.
h. Paid on account to Ferber Equipment, $700, Ck. No. 1204.
i. Received and paid the electric bill, $438, Ck. No. 1205.
j. Paid on account to Wiggins's Distributors, $315, Ck. No. 1206.
k. Sold services to customers for cash for the second half of the month, $820.
l. Received and paid the bill for the business license, $75, Ck. No. 1207 (Miscellaneous Expense).
m. Paid wages to an employee, $1,200, Ck. No. 1208.
n. Resser withdrew cash for personal use, $700, Ck. No. 1209.

Check Figure
K. Resser, Capital, July 31, 20--, $23,399

Required

1. Record the owner's name in the Capital and Drawing T accounts.
2. Correctly place the plus and minus signs for each T account and label the debit and credit sides of the accounts.
3. Record the transactions in the T accounts. Write the letter of each entry to identify the transaction.
4. Foot the T accounts and show the balances.
5. Prepare a trial balance as of July 31, 20--.
6. Prepare an income statement for July 31, 20--.
7. Prepare a statement of owner's equity for July 31, 20--.
8. Prepare a balance sheet as of July 31, 20--.

CHAPTER ASSIGNMENTS

LO 6

PROBLEM 2-5B The financial statements for Baker Custom Catering for the month of April are presented below.

Baker Custom Catering
Income Statement
(a)

Revenue:		
Professional Fees		$12,000
Expenses:		
Salary Expense	$ 800	
Rent Expense	1,200	
Utilities Expense	360	
Miscellaneous Expense	80	
Total Expenses		(b)
Net Income		$ 9,560

(c)
Statement of Owner's Equity
(d)

L. Baker, Capital, April 1, 20--		$ 0
Investments during April	$ (e)	
Net Income for April	(f)	
Subtotal	$14,560	
Less Withdrawals for April	1,000	
Increase in Capital		(g)
L. Baker, Capital, April 30, 20--		$13,560

Baker Custom Catering
Balance Sheet
(h)

Assets		
Cash	$8,000	
Accounts Receivable	800	
Office Equipment	4,000	
Office Furniture	2,000	
Total Assets		$ (i)
Liabilities		
Accounts Payable		$ 1,240
Owner's Equity		
L. Baker, Capital		(j)
Total Liabilities and Owner's Equity		$ (k)

Required

Solve for the missing information.

Try It with QuickBooks® (LO 2-7)

QB Exercise 2-1

Using the Conner's Whitewater Adventures demonstration file from Chapter 1, complete the following activities with QuickBooks. Use the dates June 1, 20--, to June 30, 20--, for all reports.

1. View and print the trial balance report for Conner's Whitewater Adventures.
   a. What is the total of the Debit column on the trial balance?
2. View and print the standard profit and loss statement for Conner's Whitewater Adventures.
   a. What is the net income or net loss for Conner's Whitewater Adventures?
3. View and print the standard balance sheet for Conner's Whitewater Adventures.
   a. What is the amount of Conner's Whitewater Adventures total assets?
4. Save the profit and loss statement as a PDF.
5. Save the profit and loss statement as an Excel file.

Activities

Why Does It Matter?

SOLID ROCK GYM, San Diego, California

Individuals and groups of all ages come to Solid Rock Gym for fun and fitness. Services include several types of indoor rock-climbing experiences such as individual and group instruction, team development, and fitness programs. Solid Rock Gym also offers bouldering (climbing close to the bottom—no rope or hardware), top-roping (climbing while protected by a rope running through anchors above the intended route), and lead climbing (climbing while protected by a rope clipped to anchors as the climber ascends a route).

List five transactions that Solid Rock Gym might record during the month. Determine what accounts are involved and whether the accounts are debited or credited.

Example: Transaction 0. Owner invested cash in the business. Accounts involved: Cash and Capital. Cash is debited, and Capital is credited.

What Would You Say?

A fellow accounting student has difficulty understanding how the fundamental accounting equation stays in balance when a compound entry with one debit and two credits is recorded. Consider, for example, that a business bought equipment for $7,000, paid $3,000 in cash, and placed the remainder on account.

This means that there are two credits and one debit—one debit and one credit on the left side of the equation and the other credit on the right side of the equation. Explain to your fellow student how the equation stays in balance.

What Would You Do?

A new bookkeeper can't find the errors that are causing the company's month-end trial balance to be out of balance. The bookkeeper is too shy to ask for help at the office, so she takes the financial records home and asks her uncle, a retired bookkeeper, to help her locate the errors. Even with the help of her uncle, the trial balance is still out of balance, and now she is too embarrassed to return to the office and ask for help. What is wrong with this practice, if anything?

chapter

3 The General Journal and the General Ledger

Learning Objectives

After you have completed this chapter, you will be able to do the following:

1. Record a group of transactions pertaining to a service business in a two-column general journal.
2. Post entries from a two-column general journal to general ledger accounts.
3. Prepare a trial balance from the ledger accounts.
4. Explain the importance of source documents.
5. Correct entries using the ruling or correcting entry method.

To: **Amy Roberts, CPA**
Subject: **Recording Transactions**

Hi Amy,
This accounting stuff can be tough! But I think I am finally getting the hang of recording transactions using T accounts. Is this how accountants actually record transactions? As I have been looking around in QuickBooks, I don't see T accounts anywhere! Help!
Thanks,
Janie

To: **Janie Conner**
Subject: **RE: Recording Transactions**

Hi Janie,
You're right—you won't find T accounts in QuickBooks. That's because recording transactions using T accounts is a beginning step. Are you ready to learn how accountants actually record transactions—in journal entries? Using what you've learned so far about T accounts and debits and credits, you're ready to move on. Here's what you'll need to do:

_____ 1. Begin recording transactions using journal entries.
_____ 2. Learn how to post journal entries into the ledger.

Your knowledge of T accounts and debits and credits is very important for this next challenge and will help you prepare the journal entries correctly. Before you get started, take some time to review the rules of debits and credits. This will really help! You are now ready to start using QuickBooks to record transactions. I will send you some hints to help you get started.
Amy

Jose Luis Pelaez Inc/Blend Images/Getty Images

Accounting Language

Cost principle (p. 115)
Cross-reference (p. 120)
General ledger (p. 118)
Journal (p. 111)
Journalizing (p. 111)
Ledger account (p. 118)
Posting (p. 120)
Source documents (p. 111)
Two-column general journal (p. 113)

In Chapter 2, we learned how to use T accounts as a tool for practicing debits and credits. We also used the trial balance as a means of making sure the debits equal the credits. In this chapter, we will further formalize our accounting procedures by learning about the general journal and the posting procedure.

Recall that *recording* is a step in the definition of accounting. Here we introduce the journal as the official record of business transactions. We have recorded business transactions as debits and credits to T accounts because it's easier to visualize these debits and credits as the plus and minus sides of the T accounts involved. **Determining the appropriate transaction debits and credits is the most important element in the accounting process.** It represents the very basic foundation of accounting, and all of the structure represented by financial statements and other reports is entirely dependent upon it. After determining the debits and credits, the accountant records the transactions in a journal.

The initial steps in the accounting process are as follows:

STEP 1. Record business transactions in a journal.

STEP 2. Post entries to accounts in the ledger.

STEP 3. Prepare a trial balance.

In this chapter, we explain all three steps.

THE GENERAL JOURNAL

Learning Objective 1 Record a group of transactions pertaining to a service business in a two-column general journal.

We have seen that an accountant must keep a record of each transaction. In Chapter 2, we recorded the transactions directly in T accounts; however, only part of the transaction would be listed in each T account. A **journal** is a book in which business transactions are recorded as they happen. In the journal, both the debits and the credits of the entire transaction are recorded in one place. Actually, the journal is a diary for the business in which you record in day-by-day or chronological order all the events involving financial affairs. A journal is called a *book of original entry*. In other words, a transaction is always recorded first in the journal. The process of recording a business transaction in the journal is called **journalizing**. The information about transactions comes from **source documents** such as checks, invoices, receipts, letters, and memos. These source documents furnish proof (objective evidence) that a transaction has taken place, and they should be identified in the journal entry whenever possible.

Remember the first transaction for Conner's Whitewater Adventures?

TRANSACTION (a). June 1: Conner deposited $90,000 in a bank account in the name of the business.

When the business receives the cash from J. Conner, the accountant creates a source document—in this case, a receipt. See Figure 1 for an example of the source document that would be created.

Figure 1
Source document

Receipt Date *June 1* 20 — No.

Received From *J. Conner* *90,000.00*

Ninety thousand and 00/100 ************************* Dollars

For *Owner investment*

Next, the accountant needs to analyze this transaction. We already know how to do this by following the steps presented in Chapter 2.

STEP 1. What accounts are involved? Cash and J. Conner, Capital are involved.

STEP 2. What are the classifications of the accounts involved? Cash is an asset account, and J. Conner, Capital is an owner's equity account.

STEP 3. Are the accounts increased or decreased? Cash is increased because Conner's Whitewater Adventures has more cash now than it had before. J. Conner, Capital is increased because Conner has a greater investment now than it had before.

STEP 4. Write the transaction as a debit to one account (or accounts) and a credit to another account (or accounts). Cash is increased, and the increase side of Cash is the left, or debit, side. J. Conner, Capital is an owner's equity account and is increased. The increase side of Capital is the right, or credit, side.

STEP 5. Is the equation in balance after the transaction has been recorded? Yes.

Let's show these entries by referring to our reliable fundamental accounting equation with the accompanying T accounts.

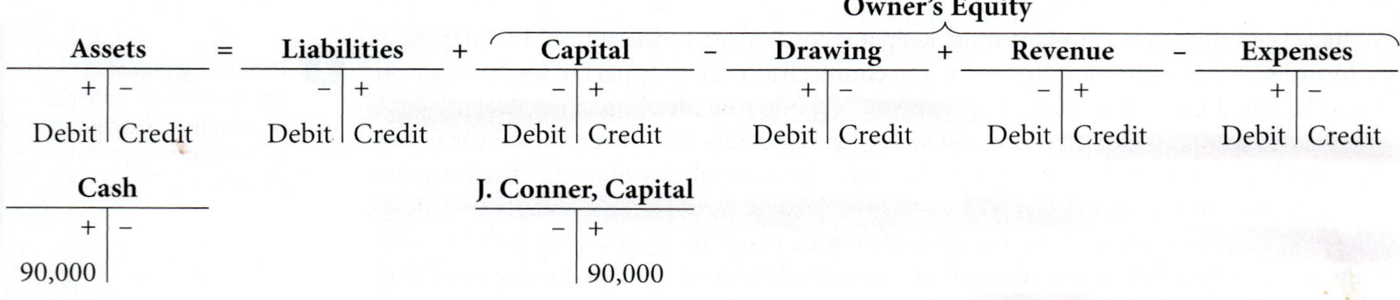

Now the accountant is ready to journalize the transaction. He or she records the business transaction in the journal. The basic form of the journal is the

two-column general journal. The term *two-column* refers to the two columns used for debit and credit amounts. The pages of the journal are numbered in consecutive order.

Let's take a look at completed transaction (a) in the journal.

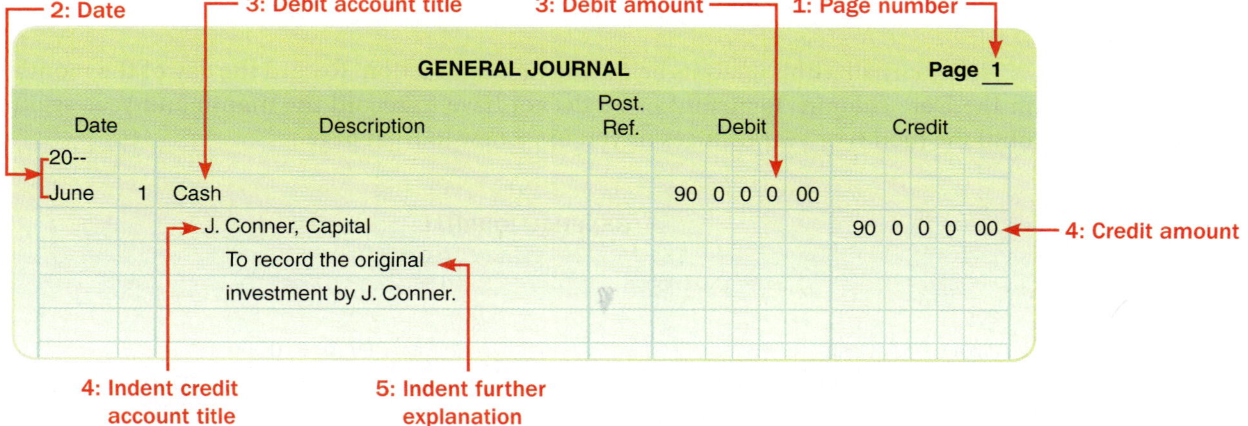

GENERAL JOURNAL — Page 1

Date		Description	Post. Ref.	Debit	Credit
20--					
June	1	Cash		90 0 0 0 00	
		J. Conner, Capital			90 0 0 0 00
		To record the original			
		investment by J. Conner.			

To explain the entry, we will break it down line by line. All journal entries contain the following:

STEP 1. *Page Number:* At the top of the page, record the page number.

STEP 2. *Date:* On the first line, record the year in the left part of the Date column. On the second line, record the month in the left part of the Date column and the day of the month in the right part of the Date column. *You don't have to repeat the year and month until you start a new page or until the year or month changes.*

STEP 3. *Debit:* **The debit part of the entry is always recorded first.** Insert the account title in the Description column and the dollar amount in the Debit column.

STEP 4. *Credit:* **The credit part of the entry is always indented and inserted on the line below the debit entry.** Insert the account title in the Description column and the dollar amount in the Credit column.

STEP 5. *Explanation:* **The explanation, indented further, is inserted on the line below the last line of the entry.** The explanation should refer to source documents, providing information such as check numbers, receipt numbers, or invoice numbers. You may also list names of charge customers or creditors or terms of payment.

For an entry in the general journal to be complete, it must contain (1) the date, (2) a debit entry, (3) a credit entry, and (4) an explanation. To anyone thoroughly familiar with the accounts, the explanation may seem obvious. Nevertheless, record the explanation as a required, integral part of the entry. To make the journal entries easier to read, leave one blank line between each transaction in your homework.

TRANSACTION (b). June 2: Conner's Whitewater Adventures bought equipment, paying cash, $38,000. Decide which accounts are involved. Then determine which of the five possible classifications each part of the transaction applies to. Visualize the plus and minus signs for each classification. Decide whether the accounts are increased or decreased. When you use T accounts to analyze the transaction, the results are as follows:

Customarily, accountants don't abbreviate account titles. If you are using accounting software, you will probably have to key only the first few letters of the name of the account before the program will recognize it or you may have to key in just the account number.

QuickBooks Tip

In accounting software, like QuickBooks, there is also space for a brief explanation. In QuickBooks, the explanation is recorded in the Memo column.

Remember

As in a trial balance, there are no dollar signs in journal entries.

Equipment	
+	−
Debit	Credit
38,000	

Cash	
+	−
Debit	Credit
	38,000

Now journalize this analysis below the first transaction. Record the day of the month in the Date column. Remember, you do not have to record the month and year again until the month or year changes or you use a new journal page.

Skip a line between entries in your homework

GENERAL JOURNAL Page 1

Date		Description	Post. Ref.	Debit	Credit
20--					
June	1	Cash		90 0 0 0 00	
		J. Conner, Capital			90 0 0 0 00
		To record the original			
		investment by J. Conner.			
	2	Equipment		38 0 0 0 00	
		Cash			38 0 0 0 00
		Bought equipment for cash.			

TRANSACTION (c). June 3: Conner's Whitewater Adventures bought equipment on account from Signal Products, $4,320. Again, start with the T accounts.

Equipment	
+	−
Debit	Credit
4,320	

Accounts Payable	
−	+
Debit	Credit
	4,320

After skipping a line in the journal, record the day of the month and then the entry. In journalizing a transaction involving Accounts Payable, state the name of the creditor in the explanation. Similarly, in journalizing a transaction involving Accounts Receivable, in the explanation, state the name of the customer who charged the amount.

Remember

In trying to figure out how a transaction should be recorded, first decide on the accounts involved. Then classify the accounts as A, L, OE, R, or E. Finally, ask yourself whether the accounts are increased or decreased and think of the related accounts with their plus and minus sides. This process will make the debits and credits of the transaction fall into place.

GENERAL JOURNAL Page 1

Date		Description	Post. Ref.	Debit	Credit
	3	Equipment		4 3 2 0 00	
		Accounts Payable			4 3 2 0 00
		Bought equipment on account			
		from Signal Products.			

When a business buys an asset, the asset should be recorded at the actual cost (the agreed amount of a transaction). This is called the **cost principle**. For example, suppose that the $4,320 that Conner's Whitewater Adventures paid for the equipment from Signal Products was a bargain price, as Signal Products had been asking $7,500 for the equipment. Conner's Whitewater Adventures *should record the cost of the equipment as the actual amount paid ($4,320) in the transaction that occurred.* This is true even though the asking price was $7,500.

TRANSACTION (d). June 4: Conner's Whitewater Adventures paid Signal Products, a creditor, $2,000. Picture the T accounts like this:

Cash	
+	−
Debit	Credit
	2,000

Accounts Payable	
−	+
Debit	Credit
2,000	

In this case, we see that cash is decreasing, so we record it on the minus side. We now have a credit to Cash and have completed half of the entry. Next, we recognize that Accounts Payable is involved. We ask ourselves, "Do we owe more or less as a result of this transaction?" The answer is "less," so we record it on the minus, or debit, side of the account.

ACCOUNTING IN YOUR FUTURE

ACCOUNTING SKILLS

If you decide to work in the field of accounting, there are a number of skills that you need to bring to the position. Of course, you will need to be able to write well and have solid communication and interpersonal skills—those skills are assumed capabilities for nearly every job. However, if you are in the accounting department, you will be expected to be skilled at analyzing transactions, debiting and crediting accounts accurately as you journalize, and posting those transactions too.

You may also be required to prepare a trial balance and financial statements. While your work will be primarily on the computer using general ledger software, you still need to understand what goes on behind the screen. This is especially important when totals don't balance or some other error needs to be uncovered and corrected. That is why the first three chapters in this textbook are particularly critical to building your accounting skills.

Get in the T account habit. Picture the T accounts in your mind, or draw T accounts on paper with their plus and minus signs. The T account habit is very helpful.

GENERAL JOURNAL Page 1

Date		Description	Post. Ref.	Debit	Credit
	4	Accounts Payable		2 0 0 0 00	
		Cash			2 0 0 0 00
		Paid Signal Products on account.			

Because you have already determined the debits and credits in Chapter 2, we will now simply list the transactions for June for Conner's Whitewater Adventures with the date of each transaction. The journal entries are illustrated in Figures 2, 3, and 4.

June 1 Conner deposited $90,000 in a bank account in the name of her business.
2 Conner's Whitewater Adventures buys equipment, paying cash, $38,000.
3 Buys equipment on account from Signal Products, $4,320.
4 Pays $2,000 on account to Signal Products, a creditor.
4 Conner invests her personal computer, with a fair market value of $5,200, in the business.
7 Conner's Whitewater Adventures sells rafting tours for cash, $8,000.

Figure 2
Journal entries for Conner's Whitewater Adventures, June 1–7

GENERAL JOURNAL Page 1

Date		Description	Post. Ref.	Debit	Credit
20--					
June	1	Cash		90 0 0 0 00	
		J. Conner, Capital			90 0 0 0 00
		To record the original			
		investment by J. Conner.			
	2	Equipment		38 0 0 0 00	
		Cash			38 0 0 0 00
		Bought equipment for cash.			
	3	Equipment		4 3 2 0 00	
		Accounts Payable			4 3 2 0 00
		Bought equipment on account			
		from Signal Products.			
	4	Accounts Payable		2 0 0 0 00	
		Cash			2 0 0 0 00
		Paid Signal Products on account.			
	4	Equipment		5 2 0 0 00	
		J. Conner, Capital			5 2 0 0 00
		To record the investment by J. Conner			
		in Conner's Whitewater Adventures.			
	7	Cash		8 0 0 0 00	
		Income from Tours			8 0 0 0 00
		Received cash for rafting tour sales.			

June 8 Conner's Whitewater Adventures pays rent for the month, $1,250.
10 Buys supplies on account from Fineman Company, $675.
10 Buys a three-month liability insurance policy, $1,875.
14 Receives a bill for newspaper advertising from *The Times*, $620.
15 Signs a contract with Crystal River Lodge to provide rafting adventures for guests. Conner's Whitewater Adventures provides 27 one-day rafting tours and bills Crystal River Lodge for $6,750.
15 Pays on account to Signal Products, $1,500.
18 Receives and pays Solar Power, Inc., for the electric bill, $225.

Remember

In recording business transactions in the journal, you must use the exact account titles as listed in the company's chart of accounts.

Figure 3
Journal entries for Conner's Whitewater Adventures, June 8–18

GENERAL JOURNAL — Page 2

Date		Description	Post. Ref.	Debit	Credit
20--					
June	8	Rent Expense		1,250.00	
		Cash			1,250.00
		Paid rent for June.			
	10	Supplies		675.00	
		Accounts Payable			675.00
		Bought supplies on account			
		from Fineman Company.			
	10	Prepaid Insurance		1,875.00	
		Cash			1,875.00
		Paid premium for three-month			
		liability insurance policy.			
	14	Advertising Expense		620.00	
		Accounts Payable			620.00
		Received bill from			
		advertising with *The Times*.			
	15	Accounts Receivable		6,750.00	
		Income from Tours			6,750.00
		Billed Crystal River Lodge for			
		services performed.			
	15	Accounts Payable		1,500.00	
		Cash			1,500.00
		Paid Signal Products on account.			
	18	Utilities Expense		225.00	
		Cash			225.00
		Paid Solar Power, Inc., bill for utilities.			

Figure 4
Journal entries for Conner's Whitewater Adventures, June 20–30

		GENERAL JOURNAL			Page 3
Date		Description	Post. Ref.	Debit	Credit
20--					
June	20	Accounts Payable		620 00	
		Cash			620 00
		Paid *The Times* in full.			
	24	Wages Expense		2,360 00	
		Cash			2,360 00
		Paid wages of part-time employee.			
	26	Equipment		3,780 00	
		Cash			1,850 00
		Accounts Payable			1,930 00
		Bought equipment on account			
		from Signal Products.			
	30	Cash		2,500 00	
		Accounts Receivable			2,500 00
		Received from Crystal River Lodge			
		to apply on account.			
	30	Cash		8,570 00	
		Income from Tours			8,570 00
		Cash revenue.			
	30	J. Conner, Drawing		3,500 00	
		Cash			3,500 00
		Withdrew cash for personal use.			

In each journal entry, debits must equal credits.

June 20 Conner's Whitewater Adventures pays on account to *The Times*, $620. (This bill was recorded previously.)

24 Pays wages of part-time employee, $2,360.

26 Buys additional equipment from Signal Products for $3,780, paying $1,850 in cash and placing the balance on account.

30 Receives $2,500 cash from Crystal River Lodge to apply against amount billed on June 15.

30 Sells tours for cash, $8,570.

30 J. Conner withdraws cash for her personal use, $3,500.

POSTING TO THE GENERAL LEDGER

You know that the journal is the *book of original entry.* Each transaction must first be recorded in the journal in full. However, it is difficult to determine the balance of any one account, such as Cash, from the general journal entries. So the **ledger account** has been devised to give a complete record of the transactions recorded in each account. The **general ledger** contains all of the ledger accounts and contains detailed information about the increases and decreases in each of those accounts.

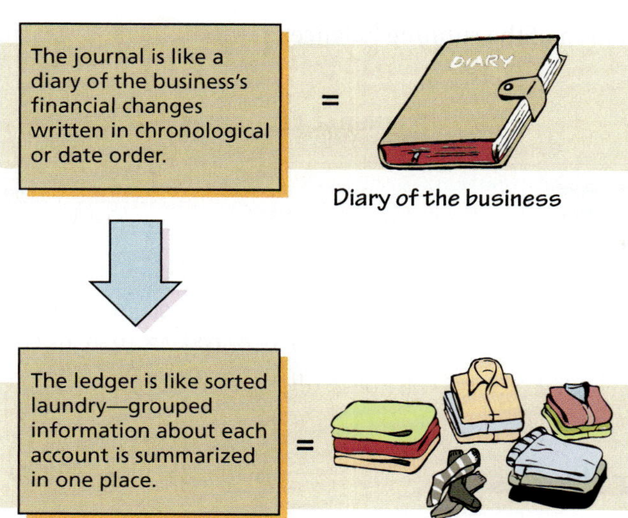

The journal is like a diary of the business's financial changes written in chronological or date order.
=
DIARY
Diary of the business
The ledger is like sorted laundry—grouped information about each account is summarized in one place.
=
A = L + Cap − Draw + R − E

The Ledger Account Form (Running Balance Format)

We have been looking at accounts in the simple T account form primarily because T accounts illustrate situations so well. The debit and credit sides are specifically labeled, making the T account form a good way to picture account activity. However, determining the balance of an account using the T account form is difficult. You must add both columns and subtract the smaller total from the larger. To overcome this disadvantage, accountants generally use the four-column account form with Balance columns in the general ledger. Let's look at the Cash account of Conner's Whitewater Adventures in four-column form (Figure 5) compared with the T account form. *Leave the Post. Ref. column blank for now.*

GENERAL LEDGER

ACCOUNT Cash **ACCOUNT NO.** 111

Date		Item	Post. Ref.	Debit	Credit	Balance Debit	Balance Credit
20--							
June	1			90,000.00		90,000.00	
	2				38,000.00	52,000.00	
	4				2,000.00	50,000.00	
	7			8,000.00		58,000.00	
	8				1,250.00	56,750.00	
	10				1,875.00	54,875.00	
	15				1,500.00	53,375.00	
	18				225.00	53,150.00	
	20				620.00	52,530.00	
	24				2,360.00	50,170.00	
	26				1,850.00	48,320.00	
	30			2,500.00		50,820.00	
	30			8,570.00		59,390.00	
	30				3,500.00	55,890.00	

Transaction amount — Running balance

Figure 5
General ledger for Conner's Whitewater Adventures

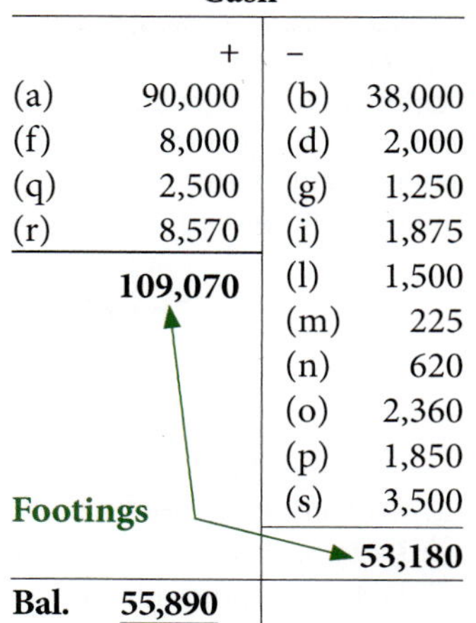

Note the calculation of the running balance. In the abbreviated form, it looks like this:

90,000 − 38,000 = 52,000
52,000 − 2,000 = 50,000

GENERAL LEDGER

ACCOUNT Cash **ACCOUNT NO.** 111

Date		Item	Post. Ref.	Debit	Credit	Balance Debit	Balance Credit
20--							
June	1			90 0 0 0 00		90 0 0 0 00	
	2				38 0 0 0 00	52 0 0 0 00	
	4				2 0 0 0 00	50 0 0 0 00	

The Posting Process

Learning Objective 2 Post entries from a two-column general journal to general ledger accounts.

The process of transferring information from the journal to the ledger accounts is called **posting**. In the posting process, you must transfer the following information from the journal to the ledger accounts: the *date of the transaction*, the *debit and credit amounts*, and the *page number* of the journal. **Post each account separately**, using the following steps. Post the debit part of the entry first.

STEP 1. Write the date of the transaction in the account's Date column.

STEP 2. Write the amount of the transaction in the Debit or Credit column and enter the new balance in the Balance columns under *Debit* or *Credit*.

STEP 3. Write the page number of the journal in the Post. Ref. column of the ledger account. (This is a **cross-reference**; it tells where the amount came from.)

STEP 4. Record the ledger account number in the Post. Ref. column of the journal. (This is also a cross-reference; it tells where the amount was posted.)

QuickBooks Tip

The Post Reference column is not used with computerized accounting software like QuickBooks.

Entering the account number in the Post. Ref. column of the journal should be the last step. It acts as a verification of the three preceding steps.

The June 1 transaction for Conner's Whitewater Adventures is illustrated in Figure 6. Let's look at the posting of the debit part of the entry.

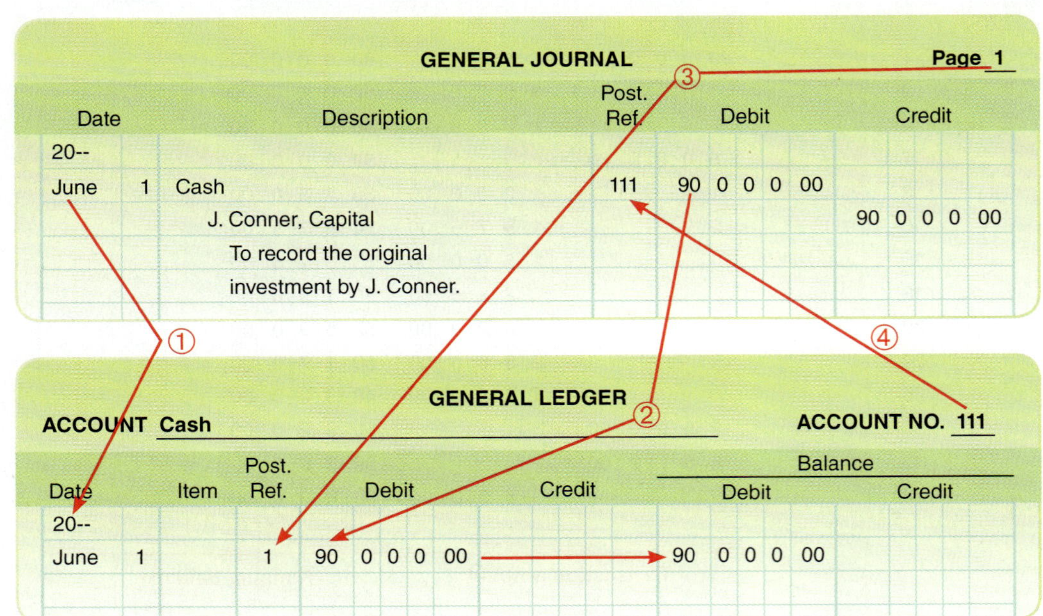

GENERAL JOURNAL Page 1

Date		Description	Post. Ref.	Debit	Credit
20--					
June	1	Cash	111	90 0 0 0 00	
		J. Conner, Capital			90 0 0 0 00
		To record the original			
		investment by J. Conner.			

GENERAL LEDGER

ACCOUNT Cash **ACCOUNT NO.** 111

Date		Item	Post. Ref.	Debit	Credit	Balance Debit	Balance Credit
20--							
June	1		1	90 0 0 0 00		90 0 0 0 00	

Figure 6
Posting from the general journal to the general ledger—debit entry (June 1 transaction)

① Date of transaction
② Amount of transaction
③ Page number of the journal
④ Ledger account number

Next, we post the credit part of the entry, as shown in Figure 7.

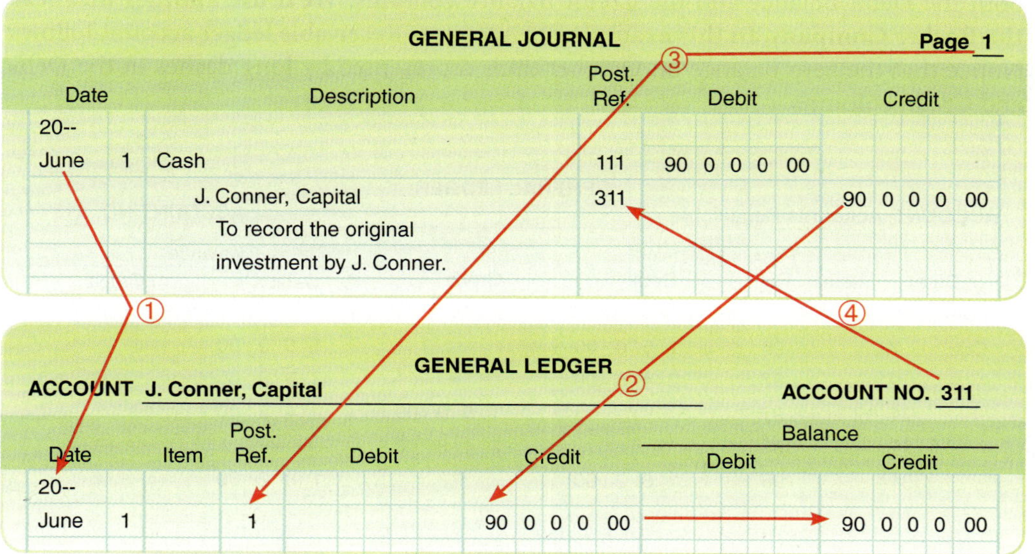

GENERAL JOURNAL — Page 1

Date		Description	Post. Ref.	Debit	Credit
20--					
June	1	Cash	111	90 0 0 0 00	
		J. Conner, Capital	311		90 0 0 0 00
		To record the original			
		investment by J. Conner.			

GENERAL LEDGER

ACCOUNT J. Conner, Capital — ACCOUNT NO. 311

Date		Item	Post. Ref.	Debit	Credit	Balance Debit	Balance Credit
20--							
June	1		1		90 0 0 0 00		90 0 0 0 00

Figure 7 Posting from the general journal to the general ledger—credit entry (June 1 transaction)

The accountant normally uses the Item column only at the end of a financial period. The following words may appear in this column: *balance, closing, adjusting,* and *reversing.* We will explain the use of these terms later.

Incidentally, some accountants use running balance-type ledger account forms that have only one balance column. However, we have used the two-balance-column arrangement to show clearly the appropriate balance of an account. For example, in Figure 6, Cash has a $90,000 balance recorded in the Debit column (normal balance). In Figure 7, J. Conner, Capital, has a $90,000 balance recorded in the Credit column (normal balance).

In the recording of the June 2 transaction, shown in Figure 8, see if you can identify in order the four steps in the posting process.

GENERAL JOURNAL — Page 1

Date		Description	Post. Ref.	Debit	Credit
	2	Equipment	124	38 0 0 0 00	
		Cash	111		38 0 0 0 00
		Bought equipment for cash.			

GENERAL LEDGER

ACCOUNT Cash — ACCOUNT NO. 111

Date		Item	Post. Ref.	Debit	Credit	Balance Debit	Balance Credit
20--							
June	1		1	90 0 0 0 00		90 0 0 0 00	
	2		1		38 0 0 0 00	52 0 0 0 00	

ACCOUNT Equipment — ACCOUNT NO. 124

Date		Item	Post. Ref.	Debit	Credit	Balance Debit	Balance Credit
20--							
June	2		1	38 0 0 0 00		38 0 0 0 00	

Figure 8 Posting from the general journal to the general ledger (June 2 transaction)

Remember

Posting is simply transferring or copying the same date and the debits and credits listed in the journal entry from the journal to the ledger.

QuickBooks Tip

Posting from the journal to the ledger is done automatically in QuickBooks.

If the temporary balance of an account happens to be zero, insert long dashes through both the Debit Balance and the Credit Balance columns. **We'll use another business, the Becker Company, in this example.** Its Accounts Receivable ledger account follows. Notice that the zero balance on October 29 is represented by long dashes in the Debit and Credit columns.

GENERAL LEDGER

ACCOUNT Accounts Receivable ACCOUNT NO. 113

Date		Item	Post. Ref.	Debit	Credit	Balance Debit	Balance Credit
20--							
Oct.	7		96	150 00		150 00	
	19		97	248 00		398 00	
	21		97		150 00	248 00	
	29		98		248 00	———	———
	31		98	182 00		182 00	

Returning to Conner's Whitewater Adventures, let's look at the journal entries for the first month of operation. As you can see in Figure 9, the Post. Ref. column has been filled in because the posting was completed. Immediately after the journal entries, the ledger accounts and entries for Conner's Whitewater Adventures are shown in Figure 10. Take a moment to review all of the journal entries and the related postings.

Figure 9
Journal entries for Conner's Whitewater Adventures (first month of operation)

GENERAL JOURNAL Page 1

Date		Description	Post. Ref.	Debit	Credit
20--					
June	1	Cash	111	90 000 00	
		J. Conner, Capital	311		90 000 00
		To record the original			
		investment by J. Conner.			
	2	Equipment	124	38 000 00	
		Cash	111		38 000 00
		Bought equipment for cash.			
	3	Equipment	124	4 320 00	
		Accounts Payable	221		4 320 00
		Bought equipment on account			
		from Signal Products.			
	4	Accounts Payable	221	2 000 00	
		Cash	111		2 000 00
		Paid Signal Products on account.			

Date		Description	Post. Ref.	Debit	Credit
	4	Equipment	124	5,200.00	
		J. Conner, Capital	311		5,200.00
		To record the investment by J. Conner in Conner's Whitewater Adventures.			
	7	Cash	111	8,000.00	
		Income from Tours	411		8,000.00
		Received cash for rafting tour sales.			

Figure 9
(Continued)

GENERAL JOURNAL Page 2

Date		Description	Post. Ref.	Debit	Credit
20--					
June	8	Rent Expense	512	1,250.00	
		Cash	111		1,250.00
		Paid rent for June.			
	10	Supplies	115	675.00	
		Accounts Payable	221		675.00
		Bought supplies on account from Fineman Company.			
	10	Prepaid Insurance	117	1,875.00	
		Cash	111		1,875.00
		Paid premium for three-month liability insurance policy.			
	14	Advertising Expense	514	620.00	
		Accounts Payable	221		620.00
		Received bill from advertising with *The Times*.			
	15	Accounts Receivable	113	6,750.00	
		Income from Tours	411		6,750.00
		Billed Crystal River Lodge for services performed.			
	15	Accounts Payable	221	1,500.00	
		Cash	111		1,500.00
		Paid Signal Products on account.			
	18	Utilities Expense	515	225.00	
		Cash	111		225.00
		Paid Solar Power, Inc., bill for utilities.			

Figure 9
(Concluded)

GENERAL JOURNAL Page 3

Date		Description	Post. Ref.	Debit	Credit
20--					
June	20	Accounts Payable	221	620.00	
		Cash	111		620.00
		Paid *The Times* in full.			
	24	Wages Expense	511	2,360.00	
		Cash	111		2,360.00
		Paid wages of part-time employee.			
	26	Equipment	124	3,780.00	
		Cash	111		1,850.00
		Accounts Payable	221		1,930.00
		Bought equipment on account from Signal Products.			
	30	Cash	111	2,500.00	
		Accounts Receivable	113		2,500.00
		Received from Crystal River Lodge to apply on account.			
	30	Cash	111	8,570.00	
		Income from Tours	411		8,570.00
		Received cash for rafting tour sales.			
	30	J. Conner, Drawing	312	3,500.00	
		Cash	111		3,500.00
		Withdrew cash for personal use.			

Figure 10
General ledger for Conner's Whitewater Adventures (first month of operation)

GENERAL LEDGER

ACCOUNT **Cash** ACCOUNT NO. **111**

Date		Item	Post. Ref.	Debit	Credit	Balance Debit	Balance Credit
20--							
June	1		1	90,000.00		90,000.00	
	2		1		38,000.00	52,000.00	
	4		1		2,000.00	50,000.00	
	7		1	8,000.00		58,000.00	
	8		2		1,250.00	56,750.00	
	10		2		1,875.00	54,875.00	
	15		2		1,500.00	53,375.00	
	18		2		225.00	53,150.00	
	20		3		620.00	52,530.00	
	24		3		2,360.00	50,170.00	
	26		3		1,850.00	48,320.00	
	30		3	2,500.00		50,820.00	
	30		3	8,570.00		59,390.00	
	30		3		3,500.00	55,890.00	

Figure 10
(Continued)

ACCOUNT **Accounts Receivable** ACCOUNT NO. **113**

Date		Item	Post. Ref.	Debit	Credit	Balance Debit	Balance Credit
20--							
June	15		2	6,750.00		6,750.00	
	30		3		2,500.00	4,250.00	

ACCOUNT **Supplies** ACCOUNT NO. **115**

Date		Item	Post. Ref.	Debit	Credit	Balance Debit	Balance Credit
20--							
June	10		2	675.00		675.00	

ACCOUNT **Prepaid Insurance** ACCOUNT NO. **117**

Date		Item	Post. Ref.	Debit	Credit	Balance Debit	Balance Credit
20--							
June	10		2	1,875.00		1,875.00	

ACCOUNT **Equipment** ACCOUNT NO. **124**

Date		Item	Post. Ref.	Debit	Credit	Balance Debit	Balance Credit
20--							
June	2		1	38,000.00		38,000.00	
	3		1	4,320.00		42,320.00	
	4		1	5,200.00		47,520.00	
	26		3	3,780.00		51,300.00	

ACCOUNT **Accounts Payable** ACCOUNT NO. **221**

Date		Item	Post. Ref.	Debit	Credit	Balance Debit	Balance Credit
20--							
June	3		1		4,320.00		4,320.00
	4		1	2,000.00			2,320.00
	10		2		675.00		2,995.00
	14		2		620.00		3,615.00
	15		2	1,500.00			2,115.00
	20		3	620.00			1,495.00
	26		3		1,930.00		3,425.00

Figure 10
(Continued)

ACCOUNT **J. Conner, Capital** ACCOUNT NO. **311**

Date		Item	Post. Ref.	Debit	Credit	Balance Debit	Balance Credit
20--							
June	1		1		90,000.00		90,000.00
	4		1		5,200.00		95,200.00

ACCOUNT **J. Conner, Drawing** ACCOUNT NO. **312**

Date		Item	Post. Ref.	Debit	Credit	Balance Debit	Balance Credit
20--							
June	30		3	3,500.00		3,500.00	

ACCOUNT **Income from Tours** ACCOUNT NO. **411**

Date		Item	Post. Ref.	Debit	Credit	Balance Debit	Balance Credit
20--							
June	7		1		8,000.00		8,000.00
	15		2		6,750.00		14,750.00
	30		3		8,570.00		23,320.00

ACCOUNT **Wages Expense** ACCOUNT NO. **511**

Date		Item	Post. Ref.	Debit	Credit	Balance Debit	Balance Credit
20--							
June	24		3	2,360.00		2,360.00	

ACCOUNT **Rent Expense** ACCOUNT NO. **512**

Date		Item	Post. Ref.	Debit	Credit	Balance Debit	Balance Credit
20--							
June	8		2	1,250.00		1,250.00	

ACCOUNT **Advertising Expense** ACCOUNT NO. **514**

Date		Item	Post. Ref.	Debit	Credit	Balance Debit	Balance Credit
20--							
June	14		2	620.00		620.00	

Figure 10
(Continued)

ACCOUNT **Utilities Expense** ACCOUNT NO. **515**

Date		Item	Post. Ref.	Debit	Credit	Balance Debit	Balance Credit
20--							
June	18		2	225.00		225.00	

THE TRIAL BALANCE

Preparation of the Trial Balance

After the journal entries have been posted, a trial balance must be prepared. The trial balance is simply a list of the ledger accounts that have balances. A trial balance is presented in Figure 11.

Learning Objective 3 Prepare a trial balance from the ledger accounts.

Remember that the trial balance proves only that the total ledger debit balances equal the total ledger credit balances. Even when the debit and credit balances are equal, other types of errors may slip through such as:

1. Posting the correct debit or credit amounts to the incorrect account or
2. Neglecting to journalize or post an entire transaction.

Conner's Whitewater Adventures
Trial Balance
June 30, 20—

Account Name	Debit	Credit
Cash	55,890	
Accounts Receivable	4,250	
Supplies	675	
Prepaid Insurance	1,875	
Equipment	51,300	
Accounts Payable		3,425
J. Conner, Capital		95,200
J. Conner, Drawing	3,500	
Income from Tours		23,320
Wages Expense	2,360	
Rent Expense	1,250	
Advertising Expense	620	
Utilities Expense	225	
	121,945	121,945

Figure 11
Trial balance for Conner's Whitewater Adventures

Steps in the Accounting Process

So far, you have learned the first three steps in the accounting process.

STEP 1. Record the transactions of a business in a journal (book of original entry or day-by-day record of the transactions of a firm). An entry should be based on some source document or evidence that a transaction has occurred, such as an invoice, a receipt, or a check.

STEP 2. Post entries to the accounts in the ledger. Transfer the amounts from the journal to the Debit or Credit columns of the specified accounts in the ledger. Use a cross-reference system. Accounts are organized in the ledger according to the account numbers assigned to them in the chart of accounts.

STEP 3. Prepare a trial balance. Record the balances of the ledger accounts in the appropriate column, Debit or Credit, of the trial balance form. Prove that the total of the debit balances equals the total of the credit balances.

SOURCE DOCUMENTS

Learning Objective 4 Explain the importance of source documents.

As mentioned earlier, a source document can be an invoice, a receipt, or a check, for example. We now add an important detail in the recording of a journal entry. This detail consists of listing the related source document number, which is used as a reference for the proof of a transaction. For example, Figure 12 is an example of a source document followed by the journal entry (Figure 13) and ledger accounts (Figure 14).

Using the source document, the accountant records the entry in the journal (Figure 13). Note how the explanation includes important information from the source document. The explanation now includes the invoice number.

The journal entry is then posted to the ledger (Figure 14).

Figure 12
Source document

INVOICE

FINEMAN COMPANY No. 4-962
220 East Ames Street, Denver CO 80012
Sold By: 203 Date: 6/10/20--
Name: Conner's Whitewater Adventures
Address: 1701 East Delaware Street
Colorado Springs, CO 80902
Terms: Net 30 days

Quantity	Description	Unit Price	Amount
10 bx	Invoice forms	12 00	120 00
5 bx	Ink cartridges	32 00	160 00
3 bx	8 x 11 copy paper	20 00	60 00
2	File cabinets, 2-drawer	32 00	64 00
4 bx	3-tab folders	12 00	48 00
3	10-key electric calculators	24 00	72 00
5 bx	12-count black ink pens	12 00	60 00
5 bx	10-count mechanical pencils	10 00	50 00
	SUBTOTAL		634 00
	SALES TAX		41 00
	SHIPPING—free		0 00
	TOTAL		675 00

GENERAL JOURNAL				Page 1
Date	Description	Post. Ref.	Debit	Credit
10	Supplies	115	6 7 5 00	
	Accounts Payable	221		6 7 5 00
	Bought supplies on account			
	from Fineman Company,			
	Invoice No. 4-962.			

Figure 13
Journal entry related to source document

SMALL BUSINESS **SUCCESS**

Paperwork—Why It's Worth Keeping Track of!

As you analyze transactions for a business, you learned that each transaction must be evidenced by a source document. Source documents, or the paperwork for transactions, are very important to all businesses. This is because all accounting transactions are developed from source documents. What are some examples of source documents? Bills from vendors, checks from customers, deposit slips, credit card receipts, bank statements, and customer invoices are all examples of source documents.

Many times businesses use accounting software to create source documents that can be printed for the businesses' or customers' records. Source documents should include the name and address of the business, as well as the date, amount, and description of the transaction. The documents should also include any customer information. The detail provided on the source documents will help the accountant record the transactions.

Source documents are also needed to substantiate the transactions should the business be audited. Internal and external auditors will review the paperwork when determining whether the transactions recorded by the business are accurate. The Internal Revenue Service (IRS) will also require the business to provide proof of transactions for income and deductions shown on the entity's tax return.

Is it necessary for the business to keep source documents forever? Well, that depends on what the source document is and to whom you talk with. Most accountants agree on the following guidelines:

Source Document	Time Period
Support for your tax return	3 years
Related to assets purchased, such as a business vehicle or computer	Keep until you sell or dispose
Documents such as accounts receivable or accounts payable ledgers, bank statements, canceled checks, and invoices	7 years
Items such as loan documents, tax returns, and financial statements	Indefinitely

Source documents are an important part of the accounting cycle. Take a moment to make sure you are comfortable with the information provided on the documents and that you are familiar with the most common documents used in accounting, such as invoices, deposit slips, receipts, and bills from vendors. As you work through the chapters of the textbook, you will be introduced to many types of source documents. Be sure to review them—important information is included on these documents!

Figure 14
Ledger posting

ACCOUNT **Supplies** ACCOUNT NO. **115**

Date		Item	Post. Ref.	Debit	Credit	Balance Debit	Balance Credit
20--							
June	10		2	6 7 5 00		6 7 5 00	

ACCOUNT **Accounts Payable** ACCOUNT NO. **221**

Date		Item	Post. Ref.	Debit	Credit	Balance Debit	Balance Credit
20--							
June	3		1		4 3 2 0 00		4 3 2 0 00
	4		1	2 0 0 0 00			2 3 2 0 00
	10		2		6 7 5 00		2 9 9 5 00

Previous Postings (June 3 and June 4 entries)

To: Amy Roberts, CPA
Subject: Errors?

Hi Amy,
I was thinking about recording transactions and wondered what happens if I make an error? Do I simply delete the error and then correct the entry?
Thanks,
Janie

To: Janie Conner
Subject: RE: Errors?

Hi Janie,
Errors happen even when you are extra careful. Once you find an error, it's important that you don't delete the error, but instead correct it using specific procedures. Using these procedures will ensure that you are properly documenting the error and the corresponding correction.
Amy

CORRECTION OF ERRORS—MANUAL AND COMPUTERIZED

Errors are occasionally made in recording journal entries and posting to the ledger accounts whether recording them manually or on a computer. Never erase or delete the errors because it may look as if you were trying to hide something. The method for correcting errors depends on how and when the errors were made. The two methods for correcting errors are as follows:

1. The ruling method (can be used only for manual entry).
2. The correcting entry method (can be used for manual and computerized entry).

Learning Objective

5 Correct entries using the ruling or correcting entry method.

The Ruling Method

You can use the ruling method to correct an error in the journal before posting or to correct an error in the ledger after an entry has been posted, but only if the entry was recorded manually (with paper and pencil).

CORRECTING ERRORS BEFORE POSTING HAS TAKEN PLACE

When an error has been made in recording an account title in a journal entry, draw a line through the incorrect account title in the journal entry and write the correct account title immediately above it. Include your initials with the correction. For example, an entry to record payment of $1,500 rent was incorrectly debited to Salary Expense.

GENERAL JOURNAL Page 1

Date		Description	Post. Ref.	Debit	Credit
20--		*Rent Expense*			
Mar.	1	~~Salary Expense~~ *DJM*		1 5 0 0 00	
		Cash			1 5 0 0 00
		Paid rent for the month.			

When an error has been made in recording an amount, draw a line through the incorrect amount in the journal entry and write the correct amount immediately above it. For example, an entry for a $120 payment for office supplies was recorded as $210. Include your initials with the correction.

GENERAL JOURNAL Page 1

Date		Description	Post. Ref.	Debit	Credit
20--				*DJM* *1 2 0 00*	
Apr.	6	Supplies		~~2 1 0 00~~	*DJM* *1 2 0 00*
		Cash			~~2 1 0 00~~
		Bought office supplies.			

CORRECTING ERRORS AFTER POSTING HAS TAKEN PLACE

When an entry was journalized correctly but one of the amounts was posted incorrectly, correct the error by drawing a single line through the amount and recording the correct amount above it. For example, an entry to record cash received for professional fees was correctly journalized as $400. However, it was posted as a debit to Cash for $400 and a credit to Professional Fees for $4,000. In the Professional Fees account, draw a line through $4,000 and insert $400 above or next to the incorrect amount. Change the running balance of the account and initial the corrections.

© iStockPhoto.com/amriphoto

In the Real World

Even large businesses make accounting errors. When a large corporation makes an error and discovers it after the financial statements have been published, the corporation is required to restate its financial statements. Some of these restatements can be huge. For example, Overstock.com once announced that it would be restating its financial statements for errors made in a previous year. Corrections of these errors affected net income by approximately $1,500,000!

ACCOUNT Professional Fees **ACCOUNT NO.** 411

Date	Item	Post. Ref.	Debit	Credit	Balance Debit	Balance Credit
				DJM 4 0 0 00		DJM 25 6 0 0 00
6		94		~~4 0 0 0 00~~		~~29 2 0 0 00~~

Correcting Entry Method—Manual or Computerized

If the transaction was journalized incorrectly and the amounts were posted, you should use the correcting entry method.

Use this entry when working with computerized accounting software. **Never delete or "fix" the original incorrect entry in a computerized accounting program.**

Following are the two correcting entry methods:

1. *One-step method.* One entry undoes the error and provides the correct account.
2. *Two-step method.* The first step reverses the error made by the original entry. The second step includes the correct entry.

Whether you are preparing accounting records manually or on computer, accuracy is of primary importance. Rapid and accurate ten-key calculator and computer keyboard skills are a must for an accountant or a bookkeeper.

When recording a correcting entry using either the one-step or two-step method, you must include an explanation. For example, on January 9, a $620 payment for advertising was incorrectly journalized and posted as a debit to Miscellaneous Expense for $620 and a credit to Cash for $620. The error was discovered and corrected on January 27 as follows using the one-step method.

GENERAL JOURNAL **Page** 1

Date		Description	Post. Ref.	Debit	Credit
20--					
Jan.	27	Advertising Expense		6 2 0 00	
		Miscellaneous Expense			6 2 0 00
		To correct error of January 9 in which			
		a payment for Advertising Expense			
		was debited to Miscellaneous Expense.			

Following the two-step method, if the original entry was recorded as a debit to Miscellaneous Expense and a credit to Cash, reverse this entry by debiting Cash and crediting Miscellaneous Expense, then record the correct entry.

GENERAL JOURNAL Page 1

Date		Description	Post. Ref.	Debit	Credit
20--					
Jan.	27	Cash		6 2 0 00	
		Miscellaneous Expense			6 2 0 00
		To reverse out an incorrect			
		entry recorded January 9.			
	27	Advertising Expense		6 2 0 00	
		Cash			6 2 0 00
		To correct error of January 9			
		in which a payment for			
		Advertising Expense was			
		debited to Miscellaneous Expense.			

YOU Make the Call

Imagine you are an accounting clerk. You find that your trial balance balances, but something doesn't seem quite right. The amount of Miscellaneous Expense is much higher than it was last month, but you don't recall making an entry that would cause this discrepancy. In checking the journal entries, you find that an entry for $724 was accidentally debited to Miscellaneous Expense and credited to Accounts Payable. The $724 should have been debited to Utilities Expense. Explain how you would correct this entry and why you chose that method.

SOLUTION

Because this is a correction after the information was posted, two methods can be used to make the correction.

1. The first method is to simply make a journal entry to correct the original error. In this case, make a journal entry to debit Utilities Expense for $724 and credit Miscellaneous Expense for $724. This is called the one-step method.
2. Another method is to "back out," or reverse, the entry that contains the error and journalize the correct entry. That is, debit Accounts Payable for $724 and credit Miscellaneous Expense for $724. Finally, the correct journal entry is to debit Utilities Expense for $724 and credit Accounts Payable for $724.

These two methods can be used in a manual or computerized system.

Accounting with QuickBooks®

Learning Objectives

After you have completed this section, you will be able to do the following:

1. Record a transaction in the general journal.
2. Record a transaction involving Accounts Payable or Accounts Receivable.
3. View and print the general journal.
4. View and print the general ledger.

In Chapter 3, you learned how to prepare journal entries manually using paper and pencil. Today, most journal entries are prepared using computerized accounting software such as QuickBooks. QuickBooks contains a journal that allows you to record transactions the same way you entered them manually for Conner's Whitewater Adventures. There's even room to include a journal explanation in the memo field.

So if the same number of steps is needed to record journal entries in the computer as is needed when using paper and pencil, why do businesses use computerized accounting programs like QuickBooks? There are several reasons. First, when entering the transaction, the user will not be required to remember the exact account name—QuickBooks allows the user to select from a list of accounts. Second, the computerized accounting software checks that the debit and credit balances are equal prior to updating a transaction. If the balances are not equal, the computer will alert the user of the error. QuickBooks does not allow out-of-balance transactions to be updated.

The best part about using a computerized accounting program, such as QuickBooks, may be that the computer automatically takes care of posting to the ledger. This means that the instant the user enters the transaction into QuickBooks and clicks **Save & Close** or **Save & New**, the transaction is posted to the ledger accounts. This saves the accountant a lot of time by eliminating repetitive data entry and helps prevent posting errors. In addition, computerized accounting programs prepare the financial statements based on the journal entries entered.

It's important to remember that even if you will be using a computerized accounting program like QuickBooks, you still need to know how to record and post journal entries as well as how to prepare financial statements. This knowledge will help ensure that you understand the information prepared, using the software, and recognize errors.

Learning Objective  Record a transaction in the general journal.

QuickBooks Tip

Journal explanations for transactions are recorded in the memo field in QuickBooks.

Recording Transactions with Quickbooks

There are two ways of recording transactions in QuickBooks. The journal entry method can be used, or a *Getting Around* screen is available on the home page. This book will demonstrate the journal entry method, but let's take a moment to discuss the *Getting Around* screen on the QuickBooks home page. The *Getting Around* screen (see Figure Q1) provides shortcuts to help users enter transactions.

QuickBooks is organized around centers such as Customers, Vendors, Employees, Banking, and Reports. Each center handles transactions related to the specific area. For example, the Customers center handles transactions related to creating invoices, statements, and sales receipts. Centers allow users to enter transactions in the accounting software without needing to know debits and credits. The software takes the information that has been entered and records the journal entry automatically.

Figure Q1
Getting Around screen

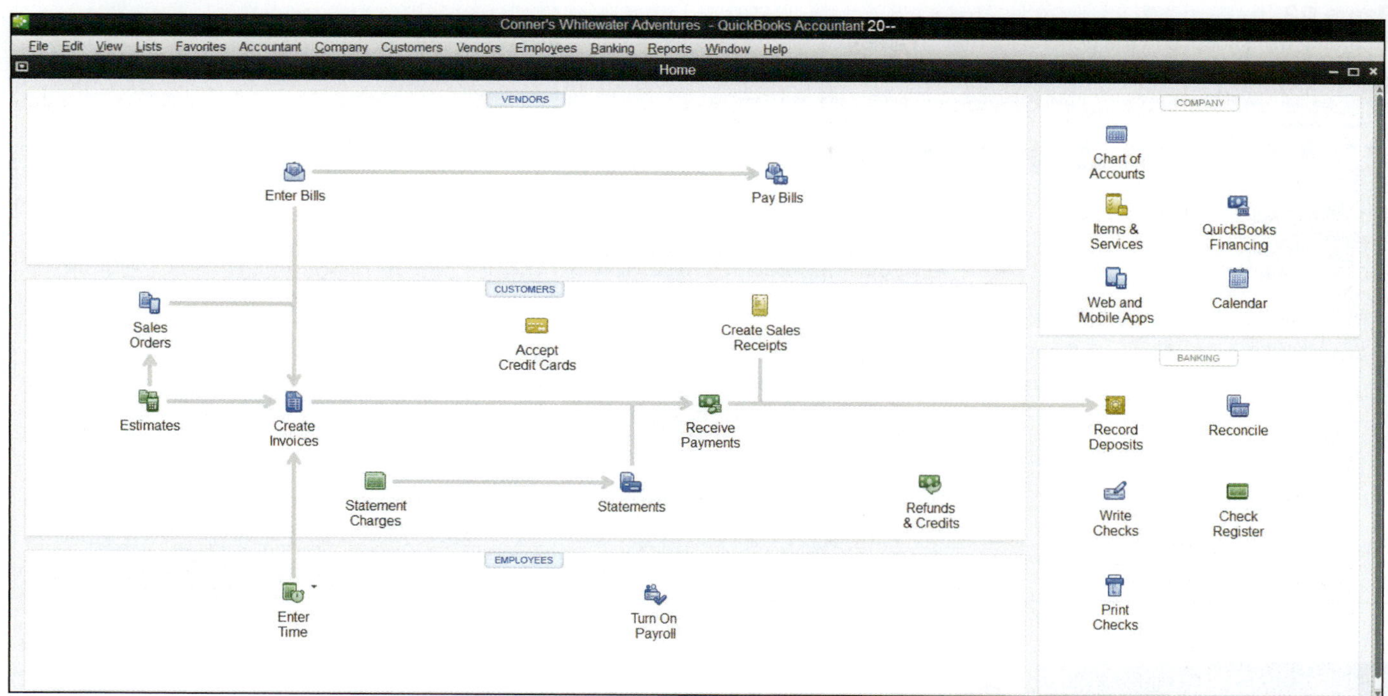

Since you know your debits and credits, you are going to learn how to enter transactions using the journal entry method. Let's analyze the first transaction for Conner's Whitewater Adventures.

June 1 Conner deposited $90,000 in a bank account in the name of the business. To record the transaction in QuickBooks, follow these steps:

STEP 1. Click the **Company** tab. Then click **Make General Journal Entries**.

STEP 2. **Enter the date.** 06/01/20-- (When preparing reports, QuickBooks will automatically default to the current date. To avoid reporting errors, be sure to verify that the report dates in QuickBooks match the actual transactions dates. For this exercise, we will use the year 2015.)

STEP 3. **Select the account to be debited using the drop-down box arrow.** 111 Cash

STEP 4. **Enter the dollar amount in the Debit column.** 90,000

STEP 5. **Enter the transaction description in the Memo box.** (You will only need to enter the description in the first memo line. QuickBooks automatically repeats the description for the next account in the transaction unless changed.)

STEP 6. **Select the account to be credited using the drop-down box arrow.** 311 J. Conner, Capital. (The debit amount is automatically filled into the Credit column. For compound transactions, the credit amount may need to be changed.)

STEP 7. **Review the transaction and click Save & New to proceed to the next entry.**

QuickBooks Tip

In QuickBooks you do not need to enter dollar signs or commas. You can also eliminate entering cents when the entry is a whole number.

The steps have been summarized for you in Figure Q2.

Figure Q2

Recording transactions in the general journal

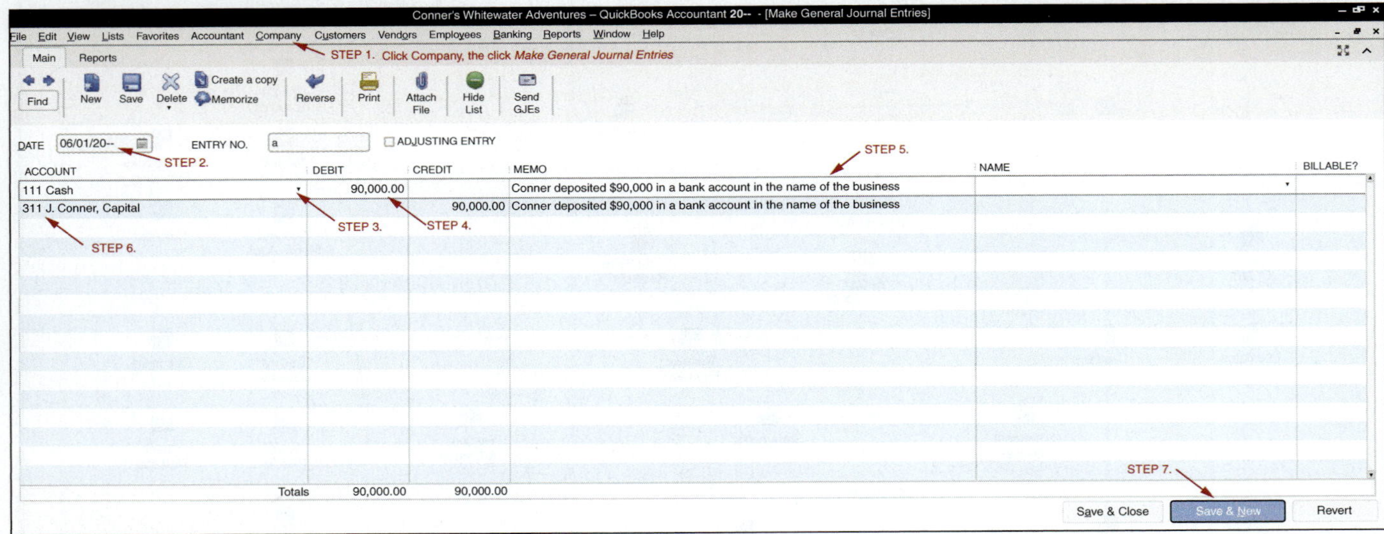

Learning Objective 2 Record a transaction involving Accounts Payable or Accounts Receivable.

When entering a transaction in QuickBooks that involves Accounts Receivable or Accounts Payable, a name must be entered for the Customer (Accounts Receivable) or the Vendor (Accounts Payable). Let's take a look at Figure Q3 for the transaction on June 3 for Conner's Whitewater Adventures.

Figure Q3

Transactions involving accounts receivable or accounts payable

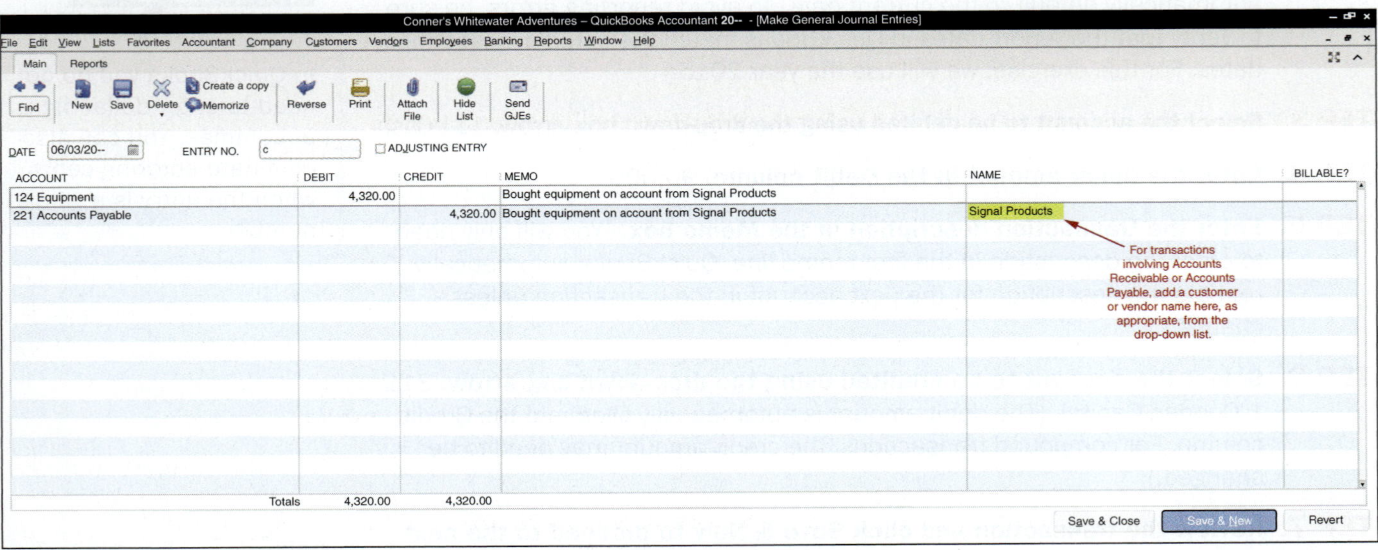

June 3 Conner's Whitewater Adventures bought equipment on account from Signal Products, $4,320. Notice that this transaction involves Accounts Payable and that the vendor is Signal Products. When the user enters the transaction in QuickBooks, he or she must select a vendor in the name box. This is completed by selecting the down arrow and then clicking the vendor name.

Learning Objective

3 View and print the general journal.

View and Print Reports

The general journal in QuickBooks is the same as the journal in a manual accounting system. Both journals contain transactions in chronological order. To view and print the transactions recorded in the general journal, follow these steps:

STEP 1. Click the **Reports** tab.

STEP 2. Click **Accountant & Taxes**.

STEP 3. Click **Journal**.

STEP 4. Adjust the **From:** and **To:** dates and click **Refresh**.

STEP 5. To print the report, click the **Print** button.

QuickBooks Tip

Want to go "green"? Print reports electronically with the Save as PDF option.

Figure Q4 shows the QuickBooks Journal report for Conner's Whitewater Adventures.

Figure Q4
General journal

Conner's Whitewater Adventures
Journal
June 20--

Trans #	Type	Date	Num	Name	Memo	Account	Debit	Credit
1	General Journal	06/01/20--	a		To record the original investment by J. Conner	111 Cash	90,000.00	
					To record the original investment by J. Conner	311 J. Conner, Capital		90,000.00
							90,000.00	90,000.00
2	General Journal	06/02/20--	b		Bought equipment for cash	124 Equipment	38,000.00	
					Bought equipment for cash	111 Cash		38,000.00
							38,000.00	38,000.00
4	General Journal	06/04/20--	d	Signal Products	Paid Signal Products on account	221 Accounts Payable	2,000.00	
				Signal Products	Paid Signal Products on account	111 Cash		2,000.00
							2,000.00	2,000.00
5	General Journal	06/04/20--	e		To record the investment by J. Conner in Conner's Whitewater Adventures	124 Equipment	5,200.00	
					To record the investment by J. Conner in Conner's Whitewater Adventures	311 J. Conner, Capital		5,200.00
							5,200.00	5,200.00
6	General Journal	06/07/20--	f		Received cash for rafting tour sales	111 Cash	8,000.00	
					Received cash for rafting tour sales	411 Income from Tours		8,000.00
							8,000.00	8,000.00

Learning Objective  View and print the general ledger.

To view and print the details of the general ledger accounts in QuickBooks, follow these steps:

STEP 1. Click the **Reports** tab.

STEP 2. Click **Accountant & Taxes.**

STEP 3. Click **General Ledger**.

STEP 4. Adjust the **From:** and **To:** dates and click **Refresh**.

STEP 5. To print the report, click the **Print** button.

Figure Q5 shows the QuickBooks General Ledger report for Conner's Whitewater Adventures.

Figure Q5
General ledger

Conner's Whitewater Adventures
General Ledger
As of June 30, 20--

Type	Date	Num	Name	Memo	Split	Debit	Credit	Balance
111 Cash								0.00
General Journal	06/01/20--	a		To record the original investment by J.Coner	311 J. Conner, Capital	90,000.00		90,000.00
General Journal	06/02/20--	b		Bought equipment for cash	124 Equipment		38,000.00	52,000.00
General Journal	06/04/20--	d	Signal Products	Paid Signal Products on account	221 Accounts Payable		2,000.00	50,000.00
General Journal	06/07/20--	f		Received cash for rafting tour sales	411 Income from Tours	8,000.00		58,000.00
General Journal	06/08/20--	g		Paid rent for June	512 Rent Expense		1,250.00	56,750.00
General Journal	06/10/20--	i		Paid premium for three-month liability insurance policy	117 Prepaid Insurance		1,875.00	54,875.00
General Journal	06/15/20--	l	Signal Products	Paid Signal Products on account	221 Accounts Payable		1,500.00	53,375.00
General Journal	06/18/20--	m		Paid Solar Power, Inc. bill for utilities	515 Utilities Expense		225.00	53,150.00
General Journal	06/20/20--	n	The Times	Paid The Times in full	221 Accounts Payable		620.00	52,530.00
General Journal	06/24/20--	o		Paid wages of part-time employee	511 Wages Expense		2,360.00	50,170.00
General Journal	06/26/20--	p		Bought equipment on account from Signal Products	124 Equipment		1,850.00	48,320.00
General Journal	06/30/20--	q		Received from Crystal River Lodge to apply on account	113 Accounts Receivable	2,500.00		50,820.00
General Journal	06/30/20--	r		Received cash for rafting tour sales	411 Income from Tours	8,570.00		59,390.00
General Journal	06/30/20--	s		Withdrew cash for personal use	312 J. Conner, Drawing		3,500.00	55,890.00
Total 111 Cash						109,070.00	53,180.00	55,890.00
113 Accounts Receivable								0.00
General Journal	06/15/20--	k	Crystal River Lodge	Billed Crystal River Lodge for services performed	411 Income from Tours	6,750.00		6,750.00
General Journal	06/30/20--	q	Crystal River Lodge	Received from Crystal River Lodge to apply on account	111 Cash		2,500.00	4,250.00
Total 113 Accounts Receivable						6,750.00	2,500.00	4,250.00

Chapter Review

Study and Practice

Record a group of transactions pertaining to a service business in a two-column general journal.

Learning Objective

Based on **source documents**, the transactions are analyzed to determine what accounts are involved and whether the accounts are debited or credited. For each transaction, total debits must equal total credits. The **journal** is a book of original entry in which a day-by-day record of business transactions is maintained. The parts of a journal entry consist of the transaction date, the title of the account(s) debited, the title of the account(s) credited, the amounts recorded in the Debit and Credit columns, and an explanation.

PRACTICE EXERCISE 1

Journalize the following transactions for the month of June:

June 1 J. Jonah deposited $35,000 in the bank in the name of the business (Jonah Company).
2 The business purchased $8,000 in equipment, paying $2,000 in cash and placing the remainder on account.
4 The business purchased supplies for cash, $250.
10 The business received cash revenue, $3,250.
20 The business paid the monthly rent, $1,800.
24 J. Jonah withdrew $500 for personal use.

PRACTICE EXERCISE 1 • SOLUTION

GENERAL JOURNAL Page 1

Date		Description	Post. Ref.	Debit	Credit
20--					
June	1	Cash		35 0 0 0 00	
		J. Jonah, Capital			35 0 0 0 00
		Jonah invested cash.			
	2	Equipment		8 0 0 0 00	
		Cash			2 0 0 0 00
		Accounts Payable			6 0 0 0 00
		Purchased equipment.			
	4	Supplies		2 5 0 00	
		Cash			2 5 0 00
		Purchased supplies.			
	10	Cash		3 2 5 0 00	
		Income from Services			3 2 5 0 00
		Cash revenue.			

(Continued)

Date	Description	Post. Ref.	Debit	Credit
20	Rent Expense		1 8 0 0 00	
	Cash			1 8 0 0 00
	Paid the monthly rent.			
24	J. Jonah, Drawing		5 0 0 00	
	Cash			5 0 0 00
	Withdrawal for personal use.			

Learning Objective  Post entries from a two-column general journal to general ledger accounts.

The **general ledger** is a book that contains all of the accounts, arranged according to the chart of accounts. **Posting** is the process of transferring information from the journal to the **ledger accounts**. The posting process consists of four steps:

STEP 1. Write the date of the transaction in the account's Date column.

STEP 2. Write the amount of the transaction in the Debit or Credit column and enter the new balance in the Balance columns under *Debit* or *Credit*.

STEP 3. Write the page number of the journal in the Post. Ref. column of the ledger account.

STEP 4. Record the ledger account number in the Post. Ref. column of the journal.

PRACTICE EXERCISE 2

Post the journal entries from Practice Exercise 1 to the following general ledger accounts:

Assets
111 Cash
115 Supplies
124 Equipment

Liabilities
221 Accounts Payable

Owner's Equity
311 J. Jonah, Capital
312 J. Jonah, Drawing

Revenue
411 Income from Services

Expenses
512 Rent Expense

PRACTICE EXERCISE 2 • SOLUTION

GENERAL LEDGER

ACCOUNT Cash **ACCOUNT NO.** 111

Date		Item	Post. Ref.	Debit	Credit	Balance Debit	Balance Credit
20--							
June	1		1	35 0 0 0 00		35 0 0 0 00	
	2		1		2 0 0 0 00	33 0 0 0 00	
	4		1		2 5 0 00	32 7 5 0 00	
	10		1	3 2 5 0 00		36 0 0 0 00	
	20		1		1 8 0 0 00	34 2 0 0 00	
	24		1		5 0 0 00	33 7 0 0 00	

ACCOUNT Supplies **ACCOUNT NO.** 115

Date		Item	Post. Ref.	Debit	Credit	Balance Debit	Balance Credit
20--							
June	4		1	250.00		250.00	

ACCOUNT Equipment **ACCOUNT NO.** 124

Date		Item	Post. Ref.	Debit	Credit	Balance Debit	Balance Credit
20--							
June	2		1	8,000.00		8,000.00	

ACCOUNT Accounts Payable **ACCOUNT NO.** 221

Date		Item	Post. Ref.	Debit	Credit	Balance Debit	Balance Credit
20--							
June	2		1		6,000.00		6,000.00

ACCOUNT J. Jonah, Capital **ACCOUNT NO.** 311

Date		Item	Post. Ref.	Debit	Credit	Balance Debit	Balance Credit
20--							
June	1		1		35,000.00		35,000.00

ACCOUNT J. Jonah, Drawing **ACCOUNT NO.** 312

Date		Item	Post. Ref.	Debit	Credit	Balance Debit	Balance Credit
20--							
June	24		1	500.00		500.00	

ACCOUNT Income from Services **ACCOUNT NO.** 411

Date		Item	Post. Ref.	Debit	Credit	Balance Debit	Balance Credit
20--							
June	10		1		3,250.00		3,250.00

ACCOUNT Rent Expense **ACCOUNT NO.** 512

Date		Item	Post. Ref.	Debit	Credit	Balance Debit	Balance Credit
20--							
June	20		1	1,800.00		1,800.00	

Learning Objective

 Prepare a trial balance from the ledger accounts.

The trial balance consists of a listing of account balances in two columns—one labeled Debit and one labeled Credit. The balances come from the ledger accounts.

PRACTICE EXERCISE 3

Prepare a trial balance from the ledger accounts in Practice Exercise 2.

PRACTICE EXERCISE 3 • SOLUTION

Jonah Company
Trial Balance
June 30, 20--

Account Name	Debit	Credit
Cash	33,700	
Supplies	250	
Equipment	8,000	
Accounts Payable		6,000
J. Jonah, Capital		35,000
J. Jonah, Drawing	500	
Income from Services		3,250
Rent Expense	1,800	
	44,250	44,250

Learning Objective

 Explain the importance of source documents.

Source documents provide proof of a transaction. Examples of source documents include invoices, receipts, checks, and deposit slips.

PRACTICE EXERCISE 4

What is a possible source document for each of the following transactions?

June 1 J. Jonah deposited $35,000 in the bank in the name of the business (Jonah Company).
2 The business purchased $8,000 in equipment, paying $2,000 in cash and placing the remainder on account.
4 The business purchased supplies for cash, $250.
10 The business received cash revenue, $3,250.
20 The business paid the monthly rent, $1,800.
24 J. Jonah withdrew $500 for personal use.

PRACTICE EXERCISE 4 • SOLUTION

June 1 Deposit slip and receipt
2 Receipt
4 Vendor invoice (bill) and check
10 Customer receipt and deposit slip
20 Vendor invoice (bill) and check
24 Withdrawal slip or ATM receipt

 Correct entries using the ruling or correcting entry method.

Learning Objective

CHAPTER REVIEW

The ruling method can be used if an error is discovered before or after an entry was posted. A line is drawn through the incorrect account title or amount and the correct account title or amount written immediately above. The person making the correction also includes his or her initials with the correction.

The correcting entry method is used if an error is discovered after an incorrectly journalized entry was posted. If the error consists of the wrong account(s), an entry is made to cancel out or reverse the incorrect account(s) and insert the correct account(s). The correcting entry must include an explanation.

PRACTICE EXERCISE 5

On July 9, a $380 payment for Supplies was incorrectly journalized and posted as a debit to Supplies Expense for $380 and a credit to Cash for $380. Provide the correcting entry following the one-step method.

PRACTICE EXERCISE 5 • SOLUTION

GENERAL JOURNAL Page 1

Date		Description	Post. Ref.	Debit	Credit
20--					
July	9	Supplies		380 00	
		Supplies Expense			380 00
		To correct error of July 9			
		in which a payment for Supplies			
		was debited to Supplies Expense.			

Glossary

Cost principle The principle that a purchased asset should be recorded at its actual cost. *(p. 115)*

Cross-reference The ledger account number in the Post. Ref. column of the journal and the journal page number in the Post. Ref. column of the ledger account. *(p. 120)*

General ledger A book or file containing the activity (by accounts), either manual or computerized, of a business. *(p. 118)*

Journal The book in which a person makes the original record of a business transaction; commonly referred to as a *book of original entry*. *(p. 111)*

Journalizing The process of recording a business transaction in a journal. *(p. 111)*

Ledger account A complete record of the transactions recorded in an individual account. *(p. 118)*

Posting The process of transferring figures from the journal to the ledger accounts. *(p. 120)*

Source documents Business papers, such as checks, invoices, receipts, letters, and memos, that furnish proof that a transaction has taken place. *(p. 111)*

Two-column general journal A general journal in which there are two amount columns, one used for debit amounts and one used for credit amounts. *(p. 113)*

Quiz Yourself

_____ 1. A ________ is a book in which business transactions are recorded.
a. journal
b. ledger
c. trial balance
d. balance sheet

_____ 2. Transferring information from the journal to the ledger is called
a. preparing the financial statements.
b. journalizing.
c. posting.
d. tracking.

_____ 3. For a journal entry to be complete, it must contain
a. the date.
b. a debit entry.
c. a credit entry.
d. an explanation.
e. all of the above.

_____ 4. The _________ is used to determine where the amount in the ledger comes from.
a. debit amount
b. posting reference (or cross-reference)
c. journal
d. none of the above

_____ 5. Which of the following is an example of source documents?
a. Canceled checks
b. Vendor invoices
c. Receipts
d. All of the above

_____ 6. A $250 payment for salaries expense was incorrectly journalized and posted as a debit to Salaries Expense for $2,500 and a credit to Cash for $2,500. Using the one-step method, how would the entry be corrected?

		Debit	Credit
a.	Cash	2,500	
	Salaries Expense		2,500
b.	Salaries Expense	250	
	Cash		250
c.	Cash	2,250	
	Salaries Expense		2,250
d.	Salaries Expense	2,250	
	Cash		2,250

Answers:
1. a 2. c 3. e 4. b 5. d 6. c

Review It with QuickBooks®

_____ 1. The general journal report is located under ____________ in QuickBooks.
a. Company & Financial
b. Accountant & Taxes
c. Custom Reports
d. All of the above

_____ 2. Transactions can be recorded in QuickBooks by _________ or __________.
a. journal entry method; general ledger method
b. *Getting Around* screen; general ledger method
c. journal entry method; *Getting Around* screen
d. scanning method; journal entry method

_____ 3. The general ledger report is located under ____________ in QuickBooks.
a. Company & Financial
b. Accountant & Taxes
c. Custom Reports
d. All of the above

_____ 4. Which of the following transactions requires using a name when recording them in QuickBooks?
a. Providing services for cash
b. Purchasing equipment for cash
c. Receiving and paying the utility bill
d. Purchasing supplies on account

Answers:
1. b 2. c 3. b 4. d

Chapter Assignments

Discussion Questions

1. Why is the journal called a book of original entry?
2. How does the journal differ from the ledger?
3. What is the purpose of providing a ledger account for each account?
4. List by account classification the order of the accounts in the general ledger.
5. Arrange the following steps in the posting process in correct order:
   a. Write the ledger account number in the Post. Ref. column of the journal.
   b. Write the amount of the transaction.
   c. Write the date of the transaction.
   d. Write the page number of the journal in the Post. Ref. column of the ledger account.
6. What does cross-referencing mean in the posting process?
7. Why is a source document important? List some examples of source documents.

Exercises

LO 1

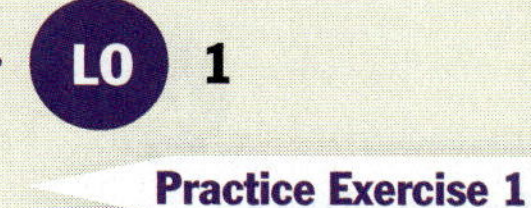

EXERCISE 3-1 In the following two-column journal, the capital letters represent where parts of a journal entry appear. Write the numbers 1 through 8 on a sheet of paper. After each number, match the capital letter where these items appear with the number of the item. (Not all letters will be used.)

GENERAL JOURNAL Page 1

Date		Description	Post. Ref.	Debit	Credit
G					
H	I	J	O	M	
		K	P		N
		L			

1. Year
2. Month
3. Explanation
4. Title of account debited
5. Ledger account number of account credited
6. Amount of debit
7. Day of the month
8. Title of account credited

CHAPTER ASSIGNMENTS

LO 1
Practice Exercise 1

EXERCISE 3-2 Decor Services completed the following transactions. Journalize the transactions in general journal form, including brief explanations.

Oct. 7 Received cash on account from Randy Hill, a customer, Inv. No. 312, $970.
15 Paid on account to Miller Ideas, a creditor, $725, Ck. No. 2242.
20 B. Brown, the owner, withdrew cash for personal use, $1,200, Ck. No. 2243.
23 Bought store supplies for $150 and office supplies for $70 on account from Williams Office Supply, Inv. No. 1040.
29 B. Brown, the owner, invested $3,000 cash and $1,500 of his personal equipment.

LO 1
Practice Exercise 1

EXERCISE 3-3 Montoya Tutoring Service completed the following transactions. Journalize the transactions in general journal form, including brief explanations.

Mar. 1 Bought equipment for $5,798 from Teaching Suppliers, paying $3,798 in cash and placing the balance on account, Ck. No. 3230.
10 Paid the wages for the first week of March, $1,536, Ck. No. 3231.
15 Sold services for cash to Mason District, $1,481, Sales Inv. 121.
26 Sold services on account to Tempe School, $1,400, Sales Inv. 122.
31 Paid on account to Teaching Suppliers, $725, Ck. No. 3232.

LO 2
Practice Exercise 2

EXERCISE 3-4 The following February journal entries all involved cash.

Increases to Cash—Debits		Decreases to Cash—Credits	
2/1	6,400	2/3	640
2/9	1,748	2/6	952
2/16	4,600	2/12	1,200
2/21	980	2/25	3,842
2/28	5,900		

Post the amounts to the ledger account for Cash, Account No. 111. Assume that all transactions appeared on page 1 of the general journal.

LO 2
Practice Exercise 2

EXERCISE 3-5 Arrange the following steps in the posting process in correct order:

a. The amount of the balance of the ledger account is recorded in the Debit Balance or Credit Balance column.
b. The amount of the transaction is recorded in the Debit or Credit column of the ledger account.
c. The ledger account number is recorded in the Post. Ref. column of the journal.
d. The date of the transaction is recorded in the Date column of the ledger account.
e. The page number of the journal is recorded in the Post. Ref. column of the ledger account.

LO 3 Practice Exercise 3

EXERCISE 3-6 The bookkeeper for Nevado Company has prepared the following trial balance:

Nevado Company
Trial Balance
June 30, 20—

Account Name	Debit	Credit
Cash		2,500
Accounts Receivable	8,300	
Supplies	600	
Prepaid Insurance	650	
Equipment	15,300	
Accounts Payable		2,700
M. Nevado, Capital		12,500
M. Nevado, Drawing	4,890	
Professional Fees		17,540
Rent Expense	500	
Miscellaneous Expense	1,800	
	32,040	35,240

The bookkeeper has asked for your help. In examining the company's journal and ledger, you discover the following errors. Use this information to construct a corrected trial balance.

a. The debits to the Cash account total $8,000, and the credits total $3,300.
b. A $500 payment to a creditor was entered in the journal correctly but was not posted to the Accounts Payable account.
c. The first two numbers in the balance of the Accounts Receivable account were transposed when the balance was copied from the ledger to the trial balance.
d. The $1,500 amount withdrawn by the owner for personal use was debited to Miscellaneous Expense by mistake—it was correctly credited to Cash.

LO 5 Practice Exercise 5

EXERCISE 3-7 Determine the effect of the following errors on a company's total revenue, total expenses, and net income. Indicate the effect by writing O for Overstated (too much), U for Understated (too little), or NA for Not Affected.

Transactions	Total Revenue	Total Expenses	Net Income
Example: A check for $325 was written to pay on account. The accountant debited Rent Expense for $325 and credited Cash for $325.	NA	O	U
a. $420 was received on account from customers. The accountant debited Cash for $420 and credited Professional Fees for $420.			
b. The owner withdrew $1,200 for personal use. The accountant debited Wages Expense for $1,200 and credited Cash for $1,200.			
c. A check was written for $1,250 to pay the rent. The accountant debited Rent Expense for $1,520 and credited Cash for $1,520.			

(*Continued*)

Transactions	Total Revenue	Total Expenses	Net Income
d. $1,800 was received on account from customers. The accountant debited Cash for $1,800 and credited the Capital account for $1,800.			
e. A check was written for $225 to pay the phone bill received and recorded earlier in the month. The accountant debited Phone Expense for $225 and credited Cash for $225.			

LO 5

EXERCISE 3-8 Journalize correcting entries for each of the following errors and include a brief explanation.

a. A cash purchase of office equipment for $680 was journalized as a cash purchase of store equipment for $680. (Use the ruling method; assume that the entry has not been posted.)
b. An entry for a $180 payment for office supplies was journalized as $810. (Use the ruling method; assume that the entry has not been posted.)
c. A $620 payment for repairs was journalized and posted as a debit to Equipment instead of a debit to Repair Expense. (Use the correcting entry method to journalize the correction.)
d. A $750 bill for vehicle insurance was received and immediately paid. It was journalized and posted as $660. (Use the correcting entry method to journalize the correction.)

Problem Set A

LO 1

PROBLEM 3-1A The chart of accounts of the Barnes School is shown here, followed by the transactions that took place during October of this year.

Assets
111 Cash
113 Accounts Receivable
115 Prepaid Insurance
124 Equipment
127 Furniture

Liabilities
221 Accounts Payable

Owner's Equity
311 R. Barnes, Capital
312 R. Barnes, Drawing

Revenue
411 Tuition Income

Expenses
511 Salary Expense
512 Rent Expense
513 Gas and Oil Expense
514 Advertising Expense
515 Repair Expense
516 Telephone Expense
517 Utilities Expense
529 Miscellaneous Expense

Oct.	1	Bought liability insurance for one year, $1,850, Ck. No. 1527.
	3	Received a bill for advertising from *Business Summary*, $415.
	4	Paid the rent for the current month, $1,870, Ck. No. 1528.
	7	Received a bill for equipment repair from Fix-It Service, $318, Inv. No. 436.

Oct. 10 Received and deposited tuition from students, $6,375.
11 Received and paid the telephone bill $312, Ck. No. 1529.
15 Bought desks and chairs from The Oak Center, $1,980, paying $980 in cash and placing the balance on account, Ck. No. 1530.
18 Paid on account to *Business Summary*, $415, Ck. No. 1531.
21 R. Barnes withdrew $1,000 for personal use, Ck. No. 1532.
24 Received a bill for gas and oil from Wagner Oil Company, $225, Inv. No. 682.
25 Received and deposited tuition from students, $6,380.
27 Paid the salary of the part-time office assistant, $1,150. Ck. No. 1533.
28 Bought a photocopier on account from Gorst Office Machines, $1,950, Inv. No. 417.
29 Received $950 tuition from a student who had charged the tuition on account in September.
30 Received and paid the bill for utilities, $623, Ck. No. 1534.
31 Paid for flower arrangements for front office, $87, Ck. No. 1535.
31 R. Barnes invested his personal computer and printer, with a fair market value of $1,549, in the business.

Required

Record these transactions in the general journal, including a brief explanation for each entry. Number the journal pages 31 and 32.

Check Figure
Equipment increased by $3,499 in October

LO 2, 3

PROBLEM 3-2A The journal entries for August, Carley's Car Care's second month of business, have been journalized in the general journal in your Working Papers and in CengageNow. The balances of the accounts as of July 31 have been recorded in the general ledger in your Working Papers and in CengageNow. Notice the word *Balance* in the Item column, the check mark in the Post. Ref. column, and the fact that the amount is in the Balance column only. This indicates a balance brought forward from a prior page or month.

Required

1. Write the owner's name, M. Carley, in the Capital and Drawing accounts.
2. Post the general journal entries to the general ledger accounts.
3. Prepare a trial balance as of August 31, 20--.
4. Prepare an income statement for the two months ended August 31, 20--.
5. Prepare a statement of owner's equity for the two months ended August 31, 20--.
6. Prepare a balance sheet as of August 31, 20--.

Check Figure
Net Income. $11,649

LO 1, 2, 3

PROBLEM 3-3A Following is the chart of accounts of the C. Lucern Clinic:

Assets
111 Cash
113 Accounts Receivable
115 Supplies
117 Prepaid Insurance
124 Equipment

Liabilities
221 Accounts Payable

Owner's Equity
311 C. Lucern, Capital
312 C. Lucern, Drawing

Revenue
411 Professional Fees

Expenses
511 Salary Expense
512 Rent Expense
513 Laboratory Expense
514 Utilities Expense

(*Continued*)

CHAPTER ASSIGNMENTS

Dr. Lucern completed the following transactions during July:

July	1	Bought laboratory equipment on account from Laser Surgical Supply Company, $3,660, paying $1,660 in cash and placing the remainder on account, Ck. No. 1730.
	3	Paid the office rent for the current month, $1,300, Ck. No. 1731.
	5	Received cash on account from patients, $360.
	6	Bought supplies on account from McRae Supply Company, $315, Inv. No. 3455.
	7	Received and paid the bill for laboratory services, $1,380, Ck. No. 1732.
	8	Bought insurance for one year, $2,650, CK. No. 1733.
	12	Performed medical services for patients on account, $5,886.
	15	Performed medical services for patients for cash, $4,793.
	16	The equipment purchased on July 1 was found to be broken. Dr. Lucern returned the damaged part and received a reduction in his bill, $518, Inv. No. 3162, Credit Memo No. 141. (Credit Equipment.)
	18	Paid the salary of the part-time nurse, $2,100, Ck. No. 1734.
	24	Received and paid the telephone bill for the month, $624, Ck. No. 1735.
	28	Performed medical services for patients on account, $7,381.
	29	Dr. Lucern withdrew cash for his personal use, $2,000, Ck. No. 1736.

Check Figure
Trial balance total, $62,679

Required

1. Journalize the transactions for July in the general journal, beginning on page 21.
2. Write the name of the owner next to the Capital and Drawing accounts in the general ledger. The balances of the accounts as of June 30 have been recorded in the general ledger in your Working Papers and in CengageNow. Notice the word *Balance* in the Item column, the check mark in the Post. Ref. column, and the fact that the amount is in the Balance column only. This indicates a balance brought forward from a prior page or month.
3. Post the entries to the general ledger accounts.
4. Prepare a trial balance.

LO 1, 2, 3

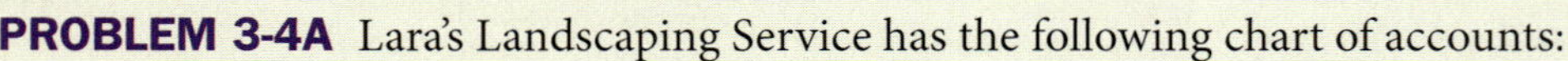

PROBLEM 3-4A Lara's Landscaping Service has the following chart of accounts:

Assets
111 Cash
113 Accounts Receivable
115 Supplies
117 Prepaid Insurance
124 Equipment

Liabilities
221 Accounts Payable

Owner's Equity
311 J. Lara, Capital
312 J. Lara, Drawing

Revenue
411 Landscaping Income

Expenses
511 Salary Expense
512 Rent Expense
513 Gas and Oil Expense
514 Utilities Expense

The following transactions were completed by Lara's Landscaping Service:

Mar.	1	Lara deposited $35,000 in a bank account in the name of the business.
	4	Lara invested his personal landscaping equipment, with a fair market value of $1,325, in the business.
	6	Bought a used trailer on account from Tow Sales, $915, Inv. No. 314.
	7	Paid the rent for the current month, $950, Ck. No. 1000.
	9	Bought a used backhoe from Digger's Equipment, $5,300, paying $3,000 in cash and placing the balance on account, Inv. 4166, Ck. No. 1001.

Mar. 10 Bought liability insurance for one year, $1,800, Ck. No. 1002.
13 Sold landscaping services on account to Fredkey's, $3,895, Inv. No. 100.
14 Bought supplies on account from Office Requip, $380, Inv. No. 5172.
15 Sold landscaping services on account to C. Endel, $2,832, Inv. No. 101.
17 Received and paid the bill from Commercial Services for gas and oil for the equipment, $180, Ck. No. 1003.
19 Sold landscaping services for cash to Riston Company, $1,864, Inv. No. 102.
22 Paid on account to Tow Sales, $500, Inv. No. 314, Ck. No. 1004.
24 Received on account from Fredkey's, $800, Inv. No. 100.
28 Sold landscaping services on account to Stevens, Inc., $1,830, Inv. No. 103.
29 Received and paid the telephone bill, $260, Ck. No. 1005.
30 Paid the salary of the employee, $1,850, Ck. No. 1006.
31 Lara withdrew cash for his personal use, $1,500, Ck. No. 1007.

Required

1. Journalize the transactions in the general journal. Provide a brief explanation for each entry.
2. Write the name of the owner on the Capital and Drawing accounts. (Skip this step if you are using QuickBooks or general ledger.)
3. Post the journal entries to the general ledger accounts. (Skip this step if you are using QuickBooks or general ledger.)
4. Prepare a trial balance dated March 31, 20--. (If you are using QuickBooks or general ledger, use the year 2015.)

Check Figure
Trial balance total, $49,841

LO 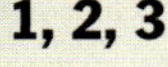 1, 2, 3

QuickBooks

PROBLEM 3-5A Following is the chart of accounts of Sanchez Realty Company:

Assets
111 Cash
113 Accounts Receivable
115 Supplies
117 Prepaid Insurance
124 Office Furniture

Liabilities
221 Accounts Payable

Owner's Equity
311 T. Sanchez, Capital
312 T. Sanchez, Drawing

Revenue
411 Professional Fees

Expenses
511 Salary Expense
512 Rent Expense
513 Advertising Expense
514 Utilities Expense

Sanchez completed the following transactions during April (the first month of business):

Apr. 1 Sanchez deposited $20,000 in a bank account in the name of the business.
5 Sold realty services on account to R. Miller, $7,500, Inv. No. 100.
7 Paid a bill for advertising, $250, Ck. No. 1001.
8 Bought supplies on account from Taylor Supply, $420, Inv. No. 2340.
9 Performed realty services for clients for cash, $2,530.
15 Received and paid the bill for utilities, $280, Ck. No. 1002.
17 Bought a desk and chair from Lewis Furniture, $1,800, paying $300 in cash and placing the balance on account, Ck. No. 1003.
20 Bought liability insurance for one year, $1,800, Ck. No. 1004.
21 Paid the rent for the current month, $1,000, Ck. No. 1005.

(*Continued*)

Apr. 25 Paid on account to Taylor Supply, $420, for supplies purchased on April 8, Ck. No. 1006.
27 Received $7,500 from R. Miller for services performed on April 5.
28 Received and paid the telephone bill for the month, $150, Ck. No. 1007.
29 Paid the salary of the office assistant, $1,030, Ck. No. 1008.
30 Sanchez withdrew cash for his personal use, $3,000, Ck. No. 1009.

Check Figure
Trial balance total, $31,530

Required

1. Journalize the transactions for April in the general journal.
2. Post the entries to the general ledger accounts. (Skip this step if you are using QuickBooks or general ledger.)
3. Prepare a trial balance as of April 30, 20--.
4. Prepare an income statement for the month ended April 30, 20--.
5. Prepare a statement of owner's equity for the month ended April 30, 20--. (Skip this step if you are using QuickBooks.)
6. Prepare a balance sheet as of April 30, 20--.

*If you are using QuickBooks or general ledger , use the year 2015 when preparing all reports.

Problem Set B

LO 1

PROBLEM 3-1B The chart of accounts of Ethan Academy is shown here, followed by the transactions that took place during December of this year.

Assets
111 Cash
113 Accounts Receivable
114 Supplies
115 Prepaid Insurance
124 Equipment
127 Furniture

Liabilities
221 Accounts Payable

Owner's Equity
311 R. Ethan, Capital
312 R. Ethan, Drawing

Revenue
411 Tuition Income

Expenses
511 Salary Expense
512 Rent Expense
513 Gas and Oil Expense
514 Advertising Expense
515 Repair Expense
516 Telephone Expense
517 Utilities Expense
529 Miscellaneous Expense

Dec. 1 Bought liability insurance for one year, $2,260, Ck. No. 1627.
11 Received a bill for advertising from the *City News*, $415, Statement No. 4267.
12 Paid the rent for the current month, $1,850, Ck. No. 1628.
13 Received a bill for equipment repair from Electronic Services, $345, Inv. No. 547.
16 Received and deposited tuition from students, $5,850.
17 Received and paid the telephone bill, $305, Ck. No. 1629.
18 Bought desks and chairs from School Furniture, $1,625, paying $625 in cash and placing the balance on account, Ck. No. 1630.
20 Paid on account to the *City News*, $415, Statement No. 4267, Ck. No. 1631.

Dec. 21 R. Ethan withdrew $1,000 for personal use, Ck. No. 1632.
26 Received a bill for gas and oil from Discount Oil Company, $210, Inv. No. 591.
27 Received and deposited tuition from students, $6,045.
31 Paid the salary of the office assistant, $1,375, Ck. No. 1633.
31 Bought a fax machine on account from EquipCo, $118, Inv. No. 529.
31 Received $1,150 tuition from a student who had charged the tuition on account last month.
31 Received and paid the bill for utilities, $470, Ck. No. 1634.
31 R. Ethan invested her personal computer and printer, with a fair market value of $1,150, in the business.
31 Bought supplies, $295, Ck. No. 1635.

Required

Record these transactions in the general journal, including a brief explanation for each entry. Number the journal pages 31 and 32.

Check Figure
Equipment increased by $1,268 in December

LO 2, 3

PROBLEM 3-2B The journal entries for May, Kiddy Day Care's second month of business, have been journalized in the general journal in your Working Papers and in CengageNow. The balances of the accounts as of April 30 have been recorded in the general ledger in your Working Papers and in CengageNow. Notice the word *Balance* in the Item column, the check mark in the Post. Ref. column, and the fact that the amount is in the Balance column only. This indicates a balance brought forward from a prior page or month.

Required

1. Write the owner's name, R. Ramirez, in the Capital and Drawing accounts.
2. Post the general journal entries to the general ledger accounts.
3. Prepare a trial balance as of May 31, 20--.
4. Prepare an income statement for the two months ended May 31, 20--.
5. Prepare a statement of owner's equity for the two months ended May 31, 20--.
6. Prepare a balance sheet as of May 31, 20--.

Check Figure
Net Income, $12,261

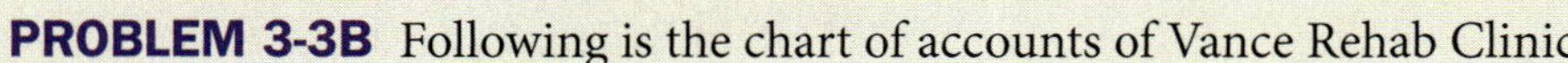

LO 1, 2, 3

PROBLEM 3-3B Following is the chart of accounts of Vance Rehab Clinic:

Assets
111 Cash
113 Accounts Receivable
115 Supplies
117 Prepaid Insurance
124 Equipment

Liabilities
221 Accounts Payable

Owner's Equity
311 J. Vance, Capital
312 J. Vance, Drawing

Revenue
411 Professional Fees

Expenses
511 Salary Expense
512 Rent Expense
513 Laboratory Expense
514 Utilities Expense

Vance completed the following transactions during July:

July 1 Bought laboratory equipment on account from Sage Surgical Supply Company, $6,520, paying $1,520 in cash and placing the remainder on account, Inv. No. 2071, Ck. No. 1930.
3 Paid the office rent for the current month, $1,550, Ck. No. 1931.

(Continued)

July	5	Received cash on account from patients, $3,045.
	6	Bought supplies on account from Allround Supply, $320, Inv. No. 3455.
	9	Received and paid the bill for laboratory services, $1,484, Ck. No. 1932.
	10	Bought insurance for one year, $2,600, Ck. No. 1933.
	12	Performed rehab services for patients on account, $5,185.
	14	Performed rehab services for patients for cash, $5,050.
	18	Part of the equipment purchased on July 1 was found to be broken. Vance returned the damaged part and received a reduction in her bill, $410, Inv. No. 2071, Credit Memo No. 218. (Credit Equipment.)
	20	Paid the salary of the part-time nurse, $2,200, Ck. No. 1934.
	22	Received and paid the telephone bill for the month, $380, Ck. No. 1935.
	24	Performed rehab services for patients on account, $4,235.
	30	Vance withdrew cash for her personal use, $2,000, Ck. No. 1936.

Check Figure
Trial balance total, $46,028

Required

1. Journalize the transactions for July in the general journal, beginning on page 21.
2. Write the name of the owner next to the Capital and Drawing accounts in the general ledger. The balances of the accounts as of June 30 have been recorded in the general ledger in your Working Papers and in CengageNow. Notice the word *Balance* in the Item column, the check mark in the Post. Ref. column, and the fact that the amount is in the Balance column only. This indicates a balance brought forward from a prior page or month.
3. Post the entries to the general ledger accounts.
4. Prepare a trial balance.

 1, 2, 3

PROBLEM 3-4B Leander's Landscaping Service maintains the following chart of accounts:

Assets
111 Cash
113 Accounts Receivable
117 Prepaid Insurance
124 Equipment

Liabilities
221 Accounts Payable

Owner's Equity
311 O. Leander, Capital
312 O. Leander, Drawing

Revenue
411 Landscaping Income

Expenses
511 Salary Expense
512 Rent Expense
513 Gas and Oil Expense
514 Utilities Expense
515 Supplies Expense

The following transactions were completed by Leander:

Apr.	1	Leander deposited $30,000 in a bank account in the name of the business.
	4	Leander invested his personal landscaping equipment, with a fair market value of $1,750, in the business.
	6	Bought a used trailer on account from Used Mart, $1,450, Inv. No. 415.
	7	Paid the rent for the current month, $925, Ck. No. 100.
	9	Bought a used bulldozer from Dray's Equipment, $5,100, paying $2,100 in cash and placing the balance on account, Inv. No. 3255, Ck. No. 101.
	10	Bought liability insurance for one year, $2,800, Ck. No. 102.
	13	Sold landscaping services on account to Fulton Homes, $4,595, Inv. No. 100.
	14	Bought supplies on account from Perry's Supply, $427, Inv. No. 4281.

Apr.	15	Sold landscaping services on account to D. D. Mau Inc., $3,997, Inv. No. 101.
	17	Received and paid the bill from Pumpers for gas and oil for the equipment, $227, Ck. No. 103.
	19	Sold landscaping services for cash to Cliff's House, $1,437, Inv. No. 102.
	22	Paid on account to Used Mart, $450, Inv. No. 415, Ck. No. 104.
	24	Received on account from Fulton Homes, $800, Inv. No. 100.
	28	Sold landscaping services on account to H. Ron, $1,785, Inv. No. 103.
	29	Received and paid the telephone bill, $321, Ck. No. 105.
	30	Paid the salary of the employee, $1,836, Ck. No. 106.
	30	Leander withdrew cash for his personal use, $1,500, Ck. No. 107.

Required

Check Figure
Trial balance total, $47,991

1. Journalize the transactions in the general journal. Prepare a brief explanation for each entry.
2. Write the name of the owner on the Capital and Drawing accounts. (Skip this step if you are using QuickBooks or general ledger.)
3. Post the journal entries to the general ledger accounts. (Skip this step if you are using QuickBooks or general ledger.)
4. Prepare a trial balance dated April 30, 20--. (If you are using QuickBooks or general ledger, use the year 2015.)

LO 1, 2, 3

PROBLEM 3-5B Following is the chart of accounts of Smith Financial Services:

Assets
111 Cash
113 Accounts Receivable
115 Supplies
117 Prepaid Insurance
124 Office Furniture

Liabilities
221 Accounts Payable

Owner's Equity
311 A. Smith, Capital
312 A. Smith, Drawing

Revenue
411 Professional Fees

Expenses
511 Salary Expense
512 Rent Expense
513 Advertising Expense
514 Utilities Expense

Smith completed the following transactions during June (the first month of business):

June	1	Smith deposited $10,000 in a bank account in the name of the business.
	3	Sold financial services on account to W. Johnson, $3,030, Inv. No. 001.
	8	Paid a bill for advertising, $100, Ck. No. 200.
	9	Bought supplies on account from Jones Supply, $75, Inv. No. 405.
	13	Performed financial services for clients for cash, $3,200.
	17	Received and paid the bill for utilities, $104, Ck. No. 201.
	19	Bought a desk and chair from Davis Furniture, $600, paying $50 in cash and placing the balance on account, Ck. No. 202.
	20	Bought liability insurance for one year, $600, Ck. No. 203.
	23	Paid the rent for the current month, $400, Ck. No. 204.
	27	Paid on account to Jones Supply, $75, for supplies purchased on June 9, Ck. No. 205.
	29	Received $3,030 from W. Johnson for services performed on June 3.

(Continued)

June 29 Received and paid the telephone bill for the month, $80, Ck. No. 206.
30 Paid the salary of the office assistant, $600, Ck. No. 207.
30 Smith withdrew cash for her personal use, $800, Ck. No. 208.

Check Figure
Trial balance total, $16,780

Required

1. Journalize the transactions for June in the general journal.
2. Post the entries to the general ledger accounts. (Skip this step if you are using QuickBooks or general ledger.)
3. Prepare a trial balance as of June 30, 20--.
4. Prepare an income statement for the month ended June 30, 20--.
5. Prepare a statement of owner's equity for the month ended June 30, 20--. (Skip this step if you are using QuickBooks.)
6. Prepare a balance sheet as of June 30, 20--.

*If you are using QuickBooks or general ledger , use the year 2015 when preparing all reports.

Try It with QuickBooks® (LO 1-4)

QB Exercise 3-1

Using the Conner's Whitewater Adventures demonstration file from Chapter 1, complete the following activities with QuickBooks. Use the dates June 1, 2015, to June 30, 2015, for all reports.

1. View and print the general journal report for Conner's Whitewater Adventures.
   a. What is the ending balance of the Debit column for the journal?
2. View and print the general ledger report for Conner's Whitewater Adventures.
   a. What is the ending balance in the Cash account? Is this balance a debit or a credit?
   b. What is the total amount of revenues during the month of June for Conner's Whitewater Adventures?
   c. What is the total amount of expenses during the month of June for Conner's Whitewater Adventures?

Activities

Why Does It Matter?

ECOTOUR EXPEDITIONS, INC., Jamestown, Rhode Island
You probably have never imagined the possibility of being an accountant who could have a direct impact on improving global ecosystems. Accountants who work for Ecotour Expeditions, Inc., an ecotourism company, might manage accounting details for guest air travel and accommodations, tour guide compensation, expedition revenue, and a variety of expenses. What type of accounting transactions would Ecotour Expeditions have? List 3 to 4 transactions and then record the journal entry for each transaction. Example: *Purchase safari jeep with cash, $42,500.*

Safari Jeep	42,500	
Cash		42,500

What Would You Say?

You are the new bookkeeper for a small business. The bookkeeper whose job you are taking is training you on the business's manual system. As he journalizes, he writes the account number in the Post. Ref. column because he believes it's easier. His thinking is that, when he posts, he won't be bothered writing the account numbers. How would you explain why he should *not* write the account number in the Post. Ref. column immediately and instead should enter the account number after he has posted the amount to the ledger?

What Do You Think?

You work as an accounting clerk. You have received the following information supplied by a client, S. Winston, from the client's bank statement, the client's tax returns, and a variety of other July documents. The client wants you to prepare an income statement, a statement of owner's equity, and a balance sheet for the month of July for Winston Company.

Income from Services	$ 9,570	Utilities Expense	$ 388
Beginning Capital	50,000	Drawing	2,500
Cash	24,940	Supplies	635
Truck	?	Equipment	16,148
Accounts Payable	?	Total Liabilities and Owner's Equity	57,473
Rent Expense	1,200		
Wages Expense	4,200		

What Would You Do?

You are responsible for preparing all of the journal entries for Regional Financial Services. You have correctly prepared the following entry for financial services provided on December 15:

Dec. 15	Cash	10,000	
	Fees Earned		10,000

Your boss has asked you to change the date from December 15 to January 15 so that the business's profit, and thus taxes, would be lower. Are you allowed to do this? What is your response to your boss? How should you handle this situation?

BEFORE A TEST CHECK

BEFORE A TEST CHECK: Chapters 1–3

PART 1 : Multiple-Choice Questions

_____ **1.** Which of the following is not considered an account?
a. Cash
b. Prepaid Insurance
c. Equipment
d. Assets
e. Accounts Receivable

_____ **2.** In which of the following transactions would an expense be recorded?
a. Received a bill for advertising.
b. Paid on an account payable for the utility bill.
c. Received and paid a bill for repairs.
d. All of these should be recorded as an expense.
e. Only a and c should be recorded as an expense.

_____ **3.** The ending capital balance appears on which of the following statements?
a. Statement of owner's equity
b. Balance sheet
c. Income statement
d. Statement of owner's equity and balance sheet
e. Statement of owner's equity and income statement

_____ **4.** On a statement of owner's equity, if beginning capital is $42,000 and there is an additional investment of $5,000, a net loss of $9,000, and owner withdrawals of $15,000, the ending capital amount would be
a. $70,000.
b. $23,000.
c. $40,000.
d. $54,000.
e. none of these.

_____ **5.** If a $260 payment of rent is recorded as a $620 debit to Rent Expense and a $620 credit to Cash, what will the result be?
a. The trial balance will be in balance.
b. The Rent Expense account will be overstated.
c. The Cash account will be understated.
d. Rent Expense will be overstated and Cash will be understated.
e. All of the above are true.

_____ **6.** A person who wanted to know the balance of an account would look in
a. the ledger.
b. the chart of accounts.
c. the journal.
d. the source documents.
e. none of these.

PART II: The Accounting Cycle

Journalizing, Posting, Trial Balance, and Financial Statements

The accounts and their balances as of December 1 of this year for Antec Services are as follows:

111 Cash	$18,900	311 J. Dunn, Capital	$49,590
113 Accounts Receivable	6,300	312 J. Dunn, Drawing	11,200
115 Supplies	870		
116 Prepaid Insurance	1,230	411 Service Income	39,600
124 Equipment	31,200		
		511 Wages Expense	10,450
221 Accounts Payable	6,340	512 Utilities Expense	2,760
		513 Rent Expense	12,620

Check Figure
Net Income, $22,315

Required

1. Journalize the following December transactions in general journal form on journal page 31.

Dec. 1 Sold services for cash, $9,500.
4 Received and paid the bill for the rent for December, $1,000, Ck. No. 2331.

Dec. 11 Received $1,750 on account from customers, Cash Receipt Nos. 1430–1438.
19 Sold services on account, $2,075, Sales Inv. No. 2591.
22 Received and paid the bill for utilities, $255, Ck. No. 2332.
23 Bought supplies on account from Office Works, $292, Inv. No. 2606.
31 Paid the wages for the month, $1,775, Ck. No. 2333.
31 Dunn withdrew $1,500 for personal use, Ck. No. 2334.

2. Label T accounts with the above account names.
3. Correctly place the plus and minus signs under all T accounts and label the debit and credit sides of each T account.
4. Post the entries to the T accounts by date and foot and balance the accounts.
5. Prepare a trial balance as of December 31.
6. Prepare an income statement for the year ended December 31.
7. Prepare a statement of owner's equity for the year ended December 31.
8. Prepare a balance sheet as of December 31.

Answers: Part I

1. d 2. e 3. d 4. b 5. e 6. a

Answers: Part II

1.

GENERAL JOURNAL **Page 3**

Date		Description	Post. Ref.	Debit	Credit
20--					
Dec.	1	Cash	111	9 5 0 0 00	
		Service Income	411		9 5 0 0 00
		Sold services for cash.			
	4	Rent Expense	513	1 0 0 0 00	
		Cash	111		1 0 0 0 00
		Ck. No. 2331.			
	11	Cash	111	1 7 5 0 00	
		Accounts Receivable	113		1 7 5 0 00
		Cash on account from customers,			
		Cash Receipt Nos. 1430–1438.			
	19	Accounts Receivable	113	2 0 7 5 00	
		Service Income	411		2 0 7 5 00
		Sales Inv. No. 2591.			
	22	Utilities Expense	512	2 5 5 00	
		Cash	111		2 5 5 00
		Ck. No. 2332.			
	23	Supplies	115	2 9 2 00	
		Accounts Payable	221		2 9 2 00
		Office Works, Inv. No. 2606.			
	31	Wages Expense	511	1 7 7 5 00	
		Cash	111		1 7 7 5 00
		Paid month's wages, Ck. No. 2333.			
	31	J. Dunn, Drawing	312	1 5 0 0 00	
		Cash	111		1 5 0 0 00
		Ck. No. 2334.			

BEFORE A TEST CHECK

2., 3., and 4.

Owner's Equity

Assets		=	Liabilities		+	Capital		−	Drawing		+	Revenue		−	Expenses	
+	−		−	+		−	+		+	−		−	+		+	−
Debit	**Credit**		**Debit**	**Credit**		**Debit**	**Credit**		**Debit**	**Credit**		**Debit**	**Credit**		**Debit**	**Credit**

Cash 111

+ Debit	− Credit
Bal. 18,900	12/4 1,000
12/1 9,500	12/22 255
12/11 1,750	12/31 1,775
30,150	12/31 1,500
	4,530
Bal. 25,620	

Accounts Receivable 113

+ Debit	− Credit
Bal. 6,300	12/11 1,750
12/19 2,075	
8,375	
Bal. 6,625	

Supplies 115

+ Debit	− Credit
Bal. 870	
12/23 292	
Bal. 1,162	

Prepaid Insurance 116

+ Debit	− Credit
Bal. 1,230	

Equipment 124

+ Debit	− Credit
Bal. 31,200	

Accounts Payable 221

− Debit	+ Credit
	Bal. 6,340
	12/23 292
	Bal. 6,632

J. Dunn. Capital 311

+ Debit	− Credit
	Bal. 49,590

J. Dunn, Drawing 312

+ Debit	
Bal. 11,200	
12/31 1,500	
Bal. 12,700	

Service Income 411

− Debit	+ Credit
	Bal. 39,600
	12/1 9,500
	12/19 2,075
	Bal. 51,175

Wages Expense 511

+ Debit	− Credit
Bal. 10,450	
12/31 1,775	
Bal. 12,225	

Utilities Expense 512

+ Debit	− Credit
Bal. 2,760	
12/22 255	
Bal. 3,015	

Rent Expense 513

+ Debit	− Credit
Bal. 12,620	
12/4 1,000	
Bal. 13,620	

5.

Antec Services
Trial Balance
December 31, 20—

Account Name	Debit	Credit
Cash	25,620	
Accounts Receivable	6,625	
Supplies	1,162	
Prepaid Insurance	1,230	
Equipment	31,200	
Accounts Payable		6,632
J. Dunn, Capital		49,590
J. Dunn, Drawing	12,700	
Service Income		51,175
Wages Expense	12,225	
Utilities Expense	3,015	
Rent Expense	13,620	
	107,397	107,397

6.

Antec Services
Income Statement
For Year Ended December 31, 20--

Revenue:		
Service Income		$51,175
Expenses:		
Wages Expense	$12,225	
Utilities Expense	3,015	
Rent Expense	13,620	
Total Expenses		28,860
Net Income		$22,315

7.

Antec Services
Statement of Owner's Equity
For Year Ended December 31, 20--

J. Dunn, Capital, January 1, 20--		$49,590
Investments during Year	$ 0	
Net Income for Year	22,315	
Subtotal	$22,315	
Less Withdrawals for Year	12,700	
Increase in Capital		9,615
J. Dunn, Capital, December 31, 20--		$59,205

8.

Antec Services Balance Sheet December 31, 20--		
Assets		
Cash	$25,620	
Accounts Receivable	6,625	
Supplies	1,162	
Prepaid Insurance	1,230	
Equipment	31,200	
Total Assets		$65,837
Liabilities		
Accounts Payable		$ 6,632
Owner's Equity		
J. Dunn, Capital		59,205
Total Liabilities and Owner's Equity		$65,837

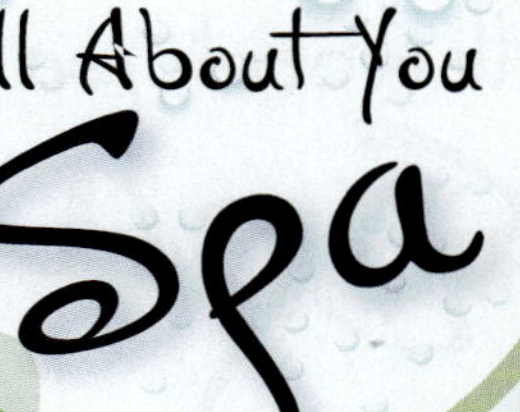

Journalizing, Posting and Preparing a Trial Balance

CONTINUING PROBLEM

A friend of yours, Anika Valli, has decided to open a spa to serve her small resort town of about 7,000 people and 4 million tourists annually. She has named the business All About You Spa to convey the idea that the business intends to pamper those who enter its doors. She will operate the spa five days a week, Tuesday through Saturday, but a phone line will always be available to answer questions and schedule appointments. Hours will be from 8 A.M. to 8 P.M. She has asked you to be the bookkeeper for this new business. At the end of the month of June, the owner, Anika Valli, would like you to provide the following:

1. General journal
2. General ledger
3. Trial balance
4. Income statement (This is the profit and loss statement in QuickBooks.)
5. Statement of owner's equity (Ignore this step if you are using QuickBooks.)
6. Balance sheet

She has kept a checkbook and a file folder with summary evidence of June's spa activity: a check register, a summary report of charges by customers for services provided, all receipts that were issued, and a summary of charges made by All About You Spa. Most of the income from services is received in cash and as charges to credit cards. No checks are accepted, except from approved clients (primarily conference planners and other organizations that book packages as prizes for attendees or gifts for employees, speakers, or other people they want to thank with a spa service or package of services). Anika deposits cash receipts on customer's accounts on the 7th, 14th, 21st, and last day of each month.

The first page in the file folder contains the following chart of accounts. Currently, you will not use or may not be familiar with some of the accounts listed here. Ignore those accounts for now; we will use them later.

CHART OF ACCOUNTS FOR ALL ABOUT YOU SPA

Assets

111 Cash
113 Accounts Receivable
114 Office Supplies
115 Spa Supplies
117 Prepaid Insurance
124 Office Equipment
125 Accum. Depr.—Office Equipment
128 Spa Equipment
129 Accum. Depr.—Spa Equipment

Liabilities

211 Accounts Payable
212 Wages Payable

Owner's Equity

311 A. Valli, Capital
312 A. Valli, Drawing
313 Income Summary

Revenue

411 Income from Services

Expenses

611 Wages Expense
612 Rent Expense
613 Office Supplies Expense
614 Spa Supplies Expense
615 Laundry Expense
616 Advertising Expense
617 Utilities Expense
618 Insurance Expense
619 Depr. Expense—Office Equipment
620 Depr. Expense—Spa Equipment
630 Miscellaneous Expense

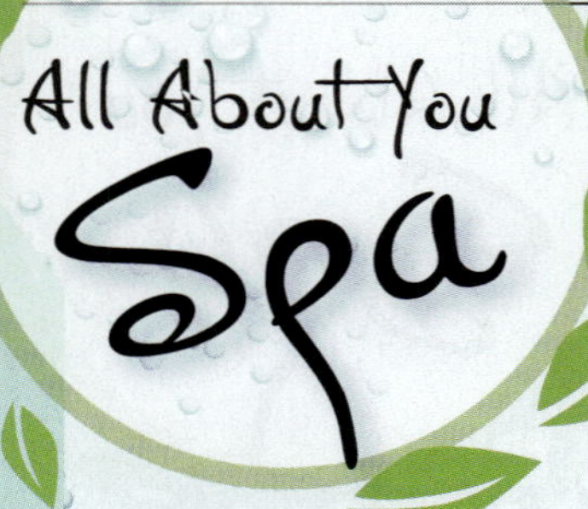

CONTINUING PROBLEM

The basis of your entries will be the following documents:

Checkbook Entries
(Deposits made and checks written)

Check No.	Date	Explanation	√	Deposits	Check Amount
	6/1	Invested cash in business.		15,000.00	
1011	6/3	Bought 6-month liability insurance policy.			960.00
1012	6/3	Bought spa equipment for $4,235, putting $2,000 cash down.			2,000.00
1013	6/3	Paid June rent.			1,650.00
1014	6/5	Bought office supplies.			248.00
1015	6/5	Purchased flowers and balloons for grand opening (Misc. Exp.).			112.00
1016	6/7	Paid first week's wages.			1,847.50
	6/7	Deposited first week's cash revenue.		2,630.00	
1017	6/11	Paid on account payable for spa equipment (June 3).			873.00
	6/14	Deposited second week's cash revenue.		3,703.00	
1018	6/14	Paid second week's wages.			1,847.50
1019	6/18	Paid on account payable for spa equipment (June 3).			1,200.00
	6/21	Deposited third week's cash revenue.		4,758.00	
1020	6/21	Paid third week's wages.			1,847.50
1021	6/25	Paid on account payable for spa equipment (June 3).			73.00
1022	6/28	Paid fourth week's wages.			1,847.50
1023	6/28	Paid month's laundry bill.			84.00
	6/30	Deposited end of month's cash revenue.		5,992.00	
1024	6/30	A. Valli withdrew $1,850 for personal use.			1,850.00
1025	6/30	Paid June telephone bill.			225.00
1026	6/30	Paid June power and water bill.			248.00

Other information that require journal entries:

Receipt

6/1 A. Valli, owner of All About You Spa, invested her personal spa equipment $3,158.00

June Accounts Payable Charges Summary Report	
6/3 Bought spa supplies on account from Spa Supplies, Inc., Inv. No. 804	$492.00
6/5 Bought office equipment on account from Office Equipment Company, Inv. No. 3415	$318.00
6/5 Bought advertising pamphlets on account from Adco, Inc., Inv. No. 512	$397.00
6/5 Bought office equipment on account from Office Equipment, Company, Inv. No. 3445	$832.00
6/5 Bought office supplies on account from Office Staples, Inv. No. 522	$120.00

If you are using QuickBooks you will need to select a vendor when recording Accounts Payable transactions.

June Sales to Customers on Account Summary Report		
6/7	Jill Anson	$325.00
6/14	Jack Morgan	$486.00
6/21	Tory Ligman	$344.00
6/30	Judy Wilcox	$109.00

If you are using QuickBooks, you will need to select a customer when recording Accounts Receivable transactions.

Required

1. Journalize the transactions for June (in date order) in the general journal.
   — If you are using QuickBooks or general ledger, review the instructions for the program on the textbook website. If you are preparing the journal entries manually, enter your transactions beginning on page 1.
2. Post the entries to the general ledger accounts.
   — Ignore this step if you are using QuickBooks or general ledger.
3. Prepare a trial balance as of June 30, 20--.
4. Prepare an income statement for the month ended June 30, 20--.
5. Prepare a statement of owner's equity for the month ended June 30, 20--. Skip this step if you are using QuickBooks.
6. Prepare a balance sheet as of June 30, 20--.

* If you are using QuickBooks or general ledger, use the year 2015 when preparing all reports.

Note: The trial balance and financial statements are unadjusted. In the next chapter, you will learn that certain accounts need to be adjusted. These adjustments will change some of the figures in these reports.

chapter

4 Adjusting Entries and the Work Sheet

Learning Objectives

After you have completed this chapter, you will be able to do the following:

1. *Define* fiscal period *and* fiscal year and explain the accounting cycle.
2. List the classifications of the accounts that occupy each column of a ten-column work sheet.
3. Complete a work sheet for a service enterprise, involving adjustments for supplies, expired insurance, depreciation, and accrued wages.
4. Journalize and post the adjusting entries.
5. Prepare an income statement, a statement of owner's equity, and a balance sheet for a service business directly from the work sheet.
6. Prepare (a) an income statement involving more than one revenue account and a net loss, (b) a statement of owner's equity with an additional investment and either a net income or a net loss, and (c) a balance sheet for a business having more than one accumulated depreciation account.

To: **Amy Roberts, CPA**
Subject: **What's Next?**

Hi Amy,
I've recorded all of my transactions for the month of June. So now I need to prepare the financial statements for the bank—I'm thinking about applying for a loan. Am I ready to prepare the financial statements because I have all of the transactions recorded?
Thanks,
Janie

To: **Janie Conner**
Subject: **RE: What's Next?**

Hi Janie,
One more step needs to take place before you can prepare the financial statements: prepare and record adjusting entries. Adjusting entries update the accounts for any internal transactions that haven't yet been recorded, such as usage of supplies, expiration of prepaid insurance, and wages that are owed. Adjusting entries need to be recorded before you can prepare the financial statements to ensure that your accounts are up to date. The easiest way to learn how to prepare adjusting entries is by using a work sheet; this will also help you learn to prepare the financial statements. So here's what you need to know before you're ready to give your financial statements to the bank:

_____ 1. Prepare a work sheet to help in recording adjusting entries
_____ 2. Record adjusting entries in the journal

Let me know if you need help!
Amy

As part of the *summarizing* step in the definition of accounting, we now introduce the work sheet and the financial statements. Now that you are familiar with the classifying and recording phases of accounting for a service business, let's look at the remaining steps in the accounting process.

Accounting Language

Accounting cycle (p. 167)
Accrual (p. 175)
Accrued wages (p. 175)
Adjusting entries (p. 181)
Adjustments (p. 170)
Book value (carrying value) (p. 173)
Contra account (p. 172)
Depreciation (p. 171)
Fiscal period (p. 167)
Fiscal year (p. 167)
Matching principle (p. 181)
Mixed accounts (p. 175)
Straight-line depreciation (p. 171)
Work sheet (p. 167)

FISCAL PERIOD

A **fiscal period** is any period of time covering a complete accounting cycle. A **fiscal year** is a fiscal period consisting of 12 consecutive months. It does not have to coincide with the calendar year. If a business has seasonal peaks, it is a good idea to complete the accounting operations at the end of the most active season. At that time, management wants to know what the results of the year are and where the business stands financially. The fiscal year of a resort that operates during the summer may be from October 1 of one year to September 30 of the next year. The government has a fiscal year from October 1 of one year to September 30 of the following year. Department stores often use a fiscal period from February 1 of one year to January 31 of the next year.

THE ACCOUNTING CYCLE

Learning Objective 1 *Define* fiscal period *and* fiscal year and explain the accounting cycle.

The **accounting cycle** represents the sequence of steps in the accounting process completed during the fiscal period. Figure 1 shows how we introduce these steps on a chapter-by-chapter basis. This outline brings you up to date on what we have accomplished so far, as well as what will be covered in Chapter 5, and how each chapter fits into the steps in the accounting cycle.

THE WORK SHEET

The **work sheet** is an optional working paper used by accountants, in a manual accounting system, to record necessary adjustments and provide up-to-date account balances needed to prepare the financial statements. **The work sheet is a tool that accountants use to help in preparing the financial statements.** As a tool, the work sheet serves as a central place for bringing together the information needed to record the adjustments. With up-to-date account balances, the accountant can then prepare the financial statements.

QuickBooks Tip

When using accounting software such as QuickBooks, the work sheet is not needed.

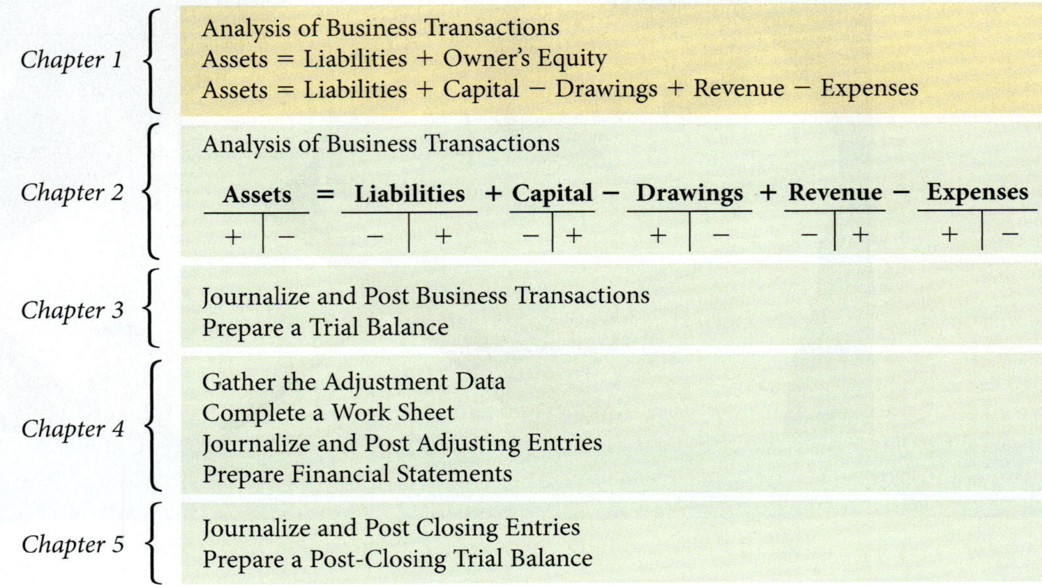

Figure 1
The accounting cycle by chapter

Accounting steps: Analyzing: *Which accounts are involved?*
Classifying: *assets, liabilities, capital, drawing, revenue, and expenses*
Recording: *journalizing*
Summarizing: *financial statements*
Interpreting: *drawing conclusions*

First, we present the work sheet form so that you can see the big picture. Then, we describe and show examples of adjustments. Finally, we show how the adjustments are entered on the work sheet and how the work sheet is completed.

We will use a ten-column work sheet—so called because two amount columns are provided for each of the work sheet's five major sections. Work sheets are most often prepared using a spreadsheet program, such as Microsoft Excel®. We will explain the function of each of these sections, again basing our discussion on the accounting activities of Conner's Whitewater Adventures. But first we need to fill in the heading, which consists of three lines: (1) the name of the company, (2) the title of the working paper, and (3) the period of time covered.

	A	B	C	D	E	F	G	H	I	J	K
1	Conner's Whitewater Adventures										
2	Work Sheet										
3	For Month Ended June 30, 20--										
4											
5		TRIAL BALANCE		ADJUSTMENTS		ADJUSTED TRIAL BALANCE		INCOME STATEMENT		BALANCE SHEET	
6	ACCOUNT NAME	DEBIT	CREDIT	DEBIT	CREDIT	DEBIT	CREDIT	DEBIT	CREDIT	DEBIT	CREDIT
7											

Next, we want to point out the account classifications that are placed in each column. We start with the Trial Balance columns and then move across the work sheet, discussing each pair of columns separately.

The Columns of the Work Sheet

TRIAL BALANCE COLUMNS

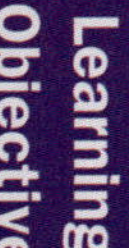

2 List the classifications of the accounts that occupy each column of a ten-column work sheet.

When you use a work sheet, you do not have to prepare a trial balance on a separate sheet of paper. Instead, you enter the account balances from the general ledger in the first two amount columns of the work sheet. List the accounts that have balances in the Account Name column in the same order in which they appear in the chart of accounts. Assuming **normal balances,** the amount of each account is listed in the Trial Balance Debit and Credit columns of the work sheet according to its classification, as shown on page 169.

	A	B	C	D	E	F	G	H	I	J	K
1						Conner's Whitewater Adventures					
2						Work Sheet					
3						For Month Ended June 30, 20--					
4											
5		TRIAL BALANCE		ADJUSTMENTS		ADJUSTED TRIAL BALANCE		INCOME STATEMENT		BALANCE SHEET	
6	ACCOUNT NAME	DEBIT	CREDIT	DEBIT	CREDIT	DEBIT	CREDIT	DEBIT	CREDIT	DEBIT	CREDIT
7		Assets →				Assets					
8			Liabilities →				Liabilities				
9			Capital →				Capital				
10		Drawing →				Drawing					
11			Revenue →				Revenue				
12		Expenses →				Expenses					
13											

As we move along in this chapter, we will discuss the adjustments. The Adjusted Trial Balance columns contain the same account classifications as the Trial Balance columns. **The Adjusted Trial Balance columns are merely extensions of the Trial Balance columns, plus or minus any adjustment amounts.** If an adjustment is required, the amounts are carried from the Trial Balance columns through the Adjustments columns and into the Adjusted Trial Balance columns.

INCOME STATEMENT COLUMNS

An income statement contains the revenues minus the expenses. Revenue accounts have credit balances, so they are recorded in the Income Statement Credit column. Expense accounts have debit balances, so they are recorded in the Income Statement Debit column.

	A	B	C	D	E	F	G	H	I	J	K
1						Conner's Whitewater Adventures					
2						Work Sheet					
3						For Month Ended June 30, 20--					
4											
5		TRIAL BALANCE		ADJUSTMENTS		ADJUSTED TRIAL BALANCE		INCOME STATEMENT		BALANCE SHEET	
6	ACCOUNT NAME	DEBIT	CREDIT	DEBIT	CREDIT	DEBIT	CREDIT	DEBIT	CREDIT	DEBIT	CREDIT
7		Assets →				Assets					
8			Liabilities →				Liabilities				
9			Capital →				Capital				
10		Drawing →				Drawing					
11			Revenue →				Revenue →		Revenue		
12		Expenses →				Expenses →		Expenses			
13											

BALANCE SHEET COLUMNS

As you may recall, the balance sheet is a statement showing assets, liabilities, and owner's equity. Asset accounts have debit balances, so they are recorded in the Balance Sheet Debit column. Liability accounts have credit balances, so they are recorded in the Balance Sheet Credit column. The Capital account has a credit balance, so it is recorded in the Balance Sheet Credit column. Because the Drawing account is a deduction from Capital, it has a debit balance and is recorded in the Balance Sheet Debit column (the opposite column from that in which Capital is recorded).

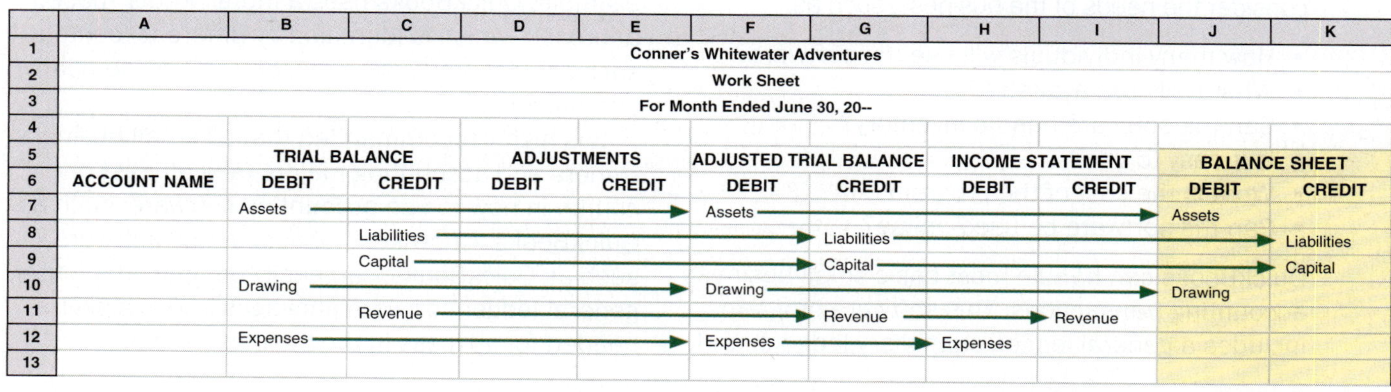

	A	B	C	D	E	F	G	H	I	J	K
1						Conner's Whitewater Adventures					
2						Work Sheet					
3						For Month Ended June 30, 20--					
4											
5		TRIAL BALANCE		ADJUSTMENTS		ADJUSTED TRIAL BALANCE		INCOME STATEMENT		BALANCE SHEET	
6	ACCOUNT NAME	DEBIT	CREDIT	DEBIT	CREDIT	DEBIT	CREDIT	DEBIT	CREDIT	DEBIT	CREDIT
7		Assets →				Assets →				Assets	
8			Liabilities →				Liabilities →				Liabilities
9			Capital →				Capital →				Capital
10		Drawing →				Drawing →				Drawing	
11			Revenue →				Revenue →		Revenue		
12		Expenses →				Expenses →		Expenses			
13											

ADJUSTMENTS

Learning Objective

3 Complete a work sheet for a service enterprise, involving adjustments for supplies, expired insurance, depreciation, and accrued wages.

Adjustments are a way of updating the ledger accounts. They may be considered *internal transactions.* They have not been recorded in the accounts up to this time because no outside party has been involved. Adjustments are determined after the trial balance has been prepared. Adjustments fine-tune the accounts to present a more accurate report of the accounts.

Only a few accounts are adjusted. To describe the reasons for making adjustments, let's return to Conner's Whitewater Adventures. First, we select the accounts that require adjustments. Then, we show the adjustments recorded in T accounts so that you can see the effect on the accounts. **However, bear in mind that the adjustments are first recorded on the work sheet when using a manual accounting system.** When using general ledger software, adjustments are recorded in the general journal. The adjustments are made at the end of the company's accounting period—in the case of Conner's Whitewater Adventures, June 30.

Without adjustments, the financial statements would be unclear.

SMALL BUSINESS **SUCCESS**

Choosing Accounting Software

Choosing accounting software is an important decision for small businesses. One popular software package designed for small businesses is QuickBooks. When picking accounting software, it's important to consider the needs of the business, such as:

- How many individuals will use the software?
- What tools are available?
- Can the software handle inventory?
- Is it easy to use?
- What is the cost of the program?
- Can the software be used online?

QuickBooks can handle most basic small business accounting transactions. This software program includes a general ledger, subsidiary ledgers, and financial statements. QuickBooks also has the ability to export data into Excel and Word. Differences in general ledger software packages typically relate to their look and how transactions are entered. For example, QuickBooks uses a more "forms"-based approach, which is identified by different "centers," such as vendors, customers, employees, company, and banking.

It is highly recommended that all small business owners and accounting majors take at least one course in how to use accounting software, such as QuickBooks. Knowledge of accounting software, such as QuickBooks, can easily be applied to other general ledger software packages and is a skill needed for success in the business world.

Supplies

Remember that when a business buys supplies for cash or on credit, the supplies account is debited. An asset is recorded because the supplies have not yet been used. At the end of the accounting period, the amount of supplies that have been used during the period must be deducted from the Supplies account and added to Supplies Expense. During June, Conner's Whitewater Adventures purchased $675 of supplies. At the end of the time period, the company counted its supplies and determined that it had $215 worth of supplies remaining. Thus, $460 ($675 − $215) worth of supplies were used during the period. The amount used, $460, must be deducted from the Supplies account and added to the Supplies Expense account.

Supplies

		+	−	
(Old)	Balance	675	**Adjusting**	**460**
(New)	Balance	215		

Supplies Expense

	+	−
Adjusting	**460**	

Notice that the new balance of the Supplies account is the amount remaining, $215 ($675 − $460). The $460 amount in Supplies Expense represents the cost of supplies used during the time period.

Prepaid Insurance

The $1,875 balance in Prepaid Insurance represents the premium paid in advance for a three-month liability insurance policy. One month ($625) of the three months of premium has now expired.

$1,875 premium ÷ 3 months = $625 per month

In the adjustment, Conner's Whitewater Adventures deducts the expired, or used, portion from Prepaid Insurance and adds it to Insurance Expense.

Prepaid Insurance

		+	−	
(Old)	Balance	1,875	**Adjusting**	**625**
(New)	Balance	1,250		

Insurance Expense

	+	−
Adjusting	**625**	

Remember

For the adjustment of insurance, you are given the amount used (expired). So in the adjusting entry, take the amount used directly out of Prepaid Insurance and put it into Insurance Expense.

The new balance of Prepaid Insurance, $1,250 ($1,875 − $625), represents the cost of insurance that remains paid in advance and should therefore appear in the Balance Sheet Debit column. The $625 amount in Insurance Expense represents the cost of insurance that has expired and should appear in the Income Statement Debit column.

Depreciation of Equipment

We have recorded durable items, such as appliances and fixtures, under Equipment because they will last longer than one year. The benefits of these assets will eventually be used up. (The assets will either wear out or become obsolete.) Therefore, we should systematically spread the cost of these assets over their useful lives. That is, we allocate the cost of the equipment as an expense *over its estimated useful life* and call this **depreciation** because, over time, such equipment loses its usefulness. A part of this depreciation expense is allotted to each fiscal period. In the case of Conner's Whitewater Adventures, the Equipment account has a balance of $51,300. Suppose we estimate that the equipment will have a useful life of seven years, with a trade-in (salvage) value of $8,292 at the end of that time. Using **straight-line depreciation**, we can allocate the cost of an asset,

There are several methods of depreciation for assets. Straight-line depreciation is shown here—equal amounts of estimated loss of usefulness are taken each year. There are also accelerated methods that assign larger amounts to expense in the early years of the life of an asset.

less any trade-in value, evenly over the useful life of the asset. Depreciation for one month is figured like this:

STEP 1. Cost − Trade-in (salvage) value = Full depreciation

$51,300 − $8,292 = $43,008 full depreciation

STEP 2. Full depreciation ÷ Number of years in the asset's useful life = Depreciation for one year

$43,008 full depreciation ÷ 7 years = $6,144 per year

STEP 3. Depreciation for one year ÷ 12 = Depreciation for one month

$6,144 per year ÷ 12 months = $512 per month

When depreciation is recorded, we do not subtract it directly from the asset account. In asset accounts, such as Equipment and Building, we must keep the original cost recorded in the account. Instead, a **contra account** is used. Such accounts are contrary to, or deducted from, other accounts and are used to provide more information to financial statement users. In this case, the amount of depreciation must be recorded in another account; that account is Accumulated Depreciation. If you were to record depreciation incorrectly by crediting the asset account, the balance of your asset account would eventually reach zero or the trade-in value, which is not correct. You would still have the equipment and need to maintain the original cost in the account. The credit should be to the contra-asset account, Accumulated Depreciation. Accumulated Depreciation, Equipment is contrary to, or a deduction from, Equipment.

Always record the adjusting entry for depreciation as a debit to Depreciation Expense (an income statement item) and a credit to Accumulated Depreciation (a balance sheet item), which increases both accounts. The adjustment in T account form would appear as follows:

Depreciation Expense, Equipment

+	−
Adjusting 512	

Accumulated Depreciation, Equipment

−	+
	Adjusting 512

To show the accounts under their proper headings, let's look at the fundamental accounting equation. Brackets indicate that Accumulated Depreciation, Equipment is a deduction from the Equipment account. Note that the plus and minus signs are opposite.

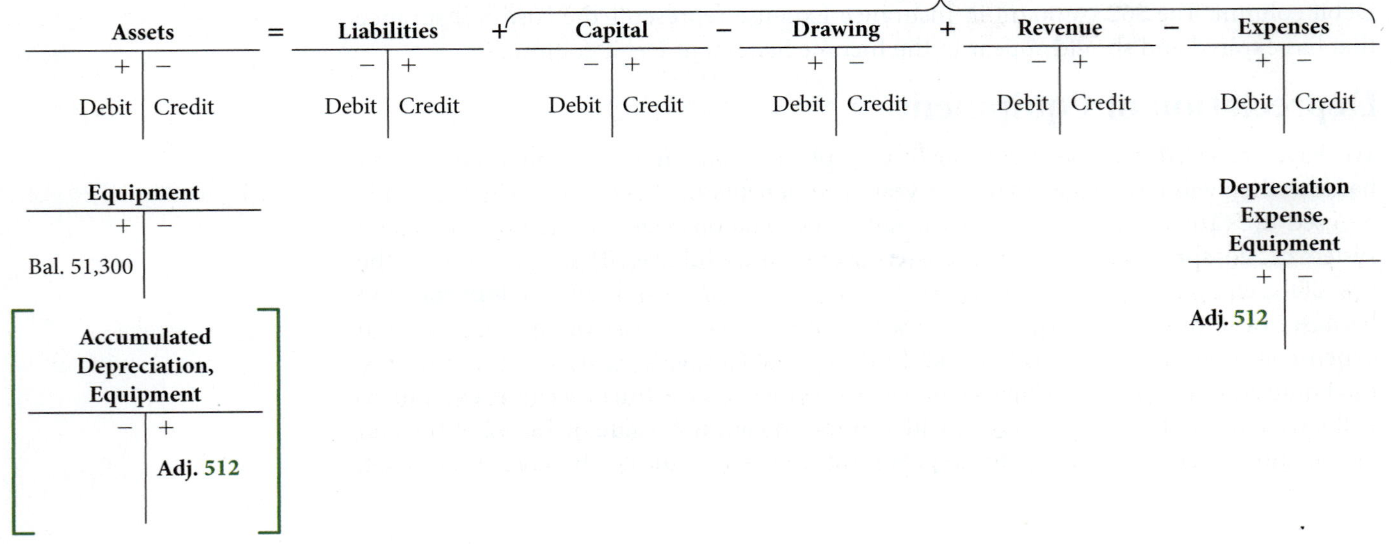

On the work sheet, Equipment (an asset) appears in the Balance Sheet Debit column. Accumulated Depreciation (a deduction from an asset) appears in the opposite column, which is the Balance Sheet Credit column.

Accumulated Depreciation, Equipment, as the title implies, is the total depreciation the company has taken since the original purchase of the asset. Rather than crediting the Equipment account, Conner's Whitewater Adventures uses a separate account to keep track of the total depreciation taken since it first acquired the asset. The maximum depreciation it could take would be the cost of the equipment, $51,300, less the trade-in value of $8,292. So for the first year, Accumulated Depreciation, Equipment will increase at the rate of $512 per month, assuming that no additional equipment has been purchased. For example, at the end of the second month, Accumulated Depreciation, Equipment will amount to $1,024 ($512 + $512).

On the balance sheet, the balance of Accumulated Depreciation is deducted from the balance of the related asset account, as illustrated on the following partial balance sheet for Conner's Whitewater Adventures. The net amount shown, $50,788, is referred to as the book value of the asset. Thus, **book value** (or **carrying value**) is the cost of an asset minus its accumulated depreciation ($51,300 − $512).

FYI

If we had a Building account, the adjusting entry would be a debit to Depreciation Expense, Building and a credit to Accumulated Depreciation, Building. Building and Accumulated Depreciation, Building would be listed separately on the balance sheet.

If we had a Land account, it would have no adjusting entry. Land is assumed to last forever, so it is not depreciated.

Conner's Whitewater Adventures
Partial Balance Sheet
June 30, 20--

Assets		
Equipment	$51,300	
Less Accumulated Depreciation	512	$50,788

Wages Expense

The end of the fiscal period and the end of the employees' payroll period rarely fall on the same day. A diagram of the situation looks like this:

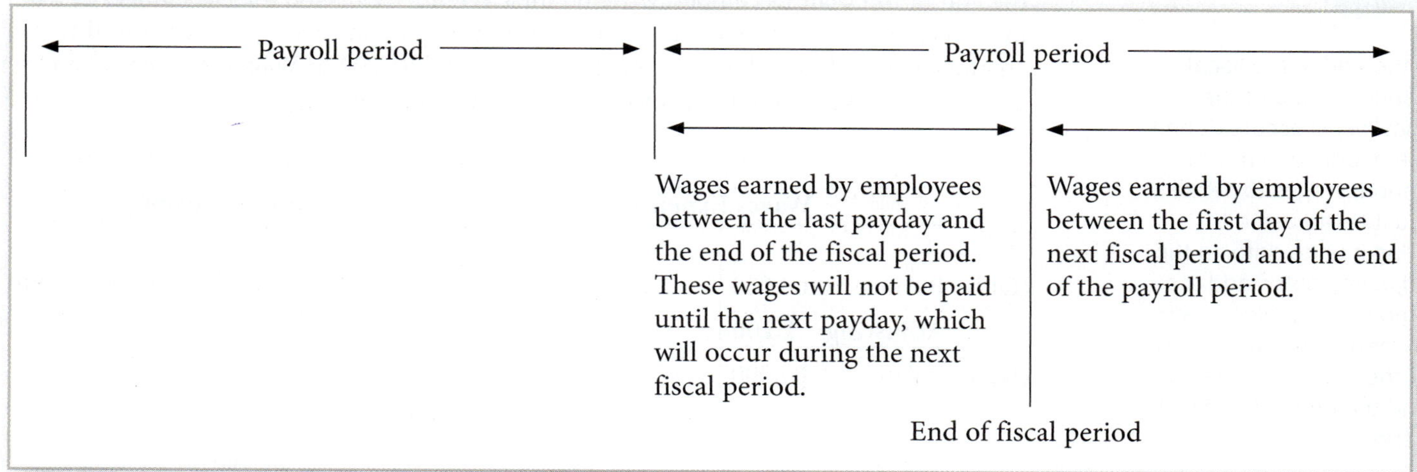

Because the last day of the fiscal period falls in the middle of the payroll period, we must split up the wages earned in that payroll period between the fiscal period just ended and the next fiscal period. We will use another company for this example.

Assume that Brown Company pays its employees $400 per day and that payday falls on Friday. The employees work a five-day week. When employees pick up their paychecks on Friday, the amount of the checks includes their wages for that day and for the preceding four days. Suppose that the last day of the fiscal period falls on Wednesday, December 31. The diagram on the next page illustrates this situation.

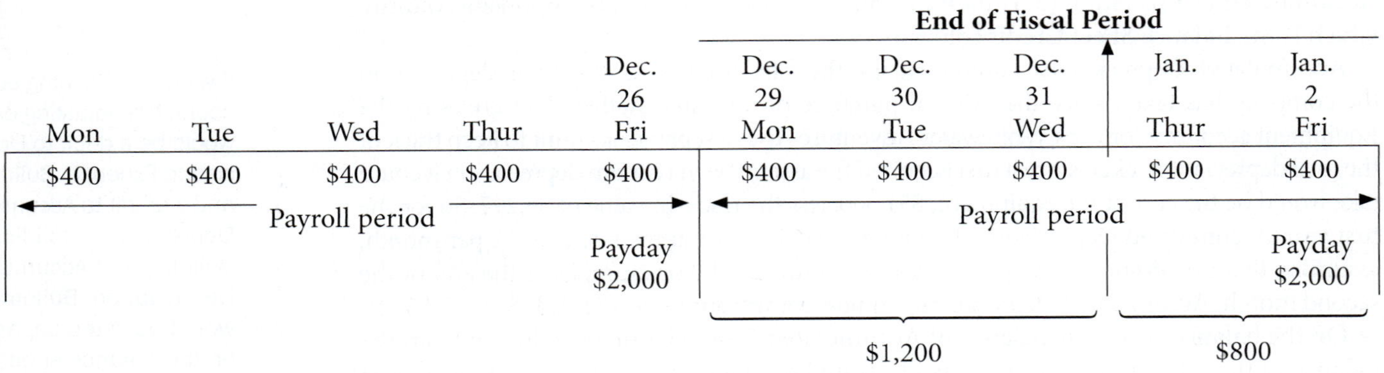

End of Fiscal Period

Mon	Tue	Wed	Thur	Dec. 26 Fri	Dec. 29 Mon	Dec. 30 Tue	Dec. 31 Wed	Jan. 1 Thur	Jan. 2 Fri
$400	$400	$400	$400	$400	$400	$400	$400	$400	$400
Payroll period					Payroll period				
				Payday $2,000					Payday $2,000
					$1,200			$800	

December						
S	M	T	W	R	F	S
	1	2	3	4	(5)	6
7	8	9	10	11	(12)	13
14	15	16	17	18	(19)	20
21	22	23	24	25	(26)	27
28	29	30	31			

Paydays

Remember

If the end of the fiscal period (or end of the fiscal year) occurs during the middle of a payroll period, Wages Expense must be adjusted to bring it up to date. In the adjusting entry, add the amount employees have earned between the end of the last payroll period and the end of the fiscal period.

So that the Wages Expense account shows an accurate balance for the fiscal period, you need to add $1,200 for the cost of labor between the last payday, December 26, and the end of the year, December 31 ($400 for December 29; $400 for December 30; $400 for December 31). Because the $1,200 will not be paid at this time but is owed to the employees as of December 31, you also need to add $1,200 to Wages Payable, a liability account, because the company owes this amount to employees.

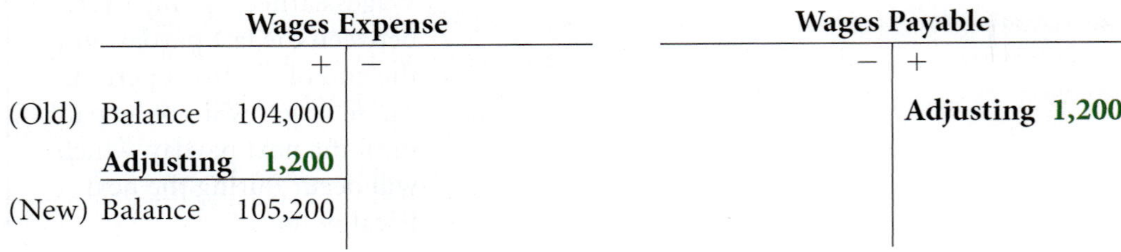

Wages Expense
+
−
(Old) Balance 104,000
Adjusting 1,200
(New) Balance 105,200
Wages Payable
−
+
Adjusting 1,200

Returning to our illustration of Conner's Whitewater Adventures, the amount of wages that has been paid so far for the month of June is $2,360. However, the last payday was June 24. Between June 24 and the end of the month, Conner's Whitewater Adventures has determined that it owes an additional $472 in wages to its employees. The additional $472 will need to be added to the Wages Expense account and also the Wages Payable. It might be tempting to decrease cash in this adjustment, but cash is not used in this case because the wages have yet not been paid.

Accountants refer to this extra amount that has not been recorded at the end of the month as **accrued wages**. In accounting terms, **accrual** means recognition of an expense or a revenue that has been incurred (expense) or earned (revenue) but has not yet been recorded.

Remember

In the adjusting entry for accrued wages, increase both the Wages Expense and the Wages Payable accounts.

Wages Expense

		+	−
(Old)	Balance	2,360	
	Adjusting	**472**	
(New)	Balance	2,832	

Wages Payable

−	+	
	Adjusting	**472**

MIXED ACCOUNTS

At this point, take special notice of the fact that each **adjusting entry contains an income statement account (revenue or expense) and a balance sheet account (asset, contra asset, or liability).** Accountants refer to these accounts as **mixed accounts**—accounts with balances that are partly income statement amounts and partly balance sheet amounts. The income statement and balance sheet accounts involved are separate accounts having a part of their name in common, such as Prepaid Insurance and Insurance Expense. Prepaid Insurance is recorded as $1,875 in the Trial Balance columns but is apportioned as $625 in Insurance Expense in the Income Statement columns and $1,250 in Prepaid Insurance in the Balance Sheet columns. In other words, portions of these trial balance amounts are recorded in each section.

Placement of Accounts on the Work Sheet

We now have to enter the adjustments on the work sheet, but before doing so, let's briefly discuss the Drawing and Accumulated Depreciation accounts, as well as net income, and their effect on the work sheet.

CAPITAL AND DRAWING ACCOUNT BALANCES

The Drawing account is a contra account (contrary to Capital). In the statement of owner's equity, Drawing is deducted from Capital. To show one account as a deduction from another, the plus and minus signs are switched. The T accounts look like this:

J. Conner, Capital

−	+
Debit	Credit
	Balance

J. Conner, Drawing

+	−
Debit	Credit
Balance	

The normal balance for the Capital account is recorded in the Credit columns of the Trial Balance, the Adjusted Trial Balance, and the Balance Sheet sections. The normal balance for the Drawing account is recorded in the Debit columns of the Trial Balance, the Adjusted Trial Balance, and the Balance Sheet sections.

EQUIPMENT AND ACCUMULATED DEPRECIATION, EQUIPMENT ACCOUNT BALANCES

The Accumulated Depreciation, Equipment account is a contra account (contrary to Equipment). On the balance sheet, Accumulated Depreciation, Equipment is deducted from Equipment. The T accounts look like this:

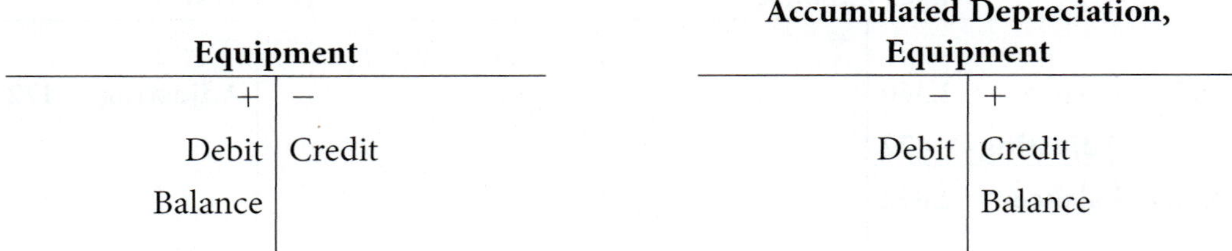

The normal balance for the Equipment account is recorded in the Debit columns of the Trial Balance, the Adjusted Trial Balance, and the Balance Sheet sections. The normal balance for the Accumulated Depreciation, Equipment account is recorded in the Credit columns of the Trial Balance, the Adjusted Trial Balance, and the Balance Sheet sections.

NET INCOME

Net income (or net loss) is the difference between revenue and expenses. It is used to balance the Income Statement columns; because revenue is normally larger than expenses, the balancing amount must be added to the expense side. Net income (or net loss) is also used to balance the Balance Sheet columns. On the statement of owner's equity, you add net income to the owner's beginning Capital balance. Because the Capital balance is located in the Balance Sheet Credit column, net income must also be added to that side. The following diagram shows these relationships:

	A	B	C	D	E	F	G	H	I	J	K
1	Conner's Whitewater Adventures										
2	Work Sheet										
3	For Month Ended June 30, 20--										
4											
5		TRIAL BALANCE		ADJUSTMENTS		ADJUSTED TRIAL BALANCE		INCOME STATEMENT		BALANCE SHEET	
6	ACCOUNT NAME	DEBIT	CREDIT	DEBIT	CREDIT	DEBIT	CREDIT	DEBIT	CREDIT	DEBIT	CREDIT
7		Assets	Accum. Depr.			Assets	Accum. Depr.			Assets	Accum. Depr.
8		+	+			+	+			+	+
9		Drawing	Liabilities			Drawing	Liabilities			Drawing	Liabilities
10		+	+			+	+				+
11		Expenses	Capital			Expenses	Capital	Expenses			Capital
12			+				+				
13			Revenue				Revenue		Revenue		
14		Total	Total			Total	Total	Total	Total	Total	Total
15	Net Income							NI ←			→ NI
16								Total =	Total	Total =	Total
17								Totals equal each other.		Totals equal each other.	
18											
19											

On the other hand, if expenses are larger than revenue, the result is a net loss. You must add net loss to the revenue side to balance the Income Statement columns. Also, because a net loss is deducted from the owner's beginning Capital balance, you must include net loss on the debit side of the Balance Sheet columns, thereby balancing these columns. To show this, let's look at the Income Statement and Balance Sheet columns diagrammed here.

		INCOME STATEMENT		BALANCE SHEET	
5		INCOME STATEMENT		BALANCE SHEET	
6	ACCOUNT NAME	DEBIT	CREDIT	DEBIT	CREDIT
7				Assets	Accum. Depr.
8				+	+
9				Drawing	Liabilities
10					+
11		Expenses			Capital
12					
13			Revenue		
14		Total	Total	Total	Total
15	Net Loss		(NL) ←	→ (NL)	
16		Total =	Total	Total =	Total
17					
18		Totals equal each other.		Totals equal each other.	
19					
20					
21					

STEPS IN THE COMPLETION OF THE WORK SHEET

The recommended steps to complete the work sheet are as follows:

STEP 1. Complete the Trial Balance columns, total, and rule (single-underline before double-underlining totals).

STEP 2. Complete the Adjustments columns, total, and rule.

STEP 3. Complete the Adjusted Trial Balance columns, total, and rule.

STEP 4. Record balances in the Income Statement and Balance Sheet columns and total each column.

STEP 5. Record net income or net loss in the Income Statement columns by subtracting the smaller side from the larger side and adding the difference to the smaller side, total, and rule.

STEP 6. Record net income or net loss in the Balance Sheet columns by subtracting the smaller side from the larger side and adding the difference to the smaller side (the amount should be the same as the difference between the Income Statement column totals—if not, there is an error), total, and rule.

The work sheet can be prepared using a computer spreadsheet program, such as Microsoft Excel®, or the work sheet can be prepared manually. Whether the work sheet is prepared manually or on a computer, the columns must be completed, totaled, and ruled.

The Trial Balance columns are the same as in the Trial Balance presented in Chapter 3.

STEP 1: TRIAL BALANCE COLUMNS

Note that the trial balance in Figure 2 is the same trial balance presented earlier for Conner's Whitewater Adventures. You will be able to follow the completion of the entire work sheet for Conner's Whitewater Adventures in Figure 3.

STEP 2: ADJUSTMENTS COLUMNS

When we write the adjustments, we identify them as (a), (b), (c), and (d) to indicate the relationships between the debit and credit sides and the sequence of the individual adjusting entries. (See Figures 2 and 3.)

Note that Supplies Expense; Insurance Expense; Depreciation Expense, Equipment; Accumulated Depreciation, Equipment; and Wages Payable did not appear in the trial balance because there were no balances in the accounts at that time. We wrote them below the Trial Balance totals to complete the work sheet. In this chapter, the business is in its first accounting period. Therefore, these accounts had no balance until the end of the fiscal period adjustments, which means they were not in the trial balance prior to adjustments. After the first fiscal period, these accounts could have a balance and would be listed in the Trial Balance columns in the order of the chart of accounts.

Here is a brief review of the adjustments:

a. To record $460 worth of supplies used during June.
b. To record the $625 cost of insurance expired during June.
c. To record $512 depreciation for the month of June.
d. To record $472 of accrued wages owed at the end of June.

Again, we emphasize that the work sheet is strictly a tool used to gather all of the up-to-date information needed to prepare the financial statements. **The adjustments must still be recorded in the journal.**

Figure 2
Partial work sheet for Conner's Whitewater Adventures

	A	B	C	D	E
1					Conner's
2					
3		Step 1		Step 2	
4					
5		TRIAL BALANCE		ADJUSTMENTS	
6	ACCOUNT NAME	DEBIT	CREDIT	DEBIT	CREDIT
7			*Accum. Depr.*		
8		*A + Draw. + E*	*+ L + Cap. + R*		
9	Cash	55,890.00			
10	Accounts Receivable	4,250.00			
11	Supplies	675.00			(a) 460.00
12	Prepaid Insurance	1,875.00			(b) 625.00
13	Equipment	51,300.00			
14	Accounts Payable		3,425.00		
15	J. Conner, Capital		95,200.00		
16	J. Conner, Drawing	3,500.00			
17	Income from Tours		23,320.00		
18	Wages Expense	2,360.00		(d) 472.00	
19	Rent Expense	1,250.00			
20	Advertising Expense	620.00			
21	Utilities Expense	225.00			
22		121,945.00	121,945.00		
23	Supplies Expense			(a) 460.00	
24	Insurance Expense			(b) 625.00	
25	Depr. Exp., Equip.			(c) 512.00	
26	Accum. Depr., Equip.				(c) 512.00
27	Wages Payable				(d) 472.00
28				2,069.00	2,069.00

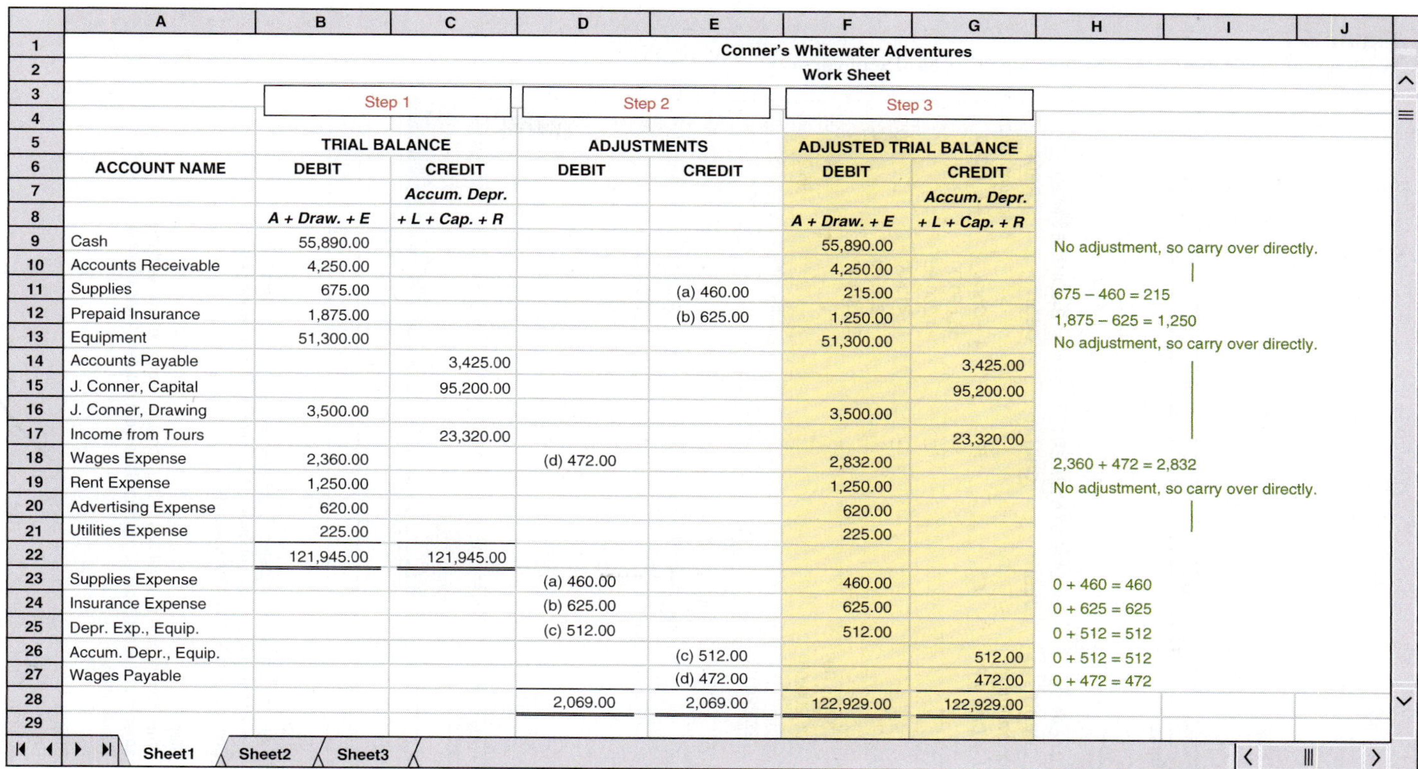

Conner's Whitewater Adventures
Work Sheet

	Step 1		Step 2		Step 3		
	TRIAL BALANCE		ADJUSTMENTS		ADJUSTED TRIAL BALANCE		
ACCOUNT NAME	DEBIT	CREDIT	DEBIT	CREDIT	DEBIT	CREDIT	
		Accum. Depr.				*Accum. Depr.*	
	A + Draw. + E	*+ L + Cap. + R*			*A + Draw. + E*	*+ L + Cap. + R*	
Cash	55,890.00				55,890.00		No adjustment, so carry over directly.
Accounts Receivable	4,250.00				4,250.00		
Supplies	675.00			(a) 460.00	215.00		675 – 460 = 215
Prepaid Insurance	1,875.00			(b) 625.00	1,250.00		1,875 – 625 = 1,250
Equipment	51,300.00				51,300.00		No adjustment, so carry over directly.
Accounts Payable		3,425.00				3,425.00	
J. Conner, Capital		95,200.00				95,200.00	
J. Conner, Drawing	3,500.00				3,500.00		
Income from Tours		23,320.00				23,320.00	
Wages Expense	2,360.00		(d) 472.00		2,832.00		2,360 + 472 = 2,832
Rent Expense	1,250.00				1,250.00		No adjustment, so carry over directly.
Advertising Expense	620.00				620.00		
Utilities Expense	225.00				225.00		
	121,945.00	121,945.00					
Supplies Expense			(a) 460.00		460.00		0 + 460 = 460
Insurance Expense			(b) 625.00		625.00		0 + 625 = 625
Depr. Exp., Equip.			(c) 512.00		512.00		0 + 512 = 512
Accum. Depr., Equip.				(c) 512.00		512.00	0 + 512 = 512
Wages Payable				(d) 472.00		472.00	0 + 472 = 472
			2,069.00	2,069.00	122,929.00	122,929.00	

Sheet1 Sheet2 Sheet3

Figure 3
Work sheet with steps of completion explained for Conner's Whitewater Adventures

STEP 3: ADJUSTED TRIAL BALANCE COLUMNS

Once the Adjustments columns are totaled and ruled, extend each Trial Balance amount, plus or minus any adjustment from the Adjustments columns, to the Adjusted Trial Balance columns as shown in Figure 3.

STEP 4: INCOME STATEMENT AND BALANCE SHEET COLUMNS

Extend the balances in the Adjusted Trial Balance columns to either the Income Statement or the Balance Sheet columns. (See Figure 4.)

STEP 5: NET INCOME OR NET LOSS—INCOME STATEMENT COLUMNS

Total each of the two Income Statement columns. Subtract the smaller side from the larger side, write the difference under the smaller Income Statement column total, and total and rule as shown in Figure 4.

If there is a net income, the credit side of the Income Statement columns will be larger than the debit side—more revenue than expenses. In this case, write *Net Income* in the Account Name column on the same line as the difference you calculated. If there is a net loss, the debit side of the Income Statement columns will be larger than the credit side—more expenses than revenue. In that case, write *Net Loss* in the Account Name column on the same line as the difference you calculated.

STEP 6: NET INCOME OR NET LOSS—BALANCE SHEET COLUMNS

Total the two Balance Sheet columns. Subtract the smaller side from the larger side, write the difference under the smaller Balance Sheet column total (the amount should equal the difference between the Income Statement column totals—if not, there is an error), and total and rule as shown in Figure 4.

Figure 4
Work sheet for Conner's Whitewater Adventures—Excel version

	A	B	C	D	E	F	G	H	I	J	K
1						Conner's Whitewater Adventures					
2						Work Sheet					
3						For Month Ended June 30, 20--					
4											
5		TRIAL BALANCE		ADJUSTMENTS		ADJUSTED TRIAL BALANCE		INCOME STATEMENT		BALANCE SHEET	
6	ACCOUNT NAME	DEBIT	CREDIT	DEBIT	CREDIT	DEBIT	CREDIT	DEBIT	CREDIT	DEBIT	CREDIT
7			*Accum. Depr.*				*Accum. Depr.*				*Accum. Depr.*
8		*A + Draw. + E*	*+ L + Cap. + R*			*A + Draw. + E*	*+ L + Cap. + R*	*E*	*R*	*A + Draw.*	*+ L + Cap.*
9	Cash	55,890.00				55,890.00				55,890.00	
10	Accounts Receivable	4,250.00				4,250.00				4,250.00	
11	Supplies	675.00			(a) 460.00	215.00				215.00	
12	Prepaid Insurance	1,875.00			(b) 625.00	1,250.00				1,250.00	
13	Equipment	51,300.00				51,300.00				51,300.00	
14	Accounts Payable		3,425.00				3,425.00				3,425.00
15	J. Conner, Capital		95,200.00				95,200.00				95,200.00
16	J. Conner, Drawing	3,500.00				3,500.00				3,500.00	
17	Income from Tours		23,320.00				23,320.00		23,320.00		
18	Wages Expense	2,360.00		(d) 472.00		2,832.00		2,832.00			
19	Rent Expense	1,250.00				1,250.00		1,250.00			
20	Advertising Expense	620.00				620.00		620.00			
21	Utilities Expense	225.00				225.00		225.00			
22		121,945.00	121,945.00								
23	Supplies Expense	Step 1		(a) 460.00		460.00		460.00			
24	Insurance Expense			(b) 625.00		625.00		625.00			
25	Depr. Exp., Equip.			(c) 512.00		512.00		512.00			
26	Accum. Depr., Equip.				(c) 512.00		512.00				512.00
27	Wages Payable				(d) 472.00		472.00				472.00
28				2,069.00	2,069.00	122,929.00	122,929.00	6,524.00	23,320.00	116,405.00	99,609.00
29	Net Income							16,796.00			16,796.00
30				Step 2		Step 3		23,320.00	23,320.00	116,405.00	116,405.00
31								Steps 4, 5, and 6			
32											

Sheet1 Sheet2 Sheet3

Step 1
In the Account name column, lists the accounts that have balances. Enter the account balances in the Trial Balance columns. Total and rule the columns.

Step 2
Enter the adjustments, labeling each adjustment as (a), (b), (c), and so on. Total and rule the columns.
(a) Supplies used, $460
(b) Insurance expired, $625
(c) Depr. of equip., $512
(d) Accrued wages, $472

Step 3
Carry amounts across from the Trial Balance columns, plus or minus any amounts appearing in the Adjustments columns. Total and rule the columns.

Step 4
From the top of the Adjusted Trial Balance columns, go down line by line, carrying each amount over to the Income Statement or Balance Sheet columns. Total the columns.

Step 5
Write *Net Income* or *Net Loss* in the Account Name column and the amount in the appropriate Income Statement column. Total and rule the columns.

Step 6
Enter the net income or loss amount in the appropriate Balance Sheet column. Total, balance, and rule the columns.

Finding Errors in the Income Statement and Balance Sheet Columns

As you have seen, the amount of the net income or net loss must be recorded in both an Income Statement column and a Balance Sheet column. Suppose that after the net income is added to the Balance Sheet Credit column, the Balance Sheet columns are not equal. To find the error, follow this procedure:

STEP 1. Check that the amount of the net income or loss is recorded in the correct columns. For example, net income is placed in the Income Statement Debit column and the Balance Sheet Credit column.

STEP 2. Verify the addition of all columns.

STEP 3. Check that the appropriate amounts have been recorded in the Income Statement and Balance Sheet columns. For example, asset amounts should be listed in the Balance Sheet Debit column, expense amounts should be listed in the Income Statement Debit column, and so on.

STEP 4. Verify by adding or subtracting across each line that the amounts carried over from the Trial Balance columns through the Adjustments columns into the Adjusted Trial Balance columns are correct.

STEP 5. Verify that the correct amounts of the revenue and expense accounts are transferred to the Income Statement columns.

STEP 6. Verify that the correct amounts of assets, liabilities, and owner's equity accounts are transferred to the Balance Sheet columns.

Generally, one of these steps will expose the error.

JOURNALIZING ADJUSTING ENTRIES

Learning Objective 4 Journalize and post the adjusting entries.

To change the balance of a ledger account, you need a journal entry as evidence of the change. So far, we have been listing adjustments only in the Adjustments columns of the work sheet. The work sheet is not a journal, so we must journalize **adjusting entries** to update the ledger accounts. **Take the information for these entries directly from the Adjustments columns of the work sheet, debiting and crediting the same accounts and amounts in the journal entries.**

In the Description column of the general journal, write *Adjusting Entries* before you begin making these entries. This eliminates the need to write an explanation for each entry. The adjusting entries for Conner's Whitewater Adventures are shown in Figure 5 on page 182.

When you post the adjusting entries to the ledger accounts, write the abbreviation *Adj.* in the Item column of the ledger account. The adjusting entry for Prepaid Insurance is posted below the adjusting entries on page 182.

In the adjusted accounts for Conner's Whitewater Adventures, notice that the intent is to make sure that the expenses recorded match up or are reported with the revenues for the same period of time. In other words, for the month of June, we record all of the revenues for June and all of the expenses for June. Thus, the revenues and expenses for the same time period are matched. This is called the **matching principle**.

Figure 5
Adjusting entries for Conner's Whitewater Adventures

GENERAL JOURNAL					Page 4
Date		Description	Post. Ref.	Debit	Credit
20--		Adjusting Entries			
June	30	Supplies Expense	513	460 00	
		Supplies	115		460 00
	30	Insurance Expense	516	625 00	
		Prepaid Insurance	117		625 00
	30	Depr. Expense, Equipment	517	512 00	
		Accum. Depr., Equipment	125		512 00
	30	Wages Expense	511	472 00	
		Wages Payable	222		472 00

Each adjusting entry consists of an income statement account and a balance sheet account.

ACCOUNT **Prepaid Insurance** ACCOUNT NO. **117**

Date		Item	Post. Ref.	Debit	Credit	Balance Debit	Balance Credit
20--							
June	10		2	1875 00		1875 00	
	30	Adj.	4		625 00	1250 00	

ACCOUNT **Insurance Expense** ACCOUNT NO. **516**

Date		Item	Post. Ref.	Debit	Credit	Balance Debit	Balance Credit
20--							
June	30	Adj.	4		625 00		625 00

In the Real World

Do large companies such as Rhapsody, a popular online music subscription service, need to make adjusting entries? You bet! All companies regardless of size are required to make adjusting entries so that their financial statements are reported accurately. Rhapsody makes similar adjusting entries to the ones we made in this chapter (for example, Prepaid Insurance, Depreciation, and Wages). So regardless of the size of the company, adjusting entries are an important part of the accounting cycle.

YOU Make the Call

Imagine that you have just been hired as an accounting clerk for a local tour bus company. Part of your job is to prepare adjusting entries prior to producing the financial statements. You have spent the week familiarizing yourself with the accounting system. You find the following preliminary adjusting notes left by the prior accounting clerk:

(a) The tour bus company pays weekly salaries of $606.65 for a five-day workweek. The end of the accounting period is on a Thursday. The amount of wages per day was computed to be $121.33.

(b) The depreciation for the buses using the straight-line method is $33,392.86 per year and $2,782.74 per month. (The buses cost $275,000, with an estimated useful life of seven years and a trade-in value of $41,250 at the end of that time.)

(c) The balance of the Prepaid Insurance account is $2,480, which covers one year. The amount of the adjusting entry for Insurance Expense for this one-month period is $206.67.

As the new accounting clerk, your job is to review these figures for accuracy and then record the appropriate adjusting entries in the general journal.

SOLUTION

(a) $606.65 ÷ 5 = $121.33
$121.33 × 4 days = $485.32 adjustment amount

(b) 1. $275,000 − $41,250 = $233,750 full depreciation
2. $233,750 full depreciation ÷ 7 years = $33,392.86 per year
3. $33,392.86 per year ÷ 12 months = $2,782.74 per month

(c) $2,480 per year ÷ 12 months = $206.67 per month

GENERAL JOURNAL Page ___

Date		Description	Post. Ref.	Debit	Credit
		Adjusting Entries			
	(a)	Wages Expense		485.32	
		Wages Payable			485.32
	(b)	Depreciation Expense, Equipment		2,782.74	
		Accumulated Depreciation, Equipment			2,782.74
	(c)	Insurance Expense		206.67	
		Prepaid Insurance			206.67

To: **Amy Roberts, CPA**
Subject: **Financial Statements Review**

Hi Amy,
I have completed the adjusting entries using the work sheet, recorded them in the general journal, and posted them to the ledger. I know we've talked before about financial statements, but I probably need a short review. Can you help?
Thanks,
Janie

To: **Janie Conner**
Subject: **RE: Financial Statements Review**

Hi Janie,
I am glad that you have the adjusting entries recorded in the general journal and also posted to the ledger. Now that the accounts are up to date, you are ready to prepare the financial statements. Remember, from what we talked about earlier, the income statement is prepared first, followed by the statement of owner's equity, and then the balance sheet. Let's review each of these statements so that you are ready to give them to the bank. Let me know if you need help.
Amy

Completion of the Financial Statements

Learning Objective

5 Prepare an income statement, a statement of owner's equity, and a balance sheet for a service business directly from the work sheet.

As we stated, the purpose of the work sheet is to help the accountant prepare the financial statements. Now that we have recorded the adjusting entries, we can use the work sheet to prepare the income statement, the statement of owner's equity, and the balance sheet. The figures for the financial statements are taken directly from the work sheet. These statements are shown in Figure 6.

Note that you record Accumulated Depreciation, Equipment in the asset section of the balance sheet as a direct deduction from Equipment. As we have said, accountants refer to this as a contra account because it is contrary to its companion asset account. The difference, $50,788, is called the book value or carrying value because it represents the cost of the asset after Accumulated Depreciation has been deducted.

When preparing the statement of owner's equity, remember to check the beginning balance of Capital against the balance shown in the Capital account in the general ledger. An additional investment may have been made during the fiscal period, and you need to report any such investment in the statement of owner's equity.

Figure 6
Financial statements for Conner's Whitewater Adventures

Conner's Whitewater Adventures
Income Statement
For Month Ended June 30, 20--

Revenue:		
Income from Tours		$23,320
Expenses:		
Wages Expense	$2,832	
Rent Expense	1,250	
Supplies Expense	460	
Advertising Expense	620	
Utilities Expense	225	
Insurance Expense	625	
Depreciation Expense, Equipment	512	
Total Expenses		6,524
Net Income		$16,796

Conner's Whitewater Adventures
Statement of Owner's Equity
For Month Ended June 30, 20--

J. Conner, Capital, June 1, 20--		$ 0
Investment during June	$ 95,200	
Net Income for June	16,796	
Subtotal	$111,996	
Less Withdrawals for June	3,500	
Increase in Capital		108,496
J. Conner, Capital, June 30, 20--		$108,496

Conner's Whitewater Adventures
Balance Sheet
June 30, 20--

Assets		
Cash		$ 55,890
Accounts Receivable		4,250
Supplies		215
Prepaid Insurance		1,250
Equipment	$51,300	
Less Accumulated Depreciation	512	50,788
Total Assets		$112,393
Liabilities		
Accounts Payable	$ 3,425	
Wages Payable	472	
Total Liabilities		$ 3,897
Owner's Equity		
J. Conner, Capital		108,496
Total Liabilities and Owner's Equity		$112,393

Remember

The columns shown on the financial statements do not represent Debit or Credit. Each column simply shows account balances. Amounts in these columns are either added or subtracted.

Remember

Total assets must always equal total liabilities and owner's equity.

Learning Objective

6a Prepare an income statement involving more than one revenue account and a net loss.

Income Statement Involving More Than One Revenue Account and a Net Loss

When an organization has more than one distinct source of revenue, a separate revenue account is set up for each source. See, for example, the income statement of Harris Miniature Golf presented in Figure 7. Also note that expenses are greater than revenues, resulting in a net loss.

Figure 7 Income statement for Harris Miniature Golf

Harris Miniature Golf
Income Statement
For Month Ended September 30, 20--

Revenues:		
Admissions Fees	$2,624	
Concession Fees	1,512	
Total Revenues		$ 4,136
Expenses:		
Wages Expense	$3,123	
Supplies Expense	317	
Advertising Expense	1,000	
Rent Expense	1,900	
Miscellaneous Expense	128	
Total Expenses		6,468
Net Loss		$(2,332)

Statement of Owner's Equity with an Additional Investment and a Net Income

Learning Objective

6b Prepare a statement of owner's equity with an additional investment and either a net income or a net loss.

Any additional investment by the owner during the period covered by the financial statements is shown on the statement of owner's equity because such a statement should show everything that has affected the Capital account from the *beginning* until the *end* of the period covered by the financial statements. For example, in Figure 8, assume that the following information is true for L. A. Grand Company, which has a net income:

Balance of L. A. Grand, Capital, on April 1	$86,000
Additional investment by L. A. Grand on April 12	8,000
Net income for the month (from income statement)	6,200
Total withdrawals for the month	4,000

Figure 8 Statement of owner's equity for L. A. Grand Company

L. A. Grand Company
Statement of Owner's Equity
For Month Ended April 30, 20--

L. A. Grand, Capital, April 1, 20--		$86,000
Investment during April	$ 8,000	
Net Income for April	6,200	
Subtotal	$14,200	
Less Withdrawals for April	4,000	
Increase in Capital		10,200
L. A. Grand, Capital, April 30, 20--		$96,200

Statement of Owner's Equity with an Additional Investment and a Net Loss

Assume the following for J. D. Ross Company, which has a net loss:

J. D. Ross, Capital, on Oct. 1	$75,000
Additional investment by J. D. Ross on Oct. 25	10,000
Net loss for the month (from income statement)	1,500
Total withdrawals for the month	5,100

The statement of owner's equity in Figure 9 shows this information. Notice that the net loss is subtracted from the additional investment during October.

FYI

The information normally shown on the statement of owner's equity is sometimes included as part of the owner's equity section of the balance sheet in computerized general ledger systems.

J. D. Ross Company
Statement of Owner's Equity
For Month Ended October 31, 20--

J. D. Ross, Capital, October 1, 20--		$75,000
Investment during October	$10,000	
Net Loss for October	1,500	
Subtotal	$ 8,500	
Less Withdrawals for October	5,100	
Increase in Capital		3,400
J. D. Ross, Capital, October 31, 20--		$78,400

Figure 9
Statement of owner's equity for J. D. Ross Company

Businesses with More Than One Depreciation Expense Account and More Than One Accumulated Depreciation Account

Figures 10 and 11 show the income statement and the balance sheet for Molen Veterinary Clinic. In Figure 11, note that the company has two assets subject to depreciation: Building and Equipment. In the financial statements, Depreciation Expense and Accumulated Depreciation must be listed for each asset.

Learning Objective

6c Prepare a balance sheet for a business having more than one accumulated depreciation account.

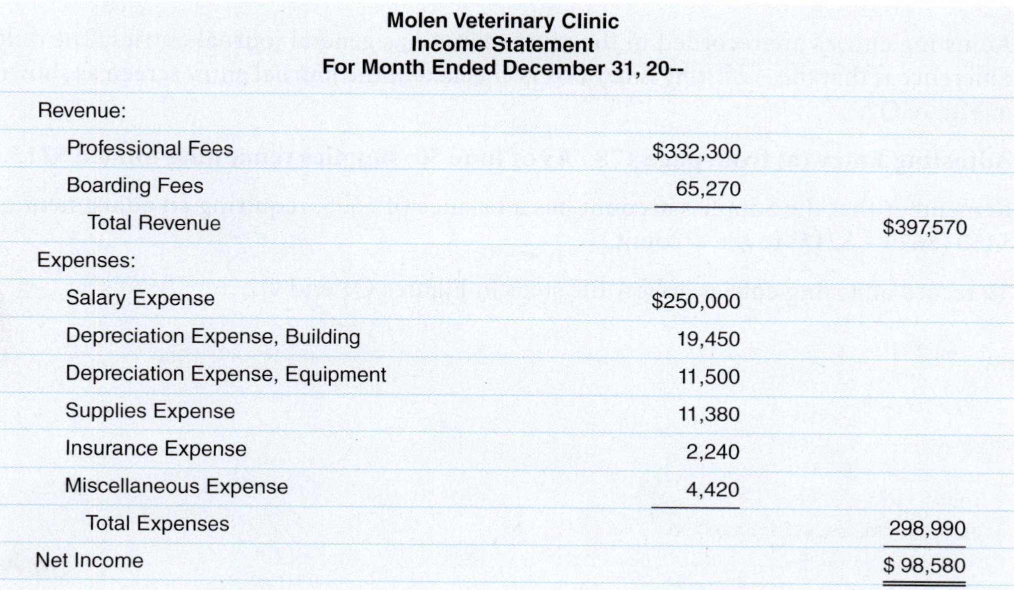

Molen Veterinary Clinic
Income Statement
For Month Ended December 31, 20--

Revenue:		
Professional Fees	$332,300	
Boarding Fees	65,270	
Total Revenue		$397,570
Expenses:		
Salary Expense	$250,000	
Depreciation Expense, Building	19,450	
Depreciation Expense, Equipment	11,500	
Supplies Expense	11,380	
Insurance Expense	2,240	
Miscellaneous Expense	4,420	
Total Expenses		298,990
Net Income		$ 98,580

Figure 10
Income statement for Molen Veterinary Clinic

Figure 11
Balance sheet for Molen Veterinary Clinic

Molen Veterinary Clinic Balance Sheet December 31, 20--		
Assets		
Cash		$ 21,320
Land		15,200
Building	$349,100	
Less Accumulated Depreciation	112,200	236,900
Equipment	$124,800	
Less Accumulated Depreciation	87,600	37,200
Total Assets		$310,620
Liabilities		
Accounts Payable		$ 7,400
Owner's Equity		
R. N. Molen, Capital		303,220
Total Liabilities and Owner's Equity		$310,620

Accounting with QuickBooks®

Adjusting Entries and Reports

Learning Objective  Record adjusting entries in QuickBooks.

Learning Objectives

After you have completed this section, you will be able to do the following:

1. Record adjusting entries in QuickBooks.
2. View and print the adjusting journal entries.
3. View and print the adjusted trial balance.
4. Memorize transactions and reports.

Adjusting entries are recorded in the same manner as general journal entries. The only difference is that the *Adjusting Entry* box is checked in the journal entry screen as shown in Figure Q2.

Adjusting Entry (a) from page 178. As of June 30, supplies remaining totaled $215.

Remember that the Supplies account has a balance of $675, requiring an adjustment of $460 ($675 – $215) to the account.

To record adjusting entries, follow the steps in Figures Q1 and Q2.

STEP 1. Click the **Company** tab. Then select **Make General Journal Entries**.

Company	Customers	Vendors	Employees

Home Page
Company Snapshot
Calendar
Documents
Lead Center
Company Information...
Advanced Service Administration...
Set Up Users and Passwords
Customer Credit Card Protection...
Set Closing Date...
Planning & Budgeting
To Do List
Reminders
Alerts Manager
Chart of Accounts Ctrl+A
Make General Journal Entries...
Manage Currency
Enter Vehicle Mileage...
Prepare Letters with Envelopes
Export Company File to QuickBooks Online

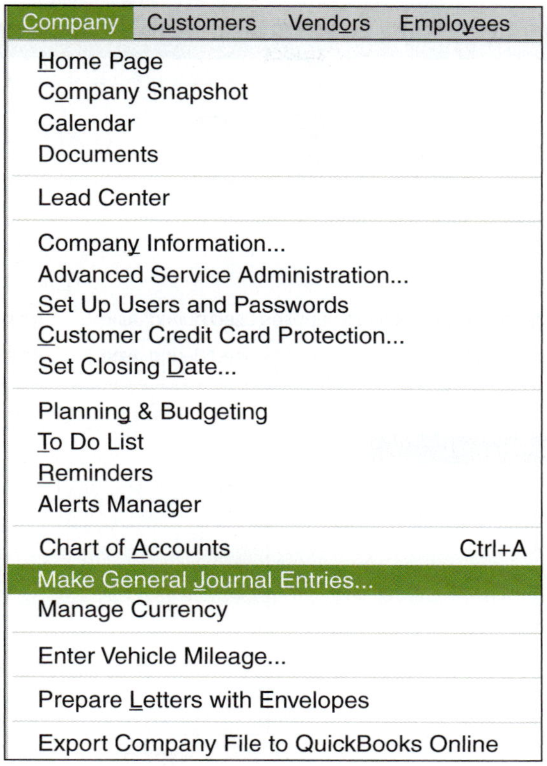

Figure Q1
Make general journal entries

QuickBooks Tip

Make General Journal Entries can also be accessed under Accountant.

STEP 2. Select or enter the **date**.
The date used for Figure Q2 (on the following page) is June 30, 20--.

STEP 3. Enter the **Entry No**.
In Figure Q2, ADJ20--.06a is used for the *Entry No.* The journal entry and adjusting journal entry numbering system can vary by company. QuickBooks has the option to automatically assign the *Entry No.*, or a company may choose to use its own system. For Conner's Whitewater Adventures, the *Entry No.* used for this adjusting entry is ADJ (for adjustment), followed by the year, then the month, and finally the adjustment transaction (a).

STEP 4. Check the **Adjusting Entry** box.

STEP 5. Select the **account to be debited**, enter the **debit amount** and then enter the **description in the memo field**.

STEP 6. Select the **account to be credited**. Then enter the **credit amount**.
The memo field should automatically appear with the information from Step 5. If not, manually enter the description in the credited account memo field.

STEP 7. Select **Save & Close** (to save the transaction and stop recording entries) or **Save & New** (to save the transaction and continue recording entries).

QuickBooks Tip

The memo field provides descriptive information in the journal, as well as other reports.

Figure Q2
Record adjusting entries in the general journal

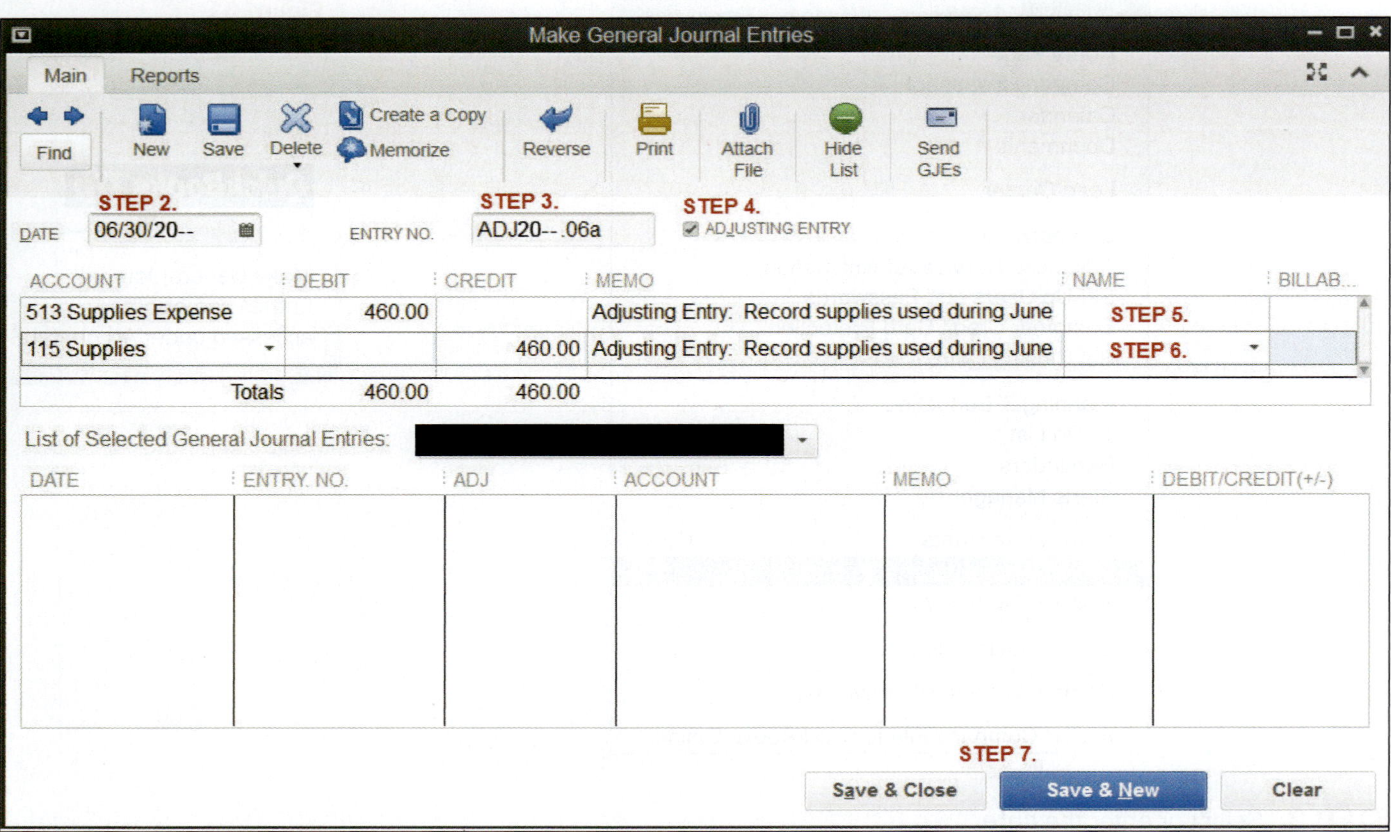

Learning Objective 2 View and print the adjusting journal entries.

To view and print the adjusting journal entries, follow the steps in Figures Q3 and Figure Q4 (on the next page), after recording the entries.

STEP 1. Select **Reports, Accountant & Taxes**, and then **Adjusting Journal Entries**.

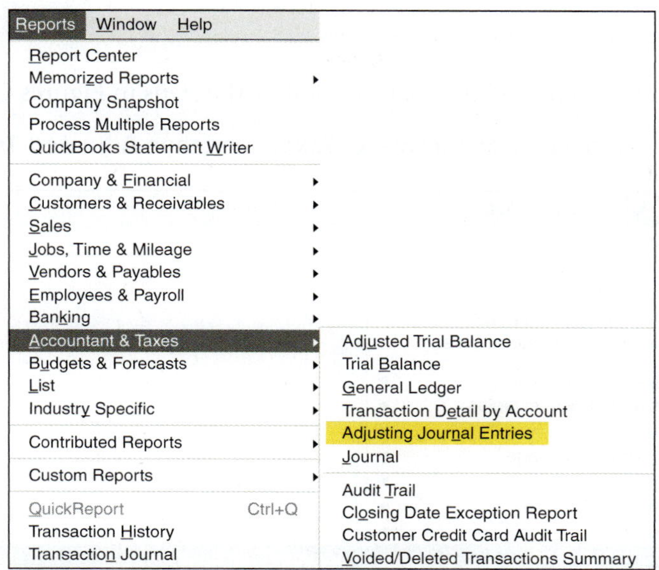

Figure Q3
View adjusting journal entries

STEP 2. Adjust the **From:** and **To:** dates and click **Refresh**.

STEP 3. To print the report, click the **Print** button.

Figure Q4 shows the adjusting journal entries report for Conner's Whitewater Adventures.

Figure Q4
View adjusting journal entries report

Conner's Whitewater Adventures
Adjusting Journal Entries
June 30, 20–

Date	Num	Memo	Account	Debit	Credit
06/30/20--	ADJ2013.06a	Adjusting Entry: Record supplies used during June	513 Supplies Expense	460.00	
		Adjusting Entry: Record supplies used during June	115 Supplies		460.00
				460.00	460.00
06/30/20--	ADJ2013.06b	Adjusting Entry: Record insurance expired during June	516 Insurance Expense	625.00	
		Adjusting Entry: Record insurance expired during June	117 Prepaid Insurance		625.00
				625.00	625.00
06/30/20--	ADJ2013.06c	Adjusting Entry: Depreciation for the month of June	517 Depreciation Expense, Equip.	512.00	
		Adjusting Entry: Depreciation for the month of June	125 Accum. Depr., Equipment		512.00
				512.00	512.00
06/30/20--	ADJ2013.06d	Adjusting Entry: Accrued wages owned at the end of June	511 Wages Expense	472.00	
		Adjusting Entry: Accrued wages owned at the end of June	222 Wages Payable		472.00
				472.00	472.00
TOTAL				2,069.00	2,069.00

Learning Objective 3 View and print the adjusted trial balance.

To view and print the adjusted trial balance, follow the steps in Figures Q5 and Q6.

STEP 1. Select **Reports, Accountant & Taxes**, and then **Adjusted Trial Balance**.

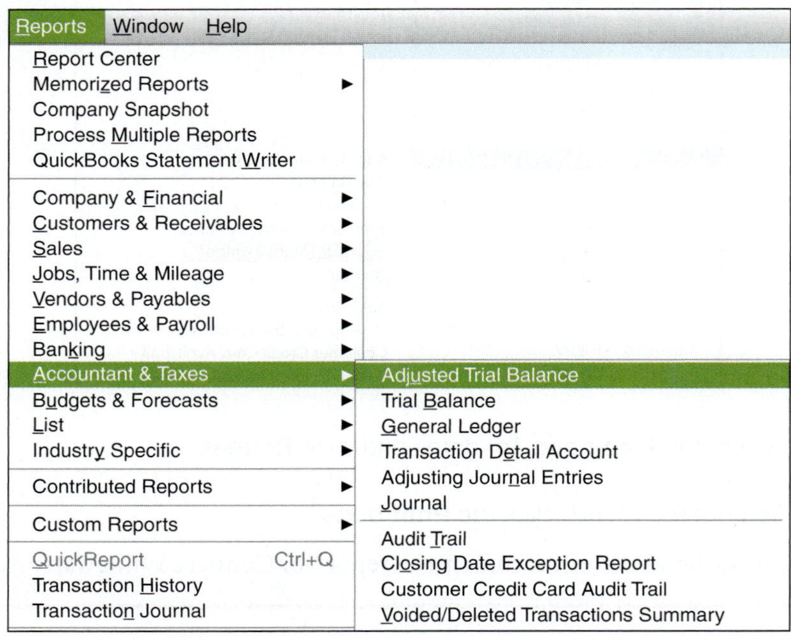

Figure Q5
View the adjusted trial balance

STEP 2. Adjust the **From:** and **To:** dates and click **Refresh**.

STEP 3. To print the report, click the **Print** button.

Figure Q6 shows the adjusted trial balance report for Conner's Whitewater Adventures.

Figure Q6
Adjusted trial balance report

Conner's Whitewater Adventures
Adjusted Trial Balance
June 30, 20--

	Unadjusted Balance		Adjustments		Adjusted Balance	
	Debit	Credit	Debit	Credit	Debit	Credit
115 Supplies				460.00		460.00
117 Prepaid Insurance				625.00		625.00
124 Equipment: 125 Accum. Depr., Equipment				512.00		512.00
222 Wages Payable				472.00		472.00
511 Wages Expenses			472.00		472.00	
513 Supplies Expenses			460.00		460.00	
516 Insurance Expenses			625.00		625.00	
517 Depreciation Expenses, Equipment			512.00		512.00	
Total	0.00	0.00	2,069.00	2,069.00	2,069.00	2,069.00

Learning Objective  4 Memorize transactions and reports.

MEMORIZE TRANSACTIONS IN THE GENERAL JOURNAL

When a transaction occurs on a regular basis, it is helpful to save or memorize the transaction to retrieve for future use. To memorize a transaction in the general journal, simply click on *Memorize* after entering the information. See Figure Q7.

Figure Q7
Memorize transactions in the general journal

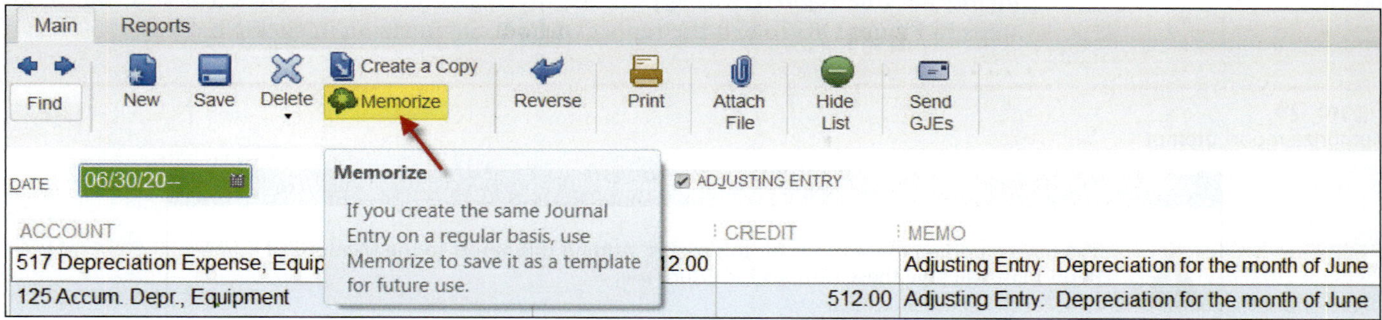

MEMORIZE REPORTS

When reports are used on a regular basis, it is also helpful to save or memorize the reports for future use. To memorize reports, follow the steps in either Figures Q8 or Q9.

STEP 1. After preparing the report, click the **Memorize** tab in the report screen.

STEP 2. Enter the **report name**.

STEP 3. Check the box **Save in Memorized Report Group**.

STEP 4. Select the **classification** where you want to save your report.

STEP 5. Click **OK**.

Figure Q8
Memorize reports

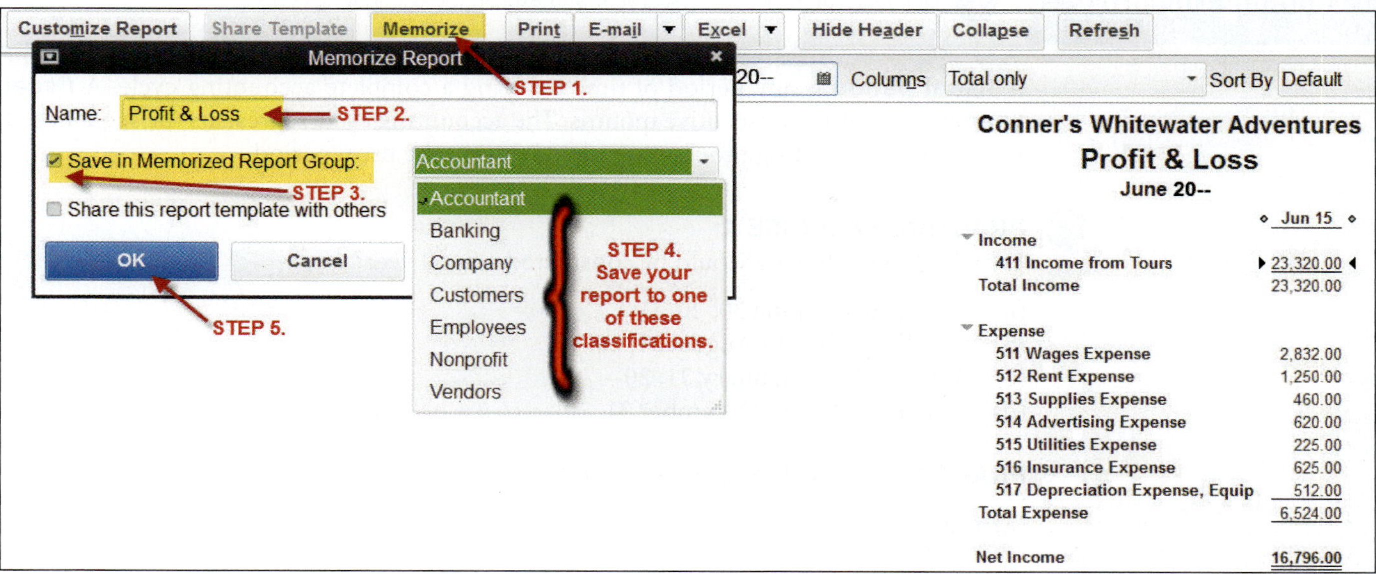

Unless disabled, QuickBooks also has a feature to remind users about memorizing reports when leaving the report area. Upon exiting any report, a message ***Would you like to memorize this report?*** will appear. To memorize the report, click Yes and follow the steps in Figure Q8. To exit the report without memorizing it, click No.

Figure Q9
Memorize report prompt

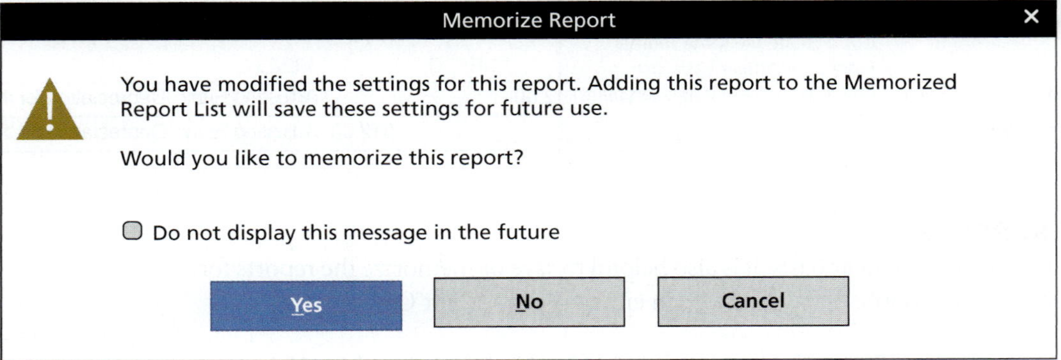

Chapter Review

Study and Practice

Learning Objective 1 *Define* fiscal period *and* fiscal year and explain the accounting cycle.

A **fiscal period** is any period of time covering a complete accounting cycle. A **fiscal year** consists of 12 consecutive months. The accounting cycle represents the sequence of steps in the accounting process completed during the fiscal period.

PRACTICE EXERCISE 1

Which of the following would be considered a fiscal year?

(a) July 1, 20-- to June 30, 20--
(b) October 1, 20-- to August 31, 20--
(c) April 1, 20-- to January 31, 20--
(d) January 1, 20-- to December 31, 20--

PRACTICE EXERCISE 1 • SOLUTION

(a) and (d)

List the classifications of the accounts that occupy each column of a ten-column work sheet.

Learning Objective

Trial Balance Debit	Assets + Drawing + Expenses
Trial Balance Credit	Accum. Depr. + Liabilities + Capital + Revenue
Adjusted Trial Balance Debit	Assets + Drawing + Expenses
Adjusted Trial Balance Credit	Accum. Depr. + Liabilities + Capital + Revenue
Income Statement Debit	Expenses
Income Statement Credit	Revenue
Balance Sheet Debit	Assets + Drawing
Balance Sheet Credit	Accum. Depr. + Liabilities + Capital

PRACTICE EXERCISE 2

Using a ten-column work sheet, list the classifications of accounts that are found in each column, with the exception of the Adjustments columns (Trial Balance, Adjusted Trial Balance, Income Statement, and Balance Sheet).

PRACTICE EXERCISE 2 • SOLUTION

	A	B	C	D	E	F	G	H	I	J	K
4											
5		TRIAL BALANCE		ADJUSTMENTS		ADJUSTED TRIAL BALANCE		INCOME STATEMENT		BALANCE SHEET	
6	ACCOUNT NAME	DEBIT	CREDIT	DEBIT	CREDIT	DEBIT	CREDIT	DEBIT	CREDIT	DEBIT	CREDIT
7		Assets	Accum. Depr.			Assets	Accum. Depr.			Assets	Accum. Depr.
8		Drawing	Liabilities			Drawing	Liabilities			Drawing	Liabilities
9		Expenses	Capital			Expenses	Capital	Expenses			Capital
10			Revenue				Revenue		Revenue		
11											

Sheet1 / Sheet2 / Sheet3

Complete a work sheet for a service enterprise, involving adjustments for supplies, expired insurance, depreciation, and accrued wages.

Learning Objective

Adjustment for supplies used: debit Supplies Expense and credit Supplies.
Adjustment for expired insurance: debit Insurance Expense and credit Prepaid Insurance.
Adjustment for **depreciation**: debit Depreciation Expense and credit Accumulated Depreciation.
Adjustment for accrued wages: debit Wages Expense and credit Wages Payable.

PRACTICE EXERCISE 3

Complete the work sheet on page 196 for Fun and Games for the month of September. Adjustment information:

(a) Supplies used during September, $500.
(b) Insurance expired during September, $175.
(c) Depreciation of equipment for the month of September, $540.
(d) Accrued wages owed at the end of September, $260.

PRACTICE EXERCISE 3 • SOLUTION

See the completed work sheet on page 197.

	A	B	C	D	E	F	G	H	I	J	K
1	Fun and Games										
2	Work Sheet										
3	For Month Ended September 30, 20--										
4											
5		TRIAL BALANCE		ADJUSTMENTS		ADJUSTED TRIAL BALANCE		INCOME STATEMENT		BALANCE SHEET	
6	ACCOUNT NAME	DEBIT	CREDIT	DEBIT	CREDIT	DEBIT	CREDIT	DEBIT	CREDIT	DEBIT	CREDIT
7	Cash	24,770.00									
8	Accounts Receivable	5,750.00									
9	Supplies	630.00									
10	Prepaid Insurance	2,100.00									
11	Equipment	36,000.00									
12	Accum. Depr., Equip.		540.00								
13	Accounts Payable		3,985.00								
14	J. Jay, Capital		54,075.00								
15	J. Jay, Drawing	5,000.00									
16	Income from Services		21,000.00								
17	Wages Expense	2,670.00									
18	Rent Expense	1,950.00									
19	Advertising Expense	450.00									
20	Utilities Expense	280.00									
21		79,600.00	79,600.00								
22	Supplies Expense										
23	Insurance Expense										
24	Depr. Exp., Equip.										
25	Wages Payable										
26											
27	Net Income										
28											
29											
30											

Sheet1 Sheet2 Sheet3

	A	B	C	D	E	F	G	H	I	J	K
1						Fun and Games					
2						Work Sheet					
3						For Month Ended September 30, 20--					
4											
5		TRIAL BALANCE		ADJUSTMENTS		ADJUSTED TRIAL BALANCE		INCOME STATEMENT		BALANCE SHEET	
6	ACCOUNT NAME	DEBIT	CREDIT	DEBIT	CREDIT	DEBIT	CREDIT	DEBIT	CREDIT	DEBIT	CREDIT
7	Cash	24,770.00				24,770.00				24,770.00	
8	Accounts Receivable	5,750.00				5,750.00				5,750.00	
9	Supplies	630.00			(a) 500.00	130.00				130.00	
10	Prepaid Insurance	2,100.00			(b) 175.00	1,925.00				1,925.00	
11	Equipment	36,000.00				36,000.00				36,000.00	
12	Accum. Depr., Equip.		540.00		(c) 540.00		1,080.00				1,080.00
13	Accounts Payable		3,985.00				3,985.00				3,985.00
14	J. Jay, Capital		54,075.00				54,075.00				54,075.00
15	J. Jay, Drawing	5,000.00				5,000.00				5,000.00	
16	Income from Services		21,000.00				21,000.00		21,000.00		
17	Wages Expense	2,670.00		(d) 260.00		2,930.00		2,930.00			
18	Rent Expense	1,950.00				1,950.00		1,950.00			
19	Advertising Expense	450.00				450.00		450.00			
20	Utilities Expense	280.00				280.00		280.00			
21		79,600.00	79,600.00								
22	Supplies Expense			(a) 500.00		500.00		500.00			
23	Insurance Expense			(b) 175.00		175.00		175.00			
24	Depr. Exp., Equip.			(c) 540.00		540.00		540.00			
25	Wages Payable				(d) 260.00		260.00				260.00
26				1,475.00	1,475.00	80,400.00	80,400.00	6,825.00	21,000.00	73,575.00	59,400.00
27	Net Income							14,175.00			14,175.00
28								21,000.00	21,000.00	73,575.00	73,575.00
29											
30											

Sheet1 Sheet2 Sheet3

CHAPTER REVIEW

CHAPTER REVIEW

Learning Objective  Journalize and post the adjusting entries.

Adjustments are a way of updating the ledger accounts. They are determined after the trial balance has been prepared. To change the balance of the ledger accounts, **adjusting entries** are needed in the general journal as evidence of the changes. The information for these entries are taken directly from the Adjustments columns of the work sheet, debiting and crediting the same accounts and amounts in the journal entries. Therefore, each adjusting entry consists of an income statement account and a balance sheet account. When the adjusting entries are posted to the ledger accounts, the abbreviation *Adj.* is written in the Item column of the ledger account.

4 PRACTICE EXERCISE 4

Journalize and post the adjusting entries for Fun and Games from Practice Exercise 3.

PRACTICE EXERCISE 4 • SOLUTION

GENERAL JOURNAL Page 4

Date		Description	Post. Ref.	Debit	Credit
20--		Adjusting Entries			
Sept.	30	Supplies Expense	513	500.00	
		Supplies	115		500.00
	30	Insurance Expense	516	175.00	
		Prepaid Insurance	117		175.00
	30	Depr. Expense, Equipment	517	540.00	
		Accum. Depr., Equipment	125		540.00
	30	Wages Expense	511	260.00	
		Wages Payable	222		260.00

ACCOUNT **Supplies** ACCOUNT NO. **115**

Date		Item	Post. Ref.	Debit	Credit	Balance Debit	Balance Credit
20--							
Sept.	*30*	*Bal.*		*630.00*		*630.00*	
		Adj.			500.00	130.00	

ACCOUNT **Prepaid Insurance** ACCOUNT NO. **117**

Date		Item	Post. Ref.	Debit	Credit	Balance Debit	Balance Credit
20--							
Sept.	*15*		*2*	*2,100.00*		*2,100.00*	
	30	Adj.	4		175.00	1,925.00	

ACCOUNT Accumulated Depreciation, Equipment **ACCOUNT NO.** 125

Date		Item	Post. Ref.	Debit	Credit	Balance Debit	Balance Credit
20--							
Sept.		Bal.			540 00		540 00
	30	Adj.	4		540 00		1,080 00

ACCOUNT Wages Payable **ACCOUNT NO.** 222

Date		Item	Post. Ref.	Debit	Credit	Balance Debit	Balance Credit
20--							
Sept.	30	Adj.	4		260 00		260 00

ACCOUNT Wages Expense **ACCOUNT NO.** 511

Date		Item	Post. Ref.	Debit	Credit	Balance Debit	Balance Credit
20--							
Sept.	15		2	2,670 00		2,670 00	
	30	Adj.	4	260 00		2,930 00	

ACCOUNT Supplies Expense **ACCOUNT NO.** 513

Date		Item	Post. Ref.	Debit	Credit	Balance Debit	Balance Credit
20--							
Sept.	30	Adj.	4	500 00		500 00	

ACCOUNT Insurance Expense **ACCOUNT NO.** 516

Date		Item	Post. Ref.	Debit	Credit	Balance Debit	Balance Credit
20--							
Sept.	30	Adj.	4	175 00		175 00	

ACCOUNT Depreciation Expense, Equipment **ACCOUNT NO.** 517

Date		Item	Post. Ref.	Debit	Credit	Balance Debit	Balance Credit
20--							
Sept.	30	Adj.	4	540 00		540 00	

5 Prepare an income statement, a statement of owner's equity, and a balance sheet for a service business directly from the work sheet. **Learning Objective**

The income statement is prepared directly from the amounts listed in the Income Statement Debit and Credit columns. The net income should equal the net income previously determined on the **work sheet**. For the statement of owner's equity, use the amount of the beginning capital listed in the Balance Sheet Credit column after checking the general ledger for any additional investment(s), the amount of the net income from the Balance Sheet Credit column, and the amount of Drawing from the Balance Sheet Debit column. Prepare the balance sheet directly from the amounts listed in the Balance Sheet Debit and Credit columns (except Drawing and Capital).

PRACTICE EXERCISE 5

Prepare an income statement, a statement of owner's equity, and a balance sheet for Fun and Games using the information from Practice Exercise 3.

PRACTICE EXERCISE 5 • SOLUTION

Fun and Games
Income Statement
For Month Ended September 30, 20--

Revenue:		
Income from Services		$21,000
Expenses:		
Wages Expense	$2,930	
Rent Expense	1,950	
Supplies Expense	500	
Advertising Expense	450	
Utilities Expense	280	
Insurance Expense	175	
Depreciation Expense, Equipment	540	
Total Expenses		6,825
Net Income		$14,175

Fun and Games
Statement of Owner's Equity
For Month Ended September 30, 20--

J. Jay, Capital, September 1, 20--		$54,075
Investment during September	$ 0	
Net Income for September	14,175	
Subtotal	$14,175	
Less Withdrawals for September	5,000	
Increase in Capital		9,175
J. Jay, Capital, September 30, 20--		$63,250

Fun and Games
Balance Sheet
September 30, 20--

Assets		
Cash		$24,770
Accounts Receivable		5,750
Supplies		130
Prepaid Insurance		1,925
Equipment	$36,000	
Less Accumulated Depreciation	1,080	34,920
Total Assets		$67,495
Liabilities		
Accounts Payable	$ 3,985	
Wages Payable	260	
Total Liabilities		$ 4,245
Owner's Equity		
J. Jay, Capital		63,250
Total Liabilities and Owner's Equity		$67,495

Learning Objective 6 Prepare (a) an income statement involving more than one revenue account and a net loss, (b) a statement of owner's equity with an additional investment and either a net income or a net loss, and (c) a balance sheet for a business having more than one accumulated depreciation account.

(a) An income statement containing more than one revenue account requires an additional line for each type of revenue, followed by a total amount of revenue.

(b) A statement of owner's equity involving an additional investment requires a line for each additional investment beneath the beginning capital amount, followed by a total amount of investment.

(c) Businesses that have more than one type of asset subject to depreciation must show a separate account for each asset on the balance sheet.

6a PRACTICE EXERCISE 6a

Using the following information, prepare an income statement for the month of September for The Swim Shack:

Depreciation Expense, Equipment	$ 525
Income from Concessions	4,000
Income from Service	1,500
Insurance Expense	200
Rent Expense	1,950
Utilities Expense	790
Wages Expense	3,580
Supplies Expense	100

PRACTICE EXERCISE 6a • SOLUTION

The Swim Shack
Income Statement
For Month Ended September 30, 20--

Revenue:		
Income from Concessions	$4,000	
Income from Services	1,500	
Total Revenue		$ 5,500
Expenses:		
Wages Expense	$3,580	
Rent Expense	1,950	
Supplies Expense	100	
Utilities Expense	790	
Insurance Expense	200	
Depreciation Expense, Equipment	525	
Total Expenses		7,145
Net Loss		$(1,645)

6b PRACTICE EXERCISE 6b

Using the following information, prepare a statement of owner's equity for the month of July for Stanley's Computers and Electronics.

P. Stanley, Capital, on July 1	$205,077
Additional investment by P. Stanley on July 21	15,500
Net loss for the month (from income statement)	1,850
Total withdrawals for the month	3,500

PRACTICE EXERCISE 6b • SOLUTION

Stanley's Computers and Electronics
Statement of Owner's Equity
For Month Ended July 31, 20--

P. Stanley, Capital, July 1, 20--		$205,077
Investment during July	$15,500	
Net Loss for July	1,850	
Subtotal	$13,650	
Less Withdrawals for July	3,500	
Increase in Capital		10,150
P. Stanley, Capital, July 31, 20--		$215,227

PRACTICE EXERCISE 6c

Using the following information, prepare a year-end balance sheet for Moreland Clinic as of December 31.

Accounts Payable	$ 7,380
Accumulated Depreciation, Building	112,200
Accumulated Depreciation, Equipment	87,600
Building	339,100
Cash	31,345
Equipment	114,800
Land	25,000
Supplies	175
W. Moreland, Capital	303,240

PRACTICE EXERCISE 6c • SOLUTION

Moreland Clinic
Balance Sheet
December 31, 20--

Assets		
Cash		$ 31,345
Supplies		175
Land		25,000
Building	$339,100	
Less Accumulated Depreciation	112,200	226,900
Equipment	$114,800	
Less Accumulated Depreciation	87,600	27,200
Total Assets		$310,620
Liabilities		
Accounts Payable		$ 7,380
Owner's Equity		
W. Moreland, Capital		303,240
Total Liabilities and Owner's Equity		$310,620

Glossary

Accounting cycle The sequence of steps in the accounting process completed during the fiscal period. *(p. 167)*

Accrual Recognition of an expense or a revenue that has been incurred or earned but has not yet been recorded. *(p. 175)*

Accrued wages Unpaid wages owed to employees for the time between the end of the last pay period and the end of the fiscal period. *(p. 175)*

Adjusting entries Entries that bring the books up to date at the end of the fiscal period. *(p. 181)*

Adjustments Internal transactions that bring ledger accounts up to date as a planned part of the accounting procedure. *(p. 170)*

Book value or carrying value The cost of an asset minus the accumulated depreciation. *(p. 173)*

Contra account An account that is contrary to, or a deduction from, another account; for example,

Accumulated Depreciation, Equipment is listed as a deduction from Equipment. *(p. 172)*

Depreciation An expense based on the expectation that an asset will gradually decline in usefulness due to time, wear and tear, or obsolescence; the cost of the asset is therefore spread out over its estimated useful life. A part of depreciation expense is apportioned to each fiscal period. *(p. 171)*

Fiscal period Any period of time covering a complete accounting cycle, generally consisting of 12 consecutive months. *(p. 167)*

Fiscal year A fiscal period consisting of 12 consecutive months. *(p. 167)*

Matching principle The principle that the expenses for one time period are matched up with the related revenues for the same time period. *(p. 181)*

Mixed accounts Certain accounts that appear on the trial balance with balances that are partly income statement amounts and partly balance sheet amounts—for example, Prepaid Insurance and Insurance Expense. *(p. 175)*

Straight-line depreciation A means of calculating depreciation in which the cost of an asset, less any trade-in value, is allocated evenly over the useful life of the asset. *(p. 171)*

Work sheet A working paper used by accountants to record necessary adjustments and provide up-to-date account balances needed to prepare the financial statements. *(p. 167)*

Quiz Yourself

_____ 1. The __________ represents the sequence of steps in the accounting process.
- a. fiscal year
- b. fiscal period
- c. accounting cycle
- d. work sheet

_____ 2. The _________ is a working paper used by accountants to record necessary adjustments and provide up-to-date account balances needed to prepare the financial statements.
- a. journal
- b. balance sheet
- c. accounting cycle
- d. work sheet

_____ 3. On the work sheet, assets are recorded in which of the following columns?
- a. Trial Balance, Credit
- b. Income Statement, Debit
- c. Balance Sheet, Debit
- d. Adjusted Trial Balance, Credit

_____ 4. Rainy Day Services had $430 of supplies reported on its unadjusted trial balance as of March 31. During the month of March, Rainy Day Services used $175 worth of supplies. What is the entry to adjust supplies?

		Debit	Credit
a.	Supplies Expense	175	
	Cash		175
b.	Supplies	430	
	Supplies Expense		430
c.	Supplies Expense	255	
	Supplies		255
d.	Supplies Expense	175	
	Supplies		175

_____ 5. On the work sheet, Accumulated Depreciation, Equipment would be recorded in which of the following columns?
- a. Adjusted Trial Balance, Credit
- b. Income Statement, Debit
- c. Balance Sheet, Debit
- d. Income Statement, Credit

_____ 6. The ___________ requires that expenses be matched up with revenue for the same period of time.
- a. matching principle
- b. expense principle
- c. revenue recognition principle
- d. separate entity concept

_____ 7. Accumulated Depreciation, Equipment is reported
- a. on the income statement as an expense.
- b. on the balance sheet as an addition to total assets.
- c. on the income statement as a revenue.
- d. on the balance sheet as a subtraction from the related asset account.

Answers:
1.c 2.d 3.c 4.d 5.a 6.a 7.d

Review It with QuickBooks®

_____ 1. Adjusting entries are recorded in the same manner as general journal entries, except for
   a. the point of entry to the general journal is different.
   b. the account name must include adjusting entry.
   c. the box marked *Adjusting Entry* is checked.
   d. All of the above

_____ 2. How is the Entry No. field in QuickBooks completed?
   a. QuickBooks can automatically assign the number.
   b. The company can have its own numbering system.
   c. Both a and b
   d. Neither a nor b

_____ 3. The Adjusted Trial Balance report is located under _____________ in QuickBooks.
   a. Company & Financial
   b. Accountant & Taxes
   c. Custom Reports
   d. All of the above

_____ 4. Which transactions and reports should be memorized in QuickBooks?
   a. Those that occur one time
   b. Those that occur every five years
   c. Those that occur on a regular basis
   d. Due to security concerns, companies should never memorize transactions or reports.

Answers:
1. c 2. c 3. b 4. c

Chapter Assignments

Discussion Questions

1. What is the purpose of a work sheet?
2. What is the purpose of adjusting entries?
3. What is a mixed account? A contra account? Give an example of each.
4. In which column of the work sheet—Income Statement (IS) or Balance Sheet (BS)—would the adjusted balances of the following accounts appear?

Account	IS or BS?	Account	IS or BS?
a. Prepaid Insurance		e. Accumulated Depreciation, Equipment	
b. Wages Expense		f. J. Karl, Drawing	
c. Wages Payable		g. Insurance Expense	
d. Income from Services		h. Depreciation Expense, Equipment	

5. Why is it necessary to make an adjustment if wages for work performed for the pay period Monday through Friday are paid on Friday and the accounting period ends on a Wednesday?
6. Define depreciation as it relates to a van you bought for your business.
7. Define an internal transaction and provide an example.
8. Why is it necessary to journalize and post adjusting entries?

CHAPTER ASSIGNMENTS

Exercises

 2

Practice Exercise 2

EXERCISE 4-1 List the following classifications of accounts in all of the columns in which they appear on the work sheet, with the exception of the Adjustments columns. (Example: Assets)

Assets	Capital
Accumulated Depreciation (with previous balance)	Drawing
Liabilities	Revenue
	Expenses

Write *Net Income* in the appropriate columns.

	A	B	C	D	E	F	G	H	I	J	K
4											
5		TRIAL BALANCE		ADJUSTMENTS		ADJUSTED TRIAL BALANCE		INCOME STATEMENT		BALANCE SHEET	
6	ACCOUNT NAME	DEBIT	CREDIT	DEBIT	CREDIT	DEBIT	CREDIT	DEBIT	CREDIT	DEBIT	CREDIT
7		Assets				Assets				Assets	
8											
9											
10											
11											
12											
13											
14											
15	Net Income										

Sheet1 Sheet2 Sheet3

LO 2

Practice Exercise 2

EXERCISE 4-2 Classify each of the accounts listed below as assets (A), liabilities (L), owner's equity (OE), revenue (R), or expenses (E). Indicate the normal debit or credit balance of each account. Indicate whether each account will appear in the Income Statement columns (IS) or the Balance Sheet columns (BS) of the work sheet. Item 0 is given as an example.

Account	Classification	Normal Balance	IS or BS Columns
0. Example: Wages Expense	E	Debit	IS
a. Prepaid Insurance			
b. Accounts Payable			
c. Wages Payable			
d. T. Bristol, Capital			
e. Accumulated Depreciation, Building			
f. T. Bristol, Drawing			
g. Rental Income			
h. Equipment			
i. Depreciation Expense, Equipment			
j. Supplies Expense			

LO 3

EXERCISE 4-3 Place a check mark next to any account(s) requiring adjustment. Explain why those accounts must be adjusted.

✓	Account Name (in trial balance order)	Reason for Adjusting This Account
	a. Cash	
	b. Prepaid Insurance	
	c. Equipment	
	d. Accumulated Depreciation, Equipment	
	e. Wages Payable	
	f. R. Wesley, Capital	
	g. R. Wesley, Drawing	
	h. Wages Expense	

LO 3

Practice Exercise 3

EXERCISE 4-4 A partial work sheet for Marge's Place is shown below. Prepare the following adjustments on this work sheet for the month ended June 30, 20--.

a. Expired or used-up insurance, $450.
b. Depreciation expense on equipment, $750. (Remember to credit the Accumulated Depreciation account for equipment, not Equipment.)
c. Wages accrued or earned since the last payday, $380 (owed and to be paid on the next payday).
d. Supplies used, $110.

	A	B	C	D	E
1	Marge's Place				
2	Work Sheet				
3	For Month Ended June 30, 20--				
4					
5		TRIAL BALANCE		ADJUSTMENTS	
6	ACCOUNT NAME	DEBIT	CREDIT	DEBIT	CREDIT
7	Cash	4,370.00			
8	Supplies	250.00			
9	Prepaid Insurance	1,800.00			
10	Equipment	4,880.00			
11	Accumulated Depreciation, Equipment		1,350.00		
12	Accounts Payable		2,539.00		
13	M. Benson, Capital		4,544.00		
14	M. Benson, Drawing	2,000.00			
15	Income from Services		6,937.00		
16	Rent Expense	1,086.00			
17	Supplies Expense	256.00			
18	Wages Expense	660.00			
19	Miscellaneous Expense	68.00			
20		15,370.00	15,370.00		
21					

Sheet1 Sheet2 Sheet3

LO 3

Practice Exercise 3

EXERCISE 4-5 Complete the work sheet for Ramey Company, dated December 31, 20--, through the adjusted trial balance using the following adjustment information:

a. Expired or used-up insurance, $460.
b. Depreciation expense on equipment, $870. (Remember to credit the Accumulated Depreciation account for equipment, not Equipment.)
c. Wages accrued or earned since the last payday, $120 (owed and to be paid on the next payday).
d. Supplies remaining, $80.

	A	B	C	D	E	F	G
1	Ramey Company						
2	Work Sheet						
3	For Month Ended December 31, 20--						
4							
5		TRIAL BALANCE		ADJUSTMENTS		ADJUSTED TRIAL BALANCE	
6	ACCOUNT NAME	DEBIT	CREDIT	DEBIT	CREDIT	DEBIT	CREDIT
7	Cash	5,190.00					
8	Supplies	430.00					
9	Prepaid Insurance	1,200.00					
10	Equipment	4,678.00					
11	Accumulated. Depr., Equip.		1,556.00				
12	Accounts Payable		1,875.00				
13	S. Ramey, Capital		6,026.00				
14	S. Ramey, Drawing	1,700.00					
15	Service Fees		5,836.00				
16	Rent Expense	965.00					
17	Supplies Expense	267.00					
18	Wages Expense	765.00					
19	Miscellaneous Expense	98.00					
20		15,293.00	15,293.00				
21							

Sheet1 Sheet2 Sheet3

LO 4

Practice Exercise 4

EXERCISE 4-6 Journalize the four adjusting entries from the partial work sheet on the next page for Brady Company for the month ended May 31. (*Hint:* Use what you know about opening new accounts for adjusting entries.)

	A	H	I	J	K
1	Brady Company				
2	Work Sheet				
3	For Month Ended May 31, 20--				
4					
5		INCOME STATEMENT		BALANCE SHEET	
6	ACCOUNT NAME	DEBIT	CREDIT	DEBIT	CREDIT
7	Cash			5,501.00	
8	Supplies			230.00	
9	Prepaid Insurance			841.00	
10	Equipment			4,832.00	
11	Accumulated Depreciation, Equipment				1,720.00
12	Accounts Payable				1,085.00
13	S. Brady, Capital				6,800.00
14	S. Brady, Drawing			2,150.00	
15	Professional Fees		9,673.00		
16	Salary Expense	3,787.00			
17	Rent Expense	1,484.00			
18	Miscellaneous Expense	134.00			
19					
20	Insurance Expense	200.00			
21	Depreciation Expense, Equipment	364.00			
22	Salaries Payable				330.00
23	Supplies Expense	85.00			
24		6,054.00	9,673.00	13,554.00	9,935.00
25	Net Income	3,619.00			3,619.00
26		9,673.00	9,673.00	13,554.00	13,554.00
27					

Sheet1 Sheet2 Sheet3

LO 4

Practice Exercise 4

EXERCISE 4-7 Journalize the adjustments for Newkirk Company as of August 31.

	A	B	C	D	E
1	Newkirk Company				
2	Work Sheet				
3	For Month Ended August 31, 20--				
4					
5		TRIAL BALANCE		ADJUSTMENTS	
6	ACCOUNT NAME	DEBIT	CREDIT	DEBIT	CREDIT
7	Cash	3,526.00			
8	Supplies	345.00			(d) 65.00
9	Prepaid Insurance	3,973.00			(a) 300.00
10	Equipment	3,678.00			
11	Accumulated Depreciation, Equipment		645.00		(b) 206.00
12	Accounts Payable		1,843.00		
13	J. Newkirk, Capital		10,752.00		
14	J. Newkirk, Drawing	3,000.00			
15	Service Fees		5,683.00		
16	Rent Expense	2,458.00			
17	Wages Expense	1,865.00		(c) 268.00	
18	Miscellaneous Expense	78.00			
19		18,923.00	18,923.00		
20	Insurance Expense			(a) 300.00	
21	Depreciation Expense, Equipment			(b) 206.00	
22	Wages Payable				(c) 268.00
23	Supplies Expense			(d) 65.00	
24				839.00	839.00
25					

Sheet1 Sheet2 Sheet3

 4

Practice Exercise 4

EXERCISE 4-8 Journalize the following adjusting entries that were included on the work sheet for the month ended December 31.

Dec. 31 Salaries for three days are unpaid at December 31, $2,700. Salaries are $4,500 for a five-day week.

31 Insurance was bought on September 1 for $3,600 for 12 months' coverage. Four months' coverage has expired, $1,200.

31 Depreciation for the month on equipment, $50, based on an asset costing $3,200 with a trade-in value of $200 and an estimated life of five years.

31 The balance in supplies before adjustment totaled $154. The amount of supplies on hand at the end of the year is $72.

LO 5

EXERCISE 4-9 Determine on which financial statement each account listed below is reported. Use the following abbreviations: Income Statement (IS), Statement of Owner's Equity (OE), and Balance Sheet (BS).

a. S. Beagle, Capital
b. Cash
c. Miscellaneous Expense
d. Accumulated Depreciation, Equipment
e. Wages Payable
f. S. Beagle, Drawing
g. Equipment
h. Supplies
i. Depreciation Expense
j. Supplies Expense
k. Service Fees
l. Accounts Receivable

Problem Set A

 3

PROBLEM 4-1A The trial balance of Morgan's Insurance Agency as of September 30, after the firm has completed its first month of operations, is as follows:

Morgan's Insurance Company
Trial Balance
September 30, 20—

Account Name	Debit	Credit
Cash	3,337	
Accounts Receivable	1,428	
Supplies	487	
Prepaid Insurance	775	
Office Equipment	5,146	
Accounts Payable		1,367
S. Morgan, Capital		9,528
S. Morgan, Drawing	1,000	
Commissions Earned		2,843
Rent Expense	885	
Travel Expense	388	
Utilities Expense	227	
Miscellaneous Expense	65	
	13,738	13,738

Required

1. Record the amounts in the Trial Balance columns of the work sheet.
2. Complete the work sheet by making the following adjustments and lettering each adjustment:
   a. Expired or used-up insurance, $300.
   b. Depreciation expense on office equipment, $600.
   c. Supplies used, $150.

Check Figure
Net Income, $228

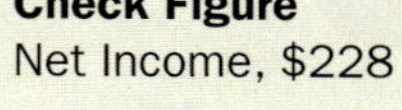

LO 3, 4

PROBLEM 4-2A The trial balance of Clayton Cleaners for the month ended September 30 is as follows:

Clayton Cleaners
Trial Balance
September 30, 20—

Account Name	Debit	Credit
Cash	2,589	
Supplies	652	
Prepaid Insurance	1,136	
Equipment	21,752	
Accumulated Depreciation, Equipment		14,357
Accounts Payable		2,647
K. Clayton, Capital		28,169
K. Clayton, Drawing	21,359	
Income from Services		40,850
Wages Expense	23,983	
Rent Expense	11,673	
Utilities Expense	1,254	
Telephone Expense	1,144	
Miscellaneous Expense	481	
	86,023	86,023

Data for the adjustments are as follows:

a. Expired or used-up insurance, $800.
b. Depreciation expense on equipment, $2,700.
c. Wages accrued or earned since the last payday, $585 (owed and to be paid on the next payday).
d. Supplies remaining at the end of month, $230.

Required

1. Complete a work sheet. (Skip this step if using QuickBooks or general ledger.)
2. Journalize the adjusting entries.

Check Figure
Net Loss, $2,192

LO 4, 5

PROBLEM 4-3A The completed work sheet for Chelsey Decorators for the month of March is in your Working Papers or in CengageNow.

Required

1. Journalize the adjusting entries.
2. If using QuickBooks, prepare an adjusting journal entries report and an adjusted trial balance.
3. Prepare an income statement.
4. Prepare a statement of owner's equity. Assume that no additional investments were made in March. (Skip this step if using QuickBooks.)
5. Prepare a balance sheet.

Check Figure
Total Assets, $15,003

 3, 4, 5, 6

PROBLEM 4-4A The trial balance for Game Time on July 31 is as follows:

Game Time Trial Balance July 31, 20—		
Account Name	**Debit**	**Credit**
Cash	14,721	
Supplies	257	
Prepaid Insurance	1,295	
Equipment	17,642	
Accumulated Depreciation, Equipment		2,287
Repair Equipment	1,265	
Accumulated Depreciation, Repair Equipment		880
Accounts Payable		942
B. Ryan, Capital		23,871
B. Ryan, Drawing	2,000	
Game Fees		7,954
Concession Fees		3,752
Wages Expense	1,068	
Rent Expense	980	
Utilities Expense	246	
Repair Expense	180	
Miscellaneous Expense	32	
	39,686	39,686

Data for month-end adjustments are as follows:

a. Expired or used-up insurance, $480.
b. Depreciation expense on equipment, $850.
c. Depreciation expense on repair equipment, $120.
d. Wages accrued or earned since the last payday, $525 (owed and to be paid on the next payday).
e. Supplies used, $70.

Check Figure
Net Income, $7,155

Required

1. Complete a work sheet for the month. (Skip this step if using QuickBooks or general ledger.)
2. Journalize the adjusting entries.
3. If using QuickBooks, prepare an adjusting journal entries report and an adjusted trial balance.
4. Prepare an income statement, a statement of owner's equity*, and a balance sheet. Assume that no additional investments were made during July.

*If using QuickBooks, skip preparing the statement of owner's equity.

LO 3, 4, 5, 6

QuickBooks

PROBLEM 4-5A The trial balance for Benner Hair Salon on March 31 is as follows:

Benner Hair Salon
Trial Balance
March 31, 20—

Account Name	Debit	Credit
Cash	4,440	
Supplies	150	
Prepaid Insurance	2,354	
Equipment	10,507	
Accumulated Depreciation, Equipment		1,000
Accounts Payable		240
A. Benner, Capital		13,449
A. Benner, Drawing	1,500	
Salon Fees		6,230
Wages Expense	1,036	
Rent Expense	650	
Utilities Expense	130	
Repair Expense	65	
Miscellaneous Expense	87	
	20,919	20,919

Data for month-end adjustments are as follows:

a. Expired or used-up insurance, $300.
b. Depreciation expense on equipment, $500.
c. Wages accrued or earned since the last payday, $235 (owed and to be paid on the next payday).
d. Supplies remaining at the end of the month, $65.

Required

1. Complete a work sheet for the month. (Skip this step if using QuickBooks or general ledger.)
2. Journalize the adjusting entries.
3. Prepare an income statement, a statement of owner's equity*, and a balance sheet. Assume that no additional investments were made during March.

Check Figure
Net Income, $3,142

*If using QuickBooks, skip preparing the statement of owner's equity.

Problem Set B

LO 3

PROBLEM 4-1B The trial balance for Mason's Insurance Agency as of August 31, after the firm has completed its first month of operations, is shown on the next page.

(*Continued*)

CHAPTER ASSIGNMENTS

Mason's Insurance Company
Trial Balance
August 31, 20—

Account Name	Debit	Credit
Cash	3,527	
Accounts Receivable	1,219	
Supplies	492	
Prepaid Insurance	1,362	
Office Equipment	3,939	
Accounts Payable		2,071
C. Mason, Capital		9,020
C. Mason, Drawing	1,900	
Commissions Earned		3,520
Rent Expense	1,695	
Travel Expense	225	
Utilities Expense	198	
Miscellaneous Expense	54	
	14,611	14,611

Check Figure
Net Loss, $12

Required

1. Record amounts in the Trial Balance columns of the work sheet.
2. Complete the work sheet by making the following adjustments and lettering each adjustment:
   a. Expired or used-up insurance, $260.
   b. Depreciation expense on office equipment, $900.
   c. Supplies used, $200.

LO 3, 4

QuickBooks

PROBLEM 4-2B The trial balance of The New Decors for the month ended September 30 is as follows:

The New Decors
Trial Balance
September 30, 20—

Account Name	Debit	Credit
Cash	4,378	
Supplies	1,864	
Prepaid Insurance	1,345	
Equipment	30,978	
Accumulated Depreciation, Equipment		15,235
Accounts Payable		3,751
R. Becker, Capital		44,208
R. Becker, Drawing	20,445	
Income from Services		44,791
Wages Expense	29,761	
Rent Expense	15,932	
Utilities Expense	1,573	
Telephone Expense	1,271	
Miscellaneous Expense	438	
	107,985	107,985

Data for the adjustments are as follows:

a. Expired or used-up insurance, $425.
b. Depreciation expense on equipment, $2,750.
c. Wages accrued or earned since the last payday, $475 (owed and to be paid on the next payday).
d. Supplies remaining at end of month, $215.

Required

1. Complete a work sheet. (Skip this step if using QuickBooks or general ledger.)
2. Journalize the adjusting entries.

Check Figure
Net Loss, $9,483

LO 4, 5

PROBLEM 4-3B The completed work sheet for Juarez Design for the month of March is in your Working Papers, CengageNow or general ledger.

QuickBooks

Required

1. Journalize the adjusting entries.
2. Prepare an income statement.
3. Prepare a statement of owner's equity*. Assume that no additional investments were made in March.
4. Prepare a balance sheet.

*If using QuickBooks, skip preparing the statement of owner's equity.

Check Figure
Total Assets, $21,997

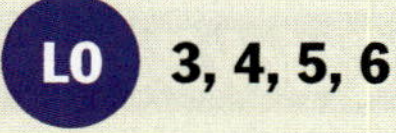
LO 3, 4, 5, 6

PROBLEM 4-4B The trial balance for Harris Pitch and Putt on June 30 is as follows: Data for month-end adjustments are as follows:

QuickBooks

Harris Pitch and Putt
Trial Balance
June 30, 20—

Account Name	Debit	Credit
Cash	5,532	
Supplies	246	
Prepaid Insurance	1,284	
Equipment	21,687	
Accumulated Depreciation, Equipment		1,478
Repair Equipment	5,289	
Accumulated Depreciation, Repair Equipment		1,285
Accounts Payable		860
W. Harris, Capital		23,110
W. Harris, Drawing	2,565	
Golf Fees		11,487
Concession Fees		3,763
Wages Expense	3,163	
Rent Expense	1,350	
Utilities Expense	457	
Repair Expense	171	
Miscellaneous Expense	239	
	41,983	41,983

a. Expired or used-up insurance, $380.
b. Depreciation expense on equipment, $1,950.
c. Depreciation expense on repair equipment, $1,650.

(Continued)

d. Wages accrued or earned since the last payday, $585 (owed and to be paid on the next payday).
e. Supplies remaining at end of month, $120.

Check Figure
Net Income, $5,179

Required

1. Complete a work sheet for the month. (Skip this step if using QuickBooks or general ledger.)
2. Journalize the adjusting entries.
3. If using QuickBooks, prepare an adjusting journal entries report and an adjusted trial balance.
4. Prepare an income statement, a statement of owner's equity*, and a balance sheet. Assume that no additional investments were made during June.

*If using QuickBooks, skip preparing the statement of owner's equity.

3, 4, 5, 6

PROBLEM 4-5B The trial balance for Wilson Financial Services on January 31 is as follows:

Wilson Financial Services
Trial Balance
January 31, 20—

Account Name	Debit	Credit
Cash	17,910	
Supplies	650	
Prepaid Insurance	4,500	
Equipment	15,400	
Accumulated Depreciation, Equipment		3,500
Accounts Payable		2,450
L. Wilson, Capital		25,800
L. Wilson, Drawing	3,000	
Financial Services Fees		15,550
Wages Expense	4,025	
Rent Expense	1,200	
Utilities Expense	430	
Repair Expense	110	
Miscellaneous Expense	75	
	47,300	47,300

Data for month-end adjustments are as follows:

a. Expired or used-up insurance, $750.
b. Depreciation expense on equipment, $300.
c. Wages accrued or earned since the last payday, $1,055 (owed and to be paid on the next payday).
d. Supplies used, $535.

Check Figure
Net Income, $7,070

Required

1. Complete a work sheet for the month. (Skip this step if using QuickBooks or general ledger.)
2. Journalize the adjusting entries.
3. If using QuickBooks, prepare an adjusting journal entries report and an adjusted trial balance.
4. Prepare an income statement, a statement of owner's equity*, and a balance sheet. Assume that no additional investments were made during January.

*If using QuickBooks, skip preparing the statement of owner's equity.

Try It with QuickBooks® (LO 1, 2, 3, 4)

QB Exercise 4-1

Using the Conner's Whitewater Adventures demonstration file from Chapter 4, complete the following activities with QuickBooks. Use the dates June 1, 2015, to June 30, 2015, for all reports.

1. Record the following adjusting entries in the QuickBooks general journal:
   a. $460 worth of supplies used during June.
   b. $625 expired insurance during June.
   c. $512 depreciation for the month of June.
   d. $472 accrued wages owed, but not recorded at the end of June.
2. View and print the adjusting entries report for Conner's Whitewater Adventures.
   a. What is the ending balance of the Debit column for this report?
3. View and print the adjusted trial balance report for Conner's Whitewater Adventures.
   a. What is the adjusted balance in the Supplies account? Is this balance a debit or a credit?
   b. What is the adjusted balance in the Wages Payable account? Is this balance a debit or a credit?
   c. What is the total debit amount of the unadjusted trial balance?
   d. What is the total credit amount of the adjusted trial balance?

Activities

Why Does It Matter?

RIDE THE DUCKS OF SEATTLE, Seattle, Washington

Ride the Ducks of Seattle may seem like an unlikely name for a thriving business—but it is the name of a real business! The year-round Seattle tour company uses vehicles that can be providing a road tour one minute and plying the waters of Elliott Bay the next. One of Ride the Ducks' employees is a bookkeeper who also serves as a reservationist, tour vehicle cleaner, and computer specialist. In addition to recording and posting journal entries each month, he makes adjusting entries. What are some of the adjusting entries this bookkeeper might make for Ride the Ducks of Seattle?

What Would You Say?

You are the bookkeeper for a small but thriving business. You have asked the owner for the information you need to make adjusting entries for depreciation, supplies, insurance, and wages. He says that he's really busy and that what you've done so far is "close enough." Explain the need for adjusting entries and their effect on the owner's balance sheet and the "bottom line" on the income statement.

What Do You Think?

Your supervisor just finished a work sheet for the month of June, but all of the columns except the following were left unreadable because of a spilled latte. You have been asked to journalize the adjusting entries using the surviving partial work sheet below.

	INCOME STATEMENT		BALANCE SHEET	
ACCOUNT NAME	DEBIT	CREDIT	DEBIT	CREDIT
Cash			8,476.00	
Accounts Receivable			1,486.00	
Equipment			12,367.00	
Accumulated Depreciation, Equipment				3,610.00
Accounts Payable				2,813.00
G. Kramer, Capital				11,707.00
G. Kramer, Drawing			1,100.00	
Income from Services		11,216.00		
Rent Expense	2,510.00			
Wages Expense	2,467.00			
Insurance Expense	210.00			
Depreciation Expense, Equipment	750.00			
Wages Payable				620.00
	5,937.00	11,216.00	24,029.00	18,750.00
Net Income	5,279.00			5,279.00
	11,216.00	11,216.00	24,029.00	24,029.00

What Would You Do?

Your client is preparing financial statements to show the bank. You know that he has incurred a refrigeration repair expense during the month, but you see no such expense on the books. When you question the client, he tells you that he has not yet paid the $1,255 bill. Your client is on the accrual basis of accounting. He does not want the refrigeration repair expense on the books as of the end of the month because he wants his profits to look good for the bank. Is your client behaving ethically by suggesting that the refrigeration repair expense not be booked until the $1,255 is paid? Are you behaving ethically if you agree to the client's request? What principle is involved here?

Adjustments

Although you printed the trial balance and financial statements to get an idea of how All About You Spa is doing financially, some accounts are not accurate. You need to make adjusting entries to provide a clearer picture of how the spa is doing.

© iStockPhoto.com/Khalus

CONTINUING PROBLEM

HOW TO COMPUTE THE ADJUSTMENTS

Compute the adjustment amounts for the month of June, using the following information:

Adjustment (a): Liability insurance for six months was purchased during the first days of the month. That protection for one month has been used or expended.

Adjustments (b) and (c): Office equipment and spa equipment have depreciated. That means they have been in use for a month and have, for accounting purposes, lost some usefulness. This is an estimate, of course, which allows us to expense the depreciation and, in effect, lowers the book value (value on the books) of both types of equipment.

(b): The owner, Anika Valli, purchased office equipment totaling $1,150. The office equipment will be depreciated using the straight-line method. The office equipment is estimated to have a salvage (trade-in) value of $550 and is expected to last five years. Remember, you want to compute the depreciation for one month, not one year.

(c): Anika Valli invested spa equipment totaling $7,393 in the business ($3,158 of her own spa equipment plus $4,235 of new spa equipment purchased). The spa equipment will be depreciated using the straight-line method. The spa equipment is estimated to have a trade-in, or salvage, value of $3,500 and is expected to last five years. Remember, you want to compute the depreciation for one month, not one year.

© iStockPhoto.com/Pixhook

Adjustment (d): All About You Spa owes one day of wages to its employees. The month's total wages paid in June amounted to $7,390. The employees worked 21 days but were paid for only 20 days because the payday for the last day worked is in the next pay period.

Adjustments (e) and (f): After a count of supplies at the end of the month, All About You Spa has $130 remaining in Office Supplies and $205 remaining in Spa Supplies.

Required

1. Complete a work sheet for the month (if required by your instructor).
2. Journalize the adjusting entries in the general journal.
   - If you are preparing the adjusting entries manually, enter your transactions beginning on page 4.

(Continued)

All About You Spa

CONTINUING PROBLEM

Check Figures
4. Adjusted trial balance total, $39,197.38
5. Net income, $7,111.62
6. A. Valli, Capital, ending balance, $23,419.62
7. Total assets, $26,037.12

3. Post the adjusting entries to the general ledger accounts.
   - Ignore this step if you are using QuickBooks or general ledger.
4. Prepare an adjusted trial balance as of June 30, 20--.
5. Prepare an income statement (after adjustment) for the month ended June 30, 20--.
6. Prepare a statement of owner's equity* (after adjustment) for the month ended June 30, 20--.
7. Prepare a balance sheet (after adjustment) as of June 30, 20--.

*If using QuickBooks, skip preparing the statement of owner's equity.

chapter 5

Closing Entries and the Post-Closing Trial Balance

Learning Objectives

After you have completed this chapter, you will be able to do the following:

1. List the steps in the accounting cycle.
2. Journalize and post closing entries for a service enterprise.
3. Prepare a post-closing trial balance.
4. Define cash basis and accrual basis accounting.
5. Prepare interim statements.

To: **Amy Roberts, CPA**
Subject: **It's the End of the Year!**

Hi Amy,
Well, I made it! The business has been successful this year, and I am even earning a profit! I can't begin to thank you enough for all the help you've given me. I guess I'll just continue to record transactions using everything we've talked about so far. Is there anything else that still needs to be completed?
Thanks,
Janie

To: **Janie Conner**
Subject: **RE: It's the End of the Year!**

Hi Janie,
I'm glad to hear the business has been successful! At the end of each fiscal period, two more steps need to take place to finish the accounting work: closing entries and post-closing trial balance. Let's start with closing entries. Closing entries are completed to prepare the accounts for next year. Like last time, we'll be looking at the work sheet to help us prepare closing entries. Here are the steps to learn:

_____ 1. Understand the steps of the accounting cycle (which is what you've been learning all along).

_____ 2. Learn how to record and post closing entries.

Let me know if you need help!
Amy

© Joshua Roper/Alamy

Accounting Language

Accrual basis of accounting (p. 235)
Cash basis of accounting (p. 234)
Closing entries (p. 224)
Income Summary account (p. 225)
Interim statements (p. 235)
Nominal (temporary-equity) accounts (p. 229)
Post-closing trial balance (p. 233)
Real (permanent) accounts (p. 229)

Let's review the steps in the accounting cycle for an entire fiscal period. Remember that a fiscal period is generally 12 consecutive months.

STEP 1. Analyze source documents and record business transactions in a journal.

STEP 2. Post journal entries to the accounts in the ledger.

STEP 3. Prepare a trial balance.

STEP 4. Gather adjustment data and record the adjusting entries on a work sheet.

STEP 5. Complete the work sheet.

STEP 6. Journalize and post the adjusting entries from the data on the work sheet.

STEP 7. Prepare financial statements from the data on the work sheet.

STEP 8. Journalize and post the closing entries.

STEP 9. Prepare a post-closing trial balance.

Learning Objective

1 List the steps in the accounting cycle.

This chapter explains the procedure for completing the final steps: journalizing and posting the closing entries and preparing the post-closing trial balance.

Adjusting entries, closing entries, and a post-closing trial balance are prepared at the end of a fiscal period. To introduce you to these final steps in the accounting cycle, we assume that the fiscal period for Conner's Whitewater Adventures ends after one month. We make this assumption so that we can thoroughly cover the material and give you a chance to practice its application. The entire accounting cycle is outlined in Figure 1 on the next page.

CLOSING ENTRIES

To help you understand the reason for the closing entries, let's take a look at a version of the fundamental accounting equation.

$$\text{Assets} = \text{Liabilities} + \text{Capital} - \text{Drawing} + \text{Revenue} - \text{Expenses}$$

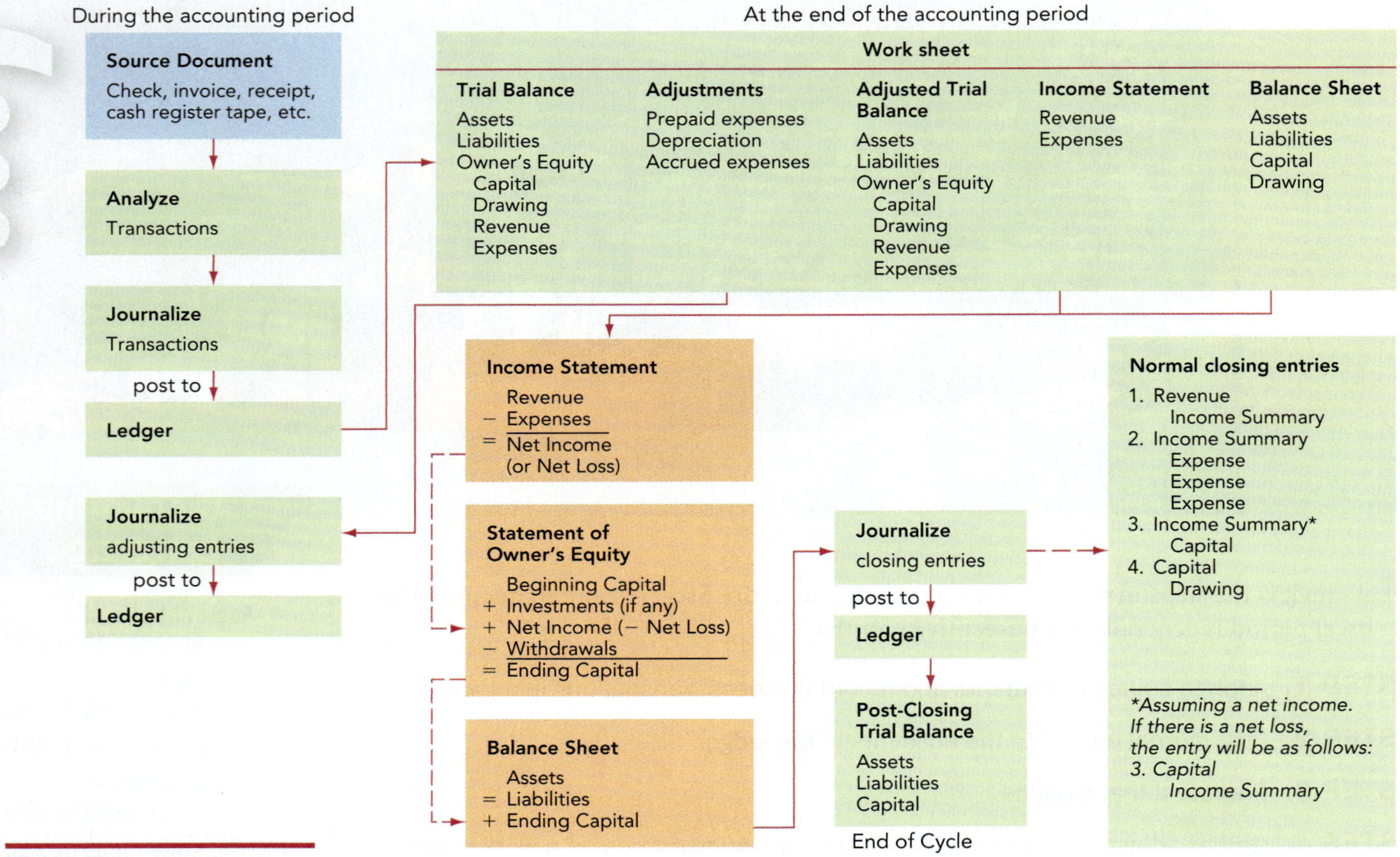

During the accounting period

Source Document
Check, invoice, receipt, cash register tape, etc.

Analyze
Transactions

Journalize
Transactions

post to

Ledger

Journalize
adjusting entries

post to

Ledger

At the end of the accounting period

Work sheet

Trial Balance	Adjustments	Adjusted Trial Balance	Income Statement	Balance Sheet
Assets Liabilities Owner's Equity Capital Drawing Revenue Expenses	Prepaid expenses Depreciation Accrued expenses	Assets Liabilities Owner's Equity Capital Drawing Revenue Expenses	Revenue Expenses	Assets Liabilities Capital Drawing

Income Statement
Revenue
− Expenses
= Net Income
(or Net Loss)

Statement of Owner's Equity
Beginning Capital
+ Investments (if any)
+ Net Income (− Net Loss)
− Withdrawals
= Ending Capital

Balance Sheet
Assets
= Liabilities
+ Ending Capital

Journalize
closing entries

post to

Ledger

Post-Closing Trial Balance
Assets
Liabilities
Capital

End of Cycle

Normal closing entries
1. Revenue
   Income Summary
2. Income Summary
   Expense
   Expense
   Expense
3. Income Summary*
   Capital
4. Capital
   Drawing

**Assuming a net income. If there is a net loss, the entry will be as follows:*
3. Capital
Income Summary

Figure 1
The accounting cycle

We know that the income statement, as stated in the third line of its heading, covers a period of time. The income statement consists of revenue minus expenses for this period of time only. So when the next fiscal period begins, we should start with zero balances. We start over again each period.

Closing entries empty, or zero out, temporary owner's equity accounts and prepare the accounts for the new accounting period—much like when you empty the information from your tax folders one year so that you can fill the folders with the new year's revenue and expense receipts.

Purpose of Closing Entries

This brings us to the *purpose* of the **closing entries**, which is to close (or zero out) revenue, expense, and Drawing accounts. We do this because their balances apply to only one fiscal period. Closing entries are made after the last adjusting entry and after the financial statements have been prepared. With the coming of the next fiscal period, we want to start from zero, recording revenue and expenses for the new fiscal period. The closing entries also update the owner's Capital account.

Accountants also refer to closing the accounts as *clearing the accounts.* For income tax purposes, this is certainly understandable. No one wants to pay income tax more than once on the same income, and the Internal Revenue Service doesn't allow you to count an expense more than once. So now we have this:

$$\text{Assets} = \text{Liabilities} + \text{Capital} - \underset{}{\overset{\text{(closed)}}{\text{Drawing}}} + \overset{\text{(closed)}}{\text{Revenue}} - \overset{\text{(closed)}}{\text{Expenses}}$$

The assets, liabilities, and owner's Capital accounts remain open. The balance sheet gives the present balances of these accounts. The accountant carries the asset, liability, and Capital account balances over to the next fiscal period.

Procedure for Closing

The procedure for closing is simply to balance off the account (in other words, to make the balance *equal to zero*). This meets our objective, which is to start from zero in the next fiscal period. Let's illustrate this first with T accounts. Suppose an account to be closed has a debit balance of $870. To make the balance equal to zero, we *credit* the account for $870.

Debit		Credit	
Balance	870	Closing	**870**
New Balance	0		

Now suppose an account to be closed has a credit balance of $1,400. To make the balance equal to zero, we *debit* the account for $1,400.

Debit		Credit	
Closing	**1,400**	Balance	1,400
		New Balance	0

Remember, every entry must have at least one debit and one credit. So to record the other half of the closing entry, we bring into existence the **Income Summary account**. The Income Summary account does not have plus and minus signs and does not have a normal balance, just debit and credit.

There are four steps in the closing procedure:

STEP 1. Close the revenue account(s) into Income Summary.

STEP 2. Close the expense account(s) into Income Summary.

STEP 3. Close the Income Summary account into the Capital account, transferring the net income or net loss to the Capital account.

STEP 4. Close the Drawing account into the Capital account.

To illustrate, we return to Conner's Whitewater Adventures. For the purpose of the illustration, assume that Conner's Whitewater Adventures' fiscal period ends after one month. We have the following T account balances in the revenue and expense accounts after the adjustments have been posted.

Income from Tours

	−	+	
		Balance	23,320

Advertising Expense

	+	−
Balance	620	

Wages Expense

	+	−
Balance	2,832	

Utilities Expense

	+	−
Balance	225	

Rent Expense

	+	−
Balance	1,250	

Insurance Expense

	+	−
Balance	625	

Supplies Expense

	+	−
Balance	460	

Depreciation Expense, Equipment

	+	−
Balance	512	

Learning Objective 2 Journalize and post closing entries for a service enterprise.

Remember

The matching principle is why we close revenue, expense, and Drawing accounts.

As a memory tool for the sequence of steps in the closing procedure, use the letters of the closing elements, **REID:** Revenue, Expenses, Income Summary, Drawing.

STEP 1. Close the revenue account(s) into Income Summary.

To make the balance of Income from Tours equal to zero, we *balance it off*, or debit it, in the amount of $23,320. Because we need an offsetting credit, we credit Income Summary for the same amount. Notice that there are no signs in Income Summary, only debit and credit.

Income from Tours			
	−	+	
Closing	**23,320**	Balance	23,320

Income Summary			
		(Revenue)	**23,320**

The balance of Income from Tours is transferred to Income Summary.

STEP 2. Close the expense account(s) into Income Summary.

To make the balances of the expense accounts equal to zero, we need to *balance them off*, or credit them. Again, the T accounts are useful for formulating this journal entry.

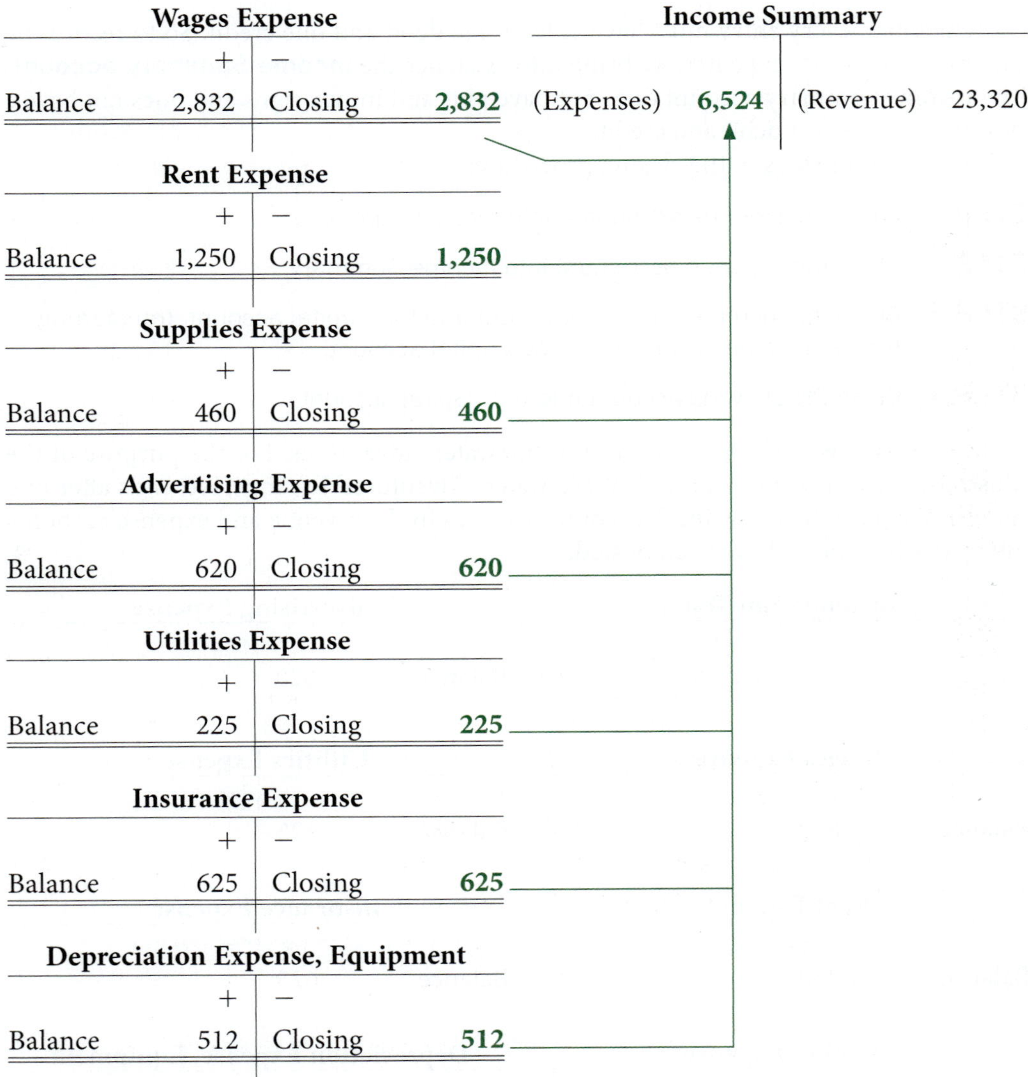

Wages Expense
+
−
Balance 2,832
Closing 2,832
Income Summary
(Expenses) 6,524
(Revenue) 23,320
Rent Expense
+
−
Balance 1,250
Closing 1,250
Supplies Expense
+
−
Balance 460
Closing 460
Advertising Expense
+
−
Balance 620
Closing 620
Utilities Expense
+
−
Balance 225
Closing 225
Insurance Expense
+
−
Balance 625
Closing 625
Depreciation Expense, Equipment
+
−
Balance 512
Closing 512

STEP 3. Close the Income Summary account into the Capital account, transferring the net income or net loss to the Capital account.

Recall that we created Income Summary so that we could have a debit and a credit in each closing entry. Now that it has done its job, we close it out. We use the same procedure as before, making the balance equal to zero, or balancing off the account. We transfer, or close, the balance of the Income Summary account into the Capital account, as shown in the T accounts below. In addition, Figure 2 shows the closing entries recorded in the general journal for steps 1 through 3.

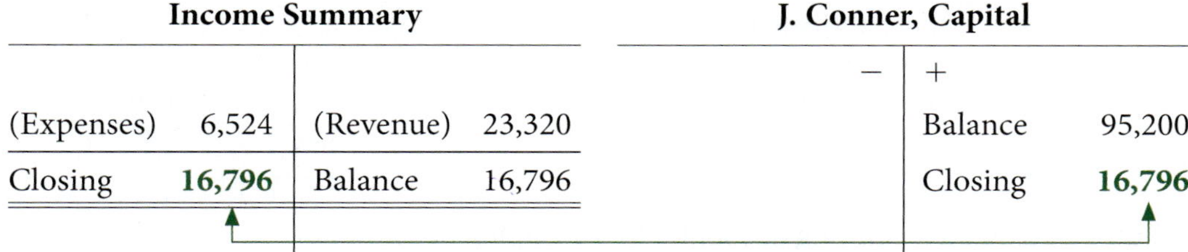

Income Summary				J. Conner, Capital			
					−	+	
(Expenses)	6,524	(Revenue)	23,320			Balance	95,200
Closing	**16,796**	Balance	16,796			Closing	**16,796**

GENERAL JOURNAL					Page 4
	Date	Description	Post. Ref.	Debit	Credit
		Closing Entries			
Step 1	30	Income from Tours		23 3 2 0 00	
		Income Summary			23 3 2 0 00
Step 2	30	Income Summary		6 5 2 4 00	
		Wages Expense			2 8 3 2 00
		Rent Expense			1 2 5 0 00
		Supplies Expense			4 6 0 00
		Advertising Expense			6 2 0 00
		Utilities Expense			2 2 5 00
		Insurance Expense			6 2 5 00
		Depreciation Expense, Equipment			5 1 2 00
Step 3	30	Income Summary		16 7 9 6 00	
		J. Conner, Capital			16 7 9 6 00

Figure 2
Closing entries for Conner's Whitewater Adventures

Income Summary is always closed into the Capital account by the amount of revenue minus expenses (the net income or the net loss). Comparing net income or net loss on the work sheet with the closing entry for Income Summary can serve as a checkpoint or verification for you.

Net income is added (credited) to the Capital account because, as shown in the statement of owner's equity, net income is treated as an addition. Net loss, on the other hand, is subtracted from (debited to) the Capital account, because net loss is treated as a deduction in the statement of owner's equity. Assuming that J. Doe Company had a net loss of $600, here's how to close Income Summary:

Income Summary				J. Doe, Capital			
					−	+	
(Expenses)	3,000	(Revenue)	**2,400**	(Net Loss)	**600**	Balance	42,000
Balance	600	Closing	**600**				

The entry to close Income Summary into J. Doe's Capital account for a net loss would look like the following:

GENERAL JOURNAL					Page 3
Date		Description	Post. Ref.	Debit	Credit
		Closing Entries			
	31	J. Doe, Capital		6 0 0 00	
		Income Summary			6 0 0 00

STEP 4. Close the Drawing account into the Capital account.

Let's return to the example of Conner's Whitewater Adventures. The Drawing account applies to only one fiscal period, so it too must be closed. Drawing is not an expense because it did not help the business generate revenue. **And because Drawing is not an expense, it cannot affect net income or net loss.** It appears in the statement of owner's equity as a deduction from the Capital account, so it is closed directly into the Capital account. We balance off the Drawing account, or make its balance equal to zero, by transferring the balance of Drawing to the Capital account.

J. Conner, Drawing

+		−	
Balance	3,500	Closing	3,500

J. Conner, Capital

−		+	
(Drawing)	3,500	Balance	95,200
		(Net Inc.)	16,796
		Balance	108,496

The entire set of journal entries in the closing procedure for Conner's Whitewater Adventures is shown below.

Figure 3
Closing entries for Conner's Whitewater Adventures

GENERAL JOURNAL						Page 4
	Date		Description	Post. Ref.	Debit	Credit
			Closing Entries			
Step 1		30	Income from Tours		23 3 2 0 00	
			Income Summary			23 3 2 0 00
Step 2		30	Income Summary		6 5 2 4 00	
			Wages Expense			2 8 3 2 00
			Rent Expense			1 2 5 0 00
			Supplies Expense			4 6 0 00
			Advertising Expense			6 2 0 00
			Utilities Expense			2 2 5 00
			Insurance Expense			6 2 5 00
			Depreciation Expense, Equipment			5 1 2 00
Step 3		30	Income Summary		16 7 9 6 00	
			J. Conner, Capital			16 7 9 6 00
Step 4		30	J. Conner, Capital		3 5 0 0 00	
			J. Conner, Drawing			3 5 0 0 00

These closing entries show that Conner's Whitewater Adventures has net income of $16,796; the owner has withdrawn $3,500 for personal expenses; and $13,296 ($16,796 − $3,500) has been retained in the business, thereby increasing capital.

Closing Entries Using Accounting Software

Making closing entries using accounting software, such as QuickBooks, is frequently an automatic procedure. The accounting software automatically updates the capital account. If you are using accounting software, at the end of each fiscal period, you should perform the following steps:

1. Make a backup copy of the file.
2. Print all financial statements.
3. Set a closing date and password-protect the books for that fiscal year.

The purpose of setting a closing date and password-protecting the books at the end of the fiscal year is to prevent changes from being made to transactions that have already been closed. This will ensure that no accidental changes are made to the previous fiscal year after it has been closed.

Closing Entries Using the Work Sheet

You can gather the information for the closing entries directly from the ledger accounts or from the work sheet. Because the Income Statement columns of the work sheet consist entirely of revenues and expenses, you can pick up the figures for three of the four closing entries from these columns. Figure 4, on page 230, shows a partial work sheet for Conner's Whitewater Adventures.

You can plan the closing entries by balancing off all of the figures that appear in the Income Statement columns. For example, in the Income Statement Credit column, there is a credit for $23,320 (Income from Tours), so we debit that account for $23,320 and credit Income Summary for $23,320.

There are debits for $2,832, $1,250, $620, $225, $460, $625, and $512 (expense accounts). So now we *credit* these accounts for the same amounts and debit Income Summary for the total ($6,524).

Next, we close Income Summary into Capital, using the net income figure ($16,796) already shown on the work sheet in Figure 4.

We do, of course, have to get the last closing entry from the Balance Sheet columns to close Drawing.

Incidentally, accountants call the accounts that are to be closed (such as revenue, expenses, and Drawing) **nominal (temporary-equity) accounts**. These accounts are temporary in that their balances apply to only one fiscal period. The *equity* aspect pertains because all of these accounts come under the umbrella of owner's equity.

On the other hand, accountants call the accounts that remain open (such as assets, liabilities, and Capital) **real (permanent) accounts**. These accounts have balances that will be carried over to the next fiscal period. They are *permanent* because as long as the company exists, these accounts will retain their balances.

Remember

The temporary-equity accounts (revenue, expenses, and Drawing) are closed out because they apply to only one fiscal period.

Posting the Closing Entries

In the Item column of the ledger account, we write the word *Closing*. To show that the balance of an account is zero, we draw a line through both the Debit Balance and the Credit Balance columns.

Figure 4

Partial work sheet for Conner's Whitewater Adventures

	A	B	C	D	E	F	G	H	I	J	K
1						Conner's Whitewater Adventures					
2						Work Sheet					
3						For Month Ended June 30, 20--					
4											
5		TRIAL BALANCE		ADJUSTMENTS		ADJUSTED TRIAL BALANCE		INCOME STATEMENT		BALANCE SHEET	
6	ACCOUNT NAME	DEBIT	CREDIT	DEBIT	CREDIT	DEBIT	CREDIT	DEBIT	CREDIT	DEBIT	CREDIT
7			*Accum. Depr.*				*Accum. Depr.*				*Accum. Depr.*
8		*A + Draw. + E*	*+ L + Cap. + R*			*A + Draw. + E*	*+ L + Cap. + R*	*E*	*R*	*A + Draw.*	*+ L + Cap.*
9	Cash	55,890.00				55,890.00				55,890.00	
10	Accounts Receivable	4,250.00				4,250.00				4,250.00	
11	Supplies	675.00			(a) 460.00	215.00				215.00	
12	Prepaid Insurance	1,875.00			(b) 625.00	1,250.00				1,250.00	
13	Equipment	51,300.00				51,300.00				51,300.00	
14	Accounts Payable		3,425.00				3,425.00				3,425.00
15	J. Conner, Capital		95,200.00				95,200.00				95,200.00
16	J. Conner, Drawing	3,500.00				3,500.00				3,500.00	
17	Income from Tours		23,320.00				23,320.00		23,320.00		
18	Wages Expense	2,360.00		(d) 472.00		2,832.00		2,832.00			
19	Rent Expense	1,250.00				1,250.00		1,250.00			
20	Advertising Expense	620.00				620.00		620.00			
21	Utilities Expense	225.00				225.00		225.00			
22		121,945.00	121,945.00								
23	Supplies Expense			(a) 460.00		460.00		460.00			
24	Insurance Expense			(b) 625.00		625.00		625.00			
25	Depr. Exp., Equip.			(c) 512.00		512.00		512.00			
26	Accum. Depr., Equip.				(c) 512.00		512.00				512.00
27	Wages Payable				(d) 472.00		472.00				472.00
28				2,069.00	2,069.00	122,929.00	122,929.00	6,524.00	23,320.00	116,405.00	99,609.00
29	Net Income							16,796.00			16,796.00
30								23,320.00	23,320.00	116,405.00	116,405.00
31											

Sheet1 Sheet2 Sheet3

After we have posted the closing entries, the Capital, Drawing, Income Summary, revenue, and expense accounts of Conner's Whitewater Adventures appear as follows:

GENERAL LEDGER

ACCOUNT J. Conner, Capital **ACCOUNT NO. 311**

Date		Item	Post. Ref.	Debit	Credit	Balance Debit	Balance Credit
20--							
June	1		1		90,000.00		90,000.00
	4		1		5,200.00		95,200.00
	30	Closing	4		16,796.00		111,996.00
	30	Closing	4	3,500.00			108,496.00

ACCOUNT J. Conner, Drawing **ACCOUNT NO. 312**

Date		Item	Post. Ref.	Debit	Credit	Balance Debit	Balance Credit
20--							
June	30		3	3,500.00		3,500.00	
	30	Closing	4		3,500.00	—	—

ACCOUNT Income Summary **ACCOUNT NO. 313**

Date		Item	Post. Ref.	Debit	Credit	Balance Debit	Balance Credit
20--							
June	30	Closing	4		23,320.00		23,320.00
	30	Closing	4	6,524.00			16,796.00
	30	Closing	4	16,796.00		—	—

ACCOUNT Income from Tours **ACCOUNT NO. 411**

Date		Item	Post. Ref.	Debit	Credit	Balance Debit	Balance Credit
20--							
June	7		1		8,000.00		8,000.00
	15		2		6,750.00		14,750.00
	30		3		8,570.00		23,320.00
	30	Closing	4	23,320.00		—	—

ACCOUNT Wages Expense **ACCOUNT NO. 511**

Date		Item	Post. Ref.	Debit	Credit	Balance Debit	Balance Credit
20--							
June	24		2	2,360.00		2,360.00	
	30	Adj.	4	472.00		2,832.00	
	30	Closing	4		2,832.00	—	—

ACCOUNT Rent Expense **ACCOUNT NO.** 512

Date		Item	Post. Ref.	Debit	Credit	Balance Debit	Balance Credit
20--							
June	8		1	1,250 00		1,250 00	
	30	Closing	4		1,250 00	—	—

ACCOUNT Supplies Expense **ACCOUNT NO.** 513

Date		Item	Post. Ref.	Debit	Credit	Balance Debit	Balance Credit
20--							
June	30	Adj.	4	460 00		460 00	
	30	Closing	4		460 00	—	—

ACCOUNT Advertising Expense **ACCOUNT NO.** 514

Date		Item	Post. Ref.	Debit	Credit	Balance Debit	Balance Credit
20--							
June	14		2	620 00		620 00	
	30	Closing	4		620 00	—	—

ACCOUNT Utilities Expense **ACCOUNT NO.** 515

Date		Item	Post. Ref.	Debit	Credit	Balance Debit	Balance Credit
20--							
June	18		2	225 00		225 00	
	30	Closing	4		225 00	—	—

ACCOUNT Insurance Expense **ACCOUNT NO.** 516

Date		Item	Post. Ref.	Debit	Credit	Balance Debit	Balance Credit
20--							
June	30	Adj.	4	625 00		625 00	
	30	Closing	4		625 00	—	—

ACCOUNT Depreciation Expense, Equipment **ACCOUNT NO.** 517

Date		Item	Post. Ref.	Debit	Credit	Balance Debit	Balance Credit
20--							
June	30	Adj.	4	512 00		512 00	
	30	Closing	4		512 00	—	—

To: **Amy Roberts, CPA**
Subject: **Closing Entries Recorded and Posted**

Hi Amy,
I have recorded and posted the closing entries. Last time we talked, you mentioned that we need to prepare a post-closing trial balance after the closing entries. What's the purpose of that trial balance?
Thanks,
Janie

To: **Janie Conner**
Subject: **RE: Closing Entries Recorded and Posted**

Hi Janie,
That's right. The post-closing trial balance is the next step. It is prepared after the closing entries have been recorded and posted, and it will help ensure the debit balances equal the credit balances. Let's take a look at the post-closing trial balance. As always, email me back if you have questions.
Amy

THE POST-CLOSING TRIAL BALANCE

Learning Objective 3 Prepare a post-closing trial balance.

After posting the closing entries and before going on to the next fiscal period, it is important to verify the balances of the accounts that remain open. To do so, prepare a **post-closing trial balance** using the final balance figures from the ledger accounts. The purpose of the post-closing trial balance is to make sure the debit balances equal the credit balances.

Note that the accounts listed in the post-closing trial balance (assets, liabilities, and Capital) are the *real*, or *permanent*, *accounts*. (See Figure 5.) The accountant carries the balances of the permanent accounts forward from one fiscal period to another.

Figure 5
Post-closing trial balance for Conner's Whitewater Adventures

Conner's Whitewater Adventures
Post-Closing Trial Balance
June 30, 20—

Account Name	Debit	Credit
Cash	55,890	
Accounts Receivable	4,250	
Supplies	215	
Prepaid Insurance	1,250	
Equipment	51,300	
Accumulated Depreciation, Equipment		512
Accounts Payable		3,425
Wages Payable		472
J. Conner, Capital		108,496
	112,905	112,905

Notice that the *nominal*, or *temporary-equity*, *accounts* (revenue, expenses, Income Summary, and Drawing), which are closed at the end of each fiscal period, are not shown on the post-closing trial balance. These accounts are not shown because they have zero balances.

If the total debits and total credits of the post-closing trial balance are not equal, here's a recommended procedure for tracking down the error.

1. Re-add the trial balance columns.
2. Check that the figures were correctly transferred from the ledger accounts to the post-closing trial balance.
3. Verify the posting of the adjusting entries and the recording of the new balances.
4. Check that the closing entries have been posted and that all revenue, expense, Income Summary, and Drawing accounts have zero balances.

THE BASES OF ACCOUNTING: CASH AND ACCRUAL

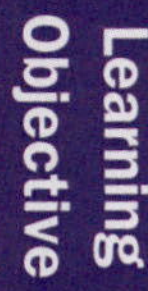

Learning Objective 4 Define cash basis and accrual basis accounting.

The basis of accounting that a company chooses has a direct effect on the company's net income and the company's income tax. The business must use the same basis of accounting from year to year, and the basis of accounting must clearly reflect the net income of the business.

Under the **cash basis of accounting**, revenue is recorded when it is received in cash and expenses are recorded when they are paid in cash. Many small businesses' and individuals' personal income taxes are recorded on the cash basis.

SMALL BUSINESS **SUCCESS**

Do I Need an Accountant?

If you are not taking this class because you want to be an accountant or a bookkeeper, you might be taking the class because you plan on owning and operating a small business. Many new small business owners take on the responsibilities of being the accountant for their business. However, at some point, your business will begin to grow, and you may need to consider hiring someone to manage your accounting books so that your time is free to run the business.

An accountant can help you in many areas of your small business, such as:

- What should my business structure be—sole proprietorship, partnership, S corporation, or corporation?
- What software should I use for my accounting?
- How do I handle the payroll for employees?
- What are my requirements for filing taxes?
- What expenses are deductible for tax purposes?
- How do I prepare financial statements when applying for a loan?

So how do you find an accountant? The best way is by referrals. Ask other businesses in your industry for references or visit your local Certified Public Accounting Society website for more recommendations (www.aicpa.org/yellow/ypascpa.htm).

Under the **accrual basis of accounting**, revenue is recorded when it is earned and expenses are recorded when they are incurred (when they occur or when the bill is received). For example, in the sale of goods, revenue is counted by the seller when the buyer accepts delivery of the goods. Expenses are recorded by the seller of the goods when the costs are incurred. Recall that this is called the matching principle because revenue in one fiscal period is matched to expenses incurred in the same period. If your business produces, purchases, or sells merchandise, the business must keep an inventory and use the accrual method for sales and purchases of merchandise.

Let's look at this example of the differences between cash and accrual. Roby Hair Salon pays $6,000 cash in July for the current month (July) and the following five months of rent (August–December). If Roby uses the cash basis of accounting, the full $6,000 will be recorded as rent expense in July. If Roby uses the accrual basis of accounting instead, the expense will be spread over the six months. The amount of $1,000 ($6,000/6) will be recorded each month.

	Cash Basis	Accrual Basis
July	$6,000	$1,000
August		1,000
September		1,000
October		1,000
November		1,000
December		1,000
TOTAL	$6,000	$6,000

Notice that the total expense recorded under both methods is the same, $6,000. The difference between the cash and the accrual basis is simply an issue of *when* the expense is recorded.

Most businesses use the same method of accounting for their financial statements and income tax reporting. Some businesses, though, are not allowed to use the cash basis method for reporting income tax. For example, corporations that average annual gross receipts of more than $5 million may not use the cash basis method. However, there are some important exceptions to this general rule. A business may use a combination of cash and accrual bases of accounting, called the *hybrid method*. Selecting a basis of accounting can often be complicated and confusing. IRS Publication 538, Accounting Periods and Methods, provides information that makes this decision less confusing. Publication 538 is available on the IRS website at www.irs.gov.

INTERIM STATEMENTS

Prepare interim statements.

Learning Objective

The owner of a business understandably does not want to wait until the end of the 12-month fiscal period to determine whether the company is making a profit or a loss. Instead, most owners want financial statements at the end of each month. Financial statements prepared during the fiscal year, for periods of less than 12 months, are called **interim statements**. (They are given this name because they are prepared within the fiscal period.) For example, a business may prepare the income statement, the statement of owner's equity, and the balance sheet *monthly*. These statements provide up-to-date

YOU Make the Call

Using the information you know about the cash basis versus the accrual basis, review the four types of businesses listed below. Consider the type of accounting transactions the following businesses might make. Then suggest whether the cash basis or the accrual basis would be a logical fit for the business.

1. An investment advisory corporation owned by outside investors with $12 million in annual gross receipts
2. A crane sales company with $1 million in annual gross receipts
3. A travel agency owned by one individual with $60,000 in annual gross receipts
4. A tractor sales company with $6 million in annual gross receipts

SOLUTION

The travel agency would probably be on the cash basis because it is a sole proprietorship. However, the investment advisory corporation would likely be on the accrual basis because its annual gross receipts exceed $5 million. The crane sales company and the tractor sales company would also use the accrual basis because both companies have inventory.

information about the results and status of operations. A company might have the following interim statements:

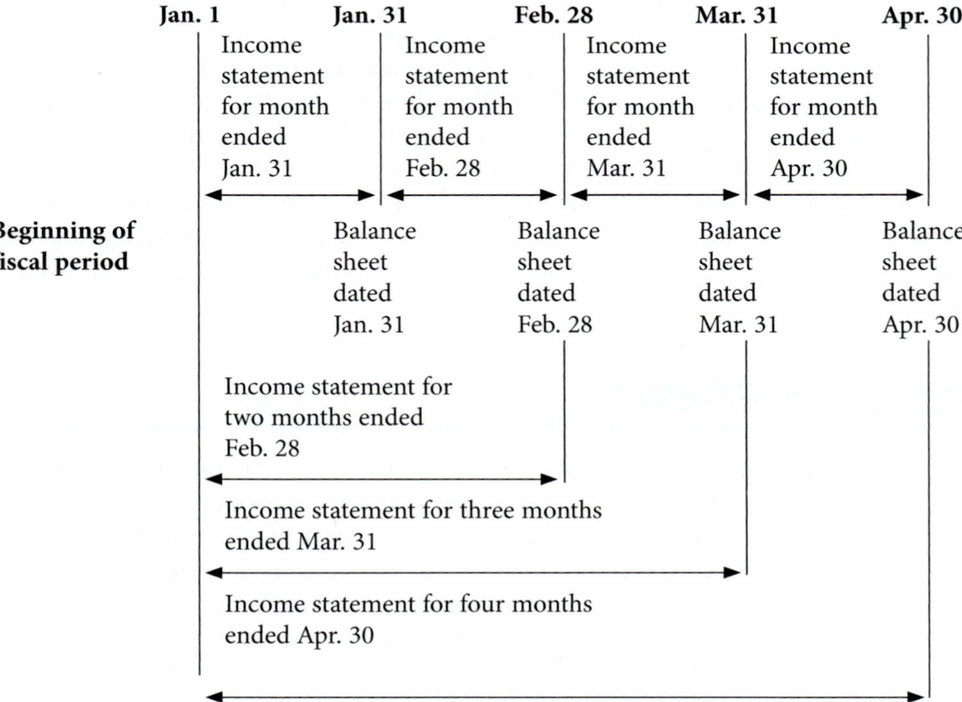

In this case, the accountant would prepare a work sheet at the end of each month. Next, based on these work sheets, he or she would journalize and post the adjusting entries and prepare the financial statements. However, the remaining steps—preparing closing entries and the post-closing trial balance—would be performed only at the end of the year.

© iStockPhoto.com/ranplett

In the Real World

Publicly traded corporations such as Electronic Arts, Inc., a leading video game publisher, are required to file interim financial statements. These interim financial statements are filed using Form 10-Q and present the quarterly (every three months) financial position of the corporation. The interim financial statements are similar to the annual financial statements but are not as detailed and are typically not verified by an auditor.

Accounting with *QuickBooks*®

Closing Entries and the Post-Closing Trial Balance

Learning Objective

 Close the fiscal period.

In QuickBooks, closing entries are completed automatically by the software. This saves users time and helps prevent errors. When using a general ledger software package, such as QuickBooks, it is important to prevent users from unintentionally posting to a prior accounting period. The QuickBooks administrator has two options to help prevent prior-period posting errors: (1) the administrator can enter a closing date in the system, which prompts QuickBooks to alert users who are entering information into a prior accounting period, or (2) the administrator can further restrict user access by requiring a password to gain access to a prior accounting period. The combination of both is recommended.

To close the fiscal period, follow the steps in Figures Q1, Q2, and Q3.

STEP 1. Click on the **Company** tab.

STEP 2. Select **Set Up Users and Passwords**.

STEP 3. Select **Set Up Users**.

Learning Objectives

After you have completed this section, you will be able to do the following:

1. Close the fiscal period.
2. View and print the post-closing trial balance.

Figure Q1
Set up users and passwords

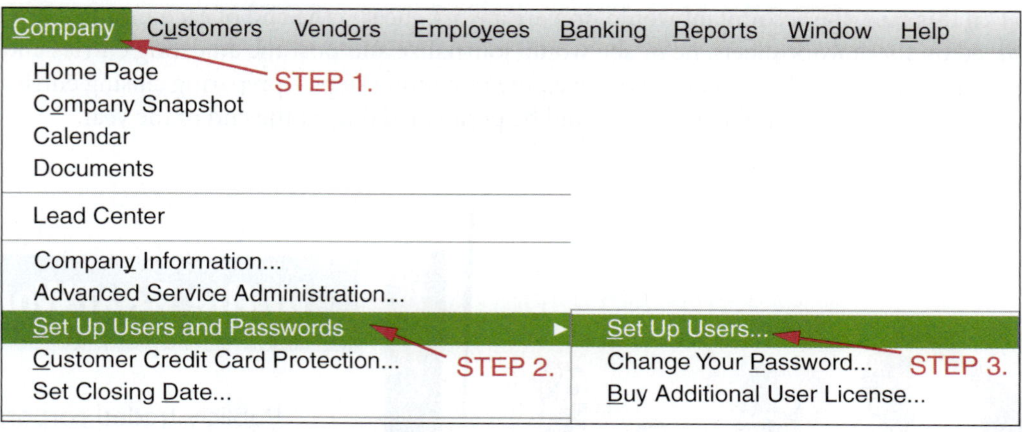

STEP 4. Click on **Closing Date**.

Figure Q2
Set the closing date

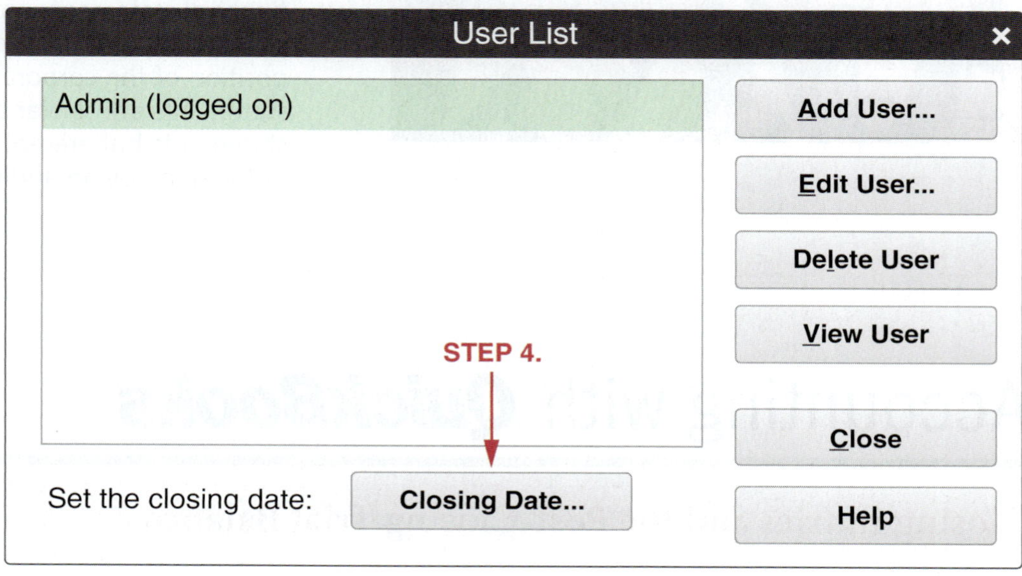

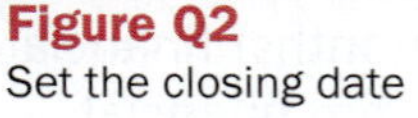

The closing date and password can also be entered from the **Accountant** tab.

STEP 5. Select **Closing Date**. This is the last day of the fiscal period.

STEP 6. Enter a **Closing Date Password** and **Confirm Password**.

STEP 7. Click **OK**.

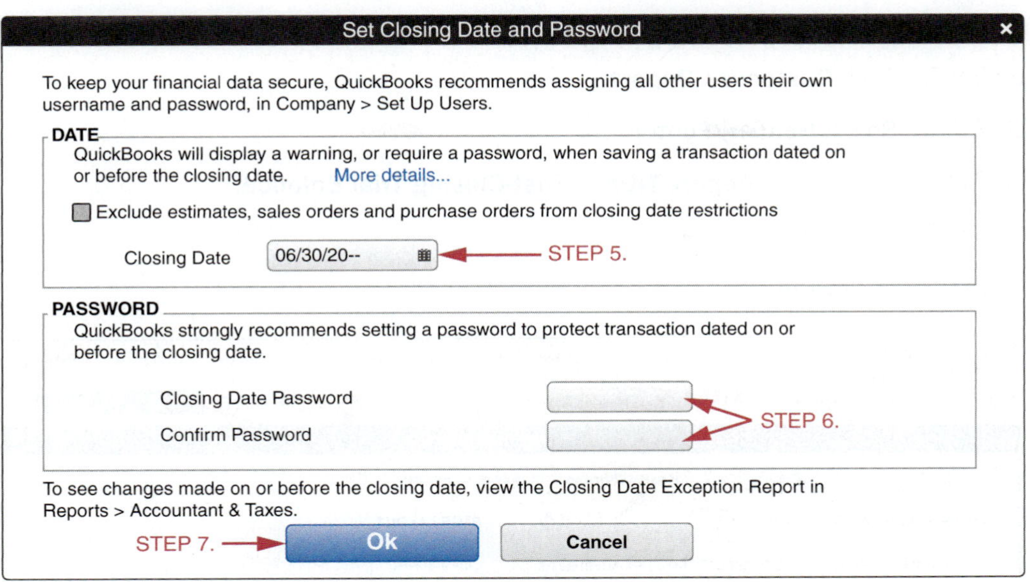

Figure Q3
Set closing date and password

Learning Objective

2 View and print the post-closing trial balance.

To view and print the post-closing trial balance, follow the steps in Figures Q4, Q5, and Q6.

STEP 1. Click **Reports**.

STEP 2. Select **Accountant & Taxes**.

STEP 3. Select **Trial Balance**.

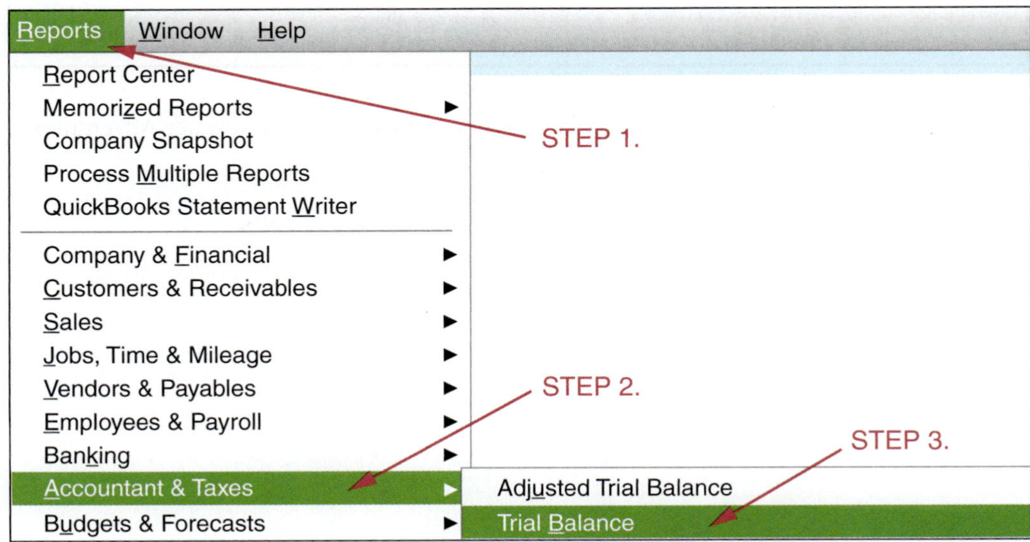

Figure Q4
View post-closing trial balance

STEP 4. Change the **From** and **To** dates and click **Refresh**.

STEP 5. Click **Customize Report**.

STEP 6. Select **Header/Footer** tab.

STEP 7. Change the **Report Title** to **Post-Closing Trial Balance**.

STEP 8. Click **OK**.

STEP 9. Click **Print**.

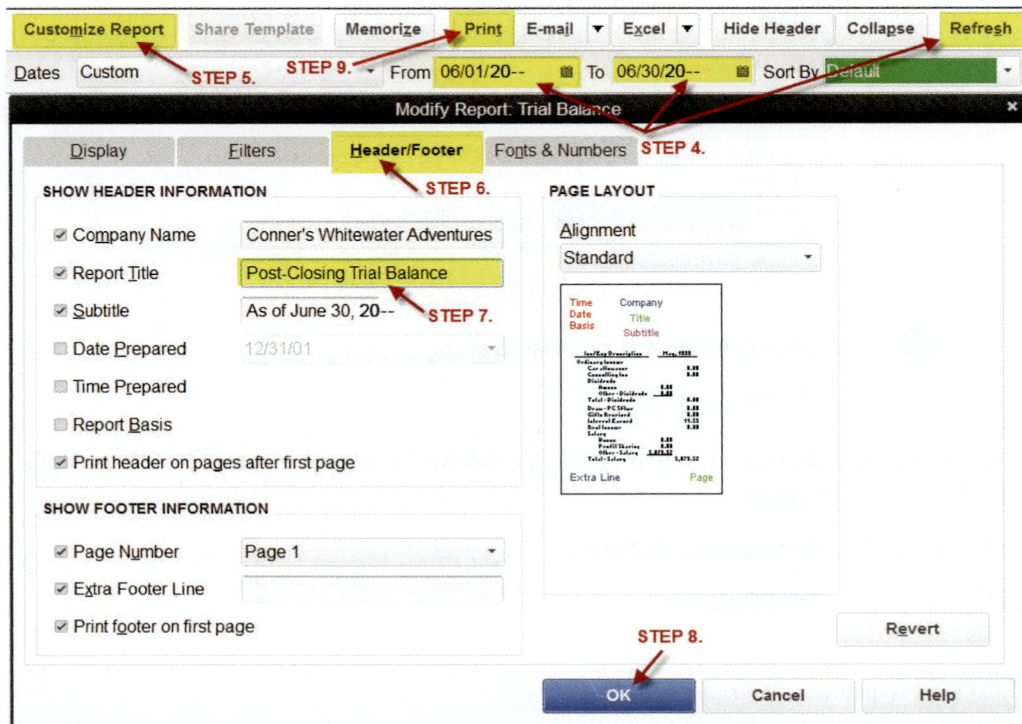

Figure Q5
Modify trial balance report to create a post-closing trial balance report

Figure Q6 shows the post-closing trial balance report for Conner's Whitewater Adventures.

Conner's Whitewater Adventures
Post-Closing Trial Balance
As of June 30, 20--

	Jun 30, 20--	
	Debit	Credit
111 Cash	55,890.00	
113 Accounts Receivable	4,250.00	
115 Supplies	215.00	
117 Prepaid Insurance	1,250.00	
124 Equipment	51,300.00	
125 Accum. Depr., Equipment		512.00
221 Accounts Payable		3,425.00
222 Wages Payable		472.00
311 J. Conner, Capital		108,496.00
312 J. Conner, Drawing	0.00	
411 Income from Tours	0.00	
511 Wages Expense	0.00	
512 Rent Expense	0.00	
513 Supplies Expense	0.00	
514 Advertising Expense	0.00	
515 Utilities Expense	0.00	
516 Insurance Expense	0.00	
517 Depreciation Expense, Equip	0.00	
TOTAL	112,905.00	112,905.00

Figure Q6
Post-closing trial balance report

ACCOUNTING WITH *QuickBooks*®

Chapter Review

Study and Practice

1 List the steps in the accounting cycle. **Learning Objective**

STEP 1. Analyze source documents and record business transactions in a journal.
STEP 2. Post journal entries to the accounts in the ledger.
STEP 3. Prepare a trial balance.
STEP 4. Gather adjustment data and record the adjusting entries on a work sheet.
STEP 5. Complete the work sheet.
STEP 6. Journalize and post the adjusting entries from the data on the work sheet.
STEP 7. Prepare financial statements from the data on the work sheet.
STEP 8. Journalize and post the **closing entries**.
STEP 9. Prepare a post-closing trial balance.

CHAPTER REVIEW

1 **PRACTICE EXERCISE 1**
Match the steps of the accounting cycle to their corresponding number.

____ 1. Step 1 a. Journalize and post the closing entries.
____ 2. Step 2 b. Prepare a trial balance.

(Continued)

____	3. Step 3	c. Analyze source documents and record business transactions in a journal.
____	4. Step 4	d. Prepare a post-closing trial balance.
____	5. Step 5	e. Prepare financial statements from the data on the work sheet.
____	6. Step 6	f. Post journal entries to the accounts in the ledger.
____	7. Step 7	g. Complete the work sheet.
____	8. Step 8	h. Journalize and post the adjusting entries from the data on the work sheet.
____	9. Step 9	i. Gather adjustment data and record the adjusting entries on a work sheet.

PRACTICE EXERCISE 1 • SOLUTION

1. c 2. f 3. b 4. i 5. g 6. h 7. e 8. a 9. d

Learning Objective  Journalize and post closing entries for a service enterprise.

The four steps in the closing procedure are as follows:

STEP 1. Close the revenue account(s) into Income Summary.

STEP 2. Close the expense account(s) into Income Summary.

STEP 3. Close the **Income Summary account** into the Capital account, transferring the net income or net loss to the Capital account.

STEP 4. Close the Drawing account into the Capital account.

2 PRACTICE EXERCISE 2

The adjusted trial balance for Larson Floral is listed below. Using this information, journalize the four closing entries.

Larson Floral
Adjusted Trial Balance
June 30, 20—

Account Name	Debit	Credit
Cash	14,600	
Accounts Receivable	500	
Supplies	335	
Prepaid Insurance	320	
Delivery Van	28,275	
Accumulated Depreciation, Delivery Van		810
Accounts Payable		750
Wages Payable		300
E. Larson, Capital		37,435
E. Larson, Drawing	1,500	
Income from Services		12,170
Wages Expense	3,600	
Rent Expense	775	
Supplies Expense	710	
Advertising Expense	270	
Utilities Expense	250	
Insurance Expense	30	
Depreciation Expense, Delivery Van	300	
	51,465	51,465

PRACTICE EXERCISE 2 • SOLUTION

GENERAL JOURNAL Page 4

Date		Description	Post. Ref.	Debit	Credit
20--		Closing Entries			
June	30	Income from Services		12,170.00	
		Income Summary			12,170.00
	30	Income Summary		5,935.00	
		Wages Expense			3,600.00
		Rent Expense			775.00
		Supplies Expense			710.00
		Advertising Expense			270.00
		Utilities Expense			250.00
		Insurance Expense			30.00
		Depreciation Expense, Delivery Van			300.00
	30	Income Summary		6,235.00	
		E. Larson, Capital			6,235.00
	30	E. Larson, Capital		1,500.00	
		E. Larson, Drawing			1,500.00

3 Prepare a post-closing trial balance. **Learning Objective**

A **post-closing trial balance** consists of the final balances of the accounts remaining open. It is the final proof that the debit balances equal the credit balances before the posting for the new fiscal period begins.

3 **PRACTICE EXERCISE 3**

Using the information in Practice Exercise 2, prepare a post-closing trial balance for Larson Floral.

PRACTICE EXERCISE 3 • SOLUTION

Larson Floral
Post-Closing Trial Balance
June 30, 20—

Account Name	Debit	Credit
Cash	14,600	
Accounts Receivable	500	
Supplies	335	
Prepaid Insurance	320	
Delivery Van	28,275	
Accumulated Depreciation, Delivery Van		810
Accounts Payable		750
Wages Payable		300
E. Larson, Capital		42,170
	44,030	44,030

Learning Objective  Define cash basis and accrual basis accounting.

Under the **cash basis of accounting**, revenue is recorded when it is received in cash, and expenses are recorded when they are paid in cash. Under the **accrual basis of accounting**, revenue is recorded when earned, even if cash is received at an earlier or a later date, and expenses are recorded when incurred, even if cash is to be paid at an earlier or a later date.

PRACTICE EXERCISE 4

Considering the following events, determine which month the revenue or expenses would be recorded using the accounting method specified.

a. Crane Company uses the *accrual basis of accounting*. Crane prepays cash in June for insurance that covers the following month, July, only.
b. Loggins & Rogers Tax Services uses the *cash basis of accounting*. Loggins & Rogers receives cash from customers in January for services to be performed in March.
c. Red Tractor Supplies Company uses the *accrual basis of accounting*. Red Tractor Supplies makes a sale to a customer in September but does not expect payment until November.
d. Norton Company uses the *cash basis of accounting*. Norton prepays cash in February for insurance that covers the following month, March, only.

PRACTICE EXERCISE 4 • SOLUTION

a. July
b. January
c. September
d. February

Learning Objective  Prepare interim statements.

Interim statements consist of year-to-date income statements, statements of owner's equity, and balance sheets as of various dates during the fiscal period.

PRACTICE EXERCISE 5

Assume that Larson Floral's fiscal period does not end on June 30 but rather December 31. Using the information from Practice Exercise 2, complete an interim balance sheet for June for Larson Floral.

PRACTICE EXERCISE 5 • SOLUTION

Larson Floral
Balance Sheet
June 30, 20--

Assets		
Cash		$14,600
Accounts Receivable		500
Supplies		335
Prepaid Insurance		320
Delivery Van	$28,275	
Less Accumulated Depreciation	810	27,465
Total Assets		$43,220
Liabilities		
Accounts Payable	$ 750	
Wages Payable	300	
Total Liabilities		$ 1,050
Owner's Equity		
E. Larson, Capital		42,170
Total Liabilities and Owner's Equity		$43,220

Glossary

Accrual basis of accounting An accounting method under which revenue is recorded when it is earned, regardless of when it is received, and expenses are recorded when they are incurred, regardless of when they are paid. (*p. 235*)

Cash basis of accounting An accounting method under which revenue is recorded only when it is received in cash, and expenses are recorded only when they are paid in cash. (*p. 234*)

Closing entries Entries made at the end of a fiscal period to close off the revenue, expense, and Drawing accounts—that is, to make the balances of the temporary-equity accounts equal to zero. Closing is also called *clearing the accounts*. (*p. 224*)

Income Summary account An account brought into existence as a debit to balance expense accounts or as a credit to balance revenue accounts in the closing entry process. The revenue and expense account balances are transferred to this account to allow calculations of net income or net loss. (*p. 225*)

Interim statements Financial statements, covering a period that is less than 12 months, that are prepared during the fiscal year. (*p. 235*)

Nominal (temporary-equity) accounts Accounts that apply to only one fiscal period and that are to be closed at the end of that fiscal period. These are the revenue, expense, and Drawing accounts. This category may also be described as all accounts except assets, liabilities, and the Capital account. (*p. 229*)

Post-closing trial balance The listing of the final balances of the real accounts at the end of the fiscal period. (*p. 233*)

Real (permanent) accounts The accounts that remain open (assets, liabilities, and the Capital account in owner's equity) and have balances that will be carried over to the next fiscal period. (*p. 229*)

CHAPTER REVIEW

Quiz Yourself

_____ 1. What is the third step in the accounting cycle?
   a. Analyze source documents and record business transactions in a journal.
   b. Prepare a post-closing trial balance.
   c. Journalize and post the closing entries.
   d. Prepare a trial balance.

_____ 2. Which of the following accounts would be closed during the closing process?
   a. Service Revenue
   b. Cash
   c. B. Williams, Capital
   d. Accumulated Depreciation, Equipment

_____ 3. If Income from Services had a $20,400 credit balance before closing entries, which of the following would be the appropriate closing entry to close revenues?

a. Income from Services	20,400	
Cash		20,400
b. Income from Services	20,400	
Income Summary		20,400
c. Income Summary	20,400	
J. Crestview, Capital		20,400
d. J. Crestview, Capital	20,400	
Income from Services		20,400

_____ 4. Which of the following accounts would appear on a post-closing trial balance?
   a. Depreciation Expense, Equipment
   b. Income from Services
   c. R. McDonald, Drawing
   d. R. McDonald, Capital

_____ 5. Under the cash basis method of accounting, which of the following statements is true?
   a. Revenue is recorded when it is earned regardless of when the cash is received.
   b. Expenses are recorded when they are paid.
   c. Expenses are recorded when they are incurred regardless of when the cash is paid.
   d. The cash basis of accounting is allowed for all corporations.

_____ 6. __________ are prepared during the fiscal year for periods of less than 12 months.
   a. Work sheets
   b. Intermediary statements
   c. Interim statements
   d. In-between statements

Answers:
1. d 2. a 3. b 4. d 5. b 6. c

Review It with QuickBooks®

_____ 1. In QuickBooks, closing entries are completed
   a. manually, using the General Journal.
   b. automatically, using the General Journal.
   c. automatically, setting the closing date.
   d. All of the above

_____ 2. The QuickBooks administrator can prevent prior-period posting errors by
   a. entering the closing date to alert users they are in a prior period.
   b. requiring a password to gain access to a prior accounting period.
   c. Both a and b
   d. Neither a nor b

_____ 3. In QuickBooks, the post-closing trial balance report is located under
   a. Company & Financial.
   b. Accountant & Taxes.
   c. Custom Reports.
   d. All of the above

_____ 4. __________ allows the modification of a report title.
   a. Lists
   b. Help
   c. Favorites
   d. Customize Report

Answers:
1. c 2. c 3. b. 4. d

Chapter Assignments

Discussion Questions

1. Number in order the following steps in the accounting cycle.
   a. Prepare a trial balance.
   b. Post journal entries to the accounts in the ledger.
   c. Journalize and post the adjusting entries from the data on the work sheet.
   d. Analyze source documents and record business transactions in a journal.
   e. Prepare financial statements from the data on the work sheet.
   f. Gather adjustment data and record the adjusting entries on a work sheet.
   g. Journalize and post the closing entries.
   h. Prepare a post-closing trial balance.
   i. Complete the work sheet.
2. List the steps in the closing procedure in the correct order.
3. What is the purpose of closing entries? What is a consequence of forgetting to make closing entries?
4. What are real accounts? What are nominal accounts? Give examples of each.
5. What is the purpose of the Income Summary account? How does it relate to the revenue and expense accounts?
6. What is the purpose of the post-closing trial balance? What is the difference between a trial balance and a post-closing trial balance?
7. Write the third closing entry to transfer the net income or net loss to the P. Hernandez, Capital account, assuming the following:
   a. A net income of $3,842 during the first quarter (Jan.–Mar.)
   b. A net loss of $1,781 during the second quarter (Apr.–Jun.)
8. When would revenue and expenses be recorded if a business used a cash basis of accounting? If a business used an accrual basis of accounting?
9. What are interim financial statements? Why would a business want to prepare them?

Exercises

LO 2
Practice Exercise 2

EXERCISE 5-1 Classify the following accounts as real (permanent) or nominal (temporary) and indicate with an X whether the account is closed. Also indicate the financial statement in which each account will appear. The Building account is given as an example.

(*Continued*)

Account Title	Real	Nominal	Closed: Yes	Closed: No	Income Statement	Balance Sheet
0. Example: Building	X			X		X
a. Prepaid Insurance						
b. Accounts Payable						
c. Wages Payable						
d. Services Revenue						
e. Rent Expense						
f. Supplies Expense						
g. Accum. Depr., Equipment						

LO 2

Practice Exercise 2

EXERCISE 5–2 The ledger accounts after adjusting entries for Cortez Services are presented below.

a. Journalize the following closing entries and number as steps 1 through 4.

b. What is the new balance of J. Cortez, Capital after closing? Show your calculations.

Owner's Equity

Assets	=	Liabilities	+	Capital	−	Drawing	+	Revenue	−	Expenses
+ Debit / − Credit		− Debit / + Credit		− Debit / + Credit		+ Debit / − Credit		− Debit / + Credit		+ Debit / − Credit

Cash

Debit	Credit
Bal. 8,500	

Wages Payable

Debit	Credit
	(a) 210

J. Cortez, Capital

Debit	Credit
	Bal. 24,000

J. Cortez, Drawing

Debit	Credit
Bal. 400	

Professional Fees

Debit	Credit
	Bal. 3,850

Wages Expense

Debit	Credit
Bal. 2,900	
(a) 210	
Bal. 3,110	

Prepaid Insurance

Debit	Credit
Bal. 990	(c) 460
Bal. 530	

Insurance Expense

Debit	Credit
(c) 460	

Equipment

Debit	Credit
Bal. 18,125	

Depr. Expense, Equipment

Debit	Credit
(b) 750	

Accum. Depr., Equipment

Debit	Credit
	Bal. 3,200
	(b) 750
	Bal. 3,950

Misc. Expense

Debit	Credit
Bal. 135	

LO 2 Practice Exercise 2

EXERCISE 5-3 As of December 31, the end of the current year, the ledger of Harris Company contained the following account balances after adjustment. All accounts have normal balances. Journalize the closing entries.

Cash	$ 8,440	C. Harris, Drawing	$1,498
Equipment	11,586	Professional Fees	7,075
Accumulated Depreciation, Equipment	2,587	Wages Expense	1,268
		Rent Expense	1,090
Accounts Payable	1,674	Depreciation Expense, Equipment	1,143
Wages Payable	658		
C. Harris, Capital	13,376	Miscellaneous Expense	345

LO 2 Practice Exercise 2

EXERCISE 5-4 The Income Statement columns of the work sheet of Dunn Company for the fiscal year ended June 30 follow. During the year, K. Dunn withdrew $4,000. Journalize the closing entries.

	A	H	I
5		INCOME STATEMENT	
6	ACCOUNT NAME	DEBIT	CREDIT
7	Service Revenue		6,797.00
8	Rental Revenue		3,576.00
9	Rent Expense	2,800.00	
10	Wages Expense	1,854.00	
11	Utilities Expense	465.00	
12	Miscellaneous Expense	59.00	
13		5,178.00	10,373.00
14	Net Income	5,195.00	
15		10,373.00	10,373.00
16			

Sheet1 Sheet2 Sheet3

LO 2 Practice Exercise 2

EXERCISE 5-5 The Income Statement columns of the work sheet of Cederblom Company for the fiscal year ended December 31 follow. During the year, S. Cederblom withdrew $17,000. Journalize the closing entries.

	A	H	I
5		INCOME STATEMENT	
6	ACCOUNT NAME	DEBIT	CREDIT
7	Service Revenue		29,960.00
8	Rental Revenue		22,000.00
9	Wages Expense	48,520.00	
10	Utilities Expense	7,130.00	
11	Miscellaneous Expense	2,200.00	
12		57,850.00	51,960.00
13	Net Income		5,890.00
14		57,850.00	57,850.00
15			

Sheet1 Sheet2 Sheet3

 2

Practice Exercise 2

EXERCISE 5-6 After all revenue and expenses have been closed at the end of the fiscal period ended December 31, Income Summary has a debit of $45,550 and a credit of $36,520. On the same date, D. Mau, Drawing has a debit balance of $12,000 and D. Mau, Capital had a beginning credit balance of $63,410.

a. Journalize the entries to close the remaining temporary accounts.

b. What is the new balance of D. Mau, Capital after closing the remaining temporary accounts? Show your calculations.

 3

Practice Exercise 3

EXERCISE 5-7 Identify whether the following accounts would be included on a post-closing trial balance.

Account Title	Post-Closing Trial Balance	
	Yes	No
0. Example: Cash	X	
a. Income from Services		
b. Prepaid Insurance		
c. Supplies Expense		
d. Accounts Payable		
e. F. Oz, Drawing		
f. Depreciation Expense, Equipment		
g. Wages Payable		
h. Accounts Receivable		
i. Wages Expense		
j. Accumulated Depreciation, Equipment		
k. F. Oz, Capital		

LO 4

Practice Exercise 4

EXERCISE 5-8 Considering the following events, determine which month the revenue or expenses would be recorded using the accounting method specified.

a. Gerber Company uses the *cash basis of accounting*. Gerber prepays cash in April for insurance that covers the following month, May, only.

b. Matthews and Dudley Attorneys uses the *accrual basis of accounting*. Matthews and Dudley Attorneys receives cash from customers in March for services to be performed in April.

c. Eckstein Company uses the *accrual basis of accounting*. Eckstein prepays cash in October for rent that covers the following month, November, only.

d. Gerbino Company uses the *cash basis of accounting*. Gerbino makes a sale to a customer in July but does not expect payment until August.

LO 5

Practice Exercise 5

EXERCISE 5-9 Indicate with an X whether each of the following would appear on the income statement, statement of owner's equity, or balance sheet. An item may appear on more than one statement. The first item is provided as an example.

Item	Income Statement	Statement of Owner's Equity	Balance Sheet
0. Example: The total liabilities of the business at the end of the year.			X
a. The amount of the owner's Capital balance at the end of the year.			
b. The amount of depreciation expense on equipment during the year.			
c. The amount of the company's net income for the year.			
d. The book value of the equipment.			
e. Total insurance expired during the year.			
f. Total accounts receivable at the end of the year.			
g. Total withdrawals by the owner.			
h. The cost of utilities used during the year.			
i. The amount of the owner's Capital balance at the beginning of the year.			

LO 5

Practice Exercise 5

EXERCISE 5-10 Prepare a statement of owner's equity for The Lindal Clinic for the year ended December 31. P. Lindal's capital amount on January 1 was $124,000, and there was an additional investment of $7,000 on May 12 and withdrawals of $31,500 for the year. Net income for the year was $20,418.

Problem Set A

LO 2

PROBLEM 5-1A After the accountant posted the adjusting entries for B. Lyon, Designer, the work sheet contained the following account balances on May 31:

	A	F	G
5		ADJUSTED TRIAL BALANCE	
6	ACCOUNT NAME	DEBIT	CREDIT
7	Cash	2,018.00	
8	Supplies	300.00	
9	Accounts Receivable	1,408.00	
10	Prepaid Insurance	987.00	
11	Office Equipment	5,790.00	
12	Accumulated Depreciation, Office Equipment		1,372.00
13	Accounts Payable		880.00
14	B. Lyon, Capital		7,520.00
15	B. Lyon, Drawing	1,550.00	
16	Commissions Earned		4,679.00
17	Rent Expense	995.00	
18	Supplies Expense	575.00	
19	Depreciation Expense, Office Equipment	462.00	
20	Utilities Expense	269.00	
21	Miscellaneous Expense	97.00	
22		14,451.00	14,451.00
23			

Sheet1 Sheet2 Sheet3

(Continued)

Check Figure
Net Income, $2,281

Required

1. Write the owner's name on the Capital and Drawing T accounts.
2. Record the account balances in the T accounts for owner's equity, revenue, and expenses.
3. Journalize the closing entries using the four steps in correct order. Number the closing entries 1 through 4.
4. Post the closing entries to the T accounts immediately after you journalize each one to see the effect of the closing entries. Number the closing entries 1 through 4.

2

PROBLEM 5-2A The partial work sheet for Ho Consulting for May follows:

	A	H	I	J	K
5		INCOME STATEMENT		BALANCE SHEET	
6	ACCOUNT NAME	DEBIT	CREDIT	DEBIT	CREDIT
7	Cash			5,710.00	
8	Supplies			209.00	
9	Prepaid Insurance			1,123.00	
10	Equipment			5,731.00	
11	Accumulated Depreciation, Equipment				1,444.00
12	Accounts Payable				1,841.00
13	G. Ho, Capital				4,302.00
14	G. Ho, Drawing			2,400.00	
15	Consulting Revenue		13,060.00		
16	Rent Expense	2,200.00			
17	Wages Expense	1,828.00			
18	Supplies Expense	422.00			
19	Miscellaneous Expense	230.00			
20					
21	Insurance Expense	325.00			
22	Depreciation Expense, Equipment	835.00			
23	Wages Payable				366.00
24		5,840.00	13,060.00	15,173.00	7,953.00
25	Net Income	7,220.00			7,220.00
26		13,060.00	13,060.00	15,173.00	15,173.00
27					

Sheet1 Sheet2 Sheet3

Check Figure
Debit to Income Summary, second entry, $5,840

Required

1. Write the owner's name on the Capital and Drawing T accounts.
2. Record the account balances in the T accounts for owner's equity, revenue, and expenses.
3. Journalize the closing entries using the four steps in correct order. Number the closing entries 1 through 4.
4. Post the closing entries to the T accounts immediately after you journalize each one to see the effect of the closing entries. Number the closing entries 1 through 4.

1, 2, 3

PROBLEM 5-3A The completed work sheet for Valerie Insurance Agency as of December 31 is presented in your Working Papers or in CengageNow, along with the general ledger as of December 31 before adjustments.

Required

1. Write the name of the owner, M. Valerie, in the Capital and Drawing accounts.
2. Write the balances from the unadjusted trial balance in the general ledger.
3. Journalize and post the adjusting entries.
4. Journalize and post the closing entries in the correct order.
5. Prepare a post-closing trial balance.

Check Figure
Post-closing trial balance total, $10,170

LO 1, 2, 3

PROBLEM 5-4A The account balances of Bryan Company as of June 30, the end of the current fiscal year, are as follows:

	A	B	C
5		TRIAL BALANCE	
6	ACCOUNT NAME	DEBIT	CREDIT
7	Cash	5,491.00	
8	Accounts Receivable	624.00	
9	Supplies	397.00	
10	Prepaid Insurance	1,280.00	
11	Equipment	6,497.00	
12	Accumulated Depreciation, Equipment		2,672.00
13	Van	10,989.00	
14	Accumulated Depreciation, Van		4,368.00
15	Accounts Payable		1,036.00
16	B. Bryan, Capital		18,583.00
17	B. Bryan, Drawing	18,000.00	
18	Fees Earned		38,417.00
19	Salary Expense	18,600.00	
20	Advertising Expense	1,887.00	
21	Van Operating Expense	462.00	
22	Utilities Expense	685.00	
23	Miscellaneous Expense	164.00	
24		65,076.00	65,076.00
25			

Sheet1 Sheet2 Sheet3

Required

1. Data for the adjustments are as follows:
   a. Expired or used up insurance, $495
   b. Depreciation expense on equipment, $670.
   c. Depreciation expense on the van, $1,190.
   d. Salary accrued (earned) since the last payday, $540 (owed and to be paid on the next payday).
   e. Supplies used during the period, $97.

   Your instructor may want you to use a work sheet for these adjustments.
2. Journalize the adjusting entries.
3. Prepare an income statement.
4. Prepare a statement of owner's equity; assume that there was an additional investment of $2,000 on June 10. (Skip this step if using QuickBooks. The additional investment assumption has already been completed in the data file.)
5. Prepare a balance sheet.
6. Journalize the closing entries using the four steps in the correct sequence.

Check Figure
Net Income, $13,627

 2, 3, 5

PROBLEM 5-5A Williams Mechanic Services prepared the following work sheet for the year ended March 31, 20--.

	A	B	C	D	E	F	G
1				Williams Mechanic Services			
2				Work Sheet			
3				For Year Ended March 31, 20—			
4							
5		TRIAL BALANCE		ADJUSTMENTS		ADJUSTED TRIAL BALANCE	
6	ACCOUNT NAME	DEBIT	CREDIT	DEBIT	CREDIT	DEBIT	CREDIT
7	Cash	6,500.00				6,500.00	
8	Accounts Receivable	1,250.00				1,250.00	
9	Supplies	415.00			(e) 200.00	215.00	
10	Prepaid Insurance	2,175.00			(a) 175.00	2,000.00	
11	Equipment	3,500.00				3,500.00	
12	Accumulated Depreciation, Equipment		1,200.00		(b) 75.00		1,275.00
13	Truck	18,300.00				18,300.00	
14	Accumulated Depreciation, Truck		4,000.00		(c) 300.00		4,300.00
15	Accounts Payable		800.00				800.00
16	J. Williams, Capital		16,940.00				16,940.00
17	J. Williams, Drawing	3,000.00				3,000.00	
18	Fees Earned		15,000.00				15,000.00
19	Salary Expense	1,200.00		(d) 125.00		1,325.00	
20	Advertising Expense	600.00				600.00	
21	Truck Operating Expense	250.00				250.00	
22	Utilities Expense	600.00				600.00	
23	Miscellaneous Expense	150.00				150.00	
24		37,940.00	37,940.00				
25	Insurance Expense			(a) 175.00		175.00	
26	Depreciation Expense, Equipment			(b) 75.00		75.00	
27	Depreciation Expense, Truck			(c) 300.00		300.00	
28	Salaries Payable				(d) 125.00		125.00
29	Supplies Expense			(e) 200.00		200.00	
30				875.00	875.00	38,440.00	38,440.00
31							

Sheet1 Sheet2 Sheet3

QuickBooks

Check Figure
Post-closing trial balance total, $31,765

Required

1. Complete the work sheet. (Skip this step if using QuickBooks or general ledger.)
2. Prepare an income statement.
3. Prepare a statement of owner's equity; assume that there was an additional investment of $5,000 on March 13. (Skip this step if using QuickBooks. The additional investment assumption has already been completed in the data file.)
4. Prepare a balance sheet.
5. Journalize the closing entries using the four steps in the correct sequence.
6. Prepare a post-closing trial balance. (For QuickBooks, select the trial balance report, then modify the report name to *Post-Closing Trial Balance*.)

Problem Set B

 2

PROBLEM 5-1B After the accountant posted the adjusting entries for M. Wally, Designer, the work sheet contained the following account balances on May 31:

	A	F	G
5		ADJUSTED TRIAL BALANCE	
6	ACCOUNT NAME	DEBIT	CREDIT
7	Cash	2,029.00	
8	Accounts Receivable	886.00	
9	Supplies	400.00	
10	Prepaid Insurance	1,460.00	
11	Office Equipment	4,672.00	
12	Accumulated Depreciation, Office Equipment		1,170.00
13	Accounts Payable		943.00
14	M. Wally, Capital		9,221.00
15	M. Wally, Drawing	1,600.00	
16	Commissions Earned		1,997.00
17	Rent Expense	990.00	
18	Supplies Expense	480.00	
19	Depreciation Expense, Office Equipment	420.00	
20	Utilities Expense	286.00	
21	Miscellaneous Expense	108.00	
22		13,331.00	13,331.00
23			

Sheet1 Sheet2 Sheet3

Required

1. Write the owner's name on the Capital and Drawing T accounts.
2. Record the account balances in the T accounts for owner's equity, revenue, and expenses.
3. Journalize the closing entries using the four steps in correct order. Number the closing entries 1 through 4.
4. Post the closing entries to the T accounts immediately after you journalize each one to see the effect of the closing entries. Number the closing entries 1 through 4.

Check Figure
Net Loss, $287

2

PROBLEM 5-2B The partial work sheet for Emil Consulting for June is as follows:

	A	H	I	J	K
5		INCOME STATEMENT		BALANCE SHEET	
6	ACCOUNT NAME	DEBIT	CREDIT	DEBIT	CREDIT
7	Cash			6,000.00	
8	Supplies			104.00	
9	Prepaid Insurance			1,344.00	
10	Equipment			6,751.00	
11	Accumulated Depreciation, Equipment				4,212.00
12	Accounts Payable				1,356.00
13	W. Emil, Capital				5,367.00
14	W. Emil, Drawing			1,700.00	
15	Consulting Fees		9,546.00		
16	Rent Expense	1,800.00			
17	Wages Expense	1,533.00			
18	Miscellaneous Expense	168.00			
19					
20	Supplies Expense	365.00			
21	Insurance Expense	364.00			
22	Depreciation Expense, Equipment	700.00			
23	Wages Payable				348.00
24		4,930.00	9,546.00	15,899.00	11,283.00
25	Net Income	4,616.00			4,616.00
26		9,546.00	9,546.00	15,899.00	15,899.00
27					

Sheet1 Sheet2 Sheet3

(*Continued*)

CHAPTER ASSIGNMENTS

Check Figure
Debit to Income Summary, second entry, $4,930

Required

1. Write the owner's name on the Capital and Drawing T accounts.
2. Record the account balances in the T accounts for owner's equity, revenue, and expenses.
3. Journalize the closing entries using the four steps in correct order. Number the closing entries 1 through 4.
4. Post the closing entries to the T accounts immediately after you journalize each one to see the effect of the closing entries. Number closing entries 1 through 4.

1, 2, 3

Check Figure
Post-closing trial balance total, $9,147

PROBLEM 5-3B The completed work sheet for Oliver Tour Company as of December 31 is presented in your Working Papers or in CengageNow, along with the general ledger as of December 31 before adjustments.

Required

1. Write the name of the owner, S. Oliver, in the Capital and Drawing accounts.
2. Write the balances from the unadjusted trial balance in the general ledger.
3. Journalize and post the adjusting entries.
4. Journalize and post the closing entries in the correct order.
5. Prepare a post-closing trial balance.

1, 2, 3

PROBLEM 5-4B The account balances of Miss Beverly's Tutoring Service as of June 30, the end of the current fiscal year, are as follows:

	A	B	C
5		TRIAL BALANCE	
6	ACCOUNT NAME	DEBIT	CREDIT
7	Cash	6,491.00	
8	Accounts Receivable	624.00	
9	Supplies	527.00	
10	Prepaid Insurance	1,280.00	
11	Equipment	5,497.00	
12	Accumulated Depreciation, Equipment		2,472.00
13	Van	13,674.00	
14	Accumulated Depreciation, Van		4,168.00
15	Accounts Payable		1,436.00
16	B. Morrow, Capital		14,848.00
17	B. Morrow, Drawing	18,000.00	
18	Fees Earned		43,680.00
19	Salary Expense	16,000.00	
20	Advertising Expense	2,200.00	
21	Van Operating Expense	705.00	
22	Utilities Expense	1,248.00	
23	Miscellaneous Expense	358.00	
24		66,604.00	66,604.00
25			

Sheet1 Sheet2 Sheet3

Check Figure
Net income, $19,567

Required

1. Data for the adjustments are as follows:
   a. Expired or used up insurance, $470.
   b. Depreciation expense on equipment, $948.
   c. Depreciation expense on the van, $1,490.
   d. Salary accrued (earned) since the last payday, $574 (owed and to be paid on the next payday).
   e. Supplies remaining as of June 30, $407.

   Your instructor may want you to use a work sheet for these adjustments.

2. Journalize the adjusting entries.
3. Prepare an income statement.
4. Prepare a statement of owner's equity; assume that there was an additional investment of $3,000 on June 10. (Skip this step if using QuickBooks. The additional investment assumption has already been completed in the data file.)
5. Prepare a balance sheet.
6. Journalize the closing entries using the four steps in the proper sequence.

LO 2, 3, 5

PROBLEM 5-5B Tom's Catering Services prepared the following work sheet for the year ended December 31, 20--.

	A	B	C	E	G	I	K
1	Tom's Catering Services						
2	Work Sheet						
3	For Year Ended December 31, 20--						
4							
5		TRIAL BALANCE		ADJUSTMENTS		ADJUSTED TRIAL BALANCE	
6	ACCOUNT NAME	DEBIT	CREDIT	DEBIT	CREDIT	DEBIT	CREDIT
7	Cash	2,400.00				2,400.00	
8	Accounts Receivable	800.00				800.00	
9	Supplies	225.00			(e) 80.00	145.00	
10	Prepaid Insurance	1,200.00			(a) 100.00	1,100.00	
11	Equipment	2,220.00				2,220.00	
12	Accumulated Depreciation, Equipment		370.00		(b) 185.00		555.00
13	Truck	25,000.00				25,000.00	
14	Accumulated Depreciation, Truck		5,000.00		(c) 1,000.00		6,000.00
15	Accounts Payable		250.00				250.00
16	Y. Tom, Capital		26,500.00				26,500.00
17	Y. Tom, Drawing	1,500.00				1,500.00	
18	Fees Earned		2,400.00				2,400.00
19	Salary Expense	640.00		(d) 80.00		720.00	
20	Advertising Expense	130.00				130.00	
21	Truck Operating Expense	125.00				125.00	
22	Utilities Expense	200.00				200.00	
23	Miscellaneous Expense	80.00				80.00	
24		34,520.00	34,520.00				
25	Insurance Expense			(a) 100.00		100.00	
26	Depreciation Expense, Equipment			(b) 185.00		185.00	
27	Depreciation Expense, Truck			(c) 1,000.00		1,000.00	
28	Salaries Payable				(d) 80.00		80.00
29	Supplies Expense			(e) 80.00		80.00	
30				1,445.00	1,445.00	35,785.00	35,785.00
31							

Sheet1 Sheet2 Sheet3

Required

1. Complete the work sheet. (Skip this step if using QuickBooks or general ledger.)
2. Prepare an income statement.
3. Prepare a statement of owner's equity; assume that there was an additional investment of $2,500 on December 1. (Skip this step if using QuickBooks. The additional investment assumption has already been completed in the data file.)
4. Prepare a balance sheet.
5. Journalize the closing entries with the four steps in the correct sequence.
6. Prepare a post-closing trial balance. (For QuickBooks, select the trial balance report, then modify the report name to *Post-Closing Trial Balance*.)

Check Figure
Post-closing trial balance total, $31,665

Try It with QuickBooks® (LO 1, 2)

QB Exercise 5-1

Using the Conner's Whitewater Adventures demonstration file for Chapter 5, complete the following activities with QuickBooks:

1. Set the closing date to June 30, 2015.
2. Record the closing entry for J. Conner, Drawing to J. Conner, Capital.
3. View and print the post-closing trial balance report for Conner's Whitewater Adventures as of July 1, 2015. (Both the From and To dates should be July 1, 2015. Be sure to change the report title to *Post-Closing Trial Balance.*)
   a. What is the ending balance of the Debit column for the post-closing trial balance?
   b. What is the ending balance in the J. Conner, Drawing account?
   c. What is the ending balance of the Wages Payable account on the post-closing trial balance? Is this a debit or a credit? What is the classification of this account?
   d. What is the total owner's equity for Conner's Whitewater Adventures as of July 1, 2015?

For the problem listed above, the QuickBooks data file is not set up to automatically close the temporary accounts. Journalize the closing entries using *Make General Journal Entries*. In the memo field, identify the entry as *Closing Entry*.

Activities

Why Does It Matter?

REAL GAP EXPERIENCE, Tunbridge Wells, Kent (UK)

Rather than going directly to college, some students take time off to travel abroad, learn new skills, or volunteer. This period is known as a "gap year." Real Gap Experience provides hundreds of gap year traveling opportunities in over 45 countries around the world. The company offers everything from volunteering to building houses in Guatemala to teaching in China (for pay) to taking a year-long, around-the-world trip. What does this have to do with accounting, and why is it important? Every company needs to keep a record of its financial activities so that financial statements can be presented and used for decision making. Real Gap Experience's accounting records are most likely computerized, but the company still needs to go through the closing process. Why is the closing process important to a company such as Real Gap Experience? What types of accounts would be used during the closing process for this company?

What Would You Say?

Your uncle owns a small sole proprietorship. He does his own bookkeeping, although he didn't finish the chapter on closing entries before he opened his business. He mentions to you that closing entries look like they take a long time. He wonders why he should bother to do them because all he really looks at is the checkbook. What would you say to convince him that closing entries are necessary?

What Do You Think?

On the next page is the post-closing trial balance submitted to you by the bookkeeper of Tafoya Consulting Company. Assume that the debit total ($41,048) is correct.

a. Analyze the work and prepare a response to what you have reviewed.
b. Journalize the closing entries.
c. What is the net income or net loss?
d. Is there an increase or a decrease in Capital?
e. What would be the ending amount of Capital?
f. What is the new balance of the post-closing trial balance?

Tafoya Consulting Company
Post-Closing Trial Balance
December 31, 20--

Account Name	Debit	Credit
Cash	3,412	
Accounts Receivable	1,693	
Prepaid Insurance	2,147	
Accounts Payable		?
C. Tafoya, Capital		13,818
C. Tafoya, Drawing	6,360	
Consulting Fees		25,603
Wages Expense	11,994	
Rent Expense	9,600	
Advertising Expense	2,582	
Supplies Expense	914	
Insurance Expense	1,610	
Miscellaneous Expense	736	
	41,048	41,048

What Would You Do?

You are preparing a post-closing trial balance for the company where you work, but it doesn't balance. You are tired, and besides, you don't think the company pays you for this much hassle and extra time. You decide to increase the balance of an asset account to make the totals balance. Discuss this action and explain whether it is ethical or illegal.

What's Wrong with This Picture?

The bookkeeper has completed a work sheet and has journalized and posted the closing entries, but he forgot to journalize and post the adjusting entries from the work sheet. What are the effects of these actions and omissions? How would these actions and omissions affect the accounting records and the resulting financial statements?

BEFORE A TEST CHECK: Chapters 4–5

PART 1: Multiple-Choice Questions

_____ 1. The net income appears on all of the following statements except
a. the statement of owner's equity.
b. the balance sheet.
c. the income statement.
d. all of the above.
e. none of the above.

_____ 2. Which of the following entries records the withdrawal of cash for personal use by Dolan, the owner of a business firm?
a. Debit Cash and credit Drawing.
b. Debit Salary Expense and credit Cash.
c. Debit Cash and credit Salary Expense.
d. Debit Drawing and credit Cash.
e. None of the above.

_____ 3. Which of the following errors, considered individually, would cause the trial balance totals to be unequal?
a. A payment of $52 for supplies was posted as a debit of $52 to Supplies Expense and a credit of $25 to Cash.
b. A payment of $625 to a creditor was posted as a debit of $625 to Accounts Payable and a debit of $625 to Cash.
c. Cash received from customers on account was posted as a debit of $380 to Cash and a credit of $38 to Accounts Receivable.
d. All of the above.
e. None of the above.

_____ 4. The balance in the Prepaid Insurance account before adjustment at the end of the year is $600. This represents six months' insurance paid on November 1. No adjusting entry was made on November 30. The adjusting entry required on December 31 is
a. debit Insurance Expense, $200; credit Prepaid Insurance, $200.
b. debit Prepaid Insurance, $100; credit Insurance Expense, $100.
c. debit Prepaid Insurance, $600; credit Insurance Expense, $600.
d. debit Insurance Expense, $600; credit Prepaid Insurance, $600.
e. none of the above.

_____ 5. If an accountant fails to make an adjusting entry to record expired insurance at the end of a fiscal period, the omission will cause
a. total expenses to be understated.
b. total revenue to be understated.
c. total assets to be understated.
d. all of the above.
e. none of the above.

_____ 6. Farmer Company bought equipment on January 2 of this year for $9,000. At the time of purchase, the equipment was estimated to have a useful life of eight years and a trade-in value of $1,000 at the end of eight years. Using the straight-line method, the amount of depreciation for the first year is
a. $900.
b. $1,000.
c. $800.
d. $950.
e. none of the above.

_____ 7. If expenses are greater than revenue, the Income Summary account will be closed by a debit to
a. Cash and a credit to Income Summary.
b. Income Summary and a credit to Cash.
c. Capital and a credit to Income Summary.
d. Income Summary and a credit to Capital.
e. none of the above.

_____ 8. In preparing closing entries, it is helpful to refer to which of the following columns of the work sheet first?
a. The Balance Sheet columns
b. The Adjusted Trial Balance columns
c. The Income Statement columns
d. Both the Adjusted Trial Balance and the Income Statement columns
e. None of the above

PART II: Practical Application

On December 31, the ledger accounts of Kristopher's Upholstery Shop have the following balances after all adjusting entries have been posted.

Cash	$ 3,600
Supplies	400
Equipment	13,000
Accumulated Depreciation, Equipment	1,100
Accounts Payable	300
K. Payton, Capital	16,500
K. Payton, Drawing	16,400
Income Summary	
Income from Services	35,900
Wages Expense	11,500
Rent Expense	2,400
Supplies Expense	4,100
Utilities Expense	1,000
Depreciation Expense, Equipment	500
Miscellaneous Expense	900

Required

Journalize the four closing entries in the proper order.

PART III: Matching Questions

____ 1. Creditor
____ 2. Business entity
____ 3. Fundamental accounting equation
____ 4. Income statement
____ 5. Owner's equity
____ 6. Accounts Receivable
____ 7. Net loss
____ 8. Ledger
____ 9. Credit
____ 10. Compound entry
____ 11. Trial balance
____ 12. Journalizing
____ 13. Posting
____ 14. Cross-reference
____ 15. Journal
____ 16. Work sheet
____ 17. Book value
____ 18. Depreciation
____ 19. Accounting cycle
____ 20. Fiscal year
____ 21. Contra account
____ 22. Mixed accounts
____ 23. Temporary-equity accounts
____ 24. Real accounts
____ 25. Debit

a. The book of original entry
b. One to whom money is owed.
c. Accounts that are partly income statement and partly balance sheet accounts
d. Assets – Liabilities
e. A listing of the ending balances of all ledger accounts that proves the equality of total debits and total credits
f. The process of recording transactions in a journal
g. The left side of a T account
h. A business enterprise, separate and distinct from the person who owns its assets.
i. The process of transferring accounts and amounts and amounts from the journal to the ledger
j. An account that is deducted from another account
k. Amounts owed by charge customers
l. Balance sheet accounts
m. Assets = Liabilities + Owner's Equity
n. A bookkeeping device for referring from journal to ledger or ledger to journal
o. The right side of a T account

(Continued)

p. Allocation of the cost of a plant asset over its estimated life
q. Financial statement that shows the net results of operations
r. Accounts that belong to only one fiscal period and are closed out at the end of each fiscal period
s. A transaction that has two or more debits and/or credits
t. Spreadsheet used to record adjustments and provide balances to prepare financial statements
u. Excess of total expenses over total revenues
v. A period of 12 consecutive months
w. A book containing all of the accounts of a business
x. The cost of an asset minus its accumulated depreciation
y. Steps in the accounting process, completed during the fiscal period

Answers: Part I

1. b 2. d 3. d 4. a 5. a 6. b 7. c 8. c

Answers: Part II

GENERAL JOURNAL Page 4

Date		Description	Post. Ref.	Debit	Credit
20--		Closing Entries			
Dec.	31	Income from Services		35 900 00	
		Income Summary			35 900 00
	31	Income Summary		20 400 00	
		Wages Expense			11 500 00
		Rent Expense			2 400 00
		Supplies Expense			4 100 00
		Utilities Expense			1 000 00
		Depreciation Expense, Equipment			500 00
		Miscellaneous Expense			900 00
	31	Income Summary		15 500 00	
		K. Payton, Capital			15 500 00
	31	K. Payton, Capital		16 400 00	
		K. Payton, Drawing			16 400 00

Answers: Part III

1. b 2. h 3. m 4. q 5. d 6. k 7. u 8. w 9. o 10. s 11. e 12. f 13. i 14. n 15. a 16. t 17. x 18. p 19. y 20. v 21. j 22. c 23. r 24. l 25. g

Accounting Cycle Review Problem A

QuickBooks

This problem is designed to enable you to apply the knowledge you have acquired in the preceding chapters. In accounting, the ultimate test is being able to handle data in real-life situations. This problem will give you valuable experience.

CHART OF ACCOUNTS

Assets

111 Cash
112 Accounts Receivable
114 Prepaid Insurance
121 Land
122 Building
123 Accumulated Depreciation, Building
124 Pool/Slide Facility
125 Accumulated Depreciation, Pool/Slide Facility
126 Pool Furniture
127 Accumulated Depreciation, Pool Furniture

Liabilities

221 Accounts Payable
222 Wages Payable
223 Mortgage Payable

Owner's Equity

311 L. Judar, Capital
312 L. Judar, Drawing
313 Income Summary

Revenue

411 Income from Services
412 Concessions Income

Expenses

511 Pool Maintenance Expense
512 Wages Expense
513 Advertising Expense
514 Utilities Expense
515 Interest Expense
517 Insurance Expense
518 Depreciation Expense, Building
519 Depreciation Expense, Pool/Slide Facility
520 Depreciation Expense, Pool Furniture
522 Miscellaneous Expense

You are to record transactions in a two-column general journal. Assume that the fiscal period is one month. You will then be able to complete all of the steps in the accounting cycle.

When you are analyzing the transactions, think them through by visualizing the T accounts or by writing them down on scratch paper. For unfamiliar types of transactions, specific instructions for recording them are included. However, reason them out for yourself as well. Check off each transaction as it is recorded.

July 1 Judar deposited $135,000 in a bank account for the purpose of buying Blast Off! The business is a recreation area offering three large waterslides (called "tubes")—one children's slide, an inner tube run, and a looping extreme slide.

2 Bought Blast Off! in its entirety for a total price of $540,800. The assets include pool furniture, $3,800; the pool/slide facility (includes filter system, pools, pump, and slides), $148,800; building, $96,200; and land, $292,000. Paid $120,000 down and signed a mortgage note for the remainder.

2 Received and paid the bill for a one-year premium for insurance, $12,240.

2 Bought 125 inner tubes from Worn Tires for $1,225, paying $500 down, with the remainder due in 20 days.

3 Signed a contract with a video game company to lease space for video games and to provide a food concession. The rental income agreed upon is 10 percent of the revenues generated from the machines and food, with the estimated monthly rental income paid in advance. Received cash payment for July, $250.

(*Continued*)

July 5 Received bills totaling $1,320 for the grand opening/Fourth of July party. The bill from Party Rentals for the promotional handouts, balloons, decorations, and prizes was $620, and the newspaper advertising bills from the *City Star* were $700. (These expenses should all be considered advertising expense.)

6 Signed a one-year contract for the pool maintenance with All-Around Maintenance and paid the maintenance fee for July of $1,600.

6 Paid cash for employee picnic food and beverages, $128. (Debit Miscellaneous Expense.)

7 Received $12,086 in cash as income for the use of the facilities.

9 Bought parts for the filter system on account from Arlen's Pool Supply, $646. (Debit Pool Maintenance Expense.)

14 Received $10,445 in cash as income for the use of the facilities.

15 Paid wages to employees for the period ended July 14, $9,460.

16 Paid $1,150 cash as partial payment on account for promotional expenses recorded on July 5. Party Rentals was paid $620 and City Star was paid the remainder of $530.

16 Judar withdrew cash for personal use, $2,500.

17 Bought additional pool furniture from Pool Suppliers for $2,100; payment due in 30 days.

18 Paid cash to seamstress for alterations and repairs to the character costumes, $328. (Debit Miscellaneous Expense.)

21 Received $10,330 in cash as income for the use of the facilities.

21 Paid cash to Worn Tires as partial payment on account, $600.

23 Received a $225 reduction of our account from Pool Suppliers for lawn chairs received in damaged condition.

25 Received and paid telephone bill, $292.

29 Paid wages for the period July 15 through 28 of $8,227.

31 Received $11,870 in cash as income for the use of the facilities.

31 Paid cash to Arlen's Pool Supply to apply on account, $360.

31 Received and paid water bill, $684.

31 Paid cash as an installment payment on the mortgage, $3,890. Of this amount, $1,910 represents a reduction in the principal and the remainder is interest.

31 Received and paid electric bill, $942.

31 Bought additional inner tubes from Worn Tires for $480, paying $100 down, with the remainder due in 30 days.

31 Judar withdrew cash for personal use, $3,200.

31 Sales for the video and food concessions amounted to $4,840, and 10 percent of $4,840 equals $484. Because you have already recorded $250 as concessions income, record the additional $234 revenue due from the concessionaire. (Cash was not received.)

Check Figure
Trial balance total, $601,941; net income, $16,293; post-closing trial balance total, $569,614

Required

1. Journalize the transactions. (Start on page 1 of the general journal if using Excel or Working Papers.)
2. Post the transactions to the ledger accounts. (Skip this step if using QuickBooks or general ledger.)
3. Prepare a trial balance. (If using a work sheet, use the first two columns.)
4. Data for the adjustments are as follows:
   a. Insurance expired during the month, $1,020.
   b. Depreciation of building for the month, $480.

c. Depreciation of pool/slide facility for the month, $675.
d. Depreciation of pool furniture for the month, $220.
e. Wages accrued at July 31, $920.
Your instructor may want you to use a work sheet for these adjustments.

5. Journalize adjusting entries.
6. Post adjusting entries to the ledger accounts. (Skip this step if using QuickBooks or general ledger.)
7. Prepare an adjusted trial balance.
8. Prepare the income statement.
9. Prepare the statement of owner's equity. (Skip this step if using QuickBooks)
10. Prepare the balance sheet.
11. Journalize closing entries.
12. Post closing entries to the ledger accounts. (Skip this step if using QuickBooks or general ledger.)
13. Prepare a post-closing trial balance. (If using QuickBooks, select the trial balance report and modify the report name to *Post-Closing Trial Balance*.)

Accounting Cycle Review Problem B

This problem is designed to enable you to apply the knowledge you have acquired in the preceding chapters. In accounting, the ultimate test is being able to handle data in real-life situations. This problem will give you valuable experience.

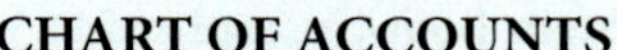

CHART OF ACCOUNTS

Assets
111 Cash
112 Accounts Receivable
114 Prepaid Insurance
121 Land
125 Pool Structure
126 Accumulated Depreciation, Pool Structure
127 Fan System
128 Accumulated Depreciation, Fan System
129 Sailboats
130 Accumulated Depreciation, Sailboats

Liabilities
221 Accounts Payable
222 Wages Payable
223 Mortgage Payable

Owner's Equity
311 R. Cury, Capital
312 R. Cury, Drawing
313 Income Summary

Revenue
411 Income from Services
412 Concessions Income

Expenses
511 Sailboat Rental Expense
512 Wages Expense
513 Advertising Expense
514 Utilities Expense
515 Interest Expense
516 Insurance Expense
517 Depreciation Expense, Pool Structure
518 Depreciation Expense, Fan System
519 Depreciation Expense, Sailboats
522 Miscellaneous Expense

You are to record transactions in a two-column general journal. Assume that the fiscal period is one month. You will then be able to complete all of the steps in the accounting cycle.

When you are analyzing the transactions, think them through by visualizing the T accounts or by writing them down on scratch paper. For unfamiliar types of transactions, specific instructions for recording them are included. However, reason them out for yourself as well. Check off each transaction as it is recorded.

June	1	Cury deposited $95,000 in a bank account for the purpose of buying Wind In Your Sails, a business offering the use of small sailboats to the public at a large indoor pool with a fan system that provides wind.
	2	Bought Wind In Your Sails in its entirety for a total price of $216,100. The assets include sailboats, $25,800; fan system, $13,300; pool structure, $140,000; and land, $37,000. Paid $60,000 down and signed a mortgage note for the remainder.
	3	Received and paid bill for newspaper advertising, $350.
	3	Received and paid bill for a one-year premium for insurance, $12,000.
	3	Bought additional boats from Louis Manufacturing Co. for $7,200, paying $3,200 down, with the remainder due in 30 days.
	3	Signed a contract with a vending machine service to lease space for vending machines. The rental income agreed upon is 10 percent of the sales generated from the machines, with the estimated total rental income payable in advance. Received estimated cash payment for June, $150.
	3	Received bill from Quick Printing for promotional handouts, $540 (Advertising Expense).
	3	Signed a contract for leasing sailboats from K. Einstein Boat Co. and paid rental fee for June, $700.
	5	Paid cash for miscellaneous expenses, $104.
	8	Received $2,855 in cash as income for the use of the boats.
	9	Bought an addition for the fan system on account from Stark Pool Supply, $745.
	15	Paid wages to employees for the period ended June 14, $3,900.
	16	Paid on account for promotional handouts already recorded on June 3, $540.
	16	Cury withdrew cash for personal use, $2,500.
	16	Bought additional sails from Canvas Products, Inc., $850; payment due in 30 days.
	16	Received $6,850 in cash as income for the use of the boats.
	19	Paid cash for miscellaneous expenses, $40.
	20	Paid cash to Louis Manufacturing Co. as part payment on account, $1,300.
	22	Received $8,260 in cash for the use of the boats.
	23	Received a reduction in the outstanding bill from Louis Manufacturing Co. for a boat received in damaged condition, $380.
	24	Received and paid telephone bill, $324.
	29	Paid wages for period June 15 through 28, $4,973.
	30	Paid cash to Stark Pool Supply to apply on account, $475.
	30	Received and paid electric bill, $345.
	30	Paid cash as an installment payment on the mortgage, $1,848. Of this amount, $497 represents a reduction in the principal and the remainder is interest.
	30	Received and paid water bill, $590.
	30	Bought additional boats from Riddle and Son for $5,320, paying $1,550 down, with the remainder due in 30 days.

(*Continued*)

June 30 Cury withdrew cash for personal use, $1,800.
30 Received $5,902 in cash as income for the use of the boats.
30 Sales from vending machines for the month amounted to $1,780. Ten percent of $1,780 equals $178. Because you have already recorded $150 as concessions income, list the additional $28 revenue earned from the vending machine operator. (Cash was not received.)

Required

1. Journalize the transactions. (Start on page 1 of the general journal if using Excel or Working Papers.)
2. Post the transactions to the ledger accounts. (Skip this step if using QuickBooks or general ledger.)
3. Prepare a trial balance. (If using a work sheet, use the first two columns.)
4. Data for the adjustments are as follows:
   a. Insurance expired during the month, $1,000.
   b. Depreciation of pool structure for the month, $715.
   c. Depreciation of fan system for the month, $260.
   d. Depreciation of sailboats for the month, $900.
   e. Wages accrued at June 30, $810.

   Your instructor may want you to use a work sheet for these adjustments.
5. Journalize adjusting entries.
6. Post adjusting entries to the ledger accounts. (Skip this step if using QuickBooks or general ledger.)
7. Prepare an adjusted trial balance.
8. Prepare the income statement.
9. Prepare the statement of owner's equity. (Skip this step if using QuickBooks.)
10. Prepare the balance sheet.
11. Journalize closing entries.
12. Post closing entries to the ledger accounts. (Skip this step if using QuickBooks or general ledger.)
13. Prepare a post-closing trial balance. (If using QuickBooks, select the trial balance report and modify the report name to *Post-Closing Trial Balance.*)

Check Figure
Trial balance total, $281,858; net income, $7,143; post-closing trial balance total, $263,341

CONTINUING PROBLEM

Closing Entries

After the adjusting entries are recorded and posted and the financial statements have been prepared, you are ready to perform the closing entries. Closing entries zero out the temporary owner's equity accounts (revenue(s), expenses(s), and Drawing). This process transfers the net income to or deducts the net loss and the withdrawals from the Capital account. In addition, the closing process prepares the records for the new fiscal period.

Check Figures

1. Debit to Income Summary second entry, $11,235.38
3. Post-closing trial balance total, $26,112

Required

1. Journalize the closing entries in the general journal.
   (If you are preparing the closing entries manually, enter your transactions beginning on page 5.)
2. Post the closing entries to the general ledger accounts.
   (Skip this step if you are using QuickBooks or general ledger.)
3. Prepare a post-closing trial balance as of June 30, 20--. (If using QuickBooks, select the trial balance report and modify the report name to *Post-Closing Trial Balance*.)

©iStockPhoto.com/Khalus

©iStockPhoto.com/Pixhook

Fuse/Jupiter Images

INTERNAL CONTROLS

A very important aspect of any financial accounting system, for an individual or for a business enterprise, is the accurate and efficient management of assets. To protect assets, a company sets up a system of policies and procedures known as **internal control**. The system is designed to:

1. Protect assets against fraud and waste.
2. Provide for accurate accounting data.
3. Promote efficient operation.
4. Encourage adherence to management policies.

Cash is one of the key assets internal control procedures are established to protect. When we talk about cash, we mean currency, coins, checks, money orders, traveler's checks, and bank drafts or bank cashier's checks. Personal checks are accepted conditionally—that is, based on the condition that they are valid. In other words, we consider checks to be good until they are otherwise proven not to be good.

Managing cash is an important aspect of business. All embezzlement starts with an employee or employees failing to follow internal control procedures. The following are some simple internal control guidelines for better management of cash receipts and payments:

Cash receipts

- Maintain separation of duties between cash handling and cash recording.
- Designate someone other than the bookkeeper to open mail.
- Make a record of cash received.
- Endorse checks immediately upon receipt with the stamp "For Deposit Only."
- Deposit cash daily.
- Journalize cash receipts as soon as possible, preferably by someone different from the person who first received the cash.
- Post cash receipts to the Accounts Receivable account as soon as possible.

Cash payments

- Make sure all cash payments are made by check (with the exception of petty cash).
- Make certain all checks are prenumbered.
- Keep check supplies in a secured area.
- Assign someone different from the check signer to prepare the checks.

Accounting Language

ATMs (automated teller machines) (p. 274)
Bank reconciliation (p. 279)
Bank routing number (p. 276)
Bank statement (p. 277)
Canceled checks (p. 279)
Cash funds (p. 272)
Change Fund (p. 293)
Collections (p. 280)
Denominations (p. 290)
Deposit in transit (p. 280)
Deposit slips (p. 273)
Drawer (p. 275)
Electronic Funds Transfer (EFT) (p. 274)
Endorsement (p. 275)
Errors (p. 280)
Interest income (p. 280)
Internal control (p. 271)
Ledger balance of cash (p. 279)
NSF (non-sufficient funds) check (p. 280)
Online banking (p. 274)
Outstanding checks (p. 280)
Payee (p. 275)
Petty Cash Fund (p. 289)
Petty cash payments record (p. 291)
Petty cash voucher (p. 290)
Personal identification number (PIN) (p. 274)
Positive pay (p. 276)
Promissory note (p. 282)
Remote deposit (p. 274)
Service charge (p. 280)
Signature card (p. 273)
Substitute check (p. 274)

Learning Objective

1 List internal controls for cash receipts and cash payments.

- Appoint someone other than the person preparing checks to prepare the bank reconciliations. (How to prepare a bank reconciliation is explained later in this chapter.)
- Keep petty cash under lock and limit access to one person other than the bookkeeper.

When cash register drawers are involved, additional security measures are required. For instance, cashiers should have their register drawer totals verified by a designated employee, manager, or owner when their shifts end. Later, we will see how the bank deposit amount is determined considering the cash in the till at the start of business.

Internal control of cash is a critical activity in any business. Divide the cash activities among several people to deter mishandling.

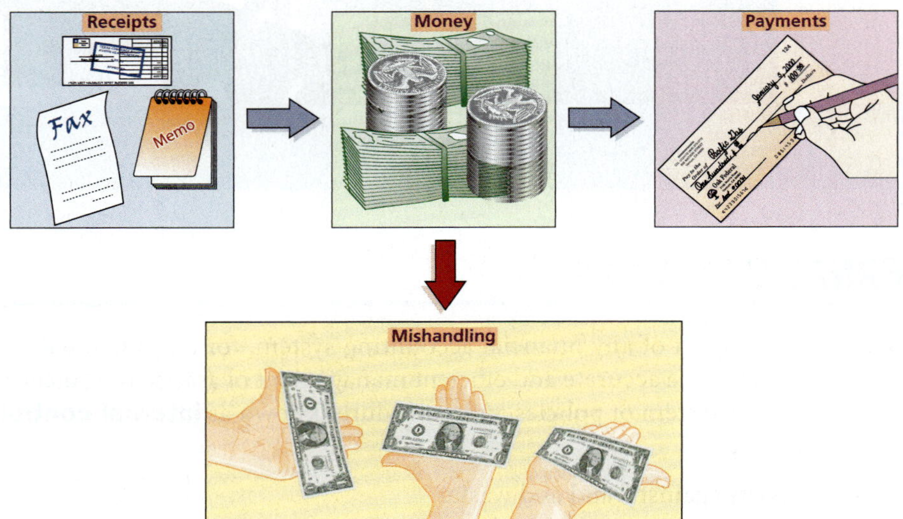

In this chapter, besides discussing bank accounts, we are going to talk about **cash funds**—Petty Cash Funds and Change Funds—which are separate cash accounts used for specific purposes.

SMALL BUSINESS **SUCCESS**

What Is Fraud?

Fraud is defined as an intentional misrepresentation of the truth. In a recent report, the Association of Certified Fraud Examiners (ACFE) estimated that "small businesses are especially vulnerable to occupational fraud, and it has become a global problem. The median loss suffered by organizations, including small businesses, was $160,000. Approximately one-fourth of all fraud cases are in excess of one million dollars." The ACFE is an organization that provides anti-fraud training and education (www.acfe.com).

A common type of fraud that occurs in small businesses involves theft of assets by employees. Theft of assets involves stealing of cash, supplies, inventory, and so on. Employees will go to such extent as to create fake employees who receive payroll and falsify invoices for payment.

The ACFE suggests several strategies to prevent fraud in small business, such as promoting honesty in the workplace and removing opportunities to commit fraud by maintaining internal controls on accounting records. In addition, companies should be especially careful when hiring employees and always conduct background checks.

USING A CHECKING ACCOUNT

Although you may be familiar with the process of opening a checking account, making deposits, and writing checks, let's review these and other procedures associated with opening and maintaining a business checking account. We will discuss signature cards, deposit slips, automated teller machines, online banking, Electronic Funds Transfer, night deposits, and endorsements.

As a means of preventing employee theft, many companies require more than one signature on checks over a certain dollar amount.

Signature Card

2 Describe the procedures for recording deposits and withdrawals.

Learning Objective

When Melinda B. Roland founded Roland's Delivery Services, she opened a checking account in the name of the business. When she opened the account, she filled out a **signature card** for the bank's files. Because Roland gave her assistant, Sheila R. Bayes, the right to sign checks too, the assistant also signed the card. The signature card gives the bank a copy of the official signatures of any persons authorized to sign checks. The bank can use it to verify the signatures on any checks Roland's Delivery Services presents for payment. This card helps the bank detect forgeries. Each banking entity has its own signature card. Figure 1 shows a typical signature card.

Title **Roland's Delivery Services** Account number 5008-3007

In consideration of the acceptance by COMPASS BANK of my/our account of the type indicated below, I/we agree to be bound by such rules and regulations and/or such schedules of interest, fees and charges applicable to such account as may now or hereafter be adopted by and in effect at said Bank, and also by the provisions printed hereon. It is understood that the acceptance by said Bank of my/our account is subject to the receipt by said Bank of satisfactory credit information.

(1) Sign Here *Melinda B. Roland*

(2) Sign Here *Sheila R. Bayes*

Address	City	State	Zip
951 Bay Road	**San Diego**	**California**	**92109**

☑ CHECKING ☐ MULTIPLE MATURITY ☐ CASH MANAGER
☐ SAVINGS ☐ GUARANTEED INTEREST (Multiple Maturity) ☐ SAFE DEPOSIT ☐ OTHER ______

IF THIS IS A JOINT ACCOUNT, BOTH OWNERS MUST SIGN ABOVE

Each of the signers guarantees the genuineness of the signature of the other. Each signer also agrees with the other and the Bank that deposits now or hereafter made to this account may be withdrawn in whole or part by either or survivor, and that each may endorse for deposit to this account any instrument payable to the order of either or both. Provisions respecting this agreement shall be modified only upon receipt by the Bank of written notice, signed by both.

Figure 1
Signature card for Roland's Delivery Services

Deposit Slips

The bank provides printed **deposit slips** on which customers record the amount of coins, currency, and checks they are depositing. Checks being deposited are listed individually. A typical deposit slip is shown in Figure 2.

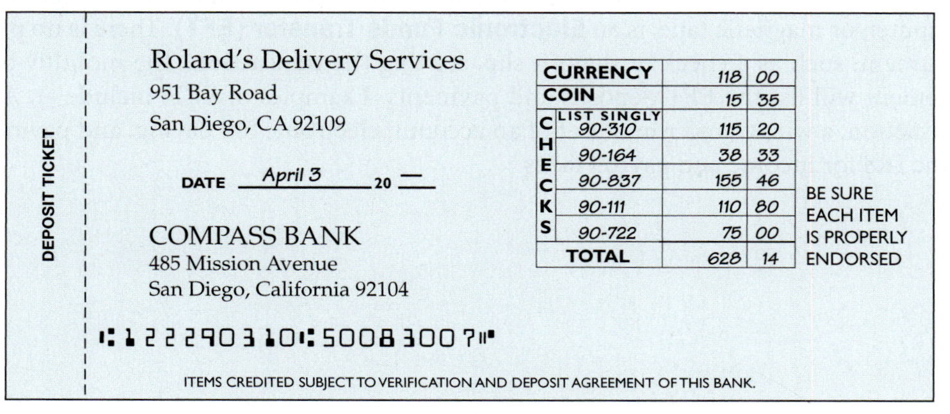

DEPOSIT TICKET

Roland's Delivery Services
951 Bay Road
San Diego, CA 92109

DATE *April 3* 20 —

COMPASS BANK
485 Mission Avenue
San Diego, California 92104

CURRENCY		118	00
COIN		15	35
CHECKS	LIST SINGLY 90-310	115	20
	90-164	38	33
	90-837	155	46
	90-111	110	80
	90-722	75	00
TOTAL		628	14

BE SURE EACH ITEM IS PROPERLY ENDORSED

⑆1222903 10⑆5008 3007⑈

ITEMS CREDITED SUBJECT TO VERIFICATION AND DEPOSIT AGREEMENT OF THIS BANK.

Figure 2
Deposit slip for Roland's Delivery Service

For a business account, the depositor fills out the deposit slip in duplicate, giving the original to the bank teller and keeping the copy. (This procedure may vary from bank to bank or company to company.)

A 2004 federal law, called The Check Clearing for the 21st Century Act (or Check 21 Act), allows banks that receive a check from a depositor to create a two-sided digital version of the original check, called a **substitute check**. This substitute check eliminates the need to handle a paper check through the banking system. One of several effects of the Check 21 Act is that consumers are no longer able to require a bank to return to them their original canceled checks with their monthly statement. Another side effect of the law is that it is now legal for anyone to use a computer scanner to capture images of checks and deposit them electronically, a process known as **remote deposit**. The Federal Reserve's website (www.federalreserve.gov/pubs/check21/consumer_guide.htm) provides more information about the Check 21 Act.

Automated Teller Machines

Deposits, withdrawals, and transfers can be made 24 hours a day, 7 days a week with **ATMs (automated teller machines)**. Each depositor uses a plastic card that contains a coded number and has a **personal identification number (PIN)**. The amount to be deposited, withdrawn, or transferred is keyed by the depositor. To make a deposit, the customer inserts into the ATM an envelope containing cash and/or checks and, if required, a copy of the deposit slip. To make a withdrawal, the customer requests an amount, the ATM dispenses it, and the customer removes the cash. In addition to deposits and withdrawals, a customer may transfer amounts from one account to another (for example, from savings to checking) as well as check the balance of his or her accounts.

Online Banking

Most transactions that can be handled at a bank location can also be completed online. With **online banking**, banks provide secure websites where customers can process transactions, such as pay bills, transfer funds, and review bank statements. Most banks also allow online banking customers to download banking transactions to a spreadsheet or accounting software. Strong internal controls are required for online banking. It is important that user names and passwords be protected. As an additional security measure, many lenders also require online banking customers to change their passwords on a regular basis.

Electronic Funds Transfer

A transfer of funds initiated through an electronic terminal, such as a telephone, a computer, or magnetic tape, is an **Electronic Funds Transfer (EFT)**. There is no paper document, such as a check or deposit slip, starting the transaction. The monthly bank statement will list the EFT deposits and payments. Examples of EFTs include an ATM transaction, a wire transfer in or out of an account, electronic bill paying, and payments to the IRS for income and payroll taxes.

Night Deposits

Most banks provide night depositories so that businesses and individuals can make deposits after regular hours. These are secured chutes into which a business's representative can insert a bag of cash and checks, knowing that the day's receipts will be safe until the bank opens in the morning.

Endorsements

The bank does not accept for deposit a check made out to a business until someone from the business has endorsed the check by signature or by stamp. The endorsement should appear on the back of the left end of a check, as it does in Figure 3. The **endorsement** (1) transfers title to the money and (2) authorizes payment of the check.

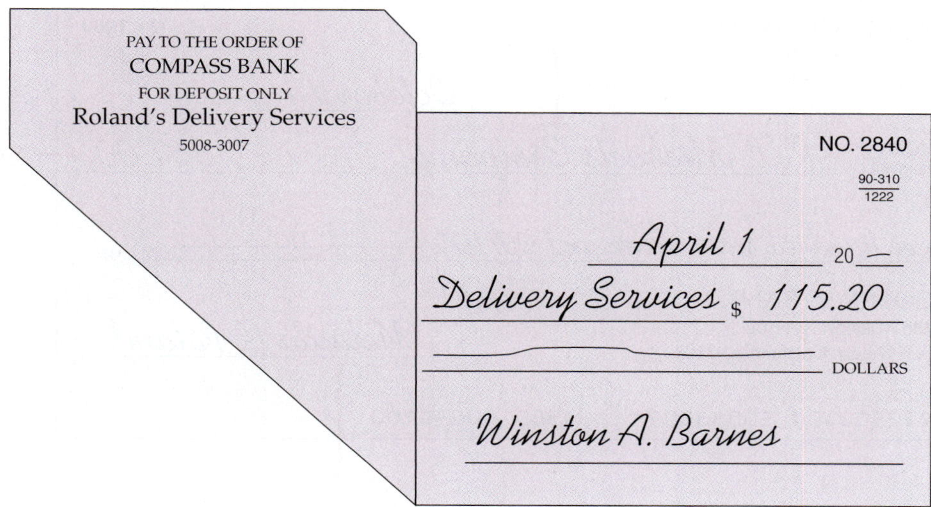

Figure 3
Endorsement for Roland's Delivery Services

WRITING CHECKS

Most people generally use a check to make payments for bills and other items. The party writing the check is called the **drawer**. A check represents an order by the drawer, directing the bank to pay a designated person or company. The party to whom payment is to be made is the **payee**.

Manual checks may be attached to check stubs. Each stub has spaces for recording the check number and amount, the date and payee, the purpose of the check, and the beginning and ending balances of cash. ***Note: The information recorded on the check stub is the basis for the journal entry, so check stubs are vitally important.*** A person in a hurry or under pressure sometimes neglects to fill in the check stubs. Therefore, it is best to record all information on the check stub ***before making out the check***. Businesses that use computerized checks do not need check stubs. One of the benefits of computerized accounting is that checks are automatically entered into the accounting system when generated.

Checks should be written carefully so that no one can successfully alter them. Figure 4 is a manual check, with the accompanying stub, drawn on the account of Roland's Delivery Services.

Follow these steps to write a manual check:

STEP 1. Write the payee's name on the first long line.

STEP 2. Write the amount of the check in figures close to the dollar sign.

STEP 3. Write the amount in words at the extreme left of the line provided for this information. Write cents as a fraction of 100. Legally, if there is a discrepancy between the amount in figures and the written amount, the written amount prevails. However, generally, the bank gets in touch with the drawer and asks what the correct amount should be.

Figure 4
Manual check with accompanying stub for Roland's Delivery Services

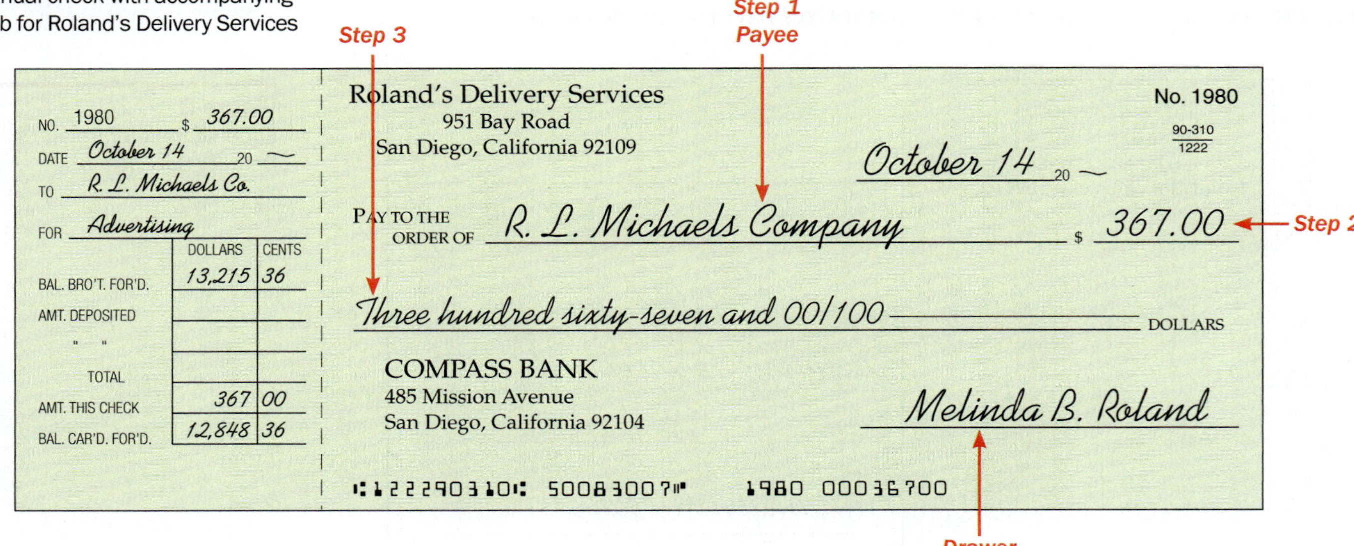

Finally, the drawer's signature on the face of the check should match the signature card on file at the drawer's bank.

The bottom of a check contains some important information such as the **bank routing number** (a nine-digit number used by the Federal Reserve Bank to identify the financial institution), the depositor account number and the check number, which are all pre-printed on the check before being sent to the account holder. Figure 5 shows where the numbers are located and what they mean.

Figure 5
Description of the script from Ck. No. 1980 in Figure 4

Positive Pay

A fraud prevention cash management program offered by banks in an attempt to protect customers and the bank is called **positive pay**. Positive pay programs require companies to submit an authorized list of checks written before the bank will allow payment. This authorized list includes information such as the payee, check number, and check amount. Many banks now require business customers to enroll in the positive pay program if they expect fraud protection from the bank. Businesses that fail to enroll in this program often do not have fraud protection coverage through the bank.

BANK STATEMENTS

The bank prepares the **bank statement**, which is created from the bank's viewpoint. Keep in mind that a customer's account is a liability to the bank and, therefore, has a credit balance. Once a month, the bank sends each of its customers the following information with the bank statement:

- The balance at the beginning of the month
- Additions in the form of deposits and credit memos
- Deductions in the form of checks and debit memos
- Electronic transactions
- The final balance at the end of the month

A bank statement for Roland's Delivery Services is shown in Figure 6 (see page 278). The following legend of symbols is listed on the bottom of the statement:

CM (credit memo) Increases or credits to the account, such as notes or accounts collected by the bank and/or interest income earned.

DM (debit memo) Decreases or debits to the account, such as NSF checks (discussed later in this chapter) and service charges. Service charges are based on the number of items processed and the average account balance. Special charges may also be levied against the account for collections and other services performed, including check printing.

OD (overdraft) The withdrawal of more than the cash balance in the account, resulting in a negative balance.

EC (error correction) Corrections of errors made by the bank, such as encoding mistakes.

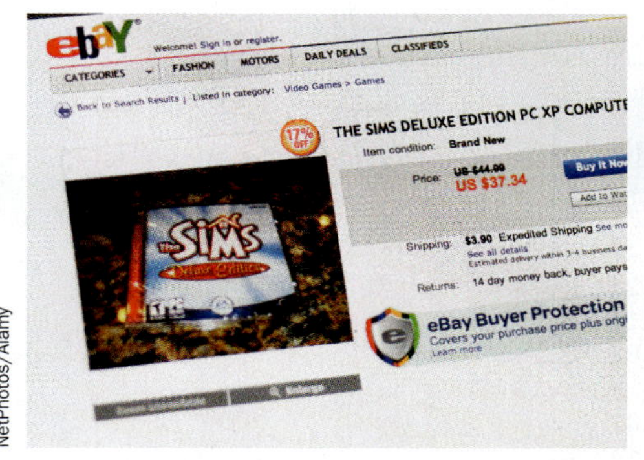

NetPhotos/Alamy

In the Real World

Internet businesses, such as eBay, Inc., understand the importance of implementing controls that protect the integrity of the service they offer. The success of eBay relies on the number of transactions between buyers and sellers; therefore, it is important that eBay users feel comfortable trading in this online marketplace.

An example of one control used by eBay to protect the integrity of the system is their feedback forum. The feedback forum helps eBay and their members uncover sellers that are misrepresenting items for sale or who fail to deliver promised goods. It also lets sellers know which buyers are not promptly paying for the items they purchased. eBay uses the feedback forum to help buyers and sellers monitor fellow users of the system. Those users who don't follow eBay's policies and procedures end up with negative feedback, which eventually hurts their reputation and may cause eBay to suspend or cancel their user access.

Figure 6
Bank statement for Roland's Delivery Services

COMPASS BANK
485 Mission Avenue
San Diego, CA 92104

STATEMENT OF ACCOUNT

Roland's Delivery Services
951 Bay Road
San Diego, CA 92109

ACCOUNT NUMBER
5008-3007
STATEMENT DATE
September 30, 20-- to October 31, 20--
TAX ID NUMBER
83-5249862

SUMMARY

Balance Last Statement	$10,403.57
Amount of Checks and Debits	$37,947.06
Number of Checks	69
Amount of Deposits and Credits	$44,793.10
Number of Deposits	21
Balance This Statement	$17,249.61

CHECKS/ OTHER DEBITS

CHECKS

CHECK NUMBER	DATE POSTED	AMOUNT	CHECK NUMBER	DATE POSTED	AMOUNT
1952	10-01	55.00	1988	10-17	65.22
1953	10-01	210.40	1989	10-17	465.30
1954	10-01	440.00	1990	10-18	560.00
1955	10-02	146.80	1991	10-19	114.57
1956	10-02	186.25	1992	10-19	24.90
1957	10-02	651.75	1993	10-19	135.36
1958	10-03	742.20	1994	10-20	118.36
1984	10-14	564.55	2018	10-30	120.75
1985	10-15	617.00	2019	10-30	843.54
1986	10-16	60.64	2020	10-31	743.20
1987	10-16	481.85	2021	10-31	123.92

OTHER DEBITS DESCRIPTION	DATE POSTED	AMOUNT
DM NSF check from B. R. Rumson	10-15	283.00
DM Automated Teller Trans. 092349 customer M3272348 at terminal 30962—cash	10-16	100.00
DM Service charge	10-31	19.50

DEPOSITS/ OTHER CREDITS

DEPOSITS

DATE POSTED	AMOUNT	DATE POSTED	AMOUNT
10-01	832.00	10-17	973.22
10-02	1,567.20	10-18	836.79
10-03	451.63	10-21	438.49
10-04	790.46	10-22	1,217.25
10-07	1,048.15	10-23	814.15
10-08	1,399.00	10-26	377.82
10-14	872.25	10-28	559.47
10-15	760.42	10-29	713.14
10-16	636.34	10-30	854.32

OTHER CREDITS DESCRIPTION	DATE POSTED	AMOUNT
CM Note collected, principal $1,000, interest $10	10-29	1,010.00

PLEASE EXAMINE THIS STATEMENT CAREFULLY. REPORT ANY POSSIBLE ERRORS WITHIN 10 DAYS.

CODE SYMBOLS

CM Credit Memo
DM Debit Memo
OD Overdraft
EC Error Correction

The bank statement is a valuable aid to efficiency and accuracy because it provides a double record of the Cash account. If a business entity deposits all cash receipts in the bank and makes all payments by check, the bank is keeping an independent record of the business's cash. You might think that the two balances—the company's and the bank's—should be equal, but this is unlikely. Some transactions may have been recorded in the company's account before being entered in the bank's records. In addition, there are unavoidable delays (by the business or the bank) in recording transactions. Ordinarily, there is a delay of one or more days between the date on which a check is written and the date it is presented to the bank for payment. Also, banks may not record deposits until the following business day. During this time lag, deposits made or checks written are recorded in the company's check register, but they are not yet listed on the bank statement.

Each month, the bank sends statements, either by mail or electronically via the Internet, to its depositors. The **canceled checks** (checks that have been paid or cleared by the bank) are listed on the bank statement. Debit or credit memos are also described on the bank statement.

Recording Deposits or Withdrawals

Each business entity keeps its accounts from its own point of view. As far as the bank is concerned, each customer's deposits are liabilities because the bank owes the customer the amount of the deposits. Using T accounts, it looks like this:

Liabilities

−	+
Debits	Credits

Deposits Payable

	−	+	
	Debits	Credits	
Debit memos	Checks written	Deposits	**Credit memos**
	Service charges	Notes collected	
	NSF checks	Interest income	
	ATM withdrawals	Wire transfers received	
	Electronic payments made		

Remember

Debit memos represent deductions from and credit memos represent additions to a bank account.

When the bank receives a cash deposit from a customer, the bank credits Deposits Payable because it owes more to its customer. When the bank cashes a check (pays out) for a customer, the bank debits Deposits Payable because it owes less to its customer.

The customer, on the other hand, uses the account titled Cash or Cash in Bank or simply the name of the bank. Deposits are recorded as debits and withdrawals are recorded as credits in the account. On a bank reconciliation, the balance of the account is listed as the **ledger balance of cash** before reconciliation with the bank statement.

Need for Reconciling Bank Balance and Ledger Balance

Learning Objective

3 Reconcile a bank statement.

Because the bank statement balance and the ledger balance of cash are not always equal, a business prepares a **bank reconciliation.** The bank reconciliation process uncovers the reasons for the difference between the two balances and corrects any errors that may have been made by the bank or the business. This makes it possible to arrive at the same balance in each account, which is called the *adjusted balance,* or *true balance,* of the Cash account.

Because identity theft and white-collar crimes are potential problems for a business, another purpose of the bank reconciliation is to make sure all of the amounts paid out from the account are proper disbursements for the business. As stated earlier, a mark of good internal control is to have the bank reconciliation prepared by someone other than the check signer (if someone other than the business owner is signing checks). The person performing the bank reconciliation will be making sure (1) the dollar amount of each canceled check matches the check entry in the ledger balance of the company's cash account; (2) all of the charges, checks, and electronic transfers belong to the company; and (3) deposits are made in a timely manner.

FYI

When a bank agrees to accept payments on behalf of a customer, the fee the bank charges does not necessarily mean that the bank will follow up on collection of a payment or notify the customer that the payment is late.

There are a variety of reasons for differences between the bank statement balance and the customer's cash balance. Here are some of the more common ones:

Deposit in transit A deposit made after the bank statement was issued. The depositor has already added the amount to the Cash account in his or her books, but the deposit has not been recorded by the bank. (This is also called a *late deposit.*)

Outstanding checks Checks that have been written by the company but not yet received for payment by the time the bank sends out its statement. The company employee, when preparing the checks, deducted the amounts from the Cash account in the company's books, which explains the difference.

Collections Money collected by the bank for the customer. When the bank acts as a collection point for its customers by accepting payments on their behalf, it adds the proceeds to the customer's bank account and either immediately sends a credit memorandum to notify the customer of the transaction or includes it on the next bank statement.

Interest income Interest earned for keeping cash in the bank account. Some checking accounts are interest-bearing or interest-earning. The depositor will not learn how much interest the bank has credited to the bank account until he or she receives the bank statement.

When a company's Cash account has a credit balance in the general ledger, the account is overdrawn.

NSF (non-sufficient funds) check A deposited check that the bank cannot process because the check writer's account does not contain enough money. When a bank customer deposits a check, it is recorded as cash on the customer's books. Occasionally, however, a check is not paid (bounces). When the bank notifies the customer of this, the customer must make a deduction from the Cash account. Simultaneously, the depositor records an increase in accounts receivable because the client's debt to the depositor remains unpaid. An NSF check is also called a *dishonored check.*

Service charge A bank charge for services rendered: for handling checks, for collecting money, for collecting payments on notes for its customers, for printing checks, and for providing other such services. The bank immediately deducts the fee from the balance of the bank account and identifies the charges on the bank statement.

Errors Mistakes made by the customer or the bank. In spite of internal controls and systems that are designed to double-check the process to prevent errors, sometimes the customer or the bank makes a mistake. Often these errors do not become evident until the bank reconciliation is performed.

Steps in Reconciling the Bank Statement

Follow these steps to reconcile a bank statement:

STEP 1. Canceled checks. Compare the amount of each canceled check on the bank statement with the ledger entries in the company's cash account. Any differences between the amount on the bank statement and the amount on the company's books should be noted.

STEP 2. Deposits.

a. Compare the deposits in transit (deposits not recorded by the bank at the time of the statement) listed on last month's bank reconciliation with the deposits shown on the bank statement. All of last month's deposits in transit should be listed on this month's bank statement. If they are not, notify the bank immediately.
b. Compare the remaining deposits listed on this month's bank statement with deposits written in the company's accounting records. Consider any deposits not shown on the bank statement as *deposits in transit*.

STEP 3. Outstanding checks.

a. Review the list of outstanding checks left over from last month's bank reconciliation and note the checks that have since been returned or cleared.
b. For each canceled check, compare the amount recorded on the bank statement with the amount recorded in the checkbook or general ledger cash account. Use a check mark (ü) to indicate that the check has been paid and that the amount is correct. Any payments that have not been marked off, including the outstanding checks from last month's bank reconciliation, are the present *outstanding checks*.

STEP 4. Bank memoranda. Trace the credit memos and debit memos to the journal. If the memos have not been recorded, make separate entries for them.

Many businesses now have computerized check registers, so the bank reconciliation will be done primarily on the computer. The procedures are similar as there is still the need to compare canceled check information, compare deposits, identify outstanding checks and deposits, and record adjustments.

Examples of Bank Reconciliations

Let's go through the reconciliation process for two businesses, W. Carson Company and Roland's Delivery Services.

W. CARSON COMPANY

The bank statement of W. Carson Company indicates a balance of $6,446 as of March 31. The balance of the Cash account in Carson's ledger as of that date is $4,650. Carson's accountant has taken the following steps:

STEP 1. Verified that canceled checks were recorded correctly on the bank statement.

STEP 2. Noted that the deposit made on March 31 was not recorded on the bank statement, $2,174.

STEP 3. Noted outstanding checks: no. 920, $1,695; no. 975, $325; no. 976, $1,279.

STEP 4. Noted credit memo: Note collected by the bank from T. Landon, $700, not recorded in the journal. Noted debit memo: Collection charge and service charge not recorded in the journal, $29.

The note received from T. Landon is called a *promissory note.* A **promissory note** is a written promise to pay a specific amount at a specific future time. Let's assume that W. Carson Company received the 60-day non-interest-bearing note from T. Landon for services performed. In recording the transaction, Carson's accountant debited Notes Receivable and credited Income from Services. (The account Notes Receivable is similar to Accounts Receivable. However, Accounts Receivable is reserved for customer charge accounts, with payments usually due in 30 days.) Then W. Carson Company turned the note over to its bank for collection.

The bank will use a credit memo form to notify W. Carson Company that the note has been collected and that the company's bank account has been increased by the amount of the note. Based on the credit memo, Carson's accountant will make a journal entry debiting Cash and crediting Notes Receivable.

Think of the bank reconciliation in terms of the following:

1. It brings the bank statement balance up to date by recognizing the activities or transactions we knew about but the bank did not know about when it prepared the statement (deposits in transit and outstanding checks as shown in our checkbook, for example).
2. It brings the balance of the Cash account up to date by recognizing the activities of transactions the bank knew about but we did not know about until we received the statement (bank fees, NSF checks, notes collected, checks cleared, interest income, debit memos and credit memos as shown on the bank statement, for example).

Figure 7 shows W. Carson Company's bank reconciliation. The items in the reconciliation that require journal entries are shown in color.

Figure 7
Bank reconciliation for W. Carson Company

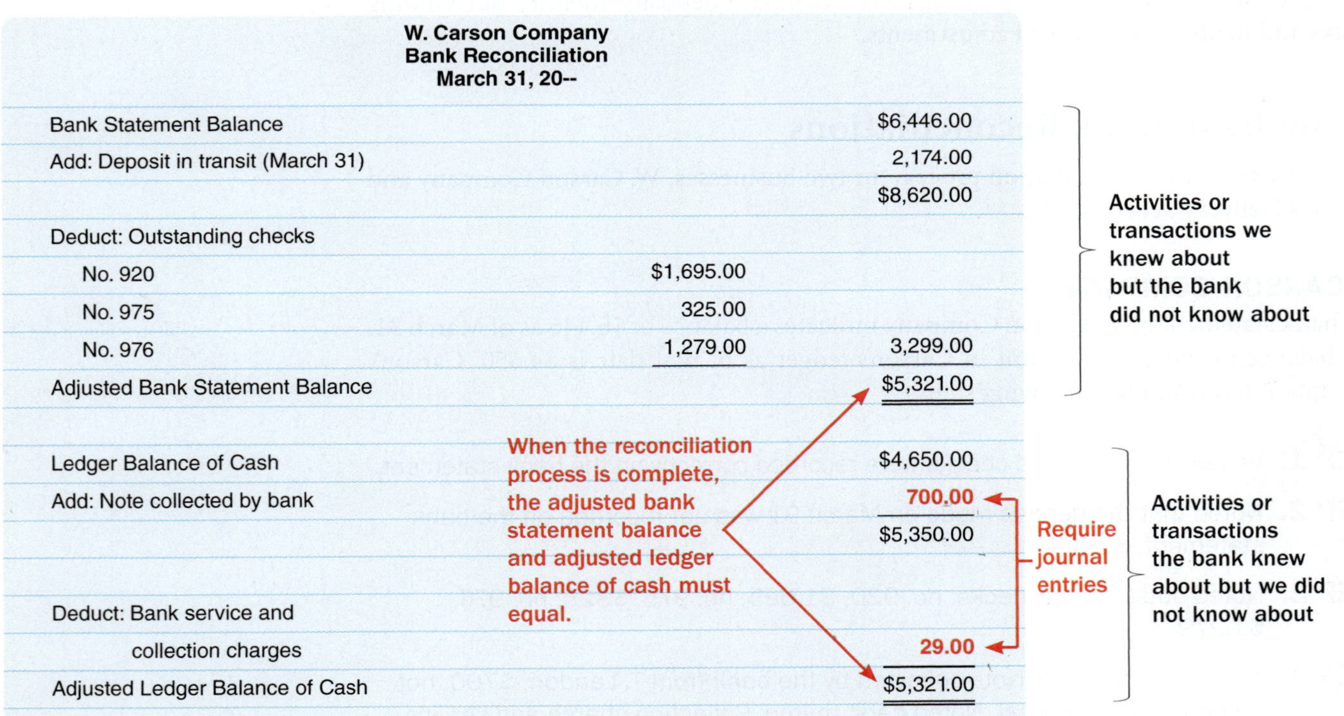

W. Carson Company
Bank Reconciliation
March 31, 20--

Bank Statement Balance		$6,446.00
Add: Deposit in transit (March 31)		2,174.00
		$8,620.00
Deduct: Outstanding checks		
No. 920	$1,695.00	
No. 975	325.00	
No. 976	1,279.00	3,299.00
Adjusted Bank Statement Balance		$5,321.00
Ledger Balance of Cash		$4,650.00
Add: Note collected by bank		700.00
		$5,350.00
Deduct: Bank service and collection charges		29.00
Adjusted Ledger Balance of Cash		$5,321.00

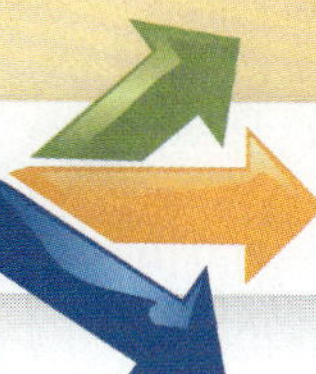

YOU Make the Call

Assume that you manage a service business that has three employees: a bookkeeper, an office manager, and a salesperson. You are so busy growing your business that you have turned over all bookkeeping and cash activities to the bookkeeper, including check-writing and signing privileges, bank reconciliation, and data entry. Your time has been so limited that you have not looked at any reports or reviewed any bank statements. Today is payday, and to your utter surprise, you are informed that there is not enough cash to make this week's payroll. When you look at the last three bank statements and compare the deposits to your cash receipts and cash payments journal, you see that things are not matching up, leading you to the conclusion that embezzlement (theft) of cash has taken place. Thinking back to how you assigned duties for your employees, what could you have done differently to have prevented this disaster?

SOLUTION

There should have been a better segregation of duties to prevent this occurrence. First, the bookkeeper should not have been assigned all cash activities, especially check-writing and signing privileges. Only you or the office manager should write and sign checks. You and no other employee in the business should mail the checks. The office manager should have the responsibility of opening and endorsing each check by stamping on the back of the check "For Deposit Only." This restricts, or limits, any further transfer of the check and forces the deposit of the check because the endorsement is not valid for any other purpose. The office manager, not the bookkeeper, should do the bank reconciliation, with you reviewing the completed statements. The bookkeeper's primary responsibilities should be to make journal entries for cash received for the general ledger as well as for the Accounts Receivable and Accounts Payable accounts.

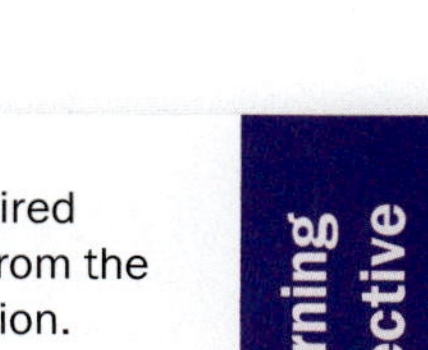

Learning Objective 4 Record the required journal entries from the bank reconciliation.

Note that the journal entries are based on the items used to adjust the ledger balance of Cash. These items represent the transactions that the bank has knowledge of but the business does not. According to the bank reconciliation, the true balance of Cash is $5,321, which is the balance we want to show on the company's books. We can't change the balance of an account unless we make a journal entry and then post the entry to the accounts involved. **Consequently, we have to make journal entries for items in the Ledger Balance of Cash section of the bank reconciliation.** The additions are debited to the Cash account, and the deductions are credited to the Cash account. W. Carson Company records the entries in its general journal as follows:

GENERAL JOURNAL					Page ___
Date		Description	Post. Ref.	Debit	Credit
20--					
Mar.	31	Cash		700 00	
		Notes Receivable			700 00
		Non-interest-bearing note signed by			
		T. Landon was collected by the bank.			
	31	Miscellaneous Expense		29 00	
		Cash			29 00
		Service charge and collection			
		charge levied by bank.			

Here bank service and collection charges are recorded in Miscellaneous Expense because the amounts are relatively small. Some accountants may use a separate expense account, such as Bank Charge Expense. After the entries have been posted, the T account for Cash looks like this:

Cash			
Balance	4,650	Mar. 31	29
Mar. 31	700		
Bal.	**5,321**		

Note that the balance in the T account is now equal to both the adjusted bank statement balance and the adjusted ledger balance of cash.

Form of Bank Reconciliation

Now that you have seen an example of a bank reconciliation, let's look at the standard form of a bank reconciliation for an imaginary company.

Bank Statement Balance (last figure on the statement)		$4,000
Add:		
Deposits in transit (deposits made after the bank statement was issued and already added to the ledger balance of Cash)	$300	
Bank errors (that understate balance)	20	320
		$4,320
Deduct:		
Outstanding checks and transfers (they have already been deducted from the Cash account)	$960	
Bank errors (that overstate balance)	40	1,000
Adjusted Bank Statement Balance (the true balance of Cash)		$3,320
Ledger Balance of Cash (the latest balance of the Cash account if it has been posted up to date; otherwise, take the beginning balance of Cash plus cash receipts minus cash payments)		$2,850
Add:		
Credit memos (additions by the bank not recorded in the Cash account, such as collections of notes and interest income earned)	$500	
Book errors (that understate balance)	40	540
		$3,390

Deduct:		
Debit memos (deductions by the bank not recorded in the Cash account, such as service charges or collection charges and NSF checks)	$ 20	
Book errors (that overstate balance)	50	70
Adjusted Ledger Balance of Cash (the true balance of Cash)		$3,320

ROLAND'S DELIVERY SERVICES

The bank statement of Roland's Delivery Services shows a final balance of $17,249.61 as of October 31. (See Figure 6, on page 278.) The present balance of the Cash account in the ledger, after Roland's Delivery Services' accountant has posted from the journal, is $16,296.11. The accountant took the following steps:

STEP 1. Verified that canceled checks were recorded correctly on the bank statement.

STEP 2. Discovered that a deposit of $1,012 made on October 31 was not recorded on the bank statement.

STEP 3. Noted outstanding checks: no. 1951, $687; no. 2022, $185; no. 2023, $367; no. 2024, $110.

STEP 4. Noted that a credit memo for a note collected by the bank from Lawson and Richards, $1,000 principal plus $10 interest, was not recorded in the journal. Found that check no. 2002 for $745, payable to Sanders, Inc., on account, was recorded in the journal as $754. (The correct amount is $745.) Noted that a debit memo for a collection charge and service charge of $19.50 was not recorded in the journal. Noted that a debit memo for an NSF check for $283 from B. R. Rumson was not recorded. Noted that a $100 personal withdrawal by Melinda B. Roland, the owner, using an ATM, was not recorded.

Look at Figure 8 (page 286) to see how each step relates to the bank reconciliation.

The accountant makes journal entries for the items indicated in Figure 8 to change the balance of the Cash account from its present balance of $16,296.11 to the true balance of $16,912.61. Again, those items that require journal entries are highlighted in Figure 8 and shown in Figure 9, on page 286.

Interest Income is classified as a revenue account. It represents the amount received on the promissory note that is over and above the face value of the note.

As for the NSF check, upon being notified by the bank, Roland's Delivery Services calls its customer (B. R. Rumson). Rumson can now take steps to cover the check. Let's review Roland's Delivery Services' transaction with B. R. Rumson: In return for services provided, Roland's Delivery Services received Rumson's check for $283. At that time, Roland's Delivery Services' accountant recorded the transaction as a debit to Cash for $283 and a credit to Income from Services for $283. Later, the bank, through its debit memorandum, notified Roland's Delivery Services about Rumson's NSF check. Then, to avoid overdrawing its own bank account, Roland's Delivery Services makes an entry crediting Cash (to correct its earlier debit to Cash) and debiting Accounts Receivable (to put the amount into Accounts Receivable). Because B. R. Rumson owes the money, it is logical to add the amount to Accounts Receivable for future collection.

Remember

When you are reconciling a bank statement, always double-check for any outstanding checks or deposits from previous statements that have been carried forward. Also double-check for any bank service charges.

Figure 8
Bank reconciliation for Roland's Delivery Services

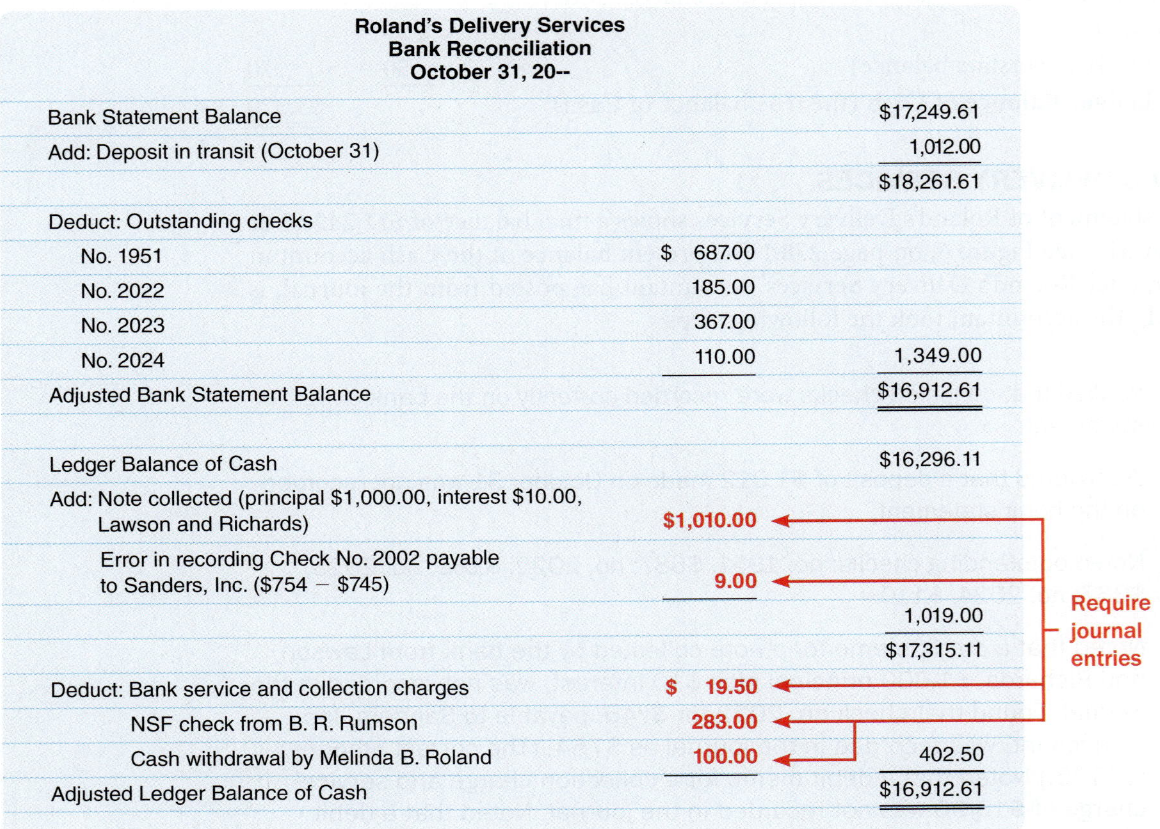

Roland's Delivery Services
Bank Reconciliation
October 31, 20--

Bank Statement Balance		$17,249.61
Add: Deposit in transit (October 31)		1,012.00
		$18,261.61
Deduct: Outstanding checks		
No. 1951	$ 687.00	
No. 2022	185.00	
No. 2023	367.00	
No. 2024	110.00	1,349.00
Adjusted Bank Statement Balance		$16,912.61
Ledger Balance of Cash		$16,296.11
Add: Note collected (principal $1,000.00, interest $10.00, Lawson and Richards)	$1,010.00	
Error in recording Check No. 2002 payable to Sanders, Inc. ($754 − $745)	9.00	
		1,019.00
		$17,315.11
Deduct: Bank service and collection charges	$ 19.50	
NSF check from B. R. Rumson	283.00	
Cash withdrawal by Melinda B. Roland	100.00	402.50
Adjusted Ledger Balance of Cash		$16,912.61

Figure 9
Journal entries for Roland's Delivery Services

GENERAL JOURNAL Page ___

Date		Description	Post. Ref.	Debit	Credit
20--					
Oct.	31	Cash		1 0 1 0 00	
		Notes Receivable			1 0 0 0 00
		Interest Income			1 0 00
		Bank collected note signed			
		by Lawson and Richards.			
	31	Cash		9 00	
		Accounts Payable			9 00
		Error in recording Ck. No. 2002			
		payable to Sanders, Inc.			
	31	Miscellaneous Expense		1 9 50	
		Cash			1 9 50
		Bank service charge and			
		collection charge.			

31	Accounts Receivable	2 8 3 00	
	Cash		2 8 3 00
	NSF check received from		
	B. R. Rumson.		
31	M. B. Roland, Drawing	1 0 0 00	
	Cash		1 0 0 00
	Withdrawal for personal use.		

Figure 9
(Concluded)

A bank reconciliation form is ordinarily printed on the back of the bank statement. The adjusted balance for the ledger balance of cash has already been determined. Consequently, the bank form is provided only for calculating the adjusted bank statement balance of the bank reconciliation. The bank form for Roland's Delivery Services is shown in Figure 10.

Figure 10
Bank form for Roland's Delivery Services

THIS FORM IS PROVIDED TO HELP YOU BALANCE
YOUR BANK STATEMENT

CHECKS OUTSTANDING—NOT CHARGED TO ACCOUNT

NO.	$	
1951	687	00
2022	185	00
2023	367	00
2024	110	00
TOTAL	$ 1,349	00

BEFORE YOU START

PLEASE BE SURE YOU HAVE ENTERED IN YOUR CHECKBOOK ALL AUTOMATIC TRANSACTIONS SHOWN ON THE FRONT OF YOUR STATEMENT.

YOU SHOULD HAVE ADDED IF ANY OCCURRED:

1. Loan advances.
2. Credit memos.
3. Other automatic deposits.

YOU SHOULD HAVE SUBTRACTED IF ANY OCCURRED:

1. Automatic loan payments.
2. Automatic savings transfers.
3. Service charges.
4. Debit memos.
5. Other automatic deductions and payments.

BANK BALANCE SHOWN ON THIS STATEMENT	$ 17,249.61
ADD	
DEPOSITS NOT SHOWN ON THIS STATEMENT *(IF ANY)*	$ 1,012.00
TOTAL	$ 18,261.61
SUBTRACT	
CHECKS OUTSTANDING	$ 1,349.00
BALANCE	$ 16,912.61

SHOULD AGREE WITH YOUR CHECKBOOK BALANCE AFTER DEDUCTING SERVICE CHARGE (IF ANY) SHOWN ON THIS STATEMENT.

Please examine immediately and report if incorrect. If no reply is received within 10 days, the account will be considered correct.

To: **Amy Roberts, CPA**
Subject: **Protecting My Cash**

Hi Amy,
I've set up my internal control guidelines and have made sure to separate the cash handling duties from the accounting activities. I have also set up a bank reconciliation schedule, so I'm sure this activity is done on a regular basis. I think I am ready for the rest of the steps you talked about. What should I look for or do next?
Thanks,
Janie

To: **Janie Conner**
Subject: **RE: Protecting My Cash**

Hi Janie,
It sounds like you are right on track. Below is a checklist for the rest of the items you should set up or monitor on a regular basis. Let me know if you have any questions.

_____ 1. Set up a Petty Cash fund for smaller purchases.
_____ 2. Set up a Change Fund to oversee your cash register funds.
_____ 3. Use the Cash Short and Over account to monitor shortages and overages when they occur.

Amy

THE PETTY CASH FUND

Day after day businesses are confronted with transactions requiring small, immediate payments, such as paying for delivery charges, birthday cards, or pizza for after-hours workers. If the business had to make all payments by check, the time required would be frustrating and the whole process would be unduly expensive. For many businesses, the cost of writing each check is more than $10; this includes the cost of an employee's time for writing and reconciling the check. Suppose you buy a few stamps from an employee for $2.20 and you want to reimburse her. To write a check would not be practical. It makes more sense to pay in cash using the **Petty Cash Fund**. *Petty* means "small," so the business sets a maximum amount that can be paid immediately out of petty cash. Payments that exceed this maximum must be processed by regular check through the journal.

ACCOUNTING IN YOUR FUTURE

FORENSIC ACCOUNTANT

© iStockPhoto.com/klikk

If the super detective Sherlock Holmes was around today and needed to investigate corporate financial crimes, he would need to rely on not only his detective skills but also his accounting knowledge. The combination of accounting and detective skills is what makes accountants such good investigators in today's financial world. Many public accountants specialize in forensic accounting—investigating and interpreting white-collar crimes such as securities fraud and embezzlement, bankruptcies and contract disputes, as well as other complex and possibly criminal financial transactions such as money laundering. Forensic accountants combine their knowledge of accounting and finance with law and investigative techniques to determine whether an activity is illegal. Many forensic accountants work closely with law enforcement personnel and lawyers during investigations and often appear as expert witnesses during trials.

Increased focus on financial crimes such as embezzlement, bribery, and securities fraud, in addition to the growing number of these occurrences, will increase the demand for forensic accountants. Computer technology has made these crimes easier to commit. At the same time, the development of new computer software and electronic surveillance technology has made tracking down financial criminals easier, thus increasing the likelihood of discovery. As success rates of investigations grow, demand for forensic accountants will increase. *U.S. News & World Report* listed forensic accounting as one of the eight most secure career tracks in America, while *SmartMoney* Magazine counted forensic accounting as one of its "ten hottest jobs" with salary amounts in six figures.

The Association of Certified Fraud Examiners offers the Certified Fraud Examiner (CFE) designation for forensic or public accountants involved in fraud prevention, detection, deterrence, and investigation. To obtain the designation, individuals must have a bachelor's degree and two years of relevant experience, pass a four-part exam, and abide by a code of ethics. Therefore, if you take the additional steps of securing your CPA status as well as education leading to your becoming a CFE, you can feed your taste for detective work while still enjoying your life as an accountant!

Establishing the Petty Cash Fund

Learning Objective

5 Record journal entries to establish a Petty Cash Fund.

After the business has set the maximum amount of a payment allowed from petty cash, the next step is to estimate how much cash will be needed during a given period of time, such as a month. It is also important to consider the element of security when keeping cash in the office. If the risk is great, the amount kept in the fund should be small. Roland's Delivery Services decides to establish a Petty Cash Fund of $100 and put it under the control of the accounting assistant. Accordingly, Roland's Delivery Services' accountant writes a check, cashes it at the bank, and records this transaction in the journal as follows:

GENERAL JOURNAL Page ___

Date		Description	Post. Ref.	Debit	Credit
20--					
Sept.	1	Petty Cash Fund		1 0 0 00	
		Cash			1 0 0 00
		Established a Petty Cash Fund,			
		Ck. No. 1880.			

T accounts for the entry look like this:

Petty Cash Fund	
+	−
100	

Cash	
+	−
	100

Remember

If no change is made in the size of the fund, the Petty Cash Fund account is debited only once, when the fund is first established.

Because the Petty Cash Fund is an asset account, it is listed on the balance sheet immediately below Cash.

Once the fund has been created, it is not debited again unless the original amount is not large enough to handle the necessary transactions. In that case, the accountant has to increase the Petty Cash Fund—perhaps from $100 to $200. **However, if no change is made in the size of the fund, the Petty Cash Fund is debited only once, when the fund is first established.**

The check is written to the accounting assistant, "Sheila R. Bayes, Petty Cash Fund." She converts it into convenient **denominations**, which are varieties of coins and currency, such as quarters and dimes and $1 and $5 bills. Then, the accounting assistant puts the money in a locked drawer and will not pay anything larger than $20 (or whatever the company determines as the agreed-upon amount) out of petty cash.

Payments from the Petty Cash Fund

Learning Objective

6 Complete petty cash vouchers, petty cash payments record and reimburse the petty cash fund.

The accounting assistant is designated as the only person who can make payments from the Petty Cash Fund. In case of her illness, another employee should be named as a backup. A **petty cash voucher** must be used to account for every payment from the fund. The voucher represents a receipt signed by the person who authorized the payment and by the person who received the payment. The voucher also explains the purpose for the payment. Thus, even for small payments of $20 or less, there would have to be collusion between the payee and the assistant for any theft to occur. Figure 11 shows an example of a petty cash voucher.

PETTY CASH VOUCHER

No. 1 Date September 2, 20--

Paid to Mason Delivery Squad $ 10.00

For Delivery

Account Delivery Expense

Approved by S. Bayes *Payment received by* R. Bates

Figure 11
Petty cash voucher

Petty Cash Payments Record

Some businesses prefer to have a written record on one sheet of paper, so they keep a **petty cash payments record**. In a petty cash payments record, petty cash vouchers and the accounts that are to be charged are listed. The purpose of the expenditure is also listed. Special columns for frequent types of expenditures are included in the Distribution of Payments section. The petty cash payments record is not a journal.

Roland's Delivery Services made the following payments from its Petty Cash Fund during September:

Sept. 2 Paid $10 for flowers for the front counter to Mason Delivery Squad, voucher no. 1.
3 Bought pencils and pens, $8.59, voucher no. 2.
5 Bought local newspapers for article related to Roland's Delivery Services, $2.50, voucher no. 3.
7 Paid postage on incoming packages, $3.70, voucher no. 4.
10 Melinda B. Roland, the owner, withdrew $10 for personal use, voucher no. 5.
14 Reimbursed employee for stamps, $2.20, voucher no. 6.
21 Bought stick-on tabs, $4.10, voucher no. 7.
22 Paid $14 for gift for retiring employee, voucher no. 8.
26 Paid for mailing packages, $3.60, voucher no. 9.
27 Paid $9 for Girl Scout cookies, voucher no. 10.
29 Bought memo pads, $4.40, voucher no. 11.
29 Paid for making duplicate keys, $8.20, voucher no. 12.
30 Paid $8 to have parking area swept, voucher no. 13.
30 Paid for trash removal, $5, voucher no. 14.

Figure 12, on page 292, shows how these payments are recorded.

Remember

The petty cash payments record is not a journal; it is simply used as a basis for compiling information for the journal entry. Remember, to change the amount of an account, we have to make a journal entry.

Reimbursement of the Petty Cash Fund

To bring the fund back up to the original amount when it is nearly exhausted (for instance, at the end of the month), the accountant reimburses the fund for expenditures made. Consequently, the Petty Cash Fund may be considered a revolving fund. If the amount initially put in the Petty Cash Fund is $100 and at the end of the month only $6.71 is left, the accountant puts $93.29 back into the fund as a reimbursement. This will bring the fund back to the original $100 to start the new month.

Bear in mind that the petty cash payments record is only a supplementary record for gathering information. A less formal way of compiling the information concerning petty cash payments might consist of collecting one month's petty cash vouchers, then sorting them by accounts (for example, Office Supplies and Delivery Expense). After the vouchers have been sorted by account, a calculator tape can be run to update account totals.

Figure 12
Petty cash payments record for Roland's Delivery Services

	A		B	C	D	E	F	G	H	I
1					Petty Cash Payments Record					
2					Month of September 20--					
3							Distribution of payments			
4										
5			Vou.			Office	Maintenance	Miscellaneous	Other Accounts	
6	Date		No.	Explanation	Payments	Supplies	Expense	Expense	Account	Amount
7	Sept.	1		Establish fund, Ck. No. 1880, $100						
8		2	1	Mason Delivery Squad	10.00			10.00		
9		3	2	Pencils and pens	8.59	8.59				
10		5	3	Local newspapers	2.50			2.50		
11		7	4	Postage on incoming packages	3.70			3.70		
12		10	5	Withdrawal by M. B. Roland	10.00				M.B. Roland, Drawing	10.00
13		14	6	Reimburse employee for stamps	2.20			2.20		
14		21	7	Stick-on tabs	4.10	4.10				
15		22	8	Gift for retiring employee	14.00			14.00		
16		26	9	Postage for mailings	3.60			3.60		
17		27	10	Girl Scout cookies	9.00			9.00		
18		29	11	Memo pads	4.40	4.40				
19		29	12	Making duplicate keys	8.20		8.20			
20		30	13	Sweeping of parking area	8.00		8.00			
21		30	14	Trash removal	5.00		5.00			
22		30		Totals	93.29	17.09	21.20	45.00		10.00
23				Balance in Fund	$ 6.71					
24				Reimburse fund, Ck. No. 1950	93.29					
25				Total	$100.00					
26										
27										
28										
29										
30										
31										

Sheet1 Sheet2 Sheet3

At the end of the month, the accountant makes a summarizing entry to officially journalize the transactions that have taken place. The general journal and T accounts of Roland's Delivery Services are shown below.

Note that in the summarizing entry, the accountant debits the accounts for which the payments were made and credits the Cash account. No entry is made to the Petty Cash Fund account. Then, the accounting assistant cashes a check for $93.29 and puts the cash in the locked Petty Cash box. The Petty Cash Fund is now restored to the original $100.

GENERAL JOURNAL Page ___

Date		Description	Post. Ref.	Debit	Credit
20--					
Sept.	30	Office Supplies		17.09	
		Maintenance Expense		21.20	
		Miscellaneous Expense		45.00	
		M. B. Roland, Drawing		10.00	
		Cash			93.29
		Reimbursed the Petty Cash			
		Fund, Ck. No. 1950.			

Cash

+	−
	93.29

Office Supplies

+	−
17.09	

M. B. Roland, Drawing

+	−
10.00	

Maintenance Expense

+	−
21.20	

Miscellaneous Expense

+	−
45.00	

THE CHANGE FUND

Anyone who has tried to pay for a small item with a $20 bill knows that any business that carries out numerous cash transactions needs a **Change Fund**.

Learning Objective 7 Record the journal entries to establish a Change Fund.

Establishing the Change Fund

Before setting up a Change Fund, you have to decide two things: (1) how much money needs to be in the fund and (2) what denominations of bills and coins are needed. Like the Petty Cash Fund, **the Change Fund is debited only once: when it is established.** It is left at the initial figure unless the person in charge decides to make it larger. The Change Fund account, like the Petty Cash Fund account, is an asset. It is recorded in the balance sheet immediately below Cash. If the Petty Cash Fund account is larger than the Change Fund account, it precedes the Change Fund.

The owner of Roland's Delivery Services, Melinda B. Roland, decides to establish a Change Fund; she decides this at the same time she sets up the company's Petty Cash Fund. The entries for the two transactions look like this:

GENERAL JOURNAL — Page___

Date		Description	Post. Ref.	Debit	Credit
20--					
Sept.	1	Petty Cash Fund		1 0 0 00	
		Cash			1 0 0 00
		Established a Petty Cash Fund,			
		Ck. No. 1880.			
	1	Change Fund		1 5 0 00	
		Cash			1 5 0 00
		Established a Change Fund,			
		Ck. No. 1881.			

The T accounts for establishing the Change Fund are as follows:

Change Fund	
+	−
150	

Cash	
+	−
	150

Roland cashes a check for $150 and gets the money in several denominations. She is now prepared to make change for any normal business transactions.

Depositing Cash

At the end of each business day, Roland's Delivery Services' accountant deposits the cash taken in during the day less the amount of the Change Fund, which should be in small denominations for the next day's business. Let's assume that on September 1, Roland's Delivery Services had $1,575 on hand at the end of the day.

$1,575	Total cash count
− 150	Change Fund
$1,425	New cash deposit

The day's receipts are journalized as follows:

GENERAL JOURNAL — Page___

Date		Description	Post. Ref.	Debit	Credit
20--					
Sept.	1	Cash		1 4 2 5 00	
		Income from Services			1 4 2 5 00
		To record revenue earned			
		during the day.			

The T accounts look like this:

Cash	
+	−
1,425	

Income from Services	
−	+
	1,425

The amount of the cash deposit is the total cash count less the amount of the Change Fund. This should be equal to the income earned.

On September 9, the cash count is $1,672. So the accountant deposits $1,522 ($1,672 − $150). Roland's Delivery Services' accountant makes the following entry to record the day's receipts:

GENERAL JOURNAL Page ___

Date		Description	Post. Ref.	Debit	Credit
20--					
Sept.	9	Cash		1 5 2 2 00	
		Income from Services			1 5 2 2 00
		To record revenue earned			
		during the day.			

Some businesses label the Cash account *Cash in Bank* and label the Change Fund *Cash on Hand.*

CASH SHORT AND OVER

There is an inherent danger in making change: Human beings make mistakes, especially when many customers need to be waited on or when the business is temporarily short-handed. Because mistakes do happen, accounting records must be set up to cope with the situation. One reason a business uses a cash register is to detect mistakes in handling cash. **If, after the Change Fund is removed, the day's receipts are less than the register reading, a cash shortage exists. Conversely, when the day's receipts are greater than the register reading, a cash overage exists.** Both shortages and overages are recorded in the same account, which is called Cash Short and Over. Shortages are considered an expense of operating a business; therefore, shortages are recorded on the debit side of the account. Overages are treated as another form of revenue; therefore, overages are recorded on the credit side of the account.

8 Record journal entries for transactions involving Cash Short and Over.

Learning Objective

Let's assume that on September 14, Roland's Delivery Services is faced with the following situation:

Cash Register Tape	Cash Count	Amount of the Change Fund
$1,515	$1,663	$150

After deducting the $150 in the Change Fund, Roland will deposit $1,513 ($1,663 − $150). Note that this amount is $2 less than the amount indicated by the cash register tape ($1,515 − $1,513); therefore, a $2 cash shortage exists. The following T accounts show how the accountant entered this transaction in the books.

The Cash Short and Over account may also be used to handle shortages and overages in the Petty Cash Fund.

Like the Income Summary account, which has no normal balance, the Cash Short and Over account has no signs.

Cash		Income from Services		Cash Short and Over	
+	−	−	+		
1,513			1,515	2	

The next day, September 15, the pendulum happens to swing in the other direction, as follows:

Cash Register Tape	Cash Count	Amount of the Change Fund
$1,578	$1,732	$150

The amount to be deposited is $1,582 ($1,732 − $150). This figure is $4 greater than the $1,578 in income from services indicated by the cash register tape. Thus, there is a $4 cash overage ($1,582 − $1,578). The analysis of this transaction is shown in the following T accounts:

Cash		Income from Services		Cash Short and Over	
+	−	−	+		
1,582			1,578		4

Roland's Delivery Services' revenue for September 14 and 15 is recorded in the general journal as follows:

GENERAL JOURNAL Page ___

Date		Description	Post. Ref.	Debit	Credit
20--					
Sept.	14	Cash		1,513.00	
		Cash Short and Over		2.00	
		Income from Services			1,515.00
		To record revenue earned for the day			
		involving a cash shortage of $2.00.			
	15	Cash		1,582.00	
		Income from Services			1,578.00
		Cash Short and Over			4.00
		To record revenue earned for the day			
		involving a cash overage of $4.00.			

As far as errors are concerned, one would think that shortages would be offset by overages. However, customers receiving change are more likely to report shortages than overages. **Consequently, the business usually experiences a greater number of shortages.** A business may set a tolerance level for the cashiers. If the shortages consistently exceed the level of tolerance, either fraud is being committed or somebody is making entirely too many careless mistakes. In the world of accounting, both cash shortages and cash overages are areas of concern.

Now let's summarize our discussion of the Cash Short and Over account by drawing the following conclusions from the illustration:

1. At the close of the business day, the business deposits the difference between the amount in the cash drawer and the amount in the Change Fund.
2. The business records the amount shown on the cash register tape as its income from services.
3. If the amount of the cash deposit disagrees with the record of receipts, Cash Short and Over makes up the difference. In the first situation just described, there was a shortage of $2, so the Cash Short and Over account was debited. In the second situation, there was an overage of $4, so the Cash Short and Over account was credited. It is apparent that as a result of these transactions, the account looks like this:

Cash Short and Over

Shortage	2	Overage	4

Throughout any fiscal period, the accountant must continually record shortages and overages in the Cash Short and Over account. Let's assume that Roland's Delivery Services' final balance is $18 on the debit side. Roland's Delivery Services winds up with a net shortage of $18. The T account would look like this:

Cash Short and Over

Shortage	2	Overage	4
	4		1
	3		1
	7		2
	5		1
	2		2
	3		1
	4		
Bal.	**18**		

At the end of the fiscal period, **if the account has a debit balance, or net shortage, the accountant classifies it as an expense, crediting Cash Short and Over and debiting Miscellaneous Expense. The amount is then reported on the income statement under Miscellaneous Expense.**

Conversely, **if the account has a credit balance, or net overage, the accountant classifies it as a revenue account and debits Cash Short and Over and credits Miscellaneous Income. The amount is then reported on the income statement under Miscellaneous Income.** This is an exception to the policy of recording accounts under their exact account title in financial statements. Rather than attaching plus and minus signs to the Cash Short and Over account immediately, we wait until we find out its final balance, then make a journal entry to send the balance to the correct account classification.

Accounting with QuickBooks®

Internal Controls in QuickBooks

Learning Objective

 List internal controls in QuickBooks.

Learning Objectives

After you have completed this section, you will be able to do the following:

1. List internal controls in QuickBooks.
2. Reconcile a bank statement with QuickBooks.
3. View and print banking reports.

USER PASSWORDS AND ACCESS

In this chapter, you learned the importance of internal controls to protect a company's assets. Different versions of QuickBooks have various internal control features available to help with fraud prevention. The QuickBooks administrator has the ability to restrict user access for various menu items by going to **Company** > **Set Up Users and Passwords** > **Set Up Users** > **User List** > **Set Up Passwords and Access**.

QuickBooks reports also can help prevent fraud. Reports such as the audit trail report, the closing date exception report, the customer credit card audit trail report, and the voided/deleted transaction summary or detail reports all can help users identify irregularities or unauthorized activity.

THE AUDIT TRAIL REPORT

The **Audit Trail Report** displays additions, deletions, and modifications to QuickBooks transactions. This report is a very useful tool to monitor unauthorized transaction activity.

CLOSING DATE EXCEPTION REPORT

The **Closing Date Exception Report** highlights changes to transactions after the accounting period has closed. Passwords can be used to restrict user access to prior accounting periods; however, the **Closing Date Exception Report** can be used to monitor prior accounting period changes that are made by authorized users.

CUSTOMER CREDIT CARD AUDIT TRAIL REPORT

The **Customer Credit Card Audit Trail Report** is only available in QuickBooks when the customer credit card protection feature is enabled. This audit report provides a record of customer credit card activity, starting when the customer's credit card is originally entered into QuickBooks, or later viewed, changed, or deleted. Unlike other QuickBooks reports, this report has limitations as it can't be filtered or memorized.

QuickBooks Tip

Using the delete option is acceptable in many companies if a check has not been printed. However, if a check has been printed, use the void option. Both deleted and voided transactions will appear on the audit reports.

VOIDED/DELETED TRANSACTIONS SUMMARY/DETAIL REPORTS

The **Voided and Deleted Transactions Reports** provide a record of voided, unvoided, or deleted transactions. There are two reports: a summary report and a detailed report. The summary report provides a quick listing of voided, unvoided, or deleted transactions, while the detailed report is useful when more information is needed. The detailed report identifies the original transaction date, the modification date(s), debit and credit information, account information, and the individual or company involved in the transaction.

To access the various audit trail reports, complete the following steps as shown in Figure Q1:

STEP 1. Click **Reports**.

STEP 2. Select **Accountant & Taxes**.

STEP 3. Select the desired report.

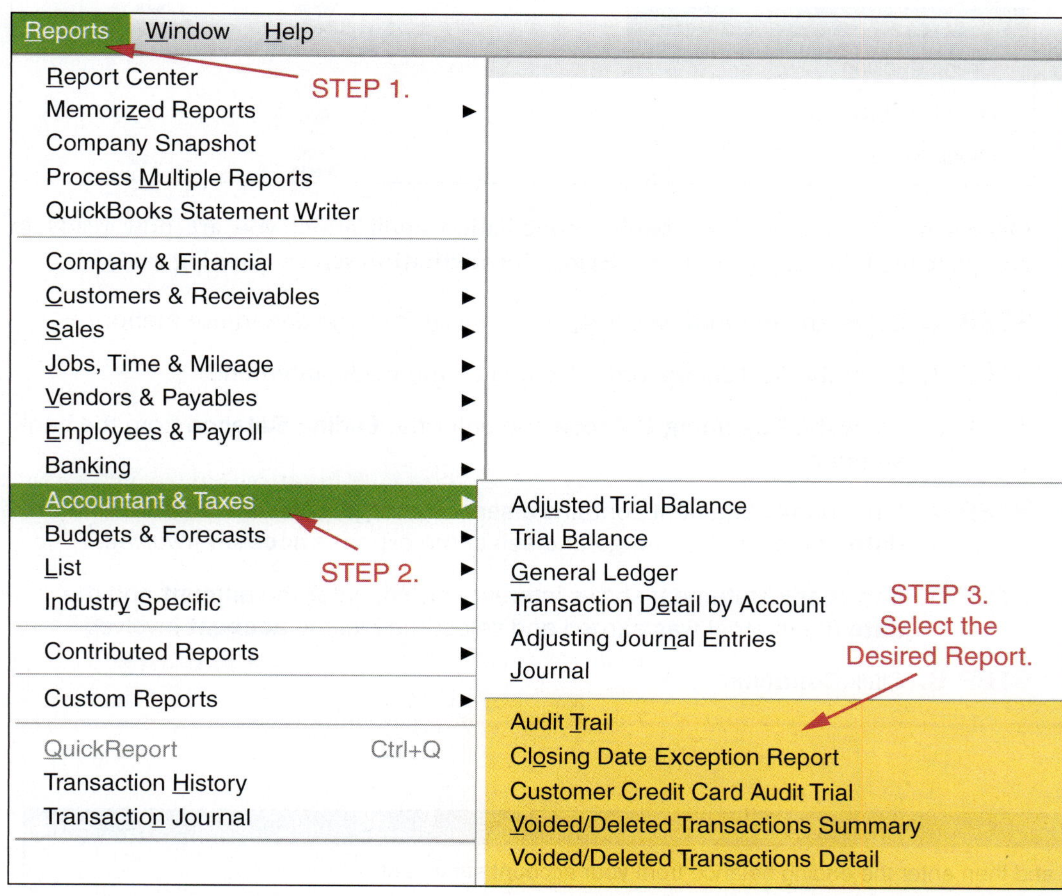

Figure Q1
Audit reports

Keep in mind that any report in QuickBooks can be used to identify irregularities. Strong internal controls involve regular monitoring of activities to identify unusual entries and take corrective action as needed.

2 Reconcile a bank statement with QuickBooks. **Learning Objective**

In this chapter, you learned the importance of reconciling the bank statement with the company's books on a regular basis. Computerized accounting software packages, such as QuickBooks, can be used to simplify this reconciliation process.

There are two ways to access the bank reconciliation feature in QuickBooks. The first option is to enter the **Banking** tab on the menu bar as shown in Figure Q2. The second option is to choose select **Reconcile**, under the **Banking Center** on the home page, as shown in Figure Q3.

Figure Q2
Accessing the bank reconciliation feature from the menu bar or the home page

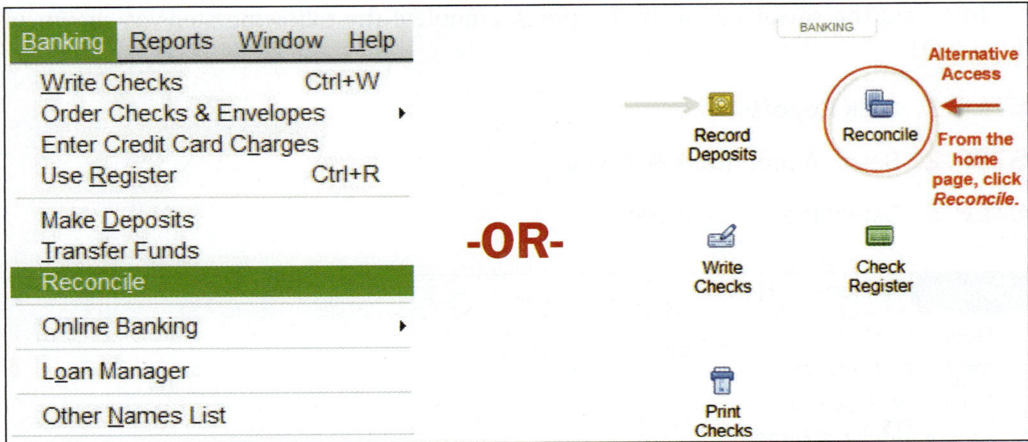

Once you have accessed the bank reconciliation application, you are now ready to complete the following steps in the **Begin Reconciliation** screen. (See Figure Q3.)

STEP 1. Select the **Account** you wish to reconcile from the drop-down menu.

STEP 2. Enter the **Statement Date**, located on the bank statement.

STEP 3. Verify the **Beginning Balance** and enter the **Ending Balance** from the bank statement.

STEP 4. If the bank statement contains a service charge, enter the **amount** and the **date** of the service charge and select the expense **account** involved.

STEP 5. If the bank statement shows interest earned, enter the **amount** and the **date** the interest was earned and select the income **account** involved.

STEP 6. Click **Continue**.

Figure Q3
Begin reconciliation

Begin Reconciliation

Select an account to reconcile, and then enter the ending balance from your account statement.

Account: Cash ← STEP 1.

Statement Date: 10/31/20-- ← STEP 2.

Beginning Balance: 16,633.11

Ending Balance: 17,249.61 ← STEP 3.

What if my beginning balance doesn't match my statement?

Enter any service charge or interest earned.

Service Charge	Date	Account	
19.50	10/31/20--	Miscellaneous Expense	← STEP 4.
Interest Earned	**Date**	**Account**	
10.00	10/31/20--	Interest Income	← STEP 5.

Locate Discrepancies | Undo Last Reconciliation | Continue ← STEP 6. | Cancel | Help

The **Reconcile – Cash** screen is where deposits and checks that have cleared the bank are marked off in QuickBooks. When all items that have cleared the bank are marked, the **Ending Balance** and the **Cleared Balance** amounts should be the same as shown in Figure Q4. If these two amounts do not match, the discrepancies need to be located.

STEP 7. When the **Difference** between the **Ending Balance** and the **Cleared Balance** in Figure 5 is **ZERO**, proceed to Step 8.

STEP 8. Click **Reconcile Now**.

Figure Q4
Reconcile cash

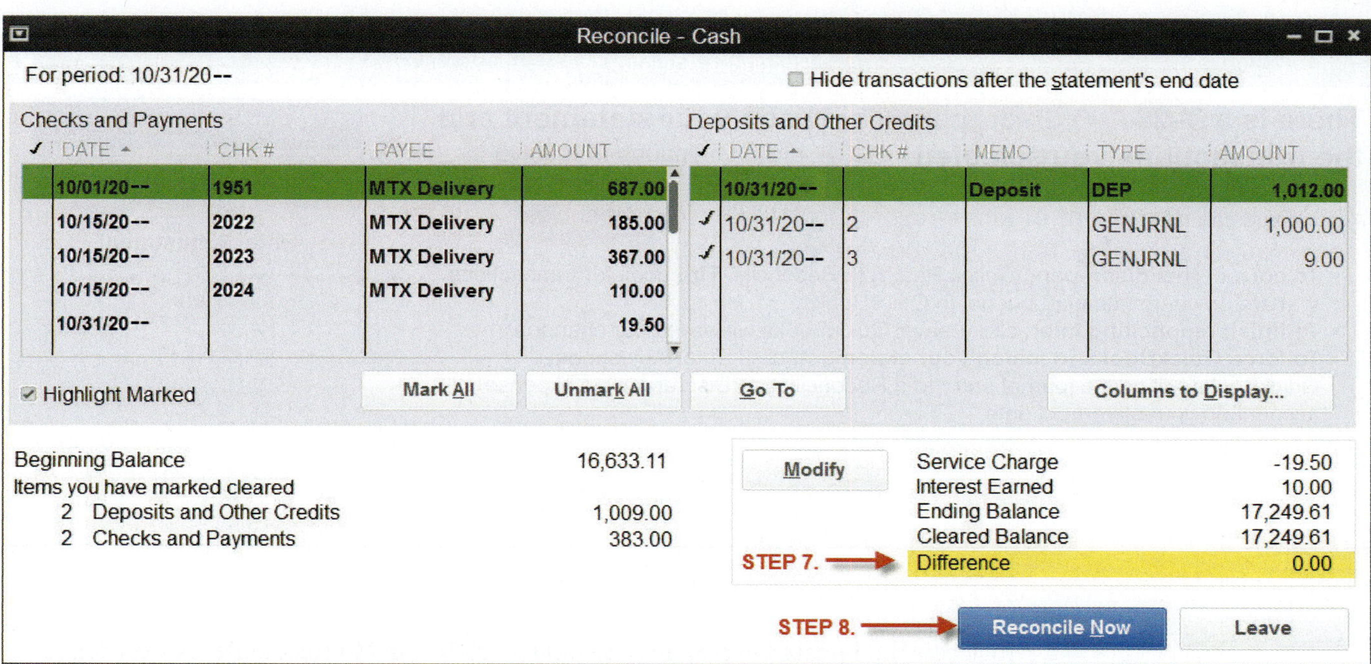

After clicking **Reconcile Now,** the **Select Reconciliation Report** window will appear, as shown in Figure Q5. Select the desired report type: **Summary**, **Detailed**, or **Both**. The selected report(s) can be viewed on the screen or printed. If reports are not desired, simply click **Close**.

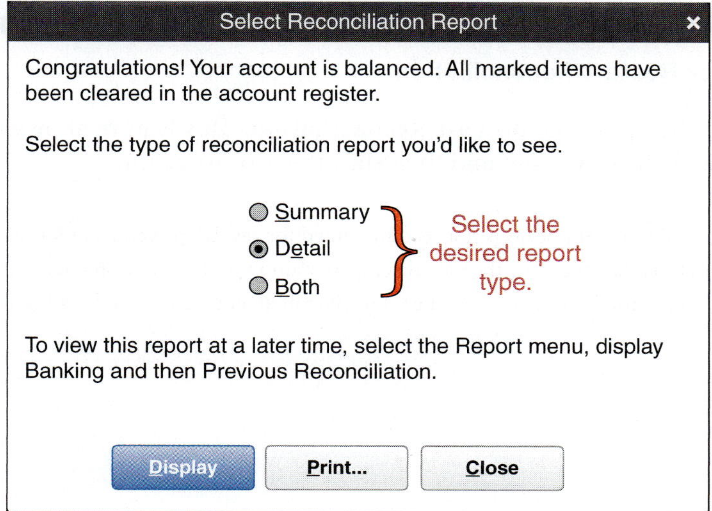

Figure Q5
Select reconciliation report

From time to time, discrepancies between the **Ending Balance** and the **Cleared Balance** will occur. QuickBooks has a feature called **Locate Discrepancies**, which can help users identify and resolve reconciliation differences. To access the **Discrepancy Report**, click on **Reconcile Now**, as shown in Step 8 of Figure Q4 on page 301. The pop-up window **Reconcile Adjustment** will appear. This window identifies reconciliation discrepancies between the bank statement and the company books. Users have three options to resolve the discrepancy: (1) **Return to Reconcile**, (2) **Leave Reconcile**, or (3) **Enter Adjustment**.* There is also a **Help** button, which provides users with more details about each of the three options.

Figure Q6
Reconcile adjustment

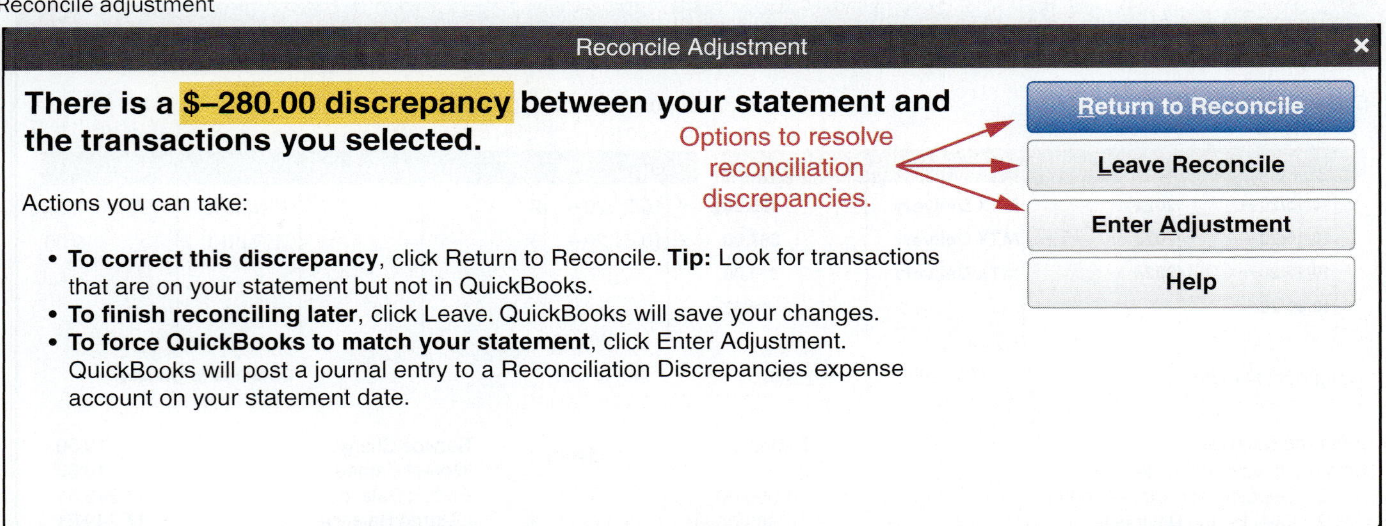

To access the **Locate Discrepancy Report**, click **Return to Reconcile**, as shown in Figure Q6 (above), and then click on **Locate Discrepancies**, as shown in Figure Q3 on page 300. When the **Locate Discrepancies** window appears, as shown in Figure Q7, follow the steps below:

STEP 1. Select the **Account**.

STEP 2. Select the type of report (**Discrepancy Report** or **Previous Reports**).

STEP 3. Click **Restart Reconciliation**.

You also have the option **Undo Last Reconciliation**. This feature allows you to clear a previous reconciliation attempt and then start the process again.

Note:* The **Enter Adjustment option is not recommended for resolving reconciliation discrepancies. This option only records an adjustment for the total discrepancy amount. If this option is used, it is still necessary to find the individual error(s) and reclassify the total adjustment entry to the appropriate accounts.

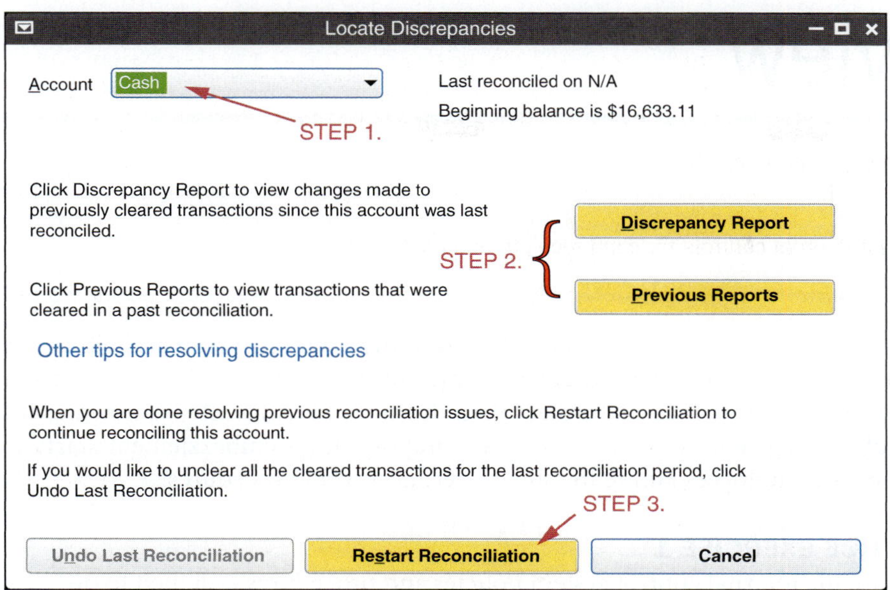

Figure Q7
Locate discrepancies

3 View and print banking reports.

Learning Objective

To view and print the banking reports, follow the steps shown below.

STEP 1. Click the **Reports** tab.

STEP 2. Click **Banking**.

STEP 3. Select the desired banking report.

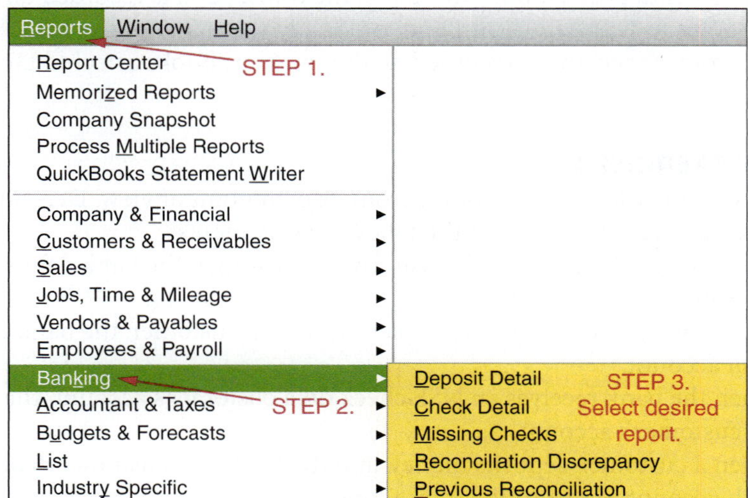

Figure Q8
Banking reports.

STEP 4. Adjust the **From:** and **To:** dates and click **Refresh**.

STEP 5. To print the report, click the **Print** button.

Chapter Review

Study and Practice

Learning Objective  List internal controls for cash receipts and cash payments.

An important aspect of any financial accounting system, for an individual or for a business enterprise, is the accurate and efficient management of assets. The handling of assets in a manner that will protect them from fraud and waste is known as **internal control**. Management of cash is especially important, as embezzlement starts with an employee or employees failing to follow internal control procedures.

PRACTICE EXERCISE 1

What are the internal control system policies and procedures designed to do?

PRACTICE EXERCISE 1 • SOLUTION

1. Protect assets against fraud and waste
2. Provide for accurate accounting data
3. Promote efficient operations
4. Encourage adherence to management policies

Learning Objective  Describe the procedures for recording deposits and withdrawals.

When a customer deposits money in a bank, the transaction is recorded on the company books as a debit to Cash, Cash in Bank, or simply the name of the bank. Withdrawals from the customer's account is recorded on the company books as a credit to the specified Cash account.

PRACTICE EXERCISE 2

Each business entity keeps its accounts from its own point of view. Determine the point of view; then answer (T) or (F) for the following statements:

___ 1. When the bank receives a deposit from a customer, the bank debits the Cash account.

___ 2. When the bank cashes a check (pays out) for a customer, the bank credits the Cash account.

___ 3. When the bank receives an NSF check on a customer's account, the bank debits the customer's account.

___ 4. When a customer deposits money into the bank, the customer debits his or her Cash account to record the transaction.

PRACTICE EXERCISE 2 • SOLUTION

1. F
2. F
3. T
4. T

3 Reconcile a bank statement.

Learning Objective

The standard form for a **bank reconciliation** is as follows:

Bank Statement Balance

Add:
Deposits in transit
Bank errors that understate the **bank statement** balance

Deduct:
Outstanding checks or electronic transfers
Bank errors that overstate the bank statement balance

Adjusted Bank Statement Balance

Ledger Balance of Cash

Add:
Notes collected
Interest income earned
Checkbook errors that understate the ledger balance of cash
Bank credit memos

Deduct:
Bank service charges
Checkbook errors that overstate the ledger balance of cash
NSF checks
Bank debit memos

Adjusted Ledger Balance of Cash

3 PRACTICE EXERCISE 3

The bank statement of M. C. Johnson Company indicates a balance of $7,428 as of July 31. The balance of the Cash account in Johnson's ledger as of that date is $6,872. Johnson's accountant has taken the following steps:

STEP 1. Verified that canceled checks were recorded correctly on the bank statement.

STEP 2. Noted that the deposit made on July 31 was not recorded on the bank statement, $2,071.

STEP 3. Noted outstanding checks: no. 1066, $1,075; no. 1099, $462; no. 1100, $605.

STEP 4. Noted credit memo: Note collected by the bank from L. Stewart, $500, not recorded in the journal. Noted debit memo: Collection charge and service charge not recorded in the journal, $15.

Based on the preceding information, prepare a bank reconciliation for M. C. Johnson Company.

(Continued)

PRACTICE EXERCISE 3 • SOLUTION

M. C. Johnson Company
Bank Reconciliation
July 31, 20--

Bank Statement Balance		$7,428.00
Add: Deposit in transit (July 31)		2,071.00
		$9,499.00
Deduct: Outstanding checks		
No. 1066	$1,075.00	
No. 1099	462.00	
No. 1100	605.00	2,142.00
Adjusted Bank Statement Balance		$7,357.00
Ledger Balance of Cash		$6,872.00
Add: Note collected by bank (L. Stewart)		500.00
		$7,372.00
Deduct: Bank service and collection charges		15.00
Adjusted Ledger Balance of Cash		$7,357.00

Learning Objective

4 Record the required journal entries from the bank reconciliation.

Journal entries for the Ledger Balance of Cash section are required. The entry for notes and interest collected is a debit to Cash and credits to Notes Receivable and Interest Income. The entry for a bank service charge is a debit to Miscellaneous Expense and a credit to Cash. The entry for an NSF check is a debit to Accounts Receivable and a credit to Cash.

PRACTICE EXERCISE 4

Prepare the necessary journal entries from the bank reconciliation in Practice Exercise 3 for M. C. Johnson Company.

PRACTICE EXERCISE 4 • SOLUTION

GENERAL JOURNAL Page ___

Date		Description	Post. Ref.	Debit	Credit
20--					
July	31	Cash		500.00	
		Notes Receivable			500.00
		Non-interest-bearing note			
		signed by L. Stewart was			
		collected by the bank.			
	31	Miscellaneous Expense		15.00	
		Cash			15.00
		Service charge and collection			
		charge levied by bank.			

5 Record journal entries to establish a Petty Cash Fund.

Learning Objective

The entry to establish a **Petty Cash Fund** is a debit to Petty Cash Fund and a credit to Cash.

5 **PRACTICE EXERCISE 5**

A Petty Cash Fund of $100 was established on October 1. At the end of the month, the following accounts were charged for expenditures from the Petty Cash Fund: Office Supplies, $13.75; Delivery Expense, $15.00; Miscellaneous Expense, $36.00; B. Thomas, Drawing, $25.00. Record the journal entries for the establishment of the Petty Cash Fund.

PRACTICE EXERCISE 5 • SOLUTION

GENERAL JOURNAL — Page ___

Date		Description	Post. Ref.	Debit	Credit
20--					
Oct.	1	Petty Cash Fund		1 0 0 00	
		Cash			1 0 0 00
		Established a Petty Cash Fund.			

6 Complete petty cash vouchers, petty cash payments record and reimburse the petty cash fund.

Learning Objective

A **petty cash voucher** is made out for each payment from the Petty Cash Fund. In the **petty cash payments record**, each voucher is listed and a notation is made concerning the accounts involved. In addition, an explanation of why the money was paid out is recorded. The petty cash payments record is used as a source of information for making the journal entry to reimburse the Petty Cash Fund. The entry to reimburse the Petty Cash Fund consists of debits to the items for which payments from the Petty Cash Fund were made and one credit to Cash for the total payments.

6 **PRACTICE EXERCISE 6**

Using the information from Practice Exercise 5, record the journal entry for the reimbursement of the Petty Cash Fund.

PRACTICE EXERCISE 6 • SOLUTION

GENERAL JOURNAL — Page ___

Date		Description	Post. Ref.	Debit	Credit
20--					
Oct.	31	Office Supplies		1 3 75	
		Delivery Expense		1 5 00	
		Miscellaneous Expense		3 6 00	
		B. Thomas, Drawing		2 5 00	
		Cash			8 9 75
		Reimbursed the Petty Cash Fund.			

CHAPTER REVIEW

Learning Objective

 Record the journal entries to establish a Change Fund.

The entry to establish the **Change Fund** is a debit to Change Fund and a credit to Cash.

PRACTICE EXERCISE 7

Journalize the entry to establish a Change Fund amounting to $150 on July 1.

PRACTICE EXERCISE 7 • SOLUTION

GENERAL JOURNAL — Page ___

Date		Description	Post. Ref.	Debit	Credit
20--					
July	1	Change Fund		150 00	
		Cash			150 00
		Established a Change Fund.			

Learning Objective

 Record journal entries for transactions involving Cash Short and Over.

The Cash Short and Over account provides a way to keep a record of errors in making change. A debit balance in Cash Short and Over denotes a shortage, which is listed as Miscellaneous Expense; the entry is a debit to Miscellaneous Expense and a credit to Cash Short and Over. A credit balance in Cash Short and Over denotes an overage, which becomes Miscellaneous Income; the entry is a debit to Cash Short and Over and a credit to Miscellaneous Income.

PRACTICE EXERCISE 8

Journalize the entries to account for two bank deposits on June 29 and June 30. The amount of the Change Fund is $100.

a. On June 29, the cash register tape showed $950.86 in income from sales. The amount in the cash drawer was $1,051.86.
b. On June 30, the cash register tape showed $1,327.44 in income from sales. The amount in the cash drawer was $1,426.12.

PRACTICE EXERCISE 8 • SOLUTION

GENERAL JOURNAL Page ___

Date		Description	Post. Ref.	Debit	Credit
20--					
June	29	Cash		951 86	
		Income from Sales			950 86
		Cash Short and Over			1 00
		To record revenue earned for the			
		day involving a cash overage			
		of $1.00.			
	30	Cash		1,326 12	
		Cash Short and Over		1 32	
		Income from Sales			1,327 44
		To record revenue earned for the			
		day involving a cash shortage			
		of $1.32.			

Glossary

ATMs (automated teller machines) Machines that enable depositors to make deposits, withdrawals, and transfers using a coded plastic card. *(p. 274)*

Bank reconciliation A process by which an accountant determines whether and why there is a difference between the balance shown on the bank statement and the balance of the Cash account in the business's general ledger. The object is to determine the adjusted (or true) balance of the Cash account. *(p. 279)*

Bank routing number A nine-digit number used by the Federal Reserve Bank to identify the financial institution of the account holder. *(p. 276)*

Bank statement A periodic statement that a bank sends to the drawer/depositor of a checking account listing deposits received and checks paid by the bank, debit and credit memos, electronic transactions, and beginning and ending balances. *(p. 277)*

Canceled checks Checks issued by the depositor that have been paid (cleared) by the bank and listed on the bank statement. They are called canceled checks because they are canceled by a stamp, indicating that they have been paid. *(p. 279)*

Cash funds Separately held reserves of cash set aside for specific purposes. *(p. 272)*

Change Fund A cash fund used by a business to make change for customers who pay cash for goods or services. *(p. 293)*

Collections Payments collected by the bank and added to the customer's bank account in the form of a credit memorandum. *(p. 280)*

Denominations Varieties of coins and currency, such as quarters, dimes, and nickels and $1 and $5 bills. *(p. 290)*

Deposit in transit A deposit not recorded on the bank statement because the deposit was made between the time of the bank's closing date for compiling items for its statement and the time the statement is received by the depositor; also known as a *late deposit*. *(p. 280)*

Deposit slips Printed forms provided by a bank on which customers can list all items being deposited; also known as *deposit tickets*. *(p. 273)*

Drawer The party who writes the check. *(p. 275)*

Electronic Funds Transfer (EFT) A transfer of funds initiated through an electronic terminal, such as a telephone, computer, or magnetic tape. *(p. 274)*

Endorsement The process by which the payee transfers ownership of the check to a bank or another party. A check must be endorsed when deposited in a bank, because the bank must have legal title to it in order to collect payment from the drawer of the check (the person or firm who wrote the check). *(p. 275)*

Errors Mistakes made by a customer or the bank. *(p. 280)*

Interest income The amount earned from lending money to another person or business. *(p. 280)*

Internal control Plans and procedures built into the accounting system with the following objectives: (1) to protect assets against fraud and waste, (2) to provide accurate accounting data, (3) to promote efficient operation, and (4) to encourage adherence to management policies. *(p. 271)*

Ledger balance of cash The balance of the Cash account in the general ledger before it is reconciled with the bank statement. *(p. 279)*

NSF (non-sufficient funds) check Check drawn against an account in which there are *not sufficient funds* and returned by the payee's bank to the drawer's bank because of nonpayment; also known as a *dishonored check. (p. 280)*

Online banking Customers conduct banking transactions, such as pay bills, transfer funds, and review bank statements through a secure website. *(p. 274)*

Outstanding checks Checks that have been written by the drawer and deducted on his or her records but have not reached the bank for payment and are not deducted from the bank balance by the time the bank issues its statement. *(p. 280)*

Payee The person to whom a check is payable. *(p. 275)*

Petty Cash Fund A cash fund used to make small, immediate cash payments. *(p. 289)*

Petty cash payments record A record indicating the amount of each petty cash voucher, the accounts to which it should be charged, and the purpose of the expenditure. *(p. 291)*

Petty cash voucher A form stating who requested cash from the Petty Cash Fund, signed by (1) the person in charge of the fund and (2) the person who received the cash, and indicating the purpose of the petty cash payment. *(p. 290)*

personal identification number (PIN) A unique *personal identification number* that is entered by the user to protect access to the user's account. *(p. 274)*

Positive pay A fraud prevention cash management program offered by banks in an attempt to protect customers and the bank. *(p. 276)*

Promissory note A written promise to pay a specific sum at a definite future time. *(p. 282)*

Remote deposit The process of capturing checks and deposits electronically for presentation to a financial institution. *(p. 274)*

Service charge The fee the bank charges for handling checks, collections, and other items. It is in the form of a debit memorandum. *(p. 280)*

Signature card The form a depositor signs to give the bank a copy of the official signatures of any persons authorized to sign checks. The bank can use it to verify the depositors' signatures on checks. *(p. 273)*

Substitute check The creation of a two-sided digital version of an original check. *(p. 274)*

Quiz Yourself

_____ 1. Which of the following is *not* an example of an internal control system?
   a. Maintain separate duties between cash handling and cash recording.
   b. Make weekly deposits.
   c. Keep petty cash locked up and under one person's control.
   d. Prenumber checks.
   e. Endorse checks immediate upon receipt.

_____ 2. Which of the following does *not* affect the bank statement?
   a. Credit memo
   b. Debit memo
   c. Overdraft
   d. Electronic transactions
   e. Endorsements

_____ 3. Which of the following does *not* explain the differences between the bank statement balance and the customer's cash balance?
   a. Deposit in transit
   b. Canceled checks
   c. An NSF check
   d. Errors
   e. Interest income

_____ 4. What is the journal entry to record an NSF check, from J. Smith for $250, that is returned with the bank statement?
   a. Cash $250 DR; NSF Check $250 CR
   b. Accounts Receivable $250 DR; Cash $250 CR
   c. NSF Check $250 DR; Accounts Receivable $250 CR
   d. Cash $250 DR; Accounts Receivable $250 CR
   e. Cash $250 DR; Miscellaneous Expense $250 DR

_____ 5. The Petty Cash account is a(n) __________.
   a. Liability
   b. Expense
   c. Asset
   d. Owner's Equity
   e. Prepaid Account

_____ 6. When the Petty Cash account is replenished at the end of the month, the journal entry includes which of the following?
   a. Debit to Cash
   b. Debit to Petty Cash
   c. Credit to Cash
   d. Credit to an Expense Account
   e. Credit to a Revenue Account

_____ 7. The entry to establish the Change Fund includes which of the following?
   a. Debit to Cash
   b. Debit to Change Fund
   c. Credit to Change Fund
   d. Debit to Petty Cash
   e. Credit to Petty Cash

_____ 8. The Cash Short and Over account covers both shortages and overages that occur in a business. What is the correct entry to record a shortage in the Cash Short and Over account? Where will the account appear on the income statement?
   a. DR Cash Short and Over; Expense
   b. CR Cash Short and Over; Income
   c. DR Cash Short and Over; Income
   d. CR Cash Short and Over; Expense
   e. None of the above; the Cash Short and Over account appears on the balance sheet.

Answers:
1.b 2.e 3.b 4.b 5.c 6.c 7.b 8.a

Review It with QuickBooks®

_____ 1. Which of the following reports can be used to prevent fraud?
   a. Audit Trail Report
   b. Closing Date Exception Report
   c. Voided/Deleted Transaction Reports
   d. All of the above

_____ 2. The ____________ screen is where deposits and checks that have cleared the bank are checked off in QuickBooks.
   a. Banking
   b. Reconcile—Cash
   c. Reconcile Adjustment
   d. Locate Discrepancies

_____ 3. Which report displays additions, deletions, and modification to QuickBooks transactions?
   a. Closing Date Exception Report
   b. Discrepancy Report
   c. Audit Trail Report
   d. None of the above

_____ 4. All of the following Reconcile Adjustment features can be used to locate bank reconciliation discrepancies, *except*:
   a. Return to Reconcile, to correct discrepancies.
   b. Leave Reconcile, to finish the reconciliation process later.
   c. Enter Adjustment, to force QuickBooks to balance with the bank statement.
   d. Reconcile—Cash, to locate cash shortages or overages.

Answers:
1.d 2.b 3.c 4.d

CHAPTER ASSIGNMENTS

Chapter Assignments

Discussion Questions

1. What are internal controls designed to do?
2. Why does a bank keep a signature card on file for customers' accounts?
3. What is the purpose of endorsing a check?
4. Why is there generally a difference between the balance in the Cash account on the company's books and the balance on the bank statement?
5. Indicate whether the following items in a bank reconciliation should be (1) added to the Cash account balance, (2) deducted from the Cash account balance, (3) added to the bank statement balance, or (4) deducted from the bank statement balance.
   a. NSF check
   b. Deposit in transit
   c. Outstanding check
   d. Bank error charging the business's account with another company's check
   e. Bank service charge
6. Why is it necessary to make general journal entries for the ledger balance side of the bank reconciliation?
7. a. Why would a business use a Petty Cash Fund?
   b. Describe the entry needed to establish a $50 Petty Cash Fund and an entry to reimburse the fund.
8. a. What does a debit balance in Cash Short and Over mean?
   b. Where does a debit balance in Cash Short and Over appear in the financial statements?
   c. What does a credit balance in Cash Short and Over mean?
   d. Where does a credit balance in Cash Short and Over appear in the financial statements?

Exercises

LO 3

Practice Exercise 3

EXERCISE 6-1 Fill in the missing amounts for the following bank reconciliation:

Bank Reconciliation
March 31, 20--

Bank Statement Balance		$3,764.00
Add: Deposit in transit		(a)
		$4,031.00
Deduct: Outstanding checks	$212.00	
No. 211	(b)	
No. 225	318.00	
No. 228		850.00
Adjusted Bank Statement Balance		(c)
Ledger Balance of Cash		$2,837.00
Add: Note collected by bank		430.00
		(d)
Deduct: Bank service and collection charges	(e)	
NSF check from customer	74.00	86.00
Adjusted Ledger Balance of Cash		(f)

LO 4
Practice Exercise 4

EXERCISE 6-2 The Ledger Balance of Cash section of the bank reconciliation for Lasha Company for July 31 follows.

Ledger Balance of Cash		$6,360.00
Add: Note collected (principal $700.00, interest $17.50, signed by D. Dansky)	$717.50	
Error in recording Ck. No. 2225 payable to Denton Company (recorded check for $12 too much)	12.00	729.50
		$ 7,089.50
Deduct: NSF check from J. Kenyon	$ 95.00	
Bank service and collection charges	29.00	124.00
Adjusted Ledger Balance of Cash		$6,965.50

Journalize the entries required to bring the general ledger up to date as of July of this year.

LO 3
Practice Exercise 3

EXERCISE 6-3 When the bank statement is received on July 3, it shows a balance, before reconciliation, of $5,200 as of June 30. After reconciliation, the adjusted balance is $3,100. If one deposit in transit amounted to $1,200, what was the total of the outstanding checks assuming that no other adjustments would be made to the bank statement?

LO 3
Practice Exercise 3

EXERCISE 6-4 Place a check mark in the column that indicates the location of each item that would be found on a bank reconciliation. Assume that the checks written by the company are written correctly.

Item	Add to Bank Statement Balance	Subtract from Bank Statement Balance	Add to Ledger Balance of Cash	Subtract from Ledger Balance of Cash
a. A check-printing charge				
b. An outstanding check				
c. A deposit for $197 listed incorrectly on the bank statement as $179				
d. A collection charge the bank made for a note it collected for its depositor				
e. A check written for $41.73 and recorded incorrectly in the checkbook as $41.37				
f. A deposit in transit				
g. An NSF check received from a customer				
h. A check written for $82.40 and recorded incorrectly in the checkbook as $820.40				

LO 3

Practice Exercise 3

EXERCISE 6-5 Hosung Company's Cash account shows a balance of $801.65 as of August 31 of this year. The balance on the bank statement on that date is $1,383. Checks for $260.50, $425.10, and $331.00 are outstanding. The bank statement shows a check issued by another depositor for $237.25 (in other words, the bank made an error and charged Hosung Company for a check written by another company). The bank statement also shows an NSF check for $180 received from one of Hosung's customers. Service charges for the month were $18. What is the adjusted ledger balance of cash as of August 31?

LO 5, 6

Practice Exercise 5

EXERCISE 6-6 Record entries in general journal form to record the following:

a. Established a Petty Cash Fund, $100. Issued Ck. No. 857.
b. Reimbursed the Petty Cash Fund for expenditures of $98: Store Supplies, $38; Office Supplies, $21; Miscellaneous Expense, $39. Issued Ck. No. 889.
c. Increased the amount of the fund by an additional $50. Issued Ck. No. 891.
d. Reimbursed the Petty Cash Fund for expenditures of $96.58: Store Supplies, $41.68; Delivery Expense, $35.00; Miscellaneous Expense, $19.90. Issued Ck. No. 936.

LO 8

Practice Exercise 8

EXERCISE 6-7 At the end of the day, the cash register tape lists $881.40 as total income from services. Cash on hand consists of $18.25 in coins, $433.60 in currency, $100.00 in traveler's checks, and $427.00 in customers' checks. The amount of the Change Fund is $100. In general journal form, record the entry to record the day's cash revenue.

LO 7, 8

Practice Exercises 7, 8

EXERCISE 6-8

a. Describe the entries that have been posted to the following accounts after the Change Fund was established.

Change Fund

Debit	Credit
200	

Sales

Debit	Credit
	Jan. 3 1,520
	4 1,421
	6 1,665

Cash

Debit	Credit
Jan. 3 1,522	
4 1,418	
6 1,664	

Cash Short and Over

Debit	Credit
Jan. 4 3	Jan. 3 2
6 1	

b. How will the balance of Cash Short and Over be reported on the income statement?

Problem Set A

LO 3, 4

PROBLEM 6-1A Arthur's Men's Shop deposits all receipts in the bank each evening and makes all payments by check. On November 30, its ledger balance of cash is $2,375.05.

The bank statement balance of cash as of November 30 is $2,784.77. Use the following information to reconcile the bank statement:

a. The reconciliation for October, the previous month, showed three checks outstanding on October 31: no. 1417 for $95.00, no. 1420 for $125.87, and no. 1422 for $136.00. Check no. 1417 and no. 1422 were returned with the November bank statement; however, check no. 1420 was not returned.
b. Check no. 1500 for $155.00, no. 1517 for $132.00, no. 1518 for $218.00, and no. 1519 for $128.85 were written during November and have not been returned by the bank.
c. A deposit of $945 was placed in the night depository on November 30 and did not appear on the bank statement.
d. The canceled checks were compared with the entries in the checkbook, and it was observed that check no. 1487, for $89, was written correctly, payable to M. A. Golden, the owner, for personal use, but was recorded in the checkbook as $98.
e. Included in the bank statement was a bank debit memo for service charges, $29.
f. A bank credit memo was also enclosed for the collection of a note signed by C.G. Tolson, $615, including $600 principal and $15 interest.

Required

1. Prepare a bank reconciliation as of November 30 assuming that the debit and credit memos have not been recorded.
2. Record the necessary entries in general journal form.

Check Figure
Adjusted ledger balance of cash, $2,970.05

LO 5, 6

PROBLEM 6-2A On May 1 of this year, Ellsworth and Company established a Petty Cash Fund. The following petty cash transactions took place during the month:

May	1	Cashed check no. 956 for $150 to establish a Petty Cash Fund and put the $150 in a locked drawer in the office.
	3	Bought postage stamps, $8.80, voucher no. 1 (Miscellaneous Expense).
	4	Issued voucher no. 2 for taxi fare, $12 (Miscellaneous Expense).
	6	Issued voucher no. 3 for delivery charges on outgoing parts, $15.
	9	B. Ellsworth, the owner, withdrew $25 for personal use, voucher no. 4.
	13	Paid $8.29 for postage, voucher no. 5 (Miscellaneous Expense).
	19	Bought pens for office, $6, voucher no. 6.
	23	Paid $3.59 for a box of staples, voucher no. 7.
	28	Paid $15 for window cleaning service, voucher no. 8 (Miscellaneous Expense).
	29	Paid $2 for pencils for office, voucher no. 9.
	31	Issued for cash check no. 1098 for $95.68 to reimburse Petty Cash Fund.

Required

1. Journalize the entry establishing the Petty Cash Fund in the general journal.
2. Record the disbursements of petty cash in the petty cash payments record.
3. Journalize the summarizing entry to reimburse the Petty Cash Fund.

Check Figure
Office Supplies, $11.59

LO 8

PROBLEM 6-3A Ellie Harrod, owner of Harrod's Dry Cleaners, makes bank deposits in the night depository at the close of each business day. The following information for the last four days of July is available.

	July			
	28	**29**	**30**	**31**
Cash register tape	$895.20	$ 977.40	$884.50	$1,027.25
Cash count	993.50	1,075.80	986.60	1,124.40

(Continued)

Check Figure
Cash Short and Over, July 31, $2.85 cash shortage

Required

In general journal form, record the cash deposit for each day assuming that there is a $100 Change Fund.

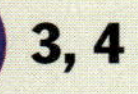
LO 3, 4

Check Figure
Adjusted ledger balance of cash, $1,480

PROBLEM 6-4A On August 31, Baginski and Company receives its bank statement (shown below). The company deposits its receipts in the bank and makes all payments by check. The debit memo for $95 is for an NSF check written by L. Pitts. Check no. 925 for $47, payable to Jardin Company (a creditor), was recorded in the checkbook and journal as $74.

The ledger balance of cash as of August 31 is $1,563. Outstanding checks as of August 31 are no. 928, $150 and no. 929, $292. The accountant notes that the deposit of August 31 for $599 did not appear on the bank statement.

Required

1. Prepare a bank reconciliation as of August 31 assuming that the debit memos have not been recorded.*
2. Record the necessary journal entries.*
3. Complete the bank form to determine the adjusted balance of cash.*

*If you are using QuickBooks, use the bank statement reconciliation application and follow the instructions provided in *Try It with QuickBooks* on page 321.

PEABODY NATIONAL BANK

STATEMENT OF ACCOUNT

Baginski and Company
416 Seneca Avenue
Kansas City, Missouri 64102

ACCOUNT NO. **152-655-217**
STATEMENT DATE **August 1 to 31, 20--**

SUMMARY	
Balance Last Statement	$961.00
Amount of Checks and Debits	$2,289.00
Number of Checks	11
Amount of Deposits and Credits	$2,651.00
Number of Deposits	7
Balance This Statement	$1,323.00

CHECKS/ OTHER DEBITS

CHECKS

CHECK NUMBER	DATE POSTED	AMOUNT	CHECK NUMBER	DATE POSTED	AMOUNT
917	8-04	172.00	923	8-09	621.00
918	8-04	76.00	924	8-17	37.00
919	8-05	146.00	925	8-17	47.00
920	8-07	206.00	926	8-23	441.00
921	8-07	139.00	927	8-28	94.00
922	8-07	200.00			

OTHER DEBITS

DESCRIPTION	DATE POSTED	AMOUNT
DM NSF check	8-31	95.00
DM Service charge	8-31	15.00

DEPOSITS/ OTHER CREDITS

DEPOSITS

DATE POSTED	AMOUNT	DATE POSTED	AMOUNT
8-02	326.00	8-18	419.00
8-05	412.00	8-24	398.00
8-09	437.00	8-28	291.00
8-14	368.00		

PLEASE EXAMINE THIS STATEMENT CAREFULLY. REPORT ANY POSSIBLE ERRORS WITHIN 10 DAYS.

CODE SYMBOLS

CM Credit Memo DM Debit Memo OD Overdraft EC Error Correction

LO 3, 4

PROBLEM 6-5A The Quilt Shop deposits all receipts in the bank each evening and makes all payments by check. On July 31, its ledger balance of cash is $2,830.15. The bank statement balance of cash as of July 31 is $3,215.20. Use the following information to reconcile the bank statement:

a. The reconciliation for June, the previous month, showed three checks outstanding on June 30: no. 1820 for $85.00, no. 1822 for $115.20, and no. 1823 for $120.00. Check no. 1820 and no. 1822 were returned with the July bank statement; however, check no. 1823 was not returned.
b. Check no. 2500 for $255.00, no. 2517 for $332.00, no. 2518 for $115.00, and no. 2519 for $28.85 were written during July and have not been returned by the bank.
c. A deposit of $446.80 was placed in the night depository on July 31 and did not appear on the bank statement.
d. The canceled checks were compared with the entries in the checkbook, and it was observed that check no. 2587, for $26, was written correctly, payable to J. L. Lang, the owner, for personal use, but was recorded in the checkbook as $62.
e. Included in the bank statement was a bank debit memo for service charges, $25.
f. Included in the bank statement was an NSF check from Jeremy Jones in the amount of $30.

Required

1. Prepare a bank reconciliation as of July 31 assuming that the debit memo and NSF check have not been recorded.
2. Record the necessary entries in general journal form.

Check Figure
Adjusted ledger balance of cash $2,811.15

Problem Set B

LO 3, 4

PROBLEM 6-1B Merkle Company deposits all receipts in the bank each evening and makes all payments by check. On November 30, its ledger balance of cash is $3,219.72. The bank statement balance of cash as of November 30, is $3,490.72. You are given the following information with which to reconcile the bank statement:

a. A deposit of $525.30 was placed in the night depository on November 30 and did not appear on the bank statement.
b. The reconciliation for October, the previous month, showed three checks outstanding on October 31: no. 728 for $80.20, no. 731 for $129.00, and no. 732 for $145.34. Check no. 728 and no. 731 were returned with the November bank statement; however, check no. 732 was not returned.
c. Check no. 743 for $42.00, no. 744 for $16.20, no. 745 for $119.00, and no. 746 for $35.26 were written during November but were not returned by the bank.
d. A $150 personal withdrawal by C. R. Merkle, the owner, using an ATM, was not recorded.
e. Included in the bank statement was a bank debit memo for service charges, $19.
f. A bank credit memo was also enclosed for the collection of a note signed by O. L. Leland, $607.50, including $600.00 principal and $7.50 interest.

Required

1. Prepare a bank reconciliation as of November 30 assuming that the debit and credit memos have not been recorded.
2. Record the necessary entries in general journal form.

Check Figure
Adjusted ledger balance of cash $3,658.22

CHAPTER ASSIGNMENTS

LO 5, 6

PROBLEM 6-2B On March 1 of this year, Stowe Company established a Petty Cash Fund, and the following petty cash transactions took place during the month:

Mar.	1	Cashed check no. 314 for $100 to establish a Petty Cash Fund and put the $100 in a locked drawer in the office.
	4	Issued voucher no. 1 for taxi fare, $7.60 (Miscellaneous Expense).
	7	Issued voucher no. 2 for memo pads, $6.50 (Office Supplies).
	9	Paid $21.50 for an advertisement in a college basketball program, voucher no. 3.
	16	Bought postage stamps, $8.80, voucher no. 4 (Miscellaneous Expense).
	20	Paid $10 to have snow removed from office front sidewalk, voucher no. 5 (Miscellaneous Expense).
	25	Issued voucher no. 6 for delivery charge, $12.
	28	R. C. Stowe, the owner, withdrew $20 for personal use, voucher no. 7.
	29	Paid $4.20 for postage, voucher no. 8 (Miscellaneous Expense).
	30	Paid $5.90 for delivery charge, voucher no. 9.
	31	Issued for cash check no. 372 for $96.50 to reimburse Petty Cash Fund.

Check Figure
Office Supplies, $6.50

Required

1. Journalize the entry establishing the Petty Cash Fund in the general journal.
2. Record the disbursements of petty cash in the petty cash payments record.
3. Journalize the summarizing entry to reimburse the Petty Cash Fund.

LO 8

PROBLEM 6-3B Roberta Felino, owner of Roberta's Beauty Salon, makes bank deposits in the night depository at the close of each business day. The following information for the first four days of April is available.

	April			
	1	2	3	4
Cash register tape	$386.75	$582.65	$586.65	$623.25
Cash count	485.50	685.75	685.75	726.15

Check Figure
Cash Short and Over, April 3, $0.90 cash shortage

Required

In general journal form, record the cash deposit for each day assuming that there is a $100 Change Fund.

LO 3, 4

QuickBooks

PROBLEM 6-4B On August 2, Northern Motel receives its bank statement (shown on the next page). The company deposits its receipts in the bank and makes all payments by check. The debit memo for $37 is for an NSF check written by T. R. Royce. Check no. 1617 for $75.50, payable to Mitchel Company (a creditor), was incorrectly recorded in the checkbook and journal as $57.50.

The ledger balance of Cash as of July 31 is $1,909.30. Outstanding checks as of July 31 are no. 1631, $118.20; no. 1632, $78.20; and no. 1633, $178.36. The accountant notes that the July 31 deposit of $630 did not appear on the bank statement.

STANTON NATIONAL BANK

STATEMENT OF ACCOUNT	Northern Motel 423 E. Long Avenue Rockford, IL 61104	ACCOUNT NO. 750-135-772 STATEMENT DATE July 1 to 31, 20--

SUMMARY		
	Balance Last Statement	$1,153.80
	Amount of Checks and Debits	$2,105.91
	Number of Checks	14
	Amount of Deposits and Credits	$2,528.17
	Number of Deposits	7
	Balance This Statement	$1,576.06

CHECKS/ OTHER DEBITS

CHECKS	CHECK NUMBER	DATE POSTED	AMOUNT	CHECK NUMBER	DATE POSTED	AMOUNT
	1617	7-03	75.50	1624	7-08	120.00
	1618	7-03	164.00	1625	7-09	409.70
	1619	7-03	124.20	1626	7-12	37.40
	1620	7-05	137.20	1627	7-14	38.49
	1621	7-06	236.25	1628	7-22	182.71
	1622	7-06	159.89	1629	7-25	96.87
	1623	7-08	244.50	1630	7-26	19.20

OTHER DEBITS	DESCRIPTION	DATE POSTED	AMOUNT
	DM NSF check	7-22	37.00
	DM Service charge	7-31	23.00

DEPOSITS/ OTHER CREDITS

DEPOSITS	DATE POSTED	AMOUNT	DATE POSTED	AMOUNT
	7-03	491.50	7-15	291.76
	7-06	415.72	7-18	142.90
	7-09	439.16	7-28	368.93
	7-11	378.20		

PLEASE EXAMINE THIS STATEMENT CAREFULLY. REPORT ANY POSSIBLE ERRORS WITHIN 10 DAYS.

CODE SYMBOLS

CM Credit Memo DM Debit Memo OD Overdraft EC Error Correction

Required

1. Prepare a bank reconciliation as of July 31 assuming that the debit memos have not been recorded.*
2. Record the necessary journal entries.*
3. Complete the bank form to determine the adjusted balance of cash.*

Check Figure
Adjusted ledger balance of cash, $1,831.30

*If you are using QuickBooks, use the bank statement reconciliation application and follow the instructions provided in *Try It with QuickBooks* on page 321.

LO 3, 4

PROBLEM 6-5B Jim's Fitness Center deposits all receipts in the bank each evening and makes all payments by check. On April 30, its ledger balance of cash is $1,515.10. The bank statement balance of cash as of April 30 is $1,920.42. Use the following information to reconcile the bank statement:

a. The reconciliation for March, the previous month, showed three checks outstanding on March 31: no. 555 for $56.00, no. 556 for $428.25, and no. 557 for $20.00. Check no. 555 and no. 557 were returned with the April bank statement; however, check no. 556 was not returned.

(*Continued*)

b. Check no. 565 for $120.00, no. 567 for $45.00, no. 569 for $15.00, and no. 570 for $18.15 were written during April and have not been returned by the bank.
c. A deposit of $119.08 was placed in the night depository on April 30 and did not appear on the bank statement.
d. The canceled checks were compared with the entries in the checkbook, and it was observed that check no. 561, for $46, was written correctly, payable to J. L. Lang, the owner, for personal use, but was recorded in the checkbook as $64.
e. Included in the bank statement was a bank debit memo for service charges, $25.
f. Included in the bank statement was an NSF check from Millie Smith in the amount of $95.

Check Figure
Adjusted ledger balance of cash $1,413.10

Required

1. Prepare a bank reconciliation as of April 30 assuming that the debit memo and NSF check have not been recorded.
2. Record the necessary entries in general journal form.

Try It with QuickBooks® (LO 1, 2, 3)

QB Exercise 6-1

Match the following report names with their appropriate uses.

1. Audit Trail Report
2. Voided/Deleted Transactions Reports
3. Customer Credit Card Audit Trail Report
4. Closing Date Exception Report

a. Provides a record of customer credit card activity.
b. Monitors unauthorized transaction activity.
c. Monitors prior accounting period changes.
d. Provides either a summary or details about voided, unvoided, or deleted transactions.

LO 2, 3

QB Exercise 6-2

Using the end-of-chapter problems 6-4A (Baginski and Company) on page 316 and 6-4B (Northern Motel) on pages 318–319, complete Steps 1–3. Then for Problem 6-4A, complete Step 4. For Problem 6-4B skip Step 4 and complete Step 5.

Required

1. Restore the appropriate company's QuickBooks data file, located at the text's website, found at www.cengagebrain.com.
2. Prepare a bank reconciliation using QuickBooks as of the date provided in the problem. Use 2015 for the year. Assume that the debit memos have not been recorded.
3. Record the service charge and interest adjustments through the bank reconciliation program. Record the necessary journal entries for any other adjustments required to eliminate discrepancies during the reconciliation process.

4. **Complete for Problem 6-4A Only:** Prepare a detailed bank reconciliation report for the current period, after the reconciliation process is complete.
   a. Enter the amount of the debit entry to cash.
   b. Enter the total amount of credit entries to cash.
5. **Complete for Problem 6-4B Only:** Prepare a detailed bank reconciliation report for the current period, after the reconciliation process is complete.
   a. Enter the total amount of credit entries to cash.
   a. Enter the amount of the error in recording Check No. 1617 payable to Mitchel Company.

Activities

Why Does It Matter?

FEELEY & DRISCOLL, Boston, Massachusetts
Based in Boston, Massachusetts, Feeley & Driscoll is a full-service consulting and forensic accounting firm. Its services range from determining contract damages to overseeing fraud examination. Its forensic accountants are experts at finding even the cleverest trails of fraudulent financial data and then providing the hard numbers needed to prove a case of fraud. The forensic accountants look beyond the numbers to analyze and reveal all relevant aspects of the situation.

Feeley & Driscoll has extensive experience in information technology for consulting audits and assessments. It also delivers complete data analysis of electronic business records and files, including e-mails, financial spreadsheets, hard drives, and tape backups.

Assume that you are a business owner concerned about preventing fraud. Explain how hiring a firm specializing in forensic accounting such as Feeley & Driscoll can help you stop fraud from occurring.

What Would You Say?

As the new bookkeeper for a small business, you find that several people access the Petty Cash Fund, usually without anyone leaving a written explanation of what the money was used for. The amount of cash does not match the recorded amount of the fund. Explain how operation of the Petty Cash Fund can be made more efficient to maintain an accurate accounting of how the money is used.

What Do You Think?

You work as a cashier for a service business. Some days you are short of cash at the end of the day, and some days you have more cash than the cash register tape says was earned. You are embarrassed when your cash is short and don't want the owner to know, so you use your own money to make up the difference. On days when you are over, you keep the difference to help pay back what you paid to cover your shortages. What do you think of this practice? Explain.

chapter

7 Employee Earnings and Deductions

Learning Objectives

After you have completed this chapter, you will be able to do the following:

1. Recognize the role of income tax laws that affect payroll deductions and contributions.
2. Calculate total earnings based on an hourly, salary, piece-rate, or commission basis.
3. Determine deductions from gross pay, such as federal income tax withheld, Social Security tax, and Medicare tax, to calculate net pay.
4. Complete a payroll register.
5. Journalize the payroll entry from a payroll register.
6. Maintain employees' individual earnings records.

To: Amy Roberts, CPA
Subject: Employee Earnings and Deductions

Hi Amy,
Thanks for all of your help with setting up my accounting system. Now I need some guidance on how to calculate and account for earnings, payroll taxes, and any other important deductions. I've been told that handling payroll in a timely and accurate manner is extremely important. Therefore, I want to make sure I know what to do. What do I need to know to calculate employee earnings and deductions?
Thanks,
Janie

To: Janie Conner
Subject: RE: Employee Earnings and Deductions

Hi Janie,
You are right. Handling payroll in a timely and accurate manner is extremely important to your employees and your company. To gain an accurate understanding of payroll, you'll need to know the following:

_____ 1. What tax laws affect payroll deductions and contributions
_____ 2. How to calculate total earnings based on hourly, salary, piece-rate, or commission basis
_____ 3. How to determine deductions and net pay
_____ 4. How to set up and use a payroll register
_____ 5. How to journalize payroll entries
_____ 6. How to maintain individual employee earnings records

Give me a call tomorrow and we can set up a meeting to discuss these items further.
Amy

© Rob Marmion/ShutterStock.com

Until now, we have been recording employees' earnings as a debit to Salary or Wages Expense and a credit to Cash, but we have been talking only about **gross pay**—the total amount of an employee's pay before deductions. We have not mentioned the various deductions that are taken out of gross pay to arrive at take-home pay, or **net pay**. In this chapter, we will talk about types of deductions and explain how to enter them in the payroll records. We also will cover the journal entries to record payroll and pay the employees.

OBJECTIVES OF PAYROLL RECORDS AND ACCOUNTING

There are two primary reasons we need to maintain accurate payroll records: First, we must collect the data necessary to compute the compensation for each employee by payroll period. Second, we must provide the information needed to complete the various government reports—federal and state—required of all employers.

All business enterprises, both large and small, are required by law to (1) withhold certain amounts from employees' pay for taxes, (2) make payments to government agencies by specific deadlines, and (3) submit reports on official forms. Because governments impose penalties if the requirements are not met, employers are vitally concerned with payroll accounting.

The employer is required to keep records of the following information:

1. **Personal data on employee:** Name, address, Social Security number, date of birth
2. **Data on wage payments:** Dates, amounts of payments, and payroll periods
3. **Amount of taxable wages paid:** Dates and amount earned (year-to-date) for the calendar year involved
4. **Amount of tax withheld from each employee's earnings by pay period**

Many companies use software, such as Excel® or QuickBooks®, or an outside payroll services, such as ADP® or Paychex®, to assist with their payroll accounting.

Accounting Language

Calendar year (p. 326)
Current Tax Payment Act (p. 324)
Employee (p. 324)
Employee's individual earnings record (p. 339)
Employee's Withholding Allowance Certificate (Form W-4) (p. 329)
Exemption (p. 329)
Fair Labor Standards Act (p. 324)
FICA taxes (p. 325)
Gross pay (p. 323)
Independent contractor (p. 324)
Medicare taxes (p. 325)
Net pay (p. 323)
Payroll bank account (p. 339)
Payroll register (p. 334)
Pre-tax deductions (p. 329)
Social Security Act of 1935 (p. 325)
Social Security taxes (p. 325)
Taxable earnings (p. 329)
Wage-bracket tax tables (p. 330)
Withholding allowance (p. 329)
Workers' compensation laws (p. 326)

EMPLOYER/EMPLOYEE RELATIONSHIPS

Payroll accounting involves employee compensation, withholdings, records, reports, and taxes. Therefore, it is important to determine who is an employee and who is an independent contractor. An **employee** is one who is under the direction and control of the employer, such as a salesperson, an administrative assistant, a vice president, and a controller. An **independent contractor** is engaged for a definite job or service and may choose his or her own means of doing the work. Payments made to independent contractors are in the form of fees or charges. Independent contractors submit bills or invoices for the work they do. The payment is not subject to withholding or payroll taxes by the person or firm paying the invoice. Such taxes are the responsibility of the independent contractor. **Businesses are required to give an independent contractor an IRS Form 1099-MISC for the year if the fees paid are $600 or more.** The IRS has published guidelines for employers to use in determining worker classification. If a worker is classified as an independent contractor and should be an employee, the IRS will impose substantial penalties on the employer. For more information about employee versus independent contractor status, go to www.irs.gov.

FYI

Examples of independent contractors include a plumber, a lawyer, or a CPA that offers his or her services to the public.

LAWS AFFECTING EMPLOYEES' PAY DEDUCTIONS

Learning Objective

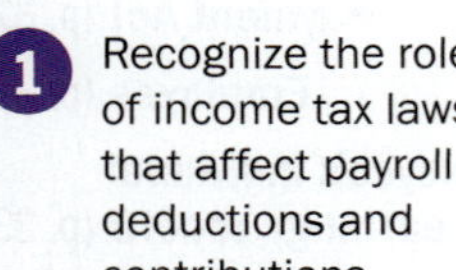

1 Recognize the role of income tax laws that affect payroll deductions and contributions.

Both federal and state laws require the employer to act as a collecting agent and deduct specified amounts from employees' gross earnings. The employer sends the withholdings to the appropriate government agencies, along with reports substantiating the figures. Let's look at some of the more important laws that pertain to employees' pay.

Fair Labor Standards Act

The **Fair Labor Standards Act** of 1938 is referred to as "the Act" or "FLSA." The Act provides minimum standards for both wages and overtime. Also included in the Act are provisions related to child labor and equal pay for equal work. In addition, the Act exempts specified employees or groups of employees from some of its provisions. Details of the Act may be found at www.opm.gov.

Federal Income Tax Withholding

The **Current Tax Payment Act**, passed in 1943, requires employers not only to withhold the tax and pay it to the U.S. Treasury but also to keep records of the names and addresses of persons employed, their earnings, withholdings, and the amounts and

In the Real World

In the real world, many companies (especially small businesses, such as this street cafe) outsource their payroll processing activities. According to Paychex®, Inc., a payroll and human resource company, businesses outsource their payroll to improve accuracy, to increase security, and to maintain compliance with tax laws and regulations. B. Thomas Golisano started Paychex in 1971 with just one employee and a $3,000 investment. In 1983, the company went public and is currently traded on the NASDAQ stock exchange.

dates of payment. The employer must submit reports to the Internal Revenue Service on a quarterly basis (Form 941) and to the employee on an annual basis (W-2 form). We will discuss these reports and the related deposits in Chapter 8.

FYI

For employees who are paid wages in excess of $200,000, an additional 0.9 percent must be withheld. Employers do not have to match the additional Medicare withholding.

FICA Taxes (Employees' Share)

The **Social Security Act of 1935** began as an attempt to provide retired workers with benefits based on their work history. Several amendments have been added (for example, benefits for spouses and minor children of retired workers, disability insurance, an increase in the age as to when benefits may be collected, Medicare, and supplemental security income).

Currently, **FICA taxes** consists of **Social Security taxes** and **Medicare taxes**. At the writing of this text, employees contribute 6.2 percent (0.062) on the first $113,700 earned in a calendar year for Social Security. Employees contribute 1.45 percent (0.0145) on all earnings in a calendar year, with no earnings limit for Medicare. Throughout this chapter, we will use these percentages and earnings limitations for our calculations.

LAWS AFFECTING EMPLOYER'S PAYROLL TAX CONTRIBUTIONS (PAYROLL TAX EXPENSE)

Certain payroll taxes are also levied on the employer. These taxes are based on the total wages paid to employees. Let's look at some of the more important laws that pertain to employees' pay.

FICA Taxes (Employer's Share)

As of the writing of this text, the employer is required to match the amount of FICA taxes withheld from the employee's wages. The employer pays 6.2% (0.062) on the first $113,700 earned by the employee for Social Security taxes and also matches the amount of Medicare taxes (1.45%, or 0.0145) withheld from the employees' wages. The employer's share of these taxes is recorded under Payroll Tax Expense. Every three months the employer must submit reports to the U.S. Treasury, using Form 941, which is the same form used to report income tax withheld. The employer's payment to the Internal Revenue Service consists of (1) the employee's share of the FICA taxes, (2) the employer's matching portion of the FICA taxes, and (3) the employee's income tax withheld. We will talk about this in detail in Chapter 8.

FYI

Certain employees may be exempt from FICA Social Security tax, such as railroad workers and some teachers.

State Unemployment Taxes (SUTA)

Each state is responsible for paying its own unemployment compensation benefits. The revenue provided by state unemployment taxes is used exclusively for this purpose. However, there is considerable variation among the states concerning the tax rates and the amount of taxable income. **This tax is paid by employers only.** A few states, under their State Unemployment Tax Act, charge their employers a percentage on the first $7,000 an employee earns. This is similar to the taxable income stipulated in the Federal Unemployment Tax Act. However, most states have a much higher taxable wage base. As of the writing of this text, Washington State, with a taxable wage base of $39,800, is the highest. In this text, we will use 5.4 percent (0.054) of the first $7,000. Most states require employers to file reports and payments on a quarterly, or three-month, basis. Included in these reports are a listing of employees' names, Social Security numbers, amounts of wages paid to each employee, and computations of unemployment taxes.

Federal Unemployment Tax Act (FUTA)

The purpose of the Federal Unemployment Tax Act is to financially support government-run employment offices, pay half of extended unemployment benefits when unemployment is high, and provide a fund that states can borrow from to pay benefits if needed. **FUTA taxes are paid by employers only**. Generally, this includes all employers except nonprofit schools and charities.

The federal unemployment tax is based on the total earnings of each employee during the **calendar year** (January 1–December 31). For the examples and problems in this text, we will use the current federal unemployment tax rate of 0.6 percent (0.006) on the first $7,000 of each employee's earnings during the calendar year. Reports to the federal government must be submitted annually on Form 940. We will discuss the SUTA and FUTA reports in Chapter 8.

Workers' Compensation Laws

Workers' compensation laws protect employees and their dependents against losses due to death or injury incurred on the job. Most states require employers to contribute to a state compensation fund or to buy similar insurance from a private insurance company. The employer ordinarily pays the cost of the insurance premiums. The premium rates vary according to the degree of danger inherent in each job category and the employer's number of accidents. The employer must keep records of job descriptions and classification, as well as claims of insured persons.

The following table presents a summary of the various payroll taxes and identifies who is responsible for each.

Employee Pays	Employer Pays
Federal income tax withholding (based on income tax rates) FICA taxes – Social Security (6.2% of earnings up to $113,700) – Medicare (1.45% of all earnings)	FICA taxes – Social Security (6.2% of earnings up to $113,700.) – Medicare (1.45% of all earnings) Federal and state unemployment taxes Workers' compensation

Employees may be paid salaries or wages depending on the type of work and the period of time covered. Money paid to a person for managerial or administrative services is usually called a salary, and the time period covered is generally a month or a year. Money paid for skilled or unskilled labor is usually called wages, and the time period covered is hours or weeks. Wages may also be paid on a piecework basis (or per-unit basis, such as number of boxes of strawberries picked). A company may also supplement an employee's salary or wage with other benefits (for example, commissions, bonuses, cost-of-living adjustments, and profit-sharing plans). As a rule, employees are paid by check or by direct deposit to their bank account. However, their compensation may also include amounts for items such as personal use of company automobiles, athletic club dues, or holiday gift cards. When the compensation is in these forms, the employer must determine the fair value of the property or service given in payment for an employee's labor. For more information on what fringe benefits are taxable and how to value them, see Publication 15-B, Employer's Tax Guide to Fringe Benefits, located on the IRS website at www.irs.gov.

Calculating Total Earnings

When compensation is based on the amount of time worked, the accountant must have a record of the number of hours that each employee worked. When there are only a few employees, this can be accomplished by means of a time book. When there are many employees, time clocks or other electronic time-keeping systems are used.

Employees may be paid weekly, biweekly, semimonthly, or monthly. Biweekly is every two weeks. Semimonthly is twice a month.

Learning Objective

2 Calculate total earnings based on an hourly, salary, piece-rate, or commission basis.

Wages

Consider Mark Anderson, who works for Green Sales Company. His regular rate of pay is $22.95 per hour. The company pays time-and-a-half for hours worked in excess of 40 per week. In addition, the company pays him double time for any work he does on Sundays and holidays. Anderson has a ½-hour lunch break during an 8½-hour day. He is not paid for the lunch break, nor is he paid for minutes before 8:00 A.M. or after 4:30 P.M. unless hours of overtime are authorized in advance. His time card for the week is shown in Figure 1.

TIME CARD

Name: Anderson, Mark
Week ended: Oct. 11, 20--

Day	In	Out	In	Out	Hours Worked	
					Regular	Overtime
Mon	7 57	12 00	12 20	4 32	8	
Tue	7 56	12 06	12 36	4 37	8	
Wed	7 57	12 02	12 31	4 31	8	
Thu	8 00	12 11	12 40	6 32	8	2
Fri	8 00	12 03	12 33	5 33	8	1
Sat	7 59	11 02				3
Sun						

Figure 1
Time card for Mark Anderson

Anderson's gross wages can be computed by one of two methods. The first method works like this:

40 hours at straight time	40 × $22.95 per hour =	$ 918.00
2 hours overtime on Thursday ($22.95 × 1.5 = $34.43)	2 × $34.43 per hour =	68.86
1 hour overtime on Friday	1 × $34.43 per hour =	34.43
3 hours overtime on Saturday	3 × $34.43 per hour =	103.29
Total hours and gross wages	46	$1,124.58

The second method of calculating gross wages is often used when it is necessary to identify or track overtime premium.

46 hours at straight time	46 × $22.95 per hour =	$1,055.70
Overtime premium:		
6 hours overtime ($22.95 × 0.5 = $11.48)	6 × $11.48 per hour =	68.88
Total gross wages		$1,124.58

Minimum wages are set by Congress or state legislature—whichever is higher. Originally, in 1938, the minimum wage was $0.25 per hour.

Salaries

Employees who are paid a regular salary may also be entitled to extra pay for overtime. It is necessary to figure out their regular hourly rate of pay before you can determine their overtime rate. Consider Madeline Huan, who receives a salary of $4,350 per month. She is entitled to overtime pay for all hours worked in excess of 40 during a week at time-and-a-half her regular hourly rate. This past week she worked 44 hours, so we calculate her gross pay as follows:

$4,350 per month × 12 months	=	$52,200 per year
$52,200 per year ÷ 52 weeks	=	$1,003.85 per week
$1,003.85 per week ÷ 40 hours	=	$25.10 per regular hour
$25.10 per regular hour × 1.5	=	$37.65 per overtime hour

Earnings for 44 hours:		
40 hours at straight time (as calculated above)		= $1,003.85
4 hours overtime	(4 × $37.65) =	150.60
Total gross earnings		$1,154.45

A shortcut to determine the hourly rate is to divide the annual salary by 2,080 (the standard work hours in a year). In this case, the calculation would be ($4,350 × 12) ÷ 2,080 = $25.10.

Piece-Rate

Workers under the piece-rate system are paid at the rate of so much per unit of production. For example, John Joseph, a strawberry picker, is paid $3 for each box of strawberries picked. If he picks 24 boxes during the day, his total earnings are 24 × $3 = $72.

Commissions

Some salespeople are paid on a purely commission basis. However, a more common arrangement is a salary plus a commission or bonus. Assume that Lora Brown receives an annual salary of $44,000. Her employer agrees to pay her a 5 percent commission on all sales during the year in excess of $200,000. Her sales for the year total $445,000. Her commission is $12,250 [($445,000 − $200,000) × 0.05]. Therefore, her total earnings are $56,250 ($44,000 + $12,250).

DEDUCTIONS FROM TOTAL EARNINGS

Learning Objective 3 Determine deductions from gross pay, such as federal income tax withheld, Social Security tax, and Medicare tax, to calculate net pay.

Anyone who has ever earned a paycheck has encountered some type of deductions. As discussed previously in this chapter, gross pay minus deductions equals net pay. Following are the most common deductions:

- Federal income tax withholding
- State income tax withholding
- FICA taxes (Social Security and Medicare), employee's share
- Union dues
- Medical insurance premiums and medical expenses under a flexible spending plan
- Contributions to a charitable organization such as United Way
- Repayment of personal loans from the company
- Savings through the company 401(k) plan
- Dependent care expenses under a flexible spending plan (subject to a $5,000 limit)

Medical insurance premiums, medical expenses, and dependent care expenses under a flexible spending plan and 401(k) deductions are usually **pre-tax deductions**. If a deduction is pre-tax, the employee does not have to pay income tax on the amount of federal income tax withheld. In certain circumstances, FICA tax also may be exempt when calculating federal income tax withholding. For example, if Lynn Langseth has a weekly salary of $4,000 and the company deducts $200 for medical premiums paid for Lynn's dependents, her payroll subject to income tax is $3,800, not $4,000. If Lynn also contributes $100 to charity, her payroll subject to income tax is still $3,800 since the charitable deduction is not a pre-tax deduction.

Employees' Federal Income Tax Withholding

Employers are required not only to withhold employees' taxes and then pay them to the U.S. Treasury but also to keep records of the names and addresses of persons employed, their **taxable earnings** (the earnings subject to tax) and withholdings, and the amounts and dates of payment.

The amount of federal income tax withheld from an employee's earnings depends on the amount of his or her total earnings, marital status, and number of withholding allowances claimed. A **withholding allowance** is used by employers to calculate the amount of income tax withheld from an employee's paycheck. The more withholding allowance's an employee claims, the less income tax an employer withholds from the employee's paycheck. An employee is entitled to one personal allowance for the taxpayer, one for his or her spouse, and one for each dependent. An **exemption** is an amount of an employee's annual earnings not subject to income tax. Each employee has to fill out an **Employee's Withholding Allowance Certificate (Form W-4)**, shown in Figure 2. The employer retains this form as authorization to withhold money for the employee's federal income tax.

Figure 2
Employee's Withholding Allowance Certificate (Form W-4) for Mark Anderson

Form **W-4** | **Employee's Withholding Allowance Certificate** | OMB No. 1545-0074

Department of the Treasury Internal Revenue Service

► Whether you are entitled to claim a certain number of allowances or exemption from withholding is subject to review by the IRS. Your employer may be required to send a copy of this form to the IRS.

20--

1 Type or print your first name and middle initial. **Mark E.** | Last name **Anderson** | 2 Your social security number **543 24 1680**

Home address (number and street or rural route) **1104 Rosewood Street**

3 ☐ Single ☒ Married ☐ Married, but withhold at higher Single rate.
Note. If married, but legally separated, or spouse is a nonresident alien, check the "Single" box.

City or town, state, and ZIP code **Bangor, Maine 04401**

4 If your last name differs from that shown on your social security card, check here. You must call 1-800-772-1213 for a new card. ► ☐

5 Total number of allowances you are claiming (from line **H** above **or** from the applicable worksheet on page 2) | 5 | 1
6 Additional amount, if any, you want withheld from each paycheck . . . . | 6 | $
7 I claim exemption from withholding for 20--, and I certify that I meet **both** of the following conditions for exemption.
• Last year I had a right to a refund of **all** federal income tax withheld because I had **no** tax liability **and**
• This year I expect a refund of **all** federal income tax withheld because I expect to have **no** tax liability.
If you meet both conditions, write "Exempt" here . . . . ► | 7 |

Under penalties of perjury, I declare that I have examined this certificate and to the best of my knowledge and belief, it is true, correct, and complete.
Employee's signature
(Form is not valid unless you sign it.) ► *Mark E. Anderson* Date ► *January 2, 20--*

8 Employer's name and address (Employer: Complete lines 8 and 10 only if sending to the IRS.) | 9 Office code (optional) | 10 Employer identification number (EIN)

For Privacy Act and Paperwork Reduction Act Notice, see page 2. Cat. No. 10220Q Form **W-4** (20--)

Publication 15 (Circular E), Employer's Tax Guide

Publication 15 (Circular E) contains the rules for depositing federal income, Social Security, and Medicare taxes, and contains the withholding tables for these taxes. This publication is regularly updated to reflect changes in tax laws and withholding rates. Publication 15 (Circular E) also describes filing requirements for official employer reports and is provided free of charge by the Internal Revenue Service (available on the Internet at www.irs.gov). Accountants responsible for preparation of payroll registers and forms should be familiar with the content in this publication.

The **wage-bracket tax tables** (found in Publication 15) cover monthly, semimonthly, biweekly, weekly, and daily payroll periods. The tables are also subdivided on the basis of marital status. To determine the federal income tax withheld, perform the following steps:

STEP 1. Locate the wage bracket in the first two columns of the table.

STEP 2. Find the column for the number of allowances claimed and read down this column until you get to the appropriate wage-bracket line.

Federal tax rates change frequently, but the procedure generally stays the same. We will use the tax table given in this chapter for all computations.

A portion of the weekly federal income tax withholding table for married persons is reproduced in Figure 3 on pages 331–332.

Assume that Mark Anderson, who claims one allowance as of the October 11 payroll, has gross wages of $1,124.58 for the week. As $1,124.58 falls in the $1,120–$1,130 bracket, you can see from the table that $116 should be withheld.

Note the headings of the bracket columns: "At least" and "But less than." A strict interpretation of the $1,120–$1,130 bracket really means $1,120–$1,129.99. Therefore, if Anderson's salary were $1,130, it would fall into the $1,130–$1,140 bracket.

Employees' State Income Tax Withholding

Many states that levy state income taxes also furnish employers with withholding tables. Other states use a fixed percentage of the federal income tax withholding as the amount to be withheld for state taxes. In our illustration, we assume that the amount of each employee's state income tax deduction is 20 percent (0.20) of that employee's federal income tax deduction.

Employees' FICA Taxes Withholding (Social Security and Medicare)

The Federal Insurance Contributions Act provides for retirement pensions after a worker reaches age 62, disability benefits for any worker who becomes disabled (and for her or his dependents), and a health insurance program after age 65 (Medicare). Both the employee and the employer must pay FICA taxes, which are commonly referred to as Social Security taxes and Medicare taxes. The employer withholds FICA taxes from employees' wages and pays them to the U.S. Treasury.

At one time, Social Security and Medicare were not separated for tax computation and there was a limit on Medicare taxable earnings. Now *all* earnings are taxable for Medicare.

FICA tax rates apply to the gross earnings of an employee during the calendar year. After an employee has paid Social Security tax on the maximum taxable earnings, the employer stops deducting Social Security tax until the next calendar year begins. Congress has frequently changed the schedule of rates and taxable incomes.

As explained earlier, in this text, we assume a Social Security rate of 6.2 percent (0.062) of the first $113,700 for each employee and a Medicare rate of 1.45 percent (0.0145) of all earnings for each employee. Both tax rates apply to earnings during the calendar year. (Tables for Social Security and Medicare tax withholdings are available in the Internal Revenue Service Publication 15.)

Figure 3
2013 federal income tax withholding table for married persons (weekly payroll period)

MARRIED Persons—WEEKLY Payroll Period
(For Wages Paid through December 2013)

And the wages are–		And the number of withholding allowances claimed is—										
At least	But less than	0	1	2	3	4	5	6	7	8	9	10
		The amount of income tax to be withheld is—										
$ 0	$160	$0	$0	$0	$0	$0	$0	$0	$0	$0	$0	$0
160	165	0	0	0	0	0	0	0	0	0	0	0
165	170	1	0	0	0	0	0	0	0	0	0	0
170	175	1	0	0	0	0	0	0	0	0	0	0
175	180	2	0	0	0	0	0	0	0	0	0	0
180	185	2	0	0	0	0	0	0	0	0	0	0
185	190	3	0	0	0	0	0	0	0	0	0	0
190	195	3	0	0	0	0	0	0	0	0	0	0
195	200	4	0	0	0	0	0	0	0	0	0	0
200	210	5	0	0	0	0	0	0	0	0	0	0
210	220	6	0	0	0	0	0	0	0	0	0	0
220	230	7	0	0	0	0	0	0	0	0	0	0
230	240	8	0	0	0	0	0	0	0	0	0	0
240	250	9	1	0	0	0	0	0	0	0	0	0
250	260	10	2	0	0	0	0	0	0	0	0	0
260	270	11	3	0	0	0	0	0	0	0	0	0
270	280	12	4	0	0	0	0	0	0	0	0	0
280	290	13	5	0	0	0	0	0	0	0	0	0
290	300	14	6	0	0	0	0	0	0	0	0	0
300	310	15	7	0	0	0	0	0	0	0	0	0
310	320	16	8	1	0	0	0	0	0	0	0	0
320	330	17	9	2	0	0	0	0	0	0	0	0
330	340	18	10	3	0	0	0	0	0	0	0	0
340	350	19	11	4	0	0	0	0	0	0	0	0
350	360	20	12	5	0	0	0	0	0	0	0	0
360	370	21	13	6	0	0	0	0	0	0	0	0
370	380	22	14	7	0	0	0	0	0	0	0	0
380	390	23	15	8	0	0	0	0	0	0	0	0
390	400	24	16	9	1	0	0	0	0	0	0	0
400	410	25	17	10	2	0	0	0	0	0	0	0
410	420	26	18	11	3	0	0	0	0	0	0	0
420	430	27	19	12	4	0	0	0	0	0	0	0
430	440	28	20	13	5	0	0	0	0	0	0	0
440	450	29	21	14	6	0	0	0	0	0	0	0
450	460	30	22	15	7	0	0	0	0	0	0	0
460	470	31	23	16	8	1	0	0	0	0	0	0
470	480	32	24	17	9	2	0	0	0	0	0	0
480	490	33	25	18	10	3	0	0	0	0	0	0
490	500	34	26	19	11	4	0	0	0	0	0	0
500	510	35	27	20	12	5	0	0	0	0	0	0
510	520	36	28	21	13	6	0	0	0	0	0	0
520	530	38	29	22	14	7	0	0	0	0	0	0
530	540	39	30	23	15	8	0	0	0	0	0	0
540	550	41	31	24	16	9	1	0	0	0	0	0
550	560	42	32	25	17	10	2	0	0	0	0	0
560	570	44	33	26	18	11	3	0	0	0	0	0
570	580	45	34	27	19	12	4	0	0	0	0	0
580	590	47	35	28	20	13	5	0	0	0	0	0
590	600	48	37	29	21	14	6	0	0	0	0	0
600	610	50	38	30	22	15	7	0	0	0	0	0
610	620	51	40	31	23	16	8	1	0	0	0	0
620	630	53	41	32	24	17	9	2	0	0	0	0
630	640	54	43	33	25	18	10	3	0	0	0	0
640	650	56	44	34	26	19	11	4	0	0	0	0
650	660	57	46	35	27	20	12	5	0	0	0	0
660	670	59	47	36	28	21	13	6	0	0	0	0
670	680	60	49	38	29	22	14	7	0	0	0	0
680	690	62	50	39	30	23	15	8	0	0	0	0
690	700	63	52	41	31	24	16	9	1	0	0	0
700	710	65	53	42	32	25	17	10	2	0	0	0
710	720	66	55	44	33	26	18	11	3	0	0	0
720	730	68	56	45	34	27	19	12	4	0	0	0
730	740	69	58	47	35	28	20	13	5	0	0	0
740	750	71	59	48	37	29	21	14	6	0	0	0
750	760	72	61	50	38	30	22	15	7	0	0	0
760	770	74	62	51	40	31	23	16	8	1	0	0
770	780	75	64	53	41	32	24	17	9	2	0	0
780	790	77	65	54	43	33	25	18	10	3	0	0
790	800	78	67	56	44	34	26	19	11	4	0	0

Figure 3
(Concluded)

MARRIED Persons—WEEKLY Payroll Period

(For Wages Paid through December 2013)

And the wages are–		And the number of withholding allowances claimed is—										
At least	But less than	0	1	2	3	4	5	6	7	8	9	10
		The amount of income tax to be withheld is—										
$800	**$810**	$80	$68	$57	$46	$35	$27	$20	$12	$5	$0	$0
810	**820**	81	70	59	47	36	28	21	13	6	0	0
820	**830**	83	71	60	49	38	29	22	14	7	0	0
830	**840**	84	73	62	50	39	30	23	15	8	0	0
840	**850**	86	74	63	52	41	31	24	16	9	1	0
850	**860**	87	76	65	53	42	32	25	17	10	2	0
860	**870**	89	77	66	55	44	33	26	18	11	3	0
870	**880**	90	79	68	56	45	34	27	19	12	4	0
880	**890**	92	80	69	58	47	35	28	20	13	5	0
890	**900**	93	82	71	59	48	37	29	21	14	6	0
900	**910**	95	83	72	61	50	38	30	22	15	7	0
910	**920**	96	85	74	62	51	40	31	23	16	8	1
920	**930**	98	86	75	64	53	41	32	24	17	9	2
930	**940**	99	88	77	65	54	43	33	25	18	10	3
940	**950**	101	89	78	67	56	44	34	26	19	11	4
950	**960**	102	91	80	68	57	46	35	27	20	12	5
960	**970**	104	92	81	70	59	47	36	28	21	13	6
970	**980**	105	94	83	71	60	49	38	29	22	14	7
980	**990**	107	95	84	73	62	50	39	30	23	15	8
990	**1,000**	108	97	86	74	63	52	41	31	24	16	9
1,000	**1,010**	110	98	87	76	65	53	42	32	25	17	10
1,010	**1,020**	111	100	89	77	66	55	44	33	26	18	11
1,020	**1,030**	113	101	90	79	68	56	45	34	27	19	12
1,030	**1,040**	114	103	92	80	69	58	47	35	28	20	13
1,040	**1,050**	116	104	93	82	71	59	48	37	29	21	14
1,050	**1,060**	117	106	95	83	72	61	50	38	30	22	15
1,060	**1,070**	119	107	96	85	74	62	51	40	31	23	16
1,070	**1,080**	120	109	98	86	75	64	53	41	32	24	17
1,080	**1,090**	122	110	99	88	77	65	54	43	33	25	18
1,090	**1,100**	123	112	101	89	78	67	56	44	34	26	19
1,100	**1,110**	125	113	102	91	80	68	57	46	35	27	20
1,110	**1,120**	126	115	104	92	81	70	59	47	36	28	21
1,120	**1,130**	128	116	105	94	83	71	60	49	38	29	22
1,130	**1,140**	129	118	107	95	84	73	62	50	39	30	23
1,140	**1,150**	131	119	108	97	86	74	63	52	41	31	24
1,150	**1,160**	132	121	110	98	87	76	65	53	42	32	25
1,160	**1,170**	134	122	111	100	89	77	66	55	44	33	26
1,170	**1,180**	135	124	113	101	90	79	68	56	45	34	27
1,180	**1,190**	137	125	114	103	92	80	69	58	47	35	28
1,190	**1,200**	138	127	116	104	93	82	71	59	48	37	29
1,200	**1,210**	140	128	117	106	95	83	72	61	50	38	30
1,210	**1,220**	141	130	119	107	96	85	74	62	51	40	31
1,220	**1,230**	143	131	120	109	98	86	75	64	53	41	32
1,230	**1,240**	144	133	122	110	99	88	77	65	54	43	33
1,240	**1,250**	146	134	123	112	101	89	78	67	56	44	34
1,250	**1,260**	147	136	125	113	102	91	80	68	57	46	35
1,260	**1,270**	149	137	126	115	104	92	81	70	59	47	36
1,270	**1,280**	150	139	128	116	105	94	83	71	60	49	38
1,280	**1,290**	152	140	129	118	107	95	84	73	62	50	39
1,290	**1,300**	153	142	131	119	108	97	86	74	63	52	41
1,300	**1,310**	155	143	132	121	110	98	87	76	65	53	42
1,310	**1,320**	156	145	134	122	111	100	89	77	66	55	44
1,320	**1,330**	158	146	135	124	113	101	90	79	68	56	45
1,330	**1,340**	159	148	137	125	114	103	92	80	69	58	47
1,340	**1,350**	161	149	138	127	116	104	93	82	71	59	48
1,350	**1,360**	162	151	140	128	117	106	95	83	72	61	50
1,360	**1,370**	164	152	141	130	119	107	96	85	74	62	51
1,370	**1,380**	165	154	143	131	120	109	98	86	75	64	53
1,380	**1,390**	167	155	144	133	122	110	99	88	77	65	54
1,390	**1,400**	168	157	146	134	123	112	101	89	78	67	56
$1,400 and over		Use Table 1(b) for a **MARRIED person** on page 44. Also see the instructions on page 42.										

Let's return to the example of Mark Anderson, who had gross wages of $1,124.58 for the week ending October 11. Suppose his total accumulated gross wages earned this year prior to this payroll period are $44,960. Anderson's total gross wages including this payroll period were $46,084.58 ($44,960 + $1,124.58). Because the Social Security tax applies to the first $113,700 and the Medicare tax applies to all earnings, Anderson's

ACCOUNTING IN YOUR FUTURE

PAYROLL DEPARTMENT

The payroll department is an important part of the accounting and finance functions at companies. Payroll personnel are responsible for ensuring that all company employees receive compensation and benefits critical to maintaining a productive and motivated workforce. Some payroll departments work closely with Information Technology, Human Resources, and other departments to ensure that the company's payroll is accurate, is up-to-date, and is serving the company's current business objectives. For these reasons, it is important to understand how payroll is determined, whether you are directly responsible for processing payroll or you are employed in another business department.

© iStockPhoto.com/klikk

earnings are subject to both taxes. For Anderson's Social Security tax, multiply $1,124.58 by 6.2 percent ($1,124.58 × 0.062 = $69.72). For Anderson's Medicare tax, multiply $1,124.58 by 1.45 percent ($1,124.58 × 0.0145 = $16.31).

Here's another example. At the beginning of the pay period, Grace Wallace had cumulative earnings of $110,800, which is $2,900 less than $113,700. During this pay period, she earned $3,010.35, which is greater than $2,900. Thus, she must pay Social Security tax of $179.80 ($2,900 × 0.062) on $2,900. However, because the Medicare tax applies to all earnings, she is not exempt from any Medicare tax. Her Medicare tax is $43.65 ($3,010.35 × 0.0145). Because Grace's cumulative earnings after this pay period are over $113,700, any remaining pay will not be subject to Social Security tax.

To: **Amy Roberts, CPA**
Subject: **Employee Earnings and Deductions**

Hi Amy,
Thanks for your help with understanding how to calculate payroll. I never knew there was so much involved. I am now ready to record my payroll entries. Can you tell me what I need to do?
Thanks,
Janie

To: **Janie Conner**
Subject: **RE: Employee Earnings and Deductions**

Hi Janie,
I'm glad you have a basic understanding of how to calculate payroll. The next steps involve the record keeping aspects of the payroll process. Below is a checklist of what you need to know. We can discuss this information further tomorrow. Can you give me a call in the morning? Let's say 10 A.M.?

_____ 1. How to set up and use a payroll register
_____ 2. How to journalize payroll entries
_____ 3. How to maintain individual employee earnings records

Amy

PAYROLL REGISTER

Learning Objective
4 Complete a payroll register.

The **payroll register** is a manual or computerized schedule prepared for each payroll period listing the earnings, deductions, and net pay for each employee. In Figure 4, we see a payroll register using Excel®. It shows the data for each employee on a separate line. This would be suitable for a firm such as Green Sales Company, which has a small number of employees.

First, we'll show the entire payroll register; then we'll break down the payroll register and explain it column by column. The number at the foot of each column refers to the related text description.

Figure 4
Payroll register for Green Sales Company

	A	B	C	D	E	F	G	H	I	J
1					EARNINGS				(7) TAXABLE EARNINGS	
2-4	NAME	TOTAL HOURS	BEGINNING CUMULATIVE EARNINGS	REGULAR	OVERTIME	TOTAL	ENDING CUMULATIVE EARNINGS	UNEMPLOYMENT	SOCIAL SECURITY	MEDICARE
5	Anderson, Mark	46	44,960.00	918.00	206.58	1,124.58	46,084.58	0.00	1,124.58	1,124.58
6	Bodell, Anna	45	5,987.00	626.20	118.00	744.20	6,731.20	744.20	744.20	744.20
7	Dorn, David	49	6,786.00	686.00	230.00	916.00	7,702.00	214.00	916.00	916.00
8	Fields, Sarah	40	38,462.00	1,084.50	0.00	1,084.50	39,546.50	0.00	1,084.50	1,084.50
9	Graham, Jason	40	68,600.00	1,798.45	0.00	1,798.45	70,398.45	0.00	1,798.45	1,798.45
10	Lee, Jeremy	40	68,500.00	1,895.58	0.00	1,895.58	70,395.58	0.00	1,895.58	1,895.58
11	Mankowitz, Hanna	55	37,850.00	1,260.00	708.75	1,968.75	39,818.75	0.00	1,968.75	1,968.75
12	Olsen, Barbara	40	45,820.00	1,487.20	0.00	1,487.20	47,307.20	0.00	1,487.20	1,487.20
13	Parker, William	44	46,430.00	1,581.58	194.70	1,776.28	48,206.28	0.00	1,776.28	1,776.28
14	Raman, Soma	45	54,867.00	1,400.00	262.50	1,662.50	56,529.50	0.00	1,662.50	1,662.50
15	Tabor, Annette	40	42,740.00	1,168.83	0.00	1,168.83	43,908.83	0.00	1,168.83	1,168.83
16	Wallace, Grace	40	110,800.00	3,010.35	0.00	3,010.35	113,810.35	0.00	2,900.00	3,010.35
17			571,802.00	16,916.69	1,720.53	18,637.22	590,439.22	958.20	18,526.87	18,637.22
18		*(1)*	*(2)*	*(3)*	*(4)*	*(5)*	*(6)*	*(7A)*	*(7B)*	*(7C)*
19										

16,916.69 + 1,720.53 = 18,637.22

571,802.00 + 18,637.22 = 590,439.22

The payroll period shown in Figure 4 covers October 5 through October 11. The first part consists of employees' names, hours worked, beginning cumulative earnings, and taxable earnings.

(1) Total Hours—Taken from employees' time records (manual or computerized).

(2) Beginning Cumulative Earnings—The amount each employee has earned between January 1 and October 4 (the last day of the previous payroll period). It is taken from each employee's individual earnings record. (See Figure 7, page 340.)

(3) Regular Earnings—Earnings for hours worked up to and including 40. In other words, the first 40 hours multiplied by each employee's regular hourly rate.

(4) Overtime Earnings—Hours in excess of 40 (relative to a 40-hour week) that each employee worked multiplied by that employee's overtime rate.

(5) Total Earnings—Regular earnings plus overtime earnings.

(6) Ending Cumulative Earnings—Beginning Cumulative Earnings plus Total Earnings.

(7) Taxable Earnings—The amount of earnings subject to taxation, **not the tax itself.** We will use these columns later to figure the amount of each tax. In other words, **Taxable Earnings is the base on which to figure the tax. Taxable Earnings multiplied by the tax rate equals the amount of the tax.**

(7A) Unemployment Taxable Earnings—In our illustration, we are using a maximum of $7,000 for unemployment tax liability on the employer for each employee. This column represents the previously untaxed portion remaining of the $7,000 for the individual employees. **Unemployment tax is paid only by the employer in most states. An unemployment tax is generally paid to both the state and federal government.** As of the writing of this text, most states use different maximum earnings and rates from the federal government's current earnings limit of $7,000. However, in this text, we will use $7,000 as the earnings limit for

Taxable earnings are the base on which to figure the tax, not the tax itself.

Figure 4
(Concluded)

PAGE 56

K	L	M	N	O	P	Q	R	S	T	U
(8) DEDUCTIONS							(9) PAYMENTS		(10) EXPENSE ACCOUNT DEBITED	
FEDERAL INCOME TAX	STATE INCOME TAX	SOCIAL SECURITY TAX	MEDICARE TAX	OTHER DEDUCTIONS		TOTAL	NET AMOUNT	CK. NO.	SALES WAGES EXPENSE	OFFICE WAGES EXPENSE
116.00	23.20	69.72	16.31		0.00	225.23	899.35	832	1,124.58	
59.00	11.80	46.14	10.79	UW	35.00	162.73	581.47	833	744.20	
85.00	17.00	56.79	13.28	UW	25.00	197.07	718.93	834	916.00	
110.00	22.00	67.24	15.72	UW	10.00	224.96	859.54	835		1,084.50
234.31	46.86	111.50	26.08		0.00	418.75	1,379.70	836	1,798.45	
258.60	51.72	117.53	27.48	AR	20.00	475.33	1,420.25	837		1,895.58
276.89	55.38	122.06	28.55		0.00	482.88	1,485.87	838	1,968.75	
170.68	34.14	92.21	21.56		0.00	318.59	1,168.61	839		1,487.20
228.77	45.75	110.13	25.76		0.00	410.41	1,365.87	840	1,776.28	
200.33	40.07	103.08	24.11	AR	30.00	397.59	1,264.91	841	1,662.50	
122.00	24.40	72.47	16.95	UW	25.00	260.82	908.01	842	1,168.83	
537.29	107.46	179.80	43.65	UW	100.00	968.20	2,042.15	843		3,010.35
2,398.87	479.78	1,148.67	270.24		245.00	4,542.56	14,094.66		11,159.59	7,477.63
(8A)	*(8B)*	*(8C)*	*(8D)*		*(8E)*	*(8F)*	*(9A)*	*(9B)*	*(10A)*	*(10B)*

2,398.87 + 479.78 + 1,148.67 + 270.24 + 245.00 = 4,542.56

4,542.56 + 14,094.66 = 18,637.22

11,159.59 + 7,477.63 = 18,637.22

all federal and state unemployment calculations. There are three possibilities for Unemployment Taxable Earnings, as follows:

a. **Employee's cumulative earnings including this pay period have not reached $7,000.** When an employee's cumulative earnings so far during the calendar year (since January 1) are less than $7,000, we record the total earnings for the payroll period in the Unemployment Taxable Earnings column. For example, Anna Bodell's cumulative earnings before this week were $5,987. Bodell's cumulative earnings after this week are $6,731.20 ($5,987 + $744.20). Because Bodell's cumulative earnings are still less than $7,000 (after the current check of $744.20), her entire $744.20 in wages earned during this pay period is listed in the Unemployment Taxable Earnings column.

Remember

Unemployment taxable earnings are used for calculating the amount of the unemployment tax, which is paid by the employer only.

b. **Employee's cumulative earnings were less than $7,000 before this week and are more than $7,000 after this week.** Look at the line for David Dorn and notice that his cumulative earnings before this week were $6,786. Dorn's new cumulative earnings (ending) are $7,702 ($6,786 + $916), putting him over the $7,000 maximum. Therefore, to bring Dorn up to the $7,000 limit, $214 ($7,000 − $6,786) of his earnings for the week are taxable. After this week, none of Dorn's earnings for the remainder of this calendar year will be taxable for unemployment.

c. **Employee's cumulative earnings before this week were more than $7,000.** After an employee's earnings top $7,000 during the calendar year, record a zero or a dash in the Unemployment Taxable Earnings column to indicate that the column has not been forgotten or overlooked. For example, Mark Anderson's total earnings before the payroll period ended October 11 (beginning) were $44,960 (as shown in his individual earnings record in Figure 7 on page 340. Because he had previously earned more than $7,000 this year, we record a zero in the Unemployment Taxable Earnings column.

Social Security and Medicare taxes are recorded separately in the payroll register because there is no limit on Medicare as there is on Social Security.

(7B) **Social Security Taxable Earnings**—The first $113,700 for each employee. We assume a Social Security tax rate of 6.2 percent of the first $113,700 paid to each employee during the calendar year.

a. **Employee's cumulative earnings including this pay period have not reached $113,700.** When an employee's cumulative earnings so far during the year are less than $113,700, we record the total earnings for the payroll period in the Social Security Taxable Earnings column. For example, Anna Bodell's cumulative earnings so far this year amount to $6,731.20. Because Bodell's total earnings are less than $113,700, the entire $744.20 of wages earned during this pay period is listed in the Social Security Taxable Earnings column. Note that this is true of all of the employees except Grace Wallace.

b. **Employee's cumulative earnings were less than $113,700 before this week and are more than $113,700 after this week.** The line for Grace Wallace shows that her cumulative earnings before the payroll period ended October 11 were $110,800. However, the cumulative earnings including those of this payroll period total $113,810.35, which is greater than the $113,700 limit. That means only $2,900 ($113,700 − $110,800) of her current pay period earnings is recorded in the Social Security Taxable Earnings column. After an employee's earnings top $113,700 during the calendar year, record a zero or a dash to indicate that the column has not been forgotten or overlooked. (Use the same procedure as that for the Unemployment Taxable Earnings column.)

(7C) **Medicare Taxable Earnings**—All earnings for this period. We have assumed a Medicare tax rate of 1.45 percent (0.0145) on all earnings that are paid to each employee during the calendar year. Therefore, all earnings for this period are taxable and are recorded in the Medicare Taxable Earnings column.

(8) **Deductions**—Amounts taken away (withheld) from total earnings.

(8A) **Federal Income Tax Deductions**—The amount of the federal income tax deduction for each employee can be located directly on the wage-bracket tables or calculated on a percentage basis. We assumed that the employees are married and have one withholding allowance.

(8B) **State Income Tax Deductions**—States that impose income taxes also provide wage-bracket tables. The state tax deduction for each employee can be located in the appropriate table. As stated previously, we are assuming a rate of 20 percent of the federal income tax.

(8C) **Social Security Tax Deductions**—For each employee's Social Security tax deduction, we go to the Social Security Taxable Earnings column and note the amount subject to tax. Then, we multiply the Social Security taxable earnings by 6.2 percent (0.062). For example, Bodell's taxable earnings are $744.20 and her Social Security tax deduction is $46.14 ($744.20 × 0.062).

Taxable earnings multiplied by the tax rate equals the tax.

(8D) **Medicare Tax Deductions**—For each employee's Medicare tax deduction, we go to the Medicare Taxable Earnings column and note the amount subject to tax. Then, we multiply the Medicare taxable earnings by 1.45 percent. For example, Bodell's taxable earnings are $744.20 and her Medicare tax deduction is $10.79 ($744.20 × 0.0145).

(8E) **Other Deductions**—Employees' voluntary withholdings. In our illustration, UW represents the United Way and AR stands for Accounts Receivable (employee pays off a loan with the company). For example, Jeremy Lee paid $20 on his loan with the company.

(8F) **Total Deductions**—The combined total of each employee's deductions for taxes and other. For example, Bodell's total deduction is $162.73 ($59.00 + $11.80 + $46.14 + $10.79 + $35.00).

(9) **Payments**—The amount of each employee's payroll check (net pay or take-home pay).

(9A) **Net Amount**—Each employee's Total Earnings minus Total Deductions. For example, Bodell's net amount is $581.47 ($744.20 − $162.73).

(9B) **Ck. No.**—The number of each employee's payroll check.

(10) **Expense Account Debited**—Columns used for distributing each amount in the appropriate wages expense account. Green Sales Company uses Sales Wages Expense and Office Wages Expense. The sum of these two columns equals the total earnings.

(10A) **Sales Wages Expense**—Amounts earned by employees involved in sales activities.

(10B) **Office Wages Expense**—Amounts earned by employees involved in office activities.

THE PAYROLL ENTRY

Learning Objective 5 Journalize the payroll entry from a payroll register.

Because the payroll register summarizes the payroll data for the period, it is used as the basis for recording the payroll in the journal. Because the payroll register does not have the status of a journal, a journal entry is necessary. Figure 5 shows the entry in general journal form.

Figure 5
Payroll journal entry for Green Sales Company

GENERAL JOURNAL — Page 31

Date		Description	Post. Ref.	Debit	Credit
20--					
Oct.	11	Sales Wages Expense		11,159.59	
		Office Wages Expense		7,477.63	
		Employees' Federal Income Tax Payable			2,398.87
		FICA Taxes Payable			1,418.91
		Employees' State Income Tax Payable			479.78
		Employees' United Way Payable			195.00
		Accounts Receivable			50.00
		Wages Payable			14,094.66
		Payroll register for the week			
		ended October 11, 20--.			
Oct.	12	Wages Payable		14,094.66	
		Cash—M. Anderson			899.35
		Cash—A. Bodell			581.47
		Cash—D. Dorn			718.93
		Cash—S. Fields			859.54
		Cash—J. Graham			1,379.70
		Cash—J. Lee			1,420.25
		Cash—H. Mankowitz			1,485.87
		Cash—B. Olson			1,168.61
		Cash—W. Parker			1,365.87
		Cash—S. Raman			1,264.91
		Cash—A. Tabor			908.01
		Cash—G. Wallace			2,042.15

$1,148.67 +
$270.24

FYI

A company with a small number of employees would probably use its regular bank account to issue a check to each employee.

Remember

The totals from the Payroll register are the amounts used in the payroll entry.

Remember

The amount shown as Wages Payable is the employees' take-home pay.

Note that the accountant records the total cost to the company for services of employees as debits to the Wages Expense accounts.

Also note that the total Social Security tax deductions ($1,148.67) and the total Medicare tax deductions ($270.24) are combined to become FICA Taxes Payable of $1,418.91 ($1,148.67 + $270.24). The two tax deductions are combined into the one liability account because they are paid together at the same time. Social Security and Medicare taxes are recorded separately in the payroll register because they must be listed separately on each employee's W-2 form (Wage and Tax Statement).

Social Security (6.2%, limited to $113,700)	+	Medicare (1.45%, unlimited)	=	FICA Taxes Payable

To pay the employees from the company's regular checking account, the accountant makes the journal entry as shown in Figure 5.

Special Payroll Bank Account—An Alternative

A firm with a large number of employees would probably open a special **payroll bank account** with its bank. One check drawn on the regular bank account is made payable to the special payroll account for the amount of the total net pay for a payroll period. All payroll checks for the period are then written on the special payroll account. To record this, the accountant makes the following journal entry. In this book, assume that the entry to debit Cash—Payroll Bank Account and to credit Cash has already been made.

GENERAL JOURNAL Page 31

Date		Description	Post. Ref.	Debit	Credit
Oct.	12	Wages Payable		14 0 9 4 66	
		Cash—Payroll Bank Account			14 0 9 4 66
		Paid wages for week ended			
		October 11.			

FYI

With the use of the special payroll bank account, if employees delay cashing their paychecks, the checks do not have to be listed on the bank reconciliation of the firm's regular bank account. Balances of Employees' United Way Payable and other employee deductions are paid out of the firm's regular bank account.

Paycheck

All of the data needed to make out a payroll check are available in the payroll register. Mark Anderson's paycheck is shown in Figure 6.

Figure 6
Paycheck for Mark Anderson

EMPLOYEE	TOTAL HOURS	O.T. HOURS	REG. PAY	O.T. PREM. PAY	GROSS PAY	FED INC. TAX	STATE INC. TAX	SOCIAL SECURITY TAX	MEDICARE TAX	OTHER	TOTAL DED.	NET PAY
Mark Anderson	46	6	918.00	206.58	1,124.58	116.00	23.20	69.72	16.31	—	225.23	899.35

Payroll Account
Green Sales Company
610 First Avenue
Bangor, Maine 04401

CENTRAL NATIONAL BANK

98-461
252

October 12 20 -- No. 832

PAY TO THE ORDER OF Mark Anderson $ 899.35

Eight hundred ninety-nine and 35/100 DOLLARS

Eileen Green

⑆121000167⑆ 1234567890⑈ 832

Employees' Individual Earnings Records

To comply with government regulations, a firm has to keep current data on each employee's accumulated earnings, deductions, and net pay. The information contained in the payroll register is recorded each payday in each **employee's individual earnings record**. Figure 7, on page 340, shows a portion of the earnings record for Mark Anderson.

Maintain employees' individual earnings records.

Learning Objective

Figure 7
Employee's individual earnings record for Mark Anderson

	A	B	C	D	E	F	G	H	I	J
1	EMPLOYEE'S INDIVIDUAL EARNINGS RECORD									
2	NAME	Mark E. Anderson				EMPLOYEE NO.		55		
3	ADDRESS	1104 Rosewood Street				SOC. SEC. NO.		543-24-1680		
4		Bangor, Maine 04401				PAY RATE		$22.95		
5	MALE	X		FEMALE		EQUIVALENT HOURLY RATE		$22.95		
6	MARRIED	X		SINGLE		DATE TERMINATED				
7	PHONE NO.	207-555-2256		DATE OF BIRTH	9/17/72	CLASSIFICATION FOR WORKERS' COMPENSATION INSURANCE Sales floor				
8			HOURS WORKED		EARNINGS				DEDUCTIONS	
9								ENDING	FEDERAL	STATE
10	PERIOD	DATE						CUMULATIVE	INCOME	INCOME
40	ENDED	PAID	REGULAR	OVERTIME	REGULAR	OVERTIME	TOTAL	EARNINGS	TAX	TAX
41	9/6	9/7	40	8	918.00	275.44	1,193.44	40,771.55	127.00	25.40
42	9/13	9/14	40	2	918.00	68.86	986.86	41,758.41	95.00	19.00
43	9/20	9/21	40	2	918.00	68.86	986.86	42,745.27	95.00	19.00
44	9/27	9/28	40	5	918.00	172.15	1,090.15	43,835.42	112.00	22.40
45	10/4	10/5	40	6	918.00	206.58	1,124.58	44,960.00	116.00	23.20
46	10/11	10/12	40	6	918.00	206.58	1,124.58	46,084.58	116.00	23.20

K	L	M	N	O	P	Q
DATE EMPLOYED	2/1/--					
NO. OF EXEMPTIONS	1					
PER HOUR	X	PER DAY	________			
PER WEEK		PER MONTH	________			
DEDUCTIONS					PAID	
SOCIAL SECURITY TAX	MEDICARE TAX	OTHER: CODE	OTHER: AMOUNT	TOTAL	NET AMOUNT	CK. NO.
73.99	17.30	UW	5.00	248.69	944.75	771
61.19	14.31	UW	0.00	189.50	797.36	783
61.19	14.31	UW	5.00	194.50	792.36	795
67.59	15.81	UW	0.00	217.80	872.35	807
69.72	16.31	UW	5.00	230.23	894.35	819
69.72	16.31	UW	0.00	225.23	899.35	832

Accounting with *QuickBooks*®

An Overview of Processing Payroll with Quickbooks

 List payroll features in QuickBooks.

Learning Objective

As you learned in Chapter 7, payroll accounting tasks are very important. Businesses are required by law to (1) withhold employee taxes, (2) pay employee and employer payroll taxes by specific deadlines, and (3) submit payroll tax reports. QuickBooks has several payroll options which can help simplify these important activities.

Learning Objectives

After you have completed this section, you will be able to do the following:

1. List payroll features in QuickBooks.
2. Pay employees using QuickBooks.
3. View and print payroll reports in QuickBooks.

QUICKBOOKS PAYROLL: SUBSCRIPTION

QuickBooks offers the following three levels of payroll subscription services:

1. **Basic** The basic payroll package calculates payroll tax deductions for processing paychecks and direct deposits; however, this package does not automatically create payroll tax forms and reports.
2. **Enhanced** The enhanced payroll package provides all of the same benefits as the basic package, plus it automatically creates payroll tax forms and reports. This option also allows the electronic submission of payroll tax liability payments.
3. **Assisted** For companies that prefer to outsource payroll activities, QuickBooks has the assisted payroll package. This full service payroll option manages paycheck processing, direct deposits, payroll tax payments, as well as payroll tax forms and reports. QuickBooks' guaranteed assurance that paychecks, tax deposits, and tax reports will be processed on time and without errors provides employers peace of mind that their important payroll activities are being properly handled.

MANUAL PAYROLL PROCESSING

Some companies want to process and maintain payroll information in a computerized environment, but they do not want to subscribe to one of the QuickBooks payroll services listed above. For these companies, QuickBooks offers a manual payroll processing option. When the manual payroll option is set up, withholding taxes and payroll taxes due from employers must be manually calculated and then recorded in QuickBooks. In this text, we will use the **process payroll manually** option, which will be covered later.

Regardless of the payroll option a company chooses, payroll is accessed one of two ways.

1. From the **Employee** home page (See Figure Q1).
2. From the **Employees** menu bar (See Figure Q2).

Figure Q1
Payroll access from the home page of the Employee Center

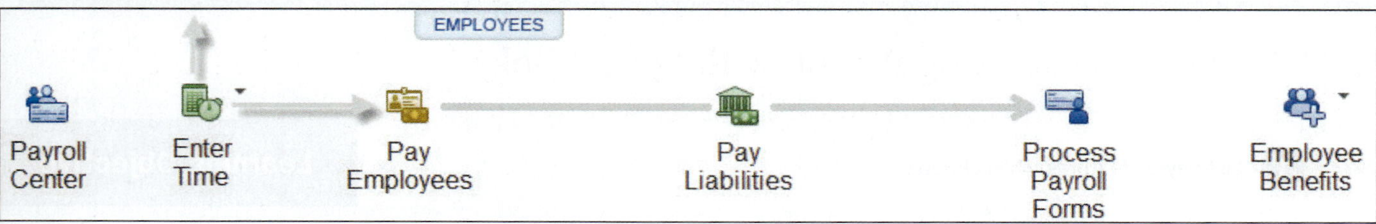

Figure Q2
Payroll access from the Employees menu bar

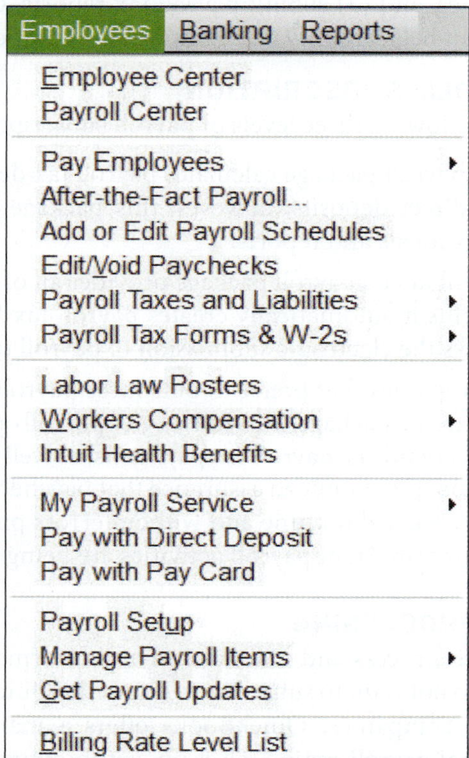

ENTER TIME

QuickBooks offers a time tracking feature that permits companies to monitor the amount of time employees work on specific jobs or for specific clients. The information collected through the **Enter Time** feature simplifies payroll processing and customer billing. Using the **Enter Time** feature for billing customers will be discussed further in Chapter 9.

Figure Q3
Enter time

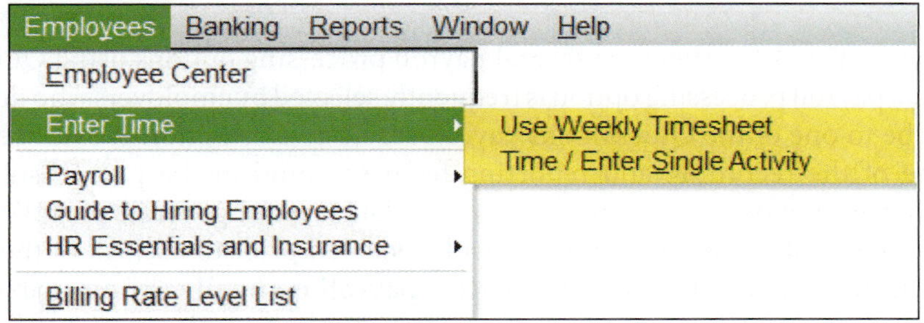

EMPLOYEE BENEFITS

QuickBooks has an **Employee Benefits** feature that employers can use to order required labor law posters, explore worker compensation insurance and health benefits, and provide employees with online payroll information. The **Employee Benefits** feature can be accessed from the **Employee** home page (Figure Q4) or from the **Employees** menu bar (Figure Q5).

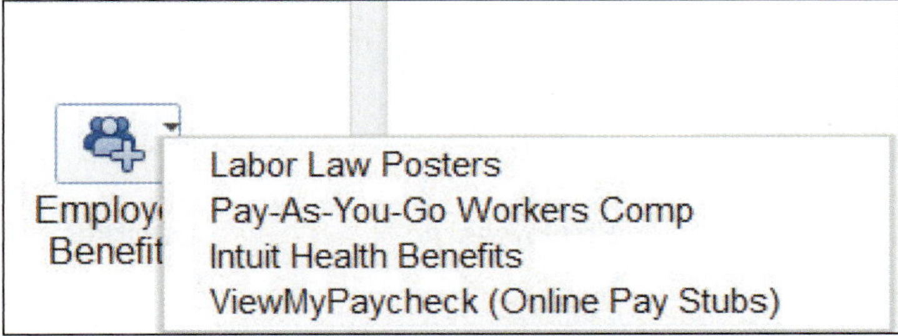

Figure Q4
Employee Benefits from home page

Figure Q5
Employee Benefits from Employees menu bar

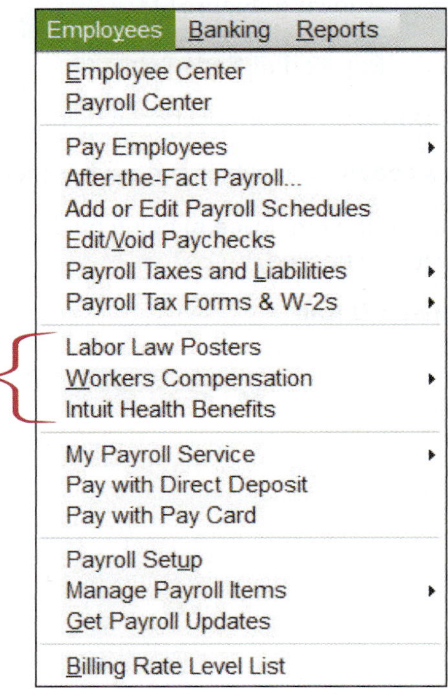

QuickBooks Tip

1. Go to **Help > QuickBooks Help**.
2. Select the **Search** tab.
3. Enter **manual payroll** in the search box and press **Enter**.
4. Click on the article titled **Calculate payroll taxes manually (without a subscription to QuickBooks Payroll).** Within this article, click **Set your company file to use the manual payroll calculations setting.**

Click **OK** on the message that is displayed and exit **Help**.

Learning Objective  Pay employees using QuickBooks.

As previously discussed, there are several payroll processing options using QuickBooks. The manual payroll processing option is frequently selected by employers who do not want to subscribe to one of the QuickBooks payroll services. This option provides employers with some of the recording and reporting features found in the payroll subscription services; however, it does not automatically calculate taxes or generate payroll tax forms. The **process payroll manually** option must be enabled prior to use. All of the data files used for this text will already have the **process payroll manually** option enabled.

Let's return to a familiar example to discuss how to pay employees using the manual payroll process in QuickBooks. In this chapter (Figure 1, page 327), Mark Anderson, an employee for Green Sales Company, submitted a time card for the week ending October 11, 20--. We will use this information to calculate gross wages for the pay period ending October 11, 20--, as shown on page 327 and withholding taxes as shown in Figure 4 on pages 334–335. Follow the steps below to pay Mark Anderson.

STEP 1. From the **Employees** center of the home page, select **Pay Employees**, as shown in Figure Q6.

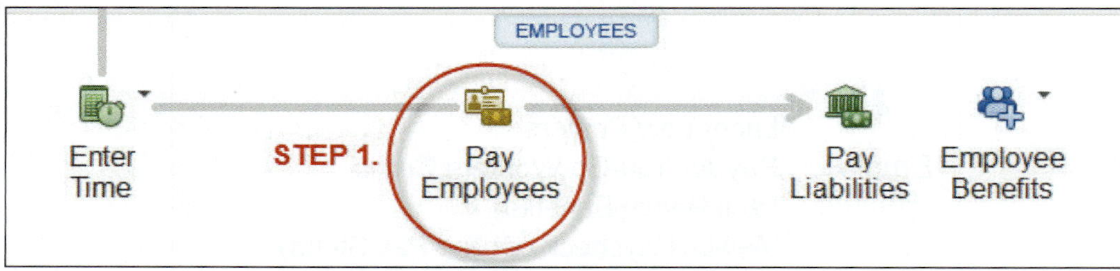

Figure Q6
Pay employees

ENTER PAYROLL INFORMATION

Complete the following steps as shown in Figure Q7.

STEP 1. Enter the date in the **Pay Period Ends** field.

STEP 2. Enter the **Check Date** for the payroll checks being processed.

STEP 3. Select the **Bank Account** from which the payroll checks will be issued.

STEP 4. Check the box next to the employee(s) being paid. In this case, Mark Anderson will be checked.

STEP 5. Click **Open Paycheck Detail**.

Figure Q7
Enter payroll information

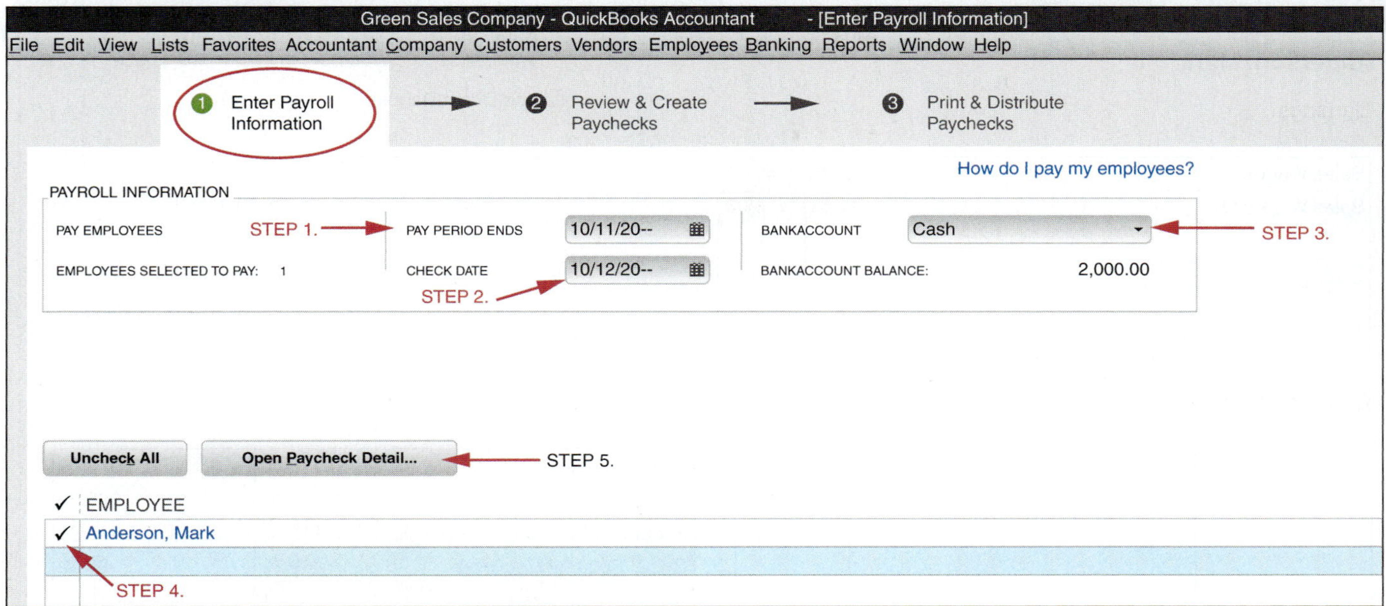

PREVIEW PAYCHECK

The preview paycheck screen allows users to manually enter the payroll information. After verifying the pay period dates in the top right-hand corner of the screen, complete the following steps as shown in Figure Q8 on page 346.

STEP 1. For hourly employees, such as Mark Anderson, enter the number of regular hours worked during this pay period. If the pay rate has previously been entered into QuickBooks, the rate will automatically appear in the **Rate** field. The rate can also be entered or modified as needed.

STEP 2. Enter the number of overtime hours worked during this pay period. The overtime rate is based on the regular wage rate and will automatically appear in the **Rate** field.

STEP 3. Manually calculate the withholding taxes and enter them in the appropriate field under the **Employee Summary** section. Notice that a minus sign appears after the amount has been entered. QuickBooks automatically places a minus sign in front of deduction fields.

STEP 4. Manually calculate the employer payroll taxes and enter them in the appropriate field under the **Company Summary** section. Employer payroll taxes will be covered further in Chapter 8.

STEP 5. Select **Save & Close** when you are finished entering payroll information. If you need to process payroll information for additional employees, you can select **Save & Next**. If you would like to view or edit information previously entered for an employee, select **Save & Previous**.

Figure Q8
Preview paycheck

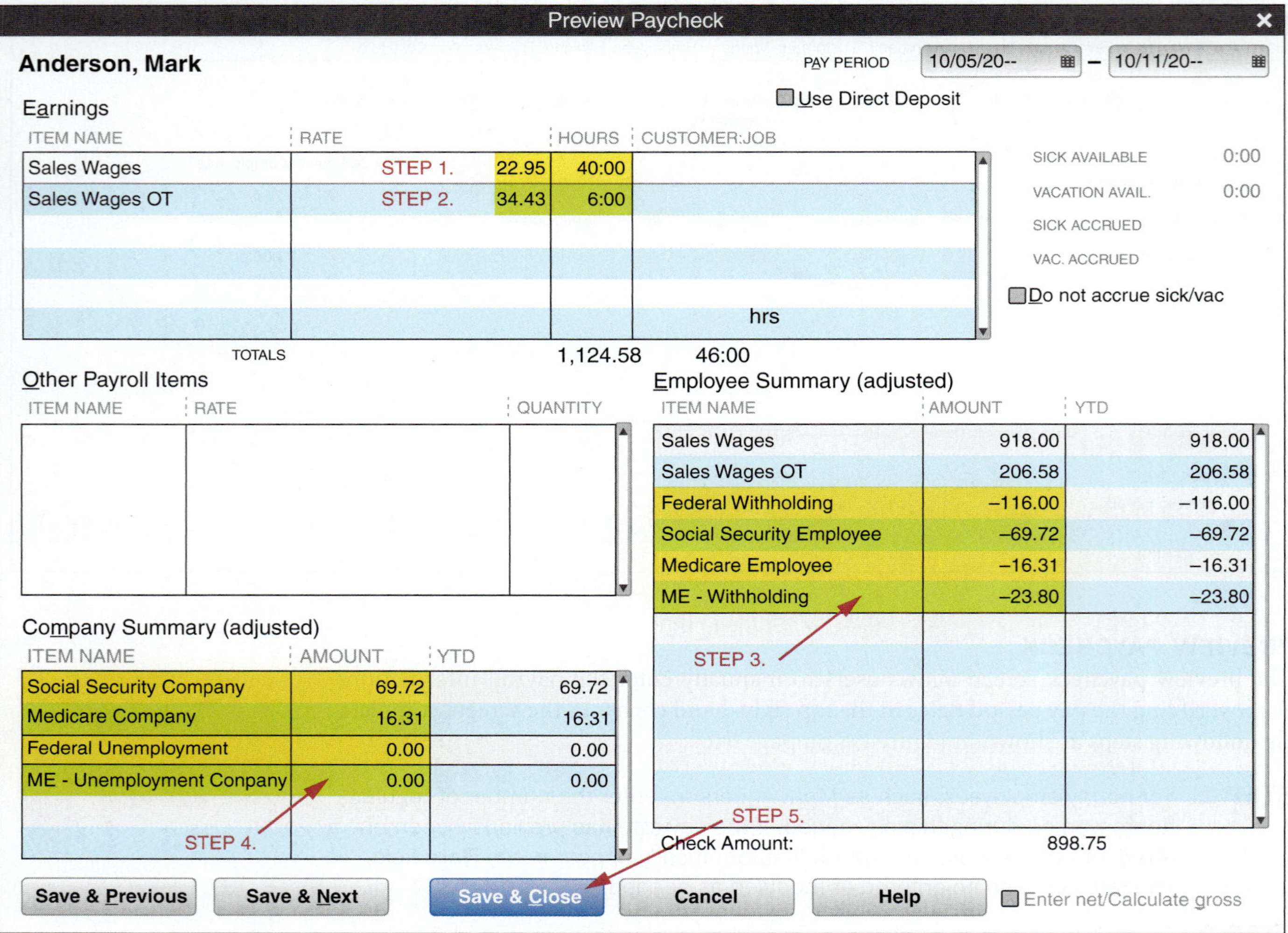

REVIEW AND CREATE PAYCHECKS

Once all of the payroll information has been entered into QuickBooks, the **Review & Create Paychecks** screen will summarize the payroll information. If the payroll information summary is correct, complete the following steps to proceed.

STEP 1. Verify the **Bank Account** information is correct.

STEP 2. Select from the **Paycheck Options** (1) **Print paychecks from QuickBooks** or (2) **Assign check numbers to handwritten checks** as shown in Figure Q9. Enter the **first check number** you will use with this payroll. For Mark Anderson, the payroll check number being used in Figure 5 on page 338 is No. 832.

STEP 3. Select **Create Paychecks**.

Figure Q9
Review and create paychecks

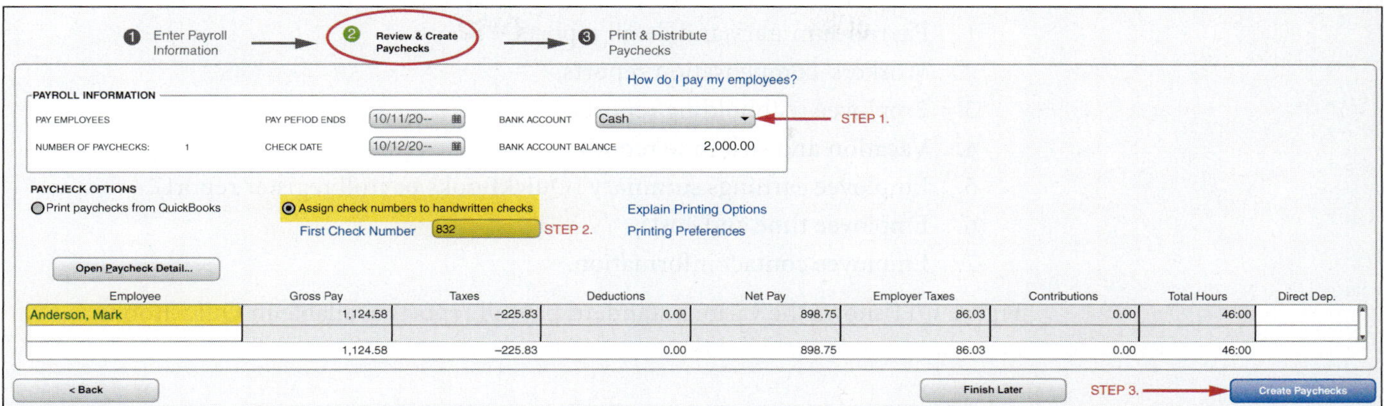

PRINT AND DISTRIBUTE PAYCHECKS

Once you have successfully created the paychecks for the pay period, you will see a confirmation message as shown in Figure Q10. Verify that all of the checks have been created and then complete the following steps to finalize the payroll process.

STEP 1. Select **Print Paychecks** or **Print Pay Stubs**. For Mark Anderson, **Print Paychecks** was selected. QuickBooks also has the option for paying employees through direct deposit. When direct deposit is used, the **Print Pay Stubs** option will provide employees with detailed information about this deposit.

STEP 2. You are now ready to distribute the paychecks or pay stubs to your employees.

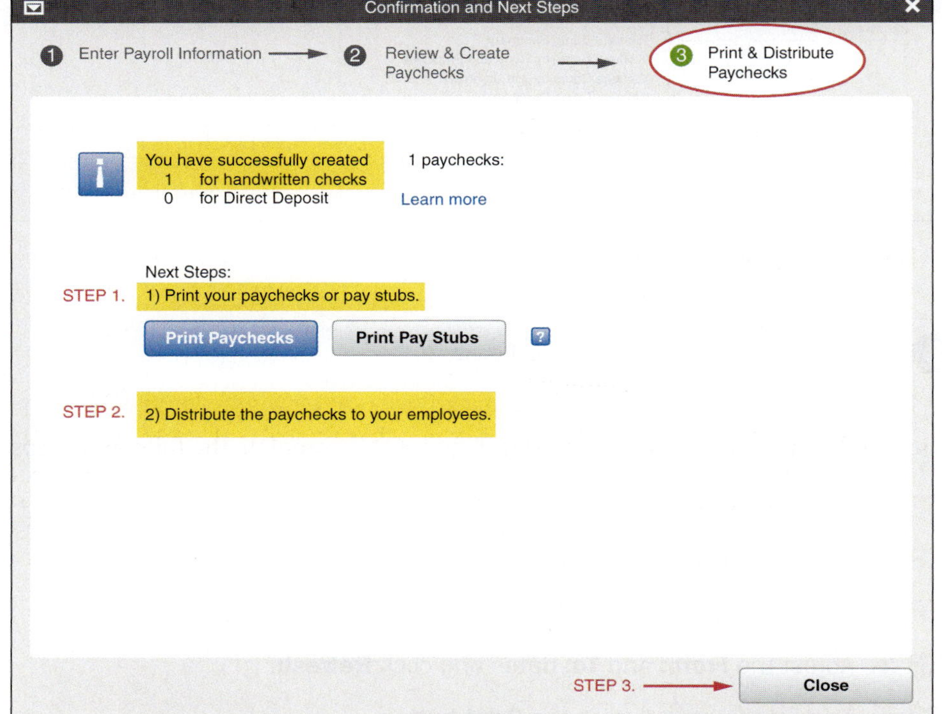

Figure Q10
Print and distribute paychecks

QUICKBOOKS PAYROLL REPORTS

QuickBooks provides numerous payroll reports, which can be viewed, printed, or exported to Excel. Standard payroll reports available in QuickBooks include the following:

1. Payroll summary and detail reports.
2. Workers' compensation reports.
3. Employee withholding reports.
4. Vacation and sick time reports.
5. Employee earnings summary (QuickBooks payroll register report).
6. Employee time and cost.
7. Employee contact information.

Figure Q11 shows the various standard payroll reports available in QuickBooks.

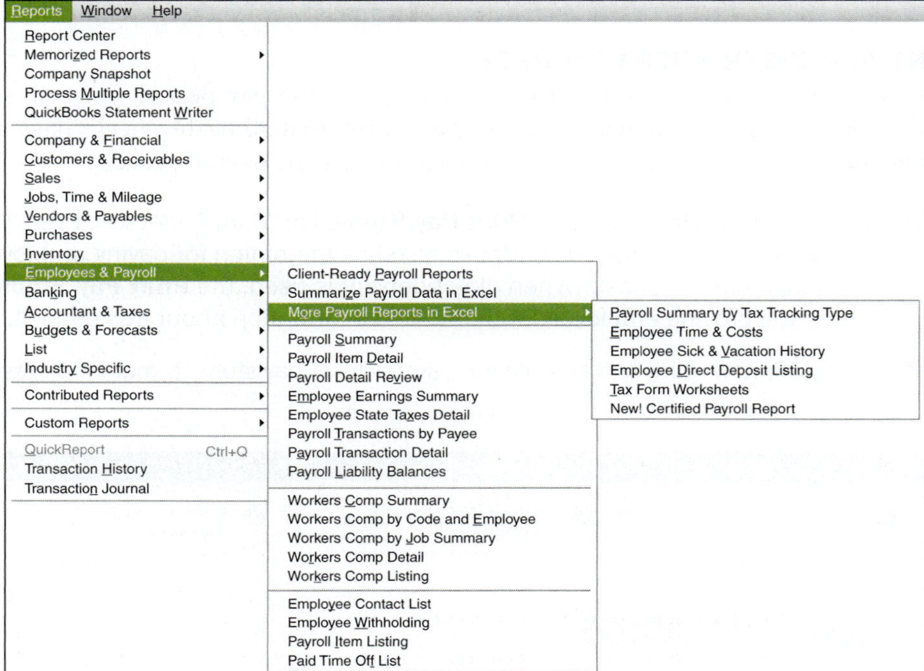

Figure Q11
QuickBooks payroll reports

Learning Objective **3** View and print payroll reports in QuickBooks.

To view and print payroll reports listed in Figure Q11, complete the following steps:

STEP 1. Click the **Reports** tab.

STEP 2. Click **Employees & Payroll**.

STEP 3. Select the desired payroll report.

STEP 4. Adjust the **From:** and **To:** dates and click **Refresh**.

STEP 5. To print the report, click the **Print** button.

Chapter Review

Study and Practice

 Recognize the role of income tax laws that affect payroll deductions and contributions. **Learning Objective**

Employees and employers involved in the computation and paying of employees for their work must understand the laws, know the percentages and limits involved, and know when and to whom to submit the funds deducted from employees and contributed by employees. The federal income tax withholding tables are provided by the IRS in Publication 15 (Circular E). FICA payroll taxes, withheld from the employee, are currently 6.2 percent (0.062) for the employee's portion of the Social Security tax, based on the first $113,700 of wages and 1.45 percent (0.0145) on all wages for Medicare.

PRACTICE EXERCISE 1

Sally Quinn earns an annual salary of $150,000. How much does she pay in FICA payroll taxes this year?

PRACTICE EXERCISE 1 • SOLUTION

Social Security taxes (limited to first $113,700)	$113,700 × 0.062 =	$7,049.40
Medicare taxes	$150,000 × 0.0145 =	2,175.00
Total FICA taxes		$9,224.40

 Calculate total earnings based on an hourly, salary, piece-rate, or commission basis. **Learning Objective**

Earnings calculated on an *hourly basis* equal the hourly rate multiplied by the number of hours worked. If an employee is paid on a *salary basis* and is entitled to extra pay for overtime, the overtime rate is the annual salary divided by 52 (weeks) divided by 40 (normal hours per week). Earnings calculated on a *piece-rate basis* equals the total number of products produced multiplied by the rate per unit of product. Earnings calculated on a *commission basis* equal the total number of units sold or the price of units sold multiplied by the commission rate.

PRACTICE EXERCISE 2

Soma Raman worked 45 hours for the week ended November 7. His hourly rate is $41.85. Determine his gross wages if he is paid time-and-a-half for all overtime hours.

PRACTICE EXERCISE 2 • SOLUTION

40 hours at straight time	40	× $41.85 per hour =	$1,674.00
5 hours overtime ($41.85 × 1.5 = $62.78)	5	× $62.78 per hour =	313.90
Total hours and gross wages	45		$1,987.90

 Determine deductions from gross pay, such as federal income tax withheld, Social Security tax, and Medicare tax, to calculate net pay. **Learning Objective**

Starting with **gross pay**, an employee's pay is reduced for federal and state income tax withholding, **FICA taxes** (**Social Security** and **Medicare taxes**), and other items such as retirement savings through a 401(k) plan and medical reimbursement plans to arrive at **net pay**.

CHAPTER REVIEW

PRACTICE EXERCISE 3

Using Figure 3 on pages 331–332, calculate the federal income tax withholding for an employee who is married and is paid weekly and whose wages are $1,360 with one withholding allowance. Then calculate the Social Security tax and Medicare tax for the employee, assuming the employee has cumulative earnings of less than $113,700 for the calendar year to date.

PRACTICE EXERCISE 3 • SOLUTION

According to Figure 3, $152 should be withheld for an employee who is married, paid weekly and whose wages are $1,360 with one withholding allowance. Social Security and Medicare taxes would be computed as follows:

$1,360 × 0.062 = $84.32 Social Security tax
$1,360 × 0.0145 = $19.72 Medicare tax

Learning Objective 4 Complete a payroll register.

To complete the **payroll register**, list the employees' names, hours worked, and beginning cumulative earnings. Add the total earnings to the beginning cumulative earnings to get ending cumulative earnings. The Unemployment Taxable Earnings column is used for the first $7,000 of each employee's earnings for FUTA and SUTA. The Social Security Taxable Earnings column is used for the first $113,700 paid to each employee during the **calendar year**. The Medicare Taxable Earnings column is used for all earnings. Under the Deductions columns, list the federal and state income taxes withheld, the Social Security taxes withheld, the Medicare taxes withheld, and other deductions. The Social Security tax deduction equals the Social Security **taxable earnings** multiplied by an assumed rate of 6.2 percent. The Medicare tax deduction equals the Medicare taxable earnings multiplied by an assumed rate of 1.45 percent. The Net Amount column equals Total Earnings minus Total Deductions.

PRACTICE EXERCISE 4

Complete the following payroll register. The employees are paid time-and-a-half for overtime.

	A	B	C	D	E	F	G	H
1				EARNINGS				
2–4	NAME	TOTAL HOURS	BEGINNING CUMULATIVE EARNINGS	REGULAR	OVERTIME	TOTAL	ENDING CUMULATIVE EARNINGS	UNEMPLOYMENT
5	Abbott, Jack	40	55,820.00	1,487.20				0.00
6	Monohan, William	44	56,430.00	1,581.60				0.00
7	Romar, Sue	45	58,967.00	1,674.16				0.00
8	Williams, Emma	40	140,000.00	3,010.35				0.00
9			311,217.00	7,753.31				0.00
10								

I	J	K	L	M	N	O	P	Q
TAXABLE EARNINGS		DEDUCTIONS					PAYMENTS	
SOCIAL SECURITY	MEDICARE	FEDERAL INCOME TAX	STATE INCOME TAX	SOCIAL SECURITY TAX	MEDICARE TAX	TOTAL	NET AMOUNT	CK. NO.
		170.68	34.14					1520
		239.41	47.88					1521
		281.72	56.34					1522
		537.29	107.46					1523
		1,229.10	245.82					

PRACTICE EXERCISE 4 • SOLUTION

	A	B	C	D	E	F	G	H
1				EARNINGS				
2			BEGINNING				ENDING	
3		TOTAL	CUMULATIVE				CUMULATIVE	
4	NAME	HOURS	EARNINGS	REGULAR	OVERTIME	TOTAL	EARNINGS	UNEMPLOYMENT
5	Abbott, Jack	40	55,820.00	1,487.20	0.00	1,487.20	57,307.20	0.00
6	Monohan, William	44	56,430.00	1,581.60	237.24	1,818.84	58,248.84	0.00
7	Romar, Sue	45	58,967.00	1,674.16	313.90	1,988.06	60,955.06	0.00
8	Williams, Emma	40	140,000.00	3,010.35	0.00	3,010.35	143,010.35	0.00
9			311,217.00	7,753.31	551.14	8,304.45	319,521.45	0.00
10								

I	J	K	L	M	N	O	P	Q
TAXABLE EARNINGS		DEDUCTIONS					PAYMENTS	
SOCIAL SECURITY	MEDICARE	FEDERAL INCOME TAX	STATE INCOME TAX	SOCIAL SECURITY TAX	MEDICARE TAX	TOTAL	NET AMOUNT	CK. NO.
1,487.20	1,487.20	170.68	34.14	92.21	21.56	318.59	1,168.61	1520
1,818.84	1,818.84	239.41	47.88	112.77	26.37	426.43	1,392.41	1521
1,988.06	1,988.06	281.72	56.34	123.26	28.83	490.15	1,497.91	1522
0.00	3,010.35	537.29	107.46	0.00	43.65	688.40	2,321.95	1523
5,294.10	8,304.45	1,229.10	245.82	328.24	120.41	1,923.57	6,380.88	

Learning Objective

5 Journalize the payroll entry from a payroll register.

Totals are taken directly from the payroll register. Refer to the general journal illustrations on pages 338–339 for an example of the first payroll entry and examples of two ways to journalize the payment of the payroll—one from the company's regular checking account and one from a special **payroll bank account**.

PRACTICE EXERCISE 5

Based on the payroll register created in Practice Exercise 4, prepare the journal entry to record the payroll for the week of December 8, 20--.

PRACTICE EXERCISE 5 • SOLUTION

GENERAL JOURNAL Page 31

Date		Description	Post. Ref.	Debit	Credit
20--					
Dec.	8	Wages Expense		8,304.45	
		Employees' Federal Income Tax Payable			1,229.10
		FICA Taxes Payable			448.65
		Employees' State Income Tax Payable			245.82
		Wages payable			6,380.88
		Payroll register for the week ended December 8, 20--.			

$328.24 + $120.41

Learning Objective  Maintain employees' individual earnings records.

In the **employees' individual earnings records**, list the personal data for each employee. Based on the information contained in the payroll register, record the earnings and deductions for each payroll period.

6 PRACTICE EXERCISE 6

Update the following employee's individual earnings record for William Monohan for the December 8 payroll from the payroll register in Practice Exercise 4.

	A	B	C	D	E	F	G	H	I
1	EMPLOYEE'S INDIVIDUAL EARNINGS RECORD								
2	NAME	William Monohan				EMPLOYEE NO.		592	
3	ADDRESS	17058 SE 97th Court				SOC. SEC. NO.		544-64-8240	
4		Miami, Florida 33158				PAY RATE		$39.54	
5	MALE	X		FEMALE		OVERTIME PAY		1½x	
6	MARRIED	X		SINGLE					
7	PHONE NO.	305-999-9001		DATE OF BIRTH 6/17/73					
8			HOURS WORKED		EARNINGS				DEDUCTIONS
9								ENDING	FEDERAL
10	PERIOD ENDED	DATE PAID	REGULAR	OVERTIME	REGULAR	OVERTIME	TOTAL	CUMULATIVE EARNINGS	INCOME TAX
11	11/17	11/18	40	8	1,581.60	474.48	2,056.08	53,029.56	298.72
12	11/24	11/25	40	2	1,581.60	118.62	1,700.22	54,729.78	209.76
13	12/1	12/2	40	2	1,581.60	118.62	1,700.22	56,430.00	209.76
14									

J	K	L	M	N	O
	DATE EMPLOYED	2/1/--			
	NO. OF EXEMPTIONS	1			
	PER HOUR	X	PER DAY	________	
	PER WEEK		PER MONTH	________	
DEDUCTIONS				PAID	
STATE INCOME TAX	SOCIAL SECURITY TAX	MEDICARE TAX	TOTAL	NET AMOUNT	CK. NO.
59.74	127.48	29.81	515.75	1,540.33	920
41.95	105.41	24.65	381.77	1,318.45	1120
41.95	105.41	24.65	381.77	1,318.45	1325

PRACTICE EXERCISE 6 • SOLUTION

	A	B	C	D	E	F	G	H	I
1	EMPLOYEE'S INDIVIDUAL EARNINGS RECORD								
2	NAME	William Monohan				EMPLOYEE NO.		592	
3	ADDRESS	17058 SE 97th Court				SOC. SEC. NO.		544-64-8240	
4		Miami, Florida 33158				PAY RATE		$39.54	
5	MALE	X		FEMALE		OVERTIME PAY		1½x	
6	MARRIED	X		SINGLE					
7	PHONE NO.	305-999-9001		DATE OF BIRTH 6/17/73					
8			HOURS WORKED		EARNINGS				DEDUCTIONS
9								ENDING	FEDERAL
10	PERIOD ENDED	DATE PAID	REGULAR	OVERTIME	REGULAR	OVERTIME	TOTAL	CUMULATIVE EARNINGS	INCOME TAX
11	11/17	11/18	40	8	1,581.60	474.48	2,056.08	53,029.56	298.72
12	11/24	11/25	40	2	1,581.60	118.62	1,700.22	54,729.78	209.76
13	12/1	12/2	40	2	1,581.60	118.62	1,700.22	56,430.00	209.76
14	12/8	12/9	40	4	1,581.60	237.24	1,818.84	58,248.84	239.41
15									

J	K	L	M	N	O
	DATE EMPLOYED	2/1/—			
	NO. OF EXEMPTIONS	1			
	PER HOUR	X	PER DAY	________	
	PER WEEK		PER MONTH	________	
DEDUCTIONS				PAID	
STATE INCOME TAX	SOCIAL SECURITY TAX	MEDICARE TAX	TOTAL	NET AMOUNT	CK. NO.
59.74	127.48	29.81	515.75	1,540.33	920
41.95	105.41	24.65	381.77	1,318.45	1120
41.95	105.41	24.65	381.77	1,318.45	1325
47.88	112.77	26.37	426.43	1,392.41	1521

Glossary

Calendar year A 12-month period beginning on January 1 and ending on December 31 of the same year. *(p. 326)*

Current Tax Payment Act (Income Tax Withholding) An act that requires employers to withhold and pay employee funds to the U.S. Treasury. *(p. 324)*

Employee One who works for compensation under the direction and control of the employer. *(p. 324)*

Employee's individual earnings record A supplementary record for each employee showing personal payroll data and yearly cumulative earnings, deductions, and net pay. *(p. 339)*

Employee's Withholding Allowance Certificate (Form W-4) A form that specifies the number of allowances claimed by each employee and gives the employer the authority to withhold money for an employee's federal income taxes. *(p. 329)*

Exemption An amount of an employee's annual earnings not subject to income tax for the taxpayer, taxpayer's spouse, and dependents *(usually children)*. *(p. 329)*

Fair Labor Standards Act The act of 1938 that provides for minimum standards for wages and overtime, including provisions related to child labor and equal pay for equal work. *(p. 324)*

FICA taxes Social Security taxes plus Medicare taxes, paid by both employee and employer under the provisions of the Federal Insurance Contributions Act. The proceeds are used to pay old-age and disability pensions and to fund the Medicare program. *(p. 325)*

Gross pay The total amount of an employee's pay before any deductions. *(p. 323)*

Independent contractor Someone who is engaged for a definite job or service and who may choose his or her own means of doing the work. This person is not an employee of the firm for which the service is provided. *(p. 324)*

Medicare taxes Federal government taxes levied on employees and employers; proceeds are used for medical insurance for eligible people aged 65 and over. *(p. 325)*

Net pay Gross pay minus deductions. Also called *take-home pay*. *(p. 323)*

Payroll bank account A special checking account used to pay a company's employees. *(p. 339)*

Payroll register A manual or computerized schedule prepared for each payroll period listing the earnings, deductions, and net pay for each employee. *(p. 334)*

Pre-tax deductions Employee deductions that are not subject to income tax. The deductions include medical insurance premiums, medical and dependent care expenses under a flexible spending plan, and 401(k) contributions. *(p. 329)*

Social Security Act of 1935 An act that provides for worker retirement funding through deductions from workers' wages and matching amounts from their employers. *(p. 325)*

Social Security taxes Federal government taxes levied on employees and employers; proceeds are used for old-age pensions and disability benefits. *(p. 325)*

Taxable earnings The amount of an employee's earnings subject to a tax. *(p. 329)*

Wage-bracket tax tables A chart providing the amounts to be deducted for income taxes based on amount of earnings, marital status, and number of allowances claimed. *(p. 330)*

Withholding allowance An allowance claimed by an employee (on a W-4), which employers use to calculate the amount of income tax withheld from an employee's paycheck. *(p. 329)*

Workers' compensation laws Laws that protect employees and dependents against losses due to death or injury incurred on the job. *(p. 326)*

Quiz Yourself

_____ 1. Which of the following is *not* usually considered an independent contractor?
a. Plumber
b. Salesperson
c. Lawyer
d. CPA
e. Electrician

_____ 2. Which of the following taxes are *not* withheld from an employee?
a. FICA Social Security
b. Federal Unemployment (FUTA)
c. FICA Medicare
d. Federal Income Tax
e. All of the above are withheld

_____ 3. Calculate an employee's total earnings if the company pays time-and-a-half when Jill Smith works 41 hours at $15 per hour.
a. $600.00
b. $615.00
c. $622.50
d. $635.00
e. None of the above

_____ 4. Which of the following is *not* a deduction from total earnings?
a. Federal income tax
b. Union dues
c. 2.5 hours of overtime
d. Medical insurance premiums
e. State income tax

_____ 5. Which of the following is *not* included in the payroll register?
a. Total hours
b. Overtime earnings
c. Unemployment taxable earnings
d. Wage-bracket tax table
e. Total earnings

_____ 6. Firms with a large number of employees generally use which of the following for disbursing payroll to employees?
   a. Payroll bank account
   b. General bank account
   c. Credit card account
   d. Accounts Receivable
   e. Accounts Payable

_____ 7. When is the payroll register updated?
   a. Annually
   b. Each payday
   c. Quarterly
   d. Monthly
   e. No set schedule—whenever there is time

Answers:
1. b 2. b 3. c 4. c 5. d 6. a 7. b

Review It with QuickBooks®

_____ 1. All of the following are QuickBooks payroll subscription services *except*
   a. basic.
   b. enhanced.
   c. assisted.
   d. manual.

_____ 2. The QuickBooks feature that permits companies to monitor the time employees work on specific jobs for processing payroll and billing customers is
   a. Pay Employees.
   b. Time Tracking.
   c. Enhanced.
   d. After-the-Fact Payroll.

_____ 3. The QuickBooks featured icon on the home page that allows employers to order labor law posters is
   a. Employee Benefits.
   b. Basic.
   c. Enhanced.
   d. Assisted.

_____ 4. Employee and payroll reports available in QuickBooks include all of the following, *except*
   a. Employee Earnings Summary.
   b. Payroll Summary.
   c. Time by Job Summary.
   d. Employee Withholding.

Answers:
1. d 2. b 3. a 4. c

Chapter Assignments

Discussion Questions

1. Why must employers maintain employees' individual earnings records?
2. What information is included in an employee's individual earnings record?
3. What is the purpose of the payroll register?
4. Explain the difference between gross earnings and net earnings for a payroll period.
5. Describe how a special payroll bank account is useful in paying the wages and salaries of employees.
6. List three required deductions and four voluntary deductions from an employee's total earnings.
7. What is the difference between an employee and an independent contractor? List two examples of an independent contractor.
8. What information is needed to use the wage-bracket withholding table? Where is the table found?

Exercises

LO 1, 2

Practice Exercises 1, 2

EXERCISE 7-1 Determine the gross pay for each employee listed below.

a. Clay Jones is paid time-and-a-half for all hours over 40. He worked 45 hours during the week. His regular pay rate is $25 per hour.

b. Mary James worked 48 hours during the week. She is entitled to time-and-a-half for all hours in excess of 40 per week. Her regular pay rate is $20 per hour.

c. Lori Terry is paid a commission of 10 percent of her sales, which amounted to $23,650.

d. Nicole Smith's yearly salary is $95,500. During the week, she worked 46 hours, and she is entitled to time-and-a-half for all hours over 40.

LO 1, 2, 3

Practice Exercises 1, 2, 3

EXERCISE 7-2 Lisa Meilo works for Pacific Company, which pays its employees time-and-a-half for all hours worked in excess of 40 per week. Meilo's pay rate is $37 per hour. Her wages are subject to federal income tax, a Social Security tax deduction at the rate of 6.2 percent, and a Medicare tax deduction at the rate of 1.45 percent. She is married and claims three allowances. Meilo has an unpaid half-hour lunch break during an 8½-hour day. In the most recent pay period, she worked 50 hours. Meilo's beginning cumulative earnings are $73,654.

Complete the following:

a.	______ hours at straight time × $ ______ per hour		$ ______
b.	______ hours overtime × $ ______ per hour		______
c.	Total gross pay		$ ______
d.	Federal income tax withholding	$ 254.66	
e.	Social Security tax withholding at 6.2 percent	______	
f.	Medicare tax withholding at 1.45 percent	______	
g.	Total withholding		______
h.	Net pay		$ ______

LO 1, 2, 3, 4

Practice Exercises 1, 2, 3, 4

EXERCISE 7-3 Using the income tax withholding table in Figure 3, pages 331–332, for each employee of Miller Company, determine the net pay for the week ended January 21. Assume a Social Security tax of 6.2 percent and a Medicare tax of 1.45 percent. All employees have cumulative earnings, including this pay period, of less than $113,700. Assume that all employees are married.

Employee	Allowances	Total Earnings	Federal Income Tax Withheld	Social Security Tax Withheld	Medicare Tax Withheld	Union Dues Withheld	United Way Contribution	Net Pay
a. Aston, F. B.	1	$ 900.00	$	$	$	$ 25.00	$ 35.00	$
b. Dwyer, S. J.	2	920.00				25.00	35.00	
c. Flynn, K. A.	3	1,110.00				25.00	40.00	
d. Harden, J. L.	0	1,025.00				25.00	40.00	
e. Nguyen, H.	2	925.00				25.00	35.00	
Totals		$4,880.00	$	$	$	$125.00	$185.00	$

LO 1, 4

Practice Exercises 1, 4

EXERCISE 7-4 For the week ended September 7, the totals of the payroll register for Benton, Inc., are presented below. The regular and overtime earnings are correct. List six errors that exist. None of the employees have earned more than $113,700, so all earnings are subject to Social Security and Medicare taxes. Assume that amounts for taxable earnings (unemployment, social security, medicare) and deductions (federal income tax, union dues, charity) are correct. Round amounts to the nearest penny.

	A	B	C	D	E	F	G	H	I
1				EARNINGS				TAXABLE EARNINGS	
2		BEGINNING				ENDING			
3		CUMULATIVE				CUMULATIVE		SOCIAL	
4	NAME	EARNINGS	REGULAR	OVERTIME	TOTAL	EARNINGS	UNEMPLOYMENT	SECURITY	MEDICARE
9		245,754.00	6,724.00	1,220.00	7,494.00	253,248.00	2,456.00	7,944.00	7,944.00
10									
11									

J	K	L	M	N	O	P	Q	R
			DEDUCTIONS			PAYMENTS		
FEDERAL INCOME TAX	SOCIAL SECURITY TAX	MEDICARE TAX	UNION DUES	CHARITY	TOTAL	NET AMOUNT	CK. NO.	WAGES EXPENSE DEBIT
949.00	314.75	115.19	193.00	292.00	1,863.94	5,630.06		7,494.00

LO 1, 4

Practice Exercises 1, 4

EXERCISE 7-5 For tax purposes, assume that the maximum taxable earnings are $113,700 for Social Security and $7,000 for the unemployment tax and that all earnings are taxable for Medicare. For the payroll register for the month of November for Shelby, Inc., determine the taxable earnings for each employee.

	A	B	C	D	E	F	G
1					TAXABLE EARNINGS		
2		BEGINNING		ENDING			
3		CUMULATIVE		CUMULATIVE			
4	NAME	EARNINGS	TOTAL EARNINGS	EARNINGS	UNEMPLOYMENT	SOCIAL SECURITY	MEDICARE
5	Axton, C.	108,000.00	7,691.00	115,691.00			
6	Edgar, E.	145,465.00	10,900.00	156,365.00			
7	Gorman, L.	36,879.00	3,064.00	39,943.00			
8	Jolson, R.	24,634.00	2,325.00	26,959.00			
9	Nixel, P.	6,850.00	2,463.00	9,313.00			
10							
11							

LO 1, 4, 5

Practice Exercises 1, 4, 5

EXERCISE 7-6 On January 21, the column totals of the payroll register for Great Products Company showed that its sales employees had earned $14,960, its truck driver employees had earned $10,692, and its office employees had earned $8,670. Social Security taxes were withheld at an assumed rate of 6.2 percent, and Medicare taxes were withheld at an assumed rate of 1.45 percent. Other deductions consisted of federal income tax, $3,975, and union dues, $560. Determine the amount of Social Security and Medicare taxes withheld and record the general journal entry for the payroll, crediting Salaries Payable for the net pay. All earnings were taxable. Round amounts to the nearest penny.

CHAPTER ASSIGNMENTS

LO 1, 2, 3

Practice Exercises 1, 2, 3

EXERCISE 7-7 Precision Labs has two employees. The following information was taken from its individual earnings records for the month of September. Determine the missing amounts assuming that the Social Security tax is 6.2 percent, the Medicare tax is 1.45 percent, and the state income tax is 20 percent of the federal income tax. Assume that the employees are married and have one withholding allowance. All earnings are subject to Social Security and Medicare taxes. Round amounts to the nearest penny.

	Brown	Ringness	Total
Regular earnings	$ 3,500.00	$?	$?
Overtime earnings	?	120.00	
Total earnings	$ 3,646.00	$?	$?
Federal income tax withheld	$ 320.00	$?	$?
State income tax withheld	?	36.76	?
Social Security tax withheld	226.05	169.76	?
Medicare tax withheld	52.87	39.70	?
Charity withheld	35.00	97.00	?
Total deductions	$ 697.92	$ 527.02	$?
Net pay	$?	$ 2,210.98	$?

LO 5

Practice Exercise 5

EXERCISE 7-8 Assume that the employees in Exercise 7-7 are paid from the company's regular bank account (check numbers 981 and 982). Prepare the entry to record and pay the payroll in general journal form, dated September 30.

Problem Set A

LO 1, 2, 3

QuickBooks

PROBLEM 7-1A Jennifer Ross, an employee of Hampton Company, worked 44 hours during the week of February 9 through 15. Her rate of pay is $30 per hour, and she receives time-and-a-half for work in excess of 40 hours per week. She is married and claims two allowances on her W-4 form. Her wages are subject to the following deductions:

a. Federal income tax (use the table in Figure 3, pages 331–332).
b. Social Security tax at 6.2 percent.
c. Medicare tax at 1.45 percent.
d. Union dues, $30.

Check Figure
Net pay, $1,100.43

Required

Compute Ross's regular pay, overtime pay, gross pay, and net pay.

PROBLEM 7-2A Highridge Homes has the following payroll information for the week ended February 21:

Name	Earnings at End of Previous Week	Daily Time							Pay Rate	Federal Income Tax
		S	M	T	W	T	F	S		
Arthur, P.	7,800.00	8	8	8	8	8			45.00	234.70
Bills, D.	2,060.00			8	8	8	8	8	12.50	27.00
Carney, W.	2,085.00	8	8	8			8	8	12.95	28.00
Dorn, J.	748.00				8	8			22.00	12.00
Edgar, L.	2,687.00	8	8	8			8	8	15.00	38.00
Fitzwilson, G.	4,150.00	8	8		8	8	8	8	23.00	127.00

Taxable earnings for Social Security are based on the first $113,700. Taxable earnings for Medicare are based on all earnings. Taxable earnings for federal and state unemployment are based on the first $7,000. Employees are paid time-and-a-half for work in excess of 40 hours per week.

Check Figure
Net amount, $4,119.41

Required

1. Complete the payroll register. The Social Security tax rate is 6.2 percent, and the Medicare tax rate is 1.45 percent. Begin payroll checks with No. 2080.
2. Prepare a general journal entry to record the payroll. The firm's general ledger contains a Wages Expense account and a Wages Payable account.
3. Assuming that the firm has transferred funds from its regular bank account to its special payroll bank account and that this entry has been made, prepare a general journal entry to record the payment of wages.

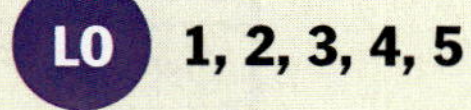

PROBLEM 7-3A Alpine Company pays its employees time-and-a-half for hours worked in excess of 40 per week. The information available from time cards and employees' individual earnings records for the pay period ended October 14 is shown in the following chart:

Name	Earnings at End of Previous Week	Daily Time						Pay Rate	Income Tax Allowances
		M	T	W	T	F	S		
Bardin, J.	43,627.00	8	8	8	8	8	2	21.30	2
Caris, A.	44,340.00	8	8	8	8	8	8	21.60	1
Drew, W.	43,845.00	8	10	10	8	8	0	21.50	1
Garen, S.	112,800.00	8	8	8	8	8	0	49.00	3
North, O.	43,875.00	8	8	8	8	8	5	21.40	3
Ovid, N.	40,150.00	8	8	8	8	8	0	21.50	1
Ross, J.	6,430.00	8	8	8	8	8	4	20.50	1
Springer, O.	44,175.00	8	8	8	8	8	3	21.25	2

Taxable earnings for Social Security are based on the first $113,700. Taxable earnings for Medicare are based on all earnings. Taxable earnings for federal and state unemployment are based on the first $7,000.

Check Figure
Net amount, $7,306.13

Required

1. Complete the payroll register using the wage-bracket income tax withholding table in Figure 3 (pages 331–332). The Social Security tax rate is 6.2 percent, and the Medicare tax rate is 1.45 percent. Assume that all employees are married. In the payroll register, begin payroll checks with No. 3945.
2. Prepare a general journal entry to record the payroll. The firm's general ledger contains a Wages Expense account and a Wages Payable account.
3. Assuming that the firm has transferred funds from its regular bank account to its special payroll bank account and that this entry has been made, prepare a general journal entry to record the payment of wages.

 **1, 3, 4, 5**

PROBLEM 7-4A The information for Titan Company, shown in the following chart, is available from Titan's time records and the employees' individual earnings records for the pay period ended December 22.

Name	Hours Worked	Earnings at End of Previous Week	Total Earnings	Class.	Federal Income Tax	Other Deductions	
Albee, C.	44	63,340.00	1,650.00	Sales	197.20	UW	25.00
Don, V.	40	136,410.00	2,841.00	Sales	494.95	AR	95.00
Fine, J.	40	76,860.00	1,507.00	Sales	173.65	UW	25.00
Ginny, N.	46	33,590.00	660.00	Office	47.00	UW	35.00
Johnson, J.	47	56,980.00	1,117.00	Office	115.00	UW	25.00
Lund, D.	43	111,800.00	2,100.00	Sales	309.70	UW	20.00
Maya, R.	42	66,860.00	1,310.00	Sales	145.00	AR	70.00
Nord, P.	41	36,750.00	720.00	Sales	56.00	UW	20.00
Oscar, T.	43	93,480.00	1,832.00	Sales	242.70	UW	25.00
Troy, B.	40	47,250.00	930.00	Sales	88.00	UW	20.00

Taxable earnings for Social Security are based on the first $113,700. Taxable earnings for Medicare are based on all earnings. Taxable earnings for federal and state unemployment are based on the first $7,000. The company does not pay for overtime hours.

Check Figure
Net amount, $11,504.32

Required

1. Complete the payroll register using a Social Security tax rate of 6.2 percent and a Medicare tax rate of 1.45 percent. Concerning Other Deductions, AR refers to Accounts Receivable and UW refers to United Way. Begin payroll checks in the payroll register with No. 2914.
2. Prepare the general journal entry to record the payroll. The firm's general ledger contains a Salary Expense account and a Salaries Payable account.
3. Prepare the general journal entry to pay the payroll. Assume that funds for this payroll have been transferred to Cash—Payroll Bank Account and that this entry has been made.

LO 2, 3

PROBLEM 7-5A Jim Moss, an employee of Jones International, worked 49 hours during the week of April 4 through 10. His rate of pay is $15 per hour, and he receives time-a-half for work in excess of 40 hours per week. Jim is married and claims four allowances on his W-4 form. Jim's YTD earnings before this pay period are $7,600, and his wages are subject to the following deductions:

a. Federal income tax (use the table in Figure 3, pages 331–332).
b. Social Security tax at 6.2 percent, with a wage limit of $113,700.
c. Medicare tax at 1.45 percent.
d. Medical insurance premium (after tax), $50.
e. United Way contribution, $10.

Required

Compute Jim's regular pay, overtime pay, gross pay, and net pay.

Check Figure
Net pay, $646.10

Problem Set B

LO 1, 2, 3

PROBLEM 7-1B Erin Chang, an employee of Solutions Company, worked 48 hours during the week of October 12 through 18. Her rate of pay is $17.50 per hour, and she receives time-and-a-half for all work in excess of 40 hours per week. Chang is married and claims two allowances on her W-4 form. Her wages are subject to the following deductions:

a. Federal income tax (use the table in Figure 3, pages 331–332).
b. Social Security tax at 6.2 percent.
c. Medicare tax at 1.45 percent.
d. Union dues, $32.

Required

Compute Chang's regular pay, overtime pay, gross pay, and net pay.

Check Figure
Net pay, $734.38

PROBLEM 7-2B Harvest Company has the following payroll information for the pay period ended April 14:

Name	Earnings at End of Previous Week	Daily Time						Pay Rate	Federal Income Tax
		M	T	W	T	F	S		
Grant, L.	7,536.00	8	8	8	8	8	0	18.00	56.00
Hamn, R.	6,496.00	8	8	8	8	8	0	18.10	56.00
Lisk, J.	6,798.00	0	8	8	8	8	8	17.80	55.00
Myre, G.	9,589.00	8	8	8	0	8	8	19.25	64.00
Segel, T.	6,585.00	8	8	8	8	8	6	17.95	79.00
Torgel, I.	7,501.00	0	8	8	8	8	8	18.70	59.00

Taxable earnings for Social Security are based on the first $113,700. Taxable earnings for Medicare are based on all earnings. Taxable earnings for federal and state unemployment are based on the first $7,000. Employees are paid time-and-a-half for work in excess of 40 hours per week.

CHAPTER ASSIGNMENTS

Check Figure
Net amount, $3,836.23

Required

1. Complete the payroll register. The Social Security tax rate is 6.2 percent, and the Medicare tax rate is 1.45 percent. Begin payroll checks with No. 2944.
2. Prepare a general journal entry to record the payroll. The firm's general ledger contains a Wages Expense account and a Wages Payable account.
3. Assuming that the firm has transferred funds from its regular bank account to its special payroll bank account and that this entry has been made, prepare a journal entry to record the payment of wages.

LO 1, 2, 3, 4, 5

PROBLEM 7-3B Williams Company pays its employees time-and-a-half for hours worked in excess of 40 per week. The information available from time records and employees' individual earnings records for the pay period ended September 21 is shown in the following chart:

Name	Earnings at End of Previous Week	Daily Time						Pay Rate	Income Tax Allowances
		M	T	W	T	F	S		
Bolt, D.	6,745.00	8	8	8	10	8	0	25.00	1
Dore, C.	136,240.00	8	8	8	8	8	0	49.50	2
Gayle, A.	32,730.00	8	10	8	8	8	0	24.50	2
Hale, R.	112,800.00	8	8	8	8	8	4	40.00	3
Jilly, B.	35,154.00	8	8	8	8	8	0	49.50	0
Karn, S.	29,938.00	8	8	9	8	8	0	20.50	2
Ober, N.	6,795.00	8	8	8	9	9	4	21.00	1
Wong, J.	27,252.00	8	8	10	8	8	0	20.00	2

Taxable earnings for Social Security are based on the first $113,700. Taxable earnings for Medicare are based on all earnings. Taxable earnings for federal and state unemployment are based on the first $7,000.

Check Figure
Net amount, 8,830.55

Required

1. Complete the payroll register using the wage-bracket income tax withholding table in Figure 3 (pages 331–332). The Social Security tax rate is 6.2 percent, and the Medicare tax rate is 1.45 percent. Assume that all employees are married. In the payroll register, begin payroll checks with No. 1863.
2. Prepare a general journal entry to record the payroll. The firm's general ledger contains a Wages Expense account and a Wages Payable account.
3. Assuming that the firm has transferred funds from its regular bank account to its special payroll bank account and that this entry has been made, prepare a general journal entry to record the payment of wages.

LO 1, 3, 4, 5

PROBLEM 7-4B The information for Best Sports Company, shown in the chart on the next page, is available from Best Sports' time records and employees' individual earnings records for the pay period ended December 29.

Name	Hours Worked	Earnings at End of Previous Week	Total Earnings	Class.	Federal Income Tax	Other Deductions	
Chang, C.	40	33,900.00	680.00	Sales	50.00	AR	80.00
Dugan, T.	42	38,270.00	2,841.00	Sales	494.95	UW	20.00
Fancher, K.	40	37,680.00	725.00	Sales	56.00	UW	25.00
Gannon, T.	40	33,245.00	660.00	Office	47.00		—
Jones, L.	40	37,789.00	750.00	Office	61.00	UW	25.00
Lange, M.	40	113,100.00	2,100.00	Office	309.70	UW	35.00
Milton, D.	40	37,684.00	1,310.00	Sales	145.00	UW	20.00
Naylor, B.	40	37,499.00	720.00	Sales	56.00		—
Orton, A.	44	94,338.00	1,780.00	Sales	342.95	AR	70.00
Tiosha, J.	42	48,120.00	1,065.00	Sales	107.00	UW	25.00

Taxable earnings for Social Security are based on the first $113,700. Taxable earnings for Medicare are based on all earnings. Taxable earnings for federal and state unemployment are based on the first $7,000. The company does not pay for overtime hours.

Required

Check Figure
Net amount, $9,788.13

1. Complete the payroll register using a Social Security tax rate of 6.2 percent and a Medicare tax rate of 1.45 percent. Concerning Other Deductions, AR refers to Accounts Receivable and UW refers to United Way. Begin payroll checks in the payroll register with No. 2914.
2. Prepare the general journal entry to record the payroll. The firm's general ledger contains a Salary Expense account and a Salaries Payable account.
3. Prepare the general journal entry to pay the payroll. Assume that funds for this payroll have been transferred to Cash—Payroll Bank Account and that this entry has been made.

LO 2, 3

PROBLEM 7-5B Rick Davis, an employee of ABC Motors, worked 42 hours during the week of September 12 through 18. His rate of pay is $30 per hour, and he receives time-a-half for work in excess of 40 hours per week. Rick is married and claims zero allowances on his W-4 form. Rick's YTD earnings before this pay period are $47,250, and his wages are subject to the following deductions:

a. Federal income tax (use the table in Figure 3, pages 331–332).
b. Social Security tax at 6.2 percent, with a wage limit of $113,700.
c. Medicare tax at 1.45 percent.
d. Medical insurance premium (after tax), $75.
e. United Way contribution, $25.

Required

Check Figure
Net pay, $938.31

Compute Rick's regular pay, overtime pay, gross pay, and net pay.

Try It with QuickBooks® (LO 1, 2)

QB Exercise 7-1

Complete the payroll for Hampton Company in QuickBooks, using Problem 7-1A on page 358. Additional information for taxes required in the Company Summary: The company matches the social security and Medicare taxes withheld. The federal unemployment tax (FUTA) is $8.28. Use the check date of February 16, 2015. The bank account for this payroll is 101—Cash.

Required

1. Restore the QuickBooks data file for Hampton Company. The data file is located on the textbook website, at www.cengagebrain.com.
2. From the **Pay Employees** icon on the home page, complete the payroll to pay Jennifer Ross.
3. Select the **Print Paychecks** option.
4. Select **Print Pay Stubs** option.
5. What are Ross's gross wages?
6. What are Ross's net wages?
7. What is the total of Ross's taxes withheld?

QB Exercise 7-2

Complete the payroll for Solutions Company in QuickBooks, using Problem 7-1B on page 361. Additional information for taxes required in the Company Summary: The company matches the social security and Medicare taxes withheld. The federal unemployment tax (FUTA) is $5.46. Use the check date of February 19, 2015. The bank account for this payroll is 101—Cash.

Required

1. Restore the QuickBooks data file for Hampton Company. The data file is located on the textbook website, at www.cengagebrain.com.
2. From the **Pay Employees** icon on the home page, complete the payroll to pay Erin Chang.
3. Select the **Print Paychecks** option.
4. Select Print **Pay Stubs** option.
5. What are Chang's gross wages?
6. What are Chang's net wages?
7. What is the total of Chang's taxes withheld?

Activities

Why Does It Matter?

RECREATIONAL EQUIPMENT INC. (REI), Sumner, Washington

Attracting and retaining the best employees is crucial to operating a business. Employees will join a company based on opportunities for advancement, training, company culture, and salary and benefits provided.

One business that is often listed in *Fortune* magazine's "100 Best Companies to Work For" is Recreational Equipment Inc. (REI). REI is committed to inspiring, educating, and outfitting its customers for a lifetime of outdoor adventure. REI offers competitive salaries as well as benefits, including paid sabbaticals, an onsite fitness center, healthcare coverage, telecommuting, and a compressed workweek.

The accounting department at REI is responsible for determining salaries/wages and benefits for employees, calculating payroll deductions for taxes and other expenses, and ensuring that company payrolls are processed in a timely and accurate manner. In this chapter, you learned how companies such as REI complete the payroll records for their employees. Why do you think timely and accurate payroll information is so important to a company such as REI?

What Would You Say?

Southern Company pays its employees weekly by issuing checks on its regular bank account. The owner thinks it would be too much trouble to have a second checking account. Explain to the owner why having this account might be worth the additional effort.

What Would You Do?

An employee who is married and has three children submits a W-4 form to his employer. He checks the box that says "Single" and writes zero in the "Deductions Claimed" box. Is this action ethical, unethical, or illegal? Explain your reasoning.

chapter 8

Employer Taxes, Payments, and Reports

Learning Objectives

After you have completed this chapter, you will be able to do the following:

1. Calculate the amount of payroll tax expense and journalize the entry.
2. Journalize the entry for the deposit of employees' federal income taxes withheld and FICA taxes (both employees' withheld and employer's share) and prepare the deposit.
3. Journalize the entries for the payment of employer's state and federal unemployment taxes.
4. Journalize the entry for the deposit of employees' state income taxes withheld.
5. Complete Employer's Quarterly Federal Tax Return, Form 941.
6. Prepare W-2 and W-3 forms and Form 940.
7. Calculate the premium for workers' compensation insurance and prepare the entry for payment in advance.
8. Determine the amount of the end-of-the-year adjustments for (a) workers' compensation insurance and (b) accrued salaries and wages and record the adjustments.

To: **Amy Roberts, CPA**
Subject: **Employee Taxes, Payments, and Reporting**

Hi Amy,
Thanks for helping me set up the payroll system for my company. I started paying my employees a few weeks ago and have been recording the payroll expenses and liabilities as you instructed. I think it is almost time to make my first payroll tax deposit(s), and I would like to review this process with you. I also am curious about how to record workers' compensation premium payments and how to handle the end-of-the-year adjustments for workers' compensation insurance and accrued salaries and wages. If you can help me better understand the payroll process, I would appreciate it. I know how important it is to handle the payroll for my company properly. I want to make sure that I'm in compliance with all tax laws, that I make deposits on time, and that I file my reports correctly when they are due. I certainly don't want to incur any penalties.
Thanks,
Janie

To: **Janie Conner**
Subject: **RE: Employee Taxes, Payments, and Reporting**

Hi Janie,
I'm glad you have a better understanding of how to handle paying your employees and recording the payroll liability. You are correct—it's time to start thinking about scheduling your payroll tax deposits and preparing for filing the appropriate reports. I would be happy to review the employer payroll taxes with you and help you set up a tax calendar to make sure you are making your deposits and filing your reports on time. Let's plan on meeting Friday to discuss the following:

_____ 1. How to calculate and record the employer payroll tax expense

_____ 2. How to prepare and record the FICA and Federal Employee Withholding payroll tax deposit

_____ 3. How to calculate and record the FUTA and SUTA liabilities and payments

_____ 4. How to journalize the payment of state income taxes withheld

Give me a call later today so that we can set up a time for our meeting.
Amy

© Fuse/Getty Images

We have talked about how to compute and record such payroll data as gross pay, employees' income tax withheld, employees' FICA taxes withheld, and various deductions requested by employees. Now we will learn how to record the transactions to pay these withholding liabilities and the taxes levied on the employer.

EMPLOYER IDENTIFICATION NUMBER

Everyone must have a Social Security number or an Individual Taxpayer Identification Number (ITIN), a vital part of federal income tax returns. An employer's counterpart to the Social Security number is the **Employer Identification Number (EIN)**, which is assigned by the Internal Revenue Service. Employers of one or more persons are required to have such a number, and it must be listed on all reports and payments of employees' federal income tax withholding and FICA taxes.

EMPLOYER'S PAYROLL TAXES

An employer's payroll taxes are based on the gross wages paid to employees. Payroll taxes—like property taxes—are an expense of doing business. Green Sales Company records these taxes in the **Payroll Tax Expense** account and debits the account for the company's portion of FICA taxes and for state and federal unemployment taxes. In T account form, Payroll Tax Expense for Green Sales Company would look like this:

Payroll Tax Expense

+	–
FICA taxes (employer's portion)	Closed at the end of the year
State unemployment tax	along with all other expense
Federal unemployment tax	accounts

As you can see, **FICA taxes (employer's share of Social Security and Medicare taxes), state unemployment tax, and federal unemployment tax are included under the Payroll Tax Expense heading.** In most states, the unemployment taxes are levied on the employer only.

Accounting Language

Electronic Federal Tax Payment System (EFTPS) (p. 371)

Employer Identification Number (EIN) (p. 367)

Federal unemployment tax (FUTA) (p. 369)

Form 940 (p. 382)

Form 941 (p. 375)

Form 941-V (p. 376)

Form W-2 (p. 380)

Form W-3 (p. 381)

Payroll Tax Expense (p. 367)

Quarter (p. 372)

State unemployment tax (SUTA) (p. 369)

Workers' compensation insurance (p. 386)

Employer's Portion of FICA Taxes

FICA taxes (the combined Social Security and Medicare taxes) are imposed equally on both the employer and employees. The employer's share is determined the same way as the employee's by multiplying the employer's tax rates [6.2 percent (0.062) for Social Security and 1.45 percent (0.0145) for Medicare] by the taxable earnings (up to a maximum wage limit of $113,700 for Social Security and all earnings for Medicare).

The accountant obtains the Social Security and Medicare taxable earnings amounts from the payroll register. Figure 1 shows the Taxable Earnings columns taken from the payroll register for Green Sales Company as prepared in the previous chapter for the week ended October 11.

Figure 1
Partial payroll register for Green Sales Company

Amount of employees' earnings for the period that has not, as of yet, been taxed as part of the $7,000 maximum liability

Amount of employees' earnings that are less than $113,700 per employee for the year

Amount of all employees' earnings

	A	B	F	G	H	I	J
1					(7) TAXABLE EARNINGS		
2				ENDING			
3		TOTAL		CUMULATIVE		SOCIAL	
4	NAME	HOURS	TOTAL	EARNINGS	UNEMPLOYMENT	SECURITY	MEDICARE
5	Anderson, Mark	46	1,124.58	46,084.58	0.00	1,124.58	1,124.58
6	Bodell, Anna	45	744.20	6,731.20	744.20	744.20	744.20
7	Dorn, David	49	916.00	7,702.00	214.00	916.00	916.00
8	Fields, Sarah	40	1,084.50	39,546.50	0.00	1,084.50	1,084.50
9	Graham, Jason	40	1,798.45	70,398.45	0.00	1,798.45	1,798.45
10	Lee, Jeremy	40	1,895.58	70,395.58	0.00	1,895.58	1,895.58
11	Mankowitz, Hanna	55	1,968.75	39,818.75	0.00	1,968.75	1,968.75
12	Olsen, Barbara	40	1,487.20	47,307.20	0.00	1,487.20	1,487.20
13	Parker, William	44	1,776.28	48,206.28	0.00	1,776.28	1,776.28
14	Raman, Soma	45	1,662.50	56,529.50	0.00	1,662.50	1,662.50
15	Tabor, Annette	40	1,168.83	43,908.83	0.00	1,168.83	1,168.83
16	Wallace, Grace	40	3,010.35	113,810.35	0.00	2,900.00	3,010.35
17			18,637.22	590,439.22	958.20	18,526.87	18,637.22
18		*(1)*	*(5)*	*(6)*	*(7A)*	*(7B)*	*(7C)*
19							

Employer's state unemployment tax
$958.20 × 0.054 = **$51.74**
(7A)

Employer's federal unemployment tax
$958.20 × 0.006 = **$5.75**
(7A)

Employer's Social Security tax
$18,526.87 × 0.062 = **$1,148.67**
(7B)

Employer's Medicare tax
$18,637.22 × 0.0145 = **$270.24**
(7C)

Combined Employer's FICA taxes
(Social Security $1,148.67 + Medicare $270.24) = **$1,418.91**

Employees' Social Security tax
$18,526.87 × 0.062 = **$1,148.67**
(7B)

Employees' Medicare tax
$18,637.22 × 0.0145 = **$270.24**
(7C)

Combined Employees' FICA taxes
(Social Security $1,148.67 + Medicare $270.24) = **$1,418.91**

Before we look at the journal entry to record the employer's share of FICA taxes, let's look at the entry in T account form.

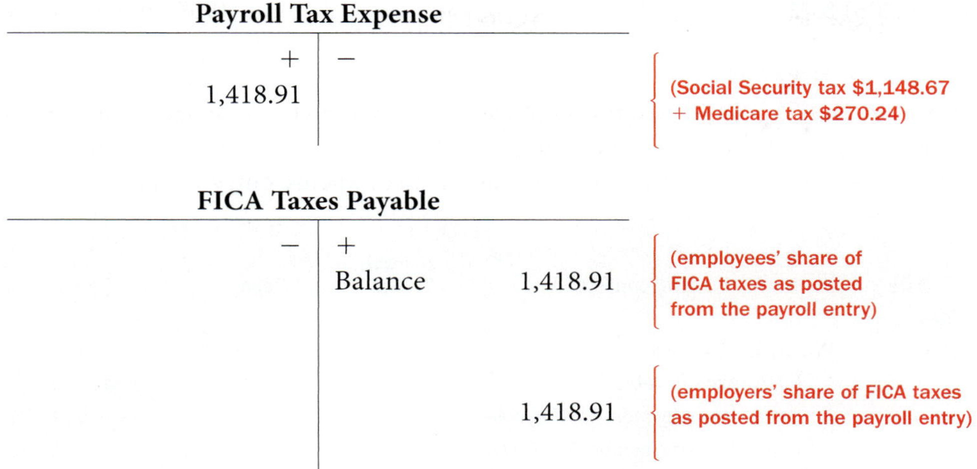

Note particularly that the FICA Taxes Payable account is often used for both the tax liability of the employer and the amounts withheld from the employees. This is logical because both FICA taxes are paid at the same time and to the same place. There may be a slight difference between the employer's and the employees' share of FICA Medicare tax because of the rounding process. For the employees' FICA taxes, the accountant uses the total of the employees' Social Security and Medicare tax deductions. For the employer's share of FICA taxes, the accountant multiplies the total taxable earnings for all employees (Social Security and Medicare) by the employer's tax rates.

Employer's State Unemployment Tax

The proceeds of the **state unemployment tax (SUTA)**, most state levy only on the employer, are used to pay subsistence benefits to unemployed workers. The rate of the state unemployment tax varies considerably among the states. Assume that Green Sales Company is subject to a rate of 5.4 percent (0.054) on the first $7,000 of each employee's earnings (the same base amount used for the federal unemployment tax). Looking at the payroll register (Figure 1), $958.20 of earnings are subject to the state unemployment tax. The following T accounts show how the state unemployment tax is calculated and posted.

Payroll Tax Expense	
+	−
(958.20 × 0.054) 51.74	

State Unemployment Tax Payable	
−	+
	(958.20 × 0.054) 51.74

Employer's Federal Unemployment Tax

The federal unemployment tax (FUTA) is paid only by the employer. From time to time, Congress may change the rate. Let's assume a rate of 0.6 percent (0.006) on the first $7,000 earned by each employee during the calendar year. For the weekly payroll period, Green Sales Company shows a tax liability of $5.75 ($958.20 of unemployment taxable earnings, taken from the payroll register, multiplied by 0.006, the tax rate). The T account is as follows:

Learning Objective

Calculate the amount of payroll tax expense and journalize the entry

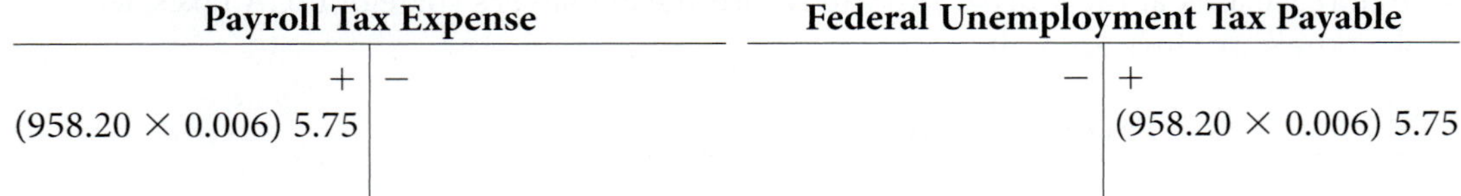

Now let's combine figures for the employer's three payroll taxes, which were previously presented separately, into the following entry. Assume that Green Sales Company pays its employees weekly, so it also makes its Payroll Tax Expense entry weekly.

Date		Description	Post. Ref.	Debit	Credit
20--					
Oct.	11	Payroll Tax Expense		1 4 7 6 40	
		FICA Taxes Payable			1 4 1 8 91
		State Unemployment Tax Payable			5 1 74
		Federal Unemployment Tax Payable			5 75
		To record employer's share of FICA			
		taxes and employer's state and federal			
		unemployment taxes.			

JOURNAL ENTRIES FOR RECORDING PAYROLL

At this point, let's restate in general journal form the entries that have already been recorded. The sequence of steps for recording the payroll entries is as follows:

STEP 1. Record the payroll for the present period in the payroll register.

STEP 2. Based on the payroll register, record the payroll entry in the journal.

STEP 3. Based on the Taxable Earnings columns of the payroll register, record Payroll Tax Expense in the journal.

STEP 4. Record a journal entry to pay the employees.

Once the payroll for the present period is recorded in the payroll register (see Chapter 7), the entry to record the payroll, which was also presented in Chapter 7, is journalized.

Date		Description	Post. Ref.	Debit	Credit
20--					
Oct.	11	Sales Wages Expense		11 1 5 9 59	
		Office Wages Expense		7 4 7 7 63	
		Employees' Federal Income Tax Payable			2 3 9 8 87
		FICA Taxes Payable			1 4 1 8 91
		Employees' State Income Tax Payable			4 7 9 78
		Employees' United Way Payable			1 9 5 00
		Accounts Receivable			5 0 00
		Wages Payable			14 0 9 4 66
		Payroll register for the week ended			
		October 11, 20--.			

Next, the entry to record the employer's payroll taxes is journalized.

Date		Description	Post. Ref.	Debit	Credit
20--					
Oct.	11	Payroll Tax Expense		1 4 7 6 40	
		FICA Taxes Payable			1 4 1 8 91
		State Unemployment Tax Payable			5 1 74
		Federal Unemployment Tax Payable			5 75
		To record employer's share of FICA taxes and employer's state and federal unemployment taxes.			

Finally, the entry to pay the employees is journalized. Green Sales Company issues one check payable to a payroll bank account. To pay its employees, it will draw separate payroll checks on this payroll account. (The entry to transfer cash to the payroll bank account is not shown here.)

Date		Description	Post. Ref.	Debit	Credit
20--					
Oct.	12	Wages Payable		14 0 9 4 66	
		Cash—Payroll Bank Account			14 0 9 4 66
		Paid wages for week ended October 11, 20--.			

As stated previously, in the first payroll entry, small employers will credit Cash directly instead of Wages Payable. These employers issue separate checks out of their regular bank accounts for each employee.

Next, we describe the entries for paying withholdings for employees' federal income tax and FICA taxes as well as the employer's share of FICA taxes. We also show the entries for paying the federal and state unemployment taxes and the withholdings for employees' state income taxes.

PAYMENTS OF FICA TAXES AND EMPLOYEES' FEDERAL INCOME TAX WITHHOLDING

After paying employees, the employer must make payments in the form of federal tax deposits. A deposit includes the combined total of three items:

- Employees' federal income taxes withheld
- Employees' FICA taxes (Social Security and Medicare) withheld
- Employer's share of FICA taxes (Social Security and Medicare)

Learning Objective 2 Journalize the entry for the deposit of employees' federal income taxes withheld and FICA taxes (both employees' withheld and employer's share) and prepare the deposit.

The timing of when the deposits must be made depends on the amount of payroll.

The IRS now requires all companies to make tax deposits electronically, using the **Electronic Federal Tax Payment System (EFTPS)**. Deposits can be submitted by computer or telephone. EFTPS allows taxpayers to make payments 24 hours a day, 7 days a week and to schedule tax payments up to 120 days in advance of the due date. See IRS

Substantial penalties are applied for late deposits of federal taxes.

Publication 15 (Circular E), Employer's Tax Guide, at www.irs.gov for more information on deposit requirements.

Employers submit a return, Form 941, every **quarter** (three consecutive months). The due dates for filing this return are as follows:

Quarter	Ending Date of Quarter	Due Date for Forms 941/941e
January–February–March	March 31	April 30
April–May–June	June 30	July 31
July–August–September	September 30	October 31
October–November–December	December 31	January 31

We will show a Form 941 later in this chapter.

Federal Tax Deposit

Let's go back to Green Sales Company, where tax payments were up-to-date. From the payroll of October 11, the following federal taxes are owed:

Employees' federal income taxes withheld	$2,398.87
Employees' FICA taxes withheld ($1,148.67 + $270.24)	1,418.91
Employer's share of FICA taxes	1,418.91
Total federal undeposited taxes	$5,236.69

Let's continue with the next payroll period, ended October 18. Assuming that the payroll information for the week is the same as it was for the week ended October 11, the two periods would be as follows:

Because of rounding differences, the employee and employer amounts of FICA taxes may differ slightly. Line 7 of Form 941 accommodates this difference.

	Oct. 11	Oct. 18	Total
Employees' federal income taxes withheld	$2,398.87	$2,398.87	$ 4,797.74
Employees' FICA taxes withheld	1,418.91	1,418.91	2,837.82
Employer's share of FICA taxes	1,418.91	1,418.91	2,837.82
Total federal undeposited taxes	$5,236.69	$5,236.69	$10,473.38

Green Sales Company, which deposits taxes semiweekly, will initiate an EFTPS tax deposit via computer or telephone. EFTPS tax deposits must be processed one calendar day in advance of the tax liability due date to be considered on time and to avoid penalties.

The following entry in general journal form records the deposit of two weeks' taxes.

Date		Description	Post. Ref.	Debit	Credit
20--					
Oct.	15	Employees' Federal Income Tax Payable		4 7 9 7 74	
		FICA Taxes Payable		5 6 7 5 64	
		($2,837.82 + $2,837.82)			
		Cash			10 4 7 3 38
		Issued check for federal tax			
		deposit, Central National Bank.			

ACCOUNTING IN YOUR FUTURE

PAYROLL CLERK

Payroll clerks perform vital functions for businesses—ensuring that employees are paid on time and that their paychecks are accurate. If mistakes are made, such as monetary errors or incorrect amounts of vacation time, these clerks research and correct the records.

Payroll clerks also perform other clerical tasks:

- Screening time cards for calculating, coding, or other errors
- Computing pay by subtracting deductions, including federal and state taxes and contributions to retirement, insurance, and savings plans, from gross earnings
- Recording changes in employees' addresses
- Closing out files when workers retire, resign, or transfer
- Advising employees on income tax withholding and other mandatory deductions

© iStockPhoto.com/klikk

For this reason, payroll clerks need to be aware of changes in tax and deduction laws so that they can implement them. Failure to do so can leave the organization exposed to penalties and other legal issues.

Payroll clerks are found in every industry. They train on the job, gaining skills by watching and learning from other workers. Those who have completed a certification program have an advantage in the job market.

As entering and recording payroll information becomes more simplified due to the increasing use of computers, the job itself is becoming more varied and complex. For example, companies now offer a greater variety of pension, 401(k), and other investment plans to their employees. These developments will contribute to job growth for payroll clerks in the years to come.

PAYMENTS OF STATE UNEMPLOYMENT TAX

Learning Objective 3 Journalize the entries for the payment of employer's state and federal unemployment taxes.

As mentioned previously, states differ with regard to both the rate and the taxable base for unemployment insurance. In our example, we assume that the state tax is 5.4 percent (0.054) of the first $7,000 paid to each employee during the calendar year. **The state tax is usually paid quarterly and is due by the end of the month following the end of the quarter (the same as the due dates for Form 941).** Here is the entry in general journal form made by Green Sales Company for the first quarter (covering January, February, and March). We assume that $70,325 was taxable for the quarter. The amount of the tax is $3,797.55 ($70,325 × 0.054).

Date		Description	Post. Ref.	Debit	Credit
20--					
Apr.	30	State Unemployment Tax Payable		3 7 9 7 55	
		Cash			3 7 9 7 55
		Issued check for payment of			
		state unemployment tax.			

The T accounts are as follows:

Cash				State Unemployment Tax Payable			
+	–			–		+	
	Apr. 30	3,797.55		Apr. 30	3,797.55	Balance	3,797.55

The balance in State Unemployment Tax Payable is the result of weekly entries recording the state unemployment portion of payroll tax expense and represents the balance on March 31. After the payment is made on April 30, the balance is shown as zero for illustrative purposes. However, throughout April, the company would be making weekly entries to record the tax liability and tax expense.

PAYMENTS OF FEDERAL UNEMPLOYMENT TAX

The FUTA tax is calculated quarterly, during the month following the end of each calendar quarter. **If the accumulated tax liability is greater than $500, the tax is deposited electronically,** similar to how deposits are handled for employees' federal income tax withholding and FICA taxes. The due date for this deposit is the last day of the month following the end of the quarter, the same as the due dates for the Employer's Quarterly Federal Tax Return and for state unemployment taxes.

Here is the entry in general journal form made by Green Sales Company for the first quarter. In our example, because the FUTA and state unemployment taxable earnings are the same (the first $7,000 for each employee), we assume that $70,325 was taxable for the quarter. The amount of the tax is $421.95 ($70,325 × 0.006).

Date		Description	Post. Ref.	Debit	Credit
20--					
Apr.	30	Federal Unemployment Tax Payable		4 2 1 95	
		Cash			4 2 1 95
		Issued check for payment of			
		federal unemployment tax.			

The T accounts are as follows:

Cash				Federal Unemployment Tax Payable			
	+	–			–	+	
		Apr. 30	421.95	Apr. 30	421.95	Balance	421.95

The balance in Federal Unemployment Tax Payable is the result of weekly entries recording the federal unemployment portion of payroll tax expense.

DEPOSITS OF EMPLOYEES' STATE INCOME TAX WITHHOLDING

Assume that the withholdings for employees' state income taxes are deposited on a quarterly basis, payable at the same time as state unemployment tax. Also, as of March 31, the credit balance of Employees' State Income Tax Payable is $1,674.10. The entry in general journal form to record the payment for the first quarter takes the following form.

4 Journalize the entry for the deposit of employees' state income taxes withheld.

Learning Objective

Date		Description	Post. Ref.	Debit	Credit
20--					
Apr.	30	Employees' State Income Tax Payable		1,674.10	
		Cash			1,674.10
		Issued check for state income tax deposit.			

The T accounts are as follows:

Cash				Employees' State Income Tax Payable			
	+	–			–	+	
		Apr. 30	1,674.10	Apr. 30	1,674.10	Balance	1,674.10

EMPLOYER'S QUARTERLY FEDERAL TAX RETURN (FORM 941)

If you are an employer, you must file a quarterly **Form 941**, Employer's Quarterly Federal Tax Return. The purpose of Form 941 is to report the tax liability for withholdings of employees' federal income tax and FICA taxes and the employer's share of FICA taxes. Total tax deposits made are also listed. As the title implies, the time period is three months. Remember that the due dates for the calendar year are first quarter, April 30; second quarter, July 31; third quarter, October 31; and fourth quarter, January 31.

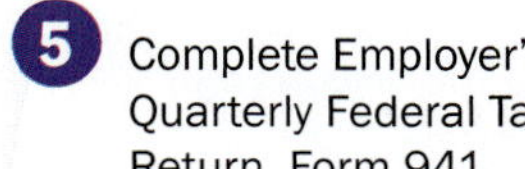

5 Complete Employer's Quarterly Federal Tax Return, Form 941.

Learning Objective

A completed Form 941 for Green Sales Company is shown in Figure 2. There are five parts to this form. Figure 2 shows the information for Green Sales Company for Parts 1 and 2. Part 3 is used when you close your business and stop paying wages—this will also stop the

To: **Amy Roberts, CPA**
Subject: **Employee Taxes, Payments, and Reporting**

Hi Amy,
I've calculated and recorded the payroll tax expenses for FICA, FUTA, and State Unemployment Taxes Payable. I've also made the appropriate tax payments and have journalized the state income taxes withheld. Is there anything else I'm missing?
Thanks,
Janie

To: **Janie Conner**
Subject: **RE: Employee Taxes, Payments, and Reporting**

Hi Janie,
Great! You are now ready to complete the payroll tax reports. We should also discuss workers' compensation insurance and adjusting for accrued salaries and wages. The following is a list of items for us to talk about when we get together:

_____ 1. Completing the 941 and 940 reports
_____ 2. Preparing W-2's and W-3's
_____ 3. Workers' Compensation Insurance
_____ 4. Adjusting for accrued salaries and wages

Can you meet on Wednesday at 1 pm?
Amy

IRS from automatically sending 941 forms. Part 4 is for you to give the IRS permission—or not—to speak with your third-party designee (employee, paid tax preparer for example). Part 5 is the signature, title, and date block for the paid preparer and/or employer. Finally, for any balance due on the 941 report, a **941-V** form accompanies the report and payment. You can find instructions or complete Form 941 online at www.irs.gov.

The top of the form contains basic information about the employer. Once an employer has secured an identification number and has filed the first return, the Internal Revenue Service automatically sends forms directly to the employer. These subsequent forms will have the employer's name, address, and identification number filled in.

Now let's look at a completed Employer's Quarterly Federal Tax Return (Form 941) as well as a 941-V form on pages 378–380.

Questions Listed on Form 941 (Figures 2a, 2b, 2c)

Tax forms can be somewhat intimidating. The best approach to completing a tax form is to have accurate and complete records and to read and complete the form line by line without skipping ahead. Green Sales Company's fourth-quarter form, shown in Figure 2, has been completed as follows. Note that the employees at Green Sales Company earn only wages. Had they also earned tips or other compensation, such as bonuses, those would have been included in the form.

Part 1:

Line 1 indicates the number of employees (12) who received wages.
Line 2 shows the total of those wages for the quarter ($197,622.00).
Line 3 shows the total income tax withheld from wages for the quarter ($35,572.00).
Line 4 is not checked because all wages during the quarter are subject to Medicare tax.
Lines 5a-d provide information that indicates how the total of the Social Security and Medicare taxes ($22,025.00 + $5,731.04 = $27,756.04) is calculated. Note that the multipliers represent the combined FICA employee and employer contributions [for Social Security, 0.062 (Employee FICA) + 0.062 (Employer FICA) = 0.124; for Medicare, 0.0145 × 2 = 0.029].
Line 5e Add column 2 on Form 941 for lines 5a-d. ($27,756.04).
Line 5f provides information about taxes due on unreported tips, which did not apply to Green Sales Company's employees.
Line 6 ($63,328.04) is the total of the income taxes withheld (line 3) plus the Social Security and Medicare taxes (line 5d), before adjustments.
Line 7 indicates tax adjustments for fraction of cents due to rounding.
Line 8 indicates adjustments for sick pay FICA taxes withheld from employees and deposited by a third-party payer.
Line 9 indicates adjustments for uncollected FICA taxes on tips and group-term life insurance.
Line 10 shows the total taxes after adjustments (lines 6–9 = $63,328.04).
Line 11 shows the total deposits ($63,328.04) made by Green Sales Company for this quarter and includes any overpayments from prior quarters. As indicated, the company has made deposits equaling the total due for this quarter.
Lines 12a and 12b disclose any premium assistance payments of COBRA for eligible individuals and the number of individuals who were provided COBRA premium assistance. COBRA provides certain former employees, retirees, spouses, former spouses, and dependent children the right to temporary continuation of health coverage at group rates when previous coverage is lost due to certain events. Qualifying events include activities such as reduction in the number of employment hours and voluntary or involuntary termination of employment for reasons other than gross misconduct. Green Sales Company did not have any COBRA payments this quarter.
Line 13 is the total of lines 11 and 12a ($63,328.04).
Lines 14 (underpayment) **and 15** (overpayment), which indicate the difference between lines 11 and 13, show that the company's balance for the quarter is zero.

Part 2:
Line 16 shows a checkmark in the third box because Green Sales Company was a semiweekly scheduled depositor for this quarter.

As stated earlier, the remaining parts of the 941 form require stating whether your business has closed (Part 3); giving permission to allow third-party inquires (Part 4); and providing signatures, titles of the preparer, and the date Form 941 is completed (Part 5). Form 941-V (Figure 2c, on page 380) is the payment voucher mailed with the 941 report when a balance is due. For instructions to assist you in filling out any IRS form, go to www.irs.gov and enter the name of the form or descriptive words into the search box.

The Form 941-V payment voucher is completed when making payments with the 941 report. To avoid a penalty, Form 941-V payments should be less than $2,500. Payment amounts over $2,500 should be filed electronically according to the depositor's required deposit schedule.

Figure 2a

Employer's Quarterly Federal Tax Return (Form 941) for Green Sales Company

Form **941 for 20--:** **Employer's QUARTERLY Federal Tax Return** 950113
(Rev. January 2013) Department of the Treasury — Internal Revenue Service OMB No. 1545-0029

Employer identification number (EIN) 9 1 – 7 2 2 8 1 6 2

Name *(not your trade name)*

Trade name *(if any)* Green Sales Company

Address 610 First Avenue
Number Street Suite or room number

Bangor ME 04401
City State ZIP code

Report for this Quarter of 20--
(Check one.)

- ☐ **1:** January, February, March
- ☐ **2:** April, May, June
- ☐ **3:** July, August, September
- ☒ **4:** October, November, December

Instructions and prior year forms are available at *www.irs.gov/form941*.

Read the separate instructions before you complete Form 941. Type or print within the boxes.

Part 1: Answer these questions for this quarter.

1	**Number of employees who received wages, tips, or other compensation for the pay period including:** ***Mar. 12*** **(Quarter 1),** ***June 12*** **(Quarter 2),** ***Sept. 12*** **(Quarter 3), or** ***Dec. 12*** **(Quarter 4)**	1	12
2	**Wages, tips, and other compensation**	2	197,622.00.00
3	**Income tax withheld from wages, tips, and other compensation**	3	35,572.00
4	**If no wages, tips, and other compensation are subject to social security or Medicare tax**	☐	**Check and go to line 6.**

		Column 1		Column 2
5a	**Taxable social security wages**	177,621.00	× .124 =	22,025.00
5b	**Taxable social security tips**	0.00	× .124 =	0.00
5c	**Taxable Medicare wages & tips**	197,622.00	× .029 =	5,731.00
5d	**Taxable wages & tips subject to Additional Medicare Tax withholding**	0.00	× .009 =	0.00

5e	**Add Column 2 from lines 5a, 5b, 5c, and 5d**	5e	27,756.04
5f	**Section 3121(q) Notice and Demand—Tax due on unreported tips** (see instructions)	5f	0.00
6	**Total taxes before adjustments** (add lines 3, 5e, and 5f)	6	63,328.04
7	**Current quarter's adjustment for fractions of cents**	7	0.00
8	**Current quarter's adjustment for sick pay**	8	0.00
9	**Current quarter's adjustments for tips and group-term life insurance**	9	0.00
10	**Total taxes after adjustments.** Combine lines 6 through 9	10	63,328.04
11	**Total deposits for this quarter, including overpayment applied from a prior quarter and overpayment applied from Form 941-X or Form 944-X filed in the current quarter**	11	63,328.04
12a	**COBRA premium assistance payments** (see instructions)	12a	0.00
12b	**Number of individuals provided COBRA premium assistance**		0
13	**Add lines 11 and 12a**	13	63,328.04
14	**Balance due.** If line 10 is more than line 13, enter the difference and see instructions	14	0.00
15	**Overpayment.** If line 13 is more than line 10, enter the difference	0.00	Check one: ☐ Apply to next return. ☐ Send a refund.

▶ **You MUST complete both pages of Form 941 and SIGN it.** Next ▶

For Privacy Act and Paperwork Reduction Act Notice, see the back of the Payment Voucher. Cat. No. 17001Z Form **941** (Rev. 1-20--)

Figure 2b

950213

Name *(not your trade name)* Green Sales Company | **Employer identification number (EIN)** 91-7228162

Part 2: Tell us about your deposit schedule and tax liability for this quarter.

If you are unsure about whether you are a monthly schedule depositor or a semiweekly schedule depositor, see Pub. 15 (Circular E), section 11.

16 Check one: ☐ **Line 10 on this return is less than $2,500 or line 10 on the return for the prior quarter was less than $2,500, and you did not incur a $100,000 next-day deposit obligation during the current quarter.** If line 10 for the prior quarter was less than $2,500 but line 10 on this return is $100,000 or more, you must provide a record of your federal tax liability. If you are a monthly schedule depositor, complete the deposit schedule below; if you are a semiweekly schedule depositor, attach Schedule B (Form 941). Go to Part 3.

☐ **You were a monthly schedule depositor for the entire quarter.** Enter your tax liability for each month and total liability for the quarter, then go to Part 3.

Tax liability: Month 1 ____ .

Month 2 ____ .

Month 3 ____ .

Total liability for quarter ____ . **Total must equal line 10.**

☒ **You were a semiweekly schedule depositor for any part of this quarter.** Complete Schedule B (Form 941), Report of Tax Liability for Semiweekly Schedule Depositors, and attach it to Form 941.

Part 3: Tell us about your business. If a question does NOT apply to your business, leave it blank.

17 If your business has closed or you stopped paying wages . . . . ☐ Check here, and

enter the final date you paid wages ___ / ___ / ___ .

18 If you are a seasonal employer and you do not have to file a return for every quarter of the year . . ☐ Check here.

Part 4: May we speak with your third-party designee?

Do you want to allow an employee, a paid tax preparer, or another person to discuss this return with the IRS? See the instructions for details.

☐ Yes. Designee's name and phone number ____ ____

Select a 5-digit Personal Identification Number (PIN) to use when talking to the IRS. ☐☐☐☐☐

☑ No.

Part 5: Sign here. You MUST complete both pages of Form 941 and SIGN it.

Under penalties of perjury, I declare that I have examined this return, including accompanying schedules and statements, and to the best of my knowledge and belief, it is true, correct, and complete. Declaration of preparer (other than taxpayer) is based on all information of which preparer has any knowledge.

✗ **Sign your name here** ____

Print your name here: R. Jones

Print your title here: Controller

Date ___ / ___ / ___

Best daytime phone: XXX-XXX-XXXX

Paid Preparer Use Only Check if you are self-employed . . . ☐

Preparer's name		PTIN	
Preparer's signature		Date	/ /
Firm's name (or yours if self-employed)		EIN	
Address		Phone	
City	State	ZIP code	

Page **2** Form **941** (Rev. 1-20--)

Figure 2c
Payment Voucher

Detach Here and Mail With Your Payment and Form 941.

Form **941-V** Department of the Treasury Internal Revenue Service	**Payment Voucher** ▶ Do not staple this voucher or your payment to Form 941.		OMB No. 1545-0029 20--
1 Enter your employer identification number (EIN). 91-7228162	2 Enter the amount of your payment. ▶	Dollars 0	Cents 00
3 Tax Period	4 Enter your business name (individual name if sole proprietor). Green Sales Company		
○ 1st Quarter ○ 3rd Quarter	Enter your address. 610 First Avenue		
○ 2nd Quarter ● 4th Quarter	Enter your city, state, and ZIP code. Bangor, ME 04401		

Learning Objective 6 Prepare W-2 and W-3 forms and Form 940.

Wage Withholding Statements for Employees (Form W-2)

After the end of a year (December 31) and by the following January 31, the employer must provide each employee a Wage and Tax Statement, known as **Form W-2**. This form contains information about the employee's earnings and tax deductions for the year. The source of the information used to complete Form W-2 is the employee's individual earnings record. The amounts used to complete Mark Anderson's W-2 form (in Figure 3) represent the amounts taken from his earnings record at the end of the calendar year, December 31.

Box 13 is used for miscellaneous items: statutory employees (workers who are independent contractors under the common-law rules but are treated by statute as employees, such as full-time life insurance sales agents and traveling salespeople), 401(k)

Figure 3
Wage and Tax Statement (Form W-2) for Mark Anderson

a Employee's social security number 543-24-1680	OMB No. 1545-0008 Safe, accurate, FAST! Use IRS e-file	Visit the IRS website at www.irs.gov/efile
b Employer identification number (EIN) 91-7228162	1 Wages, tips, other compensation 58,404.58	2 Federal income tax withheld 10,920.00
c Employer's name, address, and ZIP code Green Sales Company 610 First Avenue Bangor, Maine 04401	3 Social security wages 58,404.58	4 Social security tax withheld 3,621.08
	5 Medicare wages and tips 58,404.58	6 Medicare tax withheld 846.87
	7 Social security tips 0	8 Allocated tips 0
d Control number	9	10 Dependent care benefits 0
e Employee's first name and initial Last name Suff.	11 Nonqualified plans 0	12a See instructions for box 12
Mark E. Anderson 1104 Rosewood Street Bangor, Maine 04401	13 Statutory employee ☐ Retirement plan ☐ Third-party sick pay ☐	12b
	14 Other 0	12c
f Employee's address and ZIP code		12d

15 State	Employer's state ID number	16 State wages, tips, etc.	17 State income tax	18 Local wages, tips, etc.	19 Local income tax	20 Locality name
ME	464-729	58,404.58	2,184.00	0	0	

Form **W-2** Wage and Tax Statement 20-- Department of the Treasury—Internal Revenue Service

Copy B—To Be Filed With Employee's FEDERAL Tax Return.
This information is being furnished to the Internal Revenue Service.

plan contributions, or sick pay that is not included in income because the employee contributed to the sick pay plan. Box 14 may include the value of noncash fringe benefits, providing a vehicle for the employee, for example.

At least four copies of the W-2 form are required for each employee:

Copy A—Employer sends to the Social Security Administration.
Copy B—Employer gives to employee to be attached to the employee's individual federal income tax return.
Copy C—Employer gives to employee to be kept for his or her personal records.
Copy D—Employer keeps this copy as a record of payments made.

If state and local income taxes are withheld, the employer prepares additional copies to be sent to the appropriate tax agencies.

A copy of the W-2 is also sent (if applicable) to the state and/or local tax department, and a copy is given to the employee to attach to the state/local tax return.

Employer's Annual Federal Income Tax Reports (Form W-3)

Along with Copy A of the employees' W-2 forms, Green Sales Company sends **Form W-3**, Transmittal of Wage and Tax Statements, to the Social Security Administration. This form is due on February 28 following the end of the calendar year.

Form W-3 shows (for all employees) the total wages and tips, total federal income taxes withheld, total FICA Social Security and Medicare taxable wages, total FICA Social Security and Medicare taxes withheld, and other tax-related information. These amounts must be the same as the grand totals of the W-2 forms and the four quarterly 941 forms for the year. Green Sales Company's completed Form W-3 is presented in Figure 4.

Figure 4
Transmittal of Wage and Tax Statements (Form W-3) for Green Sales Company

DO NOT STAPLE

33333	a Control number	For Official Use Only ▶ OMB No. 1545-0008

b **Kind of Payer** (Check one): 941 [X] Military [ ] 943 [ ] 944 [ ] CT-1 [ ] Hshld. emp. [ ] Medicare govt. emp. [ ]
Kind of Employer (Check one): None apply [X] 501c non-govt. [ ] State/local non-501c [ ] State/local 501c [ ] Federal govt. [ ]
Third-party sick pay (Check if applicable) [ ]

c Total number of Forms W-2 12	d Establishment number – – – – – –	1 Wages, tips, other compensation 861,530.00	2 Federal income tax withheld 155,075.00
e Employer identification number (EIN) 91-7228162		3 Social security wages 775,358.00	4 Social security tax withheld 48,072.20
f Employer's name Green Sales Company		5 Medicare wages and tips 861,530.00	6 Medicare tax withheld 12,492.19
610 First Avenue Bangor, Maine 04401		7 Social security tips 0	8 Allocated tips 0
		9	10 Dependent care benefits 0
g Employer's address and ZIP code		11 Nonqualified plans 0	12a Deferred compensation 0
h Other EIN used this year		13 For third-party sick pay use only	12b
15 State ME	Employer's state ID number 464-729	14 Income tax withheld by payer of third-party sick pay 0	
16 State wages, tips, etc. 861,530.00	17 State income tax 31,015.00	18 Local wages, tips, etc. 0	19 Local income tax 0
Contact person Eileen Green		Telephone number (207) 555-7865	For Official Use Only
Email address egreen@emailme.net		Fax number (207) 555-1477	

Under penalties of perjury, I declare that I have examined this return and accompanying documents, and, to the best of my knowledge and belief, they are true, correct, and complete.

Signature ▶ *Eileen Green* Title ▶ *Owner* Date ▶ *2/27/20--*

Form **W-3** Transmittal of Wage and Tax Statements 20-- Department of the Treasury Internal Revenue Service

A few boxes deserve an explanation. Box d, Establishment number, may be used for a company that has separate establishments, with each establishment filing W-2 and W-3 forms separately. Box h is used by a company that had more than one employer identification number (EIN) during the year.

To summarize, the employer must submit the following at the end of the calendar year: (1) Employer's Quarterly Federal Tax Return (Form 941, for the fourth quarter by January 31); (2) Wage and Tax Statements (Form W-2, for all employees by January 31); and (3) Transmittal of Wage and Tax Statements (Form W-3 by February 28).

REPORTS AND PAYMENTS OF FEDERAL UNEMPLOYMENT TAX

If the accumulated FUTA tax liability at the end of a quarter is greater than $500, a deposit must be made.

As we stated previously, generally all employers are subject to the Federal Unemployment Tax Act. These employers must submit an Employer's Annual Federal Unemployment (FUTA) Tax Return, Form 940, no later than January 31 following the close of the calendar year. This deadline may be extended until February 10 if the employer has made deposits paying the FUTA tax liability in full. **Form 940** shows total wages paid to employees, total wages subject to federal unemployment tax, and other information.

Using Green Sales Company as an example, federal unemployment taxable earnings by quarter are as follows:

Federal Unemployment Tax	1st Quarter	2nd Quarter	3rd Quarter	4th Quarter	Cumulative Total
Taxable earnings	$85,325	$ 4,485	$ 2,816	$ 1,020	$93,646
Tax rate	× 0.006	× 0.006	× 0.006	× 0.006	× 0.006
Tax liability	$511.95	$ 26.91	$ 16.90	$ 6.12	$561.88

We now repeat the journal entry for the first quarter, in which $511.95 was deposited on April 30.

Date		Description	Post. Ref.	Debit	Credit
20--					
Apr.	30	Federal Unemployment Tax Payable		511.95	
		Cash			511.95
		Issued check for deposit of			
		federal unemployment tax.			

During the second and third quarters, many employees' total earnings passed the $7,000 limit of taxable earnings, and the firm's tax liability was reduced accordingly. Because Green Sales Company's total accumulated liability of $43.81 ($26.91 + $16.90) was less than $500, deposits covering those quarters were not made.

By the end of the fourth quarter, each of the 12 employees' earnings passed the $7,000 mark. The total accumulated liability for the second, third, and fourth quarters is $49.93

(\$26.91 + \$16.90 + \$6.12). This amount will be paid by January 31, accompanied by the completed Employer's Annual Federal Unemployment (FUTA) Tax Return, Form 940.

The T account for Federal Unemployment Tax Payable follows. The credits to the account were part of the entries to record the federal unemployment tax portion of Payroll Tax Expense for each payroll period.

Federal Unemployment Tax Payable

	−	+	
Apr. 30 deposit	511.95	1st quarter (liability)	511.95
		2nd quarter (liability)	26.91
		3rd quarter (liability)	16.90
Jan. 31 deposit	49.93	4th quarter (liability)	6.12

Employer's Annual Federal Unemployment (FUTA) Tax Return (Form 940)

Figure 5 shows a completed Form 940 for Green Sales Company. This form has seven parts. (Keep in mind that all forms change from time to time. Go to www.irs.gov for updates and detailed instructions.)

Part 1:

Line 1a indicates the abbreviation for the state in which the business was required to pay taxes, while **line 1b** is for multi-state employers.

Line 2 is for businesses that paid wages in a state that is subject to credit reduction. A credit reduction state is a state that has not repaid money it borrowed from the federal government to pay unemployment benefits. Let's assume the U.S. Department of Labor announced that there are no credit reduction states for the current tax year; in that case, Green Sales Company skips this line.

Part 2:

Line 3 lists the total wages paid during the calendar year (\$861,530.00).

Line 4 lists the amount of wages exempt from FUTA tax—this includes such items as agricultural labor, family employment, and the value of meals and lodging. It is assumed that Green Sales Company had no such wages. If it had, the appropriate box or boxes on lines 4a-e would need to be checked to show the types of payments exempt from FUTA tax.

Line 5 shows the exempt wages paid (\$767,884.00)—wages paid to each employee over and above \$7,000 for the calendar year.

Line 6 is the total exempt payments (\$767,884.00).

Line 7 shows the total taxable FUTA wages (\$93,646.00), which is computed by subtracting the total amount of exempt payments (line 6) from the total wages paid (line 3).

Line 8 indicates the total amount of FUTA tax due before adjustments (\$93,646.00 × 0.006 = \$561.88).

Part 3:

Lines 9 and 10 are to be completed if all or some of the FUTA wages paid were excluded from state unemployment tax. These lines do not apply to Green Sales Company, so they are left blank.

Line 11 is also left blank because the U.S. Department of Labor announced that there are no credit reduction states for the current tax year.

Figure 5a

Employer's Annual Federal Unemployment (FUTA) Tax Return (Form 940) for Green Sales Company

Form **940 for 20--:** **Employer's Annual Federal Unemployment (FUTA) Tax Return** 850108

Department of the Treasury — Internal Revenue Service OMB No. 1545-0028

(EIN) Employer identification number 9 1 – 7 2 2 8 1 6 2

Name *(not your trade name)*

Trade name *(if any)* Green Sales Company

Address 610 First Avenue

Number Street Suite or room number

Bangor ME 04401

City State ZIP code

Type of Return (Check all that apply.)

- ☐ **a.** Amended
- ☐ **b.** Successor employer
- ☐ **c.** No payments to employees in 20--
- ☐ **d.** Final: Business closed or stopped paying wages

Read the separate instructions before you fill out this form. Please type or print within the boxes.

Part 1: Tell us about your return. If any line does NOT apply, leave it blank.

1 If you were required to pay your state unemployment tax in ...

1a One state only, write the state abbreviation . . . **1a** ME

- OR -

1b More than one state (You are a multi-state employer) . . . **1b** ☐ Check here. Fill out Schedule A.

Skip line 2 for 20-- and go to line 3.

2 If you paid wages in a state that is subject to CREDIT REDUCTION . . . **2** ☐ Check here. Fill out Schedule A (Form 940), Part 2.

Part 2: Determine your FUTA tax before adjustments for 20--. If any line does NOT apply, leave it blank.

3 Total payments to all employees . . . **3** 861,530.00

4 Payments exempt from FUTA tax . . . **4** 0.00

Check all that apply: **4a** ☐ Fringe benefits **4b** ☐ Group-term life insurance **4c** ☐ Retirement/Pension **4d** ☐ Dependent care **4e** ☐ Other

5 Total of payments made to each employee in excess of $7,000 . . . **5** 767,884.00

6 Subtotal (line 4 + line 5 = line 6) . . . **6** 767,884.00

7 Total taxable FUTA wages (line 3 – line 6 = line 7) . . . **7** 93,646.00

8 FUTA tax before adjustments (line 7 × .006 = line 8) . . . **8** 561.88

Part 3: Determine your adjustments. If any line does NOT apply, leave it blank.

9 If ALL of the taxable FUTA wages you paid were excluded from state unemployment tax, multiply line 7 by .054 (line 7 × .054 = line 9). Then go to line 12 . . . **9** 0.00

10 If SOME of the taxable FUTA wages you paid were excluded from state unemployment tax, OR you paid ANY state unemployment tax late (after the due date for filing Form 940), fill out the worksheet in the instructions. Enter the amount from line 7 of the worksheet onto line 10 . **10** 0.00

Skip line 11 for 20-- and go to line 12.

11 If credit reduction applies, enter the amount from line 3 of Schedule A (Form 940) . . . **11** .

Part 4: Determine your FUTA tax and balance due or overpayment for 20--. If any line does NOT apply, leave it blank.

12 Total FUTA tax after adjustments (lines 8 + 9 + 10 + 11 = line 12) . . . **12** 561.88

13 FUTA tax deposited for the year, including any payment applied from a prior year . . . **13** 421.95

14 Balance due (If line 12 is more than line 13, enter the difference on line 14.)

- If line 14 is more than $500, you must deposit your tax.
- If line 14 is $500 or less, you may pay with this return. For more information on how to pay, see the separate instructions . . . **14** 139.93

15 Overpayment (If line 13 is more than line 12, enter the difference on line 15 and check a box below.) . . . **15** .

Check one: ☐ Apply to next return. ☐ Send a refund.

▶ You **MUST** fill out both pages of this form and **SIGN** it.

Next ➔

For Privacy Act and Paperwork Reduction Act Notice, see the back of Form 940-V, Payment Voucher. Cat. No. 11234O Form **940** (20--)

Figure 5b

Part 5: Report your FUTA tax liability by quarter only if line 12 is more than $500. If not, go to Part 6.

16 **Report the amount of your FUTA tax liability for each quarter; do NOT enter the amount you deposited. If you had no liability for a quarter, leave the line blank.**

16a **1st quarter** (January 1 – March 31)	**16a**	511.95
16b **2nd quarter** (April 1 – June 30)	**16b**	26.91
16c **3rd quarter** (July 1 – September 30)	**16c**	16.90
16d **4th quarter** (October 1 – December 31)	**16d**	6.12
17 **Total tax liability for the year** (lines 16a + 16b + 16c + 16d = line 17)	**17**	561.88 **Total must equal line 12.**

Part 6: May we speak with your third-party designee?

Do you want to allow an employee, a paid tax preparer, or another person to discuss this return with the IRS? See the instructions for details.

☐ **Yes.** Designee's name and phone number ( ) –

Select a 5-digit Personal Identification Number (PIN) to use when talking to IRS

☑ **No.**

Part 7: Sign here. You MUST fill out both pages of this form and SIGN it.

Under penalties of perjury, I declare that I have examined this return, including accompanying schedules and statements, and to the best of my knowledge and belief, it is true, correct, and complete, and that no part of any payment made to a state unemployment fund claimed as a credit was, or is to be, deducted from the payments made to employees. Declaration of preparer (other than taxpayer) is based on all information of which preparer has any knowledge.

✗ Sign your name here *Eileen Green*

Print your name here: **Eileen Green**

Print your title here: **Owner**

Date: 1 / 31 / 20--

Best daytime phone: (207) 555 – 7865

Figure 5c

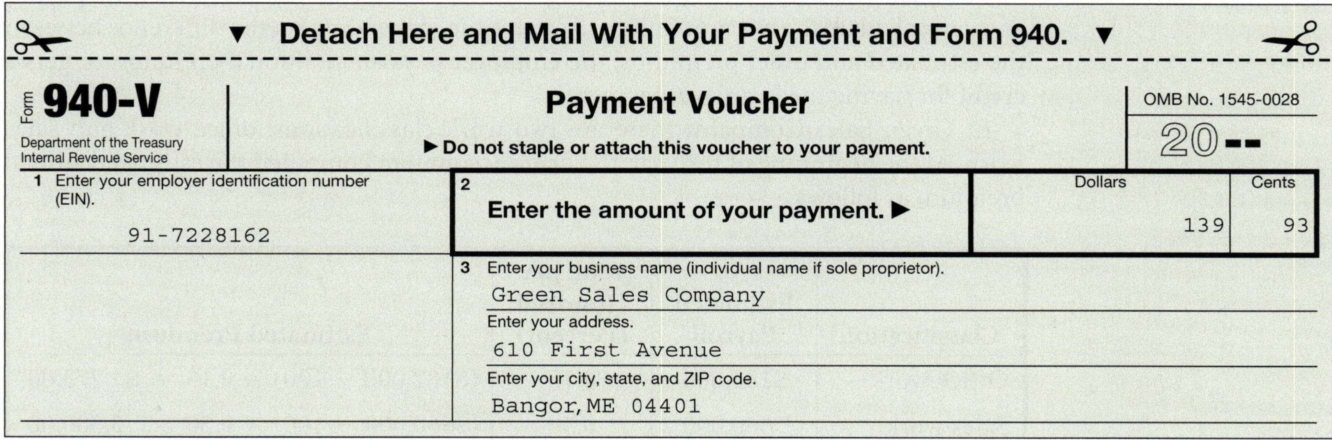

▼ **Detach Here and Mail With Your Payment and Form 940.** ▼

Form **940-V** — Department of the Treasury, Internal Revenue Service

Payment Voucher

▶ **Do not staple or attach this voucher to your payment.**

OMB No. 1545-0028 — 20--

		Dollars	Cents
1 Enter your employer identification number (EIN). 91-7228162	**2** **Enter the amount of your payment.** ▶	139	93

3 Enter your business name (individual name if sole proprietor).
Green Sales Company

Enter your address.
610 First Avenue

Enter your city, state, and ZIP code.
Bangor, ME 04401

Part 4:

Line 12 indicates the amount of total FUTA tax after adjustments ($561.88), which is the sum of line 8 + lines 9–11.

Line 13 shows the amount of total FUTA tax that was deposited for the year ($421.95).

Line 14 is the difference between line 12 and line 13 ($561.88 − $421.95 = $139.93). This represents the balance due.

Line 15 is completed if FUTA tax deposited for the year (line 13) is more than the total FUTA tax after adjustments (line 12). This indicates an overpayment.

Part 5:

Lines 16a–d ask for the amount of FUTA tax liability for each quarter.

Line 17 discloses the total tax liability for the calendar year ($561.88). It should equal the amount given on line 12 and the total of lines 16a–d.

The remaining parts of the 940 form require you to indicate whether you grant permission for third-party inquiries, requires a signature and title of the preparer, as well as the date the Form 940 is completed. There is also a Form 940-V, which is the payment voucher submitted with the 940 report when a balance is due.

WORKERS' COMPENSATION INSURANCE

Learning Objective 7 Calculate the premium for workers' compensation insurance and prepare the entry for payment in advance.

Most states require employers to provide **workers' compensation insurance** or industrial accident insurance for employees killed or injured on the job. Coverage is available to employers through private insurance companies, authorized by the state, or state-administered plans. The employer usually pays all of the premiums. The premium rate varies with the amount of risk the job entails and the company's claims history. For example, handling molten steel ingots is more dangerous than typing reports. Thus, it is important that employees be identified properly in terms of the insurance premium classifications. The rates are based as a percentage of payroll by job classification. For example, rates may be 0.15 percent on an office work payroll classification and 0.5 percent for sales work, yet industrial labor in heavy manufacturing may be 3.5 percent. These rates are typically expressed as $0.15 per $100 of the salaries or wages for office work, $0.50 per $100 for sales work, and $3.50 per $100 for industrial labor.

Generally, the employer pays a premium in advance based on the estimated payroll for the year. After the year ends, the employer knows the actual amount of the payroll and can calculate the exact premium. At that time, depending on the difference between the estimated and exact premiums, the employer pays an additional premium or gets a credit for having made an overpayment.

At Green Sales Company, there are two work classifications: office work and sales work. At the beginning of the year, the firm's accountant computed the estimated annual premium as follows:

Classification	Estimated Payroll	Rate per Hundred (Percent)	Estimated Premium	
Office work	$182,000	0.15	($182,000 ÷ 100) × 0.15 =	$ 273.00
Sales work	660,000	0.50	($660,000 ÷ 100) × 0.50 =	3,300.00
			Total estimated premium	$3,573.00

As shown by T accounts, the accountant made the following entry when payment was disbursed.

Prepaid Insurance, Workers' Compensation

+	–
Jan. 10 3,573.00	

Cash

+	–
	Jan. 10 3,573.00

Then at the end of the calendar year, the accountant calculated the exact premium as follows:

Classification	Actual Payroll	Rate per Hundred (Percent)	Exact Premium	
Office work	$188,990	0.15	($188,990 ÷ 100) × 0.15 =	$ 283.49
Sales work	672,540	0.50	($672,540 ÷ 100) × 0.50 =	3,362.70
			Total estimated premium	$3,646.19

Therefore, the amount of the unpaid premium is

$3,646.19	**Total exact premium**
3,573.00	**Less total estimated premium paid**
$ 73.19	**Additional premium owed**

8a Determine the amount of the end-of-the-year adjustment for workers' compensation insurance and record the adjustment.

Learning Objective

Now the accountant makes an adjusting entry, similar to the adjusting entry for expired insurance. This entry appears on the work sheet. The accountant also makes an additional adjusting entry for the extra premium owed. By T accounts, the entries are as follows:

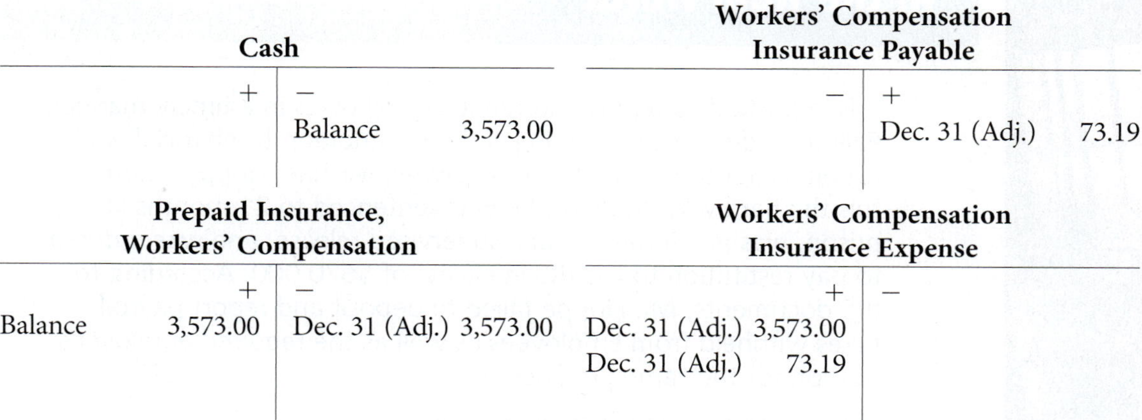

Cash

+	–
	Balance 3,573.00

Workers' Compensation Insurance Payable

–	+
	Dec. 31 (Adj.) 73.19

Prepaid Insurance, Workers' Compensation

+	–
Balance 3,573.00	Dec. 31 (Adj.) 3,573.00

Workers' Compensation Insurance Expense

+	–
Dec. 31 (Adj.) 3,573.00 Dec. 31 (Adj.) 73.19	

Green Sales Company will pay $73.19, the amount of unpaid premium, in January, together with the estimated premium for the next year.

ADJUSTING FOR ACCRUED SALARIES AND WAGES

Learning Objective

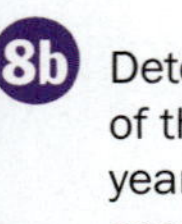

Determine the amount of the end-of-the-year adjustment for accrued salaries and wages and record the adjustment.

Now let's assume that Green Sales Company had $2,400 of wages accrue for the time between the last payday and the end of the year. An adjusting entry is necessary.

Date		Description	Post. Ref.	Debit	Credit
20--		Adjusting Entry			
Dec.	31	Wages Expense		2 4 0 0 00	
		Wages Payable			2 4 0 0 00

For the accrual adjustment, gross salary and wages are recorded, not the net salary and wages. When the accrued salary and wages are paid, the amounts withheld for federal and state taxes, FICA taxes, and other deductions are recorded.

Adjusting Entry for Accrual of Payroll Taxes

As you have seen, the following taxes come under the umbrella of the Payroll Tax Expense account: the employer's share of the FICA taxes, the state unemployment tax, and the federal unemployment tax. The employer becomes liable for these taxes only when the employees are actually paid, rather than at the time the liability to the employees is incurred. So there is no adjusting entry for Payroll Tax Expense until the wages are actually paid.

TAX CALENDAR

Now let's put it all together. To keep up with the task of paying and reporting the various taxes, the accountant compiles a chronological list of the due dates. We are including

In the Real World

It is important to report and remit payroll taxes in a timely manner. Failure to do so can result in jail time in addition to financial restitution. A South Dakota business owner, Michael Hoppe, learned this the hard way. In 2010, he was sentenced to 21 months in prison, was given three years' supervised release, and was ordered to pay restitution to the IRS in excess of $670,000. According to IRS documents, Mr. Hoppe failed to deposit and report payroll taxes withheld from employees as well as the required employer's portion for the same time period.

Source: www.irs.gov/compliance/enforcement

only the payroll taxes here, but any kind of taxes, such as sales taxes and property taxes, should also be listed. When you think about the penalties for missing tax deposit or filing due dates, this chronological list seems to be well worth the effort. We assume for this purpose that the employer is a monthly depositor for the federal tax deposit.

Jan.	10	Pay estimated annual premium for workers' compensation insurance. (This is an approximate date, as it varies among the states.)
	15	Make federal tax deposit for employees' income tax withholding, employees' FICA taxes withheld, and employer's FICA taxes for wages paid during December.
	31	Complete Employer's Quarterly Federal Tax Return, Form 941, for the fourth quarter.
	31	Issue Copies B and C of Wage and Tax Statement, Form W-2, to employees.
	31	Pay state unemployment tax liability for the previous quarter and submit state return, employer's tax report.
	31	Pay any remaining federal unemployment tax liability for the previous year and submit Form 940, Employer's Annual Federal Unemployment (FUTA) Tax Return.
	31	Make state deposit for employees' state income tax withholding and submit any required state payroll reports. (Timing and required reports may differ from state to state.)
Feb.	15	Make federal tax deposit for employees' income tax withholding, employees' FICA taxes withholding, and employer's FICA taxes for wages paid during January.
	28	Complete Transmittal of Wage and Tax Statements, Form W-3, and attach Copy A of W-2 forms for employees.
Mar.	15	Make federal tax deposit for employees' income tax withholding, employees' FICA taxes withholding, and employer's FICA taxes for wages paid during February.
Apr.	15	Make federal tax deposit for employees' income tax withholding, employees' FICA taxes withholding, and employer's FICA taxes for wages paid during March.
	30	Pay state unemployment tax liability for the previous quarter and submit state return, employer's tax report.
	30	Complete Employer's Quarterly Federal Tax Return, Form 941, for the first quarter.
	30	Make federal tax deposit for federal unemployment tax liability if it exceeds $500.
	30	Make state deposit for employees' state income tax withholding.

PAYROLL FRAUD

Payroll fraud can be a huge problem for a business in terms of monies lost and time and frustration dealing with the problem. Payroll fraud can be categorized into three general areas:

1. *Ghost employee fraud*—Someone is recorded in the payroll system who does not work for the business.

2. *False wage claim fraud*—Extra hours or other relevant factors are added to wage information to increase the amount of pay.
3. *False expense reimbursement fraud*—Improper claims are made for the reimbursement of business expenses.

Internal controls should be in place to prevent and detect payroll fraud. Some of those controls include the following:

- Require mandatory vacations for those with payroll responsibilities, having other employees perform this function in their absence.
- Use cash payments or checks minimally and increase the use of direct deposit of payroll checks.
- Have employees physically sign and show proper identification to receive their paychecks.
- Conduct periodic unannounced audits to ensure that all employees on the payroll actually work for the company.
- Cross-reference the payroll roster for duplicate addresses or Social Security numbers.
- Conduct a thorough pre-employment reference check for all payroll personnel.
- Compare payroll expense per the payroll register to the actual amounts paid. Also compare amounts to payroll deposits made.
- Outsource payroll administration.

Accounting with QuickBooks®

Payroll Liabilities and Reports

Learning Objective  View and print the payroll reports.

Learning Objectives

After you have completed this section, you will be able to do the following:

1. View and print the payroll reports.
2. Pay payroll liabilities with QuickBooks.
3. View and print information for completing payroll tax reports.

In this chapter, you learned how to calculate the employer's payroll taxes and pay the require payroll tax liabilities. You also learned how to complete several payroll related tax forms, including Form 941 and Form 940. Although completing a payroll and the associated tax forms can be done manually, as you have learned in the text, using accounting software, such as QuickBooks, simplifies this process.

Payroll Journal QuickBooks automatically records transactions to the journal from **Pay Employees**. To view and print journal transactions that involve only paychecks, the general journal can be modified by completing the steps shown in Figures Q1 and Q2.

STEP 1. Click the **Reports** tab.

STEP 2. Select **Accountant & Taxes**.

STEP 3. Select **Journal**.

STEP 4. Select the **Customize Report** tab.

STEP 5. Select the **Filters** tab.

STEP 6. Under the Filters box, select **Transaction Type**.

STEP 7. In the Transaction Type box, select **Paycheck**.

STEP 8. Click **OK**.

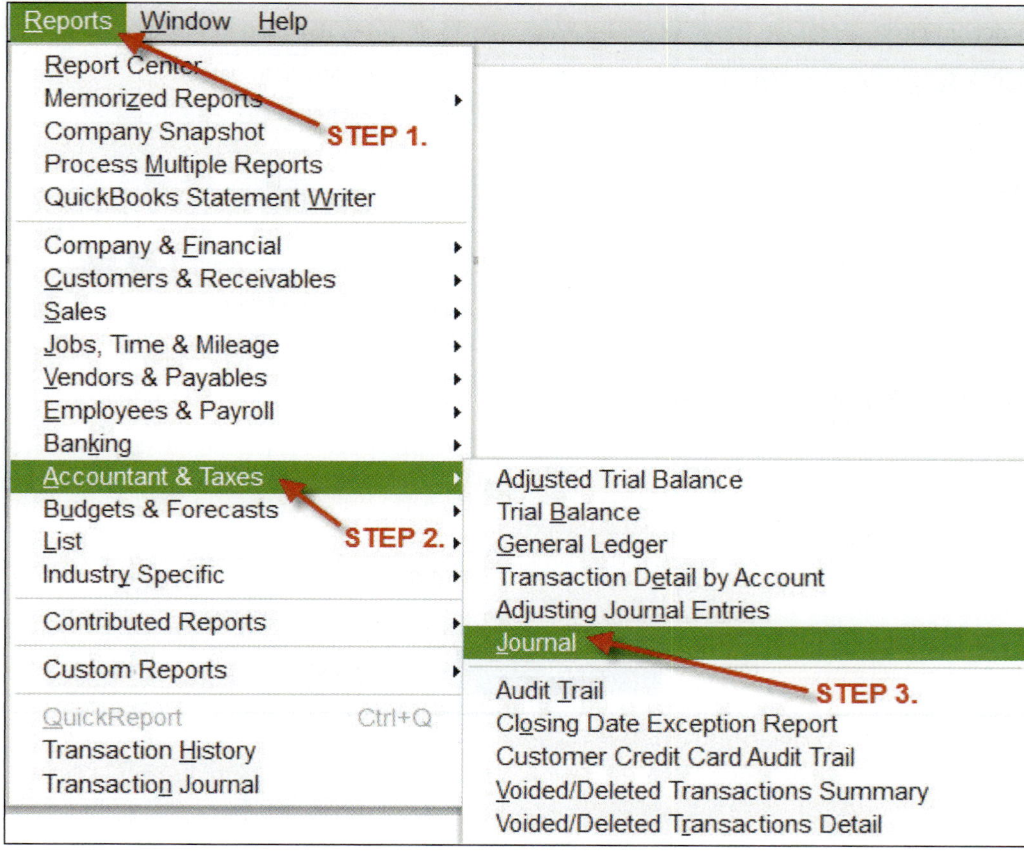

Figure Q1
Journal report access

QuickBooks Tip

Report filters appear in the **Current Filter Choices** box as shown in Figure Q2.

The journal can also be modified to view only payroll liabilities by selecting **Payroll Liabilities**, instead of **Paycheck**, in the **Transaction Type** box shown in Figure Q2, Step 7. The payroll journal report sorted by transaction type **Paycheck** for Green Sales Company is shown in Figure Q3.

Figure Q2
Modify report journal

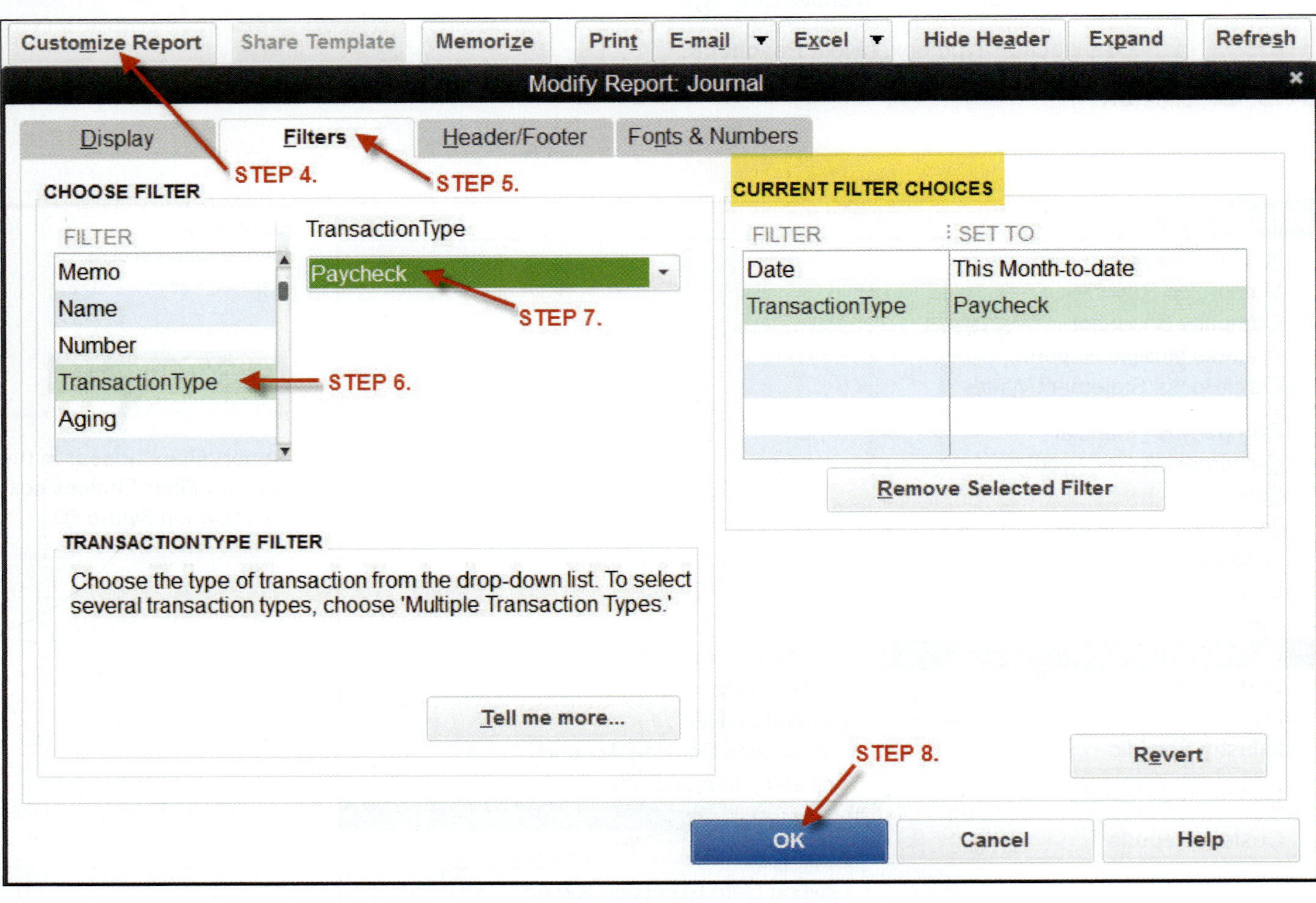

Figure Q3
Payroll journal report by paycheck

Green Sales Company
Journal
October 12, 20–

Type	Date	Num	Adj	Name	Memo	Account	Debit	Credit
Paycheck	10/12/20–	832		Anderson, Mark		Cash		899.35
				Anderson, Mark		Sales Wages Exp...	1,124.58	
				Anderson, Mark		Payroll Liabilities	0.00	
				Anderson, Mark		Payroll Liabilities		311.26
				Anderson, Mark		Payroll Expenses	86.03	
							1,210.61	1,210.61
Paycheck	10/12/20–	833		Bodell, Anna		Cash		581.47
				Bodell, Anna		Sales Wages Exp...	744.20	
				Bodell, Anna		Payroll Liabilities		264.31
				Bodell, Anna		Payroll Expenses	101.58	
							845.78	845.78
Paycheck	10/12/20–	834		Dorn, David		Cash		718.93
				Dorn, David		Sales Wages Exp...	916.00	
				Dorn, David		Payroll Liabilities		279.98
				Dorn, David		Payroll Expenses	82.91	
							998.91	998.91
Paycheck	10/12/20–	835		Fields, Sarah		Cash		859.43
				Fields, Sarah		Payroll Expenses	1,167.57	
				Fields, Sarah		Payroll Liabilities		308.14
				Fields, Sarah		Payroll Liabilities	0.00	
							1,167.57	1,167.57
Paycheck	10/12/20–	836		Graham, Jason		Cash		1,379.70
				Graham, Jason		Sales Wages Exp...	1,798.45	
				Graham, Jason		Payroll Liabilities	0.00	
				Graham, Jason		Payroll Liabilities		556.33
				Graham, Jason		Payroll Expenses	137.58	
							1,936.03	1,936.03

Payroll Summary Report The payroll summary report provides payroll details by employee, including the employer taxes and contributions. To print and view the payroll summary report shown in Figure Q5, complete the steps in Figure Q4.

STEP 1. Click the **Reports** tab.

STEP 2. Select **Employees & Payroll**.

STEP 3. Select **Payroll Summary**.

STEP 4. Adjust the **From:** and **To:** dates and click **Refresh**.

STEP 5. To print the report, click the **Print** button.

Figure Q4
Payroll summary report access

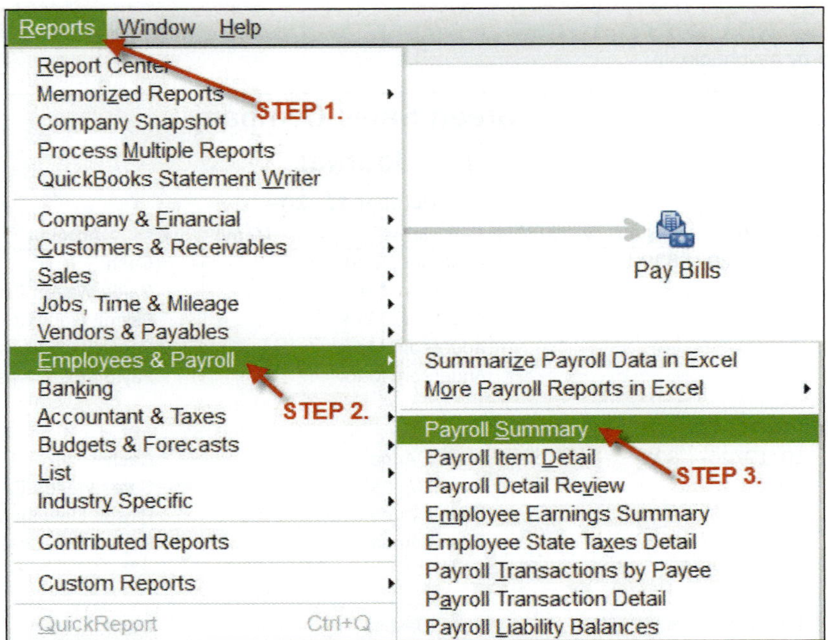

Figure Q5
Adjust report dates

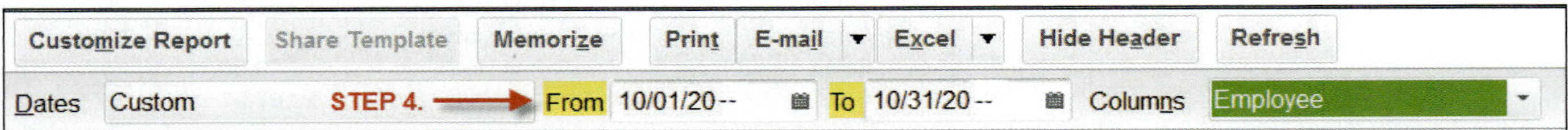

The payroll summary report for Green Sales Company's payroll ending October 11, 20-- is shown in Figure Q6 on the next page.

Figure Q6
Payroll summary report

Green Sales Company
Payroll Summary
October 11, 20--

	Anderson, Mark	Bodell, Anna	Dorn, David	Fields, Sarah	Graham, Jason	Lee, Jeremy	Mankowitz, Hanna	Olsen, Barbara
▾ Employee Wages, Taxes and Adjustments								
▾ Gross Pay								
Office Wages Expenses	0.00	0.00	0.00	1,084.50	0.00	1,895.58	0.00	1,487.20
Sales Wages Expenses	1,124.58	744.20	916.00	0.00	1,798.45	0.00	1,968.75	0.00
Total Gross Pay	1,124.58	744.20	916.00	1,084.50	1,798.45	1,895.58	1,968.75	1,487.20
Adjusted Gross Pay	1,124.58	744.20	916.00	1,084.50	1,798.45	1,895.58	1,968.75	1,487.20
▾ Taxes Withheld								
Federal Withholding	–116.00	–59.00	–85.00	–110.00	–234.31	–258.60	–276.89	–170.68
Medicare Employee	–16.31	–10.79	–13.28	–15.73	–26.08	–27.49	–28.55	–21.56
Social Security Employee	–69.72	–46.14	–56.79	–67.34	–111.50	–117.53	–122.06	–92.21
ME - Withholding	–23.20	–11.80	–17.00	–22.00	–46.86	–51.72	–55.38	–34.14
Total Taxes Withheld	–225.23	–127.73	–172.07	–215.07	–418.75	–455.34	–482.88	–318.59
▾ Deductions from NetPay								
Miscellaneous Deductions	0.00	–35.00	–25.00	–10.00	0.00	–20.00	0.00	0.00
Total Deductions from NetPay	0.00	–35.00	–25.00	–10.00	0.00	–20.00	0.00	0.00
Net Pay	899.35	581.47	718.93	859.43	1,379.70	1,420.24	1,485.87	1,168.61
▾ Employer Taxes and Contributions								
Federal Unemployment	0.00	4.46	1.28	0.00	0.00	0.00	0.00	0.00
Medicare Company	16.31	10.79	13.28	15.73	26.08	27.49	28.55	21.56
Social Security Company	69.72	46.14	56.79	67.34	111.50	117.53	122.06	92.21
ME - Unemployment	0.00	40.19	11.56	0.00	0.00	0.00	0.00	0.00
Total Employer Taxes and Contributions	86.03	101.58	82.91	83.07	137.58	145.02	150.61	113.77

Payroll Liability Balances Report To view and print the payroll liability balances reports, complete the following steps:

STEP 1. Click the **Reports** tab.

STEP 2. Select **Employees & Payroll**.

STEP 3. Select **Payroll Liability Balances**.

STEP 4. Adjust the **From**: and **To**: dates and click **Refresh**.

STEP 5. To print the report, click the **Print** button.

The payroll liability balances report for Green Sales Company's payroll ending October 11, 20--, is shown in Figure Q7.

Figure Q7
Payroll liability balances

Green Sales Company
Payroll Liability Balance
October 11, 20–

	BALANCE
Payroll Liabilities	
Federal Withholding	2,398.87
Medicare Employee	270.26
Social Security Employee	1,148.77
Federal Unemployment	5.75
Medicare Company	270.26
Social Security Company	1,148.77
ME – Withholding	479.78
ME – Unemployment	51.75
Miscellaneous Deductions	245.00
Total Payroll Liabilities	6,019.21

Learning Objective  Pay payroll liabilities with QuickBooks.

As you learned in this chapter, payroll liabilities include FICA Social Security and Medicare taxes (employee and employer), federal and state income taxes withheld from employees, and unemployment taxes (federal and state). To pay these payroll liabilities with QuickBooks, select **Pay Liabilities** from the **Employees** center on the home page as shown below. Then follow the steps in Figure Q9.

Figure Q8
Pay liabilities

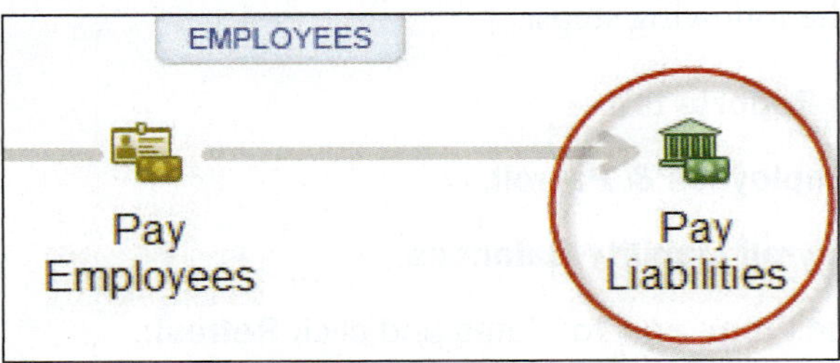

STEP 1. Make sure the box **To be printed** is checked.

STEP 2. Select the bank account the liability will be paid from.

STEP 3. Enter the **Check Date**.

STEP 4. Select the payroll items to be paid.

STEP 5. Select **Review liability check to enter expenses/penalties** or **Create liability check without reviewing**. It is strongly recommended that you always select the review option to help prevent errors.

STEP 6. Modify the dates for the payroll liability period.

STEP 7. Click **Create**.

QuickBooks Tip

The payroll liabilities report can be selected and viewed from the **Pay Liabilities** screen.

Figure Q9
Pay liabilities screen

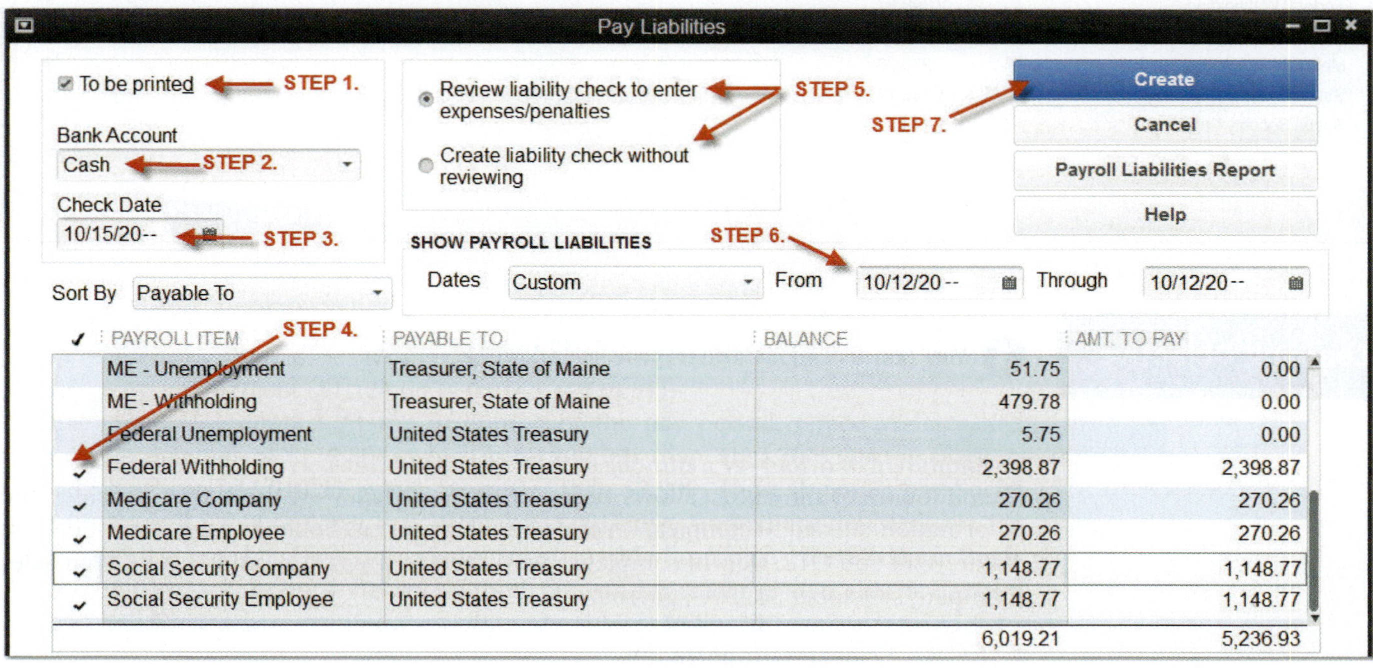

✓	PAYROLL ITEM	PAYABLE TO	BALANCE	AMT. TO PAY
	ME - Unemployment	Treasurer, State of Maine	51.75	0.00
	ME - Withholding	Treasurer, State of Maine	479.78	0.00
	Federal Unemployment	United States Treasury	5.75	0.00
✓	Federal Withholding	United States Treasury	2,398.87	2,398.87
✓	Medicare Company	United States Treasury	270.26	270.26
✓	Medicare Employee	United States Treasury	270.26	270.26
✓	Social Security Company	United States Treasury	1,148.77	1,148.77
✓	Social Security Employee	United States Treasury	1,148.77	1,148.77
			6,019.21	5,236.93

Figure Q10 is an example of a federal Form 941 tax deposit for Green Sales Company's October 11, 20--, payroll.

Figure Q10
Payroll tax liability check

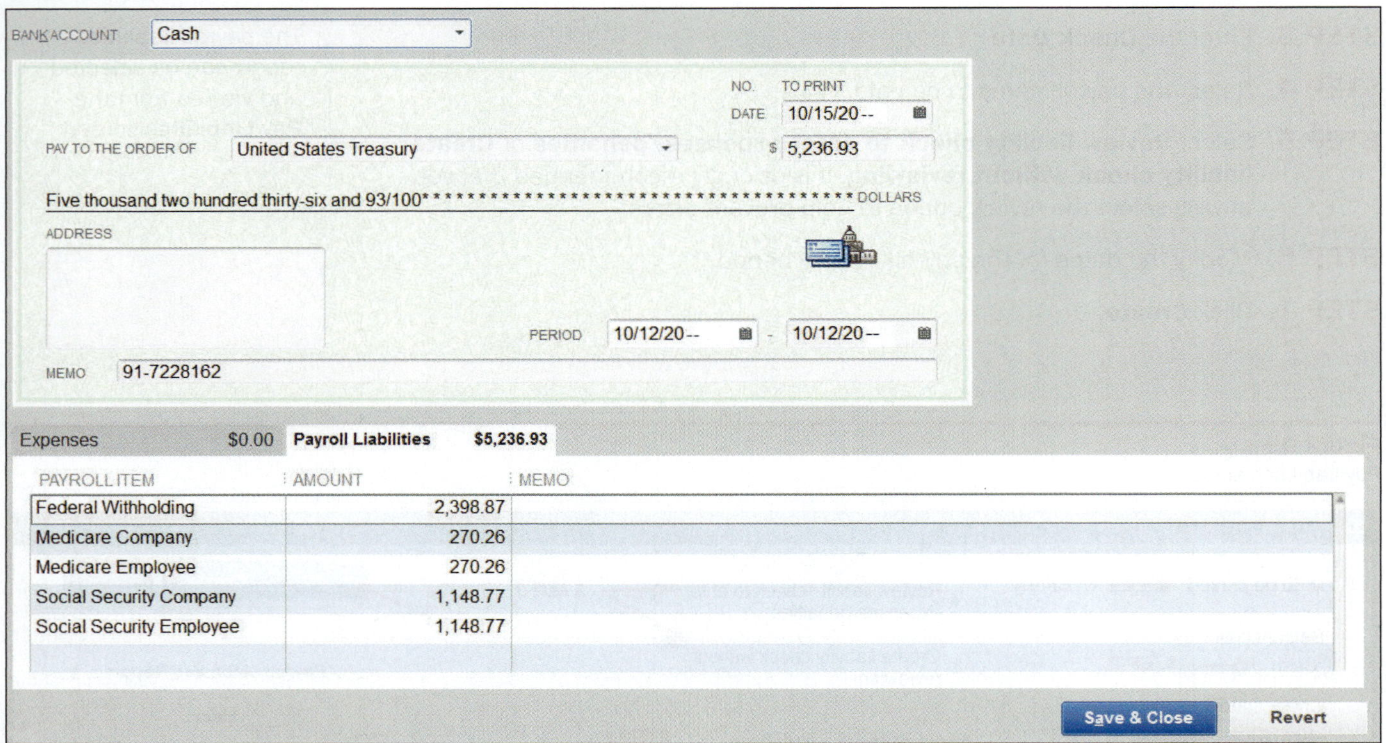

Learning Objective 3 View and print information for completing payroll tax reports.

QuickBooks, using Excel, allows users to create a tax worksheet that provides the information needed to complete several payroll tax forms. Following the steps shown in Figure Q11 and Q12, we will complete a worksheet to prepare Form 941 for Green Sales Company's October 11, 20--, payroll.

STEP 1. Select the **Reports** tab.

STEP 2. Select **Employees and Payroll**, then **More Payroll Reports in Excel**.

STEP 3. Select **Tax Form Worksheets**.

Figure Q11
Accessing the tax form worksheets

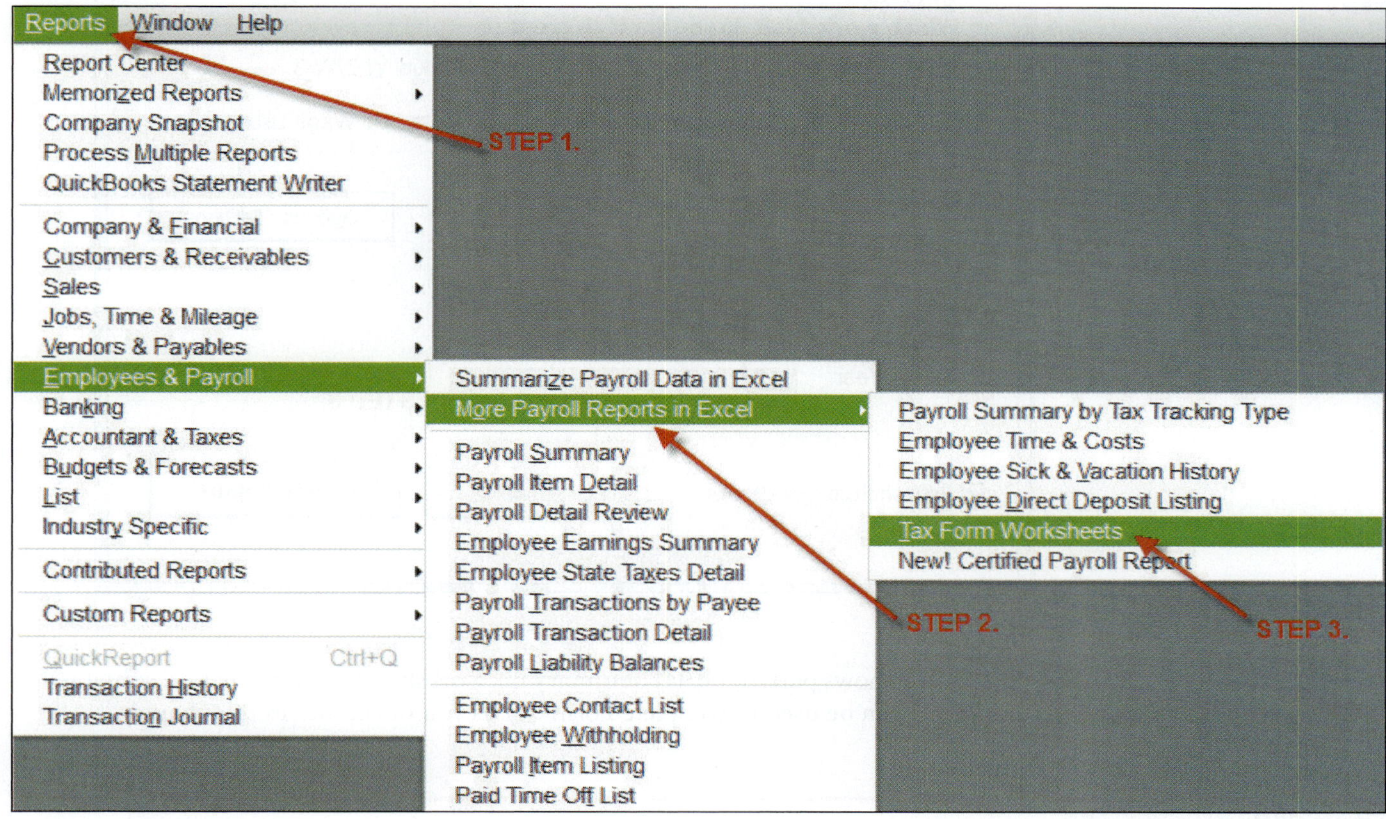

STEP 4. Select which worksheet you would like to create. For this example, we are creating Form 941.

STEP 5. Select the appropriate dates. The dates selected for Form 941 are the Last Quarter, 10/1/20-- to 12/31/20--.

STEP 6. Select **Create Report**.

QuickBooks Tip

The steps shown in Figures Q11 and Q12 can also be used to complete other payroll tax form worksheets, such as Form 940 and annual Forms W-2 and W-3.

Figure Q12
QuickBooks tax worksheet screen

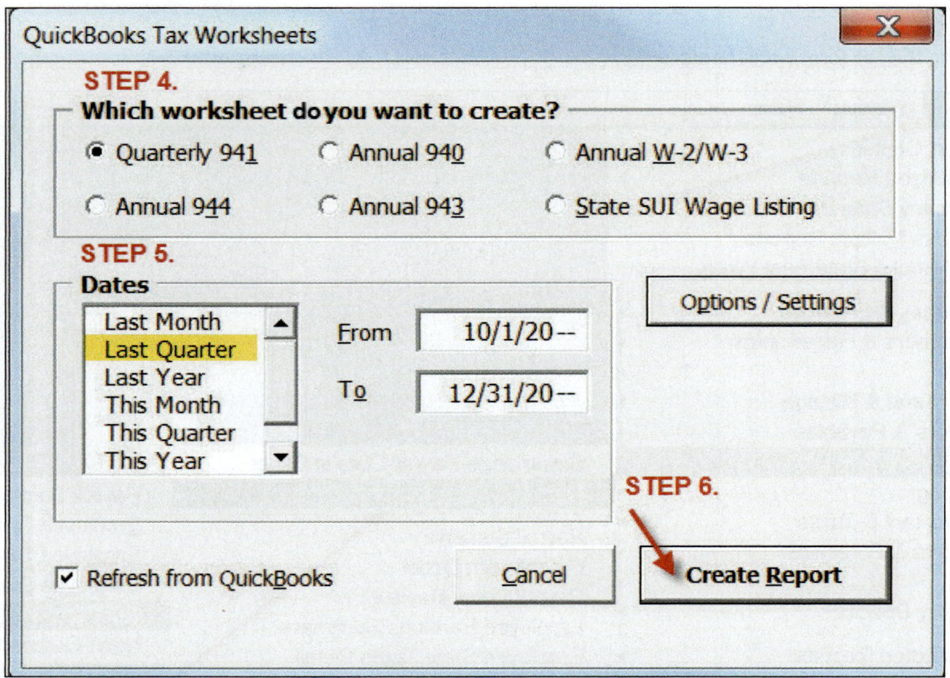

Figure Q13 shows part of the 941 summary tax worksheet. The information contained in this report can be used to complete Form 941 as you did earlier in this chapter.

Figure Q13
941 summary report

	A	B	C	D	E
1	**941 Summary**				
2	**Wages, Tips, and other Compensation**				
3	*Payroll Category*	*Item Type*	*Tax Tracking Type*		*Amount*
4	Office Wages Expense	Salary	Compensation		7,477.63
5	Sales Wages Expense	Salary	Compensation		11,159.59
6					18,637.22
7	*Federal Tax Withholding*	*Subject Income*	*Taxed Wages*		*Tax*
8	Federal Withholding	18,637.22	18,637.22		2,398.87
9	*Social Security & Medicare*	*Subject Income*	*Taxed Wages*	*Tax Rate*	*Tax*
10	Social Security	18,637.22	18,637.22	0.124	2,311.02
11	Medicare	18,637.22	18,637.22	0.029	540.48
12					2,851.50
13	**Total Tax (Calculated)**				5,250.37
14	[illegible]	[illegible]	[illegible]		[illegible]
19					

Chapter Review

Study and Practice

Calculate the amount of payroll tax expense and journalize the entry.

Learning Objective

Payroll tax expense consists of the employer's matching portion of FICA taxes plus the **state unemployment tax (SUTA)** plus the **federal unemployment tax (FUTA)**. *FICA taxes* consist of Social Security and Medicare taxes. *Employer's Social Security tax* equals total Social Security taxable earnings multiplied by 0.062 (6.2 percent assumed rate) on the taxable earnings. For this text, the maximum taxable is assumed to be $113,700. Total *Medicare tax* equals Medicare taxable earnings multiplied by 0.0145 (1.45 percent assumed rate). There is no maximum limit for Medicare—all earnings are taxable. *State unemployment tax* equals unemployment taxable earnings multiplied by 0.054 (5.4 percent assumed rate). *Federal unemployment tax* equals unemployment taxable earnings multiplied by 0.006 (0.6 percent assumed rate). Refer to the related journal entry on page 371.

PRACTICE EXERCISE 1

Quality Roofing has the following payroll information for the week ended May 31:

Total payroll	$56,000
Taxable earnings subject to Social Security	45,000
Taxable earnings subject to unemployment tax	2,000

Using the preceding tax rates, prepare the journal entry to record the employer's payroll tax liability.

PRACTICE EXERCISE 1 • SOLUTION

Date		Description	Post. Ref.	Debit	Credit
20--					
May	31	Payroll Tax Expense		3 7 2 2 00	
		FICA Taxes Payable			3 6 0 2 00
		State Unemployment Tax Payable			1 0 8 00
		Federal Unemployment Tax Payable			1 2 00
		To record employer's share of FICA			
		taxes and employer's state and			
		federal unemployment taxes.			

Computations:

FICA taxes payable:	Social Security	$45,000 × 0.062 =	$2,790.00
	Medicare	$56,000 × 0.0145 =	812.00
	Total		$3,602.00
State unemployment tax payable:		$2,000 × 0.054 =	$ 108.00
Federal unemployment tax payable:		$2,000 × 0.006 =	$ 12.00

Learning Objective

 Journalize the entry for the deposit of employees' federal income taxes withheld and FICA taxes (both employees' withheld and employer's share) and prepare the deposit.

Refer to the related journal entry on page 371.

PRACTICE EXERCISE 2

For the week ended May 31, Quality Roofing withheld the following taxes from its employees:

Federal income taxes withheld	$12,000
FICA taxes withheld	3,602

Prepare the journal entry to record the tax deposit to People's Bank. Include the employees' and the employer's share (computed in Practice Exercise 1) of FICA taxes.

PRACTICE EXERCISE 2 • SOLUTION

Date		Description	Post. Ref.	Debit	Credit
20--					
May	31	Employees' Federal Income Tax Payable		12 0 0 0 00	
		FICA Taxes Payable*		7 2 0 4 00	
		Cash			19 2 0 4 00
		Issued check for federal tax			
		deposit, People's Bank.			

*FICA taxes payable include the employees' share of $3,602 plus the employer's share of $3,602 (see Practice Exercise 1), for a total of $7,204.

Learning Objective

 Journalize the entries for the payment of employer's state and federal unemployment taxes.

State unemployment tax is paid on a quarterly basis. Payments are due by the end of the next month following the end of the calendar **quarter**. Refer to the related journal entry on the top of page 374.

If the amount of the accumulated federal unemployment tax liability exceeds $500 at the end of any quarter, the tax is due by the end of the next month following the end of the quarter. If the federal unemployment tax payable is less than $500 at the end of the year, it is due by January 31 of the next year. Refer to the related journal entry on the bottom of page 374.

PRACTICE EXERCISE 3

Assume Best Computers had $90,325 taxable earnings for the first quarter (covering January, February, and March). Assuming that the state unemployment tax rate is 5.4 percent (0.054) and the federal unemployment tax rate is 0.6 percent (0.006) of the first $7,000 paid to each employee during the calendar year, journalize the entries for the payment of Best Computers' state and federal unemployment taxes. Assume that no employee has surpassed the $7,000 limit.

PRACTICE EXERCISE 3 • SOLUTION

Date		Description	Post. Ref.	Debit	Credit
20--					
Apr.	30	State Unemployment Tax Payable		4 8 7 7 55	
		Cash			4 8 7 7 55
		Issued check for payment of			
		state unemployment tax.			
	30	Federal Unemployment Tax Payable		5 4 1 95	
		Cash			5 4 1 95
		Issued check for payment of			
		federal unemployment tax.			

4 Journalize the entry for the deposit of employees' state income taxes withheld. **Learning Objective**

Employees' state income taxes withheld are paid on a quarterly basis or as required by the state. Payment may be due by the end of the next month following the end of the calendar quarter. Refer to the related journal entry on page 375.

4

PRACTICE EXERCISE 4

For the quarter ended June 30, Quality Roofing has a credit balance of $28,000 for Employee's State Income Tax Payable. Assuming the withholdings are deposited on a quarterly basis, prepare the journal entry to record the payment.

PRACTICE EXERCISE 4 • SOLUTION

Date		Description	Post. Ref.	Debit	Credit
20--					
July	31	Employees' State Income Tax Payable		28 0 0 0 00	
		Cash			28 0 0 0 00
		Issued check for state income			
		tax deposit			

5 Complete Employer's Quarterly Federal Tax Return, Form 941. **Learning Objective**

PRACTICE EXERCISE 5

Based on the Form 941 shown on pages 378–380, what is the difference between Green Sales Company's taxable Social Security wages and taxable Medicare wages? How are the rates for each determined?

PRACTICE EXERCISE 5 • SOLUTION

For taxable Medicare wages, all wages are taxable; so the amount in Column 1 on line 5c of $197,622 is the same amount as on line 2, Wages, tips and other compensation. For taxable Social Security wages of $177,621, only the first $113,700 of wages is taxable; so in this case, some of the employees of Green Sales Company exceeded this limit. The rates of 0.124 and 0.029 represent both the employer's and employees' share of these taxes:

Social Security	6.2% + 6.2%	=	12.4%, or 0.124
Medicare	1.45% + 1.45%	=	2.9%, or 0.029

Learning Objective  Prepare W-2 and W-3 forms and Form 940.

Form W-2 (Wage and Tax Statement) is illustrated on page 380. **Form W-3** (Transmittal of Wage and Tax Statements) is illustrated on page 381. **Form 940** (Employer's Annual Federal Unemployment (FUTA) Tax Return) is illustrated on pages 384 and 385.

PRACTICE EXERCISE 6

What do Form W-2, Form W-3, and Form 940 have in common?

PRACTICE EXERCISE 6 • SOLUTION

Form W-2, Form W-3, and Form 940 all report the name, address, and Employer Identification Number of the company. (See Figures 3, 4, and 5 on pages 380, 381, and 384–385, respectively.) The total wages should be the same in Box 1 on Form W-3 and on Line 3 on Form 940. All three forms report state information, in this case for Maine.

Learning Objective  Calculate the premium for workers' compensation insurance and prepare the entry for payment in advance.

Rates for **workers' compensation insurance** vary depending on the degree of physical risk involved in different occupations. The amount of the premium equals the predicted annual payroll multiplied by the premium rate. The entry is a debit to Prepaid Insurance, Workers' Compensation and a credit to Cash.

PRACTICE EXERCISE 7

On January 15, Quality Roofing estimated the following payroll for the year:

Classification	Predicted Payroll	Rate (Percent)
Clerical/office work	$150,000	0.11
Project estimators	200,000	0.15
Roofer construction	670,000	2.20

Calculate the estimated premium and prepare the journal entry to record payment.

PRACTICE EXERCISE 7 • SOLUTION

Classification	Predicted Payroll	Rate per Hundred (Percent)	Estimated Premium	
Clerical/office work	$150,000	0.11	($150,000 ÷ 100) × 0.11 =	$ 165.00
Project estimators	200,000	0.15	($200,000 ÷ 100) × 0.15 =	300.00
Roofer construction	670,000	2.20	($670,000 ÷ 100) × 2.20 =	14,740.00
			Total estimated premium	$15,205.00

Date		Description	Post. Ref.	Debit	Credit
20--					
Jan.	15	Prepaid Insurance, Workers'			
		Compensation		15 2 0 5 00	
		Cash			15 2 0 5 00
		To record payment of estimated			
		workers' compensation premium			
		for 20--.			

8 Determine the amount of the end-of-the-year adjustments for (a) workers' compensation insurance and (b) accrued salaries and wages and record the adjustments.

Learning Objective

When the total annual payroll is known, the exact cost of workers' compensation insurance can be determined by multiplying the total payroll by the premium rate. Two adjusting entries are required. The first adjusting entry records the expired insurance as a debit to Workers' Compensation Insurance Expense and a credit to Prepaid Insurance, Workers' Compensation. The second adjusting entry records the difference between the estimated and actual premiums. If the actual premium is greater than the premium that was paid in advance, the entry is a debit to Workers' Compensation Insurance Expense and a credit to Workers' Compensation Insurance Payable. The adjustment for accrued salaries and wages accounts for the additional amount of salaries or wages paid in the next payroll that are incurred in the current fiscal period—a debit to Wages (or Salary) Expense. The credit to Wages (or Salaries) Payable accounts for the additional amount of liability incurred in the current period that will be paid with the next payroll that occurs in the following fiscal period.

PRACTICE EXERCISE 8

a. At the end of the year, Quality Roofing had the following payroll:

Classification	Actual Payroll	Rate (Percent)
Clerical/office work	$189,000	0.11
Project estimators	195,000	0.15
Roofer construction	695,000	2.20

(Continued)

Determine the amount of the end-of-the-year adjustment for workers' compensation insurance and prepare the journal entries to record the year-end adjustments for the insurance expired and the additional premium.

b. Assume that Quality Roofing had $2,000 of salaries accrue for the time between the last payday and the end of the year. Record the adjusting entry for the accrued salaries.

PRACTICE EXERCISE 8 • SOLUTION

a.

Classification	Actual Payroll	Rate per Hundred (Percent)	Exact Premium
Clerical/office work	$189,000	0.11	($189,000 ÷ 100) × 0.11 = $ 207.90
Project estimators	195,000	0.15	($195,000 ÷ 100) × 0.15 = 292.50
Roofer construction	695,000	2.20	($695,000 ÷ 100) × 2.20 = 15,290.00
			Total exact premium $15,790.40

The amount of the unpaid premium is

$15,790.40	Total exact premium
15,205.00	Less total estimated premium paid (from Practice Exercise 7)
$ 585.40	Additional premium owed

Date		Description	Post. Ref.	Debit	Credit
20--		Adjusting Entries			
Dec.	31	Workers' Compensation Insurance Expense		15 2 0 5 00	
		Prepaid Insurance, Workers' Compensation			15 2 0 5 00
	31	Workers' Compensation Insurance Expense		5 8 5 40	
		Workers' Compensation Insurance Payable			5 8 5 40

b.

Date		Description	Post. Ref.	Debit	Credit
20--		Adjusting Entry			
Dec.	31	Salary Expense		2 0 0 0 00	
		Salaries Payable			2 0 0 0 00

Glossary

Electronic Federal Tax Payment System (EFTPS) Federal tax deposits are made using this system. Payments can be made 24 hours a day, 7 days a week. Businesses can schedule payments up to 120 days in advance of the due date. To be considered on time, tax deposits must be scheduled at least one calendar day prior to the due date. (*p. 371*)

Employer Identification Number (EIN) The number assigned to each employer by the Internal Revenue Service for use in the submission of reports and payments for FICA taxes and federal income tax withheld. (*p. 367*)

Federal unemployment tax (FUTA) A tax levied only on the employer that is equal to 0.6 percent of the first $7,000 of total earnings paid to each employee during the calendar year. This tax is used to administer the funds. (*p. 369*)

Form 940 An annual report filed by employers showing total wages paid to employees, total wages subject to federal unemployment tax, total federal unemployment tax, and other information. Also called the *Employer's Annual Federal Unemployment (FUTA) Tax Return*. (*p. 382*)

Form 941 A quarterly report showing the tax liability for withholdings of employees' federal income tax and FICA taxes and the employer's share of FICA taxes. Total tax deposits made in the quarter are also listed on this Employer's Quarterly Federal Tax Return. (*p. 375*)

Form 941-V A payment voucher completed when making payments with the 941 report. (*p. 376*)

Form W-2 A form containing information about employee earnings and tax deductions for the year. Also called *Wage and Tax Statement*. (*p. 380*)

Form W-3 An annual report sent to the Social Security Administration listing the total wages and tips, total federal income tax withheld, total Social Security and Medicare taxable wages, total Social Security and Medicare tax withheld, and other information for all employees of a firm. Also called the *Transmittal of Wage and Tax Statements*. (*p. 381*)

Payroll Tax Expense A general expense account used for recording the employer's portion of the FICA taxes, the federal unemployment tax, and the state unemployment tax. (*p. 367*)

Quarter Three consecutive months. (*p. 372*)

State unemployment tax (SUTA) A tax levied against employers by most states based on a portion of employee earnings during the calendar year. Rates and earning limits vary among states. The proceeds are used to pay subsistence benefits to unemployed workers. (*p. 369*)

Workers' compensation insurance This insurance paid for by the employer provides benefits for employees injured or killed on the job. The rates vary according to the degree of risk inherent in the job. The plans may be sponsored by states or by private firms. The employer generally pays the premium in advance at the beginning of the year based on the estimated payroll. The rates are adjusted after the exact payroll is known. (*p. 386*)

Quiz Yourself

_____ 1. Which of the following is *not* considered a payroll tax expense?
   a. FICA Social Security
   b. Federal income tax withholding
   c. FICA Medicare
   d. FUTA
   e. SUTA

_____ 2. When is Form 941 submitted?
   a. Annually
   b. Semiannually
   c. Quarterly
   d. Monthly
   e. Semiweekly

_____ 3. The entry to record the payment of state unemployment tax is __________.
   a. Payroll Tax Expense DR; State Unemployment Tax Payable CR
   b. State Unemployment Tax Payable DR; Payroll Tax CR
   c. State Unemployment Tax Payable DR; Cash CR
   d. Cash DR; State Unemployment Tax Payable CR
   e. None of the above

(*Continued*)

_____ 4. The payment of employees' state income tax results in which of the following?
a. DR Cash
b. CR Employees' State Income Tax Payable
c. CR Cash
d. DR Employees' State Income Tax Expense
e. None of the above

_____ 5. The federal unemployment tax (FUTA) is paid by the _________.
a. Employee
b. State government
c. Local government
d. Employer
e. Employee and employer equally

_____ 6. The form also known as the Wage and Tax Statement is __________.
a. Form 941
b. Form 940
c. the State Income Reporting Form
d. Form W-3
e. Form W-2

_____ 7. Workers' compensation insurance premiums are based on which of the following?
a. Job risk
b. Percentage of payroll
c. Job classification
d. Company's claim history
e. All of the above

_____ 8. The adjusting entry for expired workers' compensation premium is _____.
a. Workers' Compensation Insurance Payable DR; Cash CR
b. Cash DR; Workers' Compensation Insurance Expense CR
c. Workers' Compensation Insurance Expense DR; Prepaid Insurance CR
d. Prepaid Insurance DR; Workers' Compensation Insurance Expense CR
e. Workers' Compensation Insurance Expense DR; Cash CR

_____ 9. Which of the following is *not* an internal control for preventing or detecting payroll fraud?
a. Having only one person responsible for the payroll function due to confidentiality concerns
b. Requiring mandatory vacations for payroll personnel
c. Increasing the use of direct deposits
d. Outsourcing payroll administration
e. Conducting periodic unannounced audits

Answers:
1.b 2.c 3.c 4.c 5.d 6.e 7.e 8.c 9.a

Review It with QuickBooks®

_____ 1. The general journal can be modified to only show payroll information by all of the following, *except*
a. customizing the report using transaction type filter Paycheck
b. customizing the report using transaction type filter Pay Employees
c. customizing the report using transaction type filter Payroll Liabilities
d. Both a and c

_____ 2. Payroll taxes can be paid using which QuickBooks option?
a. Pay Employees
b. Time Tracking
c. Pay Liabilities
d. After-the-Fact Payroll

_____ 3. The tax worksheet option in QuickBooks provides tax information for all of the following tax forms, *except*
a. Form 941.
b. Form 940.
c. W-4.
d. W-2/W3.

_____ 4. How do you access the tax worksheet in QuickBooks?
a. Reports > Accountant & Taxes > More Payment Reports in Excel
b. Reports > Employees & Payroll > More Payment Reports in Excel
c. Reports > Enhanced Payroll Reports
d. Reports > Employees & Payroll > Payroll Liability Balances

Answers:
1.d 2.c 3.c 4.b

CHAPTER ASSIGNMENTS

Chapter Assignments

Discussion Questions

1. What taxes are employers accounting for that increase the debit to Payroll Tax Expense?
2. Describe the journal entry to:
   a. Record the payroll.
   b. Record the employer's payroll tax contributions.
   c. Pay the payroll.
   d. Pay the state and federal unemployment taxes.
   e. Pay the FICA (Social Security and Medicare) and Federal Income Tax withholding.
   f. Pay the state income tax withholding.
3. Explain the deposit requirement for federal unemployment tax.
4. What is the purpose of Form 941? How often is it prepared, and what are the due dates?
5. How many copies are made of a Form W-2? Who uses the copies of the W-2 form?
6. What is the purpose of Form 940? How often is it prepared, and what is the due date?
7. Generally, what is the time schedule for payment of workers' compensation insurance premiums?
8. Explain the advantage of establishing a tax calendar.
9. Explain how payroll fraud can be prevented.

Exercises

LO 1

Practice Exercise 1

EXERCISE 8-1 Signature Company's partial payroll register for the week ended January 7 is as follows:

	A	C	F	G	H	I	J
1					TAXABLE EARNINGS		
2		BEGINNING		ENDING			
3		CUMULATIVE	TOTAL	CUMULATIVE		SOCIAL	
4	NAME	EARNINGS	EARNINGS	EARNINGS	UNEMPLOYMENT	SECURITY	MEDICARE
5	Barney, R. S.	—	1932.00	1932.00	1932.00	1932.00	1932.00
6	Fisk, M. C.	—	567.00	567.00	567.00	567.00	567.00
7	Hayes, W. O.	—	483.00	483.00	483.00	483.00	483.00
8	Lee, L. B.	—	679.00	679.00	679.00	679.00	679.00
9	Parks, S. J	—	578.00	578.00	578.00	578.00	578.00
10	Tempy, E. B.	—	546.00	546.00	546.00	546.00	546.00
11			4,785.00	4,785.00	4,785.00	4,785.00	4,785.00
12							

Assume that the payroll is subject to an employer's Social Security tax of 6.2 percent on the first $113,700 and a Medicare tax of 1.45 percent on all earnings. Also assume that the federal unemployment tax is 0.6 percent, and that the state unemployment tax is 5.4 percent of the first $7,000. Give the entry in general journal form to record the payroll tax expense.

CHAPTER ASSIGNMENTS

LO 1

Practice Exercise 1

EXERCISE 8-2 On January 14, at the end of the second week of the year, the totals of Castle Company's payroll register showed that its store employees' wages amounted to $33,482 and that its warehouse wages amounted to $13,560. Withholdings consisted of federal income taxes, $5,110; employer's Social Security taxes at the rate of 6.2 percent; and employees' Social Security taxes at a rate of 6.2 percent. Both the employer's and employees' Social Security taxes are based on the first $113,700, and no employee has reached the limit. Additional withholdings were Medicare taxes at the rate of 1.45 percent on all earnings and charitable contributions withheld, $845.

a. Calculate the amount of Social Security and Medicare taxes to be withheld and write the general journal entry to record the payroll. Round answers to two decimal places.
b. Write the general journal entry to record the employer's payroll taxes assuming that the federal unemployment tax is 0.6 percent of the first $7,000, that the state unemployment tax is 5.4 percent of the same base, and that no employee has surpassed the $7,000 limit.

LO 1

Practice Exercise 1

EXERCISE 8-3 Go Systems had the following payroll data for wages for the week ended February 5. The state income tax is assumed to be 20% of the federal income tax.

	F	G	H	I	J	K	L	M	N
1			TAXABLE EARNINGS			DEDUCTIONS			
2		ENDING						SOCIAL	
3	TOTAL	CUMULATIVE		SOCIAL		FEDERAL	STATE	SECURITY	MEDICARE
4	EARNINGS	EARNINGS	UNEMPLOYMENT	SECURITY	MEDICARE	INCOME TAX	INCOME TAX	TAX	TAX
5									
6	6,770.00	27,850.00	6,770.00	6,770.00	6,770.00	1,015.00	203.00	419.74	98.17
7									

a. Write the general journal entry to record the payroll.
b. Write the general journal entry to record the employer's payroll taxes. Assume rates of 0.6 percent for federal unemployment tax and 5.4 percent for state unemployment tax based on the first $7,000 for each employee. Also assume that no employee has earned more than $7,000. Round answers to two decimal places.

LO 1

Practice Exercise 1

EXERCISE 8-4 The information on earnings and deductions for the pay period ended December 14 from King Company's payroll records is as follows:

Name	Gross Pay	Beginning Cumulative Earnings
Burgess, J. L.	$ 410	$ 6,750
Clayton, M. E.	785	40,200
Drugden, T. F.	860	38,500
Lui, L. W.	990	39,700
Sparks, C. R.	4,094	110,900
Stevers, D. H.	850	6,810

For each employee, the Social Security tax is 6.2 percent of the first $113,700 and the employer's Social Security tax is 6.2 percent on the same earnings limit. The Medicare tax is 1.45 percent on all earnings. The federal unemployment tax rate is 0.6 percent of the first $7,000 of earnings of each employee. The state unemployment tax rate is 5.4 percent of the same base. Determine the total taxable earnings for unemployment, Social Security, and Medicare. Prepare a general journal entry to record the employer's payroll taxes. Round answers to the two decimal places.

LO 2
Practice Exercise 2

EXERCISE 8-5 Selected columns of Envirocon Company's payroll register for March are as follows. The employer's Social Security tax amount has already been calculated as $3,124.34. The employees' FICA Medicare tax rate is matched by the employer.

Payment Date	Employees' Federal Income Tax	Employees' Social Security Tax	Employees' Medicare Tax
March 7	1,125.00	686.43	108.75
14	1,250.00	764.22	121.08
21	1,385.00	845.22	133.91
28	1,357.00	828.47	131.25

Envirocon Company deposits taxes monthly. In general journal form, record the entry for the April 15 payment of FICA and federal income taxes for employees and employer.

LO 2, 3
Practice Exercises 2, 3

EXERCISE 8-6 On September 30, Cody Company's selected account balances are as follows:

Employees' Federal Income Tax Payable	$4,738.00
FICA Taxes Payable (employer, $2,604.46; employee, $2,604.46)	5,208.92
State Unemployment Tax Payable	2,200.00
Federal Unemployment Tax Payable	570.00

(Some employees have reached the limit.)

In general journal form, prepare the entries to record the following:

Oct. 15 Payment of liabilities for FICA taxes and the federal income tax.
31 Payment of liability for state unemployment tax.
31 Payment of liability for federal unemployment tax.

LO 2, 3
Practice Exercises 2, 3

EXERCISE 8-7 On September 30, Hilltop Company's selected payroll accounts are as follows:

FICA Taxes Payable

−	+
	Sept. 30 2,314.84 (employer)
	Sept. 30 2,314.84 (employee)

State Unemployment Tax Payable

−	+
	Sept. 30 1,183.40

Federal Unemployment Tax Payable

−	+
	Sept. 30 575.32

Employees' Federal Income Tax Payable

−	+
	Sept. 30 3,210.85

Prepare general journal entries to record the following:

Oct. 15 Payment of federal tax deposit of FICA taxes and the federal income tax.
31 Payment of state unemployment tax.
31 Payment of federal unemployment tax.

CHAPTER ASSIGNMENTS

CHAPTER ASSIGNMENTS

LO 7, 8

Practice Exercises 7, 8

EXERCISE 8-8 Great Manufacturing Company received and paid a premium notice on January 2 for workers' compensation insurance stating the rates for the new year. Estimated employees' earnings for the year are as follows:

Classification	Estimated Wages and Salaries	Rate per Hundred (Percent)	Estimated Premium
Office clerical	$ 92,000	0.11	$ 101.20
Warehouse work	29,000	0.92	266.80
Manufacturing	264,000	2.20	5,808.00
			$6,176.00

At the end of the year, the exact figures for the payroll are as follows:

Classification	Actual Wages and Salaries	Rate per Hundred (Percent)	Exact Premium
Office clerical	$ 93,000	0.11	$ 102.30
Warehouse work	30,000	0.92	276.00
Manufacturing	267,000	2.20	5,874.00
			$6,252.30

a. Record the entry in general journal form for the payment on January 2 of the estimated premium.

b. Record the adjusting entries on December 31 for the insurance expired and for the additional premium.

Problem Set A

LO 1

PROBLEM 8-1A Mooney Labs had the following payroll for the week ended February 28:

Salaries		**Deductions**	
Technicians' salaries	$6,955.00	Federal income tax withheld	$1,145.00
Office salaries	2,260.00	Social Security tax withheld	571.33
Total	$9,215.00	Medicare tax withheld	133.62
		Charity withheld	165.00
		Total	$2,014.95

Assumed tax rates are as follows:

a. FICA: Social Security (employer) 6.2 percent (0.062) and (employee) 6.2 percent (0.062) on the first $113,700 for each employee and Medicare, 1.45 percent (0.0145) on all earnings for each employee.
b. State unemployment tax, 5.4 percent (0.054) on the first $7,000 for each employee.
c. Federal unemployment tax, 0.6 percent (0.006) on the first $7,000 for each employee.

Required

Record the following entries in general journal form:

1. The payroll entry as of February 28.
2. The entry to record the employer's payroll taxes as of February 28 assuming that the total payroll is subject to the FICA taxes (combined Social Security and Medicare) and that $5,490 is subject to unemployment taxes.
3. The payment to the employees on March 2. (Assume that the company has transferred cash to Cash—Payroll Bank Account for this payroll.)

Check Figure
Payroll Tax Expense, $1,034.35

1

PROBLEM 8-2A Complete Accounting Services has the following payroll information for the week ended December 7. State income tax is computed as 20 percent of federal income tax.

	A	C	F	K	L
1				DEDUCTIONS	
2		BEGINNING			
3		CUMULATIVE		FEDERAL	STATE
4	NAME	EARNINGS	TOTAL EARNINGS	INCOME TAX	INCOME TAX
5	Denato, T.	6,820.00	480.00	11.00	2.20
6	Herrera, M.	6,840.00	470.00	10.00	2.00
7	Joyner, J.	36,320.00	740.00	47.00	9.40
8	King, L.	26,200.00	540.00	17.00	3.40
9	Wilson, M.	111,260.00	2,720.00	474.49	94.90
10	Yee, N.	28,426.00	605.00	26.00	5.20

Assumed tax rates are as follows:

a. FICA: Social Security (employer) 6.2 percent (0.062) and (employee) 6.2 percent (0.062) on the first $113,700 for each employee and Medicare, 1.45 percent (0.0145) on all earnings for each employee.
b. State unemployment tax, 5.4 percent (0.054) on the first $7,000 for each employee.
c. Federal unemployment tax, 0.6 percent (0.006) on the first $7,000 for each employee.

Required*

1. Complete the payroll register. Payroll checks begin with Ck. No. 5714 in the payroll register.
2. Prepare a general journal entry to record the payroll as of December 7. The company's general ledger contains a Salary Expense account and a Salaries Payable account.
3. Prepare a general journal entry to record the payroll taxes as of December 7.
4. Journalize the entry to pay the payroll on December 9. (Assume that the company has transferred cash to the Cash—Payroll Bank Account for this payroll.)

Check Figure
Payroll Tax Expense, $428.00

*If you are using this problem with QuickBooks, refer to the Try it with QuickBooks requirements on page 419.

LO 5

PROBLEM 8-3A For the third quarter of the year, Johnson Company, 415 Circle Avenue, Chicago, Illinois 60652, received Form 941 from the Internal Revenue Service. The identification number of Johnson Company is 91-4213171. Its payroll for the quarter ended September 30 is as follows:

	A	F	I	J	K	M	N
1			TAXABLE EARNINGS		DEDUCTIONS		
2							
3		TOTAL	SOCIAL		FEDERAL	SOCIAL	MEDICARE
4	NAME	EARNINGS	SECURITY	MEDICARE	INCOME TAX	SECURITY TAX	TAX
5	Brown, D. D.	16,629.00	16,629.00	16,629.00	2,494.00	1,031.00	241.12
6	Carey, L. R.	18,528.00	18,528.00	18,528.00	2,780.00	1,148.74	268.66
7	Domzalski, T. P.	14,665.00	14,665.00	14,665.00	2,100.00	909.23	212.64
8	Grisson, R. O.	13,721.00	13,721.00	13,721.00	2,058.00	850.70	198.95
9	Tyler, J. L.	17,406.00	17,406.00	17,406.00	2,510.00	1,079.17	252.39
10	Valdez, K. R.	15,287.00	15,287.00	15,287.00	2,295.00	947.79	221.66
11		96,236.00	96,236.00	96,236.00	14,237.00	5,966.63	1,395.42

The company has had six employees throughout the year. Assume that the FICA Social Security (employer) rate is 6.2 percent and the FICA Social Security (employee) rate is 6.2 percent on the first $113,700 and that the Medicare tax is 1.45 percent of all earnings. The employer matches the employees' FICA Medicare taxes. There are no taxable tips, adjustments, backup withholding, or earned income credits. Johnson Company has submitted the following federal tax deposits and written the accompanying checks:

On August 15 for the July Payroll		On September 15 for the August Payroll		On October 15 for the September Payroll	
Employees' income tax withheld	$4,370.00	Employees' income tax withheld	$5,122.00	Employees' income tax withheld	$4,745.00
Employees' Social Security and Medicare tax withheld	2,259.76	Employees' Social Security and Medicare tax withheld	2,326.28	Employees' Social Security and Medicare tax withheld	2,776.01
Employer's Social Security and Medicare tax contributed	2,259.76	Employer's Social Security and Medicare tax contributed	2,326.28	Employer's Social Security and Medicare tax contributed	2,776.01
	$8,889.52		$9,774.56		$10,297.02

Check Figure
Total taxes, $28,961.11

Required

Complete Part 1 of Form 941 for the third quarter for Johnson Company.

LO 1, 2, 3

PROBLEM 8-4A Lynden Company has the following balances in its general ledger as of June 1 of this year:

a. FICA Taxes Payable (liability for May), $1,719.40 (total for employee and employer).
b. Employees' Federal Income Tax Payable (liability for May), $995.00.
c. Federal Unemployment Tax Payable (liability for April and May), $380.00.
d. State Unemployment Tax Payable (liability for April and May), $1,205.75.

The company completed the following transactions involving the payroll during June and July:

June 13 Issued check for $2,714.40, payable to Security Bank, for the monthly deposit of May FICA taxes and employees' federal income tax withheld.

30 Recorded the payroll entry in the general journal from the payroll register for June. The payroll register has the following column totals:

Sales salaries	$11,490.00	
Office salaries	5,147.00	
Total earnings		$16,637.00
Employees' federal income tax deductions	$ 1,725.00	
Employees' Social Security tax deductions	1,031.49	
Employees' Medicare tax deductions	241.24	
Total deductions		2,997.73
Net pay		$13,639.27

30 Recorded payroll taxes. FICA Social Security rates are 6.2 percent (employee) and 6.2 percent (employer). The employer matches the employee's FICA Medicare rate of 1.45 percent. State unemployment tax is 5.4 percent, and federal unemployment tax is 0.6 percent. At this time, all employees' earnings are taxable for FICA and unemployment taxes.

30 Issued check for $13,639.27 from Cash—Payroll Bank Account to pay salaries for the month.

July 14 Issued check for $4,270.46, payable to Security Bank, for the monthly deposit of June FICA taxes (employee and employer) and employees' federal income tax withheld.

31 Issued check for $2,104.15, payable to the State Tax Commission, for state unemployment tax for April, May, and June. The check was accompanied by the quarterly tax return.

31 Issued check for $479.82, payable to Security Bank, for the deposit of federal unemployment tax for April, May, and June.

Check Figure
Payroll Tax Expense, $2,270.95

Required

If using Working Papers, record the transactions on pages 77–78 of the general journal.

6

Problem 8-5A Jack's Lawn Service Company has the following information related to its current year payroll as of December 31:

a. Federal Unemployment Tax Payable as of December 31, $336.00
b. FUTA taxable earnings limit of $7,000, rate 0.6 percent (0.006)
c. First-quarter FUTA taxable liability, $504.00, paid April 30
d. Second-quarter FUTA taxable liability, $168.00 (liability under $500, no payment made)
e. Third-quarter FUTA taxable liability, $112.00 (total liability under $500, no payment made)
f. Fourth-quarter FUTA taxable liability, $56.00 (payment to be made January of the following year)
g. FUTA taxable earnings for the year, $140,000
h. Total Lawn Care Wages, $310,000
i. Jack's Lawn Service Company EIN, 75-1209347
j. No exempt FUTA payments
k. Address: 1515 W. Main Street, Rice, TX 75155

(Continued)

CHAPTER ASSIGNMENTS

Check Figure
Line 14 Balance Due, 336.00

Required

Go to www.irs.gov to locate Form 940. Prepare Form 940 and the corresponding 940-V payment voucher for the year. Then record the appropriate FUTA payment entry in the journal.

Problem Set B

LO 1

PROBLEM 8-1B Kovarik Company had the following payroll for the week ended March 21:

Salaries		**Deductions**	
Sales salaries	$7,620.00	Federal income tax withheld	$1,094.00
Office salaries	1,790.00	Social Security tax withheld	583.42
Total	$9,410.00	Medicare tax withheld	136.45
		Charity withheld	153.00
		Total	$1,966.87

Assumed tax rates are as follows:

a. FICA: Social Security (employer) 6.2 percent (0.062) and (employee) 6.2 percent (0.062) on the first $113,700 for each employee and Medicare, 1.45 percent (0.0145) on all earnings for each employee.
b. State unemployment tax, 5.4 percent (0.054) on the first $7,000 for each employee.
c. Federal unemployment tax, 0.6 percent (0.006) on the first $7,000 for each employee.

Check Figure
Payroll Tax Expense, $1,017.77

Required

Record the following entries in general journal form:

1. The payroll entry as of March 21.
2. The entry to record the employer's payroll taxes as of March 21 assuming that the total payroll is subject to the FICA taxes (combined Social Security and Medicare) and that $4,965 is subject to unemployment taxes.
3. The payment of the employees on March 23. (Assume that the company has transferred cash to Cash—Payroll Bank Account for this payroll.)

LO 1

PROBLEM 8-2B Kay's Agency has the following payroll information for the week ended December 14. State income tax is computed as 20 percent of federal income tax.

	A	C	F	K	L
1				DEDUCTIONS	
2		BEGINNING			
3		CUMULATIVE		FEDERAL	STATE
4	NAME	EARNINGS	TOTAL EARNINGS	INCOME TAX	INCOME TAX
5	Arivilo, R.	10,650.00	460.00	9.00	1.80
6	Baca, T.	38,820.00	970.00	82.00	16.40
7	Eubanks, E.	111,155.00	2,790.00	494.09	98.82
8	Ling, D.	6,750.00	385.00	1.00	0.20
9	Metcalf, S.	31,670.00	694.00	40.00	8.00
10	Quinn, D.	48,961.00	1040.00	92.00	18.40

Assumed tax rates are as follows:

a. FICA: Social Security (employer) 6.2 percent (0.062) and (employee) 6.2 percent (0.062) on the first $113,700 for each employee and Medicare, 1.45 percent (0.0145) on all earnings for each employee.
b. State unemployment tax, 5.4 percent (0.054) on the first $7,000 for each employee.
c. Federal unemployment tax, 0.6 percent (0.006) on the first $7,000 for each employee.

Required*

1. Complete the payroll register. Payroll checks begin with Ck. No. 5923 in the payroll register.
2. Prepare a general journal entry to record the payroll as of December 14. The company's general ledger contains a Salary Expense account and a Salaries Payable account.
3. Prepare a general journal entry to record the payroll taxes as of December 14.
4. Journalize the entry to pay the payroll on December 16. (Assume that the company has transferred cash to the Cash—Payroll Bank Account for this payroll.)

Check Figure
Payroll Tax Expense, $484.75

*If you are using this problem with QuickBooks, refer to the Try it with QuickBooks requirements on page 419.

LO 5

PROBLEM 8-3B For the third quarter of the year, Barney Construction, 715 Red Rock Boulevard, San Francisco, California 94121, received Form 941 from the District Office of the Internal Revenue Service. The identification number for Barney Construction is 91-7382476. Its payroll for the quarter ended September 30 is as follows.

	A	F	I	J	K	M	N
1			TAXABLE EARNINGS		DEDUCTIONS		
2							
3		TOTAL	SOCIAL		FEDERAL	SOCIAL	MEDICARE
4	NAME	EARNINGS	SECURITY	MEDICARE	INCOME TAX	SECURITY TAX	TAX
5	Britton, D. L.	13,387.00	13,387.00	13,387.00	2,010.00	829.99	194.11
6	Finn, J. A.	16,753.00	16,753.00	16,753.00	2,510.00	1,038.69	242.92
7	Harrell, N. E.	17,780.00	17,780.00	17,780.00	2,767.00	1,102.36	257.81
8	Kelly, T. L.	16,243.00	16,243.00	16,243.00	2,430.00	1,007.07	235.52
9	Morton, S. M.	14,215.00	14,215.00	14,215.00	2,130.00	881.33	206.12
10	Rieck, A. J.	20,264.00	20,264.00	20,264.00	3,040.00	1,256.37	293.83
11		98,642.00	98,642.00	98,642.00	14,887.00	6,115.81	1,430.31

The company has had six employees throughout the year. Assume that the FICA Social Security (employer) is 6.2 percent and the FICA Social Security (employee) is 6.2 percent on the first $113,700 and that the Medicare tax is 1.45 percent of all earnings. The employer matches the employees' FICA Medicare taxes. There are no taxable tips, adjustments, backup withholding, or earned income credits. Barney Construction has submitted the following federal tax deposits and written the accompanying checks:

On August 15 for the July Payroll		On September 15 for the August Payroll		On October 15 for the September Payroll	
Employees' income tax withheld	$ 5,226.00	Employees' income tax withheld	$ 5,059.00	Employees' income tax withheld	$4,602.00
Employees' Social Security and Medicare tax withheld	2,597.21	Employees' Social Security and Medicare tax withheld	2,591.58	Employees' Social Security and Medicare tax withheld	2,357.33
Employer's Social Security and Medicare tax contributed	2,597.21	Employer's Social Security and Medicare tax contributed	2,591.58	Employer's Social Security and Medicare tax contributed	2,357.33
	$10,420.42		$10,242.16		$9,316.66

(*Continued*)

Check Figure
Total taxes, $29,979.23

Required

Complete Part 1 of Form 941 for the third quarter for Barney Construction.

LO 1, 2, 3

PROBLEM 8-4B Grande Company has the following balances in its general ledger as of March 1 of this year:

a. FICA Taxes Payable (liability for February), $9,180.00 (total for employee and employer).
b. Employees' Federal Income Tax Payable (liability for February), $9,000.00.
c. State Unemployment Tax Payable (liability for January and February), $3,442.50.
d. Federal Unemployment Tax Payable (liability for January and February), $510.00.

The company completed the following transactions involving the payroll during March and April:

Mar. 12 Issued check for $18,180.00, payable to Coast Bank, for the monthly deposit of February FICA taxes and employees' federal income tax withheld.

31 Recorded the payroll entry in the general journal from the payroll register for March. The payroll register had the following column totals:

Sales salaries	$47,654.00	
Office salaries	11,982.00	
Total earnings		$59,636.00
Employees' federal income tax deductions	$ 8,945.40	
Employees' Social Security tax deductions	3,697.43	
Employees' Medicare tax deductions	864.72	
Total deductions		13,507.55
Net pay		$46,128.45

31 Recorded payroll taxes. FICA Social Security rates are 6.2 percent (employee) and 6.2 percent (employer). The employer matches the employee's FICA Medicare rate of 1.45 percent. State unemployment tax is 5.4 percent. Federal unemployment tax is 0.6 percent. At this time, all employees' earnings are taxable for FICA and $1,000 of the earnings are taxable for unemployment taxes.

31 Issued check for $46,128.45 from Cash—Payroll Bank Account to pay salaries for the month.

Apr. 14 Issued check for $18,069.70, payable to Coast Bank, for the monthly deposit of March FICA taxes (employee and employer) and employees' federal income tax withheld.

30 Issued check for $3,496.50, payable to State Department of Revenue, for state unemployment tax for January, February, and March. The check was accompanied by the quarterly tax return.

30 Issued check for $516.00, payable to Coast Bank, for the deposit of federal unemployment tax for the months of January, February, and March.

Check Figure
Payroll Tax Expense, $4,622.15

Required

If using Working Papers, record the transactions on pages 77–78 of the general journal.

LO 6

Problem 8-5B Sharon's Dance Studio has the following information related to its current year payroll as of December 31:

a, Federal Unemployment Tax Payable as of December 31, $110.00
b. FUTA taxable earnings limit of $7,000, rate 0.6 percent (0.006)
c. First-quarter FUTA taxable liability, $520.00, paid April 30

d. Second-quarter FUTA taxable liability, $45.00 (liability under $500, no payment made)
e. Third-quarter FUTA taxable liability, $39.00 (total liability under $500, no payment made)
f. Fourth-quarter FUTA taxable liability, $26.00 (payment to be made January of the following year)
g. FUTA taxable earnings for the year, $105,000
h. Total Dance Instructor Wages, $195,000
i. Sharon's Dance Studio EIN, 75-9182736
j. No exempt FUTA payments
k. Address: 392 E. Michigan Ave., Smithville, TX 78957

Required

Go to www.irs.gov to locate Form 940. Prepare Form 940 and the corresponding 940-V payment voucher for the year. Then record the appropriate FUTA payment entry in the journal.

Check Figure
Line 14 Balance Due, 110.00

Try It with QuickBooks® (LO 1, 2, 3)

QB Exercise 8-1

Complete the payroll in QuickBooks for Complete Accounting Services using Problem 8-2A on page 413.

Required

1. Restore the QuickBooks data file for Complete Accounting Services. The data file is located on the textbook website. All accounts needed for this problem have been set up in the chart of accounts. Cash is the bank account for payroll.
2. From the **Pay Employees** icon on the home page, complete the payroll for December 7. Use the year 2015.
3. As you enter the payroll information for each employee, calculate the FICA Social Security and Medicare taxes (employee and employer), as well as the state and federal unemployment taxes.
4. Select the **Print paychecks** from QuickBooks option. Payroll checks begin with Ck. No. 5714.
5. Select the **Print Pay Stubs** option.
6. Prepare a payroll journal report for the paychecks from this payroll period.
   a. What is the total salary expense for this payroll period?
   b. What is the salaries payable for this payroll period?
7. Prepare a payroll summary report for this payroll period.
8. Prepare a payroll liability balances report for this payroll period.
9. Pay the payroll liabilities for FICA Social Security and Medicare taxes (employee and employer), as well as the state and federal unemployment taxes. FICA Social Security, Medicare taxes, federal taxes withheld, and federal unemployment taxes are paid to the U.S. Treasury. State unemployment taxes are paid to Treasurer, State of Maine.
10. Prepare a quarterly Form 941 tax worksheet for Complete Accounting Services.
    a. What is the total income subject to Social Security tax for this report?
    b. What is the total Form 941 tax due for this report?

(*Continued*)

QB Exercise 8-2

Complete the payroll in QuickBooks for Kay's Agency using Problem 8-2B on pages 416–417.

Required

1. Restore the QuickBooks data file for Kay's Agency. The data file is located on the textbook website. All accounts needed for this problem have been set up in the chart of accounts. Cash is the bank account for payroll.
2. From the **Pay Employees** icon on the home page, complete the payroll for December 14. Use the year 2015.
3. As you enter the payroll information for each employee, calculate the FICA Social Security and Medicare taxes (employee and employer), as well as the state and federal unemployment taxes.
4. Select the **Print paychecks** from QuickBooks option. Payroll checks begin with Ck. No. 5923.
5. Select the **Print Pay Stubs** option.
6. Prepare a payroll journal report for the paychecks from this payroll period.
   a. What is the total salary expense for this payroll period?
   b. What is the salaries payable for this payroll period?
7. Prepare a payroll summary report for this payroll period.
8. Prepare a payroll liability balances report for this payroll period.
9. Pay the payroll liabilities for FICA Social Security and Medicare taxes (employee and employer), as well as the state and federal unemployment taxes. FICA Social Security, Medicare taxes, federal taxes withheld, and federal unemployment taxes are paid to the U.S. Treasury. State unemployment taxes are paid to Treasurer, State of Maine.
10. Prepare a quarterly Form 941 tax worksheet for Kay's Agency.
    a. What is the total income subject to Social Security tax for this report?
    b. What is the total Form 941 tax due for this report?

Activities

Why Does It Matter?

TRUGREEN, Memphis, Tennessee
PAWTUCKET RED SOX, Pawtucket, Rhode Island
HOCK IT TO ME, Albuquerque, New Mexico

TruGreen is the world's largest lawn and landscape company, employing over 10,000 employees and serving more than 3.4 million customers through its 270 locations.

The Pawtucket Red Sox is a minor league baseball affiliate of the Boston Red Sox. The team's current roster consists of 24 active players, along with the team's manager, coaches, and mascots.

Hock It To Me is a privately owned pawn shop. The company has annual revenue of less than $500,000 and employs a staff of one to four people.

Even though each of these businesses has a unique payroll due to different amounts of salaries or wages, benefits, and withholdings, explain why each business needs to (a) accurately calculate the amount of payroll for each employee, (b) determine the amount of payroll taxes for which the employer is liable, (c) make the payroll tax deposits as required, and (d) file the appropriate payroll tax returns on a timely basis.

What Would You Do?

Between the end of one month and the 15th day of the next month, the balance in the employer's business bank account has been getting smaller and smaller. An employee prepares the next payroll and correctly computes the necessary withholding taxes. The employer is supposed to pay accumulated employment taxes on the 15th of the next month. Payday is the last day of the month. However, the employer has used the funds withheld from employees to pay some of the business's bills. He hopes that enough of the customers who owe him money will pay their outstanding debts. If his assumption is true, the checking account will have enough in it to pay the federal deposit on the 15th of the month. Is the employer acting ethically? After all, he says he intends to have enough money in the account for the deposit. Explain your answer.

BEFORE A TEST CHECK: Chapters 6–8

PART I: COMPLETION

1. Checks issued by the depositor that have been paid or have cleared the bank are called __________ checks.
2. A deposit that is not recorded on the bank statement because it was made after the bank's closing date for preparation of bank statements is called a(n) __________.
3. The process by which the payee transfers ownership of the check to a bank or another party is called a(n) __________.
4. The person to whom a check is payable is called the __________.
5. A cash fund used to make small immediate cash payments is called a(n) __________.

PART II: APPLICATION

1. Cheryl Chang's salary is $3,550 per month. If she works more than 40 hours in one week, she is entitled to overtime pay at the rate of 1½ times her regular hourly rate. During the current week, she worked 45 hours. Calculate her gross pay.
2. On June 30, the column totals of Expert Training's payroll register showed that its training employees had earned $18,000 and its office employees had earned $6,000. Social Security taxes were withheld at 6.2 percent, and Medicare taxes were withheld at 1.45 percent. All earnings are taxable. Other deductions consisted of federal income tax, $3,600, and charitable contributions to the United Way, $500. Determine the amount of Social Security and Medicare taxes that should be withheld. Give the general journal entry to record the payroll, crediting Salaries Payable for the net pay.
3. Roxy Company's payroll for the week ended December 31 is as follows:

Gross earnings of employees	$155,000
Social Security taxable earnings	143,000
Medicare taxable earnings	155,000
Federal unemployment taxable earnings	22,000
State unemployment taxable earnings	22,000

BEFORE A TEST CHECK

Assume that the payroll is subject to employer's Social Security tax of 6.2 percent (0.062), Medicare tax of 1.45 percent (0.0145), federal unemployment tax of 0.6 percent (0.006), and state unemployment tax of 5.4 percent (0.054). Write the entry in general journal form to record the employer's payroll tax expense.

PART III: TRUE/FALSE

T F 1. There is no limit on the amount of taxable earnings for Medicare.

T F 2. When journalizing the entry to reimburse the Petty Cash Fund, include a credit to Petty Cash Fund.

T F 3. When journalizing the entry to account for a customer's NSF check, debit Accounts Payable.

T F 4. An employee's net pay is the result of subtracting his or her deductions from gross pay.

T F 5. The gross pay for an employee who works 45 hours, earns $8.50 per hour, and receives time and a half for hours worked over 40 hours is $402.75.

Answers: Part I

1. canceled 2. deposit in transit or late deposit 3. endorsement 4. payee 5. petty cash fund

Answers: Part II

1.

$3,550 per month × 12 months = $42,600 per year

$42,600 per year ÷ 52 weeks = $819.23 per week (rounded)

$819.23 per week ÷ 40 hours = $20.48 per regular hour (rounded)

$20.48 per regular hour × 1.5 = $30.72 per overtime hour

Earnings for 45 hours:

40 hours at straight time		= $819.23
5 hours overtime	(5 × $30.72) =	153.60
Total gross earnings		$972.83

2.

GENERAL JOURNAL Page ___

Date		Description	Post. Ref.	Debit	Credit
20--					
June	30	Training Salary Expense		18 0 0 0 00	
		Office Salary Expense		6 0 0 0 00	
		Employee's Federal Income Tax			
		Payable			3 6 0 0 00
		FICA Taxes Payable			1 8 3 6 00
		($24,000 × 0.062) + ($24,000 × 0.0145)			
		Employees' United Way Payable			5 0 0 00
		Salaries Payable			18 0 6 4 00
		Payroll register for the week ended,			
		June 30, 20--.			

3.

Date		Description	Post. Ref.	Debit	Credit
20--					
Dec.	31	Payroll Tax Expense		12 4 3 3 50	
		FICA Taxes Payable ($143,000 × 0.062) + ($155,000 × 0.0145)			11 1 1 3 50
		State Unemployment Tax Payable ($22,000 × 0.054)			1 1 8 8 00
		Federal Unemployment Tax Payable ($22,000 × 0.006)			1 3 2 00
		To record employer's share of FICA Taxes and employer's state and federal unemployment taxes.			

Answers: Part III
1. T 2. F 3. F 4. T 5. F

Sales and Purchases

Learning Objectives

After you have completed this chapter, you will be able to do the following:

1. Describe the nature of a merchandising business.
2. Using a general journal and the periodic inventory system, record sales and sale-related transactions; then post to the general ledger and the accounts receivable ledger.
3. Prepare a schedule of accounts receivable.
4. Using a general journal and the periodic inventory system, record purchase and purchase-related transactions; then post to the general ledger and the accounts payable ledger.
5. Prepare a schedule of accounts payable.
6. Using a general journal and the perpetual inventory system, record sales and sale-related transactions.
7. Using a general journal and the perpetual inventory system, record purchase and purchase-related transactions.
8. Record transactions in a sales journal and post to the general ledger and accounts receivable ledger.
9. Record transactions in a three-column purchases journal and post to the general ledger and accounts payable ledger.

To: **Amy Roberts, CPA**
Subject: **Sales and Purchases**

Hi Amy,
So far things are going well with the business. Thanks for all of your help and advice. I think I'm ready to expand into the next stage of my business plan. Up until now, I have been offering services, but I would like to start selling products as well. When you get some time, can you help me understand the accounting process for recording sales and purchases of merchandise?
Thanks,
Janie

To: **Janie Conner**
Subject: **RE: Sales and Purchases**

Hi Janie,
Because you are expanding into a merchandising business, you need to use some new accounts for recording sales and purchases and to understand how to record sales tax, merchandise returns, and freight. Let's plan on meeting next week to discuss the following:

_____ 1. What specific accounts you will use with your new merchandise line.
_____ 2. How to journalize sales transactions, sales tax, and sales returns and allowances in the general journal.
_____ 3. How to post to the accounts receivable ledger and general ledger.
_____ 4. How to journalize purchase-related transactions in the general journal.
_____ 5. How to post to the accounts payable ledger and general ledger.
_____ 6. How to handle freight charges on merchandise.
_____ 7. How to prepare schedules for accounts receivables and accounts payable.

I'll give you a call the first of next week to set up a meeting.
Amy

In the previous chapters, we discussed companies that specialized in providing a service, such as Conner's Whitewater Adventures. Now we will turn our focus to companies that buy and sell goods. These types of companies are known as **merchandising businesses**. A merchandising business can be a wholesale or retail business. A wholesale business, which is sometimes called a middleman or a distributor, buys goods from manufacturers and sells them to retailers. A retail business sells goods directly to consumers (the public). Before we begin analyzing transactions, let's take a moment to review the specific accounts for merchandising firms.

Accounting Language

Accounts payable ledger (p. 439)
Accounts receivable ledger (p. 431)
Controlling account (p. 431)
Cost of Goods Sold account (p. 443)
Credit memorandum (p. 429)
FOB destination (p. 437)
FOB shipping point (p. 437)
Invoices (p. 426)
Merchandise inventory (p. 425)
Merchandising businesses (p. 425)
Periodic inventory system (p. 425)
Perpetual inventory system (p. 425)
Purchases account (p. 433)
Purchases journal (p. 447)
Purchases Returns and Allowances account (p. 436)
Sales account (p. 425)
Sales journal (p. 447)
Sales Returns and Allowances account (p. 428)
Sales Tax Payable account (p. 429)
Special journals (p. 447)
Subsidiary ledger (p. 431)

NATURE OF MERCHANDISING BUSINESS

Merchandise inventory consists of a stock of goods that a company buys and intends to resell at a profit. Merchandise should be differentiated from other assets, such as furniture and equipment, that are acquired for use in the business and are not for resale.

Merchandise inventory can be recorded using the periodic inventory system or the perpetual inventory system. The **periodic inventory system** requires that companies periodically take a physical count of merchandise on hand and then attach a value to it. Under the **perpetual inventory system**, companies keep continuous records of inventories so that at any given time they know what they should have on hand and the current cost of each item. In the first part of this chapter, we will assume that the company records merchandise inventory using the periodic inventory system. Later in the chapter, we will demonstrate how to record the journal entries for merchandise inventory under the perpetual inventory system.

Learning Objective

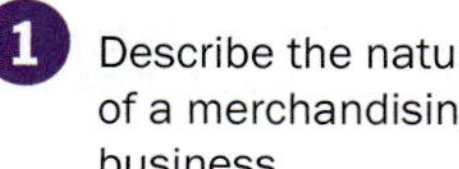
1 Describe the nature of a merchandising business.

SALES TRANSACTIONS

When merchandising firms record sales of merchandise, they use the **Sales account**. The Sales account is a revenue account, has a normal credit balance, and appears on the Income Statement.

Source Documents Related to Sales

In a retail business, a salesperson usually prepares a sales ticket in duplicate or triplicate for a sale on account. One copy goes to the customer, and another copy goes to the accounting department, where it serves as the basis for an entry in the journal. A third copy may be used as a record of sales—to compute sales commissions or control inventory, for example.

In a wholesale business, the company usually receives a written order directly from a customer or through a salesperson who obtained the order from the customer. The credit department approves the order and then sends it to the billing department, where the sales invoice is prepared.

Invoices are prepared in multiple copies and serve as evidence for recording the transaction. Invoice copies should be sent to multiple parties throughout the business such as the sales department, accounting, and the credit department. In addition, the customer should receive a copy of the invoice. The sales invoice for Whitewater Raft Supply's sale of merchandise to Mesa River Raft Company is shown in Figure 1.

Figure 1
Sales invoice

Whitewater Raft Supply

Whitewater Raft Supply
1400 Front Street
Seattle, WA 98101
419-555-6123

Invoice

DATE	INVOICE #
08/01/20--	9384
TERMS	**DUE DATE**
2/10, n/30	08/31/20--

BILL TO
Mesa River Raft Company
5120 Gilman Avenue
Portland, OR 97202
503-555-6123

AMOUNT DUE	ENCLOSED
$1,933.50	

Please detach top portion and return with your payment.

Activity	Description	Quantity	Rate	Discount	Amount
15' Self Bailing Outfitter Raft #22B652		1	1,599.00		1,599.00
8" Outfitter Blades #37B411		2	63.00		126.00
Boat Bags #42B782		3	69.50		208.50
			Total Discount:	$0.00	
				Subtotal:	*$1,933.50*
				Sales Tax:	*$0.00*
				Total:	*$1,933.50*
				Payments:	*$0.00*
				Balance Due:	*$1,933.50*
			TOTAL		**$1,933.50**

Recording Sales Transactions in a General Journal

Sales transactions can be recorded two ways—by recording directly into the general journal or by using a special journal called the sales journal. We will introduce sales transactions using the general journal first. Then, because of the importance of understanding accounting systems, we will introduce the use of the sales journal later in this chapter.

Learning Objective 2 Using a general journal and the periodic inventory system, record sales and sale-related transactions; then post to the general ledger and the accounts receivable ledger.

In the previous chapters, we examined the transactions for Conner's Whitewater Adventures. Conner purchases the Whitewater rafts she uses on her tours from Whitewater Raft Supply. Whitewater Raft Supply is a wholesaler specializing in selling rafts, kayaks, oars, paddles, and other accessories to businesses across the nation.

We will introduce recording sales by looking at five transactions on the books of Whitewater Raft Supply for August.

Aug. 1 Sold merchandise on account to Mesa River Raft Company, invoice no. 9384, $1,933.50.

8 Sold merchandise on account to Green River Rafts, invoice no. 9385, $1,116.

14 Sold merchandise on account to Marty's Fly Fishing Adventures, invoice no. 9386, $1,594.

19 Sold merchandise on account to Hi-Flying Adventures, Inc., invoice no. 9387, $552.30.

25 Sold merchandise on account to Hi-Flying Adventures, Inc., invoice no. 9388, $1,674.

Whitewater Raft Supply will record the transactions into the general journal as follows:

GENERAL JOURNAL Page 26

Date		Description	Post. Ref.	Debit	Credit
20--					
Aug.	1	Accounts Receivable, Mesa River			
		Raft Company		1 9 3 3 50	
		Sales			1 9 3 3 50
		Sold merchandise to Mesa			
		River Raft Company,			
		invoice no. 9384.			
	8	Accounts Receivable, Green			
		River Rafts		1 1 1 6 00	
		Sales			1 1 1 6 00
		Sold merchandise to Green			
		River Rafts, invoice no. 9385.			
	14	Accounts Receivable, Marty's Fly			
		Fishing Adventures		1 5 9 4 00	
		Sales			1 5 9 4 00
		Sold merchandise to Marty's			
		Fly Fishing Adventures,			
		invoice no. 9386.			

(Continued)

GENERAL JOURNAL Page 26

Date		Description	Post. Ref.	Debit	Credit
20--					
Aug.	19	Accounts Receivable, Hi-Flying			
		Adventures, Inc.		552.30	
		Sales			552.30
		Sold merchandise to			
		Hi-Flying Adventures, Inc.,			
		invoice no. 9387.			
	25	Accounts Receivable, Hi-Flying			
		Adventures, Inc.		1,674.00	
		Sales			1,674.00
		Sold merchandise to			
		Hi-Flying Adventures, Inc.,			
		invoice no. 9388.			

Whitewater Raft Supply's accountant records a debit to Accounts Receivable to record the amount each customer owes the company and a credit to Sales for each transaction. The Sales account is credited because it is a revenue account that is used for recording sales of merchandise.

Here's how the accounts appear in the fundamental accounting equation:

Assets		=	Liabilities		+	Capital		−	Drawing		+	Revenue		−	Expenses	
+	−		−	+		−	+		+	−		−	+		+	−
Debit	Credit		Debit	Credit		Debit	Credit		Debit	Credit		Debit	Credit		Debit	Credit

Accounts Receivable	
+	−
1,933.50	
1,116.00	
1,594.00	
552.30	
1,674.00	

Sales	
−	+
	1,933.50
	1,116.00
	1,594.00
	552.30
	1,674.00

Remember that the transactions are recorded assuming that Whitewater Raft Supply records merchandise inventory using the periodic inventory method. If Whitewater Raft Supply used the perpetual inventory method instead, an additional journal entry would be required. This additional journal entry will be discussed later in this chapter.

Sales Returns and Allowances

Occasionally customers will need to return inventory or will ask for a reduction in the original price for a specific reason, such as damaged or defective goods. The **Sales Returns and Allowances account** handles these types of transactions. A *return* is a physical return of the goods. An *allowance* is a reduction from the original price for an agreed-upon reason, such as goods that were defective or damaged. To avoid writing a formal business letter each time to inform customers of their account adjustments, businesses use a special form called a **credit memorandum**. A credit memorandum is a written statement indicating a seller's willingness to reduce the amount of a buyer's debt.

The Sales Returns and Allowances account is a contra account that is deducted from Sales. Using an account separate from Sales provides a better record of the total returns and allowances. Accountants deduct Sales Returns and Allowances from Sales on the income statement to determine net sales.

Returning to the Whitewater Raft Supply example, here's an example of a return. The original sale is repeated here for reference, followed by the issuance of a credit memorandum.

TRANSACTION (a). On August 14, Whitewater Raft Supply sold merchandise on account to Marty's Fly Fishing Adventures, $1,594, and recorded the sale in the general journal.

TRANSACTION (b). On September 5, Marty's Fly Fishing Adventures returned $254 worth of the merchandise. Whitewater Raft Supply issued credit memorandum no. 1069.

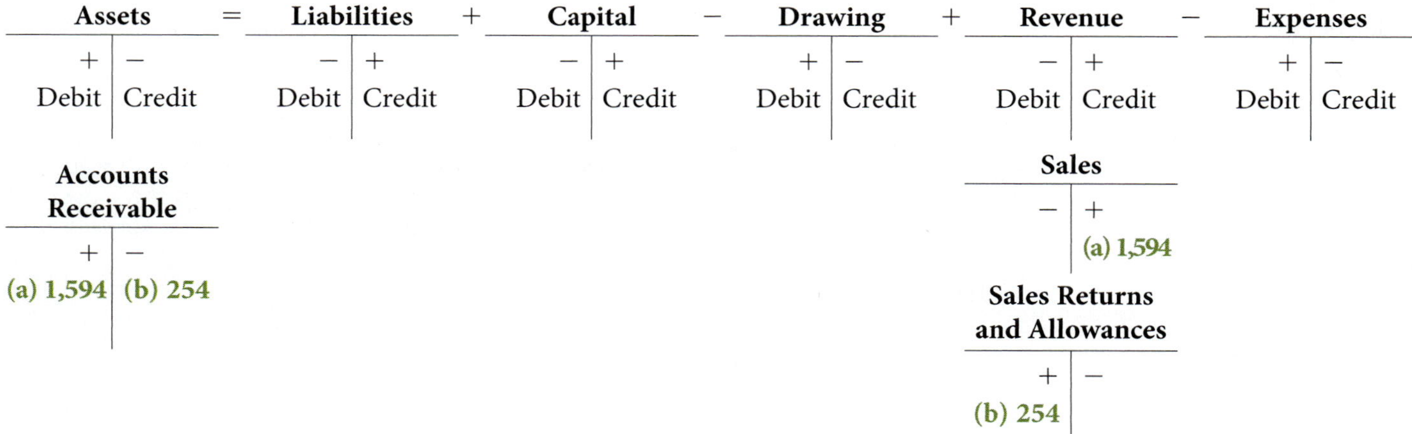

Whitewater Raft Supply's accountant debits Sales Returns and Allowances to increase it. Then, the accountant credits Accounts Receivable to decrease it because the credit customer, Marty's Fly Fishing Adventures, owes less than before.

GENERAL JOURNAL Page 27

Date		Description	Post. Ref.	Debit	Credit
20--					
Sept.	5	Sales Returns and Allowances		254.00	
		Accounts Receivable, Marty's			
		Fly Fishing Adventures			254.00
		Issued credit memo no. 1069.			

Sales Transactions Involving Sales Tax

Most states and some cities levy a sales tax on retail sales of goods and services. The retailer collects the sales tax from customers and later pays it to the tax authorities.

When goods or services are sold, the sales tax is charged to the customer and recorded at the time of the sale. The amount of the sales tax must be computed and included for each transaction and is recorded in the **Sales Tax Payable account**. The customer owes the amount of the sale plus the applicable sales tax.

Assume that David Fly Fishing Outfitters, a retail store, had the following transaction, which includes sales tax computed on the amount of the sale of merchandise:

Jan. 3 Sold merchandise on account to R. Martinez, invoice no. 101, $153.50 plus sales tax of $12.28.

The transaction would be recorded in T accounts and in the general journal as follows:

Assets	=	Liabilities	+	Capital	−	Drawing	+	Revenue	−	Expenses
+ Debit | − Credit		− Debit | + Credit		− Debit | + Credit		+ Debit | − Credit		− Debit | + Credit		+ Debit | − Credit

Accounts Receivable	Sales Tax Payable	Sales
+ | −	− | +	− | +
165.78 |	| 12.28	| 153.50

GENERAL JOURNAL Page 5

Date		Description	Post. Ref.	Debit	Credit
20--					
Jan.	3	Accounts Receivable, R. Martinez		1 6 5 78	
		Sales			1 5 3 50
		Sales Tax Payable			1 2 28
		Sold merchandise to			
		R. Martinez, invoice no. 101.			

At the end of the first quarter, the accountant for David Fly Fishing Outfitters determines that the total sales tax payable for the quarter is $3,240.50. When the sales tax is paid to the state, the accountant debits Sales Tax Payable and credits Cash for the total amount due.

GENERAL JOURNAL Page 8

Date		Description	Post. Ref.	Debit	Credit
20--					
Apr.	20	Sales Tax Payable		3 2 4 0 50	
		Cash			3 2 4 0 50
		Paid sales tax due for first			
		quarter.			

SALES RETURNS INVOLVING SALES TAX

If a customer who returns merchandise to a retail store was originally charged a sales tax, the amount of the sale and the sales tax must be returned to the customer. Review the following two transactions for David Fly Fishing Outfitters.

TRANSACTION (a). On May 1, David Fly Fishing Outfitters sold merchandise on account to B. Hill, $1,550, plus $124 sales tax.

TRANSACTION (b). On May 5, B. Hill returned the merchandise and David Fly Fishing Outfitters issued credit memorandum no. 1152.

Following is the general journal entry required for this type of return:

GENERAL JOURNAL					Page 9
Date		Description	Post. Ref.	Debit	Credit
20--					
May	5	Sales Returns and Allowances		1 5 5 0 00	
		Sales Tax Payable		1 2 4 00	
		Accounts Receivable, B. Hill			1 6 7 4 00
		Issued credit memo no. 1152.			

Notice that David Fly Fishing Outfitters credited B. Hill's account for the amount of the sale ($1,550) and the amount of the sales tax payable ($124).

The Accounts Receivable Ledger

In the sales transactions for Whitewater Raft Supply, we recorded the receivable directly into the Accounts Receivable account. The general journal entry serves as the posting source for crediting the Accounts Receivable account in the general ledger. In addition, to know how much each credit customer owes a business, the firm also maintains an **accounts receivable ledger**. This ledger is a separate record containing a list of the credit customers, in alphabetical order or by account number, with their respective balances. It is important to maintain an accounts receivable ledger so that the company will know at any point in time what amount is owed by the customer, whether the amount is past due, and what payments have been made on the account.

Even though an accounts receivable ledger is maintained, the Accounts Receivable account in the general ledger should still be maintained. When all of the postings are up-to-date, the balance of the Accounts Receivable account should equal the total of all of the credit customers' individual account balances. This means that the accountant must post to *both* the Accounts Receivable account in the general ledger *and* the accounts receivable ledger. The Accounts Receivable *account* in the general ledger is called a **controlling account**. The accounts receivable *ledger,* containing the accounts of all credit customers, is a special type of ledger called a **subsidiary ledger**.

If the accountant was using a computerized accounting system, the software would automatically post the transaction to the Accounts Receivable controlling account and the customer's account in the accounts receivable ledger. In a manual system, to take care of this double posting for Accounts Receivable, the accountant draws a slanted line in the Post. Ref. column. When the amount has been posted as a debit to the general ledger account, the accountant writes the account number of Accounts Receivable in the left part of the Post. Ref. column. After the debit has been posted to the customer's account in the subsidiary ledger, the accountant puts a check mark in the right portion of the Post. Ref. column. The following entries in the general journal, general ledger, and accounts receivable ledger are shown for Mesa River Raft Company's August 1st transaction after posting is complete.

GENERAL JOURNAL Page 26

Date		Description	Post. Ref.	Debit	Credit
20--					
Aug.	1	Accounts Receivable, Mesa River			
		Raft Company	113/✓	1 9 3 3 50	
		Sales	411		1 9 3 3 50
		Sold merchandise to Mesa			
		River Raft Company,			
		invoice no. 9384.			

GENERAL LEDGER

ACCOUNT **Accounts Receivable** ACCOUNT NO. 113

Date		Item	Post. Ref.	Debit	Credit	Balance Debit	Balance Credit
20--							
Aug.	1		J26	1 9 3 3 50		1 9 3 3 50	

ACCOUNTS RECEIVABLE LEDGER

NAME **Mesa River Raft Company**
ADDRESS **5120 Gilman Avenue**
Portland, OR 97202

Date		Item	Post. Ref.	Debit	Credit	Balance
20--						
Aug.	1		J26	1 9 3 3 50		1 9 3 3 50

Learning Objective 3 Prepare a schedule of accounts receivable.

SCHEDULE OF ACCOUNTS RECEIVABLE

From the information contained in the accounts receivable subsidiary ledger, the accountant can prepare a schedule of accounts receivable, such as the one shown in Figure 2, listing each credit customer's account balance.

Figure 2 Schedule of accounts receivable

Whitewater Raft Supply
Schedule of Accounts Receivable
August 31, 20--

Green River Rafts	$1,116.00
Hi-Flying Adventures, Inc.	2,226.30
Marty's Fly Fishing Adventures	1,594.00
Mesa River Raft Company	1,933.50
Total Accounts Receivable	$6,869.80

Figure 3 diagrams the interrelationships of the subsidiary ledger, general ledger, and schedule of accounts receivable for Whitewater Raft Supply for August. Notice that each entry is posted to Accounts Receivable and Sales in the general ledger. Also, the

Figure 3
Interrelationship of the accounts receivable ledger, general ledger, and schedule of accounts receivable

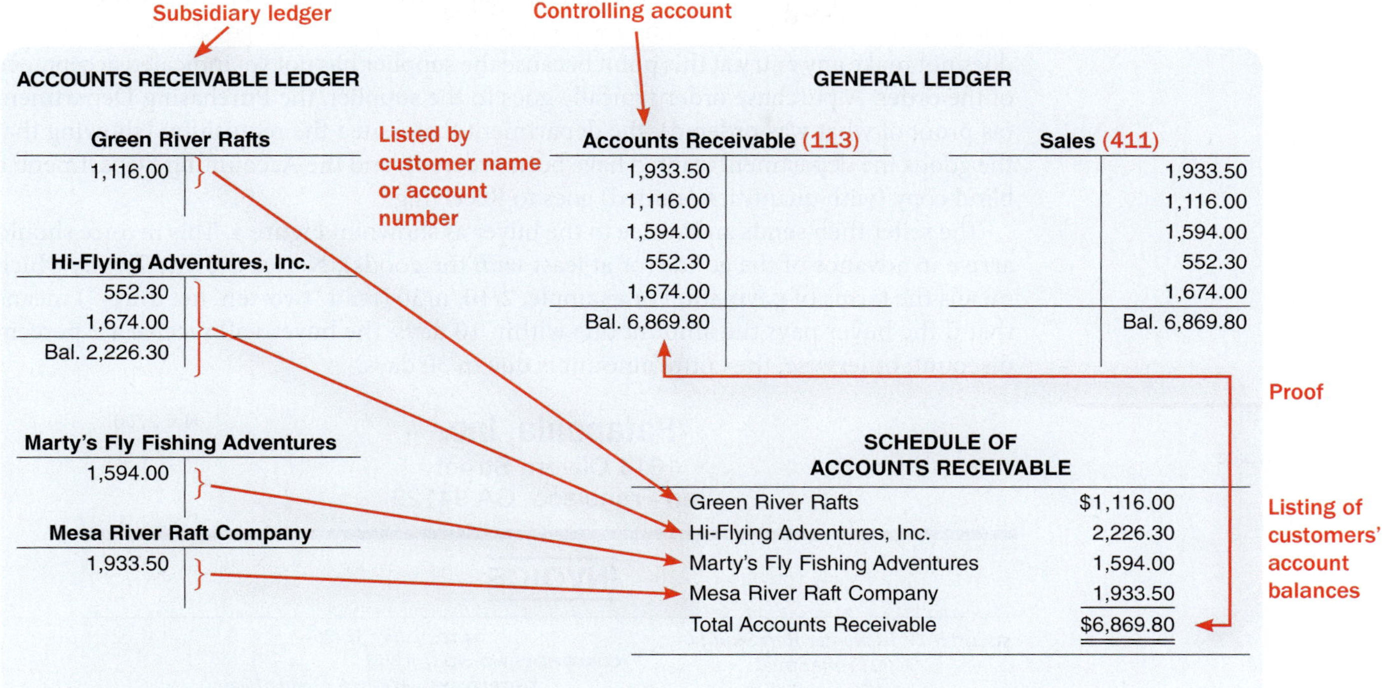

amount owed by the customer is posted to the subsidiary accounts receivable ledger to maintain a running balance of the amount that each customer owes. If performing the posting manually, the accountant should post the individual amounts to the accounts receivable ledger every day so that this ledger will have up-to-date information. Finally, the Accounts Receivable controlling account in the general ledger will have the same balance, $6,869.80, as the schedule of accounts receivable.

In the simplified illustration in Figure 2, it just so happens that because no payments were received from credit customers, the total of the Sales account equals the balance of Accounts Receivable. However, if $1,200 had been received from credit customers, both the balance of the Accounts Receivable controlling account and the total of the schedule of accounts receivable would be $5,669.80 ($6,869.80 – $1,200.00). The total of the Sales account would still be $6,869.80. Also, if some sales were cash only transactions, this would cause a difference between total Sales and the balance of Accounts Receivable.

PURCHASE TRANSACTIONS

The **Purchases account** is used to record the cost of merchandise bought for resale. The Purchases account is considered an expense and has a normal debit balance.

Source Documents Related to Purchases

In a small retail store, the owner may do the buying. In large retail and wholesale businesses, department heads or division managers do the buying, after which the Purchasing Department goes into action: It places purchase orders, follows up on the orders, and sees that deliveries are made to the correct departments. The Purchasing Department also acts as a source of information on current prices, price trends, quality of goods, prospective suppliers, and reliability of suppliers.

The Purchasing Department normally requires that any requests to buy merchandise be in writing in the form of a purchase requisition. After the purchase requisition is approved, the Purchasing Department sends a purchase order to the supplier. A purchase order (often referred to as a "PO") is the company's written offer to buy certain goods. The accountant does not make any entry at this point because the supplier has not yet indicated acceptance of the order. A purchase order typically goes to the supplier, the Purchasing Department (as proof of what was ordered), the department that issued the requisition (showing that the goods the department wanted have been ordered), and the Accounting Department; a blind copy (with quantities omitted) goes to Receiving.

The seller then sends an invoice to the buyer as shown in Figure 4. This invoice should arrive in advance of the goods (or at least *with* the goods). Notice the line *Terms*, which means the terms of payment. For example, 2/10, n/30 (read "two-ten, net thirty") means that if the buyer pays the amount due within 10 days, the buyer will receive a 2 percent discount; otherwise, the entire amount is due in 30 days.

Figure 4
Purchase invoice

Pataponia, Inc.
1614 Olivera Street
San Francisco, CA 94129

No. 2706

INVOICE

SOLD TO *Whitewater Raft Supply*
1400 Front Street
Seattle, WA 98101

DATE: *July 31, 20--*
CUSTOMER'S P.O. NO.: *7918*
SHIPPED BY: *Western Freight Line*
TERMS: *2/10, n/30*

YOUR ORDER NO.	SALESPERSON	TERMS
7918	*C.L.*	*2/10, n/30*
DATE SHIPPED	**SHIPPED BY**	**FOB**
July 31, 20--	*Western Freight Line*	*San Francisco*

QUANTITY	DESCRIPTION	UNIT PRICE	TOTAL
12	*Rio Frio Personal Flotation Device (PFD) #772R*	*142.50*	*1,710.00*
	Freight		*85.50*
	Total		*1,795.50*

Pataponia, Inc. (the seller) prepaid the freight cost and added the $85.50 to the bill, listing it separately. This is similar to buying something by mail order or online. Accounting for freight charges is discussed in more detail below and later in the chapter.

Recording Purchase Transactions in a General Journal

Learning Objective 4 Using a general journal and the periodic inventory system, record purchase and purchase-related transactions; then post to the general ledger and the accounts payable ledger.

Now that we have reviewed the source documents for purchase transactions, let's move on to recording purchase transactions. Purchase transactions can be recorded in two ways—by recording directly into the general journal or by using a special journal called the purchases journal. We will introduce purchase transactions using the general journal first. Then we will discuss how to record the transactions into the purchases journal later in this chapter.

Let's look at four purchase transactions on the books of Whitewater Raft Supply for August. Some of these transactions include the cost of delivering the merchandise, called Freight In. The Freight In account is used to record the transportation charges on incoming merchandise intended for resale.

Aug. 2 Bought merchandise on account from Pataponia, Inc., invoice no. 2706, \$1,710; terms 2/10, n/30; dated July 31; freight prepaid and added to the invoice, \$85.50 (total \$1,795.50).

10 Bought merchandise on account from Langseth and Son, invoice no. 982, \$2,772; terms net 30 days; dated August 8; freight prepaid and added to the invoice, \$157 (total \$2,929).

17 Bought merchandise on account from Dana Manufacturing Company, invoice no. 10611, \$564; terms 2/10, n/30; dated August 15; freight paid by the seller.

26 Bought merchandise on account from Pataponia, Inc., invoice no. 2801, \$2,503.70; terms 2/10, n/30; dated August 24; freight prepaid and added to the invoice, \$102.30 (total \$2,606).

Whitewater Raft Supply will record the transactions into the general journal as follows:

GENERAL JOURNAL **Page 26**

Date		Description	Post. Ref.	Debit	Credit
20--					
Aug.	2	Purchases		1 7 1 0 00	
		Freight In		8 5 50	
		Accounts Payable, Pataponia, Inc.			1 7 9 5 50
		Purchased merchandise from			
		Pataponia, Inc., invoice no.			
		2706, invoice dated 7/31,			
		terms 2/10, n/30.			
	10	Purchases		2 7 7 2 00	
		Freight In		1 5 7 00	
		Accounts Payable, Langseth			
		and Son			2 9 2 9 00
		Purchased merchandise from			
		Langseth and Son, invoice			
		no. 982, invoice dated 8/8,			
		terms n/30.			
	17	Purchases		5 6 4 00	
		Accounts Payable, Dana			
		Manufacturing Company			5 6 4 00
		Purchased merchandise from			
		Dana Manufacturing Company,			
		invoice no. 10611, invoice dated			
		8/15, terms 2/10, n/30.			
	26	Purchases		2 5 0 3 70	
		Freight In		1 0 2 30	
		Accounts Payable, Pataponia, Inc.			2 6 0 6 00
		Purchased merchandise from			
		Pataponia, Inc., invoice no.			
		2801, invoice dated 8/24,			
		terms 2/10, n/30.			

Whitewater Raft Supply's accountant records a debit to the Purchases account to record the cost of merchandise bought for resale. Remember that the Purchases account is similar to an expense account and therefore has a normal debit balance. Freight In (if applied) is also debited to record the increase to the cost of purchases for the transportation charges on incoming merchandise. The corresponding credit is to the Accounts Payable account. Note that the transactions are recorded on the day the merchandise is received.

Here's how the accounts appear in the fundamental accounting equation:

Assets		=	**Liabilities**		+	**Capital**		−	**Drawing**		+	**Revenue**		−	**Expenses**	
+	−		−	+		−	+		+	−		−	+		+	−
Debit	Credit		Debit	Credit		Debit	Credit		Debit	Credit		Debit	Credit		Debit	Credit

Accounts Payable

−	+
	1,795.50
	2,929.00
	564.00
	2,606.00

Purchases

+	−
1,710.00	
2,772.00	
564.00	
2,503.70	

Freight In

+	−
85.50	
157.00	
102.30	

Purchases Returns and Allowances

Occasionally a business will need to return merchandise or request an allowance for reasons such as damaged merchandise. The **Purchases Returns and Allowances account** handles these types of transactions. In both cases, there is a reduction in the amount owed to the supplier. The buyer sends a letter or printed form to the supplier, who acknowledges the reduction by sending a credit memorandum. The buyer should wait for notice of the agreed deduction before making an entry.

The Purchases Returns and Allowances account is a contra account to Purchases and is considered to be a deduction from Purchases. Using a separate account provides a better record of the total returns and allowances. Purchases Returns and Allowances is deducted from the Purchases account on the income statement. Let's look at an example consisting of a return on the books of Whitewater Raft Supply. The original transaction is shown here for review and then the credit memorandum is shown.

TRANSACTION (a). On September 2, bought merchandise on account from Dana Manufacturing Company, $830.

TRANSACTION (b). On September 8, Whitewater Raft Supply returned some merchandise and received credit memorandum no. 1629 from Dana Manufacturing Company for $270.

First, here is how the transcriptions appear in the fundamental accounting equation:

Assets		=	Liabilities		+	Capital		−	Drawing		+	Revenue		−	Expenses	
+	−		−	+		−	+		+	−		−	+		+	−
Debit	Credit		Debit	Credit		Debit	Credit		Debit	Credit		Debit	Credit		Debit	Credit

Accounts Payable	
−	+
(b) 270	(a) 830

Purchases	
+	−
(a) 830	

Purchases Returns and Allowances	
−	+
	(b) 270

In the general journal, transaction (a) was journalized as a debit to Purchases and a credit to Accounts Payable. Transaction (b) is journalized as follows:

GENERAL JOURNAL — Page 27

Date		Description	Post. Ref.	Debit	Credit
20--					
Sept.	8	Accounts Payable, Dana Manufacturing Company		270 00	
		Purchases Returns and Allowances			270 00
		Credit memo no. 1629 for return of merchandise.			

Purchases Returns and Allowances is credited because Whitewater Raft Supply's amount of returns and allowances has increased. Accounts Payable is debited because Whitewater Raft Supply owes less than before.

Freight Charges on Incoming Merchandise

Companies use the Freight In account to keep a record of all separately charged delivery costs on incoming merchandise.

Freight costs are expressed as FOB (free on board) destination or shipping point. **(Destination is the buyer's location; shipping point is the seller's location.)** In both cases, the supplier loads the goods on board the carrier. Beyond that point, there must be an understanding as to who is responsible for paying the freight charges. **If the seller assumes the entire cost of transportation, without any reimbursement from the buyer, the terms are FOB destination**. In this case, title or ownership changes hands when the buyer receives the goods. **If the buyer is responsible for paying the freight cost, the shipping terms are called FOB shipping point**. In this case, title or ownership changes hands when goods are transferred to a common carrier (freight company).

Briefly, when goods are shipped FOB destination, the freight charges are not stated and the seller simply pays the amount of the freight. Suppose Whitewater Raft Supply, which

FYI

Unless the title to the goods is expressly reserved by the seller, whoever pays the freight charges customarily has title to the goods.

is in Seattle, buys merchandise from a supplier in Chicago with shipping terms of FOB Seattle listed on the invoice. The total of the invoice is $1,740, and there is no separate listing of freight charges. In other words, the seller has included the transportation costs in the price.

When goods are shipped FOB shipping point, with the buyer responsible for paying the freight charges, transportation costs may be handled in two ways:

1. The buyer may pay the freight charges directly to the transportation company. For example, an automobile dealer in Houston buys cars FOB Detroit. In this case, the automobile dealer makes one check payable to the manufacturer and another check payable to the carrier for the freight charges. (FOB Detroit is the same as FOB shipping point.)
2. The transportation or shipping costs may be listed separately on the invoice. For example, suppose a person orders a computer from a company online. The company has prepaid (paid in advance) the freight charges as a favor or convenience for the buyer. However, the freight charges are listed on the bill or invoice, and the buyer is responsible for reimbursing the company for the freight charges. Similarly, when a business buys merchandise, the amount of the freight charges may be prepaid by the seller and listed separately on the invoice.

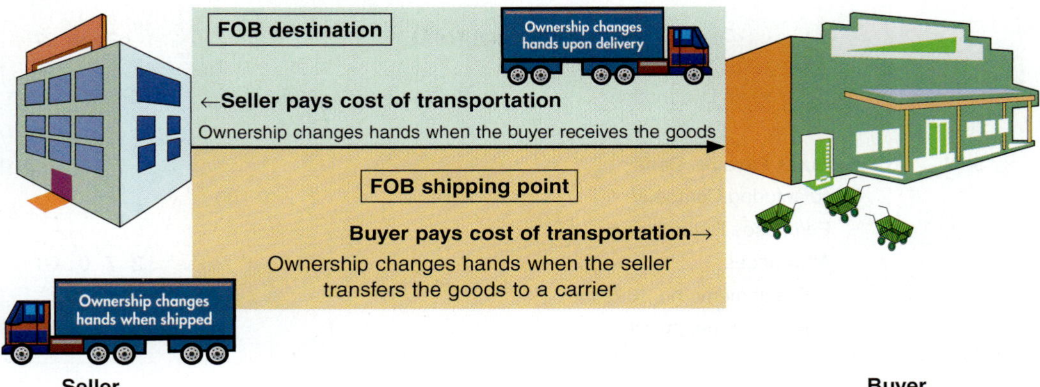

Look again at the invoice from Pataponia, Inc., on page 434. Note that the freight cost is listed separately, and the terms are FOB shipping point (San Francisco). Pataponia paid the transportation cost; Whitewater Raft Supply must reimburse Pataponia for this cost.

The transaction for the purchase from Pataponia, Inc., was recorded as follows:

GENERAL JOURNAL Page 26

Date		Description	Post. Ref.	Debit	Credit
20--					
Aug.	2	Purchases		1 7 1 0 00	
		Freight In		8 5 50	
		Accounts Payable, Pataponia, Inc.			1 7 9 5 50
		Purchased merchandise from			
		Pataponia, Inc., invoice no.			
		2706, invoice dated 7/31,			
		terms 2/10, n/30.			

Notice that the transportation cost is recorded separately as a debit to the Freight In account for $85.50. Also notice that because this purchase was FOB shipping point, the buyer (Whitewater Raft Supply) must reimburse the seller for the transportation costs by paying the total invoice cost of $1,795.50.

When the buyer pays for the cost of freight, the buyer records the cost as Freight In, which is included in the cost of purchases and reported on the income statement. If the seller pays for the cost of freight, the seller records the cost as a selling expense in the Delivery Expense or Freight Out account.

Freight Charges on the Buying of Goods and Services Other Than Merchandise

Any freight charges incurred when buying other assets, such as supplies or equipment, should be debited to the respective asset accounts. The Freight In account is used only to record the incoming transportation charges on merchandise intended for resale. For example, assume that Whitewater Raft Supply bought display cases on account from Carter Cabinet Shop at a cost of $2,700 plus freight charges of $290. The seller of the display cases prepaid the transportation costs for Whitewater Raft Supply and then added the $290 to the invoice price of the cases. Let's visualize this with T accounts.

Store Equipment	
+	−
2,990	

Accounts Payable	
−	+
	2,990

Notice that Whitewater Raft Supply did not use the Freight In account to record the transportation costs. Instead, the company recorded the transportation costs directly into the Store Equipment account.

The Accounts Payable Ledger

Previously, we called the Accounts Receivable account in the general ledger a controlling account, and we saw that the accounts receivable ledger consists of an individual account for each credit customer.

Accounts Payable is a parallel case; it, too, is a controlling account in the general ledger. The **accounts payable ledger** is a subsidiary ledger, and it consists of individual accounts for all of the creditors listed in either alphabetical or numerical order.

Even though an accounts payable ledger is used, the Accounts Payable account in the general ledger should still be maintained. When all of the postings are up-to-date, the balance of the Accounts Payable account should equal the total of all of the creditors' individual account balances. As in sales transactions, the accountant must post purchase transactions daily to both the general ledger and the accounts payable ledger.

In a computerized accounting system, when the purchase is recorded, the software automatically posts to the appropriate accounts payable ledger. When posting manually for Accounts Payable, the accountant draws a slanted line in the Post. Ref. column. The account number of Accounts Payable is shown in the left portion to signify the posting to the general ledger and a check mark is shown in the right portion to signify posting to the accounts payable ledger.

The following entries in the general journal, general ledger, and accounts payable ledger are shown for the August 2 transaction after posting is complete.

Remember

Creditors are companies or individuals to whom we owe money.

GENERAL JOURNAL Page 26

Date		Description	Post. Ref.	Debit	Credit
20--					
Aug.	2	Purchases	511	1 7 1 0 00	
		Freight In	514	8 5 50	
		Accounts Payable, Pataponia, Inc.	212/✓		1 7 9 5 50
		Purchased merchandise from			
		Pataponia, Inc., invoice no.			
		2706, invoice dated 7/31,			
		terms 2/10, n/30.			

GENERAL LEDGER

ACCOUNT Accounts Payable **ACCOUNT NO.** 212

Date		Item	Post. Ref.	Debit	Credit	Balance Debit	Balance Credit
20--							
Aug.	2				1 7 9 5 50		1 7 9 5 50

ACCOUNTS PAYABLE LEDGER

NAME Pataponia, Inc.
ADDRESS 1614 Olivera Street
San Francisco, CA 94129

Date		Item	Post. Ref.	Debit	Credit	Balance
20--						
Aug.	2		J26		1 7 9 5 50	1 7 9 5 50

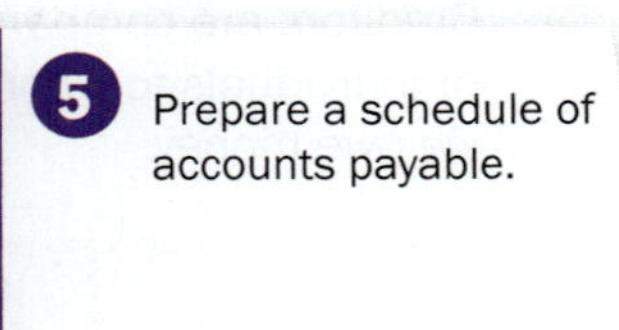

SCHEDULE OF ACCOUNTS PAYABLE

Assuming that there were no previous balances in the creditors' accounts and that no other transactions for Whitewater Raft Supply involved Accounts Payable, the schedule of accounts payable, as of the end of August, would appear as shown in Figure 5. Note that the schedule of accounts payable lists each creditor's account balance and that it equals the Accounts Payable account shown in the general ledger (Figure 6).

Figure 5
Schedule of accounts payable

Whitewater Raft Supply
Schedule of Accounts Payable
August 31, 20--

Assets	
Dana Manufacturing Company	$ 564.00
Langseth and Son	2,929.00
Pataponia, Inc.	4,401.50
Total Accounts Payable	$7,894.50

GENERAL LEDGER

ACCOUNT Accounts Payable ACCOUNT NO. 212

Date		Item	Post. Ref.	Debit	Credit	Balance Debit	Balance Credit
20--							
Aug.	2		J26		1 7 9 5 50		1 7 9 5 50
	10		J26		2 9 2 9 00		4 7 2 4 50
	17		J26		5 6 4 00		5 2 8 8 50
	26		J26		2 6 0 6 00		7 8 9 4 50

Figure 6
Accounts Payable controlling account

Internal Control of Purchases

Purchases is one of the areas in which internal control is essential. Efficiency and security require most companies to work out careful procedures for buying and paying for goods. This is understandable, as large sums of money are usually involved. The control aspect generally involves the following measures:

1. Purchases are made only after proper authorization is given. Purchase requisitions and purchase orders are prenumbered so that each form can be accounted for.
2. The receiving department, which received a copy of the purchase order without quantities listed, carefully checks all goods upon receipt for count, damages, and description. Later, the report of the receiving department is verified against the purchase order and the purchase invoice.
3. The person who authorizes the payment is neither the person doing the ordering nor the person writing the check. Payment is authorized only after the purchase invoice data are verified against the receiving report and purchase order.
4. The person who actually writes the check has not been involved in any of the foregoing purchasing procedures.

To: **Amy Roberts, CPA**
Subject: **Sales and Purchases**

Hi Amy
Well, I can see there are some differences between a merchandising business and a service business. I believe I now understand how to record my merchandising sales and purchases transactions. What should we discuss next?
Thanks,
Janie

(*Continued*)

To: **Janie Conner**
Subject: **RE: Sales and Purchases**

Hi Janie,
Now that you understand how to handle various activities for the merchandising side of your business, we should discuss what type of inventory system you should use (periodic or perpetual). It would also be a good time to discuss whether you should record transactions in the general journal or special journals. Are you available later this week for a conference call on the following topics?

_______ 1. Periodic versus perpetual inventory systems.
_______ 2. Special journals versus the general journal for recording transactions.

I will be in the office the rest of the week. Just let me know what time works best for you.
Amy

THE PERPETUAL INVENTORY SYSTEM

Up until now, we have discussed how to record sales and purchases transactions in the general journal using the periodic inventory system. The periodic inventory system requires that companies periodically take a physical count of inventory at the end of the period to determine the amount of inventory on hand.

On the other hand, the perpetual inventory system keeps continuous records of inventories by recording all transactions so that at any given time, companies know the current amount of inventory on hand and have a better understanding of their profits. Under the perpetual inventory system, sales and purchases are recorded differently than they are under the periodic inventory system.

Sales Transactions

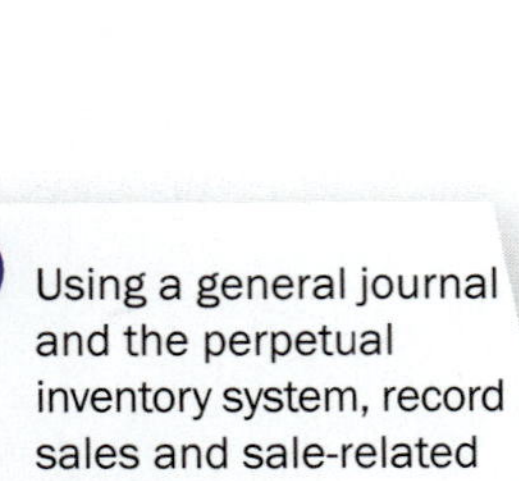
Learning Objective 6 Using a general journal and the perpetual inventory system, record sales and sale-related transactions.

Let's review the first two sales transactions on the books of Whitewater Raft Supply for August.

Aug. 1 Sold merchandise on account to Mesa River Raft Company, invoice no. 9384, $1,933.50. *Cost of inventory sold is $1,643.48.*

8 Sold merchandise on account to Green River Rafts, invoice no. 9385, $1,116. *Cost of inventory sold is $948.60.*

Note that the new information regarding the cost of inventory sold is shown in italics. This information concerning the cost of the inventory sold is needed when sales transactions are recorded using the perpetual inventory system.

Whitewater Raft Supply's accountant would record the transactions in the general journal as follows:

GENERAL JOURNAL **Page 26**

Date		Description	Post. Ref.	Debit	Credit
20--					
Aug.	1	Accounts Receivable, Mesa River			
		Raft Company		1 9 3 3 50	
		Sales			1 9 3 3 50
		Sold merchandise to Mesa			
		River Raft Company, invoice			
		no. 9384.			
		Cost of Goods Sold		1 6 4 3 48	
		Merchandise Inventory			1 6 4 3 48
		Cost of merchandise sold to			
		Mesa River Raft Company, invoice			
		no. 9384.			
	8	Accounts Receivable, Green			
		River Rafts		1 1 1 6 00	
		Sales			1 1 1 6 00
		Sold merchandise to Green			
		River Rafts, invoice no. 9385.			
		Cost of Goods Sold		9 4 8 60	
		Merchandise Inventory			9 4 8 60
		Cost of merchandise sold to			
		Green River Rafts, invoice			
		no. 9385.			

The sales portion of the transaction is recorded the same under either method. Whitewater Raft Supply's accountant records a debit to Accounts Receivable to record the amount that each customer owes the company and a credit to Sales for each transaction. **However, using the perpetual inventory system, the accountant must also record a debit to Cost of Goods Sold for the cost of the inventory sold and a credit to Merchandise Inventory**. The **Cost of Goods Sold account** represents the cost of the inventory sold and is an expense account that is reported on the income statement. Cost of Goods Sold increases when there is a sale and, therefore, is debited. The Merchandise Inventory account must decrease by the cost of the inventory sold, so the accountant records a credit to Merchandise Inventory.

By recording sales transactions in this manner, the company can easily calculate the profit on the sale of the inventory by subtracting Cost of Goods Sold from Sales. Whitewater Raft Supply's gross profit is $290.02 ($1,933.50 – $1,643.48) on the August 1 sale.

Only returned merchandise that can be resold is debited to Merchandise Inventory. Damaged goods that are returned but cannot be resold should be expensed.

Sales Returns and Allowances

Sales returns and allowances is also recorded differently under the perpetual inventory system. Let's look at Whitewater Raft Supply's return on September 5, with the original sale described first.

TRANSACTION (a). On August 14, Whitewater Raft Supply sold merchandise on account to Marty's Fly Fishing Adventures, $1,594, and recorded the sale in the general journal. *Cost of inventory sold is $1,354.90.*

TRANSACTION (b). On September 5, Marty's Fly Fishing Adventures returned $254 worth of the merchandise *having a cost of $215.90.* Whitewater Raft Supply issued credit memorandum no. 1069.

Again, note the additional information provided describing the cost of the inventory sold and returned. This information is necessary to record the transactions using the perpetual inventory system.

Whitewater Raft Supply's accountant would record the return on September 5 as follows:

GENERAL JOURNAL Page 27

Date		Description	Post. Ref.	Debit	Credit
20--					
Sept.	5	Sales Returns and Allowances		254 00	
		Accounts Receivable, Marty's			
		Fly Fishing Adventures			254 00
		Issued credit memo no. 1069.			
		Merchandise Inventory		215 90	
		Cost of Goods Sold			215 90
		Cost of merchandise returned,			
		credit memo no. 1069.			

The first part of the journal entry is the same as when using the periodic inventory system. The accountant debits Sales Returns and Allowances and credits Accounts Receivable to decrease it because the customer owes less than before. However, because Whitewater Raft Supply is using the perpetual inventory system, the company must also record the effect of this return on merchandise inventory by debiting Merchandise Inventory to increase it for the returned items and crediting Cost of Goods Sold to decrease the expense.

Purchase Transactions

Learning Objective 7 Using a general journal and the perpetual inventory system, record purchase and purchase-related transactions.

As we learned earlier in the chapter, when using the periodic inventory system, the accountant uses the Purchases and Freight In (if applied) accounts to record transactions involving purchases. **Under the perpetual inventory system, all transactions related to the purchase of inventory are recorded in the Merchandise Inventory account.** The accountant never uses the Purchases and Freight In accounts when recording purchase transactions under the perpetual inventory system because *all* costs of merchandise inventory (including freight) are included in the Merchandise Inventory account.

Let's look at two purchase transactions on the books of Whitewater Raft Supply for August.

Aug. 2 Bought merchandise on account from Pataponia, Inc., invoice no. 2706, $1,710; terms 2/10, n/30; dated July 31; FOB San Francisco, freight prepaid and added to the invoice, $85.50 (total $1,795.50).

10 Bought merchandise on account from Langseth and Son, invoice no. 982, $2,772; terms net 30 days; dated August 8; FOB Cleveland, freight prepaid and added to the invoice, $157 (total $2,929).

Whitewater Raft Supply's accountant will record the transactions in the general journal as follows:

GENERAL JOURNAL Page 26

Date		Description	Post. Ref.	Debit	Credit
20--					
Aug.	2	Merchandise Inventory		1 7 9 5 50	
		Accounts Payable, Pataponia, Inc.			1 7 9 5 50
		Purchased merchandise from			
		Pataponia, Inc., invoice no.			
		2706, invoice dated 7/31,			
		terms 2/10, n/30.			
	10	Merchandise Inventory		2 9 2 9 00	
		Accounts Payable, Langseth and Son			2 9 2 9 00
		Purchased merchandise from			
		Langseth and Son, invoice			
		no. 982, invoice dated 8/8,			
		terms n/30.			

Note that Whitewater Raft Supply records a debit to the Merchandise Inventory account (not Purchases and Freight In) to record the cost of merchandise, including freight, bought for resale.

Purchases Returns and Allowances

Under the perpetual inventory system, purchases returns and allowances transactions are recorded directly into the Merchandise Inventory account, and the Purchases Returns and Allowances account is not used.

Let's look at a return on September 8 for Whitewater Raft Supply, with the original purchase described first.

TRANSACTION (a). On September 2, bought merchandise on account from Dana Manufacturing Company, $830.

TRANSACTION (b). On September 8, Whitewater Raft Supply returned some merchandise and received credit memorandum no. 1629 from Dana Manufacturing Company for $270.

Under the perpetual inventory system, the accountant would record the return on September 8 as follows:

GENERAL JOURNAL Page 27

Date		Description	Post. Ref.	Debit	Credit
20--					
Sept.	8	Accounts Payable, Dana			
		Manufacturing Company		2 7 0 00	
		Merchandise Inventory			2 7 0 00
		Credit memo no. 1629 for			
		return of merchandise.			

Whitewater Raft Supply's accountant debits the creditor's Accounts Payable account to decrease it and credits Merchandise Inventory (not Purchases Returns and Allowances) to decrease it. Recording the credit to the Merchandise Inventory account automatically decreases it for the cost of the inventory returned.

Periodic Inventory System versus Perpetual Inventory System

Following is an abbreviated version of the chart of accounts for both the periodic and perpetual inventory systems. Note that in the periodic inventory system, the company uses accounts such as Purchases, Purchases Returns and Allowances, and Freight In that are not used in the perpetual inventory system.

PERIODIC INVENTORY SYSTEM

Revenue (400–499)

411 Sales
412 Sales Returns and Allowances

Cost of Goods Sold (500–599)

511 Purchases
512 Purchases Returns and Allowances
514 Freight In

PERPETUAL INVENTORY SYSTEM

Revenue (400–499)

411 Sales
412 Sales Returns and Allowances

Cost of Goods Sold (500–599)

511 Cost of Goods Sold

Now that we have reviewed the main differences between the periodic and perpetual inventory systems, let's take a moment to reflect on those differences. Figure 7 shows a comparison of the transactions we learned for both inventory systems. Make sure you are familiar with each system and their differences.

Figure 7
Comparison of journal entries for periodic and perpetual inventory systems

Comparison: Periodic Versus Perpetual Inventory Systems						
Transaction	**Periodic Inventory System**			**Perpetual Inventory System**		
Sold merchandise, having a cost of $1,643.48, to customer on account, $1,933.50.	Accounts Receivable, Mesa River Raft Company Sales	1,933.50	1,933.50	Accounts Receivable, Mesa River Raft Company Sales	1,933.50	1,933.50
				Cost of Goods Sold Merchandise Inventory	1,643.48	1,643.48
Customer returned merchandise, $254, having a cost of $215.90.	Sales Returns and Allowances Accounts Receivable, Rugged River Company	254.00	254.00	Sales Returns and Allowances Accounts Receivable, Rugged River Company	254.00	254.00
				Merchandise Inventory Cost of Goods Sold	215.90	215.90
Purchased merchandise from supplier on account, $1,710, with prepaid freight of $85.50.	Purchases Freight In Accounts Payable, Pataponia, Inc.	1,710.00 85.50	1,795.50	Merchandise Inventory Accounts Payable, Pataponia, Inc.	1,795.50	1,795.50
Returned merchandise to supplier, $270.	Accounts Payable, Dana Manufacturing Company Purchases Returns and Allowances	270.00	270.00	Accounts Payable, Dana Manufacturing Company Merchandise Inventory	270.00	270.00

© iStockPhoto.com/RiverNorthPhotography

In the Real World

In order to be profitable, low margin, discount merchandising companies such as Dollar Tree, need to carefully track their sales, purchases, cost of goods sold, sales discounts, and sales returns and allowances. With over 4,000 store locations across the country, it is also important for companies like Dollar Tree to know what inventory is on hand and where that inventory is located. With a fixed sales price of $1 per item sold, there is little room for purchasing mistakes or inventory discrepancies.

SPECIAL JOURNALS

We have demonstrated sales and purchases by recording the transactions directly into the general journal. Companies can, however, also record sales and purchases into a special journal. **Special journals** are books of original entry used to simplify the recording process. One or more of these journals may be used in a manual accounting system, or they may be used in certain computerized systems designed to facilitate specialized types of repetitive transactions. The four most commonly used special journals are as follows:

Sales journal (S) Used to record sales of merchandise sold on account *only*. For example, if Whitewater Raft Supply sold a kayak to a customer on account, Whitewater Raft Supply could use this journal to record the sale. However, if the customer paid cash for the kayak, the sale would not be recorded in this journal. Also, if Whitewater Raft Supply sold an old computer equipment on account, this journal would not be used because the equipment was not part of the business's merchandise sales.

Purchases journal (P) Used to record purchases of merchandise purchased on account for resale *only*. For example, Whitewater Raft Supply could use this journal for its purchase, on account, of rafts to resell to customers. However, Whitewater Raft Supply would not use this journal when buying a copy machine or supplies for the office, even though they are purchased on account, because those goods are not intended for resale to customers.

Cash receipts journal (CR) Used to record all transactions that include a debit to Cash, such as cash sales, checks received, or interest earned on a checking account.

Cash payments journal (CP) Used to record all transactions that include a credit to Cash, such as payments by check or bank service charges.

In this chapter, we will demonstrate how Whitewater Raft Supply records sales and purchases transactions using the sales journal and purchases journal. In the next chapter, we will discuss the cash receipts journal and cash payments journal.

The Sales Journal

Learning Objective 8 Record transactions in a sales journal and post to the general ledger and accounts receivable ledger.

The sales journal records sales of merchandise **on account only.** This specialized type of transaction calls for debits to Accounts Receivable and credits to Sales.

Recall the sales transactions introduced for Whitewater Raft Supply for August:

Aug. 1 Sold merchandise on account to Mesa River Raft Company, invoice no. 9384, $1,933.50.

8 Sold merchandise on account to Green River Rafts, invoice no. 9385, $1,116.

14 Sold merchandise on account to Marty's Fly Fishing Adventures, invoice no. 9386, $1,594.

19 Sold merchandise on account to Hi-Flying Adventures, Inc., invoice no. 9387, $552.30.

25 Sold merchandise on account to Hi-Flying Adventures, Inc., invoice no. 9388, $1,674.

Assume that Whitewater Raft Supply uses the sales journal *instead of* the general journal to record the five transactions. The accountant will record each transaction into the sales journal only.

The sales journal is a book of original entry. Do not duplicate the transaction in the general journal.

SALES JOURNAL Page 38

Date		Inv. No.	Customer's Name	Post. Ref.	Accounts Receivable Dr. Sales Cr.	
20--						
Aug.	1	9384	Mesa River Raft Company		1 9 3 3	50
	8	9385	Green River Rafts		1 1 1 6	00
	14	9386	Marty's Fly Fishing Adventures		1 5 9 4	00
	19	9387	Hi-Flying Adventures, Inc.		5 5 2	30
	25	9388	Hi-Flying Adventures, Inc.		1 6 7 4	00

Because *one* column is labeled "Accounts Receivable Dr./Sales Cr.," each transaction requires only a single line. Repetition is avoided, and all entries for sales of merchandise on account are found in one place. Listing the invoice number makes it easier to check the details of a particular sale at a later date. It also ensures that no invoice is missed since they are clearly listed in number order.

As with the general journal, the amount of each sale should be posted daily to the account of each credit customer in the accounts receivable ledger. After you post an amount from the sales journal to a credit customer's account in the accounts receivable ledger, put a check mark in the Post. Ref. column of the sales journal.

POSTING FROM THE SALES JOURNAL TO THE GENERAL LEDGER

Using the sales journal also saves time and space in posting to the ledger accounts. Because every entry is a debit to Accounts Receivable and a credit to Sales, you can make a single posting to these accounts for the amount of the total as of the last day of the month. This entry is called a summarizing entry because it summarizes one month's transactions. Because Whitewater Raft Supply had no more sales transactions after August 25, the amounts in the Accounts Receivable Dr./Sales Cr. Column from the sales journal are added up and totaled. The total ($6,869.80) is then posted to the Accounts Receivable and Sales accounts in the general ledger. In the Post. Ref. columns of the ledger accounts, the letter *S* designates the sales journal.

GENERAL LEDGER

ACCOUNT Accounts Receivable ACCOUNT NO. 113

Date		Item	Post. Ref.	Debit	Credit	Balance Debit	Balance Credit
20--							
Aug.	31		S38	6 8 6 9 80		6 8 6 9 80	

GENERAL LEDGER

ACCOUNT Sales ACCOUNT NO. 411

Date		Item	Post. Ref.	Debit	Credit	Balance Debit	Balance Credit
20--							
Aug.	31		S38		6 8 6 9 80		6 8 6 9 80

Remember

The purpose of posting reference numbers is to tell where in the ledger an amount was posted or from which journal it came.

After posting the total of the sales journal to the Accounts Receivable account in the general ledger, write the account number of Accounts Receivable at the left below the total of the sales journal. Repeat the process of posting for the total of the sales journal to the Sales account in the general ledger, placing the account number of Sales at the right below the total of the sales journal. **Don't record these account numbers until you have completed the postings.** Figure 8 shows the completed sales journal for Whitewater Raft Supply for August.

SALES JOURNAL Page 38

Date		Inv. No.	Customer's Name	Post. Ref.	Accounts Receivable Dr. Sales Cr.
20--					
Aug.	1	9384	Mesa River Raft Company	✓	1 9 3 3 50
	8	9385	Green River Rafts	✓	1 1 1 6 00
	14	9386	Marty's Fly Fishing Adventures	✓	1 5 9 4 00
	19	9387	Hi-Flying Adventures, Inc.	✓	5 5 2 30
	25	9388	Hi-Flying Adventures, Inc.	✓	1 6 7 4 00
	31		Total		6 8 6 9 80
					(113) (411)

Figure 8
Sales journal

SALES JOURNAL WITH SALES TAX PAYABLE

When recording sales transactions that involve sales tax, the sales journal will need to include three columns: Accounts Receivable Debit, Sales Tax Payable Credit, and Sales Credit.

Recall the transaction given for David Fly Fishing Outfitters earlier in the chapter.

Jan. 3 Sold merchandise on account to R. Martinez, invoice no. 101, \$153.50 plus sales tax of \$12.28.

The sales journal is used to record only the sales of merchandise (goods) on account.

As shown below, David Fly Fishing Outfitters would record the transaction in the sales journal as follows:

SALES JOURNAL Page 3

Date		Inv. No.	Customer's Name	Post. Ref.	Accounts Receivable Debit	Sales Tax Payable Credit	Sales Credit
20--							
Jan.	3	101	R. Martinez		165.78	12.28	153.50

At the end of the month, the accountant for David Fly Fishing Outfitters would total the columns and post them as a debit to Accounts Receivable, a credit to Sales Tax Payable, and a credit to Sales. However, with a journal that has more than one column, before posting to the general ledger accounts you should use the column totals to prove that the total debits equal the total credits. After posting, the respective account numbers are recorded in parentheses below the totals.

Purchases Journal (Three-Column)

Learning Objective 9 Record transactions in a three-column purchases journal and post to the general ledger and accounts payable ledger.

Following are the purchase transactions for Whitewater Raft Supply for August. We will use these transactions to demonstrate the purchases journal.

Aug. 2 Bought merchandise on account from Pataponia, Inc., invoice no. 2706, $1,710; terms 2/10, n/30; dated July 31; FOB San Francisco, freight prepaid and added to the invoice, $85.50 (total $1,795.50).

10 Bought merchandise on account from Langseth and Son, invoice no. 982, $2,772; terms net 30 days; dated August 8; FOB Cleveland, freight prepaid and added to the invoice, $157 (total $2,929).

17 Bought merchandise on account from Dana Manufacturing Company, invoice no. 10611, $564; terms 2/10, n/30; dated August 15; FOB Los Angeles.

26 Bought merchandise on account from Pataponia, Inc., invoice no. 2801, $2,503.70; terms 2/10, n/30; dated August 24; FOB San Francisco, freight prepaid and added to the invoice, $102.30 (total $2,606).

As shown below, Whitewater Raft Supply's accountant will record each transaction into the purchases journal. Notice that by including a separate column for each account, Whitewater Raft Supply can record a typical purchase of merchandise on account on one line.

PURCHASES JOURNAL Page 29

Date		Supplier's Name	Inv. No.	Inv. Date	Terms	Post. Ref.	Accounts Payable Credit	Freight In Debit	Purchases Debit
20--									
Aug.	2	Pataponia, Inc.	2706	7/31	2/10, n/30		1795.50	85.50	1710.00
	10	Langseth and Son	982	8/8	n/30		2929.00	157.00	2772.00
	17	Dana Manufacturing Co.	10611	8/15	2/10, n/30		564.00		564.00
	26	Pataponia, Inc.	2801	8/24	2/10, n/30		2606.00	102.30	2503.70

POSTING FROM THE PURCHASES JOURNAL TO THE GENERAL LEDGER

If using a manual system, each purchase should be posted daily to the accounts payable ledger. After you post an amount from the purchases journal to the accounts payable ledger, put a check mark in the Post. Ref. column of the purchases journal. The accountant also posts the totals of each column into the appropriate general ledger accounts at the end of each month. Figure 9 shows the journal entries in the purchases journal for Whitewater Raft Supply for all transactions involving the purchase of merchandise on account for August and the related ledger accounts for the same time period. In the Post. Ref. column of the ledger accounts, *P* designates the purchases journal. After posting the column totals for the month to the ledger accounts, the accountant goes back to the purchases journal and records the account numbers in parentheses directly below the total.

Transactions involving the buying of supplies or other assets should not be journalized in the three-column purchases journal. This purchases journal may be used only for purchases of merchandise for resale.

PURCHASES JOURNAL — Page 29

Date		Supplier's Name	Inv. No.	Inv. Date	Terms	Post. Ref.	Accounts Payable Credit	Freight In Debit	Purchases Debit
20--									
Aug.	2	Pataponia, Inc.	2706	7/31	2/10, n/30	✓	1 7 9 5 50	8 5 50	1 7 1 0 00
	10	Langseth and Son	982	8/8	n/30	✓	2 9 2 9 00	1 5 7 00	2 7 7 2 00
	17	Dana Manufacturing Co.	10611	8/15	2/10, n/30	✓	5 6 4 00		5 6 4 00
	26	Pataponia, Inc.	2801	8/24	2/10, n/30	✓	2 6 0 6 00	1 0 2 30	2 5 0 3 70
	31	Totals					7 8 9 4 50	3 4 4 80	7 5 4 9 70
							(2 1 2)	(5 1 4)	(5 1 1)

GENERAL LEDGER

ACCOUNT **Accounts Payable** — ACCOUNT NO. **212**

Date		Item	Post. Ref.	Debit	Credit	Balance Debit	Balance Credit
20--							
Aug.	31		P29		7 8 9 4 50		7 8 9 4 50

ACCOUNT **Purchases** — ACCOUNT NO. **511**

Date		Item	Post. Ref.	Debit	Credit	Balance Debit	Balance Credit
20--							
Aug.	31		P29	7 5 4 9 70		7 5 4 9 70	

ACCOUNT **Freight In** — ACCOUNT NO. **514**

Date		Item	Post. Ref.	Debit	Credit	Balance Debit	Balance Credit
20--							
Aug.	31		P29	3 4 4 80		3 4 4 80	

Figure 9
Purchases journal and general ledger accounts

Accounting with QuickBooks®

Sales and Purchases with QuickBooks

Learning Objective

 List QuickBooks centers.

Learning Objectives

After you have completed this section, you will be able to do the following:

1. List QuickBooks centers.
2. Create invoices.
3. Create credit memo/ refunds.
4. Create purchase orders.
5. Enter bills.
6. View and print accounts receivable and accounts payable reports.

Transactions can be recorded two ways in QuickBooks: the journal entry method, as you learned in Chapter 3, or the forms-based approach accessed through the QuickBooks home page, as shown in Figure Q1. The QuickBooks home page is organized into five centers: (1) Vendors, (2) Customers, (3) Employees, (4) Company, and (5) Banking. These centers allow users to quickly enter transactions without the need to know debits and credits. The software takes the information that has been entered through the center applications and records the journal entry automatically. Each center handles transaction activity related to a specific area. For example, the Customers center handles transactions related to creating invoices, sales receipts, and statements. In Chapters 3–5, you used the journal entry method with Conner's Whitewater Adventures, a service business. For Chapters 9–12, you will use the forms-based approach with Whitewater Raft Supply, a merchandising business. Let's get started.

Figure Q1
QuickBooks home page and centers

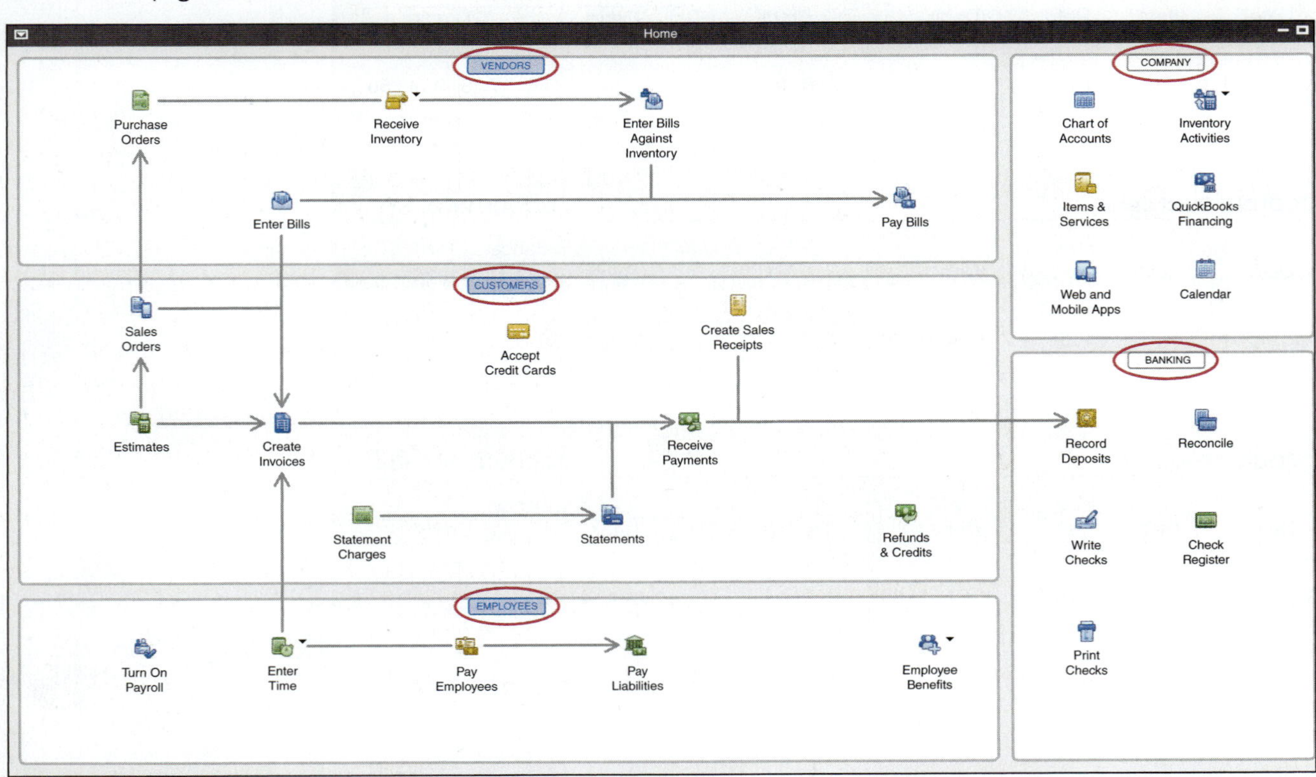

2 Create invoices.

Learning Objective

Sales can be recorded in QuickBooks in one of three ways: (1) using the journal entry method, (2) creating a sales receipt, or (3) creating an invoice. In Chapters 3–5, you recorded sales for Conner's Whitewater Adventures using the journal entry method. For Chapters 9–12, you will be using a forms-based approach where sales receipts can record sales transactions for customers making payment at the time of the sale with cash, check, money order, credit card, debit card, or gift card and invoices can record sales transactions for customers making purchases on credit. We will discuss cash sales and sales receipts more in Chapter 10. For now, we will focus on creating invoices for customers making purchases on credit. To create an invoice in QuickBooks, complete the steps in Figures Q2 and Q3.

QuickBooks Tip

Many applications in QuickBooks are integrated. Notice in Figure Q2 that the **Enter Bills** and **Enter Time** applications are linked to **Create Invoices**.

STEP 1. Select **Create Invoices** from the home page, under the **Customers** center.

Figure Q2
Create Invoices icon on home page

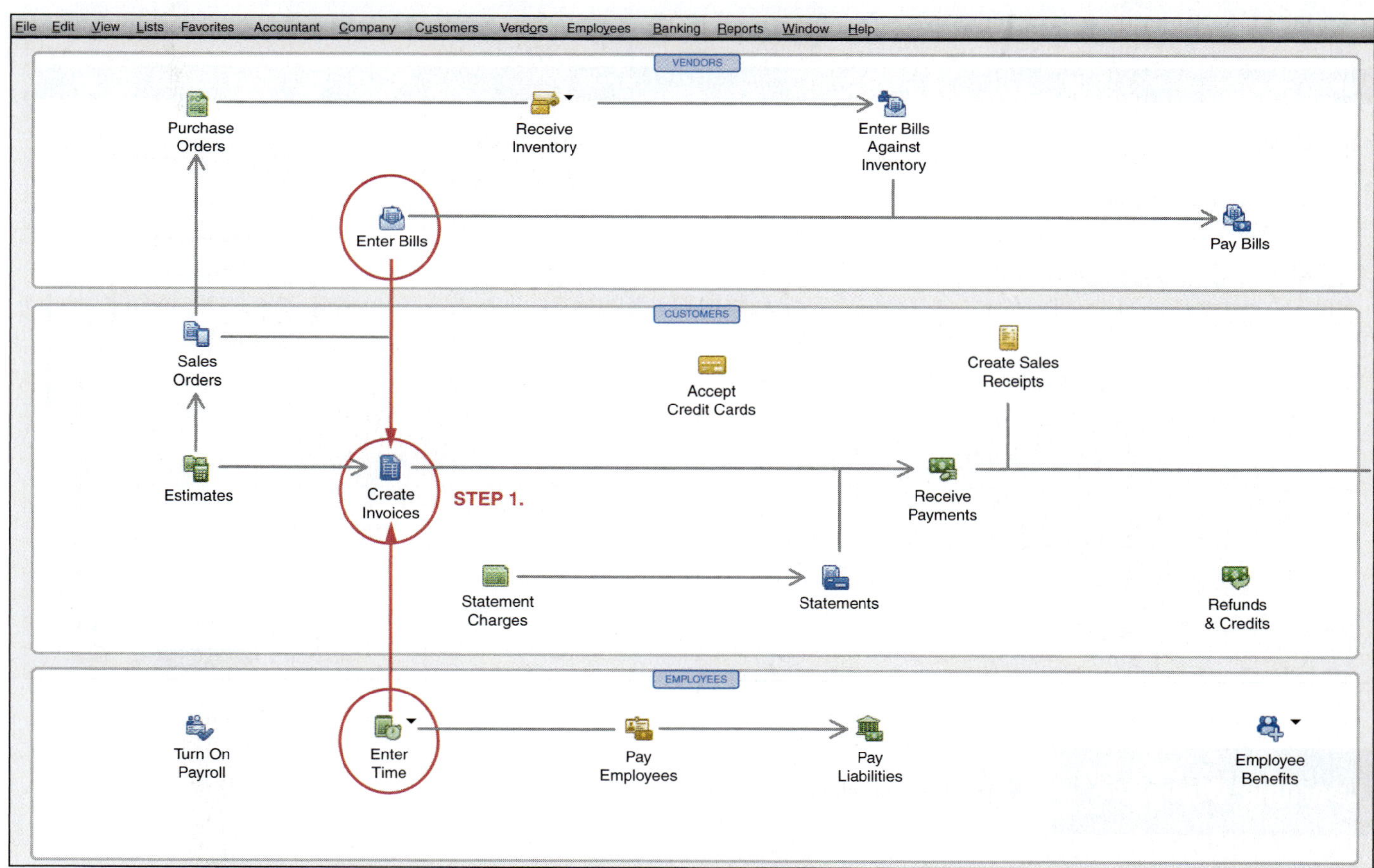

STEP 2. Select **Customer** from the drop-down menu. In this example, the customer is Mesa River Raft Company.

STEP 3. Select or enter the **Date**.

STEP 4. Enter the **Invoice** #. The system may assign this number automatically.

ACCOUNTING WITH QuickBooks®

QuickBooks Tip

Item lists can be created under **Lists** or within the invoice by selecting **Add New**.

STEP 5. Verify the **Bill To** information. Modify as necessary.

STEP 6. Select the **Terms**.

STEP 7. Select the **Item**.

STEP 8. Enter the **Description**. The system may complete this information automatically.

STEP 9. Enter the **QTY** (Quantity).

STEP 10. Enter the **Rate**. The system may complete this information automatically.

STEP 11. Verify the **Amount**.This information will automatically be filled in based on the quantity and rate entered.

STEP 12. Select **Save & New** if you want to create another invoice or **Save & Close** to leave the **Create Invoices** application.

Figure Q3
Invoice entry screen

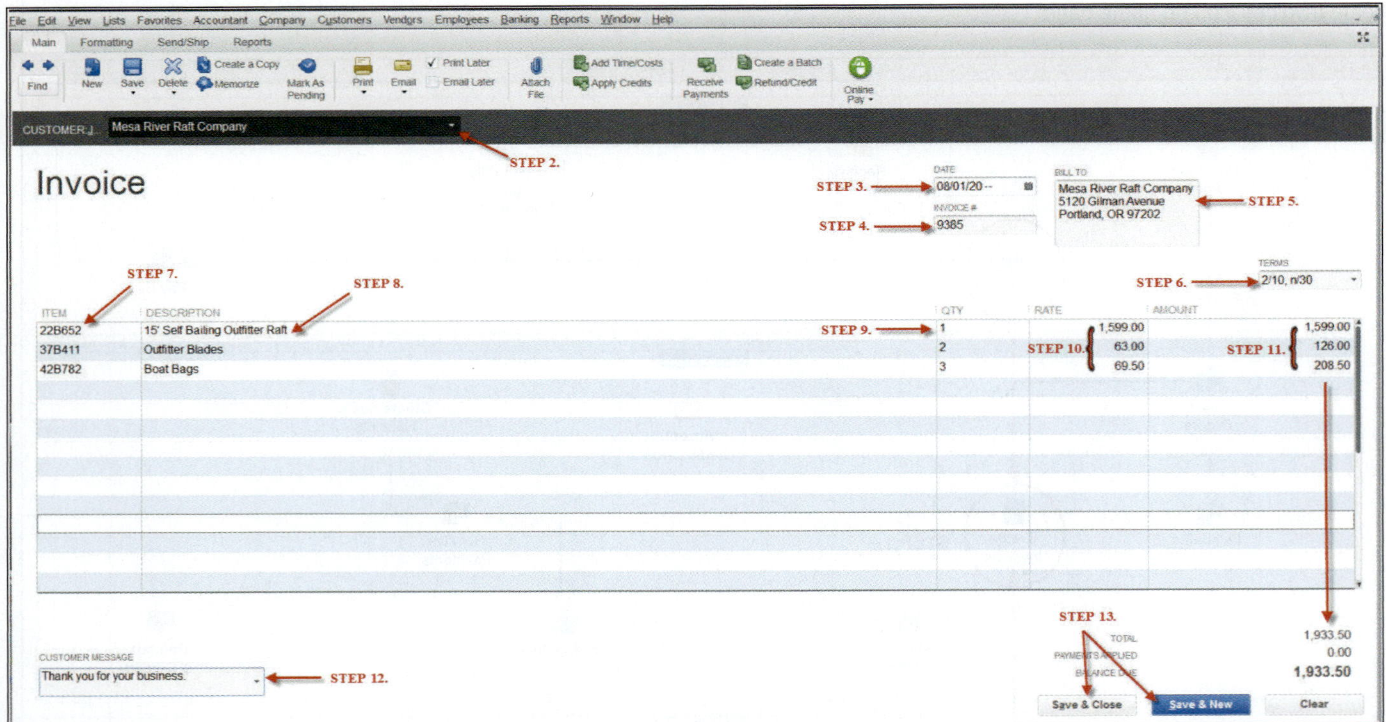

Learning Objective

3 Create credit memo/refunds.

As you learned in this chapter, occasionally customers will need to return inventory or will ask for a reduction in the original price for a specific reason, such as damaged or defective goods. QuickBooks uses the **Refunds & Credits** application to handle returned merchandise. To create a credit memo or refund, complete the following steps as shown in Figures Q4 and Q5.

STEP 1. Select **Refunds & Credits** from the home page, under the **Customers** center.

Figure Q4
Refunds & Credits icon on home page

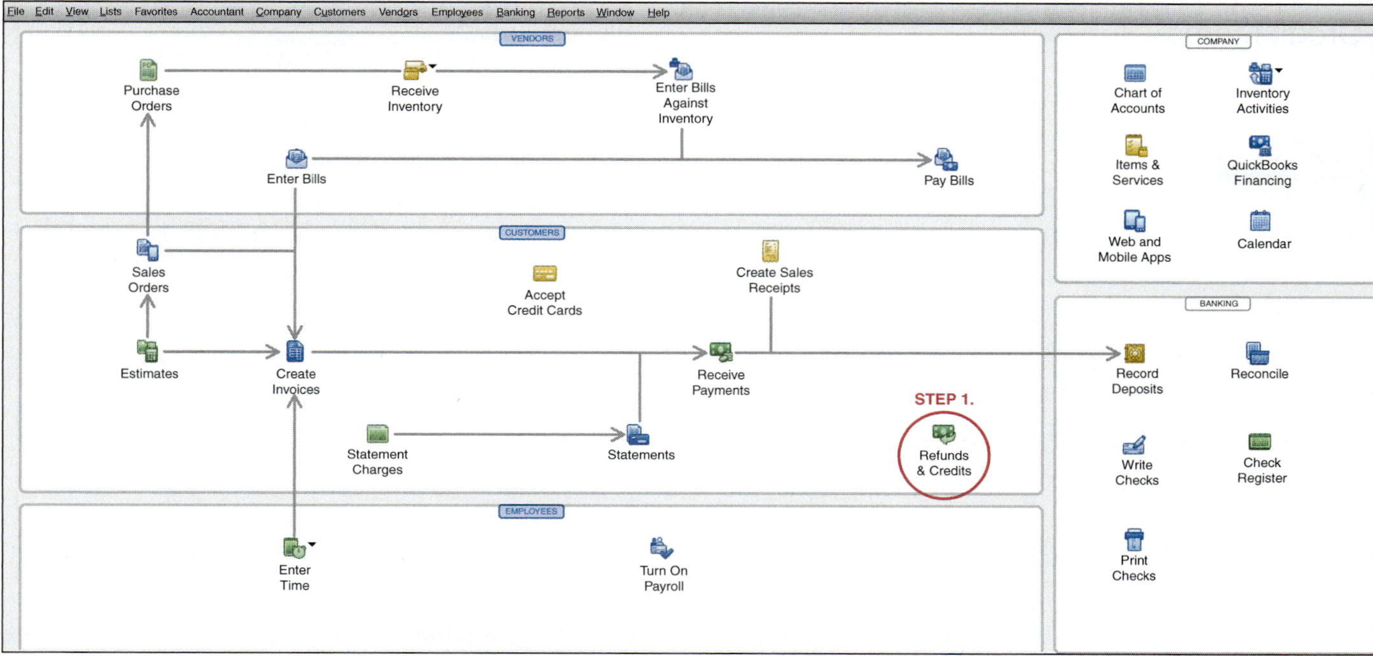

STEP 2. Select **Customer: Job** from the drop-down menu. In this example, the customer is Marty's Fly Fishing Adventures.

STEP 3. Select or enter the **Date**.

STEP 4. Enter the **Credit No.** The system may assign a number automatically.

STEP 5. Verify the **Customer** information. The system should fill in this information automatically from the **Customers** center.

STEP 6. Select the **Item**.

STEP 7. Enter the **Decription**. The system may complete this information automatically.

STEP 8. Enter the **QTY** (Quantity).

STEP 9. Enter the **Rate**. The system may complete this information automatically.

STEP 10. Verify the **Amount**. This information will automatically be filled in based on the quantity and rate.

STEP 11. Select **Save & New** if you want to create another credit memo or **Save & Close** to leave the **Credit Memo** application.

Figure Q5
Credit memo entry screen

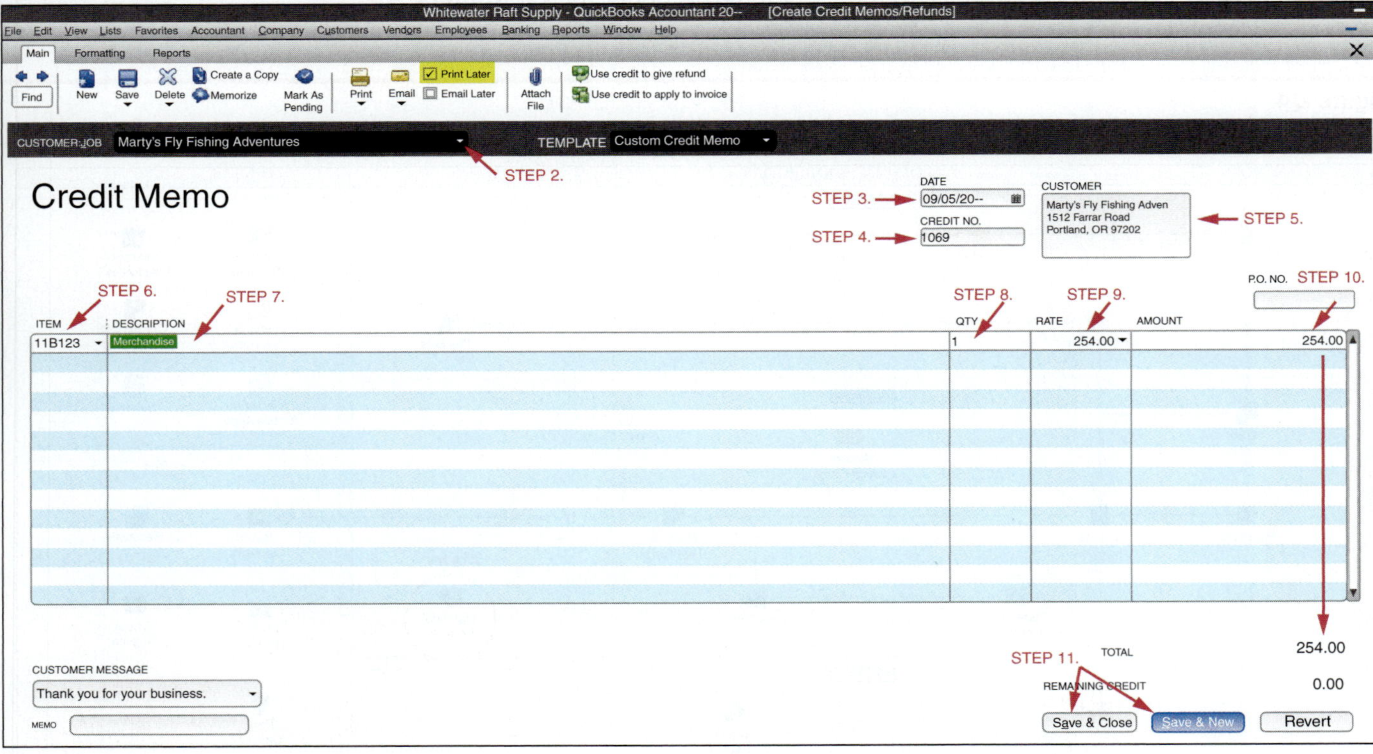

After you have created a credit memo, the **Available Credit** window, as shown in Figure Q6, may appear. Select how you would like to apply this credit, and then click **OK**. Credit memos can be retained as an available credit for future use, refunded, or applied to an existing invoice. For Marty's Fly Fishing Adventures, credit memo 1069 was applied to invoice 9386, as shown in Figure Q7.

Figure Q6
Available Credit

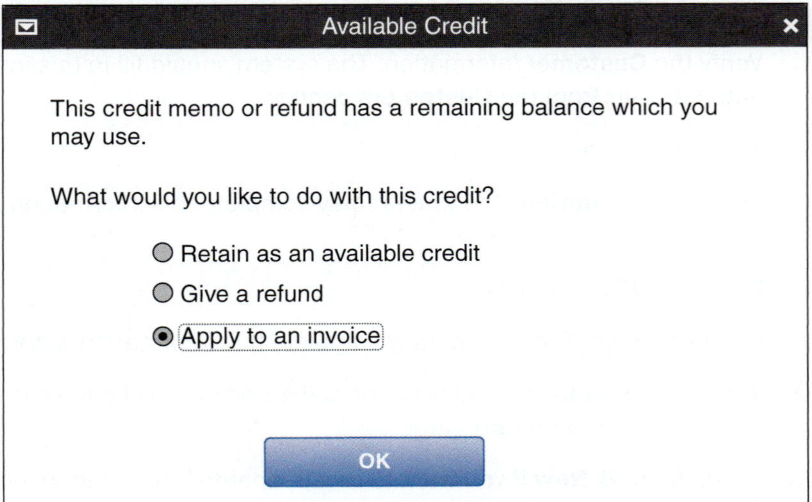

Figure Q7
Apply Credit to Invoices screen

Apply Credit to Invoices

CREDIT MEMO

Customer:Job Marty's Fly Fishing Adventures

Ref. No. 1069 Original Amt. 254.00

Date 09/05/20-- Remaining Credit 0.00

✓	DATE	JOB	NUMBER	ORIG. AMT.	AMT. DUE	AMT. APPLIED
✓	08/14/20--		9386	1,594.00	1,594.00	254.00
			Totals	1,594.00	0.00	254.00

Clear Selections

Done Cancel

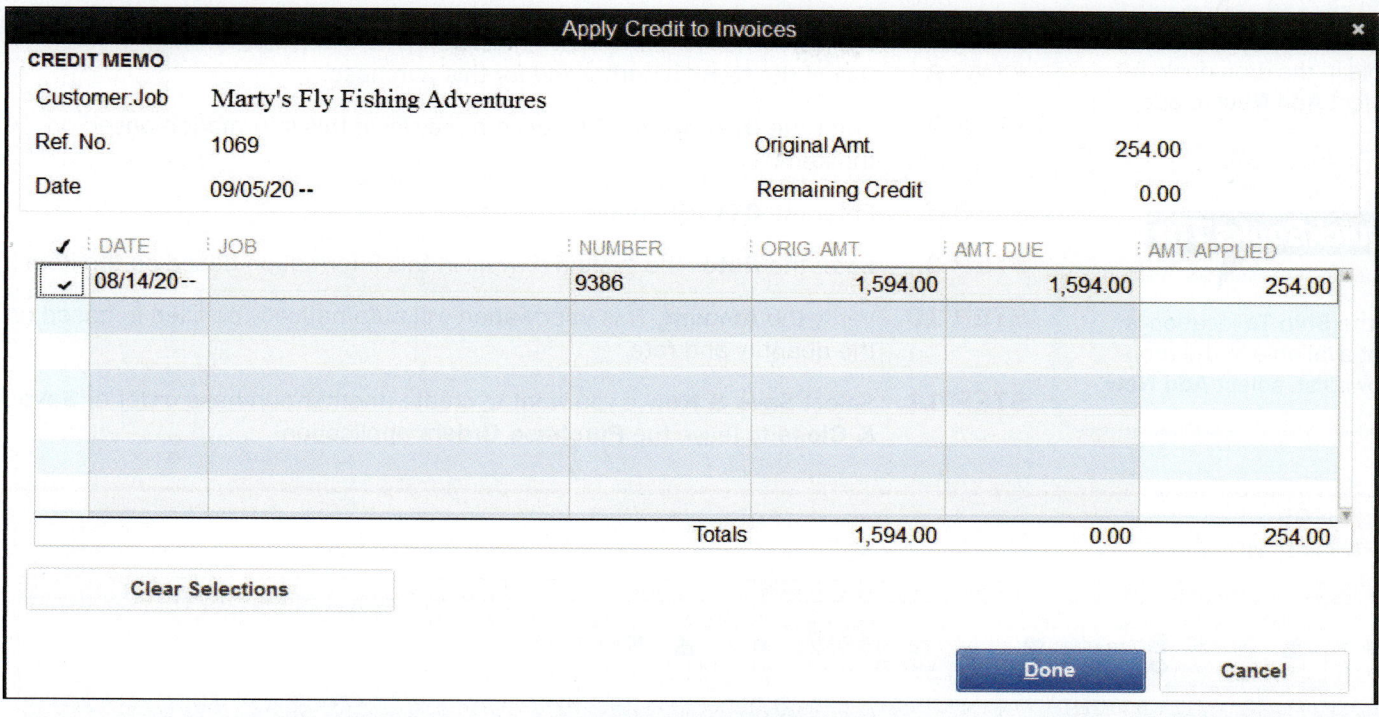

4 Create purchase orders. **Learning Objective**

As discussed in this chapter, purchases require strong internal controls. Organizations use purchase orders as one form of internal control to authorize and monitor purchases. QuickBooks has a **Purchase Orders** feature that is integrated with inventory and bill paying. To create purchase orders, complete the steps shown in Figures Q8 and Q9.

Figure Q8
Purchase Orders icon on home page

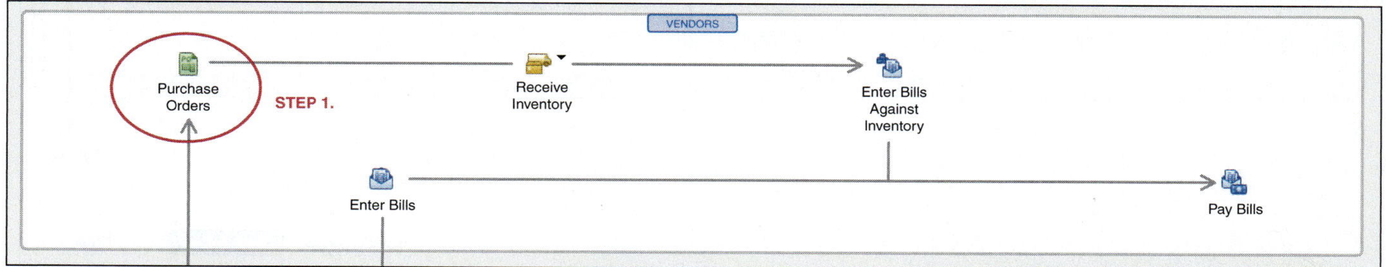

STEP 1. Select **Purchase Orders** from the home page, under the **Vendors** center.

STEP 2. Select **Vendor**. In this example, the vendor is Pataponia, Inc.

STEP 3. Select or enter the **Date**.

ACCOUNTING WITH QuickBooks®

QuickBooks Tip

If the vendor is not available in the drop-down list, select **Add New** to add.

QuickBooks Tip

If the **Ship To** location is not available in the drop-down list, select **Add New**.

STEP 4. Enter the **PO. No.** (Purchase Order Number). The system may assign a number.

STEP 5. Select the **Ship To** location.

STEP 6. Select the **Item**(s) authorized for this purchase.

STEP 7. Enter the **Description**. The system may fill in this information based on the item.

STEP 8. Enter the **QTY** (Quantity).

STEP 9. Enter the **Rate**. The system may fill in this information based on the item.

STEP 10. Verify the **Amount**. This information will automatically be filled in based on the quantity and rate.

STEP 11. Select **Save & New** if you want to create another purchase order or **Save & Close** to leave the **Purchase Orders** application.

Figure Q9

Purchase Order

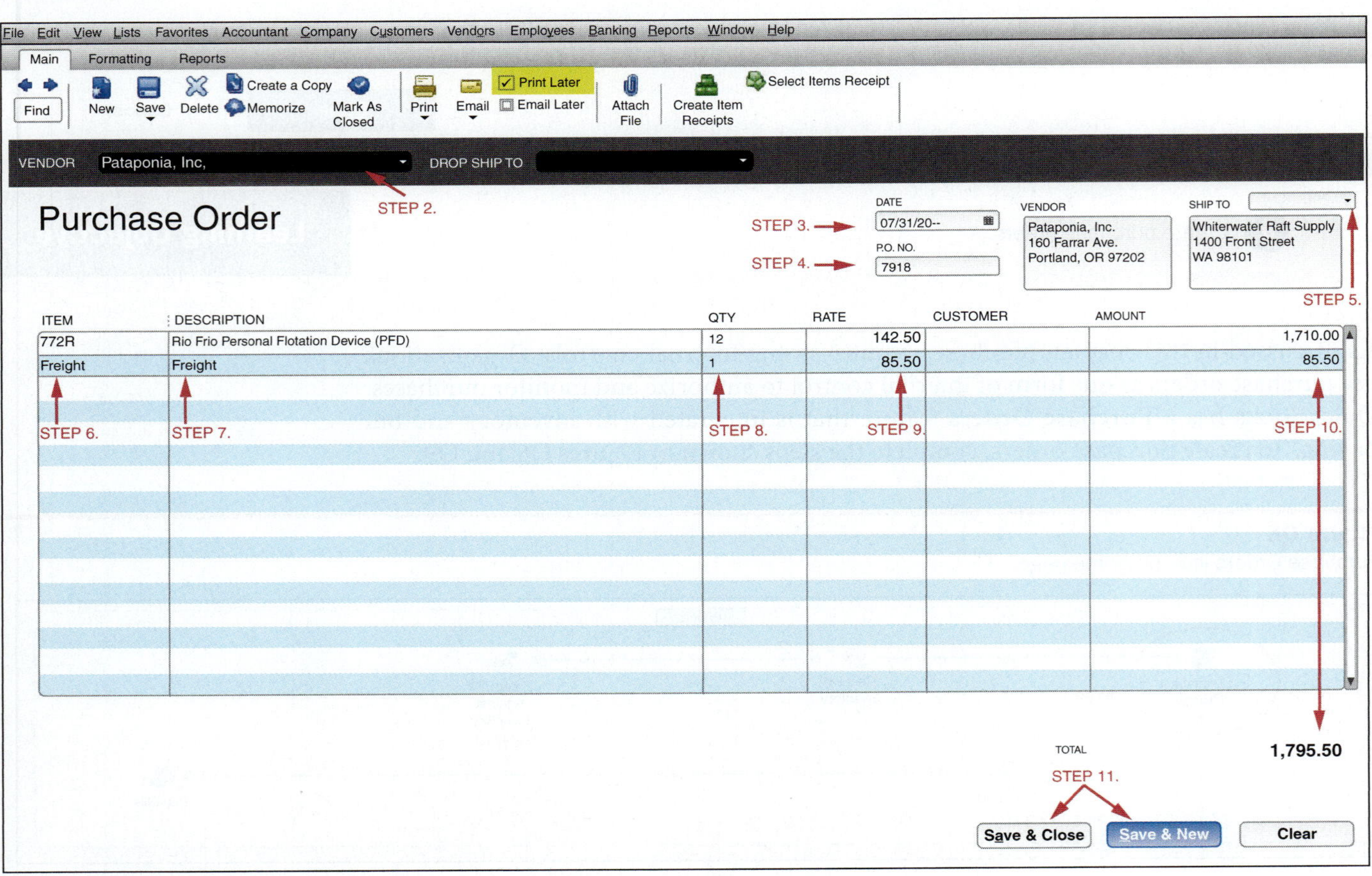

Learning Objective

5 Enter bills.

The **Enter Bills** feature in QuickBooks allows users to enter bills upon receipt. This feature assists users in monitoring amounts owed by vendors, payment discounts, and due dates. To use the **Enter Bills** feature, follow the steps in Figures Q10 and Q11.

STEP 1. Select **Enter Bills** from the home page, under the **Vendors** center.

Figure Q10
Enter Bills icon on home page

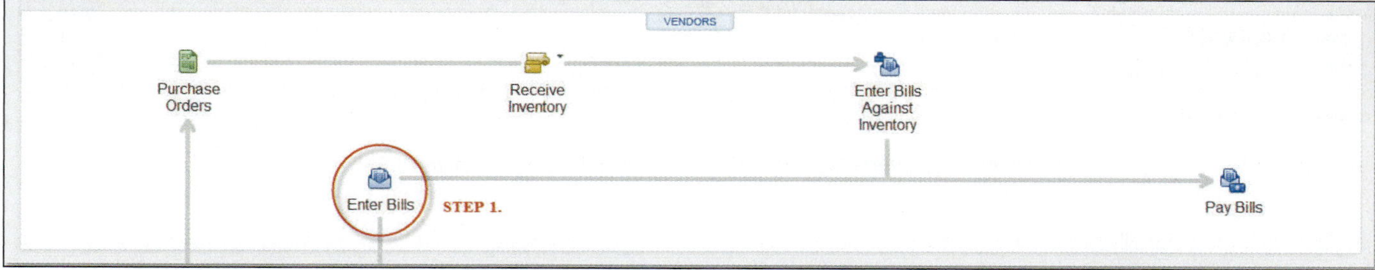

STEP 2. Select **Vendor**. In this example, the vendor is Pataponia, Inc.

STEP 3. Verify the **Address**. This information should be filled in automatically from the vendor information, but it can be added to or modified as needed.

STEP 4. Select or enter the **Date**.

STEP 5. Enter the **Ref. No.** This is typically the invoice number.

STEP 6. Enter the **Amount Due**. This is the total amount of the invoice.

STEP 7. Select the **Terms**. The **Terms** field will automatically fill in the **Discount Date** and **Bill Due** date.

STEP 8. Enter descriptive information in the **Memo** field as desired. In this example, the invoice number was entered.

STEP 9. Select the **Account**.

STEP 10. The invoice **Amount** will be filled in automatically from the **Amount Due** field. If more than one account is required in Step 9, you can modifiy the amount(s) in Step 10 as needed.

STEP 11. Enter descriptive information about the transaction in this **Memo** field. The information in this field will be recorded in the journal.

STEP 12. Select **Save & New** if you want to enter another bill or **Save & Close** to leave the **Enter Bills** application.

QuickBooks Tip

Purchase orders can be printed or e-mailed immediately upon completion, or they can be marked to print or e-mail later. Figure Q9 shows the **Print Later** option selected.

Figure Q11
Enter Bills entry screen

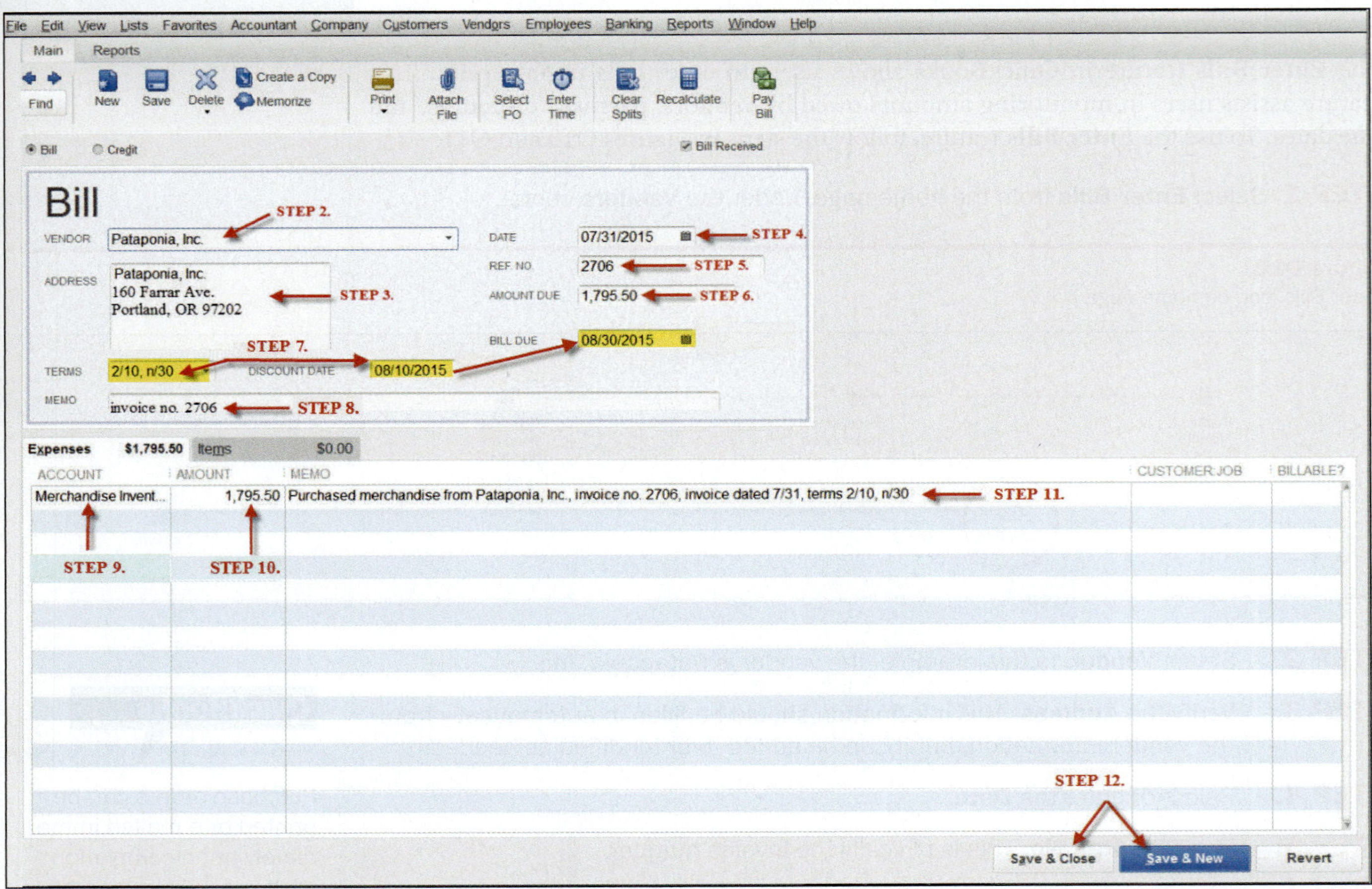

Learning Objective

6 View and print accounts receivable and accounts payable reports.

VIEW AND PRINT ACCOUNTS RECEIVABLE REPORTS

To view and print the accounts receivable reports, follow the steps below and as shown in Figure Q12.

STEP 1. Click the **Reports** tab.

STEP 2. Click **Customers & Receivables**.

STEP 3. Select the desired accounts receivable report. For this example, the A/R Aging Summary report was prepared in Figure Q13.

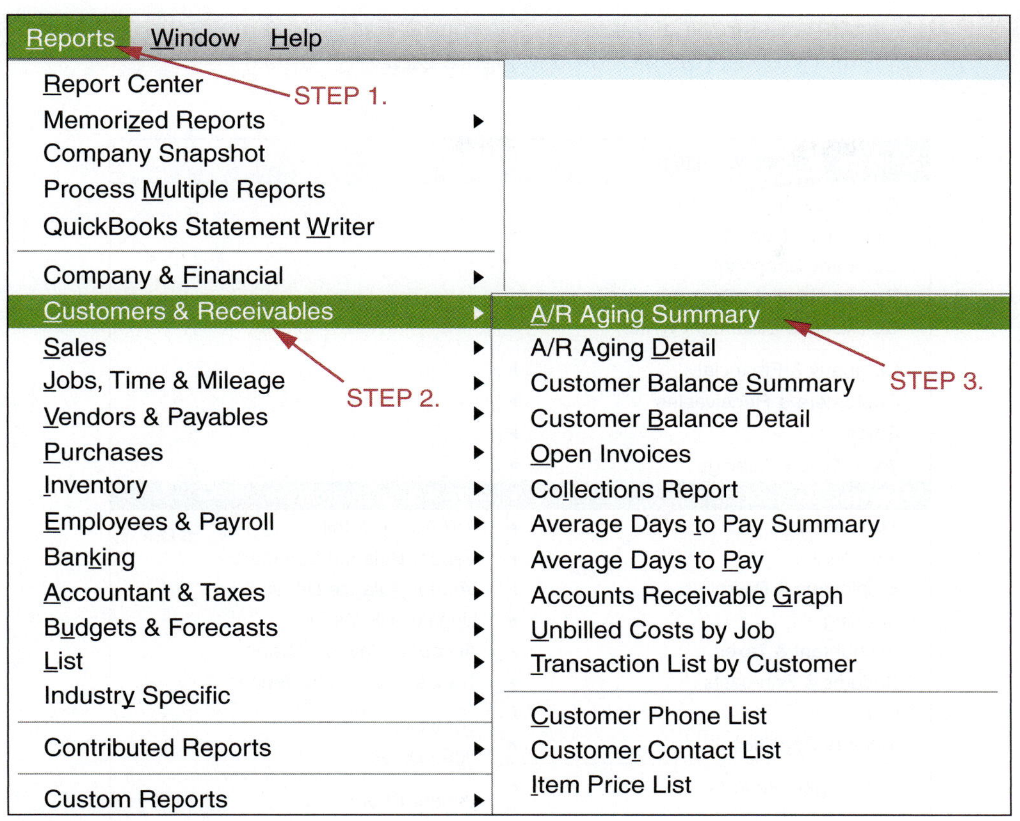

Figure Q12
Accounts Receivable report menu

The A/R Aging Summary report prepared in QuickBooks, as shown in Figure Q13, is the same information as the schedule of accounts receivable from page 432.

Whitewater Raft Supply
A/R Aging Summary
As of August 31, 20--

	Current	1–30	31–60	61–90	> 90	TOTAL
Green River Rafts	0.00	1,116.00	0.00	0.00	0.00	1,116.00
Hi-Flying Adventures, Inc.	0.00	2,226.30	0.00	0.00	0.00	2,226.30
Marty's Fly Fishing Adventures	1,594.00	0.00	0.00	0.00	0.00	1,594.00
Mesa River Raft Company	1,933.50	0.00	0.00	0.00	0.00	1,933.50
TOTAL	**3,527.50**	**3,342.30**	**0.00**	**0.00**	**0.00**	**6,869.80**

Figure Q13
A/R Aging Summary report

VIEW AND PRINT ACCOUNTS PAYABLE REPORTS

To view and print the accounts payable reports, follow the steps below and as shown in Figure Q14.

STEP 1. Click the **Reports** tab.

STEP 2. Click **Vendors & Payables**.

STEP 3. Select the desired accounts payable report. For this example, the A/P Aging Summary report was prepared in Figure Q15.

Figure Q14
Accounts Payable report menu

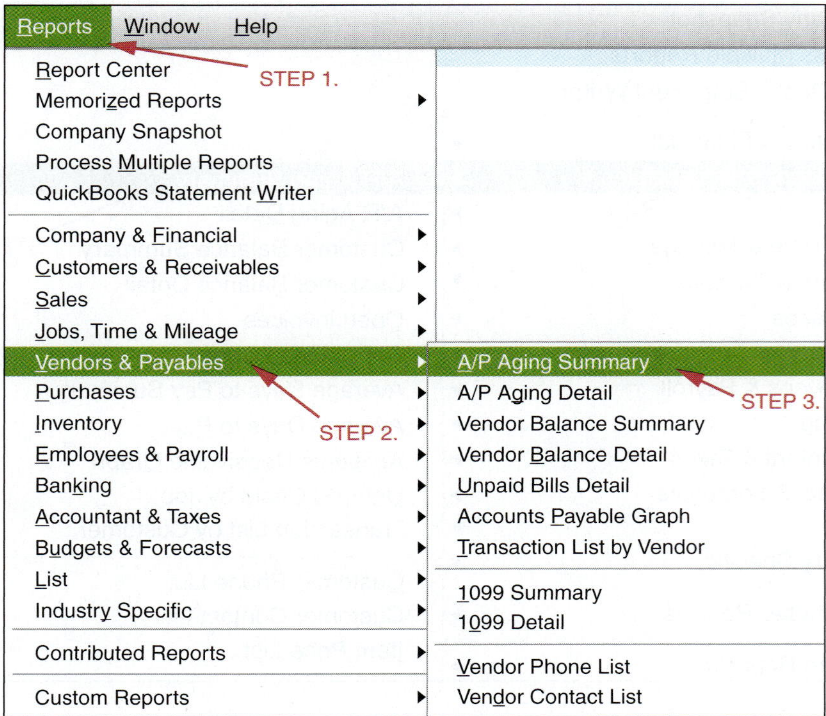

The A/P Aging Summary report prepared in QuickBooks, as shown in Figure Q15, is the same information as the schedule of accounts payable from page 440.

Figure Q15
A/P Aging Summary report

Whitewater Raft Supply
A/P Aging Summary
As of August 31, 20--

	Current	1–30	31–60	61–90	> 90	TOTAL
Dana Manufacturing Company	564.00	0.00	0.00	0.00	0.00	564.00
Langseth and Son	2,929.00	0.00	0.00	0.00	0.00	2,929.00
Pataponia, Inc.	2,606.00	1,795.50	0.00	0.00	0.00	4,401.50
TOTAL	**6,099.00**	**1,795.50**	**0.00**	**0.00**	**0.00**	**7,894.50**

Chapter Review

Study and Practice

1 Describe the nature of a merchandising business. **Learning Objective**

A **merchandising business** is a company that buys and sells inventory.

The **Merchandise Inventory** account is an asset account representing the cost of goods bought for resale.

Merchandise inventory can be recorded using the **periodic inventory system** or the **perpetual inventory system**.

Practice Exercise 1

Identify the appropriate inventory system (periodic or perpetual) below.

In the ________________ inventory system, companies keep continuous records of inventories.

The ________________ inventory system requires companies periodically to take a physical count of merchandise.

Practice Exercise 1 • SOLUTION

In the *perpetual* inventory system, companies keep continuous records of inventories.

The *periodic* inventory system requires companies periodically to take a physical count of merchandise.

2 Using a general journal and the periodic inventory system, record sales and sale-related transactions; then post to the general ledger and the accounts receivable ledger. **Learning Objective**

Sales transactions are recorded in the general journal by debiting Accounts Receivable and crediting Sales. The entry is posted to the Accounts Receivable and Sales accounts in the general ledger. The entries are also posted daily to the **accounts receivable ledger**.

When a customer returns merchandise, or when his or her bill is reduced by an allowance for defective or damaged merchandise, the Sales Returns and Allowances account is debited and the Accounts Receivable account is credited. The entry is recorded in the general journal and posted to both the general ledger and the accounts receivable ledger.

Where required, sales tax is collected from customers by the retailer and later paid to the appropriate tax authorities. When goods are sold, the sales tax is charged to the customer and recorded at the time of sale. The entry involves recording a debit to Accounts Receivable or Cash and credits to Sales and Sales Tax Payable.

PRACTICE EXERCISE 2

Record the following transactions for Rodgers Refrigerator Supply in general journal form.

Aug.	23	Sold merchandise on account to Robbins Hardware Store, invoice no. 3209, $1,340.
Sept.	1	Robbins Hardware Store returned $81 of the merchandise. Rodgers Refrigerator Supply issued credit memo no. 114.
	14	Sold merchandise on account to C. Heald, invoice no. 3210, $560 plus $44.80 sales tax.

PRACTICE EXERCISE 2 • SOLUTION

GENERAL JOURNAL Page ___

Date		Description	Post. Ref.	Debit	Credit
20--					
Aug.	23	Accounts Receivable, Robbins			
		Hardware Store		1,340.00	
		Sales			1,340.00
		Sold merchandise to Robbins			
		Hardware Store, invoice			
		no. 3209.			
Sept.	1	Sales Returns and Allowances		81.00	
		Accounts Receivable, Robbins			
		Hardware Store			81.00
		Issued credit memo no. 114.			
	14	Accounts Receivable, C. Heald		604.80	
		Sales			560.00
		Sales Tax Payable			44.80
		Sold merchandise to C. Heald,			
		invoice no. 3210.			

Learning Objective

Prepare a schedule of accounts receivable.

The schedule of accounts receivable consists of a listing of the individual account balances of the credit customers taken from the accounts receivable ledger.

PRACTICE EXERCISE 3

Fill in the missing amounts in the accounts receivable subsidiary ledgers for Willis Spas and Pools. Then, using the information from the ledgers, prepare a schedule of accounts receivable as of May 31.

ACCOUNTS RECEIVABLE LEDGER

NAME J. Hersch
ADDRESS 3540 Key Avenue
Lampasas, TX 76550

Date		Item	Post. Ref.	Debit	Credit	Balance
20--						
May	2		J26	781.40		781.40
	8		J26	1,780.00		(a)
	22		J26		1,205.00	(b)

NAME M. Hill
ADDRESS 220 Lawrence Avenue
Copperas Cove, TX 76522

Date		Item	Post. Ref.	Debit	Credit	Balance
20--						
May	15		J26	481.40		481.40
	18		J26		204.80	(c)

NAME R. D. Moen
ADDRESS 416 Fifth Avenue
Dallas, TX 75204

Date		Item	Post. Ref.	Debit	Credit	Balance
20--						
May	31		J26	312.60		312.60

PRACTICE EXERCISE 3 • SOLUTION

(a) $2,561.40
(b) $1,356.40
(c) $276.60

Willis Spas and Pools
Schedule of Accounts Receivable
May 31, 20--

J. Hersch	$1,356.40
M. Hill	276.60
R. D. Moen	312.60
Total Accounts Receivable	$1,945.60

Learning Objective 4 Using a general journal and the periodic inventory system, record purchase and purchase-related transactions; then post to the general ledger and the accounts payable ledger.

Purchase transactions are recorded in the general journal by debiting the Purchases account and crediting Accounts Payable. If the company pays for freight, the company will also record a debit to Freight In. The purchase transactions are posted to the general ledger as a debit to Purchases, a debit to Freight In, and a credit to Accounts Payable. Each transaction must also be posted daily to the **accounts payable ledger**.

When a credit memo is received for the return of merchandise or as an allowance for damaged goods, the buyer credits Purchases Returns and Allowances. If the merchandise was bought on account, the buyer debits Accounts Payable. The entry is recorded in the general journal and posted to both the general ledger and the accounts payable ledger.

The Freight In account is debited for the cost of transportation charges on incoming merchandise intended for resale. Freight costs that apply to non-merchandise assets purchased are added to the asset account that applies.

4 PRACTICE EXERCISE 4

Record the following transaction for Byrne Corporation in general journal form.

Apr. 14 Bought merchandise on account from Jabari, Inc., invoice no. C3009, $1,125; terms net 30 days; dated April 12; FOB shipping point, freight prepaid and added to the invoice, $72.50 (total $1,197.50).

24 Byrne Corporation received credit memo no. 117 from Jabari, Inc., for merchandise returned, $127.

PRACTICE EXERCISE 4 • SOLUTION

GENERAL JOURNAL Page ___

Date		Description	Post. Ref.	Debit	Credit
20--					
Apr.	14	Purchases		1 1 2 5 00	
		Freight In		7 2 50	
		Accounts Payable, Jabari, Inc.			1 1 9 7 50
		Purchased merchandise from			
		Jabari, Inc., invoice no. C3009,			
		invoice dated 4/12, terms n/30.			
	24	Accounts Payable, Jabari, Inc.		1 2 7 00	
		Purchases Returns and Allowances			1 2 7 00
		Credit memo no. 117 for			
		return of merchandise.			

Learning Objective  5 Prepare a schedule of accounts payable.

A schedule of accounts payable, which lists the balance of each creditor's account, is prepared from the accounts payable ledger.

5 PRACTICE EXERCISE 5

Fill in the missing amounts in the accounts payable subsidiary ledgers for Updike Train Supply. Then, using the information from the ledgers, prepare a schedule of accounts payable as of June 30.

ACCOUNTS PAYABLE LEDGER

NAME J. Fletcher and Sons
ADDRESS 326 Fairway Drive
Richmond, CA 94805

Date		Item	Post. Ref.	Debit	Credit	Balance
20--						
June	1		J73		1 7 5 1 55	1 7 5 1 55
	14		J73	1 5 7 6 15		(a)

NAME Rocky and Schlink
ADDRESS 542 Roselle Blvd.
Oakland, CA 94601

Date		Item	Post. Ref.	Debit	Credit	Balance
20--						
June	13		J73		2 1 8 00	2 1 8 00

NAME Tan Supplies
ADDRESS 120 Fish Road
Berkeley, CA 94720

Date		Item	Post. Ref.	Debit	Credit	Balance
20--						
June	5		J73		2 7 1 0 00	2 7 1 0 00
	23		J73		1 7 4 0 25	(b)
	29		J73	1 5 0 0 00		(c)

PRACTICE EXERCISE 5 • SOLUTION

(a) $175.40
(b) $4,450.25
(c) $2,950.25

Updike Train Supply
Schedule of Accounts Payable
June 30, 20--

J. Fletcher and Sons	$ 175.40
Rocky and Schlink	218.00
Tan Supplies	2,950.25
Total Accounts Payable	$3,343.65

6 Using a general journal and the perpetual inventory system, record sales and sale-related transactions.

Learning Objective

The perpetual inventory system keeps continuous records of inventories by recording all transactions. This system allows companies, at any given time, to know the current cost of inventory on hand and provides them with a better understanding of their sales profits. With the perpetual inventory system, sales, sales returns and allowances, and purchases are recorded differently than in the periodic inventory system. While the actual sales portion of the sales transaction is recorded the same under both methods, the perpetual inventory system requires an additional step in the recording process. To track the inventory and costs, accountants using the perpetual inventory system debit Cost of Goods Sold and credit Merchandise Inventory.

6 PRACTICE EXERCISE 6

Record the following transactions for North Company in general journal form. North Company uses the perpetual inventory system.

July 1 Sold merchandise on account to Ryder, Inc., invoice no. 5865, $1,450.50. Cost of inventory sold is $1,125.40.

6 Sold merchandise on account to Dean Co., invoice no. 5866, $2,240.25. Cost of inventory sold is $1,950.30.

8 Ryder, Inc., returned $475.00 worth of merchandise purchased on July 1, with a cost of $230.25. North Company issued credit memorandum no. 149.

PRACTICE EXERCISE 6 • SOLUTION

GENERAL JOURNAL Page ___

Date		Description	Post. Ref.	Debit	Credit
20--					
July	1	Accounts Receivable, Ryder, Inc.		1 4 5 0 50	
		Sales			1 4 5 0 50
		Sold merchandise on account to			
		Ryder, Inc., invoice no. 5865.			
		Cost of Goods Sold		1 1 2 5 40	
		Merchandise Inventory			1 1 2 5 40
		Cost of merchandise sold			
		to Ryder, Inc., invoice no. 5865			
	6	Accounts Receivable, Dean Co.		2 2 4 0 25	
		Sales			2 2 4 0 25
		Sold merchandise to Dean Co.,			
		invoice no. 5866			
		Cost of Goods Sold		1 9 5 0 30	
		Merchandise Inventory			1 9 5 0 30
		Cost of merchandise sold to Dean Co.,			
		invoice no. 5866			
	8	Sales Returns and Allowances		4 7 5 00	
		Accounts Receivable, Ryder, Inc.			4 7 5 00
		Issued credit memo no. 149			
		Merchandise Inventory		2 3 0 25	
		Cost of Goods Sold			2 3 0 25
		Cost of merchandise returned credit			
		memo no. 149			

7 Using a general journal and the perpetual inventory system, record purchase and purchase-related transactions.

Learning Objective

Under the perpetual inventory system, all transactions related to the purchase of inventory (including freight in) are recorded in the Merchandise Inventory account. In addition, the purchase return and allowance of merchandise is recorded as a credit to Merchandise Inventory.

PRACTICE EXERCISE 7

Record the following transactions for Mitchell Co., in general journal form. Mitchell Co. uses the perpetual inventory system.

Aug. 1 Bought merchandise on account from Engel Industries, invoice no. 2516, $3,542.15; terms 2/10, n/30; FOB Detroit, freight prepaid and added to the invoice, $115.00 (total $3,657.15).

10 Received credit memorandum no. 1115 from Engel Industries for $450.00.

PRACTICE EXERCISE 7 • SOLUTION

GENERAL JOURNAL Page ___

Date		Description	Post. Ref.	Debit	Credit
20--					
Aug.	1	Merchandise Inventory		3 6 5 7 15	
		Accounts Payable, Engel Industries			3 6 5 7 15
		Purchased merchandise from Engel			
		Industries, invoice no. 2516,			
		invoice dated 8/1, terms 2/10, n/30			
	10	Accounts Payable, Engel Industries		4 5 0 00	
		Merchandise Inventory			4 5 0 00
		Credit memo no. 1115 for return of			
		merchandise.			

8 Record transactions in a sales journal and post to the general ledger and accounts receivable ledger.

Learning Objective

The **sales journal** is used to record only sales of merchandise on account. The entries are posted daily to the accounts receivable ledger. At the end of the month, the total is posted to the general ledger as a debit to the Accounts Receivable controlling account and a credit to the Sales account.

PRACTICE EXERCISE 8

Record the following sales of merchandise on account on page 25 of the sales journal and then post to the general ledger. (The company uses the same account numbers as Whitewater Raft Supply.)

Apr. 1 Sold merchandise on account to West Company, invoice no. 1054, $1,378.95.

15 Sold merchandise on account to Ruiz Company, invoice no. 1055, $578.15.

PRACTICE EXERCISE 8 • SOLUTION

SALES JOURNAL — Page 25

Date		Inv. No.	Customer's Name	Post. Ref.	Accounts Receivable Dr. Sales Cr.
20--					
Apr.	1	1054	West Company		1,378.95
	15	1055	Ruiz Company		578.15
	30		Total		1,957.10
					(113) (411)

GENERAL LEDGER

ACCOUNT **Accounts Receivable** — ACCOUNT NO. 113

Date		Item	Post. Ref.	Debit	Credit	Balance Debit	Balance Credit
20--							
Apr.	30		S25	1,957.10		1,957.10	

ACCOUNT **Sales** — ACCOUNT NO. 411

Date		Item	Post. Ref.	Debit	Credit	Balance Debit	Balance Credit
20--							
Apr.	30		S25		1,957.10		1,957.10

Learning Objective  Record transactions in a three-column purchases journal and post to the general ledger and accounts payable ledger.

The three-column **purchases journal** handles the purchase of merchandise on account and freight charges that are prepaid by the seller and included in the invoice total. Amounts in the Accounts Payable credit column are posted daily to the accounts payable ledger. At the end of the month, the totals are posted to the general ledger as a debit to Purchases, a debit to Freight In, and a credit to Accounts Payable.

9 PRACTICE EXERCISE 9

Record the following purchases of merchandise on account on page 52 of the purchases journal and then post to the general ledger. (The company uses the same account numbers as Whitewater Raft Supply.)

Jan. 4 Bought merchandise on account from Switzer Corporation, invoice no. A459, $578; terms net 60 days; dated January 2; FOB destination.

24 Bought merchandise on account from Stevens Company, invoice no. 48512, $799.80; terms 2/10, n/30; dated January 22; FOB shipping point, freight prepaid and added to the invoice, $50 (total $849.80).

PRACTICE EXERCISE 9 • SOLUTION

PURCHASES JOURNAL Page 52

Date		Supplier's Name	Inv. No.	Inv. Date	Terms	Post. Ref.	Accounts Payable Credit	Freight In Debit	Purchases Debit
20--									
Jan.	4	Switzer Corporation	A459	1/2	n/60		578 00		578 00
	24	Stevens Company	48512	1/22	2/10, n/30		849 80	50 00	799 80
	31	Totals					1,427 80	50 00	1,377 80
							(212)	(514)	(511)

GENERAL LEDGER

ACCOUNT Accounts Payable **ACCOUNT NO.** 212

Date		Item	Post. Ref.	Debit	Credit	Balance Debit	Balance Credit
20--							
Jan.	31		P52		1,427 80		1,427 80

ACCOUNT Purchases **ACCOUNT NO.** 511

Date		Item	Post. Ref.	Debit	Credit	Balance Debit	Balance Credit
20--							
Jan.	31		P52	1,377 80		1,377 80	

ACCOUNT Freight In **ACCOUNT NO.** 514

Date		Item	Post. Ref.	Debit	Credit	Balance Debit	Balance Credit
20--							
Jan.	31		P52	50 00		50 00	

Glossary

Accounts payable ledger A subsidiary ledger that lists the individual accounts of creditors in alphabetical or numerical order with their respective balances. *(p. 439)*

Accounts receivable ledger A subsidiary ledger that lists the individual accounts of credit customers in alphabetical or numerical order, with their respective transactions and balances. *(p. 431)*

Controlling account An account in the general ledger that summarizes the balances of a subsidiary ledger. *(p. 431)*

Cost of Goods Sold account An account, used in the perpetual inventory system, that represents the cost of the inventory sold. *(p. 443)*

Credit memorandum A written statement indicating a seller's willingness to reduce the amount of a buyer's debt. The seller records the amount of the credit memorandum in the Sales Returns and Allowances account. *(p. 429)*

FOB destination Shipping terms under which the seller pays the freight charges and includes them in the selling price. Title or ownership changes hands when the buyer receives the goods. *(p. 437)*

FOB shipping point Shipping terms under which the buyer pays the freight charges between the point of shipment and the destination. Payment may be made directly to the carrier upon receiving the goods or to the supplier if the supplier prepaid the freight charges on behalf of the buyer. Title or ownership changes hands when goods are transferred to the freight company. *(p. 437)*

Invoices Business forms prepared by the seller that list the items shipped, their cost, the terms of the sale, and the mode of shipment. They may also state the freight charges. The buyer considers them purchase invoices; the seller considers them sales invoices. *(p. 426)*

Merchandise inventory Goods (an asset account) that a company buys and intends to resell at a profit. *(p. 425)*

Merchandising businesses Businesses that buy and sell goods. *(p. 425)*

Periodic inventory system A method of recording inventory that requires the company to determine the amount of goods on hand by periodically taking a physical count and then attaching a value to it. *(p. 425)*

Perpetual inventory system A method of recording inventory that provides the firm with a running balance of inventory. *(p. 425)*

Purchases account An account for recording the cost of merchandise acquired for resale. *(p. 433)*

Purchases journal A special journal used to record only the buying of goods on account. It may be used to record the purchase of merchandise only. *(p. 447)*

Purchases Returns and Allowances account An account that records a company's return of merchandise it has purchased or a reduction in the bill for an agreed-upon reason; it is treated as a deduction from Purchases. *(p. 436)*

Sales account A revenue account for recording the sale of merchandise. *(p. 425)*

Sales journal A special journal for recording only the sale of merchandise on account. *(p. 447)*

Sales Returns and Allowances account The account a seller uses to record the physical return of merchandise by customers or a reduction in a bill for an agreed-upon reason. Sales Returns and Allowances is treated as a deduction from Sales. This account is usually evidenced by a credit memorandum issued by the seller. *(p. 428)*

Sales Tax Payable account An account used to record a tax levied by a state or city government on the retail sale of goods and services. The tax is paid by the consumer but collected by the retailer. *(p. 429)*

Special journals Books of original entry in which specialized types of repetitive transactions are recorded. *(p. 447)*

Subsidiary ledger A group of accounts representing individual subdivisions showing the debits and credits of a controlling account. *(p. 431)*

Quiz Yourself

_____ 1. Which of the following is true about the Sales Returns and Allowances account?
   a. It is used to record the sale of merchandise.
   b. It is used to record the reduction of inventory.
   c. It is a contra account, deducted from sales.
   d. It is used to record discounts for prompt payment.
   e. None of the above.

_____ 2. What is the accounts receivable ledger?
   a. A record of credit customers and their balances
   b. A record of vendors and their balances
   c. Part of the sales journal
   d. Part of the general journal
   e. Part of the general ledger

_____ 3. Using the information contained in the accounts receivable ledger, the accountant can prepare __________.
   a. The general ledger balance
   b. The balance sheet
   c. The income statement
   d. A schedule of accounts receivable
   e. None of the above

_____ 4. Which of the following is a written statement indicating a seller's willingness to reduce the amount of a buyer's debt?
   a. Debit memorandum
   b. Credit memorandum
   c. Letter of intent
   d. Sales Returns and Allowances memorandum
   e. None of the above

_____ 5. What does the "2" in 2/10, n/30 mean?
   a. Pay in 2 days to ensure early payment
   b. 2% discount for early payment within 10 days
   c. 2% extra payment due if paid between 10 days and 30 days
   d. $2 discount if paid within 10 days
   e. None of the above

_____ 6. Which of the following is a subsidiary ledger that consists of individual accounts for all creditors?
   a. Accounts receivable ledger
   b. Controlling ledger
   c. Accounts payable ledger
   d. Inventory ledger
   e. Purchase ledger

_____ 7. The schedule of accounts payable lists each creditor's account balance, and the total equals the ______________.
   a. Controlling account in the journal
   b. Accounts Payable account in the general ledger
   c. Accounts Receivable account in the general ledger
   d. Purchases account in the general ledger
   e. Sales account in the general ledger

_____ 8. If the seller assumes the entire cost of transportation, without any reimbursement from the buyer, the freight terms are considered ______________.
   a. FOB shipping point
   b. FOB destination
   c. Freight in
   d. Freight out
   e. FOB freight

_____ 9. Under the perpetual inventory system, how does the seller record sales made on account?

a. Accounts Payable	DR	
Sales		CR
b. Sales	DR	
Accounts Payable		CR
c. Accounts Receivable	DR	
Sales		CR
d. Accounts Receivable	DR	
Sales		CR
Cost of Goods Sold	DR	
Merchandise Inventory		CR
e. Sales	DR	
Accounts Receivable		CR
Merchandise Inventory	DR	
Cost of Goods Sold		CR

_____ 10. Purchases on account of merchandise for resale would be recorded in the ______________.
   a. Sales journal
   b. Purchases journal
   c. Cash receipts journal
   d. Cash payments journal
   e. None of the above

Answers:
1. c 2. a 3. d 4. b 5. b 6. c 7. b
8. b 9. d 10. b

Review It with QuickBooks®

_____ 1. All of the following are QuickBooks centers, *except*
   a. Vendors.
   b. Suppliers.
   c. Customers.
   d. Banking.

_____ 2. Sales can be recorded in QuickBooks by all of the following methods, *except*
   a. using the journal entry method.
   b. by creating a sales receipt.
   c. by creating sales.
   d. by creating an invoice.

_____ 3. The Amount field in Credit Memos
   a. is calculated by the rate.
   b. is calculated by the quantity.
   c. must be manually entered in QuickBooks.
   d. Both a and b

_____ 4. The A/R Aging Summary report in QuickBooks is similar to the __________ in a manual accounting system.
   a. schedule of accounts receivable
   b. A/P Aging Summary report
   c. schedule of accounts payable
   d. Accounts Receivable general ledger account

Answers:
1. b 2. c 3. d 4. a

Chapter Assignments

Discussion Questions

1. What is the difference between a wholesale business and a retail business?
2. For each of the following accounts, identify whether the normal balance is a debit or a credit. Also specify whether the account is a contra account.
   a. Sales Returns and Allowances
   b. Merchandise Inventory
   c. Sales
   d. Freight In
   e. Purchases Returns and Allowances
   f. Sales Tax Payable
   g. Purchases
3. What is the purpose of each of the following?
   a. Schedule of accounts receivable
   b. Schedule of accounts payable
4. Why is an accounts receivable ledger or an accounts payable ledger necessary for a business with large numbers of credit customers or large numbers of vendors/suppliers?
5. Why is it a good practice to post daily to the accounts receivable or accounts payable ledgers?
6. With regard to goods sold and purchased, explain how sales returns and allowances and purchases returns and allowances are different from each other.
7. Explain the meaning and importance of the shipping terms FOB destination and FOB shipping point. Who has title to the goods once they have been shipped?
8. Describe the four procedures that most companies follow to maintain internal control of purchases of merchandise.
9. Describe the posting procedures to the general ledger and the rules for totaling and ruling the following.
   a. Sales journal
   b. Purchases journal
10. Describe the procedure for posting each of the following:
    a. From the sales journal to the accounts receivable ledger
    b. From the purchases journal to the accounts payable ledger
11. Who issues a credit memorandum and why?
12. What is the difference between a periodic inventory system and a perpetual inventory system?

Exercises

LO 2

Practice Exercise 2

QuickBooks

EXERCISE 9-1 Record the following transactions in general journal form.

a. Sold merchandise on account to D. North, invoice no. 4556, $2,515.25.
b. Sold merchandise on account to NexStar Industries, invoice no. 4557, $775.00.
c. NexStar Industries returned $225.50 worth of the merchandise. Issued credit memo no. 101.

*Follow the instructions on pages 453–457 when using QuickBooks.

LO 2

Practice Exercises 2, 3

EXERCISE 9-2 Post the following entry to the general ledger and subsidiary ledger.

GENERAL JOURNAL — Page 52

Date		Description	Post. Ref.	Debit	Credit
20--					
June	16	Sales Returns and Allowances		241 27	
		Accounts Receivable, F. E. Dixon			241 27
		Issued credit memo no. 131.			

GENERAL LEDGER

ACCOUNT Accounts Receivable — ACCOUNT NO. 113

Date		Item	Post. Ref.	Debit	Credit	Balance Debit	Balance Credit
20--							
June	1	Balance	✓			6511 19	

ACCOUNT Sales Returns and Allowances — ACCOUNT NO. 412

Date		Item	Post. Ref.	Debit	Credit	Balance Debit	Balance Credit
20--							
June	1	Balance	✓			314 60	

ACCOUNTS RECEIVABLE LEDGER

NAME F. E. Dixon
ADDRESS 416 Fifth Avenue
Dallas, TX 75204

Date		Item	Post. Ref.	Debit	Credit	Balance
20--						
May	31		J51	312 60		312 60

LO 2

Practice Exercise 2

EXERCISE 9-3 Record the following transactions in general journal form.

a. Sold merchandise on account to A. Bauer, $680 plus $54.40 sales tax (invoice no. D446).

b. Bauer returned $105.50 of the merchandise. Issued credit memo no. 114 for $113.94 ($105.50 for the amount of the sale plus $8.44 for the amount of the sales tax).

LO 4

Practice Exercise 4

EXERCISE 9-4 Journalize the following transactions in general journal form.

a. Bought merchandise on account from Brewer, Inc., invoice no. B2997, $914; terms net 30 days; FOB destination.

b. Received credit memo no. 96 from Brewer, Inc., for merchandise returned, $238.

CHAPTER ASSIGNMENTS

4

Practice Exercises 4, 5

EXERCISE 9-5 Post the following entry to the general ledger and the subsidiary ledger.

GENERAL JOURNAL — Page 92

Date		Description	Post. Ref.	Debit	Credit
20--					
July	14	Accounts Payable, Jensen and Silva		1 9 2 30	
		Purchases Returns and			
		Allowances			1 9 2 30
		Credit memo no. 942 for			
		return of merchandise.			

GENERAL LEDGER

ACCOUNT Accounts Payable — **ACCOUNT NO. 212**

Date		Item	Post. Ref.	Debit	Credit	Balance Debit	Balance Credit
20--							
July	1	Balance	✓				2 7 6 1 24

ACCOUNT Purchases Returns and Allowances — **ACCOUNT NO. 512**

Date		Item	Post. Ref.	Debit	Credit	Balance Debit	Balance Credit
20--							
July	1	Balance	✓				2 3 0 16

ACCOUNTS PAYABLE LEDGER

NAME Jensen and Silva

ADDRESS 542 Roselle Blvd.

Chicago, IL 60141

Date		Item	Post. Ref.	Debit	Credit	Balance
20--						
July	5		J92		2 1 8 00	2 1 8 00

LO 2, 4

Practice Exercises 2, 4

EXERCISE 9-6 Record the following transactions in general journal form for Ford Education Outfitters and Romero Textbooks, Inc.

a. Ford Educational Outfitters bought merchandise on account from Romero Textbooks, Inc., invoice no. 10594, $1,875.34; terms net 30 days; FOB destination. Romero Textbooks, Inc., paid $93.80 for shipping.

b. Ford Education Outfitters received credit memo no. 513A from Romero Textbooks, Inc., for merchandise returned, $135.78.

LO 6, 7

Practice Exercises 6, 7

EXERCISE 9-7 Record the following transactions for a perpetual inventory system in general journal form.

a. Sold merchandise on account to Southridge Manufacturing, Inc., invoice no. 6910, $1,815.24. The cost of merchandise was $1,320.
b. Issued credit memorandum no. 56 to Southridge Manufacturing, Inc., for merchandise returned, $622. The cost of the merchandise was $485.
c. Bought merchandise on account from Michal's Inc., invoice no. 1685, $850; terms 1/10, n/30; dated April 14; FOB Dallas, freight prepaid and added to the invoice, $65.00 (total $915).
d. Received credit memorandum no. 219 from Michal's Inc. for merchandise returned, $210.

LO 8

Practice Exercise 8

EXERCISE 9-8 Toby Company had the following sales transactions for March:

Mar. 6 Sold merchandise on account to Osbourne, Inc., invoice no. 1128, $563.17.
14 Sold merchandise on account to Ortiz Company, invoice no. 1129, $823.50.
20 Sold merchandise on account to Bailey Corporation, invoice no. 1130, $2,350.98.
24 Sold merchandise on account to Shannon Corporation, invoice no. 1131, $1,547.07.

Assume that Toby Company had beginning balances on March 1 of $3,569.80 (Sales 411) and $2,450.39 (Accounts Receivable 113). Record the sales of merchandise on account in the sales journal (page 24) and then post to the general ledger.

LO 9

Practice Exercise 9

EXERCISE 9-9 Williams Corporation had the following purchases for May:

May 3 Bought ten lawn rakes from Owens Company, invoice no. J34Y9, $250.25; terms net 15 days; dated May 1; FOB shipping point, freight prepaid and added to the invoice, $15 (total $265.25).
11 Bought one weed trimmer from Lionel's Lawn & Landscaping, invoice no. R7740, $219.72; terms 2/10, n/30; dated May 9; FOB shipping point, freight prepaid and added to the invoice, $35 (total $254.72).
15 Bought five bags of fertilizer from Wright's Farm Supplies, invoice no. 478, $210.97; terms net 30 days; dated May 13; FOB destination.
25 Bought one lawn mower from Gutierrez Corporation, invoice no. 2458, $425.39; terms net 30 days; dated May 22; FOB destination.

Assume that Williams Corporation had beginning balances on May 1 of $3,492.29 (Accounts Payable 212), $4,239.49 (Purchases 511), and $234.89 (Freight In 514). Record the purchases of merchandise on account in the purchases journal (page 13) and then post to the general ledger.

LO 8, 9

Practice Exercises 8, 9

QuickBooks

EXERCISE 9-10 Kelley Company has completed October's sales and purchases journals (on the following page).

a. Total and post the journals to T accounts for the general ledger and the accounts receivable and accounts payable ledgers. Skip this step if using QuickBooks.
b. Complete a schedule of accounts receivable for October 31, 20--.
c. Complete a schedule of accounts payable for October 31, 20--.
d. Compare the balances of the schedules with their respective general ledger accounts. If they are not the same, find and correct the error(s).

*Follow the instructions on pages 460–462 when using QuickBooks.

CHAPTER ASSIGNMENTS

SALES JOURNAL **Page 18**

Date		Inv. No.	Customer's Name	Post. Ref.	Accounts Receivable Dr. Sales Cr.
20--					
Oct.	3	414	Anderson Company		443 24
	4	415	R. T. Holcomb		1426 90
	7	416	Gray and Malo		1647 00
	11	417	Mercer Mobil		3112 16
	16	418	J. L. Anthony		2130 00
	22	419	C. A. Goldschmidt		1944 05
	31	420	F. A. Baumann		2791 00
	31		Total		
					( ) ( )

PURCHASES JOURNAL **Page 10**

Date		Supplier's Name	Inv. No.	Inv. Date	Terms	Post. Ref.	Accounts Payable Credit	Freight In Debit	Purchases Debit
20--									
Oct.	2	Colter, Inc.	2706	7/31	2/10, n/30		759 00	49 00	710 00
	3	Thomas and Son	982	8/2	n/30		829 00	57 00	772 00
	5	Archer Manufacturing Co.	10611	8/3	2/10, n/30		564 00		564 00
	9	Spence Products Co.	B643	8/6	1/10, n/30		165 00	10 00	155 00
	18	L. C. Walter	46812	8/17	n/60		228 00		228 00
	25	Delaney and Cox	1024	8/23	2/10, n/30		376 00	14 00	362 00
	26	Colter, Inc.	2801	8/25	2/10, n/30		406 00	22 00	384 00
	31	Totals							
							( )	( )	( )

Problem Set A

LO 2, 3

PROBLEM 9-1A Bell Florists sells flowers on a retail basis. Most of the sales are for cash; however, a few steady customers have credit accounts. Bell's sales staff fills out a sales slip for each sale. There is a state retail sales tax of 5 percent, which is collected by the retailer and submitted to the state. The balances of the accounts as of March 1 have been recorded in the general ledger in your Working Papers or in CengageNow. The following represent Bell Florists' charge sales for March:

Mar. 4 Sold potted plant on account to C. Morales, sales slip no. 242, \$27, plus sales tax of \$1.35, total \$28.35.

6 Sold floral arrangement on account to R. Dixon, sales slip no. 267, \$54, plus sales tax of \$2.70, total \$56.70.

12 Sold corsage on account to B. Cox, sales slip no. 279, \$16, plus sales tax of \$0.80, total \$16.80.

Mar. 16 Sold wreath on account to All-Star Legion, sales slip no. 296, $104, plus sales tax of $5.20, total $109.20.

18 Sold floral arrangements on account to Tucker Funeral Home, sales slip no. 314, $260, plus sales tax of $13, total $273.

21 Tucker Funeral Home complained about a wrinkled ribbon on the floral arrangement. Bell Florists allowed a $30 credit plus sales tax of $1.50, credit memo no. 27.

23 Sold flower arrangements on account to Price Savings and Loan Association for their fifth anniversary, sales slip no. 337, $180, plus sales tax of $9, total $189.

24 Allowed Price Savings and Loan Association credit, $25, plus sales tax of $1.25, because of a few withered blossoms in floral arrangements, credit memo no. 28.

Required

1. Record these transactions in the general journal (pages 57 and 58).
2. Post the amounts from the general journal to the general ledger and accounts receivable ledger: Accounts Receivable 113, Sales Tax Payable 214, Sales 411, Sales Returns and Allowances 412.
3. Prepare a schedule of accounts receivable and compare its total with the balance of the Accounts Receivable controlling account.

Check Figure
Schedule of Accounts Receivable total, $726.52

LO 4, 5

PROBLEM 9-2A Berry's Pet Store records purchase transactions in the general journal. The company is located in Boston, Massachusetts. In addition to a general ledger, Berry's Pet Store also uses an accounts payable ledger. Transactions for April related to the purchase of merchandise are as follows:

Apr. 2 Bought ten Carefree Pet Bedding bags from Blackburn Company, $399.90, invoice no. 4R48, dated April 1; terms net 30 days; FOB destination.

5 Bought seven Marine Betta Kits from Herrera Company, $83.93, invoice no. 4851, dated April 3; terms 2/10, n/30; FOB shipping point, freight prepaid and added to the invoice, $15 (total $98.93).

6 Bought 15 Two Door Deluxe Kennels from Barrett, Inc., $719.85, invoice no. 1845R, dated April 5; terms 1/10, n/30; FOB destination.

8 Bought five Dome Top Bird Cages from Faulkner Company, $1,849.95, invoice no. 1485, dated April 7; terms 2/10, n/30; FOB shipping point, freight prepaid and added to the invoice, $76 (total $1,925.95).

13 Received credit memo no. 415 from Faulkner Company for merchandise returned, $589.13.

23 Bought three Five Tiered Cat Trees from Rhodes Manufacturing, $1,107, invoice no. 246J, dated April 21; terms net 60 days; FOB destination.

27 Bought 30 Glitter Collection Leashes from Solomon Products Company, $299.70, invoice no. 2675, dated April 25; terms net 30 days; FOB destination.

30 Received credit memo no. 861 from Solomon Products Company for merchandise returned, $76.25.

Required

1. Open the following accounts in the accounts payable ledger and record the April 1 balances, if any, as given: Barrett, Inc., $185.25; Blackburn Company, $254.64; Faulkner Company, $485.12; Herrera Company; Rhodes Manufacturing, $452.31;

Check Figure
Accounts Payable account balance, $7,048.50 credit

(Continued)

Solomon Products Company, $1,785.23. For the accounts having balances, write *Balance* in the Item column and place a check mark in the Post. Ref. column.

2. Record the April 1 balances in the general ledger as given: Accounts Payable 212 controlling account, $3,162.55; Purchases 511, $559.06; Purchases Returns and Allowances 512, $123.50; Freight In 514, $15.20. Write *Balance* in the Item column and place a check mark in the Post. Ref. column.
3. Record the transactions in the general journal beginning on page 115.
4. Post to the general ledger and the accounts payable ledger.
5. Prepare a schedule of accounts payable and compare the balance of the Accounts Payable controlling account with the total of the schedule of accounts payable.

LO 2, 3, 4, 5

PROBLEM 9-3A Shirley's Beauty Store records sales and purchase transactions in the general journal. In addition to a general ledger, Shirley's Beauty Store also uses an accounts receivable ledger and an accounts payable ledger. Transactions for January related to the sales and purchase of merchandise are as follows:

Jan.	3	Bought 30 Mango Bath and Shower Gels from Madden, Inc., $660, invoice no. 3487, dated January 1; terms 2/10, n/30; FOB shipping point, freight prepaid and added to the invoice, $125.43 (total $785.43).
	4	Bought ten Beauty Candle Travel Sets from Calhoun Candles, Inc., $420, invoice no. 4513, dated January 1; terms net 45; FOB destination.
	12	Sold four Mango Bath and Shower Gels on account to R. Kielman, sales slip no. 1456, $120, plus sales tax of $9.60, total $129.60.
	13	Received credit memo no. 8715 from Calhoun Candles, Inc., for merchandise returned, $84.
	21	Bought five Winter Skin Essentials Kits from Whitney and Waters, $197.50, invoice no. A875, dated January 18; terms 2/15, n/45; FOB destination.
	25	Sold three Winter Skin Essentials on account to A. Benner, sales slip no. 1457, $135.75, plus sales tax of $10.86, total $146.61.
	27	Issued credit memo no. 33 to A. Benner for merchandise returned, $45.25 plus $3.62 sales tax, total $48.87.

Check Figure
Schedule of Accounts Payable total, $2,297.56

Required

1. Open the following accounts in the accounts receivable ledger and record the balances as of January 1: A. Benner, $45.77; R. Kielman, $175.39. Write *Balance* in the Item column and place a check mark in the Post. Ref. column.
2. Open the following accounts in the accounts payable ledger and record the balances as of January 1: Calhoun Candles, Inc., $355.23; Madden, Inc., $573.15; Whitney and Waters, $50.25. Write *Balance* in the Item column and place a check mark in the Post. Ref. column.
3. Record the January 1 balances in the general ledger as given: Accounts Receivable 113 controlling account, $221.16; Accounts Payable 212 controlling account, $978.63; Sales Tax Payable 214, $128.45. Write *Balance* in the Item column and place a check mark in the Post. Ref. column.
4. Record the transactions in the general journal beginning on page 25.
5. Post the entries to the general journal and accounts receivable ledger or accounts payable ledger as appropriate.
6. Prepare a schedule of accounts receivable.
7. Prepare a schedule of accounts payable.
8. Compare the totals of the schedules with the balances of the controlling accounts.

LO 6, 7

PROBLEM 9-4A The following transactions relate to Hawkins, Inc., an office store wholesaler, during June of this year. Terms of sale are 2/10, n/30. The company is located in Los Angeles, California.

June 1 Sold merchandise on account to Hendrix Office Store, invoice no. 1001, $451.20. The cost of the merchandise was $397.06.
3 Bought merchandise on account from Krueger, Inc., invoice no. 845A, $485.15; terms 1/10, n/30; dated June 1; FOB San Diego, freight prepaid and added to the invoice, $15 (total $500.15).
10 Sold merchandise on account to Ballard Stores, invoice no. 1002, $2,483.65. The cost of the merchandise was $2,235.29.
13 Bought merchandise on account from Kennedy, Inc., invoice no. 4833, $2,450.13; terms 2/10, n/30; dated June 11; FOB San Francisco, freight prepaid and added to the invoice, $123 (total $2,573.13).
18 Sold merchandise on account to Lawson Office Store, invoice no. 1003, $754.99. The cost of the merchandise was $671.94.
20 Issued credit memo no. 33 to Lawson Office Store for merchandise returned, $103.25. The cost of the merchandise was $91.89.
25 Bought merchandise on account from Villarreal, Inc., invoice no. 4R32, $1,552.30; terms net 30; dated June 18; FOB Santa Rosa, freight prepaid and added to the invoice, $84 (total $1,636.30).
30 Received credit memo no. 44 for merchandise returned to Villarreal, Inc., for $224.50.

Required

Record the transactions in the general journal (pages 25 and 26) using the perpetual inventory system.

Check Figure
Net Merchandise Inventory, $1,272.68 debit

LO 2, 3, 8

PROBLEM 9-5A Gomez Company sells electrical supplies on a wholesale basis. The balances of the accounts as of April 1 have been recorded in the general ledger in your Working Papers, CengageNow, or QuickBooks. The following transactions took place during April of this year:

Apr. 1 Sold merchandise on account to Myers Company, invoice no. 761, $570.40.
5 Sold merchandise on account to L. R. Foster Company, invoice no. 762, $486.10.
6 Issued credit memo no. 50 to Myers Company for merchandise returned, $40.70.
10 Sold merchandise on account to Diaz Hardware, invoice no. 763, $293.35.
14 Sold merchandise on account to Brooks and Bennett, invoice no. 764, $640.16.
17 Sold merchandise on account to Powell and Reyes, invoice no. 765, $582.12.
21 Issued credit memo no. 51 to Brooks and Bennett for merchandise returned, $68.44.
24 Sold merchandise on account to Ortiz Company, invoice no. 766, $652.87.
26 Sold merchandise on account to Diaz Hardware, invoice no. 767, $832.19.
30 Issued credit memo no. 52 to Diaz Hardware for damage to merchandise, $98.50.

Required

1. Record these sales of merchandise on account in the sales journal (page 39). If using QuickBooks, create invoices for all sales of merchandise on account. Record the sales returns and allowances in the general journal (page 74). If using QuickBooks, create credit memos for all sales returns and allowances.
2. Immediately after recording each transaction, post to the accounts receivable ledger. Skip this step if using QuickBooks.

Check Figure
Accounts Receivable account balance, $5,018.97 debit

(Continued)

CHAPTER ASSIGNMENTS

3. Post the amounts from the general journal daily. Post the sales journal amount as a total at the end of the month: Accounts Receivable 113, Sales 411, Sales Returns and Allowances 412. Skip this step if using QuickBooks.
4. Prepare a schedule of accounts receivable (A/R Aging Detail report if using QuickBooks). Compare the balance of the Accounts Receivable controlling account with the total of the schedule of accounts receivable.

PROBLEM 9-6A Patterson Appliance uses a three-column purchases journal. The company is located in Fresno, California. In addition to a general ledger, Patterson Appliance also uses an accounts payable ledger. Transactions for January related to the purchase of merchandise are as follows:

Jan.	2	Bought eighty 12-inch, 3-speed Brighton Oscillating Fans from Snyder and Jordan, $1,890, invoice no. 268J, dated January 2; terms net 60 days; FOB Fresno.
	4	Bought ten 35-pint-capacity Crystal Humidifiers from Simpson Company, $2,300, invoice no. 39426, dated January 2; terms 2/10, n/30; FOB Durango, freight prepaid and added to the invoice, $90 (total $2,390).
	7	Bought ten 16-inch Axel Window Fans from Tran, Inc., $360, invoice no. 452AD, dated January 6; terms 1/10, n/30; FOB Fresno.
	10	Bought twenty-four 4-blade Tiempo Ceiling Fans, Model 2760, from Ukele Company, $3,550, invoice no. D7742, dated January 7; terms 2/10, n/30; FOB Sacramento, freight prepaid and added to the invoice, $84 (total $3,634).
	14	Bought four Charger Electric Hedge Trimmers from Fernandez Products Company, $186, invoice no. 2542, dated January 13; terms net 30 days; FOB Fresno.
	22	Bought 40 Lindon Electric Bug Killers from Snyder and Jordan, $2,265, invoice no. 392J, dated January 22; terms net 60 days; FOB Fresno.
	28	Bought ten Charger Electric Blowers from Fernandez Products Company, $830, invoice no. 2691, dated January 27; terms net 30 days; FOB Fresno.
	30	Bought ten Kole Powered Attic Ventilators from Porter Company, $446, invoice no. 664CC, dated January 27; terms 2/10, n/30; FOB Seattle, freight prepaid and added to the invoice, $48 (total $494).

Check Figure
Accounts Payable account balance, $12,608.06 credit

Required

1. Open the following accounts in the accounts payable ledger and record the January 1 balances, if any, as given: Fernandez Products Company; Porter Company, $163.17; Simpson Company, $167.19; Snyder and Jordan; Tran, Inc., $228.70; Ukele Company. For the accounts having balances, write *Balance* in the Item column and place a check mark in the Post. Ref. column. Skip this step if using QuickBooks or general ledger.
2. Record the balance of $559.06 in the Accounts Payable 212 controlling account as of January 1. Write *Balance* in the Item column and place a check mark in the Post. Ref. column. Skip this step if using QuickBooks or general ledger.
3. Record the transactions in the purchases journal beginning on page 81. Enter bills for each transaction if using QuickBooks.
4. Post to the accounts payable ledger daily. Skip this step if using QuickBooks or general ledger.
5. Post to the general ledger at the end of the month. Skip this step if using QuickBooks or general ledger.
6. Prepare a schedule of accounts payable (A/P Aging Detail report if using QuickBooks) and compare the balance of the Accounts Payable controlling account with the total of the schedule of accounts payable.

Problem Set B

LO 2, 3

PROBLEM 9-1B Abbott Florists sells flowers on a retail basis. Most of the sales are for cash; however, a few steady customers have credit accounts. Abbott's sales staff fills out a sales slip for each sale. There is a state retail tax of 5 percent, which is collected by the retailer and submitted to the state. The balances of the accounts as of March 1 have been recorded in the general ledger in your Working Papers or in CengageNow. Abbott Florists' charge sales for March are as follows:

Mar. 4 Sold floral arrangement on account to R. Duarte, sales slip no. 236, $45, plus sales tax of $2.25, total $47.25.

7 Sold potted plant on account to C. Meadows, sales slip no. 272, $61, plus sales tax of $3.05, total $64.05.

12 Sold wreath on account to Anthony Realty, sales slip no. 294, $63, plus sales tax of $3.15, total $66.15.

17 Sold floral arrangements on account to Travis Dress Shop, sales slip no. 299, $170, plus sales tax of $8.50, total $178.50.

20 Travis Dress Shop returned a flower spray, complaining that there were dead blooms. Abbott Florists allowed a credit of $36, plus sales tax of $1.80, credit memo no. 27.

21 Sold flower arrangements on account to Porter Computers for its anniversary, sales slip no. 310, $236, plus sales tax of $11.80, total $247.80.

22 Allowed Porter Computers credit, $25, plus sales tax of $1.25, because of withered blossoms in floral arrangements, credit memo no. 28.

27 Sold corsage on account to B. Crosby, sales slip no. 332, $30, plus sales tax of $1.50, total $31.50.

Required

1. Record these transactions in the general journal (pages 57 and 58).
2. Post the amounts from the general journal to the general ledger and accounts receivable ledger: Accounts Receivable 113, Sales Tax Payable 214, Sales 411, Sales Returns and Allowances 412.
3. Prepare a schedule of accounts receivable and compare its total with the balance of the Accounts Receivable controlling account.

Check Figure
Schedule of Accounts Receivable total, $682.42

LO 4, 5

PROBLEM 9-2B Lowery's Pet Depot records purchase transactions in the general journal. The company is located in Cleveland, Ohio. In addition to a general ledger, Lowery's Pet Depot also uses an accounts payable ledger. Transactions for October related to the purchase of merchandise are as follows:

Oct. 3 Bought 12 Automatic Fish Feeders from Barrera Company, $959.88, invoice no. 5493, dated October 2; terms net 30 days; FOB shipping point, freight prepaid and added to the invoice, $79.45 (total $1,039.33).

4 Bought two 18 x 18 Terrarium Stands from Hickman Company, $259.98, invoice no. 2JYX, dated October 2; terms 2/10, n/30; FOB destination.

7 Bought four Chinchilla Bath Houses from Baldwin, Inc., $67.96, invoice no. 4183, dated October 6; terms 1/10, n/30; FOB destination.

10 Received credit memo no. 123 from Baldwin, Inc., for merchandise returned, $13.94.

(*Continued*)

Oct. 14 Bought 20 Zoo Slider Hoods from Douglas, Inc., $2,599.80, invoice no. X431, dated October 12; terms 2/10, n/30; FOB shipping point, freight prepaid and added to the invoice, $140.50 (total $2,740.30).

15 Bought four Hanging Bird Baths from Krause, Inc., $71.96, invoice no. A499, dated October 11; terms net 60 days; FOB destination.

24 Bought eight Automatic Cat Litter Boxes from Villa Manufacturing, $2,399.92, invoice no. 4429, dated October 21; terms net 30 days; FOB destination.

27 Received credit memo no. 452 from Villa Manufacturing for merchandise returned, $346.78.

Check Figure
Accounts Payable account balance, $8,372.74 credit

Required

1. Open the following accounts in the accounts payable ledger and record the October 1 balances, if any, as given: Baldwin, Inc., $46.57; Barrera Company, $743.15; Douglas, Inc., $615.20; Hickman Company; Krause, Inc., $23.45; Villa Manufacturing, $725.64. For the accounts having balances, write *Balance* in the Item column and place a check mark in the Post. Ref. column.
2. Record the October 1 balances in the general ledger as given: Accounts Payable 212 controlling account, $2,154.01; Purchases 511, $2,485.12; Purchases Returns and Allowances 512, $287.52; Freight In 514, $48.57. Write *Balance* in the Item column and place a check mark in the Post. Ref. column.
3. Record the transactions in the general journal beginning on page 95.
4. Post to the general ledger and the accounts payable ledger.
5. Prepare a schedule of accounts payable, and compare the balance of the Accounts Payable controlling account with the total of the schedule of accounts payable.

LO 2, 3, 4, 5

PROBLEM 9-3B May's Beauty Store records sales and purchase transactions in the general journal. In addition to a general ledger, May's Beauty Store also uses an accounts receivable ledger and an accounts payable ledger. Transactions for January related to the sales and purchase of merchandise are as follows:

Jan. 2 Bought nine Matte Nail Color Kits from Mejia, Inc., $450, invoice no. 4521, dated January 1; terms 2/10, n/30; FOB shipping point, freight prepaid and added to the invoice, $87.50 (total $537.50).

5 Bought 30 Perfume Cocktail Rings from Braun, Inc., $1,200, invoice no. 37A, dated January 3; terms 2/10, n/30; FOB destination.

8 Sold two Matte Nail Color Kits on account to J. Herbert, sales slip no. 113, $110, plus sales tax of $8.80, total $118.80.

11 Received credit memo no. 455 from Braun, Inc., for merchandise returned, $315.25.

18 Bought 15 Eye Palettes from Vargas, Inc., $660, invoice no. 910, dated January 14; terms net 30; FOB destination.

23 Sold four Eye Palettes on account to T. Cantrell, sales slip no. 114, $200, plus sales tax of $16, total $216.

26 Issued credit memo no. 12 to T. Cantrell for merchandise returned, $50 plus $4 sales tax, total $54.

Check Figure
Schedule of Accounts Payable balance, $2,776

Required

1. Open the following accounts in the accounts receivable ledger and record the balances as of January 1: T. Cantrell, $86.99; J. Hebert, $63.47. Write *Balance* in the Item column and place a check mark in the Post. Ref. column.
2. Open the following accounts in the accounts payable ledger and record the balances as of January 1: Braun, Inc., $513.20; Mejia, Inc., $113.40; Vargas, Inc., $67.15. Write *Balance* in the Item column and place a check mark in the Post. Ref. column.

3. Record the January 1 balances in the general ledger as given: Accounts Receivable 113 controlling account, $150.46; Accounts Payable 212 controlling account, $693.75; Sales Tax Payable 214, $237.89. Write *Balance* in the Item column and place a check mark in the Post. Ref. column.
4. Record the transactions in the general journal beginning on page 17.
5. Post the entries to the general journal and accounts receivable ledger or accounts payable ledger as appropriate.
6. Prepare a schedule of accounts receivable.
7. Prepare a schedule of accounts payable.
8. Compare the totals of the schedules with the balances of the controlling accounts.

6, 7

PROBLEM 9-4B The following transactions relate to Khan, Inc., a sporting goods wholesaler, during November of this year. Terms of sale are 2/10, n/30. The company is located in Denver, Colorado.

Nov.	3	Sold merchandise on account to Spence Tennis Shop, invoice no. 5420, $2,482.51. The cost of the merchandise was $1,961.18.
	5	Issued credit memo no. 38 to Spence Tennis Shop for merchandise returned, $287.45. The cost of the merchandise was $227.09.
	7	Bought merchandise on account from Maldonado Manufacturing, Inc., invoice no. 1548, $3,854.16; terms n/45; dated November 4; FOB Memphis, freight prepaid and added to the invoice, $135 (total $3,989.16).
	9	Bought merchandise on account from Lozano, Inc., invoice no. 8755, $426.65; terms 1/15, n/30; dated November 5; FOB New York City, freight prepaid and added to the invoice, $67 (total $493.65).
	12	Received credit memo no. 542 to Lozano, Inc., for merchandise returned, $102.20.
	17	Sold merchandise on account to Jack's Golfing Shop, invoice no. 5421, $486.35. The cost of the merchandise was $432.85.
	23	Sold merchandise on account to Yates Sporting Goods, invoice no. 5422, $2,465.99. The cost of the merchandise was $1,972.79.
	28	Bought merchandise on account from Fields, Inc., invoice no. 4599, $441.29; terms 2/10, n/30; dated November 25; FOB Austin, freight prepaid and added to the invoice, $102 (total $543.29).

Required
Record the transactions in the general journal (pages 84 and 85) using the perpetual inventory system.

Check Figure
Total Gross Sales, $5,434.85 credit

LO 2, 3, 8

PROBLEM 9-5B R. J. Hinton Company sells electrical supplies on a wholesale basis. The balances of the accounts as of April 1 have been recorded in the general ledger in your Working Papers, CengageNow, or QuickBooks. The following transactions took place during April of this year:

Apr.	3	Sold merchandise on account to Maxwell Company, invoice no. 822, $652.80.
	7	Sold merchandise on account to B. A. Fitzpatrick Company, invoice no. 823, $462.15.
	8	Sold merchandise on account to Durham Hardware, invoice no. 824, $205.60.
	13	Issued credit memo no. 61 to B. A. Fitzpatrick Company for merchandise returned, $136.50.
	15	Sold merchandise on account to Briggs and Campos, invoice no. 825, $831.47.
	21	Sold merchandise on account to Pena and Carr, invoice no. 826, $590.34.
	24	Issued credit memo no. 62 to Briggs and Campos for merchandise returned, $80.45.

(*Continued*)

Apr. 26 Sold merchandise on account to O'Neill Company, invoice no. 827, $569.90.
28 Issued credit memo no. 63 to Durham Hardware for damage to merchandise, $52.48.
30 Sold merchandise on account to Durham Hardware, invoice no. 828, $735.50.

Check Figure
Accounts Receivable account balance, $4,947.75 debit

Required

1. Record these sales of merchandise on account in the sales journal (page 39). If using QuickBooks, create invoices for all sales of merchandise on account. Record the sales returns and allowances in the general journal (page 74). If using QuickBooks, create credit memos for all sales returns and allowances.
2. Immediately after recording each transaction, post to the accounts receivable ledger. Skip this step if using QuickBooks.
3. Post the amounts from the general journal daily. Post the sales journal amount as a total at the end of the month: Accounts Receivable 113, Sales 411, Sales Returns and Allowances 412. Skip this step if using QuickBooks.
4. Prepare a schedule of accounts receivable. (A/R Aging Detail report if using QuickBooks). Compare the balance of the Accounts Receivable controlling account with the total of the schedule of accounts receivable.

LO 5, 9

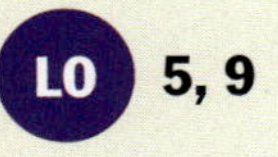

QuickBooks

PROBLEM 9-6B West Bicycle Shop uses a three-column purchases journal. The company is located in Topeka, Kansas. In addition to a general ledger, the company also uses an accounts payable ledger. Transactions for January related to the purchase of merchandise are as follows:

Jan. 4 Bought fifty 10-speed bicycles from Nielsen Company, $4,775, invoice no. 26145, dated January 3; terms net 60 days; FOB Topeka.
7 Bought tires from Barton Tire Company, $792, invoice no. 9763, dated January 5; terms 2/10, n/30; FOB Topeka.
8 Bought bicycle lights and reflectors from Gross Products Company, $384, invoice no. 17317, dated January 6; terms net 30 days; FOB Topeka.
11 Bought hand brakes from Bray, Inc., $470, invoice no. 291GE, dated January 9; terms 1/10, n/30; FOB Kansas City, freight prepaid and added to the invoice, $36 (total $506).
19 Bought handle grips from Gross Products Company, $96.50, invoice no. 17520, dated January 17; terms net 30 days; FOB Topeka.
24 Bought thirty 5-speed bicycles from Nielsen Company, $1,487, invoice no. 26942, dated January 23; terms net 60 days; FOB Topeka.
29 Bought knapsacks from Davila Manufacturing Company, $304.80, invoice no. 762AC, dated January 26; terms 2/10, n/30; FOB Topeka.
31 Bought locks from Lamb Safety Net, $415.47, invoice no. 27712, dated January 26; terms 2/10, n/30; FOB Dodge City, freight prepaid and added to the invoice, $22 (total $437.47).

Check Figure
Accounts Payable account balance, $9,205.85 credit

Required

1. Open the following accounts in the accounts payable ledger and record the January 1 balances, if any, as given: Barton Tire Company, $156; Bray, Inc.; Davila Manufacturing Company, $82.88; Gross Products Company; Lamb Safety Net, $184.20; Nielsen Company. For the accounts having balances, write *Balance* in the Item column and place a check mark in the Post. Ref. column. Skip this step if using QuickBooks or general ledger.

2. Record the balance of $423.08 in the Accounts Payable 212 controlling account as of January 1. Write *Balance* in the Item column and place a check mark in the Post. Ref. column. Skip this step if using QuickBooks or general ledger.
3. Record the transactions in the purchases journal beginning with page 81. Enter bills for each transaction if using QuickBooks.
4. Post to the accounts payable ledger daily. Skip this step if using QuickBooks or general ledger.
5. Post to the general ledger at the end of the month. Skip this step if using QuickBooks or general ledger.
6. Prepare a schedule of accounts payable, (A/P Aging Detail report if using QuickBooks) and compare the balance of the Accounts Payable controlling account with the total of the schedule of accounts payable.

Try It with QuickBooks® (LO 2, 3, 5, 6)

QB Exercise 9-1 (LO 2, 3, 6)

Using the information in Exercise 9-1 on page 474 and the QuickBooks data file labeled Exercise 9-1 on the textbook website, complete the following activities:

1. Create an invoice for transactions (a) and (b).
2. Prepare a credit memo for transaction (c).
3. Prepare an A/R Aging Summary report.
   a. What is the amount in the total column for NexStar?

QB Exercise 9-2 (LO 5,6)

Using the information in Exercise 9-10 on page 477–478 and the QuickBooks data file labeled Exercise 9-10 on the textbook website, complete the following activities:

1. Use Enter Bills to complete the October transactions for the purchases journal.
2. Prepare an A/P Aging Summary report.
   a. What is the amount in the Total column for Delaney and Cox?
   b. What is the total for the A/P Aging Summary report?

Activities

Why Does It Matter?

Jax Mercantile Co. has been northern Colorado's premier outdoor gear source for over 50 years. Jax sells men's, women's, and children's clothing for any outdoor activity. Customers can also find camping and fishing gear, mountaineering tools, and hunting items. If a customer is not the outdoor type, Jax still offers plenty of other products, such as specialty kitchenware and household decorative items. Jax also carries a full line of optics and photography products, agricultural and automotive accessories, animal care products, and lawn and garden accessories.

Jax has succeeded in stocking a large inventory that meets customers' outdoor and indoor gear needs. When Jax purchases inventory for resale, it must have a way of recording these purchases. Jax also must have a way to record the sales of goods to customers and be able to handle returns and discounts. Considering the size of Jax's inventory (in items and in dollar amount), would Jax use a periodic or perpetual inventory system? Explain your answer.

What Would You Say?

You are the bookkeeper at a small merchandising firm. You are comparing the income statements from the last three years. You notice that the Purchases Returns and Allowances account (as a percentage of net sales) has been increasing at an alarming rate. If you were a manager, to whom would you speak in the organization to help you understand why so much merchandise is being returned? What types of questions would you ask?

What Do You Think?

TO: Accounting Clerk DATE: April 1, 20--

FROM: Senior Accountant SUBJECT: Errors in trial balance

Following is a trial balance prepared just before you were hired. Two accounts are missing, and the amount for Sales is off. Here are a few facts to consider. Our business is in a state that collects sales tax. I ran some totals, and we collected $1,800 in sales tax. Customers returned $900 in goods, which would reduce the above sales tax by $70. Our books need to reflect these events. The former accounting clerk said that she recorded everything—somewhere. She said that she may have credited the $1,800 sales tax to Sales and not to Sales Tax Payable. And she looked confused when Sales Returns and Allowances was mentioned. She asked, "Why not just debit Sales?" Determine the two missing accounts and correct the accounts that are off.

Pierce Retail Outlet
Trial Balance
March 31, 20--

Account Name	Debit	Credit
Cash	8,940	
Accounts Receivable	480	
Store Equipment	9,460	
Accounts Payable		958
D. Pierce, Capital		11,959
D. Pierce, Drawing	4,480	
Sales		18,000
Rent Expense	2,400	
Wages Expense	4,864	
Supplies Expense	175	
Miscellaneous Expense	118	
	30,917	30,917

1. Think about where these amounts might have been put, think about what accounts are missing, and use T accounts to solve the problems.
2. Prepare a corrected trial balance.

All About You Spa

Sales and Purchases

Ms. Valli of All About You Spa has decided to expand her business by adding two lines of merchandise—a selection of products used in the salon for the body, the feet, and the face, as well as logo mugs, T-shirts, and baseball caps that can provide advertising benefits. She believes she will be able to increase her profits significantly.

July Journal Entries

QuickBooks

So that you can complete the journal entries for the month of July, Ms. Valli has also left the information you will need and directions on how to proceed.

Note that with the expansion of the business into merchandising, new accounts have been added to the chart of accounts. For example, an additional revenue account, Merchandise Sales, is needed. Because All About You Spa now needs a Purchases account, the chart of accounts needs to be modified as follows: The 500–599 range is used for the purchase-related accounts (for example, Purchases 511 and Freight In 515). Your new chart of accounts is as follows:

CHART OF ACCOUNTS FOR ALL ABOUT YOU SPA

Assets
- 111 Cash
- 113 Accounts Receivable
- 114 Office Supplies
- 115 Spa Supplies
- 116 Merchandise Inventory
- 117 Prepaid Insurance
- 124 Office Equipment
- 125 Accum. Depr., Office Equip.
- 128 Spa Equipment
- 129 Accum. Depr., Spa Equip.

Liabilities
- 211 Accounts Payable
- 212 Wages Payable
- 215 Sales Tax Payable

Owner's Equity
- 311 A. Valli, Capital
- 312 A. Valli, Drawing
- 313 Income Summary

Revenue
- 411 Income from Services
- 412 Merchandise Sales
- 413 Sales Discounts
- 414 Sales Returns & Allow.

Purchases
- 511 Purchases
- 512 Purchases Discounts
- 513 Purch. Returns & Allow.
- 515 Freight In

Expenses
- 611 Wages Expense
- 612 Rent Expense
- 613 Office Supplies Expense
- 614 Spa Supplies Expense
- 615 Laundry Expense
- 616 Advertising Expense
- 617 Utilities Expense
- 618 Insurance Expense
- 619 Depr. Expense, Office Equip.
- 620 Depr. Expense, Spa Equip.
- 630 Miscellaneous Expense

Also note that because you will be making purchases on account and sales on account, subsidiary ledgers will be needed to track what is due from individual customers and owed to individual vendors. A listing of customers and vendors with current balances are as follows:

ACCOUNTS RECEIVABLE LEDGER	
About Face Spa	$ 0.00
Jill Anson	325.00
Chaco's	0.00
Holmes Condos	0.00
Tory Ligman	344.00
Los Obrigados Lodge	0.00
Mini Spa	0.00
Jack Morgan	486.00
Pleasant Spa	0.00
Judy Wilcox	109.00

ACCOUNTS PAYABLE LEDGER	
Adco, Inc.	$ 397.00
Giftco	0.00
Golden Spa Supplies	492.00
Logo Products	0.00
Office Staples	120.00
Spa Equipment, Inc.	89.00
Spa Goods	0.00
Spa Magic	0.00
Superior Equipment	1,150.00

Checkbook Register

All About You Spa

*If using QuickBooks, record the following transactions in the general journal.

Check No.	Date	Explanation	✓	Deposits	Check Amount
	7/1	Owner invested cash in business.		25,000.00	
1027	7/3	Bought additional spa equipment from Spa Equipment, Inc., for $8,235.00, paying $2,000.00 cash down, invoice no. 2731, dated 7/3; terms 2/10, n/60.			2,000.00
1028	7/3	Paid July's rent.			1,650.00
1029	7/3	Paid on account to Spa Equipment, Inc., invoice no. 2013, dated June 3 (no discount). Paid in full.			89.00
1030	7/5	Paid on account to Golden Spa Supplies, invoice no. 804, dated June 3 (no discount). Paid in full.			492.00
1031	7/5	Paid on account to Office Staples, invoice no. 522, dated June 5 (no discount). Paid in full.			120.00
1032	7/5	Paid Celebrate, Inc., for flowers and balloons for lobby (Miscellaneous Expense).			98.00
1033	7/5	Paid on account to Adco, Inc., invoice no. 512, dated June 5 (no discount). Paid in full.			397.00
1034	7/5	Paid week's wages. (A portion of this payment was recorded as an adjusting entry on June 30.) *Note:* Payroll taxes related to wages will be ignored here for purposes of simplification.			1,845.50
	7/7	Deposited first week's cash sales: merchandise, $1,410.00; services, $3,110.00; sales tax collected, $361.60. (Use the new accounts Merchandise Sales 412 and Sales Tax Payable 215.)		4,881.60	
	7/7	Deposited check from Jill Anson, invoice no. 10, dated June 7 (balance due in August, $175.00).		150.00	
1035	7/12	Paid week's wages.			1,845.50
	7/14	Deposited check from Jack Morgan, invoice no. 11, dated June 14 (balance due in August, $286.00).		200.00	

(Continued)

CONTINUING PROBLEM

Check No.	Date	Explanation	✓	Deposits	Check Amount
	7/14	Deposited second week's cash sales: merchandise, $1,220.00; services, $2,630.00; sales tax collected, $308.00.		4,158.00	
1036	7/18	Paid on account to Superior Equipment, invoice no. 3140, dated June 5 (no discount). Paid in full.			1,150.00
1037	7/19	Paid week's wages.			1,840.50
	7/21	Deposited check from Tory Ligman, invoice no. 12, dated June 21 (balance due in August, $164.00).		180.00	
	7/21	Deposited third week's cash sales: merchandise, $1,940.00; services, $2,920.00; sales tax collected, $388.80.		5,248.80	
1038	7/25	Bought new nail cart for cash (debit Spa Equipment).			173.00
1039	7/26	Paid week's wages.			1,842.00
1040	7/28	Paid month's laundry bill.			84.00
	7/28	Deposited check from Judy Wilcox, invoice no. 13, dated June 28 (paid in full).		109.00	
	7/31	Deposited end of month's cash sales: merchandise, $1,930.00; services, $4,062.00; sales tax collected, $479.36.		6,471.36	
1041	7/31	Owner withdrew cash for personal use.			2,500.00
1042	7/31	Paid July telephone bill.			225.00
1043	7/31	Paid July power and water bill.			248.00

Purchases Invoices for Merchandise Bought on Account During July

All About You Spa will pay all freight costs associated with purchases of merchandise to the supplier. Use the new accounts Purchases 511 and Freight In 515.

Date of Purchase	Transaction Information	Amount
July 1	Bought aromatherapy products from Spa Goods; invoice no. 312, dated 7/1; terms 2/10, n/60.	$5,300.00 plus $145.00 freight
1	Bought logo merchandise from Logo Products; invoice no. 1579, dated 7/1; terms 2/10, n/60.	$3,692.00 plus $104.00 freight
2	Bought bath and beauty products from Spa Magic; invoice no. 5033, dated 7/2; terms 2/10, n/30.	$2,623.00 plus $98.00 freight
5	Bought logo merchandise from Giftco; invoice no. 316, dated 7/5; terms 2/10, n/60.	$1,253.00 plus $56.00 freight

*If using QuickBooks, you can record the purchase invoices in the general journal or use the Enter Bills application from the home page.

Sales Invoices for Gift Certificates Sold on Account During July

All About You Spa is responsible for collecting and paying the sales tax on merchandise that it sells. The sales tax rate where All About You Spa does business is 8 percent of each sale (for example, $325.00 × 0.08 = $26.00).

Date of Sale	Transaction Information	Sales Amount (Before Tax)
July 2	Los Obrigados Lodge, invoice no. 14.	$ 325.00
4	Chaco's, invoice no. 15.	481.50
5	Pleasant Spa, invoice no. 16.	1,815.95
10	Holmes Condos, invoice no. 17.	340.25
10	Mini Spa, invoice no. 18.	206.00
12	About Face Spa, invoice no. 19.	482.95

Note: All gift certificates were redeemed for merchandise by the end of the month.

*If using QuickBooks, you can record the sales invoices in the general journal or use the Create Invoices application from the home page.

Other July Transactions

There were five other transactions in July. None involved cash.

If using QuickBooks, you can record the other July transactions in the general journal or use the Enter Bills application from the home page to record purchases. Owner investments should be recorded in the general journal.

Date	Transaction Information	Amount
July 1	Bought spa supplies on account from Golden Spa Supplies, invoice no. 1836, dated 7/1; terms n/45.	$ 490.00
5	Bought office equipment on account from Superior Equipment, invoice no. 3608, dated 7/5; terms 2/10, n/60.	420.00
5	Bought self-help books for the waiting room on account (Miscellaneous Expense) from Office Staples, invoice no. 1417, dated 7/5; terms n/30.	186.00
5	Bought office supplies on account from Office Staples, invoice no. 1418, dated 7/5; terms n/30.	118.00
31	Owner invested additional personal spa equipment (treadmill and bicycle) valued at $1,800.00.	1,800.00

Check Figures

3. Trial balance total, July 31, $95,718.05
4. Schedule of accounts receivable total, July 31, $4,568.79
5. Schedule of accounts payable total, July 31, $20,720.00

Required

1. Journalize the transactions for July (in date order), or if you are using QuickBooks you can use the forms-based approach from the home page as appropriate to record transactions. Ask your instructor whether you should use the special journals, the general journal, or the forms-based approach with QuickBooks.
    - If you are preparing the journal entries using Working Papers, enter your transactions beginning on page 6.

All About You Spa

CONTINUING PROBLEM

2. Post the entries to the accounts receivable, accounts payable, and general ledger.
   - Ignore this step if you are using QuickBooks or general ledger.
3. Prepare a trial balance as of July 31, 20--.
4. Prepare a schedule of accounts receivable or A/R Aging Summary report if using QuickBooks as of July 31, 20--.
5. Prepare a schedule of accounts payable or A/P Aging Summary report if using QuickBooks as of July 31, 20--.

chapter

10 Cash Receipts and Cash Payments

Learning Objectives

After you have completed this chapter, you will be able to do the following:

1. Determine cash discounts according to credit terms.
2. In the general journal, record sales transactions involving cash receipts and cash discounts.
3. In the general journal, record purchase transactions involving cash payments and cash discounts.
4. Record transactions involving trade discounts.
5. In the cash receipts journal, record transactions for a merchandising business and post from a cash receipts journal to a general ledger and an accounts receivable ledger.
6. In the cash payments journal, record transactions for a merchandising business and post from a cash payments journal to a general ledger and an accounts payable ledger.

To: **Amy Roberts, CPA**
Subject: **Cash Receipts and Cash Payments**

Hi Amy,
Well, the business continues to grow. Thanks again for all of your help. I do have a couple more questions. Is there any way I can speed up the collection of my Accounts Receivable? At certain times during the month, I'm finding that my cash flow is a little tight. Also, some customers have talked to me about trade discounts. What are these? Are they something I should be using in my business?
Thanks,
Janie

To: **Janie Conner**
Subject: **RE: Cash Receipts and Cash Payments**

Hi Janie,
I'm happy to hear that your business continues to grow. I do have some suggestions for you. First, implementing sales discounts with your charge customers may help encourage early payment. Sales discounts could significantly improve your cash flow situation. As a buyer, you may also want to deal with companies that offer you a purchases discount. Purchases discounts can save you money as well. Regarding trade discounts, these are a reduction from your list prices. The amount of the discount can vary. Trade discounts are not journalized; they are simply a reduction in the published price for certain customers. To be more competitive, you may want to consider offering some type of trade discount to your larger customers. Below is a summary of the agenda we can use when we talk.

_____ 1. Using cash discounts according to credit terms
_____ 2. Journalizing sales transactions and cash receipts from customers entitled to cash discounts
_____ 3. Journalizing purchase transactions and cash payments when you are entitled to cash discounts
_____ 4. Using trade discounts

Janie, let's talk on Friday afternoon. Give me a call anytime after 1 P.M.
Amy

© igor kisselev/Shutterstock.com

In the previous chapter, we discussed sales and purchases on account. Now we will learn how a company records cash receipts and cash payments for those transactions. We will begin by reviewing discounts and terms available to purchasers and sellers and then discuss recording the cash associated with merchandising transactions.

Accounting Language

Cash discount (p. 497)
Cash payments journal (p. 516)
Cash receipts journal (p. 511)
Credit period (p. 497)
Notes Payable (p. 514)
Promissory note (p. 514)
Purchases discount (p. 504)
Sales discount (p. 498)
Trade discounts (p. 508)

CREDIT TERMS

When we discussed sales and purchases of merchandise in Chapter 9, we noted that each sale or purchase was associated with a *term*. The seller stipulates the *terms*—how much credit a customer is allowed and how much time a customer is given to pay in full. The **credit period** is the time the seller allows the buyer before full payment has to be made. Retailers generally allow 25 to 30 days for payment.

Learning Objective

1 Determine cash discounts according to credit terms.

Wholesalers and manufacturers often specify a **cash discount** in their credit terms. A cash discount is an amount that a customer can deduct if a bill is paid within a specified time. The discount is based on the *total amount of the invoice after any returns and allowances and freight charges billed on the invoice have been deducted.* Naturally, this discount acts as an incentive for credit customers to pay their bills promptly.

Let's say that a wholesaler offers customers credit terms of 2/10, n/30. In Chapter 9, we discussed that these terms mean that the customer gets a 2 percent discount if the bill is paid within 10 days after the invoice date. The discount period begins the day after the invoice date. If the bill is not paid within the 10 days, the entire amount is due within 30 days after the invoice date. Other types of cash discounts may be used, such as:

- **1/15, n/60**—The seller offers a 1 percent discount if the bill is paid within 15 days after the invoice date, and the whole bill must be paid within 60 days after the invoice date.
- **2/10, EOM, n/60**—The seller offers a 2 percent discount if the bill is paid within 10 days after the end of the month, and the whole bill must be paid within 60 days after the last day of the month.

A wholesaler or manufacturer that offers a cash discount adopts a single cash discount as a credit policy and makes this available to all of its customers. The seller considers cash discounts as sales discounts under both the periodic and perpetual inventory systems; the buyer, on the other hand, considers cash discounts as purchases discounts under the periodic inventory system and a reduction to Merchandise Inventory under the perpetual inventory system.

RECORDING TRANSACTIONS INTO THE GENERAL JOURNAL

Learning Objective 2 In the general journal, record sales transactions involving cash receipts and cash discounts.

Occasionally, sales or purchases of merchandise will involve various discounts. In this section, we will discuss discounts and learn how they are recorded in the general journal.

Sales Discounts

First, we will concentrate on the **sales discount**. *The Sales Discounts account, like Sales Returns and Allowances, is a contra revenue account and is, therefore, deducted from Sales.*

To illustrate, we return to Whitewater Raft Supply. We will record the following transactions in the general journal and T accounts.

TRANSACTION (a). On August 1, Whitewater Raft Supply sold merchandise on account to Mesa River Raft Company, invoice no. 9384, $1,933.50; terms 2/10, n/30. (Take a moment to review the source document on page 426 in Chapter 9 and identify the terms on the invoice.)

TRANSACTION (b). On August 10, received check from Mesa River Raft Company for $1,894.83 in payment of invoice no. 9384, less cash discount ($1,933.50 × 0.02 = $38.67; $1,933.50 − $38.67 = $1,894.83).

GENERAL JOURNAL Page 26

Date		Description	Post. Ref.	Debit	Credit
20--					
Aug.	1	Accounts Receivable, Mesa River			
		Raft Company		1,933.50	
		Sales			1,933.50
		Sold merchandise to Mesa River			
		Raft Company, invoice no. 9384.			
	10	Cash		1,894.83	
		Sales Discounts		38.67	
		Accounts Receivable, Mesa River			
		Raft Company			1,933.50
		Collected cash on account,			
		invoice no. 9384.			

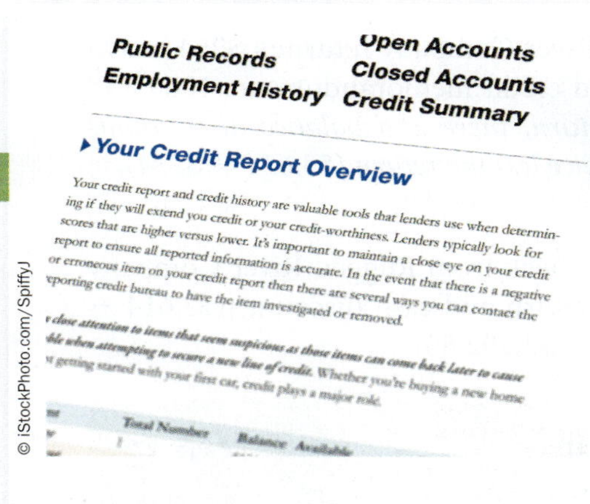

In the Real World

Dun & Bradstreet is a business credit rating organization that looks at a company's collection period ratio as one of its rating measurements. Therefore, businesses should make sure credit periods and terms encourage prompt payment.

Remember

When recording a cash receipt involving a sales discount, be sure to credit Accounts Receivable for the total amount of the sales transaction.

To record the receipt of payment from the customer on August 10, the accountant records a debit to Cash for the amount of cash received. The amount of discount granted is recorded as a debit to Sales Discounts. The Accounts Receivable account is credited so that the customer's account will decrease. Notice that the accountant records a credit to Accounts Receivable, Mesa River Raft Company for the total invoice amount, $1,933.50. This is important because if the receivable was credited for only the cash received, the customer's account would still show a balance owed.

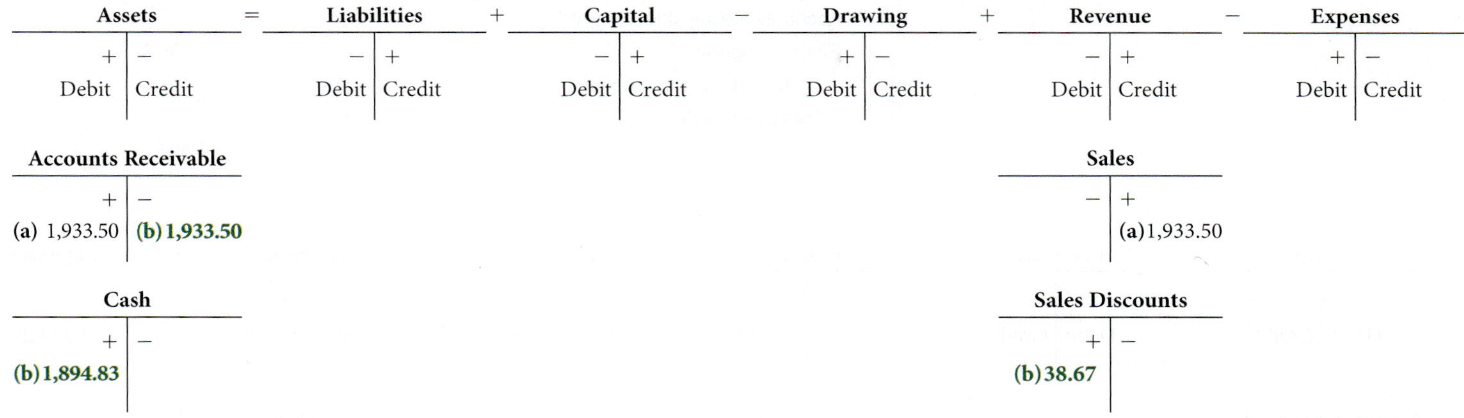

When a company receives a return of merchandise sold, the sales discount is calculated by excluding the amount of the returned items. Let's take a look at this example. The journal and T accounts for the following transactions are shown on the next page.

TRANSACTION (a). On September 1, Whitewater Raft Supply sold merchandise on account to Rugged River Company, invoice no. 9391; $3,614, terms 2/10, n/30; and recorded the sale in the general journal.

TRANSACTION (b). On September 5, Rugged River Company returned $254 worth of the merchandise. Whitewater Raft Supply issued credit memorandum no. 1069 and recorded the transaction. *Notice that after the return, there is a balance in Accounts Receivable of $3,360, the amount of the original invoice less the return ($3,614 − $254).*

TRANSACTION (c). On September 8, received check from Rugged River Company for $3,292.80 in payment of invoice no. 9391, less return and cash discount [($3,614 − $254) × 0.02 = $67.20; ($3,614 − $254) − $67.20 = $3,292.80].

GENERAL JOURNAL Page 27

Date		Description	Post. Ref.	Debit	Credit
20--					
Sept.	1	Accounts Receivable, Rugged River			
		Company		3 6 1 4 00	
		Sales			3 6 1 4 00
		Sold merchandise to Rugged			
		River Company, invoice no. 9391.			
	5	Sales Returns and Allowances		2 5 4 00	
		Accounts Receivable, Rugged			
		River Company			2 5 4 00
		Issued credit memo no. 1069.			
	8	Cash		3 2 9 2 80	
		Sales Discounts		6 7 20	
		Accounts Receivable, Rugged			
		River Company			3 3 6 0 00
		Collected cash on account,			
		invoice no. 9391.			

Assets	=	Liabilities	+	Capital	−	Drawing	+	Revenue	−	Expenses
+ | −		− | +		− | +		+ | −		− | +		+ | −
Debit | Credit		Debit | Credit		Debit | Credit		Debit | Credit		Debit | Credit		Debit | Credit

Accounts Receivable

+	−
(a) 3,614.00	(b) 254.00
	(c) **3,360.00**

Cash

+	−
(c) **3,292.80**	

Sales

−	+
	(a) 3,614.00

Sales Returns and Allowances

+	−
(b) 254.00	

Sales Discounts

+	−
(c) **67.20**	

Notice that when the accountant records the receipt of cash, the discount is calculated less the sales return. This is because the company would grant a discount only on the remaining amount owed, not for the original sale amount.

No Sales Discounts Involved

When a transaction does not involve a sales discount or the discount has expired, the seller records the receipt of payment on account by debiting Cash and crediting Accounts Receivable. Assume that Blue Merchandise Company recorded the following transactions:

TRANSACTION (a). On April 1, Blue Merchandise Company sold merchandise on account to Yellow Company, invoice no. 1294, $9,450; terms 2/10, n/30; and recorded the sale in the general journal.

TRANSACTION (b). On April 26, received check from Yellow Company for $9,450 in payment of invoice no. 1294.

Blue Merchandise Company's accountant would record the transactions in the general journal as follows:

GENERAL JOURNAL					Page 65
Date		Description	Post. Ref.	Debit	Credit
20--					
Apr.	1	Accounts Receivable, Yellow			
		Company		9 4 5 0 00	
		Sales			9 4 5 0 00
		Sold merchandise to Yellow			
		Company, invoice no. 1294.			
	26	Cash		9 4 5 0 00	
		Accounts Receivable, Yellow			
		Company			9 4 5 0 00
		Collected cash on account,			
		invoice no. 1294.			

Notice that because Yellow Company did not make payment within ten days, the discount was not applied to the invoice amount. Yellow Company paid the invoice in full.

POSTING TO THE GENERAL LEDGER AND SUBSIDIARY LEDGER

To post cash receipts of sales, post each entry to Cash and any other accounts involved in the general ledger. Also post the amounts paid by customers to the subsidiary accounts receivable ledger to maintain a running balance of the amount each customer owes.

POSTING TO THE GENERAL LEDGER AND SUBSIDIARY LEDGER—A COMPUTERIZED APPROACH

Most computer accounting software allows businesses to post cash receipts for sales and apply discounts. In Figure 1, the cash receipt of $1,894.83 in payment of invoice no. 9384 is being recorded into the accounting software.

Figure 1
Recording a cash receipt using accounting software

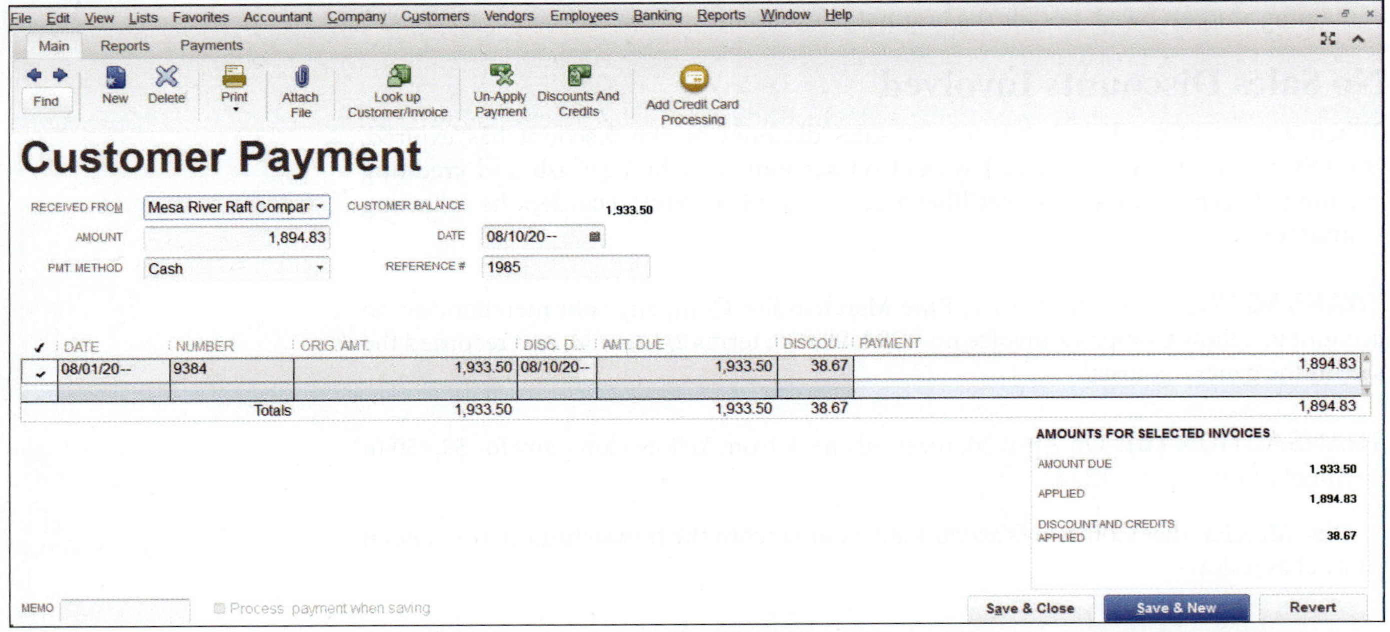

Figure 2
Recording a cash discount using accounting software

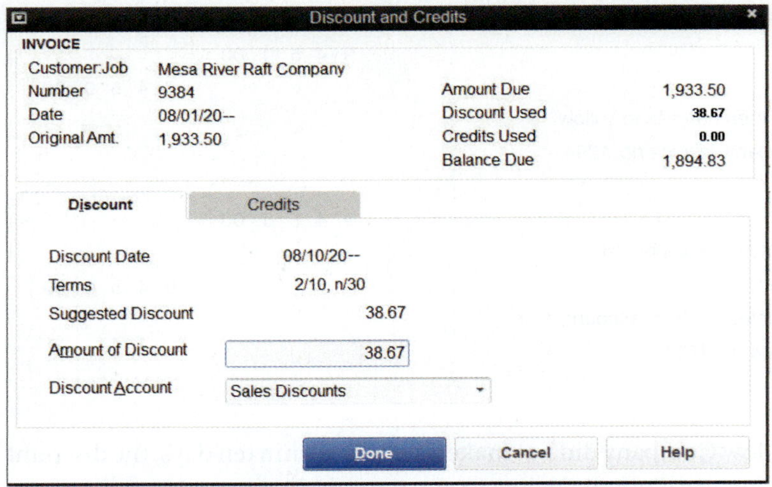

Notice that this software system allows the accountant to apply a discount. Look in the lower right corner to see the discount application button. In Figure 2, the accountant is recording the discount into the system.

After the discount has been applied, the invoice is shown as having been paid (Figure 3) and the balance due is $0.00. Using a computerized accounting system is an excellent way for businesses to keep track of cash receipts and discounts. Most computerized accounting software can also handle returns and allowances of merchandise that has been sold.

Sales Returns and Allowances and Sales Discounts on an Income Statement

On the income statement, the Sales Returns and Allowances and Sales Discounts are placed under Sales. Both accounts are contra accounts, so we subtract their totals from Sales. The Revenue from Sales section of the annual income statement of Whitewater Raft Supply is shown in Figure 4.

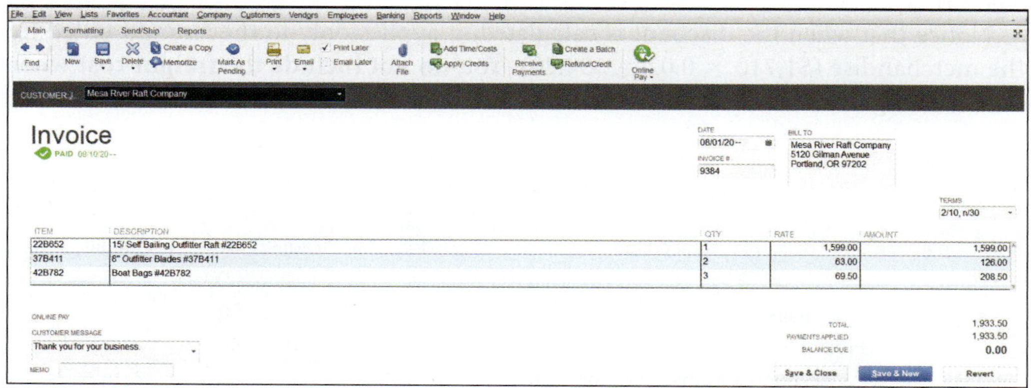

Figure 3
Paid invoice

Whitewater Raft Supply
Income Statement
For the Year Ended December 31, 20--

Revenue from Sales:			
Sales		$257,180	
Less: Sales Returns and Allowances	$ 940		
Sales Discounts	1,980	2,920	
Net Sales			$254,260

Figure 4
Revenue from Sales section of income statement

Purchases Discounts

Learning Objective 3 In the general journal, record purchase transactions involving cash payments and cash discounts.

Recall that a cash discount is the amount the buyer may deduct from the bill; this acts as an incentive to get the buyer to pay the bill promptly. The buyer considers the cash discount to be a **purchases discount** because it relates to the buyer's purchase of merchandise. *Under the periodic inventory system, the Purchases Discounts account, like Purchases Returns and Allowances, is a contra account and is treated as a deduction from Purchases on the buyer's income statement.*

Let's return to Whitewater Raft Supply and assume that the following transactions take place.

Remember The cash discount does not apply to freight charges billed separately on an invoice.

TRANSACTION (a). On August 2, Whitewater Raft Supply bought merchandise on account from Pataponia, Inc., invoice no. 2706, $1,710; terms 2/10, n/30; dated July 31; FOB San Francisco, freight prepaid and added to the invoice, $85.50 (total $1,795.50).

TRANSACTION (b). On August 8, issued Ck. No. 2076 to Pataponia, Inc., in payment of invoice no. 2706, less cash discount of $34.20, $1,761.30 ($1,795.50 − $34.20).

Notice that when the discount is calculated, it applies only to the amount billed for the merchandise ($1,710 × 0.02 = $34.20). **You do not include the freight cost when determining the discount.**

GENERAL JOURNAL Page 26

Date		Description	Post. Ref.	Debit	Credit
20--					
Aug.	2	Purchases		1 7 1 0 00	
		Freight In		8 5 50	
		Accounts Payable, Pataponia, Inc.			1 7 9 5 50
		Purchased merchandise from			
		Pataponia, Inc., invoice no. 2706,			
		invoice dated 7/31,			
		terms 2/10, n/30.			
	8	Accounts Payable, Pataponia, Inc.		1 7 9 5 50	
		Cash			1 7 6 1 30
		Purchases Discounts			3 4 20
		Paid Pataponia, Inc., for			
		invoice no. 2706, Ck. No. 2076.			

To record the payment to Pataponia, Inc., the accountant records a debit to Accounts Payable and a credit to Cash for the amount of cash paid. The amount of discount received is recorded as a credit to Purchases Discounts. Notice that the accountant records a debit to Accounts Payable, Pataponia, Inc., for the total invoice amount, $1,795.50. This is important because if the payable was debited for only the cash paid, the account would still show a balance due.

Assets		=	Liabilities		+	Capital		−	Drawing		+	Revenue		−	Expenses	
+	−		−	+		−	+		+	−		−	+		+	−
Debit	Credit		Debit	Credit		Debit	Credit		Debit	Credit		Debit	Credit		Debit	Credit

Cash	
+	−
	(b) 1,761.30

Accounts Payable	
−	+
(b) 1,795.50	(a) 1,795.50

Purchases	
+	−
(a) 1,710.00	

Purchases Discounts	
−	+
	(b) 34.20

Freight In	
+	−
(a) 85.50	

Similar to sales returns, purchase returns and allowances are also not included when calculating the discount. Remember to omit any prepaid freight and returns and allowances when determining the amount of the discount.

No Purchases Discounts Involved

When a transaction does not involve a purchases discount or the discount has expired, the buyer will record the payment by debiting Accounts Payable and crediting Cash. Assume that Blue Merchandise Company recorded the following transactions:

TRANSACTION (a). On November 1, Blue Merchandise Company bought merchandise on account from Grey, Inc., invoice no. 3901, $4,600; terms 2/10, n/30; dated October 31.

TRANSACTION (b). On November 28, issued Ck. No. 1151 to Grey, Inc., in payment of invoice no. 3901, $4,600.

Blue Merchandise Company's accountant would record the transactions in the general journal as follows:

GENERAL JOURNAL — Page 81

Date		Description	Post. Ref.	Debit	Credit
20--					
Nov.	1	Purchases		4 6 0 0 00	
		Accounts Payable, Grey, Inc.			4 6 0 0 00
		Purchased merchandise from			
		Grey, Inc., invoice no. 3901,			
		invoice dated 10/31,			
		terms 2/10, n/30.			
	28	Accounts Payable, Grey, Inc.		4 6 0 0 00	
		Cash			4 6 0 0 00
		Paid Grey, Inc., for invoice no. 3901,			
		Ck. No. 1151.			

Notice that because Blue Merchandise Company did not make payment within ten days, the discount was not applied to the invoice amount. Blue Merchandise Company paid the invoice in full.

POSTING TO THE GENERAL LEDGER AND SUBSIDIARY LEDGER

To post cash payments of purchases, post each entry to Cash, Accounts Payable, and any other accounts involved in the general ledger. Also post the amounts owed to vendors to the subsidiary accounts payable ledger to maintain a running balance of the amount owed to each vendor.

POSTING TO THE GENERAL LEDGER AND SUBSIDIARY LEDGER—A COMPUTERIZED APPROACH

Businesses can use a computerized accounting program to enter cash payments to vendors. Cash payments are applied to vendor invoices that are created by the accountant in the software. In Figure 5, the accountant is beginning to record the payment of the invoice by selecting the correct invoice due.

After the accountant has selected the bill on which to make payment, he or she can apply any discount granted and process the payment. Figure 6 shows the bill payment verification screen showing that payment has been applied to the invoice.

Purchases Returns and Allowances, Purchases Discounts, and Freight In on an Income Statement

On the income statement, the Purchases Returns and Allowances and Purchases Discounts are placed under Purchases. Both accounts are contra accounts, so we subtract their totals from Purchases. Because Freight In increases the cost of purchases, it must be added. A portion of the Cost of Goods Sold section of the annual income statement of Whitewater Raft Supply, as well as the Revenue from Sales section (taken from Figure 4, on page 503), is shown in Figure 7.

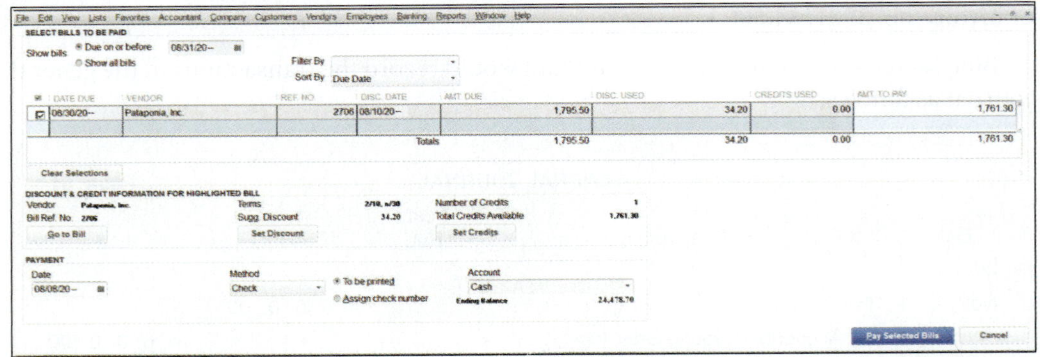

Figure 5
Recording a cash payment using accounting software

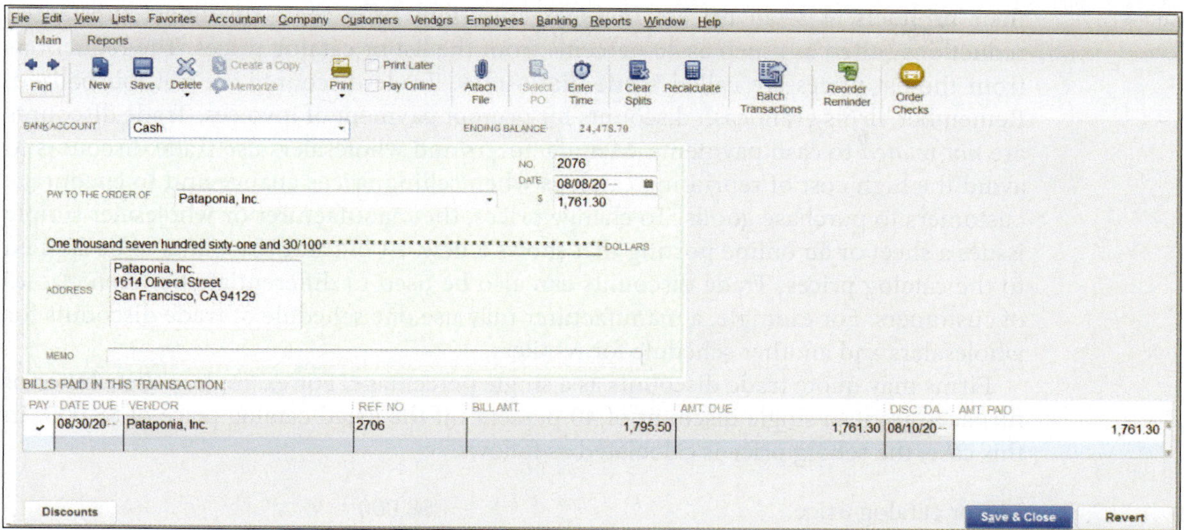

Figure 6
Bill payment

Whitewater Raft Supply
Income Statement
For the Year Ended December 31, 20--

Revenue from Sales:				
Sales			$ 257,180	
Less: Sales Returns and Allowances		$ 940		
Sales Discounts		1,980	2,920	
Net Sales				$254,260
Cost of Goods Sold:				
Merchandise Inventory, January 1, 20--			$ 67,000	
Purchases		$87,840		
Less: Purchases Returns and Allowances	$ 932			
Purchases Discounts	1,348	2,280		
Net Purchases		$85,560		
Add Freight In		2,360		
Delivered Cost of Purchases			87,920	
Cost of Goods Available for Sale			$154,920	

Figure 7
Partial income statement for Whitewater Raft Supply

Trade Discounts

Learning Objective

Record transactions involving trade discounts.

Manufacturers and wholesalers of many lines of products publish annual catalogs listing their products at retail prices. These organizations offer their customers substantial reductions (often as much as 40 percent) from the list or catalog prices. The reductions from the list prices are called **trade discounts**. Trade discounts are not journalized. Remember, firms grant cash discounts for prompt payment of invoices. Trade discounts are *not related* to cash payments. Manufacturers and wholesalers use trade discounts to avoid the high cost of reprinting catalogs when selling prices change and to encourage customers to purchase goods. To change prices, the manufacturer or wholesaler simply issues a sheet or an online posting that shows a new list of trade discounts to be applied to the catalog prices. Trade discounts can also be used to differentiate between classes of customers. For example, a manufacturer may use one schedule of trade discounts for wholesalers and another schedule for retailers.

Firms may quote trade discounts as a single percentage. For example, a distributor of furnaces grants a single discount of 40 percent off the listed catalog price of $8,000. In this case, the selling price is calculated as follows:

List or catalog price	$8,000
Less trade discount of 40% ($8,000 × 0.40)	3,200
Selling price	$4,800

Neither the seller nor the buyer records trade discounts in the accounts; they enter only the selling price. Using T accounts, the furnace distributor records the sale like this:

Accounts Receivable			Sales	
+	−		−	+
4,800				4,800

The buyer records the purchase as follows:

Purchases			Accounts Payable	
+	−		−	+
4,800				4,800

Firms may also quote trade discounts as a chain, or series, of percentages. For example, a distributor of automobile parts grants discounts of 30 percent, 10 percent, and 10 percent off the listed catalog price of $900. In this case, the selling price is calculated as follows:

List or catalog price	$900.00
Less first trade discount of 30% ($900 × 0.30)	270.00
Remainder after first discount	$630.00
Less second trade discount of 10% ($630 × 0.10)	63.00
Remainder after second discount	$567.00
Less third discount of 10% ($567 × 0.10)	56.70
Selling price	$510.30

Using T accounts, the automobile parts distributor records the sale as follows:

Accounts Receivable			Sales	
+	−		−	+
510.30				510.30

The buyer records the purchase as follows:

In the situation involving a chain of discounts, the additional discounts are granted for large-volume transactions, in either dollar amount or size of shipment, such as carload lots.

Cash discounts could also apply in situations involving trade discounts. *Example:* Suppose the credit terms of the preceding sale include a cash discount of 2/10, n/30 and the buyer pays the invoice within ten days. The seller applies the cash discount to the selling price. The seller records the transaction as shown in the following T accounts:

Cash		Sales Discounts		Accounts Receivable	
+	–	+	–	+	–
500.09		10.21			510.30

The buyer records the transaction as follows:

Cash		Purchases Discounts		Accounts Payable	
+	–	–	+	–	+
	500.09		10.21	510.30	

A Review of Purchases and Sales Transactions

Now that we have covered all of the transactions involving purchases and sales, let's take a moment to review. Remember that each transaction affects a purchaser and a seller. In Figure 8, we show how each transaction would be recorded by a purchaser (Able Company) and a seller (Baker Company). Note that Able Company is using a periodic inventory system. For companies using a perpetual inventory system, Merchandise Inventory would be debited for purchases and credited for purchases returns and allowances and purchases discounts.

Remember

To the seller, a cash discount is a sales discount, and to the purchaser, a cash discount is a purchases discount.

Purchaser's Books—Able Company			Seller's Books—Baker Company		
Bought merchandise from Baker Company, $500; terms 2/10, n/30.			Sold merchandise to Able Company, $500; terms 2/10, n/30.		
Purchases	500		Accounts Receivable	500	
Accounts Payable		500	Sales		500
Received credit memo from Baker Company for return of merchandise, $100.			Issued credit memo to Able Company for return of merchandise, $100.		
Accounts Payable	100		Sales Returns and Allowances	100	
Purchases Returns and Allowances		100	Accounts Receivable		100
Paid Baker Company within the discount period, $392 ($500 − $100 = $400; $400 × 0.02 = $8; $400 − $8 = $392).			Received cash from Able Company within the discount period, $392.		
Accounts Payable	400		Cash	392	
Cash		392	Sales Discounts	8	
Purchases Discounts		8	Accounts Receivable		400

Figure 8
Transactions for two companies' purchases and sales

To: **Amy Roberts, CPA**
Subject: **Cash Receipts and Cash Payments**

Hi Amy,

I think I understand discounts. Thanks again for your help. I did come up with another question. Is there any way to speed up the journalizing process for cash receipts and cash payments? It seems like I spend a lot of time posting to the same accounts. Can you suggest something that might reduce the time I spend recording transactions?

Thanks,
Janie

To: **Janie Conner**
Subject: **RE: Cash Receipts and Cash Payments**

Hi Janie,

I do have a few suggestions regarding your process for recording cash receipts and cash payments. We can discuss the benefits of using the cash receipts and cash payment journals, as well as, using the accounts receivable and accounts payable ledgers.

Below is a summary of the items for us to discuss the next time we talk.

____ 1. Journalizing transactions using the cash receipts journal and posting to the accounts receivable ledger

____ 2. Journalizing transactions using the cash payments journal and posting to the accounts payable ledger

Just give me a call when you have some time later this week.

Amy

RECORDING TRANSACTIONS INTO THE CASH RECEIPTS JOURNAL AND CASH PAYMENTS JOURNAL

In Chapter 9, we saw that using a sales journal and a purchases journal enables an accountant to carry out the journalizing and posting processes more efficiently. These special journals make it possible to post column totals rather than individual figures. They also make the division of labor more efficient because the journalizing functions can be delegated to different people. The *cash receipts journal* and the *cash payments journal* further extend these advantages.

The Cash Receipts Journal

The **cash receipts journal** contains all transactions in which cash is received, or increased. When a cash receipts journal is used, all transactions in which cash is debited *must* be recorded in it. It may be used for a service as well as a merchandising business. Let's list some typical transactions of a merchandising business, Whitewater Raft Supply, that result in an increase in cash. To get a better picture of the transactions, let's record them in T accounts and then in the general journal.

> **Learning Objective 5** In the cash receipts journal, record transactions for a merchandising business and post from a cash receipts journal to a general ledger and an accounts receivable ledger.

Oct. 1 Sold merchandise on account to Green River Rafts, invoice no. 10050, $3,500; terms 2/10, n/30.

Oct. 4 Sold merchandise, $500, and the customer used a credit card.

The bank issuing the card bills the customer directly each month. The business, on the other hand, deposits the bank credit card receipts every day. The bank *deducts a discount* and credits the firm's account for the cash difference. We will assume that the discount is 4 percent. The firm therefore records the amount of the discount under Credit Card Expense: $500 × 0.04 = $20 credit card expense; $500 − $20 = $480.

Cash		Credit Card Expense		Sales	
+	–	+	–	–	+
480		20			500

As an alternative, many businesses postpone recording the amount of bank credit card expense until they receive notification from their bank on their bank statement. For example, total credit card sales for a restaurant for a time period amount to $10,600 plus 8 percent sales tax. The entry is as follows:

Cash		Sales Tax Payable		Sales	
+	–	–	+	–	+
11,448			848		10,600

The restaurant's next bank statement includes a debit memorandum for credit card charges of $457.92, using an assumed 4 percent discount rate ($11,448 × 0.04). The business handles this in a similar manner to a check service charge.

Credit Card Expense		Cash	
+	–	+	–
457.92			457.92

Oct. 5 Collected cash on account from L. R. Ray, a charge customer, $416.

Cash		Accounts Receivable	
+	–	+	–
416			416

SMALL BUSINESS **SUCCESS**

Credit Cards: Are They Worth It?

Accepting credit cards for sales of merchandise or services has become a natural part of business for most companies. However, some small businesses still don't accept credit cards and rely only on cash sales. The decision to accept credit cards comes at a cost to the business in the form of a fee. The bank that processes your credit card sales will charge your company a fee for any credit card sales. The amount of the fee varies based on the bank you are using and the amount of transactions your company processes. In addition to banks, specific companies, often called merchant service companies, offer credit card processing services.

Why would a company choose to accept credit cards in the form of payment? There are many reasons. One is that it may increase sales by allowing customers more flexibility in payment methods. Also, the bank or processing company assumes all risk associated with non-paying customers. Unlike uncollectible accounts receivables, the company always gets paid when a transaction involves a credit card sale.

How does a company begin accepting credit cards? The first step is to apply for merchant status. Applying for merchant status is similar to applying for a loan. Your company must fill out an application and have its financial records reviewed. Once merchant status is approved for your company, you will be able to accept most common credit cards. The bank or merchant services company that you partner with will transfer the cash proceeds, less the fee, for each credit card sale to your bank account. The transaction fee or service charge usually ranges from 1.5 to 5 percent of the sale. In addition, there may be monthly or other fees associated with credit card transactions.

Oct. 7 The owner, D. M. Bruce, invested cash in the business, $9,000.

Cash

+	−
9,000	

D. M. Bruce, Capital

−	+
	9,000

Oct. 8 Sold equipment at cost for cash, $500.

Cash

+	−
500	

Equipment

+	−
	500

Oct. 10 Received check from Green River Rafts for $3,430 in payment of invoice no. 10050, less cash discount ($3,500 × 0.02 = $70; $3,500 − $70 = $3,430).

Cash

+	−
3,430	

Sales Discounts

+	−
70	

Accounts Receivable

+	−
	3,500

Oct. 15 Cash sales for first half of the month, $2,460.

Cash

+	−
2,460	

Sales

−	+
	2,460

The same transactions are shown in general journal form as follows:

GENERAL JOURNAL Page 29

Date		Description	Post. Ref.	Debit	Credit
20--					
Oct.	1	Accounts Receivable, Green River Rafts		3,500.00	
		Sales			3,500.00
		Sold merchandise to Green River Rafts, invoice no. 10050.			
	4	Cash		480.00	
		Credit Card Expense		20.00	
		Sales			500.00
		Sold merchandise involving a credit card.			
	5	Cash		416.00	
		Accounts Receivable, L. R. Ray			416.00
		Collected cash on account.			
	7	Cash		9,000.00	
		D. M. Bruce, Capital			9,000.00
		Owner invested cash.			
	8	Cash		500.00	
		Equipment			500.00
		Sold equipment at cost.			
	10	Cash		3,430.00	
		Sales Discounts		70.00	
		Accounts Receivable, Green River Rafts			3,500.00
		Received a check in payment of invoice no. 10050, less cash discount.			
	15	Cash		2,460.00	
		Sales			2,460.00
		Cash sales for the first half of the month.			

Now let's analyze these seven transactions: The transaction on October 1 does not involve cash; therefore, it would not be recorded in the cash receipts journal. Instead, this transaction would be recorded in either the general journal or the sales journal. The transactions occurring on 10/4, 10/5, 10/10, and 10/15 would occur frequently; the transactions on 10/7 and 10/8 would occur less frequently. When designing a cash receipts journal, it is logical to include a Cash Debit column because all of the transactions involve an increase in cash. If a business regularly collects cash from credit customers, there should be an Accounts Receivable Credit column and Sales Discounts Debit column. If a firm often sells merchandise for cash and collects a sales tax, there should be a Sales Credit column and a Sales Tax Payable Credit column. If the business accepts credit cards and wants to record the amount of the discount at the time of each transaction, there should be a Credit Card Expense Debit column for the amount deducted by the bank.

However, the credit to D. M. Bruce, Capital and the credit to Equipment do not occur very often, so it would not be practical to set up special columns for these credits. They can be handled adequately by an Other Accounts Credit column, which can be used for credits to all accounts that have no special column.

The accountant would record these transactions in a cash receipts journal. (See Figure 9.) Notice that there are columns for each of the most common cash transactions. The accountant would record each transaction directly into the cash receipts journal by placing each amount in the appropriate column.

Figure 9
Cash receipts journal

CASH RECEIPTS JOURNAL **Page 41**

Date		Account Credited	Post. Ref.	Cash Debit	Credit Card Expense Debit	Sales Discounts Debit	Accounts Receivable Credit	Sales Credit	Other Accounts Credit
20—									
Oct.	4	________		480 00	20 00			500 00	
	5	L. R. Ray		416 00			416 00		
	7	D. M. Bruce,							
		Capital		9000 00					9000 00
	8	Equipment		500 00					500 00
	10	Green							
		River Rafts		3430 00		70 00	3500 00		
	15	________		2460 00				2460 00	

Posting from the Cash Receipts Journal

Special journals include a sales journal (S), a purchases journal (P), a cash receipts journal (CR), and a cash payments journal (CP). Using these special journals saves time in posting totals of the special columns rather than individual amounts to the general ledger.

Here are some other transactions made during the month that involve increases in cash.

Oct. 16 Received check from Floyd Mercantile for $1,366.12 in payment of invoice no. 10052, less cash discount ($1,394.00 − $27.88 = $1,366.12).

17 Borrowed $9,000 from the bank, receiving cash and giving the bank a promissory note.

21 Received check from Hartman Guides for $3,696.80 in payment of invoice no. 10055, less cash discount ($3,772.24 − $75.44 = $3,696.80).

30 Received check from Bowers River Co. for $1,710 in payment of invoice no. 10054. (This is longer than the 10-day period, so the cash discount is not allowed.)

31 Cash sales for second half of the month, $2,620.

In the transaction of October 17, in which $9,000 was borrowed from the bank, the bank was given a **promissory note** (a written promise to pay a specified amount at a specified time) as evidence of the debt. The account **Notes Payable**, instead of Accounts Payable, is used to represent the amount owed on the promissory note. The Accounts Payable account is reserved for charge accounts with creditors, which are normally paid on a 30-day basis.

Let's assume that all of the month's transactions involving debits to Cash have been recorded in the cash receipts journal. The cash receipts journal (see Figure 10) and the T accounts following it illustrate the postings to the general ledger and the accounts receivable ledger.

Figure 10

Posting from the cash receipts journal to the general ledger and accounts receivable ledger

CASH RECEIPTS JOURNAL — Page 41

Date		Account Credited	Post. Ref.	Cash Debit	Credit Card Expense Debit	Sales Discounts Debit	Accounts Receivable Credit	Sales Credit	Other Accounts Credit
20--									
Oct.	4	________	—	480 00	20 00			500 00	
	5	L. R. Ray	✓	416 00			416 00		
	7	D. M. Bruce, Capital	311	9,000 00					9,000 00
	8	Equipment	124	500 00					500 00
	10	Green River Rafts	✓	3,430 00		70 00	3,500 00		
	15	________	—	2,460 00				2,460 00	
	16	Floyd Mercantile	✓	1,366 12		27 88	1,394 00		
	17	Notes Payable	211	9,000 00					9,000 00
	21	Hartman Guides	✓	3,696 80		75 44	3,772 24		
	30	Bowers River Co.	✓	1,710 00			1,710 00		
	31	________	—	2,620 00				2,620 00	
	31	Total		34,678 92	20 00	173 32	10,792 24	5,580 00	18,500 00
				(111)	(615)	(413)	(113)	(411)	(X)

Accounts Receivable Ledger

Bowers River Co.

	+	−	
Beg. Bal.	2,500.00	Oct. 30	1,710.00
End. Bal.	790.00		

Floyd Mercantile

	+	−	
Beg. Bal.	1,394.00	Oct. 16	1,394.00

Green River Rafts

	+	−	
Beg. Bal.	5,000.00	Oct. 10	3,500.00
End Bal.	1,500.00		

Hartman Guides

	+	−	
Beg. Bal.	3,772.24	Oct. 21	3,772.24

L. R. Ray

	+	−	
Beg. Bal.	416.00	Oct. 5	416.00

General Ledger

Cash 111

	+	−	
Oct. 31	34,678.92		

Accounts Receivable 113

	+	−	
		Oct. 31	10,792.24

Equipment 124

	+	−	
		Oct. 8	500.00

Notes Payable 211

	−	+	
		Oct. 17	9,000.00

D. M. Bruce, Capital 311

	−	+	
		Oct. 7	9,000.00

Sales 411

	−	+	
Oct. 31	5,580.00		

Sales Discounts 413

	+	−	
Oct. 31	173.32		

Credit Card Expense 615

	+	−	
Oct. 31	20.00		

Individual amounts in the Accounts Receivable Credit column of the cash receipts journal are usually posted daily to the accounts receivable ledger. Individual amounts in the Other Accounts Credit column are usually posted daily.

At the end of the month, we can post the special column totals in the cash receipts journal to the general ledger accounts. These columns include Cash Debit, Credit Card Expense Debit, Sales Discounts Debit, Accounts Receivable Credit, and Sales Credit.

In the Post. Ref. column, the check marks (✓) indicate that the amounts in the Accounts Receivable Credit column have been posted to the individual credit customers' accounts as credits. The account numbers show that the amounts in the Other Accounts Credit column have been posted separately to the accounts described in the Account Credited column. An (X) goes under the total of the Other Accounts Credit column; it means "do not post—the figures have already been posted separately." This column is totaled to make it easier to prove that the debits equal the credits.

Debit Totals		Credit Totals	
Cash	$34,678.92	Accounts Receivable	$10,792.24
Credit Card Expense	20.00	Sales	5,580.00
Sales Discounts	173.32	Other Accounts	18,500.00
	$34,872.24		$34,872.24

ADVANTAGES OF A CASH RECEIPTS JOURNAL

The advantages of using a cash receipts journal are as follows:

- Transactions generally can be recorded on one line.
- All transactions involving debits to Cash are recorded in one place.
- It eliminates much repetition in posting to the general ledger when there are numerous transactions involving Cash debits. The Cash Debit side can be posted as one total.
- Special columns can be used for similar transactions and posted as one total.

The Cash Payments Journal

Learning Objective 6: In the cash payments journal, record transactions for a merchandising business and post from a cash payments journal to a general ledger and an accounts payable ledger.

The **cash payments journal**, as the name implies, is a special journal used to record all transactions in which cash goes out, or decreases. When the cash payments journal is used, all transactions in which cash is credited *must* be recorded in it. This journal may be used for either a service or a merchandising business.

To get acquainted with the cash payments journal, let's list some typical transactions of a merchandising business that result in a decrease in cash. To illustrate, we record the following transactions in T accounts:

Oct. 2 Bought merchandise on account from Pataponia, Inc., invoice no. 2746, $2,500; terms 2/10, n/30; dated September 30; FOB San Francisco, freight prepaid and added to the invoice, $100.25 (total $2,600.25).

Accounts Payable		Purchases		Freight In	
−	+	+	−	+	−
	2,600.25	2,500.00		100.25	

Oct. 8 Issued Ck. No. 2226 to Pataponia, Inc., in payment of invoice no. 2746, less cash discount of $50.00, $2,550.25 ($2,600.25 − $50.00). [Notice that the discount applies only to the amount billed for the merchandise (2 percent of $2,500).]

Cash		Accounts Payable		Purchases Discounts	
+	−	−	+	−	+
	2,550.25	2,600.25			50.00

Oct. 10 Paid cash for liability insurance, Ck. No. 2227 $4,890.

Prepaid Insurance		Cash	
+	−	+	−
4,890			4,890

Oct. 12 Paid wages for two weeks, Ck. No. 2228, $6,220 (previously recorded in the payroll entry).

Wages Payable		Cash	
−	+	+	−
6,220			6,220

Oct. 14 Paid rent for the month, Ck. No. 2229, $2,950.

Rent Expense		Cash	
+	−	+	−
2,950			2,950

The same transactions are shown in general journal form as follows:

GENERAL JOURNAL Page 29

Date		Description	Post. Ref.	Debit	Credit
20--					
Oct.	2	Purchases		2 5 0 0 00	
		Freight In		1 0 0 25	
		Accounts Payable, Pataponia, Inc.			2 6 0 0 25
		Purchased merchandise from			
		Pataponia, Inc., invoice no. 2746,			
		invoice dated 9/30, terms 2/10, n/30.			
	8	Accounts Payable, Pataponia, Inc.		2 6 0 0 25	
		Cash			2 5 5 0 25
		Purchases Discounts			5 0 00
		Paid on account, Ck. No. 2226.			
	10	Prepaid Insurance		4 8 9 0 00	
		Cash			4 8 9 0 00
		Paid liability insurance,			
		Ck. No. 2227.			
	12	Wages Payable		6 2 2 0 00	
		Cash			6 2 2 0 00
		Paid wages for two weeks,			
		Ck. No. 2228.			
	14	Rent Expense		2 9 5 0 00	
		Cash			2 9 5 0 00
		Paid rent for month, Ck. No. 2229.			

Now let's analyze these five transactions. The transaction on October 2 does not involve cash; therefore, it would not be recorded in the cash payments journal. Instead, this transaction would be recorded in either the general journal or the purchases journal. The transaction on October 8 would occur frequently, as payments to creditors are made several times a month. Of the other transactions, the debit to Wages Payable might occur only twice a month, the debit to Rent Expense once a month, and the debit to Prepaid Insurance only occasionally.

It is logical to include a Cash Credit column in a cash payments journal because all transactions recorded in this journal involve a decrease in cash. Because payments to creditors are made often, there should also be an Accounts Payable Debit column and a Purchases Discounts Credit column. You can set up any other column that is used often enough to warrant it. Otherwise, an Other Accounts Debit column takes care of all other transactions.

Now let's record these same transactions in a cash payments journal and include a column titled Ck. No. (See Figure 11.) If you think for a moment, you will see that this is consistent with good management of cash. All expenditures except Petty Cash expenditures should be paid for by check.

Figure 11
Cash payments journal

CASH PAYMENTS JOURNAL — Page 62

Date		Ck. No.	Account Debited	Post. Ref.	Other Accounts Debit	Accounts Payable Debit	Purchases Discounts Credit	Cash Credit
20--								
Oct.	8	2226	Pataponia, Inc.			2 6 0 0 25	5 0 00	2 5 5 0 25
	10	2227	Prepaid Insurance		4 8 9 0 00			4 8 9 0 00
	12	2228	Wages Payable		6 2 2 0 00			6 2 2 0 00
	14	2229	Rent Expense		2 9 5 0 00			2 9 5 0 00

Here are some other transactions of Whitewater Raft Supply involving decreases in cash during October. Note that credit terms vary among the different creditors.

Oct. 15 Issued Ck. No. 2230 to Gibbs Company in payment of invoice no. 10611 (\$564), less return (\$270); less cash discount, terms 2/10, n/30; \$288.12 [\$564 − \$270 = \$294; \$294.00 × 0.02 = \$5.88; \$294.00 − \$5.88 = \$288.12].

16 Issued Ck. No. 2231 to Gardner Products Company in payment of invoice no. B643 (\$1,245), less return (\$315); less cash discount, terms 1/10, n/30; \$921.60 [\$1,245 − \$315 = \$930. Freight charges totaled \$90 (\$930 − \$90 = \$840); \$840.00 × 0.01 = \$8.40; \$930.00 − \$8.40 = \$921.60].

17 Bought merchandise for cash, Ck. No. 2232, payable to Jones and Son, \$200.

19 Received bill and issued Ck. No. 2233 to Monroe Express for freight charges on merchandise purchased earlier from Gibbs Company, \$60.

23 Voided Ck. No. 2234.

25 Paid wages for two-week period, Ck. No. 2235, \$1,750 (previously recorded in the payroll entry).

27 Paid F. P. Franz for merchandise returned on a cash sale, Ck. No. 2236, \$51.

27 Issued Ck. No. 2237 to Langseth and Son in payment of invoice no. 902, \$1,180; terms net 30 days.

The transaction of October 19 paying the freight bill to Monroe Express increases the Freight In account, as the transportation charges are for merchandise purchased.

Figure 12
Cash payments journal

CASH PAYMENTS JOURNAL — Page 62

Date		Ck. No.	Account Debited	Post. Ref.	Other Accounts Debit	Accounts Payable Debit	Purchases Discounts Credit	Cash Credit
20--								
Oct.	8	2226	Pataponia, Inc.	✓		2,600.25	50.00	2,550.25
	10	2227	Prepaid Insurance	116	4,890.00			4,890.00
	12	2228	Wages Payable	213	6,220.00			6,220.00
	14	2229	Rent Expense	612	2,950.00			2,950.00
	15	2230	Gibbs Company	✓		294.00	5.88	288.12
	16	2231	Gardner Products Company	✓		930.00	8.40	921.60
	17	2232	Purchases	511	200.00			200.00
	19	2233	Freight In	514	60.00			60.00
	23	2234	Void	—				
	25	2235	Wages Payable	213	1,750.00			1,750.00
	27	2236	Sales Returns and Allowances	412	51.00			51.00
	27	2237	Langseth and Son	✓		1,180.00		1,180.00
	31		Totals		16,121.00	5,004.25	64.28	21,060.97
					(X)	(212)	(513)	(111)

You should list all checks in consecutive order, even those checks that must be voided. In this way, *every* check is accounted for, which is necessary for internal control.

These transactions are recorded in the cash payments journal illustrated in Figure 12. Notice that an (X) is placed under the Other Accounts column. That means "do not post—the figures have already been posted separately."

The posting process for the cash payments journal is similar to the posting process for the cash receipts journal. Individual amounts in the Accounts Payable Debit column are usually posted daily to the subsidiary ledger. After posting, put a check mark (✓) in the Post. Ref. column. Individual amounts in the Other Accounts Debit column are usually posted daily to the general ledger. Post these figures individually; then place the account number in the Post. Ref. column. Totals of the Cash Credit column, Purchases Discounts Credit column, and Accounts Payable Debit column are posted to the general ledger accounts at the end of the month. Write the appropriate general ledger account number in parentheses below the column totals. Put an (X) below the total of the Other Accounts Debit column to indicate that the total amount is not posted.

Remember

The (X) below the total of the Other Accounts Debit column means "do not post total."

At the end of the month, after totaling the columns, check the accuracy of the footings by proving that the sum of the debit totals equals the sum of the credit totals. Because you have posted the individual amounts in the Other Accounts Debit column to the general ledger, the only posting that remains is the credit to the Cash account for $21,060.97, the credit to the Purchases Discounts account for $64.28, and the debit to the Accounts Payable (controlling) account for $5,004.25.

Debit Totals		Credit Totals	
Accounts Payable	$ 5,004.25	Cash	$21,060.97
Other Accounts	16,121.00	Purchases Discounts	64.28
	$21,125.25		$21,125.25

Advantages of a Cash Payments Journal

The advantages of the cash payments journal are similar to the advantages of the cash receipts journal.

- Transactions generally can be recorded on one line.
- All transactions involving credits to Cash are recorded in one place.
- For numerous transactions involving Cash credits, the Cash Credit side can be posted in the general ledger as one total.
- Special columns can be used for similar transactions and posted as one total.

COMPARISON OF THE FIVE TYPES OF JOURNALS

We have now looked at four special journals and the general journal. It is important for a business to select and use the journals that provide the most efficient accounting system possible. Figure 13 summarizes the applications of the journals we have discussed and the correct procedures for using them.

Figure 13
Using special journals

Types of Transactions

Sale of merchandise on account	Purchase of merchandise on account	Receipt of cash	Payment of cash	All other

Evidenced by Source Documents

Sales invoice	Purchase invoice	Credit card receipts Cash Checks Electronic funds transfers	Check stub Electronic funds transfers	Miscellaneous

Types of Journals

Sales journal	Purchases journal	Cash receipts journal	Cash payments journal	General journal

Posting to Ledger Accounts

Individual amounts posted daily to the accounts receivable ledger and the total posted monthly to the general ledger.	*Individual amounts posted daily to the accounts payable ledger and the totals of the special columns posted monthly to the general ledger.*	*Individual amounts in the Accounts Receivable Credit column posted daily to the accounts receivable ledger.* *Individual amounts in the Other Accounts columns posted daily to the general ledger.* *Totals of special columns posted monthly to the general ledger.*	*Individual amounts in the Accounts Payable Debit column posted daily to the accounts payable ledger.* *Individual amounts in the Other Accounts columns posted daily to the general ledger.* *Totals of special columns posted monthly to the general ledger.*	*Entries posted daily to the subsidiary ledgers and the general ledger.*

Recommended Order of Posting to the Subsidiary Ledgers and the General Ledger

To avoid errors and negative balances in accounts, post from the special journals in this order:

1. Sales journal
2. Purchases journal
3. Cash receipts journal
4. Cash payments journal

Accounting with QuickBooks®

Cash Receipts and Cash Payments

1 Create sales receipts — **Learning Objective**

In Chapter 9, you learned how to create invoices for sales made to customers on account. Now we will look at creating sales receipts to record sales made to customers for cash. Cash sales include methods of payment such as cash, checks, money orders, credit cards, debit cards, or gift cards. To create a sales receipt in QuickBooks that records cash sales, complete the steps in Figures Q1 and Q2.

STEP 1. Select **Create Sales Receipts** from the home page, under the **Customers** center.

Learning Objectives

After you have completed this section, you will be able to do the following:

1. Create sales receipts.
2. Receive payments.
3. Record deposits.
4. Pay bills.
5. Write checks.

Figure Q1
Create sales receipts

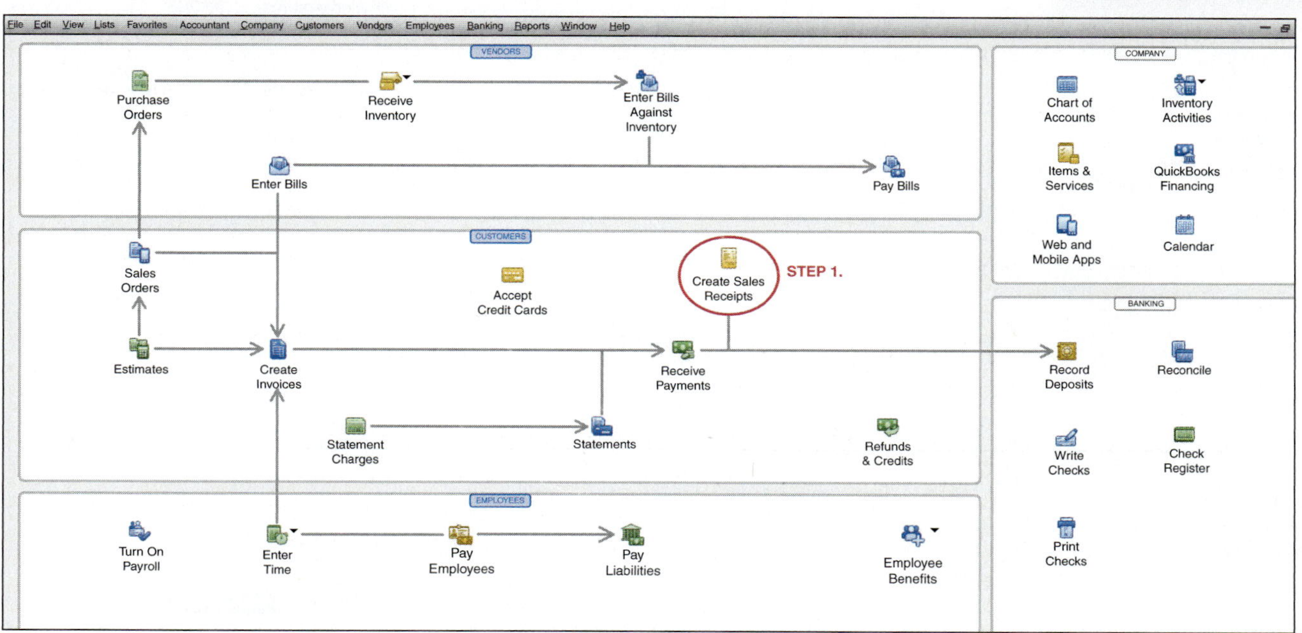

QuickBooks Tip

When companies do not want to track cash sales by individual customers, they can set up a generic customer name, such as *Cash Sales*, to use for all cash sales transactions in the sales receipt application.

STEP 2. Select **Customer** from the drop-down menu. In Figure Q2, the customer selected is Red River Raft, Inc.

STEP 3. Select or enter the **Date**.

STEP 4. Enter the **Sale No**. The system may assign this number automatically.

STEP 5. Verify the **Sold To** information.

STEP 6. If the customer is paying by check, enter the **Check No**.

STEP 7. Select the **Payment Method**.

STEP 8. Select or enter the **Item**.

STEP 9. Enter the **Description**. The system may complete this information automatically.

STEP 10. Enter the **QTY** (Quantity).

STEP 11. Enter the **Rate**. The Rate is the unit cost for the product or service. At times the software may be set up to complete this information automatically.

STEP 12. Verify the **Amount**. This information will automatically be filled in based on the quantity and rate entered.

STEP 13. Select **Save & New** if you want to create another sales receipt or **Save & Close** to leave the **Create Sales Receipt** application.

Figure Q2
Sales receipt

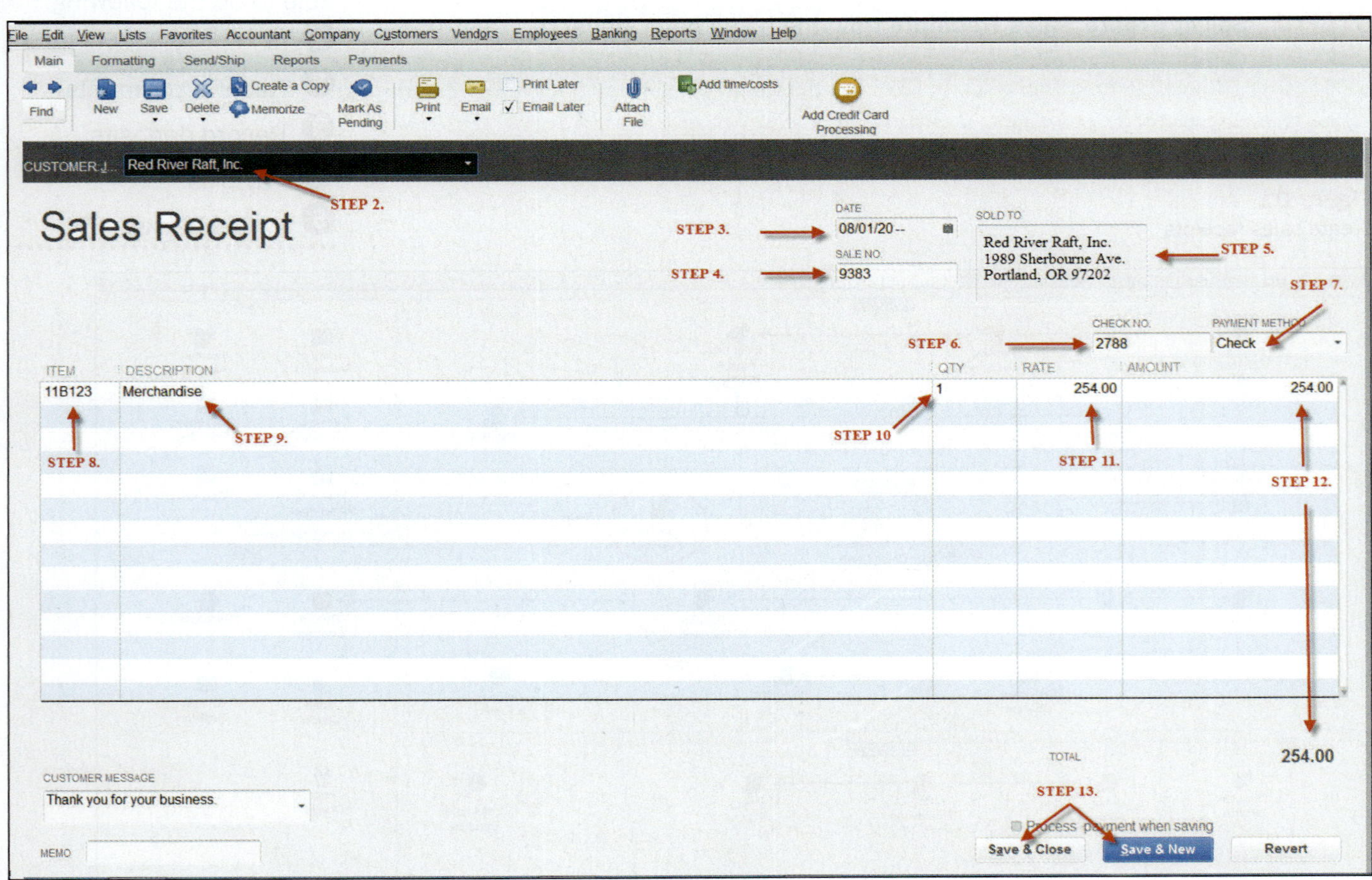

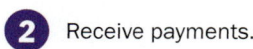

2 Receive payments.

Learning Objective

As you just learned, the sales receipts application in QuickBooks allows users to record cash sales and receive payment at the same time. However, remember that in Chapter 9, you created invoices to record sales made to customers on account. The **Receive Payments** application in QuickBooks allows users to record payments on those previously generated invoices. To receive payments on invoices in QuickBooks, complete the steps in Figures Q3 through Q5.

STEP 1. Select **Receive Payments** from the home page, under the **Customers** center.

Figure Q3
Receive payments

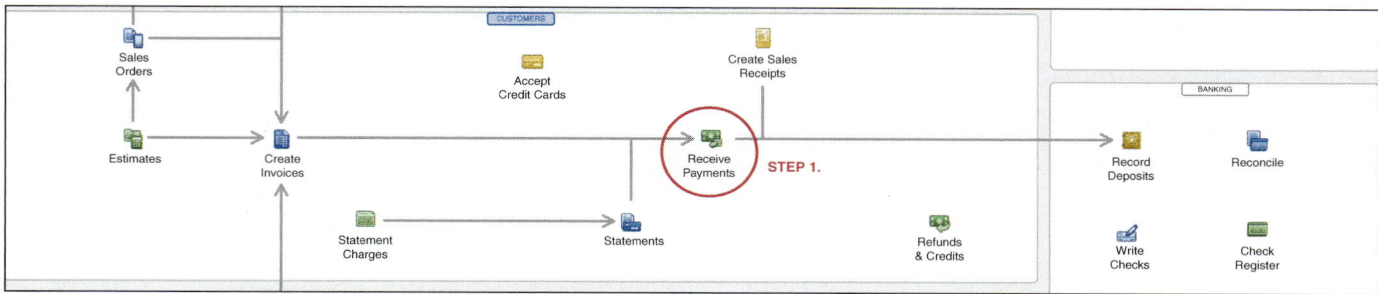

STEP 2. Select the customer's name from the drop-down menu in the **Received From** field. In Figure Q4, Mesa River Raft Company is making the payment.

STEP 3. Enter the **Amount** received.

STEP 4. Select or enter the **PMT Method**.

STEP 5. Select or enter the **Date**.

STEP 6. Enter the **Reference** #. The system may assign this number automatically.

STEP 7. Check the invoice(s) the customer is paying.

STEP 8. Apply **Discounts And Credits**. (See Figure Q5 for Steps 8a–8c.)

STEP 8a. Verify or enter the **Amount of Discount**.

STEP 8b. Select the **Discount Account**. In Figure Q5, payment was received within the discount period; therefore, the account, **Sales Discounts**, was selected.

STEP 8c. Click **Done**.

STEP 9. Verify the amount. This information will automatically be filled in based on the quantity and rate entered.

STEP 10. Select **Save & New** if you want to create another customer payment or **Save & Close** to leave the **Receive Payments** application.

Figure Q4
Customer payment

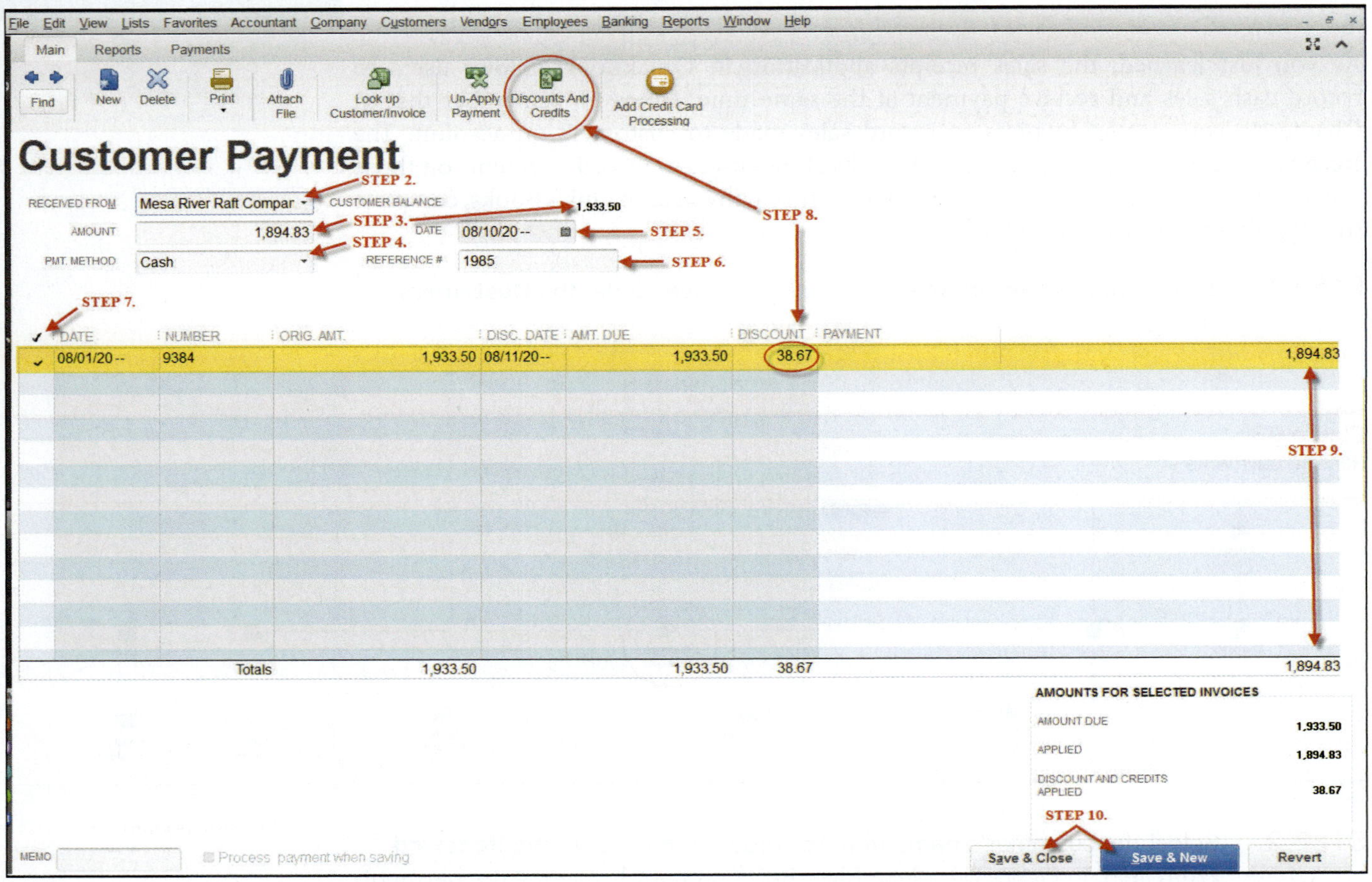

File Edit View Lists Favorites Accountant Company Customers Vendors Employees Banking Reports Window Help
Main Reports Payments
Find New Delete Print Attach File Look up Customer/Invoice Un-Apply Payment Discounts And Credits Add Credit Card Processing
Customer Payment
RECEIVED FROM Mesa River Raft Compar
CUSTOMER BALANCE 1,933.50
AMOUNT 1,894.83
DATE 08/10/20--
PMT. METHOD Cash
REFERENCE # 1985
STEP 2.
STEP 3.
STEP 4.
STEP 5.
STEP 6.
STEP 7.
STEP 8.
DATE NUMBER ORIG. AMT. DISC. DATE AMT. DUE DISCOUNT PAYMENT
08/01/20-- 9384 1,933.50 08/11/20-- 1,933.50 38.67 1,894.83
STEP 9.
Totals 1,933.50 1,933.50 38.67 1,894.83
AMOUNTS FOR SELECTED INVOICES
AMOUNT DUE 1,933.50
APPLIED 1,894.83
DISCOUNT AND CREDITS APPLIED 38.67
STEP 10.
MEMO
Process payment when saving
Save & Close Save & New Revert

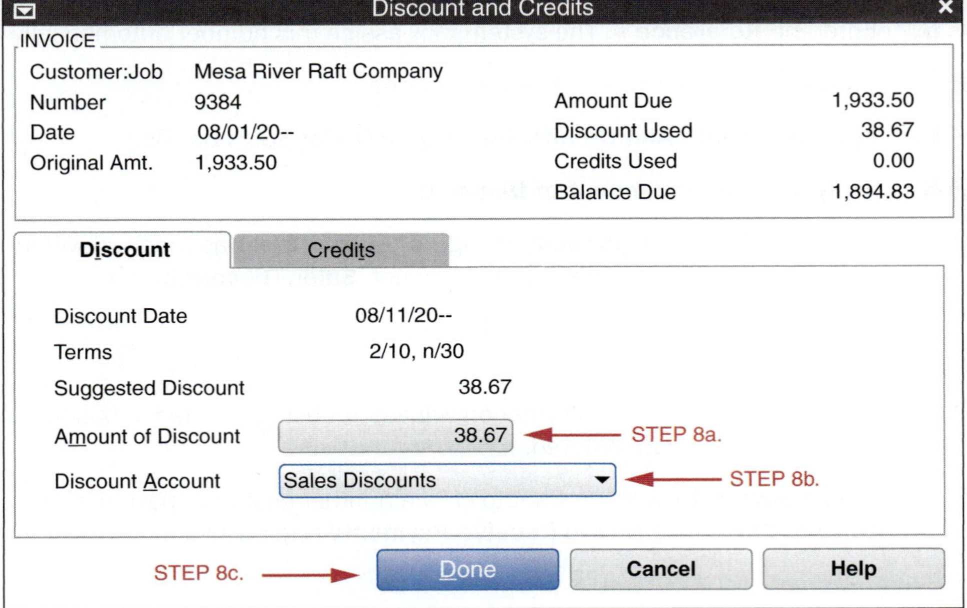

Figure Q5
Discounts and credits: sales discounts

Discount and Credits
INVOICE
Customer:Job Mesa River Raft Company
Number 9384
Date 08/01/20--
Original Amt. 1,933.50
Amount Due 1,933.50
Discount Used 38.67
Credits Used 0.00
Balance Due 1,894.83
Discount Credits
Discount Date 08/11/20--
Terms 2/10, n/30
Suggested Discount 38.67
Amount of Discount 38.67
STEP 8a.
Discount Account Sales Discounts
STEP 8b.
STEP 8c.
Done Cancel Help

3 Make deposits.

Learning Objective

After payments have been recorded in the **Receive Payments** application, the next step is depositing the money to the bank. Some companies may make multiple deposits in one day, while others may make deposits less frequently. The **Record Deposits** application in QuickBooks helps users keep track of undeposited funds. To record deposits, complete the steps in Figures Q6 through Q8.

QuickBooks Tip

Deposits can also be recorded from the Banking tab by selecting Make Deposits.

STEP 1. Select **Record Deposits** from the home page, under the **Banking** center.

Figure Q6
Record deposits

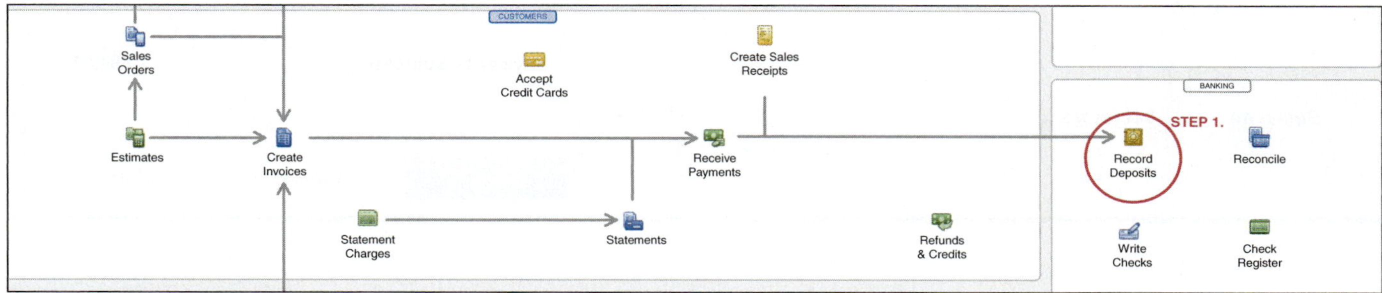

STEP 2. Select the payment method using **View payment method type** and select how payments will be displayed in the **Select Payments to Deposit** area using the **Sort payments by** field.

STEP 3. Check the payments to be deposited in the **Select Payments to Deposit** window.

STEP 4. Click **OK**.

STEP 5. In the **Deposit To** field, select the bank account where the funds will be deposited.

STEP 6. Select or enter the **Date**.

STEP 7. Enter a brief description in the **Memo** field.

STEP 8. Verify the **Deposit Total.**

STEP 9. Select **Save & New** if you want to create another deposit or **Save & Close** to leave the **Record Deposits** application.

QuickBooks Tip

The Undeposited Funds account is a holding account, similar to holding money in a drawer until you make a deposit to your financial institution. This account should not carry a balance and should be cleared when you make a deposit in QuickBooks.

Figure Q7
Payments to deposit

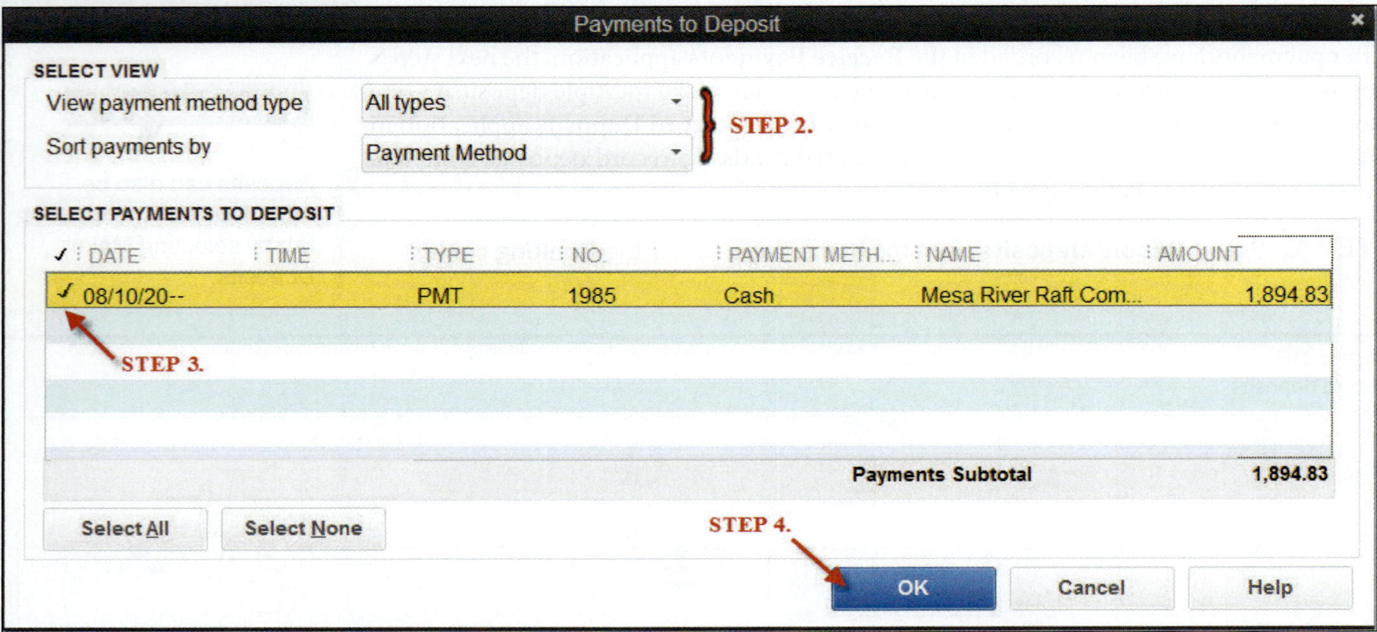

Figure Q8
Deposit undeposited funds

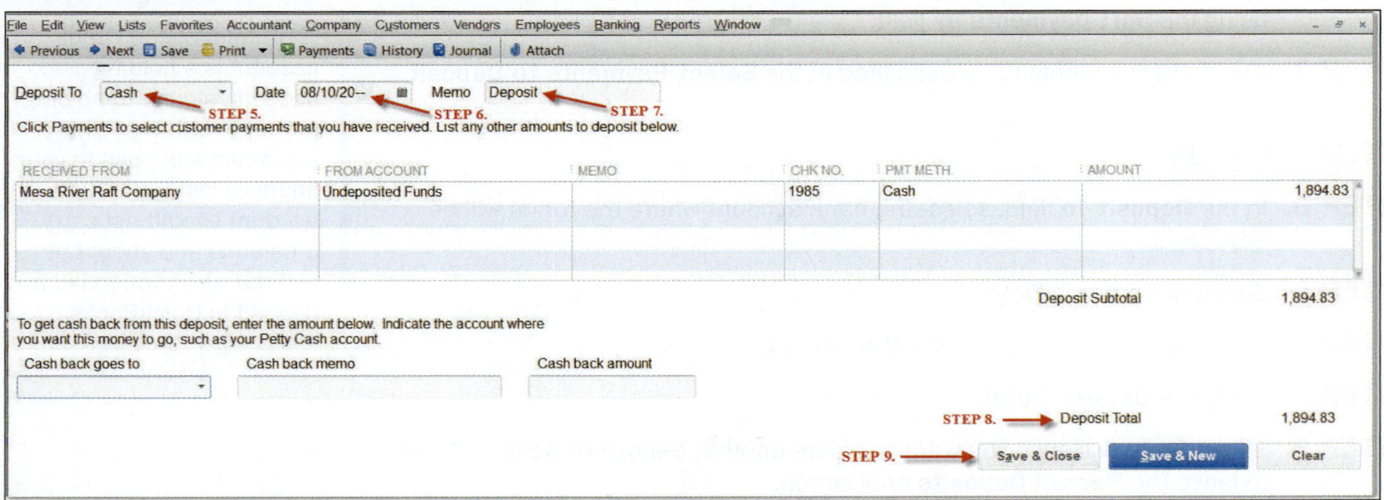

4 Pay bills.

Learning Objective

In Chapter 9, you learned to use the **Enter Bills** application to record invoices received, when payments will be made later. The **Pay Bills** application uses the information entered in **Enter Bills** to track available purchase discounts and credits, as well as due dates. The **Pay Bills** application also contains the necessary information to process payments. To pay bills, complete the steps in Figures Q9 through Q13.

STEP 1. Select **Pay Bills** from the home page, under the **Vendors** center.

Figure Q9
Pay bills

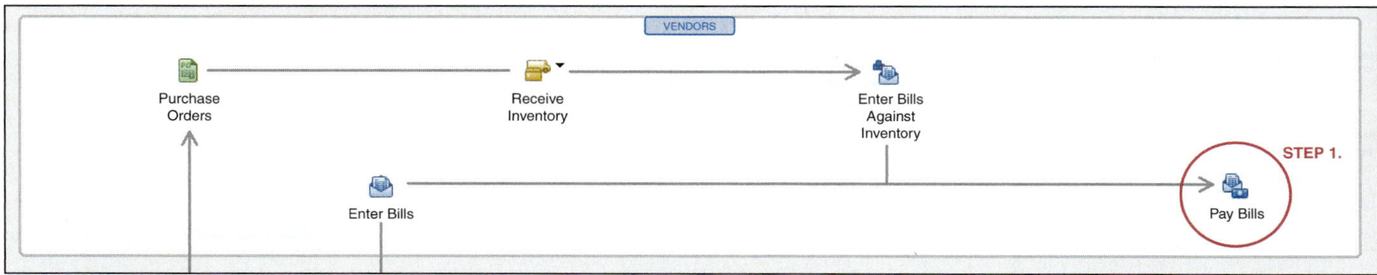

STEP 2. Go to **Select Bills To Be Paid > Show bills** and then select **Show all bills** for viewing as seen in Figure Q10, or narrow your search by selecting **Due on or before**.

STEP 3. Select the desired **Filter By** and **Sort By** options for displaying the bills to be paid.

STEP 4. Select the bill(s) to be paid by checking the box to the left of the invoice. To pay all of the invoices listed, check the box at the top of the column.

STEP 5. To view invoice details, click **Go to Bill**.

STEP 6. Click **Set Discount** to view or modify discount amounts. (See Figure Q11 for Steps 6a–6c.)

STEP 6a. Verify or modify **Amount of Discount**.

STEP 6b. Select **Discount Account**. In Figure Q11, **Purchase Discounts** was selected.

STEP 6c. Click **Done**.

STEP 7. Click **Set Credits** to view or modify credit amounts.

STEP 8. Select or enter the **Payment Date**.

STEP 9. Select the payment **Method**. In Figure Q10, the method of payment is listed as **Check**. Select **To be printed or Assign check number**. The **To be printed** option will automatically assign the check number.

STEP 10. Select the bank account name to record the payment.

STEP 11. Click **Pay Selected Bills**.

QuickBooks Tip

Use the **Set Credits** option for recording credit memos received for returned merchandise.

ACCOUNTING WITH *QuickBooks*®

Figure Q10
Select bills to be paid

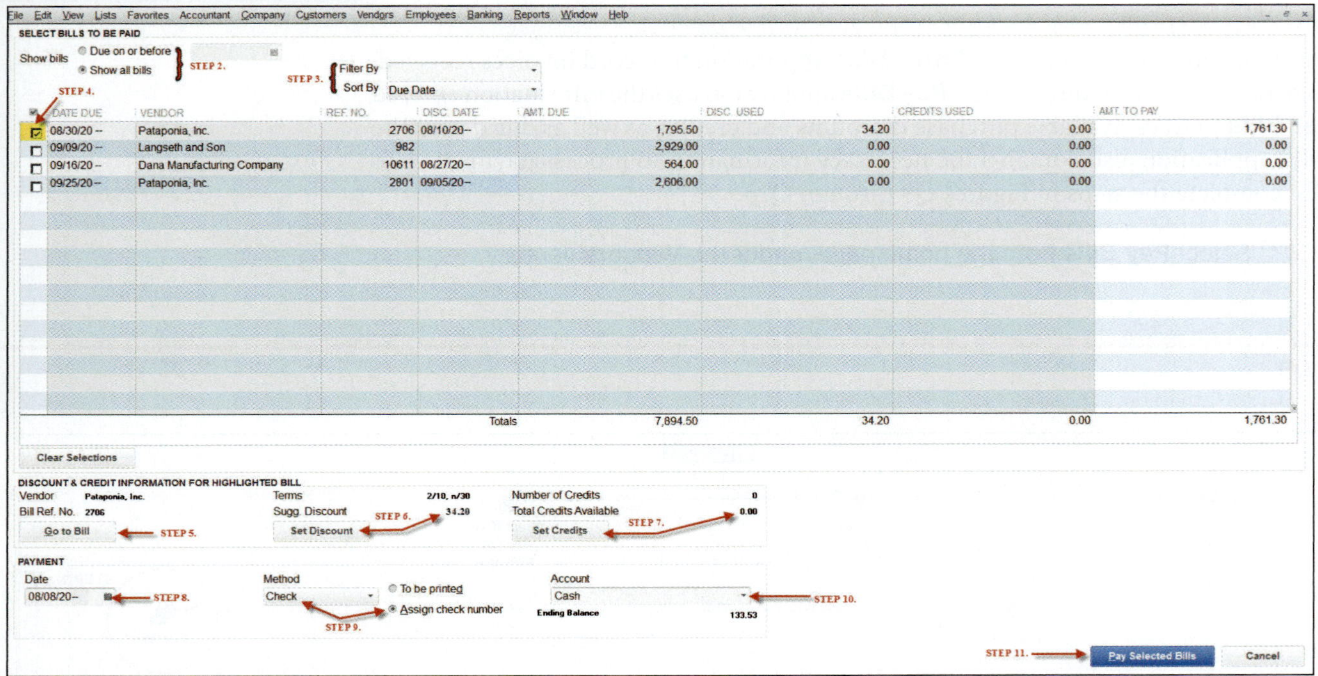

Figure Q11
Discounts and credits for purchases

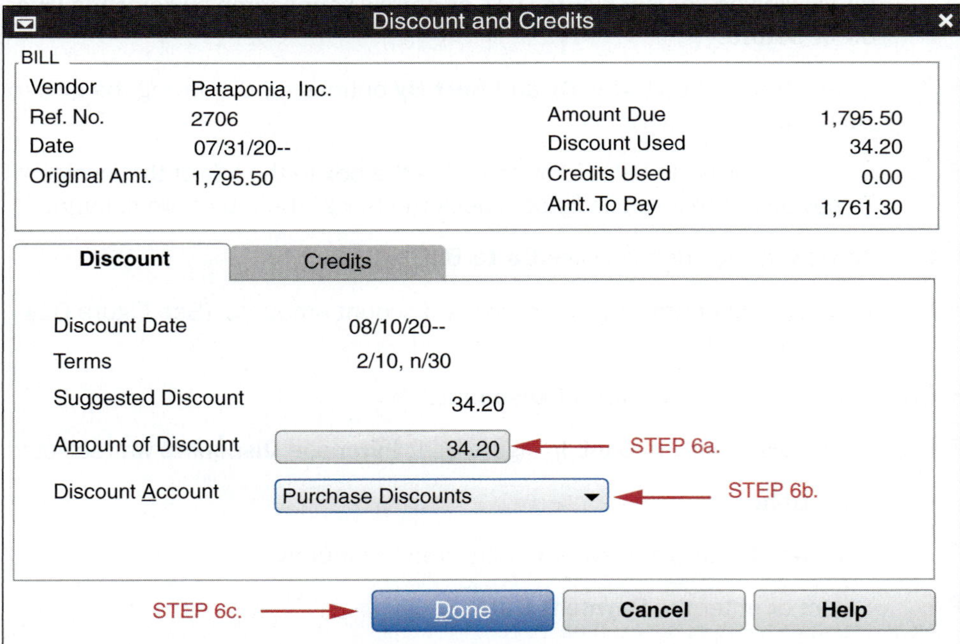

STEP 12. Select either **Let QuickBooks assign check numbers** or **Let me assign the check numbers below** (See Figure Q12).

STEP 13. In Figure Q12, the **Let me assign the check numbers below** option was selected and number **2076** was manually entered.

STEP 14. Click **OK**.

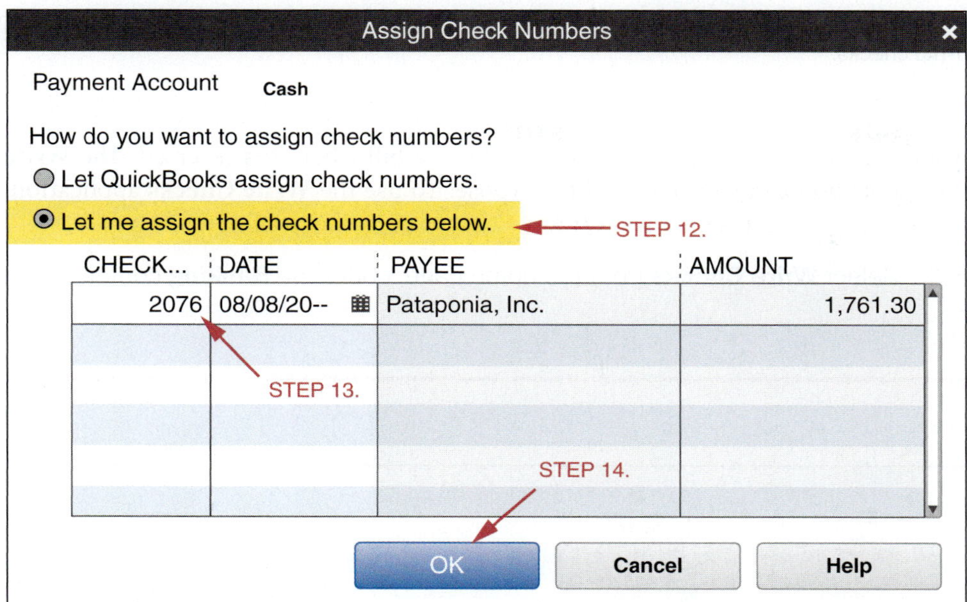

Figure Q12
Assignment of check numbers

STEP 15. Select **Pay More Bills** to continue or **Done** to exit the **Pay Bills** application (See Figure Q13).

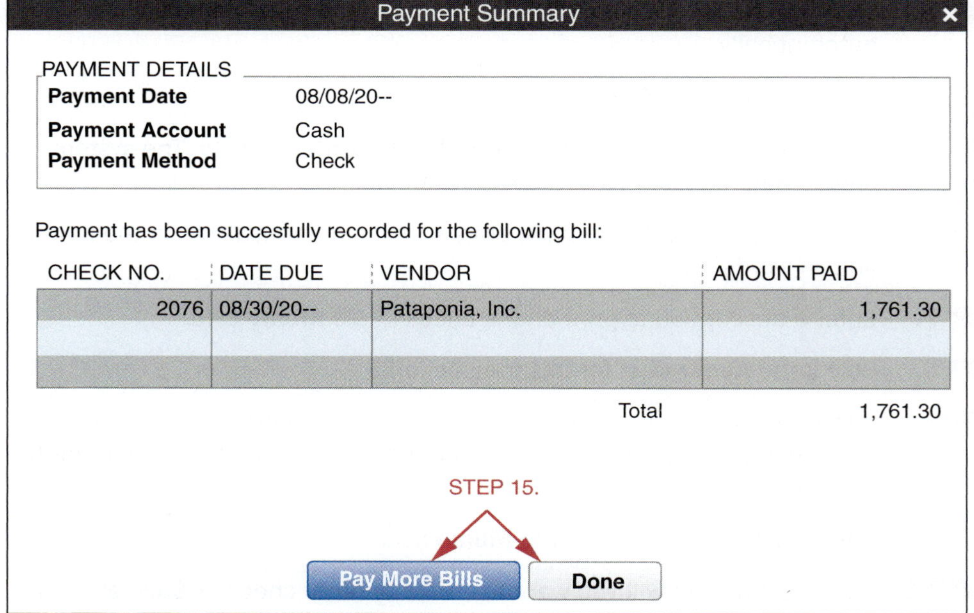

Figure Q13
Payment summary

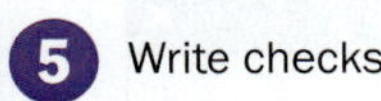

Learning Objective 5 Write checks.

At certain times, you may want to record and pay a bill when it is received. The **Write Checks** application can be used for this purpose. To use the **Write Checks** application, follow the steps in Figures Q14 and Q15.

STEP 1. Select **Write Checks** from the home page, under the **Banking** center.

Figure Q14
Write checks

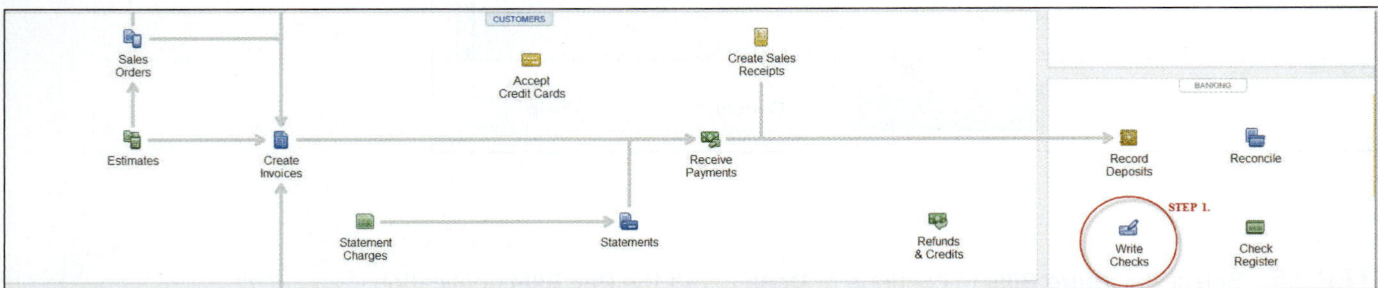

STEP 2. Select **Bank Account** from the drop-down menu. In Figure Q15, the bank account selected is Cash.

STEP 3. Enter the **No**. of the check. The system may assign this number automatically.

STEP 4. Select or enter the **Date**.

STEP 5. Select or enter the payee in the **Pay To The Order Of** field. The system should automatically fill in the **Address** field.

STEP 6. Enter the amount.The numeric amount will automatically fill in the amount field in words.

STEP 7. Enter a description to print on the check in the **Memo** field.

STEP 8. Select the **Account**(s) for this transaction.

STEP 9. If the transaction only uses one account, this **Amount** field will automatically be filled in by the system. If more than one account is used, enter the correct amount for each account.

STEP 10. Enter a brief description in the **Memo** field.

STEP 11. Select **Save & New** if you want to create another check or **Save & Close** to leave the **Write Checks** application.

Figure Q15
Write checks screen

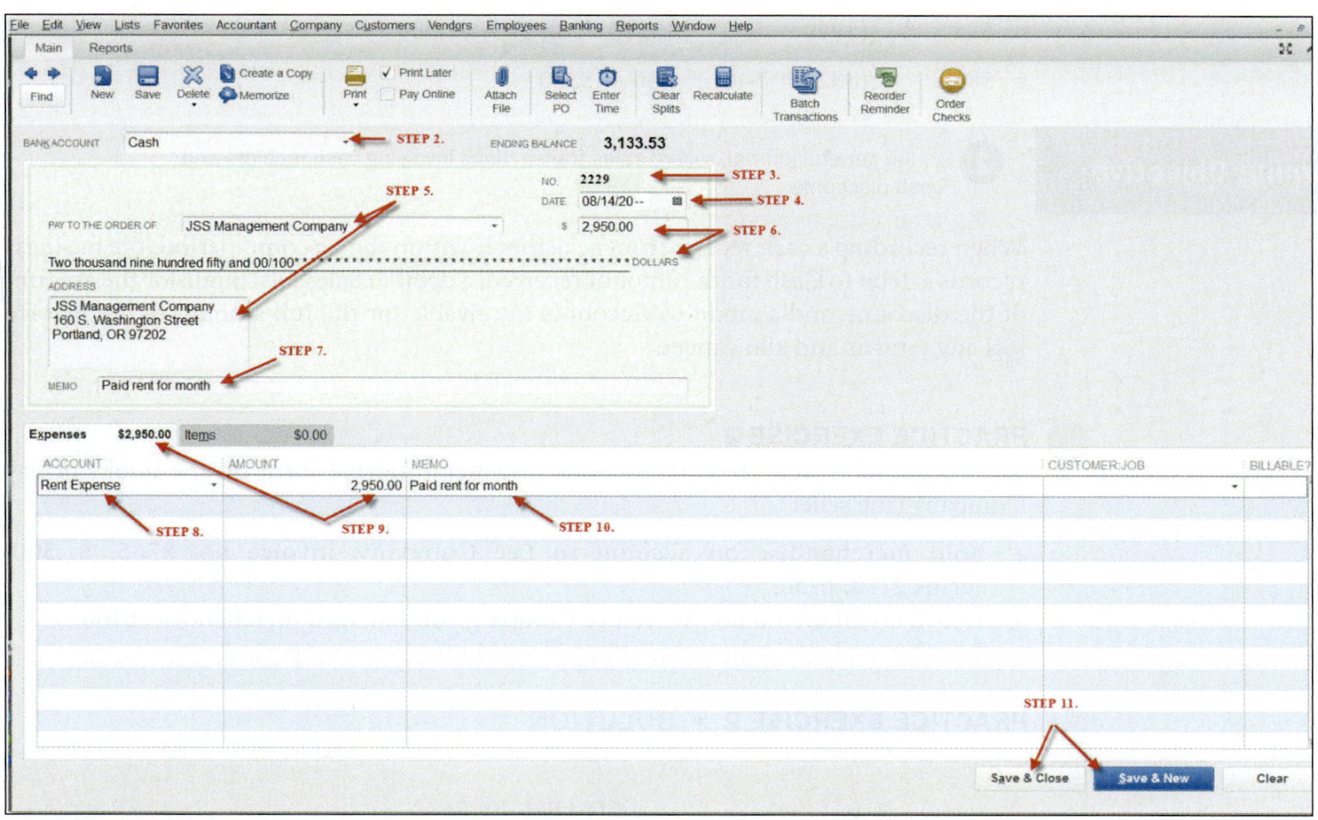

Chapter Review

Study and Practice

 Determine cash discounts according to credit terms.

Learning Objective

The amount of the discount is determined by multiplying the invoice total (excluding freight charges and any returns and allowances) by the **cash discount** rate.

PRACTICE EXERCISE 1

For the following purchases of merchandise, determine the amount of cash to be paid.

Purchase	Invoice Date	Credit Terms	FOB	Amount of Purchase	Freight Charges	Total Invoice Amount	Returns and Allowances	Date Paid
a.	June 12	1/10, n/30	Destination	$700	—	$ 700	$100	June 21
b.	June 14	2/10, n/30	Shipping point	940	$60	1,000	—	June 20
c.	June 18	n/30	Shipping point	820	40	860	30	July 17

PRACTICE EXERCISE 1 • SOLUTION

a. $594 ($700 − $100) − ($600 × 0.01) = $600 − $6 = $594

b. $981.20 ($940 + $60) − ($940 × 0.02) = $1,000 − $18.80 = $981.20

c. $830 ($820 + $40) − $30 = $830

Learning Objective  2 In the general journal, record sales transactions involving cash receipts and cash discounts.

When recording a cash receipt from a customer within the discount period, the business records a debit to Cash for the amount received, a debit to Sales Discounts for the amount of the discount, and a credit to Accounts Receivable for the full amount of the invoice less any returns and allowances.

PRACTICE EXERCISE 2

Record the following sales transactions in general journal form on the books of Fry Company (the seller).

a. Sold merchandise on account to Lee Company, invoice no. 8765, $1,500; terms 2/10, n/30.
b. Issued credit memo no. 967 to Lee Company for damaged merchandise, $100.
c. Lee Company paid the account in full within the discount period.

PRACTICE EXERCISE 2 • SOLUTION

GENERAL JOURNAL Page ___

Date	Description	Post. Ref.	Debit	Credit
a.	Accounts Receivable, Lee Company		1 5 0 0 00	
	Sales			1 5 0 0 00
	Sold merchandise to Lee			
	Company, invoice no. 8765.			
b.	Sales Returns and Allowances		1 0 0 00	
	Accounts Receivable, Lee Company			1 0 0 00
	Issued credit memo no. 967.			
c.	Cash		1 3 7 2 00	
	Sales Discounts		2 8 00	
	Accounts Receivable, Lee Company			1 4 0 0 00
	Received payment in full.			
	[($1,500 − $100) × 0.02]			

Learning Objective  3 In the general journal, record purchase transactions involving cash payments and cash discounts.

When recording a payment to a vendor within the discount period, the business records a debit to Accounts Payable for the full amount of the invoice less any returns and allowances, a credit to Purchases Discounts for the amount of the discount, and a credit to Cash for the amount paid.

PRACTICE EXERCISE 3

Record the following purchase transactions in general journal form on the books of Lee Company (the buyer).

a. Purchased merchandise on account from Fry Company, invoice no. 8765, $1,500; terms 2/10, n/30.
b. Received credit memo no. 967 from Fry Company for damaged merchandise, $100.
c. Paid Fry Company in full within the discount period.

PRACTICE EXERCISE 3 • SOLUTION

GENERAL JOURNAL Page ___

Date		Description	Post. Ref.	Debit	Credit
	a.	Purchases		1 5 0 0 00	
		Accounts Payable, Fry Company			1 5 0 0 00
		Purchased merchandise from			
		Fry Company, invoice no. 8765.			
	b.	Accounts Payable, Fry Company		1 0 0 00	
		Purchases Returns and Allowances			1 0 0 00
		Received credit memo no. 967.			
	c.	Accounts Payable, Fry Company		1 4 0 0 00	
		Purchases Discounts			2 8 00
		Cash			1 3 7 2 00
		Paid invoice no. 8765 in full.			
		[($1,500 − $100) × 0.02]			

4 Record transactions involving trade discounts. **Learning Objective**

In transactions involving **trade discounts**, the trade discounts are deducted from the list prices to arrive at the selling prices. Both sellers and buyers record the transactions at the selling prices.

PRACTICE EXERCISE 4

Record the following transaction involving a trade discount.

Feb. 2 Bought merchandise on account from Coffee Company, $3,500, received a 40% trade discount, invoice no. 234C, dated Jan. 31; terms 2/10, n/EOM.

PRACTICE EXERCISE 4 • SOLUTION

GENERAL JOURNAL Page ___

Date		Description	Post. Ref.	Debit	Credit
20--					
Feb.	2	Purchases		2 1 0 0 00	
		Accounts Payable, Coffee Company			2 1 0 0 00
		Purchased merchandise from			
		Coffee Company, invoice no. 234C.			
		[$3,500 − ($3,500 × 0.40)]			

Learning Objective  In the cash receipts journal, record transactions for a merchandising business and post from a cash receipts journal to a general ledger and an accounts receivable ledger.

CHAPTER REVIEW

A transaction for a merchandising business can be recorded on one line in a **cash receipts journal.** The cash receipts journal usually contains the following columns: Date, Account Credited, Post. Ref., Cash Debit, Credit Card Expense Debit, Sales Discounts Debit, Accounts Receivable Credit, Sales Credit, Sales Tax Payable Credit, and Other Accounts Credit.

The accountant posts daily from the Accounts Receivable Credit column to the individual credit customers' accounts in the accounts receivable ledger. After posting, the accountant puts a check mark (✓) in the Post. Ref. column. The accountant also posts the amounts daily in the Other Accounts Credit column and records the account numbers in the Post. Ref. column. The special columns are posted as totals at the end of the month. The accountant then writes the account numbers in parentheses under the totals. An (X) below the total of the Other Accounts Credit column shows that amounts are posted individually and the total is not posted.

PRACTICE EXERCISE 5

Indicate the appropriate columns in which each of the following transactions would be recorded in the cash receipts journal.

Transaction	Cash Debit	Credit Card Expense Debit	Sales Discounts Debit	Accounts Receivable Credit	Sales Credit	Other Accounts Credit
a. Collected cash on account from a charge customer.						
b. Received check from a charge customer in payment of an invoice within the discount period.						
c. Borrowed money from the bank, receiving cash and giving the bank a promissory note.						
d. Received check from a charge customer in payment of an invoice past the discount period.						
e. Recorded cash sales for the month.						

PRACTICE EXERCISE 5 • SOLUTION

Transaction	Cash Debit	Credit Card Expense Debit	Sales Discounts Debit	Accounts Receivable Credit	Sales Credit	Other Accounts Credit
a. Collected cash on account from a charge customer.	✓			✓		
b. Received check from a charge customer in payment of an invoice within the discount period.	✓		✓	✓		
c. Borrowed money from the bank, receiving cash and giving the bank a promissory note.	✓					✓
d. Received check from a charge customer in payment of an invoice past the discount period.	✓			✓		
e. Recorded cash sales for the month.	✓				✓	

6 In the cash payments journal, record transactions for a merchandising business and post from a cash payments journal to a general ledger and an accounts payable ledger.

Learning Objective

A cash payment by a merchandising business that includes a purchases discount can be recorded on one line in a **cash payments journal**. The cash payments journal usually contains the following columns: Date, Ck. No., Account Debited, Post. Ref., Other Accounts Debit, Accounts Payable Debit, Purchases Discounts Credit, and Cash Credit.

The accountant posts daily from the Accounts Payable Debit column to the individual suppliers' accounts in the accounts payable ledger. After posting, the accountant puts a check mark (✓) in the Post. Ref. column. The accountant also posts the amounts daily in the Other Accounts Debit column and records the account numbers in the Post. Ref. column. The special columns are posted as totals at the end of the month. The accountant then writes the account numbers in parentheses under the totals. An (X) below the total of the Other Accounts Debit column shows that amounts are posted individually and the total is not posted.

PRACTICE EXERCISE 6

Indicate the appropriate columns in which each of the following transactions would be recorded in the cash payments journal.

Transaction	Other Accounts Debit	Accounts Payable Debit	Purchases Discounts Credit	Cash Credit
a. Issued check to vendor in payment of an invoice within the discount period.				
b. Paid customer for merchandise returned on a cash sale.				
c. Paid wages for two weeks.				
d. Issued check to vendor in payment of an invoice past the discount period.				
e. Paid rent for the month.				

PRACTICE EXERCISE 6 • SOLUTION

Transaction	Other Accounts Debit	Accounts Payable Debit	Purchases Discounts Credit	Cash Credit
a. Issued check to vendor in payment of an invoice within the discount period.		✓	✓	✓
b. Paid customer for merchandise returned on a cash sale.	✓			✓
c. Paid wages for two weeks.	✓			✓
d. Issued check to vendor in payment of an invoice past the discount period.		✓		✓
e. Paid rent for the month.	✓			✓

Glossary

Cash discount The amount a customer can deduct for paying a bill within a specified period of time; used to encourage prompt payment. Not all sellers offer cash discounts. *(p. 497)*

Cash payments journal A special journal used to record all transactions involving cash payments or decreases to the Cash account. *(p. 516)*

Cash receipts journal A special journal used to record all transactions involving cash receipts or increases to the Cash account. *(p. 511)*

Credit period The time the seller allows the buyer before full payment on a charge sale has to be made. *(p. 497)*

Notes Payable The account containing the balance of promissory notes. *(p. 514)*

Promissory note A written promise to pay a specified amount at a specified time. *(p. 514)*

Purchases discount A cash discount granted by suppliers in return for prompt payment; it is treated as a deduction from Purchases. *(p. 504)*

Sales discount A deduction from the original price granted by the seller to the buyer for the prompt payment of an invoice. *(p. 498)*

Trade discounts Substantial discounts from the list or catalog prices of goods, granted by the seller; not recorded by the buyer or the seller. *(p. 508)*

Quiz Yourself

_____ 1. What do credit terms of 2/10, n/30 mean?
   a. 2–10 days to pay on time or 30 days before going to collection.
   b. 2 percent discount if paid within 10 days, but 30 days to pay on time
   c. 2–10 days to pay with a discount, net 30 days to pay after the discount period
   d. 2–10 percent discount if paid within 30 days
   e. None of the above

_____ 2. What is the entry to record the cash received on a sale of $500, credit terms 1/15, n/30, if the payment is received within the discount period?
   a. Accounts Receivable 500 DR; Cash 500 CR
   b. Cash 500 DR; Accounts Receivable 500 CR
   c. Cash 495 DR, Sales Discount 5 DR; Accounts Receivable 500 CR
   d. Accounts Receivable 500 DR; Cash 495 CR, Sales Discount 5 CR
   e. Cash 500 DR; Sales Discount 5 CR, Accounts Receivable 495 CR

_____ 3. Which of the following statements is true?
   a. Sales discounts are taken on freight charges.
   b. Credit terms are established by the buyer.
   c. Purchases discounts are taken on returns.
   d. Purchases discounts are not taken on freight costs.
   e. None of the above.

_____ 4. Which of the following is *not* an advantage of the cash receipts journal?
   a. Transactions do not have to be posted on a regular basis.
   b. Transactions can be recorded on one line.
   c. Transactions involving debits to Cash are recorded in one place.
   d. Repetition in posting is eliminated.
   e. Special columns can be used for similar transactions.

_____ 5. Which of the following is an advantage of the cash payments journal?
   a. It provides notification of early payment.
   b. Transactions do not have to be posted on a regular basis.
   c. Purchases and payments are recorded in the same place.
   d. Transactions involving credits to Cash are recorded in one place.
   e. None of the above.

Answers:
1. b 2. c 3. d 4. a 5. d

Review It with QuickBooks®

_____ 1. Which QuickBooks application is used to record payments on invoices?
a. Create Sales Receipts
b. Receive Payments
c. Create Invoices
d. All of the above

_____ 2. Which QuickBooks application is used to record cash sales?
a. Create Sales Receipts
b. Receive Payments
c. Create Invoices
d. All of the above

_____ 3. In which QuickBooks application are undeposited funds displayed?
a. Create Sales Receipts
b. Create Invoices
c. Receive Payments
d. Record Deposits

_____ 4. Which QuickBooks application is used to record and pay invoices at the same time?
a. Enter Bills
b. Pay Bills
c. Write Checks
d. All of the above

Answers:
1. b 2. a 3. d 4. c

Chapter Assignments

Discussion Questions

1. What is the normal balance for each of the following accounts: (a) Purchases? (b) Sales Discounts? (c) Purchases Returns and Allowances? (d) Sales? (e) Purchases Discounts? (f) Sales Returns and Allowances?
2. What does an X under the total of a special journal's Other Accounts column signify?
3. Explain the following credit terms: (a) n/30; (b) 2/10, n/60; (c) 1/15, EOM, n/30.
4. In a cash receipts journal, both the Accounts Receivable Credit column and the Cash Debit column were mistakenly underadded by $700. How will this error be discovered?
5. If a cash payments journal is supposed to save time spent writing, why are there so many entries in the Other Accounts Debit column?
6. Describe the posting procedure for a cash payments journal with an Other Accounts Debit column and several special columns, including an Accounts Payable Debit column.
7. An electronics business purchased speakers for resale. The total of the invoice is $2,580, and it is subject to trade discounts of 15 percent, 10 percent, and 5 percent. Compute the amount the dealer will pay for the speakers.
8. What is the difference between a cash discount and a trade discount?

CHAPTER ASSIGNMENTS

Exercises

LO 1, 3

Practice Exercises 1, 3

EXERCISE 10-1 For the following purchases of merchandise, determine the amount of cash to be paid:

Purchase	Invoice Date	Credit Terms	FOB	Amount of Purchase	Freight Charges	Total Invoice Amount	Returns and Allowances	Date Paid
a.	June 1	2/10, n/30	Destination	$550	—	$ 550	—	June 30
b.	June 12	1/10, n/30	Destination	700	—	700	$100	June 21
c.	June 14	2/10, n/30	Shipping point	940	$60	1,000	—	June 23
d.	June 21	n/30	Shipping point	830	70	900	130	July 20
e.	June 24	1/10, n/30	Shipping point	760	50	810	90	July 3

LO 2

Practice Exercise 2

EXERCISE 10-2 Describe the transactions recorded in the following T accounts:

Cash

Debit	Credit
(c) 5,042.10	

Accounts Receivable

Debit	Credit
(a) 5,320	(b) 175
	(c) 5,145

Sales

Debit	Credit
	(a) 5,320

Sales Returns and Allowances

Debit	Credit
(b) 175	

Sales Discounts

Debit	Credit
(c) 102.90	

LO 3

Practice Exercise 3

EXERCISE 10-3 Describe the transactions recorded in the following T accounts:

Cash

Debit	Credit
	(c) 1,176

Accounts Payable

Debit	Credit
(b) 150	(a) 1,350
(c) 1,200	

Purchases

Debit	Credit
(a) 1,350	

Purchases Returns and Allowances

Debit	Credit
	(b) 150

Purchases Discounts

Debit	Credit
	(c) 24

LO 2, 3

Practice Exercises 2, 3

EXERCISE 10-4 Record the following transactions in general journal form using the periodic inventory system:

June 5 Sold merchandise on account to Wilson, Inc., $520; terms 1/10, n/30.
12 Bought merchandise on account from Mastercraft Company, $425; terms 2/10, n/45; FOB shipping point.
15 Paid Alliance Freight Lines for freight charges on merchandise purchased from Mastercraft Company, $45.
17 Received full payment from Wilson, Inc.

June 20 Received a credit memo from Mastercraft Company for defective merchandise returned, $75.
25 Paid Mastercraft Company in full within the discount period.
29 Bought merchandise on account from Boze Industries, $1,090; terms 1/15, n/30; freight prepaid and added to the invoice, $52 (total $1,142).

LO 2, 3

Practice Exercises 2, 3

QuickBooks

EXERCISE 10-5 Record the following transactions in general journal form on the books of the seller (Fuentes Company) and then on the books of the buyer (Lowe Company) using the periodic inventory system.

*Follow the instructions on page 548 when using QuickBooks.

Fuentes Company

a. Sold merchandise on account to Lowe Company, $1,500; terms 2/10, n/30.
b. Issued a credit memo to Lowe Company for damaged merchandise, $100.
c. Lowe Company paid the account in full within the discount period.

Lowe Company

a. Purchased merchandise on account from Fuentes Company, $1,500; terms 2/10, n/30.
b. Received a credit memo from Fuentes Company for damaged merchandise, $100.
c. Paid Fuentes Company in full within the discount period.

LO 2, 3, 4

Practice Exercises 2, 3, 4

EXERCISE 10-6 Record general journal entries to correct the errors described below. Assume that the incorrect entries were posted in the same period in which the errors occurred and were recorded using the periodic inventory system.

a. A freight cost of $85 incurred on equipment purchased for use in the business was debited to Freight In.
b. The issuance of a credit memo to Lang Company for $119 for merchandise returned was recorded as a debit to Purchases Returns and Allowances and a credit to Accounts Receivable, Lang Company.
c. A cash sale of $68 to J. L. LaSalle was recorded as a sale on account.
d. A purchase of merchandise from James Company in the amount of $750 with a 25 percent trade discount was recorded as a debit to Purchases and a credit to Accounts Payable of $750 each.

LO 5

Practice Exercise 5

EXERCISE 10-7 Label the blanks in the column heads as either Debit or Credit.

CASH RECEIPTS JOURNAL — Page ___

Date	Account Credited	Post. Ref.	Cash ______	Sales Discounts ______	Accounts Receivable ______	Sales ______	Other Accounts ______

LO 5

Practice Exercise 5

EXERCISE 10-8 Describe the transaction recorded.

Cash		Sales Tax Payable		Sales		Credit Card Expense	
322.56			16.00		320.00	13.44	

CHAPTER ASSIGNMENTS

LO 6

Practice Exercise 6

EXERCISE 10-9 Label the blanks in the column heads as either Debit or Credit.

CASH PAYMENTS JOURNAL							Page ___
Date	Ck. No.	Account Debited	Post. Ref.	Other Accounts ______	Accounts Payable ______	Purchases Discounts ______	Cash ______

LO 5, 6

Practice Exercises 5, 6

EXERCISE 10-10 Indicate the journal in which each of the following transactions should be recorded. Assume a three-column purchases journal.

Transaction	Journal S	P	CR	CP	J
a. Paid a creditor on account.					
b. Bought merchandise on account.					
c. Sold merchandise for cash.					
d. Adjusted for insurance expired.					
e. Received payment on account from a charge customer.					
f. Received a credit memo for merchandise returned.					
g. Bought equipment on credit.					
h. Sold merchandise on account.					
i. Recorded a customer's NSF check.					
j. Invested personal noncash assets in the business.					
k. Withdrew cash for personal use.					

Problem Set A

LO 1, 2, 3

QuickBooks

PROBLEM 10-1A The following transactions were completed by Hammond Auto Supply during January, which is the first month of this fiscal year. Terms of sale are 2/10, n/30. The balances of the accounts as of January 1 have been recorded in the general ledger in your Working Papers or in CengageNow. Hammond Auto Supply does not track cash sales by customer. If you are using the form-based approach with QuickBooks or general ledger, select "Cash Sales" as the customer for all cash sales transactions.

Jan.	2	Issued Ck. No. 6981 to JSS Management Company for monthly rent, $775.
	2	J. Hammond, the owner, invested an additional $3,500 in the business.
	4	Bought merchandise on account from Valencia and Company, invoice no. A691, $2,930; terms 2/10, n/30; dated January 2.
	4	Received check from Vega Appliance for $980 in payment of $1,000 invoice less discount.
	4	Sold merchandise on account to L. Paul, invoice no. 6483, $850.
	6	Received check from Petty, Inc., $637, in payment of $650 invoice less discount.
	7	Issued Ck. No. 6982, $588, to Fischer and Son, in payment of invoice no. C1272 for $600 less discount.
Jan.	7	Bought supplies on account from Doyle Office Supply, invoice no. 1906B, $108; terms net 30 days.

7 Sold merchandise on account to Ellison and Clay, invoice no. 6484, $787.
9 Issued credit memo no. 43 to L. Paul, $54, for merchandise returned.
11 Cash sales for January 1 through January 10, $4,863.20.
11 Issued Ck. No. 6983, $2,871.40, to Valencia and Company, in payment of $2,930 invoice less discount.
14 Sold merchandise on account to Vega Appliance, invoice no. 6485, $2,050.
18 Bought merchandise on account from Costa Products, invoice no. 7281D, $4,854; terms 2/10, n/60; dated January 16; FOB shipping point, freight prepaid and added to the invoice, $147 (total $5,001).
21 Issued Ck. No. 6984, $194, to M. Miller for miscellaneous expenses not recorded previously.
21 Cash sales for January 11 through January 20, $4,591.
23 Issued Ck. No. 6985 to Forbes Freight, $96, for freight charges on merchandise purchased on January 4.
23 Received credit memo no. 163, $376, from Costa Products for merchandise returned.
29 Sold merchandise on account to Bruce Supply, invoice no. 6486, $1,835.
31 Cash sales for January 21 through January 31, $4,428.
31 Issued Ck. No. 6986, $53, to M. Miller for miscellaneous expenses not recorded previously.
31 Recorded payroll entry from the payroll register: total salaries, $6,200; employees' federal income tax withheld, $872; FICA taxes withheld, $474.30.*
31 Recorded the payroll taxes: FICA taxes, $474.30; state unemployment tax, $334.80; federal unemployment tax, $49.60.
31 Issued Ck. No. 6987, $4,853.70, for salaries for the month.*
31 J. Hammond, the owner, withdrew $1,000 for personal use, Ck. No. 6988.

*If using QuickBooks, record transactions in the general journal.

Check Figure
Trial balance totals, $65,288.80

Required

1. Record the transactions for January using a general journal, page 1. Assume the periodic inventory method is used.*

*If using QuickBooks, record transactions using either the journal entry method or the forms-based approach as directed by your instructor.

The chart of accounts is as follows:

111 Cash
113 Accounts Receivable
114 Merchandise Inventory
115 Supplies
116 Prepaid Insurance
121 Equipment

212 Accounts Payable
215 Salaries Payable
216 Employees' Federal Income Tax Payable
217 FICA Taxes Payable
218 State Unemployment Tax Payable
219 Federal Unemployment Tax Payable

311 J. Hammond, Capital
312 J. Hammond, Drawing

411 Sales
412 Sales Returns and Allowances
413 Sales Discounts

511 Purchases
512 Purchases Returns and Allowances
513 Purchases Discounts
514 Freight In

621 Salary Expense
622 Payroll Tax Expense
627 Rent Expense
631 Miscellaneous Expense

2. Post daily all entries involving customer accounts to the accounts receivable ledger.*
3. Post daily all entries involving creditor accounts to the accounts payable ledger.*
4. Post daily the general journal entries to the general ledger. Write the owner's name in the Capital and Drawing accounts.*

*If using QuickBooks or general ledger, ignore Steps 2, 3, and 4.

(*Continued*)

5. Prepare a trial balance.
6. Prepare a schedule of accounts receivable (A/R Aging Detail report in QuickBooks) and a schedule of accounts payable (A/P Summary Detail report in QuickBooks). Do the totals equal the balances of the related controlling accounts?

1, 5

PROBLEM 10-2A Preston Company sells candy wholesale, primarily to vending machine operators. Terms of sales on account are 2/10, n/30, FOB shipping point. The following transactions involving cash receipts and sales of merchandise took place in May of this year:

May	1	Received $2,156 cash from L. Reilly in payment of April 22 invoice of $2,200, less cash discount.
	4	Received $1,096 cash in payment of $1,000 note receivable and interest of $96.
	7	Received $588 cash from K. L. Shannon in payment of April 29 invoice of $600, less cash discount.
	8	Sold merchandise on account to D. Padilla, invoice no. 272, $489.
	16	Cash sales for first half of May, $2,265.
	17	Received cash from D. Padilla in payment of invoice no. 272, less cash discount.
	20	Received $325 cash from L. N. Salas in payment of April 16 invoice, no discount.
	21	Sold merchandise on account to R. O. Wilcox, invoice no. 273, $935.
	24	Received $220 cash refund for return of defective equipment that was originally bought for cash.
	27	Sold merchandise on account to R. Jarvis, invoice no. 274, $450.
	31	Cash sales for second half of May, $2,845.

Check Figure
Total Cash Debit, $9,974.22

Required

1. Journalize the transactions for May in the cash receipts journal and the sales journal. Assume the periodic inventory method is used.
2. Total and rule the journals.
3. Prove the equality of the debit and credit totals.

1, 6

PROBLEM 10-3A MacDonald Bookshop had the following transactions that occurred during February of this year:

Feb.	3	Issued Ck. No. 4312, $892, to Kent Company for invoice no. 68172, recorded previously for $910.20, less 2 percent cash discount.
	4	Issued Ck. No. 4313 to Kirby Express Company for freight charges, $35, for books purchased.
	6	Issued Ck. No. 4314 to Morse Land Company for monthly rent, $590.
	11	Received and paid bill for advertising in the *Ballard News*, $105.79, Ck. No. 4315.
	11	Issued Ck. No. 4316, $1,078.11, to Contreras Book Company for invoice no. A3322, recorded previously for $1,089, less 1 percent cash discount.
	17	Paid wages recorded previously for first half of February, $487; Ck. No. 4317.
	21	R. D. MacDonald, the owner, withdrew $1,200 for personal use; Ck. No. 4318.
	26	Issued Ck. No. 4319 to First National Bank for payment on bank loan, $560, consisting of $500 on the principal and $60 interest.
	27	Issued Ck. No. 4320, $645, to Graham Publishing Company for invoice no. 7768, recorded previously (no discount).
	28	Voided Ck. No. 4321.
	28	Paid wages recorded previously for second half of February, $641; Ck. No. 4322.

Check Figure
Total Cash Credit, $6,233.90

Required

1. Journalize the transactions for February in the cash payments journal. Assume the periodic inventory method is used.
2. Total and rule the journal.
3. Prove the equality of the debit and credit totals.

LO 1, 2, 3, 5, 6

PROBLEM 10-4A Refer to the information for Problem 10-1A on pages 540–542.

Required

1. Record the transactions for January using a sales journal, page 73; a purchases journal, page 56; a cash receipts journal, page 38; a cash payments journal, page 45; and a general journal, page 100. Assume the periodic inventory method is used.

Check Figure
Schedule of Accounts Receivable total, $5,468.00

111 Cash
113 Accounts Receivable
114 Merchandise Inventory
115 Supplies
116 Prepaid Insurance
121 Equipment

212 Accounts Payable
215 Salaries Payable
216 Employees' Federal Income Tax Payable
217 FICA Taxes Payable
218 State Unemployment Tax Payable
219 Federal Unemployment Tax Payable

311 J. Hammond, Capital
312 J. Hammond, Drawing

411 Sales
412 Sales Returns and Allowances
413 Sales Discounts

511 Purchases
512 Purchases Returns and Allowances
513 Purchases Discounts
514 Freight In

621 Salary Expense
622 Payroll Tax Expense
627 Rent Expense
631 Miscellaneous Expense

2. Post daily all entries involving customer accounts to the accounts receivable ledger.
3. Post daily all entries involving creditor accounts to the accounts payable ledger.
4. Post daily those entries involving the Other Accounts columns and the general journal to the general ledger. Write the owner's name in the Capital and Drawing accounts.
5. Add the columns of the special journals and prove the equality of the debit and credit totals on scratch paper.
6. Post the appropriate totals of the special journals to the general ledger.
7. Prepare a trial balance.
8. Prepare a schedule of accounts receivable and a schedule of accounts payable. Do the totals equal the balances of the related controlling accounts?

LO 1, 2, 3, 4, 5, 6

Problem 10-5A The following transactions were completed by Nelson's Boutique, a retailer, during July. Terms on sales on account are 2/10, n/30, FOB shipping point.

July 3 Received cash from J. Smith in payment of June 29 invoice of $350, less cash discount.
6 Issued Ck. No. 1718, $742.50, to Designer, Inc., for invoice. no. 2256, recorded previously for $750, less cash discount of $7.50.
9 Sold merchandise in the amount of $250 on a credit card. Sales tax on this sale is 6%. The credit card fee the bank deducted for this transaction is $5.
10 Issued Ck. No. 1719, $764.40, to Smart Style, Inc., for invoice no. 1825, recorded previously on account for $780. A trade discount of 25% was applied at the time of purchase, and Smart Style, Inc.'s credit terms are 2/10, n/30.
12 Received $180 cash in payment of June 20 invoice from R. Matthews. No cash discount applied.
18 Received $1,575 cash in payment of a $1,500 note receivable and interest of $75.
21 Voided Ck. No. 1720 due to error.
25 Received and paid utility bill, $152; Ck. No. 1721, payable to City Utilities Company.
31 Paid wages recorded previously for the month, $2,586, Ck. No. 1722.

CHAPTER ASSIGNMENTS

Check Figure
Total Cash Credits, $4,244.90

Required

1. Journalize the transactions for July in the cash receipts journal, the general journal (for the transaction on July 9th), or the cash payment journal as appropriate. Assume the periodic inventory method is used.
2. Total and rule the journals.
3. Prove the equality of debit and credit totals.

Problem Set B

LO 1, 2, 3

PROBLEM 10-1B The following transactions were completed by Yang Restaurant Equipment during January, the first month of this fiscal year. Terms of sale are 2/10, n/30. The balances of the accounts as of January 1 have been recorded in the general ledger in your Working Papers or in CengageNow. Yang Restaurant Equipment does not track cash sales by customer. If you are using the form-based approach with QuickBooks or general ledger, select "Cash Sales" as the customer for all cash sales transactions.

Jan. 2 Issued Ck. No. 6981 to Tri-County Management Company for monthly rent, $850.
2 L. Yang, the owner, invested an additional $4,500 in the business.
4 Bought merchandise on account from Valentine and Company, invoice no. A694, $2,830; terms 2/10, n/30; dated January 2.
4 Received check from Velez Appliance for $980 in payment of invoice for $1,000 less discount.
4 Sold merchandise on account to L. Parrish, invoice no. 6483, $755.
6 Received check from Peck, Inc., $637, in payment of $650 invoice less discount.
7 Issued Ck. No. 6982, $588, to Frost and Son, in payment of invoice no. C127 for $600 less discount.
7 Bought supplies on account from Dudley Office Supply, invoice no. 190B, $93.54; terms net 30 days.
7 Sold merchandise on account to Ewing and Charles, invoice no. 6484, $1,115.
9 Issued credit memo no. 43 to L. Parrish, $47, for merchandise returned.
11 Cash sales for January 1 through January 10, $4,454.87.
11 Issued Ck. No. 6983, $2,773.40, to Valentine and Company, in payment of $2,830 invoice less discount.
14 Sold merchandise on account to Velez Appliance, invoice no. 6485, $2,100.
14 Received check from L. Parrish, $693.84, in payment of $755 invoice, less return of $47 and less discount.
19 Bought merchandise on account from Crawford Products, invoice no. 7281, $3,700; terms 2/10, n/60; dated January 16; FOB shipping point, freight prepaid and added to invoice, $142 (total $3,842).
21 Issued Ck. No. 6984, $245, to A. Bautista for miscellaneous expenses not recorded previously.
21 Cash sales for January 11 through January 20, $3,689.
23 Received credit memo no. 163, $87, from Crawford Products for merchandise returned.
29 Sold merchandise on account to Bradford Supply, invoice no. 6486, $1,697.20.
29 Issued Ck. No. 6985 to Western Freight, $64, for freight charges on merchandise purchased January 4.
31 Cash sales for January 21 through January 31, $3,862.
31 Issued Ck. No. 6986, $65, to M. Pineda for miscellaneous expenses not recorded previously.
31 Recorded payroll entry from the payroll register: total salaries, $5,900; employees' federal income tax withheld, $795; FICA taxes withheld, $451.35.*

Jan. 31 Recorded the payroll taxes: FICA taxes, $451.35; state unemployment tax, $265.50; federal unemployment tax, $47.20.
31 Issued Ck. No. 6987, $4,653.65, for salaries for the month.*
31 L. Yang, the owner, withdrew $1,000 for personal use, Ck. No. 6988.

*If using QuickBooks, record transactions in the general journal.

Required

Check Figure
Trial balance totals, $63,187.61

1. Record the transactions for January using a general journal, page 1. Assume the periodic inventory method is used.*

*If using QuickBooks, record transactions using either the journal entry method or the forms-based approach, as directed by your instructor.

The chart of accounts is as follows:

111 Cash
113 Accounts Receivable
114 Merchandise Inventory
115 Supplies
116 Prepaid Insurance
121 Equipment

212 Accounts Payable
215 Salaries Payable
216 Employees' Federal Income Tax Payable
217 FICA Taxes Payable
218 State Unemployment Tax Payable
219 Federal Unemployment Tax Payable

311 L. Yang, Capital
312 L. Yang, Drawing

411 Sales
412 Sales Returns and Allowances
413 Sales Discounts

511 Purchases
512 Purchases Returns and Allowances
513 Purchases Discounts
514 Freight In

621 Salary Expense
622 Payroll Tax Expense
627 Rent Expense
631 Miscellaneous Expense

2. Post daily all entries involving customer accounts to the accounts receivable ledger.*
3. Post daily all entries involving creditor accounts to the accounts payable ledger.*
4. Post daily the general journal entries to the general ledger. Write the owner's name in the Capital and Drawing accounts.*
5. Prepare a trial balance.
6. Prepare a schedule of accounts receivable (A/R Aging Detail report in QuickBooks) and a schedule of accounts payable (A/P Aging Detail report in QuickBooks). Do the totals equal the balances of the related controlling accounts?

*If using QuickBooks or general ledger, ignore Steps 2, 3, and 4.

1, 5

PROBLEM 10-2B C. R. McIntyre Company sells candy wholesale, primarily to vending machine operators. Terms of sales on account are 2/10, n/30, FOB shipping point. The following transactions involving cash receipts and sales of merchandise took place in May of this year:

May 2 Received $411.60 cash from N. Rojas in payment of April 23 invoice of $420, less cash discount.
5 Received $2,085 cash in payment of $2,000 note receivable and interest of $85.
8 Sold merchandise on account to G. Soto, invoice no. 862, $830.
9 Received $11,838.40 cash from D. Maddox in payment of April 30 invoice of $12,080, less cash discount.
15 Received cash from G. Soto in payment of invoice no. 862, less cash discount.
16 Cash sales for first half of May, $3,259.
19 Received $296 cash from R. O. Higgins in payment of April 14 invoice, no discount.
22 Sold merchandise on account to N. T. Jennings, invoice no. 863, $753.
25 Received $239 cash refund for return of defective equipment bought in April for cash.

(Continued)

May 28 Sold merchandise on account to M. E. Mueller, invoice no. 864, $964.
31 Cash sales for second half of May, $4,728.

Check Figure Total Cash Debit, $23,670.40

Required

1. Journalize the transactions for May in the cash receipts journal and the sales journal. Assume the periodic inventory method is used.
2. Total and rule the journals.
3. Prove the equality of the debit and credit totals.

 **1, 6**

PROBLEM 10-3B Jacobs Company had the following transactions that occurred during February of this year:

Feb. 1 Issued Ck. No. 4311, $637, to Barker Company for invoice no. 3113E, recorded previously for $650, less cash discount of $13.
2 Issued Ck. No. 4312 to Bonilla Express Company for freight charges, $48, for merchandise purchased.
4 Issued Ck. No. 4313 to Dillon Realty for monthly rent, $560.
9 Received and paid bill for advertising in *The Nickel News*, $84, Ck. No. 4314.
10 Issued Ck. No. 4315, $990, to Dorsey Company for invoice no. D642, recorded previously for $1,000, less 1 percent cash discount.
15 Paid wages recorded previously for first half of month, $1,678; Ck. No. 4316.
19 R. Jacobs, the owner, withdrew $900 for personal use; Ck. No. 4317.
25 Issued Ck. No. 4318 to First National Bank for payment on bank loan, $896, consisting of $800 on principal and $96 interest.
27 Issued Ck. No. 4319, $430, to Long Company for invoice no. 6317, recorded previously (no discount).
28 Voided Ck. No. 4320.
28 Paid wages recorded previously for second half of month, $1,648; Ck. No. 4321.
28 Received and paid telephone bill, $86; Ck. No. 4322, payable to Southwestern Telephone Company.

Check Figure Total Cash Credit, $7,957

Required

1. Journalize the transactions for February in the cash payments journal. Assume the periodic inventory method is used.
2. Total and rule the journal.
3. Prove the equality of the debit and credit totals.

LO **1, 2, 3, 5, 6**

PROBLEM 10-4B Refer to the information for Problem 10-1B on pages 544–545.

Check Figure Schedule of Accounts Receivable total, $4,912.20

Required

1. Record the transactions for January using a sales journal, page 91; a purchases journal, page 74; a cash receipts journal, page 56; a cash payments journal, page 63; and a general journal, page 119. Assume the periodic inventory method is used.

111 Cash
113 Accounts Receivable
114 Merchandise Inventory
115 Supplies
116 Prepaid Insurance
121 Equipment
212 Accounts Payable
215 Salaries Payable
216 Employees' Federal Income Tax Payable
217 FICA Taxes Payable
218 State Unemployment Tax Payable

219 Federal Unemployment Tax Payable	511 Purchases
311 L. Yang, Capital	512 Purchases Returns and Allowances
312 L. Yang, Drawing	513 Purchases Discounts
	514 Freight In
411 Sales	621 Salary Expense
412 Sales Returns and Allowances	622 Payroll Tax Expense
413 Sales Discounts	627 Rent Expense
	631 Miscellaneous Expense

2. Post daily all entries involving customer accounts to the accounts receivable ledger.
3. Post daily all entries involving creditor accounts to the accounts payable ledger.
4. Post daily those entries involving the Other Accounts columns and the general journal to the general ledger. Write the owner's name in the Capital and Drawing accounts.
5. Add the columns of the special journals and prove the equality of the debit and credit totals on scratch paper.
6. Post the appropriate totals of the special journals to the general ledger.
7. Prepare a trial balance.
8. Prepare a schedule of accounts receivable and a schedule of accounts payable. Do the totals equal the balances of the related controlling accounts?

LO 1, 2, 3, 4, 5, 6

Problem 10-5B The following transactions were completed by Nelson's Hardware, a retailer, during September. Terms on sales on account are 1/10, n/30, FOB shipping point.

Sept.	4	Received cash from M. Alex in payment of August 25 invoice of $275, less cash discount.
	7	Issued Ck. No. 8175, $915.75, to Top Tools, Inc., for invoice. no. 2256, recorded previously for $925, less cash discount of $9.25.
	10	Sold merchandise in the amount of $175 on a credit card. Sales tax on this sale is 8%. The credit card fee the bank deducted for this transaction is $5.
	11	Issued Ck. No. 8176, $653.40, to Snap Tools, Inc. for invoice no. 726, recorded previously on account for $660. A trade discount of 15% was applied at the time of purchase, and Snap Tools, Inc.'s credit terms are 1/10, n/45.
	15	Received $95 cash in payment of August 20 invoice from N. Johnson. No cash discount applied.
	19	Received $1,165 cash in payment of a $1,100 note receivable and interest of $65.
	22	Voided Ck. No. 8177 due to error.
	26	Received and paid telephone bill, $62; Ck. No. 8178, payable to Southern Telephone Company.
	30	Paid wages recorded previously for the month, $3,266, Ck. No. 8179.

Required

1. Journalize the transactions for September in the cash receipts journal, the general journal (for the transaction on Sept. 10th), or the cash payment journal as appropriate. Assume the periodic inventory method is used.
2. Total and rule the journals.
3. Prove the equality of debit and credit totals.

Check Figure
Total Cash Credit, $4,897.15

Try It with QuickBooks® (LO2, 3, 4)

QB Exercise 10-1

Using the information in Exercise 10-5 on page 539 and the QuickBooks data file labeled Exercise 10-5 on the textbook website, complete entries for Fuentes Company and Lowe Company using the form-based approach in QuickBooks. Use the year 2015 for all transactions.

Fuentes Company

1. Using the forms-based approach, which QuickBooks application is used to record transaction (a)?
2. Using the forms-based approach, which two QuickBooks applications are required to record transaction (c)?
3. What is the amount of cash received by Fuentes Company in transaction (c)?
4. What is the amount of the sales discount recorded by Fuentes Company in transaction (c)?

Lowe Company

5. Using the forms-based approach, which QuickBooks application is used to record transaction (a)?
6. Using the forms-based approach, which QuickBooks application is used to pay Fuentes Company in transaction (c) and apply the credit received in transaction (b)?
7. What is the amount recorded for purchases by Lowe Company in transaction (a)?

Activities

Why Does It Matter?

BOOKSHOP SANTA CRUZ, Santa Cruz, California

If you're ever in Santa Cruz, California, take some time to visit Bookshop Santa Cruz. You'll find books "that entertain, help solve problems, or occasionally, change a life."

Since opening in 1966, Bookshop Santa Cruz has been a vital part of the Bay Area. The bookstore takes immense pride in being an independent bookseller, a rare commodity in today's world of large corporate booksellers such as Barnes & Nobles.

The bookstore has several buyers who are responsible for spotting reading trends, reordering current books, and purchasing the newest and hottest books on the market. Each time a buyer makes a purchase and every time Bookshop Santa Cruz makes a sale, a transaction must be recorded. Discuss the advantages a store such as Bookshop Santa Cruz would gain by recording the receipt of cash from sales in the cash receipts journal and the payment of cash for purchases in the cash payments journal?

What Would You Say?

You are the manager of the Accounts Receivable Department for a merchandising business. Your billing clerk sent a bill for $2 to a customer who had charged $100 in goods (including sales tax) with terms 2/10, n/30. The customer called and indicated his displeasure; he can't understand an error like this because he paid on time. Explain to your billing clerk why Accounts Receivable is credited for $100 and not $98. How was permission given to send less than the full amount?

What Do You Think?

You work for Gregory Plumbing Supply. You are responsible for training a new accounting clerk. She has the following questions for you to answer about this invoice.

Gregory Plumbing Supply
14 Indiana Avenue
Chicago, Illinois 60612

No. 320

INVOICE

SOLD TO: *C. P. Lund Company*
5210 Gilman Avenue
San Diego, CA 92102

DATE: *August 1, 20--*
CUSTOMER'S P.O. NO.: *5384*
SHIPPED BY: *Faster Freight*
TERMS: *2/10, n/30*
SALESPERSON: *H. T.*

QUANTITY	DESCRIPTION	UNIT PRICE		TOTAL	
6	*Olin single-control tub shower faucet #44B652*	*51*	*50*	*309*	*00*
6	*Olin dual-control washerless lavatory faucet #59B641*	*22*	*20*	*133*	*20*
12	*Olin massage shower head, antique brass #37B411*	*11*	*56*	*138*	*72*
	Subtotal			*580*	*92*
	Freight			*63*	*80*
	Total			*644*	*72*

1. Who is the buyer?
2. Who is paying the freight?
3. What is the customer's order number?
4. What percentage of the goods bought is the cost of the freight?
5. What are the credit terms? What do they mean?
6. How much will the buyer actually have to pay if the money is received within ten days?
7. What is the dollar amount of the discount?
8. Who receives the discount?
9. What is the due date for payment to get the discount?
10. Why would a seller give a buyer a discount?

What's Wrong with This Picture?

Suppose we collected cash from a charge customer and the debit was to Cash and the credit to Sales. How and when would this error be discovered?

BEFORE A TEST CHECK

BEFORE A TEST CHECK: Chapters 9–10

PART I: Completion

1. The normal balance of the Purchases Discounts account is on the ______ side.
2. Entries in the Accounts Payable Debit column of a cash payments journal are posted daily to the ______.
3. A(n) ______ is the amount a customer may deduct for paying a bill within a specified period of time.
4. The form sent to the supplier of merchandise is called a(n) ______.
5. The ______ account is used to record the buying of merchandise only.
6. If the freight charges are FOB shipping point, the ______ pays the transportation charges.
7. The time the seller allows the buyer before full payment has to be made is the ______.
8. Increases in Sales Returns and Allowances are recorded on the ______ side.
9. The sales journal is used to record all ______.
10. The schedule of accounts receivable lists the balances of all ______ accounts at the end of the month.

PART II: Matching

____ 1. Paid freight bill on merchandise purchased.
____ 2. Bought office equipment on account.
____ 3. Received a credit memo for merchandise returned.
____ 4. Bought office equipment for cash.
____ 5. Sold merchandise on account.
____ 6. Journalized the closing entries.
____ 7. Paid state sales tax to the state revenue department.
____ 8. Bought merchandise on account.
____ 9. Sold merchandise for cash.
____ 10. Bought merchandise for cash.

S Sales journal
P Purchases journal
CR Cash receipts journal
CP Cash payments journal
J General journal

PART III: True/False

T F 1. The Purchases Discounts account is classified as a revenue account.
T F 2. The normal balance of the Sales Discounts account is on the debit side.
T F 3. Check marks in the Posting Reference column of the sales journal indicate that the amounts are not to be posted.
T F 4. The purchases journal is used for buying merchandise for cash and on account.
T F 5. On the income statement, Freight In is subtracted from Purchases.

Answers: Part I
1. credit 2. accounts payable ledger 3. cash discount 4. purchase order 5. Purchases 6. buyer 7. credit period 8. debit 9. sales of merchandise on account 10. credit customers'

Answers: Part II
1. CP 2. J 3. J 4. CP 5. S 6. J 7. CP 8. P 9. CR 10. CP

Answers: Part III
1. F 2. T 3. F 4. F 5. F

August Journal Entries

Ms. Valli has provided the transactions for the month of August to be entered in the system. All About You Spa does not track cash sales by customer. If you are using the form-based approach with QuickBooks or general ledger, select "Cash Sales" as the customer for all cash sales transactions.

Checkbook Register

*If using QuickBooks, record the following transactions in the general journal.

Check No.	Date	Explanation	✓	Deposits	Check Amount
1044	8/1	Paid August's rent.			1,650.00
	8/1	Deposited Chaco's payment received on account, invoice no. 15.		400.00	
	8/1	Deposited Mini Spa's payment received on account, invoice no. 18. Paid in full.		222.48	
1045	8/1	Paid accumulated sales tax payable to State Revenue Dept.			1,829.90
1046	8/2	Paid advertising expense for August photo ad.			455.00
1047	8/2	Paid week's wages.			1,845.50
1048	8/2	Paid Spa Magic for invoice no. 5033, dated June 2. Paid in full.			2,721.00
1049	8/3	Bought silk flower arrangement for the salon (Miscellaneous Expense).			87.90
	8/3	Deposited Tory Ligman's payment received on account. Paid in full.		164.00	
1050	8/4	Bought spa supplies—5 cases of bottled water for clients (debit Spa Supplies).			45.00
	8/4	Deposited Jill Anson's payment received on account.		87.50	
1051	8/5	Bought a digital camera for confidential before-and-after pictures (debit Spa Equipment).			482.00
1052	8/5	Paid Office Staples for invoice 1417, dated July 5. Paid in full.			186.00
1053	8/5	Paid on Giftco for invoice no. 316, dated July 5. Paid in full.			1,309.00
	8/6	Deposited Pleasant Spa's payment received on account, invoice no. 16.		997.42	
1054	8/6	Paid Golden Spa Supplies for invoice no. 1836, dated July 1. Paid in full.			490.00
	8/7	Deposited first week's cash sales: merchandise $1,630.00; services $3,350.00; sales tax collected $398.40.		5,378.40	

Check No.	Date	Explanation	✓	Deposits	Check Amount
	8/8	Deposited Los Obrigados Lodge's payment received on account, invoice no. 14.		200.00	
	8/9	Deposited Holmes Condo's payment received on account, invoice no. 17.		200.00	
1055	8/9	Paid week's wages.			1,850.00
1056	8/10	Paid Giftco for invoice no. 416, dated August 1. Paid in full less applicable discount.			4,198.00
	8/14	Deposited second week's cash sales: merchandise $1,330.00; services $2,340.00; sales tax collected $293.60.		3,963.60	
	8/15	Deposited About Face Spa's payment received on account, invoice no. 19.		265.00	
1057	8/16	Paid week's wages.			1,853.00
1058	8/18	Paid Superior Equipment for invoice no. 3608, dated July 5. Paid in full.			420.00
	8/19	Deposited Jack Morgan's payment received on account. Paid in full.		286.00	
	8/21	Deposited third week's cash sales: merchandise $2,220.00; services $2,810.00; sales tax collected $402.40.		5,432.40	
1059	8/22	Paid on account to Logo Products, invoice no. 1579, dated July 1.			2,500.00
	8/23	Deposited Mini Spa's payment received on account. Paid in full less applicable discount.		925.38	
1060	8/23	Paid on account to Spa Goods, invoice no. 312, dated July 1.			2,000.00
1061	8/23	Paid week's wages.			1,847.50
1062	8/28	Paid month's laundry bill.			95.00
1063	8/28	Owner withdrew cash for personal use.			2,500.00
1064	8/30	Paid week's wages.			1,850.00
	8/31	Deposited end of month's cash sales: merchandise $2,030.00; services $4,176.00; $496.48 sales tax.		6,702.48	
1065	8/31	Paid August telephone bill.			235.00
1066	8/31	Paid on account to Spa Equipment, Inc., invoice no. 2731, dated July 3.			3,000.00
1067	8/31	Paid August power and water bill.			255.00

Purchases Invoices for Merchandise Bought on Account During August

All About You Spa will pay all freight costs associated with purchases of merchandise to the supplier. Invoice 416 was paid within the discount period on 8/10. The remaining August purchases were not paid until September.

Date of Purchase	Transaction Information	Amount
Aug. 1	Bought logo merchandise from Giftco; invoice no. 416, dated 8/1; terms 2/10, n/30.	\$4,100.00 plus \$180.00 freight
1	Bought bath and beauty products from Spa Magic; invoice no. 5235, dated 8/1; terms 2/10, n/30.	\$3,562.00 plus \$155.00 freight
2	Bought logo merchandise from Logo Products; invoice no. 1680, dated 8/2; terms 2/10, n/30.	\$2,451.00 plus \$144.00 freight
5	Bought spa accessories from Spa Goods; invoice no. 387, dated 8/5; terms 2/10, n/30.	\$1,120.00 plus \$110.00 freight

*If using QuickBooks, you can record the purchase invoices in the general journal or use the Enter Bills application from the home page.

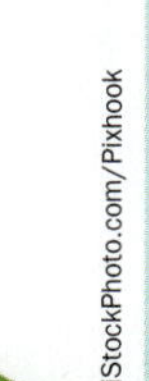

Sales Invoices for Gift Certificates Sold on Account During August

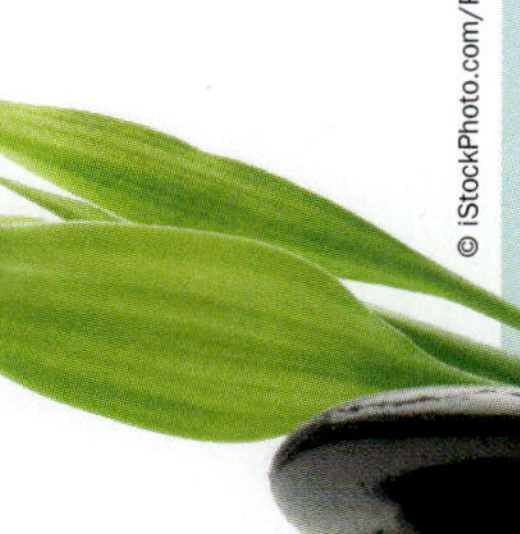

All About You Spa is responsible for collecting and paying the sales tax on merchandise that it sells. The sales tax rate where All About You Spa does business is 8 percent of each sale (for example, \$650.00 × 0.08 = \$52.00). Invoice 25 was received within the discount period on 8/23. (Apply the discount to the invoice amount. Disregard the sales tax when calculating the discount.) The remaining August sales were not received until September.

Date of Sale	Transaction Information	Sales Amount (Before Tax)
Aug. 1	About Face Spa, invoice no. 20; terms 2/10, n/45.	\$ 650.00
5	Chaco's, invoice no. 21; terms 2/10, n/45.	395.00
8	Holmes Condos, invoice no. 22; terms 2/10, n/45.	1,294.00
9	Pleasant Spa, invoice no. 23; terms 2/10, n/45.	1,560.00
11	Los Obrigados Lodge, invoice no. 24; terms 2/10, n/45.	356.00
14	Mini Spa, invoice no. 25; terms 2/10, n/45.	873.00

Note: All gift certificates were redeemed for merchandise by the end of the month.

*If using QuickBooks, you can record the sales invoices in the general journal or use the Create Invoices application from the home page.

All About You Spa

CONTINUING PROBLEM

Other August Transactions

There were two other transactions in August. Neither involved cash.

Date	Transaction Information	Amount
Aug. 9	Issued credit memorandum no. 1 to About Face Spa for an allowance for damaged goods. (Debit the new account Sales Returns and Allowances 414.)	$ 88.00
29	Received a credit memorandum for damaged spa accessories from Spa Magic. (Credit the new account Purchases Returns and Allowances 513.)	123.00

*If using QuickBooks, you can record the other July transactions in the general journal or use the Enter Bills application from the home page to record purchases. Owner investments should be recorded in the general journal.

Check Figures

3. Trial balance total, August 31, $115,901.27
4. Schedule of accounts receivable total, August 31, $6,253.79
5. Schedule of accounts payable total, August 31, $15,513.00

Required

1. Journalize the transactions for August (in date order), or if you are using QuickBooks, you can use the forms-based approach from the home page as appropriate to record transactions. Ask your instructor whether you should use the special journals, the general journal, or the forms-based approach with QuickBooks.

   * If you are preparing the journal entries manually, enter your transactions beginning on page 11.

2. Post the entries to the accounts receivable, accounts payable, and general ledger.

   * Ignore this step if you are using QuickBooks or general ledger.

3. Prepare a trial balance as of August 31, 20--.
4. Prepare a schedule of accounts receivable or A/R Aging Detail report if using QuickBooks as of August 31, 20--.
5. Prepare a schedule of accounts payable or A/P Aging Detail report if using QuickBooks as of August 31, 20--.

APPENDIX

The Voucher System of Accounting

Learning Objectives After you have completed this appendix, you will be able to do the following:

1. Prepare vouchers.
2. Record vouchers in a voucher register.
3. Record payment of vouchers in a check register.
4. Record transactions involving canceling or altering an original voucher.

Accounting Language

Voucher (p. 555)
Voucher register (p. 559)

The voucher system is a means of achieving internal control and enabling the owner or manager to maintain contact with day-to-day transactions. This system promotes the delegation of duties and responsibilities.

OBJECTIVE OF THE VOUCHER SYSTEM

The objective of the voucher system is to control the incurrence of all liabilities and the payment of all expenditures—in other words, to control the purchase of (1) merchandise or materials, (2) other assets, and (3) services. The voucher system is suitable for companies of varying sizes that require a clear separation of duties. The voucher system has the following components: vouchers, voucher register, check register, unpaid voucher file, paid voucher file, and general journal.

VOUCHERS

A **voucher** is a document that serves as proof of a transaction and, from a business point of view, also serves as a full description of the transaction. **When a business is using the voucher system, a voucher must be filled out for every invoice or bill received, whether it is to be paid immediately or in the future. The invoice or bill is usually stapled to the voucher.**

Characteristics of Vouchers

Just as the form of invoices varies from one company to another, so too the form of vouchers varies from one company to another. However, the following characteristics are usually present:

- Vouchers are numbered consecutively.
- The name and address of the payee or creditor appear on the voucher.
- The amount and credit terms of the invoice appear on the voucher.
- Vouchers state due dates so that firms can take advantage of any cash discounts.
- For internal control, vouchers require signatures approving payment.
- Vouchers record payment: date paid and check number.

Figure 1
Steps for processing a voucher for a purchase of merchandise

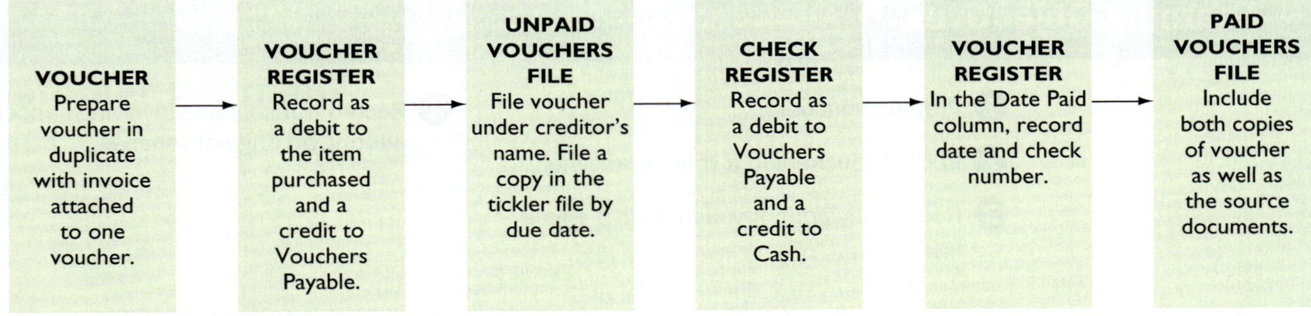
VOUCHER
Prepare voucher in duplicate with invoice attached to one voucher.
VOUCHER REGISTER
Record as a debit to the item purchased and a credit to Vouchers Payable.
UNPAID VOUCHERS FILE
File voucher under creditor's name. File a copy in the tickler file by due date.
CHECK REGISTER
Record as a debit to Vouchers Payable and a credit to Cash.
VOUCHER REGISTER
In the Date Paid column, record date and check number.
PAID VOUCHERS FILE
Include both copies of voucher as well as the source documents.

A completed voucher, with the invoice or bill stapled to it, describes an entire transaction as well as the procedure for processing the voucher. So that you can see the big picture, Figure 1 presents the steps involved in processing a voucher for a purchase of merchandise.

Preparation and Approval of Vouchers

Learning Objective

1 Prepare vouchers.

To cite a familiar example, let's assume that Whitewater Raft Supply has now achieved such a volume of business that it is using a voucher system. Let's also assume that Whitewater Raft Supply has received from its supplier, Pataponia, Inc., the invoice shown here.

Pataponia, Inc.
1614 Olivera Street
San Francisco, CA 94129

No. 3101

INVOICE

SOLD TO: *Whitewater Raft Supply*
1400 Front Street
Seattle, WA 98101

DATE: *December 1, 20--*
CUSTOMER'S P.O. NO.: *9103*
SHIPPED BY: *Western Freight Line*
TERMS: *2/10, n/30*

YOUR ORDER NO.	SALESPERSON	TERMS
9103	*C.L.*	*2/10, n/30*
DATE SHIPPED	**SHIPPED BY**	**FOB**
December 1, 20--	*Western Freight Line*	*San Francisco*

QUANTITY	DESCRIPTION	UNIT PRICE	TOTAL
12	*Reinforced Whitewater Spray Skirt #6020*	118 95	1,427 40
	Freight		42 82
	Total		1,470 22

Whitewater Raft Supply's accountant, using the invoice as the source of information, fills out the following voucher. The face of the voucher lists the details of the transaction.

WHITEWATER RAFT SUPPLY
1400 Front Street
Seattle, WA 98101

No. 118

VOUCHER

PAY TO: *Pataponia, Inc.*
1614 Olivera St.
San Francisco, CA 94129

DATE *12/1/20--*

DATE OF INVOICE	TERMS	DESCRIPTION	AMOUNT
12/1	*2/10, n/30*	*Invoice No. 3101*	*1,427 40*
		Less discount	*28 55*
		Freight	*42 82*
		Net amount payable	*1,441 67*

APPROVAL	DATES	APPROVED BY
Extensions and footings verified	*12/2*	*M. C. L.*
Prices in agreement with purchase order	*12/2*	*S. T.*
Credit terms in agreement with purchase order	*12/2*	*S. T.*
Quantities in agreement with receiving report	*12/2*	*J. D. S.*
Approved for payment	*12/7*	*R. L. R.*

ACCOUNT DISTRIBUTION

ACCOUNT DEBITED	AMOUNT
Purchases	*1,427.40*
Freight In	*42.82*
Wages Payable	
Supplies	
Miscellaneous Expense	
Total Vouchers Payable Cr.	*1,470.22*

ACCOUNT DISTRIBUTION by *R. R. H.*

VOUCHER NO. *118*

DUE DATE: *12/8*

PAY TO: *Pataponia, Inc.*
1614 Olivera Street
San Francisco, CA 94129

SUMMARY OF CHARGES

Amount of invoice	*1,470.22*
Less cash discount	*28.55*
Net amount	*1,441.67*

RECORD OF PAYMENT

Paid by check no.	*2815*
Date of check	*12/8*
Amount of check	*1,441.67*

ENTERED IN VOUCHER REG. by *M. C. L.*

Remember

Because the check register replaces the cash payments journal and the voucher register replaces the purchases journal, the special-column totals from the voucher register must be posted before those from the check register.

The *due date* represents the last day on which a company can take advantage of the cash discount. For example, the invoice of Pataponia, Inc., was dated December 1, with terms of 2/10, n/30. The discount period ends on December 11. Therefore, at the latest, the check must be sent on December 8 to receive the discount.

The Account Distribution section is used to record the account titles and amounts to be debited, the total amount to be credited to Vouchers Payable, and the initials of the person authorized to determine the distribution.

THE VOUCHERS PAYABLE ACCOUNT

When you use a voucher system, you substitute the Vouchers Payable account for Accounts Payable. For example, when a firm buys merchandise on account, the accountant enters it as a debit to Purchases and a credit to Vouchers Payable. Similarly, when a firm buys store equipment on account, the accountant records it as a debit to Store Equipment and a credit to Vouchers Payable. Also, if a company incurs an expense on account, such as Advertising, the entry is a debit to Advertising Expense and a credit to Vouchers Payable.

When a check is issued in payment of a voucher, record the entry in the check register as a debit to Vouchers Payable and a credit to Cash. Remember that *all* liabilities are recorded in the Vouchers Payable account.

Date		Vou. No.	Creditor	Payment Date		Ck. No.	Vouchers Payable Credit	Purchases Debit
20--								
Dec.	1	117	Fast-Way Freight	12	1	2808	63 00	
	1	118	Pataponia, Inc.	12	8	2815	1470 22	1427 40
	3	119	Dell Office Supply	12	3	2809	48 72	
	5	120	Stable Ins. Company	12	5	2812	174 00	
	9	121	Langseth and Son	12	18	2829	328 00	306 00
	10	122	Payroll Bank Account	12	10	2818	1690 00	
	12	123	Southland Journal				176 00	
	12	124	Bradley Construction	12	12	2820	116 00	
	15	125	D. M. Bruce	12	15	2824	500 00	
	15	126	C. A. Waters, Inc.	12	18	Note	421 00	421 00
	29	149	Dana Mfg. Company				714 00	714 00
	30	150	Safety National Bank	12	30	2837	1507 50	
	31		Totals				11674 90	5095 10
							(212)	(511)

	Debits		Credit
Purchases	*$ 5,095.10*	*Vouchers Payable*	*$11,674.90*
Freight In	*234.32*		
Wages Payable	*3,314.00*		
Supplies	*121.79*		
Miscellaneous Expense	*83.69*		
Other Accounts	*2,826.00*		
	$11,674.90		

THE VOUCHER REGISTER

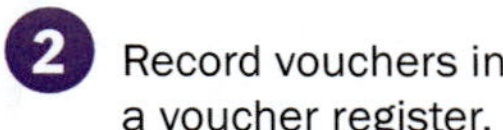

Learning Objective 2: Record vouchers in a voucher register.

The **voucher register** has the status of a journal; it is a book of original entry. All vouchers must be recorded in it, in numerical order. Think of it as a multicolumn purchases journal. The voucher register has only one credit column, Vouchers Payable Credit, but a number of debit columns. Headings for the debit columns are selected on the basis of their frequency of use. In addition to the special columns, the voucher register also has space for recording the voucher number, the name of the creditor, the date of payment, and the check number. The voucher register for Whitewater Raft Supply appears below.

When you first record the voucher, leave the Payment Date and Ck. No. columns blank. After you have recorded the payment in the check register, go back to the voucher register and enter the date of payment and the number of the check.

Remember

A voucher is prepared for every invoice or bill the company receives.

Posting from the Voucher Register

The entries in the Other Accounts columns are posted *daily* to the general ledger, just as the Other Accounts columns of the other special journals are posted daily.

VOUCHER REGISTER Page 3

Freight In Debit	Wages Payable Debit	Supplies Debit	Miscellaneous Expense Debit	Other Accounts Debit: Account	Post. Ref.	Amount
63 00						
42 82						
		48 72				
				Prepaid Insurance	116	174 00
22 00						
	1,690 00					
				Advertising Expense	618	176 00
				Sales Returns and Allowances	412	116 00
				D. M. Bruce, Drawing	312	500 00
				Notes Payable	211	1,500 00
				Interest Expense	634	7 50
234 32	3,314 00	121 79	83 69			2,826 00
(514)	(213)	(622)	(619)			(X)

The (X) under the column total means "do not post." At the end of the month, total all of the columns, and prove the equality of the debit and credit entries by comparing the combined total of the debit columns with the total of the Vouchers Payable Credit column.

THE CHECK REGISTER

Learning Objective 3 Record payment of vouchers in a check register.

Any company or organization using a voucher system uses both the voucher register and the check register as books of original entry. Now let's look at the procedure for the check register. Because checks are issued only in payment of approved and recorded vouchers, the entry in the check register is always a debit to Vouchers Payable and a credit to Cash. A Vouchers Payable Debit column in the check register offsets the Vouchers Payable Credit column in the voucher register. Recall that after you record the entry in the check register, you enter the date and check number on the appropriate line in the voucher register and on the outside of the voucher in the Record of Payment section.

CHECK REGISTER — Page 11

Date		Ck. No.	Payee	Vou. No.	Vouchers Payable Debit	Purchases Discounts Credit	Cash Credit
20--							
Dec.	1	2808	Fast-Way Freight	117	63.00		63.00
	3	2809	Dell Office Supply	119	48.72		48.72
	3	2810	Gardner Products Company	114	206.00	2.06	203.94
	4	2811	Dana Manufacturing Company	115	540.00	10.80	529.20
	5	2812	Stable Insurance Company	120	174.00		174.00
	6	2813	Void				
	6	2814	Langseth and Son	116	464.00	9.28	454.72
	8	2815	Pataponia, Inc.	118	1,470.22	28.55	1,441.67
	30	2837	Safety National Bank	150	1,507.50		1,507.50
	31		Totals		7,281.20	90.09	7,191.11
					(212)	(513)	(111)

Debit	Credit
$7,281.20	$ 90.09
	7,191.11
	$7,281.20

HANDLING OF UNPAID VOUCHERS

Firms usually prepare vouchers in duplicate. In the system used by Whitewater Raft Supply, the invoice is attached to the original copy of the voucher. Then the voucher is circulated within the company for the necessary signatures. After a voucher is recorded in the voucher register, it is filed under the name of the creditor. (Other companies may prepare only one copy of the voucher and file it under the date on which it is supposed to be paid.)

At Whitewater Raft Supply, the Unpaid Vouchers file contains all outstanding vouchers or credit memos. This file, organized by names of creditors, now acts as a subsidiary ledger. In fact, at Whitewater Raft Supply, this file substitutes for the accounts payable ledger.

The *second* copy of the voucher goes to the treasurer, who files it chronologically by due date. This tickler file (a file of unpaid vouchers filed by due date) helps the treasurer forecast the amount of cash that will be needed to pay outstanding bills and take advantage of cash discounts.

The Vouchers Payable account is a controlling account, similar to Accounts Payable being a controlling account.

Whitewater Raft Supply
Schedule of Vouchers Payable
December 31, 20--

Vou. No.	Name of Creditor	Amount
123	Southland Journal	$176
149	Dana Manufacturing Company	714
	Total Vouchers Payable	$890

At the end of the month, the accountant lists all of the vouchers payable, taking the information directly from the Unpaid Vouchers file.

FILING PAID VOUCHERS

Now let's assume that the firm has paid its bill. The payment is recorded in the check register and in the Payment columns of the voucher register. Then the voucher is stapled to the copy in the tickler file, marked paid, and filed in numerical order in a Paid Vouchers file.

SITUATIONS REQUIRING SPECIAL TREATMENT

When a firm is using the voucher system, it inevitably runs into an occasional nonroutine transaction that does not fit in the fixed channels of the voucher system and therefore may require an entry in the general journal. You can consider such treatment as an adjustment to the voucher system.

Learning Objective 4 Record transactions involving canceling or altering an original voucher.

Return of a Purchase Before Original Voucher Has Been Recorded

Normally, if a business with an efficient purchasing department is going to return any merchandise, it returns the merchandise before the vouchers are recorded in the voucher register. The accountant records the deduction directly on the invoice and records the invoice in the voucher register for the net amount.

Return of a Purchase After Original Voucher Has Been Recorded

Assume that a business purchased merchandise for $566. The transaction was recorded in the voucher register as a debit to Purchases and a credit to Vouchers Payable. Later, the company returns $26 worth of defective merchandise. The return is recorded in the general journal as a debit to Vouchers Payable and a credit to Purchases Returns and Allowances. The notation "Return" is entered in the Payment column of the voucher register.

Installment Payments Planned at Time of Original Purchase

In a voucher system, invoices not subject to cash discounts are generally paid in full. Sometimes, however, management prefers to pay for an item in installments. When this happens, the company's accountant prepares a separate voucher for each installment and records each of these vouchers in the voucher register. Each voucher's due date corresponds to the date on which that installment is to be paid.

Installment Payments After Original Voucher Has Been Recorded

However, suppose the buyer records the entire amount of the invoice on one voucher and *later* decides to pay the invoice in installments. The accountant must now cancel the original voucher by means of a general journal entry and issue a new voucher for each installment. A notation listing the new voucher numbers is made in the Payment column of the voucher register.

Correcting an Amount After Original Voucher Has Been Recorded

If an error in the purchase of merchandise is discovered after the voucher has been recorded in the voucher register, the original voucher must be canceled by means of a general journal entry debiting Vouchers Payable and crediting Purchases. Next, a new entry is made in the voucher register for the correct amount, debiting Purchases and crediting Vouchers Payable. A notation listing the new voucher number is made in the Payment column of the voucher register.

Issuing a Note Payable After Original Voucher Has Been Recorded

If a note is issued for the amount of an unpaid invoice after the voucher has been recorded, an entry must be made in the general journal to cancel the original voucher. The entry is a debit to Vouchers Payable and a credit to Notes Payable. The notation "Note" is made in the Date Paid column of the voucher register. When the note is to be paid, a new voucher is issued for the amount of the principal and interest, debiting Notes Payable and Interest Expense and crediting Vouchers Payable.

Glossary

Voucher A document that serves as proof of a transaction and, from a business point of view, also serves as a full description of the transaction. *(p. 555)*

Voucher register A book of original entry in which all vouchers are recorded in numerical order. *(p. 559)*

Problems

LO 2, 3

PROBLEM 10A-1 Saenz Company uses a voucher system in which it records invoices at the gross amount. The following vouchers were issued during February and were unpaid on March 1:

Voucher Number	Company	For	Date of Voucher	Amount
1729	Kipley Company	Merchandise, FOB destination	Feb. 26	$3,436
1732	J. R. Steven	Merchandise, FOB destination	Feb. 28	4,710

The following transactions were completed during March:

Mar. 3 Issued voucher no. 1734 in favor of Larry Company for March rent, $1,220.
3 Issued Ck. No. 1829 in payment of voucher no. 1734, $1,220.
5 Bought merchandise on account from Lorenzo, Inc., $3,890; terms 2/10, n/30; FOB shipping point; freight prepaid and added to the invoice, $72 (total, $3,962). Issued voucher no. 1735.
5 Issued Ck. No. 1830 in payment of voucher no. 1729, $3,401.64 ($3,436 less 1 percent cash discount).
9 Issued voucher no. 1736 in favor of Mario Electric Company for electric bill, $216.
9 Issued Ck. No. 1831 in payment of voucher no. 1736, $216.
9 Issued Ck. No. 1832 in payment of voucher no. 1732, $4,615.80 ($4,710 less 2 percent cash discount).
13 Issued Ck. No. 1833 in payment of voucher no. 1735, less the cash discount, $3,884.20. Recall that the freight portion is not eligible for discount.
16 Bought merchandise on account from McGinnis Manufacturing Company, $6,260; terms 2/10 EOM; FOB destination. Issued voucher no. 1737.
25 Issued voucher no. 1738 for note payable previously recorded in the general journal: principal, $4,000, plus $30 interest. The note is payable to the Keller State Bank.
25 Issued Ck. No. 1834 in payment of voucher no. 1737, $6,134.80 ($6,260 less 2 percent cash discount).
31 Issued voucher no. 1739 for wages payable, $4,985, in favor of the payroll bank account. (Assume that the payroll entry was previously recorded in the general journal.)
31 Paid voucher no. 1739 by issuing Ck. No. 1835, $4,985, payable to Payroll Bank Account.

Required

1. Using the voucher issue date, enter the unpaid invoices in the voucher register (page 65) beginning with voucher no. 1729. Then draw double lines across all columns to separate the vouchers of February from those of March.
2. Record the transactions for March in the voucher register. Also record the appropriate transactions in the check register (page 71).
3. Total and rule the voucher register and the check register.
4. Prove the equality of the debits and credits in the voucher register and the check register.

Check Figure
Voucher Register, Vouchers Payable Credit total, $20,673

LO 2, 3, 4

PROBLEM 10A-2 Hartman Company, which uses a voucher system, has the following unpaid vouchers on July 1. The firm follows the practice of recording vouchers at the gross amount.

Voucher Number	Company	For	Date of Voucher	Amount
4789	Garrison and Son	Store equipment	June 15	$ 4,996
4795	Fenner and Company	Merchandise, FOB destination	June 28	8,571
4797	J. R. Paige Company	Merchandise, FOB destination	June 28	10,710

The company completed the following transactions during July:

July 1 Issued voucher no. 4800 in favor of Mortenson Insurance Company for a premium on a 12-month fire insurance policy, $890.
2 Paid voucher no. 4789 by issuing Ck. No. 8219, $4,996.
2 Issued Ck. No. 8220 in payment of voucher no. 4800, $890.
3 Issued voucher no. 4801 in favor of Quinn Quick Freight for transportation charges on merchandise purchases, $223.
5 Paid voucher no. 4801 by issuing Ck. No. 8221, $223.
7 Issued Ck. No. 8222 in payment of voucher no. 4795, $8,485.29 ($8,571 less 1 percent cash discount).
8 Issued Ck. No. 8223 in payment of voucher no. 4797, $10,602.90 ($10,710 less 1 percent cash discount).
11 Established a petty cash fund of $250. Issued voucher no. 4802.
11 Paid voucher no. 4802 by issuing Ck. No. 8224, $250.
13 Issued voucher no. 4803 in favor of Mohammad Company for merchandise, $14,708; terms 2/10, n/30; FOB shipping point; freight prepaid and added to the invoice, $384 (total, $15,092).
15 Received bill for advertising in the *Weekly Ads*. Issued voucher no. 4804 in the amount of $410.
17 Received a credit memo for $764 from Mohammad Company for merchandise returned to it, credit memo no. 540 (pertaining to voucher no. 4803).
20 Issued voucher no. 4805 in favor of Vinson County for six months' property tax (Prepaid Property Taxes), $2,272.
20 Paid voucher no. 4805 by issuing Ck. No. 8225, $2,272.
21 Issued Ck. No. 8226 in payment of voucher no. 4803, $14,049.12 ($14,708 less $764 return, less cash discount, plus freight).
23 Bought merchandise on account from Summers and Company, $6,039; terms 1/10, n/30; FOB destination. Issued voucher no. 4806.
27 Received a credit memo for $984 from Summers and Company for damaged merchandise, credit memo no. 437 (pertaining to voucher no. 4806).
31 Issued voucher no. 4807 to reimburse petty cash fund. The charges were:

Supplies Expense	$110.43
H. Hartman, Drawing	75.00
Miscellaneous Expense	39.67

31 Issued Ck. No. 8227 in payment of voucher no. 4807, $225.10.

July 31 Issued voucher no. 4808 for wages payable, $8,448, in favor of the payroll bank account. (Assume that the payroll entry was recorded previously in the general journal.)

31 Paid voucher no. 4808 by issuing Ck. No. 8228, payable to Payroll Bank Account.

Required

Check Figure
Check Register, Cash Credit total, $50,441.41

1. Using the voucher issue date, enter the unpaid invoices in the voucher register (page 75) beginning with voucher no. 4789. Then draw double lines across all columns to separate the vouchers of June from those of July.
2. Enter the transactions for July in the voucher register at the gross amount. Also record the appropriate transactions in the check register (page 86) and the general journal (page 41).
3. Total and rule the voucher register and the check register for the transactions recorded during July.
4. Prove the equality of the debits and credits on the voucher register and the check register.

LO 2, 3, 4

PROBLEM 10A-3 Nathan Systems uses a voucher system in which it records invoices at the **gross amount**. During October, it completed the following transactions:

Oct. 2 Issued voucher no. 2632 in favor of Myers and Horn for the purchase of merchandise with an invoice price of $5,831; terms n/30; FOB shipping point; freight prepaid and added to the invoice, $192 (total, $6,023). Leave an extra line after this entry.

3 Issued voucher no. 2633 for $1,010, no. 2634 for $1,010, and no. 2635 for $1,010. The debt arose because Nathan Systems bought a laptop and printer from Fitzpatrick, Inc. The terms are $1,010 cash on delivery, $1,010 in 30 days, and $1,010 in 60 days. (Use three lines.)

5 Issued Ck. No. 2725 in payment of voucher no. 2633, $1,010.

9 Issued voucher no. 2636 in favor of Cordero Company for the purchase of supplies, $360.50; terms n/30.

12 Issued voucher no. 2637 in favor of Goode Realty for rent for the month, $1,650.

12 Issued Ck. No. 2726 in payment of voucher no. 2637, $1,650.

16 Issued voucher no. 2638 in favor of French Cargo for freight charges on merchandise purchased, $104.

16 Issued voucher no. 2639 in favor of Holley Company for the purchase of merchandise having a list price of $6,512 with a 25 percent trade discount (record voucher for $4,884); terms 2/10, n/30; FOB shipping point. Leave an extra line after this entry.

16 Issued Ck. No. 2727 in payment of voucher no. 2638, $104.

16 Canceled voucher no. 2632 because the invoice will be paid in two installments as follows: voucher no. 2640, payable November 1, $3,011.50; voucher no. 2641, payable November 15, $3,011.50. Issued voucher no. 2640 and no. 2641.

17 Received a credit memo from Holley Company for merchandise returned, $352, credit memo no. 580, voucher no. 2639.

22 Issued voucher no. 2642 in favor of Pardo Telephone Company for telephone bill, $164.90.

22 Issued Ck. No. 2728 in payment of voucher no. 2642, $164.90.

23 Issued Ck. No. 2729 in payment of voucher no. 2639, $4,441.36. ($4,884 less $352 return, less cash discount.)

(*Continued*)

Oct. 31 Issued voucher no. 2643 for wages payable, $4,550, in favor of Payroll Bank Account. (Assume that the payroll entry was recorded previously in the general journal.)

31 Issued Ck. No. 2730 in payment of voucher no. 2643, $4,550.

31 Issued voucher no. 2644 in favor of N. S. Nathan, the owner, for personal withdrawal, $1,400.

31 Issued Ck. No. 2731 in payment of voucher no. 2644, $1,400.

Check Figure
Schedule of Vouchers Payable total, $8,403.50

Required

1. Record the transactions for October in the voucher register (page 32), the check register (page 34), and the general journal (page 18).
2. Total and rule the voucher register and the check register.
3. Prove the equality of the debits and credits on the voucher register and the check register.
4. Post the amounts from the registers and the general journal to the Vouchers Payable account, No. 212. Assume no previous balance in the account. (Posting from the voucher register should be marked as VR32. Posting from the check register should be marked as CkR34.)
5. Prepare a schedule of vouchers payable. Compare this total with the balance of the Vouchers Payable account.

chapter 11

Work Sheet and Adjusting Entries

Learning Objectives

After you have completed this chapter, you will be able to do the following:

1. Prepare an adjustment for unearned revenue.
2. Prepare an adjustment for merchandise inventory under the periodic inventory system.
3. Record adjustment data in a work sheet including merchandise inventory, unearned revenue, supplies used, expired insurance, depreciation, and accrued wages or salaries.
4. Complete the work sheet.
5. Journalize the adjusting entries for a merchandising business under the periodic inventory system.
6. Prepare and journalize the adjusting entry for merchandise inventory under the perpetual inventory system.

To: **Amy Roberts, CPA**
Subject: **Work Sheet and Adjusting Entries**

Hi Amy,
A while back you helped me understand adjusting entries for the service side of my business. Are there any differences regarding adjusting entries for the merchandising side of my business that I should know about?
Thanks,
Janie

To: **Janie Conner**
Subject: **RE: Work Sheet and Adjusting Entries**

Hi Janie,
For the merchandising side of your business, you will still do adjustments for items such as insurance, depreciation, supplies, and accrued wages as we talked about before. However, there are two more adjusting entries that you will need to learn. One involves unearned revenues; the other involves merchandise inventory. The adjustment for unearned revenues can be used with the service side or the merchandising side of your business. The adjusting entry for merchandise inventory applies only to the merchandising side of your business, and the entry you make will depend on the inventory method you use (periodic or perpetual).

Take some time to review the following concepts and let's talk again next week.

_____ 1. Adjusting entries for insurance, depreciation, supplies, and accrued wages
_____ 2. Adjusting entries for unearned revenues
_____ 3. Adjusting entries for merchandise inventory

Amy

© Vladimir Daragan/Shutterstock.com

Accounting Language

Inventory shrinkage (p. 580)
Physical inventory (p. 571)
Revenue recognition principle (p. 570)
Unearned revenue (p. 570)

We have talked about the journals and accounts that a merchandising business keeps. Now we take another step toward completing the accounting cycle by presenting the related adjustments and the work sheet. First, let's briefly review the adjusting entries you have learned so far. The data and related adjusting entries are below.

Supplies

	+		−
Bal.	1,540	Adj.	1,125
Bal.	415		

Supplies Expense

	+		−
Adj.	1,125		

Supplies used, $1,125. (Used supplies become supplies expense)

Prepaid Insurance

	+		−
Bal.	4,000	Adj.	3,600
Bal.	400		

Insurance Expense

	+		−
Adj.	3,600		

Insurance expired, $3,600. (The amount expired is the amount used.)

Depreciation Expense, Equipment

	+		−
Adj.	1,800		

Accumulated Depreciation Equipment

	−		+
		Bal.	11,000
		Adj.	1,800
		Bal.	12,800

Additional depreciation, $1,800. (Add to both accounts.)

Wages Expense

	+		−
Bal.	25,000		
Adj.	2,900		
Bal.	27,900		

Wages Payable

	−		+
		Adj.	2,900

Accrued wages (owed but not yet paid), $2,900. (Add to both accounts.)

This chapter introduces two more adjusting entries:

1. **Unearned revenue.** This adjustment could apply to a merchandising, manufacturing, or service business.
2. **Merchandise inventory.** This adjustment is used exclusively for a merchandising business. We will show adjusting entries for both the periodic and perpetual inventory methods.

ADJUSTMENT FOR UNEARNED REVENUE

Learning Objective 1 Prepare an adjustment for unearned revenue.

Another type of adjusting entry occurs when previously unearned revenues are earned. **Unearned revenue** occurs when cash is received in advanced for goods that will be delivered or services that will be performed later. This entry could pertain to a service business as well as to a merchandising or manufacturing business. Frequently, cash is received in advance for services to be performed in the future. For example, a professional sports team sells tickets in advance, a concert association sells season tickets in advance, a magazine publisher sells subscriptions in advance, and an insurance company receives premiums in advance. According to the **revenue recognition principle**, revenues are recorded when they are earned, which may occur at a time different from when cash is received. Therefore, if the cash amounts received by each of these organizations are earned during the present fiscal period, the amounts should be credited to revenue accounts. On the other hand, if some or all of the amounts received are *not* earned during the current fiscal period, the amounts should be credited to unearned revenue accounts. **An unearned revenue account is classified as a liability** because an organization is liable for (owes) the amount received in advance until it is earned.

To illustrate, assume that on April 1, Ressor Publishing Company receives $73,000 in cash for subscriptions paid in advance and records them originally as debits to Cash and credits to Unearned Subscriptions. At the end of the year, Ressor finds that $32,400 of the subscriptions has been earned. Accordingly, Ressor's accountant makes an adjusting entry, debiting Unearned Subscriptions and crediting Subscriptions Income. In other words, the accountant takes the earned portion out of Unearned Subscriptions and adds it to Subscriptions Income. The T accounts below show how this situation would be recorded.

Cash

	+	–	
Apr. 1	73,000		

Unearned Subscriptions

	–	+	
Adj.	**32,400**	Apr. 1	73,000
		Bal.	40,600

Subscriptions Income

	–	+	
		Adj.	**32,400**

As another example, suppose Trey's Landscape Supply offers a how-to course in landscape maintenance. On November 1, Trey's Landscape Supply receives $2,400 in fees for a three-month course. Because Trey's Landscape Supply's fiscal period ends on December 31, only two of the three months' worth of fees received in advance will be earned during this fiscal period. Therefore, Trey's Landscape Supply's accountant records the transaction as a debit to Cash of $2,400 and a credit to Unearned Course Fees of $2,400. Unearned Course Fees is a liability account because Trey's Landscape Supply must complete the how-to course or refund a portion of the money it collected. **Any account beginning with the word *Unearned* is a liability.**

On December 31, because two months' worth of course fees have now been earned, Trey's Landscape Supply's accountant makes an adjusting entry to transfer $1,600 ($^2/_3$ of $2,400) from Unearned Course Fees to Course Fees Income. T accounts for the entries look like this:

Cash

	+	−	
Nov. 1	2,400		

Unearned Course Fees

	−	+	
Adj.	1,600	Nov. 1	2,400
		Bal.	800

Course Fees Income

	−	+	
		Adj.	1,600

ADJUSTMENT FOR MERCHANDISE INVENTORY USING THE PERIODIC INVENTORY SYSTEM

Under the periodic inventory system, we do not make an entry in the Merchandise Inventory account until an actual **physical inventory** or count of the stock of goods on hand has been taken. Instead, we record the purchase of merchandise as a debit to Purchases for the cost amount and the sale of the merchandise as a credit to Sales for the amount of the selling price. Finally, after a physical count of merchandise has been taken, one method of adjusting inventory is to make two entries to record the dollar amount of the inventory. The first adjusting entry is to remove the beginning inventory. The second entry is to enter the ending inventory.

Learning Objective 2 Prepare an adjustment for merchandise inventory under the periodic inventory system.

Consider this example. A firm has a Merchandise Inventory balance of $183,000, which represents the cost of the inventory at the beginning of the fiscal period. At the end of the fiscal period, the firm takes an actual count of the stock on hand and determines the cost of the ending inventory to be $186,000. Naturally, in any business, goods are constantly being bought, sold, and replaced. The cost of the ending inventory is larger than the cost of the beginning inventory because the firm bought more than it sold. When we adjust the Merchandise Inventory account, we place the new figure of $186,000 in the account. This method requires two steps.

Remember

The Income Summary account is the same Income Summary account we used to record closing entries for service businesses. Income Summary now has the extra function of being the balancing or offsetting account in the adjustment of Merchandise Inventory.

STEP 1. Eliminate the amount of the beginning inventory from the Merchandise Inventory account by transferring the amount into Income Summary. (Remove the beginning inventory.)

Merchandise Inventory

	+	−	
Bal.	183,000	Adj.	183,000 ①

Income Summary

Adj.	183,000 ①		

We debit Income Summary and then credit Merchandise Inventory.

STEP 2. Enter the ending or latest physical count of Merchandise Inventory because you must record on the books the cost of the asset remaining on hand. (Enter the ending inventory.)

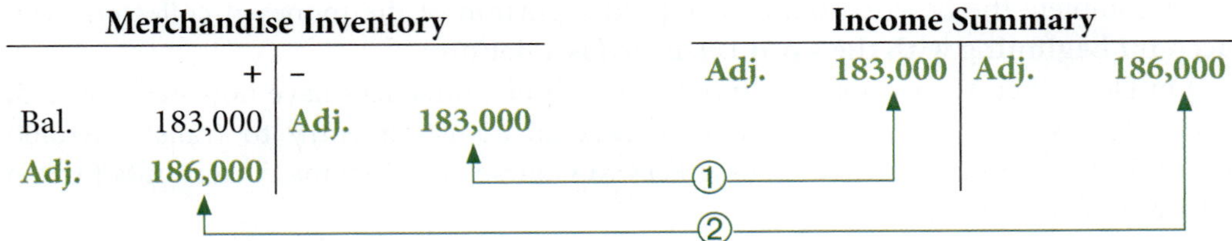

In Step 2, we debit Merchandise Inventory (recording the asset on the plus side of the account) and credit Income Summary.

The reason for adjusting the Merchandise Inventory account in these two steps is that both the beginning and ending amounts appear as distinct figures in the Income Statement columns of a work sheet, and these columns are used as the basis for preparing the income statement.

Whitewater Raft Supply's chart of accounts follows. Notice that Whitewater Raft Supply has an account titled Unearned Course Fees. In addition to selling rafting supplies, Whitewater Raft Supply provides courses to small business owners on how to start and run a successful rafting company. If the small business owner pays in advance for the course before it is offered, the receipt of cash is recorded as Unearned Course Fees. The account number arrangement will be discussed in Chapter 12.

Assets (100–199)
111 Cash
112 Notes Receivable
113 Accounts Receivable
114 Merchandise Inventory
116 Prepaid Insurance
121 Land
122 Building
123 Accumulated Depreciation, Building
124 Equipment
125 Accumulated Depreciation, Equipment

Liabilities (200–299)
211 Notes Payable
212 Accounts Payable
213 Wages Payable
217 Unearned Course Fees
221 Mortgage Payable

Owner's Equity (300–399)
311 J. Conner, Capital
312 J. Conner, Drawing
313 Income Summary

Revenue (400–499)
411 Sales
412 Sales Returns and Allowances
413 Sales Discounts
421 Course Fees Income
422 Interest Income

Cost of Goods Sold (500–599)
511 Purchases
512 Purchases Returns and Allowances
513 Purchases Discounts
514 Freight In

Expenses (600–699)
611 Wages Expense
622 Supplies Expense
623 Insurance Expense
624 Depreciation Expense, Building
625 Depreciation Expense, Equipment
626 Property Tax Expense
634 Interest Expense

In the Real World

Companies such as Walmart utilize RFID (radio frequency identification) systems to improve inventory accuracy. RFID systems help retailers identify and track their merchandise. By using RFID technology, Walmart has improved inventory accuracy, noting the need for fewer manual inventory adjustments and eliminating some unnecessary inventory. When retailers have better control over their merchandise inventory, they are able to maintain more affordable prices for their customers.

Before we demonstrate how to record adjustments, let's look at the trial balance section of Whitewater Raft Supply's work sheet (Figure 1).

Figure 1
Trial balance section of Whitewater Raft Supply's work sheet

	A	B	C	D	E
1	Whitewater Raft Supply				
2	Work Sheet				
3	For Month Ended December 31, 20--				
4					
5		TRIAL BALANCE		ADJUSTMENTS	
6	ACCOUNT NAME	DEBIT	CREDIT	DEBIT	CREDIT
7	Cash	24,154.00			
8	Notes Receivable	4,000.00			
9	Accounts Receivable	29,546.00			
10	Merchandise Inventory	67,000.00			
11	Supplies	1,540.00			
12	Prepaid Insurance	960.00			
13	Land	122,100.00			
14	Building	129,000.00			
15	Accumulated Depreciation, Building		51,000.00		
16	Equipment	33,100.00			
17	Accumulated Depreciation, Equipment		16,400.00		
18	Notes Payable		36,600.00		
19	Accounts Payable		3,300.00		
20	Unearned Course Fees		1,200.00		
21	Mortgage Payable		7,800.00		
22	J. Conner, Capital		253,774.00		
23	J. Conner, Drawing	77,000.00			
24	Sales		257,180.00		
25	Sales Returns and Allowances	940.00			
26	Sales Discounts	1,980.00			
27	Interest Income		220.00		
28	Purchases	87,840.00			
29	Purchases Returns and Allowances		932.00		
30	Purchases Discounts		1,348.00		
31	Freight In	2,360.00			
32	Wages Expense	45,900.00			
33	Property Tax Expense	1,860.00			
34	Interest Expense	474.00			
35		629,754.00	629,754.00		
36					
37					

Sheet1 Sheet2 Sheet3

DATA FOR THE ADJUSTMENTS

Learning Objective 3 Record adjustment data in a work sheet including merchandise inventory, unearned revenue, supplies used, expired insurance, depreciation, and accrued wages or salaries.

Listing the adjustment data appears to be a relatively minor task. In a business situation, however, someone must take actual physical counts of the inventories and match them up with costs. Someone must check insurance policies to determine the amount of insurance that has expired. In addition, it is important to determine the actual supplies on hand versus those that have been used. Finally, someone must systematically write off, or depreciate, the *used-up* portion of costs on fixed assets, such as buildings and equipment.

Here are the adjustment data for Whitewater Raft Supply. We will show the adjustments recorded in T accounts.

a–b. Ending merchandise inventory, $64,800.

Merchandise Inventory

	+	–	
Bal.	67,000	(a) Adj.	67,000
(b) Adj.	64,800		

Income Summary

(a) Adj.	67,000	(b) Adj.	64,800

Remember

The ending balance of the Supplies account after the adjusting entry equals the amount of supplies *on hand* in the ending supplies inventory.

c. Course fees earned, $800.

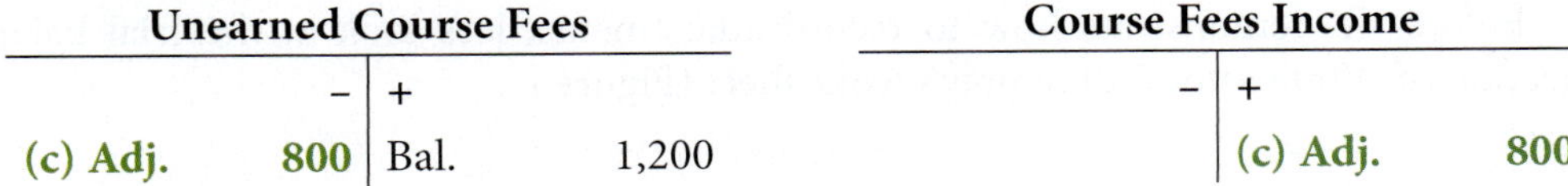

Unearned Course Fees

	–	+	
(c) Adj.	800	Bal.	1,200

Course Fees Income

	–	+	
		(c) Adj.	800

d. Supplies used, $1,125.

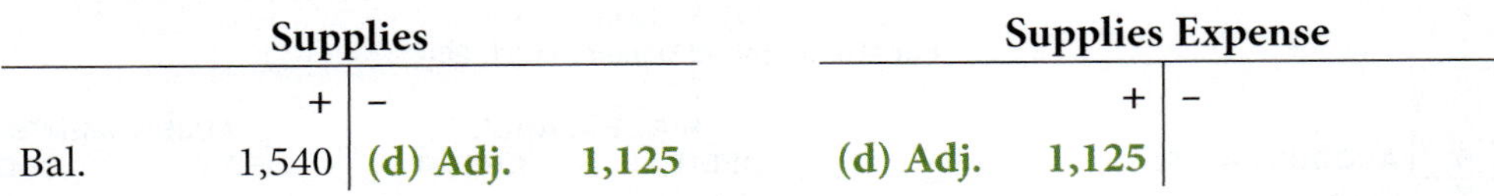

Supplies

	+	–	
Bal.	1,540	(d) Adj.	1,125

Supplies Expense

	+	–	
(d) Adj.	1,125		

e. Insurance expired, $520.

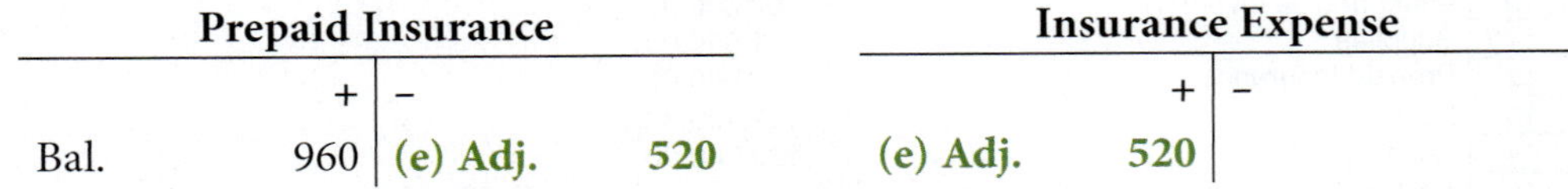

Prepaid Insurance

	+	–	
Bal.	960	(e) Adj.	520

Insurance Expense

	+	–	
(e) Adj.	520		

f. Additional year's depreciation of building, $3,500.

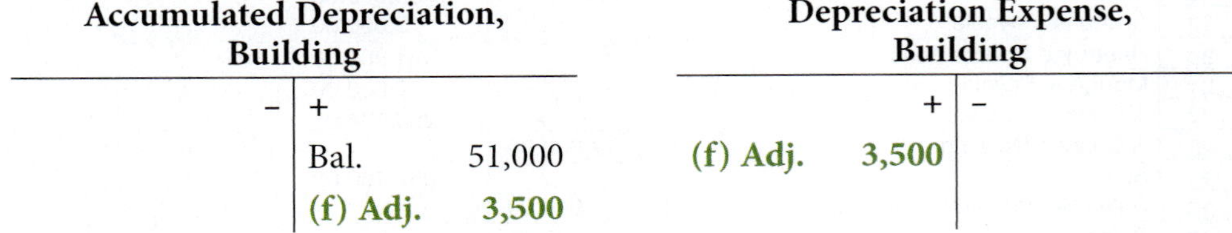

Accumulated Depreciation, Building

	–	+	
		Bal.	51,000
		(f) Adj.	3,500

Depreciation Expense, Building

	+	–	
(f) Adj.	3,500		

g. Additional year's depreciation of equipment, $4,900.

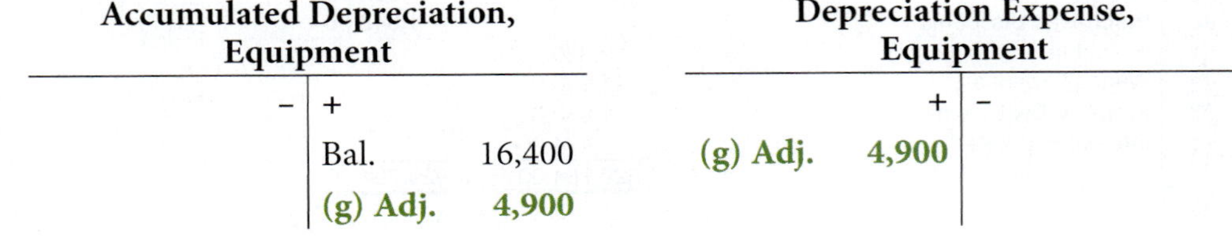

Accumulated Depreciation, Equipment

	–	+	
		Bal.	16,400
		(g) Adj.	4,900

Depreciation Expense, Equipment

	+	–	
(g) Adj.	4,900		

h. Wages owed but not paid to employees at end of year, $1,030

Wages Payable				Wages Expense			
−	+					+	−
	(h) Adj.	1,030		Bal.		45,900	
				(h) Adj.		1,030	

We now record these in the Adjustments columns of the work sheet, using the same letters to identify the adjustments. (See Figure 2.)

Figure 2

Trial balance and adjustments sections of Whitewater Raft Supply's work sheet

	A	B	C	D	E
1		Whitewater Raft Supply			
2		Work Sheet			
3		For Month Ended December 31, 20--			
4					
5		TRIAL BALANCE		ADJUSTMENTS	
6	ACCOUNT NAME	DEBIT	CREDIT	DEBIT	CREDIT
7	Cash	24,154.00			
8	Notes Receivable	4,000.00			
9	Accounts Receivable	29,546.00			
10	Merchandise Inventory	67,000.00		(b) 64,800.00	(a) 67,000.00
11	Supplies	1,540.00			(d) 1,125.00
12	Prepaid Insurance	960.00			(e) 520.00
13	Land	122,100.00			
14	Building	129,000.00			
15	Accumulated Depreciation, Building		51,000.00		(f) 3,500.00
16	Equipment	33,100.00			
17	Accumulated Depreciation, Equipment		16,400.00		(g) 4,900.00
18	Notes Payable		36,600.00		
19	Accounts Payable		3,300.00		
20	Unearned Course Fees		1,200.00	(c) 800.00	
21	Mortage Payable		7,800.00		
22	J. Conner, Capital		253,774.00		
23	J. Conner, Drawing	77,000.00			
24	Sales		257,180.00		
25	Sales Returns and Alllowances	940.00			
26	Sales Discounts	1,980.00			
27	Interest Income		220.00		
28	Purchases	87,840.00			
29	Purchases Returns and Allowances		932.00		
30	Purchases Discounts		1,348.00		
31	Freight In	2,360.00			
32	Wages Expense	45,900.00		(h) 1,030.00	
33	Property Tax Expense	1,860.00			
34	Interest Expense	474.00			
35		629,754.00	629,754.00		
36	Income Summary			(a) 67,000.00	(b) 64,800.00
37	Course Fees Income				(c) 800.00
38	Supplies Expense			(d) 1,125.00	
39	Insurance Expense			(e) 520.00	
40	Depreciation Expense, Building			(f) 3,500.00	
41	Depreciation Expense, Equipment			(g) 4,900.00	
42	Wages Payable				(h) 1,030.00
43				143,675.00	143,675.00
44					
45					

Sheet1 Sheet2 Sheet3

COMPLETION OF THE WORK SHEET

Learning Objective 4 Complete the work sheet.

Previously, in introducing work sheets, we included the Adjusted Trial Balance columns as a means of verifying that the accounts were in balance after the adjusting entries were recorded. At this time, to reduce the number of columns in the work sheet, we will eliminate the Adjusted Trial Balance columns. The account balances after the adjusting entries will be carried directly into the Income Statement and Balance Sheet columns.

Figure 3 shows the completed work sheet.

Figure 3
Completed work sheet for Whitewater Raft Supply

	A	B	C	D	E
1				Whitewater Raft Supply	
2				Work Sheet	
3				For Month Ended December 31, 20--	
4					
5		TRIAL BALANCE		ADJUSTMENTS	
6	ACCOUNT NAME	DEBIT	CREDIT	DEBIT	CREDIT
7	Cash	24,154.00			
8	Notes receivable	4,000.00			
9	Accounts Receivable	29,546.00			
10	Merchandise Inventory	67,000.00		(b) 64,800.00	(a) 67,000.00
11	Supplies	1,540.00			(d) 1,125.00
12	Prepaid Insurance	960.00			(e) 520.00
13	Land	122,100.00			
14	Building	129,000.00			
15	Accumulated Depreciation, Building		51,000.00		(f) 3,500.00
16	Equipment	33,100.00			
17	Accumulated Depreciation, Equipment		16,400.00		(g) 4,900.00
18	Notes Payable		36,600.00		
19	Accounts Payable		3,300.00		
20	Unearned Course Fees		1,200.00	(c) 800.00	
21	Mortgage Payable		7,800.00		
22	J. Conner, Capital		253,774.00		
23	J. Conner, Drawing	77,000.00			
24	Sales		257,180.00		
25	Sales Returns and Alllowances	940.00			
26	Sales Discounts	1,980.00			
27	Interest Income		220.00		
28	Purchases	87,840.00			
29	Purchases Returns and Allowances		932.00		
30	Purchases Discounts		1,348.00		
31	Freight In	2,360.00			
32	Wages Expense	45,900.00		(h) 1,030.00	
33	Property Tax Expense	1,860.00			
34	Interest Expense	474.00			
35		629,754.00	629,754.00		
36	Income Summary			(a) 67,000.00	(b) 64,800.00
37	Course Fees Income				(c) 800.00
38	Supplies Expense			(d) 1,125.00	
39	Insurance Expense			(e) 520.00	
40	Depreciation Expense, Building			(f) 3,500.00	
41	Depreciation Expense, Equipment			(g) 4,900.00	
42	Wages Payable				(h) 1,030.00
43				143,675.00	143,675.00
44	Net Income				
45					
46					

Sheet1 Sheet2 Sheet3

Observe in particular the way we carry forward the figures for Merchandise Inventory and Income Summary. **Income Summary is the only account in which we don't combine the debit and credit figures. Instead, we carry them into the Income Statement columns in Figure 3 as two distinct figures—move the two figures as a pair to the Income Statement columns.** The reason for moving them as a pair is that both figures are needed for completion of the income statement. The debit amount in Income Summary in the Income Statement Debit column is the *beginning* merchandise inventory. The credit amount in Income Summary in the Income Statement Credit column is the *ending* merchandise inventory. We will talk about this topic in greater detail in Chapter 12 when we formulate the income statement for a merchandising entity.

F	G	H	I
INCOME STATEMENT		BALANCE SHEET	
DEBIT	CREDIT	DEBIT	CREDIT
		24,154.00	
		4,000.00	
		29,546.00	
		64,800.00	
		415.00	
		440.00	
		122,100.00	
		129,000.00	
			54,500.00
		33,100.00	
			21,300.00
			36,600.00
			3,300.00
			400.00
			7,800.00
			253,774.00
		77,000.00	
	257,180.00		
940.00			
1,980.00			
	220.00		
87,840.00			
	932.00		
	1,348.00		
2,360.00			
46,930.00			
1,860.00			
474.00			
67,000.00	64,800.00		
	800.00		
1,125.00			
520.00			
3,500.00			
4,900.00			
			1,030.00
219,429.00	325,280.00	484,555.00	378,704.00
105,851.00			105,851.00
325,280.00	325,280.00	484,555.00	484,555.00

When completing a work sheet, complete one stage at a time before moving to the next stage:

STEP 1. Record the trial balance and make sure the total of the Debit column equals the total of the Credit column before going to the adjustments.

STEP 2. Record the adjustments in the Adjustments columns, and make sure the totals are equal before extending the new totals into the Income Statement and Balance Sheet columns.

STEP 3. Complete the Income Statement and Balance Sheet columns by recording the adjusted balance of each account. The accounts and classifications pertaining to a merchandising business using the periodic inventory system appear in these columns:

Income Statement		Balance Sheet	
Debit	**Credit**	**Debit**	**Credit**
Expenses + Sales Returns and Allowances + Sales Discounts + Purchases + Freight In + Income Summary	Revenues + Purchases Returns and Allowances + Purchases Discounts + Income Summary	Assets + Drawing	Accumulated Depreciation + Liabilities + Capital

Study the following example of a work sheet, noting in particular the way we treat these accounts for a merchandising business using the periodic inventory system.

	Location on Work Sheet			
	Income Statement		Balance Sheet	
Account Name	**Debit**	**Credit**	**Debit**	**Credit**
Merchandise Inventory			64,800.00	
Sales		257,180.00		
Sales Returns and Allowances	940.00			
Sales Discounts	1,980.00			
Purchases	87,840.00			
Purchases Returns and Allowances		932.00		
Purchases Discounts		1,348.00		
Freight In	2,360.00			
Income Summary	67,000.00	64,800.00		

ADJUSTING ENTRIES USING THE PERIODIC INVENTORY SYSTEM

Figure 4 shows the adjusting entries as taken from the Adjustments columns of the work sheet and recorded in the general journal.

Learning Objective

5 Journalize the adjusting entries for a merchandising business under the periodic inventory system.

Figure 4
Adjusting entries for Whitewater Raft Supply

GENERAL JOURNAL — Page 96

Date		Description	Post. Ref.	Debit	Credit
20--		Adjusting Entries			
Dec.	31	Income Summary		67 0 0 0 00	
(a)		Merchandise Inventory			67 0 0 0 00
(b)	31	Merchandise Inventory		64 8 0 0 00	
		Income Summary			64 8 0 0 00
(c)	31	Unearned Course Fees		8 0 0 00	
		Course Fees Income			8 0 0 00
(d)	31	Supplies Expense		1 1 2 5 00	
		Supplies			1 1 2 5 00
(e)	31	Insurance Expense		5 2 0 00	
		Prepaid Insurance			5 2 0 00
(f)	31	Depreciation Expense, Building		3 5 0 0 00	
		Accumulated Depreciation, Building			3 5 0 0 00
(g)	31	Depreciation Expense, Equipment		4 9 0 0 00	
		Accumulated Depreciation,			
		Equipment			4 9 0 0 00
(h)	31	Wages Expense		1 0 3 0 00	
		Wages Payable			1 0 3 0 00

ADJUSTMENT FOR MERCHANDISE INVENTORY UNDER THE PERPETUAL INVENTORY SYSTEM

Before we demonstrate how to record the adjustment for the perpetual inventory system, let's look at a portion of the trial balance section of Whitewater Raft Supply's work sheet (Figure 5 on the next page) assuming the company used the perpetual inventory system.

Under the perpetual inventory system, a business continually maintains a record of each item in stock. **When merchandise is purchased, the Merchandise Inventory account (not the Purchases account) is debited for the cost of the merchandise and Accounts Payable or Cash is credited. When merchandise is sold, two journal entries are required. First, debit Accounts Receivable or Cash and credit Sales. Second, debit the Cost of Goods Sold account for the cost of merchandise and credit the Merchandise Inventory account for the same amount.**

Learning Objective

Prepare and journalize the adjusting entry for merchandise inventory under the perpetual inventory system.

Figure 5
A portion of the trial balance section of Whitewater Raft Supply's work sheet (perpetual inventory system)

	A	B	C
24	Sales		257,180.00
25	Sales Returns and Allowances	940.00	
26	Sales Discounts	1,980.00	
27	Interest Income		220.00
28	Cost of Goods Sold	90,120.00	
29	Wages Expense	46,930.00	

Sheet1 Sheet2 Sheet3

Many firms use electronic devices to keep track of stock items under the perpetual inventory system. For example, when a sale is made at a supermarket checkout counter, as the bar code on each item is scanned, the price and stock number are recorded. The cash register is connected to a computer that updates the inventory record and records the cost of the item. So the business perpetually (always) knows how much inventory it should have on hand.

However, to verify the inventory record, a physical count should be taken from time to time. The amount shown by the physical count may be less than the computer record as a result of errors, shrinkage, or shoplifting. This difference is called **inventory shrinkage**, and an adjusting entry must be made. This entry is a debit to the Cost of Goods Sold account (an expense account) and a credit to the Merchandise Inventory account. The opposite is true if the physical count is more than the computer record; the adjusting entry would be a debit to Merchandise Inventory and a credit to Cost of Goods Sold.

ADJUSTING ENTRY UNDER THE PERPETUAL INVENTORY SYSTEM

Here are examples of entries under the perpetual inventory system when the physical count does not agree with the computer record of merchandise inventory. Assume a beginning inventory of $75,000.

1. Bought merchandise on account, $50,000.

Merchandise Inventory

	+	–	
Bal.	75,000		
(1)	50,000		

Accounts Payable

	–	+	
		(1)	50,000

2. Sold merchandise for $84,000 having a cost of $60,300.

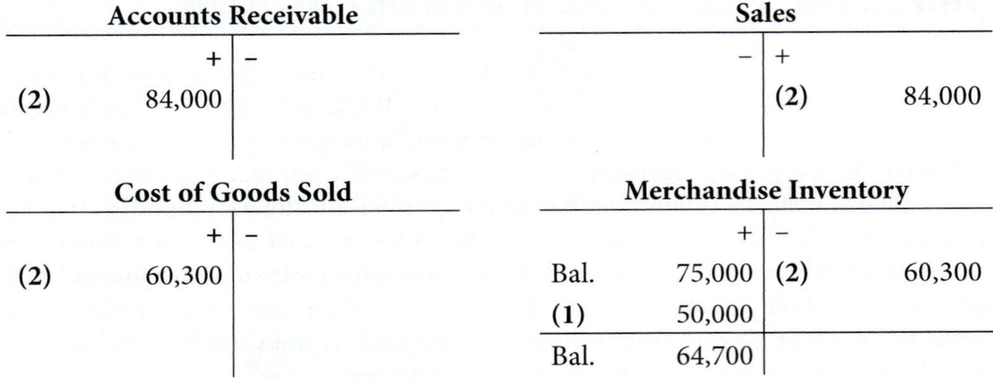

Accounts Receivable

	+	–	
(2)	84,000		

Sales

	–	+	
		(2)	84,000

Cost of Goods Sold

	+	–	
(2)	60,300		

Merchandise Inventory

	+	–	
Bal.	75,000	(2)	60,300
(1)	50,000		
Bal.	64,700		

3a. The adjusting entry for the perpetual inventory system is computed by determining the difference between the computer record and the physical count for ending inventory, $63,200. The recorded balance of the perpetual inventory is $64,700 ($75,000 + $50,000 − $60,300).

The difference of $1,500 ($64,700 − $63,200) is the adjustment amount under the perpetual inventory system. The adjusting entry required to record the $1,500 loss involves a debit to Cost of Goods Sold and a credit to Merchandise Inventory (shown in Figure 6).

Remember

The ending inventory of one period becomes the beginning inventory of the next period.

Cost of Goods Sold

	+		−
(2)	60,300		
(3) Adj.	1,500		
Bal.	61,800		

Merchandise Inventory

	+		−
Bal.	75,000	(2)	60,300
(1)	50,000	(3) Adj.	1,500
Bal.	63,200		

3b. Suppose, on the other hand, that the physical count of the stock of merchandise ($65,200) was more than the recorded amount ($64,700). The adjusting entry would need to increase the Merchandise Inventory account with a debit to Merchandise Inventory and corresponding credit to Cost of Goods Sold (account) for the difference ($65,200 − $64,700 = $500). (Refer to Figure 6.)

On the income statement under the perpetual inventory system, the Cost of Goods Sold account is listed under one line rather than there being a Cost of Goods Sold section. The following is a comparison of income statements under the periodic and perpetual inventory systems assuming scenario 3a from above.

Periodic

Sales (net)		$84,000
Cost of Goods Sold:		
Merchandise Inventory (beginning)	$ 75,000	
Purchases (net)	50,000	
Cost of Goods Available for Sale	$125,000	
Less Merchandise Inventory (ending)	63,200	
Cost of Goods Sold		61,800
Gross Profit		$22,200

Perpetual

Sales (net)	$84,000
Cost of Goods Sold	61,800
Gross Profit	$22,200

GENERAL JOURNAL Page 96

Date		Description	Post. Ref.	Debit	Credit
20--		Adjusting Entries			
Dec.	31	Cost of Goods Sold		1 5 0 0 00	
3a.		Merchandise Inventory			1 5 0 0 00
3b.	31	Merchandise Inventory		5 0 0 00	
		Cost of Goods Sold			5 0 0 00

Figure 6
Adjusting entry for ending inventory under the perpetual inventory system

YOU Make the Call

You and a college friend have decided to start a merchandising business that markets green products: people- and earth-friendly products for the home and business. You have identified approximately 100 different items, including bath soaps, home cleaning products, plant-friendly foods and pesticides, and a line of organic canned foods. Both of you have taken accounting courses and are trying to decide whether to use the periodic or perpetual inventory system. What are the advantages, disadvantages, and implications of each system?

SOLUTION

For simplicity, using the periodic inventory system would be the way to go. It is less complicated than the perpetual inventory system, requires fewer accounting entries, and is less costly than the perpetual inventory system because you do not have to buy software, hardware, or other electronic inventory tracking devices. However, the perpetual inventory system offers a higher degree of control. It is a better way to manage proper inventory levels because it provides up-to-the-minute data for determining purchasing needs—an advantage that may very well outweigh the disadvantages.

Accounting with QuickBooks®

ACCOUNTING WITH QuickBooks®

Adjusting Entries for a Merchandising Company

Learning Objective

1 Record adjusting entries for a merchandising company in QuickBooks.

Learning Objective

After you have completed this section, you will be able to do the following with QuickBooks:

1. Record adjusting entries for a merchandising company in QuickBooks.

As you originally learned in Chapter 4, adjusting entries are recorded in the same manner as general journal entries. The only difference is that the *Adjusting Entry* box is checked in the journal entry screen as shown in Figure Q2. Let's review how to record adjusting entries, using the following adjustment data for Whitewater Raft Supply.

Adjusting Entry (d) from page 579. As of December 31, 20--, Whitewater Raft Supply used $1,125 worth of supplies.

To record the adjusting entry, follow the steps in Figures Q1 and Q2.

STEP 1. Click the **Company** tab. Then select **Make General Journal Entries**.

Company	Customers	Vendors	Employees
Home Page			
Company Snapshot			
Calendar			
Documents			
Lead Center			
Company Information...			
Advanced Service Administration...			
Set Up Users and Passwords			
Customer Credit Card Protection...			
Set Closing Date...			
Planning & Budgeting			
To Do List			
Reminders			
Alerts Manager			
Chart of Accounts			Ctrl+A
Make General Journal Entries...			
Manage Currency			
Enter Vehicle Mileage...			
Prepare Letters with Envelopes			
Export Company File to QuickBooks Online			

Figure Q1
Make general journal entries.

STEP 2. Select or enter the **date**. The date used in Figure Q2 is December 31, 20- -.

STEP 3. Enter the **Entry No.** In Figure Q2, ADJ20- -.12d is used for the **Entry No.** The journal entry and adjusting journal entry numbering system can vary by company. QuickBooks has the option to automatically assign the **Entry No.**, or a company may choose to use its own system. For Whitewater Raft Supply, the **Entry No.** used for the adjusting entry in Figure Q2 is ADJ (for adjustment), followed by the year, then the month, and finally the adjustment transaction (d).

STEP 4. Check the **Adjusting Entry** box.

STEP 5. Select the **Debit Account**, enter the **Debit Amount**, and then enter the **Description** in the **Memo** field.

STEP 6. Select the **Credit Account**. Then enter the **Credit Amount**. The **Memo** field should automatically appear with the information from **STEP 5**. If not, manually enter the **Description** in the **Credit Account Memo** field.

QuickBooks Tip

QuickBooks may automatically complete the credit amount in the journal. For journal entries involving multiple accounts, the suggested credit amount could require modification.

STEP 7. Select **Save & New** to save the transaction and continue recording adjusting entries or **Save & Close** to save the transaction and leave the general journal application.

Figure Q2
Adjusting journal entry

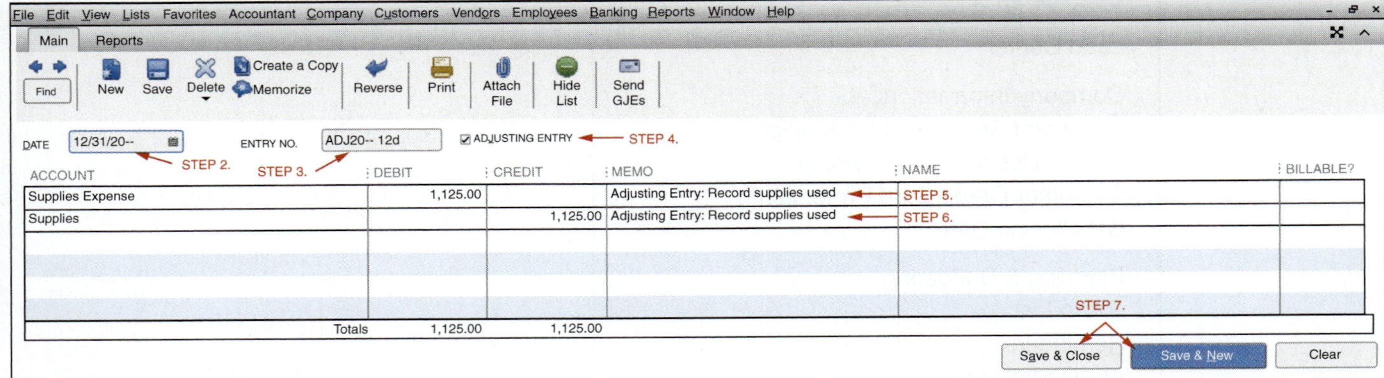

Chapter Review

Study and Practice

Learning Objective 1 Prepare an adjustment for unearned revenue.

According to the **revenue recognition principle**, revenues are recorded when they are earned. The receipt of cash and the earning of revenue may occur at different times. For revenue received in advance, an adjustment is required to separate the portion that has been earned from the portion that is unearned. We assume that the amount of cash received in advance was originally recorded as **unearned revenue**, which is a liability. In the adjusting entry for the amount actually earned, debit the unearned revenue account (for example, Unearned Course Fees) and credit the revenue account (such as Course Fees Income).

PRACTICE EXERCISE 1

On June 1, Thompson Company receives $148,540 in cash for subscriptions covering two years. At the end of the year, December 31, Thompson finds that $94,302 of the subscriptions have been earned. Record in general journal form (a) the original receipt of cash on June 1 and (b) the year-end adjusting entry for Thompson Company.

PRACTICE EXERCISE 1 • SOLUTION

GENERAL JOURNAL — Page ___

Date		Description	Post. Ref.	Debit	Credit
20--					
June	1	Cash		148 5 4 0 00	
(a)		Unearned Subscriptions			148 5 4 0 00
		Adjusting Entries			
Dec.	31	Unearned Subscriptions		94 3 0 2 00	
(b)		Subscriptions Income			94 3 0 2 00

2 Prepare an adjustment for merchandise inventory under the periodic inventory system. **Learning Objective**

The adjustment for merchandise inventory under the periodic inventory system requires two adjusting entries. In the first adjusting entry (to remove the beginning inventory), debit Income Summary and credit Merchandise Inventory. In the second adjusting entry (to enter the ending inventory), debit Merchandise Inventory and credit Income Summary.

PRACTICE EXERCISE 2

Morkin Company's beginning inventory amounted to $264,072. A physical count at the end of the year reveals that the ending inventory amount is $267,322. Record the necessary adjustments in the T accounts.

PRACTICE EXERCISE 2 • SOLUTION

Merchandise Inventory

	+	–
Bal.	264,072	(a) Adj. 264,072
(b) Adj.	267,322	

Income Summary

(a) Adj. 264,072	(b) Adj. 267,322

Record adjustment data in a work sheet including merchandise inventory, unearned revenue, supplies used, expired insurance, depreciation, and accrued wages or salaries. **Learning Objective**

In the Adjustments columns of the work sheet, record the following adjusting entries:

For merchandise inventory: Debit Income Summary and credit Merchandise Inventory (to remove the beginning inventory); then debit Merchandise Inventory and credit Income Summary (to enter the ending inventory).

For unearned revenue: Debit the unearned revenue account and credit the revenue account (to record revenue earned).

For supplies used: Debit Supplies Expense and credit Supplies.

For expired insurance: Debit Insurance Expense and credit Prepaid Insurance.

For depreciation: Debit Depreciation Expense and credit Accumulated Depreciation.

For accrued wages or salaries: Debit Wages Expense or Salaries Expense and credit Wages Payable or Salaries Payable.

PRACTICE EXERCISE 3

Following are the adjustment data for Majors Company:

a–b. Merchandise inventory (ending), $64,800.
c. Course fees earned, $1,800.
d. Supplies inventory (on hand), $2,415.
e. Insurance expired, $1,520.
f. Depreciation of building, $13,500.
g. Depreciation of equipment, $5,900.
h. Wages accrued, $2,030.

Record these data in the Adjustments column of the following work sheet.

	A	B	C	D	E
1	Majors Company				
2	Work Sheet				
3	For Year Ended December 31, 20--				
4					
5		TRIAL BALANCE		ADJUSTMENTS	
6	ACCOUNT NAME	DEBIT	CREDIT	DEBIT	CREDIT
7	Cash	23,010.00			
8	Notes Receivable	6,000.00			
9	Accounts Receivable	28,540.00			
10	Merchandise Inventory	68,000.00			
11	Supplies	12,440.00			
12	Prepaid Insurance	2,110.00			
13	Land	120,100.00			
14	Building	128,000.00			
15	Accumulated Depreciation, Building		50,000.00		
16	Equipment	34,100.00			
17	Accumulated Depreciation, Equipment		19,600.00		
18	Notes Payable		34,600.00		
19	Accounts Payable		4,300.00		
20	Unearned Course Fees		2,200.00		
21	Mortgage Payable		8,800.00		
22	R. L. Majors, Capital		252,774.00		
23	R. L. Majors, Drawing	65,000.00			
24	Sales		253,980.00		
25	Sales Returns and Alllowances	940.00			
26	Sales Discounts	1,880.00			
27	Interest Income		1,220.00		
28	Purchases	88,840.00			
29	Purchases Returns and Allowances		832.00		
30	Purchases Discounts		1,448.00		
31	Freight In	2,460.00			
32	Wages Expense	44,900.00			
33	Property Tax Expense	2,860.00			
34	Interest Expense	574.00			
35		629,754.00	629,754.00		
36	Income Summary				
37	Course Fees Income				
38	Supplies Expense				
39	Insurance Expense				
40	Depreciation Expense, Building				
41	Depreciation Expense, Equipment				
42	Wages Payable				
43					
44					

Sheet1 Sheet2 Sheet3

PRACTICE EXERCISE 3 • SOLUTION

	A	B	C	D	E
1	Majors Company				
2	Work Sheet				
3	For Year Ended December 31, 20--				
4					
5		TRIAL BALANCE		ADJUSTMENTS	
6	ACCOUNT NAME	DEBIT	CREDIT	DEBIT	CREDIT
7	Cash	23,010.00			
8	Notes Receivable	6,000.00			
9	Accounts Receivable	28,540.00			
10	Merchandise Inventory	68,000.00		(b) 64,800.00	(a) 68,000.00
11	Supplies	12,440.00			(d) 10,025.00
12	Prepaid Insurance	2,110.00			(e) 1,520.00
13	Land	120,100.00			
14	Building	128,000.00			
15	Accumulated Depreciation, Building		50,000.00		(f) 13,500.00
16	Equipment	34,100.00			
17	Accumulated Depreciation, Equipment		19,600.00		(g) 5,900.00
18	Notes Payable		34,600.00		
19	Accounts Payable		4,300.00		
20	Unearned Course Fees		2,200.00	(c) 1,800.00	
21	Mortgage Payable		8,800.00		
22	R. L. Majors, Capital		252,774.00		
23	R. L. Majors, Drawing	65,000.00			
24	Sales		253,980.00		
25	Sales Returns and Allowances	940.00			
26	Sales Discounts	1,880.00			
27	Interest Income		1,220.00		
28	Purchases	88,840.00			
29	Purchases Returns and Allowances		832.00		
30	Purchases Discounts		1,448.00		
31	Freight In	2,460.00			
32	Wages Expense	44,900.00		(h) 2,030.00	
33	Property Tax Expense	2,860.00			
34	Interest Expense	574.00			
35		629,754.00	629,754.00		
36	Income Summary			(a) 68,000.00	(b) 64,800.00
37	Course Fees Income				(c) 1,800.00
38	Supplies Expense			(d) 10,025.00	
39	Insurance Expense			(e) 1,520.00	
40	Depreciation Expense, Building			(f) 13,500.00	
41	Depreciation Expense, Equipment			(g) 5,900.00	
42	Wages Payable				(h) 2,030.00
43				167,575.00	167,575.00
44					

Sheet1 Sheet2 Sheet3

Complete the work sheet.

Learning Objective

Carry the Income Summary account from the Adjustments columns into the Income Statement columns as two separate figures. For merchandise inventory, record the amount of the ending inventory in the Balance Sheet Debit column. For unearned revenue, record the unearned revenue account in the Balance Sheet Credit column and the revenue account in the Income Statement Credit column.

PRACTICE EXERCISE 4

Complete the Income Statement and Balance Sheet columns of the work sheet for Majors Company from Practice Exercise 3.

(Continued)

PRACTICE EXERCISE 4 • SOLUTION

	A	B	C	D	E
1				Majors Company	
2				Work Sheet	
3				For Year Ended December 31, 20--	
4					
5		TRIAL BALANCE		ADJUSTMENTS	
6	ACCOUNT NAME	DEBIT	CREDIT	DEBIT	CREDIT
7	Cash	23,010.00			
8	Notes Receivable	6,000.00			
9	Accounts Receivable	28,540.00			
10	Merchandise Inventory	68,000.00		(b) 64,800.00	(a) 68,000.00
11	Supplies	12,440.00			(d) 10,025.00
12	Prepaid Insurance	2,110.00			(e) 1,520.00
13	Land	120,100.00			
14	Building	128,000.00			
15	Accumulated Depreciation, Building		50,000.00		(f) 13,500.00
16	Equipment	34,100.00			
17	Accumulated Depreciation, Equipment		19,600.00		(g) 5,900.00
18	Notes Payable		34,600.00		
19	Accounts Payable		4,300.00		
20	Unearned Course Fees		2,200.00	(c) 1,800.00	
21	Mortgage Payable		8,800.00		
22	R. L. Majors, Capital		252,774.00		
23	R. L. Majors, Drawing	65,000.00			
24	Sales		253,980.00		
25	Sales Returns and Alllowances	940.00			
26	Sales Discounts	1,880.00			
27	Interest Income		1,220.00		
28	Purchases	88,840.00			
29	Purchases Returns and Allowances		832.00		
30	Purchases Discounts		1,448.00		
31	Freight In	2,460.00			
32	Wages Expense	44,900.00		(h) 2,030.00	
33	Property Tax Expense	2,860.00			
34	Interest Expense	574.00			
35		629,754.00	629,754.00		
36	Income Summary			(a) 68,000.00	(b) 64,800.00
37	Course Fees Income				(c) 1,800.00
38	Supplies Expense			(d) 10,025.00	
39	Insurance Expense			(e) 1,520.00	
40	Depreciation Expense, Building			(f) 13,500.00	
41	Depreciation Expense, Equipment			(g) 5,900.00	
42	Wages Payable				(h) 2,030.00
43				167,575.00	167,575.00
44	Net Income				
45					
46					

Sheet1 Sheet2 Sheet3

F	G	H	I
INCOME STATEMENT		BALANCE SHEET	
DEBIT	CREDIT	DEBIT	CREDIT
		23,010.00	
		6,000.00	
		28,540.00	
		64,800.00	
		2,415.00	
		590.00	
		120,100.00	
		128,000.00	
			63,500.00
		34,100.00	
			25,500.00
			34,600.00
			4,300.00
			400.00
			8,800.00
			252,774.00
		65,000.00	
	253,980.00		
940.00			
1,880.00			
	1,220.00		
88,840.00			
	832.00		
	1,448.00		
2,460.00			
46,930.00			
2,860.00			
574.00			
68,000.00	64,800.00		
	1,800.00		
10,025.00			
1,520.00			
13,500.00			
5,900.00			
			2,030.00
243,429.00	324,080.00	472,555.00	391,904.00
80,651.00			80,651.00
324,080.00	324,080.00	472,555.00	472,555.00

Learning Objective  Journalize the adjusting entries for a merchandising business under the periodic inventory system.

Take the adjusting entries recorded in the journal directly from the Adjustments columns of the work sheet.

5 PRACTICE EXERCISE 5

Prepare the year-end adjusting entries from the Adjustments column of Majors Company's work sheet from Practice Exercise 3.

PRACTICE EXERCISE 5 • SOLUTION

GENERAL JOURNAL Page ___

Date		Description	Post. Ref.	Debit	Credit
20--		Adjusting Entries			
Dec.	31	Income Summary		68000 00	
(a)		Merchandise Inventory			68000 00
(b)	31	Merchandise Inventory		64800 00	
		Income Summary			64800 00
(c)	31	Unearned Course Fees		1800 00	
		Course Fees Income			1800 00
(d)	31	Supplies Expense		10025 00	
		Supplies			10025 00
(e)	31	Insurance Expense		1520 00	
		Prepaid Insurance			1520 00
(f)	31	Depreciation Expense, Building		13500 00	
		Accumulated Depreciation, Building			13500 00
(g)	31	Depreciation Expense, Equipment		5900 00	
		Accumulated Depreciation,			
		Equipment			5900 00
(h)	31	Wages Expense		2030 00	
		Wages Payable			2030 00

Learning Objective  Prepare and journalize the adjusting entry for merchandise inventory under the perpetual inventory system.

Assuming that the amount of the physical count of the stock of merchandise is less than the recorded amount, the adjusting entry is a debit to Cost of Goods Sold and a credit to Merchandise Inventory for the amount of the difference. On the other hand, if the physical count of the stock of merchandise is more than the recorded amount, the adjusting entry is to debit Merchandise Inventory and credit Cost of Goods Sold for the amount of the difference.

PRACTICE EXERCISE 6

Larkin Company employs the perpetual inventory system. Cost of Goods Sold for the year before any adjustment is $553,250. The computer record shows the amount of ending inventory to be $369,583, while the physical count shows ending inventory to be $362,720. Record the adjustment into T accounts and then journalize the adjusting entry.

PRACTICE EXERCISE 6 • SOLUTION

Cost of Goods Sold

	+	–
Bal.	553,250	
Adj.	6,863	

Merchandise Inventory

	+	–	
Bal.	369,583	Adj.	6,863*

*Adjustment = $362,720 – $369,583 = $(6,863)

GENERAL JOURNAL Page ___

Date		Description	Post. Ref.	Debit	Credit
20--		Adjusting Entries			
Dec.	31	Cost of Goods Sold		6 8 6 3 00	
		Merchandise Inventory			6 8 6 3 00

Glossary

Inventory shrinkage The amount by which inventory diminishes due to theft, misplacement, loss, or mismarking. *(p. 580)*

Physical inventory An actual count of the stock of goods on hand. *(p. 571)*

Revenue recognition principle An accrual-based accounting principle that requires revenue to be recognized when it is earned regardless of when payment is received. *(p. 570)*

Unearned revenue Cash received in advance for goods or services to be delivered later; considered to be a liability until the revenue is earned. *(p. 570)*

Quiz Yourself

_____ 1. Which of the following is the adjusting entry for depreciation on Equipment?
   a. Debit Depreciation Expense, Equipment and credit Equipment
   b. Debit Equipment and credit Depreciation Expense, Equipment
   c. Debit Depreciation Expense, Equipment and credit Accumulated Depreciation, Equipment
   d. Debit Accumulated Depreciation, Equipment and credit Depreciation Expense, Equipment
   e. None of the above

(Continued)

_____ 2. The adjusting entry for unearned revenue pertains to which of the following types of businesses?
   a. Service
   b. Merchandising
   c. Manufacturing
   d. Service and merchandising
   e. All of the above

_____ 3 An account that has *unearned* in its name is classified as what type of account?
   a. Asset
   b. Liability
   c. Revenue
   d. Owner's equity
   e. Expense

_____ 4. This type of inventory system does not require an entry to Merchandise Inventory until a physical inventory has been taken.
   a. Periodic inventory system
   b. Perpetual inventory system
   c. Merchandise inventory system
   d. Beginning inventory system
   e. Ending inventory system

_____ 5 The Supplies account has a $1,400 balance. A physical inventory is taken at the end of the fiscal year, and the amount on hand is determined to be $300. What adjusting entry is required to record the supplies used?
   a. Supplies 300 DR, Cash 300 CR
   b. Supplies Expense 1,400 DR, Supplies 1,400 CR
   c. Supplies 1,100 DR, Supplies Expense 1,100 CR
   d. Supplies Expense 1,100 DR, Supplies 1,100 CR
   e. None of the above

_____ 6. Which of the following accounts would *not* be listed in the Income Statement column(s) of the work sheet?
   a. Income Summary
   b. Freight In
   c. Sales Returns and Allowances
   d. Purchases Discounts
   e. Merchandise Inventory

_____ 7. The amount of inventory shown on the company books may be different than the physical inventory count. Which of the following is *not* a reason for this difference?
   a. Errors in accounting
   b. Shrinkage
   c. Shoplifting
   d. Errors in receiving merchandise
   e. A change in supplier

Answers:
1. c 2. e 3. b 4. a 5. d 6. e 7. e

Review It with QuickBooks®

_____ 1. Adjusting entries for a merchandising company are recorded in the same manner as general journal entries, except
   a. the point of entry to the general journal is different.
   b. the box marked Adjusting Entry is checked.
   c. the account name must include an adjusting entry.
   d. the journal entry numbering system is optional.

_____ 2. Make General Journal Entries is located under which tab in QuickBooks?
   a. Customers
   b. Vendors
   c. Banking
   d. Company

Answers:
1. b 2. d

Chapter Assignments

Discussion Questions

1. What is a physical inventory? What does the word *periodic* mean in the term *periodic inventory*?
2. On the Income Summary line of a work sheet, $126,220 appears in the Income Statement Debit column and $123,300 appears in the Income Statement Credit column. Which figure represents the beginning inventory?
3. Using the perpetual inventory system, what account is debited when a business finds that its physical count of inventory is greater than the recorded amount?
4. On a work sheet, where will the amount of the ending merchandise inventory be recorded?
5. Explain what is meant by unearned revenue. Why it is treated as a liability?
6. Why is it necessary to adjust the Merchandise Inventory account under a periodic inventory system?
7. A merchandising company shows $8,842 in the Supplies account on the preadjusted trial balance. After taking inventory of the actual supplies, the company still owns $3,638.
   a. How much was used or expired?
   b. Write the adjusting entry.
8. Assume that a college receives $84,000 for one semester's dormitory rent in advance and an entry is made debiting Cash and crediting Unearned Rent. At the end of the year, $68,000 of the rent has been earned. What adjusting entry would be made?

Exercises

LO 1 — Practice Exercise 1

EXERCISE 11-1 For the university football program's Unearned Season Tickets account, list the debits and credits for each amount posted to the account and briefly describe each transaction.

ACCOUNT Unearned Season Tickets — **ACCOUNT NO.** 214

Date		Item	Post. Ref.	Debit	Credit	Balance Debit	Balance Credit
20--							
Jan.	1	Balance	✓				12 9 0 0 00
Oct.	15		J42		36 7 8 0 00		49 6 8 0 00
Nov.	1		J43		42 6 0 0 00		92 2 8 0 00
Dec.	31	Adj.	J52	43 1 2 5 00			49 1 5 5 00

LO 1 — Practice Exercise 1

EXERCISE 11-2 On October 31, the Vermillion Igloos Hockey Club received $800,000 in cash in advance for season tickets for eight home games. The transaction was recorded as a debit to Cash and a credit to Unearned Admissions. By December 31, the end of the fiscal year, the team had played three home games and received an additional $450,000 cash admissions income at the gate.

(*Continued*)

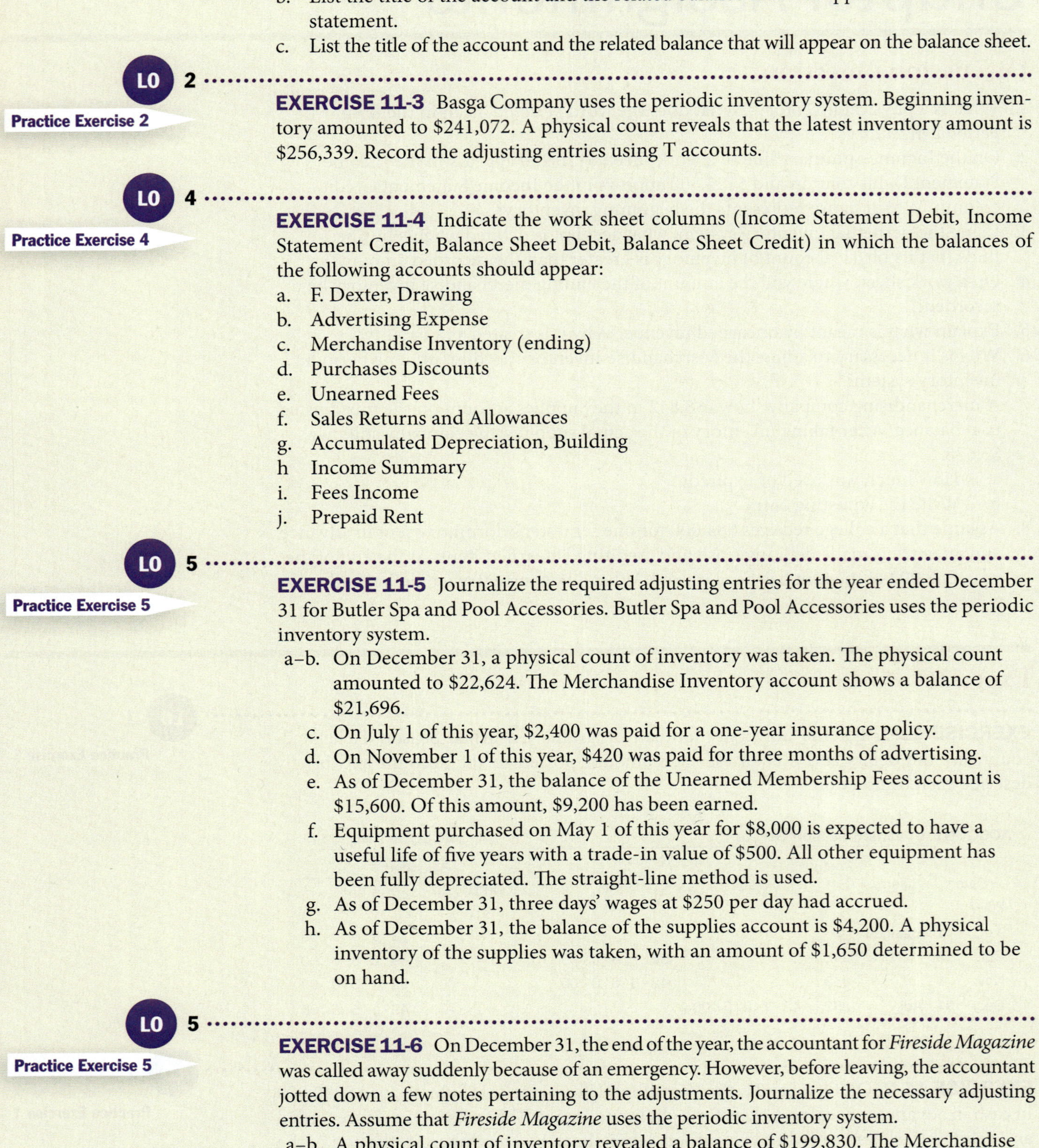

a. Journalize the adjusting entry as of December 31.
b. List the title of the account and the related balance that will appear on the income statement.
c. List the title of the account and the related balance that will appear on the balance sheet.

LO 2
Practice Exercise 2

EXERCISE 11-3 Basga Company uses the periodic inventory system. Beginning inventory amounted to $241,072. A physical count reveals that the latest inventory amount is $256,339. Record the adjusting entries using T accounts.

LO 4
Practice Exercise 4

EXERCISE 11-4 Indicate the work sheet columns (Income Statement Debit, Income Statement Credit, Balance Sheet Debit, Balance Sheet Credit) in which the balances of the following accounts should appear:

a. F. Dexter, Drawing
b. Advertising Expense
c. Merchandise Inventory (ending)
d. Purchases Discounts
e. Unearned Fees
f. Sales Returns and Allowances
g. Accumulated Depreciation, Building
h Income Summary
i. Fees Income
j. Prepaid Rent

LO 5
Practice Exercise 5

EXERCISE 11-5 Journalize the required adjusting entries for the year ended December 31 for Butler Spa and Pool Accessories. Butler Spa and Pool Accessories uses the periodic inventory system.

a–b. On December 31, a physical count of inventory was taken. The physical count amounted to $22,624. The Merchandise Inventory account shows a balance of $21,696.
c. On July 1 of this year, $2,400 was paid for a one-year insurance policy.
d. On November 1 of this year, $420 was paid for three months of advertising.
e. As of December 31, the balance of the Unearned Membership Fees account is $15,600. Of this amount, $9,200 has been earned.
f. Equipment purchased on May 1 of this year for $8,000 is expected to have a useful life of five years with a trade-in value of $500. All other equipment has been fully depreciated. The straight-line method is used.
g. As of December 31, three days' wages at $250 per day had accrued.
h. As of December 31, the balance of the supplies account is $4,200. A physical inventory of the supplies was taken, with an amount of $1,650 determined to be on hand.

LO 5
Practice Exercise 5

EXERCISE 11-6 On December 31, the end of the year, the accountant for *Fireside Magazine* was called away suddenly because of an emergency. However, before leaving, the accountant jotted down a few notes pertaining to the adjustments. Journalize the necessary adjusting entries. Assume that *Fireside Magazine* uses the periodic inventory system.

a–b. A physical count of inventory revealed a balance of $199,830. The Merchandise Inventory account shows a balance of $202,839.
c. Subscriptions received in advance amounting to $156,200 were recorded as Unearned Subscriptions. At year-end, $103,120 has been earned.

d. Depreciation of equipment for the year is $12,300.
e. The amount of expired insurance for the year is $1,612.
f. The balance of Prepaid Rent is $2,400, representing four months' rent. Three months' rent has expired.
g. Three days' salaries will be unpaid at the end of the year; total weekly (five days') salaries are $4,000.
h. As of December 31, the balance of the supplies account is $1,800. A physical inventory of the supplies was taken, with an amount of $920 determined to be on hand.

LO 6

Practice Exercise 6

EXERCISE 11-7 On December 31, Marchant Company took a physical count of its merchandise inventory. It operates under the perpetual inventory system. The physical count amounted to $185,294. The Merchandise Inventory account shows a balance of $187,936. Journalize the adjusting entry.

Problem Set A

LO 3, 4

PROBLEM 11–1A The trial balance of Hadden Company as of December 31, the end of its current fiscal year, is as follows:

Hadden Company
Trial Balance
December 31, 20--

Account Name	Debit	Credit
Cash	9,246.52	
Merchandise Inventory	63,674.80	
Supplies	1,466.34	
Prepaid Insurance	1,420.00	
Store Equipment	36,230.00	
Accumulated Depreciation, Store Equipment		22,726.00
Accounts Payable		13,196.96
Sales Tax Payable		1,236.98
R. M. Hadden, Capital		56,339.32
R. M. Hadden, Drawing	28,000.00	
Sales		175,864.31
Sales Returns and Allowances	1,573.72	
Purchases	77,300.04	
Purchases Returns and Allowances		1,744.32
Purchases Discounts		1,413.62
Freight In	2,427.00	
Salary Expense	35,458.85	
Rent Expense	14,600.00	
Miscellaneous Expense	1,124.24	
	272,521.51	272,521.51

(*Continued*)

Here are the data for the adjustments.

a–b. Merchandise Inventory at December 31, $64,742.80.
c. Store supplies inventory (on hand), $420.20.
d. Insurance expired, $738.
e. Salaries accrued, $684.50.
f. Depreciation of store equipment, $3,620.

Check Figure
Net income, $41,517.76

Required

Complete the work sheet after entering the account names and balances onto the work sheet.

1, 3, 4, 5

PROBLEM 11–2A The balances of the ledger accounts of Beldren Home Center as of December 31, the end of its fiscal year, are as follows:

Cash	$ 10,592
Accounts Receivable	43,962
Merchandise Inventory	120,838
Supplies	1,570
Prepaid Insurance	2,628
Store Equipment	35,924
Accumulated Depreciation, Store Equipment	29,420
Office Equipment	10,436
Accumulated Depreciation, Office Equipment	1,720
Notes Payable	5,000
Accounts Payable	29,822
Unearned Rent	3,200
A. P. Beldren, Capital	120,532
A. P. Beldren, Drawing	29,000
Sales	653,000
Sales Returns and Allowances	9,748
Purchases	519,374
Purchases Returns and Allowances	12,440
Purchases Discounts	8,634
Freight In	24,724
Wages Expense	54,200
Interest Expense	772

Data for the adjustments are as follows:

a–b. Merchandise Inventory at December 31, $102,765.
c. Wages accrued at December 31, $1,834.
d. Supplies inventory (on hand) at December 31, $645.
e. Depreciation of store equipment, $5,782.
f. Depreciation of office equipment, $1,791.
g. Insurance expired during the year, $845.
h. Rent earned, $2,500.

Check Figure
Net income, $38,506

Required

1. Complete the work sheet after entering the account names and balances onto the work sheet. Ignore this step if using QuickBooks or general ledger.
2. Journalize the adjusting entries. If using manual working papers, record adjusting entries on journal page 16.

LO 3, 4, 5

PROBLEM 11-3A A portion of the work sheet of Sadie's Flowers for the year ended December 31 is as follows:

	A	F	G	H	I
4					
5		INCOME STATEMENT		BALANCE SHEET	
6	ACCOUNT NAME	DEBIT	CREDIT	DEBIT	CREDIT
7	Cash			9,340.00	
8	Merchandise Inventory			76,940.00	
9	Supplies			256.00	
10	Prepaid Insurance			240.00	
11	Store Equipment			39,280.00	
12	Accumulated Depreciation, Store Equipment				26,220.00
13	Accounts Payable				14,600.00
14	S. R. Rodriguez, Capital				68,940.00
15	S. R. Rodriguez, Drawing			27,600.00	
16	Sales		173,420.00		
17	Sales Returns and Allowances	1,520.00			
18	Purchases	82,312.00			
19	Purchases Returns and Allowances		940.00		
20	Purchases Discounts		1,600.00		
21	Freight In	1,948.00			
22	Salary Expense	37,560.00			
23	Rent Expense	14,800.00			
24					
25	Income Summary	65,680.00	76,940.00		
26	Depreciation Expense, Store Equipment	4,040.00			
27	Insurance Expense	760.00			
28	Supplies Expense	944.00			
29	Salaries Payable				560.00
30		209,564.00	252,900.00	153,656.00	110,320.00
31					

Sheet1 Sheet2 Sheet3

Required

1. Determine the entries that appeared in the Adjustments columns and present them in general journal form on page 41.
2. Determine the net income for the year.
3. What is the amount of the ending capital?

Check Figure
Increase in Capital, $15,736

LO 3, 4, 6

PROBLEM 11–4A Here are the accounts in the ledger of Misha's Jewel Box, with the balances as of December 31, the end of its fiscal year.

Cash	$ 13,242
Accounts Receivable	3,984
Merchandise Inventory	126,540
Supplies	2,484
Prepaid Insurance	2,655
Land	18,000
Building	97,000
Accumulated Depreciation, Building	38,240
Store Equipment	46,170
Accumulated Depreciation, Store Equipment	16,250
Accounts Payable	8,270
Sales Tax Payable	2,371
Mortgage Payable	77,871
M. Beloit, Capital	185,000
M. Beloit, Drawing	48,000

(*Continued*)

Sales	$379,354
Sales Returns and Allowances	3,892
Cost of Goods Sold	279,198
Salary Expense	54,400
Advertising Expense	3,526
Utilities Expense	2,538
Property Tax Expense	1,162
Miscellaneous Expense	1,613
Interest Expense	2,952

Here are the data for the adjustments. Assume that Misha's Jewel Box uses the perpetual inventory system.

a. Merchandise Inventory at December 31, $124,630.
b. Insurance expired during the year, $1,294.
c. Depreciation of building, $3,300.
d. Depreciation of store equipment, $6,470.
e. Salaries accrued at December 31, $2,470.
f. Store supplies inventory (on hand) at December 31, $1,959.

Check Figure
Net income, $14,104

Required

1. Complete the work sheet after entering the account names and balances onto the work sheet. Ignore this step if using QuickBooks or general ledger.
2. Journalize the adjusting entries . If using manual working papers, record adjusting entries on journal page 63.

LO 1, 3, 4, 5

PROBLEM 11–5A A portion of Anderson Publishing's work sheet for the year ended December 31 follows:

	A	F	G	H	I
4					
5		INCOME STATEMENT		BALANCE SHEET	
6	ACCOUNT NAME	DEBIT	CREDIT	DEBIT	CREDIT
7	Cash			100,000.00	
8	Accounts Receivable			114,050.00	
9	Publishing Supplies			1,480.00	
10	Merchandise Inventory			15,000.00	
11	Prepaid Insurance			2,000.00	
12	Publishing Equipment			42,250.00	
13	Accumulated Depreciation, Publishing Equipment				16,900.00
14	Accounts Payable				5,562.00
15	Unearned Subscription Renewals				9,050.00
16	J. Anderson, Capital				218,450.00
17	J. Anderson, Drawing			48,000.00	
18	Magazine Sales		125,000.00		
19	Subscription Renewals		92,000.00		
20	Sales Returns and Allowances	5,425.00			
21	Purchases	65,000.00			
22	Purchases Returns and Allowances		4,500.00		
23	Purchases Discounts		9,000.00		
24	Freight In	7,500.00			
25	Salaries Expense	57,825.00			
26	Rent Expense	9,600.00			
27					
28	Income Summary	16,325.00	15,000.00		
29	Depreciation Expense, Publishing Equipment	8,950.00			
30	Insurance Expense	2,800.00			
31	Salaries Payable				1,113.00
32	Publishing Supplies Expense	370.00			
33		173,795.00	245,500.00	322,780.00	251,075.00

Sheet1 Sheet2 Sheet3

Required

1. Determine the entries that appeared in the Adjustments columns and prepare the general journal entries for the adjustments in the general journal, page 120.
2. Determine the net income for the year.
3. What is the amount of ending capital?

Check Figure
Increase in Capital, $23,705

Problem Set B

LO 3, 4

PROBLEM 11-1B The trial balance of Jillson Company as of December 31, the end of its current fiscal year, is as follows:

Jillson Company
Trial Balance
December 31, 20--

Account Name	Debit	Credit
Cash	8,463.92	
Merchandise Inventory	47,356.00	
Supplies	1,321.12	
Prepaid Insurance	1,660.00	
Store Equipment	26,580.00	
Accumulated Depreciation, Store Equipment		15,320.00
Accounts Payable		25,578.80
Sales Tax Payable		1,243.36
G. L. Jillson, Capital		75,630.00
G. L. Jillson, Drawing	28,440.00	
Sales		82,026.74
Sales Returns and Allowances	1,542.04	
Purchases	43,348.45	
Purchases Returns and Allowances		1,748.09
Purchases Discounts		1,987.90
Freight In	2,775.00	
Salary Expense	25,758.80	
Rent Expense	15,300.00	
Miscellaneous Expense	989.56	
	203,534.89	203,534.89

Here are the data for the adjustments.

a–b. Merchandise Inventory at December 31, $54,845.00.
c. Store supplies inventory (on hand), $488.50.
d. Insurance expired, $680.
e. Salaries accrued, $692.
f. Depreciation of store equipment, $3,760.

(*Continued*)

Check Figure
Net loss, $2,426.74

Required

Complete the work sheet after entering the account names and balances onto the work sheet.

1, 3, 4, 5

PROBLEM 11-2B The balances of the ledger accounts of Pelango Furniture as of December 31, the end of its fiscal year, are as follows:

Cash	$ 12,482
Accounts Receivable	38,962
Merchandise Inventory	118,628
Supplies	1,850
Prepaid Insurance	2,488
Store Equipment	32,824
Accumulated Depreciation, Store Equipment	26,420
Office Equipment	11,236
Accumulated Depreciation, Office Equipment	3,410
Notes Payable	6,000
Accounts Payable	23,420
Unearned Rent	3,150
L. Pelango, Capital	120,532
L. Pelango, Drawing	28,000
Sales	647,090
Sales Returns and Allowances	8,848
Purchases	519,374
Purchases Returns and Allowances	12,440
Purchases Discounts	8,634
Freight In	22,824
Wages Expense	52,800
Interest Expense	780

Data for the adjustments are as follows:

a–b. Merchandise Inventory at December 31, $104,565.
c. Wages accrued at December 31, $934.
d. Supplies inventory (on hand) at December 31, $755.
e. Depreciation of store equipment, $4,982.
f. Depreciation of office equipment, $1,531.
g. Insurance expired during the year, $935.
h. Rent earned, $2,450.

Check Figure
Net income, $42,448

Required

1. Complete the work sheet after entering the account names and balances onto the work sheet. Ignore this step if using QuickBooks or general ledger.
2. Journalize the adjusting entries. If using manual working papers, record adjusting entries on journal page 16.

LO 3, 4, 5

PROBLEM 11-3B A portion of the work sheet of Habib Company for the year ended December 31 follows.

(Continued)

	A	F	G	H	I
4					
5		INCOME STATEMENT		BALANCE SHEET	
6	ACCOUNT NAME	DEBIT	CREDIT	DEBIT	CREDIT
7	Cash			7,736.00	
8	Merchandise Inventory			74,298.00	
9	Supplies			298.00	
10	Prepaid Insurance			250.00	
11	Store Equipment			37,960.00	
12	Accumulated Depreciation, Store Equipment				29,440.00
13	Accounts Payable				13,760.00
14	O. B. Habib, Capital				75,142.00
15	O. B. Habib, Drawing			30,800.00	
16	Sales		171,816.00		
17	Sales Returns and Allowances	1,434.00			
18	Purchases	85,934.00			
19	Purchases Returns and Allowances		964.00		
20	Purchases Discounts		1,636.00		
21	Freight In	2,658.00			
22	Salary Expense	37,852.00			
23	Rent Expense	14,400.00			
24					
25	Income Summary	68,228.00	74,298.00		
26	Depreciation Expense, Store Equipment	4,360.00			
27	Insurance Expense	552.00			
28	Supplies Expense	884.00			
29	Salaries Payable				588.00
30		216,302.00	248,714.00	151,342.00	118,930.00
31					

Sheet1 Sheet2 Sheet3

Required

1. Determine the entries that appeared in the Adjustments columns and present them in general journal form on page 41.
2. Determine the net income for the year.
3. What is the amount of the ending capital?

Check Figure
Increase in capital, $1,612

LO 3, 4, 6

PROBLEM 11-4B The accounts in the ledger of Markey's Mountain Shop with the balances as of December 31, the end of its fiscal year, are as follows:

Cash	$ 12,840
Accounts Receivable	3,242
Merchandise Inventory	137,757
Store Supplies	1,530
Prepaid Insurance	2,845
Land	22,000
Building	86,000
Accumulated Depreciation, Building	36,940
Store Equipment	54,952
Accumulated Depreciation, Store Equipment	13,348
Notes Payable	10,500
Accounts Payable	18,540
Sales Tax Payable	5,706
B. Markey, Capital	171,000
B. Markey, Drawing	52,000
Sales	458,905
Sales Returns and Allowances	7,590
Cost of Goods Sold	265,315
Salary Expense	52,973

(Continued)

CHAPTER ASSIGNMENTS

Advertising Expense	$6,288
Utilities Expense	7,355
Property Tax Expense	800
Miscellaneous Expense	775
Interest Expense	677

Data for the adjustments are as follows. Assume that Markey's Mountain Shop uses the perpetual inventory system.

a. Merchandise Inventory at December 31, $140,357.
b. Store supplies inventory (on hand) at December 31, $540.
c. Depreciation of building, $3,400.
d. Depreciation of store equipment, $3,800.
e. Salaries accrued at December 31, $1,250.
f. Insurance expired during the year, $1,480.

Check Figure
Net income, $108,812

Required

1. Complete the work sheet after entering the account names and balances onto the work sheet. Ignore this step if using QuickBooks or general ledger.
2. Journalize the adjusting entries. If using manual working papers, record adjusting entries on journal page 63.

LO 1, 3, 4, 5

PROBLEM 11-5B A portion of Johnson's Farm Supply work sheet for the year ended December 31 follows:

	A	F	G	H	I
4		INCOME STATEMENT		BALANCE SHEET	
5	ACCOUNT NAME	DEBIT	CREDIT	DEBIT	CREDIT
6	Cash			95,000.00	
7	Accounts Receivable			75,250.00	
8	Supplies			750.00	
9	Merchandise Inventory			75,262.00	
10	Prepaid Insurance			400.00	
11	Equipment			96,375.00	
12	Accumulated Depreciation, Equipment				38,550.00
13	Accounts Payable				12,446.00
14	Unearned Revenues				3,600.00
15	V. Johnson, Capital				268,933.75
16	V. Johnson, Drawing			27,250.00	
17	Sales		325,024.00		
18	Sales Returns and Allowances	7,526.20			
19	Purchases	205,576.00			
20	Purchases Returns and Allowances		38,026.00		
21	Purchases Discounts		2,500.00		
22	Freight In	10,836.40			
23	Salaries Expense	62,185.00			
24	Rent Expense	11,400.00			
25					
26	Income Summary	74,852.00	75,262.00		
27	Depreciation Expense, Equipment	19,275.00			
28	Insurance Expense	3,600.00			
29	Salaries Payable				1,195.85
30		395,250.60	440,812.00	370,287.00	324,725.60
31					

Sheet1 Sheet2 Sheet3

Check Figure
Increase in Capital, $18,311.40

Required

1. Determine the entries that appeared in the Adjustments columns and prepare the general journal entries for the adjustments in the general journal, page 19.
2. Determine the net income for the year.
3. What is the amount of the ending capital?

Try It with *QuickBooks*® (LO 1)

QB Exercise 11-1

Using the information in Problem 11-2A on page 596 and the QuickBooks data file labeled QB Exercise 11-1 on the textbook website at www.cengagebrain.com, complete the following activities:

1. Journalize the adjusting entries for Beldren Home Center as of December 31, 2015.
2. Prepare an adjusted trial balance report.
3. Prepare an income statement (profit and loss statement standard format).
   a. What is the net income for Beldren Home Center as of December 31?
4. Prepare a balance sheet (standard format).
   a. What is the ending balance for Unearned Rent?

QB Exercise 11-2

Using the information in Problem 11–4A on page 597–598 and the QuickBooks data file labeled QB Exercise 11-2 on the textbook website, complete the following activities:

1. Journalize the adjusting entries for Misha's Jewel Box as of December 31, 2015.
2. Prepare an adjusted trial balance report.
3. Prepare an income statement (profit and loss statement standard format).
   a. What is the net income for Misha's Jewel Box as of December 31?
4. Prepare a balance sheet (standard format).
   a. What is the ending balance for Prepaid Insurance?

Activities

Why Does It Matter?

BURT'S BEES, Durham, North Carolina

Burt's Bees describes itself as an "Earth-Friendly, Natural Personal Care Company" that produces products for health, beauty, and personal hygiene. The company manufactures over 150 products distributed in nearly 30,000 retail outlets worldwide. As a merchandising company, Burt's Bees follows its inventory closely. This requires monitoring the receipt, production, purchasing, and planning of inventory. At the end of each time period, Burt's Bees must make adjusting entries to prepare its financial statements accurately. Many of the adjustments are entries you have already learned, such as depreciation, expiration of prepaid expenses, adjustment of supplies used, and recording of accrued expenses. However, merchandising companies also require adjusting entries related to merchandise inventory. Companies such as Burt's Bees monitor inventory, prepare a worksheet, and record adjusting entries using either the perpetual or periodic inventory system. Using your book and/or conducting a brief Internet search to find the differences between perpetual and periodic inventory systems, answer the following questions:

1. What type of inventory system do you think Burt's Bees uses? Why?
2. Using the inventory system you selected in no. 1, what is an example of the type of journal entry Burt's Bees would make when purchasing merchandise on account?
3. Using the inventory system you selected in no. 1, what journal entry would Burt's Bees use to record the sale of merchandise on account?

What Would You Say?

You have a friend who is a seamstress specializing in Renaissance costumes. She receives cash well in advance of the required date, often in the fiscal period prior to the date of delivery of the costume, not only to enable her to purchase material but also to cover her labor. She always debits Cash and credits Costume Income. First, explain to her why this entry violates the revenue recognition principle. Second, identify the classification of Unearned Revenue. Third, explain when the Unearned Revenue account is used.

What Do You Think?

On November 1, an exterior painting company received $5,310 for a paint job that will not be finished for a few months. As of December 31, which is the end of the fiscal period, $2,400 worth of painting will not have been completed. The bookkeeper completed the following entries prior to leaving on vacation:

Cash

11/1	5,310		

Painting Income

12/31	2,400	11/1	5,310

Unearned Painting Income

		12/31	2,400

The owner wants to get a bank loan by December 1. The bank requires interim financial statements to be submitted as of December 1. How will the bookkeeper's entries affect the accuracy of the interim balance sheet and income statements? What difference will the bookkeeper's methods make in the December 31 balance sheet and income statement?

What Would You Do?

The owner of a motorcycle shop allows his two sons to take motorcycles home to try them out on different types of surfaces because he believes that his sons need to be familiar with the products they sell. Sometimes the motorcycles are not returned to the store by the time the physical count of inventory takes place. Respond to this practice.

What's Wrong with This Picture?

What could happen if a business spent the cash it received in advance for services it promised to perform at a later date?

Adjusting Entries

Two months (July and August) have passed since Ms. Valli has seen the financial statements for All About You Spa. It is time to begin their preparation. Several accounts need adjusting. These include the accounts you adjusted in Chapter 4 as well as any accounts involved with merchandising.

Adjusting Entry Information

Merchandise Inventory Adjustment (a)

A physical count of inventory was taken, and the inventory was valued at $13,110.

Supplies Adjustments (b) and (c)

A physical count has been taken of the two supplies accounts. The values of the remaining inventories of supplies are as follows:

Office Supplies	$ 75.00
Spa Supplies	345.00

Prepaid Insurance Adjustment (d)

A review of the insurance records determined that $281.67 in liability insurance coverage had been used during the last two months.

Depreciation Adjustments (e) and (f)

Estimated depreciation amounts for the two equipment accounts are as follows:

Office Equipment	$ 20.00
Spa Equipment	129.76

Wages Expense/Wages Payable Adjustment

There is no need for a Wages Expense/Wages Payable adjustment because the end of the fiscal period did not come in the middle of a pay period.

Check Figures

3. Adjusting Entries General Journal report total, $14,109.43
4. Adjusted trial balance total, $129,161.03

Required

1. Complete a work sheet (if required by your instructor). Ignore this step if using QuickBooks or general ledger.
2. Journalize the adjusting entries in the general journal.
   - If you are preparing the adjusting entries manually, enter your transactions beginning on page 16.
3. Post the adjusting entries to the general ledger accounts.
   - Ignore this step if you are using QuickBooks or general ledger.
4. Prepare an adjusted trial balance as of August 31, 20--.

Financial Statements, Closing Entries, and Reversing Entries

Learning Objectives

After you have completed this chapter, you will be able to do the following:

1. Prepare a classified income statement for a merchandising firm.
2. Prepare a classified balance sheet for any type of business.
3. Compute working capital and current ratio.
4. Record the closing entries for a merchandising firm.
5. Determine which adjusting entries can be reversed and record the reversing entries.

To: **Amy Roberts, CPA**
Subject: **Financial Statements, Working Capital, and Current Ratio**

Hi Amy,
I am talking to my bank about obtaining a line of credit, and the loan officer asked for a classified income statement and balance sheet. Can you explain to me how these are prepared? I was also asked for Whitewater Raft Supply's working capital and current ratio. What are these?
Thanks,
Janie

To: **Janie Conner**
Subject: **RE: Financial Statements, Working Capital, and Current Ratio**

Hi Janie,
A classified income statement and balance sheet is just a more detailed version of the income statement and balance sheet you currently use. The additional breakdown of information will give you and the bank a better idea of your financial position. Here is a list of items that we will need to talk about at our next meeting so that you will be prepared to meet with the bank. I've also attached a copy of a classified income statement and balance sheet for you to review before our meeting.

_____ 1. Prepare a classified income statement.
_____ 2. Prepare a classified balance sheet.
_____ 3. Compute working capital and current ratio.

Let's get started with these items. Let me know if you have any questions.
Amy

Imagesource/Glow Images

Accounting Language

Cash equivalents (p. 633)
Common-sized statement (p. 629)
Current Assets (p. 616)
Current Liabilities (p. 617)
Current ratio (p. 618)
Delivered Cost of Purchases (p. 613)
Financing activities (p. 633)
General Expenses (p. 613)
Gross Profit (p. 609)
Horizontal analysis (p. 629)
Indirect method (p. 634)
Investing activities (p. 633)
Liquidity (p. 617)
Long-Term Liabilities (p. 617)
Net Income or Net Profit (p. 609)
Net Purchases (p. 613)
Net Sales (p. 611)
Notes Receivable (current) (p. 617)
Operating activities (p. 633)
Property and Equipment (p. 617)
Reversing entries (p. 625)
Selling Expenses (p. 613)
Statement of cash flows (p. 633)
Temporary-equity accounts (p. 622)
Vertical analysis (p. 629)
Working capital (p. 618)

In this chapter, we review how to prepare financial statements directly from a work sheet. We will also look at financial statements in their entirety and explain their various subdivisions. Finally, we will explain the functions of closing entries and reversing entries as means of completing the accounting cycle.

First, here is the chart of accounts for Whitewater Raft Supply.

PERIODIC INVENTORY CHART OF ACCOUNTS	PERPETUAL INVENTORY CHART OF ACCOUNTS
Assets (100–199)	**Assets (100–199)**
111 Cash	111 Cash
112 Notes Receivable	112 Notes Receivable
113 Accounts Receivable	113 Accounts Receivable
114 Merchandise Inventory	114 Merchandise Inventory
115 Supplies	115 Supplies
116 Prepaid Insurance	116 Prepaid Insurance
121 Land	121 Land
122 Building	122 Building
123 Accumulated Depreciation, Building	123 Accumulated Depreciation, Building
124 Equipment	124 Equipment
125 Accumulated Depreciation, Equipment	125 Accumulated Depreciation, Equipment
Liabilities (200–299)	**Liabilities (200–299)**
211 Notes Payable	211 Notes Payable
212 Accounts Payable	212 Accounts Payable
213 Wages Payable	213 Wages Payable
217 Unearned Course Fees	217 Unearned Course Fees
221 Mortgage Payable	221 Mortgage Payable
Owner's Equity (300–399)	**Owner's Equity (300–399)**
311 J. Conner, Capital	311 J. Conner, Capital
312 J. Conner, Drawing	312 J. Conner, Drawing
313 Income Summary	313 Income Summary

PERIODIC INVENTORY CHART OF ACCOUNTS	PERPETUAL INVENTORY CHART OF ACCOUNTS
Revenue (400–499)	**Revenue (400–499)**
411 Sales	411 Sales
412 Sales Returns and Allowances	412 Sales Returns and Allowances
413 Sales Discounts	413 Sales Discounts
421 Course Fees Income	421 Course Fees Income
422 Interest Income	422 Interest Income
Cost of Goods Sold (500–599)	**Cost of Goods Sold (500–599)**
511 Purchases	511 Cost of Goods Sold
512 Purchases Returns and Allowances	**Expenses (600–699)**
513 Purchases Discounts	611 Wages Expense
514 Freight In	622 Supplies Expense
Expenses (600–699)	623 Insurance Expense
611 Wages Expense	624 Depreciation Expense, Building
622 Supplies Expense	625 Depreciation Expense, Equipment
623 Insurance Expense	626 Property Tax Expense
624 Depreciation Expense, Building	634 Interest Expense
625 Depreciation Expense, Equipment	
626 Property Tax Expense	
634 Interest Expense	

FYI

Accountants sometimes number contra accounts as subaccounts. For example, Accumulated Depreciation, Building is 122.1, Sales Returns and Allowances is 411.1, Sales Discounts is 411.2, Purchases Returns and Allowances is 511.1, and so on.

THE INCOME STATEMENT

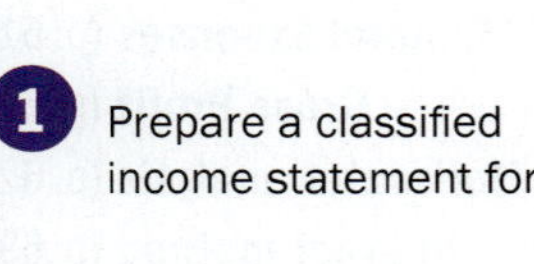

Learning Objective 1: Prepare a classified income statement for

As you know, the work sheet is merely a tool that accountants use to prepare the financial statements. In Figure 1 (on the next page), we present the part of the work sheet for Whitewater Raft Supply that includes the Income Statement columns. Of course, **each of the amounts that appear in the Income Statement columns of the work sheet will be used in the income statement**. Notice that the amounts for the beginning and ending merchandise inventory appear separately on the Income Summary line. Recall that, in Chapter 11, you were asked to pick up the two figures and move them—not to take the difference between the two. Figure 2 (on page 610) shows the entire income statement. Take your time to look it over carefully; then we will break it down into its components.

The income statement follows a logical pattern that is much the same for any type of merchandising business. The ability to interpret the income statement and extract parts from it is very useful when gathering information for decision making. To realize the full value of an income statement, however, you need to know the basic format of an income statement. Let's look at the statement section by section.

Net Sales	$254,260
– Cost of Goods Sold	90,120
Gross Profit	$164,140
– Operating Expenses	58,835
Income from Operations	$105,305

To illustrate the concepts of **gross** and **net**, the following is an example of a simple single-sale transaction.

Figure 1
Partial work sheet for Whitewater Raft Supply

	A	B	C	D	E	H	I
1			Whitewater Raft Supply				
2			Work Sheet				
3			For Month Ended December 31, 20--				
4							
5		TRIAL BALANCE		ADJUSTMENTS		INCOME STATEMENT	
6	ACCOUNT NAME	DEBIT	CREDIT	DEBIT	CREDIT	DEBIT	CREDIT
7	Cash	24,154.00					
8	Notes Receivable	4,000.00					
9	Accounts Receivable	29,546.00					
10	Merchandise Inventory	67,000.00		(b) 64,800.00	(a) 67,000.00		
11	Supplies	1,540.00			(d) 1,125.00		
12	Prepaid Insurance	960.00			(e) 520.00		
13	Land	122,100.00					
14	Building	129,000.00					
15	Accumulated Depreciation, Building		51,000.00		(f) 3,500.00		
16	Equipment	33,100.00					
17	Accumulated Depreciation, Equipment		16,400.00		(g) 4,900.00		
18	Notes Payable		36,600.00				
19	Accounts Payable		3,300.00				
20	Unearned Course Fees		1,200.00	(c) 800.00			
21	Mortgage Payable		7,800.00				
22	J. Conner, Capital		253,774.00				
23	J. Conner, Drawing	77,000.00					
24	Sales		257,180.00				257,180.00
25	Sales Returns and Allowances	940.00				940.00	
26	Sales Discounts	1,980.00				1,980.00	
27	Interest Income		220.00				220.00
28	Purchases	87,840.00				87,840.00	
29	Purchases Returns and Allowances		932.00				932.00
30	Purchases Discounts		1,348.00				1,348.00
31	Freight In	2,360.00				2,360.00	
32	Wages Expense	45,900.00		(h) 1,030.00		46,930.00	
33	Property Tax Expense	1,860.00				1,860.00	
34	Interest Expense	474.00				474.00	
35		629,754.00	629,754.00				
36	Income Summary			(a) 67,000.00	(b) 64,800.00	67,000.00	64,800.00
37	Course Fees Income				(c) 800.00		800.00
38	Supplies Expense			(d) 1,125.00		1,125.00	
39	Insurance Expense			(e) 520.00		520.00	
40	Depreciation Expense, Building			(f) 3,500.00		3,500.00	
41	Depreciation Expense, Equipment			(g) 4,900.00		4,900.00	
42	Wages Payable				(h) 1,030.00		
43				143,675.00	143,675.00	219,429.00	325,280.00
44	Net Income					105,851.00	
45						325,280.00	325,280.00
46							

Sheet1 Sheet2 Sheet3

Several years ago Della Reyes bought an antique table at a secondhand store for $800. She sold the table for $1,850. She advertised it in the daily newspaper at a cost of $73. How much did she make as clear profit?

Sale of Table	$1,850
Less Cost of Table	800
Gross Profit	$1,050
Less Advertising Expense	73
Net Income or Net Profit (gain on the sale)	$ 977

Gross Profit is the profit on the sale of the table before any operating expenses have been deducted; in this case, Gross Profit is $1,050. **Net Income,** or **Net Profit,** is the final or clear profit after all operating expenses have been deducted. In a single-sale situation such as this, we refer to the final outcome as the net profit. But for a business that has many sales and expenses, most accountants prefer the term *net income.* Regardless of which word you use, *net* refers to clear profit—after all expenses have been deducted.

Figure 2
Income statement for Whitewater Raft Supply

Whitewater Raft Supply Income Statement For Year Ended December 31, 20--				
Revenue from Sales:				
Sales			$ 257,180	
Less: Sales Returns and Allowances		$ 940		
Sales Discounts		1,980	2,920	
Net Sales				$254,260
Cost of Goods Sold:				
Merchandise Inventory, January 1, 20--			$ 67,000	
Purchases		$ 87,840		
Less: Purchases Returns and Allowances	$ 932			
Purchases Discounts	1,348	2,280		
Net Purchases		$85,560		
Add Freight In		2,360		
Delivered Cost of Purchases			87,920	
Cost of Goods Available for Sale			$154,920	
Less Merchandise Inventory, December 31, 20--			64,800	
Cost of Goods Sold				90,120
Gross Profit				$164,140
Operating Expenses:				
Wages Expense			$ 46,930	
Supplies Expense			1,125	
Insurance Expense			520	
Depreciation Expense, Building			3,500	
Depreciation Expense, Equipment			4,900	
Property Tax Expense			1,860	
Total Operating Expenses				58,835
Income from Operations				$105,305
Other Income:				
Course Fees Income			$ 800	
Interest Income			220	
Total Other Income			$ 1,020	
Other Expenses:				
Interest Expense			474	546
Net Income				$105,851

Revenue from Sales

Now let's look at the Revenue from Sales section of the income statement for Whitewater Raft Supply:

Revenue from Sales:			
Sales		$ 257,180	
Less: Sales Returns and Allowances	$ 940		
Sales Discounts	1,980	2,920	
Net Sales			$254,260

When we introduced Sales Returns and Allowances and Sales Discounts, we treated them as deductions from Sales. You can see that on the income statement, they are deducted from Sales to give us **Net Sales**. Note that we record these items in the same order in which they appear in the ledger.

Remember

Returns and Allowances (Sales or Purchases) is listed on one line, and Discounts (Sales or Purchases) is listed below.

RATIO ANALYSIS

GROSS PROFIT PERCENTAGE

An important function of accounting is to provide tools for interpreting the financial statements or the results of operations. One ratio that is frequently used to analyze financial statements is *gross profit percentage.*

Southern Office Furniture will serve as our example. (See the comparative income statement below.)

Southern Office Furniture
Comparative Income Statement
For Years Ended January 31, 2015, and January 31, 2014

	2015		2014	
	Amount	**Percent**	**Amount**	**Percent**
Revenue from Sales:				
Sales	$533,600	101%	$510,000	102%
Less Sales Returns and Allowances	5,600	1	10,000	2
Net Sales	$528,000	100%	$500,000	100%
Cost of Goods Sold:				
Merchandise Inventory, February 1	$ 46,000	9%	$ 64,000	13%
Delivered Cost of Purchases	290,000	55	230,000	46
Cost of Goods Available for Sale	$336,000	64%	$294,000	59%
Less Merchandise Inventory, January 31	58,000	11	46,000	9
Cost of Goods Sold	$278,000	53%	$248,000	50%
Gross Profit	$250,000	47%	$252,000	50%
Operating Expenses:				
Sales Salary Expense	$ 63,600	12%	$ 58,000	12%
Rent Expense	24,000	5	24,000	5
Advertising Expense	21,400	4	16,000	3
Depreciation Expense, Equipment	20,000	4	18,000	4
Insurance Expense	2,000	—	2,000	—
Store Supplies Expense	1,000	—	1,000	—
Miscellaneous Expense	1,000	—	1,000	—
Total Operating Expenses	$133,000	25%	$120,000	24%
Net Income	$117,000	22%	$132,000	26%

(*Continued*)

For each year, net sales is the base (100 percent). All other items on the income statement can be expressed as a percentage of net sales for the particular year involved. For example, let's look at the following percentages:

$$\text{Gross Profit \% (2015)} = \frac{\text{Gross Profit for 2015}}{\text{Net Sales for 2015}} = \frac{\$250{,}000}{\$528{,}000} = 0.473 = 47\%$$

$$\text{Gross Profit \% (2014)} = \frac{\text{Gross Profit for 2014}}{\text{Net Sales for 2014}} = \frac{\$252{,}000}{\$500{,}000} = 0.504 = 50\%$$

$$\text{Sales Salary Expense \% (2015)} = \frac{\text{Sales Salary Expense for 2015}}{\text{Net Sales for 2015}}$$

$$= \frac{\$63{,}600}{\$528{,}000} = 0.120 = 12\%$$

$$\text{Sales Salary Expense \% (2014)} = \frac{\text{Sales Salary Expense for 2014}}{\text{Net Sales for 2014}}$$

$$= \frac{\$58{,}000}{\$500{,}000} = 0.116 = 12\%$$

Here's how you might interpret a few of the percentages.

2015

- For every $100 in net sales, gross profit amounted to $47.
- For every $100 in net sales, sales salary expense amounted to $12.
- For every $100 in net sales, net income amounted to $22.

2014

- For every $100 in net sales, gross profit amounted to $50.
- For every $100 in net sales, sales salary expense amounted to $12.
- For every $100 in net sales, net income amounted to $26.

The gross profit percentage declined from 50% in 2012 to 47% in 2015 because the Cost of Goods Sold percentage increased from 50% in 2014 to 53% in 2015.

Cost of Goods Sold

The section of the income statement that requires the greatest amount of concentration is the Cost of Goods Sold section, where the cost of the goods we sold is computed. We've repeated the section below.

Cost of Goods Sold:				
Merchandise Inventory, January 1, 20--			$ 67,000	
Purchases		$87,840		
Less: Purchases Returns and Allowances	$ 932			
Purchases Discounts	1,348	2,280		
Net Purchases		$85,560		
Add Freight In		2,360		
Delivered Cost of Purchases			87,920	
Cost of Goods Available for Sale			$154,920	
Less Merchandise Inventory, December 31, 20--			64,800	
Cost of Goods Sold				90,120

First, let's look closely at the Purchases section.

Purchases		$ 87,840	
Less: Purchases Returns and Allowances	$ 932		
Purchases Discounts	1,348	2,280	
Net Purchases		$85,560	
Add Freight In		2,360	
Delivered Cost of Purchases			87,920

Note the parallel to the Revenue from Sales section. To arrive at **Net Purchases**, we deduct the sum of Purchases Returns and Allowances and Purchases Discounts from Purchases. To complete the Purchases section, we add Freight In to Net Purchases to get **Delivered Cost of Purchases**.

Now let's look at the full Cost of Goods Sold section. You might think of Cost of Goods Sold like this:

	Amount we started with (beginning inventory)	$ 67,000
+	Net amount we purchased, including freight charges	87,920
	Total amount that could have been sold (available)	$154,920
–	Amount left over (ending inventory)	64,800
	Cost of the goods that were actually sold	$ 90,120

Here's the Cost of Goods Sold expressed in proper wording.

	Merchandise Inventory, January 1, 20--	$ 67,000
+	Delivered Cost of Purchases	87,920
	Cost of Goods Available for Sale	$154,920
–	Merchandise Inventory, December 31, 20--	64,800
	Cost of Goods Sold	$ 90,120

Operating Expenses

Operating expenses, as the name implies, are the regular expenses of doing business. We list the accounts and their respective balances in the order in which they appear in the ledger.

Many firms use subclassifications of operating expenses, such as the following:

1. **Selling Expenses** Any expenses directly connected with the selling activity:
   - Sales Salary Expense
   - Sales Commissions Expense
   - Advertising Expense
   - Store Supplies Expense
   - Delivery Expense
   - Depreciation Expense, Store Equipment
2. **General Expenses** Any expenses related to the office or administration, or any expense that cannot be directly connected with a selling activity:
   - Office Salary Expense
   - Property Tax Expense
   - Depreciation Expense, Office Equipment
   - Rent Expense
   - Insurance Expense
   - Office Supplies Expense
   - Miscellaneous General Expense

FYI

In preparing the income statement, classifying expense accounts as selling expenses or general expenses is a matter of judgment.

If the Cash Short and Over account has a debit balance (net shortage), the balance is added to and reported as Miscellaneous General Expense. Conversely, if the Cash Short and Over account has a credit balance (net overage), the balance is added to and reported as Miscellaneous Income, which is classified as Other Income.

Income from Operations

Now let's repeat the skeleton outline:

Net Sales
– Cost of Goods Sold

Gross Profit
– Operating Expenses

Income from Operations

If Operating Expenses are the regular, recurring expenses of doing business, Income from Operations should be the regular or recurring income from normal business operations. When you compare the results of operations over a number of years, Income from Operations is the figure to use as a basis for comparison.

Other Income and Other Expenses

The Other Income classification, as the name implies, includes any revenue account other than Revenue from Sales. We are trying to isolate Sales at the top of the income statement as the major revenue account so that the Gross Profit figure represents the profit made on the sale of merchandise *only*. Additional accounts that may appear under the heading Other Income are Rent Income (the firm is subletting part of its premises), Interest Income (the firm holds an interest-bearing note or contract), Gain on Disposal of Property and Equipment (the firm makes a profit on the sale of property and equipment), and Miscellaneous Income (the firm has an overage recorded in the Cash Short and Over account).

The classification Other Expenses records various nonoperating expenses such as Interest Expense or Loss on Disposal of Property and Equipment.

Remember

Net income appears on both the income statement and the statement of owner's equity.

THE STATEMENT OF OWNER'S EQUITY

Figure 3 is a partial work sheet for Whitewater Raft Supply. Here again we find that **every figure in the Balance Sheet columns of the work sheet is used in the statement of owner's equity or the balance sheet.**

Preparation of the financial statements follows the same order we presented before: first, the income statement; second, the statement of owner's equity; third, the balance sheet. The statement of owner's equity shows why the balance of the Capital account has changed from the beginning of the fiscal period to the end of it. In preparing the statement of owner's equity, always look in the ledger for the owner's Capital account to find any changes, such as additional investments, made during the year.

Remember

The columns on the financial statements *do not* represent debit or credit columns. The columns are for making computations and listing totals.

Figure 3
Partial work sheet for Whitewater Raft Supply

	A	B	C	D	E	J	K
1			Whitewater Raft Supply				
2			Work Sheet				
3			For Month Ended December 31, 20--				
4							
5		TRIAL BALANCE		ADJUSTMENTS		BALANCE SHEET	
6	ACCOUNT NAME	DEBIT	CREDIT	DEBIT	CREDIT	DEBIT	CREDIT
7	Cash	24,154.00				24,154.00	
8	Notes Receivable	4,000.00				4,000.00	
9	Accounts Receivable	29,546.00				29,546.00	
10	Merchandise Inventory	67,000.00		(b) 64,800.00	(a) 67,000.00	64,800.00	
11	Supplies	1,540.00			(d) 1,125.00	415.00	
12	Prepaid Insurance	960.00			(e) 520.00	440.00	
13	Land	122,100.00				122,100.00	
14	Building	129,000.00				129,000.00	
15	Accumulated Depreciation, Building		51,000.00		(f) 3,500.00		54,500.00
16	Equipment	33,100.00				33,100.00	
17	Accumulated Depreciation, Equipment		16,400.00		(g) 4,900.00		21,300.00
18	Notes Payable		36,600.00				36,600.00
19	Accounts Payable		3,300.00				3,300.00
20	Unearned Course Fees		1,200.00	(c) 800.00			400.00
21	Mortgage Payable		7,800.00				7,800.00
22	J. Conner, Capital		253,774.00				253,774.00
23	J. Conner, Drawing	77,000.00				77,000.00	
24	Sales		257,180.00				
25	Sales Returns and Allowances	940.00					
26	Sales Discounts	1,980.00					
27	Interest Income		220.00				
28	Purchases	87,840.00					
29	Purchases Returns and Allowances		932.00				
30	Purchases Discounts		1,348.00				
31	Freight In	2,360.00					
32	Wages Expense	45,900.00		(h) 1,030.00			
33	Property Tax Expense	1,860.00					
34	Interest Expense	474.00					
35		629,754.00	629,754.00				
36	Income Summary			(a) 67,000.00	(b) 64,800.00		
37	Course Fees Income				(c) 800.00		
38	Supplies Expense			(d) 1,125.00			
39	Insurance Expense			(e) 520.00			
40	Depreciation Expense, Building			(f) 3,500.00			
41	Depreciation Expense, Equipment			(g) 4,900.00			
42	Wages Payable				(h) 1,030.00		1,030.00
43				143,675.00	143,675.00	484,555.00	378,704.00
44	Net Income						105,851.00
45						484,555.00	484,555.00
46							

Sheet1 Sheet2 Sheet3

In Figure 3, we observe the balance of J. Conner, Capital listed on the work sheet as $253,774. We note from the ledger account a credit of $9,000 representing an additional investment. Therefore, the beginning balance of J. Conner, Capital was $244,774 ($253,774 − $9,000).

Figure 4
Statement of owner's equity for Whitewater Raft Supply

Whitewater Raft Supply Statement of Owner's Equity For Year Ended December 31, 20--		
J. Conner, Capital, January 1, 20--		$244,774
Investment during the Year	$ 9,000	
Net Income for the Year	105,851	
Subtotal	$114,851	
Less Withdrawals for the Year	77,000	
Increase in Capital		37,851
J. Conner, Capital, December 31, 20--		$282,625

BALANCE SHEET

Learning Objective

Prepare a classified balance sheet for any type of business.

Balance sheet classifications are generally uniform for all types of business enterprises. You are strongly urged to take the time to learn the following definitions of the classifications and the order of accounts within them. As you read, refer to Figure 5.

Current Assets

Current Assets consist of cash and any other assets or resources that are expected to be realized in cash or to be sold or consumed during the normal operating cycle of the business (or one year if the normal operating cycle is less than 12 months).

Figure 5
Balance sheet for Whitewater Raft Supply

Whitewater Raft Supply
Balance Sheet
December 31, 20--

Assets			
Current Assets:			
Cash		$ 24,154	
Notes Receivable		4,000	
Accounts Receivable		29,546	
Merchandise Inventory		64,800	
Supplies		415	
Prepaid Insurance		440	
Total Current Assets			$123,355
Property and Equipment:			
Land		$122,100	
Building	$129,000		
Less Accumulated Depreciation	54,500	74,500	
Equipment	$ 33,100		
Less Accumulated Depreciation	21,300	11,800	
Total Property and Equipment			208,400
Total Assets			$331,755
Liabilities			
Current Liabilities:			
Notes Payable		$ 36,600	
Mortgage Payable (current portion)		2,000	
Accounts Payable		3,300	
Wages Payable		1,030	
Unearned Course Fees		400	
Total Current Liabilities			$ 43,330
Long-Term Liabilities:			
Mortgage Payable			5,800
Total Liabilities			$ 49,130
Owner's Equity			
J. Conner, Capital			282,625
Total Liabilities and Owner's Equity			$331,755

Accountants list current assets in the order of their convertibility into cash—in other words, their **liquidity**. (If you have an asset, such as a car or a stereo, and you sell it quickly and turn it into cash, you are said to be turning it into a *liquid* state.) If a company has the first four accounts shown under Current Assets in Figure 5, they are presented in the following order: (1) Cash, (2) Notes Receivable, (3) Accounts Receivable, and (4) Merchandise Inventory.

Notes Receivable (current) are short-term (one year or less) promissory notes (promise-to-pay notes) held by the firm. A note is generally received from a customer as a substitute for a charge account.

Prepaid Insurance and Supplies are considered prepaid items that will be used up or will expire within the following operating cycle or year. Generally, these prepaid items are not converted into cash, which is why they appear at the bottom of the Current Assets section.

Some companies are so successful that they accumulate cash from earnings that are not needed to pay current obligations. Rather than leaving the cash in a bank account, companies may prefer to invest it in short-term government or corporate notes or bonds. These are called marketable securities. On the balance sheet, Marketable Securities is a separate account listed just below Cash.

Property and Equipment

Property and Equipment are relatively long-lived assets that are held for use in the production or sale of other assets or services; some accountants refer to them as *fixed assets*. The three types of accounts that usually appear in this category are Land, Building, and Equipment. (Refer to Figure 5.) Note that the Building and Equipment accounts are followed by their respective Accumulated Depreciation accounts. We list these assets in order of their length of life, with the longest-lived asset placed first.

Remember

Because Accumulated Depreciation is a contra account, it is deducted from the appropriate asset.

Current Liabilities

Current Liabilities are debts that will become due within the normal operating cycle of the business, usually within one year; they normally will be paid, when due, from current assets. List current liabilities in the order of their expected payment. Notes Payable represents the amount owed on promissory notes. Mortgage Payable is the payment made to reduce the principal of the mortgage in a given year. Accounts Payable are debts owed to creditors. Wages Payable and any other accrued liabilities, such as Commissions Payable and the current portion of unearned revenue accounts, usually fall at the bottom of the list of current liabilities.

Long-Term Liabilities

Long-Term Liabilities are debts that are payable over a comparatively long period, usually longer than one year. The current portion of notes, contracts, and loans (the amount of principal due within the next year) is shown as a current liability. The remaining amount is shown as a long-term liability. Note that for Whitewater Raft Supply, $2,000 of the Mortgage Payable represents the current portion and is shown as a current liability. The remaining $5,800 is shown as a long-term liability. (Refer to Figure 5.)

WORKING CAPITAL AND CURRENT RATIO

3 Compute working capital and current ratio.

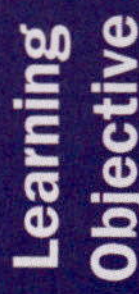

Both the management and the short-term creditors of a firm are vitally interested in two questions:

1. Does the firm have a sufficient amount of capital to operate?
2. Does the firm have the ability to pay its debts?

Two measures used to answer these questions are a firm's working capital and its current ratio; the necessary data are taken from a classified balance sheet.

Working capital is determined by subtracting current liabilities from current assets; thus,

$$\text{Working capital} = \text{Current assets} - \text{Current liabilities}$$

The normal operating cycle for most firms is less than one year. Because current assets equal cash—or items that can be converted into cash or used up within one year—and current liabilities equal the total amount the company must pay out within one year, working capital is appropriately named. It is the amount of capital the company has available to use or to work with. The working capital for Whitewater Raft Supply is as follows:

$$\text{Working capital} = \$123{,}355 - \$43{,}330 = \$80{,}025$$

The **current ratio** is useful in revealing a firm's ability to pay its bills. It is determined by dividing current assets by current liabilities.

The current ratio has a weakness. It favors companies with many current assets. However, the current ratio does not attempt to measure the overall strength of a company.

$$\text{Current ratio} = \frac{\text{Current assets (amount of cash coming in within one year)}}{\text{Current liabilities (amount of cash going out within one year)}}$$

The current ratio for Whitewater Raft Supply is calculated like this:

$$\text{Current ratio} = \frac{\$123{,}355}{\$43{,}330} = 2.85$$

In the case of Whitewater Raft Supply, $2.85 in current assets is available to pay every dollar currently due on December 31.

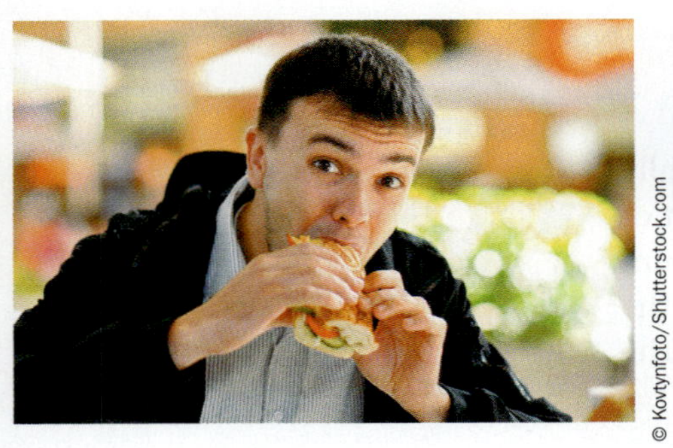

In the Real World

In franchises such as Subway, minimum working capital standards are used to make sure franchisees have adequate financial resources to run their businesses successfully. Each franchise-granting organization has its own financial requirements regarding minimum working capital standards. These standards are typically based on the location of the business and on minimum performance standards.

YOU Make the Call

J. J. Marston owns Woodland Toys, a small business selling handmade wooden toys. Sales have been a bit slow, so he has come up with some strategies to increase sales as well as to begin exporting his specialty toys. The problem is that he needs cash to hire assistants and to purchase several woodworking tools to increase production. He has tried to figure out how he can manage the investment. He has no idea how to analyze his financial statements to provide valuable decision-making information. How would you recommend that he use his most recent balance sheet (shown below) and the two formulas discussed in the chapter to help him decide whether to expand his operation?

Woodland Toys
Balance Sheet
December 31, 20--

Assets		
Current Assets:		
Cash	$22,751	
Accounts Receivable	7,692	
Merchandise Inventory	45,018	
Prepaid Insurance	1,265	
Total Current Assets		$76,726
Property and Equipment:		
Shop Equipment	$18,357	
Less Accumulated Depreciation	6,020	
Total Property and Equipment		12,337
Total Assets		$89,063
Liabilities		
Current Liabilities:		
Accounts Payable	$10,340	
Total Current Liabilities		$10,340
Long-Term Liabilities:		
Mortgage Payable		3,500
Total Liabilities		$13,840
Owner's Equity		
J. J. Marston, Capital		75,223
Total Liabilities and Owner's Equity		$89,063

(Continued)

YOU Make the Call

SOLUTION

While many more tools are available for analyzing financial statements than have been introduced, you have learned two formulas in this chapter that can assist Mr. Marston in determining his ability to expand his business—working capital and current ratio.

Working capital is the amount of capital the company has available to use or to work with. To compute Woodland Toys' working capital, subtract its current liabilities from its current assets:

$$\text{Working capital} = \$76{,}726 - \$10{,}340 = \$66{,}386$$

While J. J. Marston does not want to liquidate all of his assets, he can see that there is adequate capital to begin planning his business expansion.

A second formula that can help in making the decision to expand is the current ratio. It is useful in revealing a firm's ability to pay its bills. To compute Woodland Toys' current ratio, divide its current assets by its current liabilities.

$$\text{Current ratio} = \frac{\$76{,}726}{\$10{,}340} = 7.42$$

This means that $7.42 in current asset is available to pay every dollar of debt currently due on December 31. The higher the current ratio, the better position the company is in to pay short-term debt. A current ratio of 7.42 shows that Woodland Toys is in a very favorable position.

Chart of Accounts

Remember

A common organization for the chart of accounts is

Assets	1--
Liabilities	2--
Owner's Equity	3--
Revenue	4--
Cost of Goods Sold	5--
Expenses	6--

When we introduced the chart of accounts and the account number arrangement, we said that the first digit represents the classification of an account. Because we are now acquainted with classified income statements and balance sheets, we can introduce the second digit. The second digit stands for the subclassification.

Assets	1--	Revenue	4--
Current Assets	11-	Revenue from Sales	41-
Property and Equipment	12-	Other Income	42-
Liabilities	2--	Cost of Goods Sold	5--
Current Liabilities	21-	Purchases	51-
Long-Term Liabilities	22-	Expenses	6--
Owner's Equity	3--	Selling Expenses	61-
Capital	31-	General Expenses	62-
		Other Expenses	63-

The third digit indicates the placement of the account within the subclassification. For example, account number 411 represents Sales, which is the first account listed under Revenue. Account number 512 represents Purchases Returns and Allowances, which is the second account listed under Cost of Goods Sold. Account number 312 represents Drawing, which is the second account listed under Owner's Equity.

To: **Amy Roberts, CPA**
Subject: **End of the Year**

Hi Amy,
Thanks for sending the examples of a classified income statement and balance sheet. These were very helpful. Now that we are approaching the end of the year, do you have time to discuss the closing entries that I need to do for Whitewater Raft Supply? Are these entries different for a merchandising business?
Janie

To: **Janie Conner**
Subject: **RE: End of the Year**

Hi Janie,
Closing entries for your merchandising business are handled in the same way as the entries you completed for your service business. The closing process involves the same four steps, which include resetting your temporary accounts to a zero balance.

In addition to closing entries, you may also need to do reversing entries. Reversing entries let routine transactions continue to be posted in their usual manner without worrying about how the adjusting entry may interfere. Here's what we'll talk about at our next meeting.

_____ 1. Review closing entries.

_____ 2. Record reversing entries and understand why your company might use them.

Congratulations on wrapping up your first year. Let me know if I can help you with anything else.
Amy

CLOSING ENTRIES

Learning Objective

 Record the closing entries for a merchandising firm.

Now let's look at closing entries for a merchandising business. You follow the same four steps to close, or zero out, the revenue, expense, and Drawing accounts as you do for a service business.

At the end of a fiscal period, you close the revenue and expense accounts so that you can start the next fiscal period with zero balances. You close the Drawing account because it, too, applies to one fiscal period. Recall in Chapter 5 we discussed that these accounts are called **temporary-equity accounts**, or *nominal accounts*.

Figure 6 shows the isolated Income Statement columns. After you have looked them over, we'll discuss at the four steps of the closing procedure.

Figure 6
Partial work sheet for Whitewater Raft Supply

	A	B	C	H	I
1	Whitewater Raft Supply				
2	Work Sheet				
3	For Month Ended December 31, 20--				
4					
5		TRIAL BALANCE		INCOME STATEMENT	
6	ACCOUNT NAME	DEBIT	CREDIT	DEBIT	CREDIT
7	Cash	24,154.00			
8	Notes Receivable	4,000.00			
9	Accounts Receivable	29,546.00			
10	Merchandise Inventory	67,000.00			
11	Supplies	1,540.00			
12	Prepaid Insurance	960.00			
13	Land	122,100.00			
14	Building	129,000.00			
15	Accumulated Depreciation, Building		51,000.00		
16	Equipment	33,100.00			
17	Accumulated Depreciation, Equipment		16,400.00		
18	Notes Payable		36,600.00		
19	Accounts Payable		3,300.00		
20	Unearned Course Fees		1,200.00		
21	Mortgage Payable		7,800.00		
22	J. Conner, Capital		253,774.00		
23	J. Conner, Drawing	77,000.00			
24	Sales		257,180.00		257,180.00
25	Sales Returns and Allowances	940.00		940.00	
26	Sales Discounts	1,980.00		1,980.00	
27	Interest Income		220.00		220.00
28	Purchases	87,840.00		87,840.00	
29	Purchases Returns and Allowances		932.00		932.00
30	Purchases Discounts		1,348.00		1,348.00
31	Freight In	2,360.00		2,360.00	
32	Wages Expense	45,900.00		46,930.00	
33	Property Tax Expense	1,860.00		1,860.00	
34	Interest Expense	474.00		474.00	
35		629,754.00	629,754.00		
36	Income Summary			67,000.00	64,800.00
37	Course Fees Income				800.00
38	Supplies Expense			1,125.00	
39	Insurance Expense			520.00	
40	Depreciation Expense, Building			3,500.00	
41	Depreciation Expense, Equipment			4,900.00	
42	Wages Payable				
43				219,429.00	325,280.00
44	Net Income			105,851.00	
45				325,280.00	325,280.00
46					

Sheet1 Sheet2 Sheet3

Four Steps in the Closing Procedure

These four steps should be followed when closing:

STEP 1. Close the revenue accounts and the other accounts that appear on the income statement and that have credit balances (all temporary or nominal accounts with credit balances) into Income Summary. **(Debit the figures that are credited in the Income Statement columns of the work sheet, except the figure on the Income Summary line.)** This entry is illustrated for Whitewater Raft Supply as follows:

GENERAL JOURNAL — Page 97

Date		Description	Post. Ref.	Debit	Credit
20--		Closing Entries			
Dec.	31	Sales		257 1 8 0 00	
		Interest Income		2 2 0 00	
		Purchases Returns and Allowances		9 3 2 00	
		Purchases Discounts		1 3 4 8 00	
		Course Fees Income		8 0 0 00	
		Income Summary			260 4 8 0 00

STEP 2. Close the expense accounts and the other accounts appearing on the income statement that have debit balances (all temporary or nominal accounts with debit balances) into Income Summary. **(Credit the figures that are debited in the Income Statement columns of the work sheet, except the figure on the Income Summary line.)**

Note that you close Purchases Discounts and Purchases Returns and Allowances in Step 1 along with the revenue accounts. Note also that in Step 2, you close Sales Discounts and Sales Returns and Allowances along with the expense accounts.

GENERAL JOURNAL — Page 97

Date		Description	Post. Ref.	Debit	Credit
Dec.	31	Income Summary		152 4 2 9 00	
		Sales Returns and Allowances			9 4 0 00
		Sales Discounts			1 9 8 0 00
		Purchases			87 8 4 0 00
		Freight In			2 3 6 0 00
		Wages Expense			46 9 3 0 00
		Supplies Expense			1 1 2 5 00
		Property Tax Expense			1 8 6 0 00
		Interest Expense			4 7 4 00
		Insurance Expense			5 2 0 00
		Depreciation Expense, Building			3 5 0 0 00
		Depreciation Expense, Equipment			4 9 0 0 00

STEP 3. Close the Income Summary account into the Capital account, transferring the net income or loss to the Capital account.

GENERAL JOURNAL — Page 97

Date		Description	Post. Ref.	Debit	Credit
Dec.	31	Income Summary		105 8 5 1 00	
		J. Conner, Capital			105 8 5 1 00

Here is what the T accounts look like. Note that the Income Summary account already contains adjusting entries for merchandise inventory.

Income Summary

Debit		Credit	
Adj. (Beginning Merchandise Inventory)	67,000	Adj. (Ending Merchandise Inventory)	64,800
Closing (Expenses and other debit balance accounts)	152,429	Closing (Revenue and other credit balance accounts)	260,480
Closing (Net Income)	105,851		

J. Conner, Capital

−		+	
		Bal.	253,774
		Closing (Net Income)	105,851

STEP 4. Close the Drawing account into the Capital account.

GENERAL JOURNAL — Page 97

Date		Description	Post. Ref.	Debit	Credit
Dec.	31	J. Conner, Capital		77 0 0 0 00	
		J. Conner, Drawing			77 0 0 0 00

Here is what the T accounts would look like.

J. Conner, Drawing

+		−	
Bal.	77,000	Closing	77,000

J. Conner, Capital

−		+	
Closing (Drawing)	77,000	Bal.	253,774
		Closing (Net Income)	105,851
		Bal.	282,625

REVERSING ENTRIES

5 Determine which adjusting entries can be reversed and record the reversing entries.

Learning Objective

Reversing entries are general journal entries that are the exact reverse of certain adjusting entries. A reversing entry enables the accountant to record routine transactions in the usual manner *even though* an adjusting entry affecting one of the accounts involved in the transaction has intervened. We can understand this concept best by looking at an example.

Suppose there is an adjusting entry for accrued wages owed to employees at the end of the fiscal year. Assume that, altogether, the employees of Mason Company earn $400 per day for a five-day week and that payday occurs every Friday throughout the year. When the employees get their checks at 5 P.M. on Friday, the checks include their wages for that day and for the preceding four days. And assume that December 31, the last day of the fiscal year, falls on a Wednesday. A diagram of this situation would look like this:

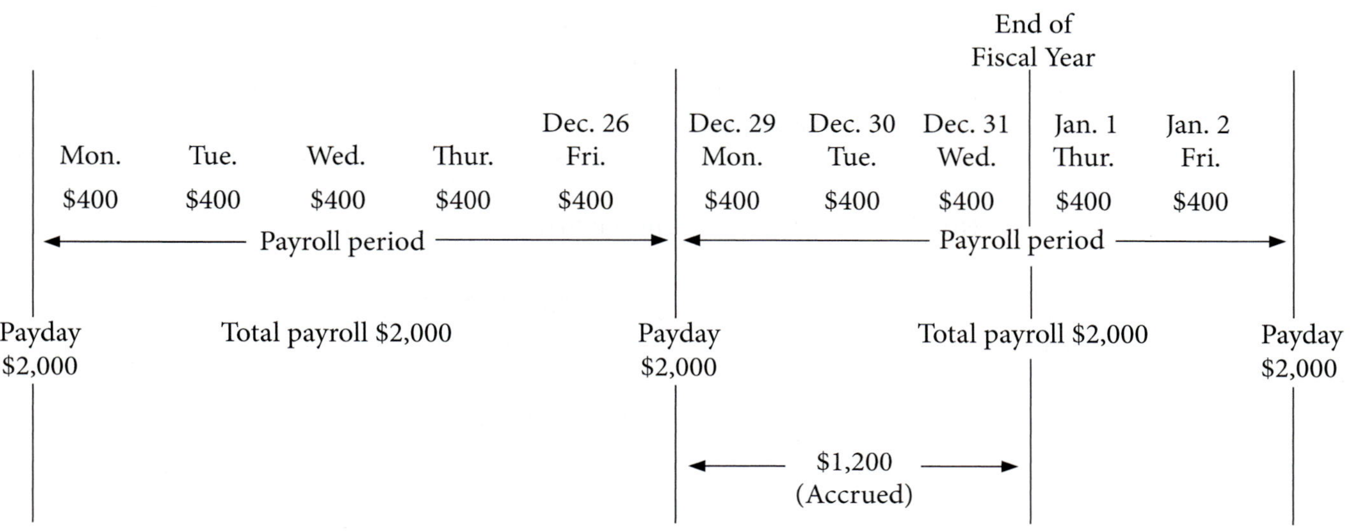

Each Friday during the year, the payroll has been debited to the Wages Expense account and credited to the Cash account. As a result, Wages Expense has a debit balance of $102,000 as of December 26. The year-end adjusting entry, in T account form, would be:

Wages Expense

	+	−	
Bal.	102,000		
Dec. 31 Adj.	1,200		

Wages Payable

	−	+	
		Dec. 31 Adj.	1,200

Next, when all of the expense accounts are closed, Wages Expense is closed by crediting it for $103,200. However, Wages Payable continues to have a credit balance of $1,200. The $2,000 payroll on January 2 must be allocated by debiting Wages Payable $1,200, debiting Wages Expense $800, and crediting Cash $2,000.

FYI

The use of reversing entries is optional.

The employee who records the payroll not only has to record this particular payroll differently from all other weekly payrolls for the year but also has to refer back to the adjusting entry to determine what portion of the $2,000 is debited to Wages Payable and what portion is debited to Wages Expense. In many companies, however, the employee who records the payroll does not have access to the adjusting entries.

There is a solution to this problem. The need to refer to the earlier entry and allocate the debit total between the two accounts is eliminated *if a reversing entry is made on the first day of the following fiscal period.* You make an entry that is the reverse of the adjusting entry as follows:

GENERAL JOURNAL Page 118

Date		Description	Post. Ref.	Debit	Credit
20--		Reversing Entries			
Jan.	1	Wages Payable		1 2 0 0 00	
		Wages Expense			1 2 0 0 00

Now let's bring the T accounts up to date.

Wages Expense

	+	–	
Bal.	102,000		
Dec. 31 Adj.	1,200	Dec. 31 Closing	103,200
Bal.	——	Jan. 1 Reversing	1,200

Wages Payable

	–	+	
Jan. 1 Reversing	1,200	Dec. 31 Adj.	1,200

The reversing entry has the effect of transferring the $1,200 liability from Wages Payable to the credit side of Wages Expense. Wages Expense will temporarily have a credit balance until the next payroll is recorded in the routine manner. In our example, this occurs on January 2 as follows:

Wages Expense

	+	–	
Bal.	102,000		
Dec. 31 Adj.	1,200	Dec. 31 Closing	103,200
Bal.	——		
Jan. 2	2,000	Jan. 1 Reversing	1,200
Bal.	800		

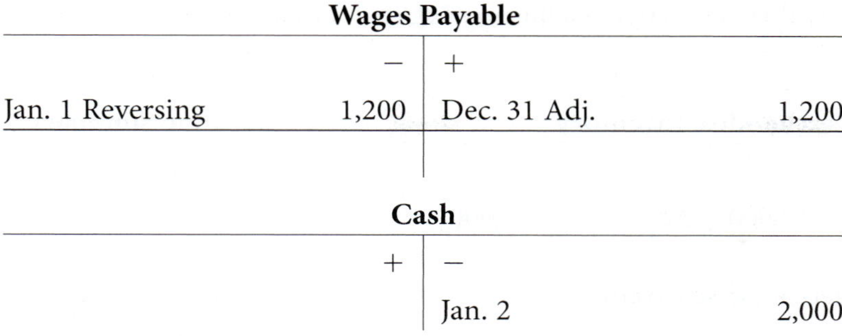

There is now a *net debit balance* of $800 in Wages Expense, which is the correct amount ($400 for January 1 and $400 for January 2). To see this, look at the following ledger accounts. December 26 was the last payday of one year, and January 2 is the first payday of the next year.

GENERAL LEDGER

ACCOUNT **Wages Expense** **ACCOUNT NO.** **611**

Date		Item	Post. Ref.	Debit	Credit	Balance Debit	Balance Credit
20--							
Dec.	26		CP16	2 0 0 0 00		102 0 0 0 00	
	31	Adjusting	J116	1 2 0 0 00		103 2 0 0 00	
	31	Closing	J117		103 2 0 0 00	———	———
20--							
Jan.	1	Reversing	J118		1 2 0 0 00		1 2 0 0 00
	2		CP17	2 0 0 0 00		8 0 0 00	

ACCOUNT **Wages Payable** **ACCOUNT NO.** **213**

Date		Item	Post. Ref.	Debit	Credit	Balance Debit	Balance Credit
20--							
Dec.	31	Adjusting	J116		1 2 0 0 00		1 2 0 0 00
20--							
Jan.	1	Reversing	J118	1 2 0 0 00		———	———

The reversing entry for accrued salaries or wages applies to service as well as merchandising companies. You can see that a reversing entry simply switches an adjusting entry. The question is, Which adjusting entries should be reversed? Here are two handy rules for reversing. **If an adjusting entry is to be reversed, it must meet both of the following qualifications:**

1. **The adjusting entry increases an asset or liability account.**
2. **The asset or liability account did not have a previous balance.**

With the exception of the first year of operations, Merchandise Inventory and contra accounts—such as Accumulated Depreciation—always have previous balances. Consequently, adjusting entries involving these accounts should never be reversed.

Let's apply these rules to the adjusting entries for Whitewater Raft Supply.

Do not reverse: Merchandise Inventory is an asset, but it was decreased and has a previous balance.

Merchandise Inventory			
	+	−	
Bal.	67,000	Adj.	67,000

Income Summary			
Adj.	67,000		

Do not reverse: Merchandise Inventory is an asset, but it has a previous balance.

Merchandise Inventory			
	+	−	
Bal.	67,000	Adj.	67,000
Adj.	64,800		

Income Summary			
Adj.	67,000	Adj.	64,800

Do not reverse: Unearned Course Fees is a liability, but it was decreased and has a previous balance.

Course Fees Income			
	−	+	
		Adj.	800

Unearned Course Fees			
	−	+	
Adj.	800	Bal.	1,200

Do not reverse: Supplies is an asset account, but it was decreased and has a previous balance.

Supplies			
	+	−	
Bal.	1,540	Adj.	1,125

Supplies Expense			
	+	−	
Adj.	1,125		

Do not reverse: Prepaid Insurance is an asset account, but it was decreased and has a previous balance.

Insurance Expense			
	+	−	
Adj.	520		

Prepaid Insurance			
	+	−	
Bal.	960	Adj.	520

Do not reverse: Accumulated Depreciation is a contra asset, and it always has a previous balance after the first year.

Depreciation Expense, Building			
	+	−	
Adj.	3,500		

Accumulated Depreciation, Building			
	−	+	
		Bal.	51,000
		Adj.	3,500

Do not reverse: Accumulated Depreciation is a contra asset, and it always has a previous balance after the first year.

Depreciation Expense, Equipment			
	+	−	
Adj.	4,900		

Accumulated Depreciation, Equipment			
	−	+	
		Bal.	16,400
		Adj.	4,900

Reverse: Wages Payable is a liability account. It was increased, and it had no previous balance.

Wages Expense			
	+	−	
Bal.	45,900		
Adj.	1,030		

Wages Payable			
	−	+	
		Adj.	1,030

Remember

Reversing entries are optional.

Whenever additional adjusting entries are introduced, we make it a point to state whether they can be reversed.

Accounting with QuickBooks®

Financial Statement Reporting and Analysis

Learning Objective

1 View and print comparison financial statements.

Learning Objectives

After you have completed this section, you will be able to do the following:

1. View and print comparison financial statements.
2. View and print graphs.
3. View and print the statement of cash flows.
4. Find and correct accounting errors with QuickBooks.
5. Complete reversing entries.
6. Complete closing entries for a merchandising company.

Accounting is the process of analyzing, classifying, recording, summarizing, and *interpreting* business transactions. The financial condition of a company is of interest not only to owners, employers, and mangers, but also to creditors. We are now ready to prepare and use financial statements, with QuickBooks, that will help us interpret information about various companies.

One technique for analyzing and interpreting financial data is the preparation of comparative financial statements. Two types of analysis—horizontal and vertical—are commonly used. **Horizontal analysis** is the comparison of the same item in a company's financial statements for two or more periods. **Vertical analysis**, on the other hand, compares one account as a percentage of the total within the same financial statement. For example, a comparative balance sheet, using vertical analysis, may express Cash as a percentage of total assets. A financial statement using vertical analysis percentages is known as a **common-size statement**. Common-size statements can be used to compare one company with another or to compare a company against industry averages. Trade and marketing associations often gather information and publish common-size statements.

To view and print a comparative financial statement, follow the steps in Figures Q1 and Q2.

STEP 1. Click **Reports**.

STEP 2. Select **Company & Financial**.

STEP 3. Select **Profit & Loss Prev Year Comparison** for this example.

STEP 4. Click **Customize Report**.

STEP 5. Adjust the **From**: and **To**: dates and then click **Refresh**.

STEP 6. To complete a horizontal analysis of any financial statement, check **Previous Year** and then check **$ Change** or **% Change** based on the desired report information.

STEP 7. To complete a vertical analysis of any financial statement, select any of the following options: **% of Row; % of Column; % of Income; or % of Expense**.

STEP 8. To print the report, click the **Print** button.

STEP 9. Click **OK**.

QuickBooks Tip

An accurate vertical analysis cannot be completed using the QuickBooks balance sheet reports. To complete a vertical analysis of balance sheet information, export a QuickBooks balance sheet report into Excel, as shown in Step 7 of Figure Q2.

Figure Q1
Comparative financial statement report access

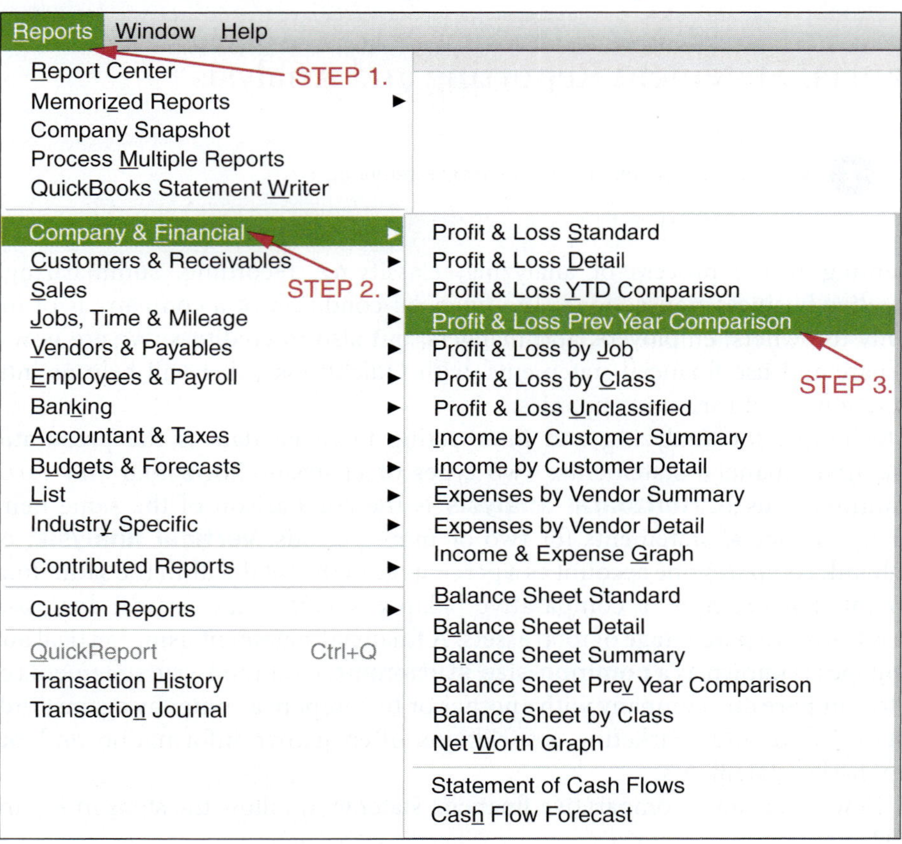

Figure Q2
Modify reports for horizontal and vertical analyses

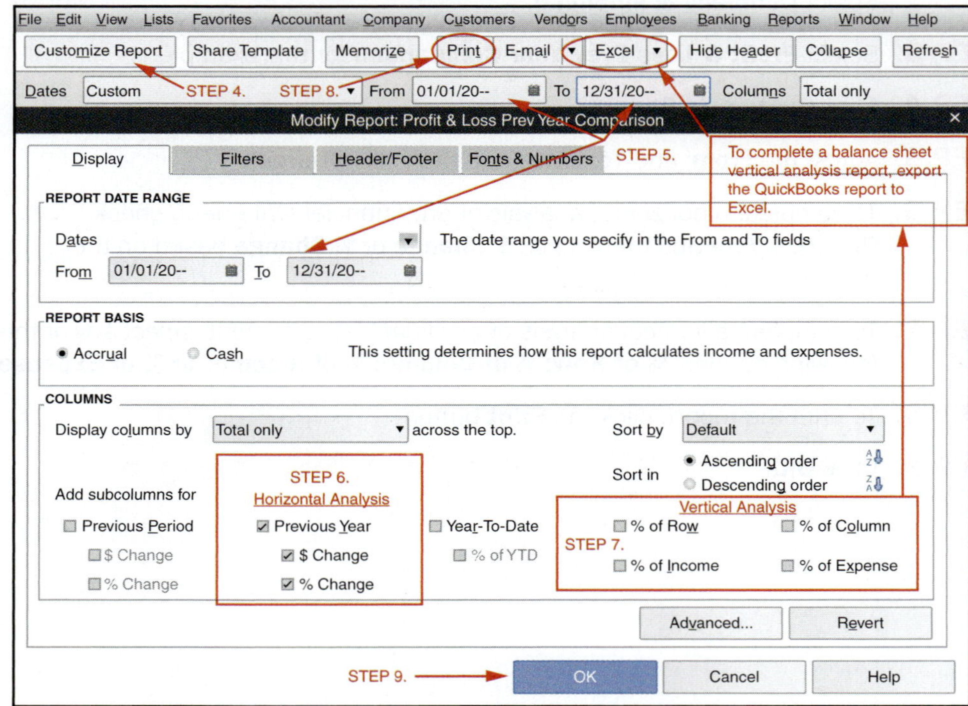

Figure Q3 shows the **Profit & Loss Prev Year Comparison** report for Southern Office Furniture, using horizontal analysis.

Figure Q3
Profit and loss previous year comparison horizontal analysis report

Southern Office Furniture
Profit & Loss Prev Year Comparison
January through December 2015

	Jan – Dec 15	Jan – Dec 14	$ Change	% Change
Income				
Sales	533,600.00	510,000.00	23,600.00	4.6%
Sales Returns and Allowances	–5,600.00	–10,000.00	4,400.00	44.0%
Total Income	528,000.00	500,000.00	28,000.00	5.6%
Cost of Goods Sold				
Cost of Goods Sold	278,000.00	248,000.00	30,000.00	12.1%
Total COGS	278,000.00	248,000.00	30,000.00	12.1%
Gross Profit	250,000.00	252,000.00	–2,000.00	–0.8%
Expense				
Sales Salary Expense	63,600.00	58,000.00	5,600.00	9.7%
Rent Expense	24,000.00	24,000.00	0.00	0.0%
Advertising Expense	21,400.00	16,000.00	5,400.00	33.8%
Depreciation Expense, Equipment	20,000.00	18,000.00	2,000.00	11.1%
Insurance Expense	2,000.00	2,000.00	0.00	0.0%
Store Supplies Expense	1000.00	1,000.00	0.00	0.0%
Miscellaneous Expense	1000.00	1,000.00	0.00	0.0%
Total Expense	133,000.00	120,000.00	13,000.00	10.8%
Net Income	**117,000.00**	**132, 000.00**	**–15,000.00**	**–11.4%**

Learning Objective

2 View and print graphs.

Sometimes it is easier to explain financial information with a picture, rather than numbers. QuickBooks has several reports that can be displayed as a graph. To view and print graphs with QuickBooks, follow the steps in Figures Q4 and Q5.

STEP 1. Click **Reports**.

STEP 2. Select **Company & Financial**.

STEP 3. Select **Income & Expense Graph** for this example.

QuickBooks Tip

Exporting QuickBooks' report data to Excel provides additional graphing features and formatting options.

Figure Q4
Graph report access

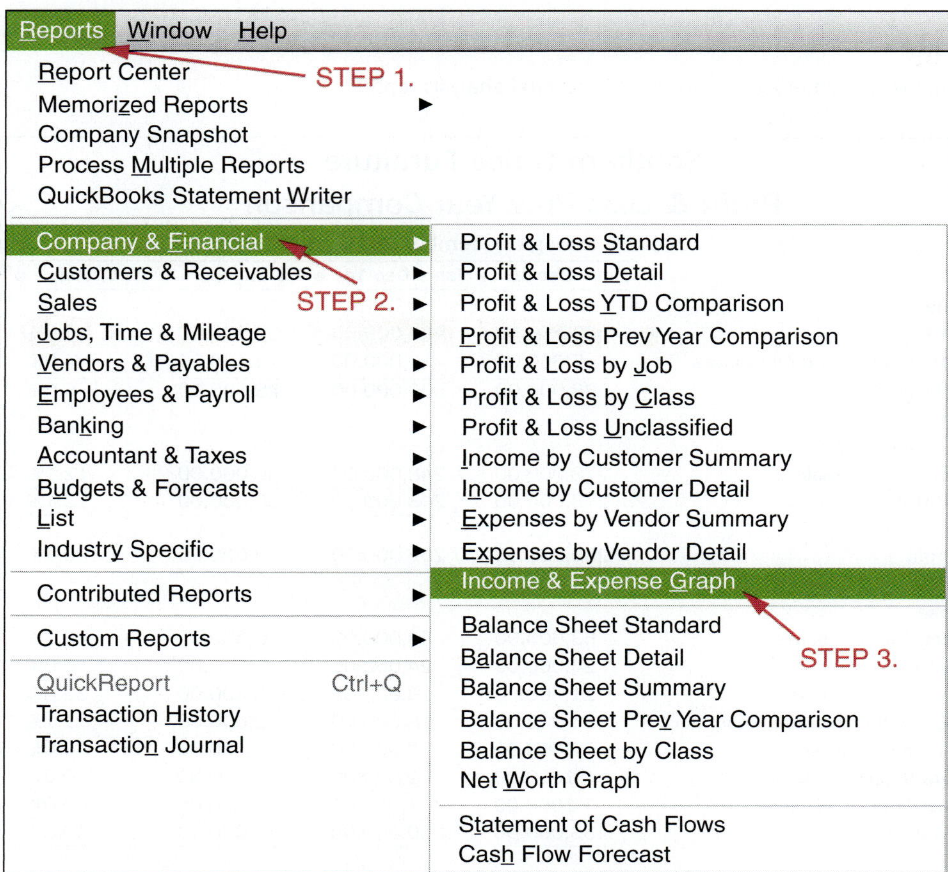

STEP 4. Click **Dates**.

STEP 5. In the **Change Graph Dates** window, adjust the **From**: and **To**: dates and then click **Refresh**.

STEP 6. Click **OK**.

Figure Q5
Change graph dates window

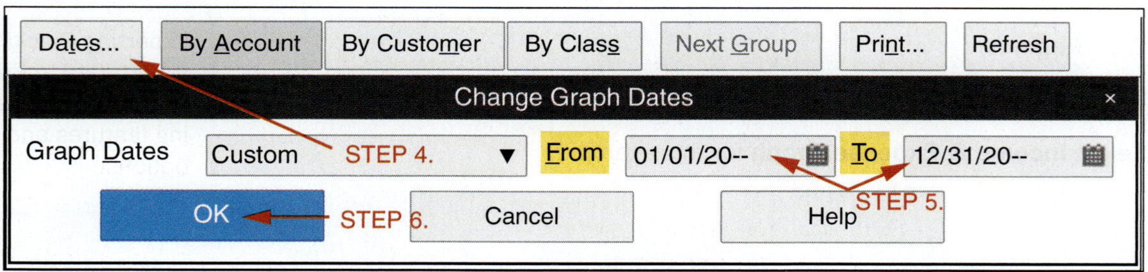

Figure Q6 shows an example of an **Income and Expense Graph** report.

Figure Q6
Income and expense graph report

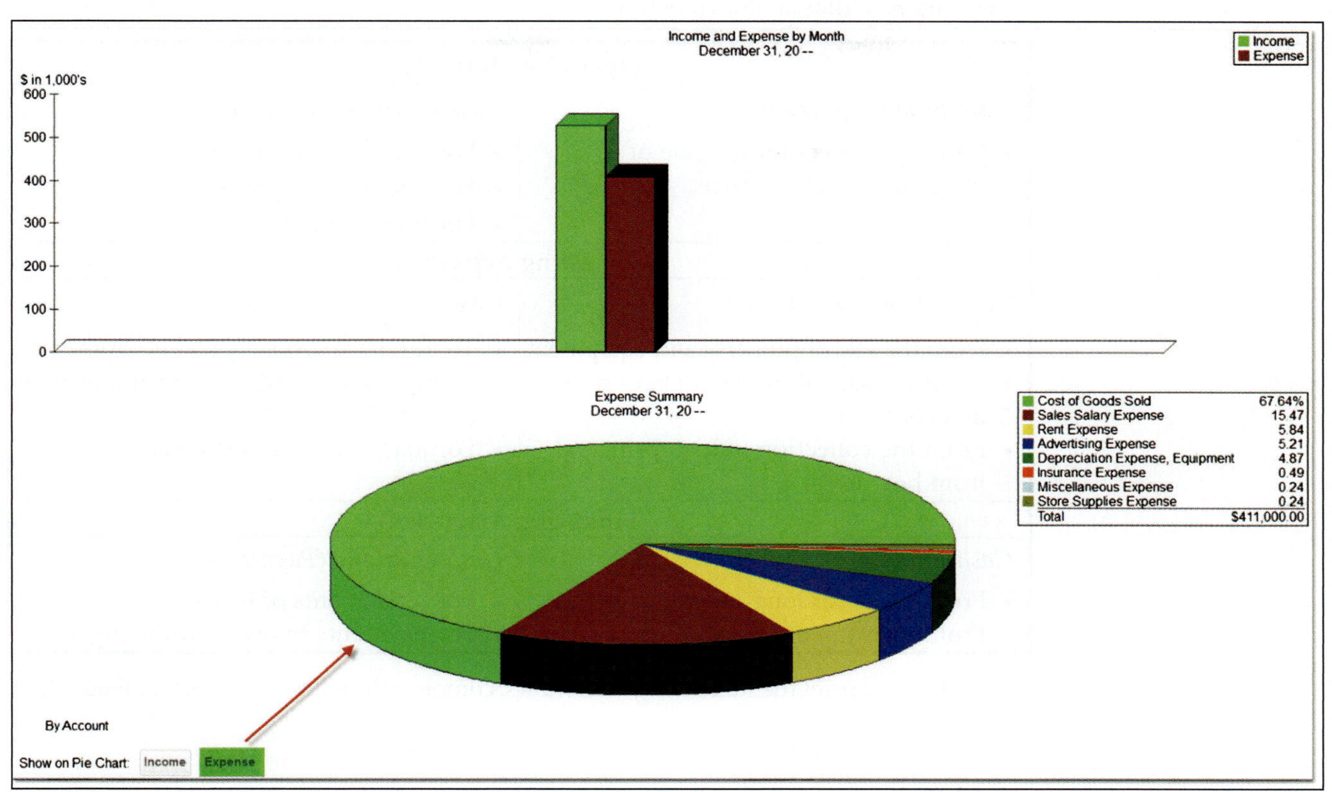

Learning Objective

3 View and print the statement of cash flows.

The fourth major financial statement is the **statement of cash flows**. This statement explains in detail how the balance of Cash has changed between the beginning and the end of the fiscal period. A profitable company can still go out of business if it runs out of cash. Therefore, the statement of cash flows is as important to a company as an income statement.

The main purpose of the statement of cash flows is to provide a summary of information concerning a company's cash receipts and payments during a fiscal period. A secondary purpose is to provide information about a firm's operating, investing, and financing activities during a fiscal period. The statement of cash flows also serves to reconcile the beginning and ending cash balance for the period. The statement of cash flows has three main sections: **Operating Activities**, **Investing Activities**, and **Financing Activities**. Cash flows are subdivided into cash inflows and cash outflows.

Cash, for purposes of the cash flow statement, includes checking and savings accounts as well as **cash equivalents**. A company that has idle cash temporarily during the year may prefer to invest in short-term interest-bearing notes or money market funds. These short-term funds are considered to be cash equivalents.

Preparing a statement of cash flows is easy with QuickBooks. QuickBooks uses the **indirect method**, which involves adjusting net income to determine cash flows from operating activities as shown below.

Operating Activities	
Cash Inflows (Receipts): • From customers for the sale of merchandise and services	*Cash Outflows (Payments):* • For merchandise purchases • For operating expenses • For interest paid
Investing Activities	
Cash Inflows (Receipts): • From the sale of property and equipment • From the sale of investments or bonds in a corporation • From the collection of loan principal from borrowers	*Cash Outflows (Payments):* • To purchase property and equipment • To purchase investments or bonds in a corporation • For loans made to borrowers
Financing Activities	
Cash Inflows (Receipts): • From short- or long-term borrowings • From investment of cash by owner	*Cash Outflows (Payments):* • For repayments of loans • For payments to owner (drawings)

To view and print the statement of cash flows, complete the following steps (see Figure Q7):

STEP 1. Click **Reports**.

STEP 2. Select **Company & Financial**.

Figure Q7
Statement of cash flows report access

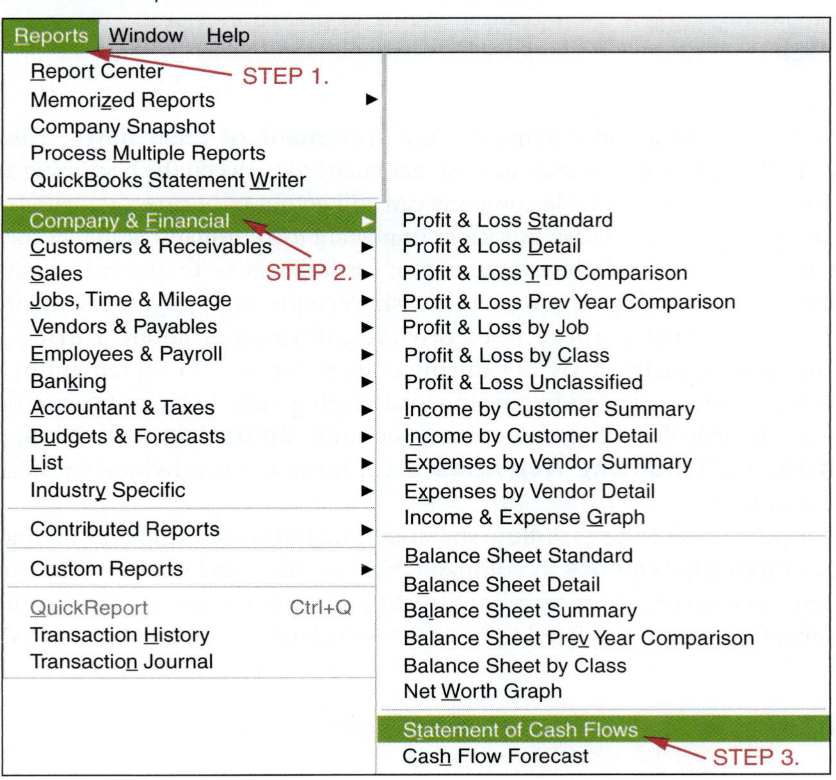

STEP 3. Select **Statement of Cash Flows**.

STEP 4. Adjust the **From:** and **To:** dates and then click Refresh.

STEP 5. To print the report, click the Print button.

STEP 6. Click OK.

Figure Q8 shows an example of a **Statement of Cash Flows** report for Conner's Whitewater Adventures.

Figure Q8
Statement of cash flows

Conner's Whitewater Adventures
Statement of Cash Flows
January through December 20--

	Jan - Dec
▾ OPERATING ACTIVITIES	
Net Income	16,796.00
▾ Adjustments to reconcile Net Income	
▾ to net cash provided by operations:	
113 Accounts Receivable	–4,250.00
115 Supplies	–215.00
117 Prepaid Insurance	–1,250.00
221 Accounts Payable	3,425.00
222 Wages Payable	472.00
Net cash provided by Operating Activites	14,978.000
▾ INVESTING ACTIVITIES	
124 Equipment	–51,300.00
125 Accum. Depr., Equipment	512.00
Net cash provided by Investing Activites	–50,788.00
▾ FINANCING ACTIVITIES	
311 J. Conner, Capital	91,700.00
Net cash provided by Financing Activites	91,700.00
Net cash increase for period	55,890.00
Cash at end of period	**55,890.00**

Find and correct accounting errors with QuickBooks.

Learning Objective

Ideally, errors will be noticed before transactions are saved in QuickBooks; however, occasionally errors are not detected until after a transaction has been updated. There are two ways to identify errors in QuickBooks:

1. From the original entry source.
2. By reviewing reports.

Let's look at an example of how to delete or void a transaction from the original entry source of **Write Checks**. (See Figures Q9 through Q11.)

STEP 1. Click **Write Checks** from the home page as shown in Figure Q9. Then locate the check you want to delete or void.

QuickBooks Tip

Company policies vary as to whether documents can be deleted or voided. QuickBooks allows the administrator to restrict user access to the Delete and Void options. Regardless of a company's policy, it is important to track deleted or voided documents for audit and internal control purposes.

Figure Q9
Write Checks

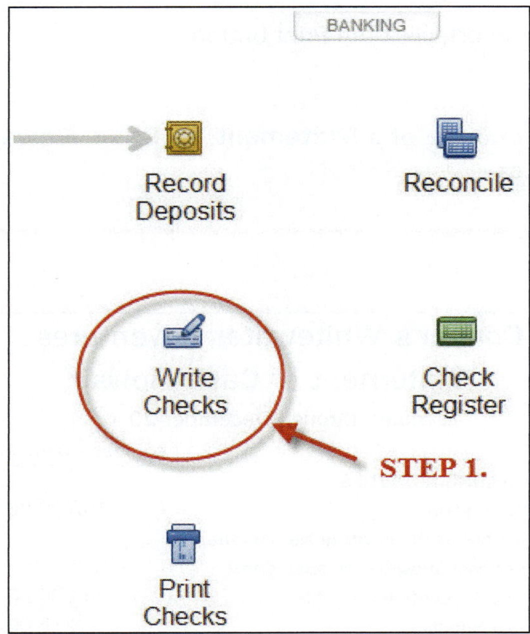

STEP 2. Click the **Edit** tab.

STEP 3. Select either **Delete Check** or **Void Check**.

Figure Q10
Delete or void check from edit tab

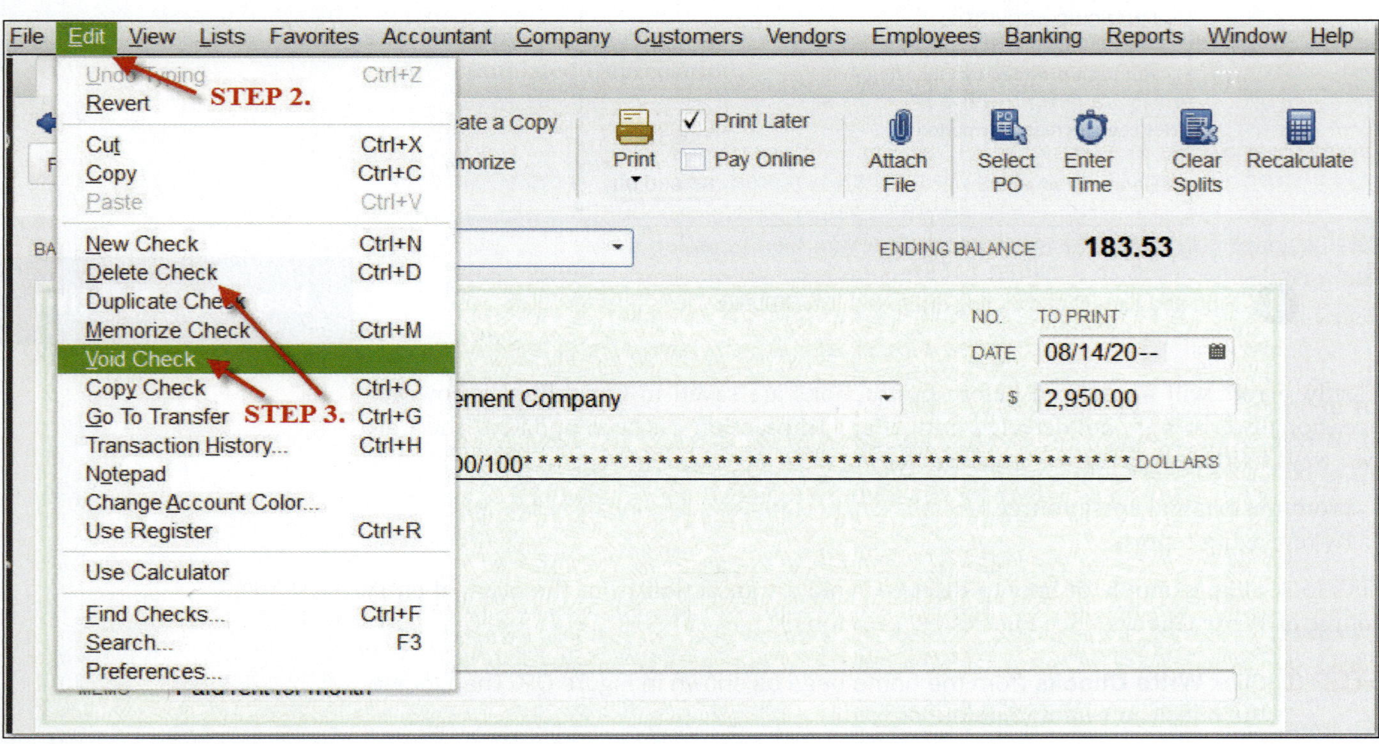

An alternative method to access the Delete or Void feature is located under the **X (Delete)** option within the check document, as shown in Figure Q11.

Figure Q11
An alternative method for deleting or voiding checks

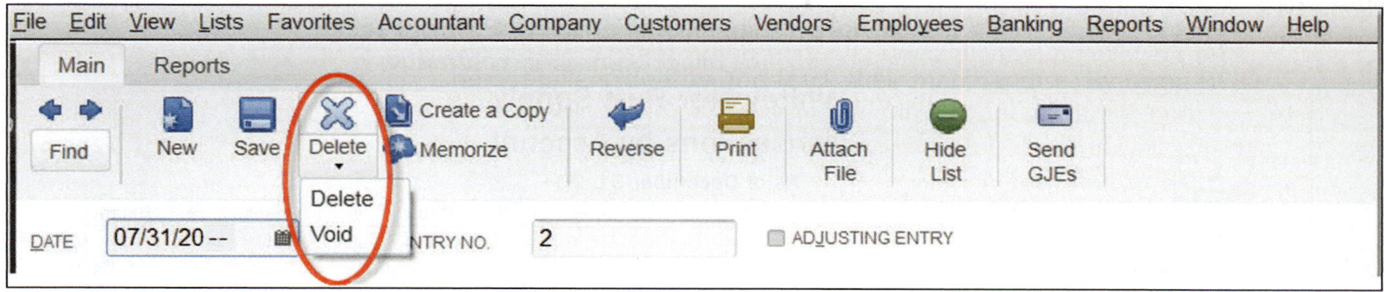

Now let's look at an example of how to find and correct errors in QuickBooks, using a report such as the trial balance. The process shown in Figures Q12 through Q15 can be applied with any QuickBooks report. We will use the financial information from December 31, 20--, for Whitewater Raft Supply, from the partial work sheet in Figure 3 on page 615.

QuickBooks Tip

Ctrl R provides quick access to the register from the home screen or any application. Transactions can be voided or deleted using the Register Edit feature.

STEP 1. Click **Reports > Accountant & Taxes > Trial Balance**.

STEP 2. Review the balance sheet columns for the work sheet on page 615 against the trial balance information shown in Figure Q12. Notice the Supplies account amount of $440.00 on the trial balance does not match the Supplies account amount of $415.00 on the worksheet. There is a $25 discrepancy. To research this discrepancy, double click on the Supplies amount of $440.00 from the trial balance report. The **Transactions by Account** report shown in Figure Q13 will appear.

Figure Q12
Locating errors using the trial balance

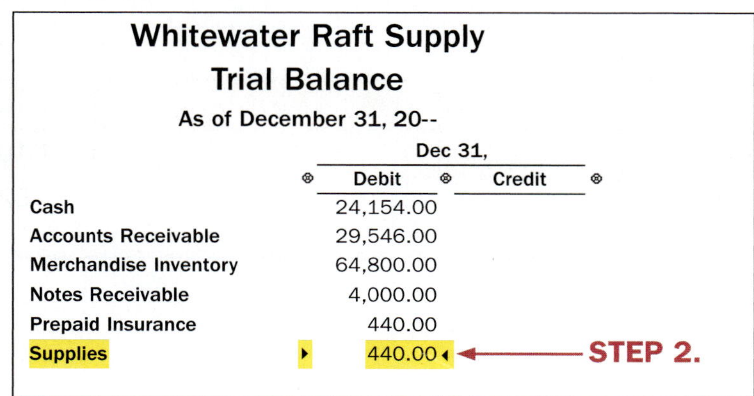

Whitewater Raft Supply
Trial Balance
As of December 31, 20--

	Dec 31, Debit	Credit
Cash	24,154.00	
Accounts Receivable	29,546.00	
Merchandise Inventory	64,800.00	
Notes Receivable	4,000.00	
Prepaid Insurance	440.00	
Supplies	440.00	

STEP 3. Click the transaction amount, in this case $440.00, from the **Transactions by Account** report. The source document window will appear. The source type shown for this transaction is the general journal.

Figure Q13
Transactions by account report

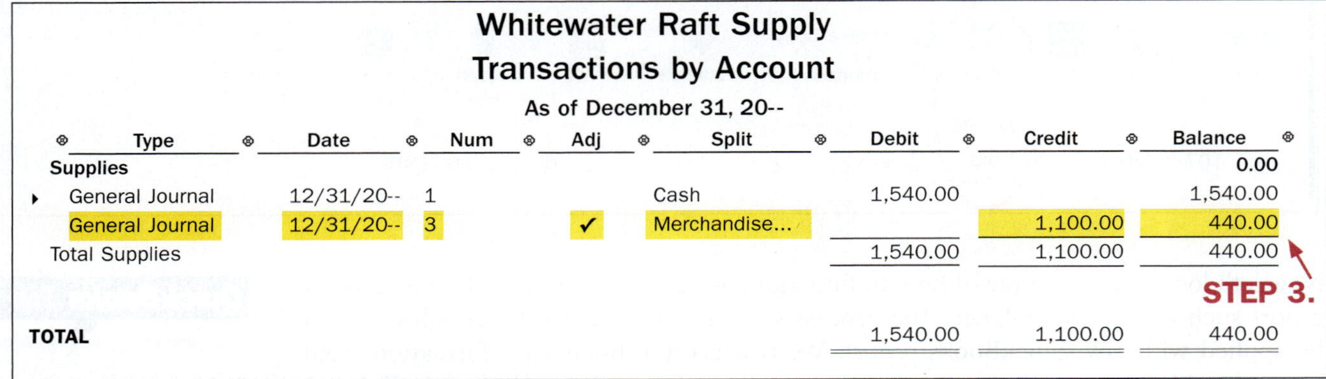

Whitewater Raft Supply
Transactions by Account
As of December 31, 20--

Type	Date	Num	Adj	Split	Debit	Credit	Balance
Supplies							0.00
General Journal	12/31/20--	1		Cash	1,540.00		1,540.00
General Journal	12/31/20--	3	✓	Merchandise...		1,100.00	440.00
Total Supplies					1,540.00	1,100.00	440.00
TOTAL					1,540.00	1,100.00	440.00

STEP 4. Notice that adjusting entry (d) for Supplies Expense and Supplies on page 615, Figure 3 was $1,125.00, not $1,100.00 as shown in Figure Q14.

Figure Q14
Identifying an error

12/31/20--	3	Payee
	GENJRNL	-split-

ACCOUNT	AMOUNT
Merchandise Inventory	67,000.00
Supplies	1,100.00
Supplies Expense	1,100.00
Prepaid Insurance	520.00

STEP 4.

STEP 5. Correct the amount for Supplies Expense and Supplies as shown in Figure Q15.

Figure Q15
Correcting an error

12/31/20--	3	Payee
	GENJRNL	-split-

ACCOUNT	AMOUNT
Merchandise Inventory	67,000.00
Supplies	STEP 5. 1,125.00
Supplies Expense	1,125.00
Prepaid Insurance	520.00

STEP 6. To update the corrected entry, click Record.

Learning Objective

5 Complete reversing entries.

As you learned in this chapter, reversing entries are general journal entries that reverse prior adjusting entries. To make a reversing entry in QuickBooks, complete the following steps:

STEP 1. Click **Company**.

STEP 2. Select **Make General Journal Entries**.

STEP 3. Locate the adjusting entry to reverse as shown in Figure Q16.

Figure Q16
Adjusting entry to reverse

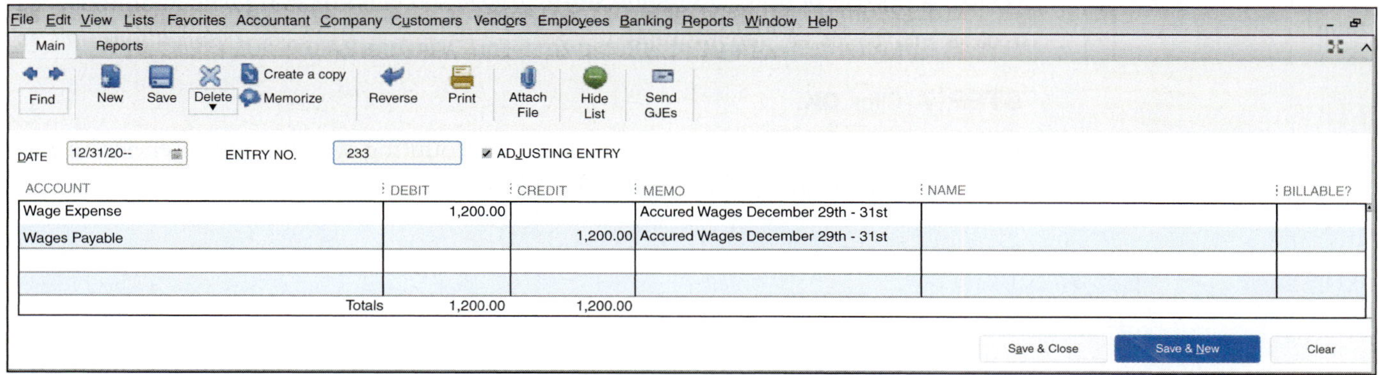

STEP 4. Click the Reverse option as shown in Figure Q17. Be sure to verify the date and then select Save & Close or Save & New.

Figure Q17
Reversing entry

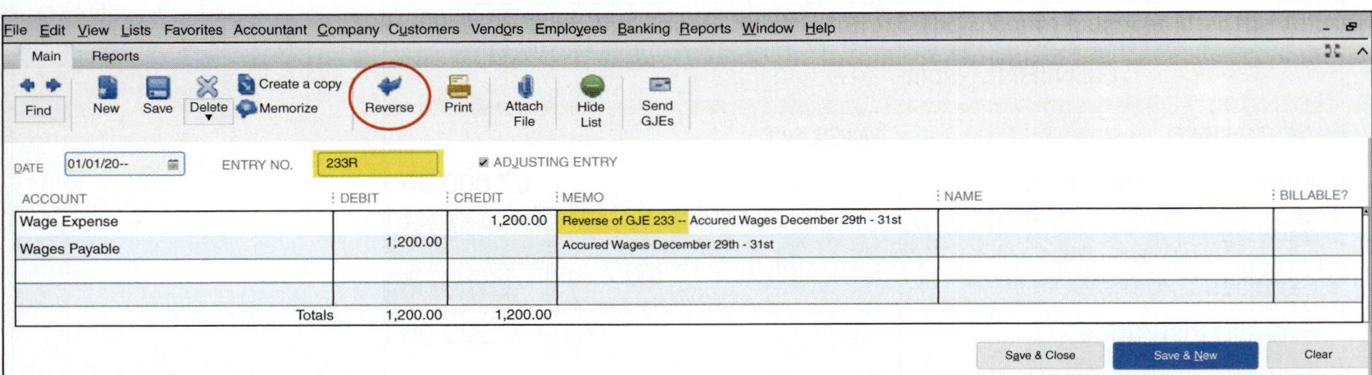

Learning Objective

Complete closing entries for a merchandising company.

In Chapter 5, you learned the automatic closing process with QuickBooks for a service company. The process for closing a merchandising company is identical. Remember, the QuickBooks administrator has two options to help prevent prior period posting errors: (1) the administrator can enter a closing date in the system, which prompts QuickBooks to alert users who are entering information into a prior accounting period, or (2) the administrator can further restrict user access by requiring a password to gain access to a prior accounting period. The combination of both is recommended.

Let's review the following steps in closing a merchandising company.

STEP 1. Click the **Company** tab.

STEP 2. Select **Set Up Users and Passwords**.

STEP 3. Select **Set Up Users**.

STEP 4. Click **Closing Date**.

STEP 5. Select or enter a **closing date.** This is the last day of the fiscal period.

STEP 6. Enter a **Closing Date Password** and **Confirm Password**.

STEP 7. Click **OK**.

Congratulations, you have now completed the accounting cycle for both a service business and a merchandising business using QuickBooks!

Chapter Review

Study and Practice

Learning Objective

1 Prepare a classified income statement for a merchandising firm.

The outline of the income statement looks like this:

Revenue from Sales
- Gross Sales
- − Sales Returns and Allowances
- − Sales Discounts
- = **Net Sales**

− Cost of Goods Sold
- Beginning Merchandise Inventory
- + **Delivered Cost of Purchases**
  - Gross Purchases
  - − Purchases Returns and Allowances
  - − Purchases Discounts
  - + Freight In
  - = Delivered Cost of Purchases
- = Cost of Goods Available for Sale
- − Ending Merchandise Inventory
- = Cost of Goods Sold

= **Gross Profit**

− Operating Expenses
- **Selling Expenses**
- **General Expenses**

= **Income from Operations**

+ Other Income
- Interest Income
- Rent Income
- Gain on Disposal of Property and Equipment

− Other Expenses
- Interest Expense
- Loss on Disposal of Property and Equipment

= **Net Income**

PRACTICE EXERCISE 1

Using the following information, prepare the Cost of Goods Sold section of an income statement.

Purchases Discounts	$ 9,000
Merchandise Inventory, December 31	192,000
Purchases	480,000
Merchandise Inventory, January 1	188,000
Purchases Returns and Allowances	16,000
Freight In	27,000

PRACTICE EXERCISE 1 • SOLUTION

Cost of Goods Sold:				
Merchandise Inventory, January 1, 20--			$188,000	
Purchases		$480,000		
Less: Purchases Returns and Allowances	$16,000			
Purchases Discounts	9,000	25,000		
Net Purchases		$455,000		
Add Freight In		27,000		
Delivered Cost of Purchases			482,000	
Cost of Goods Available for Sale			$670,000	
Less Merchandise Inventory, December 31, 20--			192,000	
Cost of Goods Sold				478,000

Learning Objective  Prepare a classified balance sheet for any type of business.

The outline of the balance sheet looks like this:

Assets

Current Assets (listed in the order of their convertibility into cash; the most liquid asset is listed first)

1. Cash
2. Notes Receivable
3. Accounts Receivable
4. Merchandise Inventory
5. Prepaid items (Supplies; Prepaid Insurance)

Property and Equipment (listed in the order of their length of life; the asset with the longest life is placed first)

1. Land
2. Buildings
3. Equipment

Liabilities

Current Liabilities (listed in the order of their urgency of payment; the most pressing obligation is placed first)

1. Notes Payable
2. Mortgage Payable or Contracts Payable (current portion)
3. Accounts Payable
4. Accrued liabilities (Wages Payable; Commissions Payable)
5. Unearned Revenue

Long-Term Liabilities (Contracts Payable; Mortgage Payable)

Owner's Equity Capital balance at end of the fiscal year

2 PRACTICE EXERCISE 2

Identify each of the following items relating to sections of a balance sheet as Current Assets (CA), Property and Equipment (PE), Current Liabilities (CL), Long-Term Liabilities (LTL), or Owner's Equity (OE).

a. Land
b. Unearned Course Fees
c. Merchandise Inventory
d. Cash
e. Salaries Payable
f. Accumulated Depreciation, Building
g. Note Payable (current)
h. Note Payable (due in ten years)
i. F. R. Fred, Capital

PRACTICE EXERCISE 2 • SOLUTION

a. Land, PE
b. Unearned Course Fees, CL
c. Merchandise Inventory, CA
d. Cash, CA
e. Salaries Payable, CL
f. Accumulated Depreciation, Building, PE
g. Note Payable (current), CL
h. Note Payable (due in ten years), LTL
i. F. R. Fred, Capital, OE

Compute working capital and current ratio.

Learning Objective

These two measures help analysts determine whether a firm has enough capital to operate and whether it can pay its debts.

$$\textbf{Working capital} = \text{Current assets} - \text{Current liabilities}$$

$$\textbf{Current ratio} = \frac{\text{Current assets}}{\text{Current liablities}}$$

3 **PRACTICE EXERCISE 3**

On December 31, 20--, Laredo Company's balance sheet shows that total current assets equal $450,784 and that total current liabilities equal $435,209. Determine the amount of Laredo Company's working capital and current ratio and explain what these measures mean.

PRACTICE EXERCISE 3 • SOLUTION

$$\text{Working capital} = \$450{,}784 - \$435{,}209 = \$15{,}575$$

$$\text{Current ratio} = \frac{\$450{,}784}{\$435{,}209} = 1.04$$

Laredo Company's working capital shows that it has $15,575 to use or to work with (for example, for expansion or other improvements). Its current ratio shows that the company has $1.04 available to pay for every dollar currently due.

Record the closing entries for a merchandising firm.

Learning Objective

There are four steps in making closing entries for a merchandising business:

STEP 1. Close the revenue accounts and the other accounts that appear on the income statement and that have credit balances (all temporary or nominal accounts with credit balances) into Income Summary.

STEP 2. Close the expense accounts and the other accounts appearing on the income statement that have debit balances (all temporary or nominal accounts with debit balances) into Income Summary.

STEP 3. Close the Income Summary account into the Capital account, transferring the net income or loss to the Capital account.

STEP 4. Close the Drawing account into the Capital account.

4 PRACTICE EXERCISE 4

From the following partial work sheet for Glasco Company, journalize the closing entries dated December 31.

	A	B	C	H	I
4					
5		TRIAL BALANCE		INCOME STATEMENT	
6	ACCOUNT NAME	DEBIT	CREDIT	DEBIT	CREDIT
7					
22	O. E. Glasco, Capital		250,800.00		
23	O. E. Glasco, Drawing	77,000.00			
24	Sales		256,150.00		256,150.00
25	Sales Returns and Allowances	960.00		960.00	
26	Sales Discounts	1,860.00		1,860.00	
27	Interest Income		1,230.00		1,230.00
28	Purchases	87,840.00		87,840.00	
29	Purchases Returns and Allowances		922.00		922.00
30	Purchases Discounts		1,348.00		1,348.00
31	Freight In	2,460.00		2,460.00	
32	Wages Expense	45,900.00		46,930.00	
33	Supplies Expense	1,540.00		1,125.00	
34	Property Tax Expense	1,960.00		1,960.00	
35	Interest Expense	344.00		344.00	
36		630,631.00	630,631.00		
37	Income Summary			65,740.00	62,700.00
38	Course Fees Income				730.00
39	Supplies				
40	Insurance Expense			550.00	
41	Depreciation Expense, Building			5,000.00	
42	Depreciation Expense, Equipment			3,400.00	
43	Wages Payable				
44				218,169.00	323,080.00
45	Net Income			104,911.00	
46				323,080.00	323,080.00
47					

Sheet1 Sheet2 Sheet3

PRACTICE EXERCISE 4 • SOLUTION

GENERAL JOURNAL Page ___

Date		Description	Post. Ref.	Debit	Credit
20--		Closing Entries			
Dec.	31	Sales		256 1 5 0 00	
		Interest Income		1 2 3 0 00	
		Purchases Returns and Allowances		9 2 2 00	
		Purchases Discounts		1 3 4 8 00	
		Course Fees Income		7 3 0 00	
		Income Summary			260 3 8 0 00
	31	Income Summary		152 4 2 9 00	
		Sales Returns and Allowances			9 6 0 00
		Sales Discounts			1 8 6 0 00
		Purchases			87 8 4 0 00
		Freight In			2 4 6 0 00
		Wages Expense			46 9 3 0 00
		Supplies Expense			1 1 2 5 00
		Property Tax Expense			1 9 6 0 00
		Interest Expense			3 4 4 00
		Insurance Expense			5 5 0 00
		Depreciation Expense, Building			5 0 0 0 00
		Depreciation Expense, Equipment			3 4 0 0 00

CHAPTER REVIEW

31	Income Summary*		104 9 1 1 00	
	O. E. Glasco, Capital			104 9 1 1 00
	*($62,700 + $260,380) −			
	($65,740 + $152,429)			
31	O. E. Glasco, Capital		77 0 0 0 00	
	O. E. Glasco, Drawing			77 0 0 0 00

Learning Objective

5 Determine which adjusting entries can be reversed and record the reversing entries.

The use of **reversing entries** is optional. Reverse the adjusting entries that increase asset or liability accounts that do not have previous balances. A contra account, such as Accumulated Depreciation, should not be reversed. Reversing entries are dated as of the first day of the next fiscal period.

5 PRACTICE EXERCISE 5

From the following T accounts, determine which adjusting entries can be reversed and journalize the reversing entries.

Merchandise Inventory

	+		−
Bal.	68,500	Adj.	68,500

Income Summary

Adj.	68,500		

Merchandise Inventory

	+		−
Bal.	68,500	Adj.	68,500
Adj.	70,320		

Income Summary

Adj.	68,500	Adj.	70,320

Course Fees Income

	−		+
		Adj.	800

Unearned Course Fees

	−		+
Adj.	800	Bal.	850

Supplies

	+		−
Bal.	1,620	Adj.	735

Supplies Expense

	+		−
Adj.	735		

Insurance Expense

	+		−
Adj.	1,620		

Prepaid Insurance

	+		−
Bal.	2,110	Adj.	1,620

Depreciation Expense, Building

	+		−
Adj.	3,200		

Accumulated Depreciation, Building

	−		+
		Bal.	46,000
		Adj.	3,200

(*Continued*)

Depreciation Expense, Equipment

	+	−
Adj.	4,300	

Accumulated Depreciation, Equipment

−	+	
	Bal.	21,400
	Adj.	4,300

Wages Expense

	+	−
Bal.	32,560	
Adj.	2,230	

Wages Payable

−	+	
	Adj.	2,230

PRACTICE EXERCISE 5 • SOLUTION

GENERAL JOURNAL Page ___

Date		Description	Post. Ref.	Debit	Credit
20--		Reversing Entries			
Jan.	1	Wages Payable		2 2 3 0 00	
		Wages Expense			2 2 3 0 00

Glossary

Cash equivalents Items included in the broad definition of cash. Included are short-term, highly liquid investments (for example, money market accounts, U.S. Treasury bills, and commercial paper) having maturities with a maximum of 90 days from the date acquired. *(p. 633)*

Common-sized statement A financial statement using vertical analysis with all items expressed as percentages; allows comparison of one company with another as well as with industry averages. *(p. 629)*

Current Assets Cash and any other assets or resources that are expected to be realized in cash or to be sold or consumed during the normal operating cycle of the business (or one year if the normal operating cycle is less than 12 months). *(p. 616)*

Current Liabilities Debts that will become due within the normal operating cycle of a business, usually within one year, and that are normally paid from current assets. *(p. 617)*

Current ratio A firm's current assets divided by its current liabilities. Portrays a firm's short-term debt-paying ability. *(p. 618)*

Delivered Cost of Purchases Net Purchases plus Freight In:

Net Purchases
+ Freight In
Delivered Cost of Purchases *(p. 613)*

Financing activities A category on the statement of cash flows (involving inflows and outflows) that includes the borrowing of money or the repaying of loans and additional cash investments or reductions of owners' investments through cash dividends or owners withdrawals. *(p. 633)*

General Expenses Expenses incurred in the administration of a business, including office expenses and any expenses that are not completely classified as Selling Expenses or Other Expenses. *(p. 613)*

Gross Profit Net Sales minus Cost of Goods Sold, or profit before deducting operating expenses:

Net Sales
− Cost of Goods Sold
Gross Profit *(p. 609)*

Horizontal analysis Comparing the same item in the financial statements of an enterprise for two or more periods. *(p. 629)*

Indirect method A method used to prepare the Operating Activities section of the statement of cash flows that involves adjustments made to net income for noncash operating income and expense items and changes in current assets (other than Cash) and current liabilities. *(p. 634)*

Investing activities A category on the statement of cash flows (involving inflows and outflows) that includes the buying and selling of property and equipment, the acquiring and selling of investments other than cash equivalents, and the making and collecting of loans. *(p. 633)*

Liquidity The ability of an asset to be quickly turned into cash by selling it or by putting it up as security for a loan. *(p. 617)*

Long-Term Liabilities Debts payable over a comparatively long period, usually more than one year. *(p. 617)*

Net Income or **Net Profit** The final figure on an income statement after all expenses have been deducted from revenues. *(p. 609)*

Net Purchases Purchases minus Purchases Returns and Allowances, minus Purchases Discounts:

Purchases
– Purchases Returns and Allowances
– Purchases Discounts

Net Purchases *(p. 613)*

Net Sales Sales minus Sales Returns and Allowances, minus Sales Discounts:

Sales
– Sales Returns and Allowances
– Sales Discounts

Net Sales *(p. 611)*

Notes Receivable (current) Written promises to pay the seller/lender the amount due in a period of less than one year. *(p. 617)*

Operating activities A category on the statement of cash flows (involving inflows and outflows) that includes cash receipts from customers for the sale of merchandise and services, cash receipts from interest and dividends, cash payments for merchandise purchases, cash payments for operating expenses, cash payments for interest, and cash payments for income taxes. *(p. 633)*

Property and Equipment Long-lived assets that are held for use in the production or sale of other assets or services; also called *fixed assets. (p. 617)*

Reversing entries The reverse of certain adjusting entries, reversing entries are recorded as of the first day of the following fiscal period. The use of reversing entries is optional. *(p. 625)*

Selling Expenses Expenses directly connected with the selling activity, such as salaries of sales staff, advertising expenses, and delivery expenses. *(p. 613)*

Statement of cash flows A financial statement that explains in detail how the balance of cash and cash equivalents has changed between the beginning and the end of a fiscal period. A schedule on the statement presents important noncash investing and financing activities that occurred during the same period. *(p. 633)*

Temporary-equity accounts Accounts whose balances apply to one fiscal period only, such as revenues, expenses, and the Drawing account. Temporary-equity accounts are also called *nominal accounts. (p. 622)*

Vertical analysis Portraying items in financial statements as percentages (or proportional parts) of a given item on the same financial statement. *(p. 629)*

Working capital A firm's current assets less its current liabilities. The amount of capital a firm has available to use or to work with during a normal operating cycle. *(p. 618)*

CHAPTER REVIEW

Quiz Yourself

_____ 1. What is the term used for the profit on a sale before any operating expenses have been deducted?
  a. Net Income
  b. Net Profit
  c. Gross Profit
  d. Gain on Sale
  e. All of the above

_____ 2. Which of the following is *not* an example of a current asset?
  a. Cash
  b. Merchandising Inventory
  c. Prepaid Expenses
  d. Equipment
  e. Supplies

_____ 3. The data needed to calculate working capital and its current ratio can be found on which of the following?
  a. Classified balance sheet
  b. Statement of owner's equity
  c. Classified income statement
  d. Chart of accounts
  e. All of the above

_____ 4. What is the third entry of the closing procedure for a merchandising business?
  a. Sales to Income Summary
  b. Income Summary to Capital
  c. Expenses to Income Summary
  d. Drawing to Capital
  e. Capital to Income Summary

_____ 5. What general journal entry is used to undo a previously made adjusting entry?
  a. Adjusting entry
  b. Closing entry
  c. Special journal entry
  d. Correcting entry
  e. Reversing entry

Answers:
1. c 2. d 3. a 4. b 5. e

Review It with QuickBooks®

_____ 1. Comparative financial reports in QuickBooks have the option to calculate reports for _____ or _____ analysis.
  a. horizontal, comparative
  b. horizontal, vertical
  c. percentage, vertical
  d. None of the above

_____ 2. Which QuickBooks report feature provides financial information in a picture format?
  a. Profit & Loss Statement
  b. Balance Sheet
  c. Company & Financial
  d. Income & Expense Graph

_____ 3. Which is not one of the four major financial statements that are standard in QuickBooks?
  a. Profit & loss statement
  b. Statement of owner's equity
  c. Balance sheet
  d. Statement of cash flows

_____ 4. All of the following are options for correcting errors in QuickBooks except
  a. void a transaction.
  b. delete a transaction.
  c. edit a transaction.
  d. reverse entries.

Answers:
1. b 2. d 3. b 4. d

Chapter Assignments

Discussion Questions

1. What is the order for listing accounts in the Current Assets section of the balance sheet?
2. What is the difference between the cost of goods available for sale and the cost of goods sold?
3. What are the basic classifications found on an income statement for a merchandising business as compared to a service business?
4. On a balance sheet, what is the difference between Current Liabilities and Long-Term Liabilities? Give an example of an account in each classification.
5. On an income statement, what is the difference between income from operations and net income? Which is more useful in comparing the results of operations over a number of years?
6. Explain the calculation of net sales and net purchases.
7. In the closing procedure, what happens to (a) Purchases Discounts, (b) Sales Returns and Allowances, (c) Freight In, and (d) Gain on Disposal of Property and Equipment?
8. What are the rules for recognizing whether an adjusting entry should be reversed?
9. What two measures are used to determine whether a firm has sufficient capital to operate and whether the firm has the ability to pay its debts?

Exercises

LO 1 Practice Exercise 1

EXERCISE 12-1 Calculate the missing items in the following:

Sales	Sales Returns and Allowances	Net Sales	Beginning Merchandise Inventory	Net Purchases	Cost of Goods Available for Sale	Ending Merchandise Inventory	Cost of Goods Sold	Gross Profit
a. $242,000	$ 6,000	______	$152,000	$170,000	______	$136,000	$186,000	______
b. 304,000	______	$297,000	134,000	______	$404,000	176,000	228,000	______
c. ______	10,000	628,000	______	416,000	486,000	89,000	______	______

LO 1 Practice Exercise 1

EXERCISE 12-2 Using the following information, prepare the Cost of Goods Sold section of an income statement.

Purchases Discounts	$ 8,500
Merchandise Inventory, December 31	189,000
Purchases	476,000
Merchandise Inventory, January 1	185,000
Purchases Returns and Allowances	9,000
Freight In	12,000

LO 1

Practice Exercise 1

EXERCISE 12-3 Identify each of the following items relating to sections of an income statement as Revenue from Sales (S), Cost of Goods Sold (CGS), Selling Expenses (SE), General Expenses (GE), Other Income (OI), or Other Expenses (OE).

a. Advertising Expense
b. Rent Expense
c. Purchases Discounts
d. Sales Returns and Allowances
e. Interest Income
f. Freight In
g. Depreciation Expense, Building
h. Interest Expense
i. Insurance Expense
j. Delivery Expense

LO 1

Practice Exercise 1

EXERCISE 12-4 The Income Statement columns of the August 31 (year-end) work sheet for Ralley Company are shown here. From the information given, prepare an income statement for the company. To save time and space, the expenses have been grouped together into two categories.

	A	H	I
4			
5		INCOME STATEMENT	
6	ACCOUNT NAME	DEBIT	CREDIT
7			
23	Income Summary	32,000.00	31,000.00
24	Sales		324,000.00
25	Sales Returns and Allowances	13,310.00	
26	Sales Discounts	7,700.00	
27	Purchases	126,360.00	
28	Purchases Returns and Allowances		1,200.00
29	Purchases Discounts		1,300.00
30	Freight In	7,500.00	
31	Selling Expenses	61,560.00	
32	General Expenses	50,884.00	
33		299,314.00	357,500.00
34	Net Income	58,186.00	
35		357,500.00	357,500.00
36			

Sheet1 Sheet2 Sheet3

LO 2

Practice Exercise 2

EXERCISE 12-5 Identify each of the following items relating to sections of a balance sheet as Current Assets (CA), Property and Equipment (PE), Current Liabilities (CL), Long-Term Liabilities (LTL), or Owner's Equity (OE).

a. Accounts Receivable
b. Building
c. Wages Payable
d. Prepaid Property Taxes
e. Mortgage Payable (current)
f. Supplies
g. Mortgage Payable (due in 3 years)
h. Unearned Fees
i D. Marlor, Capital
j. Notes Payable (due in 3 months)

LO 3

Practice Exercise 3

EXERCISE 12-6 On December 31, 20--, the following selected accounts and amounts appeared on the balance sheet for Duncan Company. Determine the amount of the working capital and the current ratio. (Round to two decimal places.)

Building	$180,000
Prepaid Insurance	1,800
Merchandise Inventory	85,000
Store Equipment	11,000
Unearned Fees	1,200
Notes Payable (due in six months)	6,000
Accumulated Depreciation, Building	62,000
Accounts Payable	25,000
Land	50,000
Cash	50,000
Store Supplies	1,400
Accumulated Depreciation, Store Equipment	8,000
Notes Receivable (due in four months)	1,500
Mortgage Payable (current portion)	4,400
Salaries Payable	1,600
M. Duncan, Capital	161,500
Mortgage Payable (due in four years)	86,000

LO 4

Practice Exercise 4

EXERCISE 12-7 From the following T accounts, journalize the closing entries dated December 31 for Baylor Company.

Salary Expense	
+	−
65,000	

H. Baylor, Drawing	
+	−
55,000	

Purchases Returns and Allowances	
−	+
	8,600

Purchases	
+	−
235,600	

Miscellaneous Expense	
+	−
12,200	

Rent Expense	
+	−
22,000	

Sales Returns and Allowances	
+	−
7,400	

Freight In	
+	−
11,200	

Sales	
−	+
	502,000

Income Summary	
87,000	103,000

H. Baylor, Capital	
−	+
	335,000

Purchases Discounts	
−	+
	4,300

CHAPTER ASSIGNMENTS

CHAPTER ASSIGNMENTS

 4

Practice Exercise 4

EXERCISE 12-8 From the following information, journalize the last two closing entries and present a statement of owner's equity for Nishimoto Company.

H. Nishimoto, Capital

−		+	
		Jan. 1 Bal.	450,000
		Apr. 7	18,000

H. Nishimoto, Drawing

+		−	
Mar. 1	35,000		
Dec. 9	40,000		

Income Summary

Dec. 31 Adj.	190,000	Dec. 31 Adj.	206,000
Dec. 31 Closing	415,000	Dec. 31 Closing	492,000

Problem Set A

LO 1, 4

PROBLEM 12-1A A partial work sheet for The Fan Shop is presented here. The merchandise inventory at the beginning of the year was $52,300. P. G. Ochoa, the owner, withdrew $30,500 during the year.

	A	H	I
1	The Fan Shop		
2	Work Sheet		
3	For Year Ended December 31, 20--		
4			
5		INCOME STATEMENT	
6	ACCOUNT NAME	DEBIT	CREDIT
7			
24	Sales		324,000.00
25	Sales Returns and Allowances	3,400.00	
26	Sales Discounts	2,707.00	
27	Interest Income		1,830.00
28	Purchases	201,490.00	
29	Purchase Returns and Allowances		2,880.00
30	Freight In	9,790.00	
31	Wages Expense	46,240.00	
32	Rent Expense	12,610.00	
33	Commissions Expense	8,310.00	
34	Supplies Expense	1,842.00	
35	Interest Expense	854.00	
36	Income Summary	52,300.00	54,580.00
37	Insurance Expense	1,240.00	
38	Depreciation Expense, Building	4,600.00	
39	Depreciation Expense, Equipment	2,600.00	
40			
41		347,983.00	383,290.00
42	Net Income	35,307.00	
43		383,290.00	383,290.00
44			

Sheet1 Sheet2 Sheet3

Check Figure
Cost of Goods Sold, $206,120

Required

1. Prepare an income statement.
2. Journalize the closing entries.

LO 2, 3

PROBLEM 12-2A Here is the partial work sheet for Eckland Stereo.

	A	J	K
1	Eckland Stereo		
2	Work Sheet		
3	For Year Ended December 31, 20--		
4			
5		BALANCE SHEET	
6	ACCOUNT NAME	DEBIT	CREDIT
7	Cash	14,815.00	
8	Notes Receivable	7,500.00	
9	Accounts Receivable	30,170.00	
10	Merchandise Inventory	50,244.00	
11	Prepaid Property Taxes	2,115.00	
12	Prepaid Insurance	1,640.00	
13	Land	16,700.00	
14	Building	50,000.00	
15	Accumulated Depreciation, Building		15,900.00
16	Computer Equipment	6,892.00	
17	Accumulated Depreciation, Computer Equipment		5,674.00
18	Store Equipment	7,230.00	
19	Accumulated Depreciation, Store Equipment		4,424.00
20	Delivery Equipment	4,300.00	
21	Accumulated Depreciation, Delivery Equipment		3,470.00
22	Notes Payable		5,215.00
23	Accounts Payable		27,140.00
24	Mortgage Payable (current portion)		2,800.00
25	Mortgage Payable		65,200.00
26	M. J. Eckland, Capital		57,314.00
27	M. J. Eckland, Drawing	23,000.00	
28			
41	Wages Payable		1,984.00
42		214,606.00	189,121.00
43	Net Income		25,485.00
44		214,606.00	214,606.00
45			

Sheet1 Sheet2 Sheet3

Check Figure
Working capital, $69,345

Required

1. Prepare a statement of owner's equity (no additional investment).
2. Prepare a balance sheet.
3. Determine the amount of the working capital.
4. Determine the current ratio (carry to two decimal places).

CHAPTER ASSIGNMENTS

LO 4, 5

PROBLEM 12-3A The following partial work sheet covers the affairs of Masanto and Company for the year ended June 30.

	A	H	I	J	K
1	Masanto and Company				
2	Work Sheet				
3	For Year Ended June 30, 20--				
4					
5		INCOME STATEMENT		BALANCE SHEET	
6	ACCOUNT NAME	DEBIT	CREDIT	DEBIT	CREDIT
7	Cash			21,034.00	
8	Accounts Receivable			89,016.00	
9	Merchandise Inventory			116,400.00	
10	Prepaid Insurance			3,210.00	
11	Delivery Equipment			12,400.00	
12	Accumulated Depreciation, Delivery Equipment				4,600.00
13	Store Equipment			30,400.00	
14	Accumulated Depreciation, Store Equipment				8,700.00
15	Accounts Payable				55,300.00
16	P. R. Masanto, Capital				172,720.00
17	P. R. Masanto, Drawing			26,000.00	
18	Sales		516,000.00		
19	Purchases	399,101.00			
20	Purchases Returns and Allowances		9,600.00		
21	Purchases Discounts		6,800.00		
22	Freight In	14,000.00			
23	Salary Expense	46,000.00			
24	Delivery Equipment Expense	10,600.00			
25	Supplies Expense	2,700.00			
26	Miscellaneous Expense	1,459.00			
27					
28	Income Summary	112,200.00	116,400.00		
29	Salaries Payable				1,240.00
30	Insurance Expense	2,840.00			
31	Depreciation Expense, Delivery Equipment	1,400.00			
32	Depreciation Expense, Store Equipment	2,600.00			
33		592,900.00	648,800.00	298,460.00	242,560.00
34	Net Income	55,900.00			55,900.00
35		648,800.00	648,800.00	298,460.00	298,460.00
36					

Sheet1 Sheet2 Sheet3

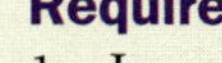

Check Figure
Reversing entry amount, $1,240

Required

1. Journalize the six adjusting entries.
2. Journalize the closing entries.
3. Journalize the reversing entry.

LO 1, 2, 4, 5

PROBLEM 12-4A The following accounts appear in the ledger of Celso and Company as of June 30, the end of this fiscal year.

Cash	$ 15,349
Accounts Receivable	13,810
Merchandise Inventory	50,280
Store Supplies	1,935
Prepaid Insurance	1,385
Store Equipment	18,640
Accumulated Depreciation, Store Equipment	6,882
Accounts Payable	10,065
B. E. Celso, Capital	96,524
B. E. Celso, Drawing	30,000
Sales	208,030
Sales Returns and Allowances	1,740
Purchases	133,050
Purchases Returns and Allowances	4,295

Purchases Discounts	$ 3,853
Freight In	8,350
Wages Expense	35,400
Advertising Expense	7,710
Rent Expense	12,000

The data needed for the adjustments on June 30 are as follows:

a–b. Merchandise inventory, June 30, $54,600.
c. Insurance expired for the year, $475.
d. Depreciation for the year, $4,380.
e. Accrued wages on June 30, $1,492.
f. Supplies on hand at the end of the year, $100.

Required

Check Figure
Net income, $14,066

1. Prepare a work sheet for the fiscal year ended June 30. Ignore this step if using QuickBooks or general ledger.
2. Prepare an income statement.
3. Prepare a statement of owner's equity. No additional investments were made during the year. Ignore this step if using QuickBooks.
4. Prepare a balance sheet.
5. Journalize the adjusting entries.
6. Journalize the closing entries.
7. Journalize the reversing entry.

Problem Set B

LO 1, 4

PROBLEM 12-1B A partial work sheet for McKnight Music Store is presented here. The merchandise inventory at the beginning of the fiscal period was $48,473. W. J. McKnight, the owner, withdrew $40,000 during the year.

	A	H	I
1	McKnight Music Store		
2	Work Sheet		
3	For Year Ended December 31, 20--		
4			
5		INCOME STATEMENT	
6	ACCOUNT NAME	DEBIT	CREDIT
7			
24	Sales		315,483.00
25	Sales Returns and Allowances	4,348.00	
26	Sales Discounts	1,817.00	
27	Interest Income		925.00
28	Purchases	185,272.00	
29	Purchases Returns and Allowances		1,547.00
30	Freight In	9,173.00	
31	Wages Expense	40,615.00	
32	Rent Expense	10,840.00	
33	Commissions Expense	8,220.00	
34	Supplies Expense	1,826.00	
35	Interest Expense	1,258.00	
36	Income Summary	48,473.00	48,850.00
37	Insurance Expense	2,624.00	
38	Depreciation Expense, Building	4,220.00	
39	Depreciation Expense, Equipment	4,500.00	
40			
41		323,186.00	366,805.00
42	Net Income	43,619.00	
43		366,805.00	366,805.00
44			

Sheet1 Sheet2 Sheet3

(Continued)

Check Figure
Cost of Goods Sold, $192,521

Required

1. Prepare an income statement.
2. Journalize the closing entries.

 2, 3

PROBLEM 12-2B Here is the partial work sheet for Meyer Mountain Shop.

	A	J	K
1	Meyer Mountain Shop		
2	Work Sheet		
3	For Year Ended December 31, 20--		
4			
5		BALANCE SHEET	
6	ACCOUNT NAME	DEBIT	CREDIT
7	Cash	18,525.00	
8	Notes Receivable	4,500.00	
9	Accounts Receivable	22,680.00	
10	Merchandise Inventory	53,542.00	
11	Prepaid Property Taxes	1,820.00	
12	Prepaid Insurance	2,450.00	
13	Land	18,600.00	
14	Building	42,000.00	
15	Accumulated Depreciation, Building		22,500.00
16	Computer Equipment	4,424.00	
17	Accumulated Depreciation, Computer Equipment		2,250.00
18	Store Equipment	7,480.00	
19	Accumulated Depreciation, Store Equipment		5,085.00
20	Delivery Equipment	5,740.00	
21	Accumulated Depreciation, Delivery Equipment		3,225.00
22	Notes Payable		6,500.00
23	Accounts Payable		19,455.00
24	Mortgage Payable (current portion)		2,500.00
25	Mortgage Payable		54,600.00
26	M. E. Meyer, Capital		75,085.00
27	M. E. Meyer, Drawing	35,250.00	
28			
41	Wages Payable		1,460.00
42		217,011.00	192,660.00
43	Net Income		24,351.00
44		217,011.00	217,011.00
45			

Sheet1 Sheet2 Sheet3

Check Figure
Working capital, $73,602

Required

1. Prepare a statement of owner's equity (no additional investment).
2. Prepare a balance sheet.
3. Determine the amount of the working capital.
4. Determine the current ratio (carry to two decimal places).

LO 4, 5

PROBLEM 12-3B The following partial work sheet covers the affairs of Ketcher and Company for the year ended June 30.

	A	H	I	J	K
1	Ketcher and Company				
2	Work Sheet				
3	For Year Ended June 30, 20--				
4					
5		INCOME STATEMENT		BALANCE SHEET	
6	ACCOUNT NAME	DEBIT	CREDIT	DEBIT	CREDIT
7	Cash			37,302.00	
8	Accounts Receivable			97,557.00	
9	Merchandise Inventory			117,274.00	
10	Prepaid Insurance			2,410.00	
11	Delivery Equipment			12,700.00	
12	Accumulated Depreciation, Delivery Equipment				6,240.00
13	Store Equipment			35,900.00	
14	Accumulated Depreciation, Store Equipment				10,480.00
15	Accounts Payable				77,328.00
16	J. Ketcher, Capital				193,810.00
17	J. Ketcher, Drawing			40,350.00	
18	Sales		532,262.00		
19	Purchases	397,830.00			
20	Purchases Returns and Allowances		8,817.00		
21	Purchases Discounts		6,935.00		
22	Freight In	23,400.00			
23	Salary Expense	54,700.00			
24	Delivery Equipment Expense	9,492.00			
25	Supplies Expense	2,416.00			
26	Miscellaneous Expense	1,800.00			
27					
28	Income Summary	113,202.00	117,274.00		
29	Salaries Payable				1,645.00
30	Insurance Expense	2,940.00			
31	Depreciation Expense, Delivery Equipment	2,800.00			
32	Depreciation Expense, Store Equipment	2,718.00			
33		611,298.00	665,288.00	343,493.00	289,503.00
34	Net Income	53,990.00			53,990.00
35		665,288.00	665,288.00	343,493.00	343,493.00
36					

Sheet1 Sheet2 Sheet3

Required

1. Journalize the six adjusting entries.
2. Journalize the closing entries.
3. Journalize the reversing entry.

Check Figure
Reversing entry amount, $1,645

LO 1, 2, 4, 5

QuickBooks

PROBLEM 12-4B The following accounts appear in the ledger of Sheldon Company on January 31, the end of this fiscal year.

Cash	$ 16,400
Accounts Receivable	15,100
Merchandise Inventory	55,500
Store Supplies	1,603
Prepaid Insurance	3,080
Store Equipment	24,900
Accumulated Depreciation, Store Equipment	3,860
Accounts Payable	14,400
M. E. Sheldon, Capital	126,484
M. E. Sheldon, Drawing	36,000
Sales	227,000
Sales Returns and Allowances	2,000
Purchases	172,000
Purchases Returns and Allowances	2,375

(*Continued*)

Purchases Discounts	$ 3,567
Freight In	7,491
Wages Expense	24,800
Advertising Expense	5,912
Rent Expense	12,900

The data needed for adjustments on January 31 are as follows:

a–b. Merchandise inventory, January 31, $55,750.
c. Insurance expired for the year, $1,285.
d. Depreciation for the year, $5,482.
e. Accrued wages on January 31, $1,556.
f. Supplies used during the year $1,503.

Check Figure
Net loss, $1,737

Required

1. Prepare a work sheet for the fiscal year ended January 31. Ignore this step if using QuickBooks or general ledger.
2. Prepare an income statement.
3. Prepare a statement of owner's equity. No additional investments were made during the year. Ignore this step if using QuickBooks.
4. Prepare a balance sheet.
5. Journalize the adjusting entries.
6. Journalize the closing entries.

Try It with *QuickBooks*® (LO 1, 2, 3, 5, 6)

LO 1

QB Exercise 12-1

Using the QuickBooks data file labeled Ortiz's Jewelry Store, Inc., located on the textbook website at www.cengagebrain.com, prepare a two-year, comparative income statement for the years 2014 and 2015, using horizontal analysis.

1. What is the percent of increase or (decrease) in sales?
2. What is the percent of increase or (decrease) in net income?
3. Comment on what you think the percentages of increase or decrease mean.

LO 1

QB Exercise 12-2

Using the QuickBooks data file labeled Ortiz's Jewelry Store, Inc., located on the textbook website at www.cengagebrain.com, prepare a two-year, comparative income statement for the years 2014 and 2015, using vertical analysis.

1. What is the percent of net income to net sales for 2014?
2. What is the percent of net income to net sales for 2015?
3. Comment on what you think the percentage figures mean.

QB Exercise 12-3

LO 2, 5, 6

Using the information in Problem 12-4A on page 654–655 and the QuickBooks data file labeled Celso and Company located on the textbook website, complete parts (2), (4), (5), (6), and (7) on page 655 and then answer the following questions.

1. What are the total assets on the balance sheet?
2. What is the adjusting entry for supplies?
3. View and print an expense graph.
   a. What expense is the largest percentage of total expense?
   b. What is the percent amount?

QB Exercise 12-4

LO 2, 5, 6

Using the information in Problem 12-4B on page 657–658 and the QuickBooks data file labeled Sheldon Company located on the textbook website, complete parts (2), (4), (5), (6), and (7) on page 658 and then answer the following questions.

1. What are the total assets on the balance sheet?
2. What are the total liabilities on the balance sheet?
3. View and print an expense graph.
   a. What expense is the largest percentage of total expense?
   b. What is the percent amount?

QB Exercise 12-5

LO 3

Using the QuickBooks data file labeled Salinas Marine Sales located on the textbook website, prepare a statement of cash flows report with QuickBooks for 2015.

1. What is the net increase (decrease) in cash?

Activities

Why Does It Matter?

COSTCO WHOLESALE CORPORATION, Issaquah, Washington

Costco is the largest chain of membership warehouse clubs in the world based on sales volume, and it is the fifth largest general retailer in the United States. Costco focuses on selling products at low prices, often at a very high volume. These goods are usually bulk-packaged and marketed primarily to large families and businesses. Costco became the first company to grow from zero to $3 billion in sales in less than six years. In a recent fiscal year, Costco's sales totaled $76.3 billion, a 29.3 percent increase from 2006, and its net income reached $1.30 billion, an 18.1 percent increase from 2006. This information, and much more, can be derived from the financial statements that merchandising firms such as Costco prepare on a regular basis to provide shareholders and other interested parties information about the company's activities and financial performance.

1. What type of information would a classified income statement provide to shareholders and other interested parties?
2. What type of information would a classified balance sheet provide to shareholders and other interested parties? Why would this information be important for calculating the working capital and the current ratio, for example?

What Would You Say?

A music store sells new instruments. The store also sells used instruments for people who are willing to give the store part of the sales price. The sales of used instruments, called commissions, amount to about one-fourth of total sales. On the firm's classified income statement under the Revenue heading are both New Instrument Sales and Sales Commissions. Comment on this practice.

What Do You Think?

You are an owner/bookkeeper in a country whose economy has been nearly destroyed. Goods are scarce; in fact, you have no goods to sell at the start of each day. You go out early each morning to purchase goods and haul them back to sell. At the end of the day, you have sold everything. Prepare a Cost of Goods Sold section for a day when you purchased $400 in goods. What conclusion can you draw?

What Would You Do?

Marty is an accountant. Sometimes printouts of financial statements contain errors, making the financial statements unusable. Marty doesn't like to waste anything, so he takes the unusable financial statements to his son's day care center to use for drawing paper. Explain why you think this is or is not unethical behavior.

What's Wrong with This Picture?

What if the freight charges on a new desk for the owner were journalized and posted to the Freight In account? Would this affect the Cost of Goods Sold section? If so, how?

BEFORE A TEST CHECK: Chapters 11–12

PART I: Completion

1. An actual count of a stock of goods is called a(n) ______.
2. Under the ______ system, entries to record the purchase of merchandise are recorded in the Merchandise Inventory account.
3. Unearned revenue is classified as a(n) ______.
4. Under the periodic inventory system, the first adjustment is to debit ______ for the amount of the beginning inventory.
5. Under the perpetual inventory system, after recording the sale of the goods, the accountant debits ______ and credits ______.
6. An increase in Rent Expense results in a(n) ______ to net income.
7. Gross Profit is calculated by subtracting ______ from Net Sales.
8. Current Assets minus Current Liabilities equals ______.
9. Gross Profit minus Total Operating Expenses equals ______.
10. Net Purchases plus ______ equals Delivered Cost of Purchases.

PART II: True/False

T F 1. The second adjustment for Merchandise Inventory under the periodic inventory system is to debit Cost of Goods Sold and credit Merchandise Inventory.

T F 2. Unearned Rent Income is classified as a revenue.

T F 3. The perpetual inventory system requires that each sale of goods has two entries: one to reduce inventory and affix the cost of the goods sold and one to record the sale.

T F 4. The periodic inventory system requires two adjusting entries: one to remove the old inventory amount and one to enter the latest inventory amount.

T F 5. The adjustment to unearned revenue allows the correct amount of liability and revenue to be applied to each fiscal period involved.

T F 6. Freight In is classified in the Operating Expenses section of an income statement.

T F 7. Under the perpetual inventory system, the cost of goods sold is calculated by subtracting ending inventory from the cost of goods available for sale.

T F 8. Reversing entries are optional, and only some adjusting entries are reversed.

T F 9. Delivery Expense is added to Net Purchases to arrive at Delivered Cost of Purchases.

T F 10. Purchases Returns and Allowances increases Income from Operations.

PART III: Application

1. Alphonse Company uses the periodic inventory system. Employees have just taken a physical count of its inventory. This ending inventory has been valued at $136,000. The company's accounting records show the Merchandise Inventory account with a debit balance of $132,000. Journalize the entries on December 31 to adjust the records for this situation.
2. Regletto Company uses the perpetual inventory system. Employees have just taken a physical count of its inventory. This ending inventory has been valued at $146,000. The company's accounting records show the Merchandise Inventory account with a debit balance of $148,000. Journalize the entry on December 31 to adjust the records for this situation.
3. On December 1, Wesley Company collected $20,000 for a remodeling job that will be completed on March 31 of the following year. The revenue will be earned evenly over four months. Wesley Company's fiscal period ends December 31. Make the

entries to record the collection of the cash and the year-end adjustment to reflect the amount of revenue earned in December.

4. Yorkland Company has total assets of $250,000, of which noncurrent assets amount to $140,000. The company also has total liabilities of $130,000, of which $80,000 are long-term liabilities. Calculate (a) working capital and (b) current ratio.

Answers: Part I

1. physical inventory 2. perpetual inventory 3. current liability 4. Income Summary 5. Cost of Goods Sold; Merchandise Inventory 6. decrease 7. Cost of Goods Sold 8. Working Capital 9. Income from Operations 10. Freight In

Answers: Part II

1. F 2. F 3. T 4. T 5. T 6. F 7. F 8. T 9. F 10. T

Answers: Part III

1.

GENERAL JOURNAL Page ___

Date		Description	Post. Ref.	Debit	Credit
20--		Adjusting Entries			
Dec.	31	Income Summary		132 0 0 0 00	
		Merchandise Inventory			132 0 0 0 00
	31	Merchandise Inventory		136 0 0 0 00	
		Income Summary			136 0 0 0 00

2.

GENERAL JOURNAL Page ___

Date		Description	Post. Ref.	Debit	Credit
20--		Adjusting Entries			
Dec.	31	Cost of Goods Sold		2 0 0 0 00	
		Merchandise Inventory			2 0 0 0 00

3.

GENERAL JOURNAL Page ___

Date		Description	Post. Ref.	Debit	Credit
20--					
Dec.	1	Cash		20 0 0 0 00	
		Unearned Revenue			20 0 0 0 00
		To record collection of cash for a			
		four-month job.			
		Adjusting Entry			
	31	Unearned Revenue		5 0 0 0 00	
		Remodeling Revenue			5 0 0 0 00
		To record one month's revenue			
		earned.			

4. a. \$250,000 total assets − \$140,000 noncurrent assets = \$110,000 current assets

\$130,000 total liabilities − \$80,000 long-term liabilities = \$50,000 current liabilities

\$110,000 current assets − \$50,000 current liabilities = \$60,000 working capital

b. $\frac{\$110{,}000 \text{ current assets}}{\$50{,}000 \text{ current liabilities}} = 2.20$ current ratio

Comprehensive Review Problem

You are to record transactions completed by Fabulous Furnishings during February of this year. Beginning balances for the accounts listed below have been provided in your Working Papers. This company is located in Dallas. To gain practice in completing the steps in the accounting cycle, assume that the fiscal period consists of one month.

QuickBooks

CHART OF ACCOUNTS

Assets (100–199)
111 Cash
112 Petty Cash Fund
113 Accounts Receivable
114 Merchandise Inventory
116 Supplies
118 Prepaid Insurance
122 Equipment
123 Accumulated Depreciation, Equipment

Liabilities (200–299)
221 Accounts Payable
226 Employees' Income Tax Payable
227 FICA Tax Payable
228 State Unemployment Tax Payable
229 Federal Unemployment Tax Payable
230 Salaries Payable

Owner's Equity (300–399)
311 M. L. Langdon, Capital
312 M. L. Langdon, Drawing
313 Income Summary

Revenue (400–499)
411 Sales
412 Sales Returns and Allowances

Cost of Goods Sold (500–599)
511 Purchases
512 Purchases Returns and Allowances
513 Purchases Discounts
514 Freight In

Expenses (600–699)
611 Salary Expense
612 Payroll Tax Expense
613 Rent Expense
614 Utilities Expense
616 Supplies Expense
617 Insurance Expense
618 Depreciation Expense, Equipment
619 Miscellaneous Expense

(Continued)

JOURNALS

Sales Journal, page 56
Purchases Journal, page 62
Cash Receipts Journal, page 69
Cash Payments Journal, page 75
General Journal, pages 89–95

*If using manual journals, reference the journal page numbers listed above. If using QuickBooks, record transactions using either the journal entry method or the forms-based approach (unless otherwise specified).

ACCOUNTS RECEIVABLE

Fashion Decor
Hotel Beritz
Jason and Waldon

ACCOUNTS PAYABLE

Brandon, Inc.
Kingston Fabrics
Magnuson Textiles
Tyson Manufacturing Company

TRANSACTIONS

The following transactions were completed during February of this year.

Fabulous Furnishings does not track cash sales by customer. If you are using the forms-based approach with QuickBooks or using general ledger, select "Cash Sales" as the customer for all cash sales transactions.

Feb. 1 Reversed the adjusting entry for accrued salaries, $620.*

1 Sold merchandise on account to Hotel Beritz, $12,520.86, invoice no. 5221.

2 Issued Ck. No. 7216, $16,593.46, to Kingston Fabrics, in payment of its invoice no. D1739 for $16,932.10 less 2 percent discount.

5 Bought merchandise on account from Magnuson Textiles, $4,874.80, invoice no. RE275, dated February 2; terms 1/10, n/30; FOB Louisville; freight prepaid and added to the invoice, $158 (total, $5,032.80).

5 Received an electric bill and paid Countywide Power, Ck. No. 7217, $358.

6 Received check from Jason and Waldon, $10,780.51, in payment of account.

7 Issued Ck. No. 7218, $9,684.18, to Magnuson Textiles, in payment of its invoice no. RE64 for $9,782 less 1 percent discount.

9 Cash sales for February 1 through February 9, $9,745.40.

12 Recorded the payroll in the payroll register* for regular biweekly salaries for period ended February 12. Salaries: R. W. Harris, $2,840; T. L. Newkirk, $2,374. Income tax withholdings are $287 for Harris and $216 for Newkirk. Assume the following tax rates and taxable earnings limits (see the payroll register for beginning cumulative earnings in your Working Papers. This information is also provided in CengageNow, QuickBooks or general ledger.):

- Social Security taxable earnings, $113,700, with a rate of 6.2 percent for employees and 6.2 percent for employers.
- Medicare taxable earnings, all earnings, with a rate of 1.45 percent (for both employees and employers).

12 Recorded the payroll entry, crediting Salaries Payable.

12 Issued Ck. No. 7219, $2,335.74, to R. W. Harris. Issued Ck. No. 7220, $1,976.39, to T. L. Newkirk. Use two lines and debit Salaries Payable. (Verify these amounts.)

Feb. 12 Recorded payroll taxes.* Assume the following tax rates and taxable earnings:
- Federal unemployment taxable earnings, $7,000, with a rate of 0.6 percent.
- State unemployment taxable earnings, $7,000, with a rate of 5.4 percent.

12 Received a credit memo from Magnuson Textiles for defective merchandise, $692, credit memo no. 916.

14 Issued Ck. No. 7221, $2,900.80, to Mid-State Bank for monthly deposit of January employees' federal income tax withheld, $1,285, and FICA taxes, $1,615.80.

14 Sold merchandise on account to Jason and Waldon, $15,781.30, invoice no. 5222.

14 Issued Ck. No. 7222, $4,298.97, to Magnuson Textiles, in payment of its invoice no. RE275 less the credit memo for defective merchandise and less the discount ($41.83).

18 Bought merchandise on account from Brandon, Inc., $21,375.20, invoice no. 164M, dated February 14; terms 2/10, n/30; FOB Miami; freight prepaid and added to the invoice, $1,242 (total, $22,617.20).

18 Cash sales for February 10 through February 18, $7,889.24.

19 Issued Ck. No. 7223 payable to Quicker Printing for invoice forms, $336 (not previously recorded).

19 Received check from Fashion Decor, $4,830.65, in payment of account.

22 Issued Ck. No. 7224, $12,540, to Tyson Manufacturing Company, in payment of its invoice no. 9264D.

22 Sold merchandise on account to Fashion Decor, $17,435.32, invoice no. 5223.

24 Issued credit memo no. 214 to Fashion Decor, $185, for merchandise returned.

24 Bought merchandise on account from Kingston Fabrics, $16,536.90, invoice no. D1797, dated February 22; terms 2/10, n/30; FOB Dallas.

26 Recorded the payroll in the payroll register* for regular biweekly salaries for period ended February 26. Salaries: R. W. Harris, $2,840; T. L. Newkirk, $2,374. Income tax withholdings are $287 for Harris and $216 for Newkirk. Note: See the entry of February 12 for taxable earnings limits and tax rates. See the payroll register this payroll's beginning cumulative earnings.

26 Recorded the payroll entry, crediting Salaries Payable.

26 Issued Ck. No. 7225, $2,392.54, to R. W. Harris. Issued Ck. No. 7226, $2,023.87, to T. L. Newkirk. Use two lines and debit Salaries Payable.

26 Ck. No. 7227 voided.

26 Recorded payroll taxes.* Assume the following tax rates and taxable earnings:
- Federal unemployment taxable earnings, $7,000, with a rate of 0.6 percent.
- State unemployment taxable earnings, $7,000, with a rate of 5.4 percent.

27 Issued Ck. No. 7228, $1,035, to JIT Freight Line for transportation charge on merchandise purchased from Kingston Fabrics.

28 Issued Ck. No. 7229, $155.60, payable to Cash to reimburse the petty cash fund. Petty cash payments consist of Supplies, $130.24, and Miscellaneous Expense, $25.36.

28 Cash sales for February 19 through February 28, $8,986.60.

28 Issued Ck. No. 7230, $2,290, to Global Rental Agency for monthly rent.

28 M. L. Langdon (owner) withdrew $5,000 for personal use, Ck. No. 7231.

(Continued)

Required

1. Journalize and post the transactions completed during February using either a general journal or special journals or both. (Your instructor will assign you which one(s) to use.)

If using QuickBooks, use the journal entry method or forms-based approach (unless otherwise specified). *Transactions with an asterisk must be recorded in the general journal.

General Journal. Ignore this section if using QuickBooks or general ledger.
   a. Post daily all entries involving customer accounts to the accounts receivable ledger.
   b. Post daily all entries involving creditor accounts to the accounts payable ledger.
   c. Post daily the general journal entries to the general ledger.

Special Journals. Ignore this section if using QuickBooks or general ledger.
   a. Post daily the amounts in the Other Accounts columns of the special journals.
   b. Post daily the general journal.
   c. Post the totals of the special columns of the special journals at the end of the month.

2. Prepare a schedule of accounts receivable (A/R Summary Detail if using QuickBooks) and a schedule of accounts payable (A/P Summary Detail if using QuickBooks).
3. Complete the work sheet for February. Ignore this step if using QuickBooks or general ledger.
   Data for the month-end adjustments are as follows:
   a–b. Merchandise inventory at February 28, $45,484.
   c. Salaries accrued at February 28, $2,084.
   d. Insurance expired during February, $210.
   e. Depreciation of equipment during February, $1,885.
   f. Supplies on hand, $100.
4. Journalize the adjusting entries. If using manual Working Papers, post the adjusting entries to the general ledger.
5. Prepare an income statement.
6. Prepare a statement of owner's equity. (No additional investment was made during the month.) Ignore this step if using QuickBooks.
7. Prepare a balance sheet.
8. Journalize the closing entries. If using manual Working Papers, post to the general ledger.
9. Prepare a post-closing trial balance.

QuickBooks GL GENERAL LEDGER

All About You Spa

CONTINUING PROBLEM

Closing Entries and Financial Statements

It is now August 31. You have journalized and posted the adjustments in the All About You Spa accounting records, and Ms. Valli wants to see financial statements for the last two months (July and August). Then she would like you to prepare the closing entries.

Required

1. Prepare an income statement for the two months ended August 31, 20--.

2. Prepare a statement of owner's equity for the two months ended August 31, 20--. Ignore this step if using QuickBooks.

3. Prepare a balance sheet as of August 31, 20--.

4. Journalize the closing entries in the general journal.

- If you are preparing the closing entries manually, enter your transactions beginning on page 5.

5. Post the closing entries to the general ledger accounts.

- Ignore this step if you are using QuickBooks or general ledger.

6. Prepare a post-closing trial balance as of August 31, 20--.

Congratulations! You have completed your work with All About You Spa.

Check Figures

1. Net income, $13,485.86
2. A. Valli, Capital (end of period), $58,705.48
3. Balance Sheet report total assets, $76,219.60
4. Closing Journal Entries report total, $114,295.30
6. Post-closing trial balance total, $76,444.24

QuickBooks Analysis Activities

QB ANALYSIS ACTIVITY 1

Using the information in the Comprehensive Review Problem on pages 663–666 and the QuickBooks data file labeled Fabulous Furnishing on the textbook website at www.cengagebrain.com, complete the following activities. Be sure to prepare and print (or save as a PDF) your reports as you complete the steps below.

1. Record the transactions completed during February using either the journal entry method or the forms-based approach (unless otherwise specified in the problem).
2. Prepare a trial balance (unadjusted).
3. Prepare an A/R Summary—Detail report.
4. Prepare an A/P Summary—Detail report.
5. Journalize the adjusting entries.
6. Prepare a trial balance (adjusted).
7. Prepare an income statement (Profit & Loss—standard).
8. Prepare an income statement (Profit & Loss—comparative financial statement, using vertical analysis).
9. Prepare a balance sheet.
10. Prepare a statement of cash flows.
11. Journalize the closing entries.
12. Prepare a post-closing trial balance.
13. Prepare a journal report.
14. Prepare a ledger report.

Answer the following questions:

1. What is the amount of total accounts receivable?
2. What is the amount of total accounts payable?
3. What is Fabulous Furnishings' net income as of February 28, 20--?
4. What is the percentage of net income to net sales?
5. What is the amount of total assets?
6. What is the amount of total liabilities?
7. What is the increase (decrease) in cash flow?
8. What is the total for the Debit column on the post-closing trial balance?

QB ANALYSIS ACTIVITY 2

Using the QuickBooks data file labeled New Age Design, Inc., located on the textbook website at www.cengagebrain.com, prepare a two-year, comparative income statement for the years 2014 and 2015, using horizontal and vertical analysis.

Horizontal Analysis

1. What is the percent of increase or (decrease) in sales?
2. What is the percent of increase or (decrease) in net income?
3. Comment on what you think the percentages of increase or decrease mean.

Vertical Analysis

1. What is the percent of net income to net sales for 2014?
2. What is the percent of net income to net sales for 2015?
3. Comment on what you think the percentage figures mean.

QB ANALYSIS ACTIVITY 3

The income statement (Figure QA1) and balance sheet (Figure QA2) reflect the correct financial information for Dynamo Bike Shop. Using the QuickBooks data file labeled

Dynamo Bike Shop that is located on the textbook website at www.cengagebrain.com, complete the following activities as of December 31, 2015:

1. Prepare an income statement (profit and loss—standard) with QuickBooks.
2. Prepare a balance sheet with QuickBooks.
3. Compare the QuickBooks financial statements you prepared with the financial statements in Figures QA1 and QA2.
4. Identify all discrepancies.
5. Journalize the adjusting entries.
6. Explain how you identified the discrepancies.

Figure QA1

Dynamo Bike Shop, Inc.
Profit & Loss
January through December 2015

▾ Ordinary Income/Expense	
▾ Income	
Sales	982,100.00
Sales Returns and Allowances	−12,500.00
Total Income	969,600.00
▾ Cost of Good Sold	
Cost of Goods Sold	662,900.00
Total COGS	662,900.00
Gross profit	306,700.00
▾ Expense	
Advertising Expense	7,900.00
Bad Debts Expense	6,200.00
Delivery Expense	12,950.00
Depreciation Expense, Building	14,200.00
Depreciation Expense, Equipment	6,800.00
Insurance Expense	1,100.00
Misc. General Expense	680.00
Office Salary Expense	33,440.00
Property Taxes Expense	6,100.00
Sales Salary Expense	114,650.00
Store Suppies Expense	450.00
Total Expense	204,470.00
Net Ordinary Income	102,230.00
▾ Other Income/Expense	
▾ Other Expense	
Income Tax Expense	18,420.00
Interest Expense	7,920.00
Total Other Expense	26,340.00
Net Other Income	−26,340.00
Net Income	75,890.00

Figure QA2

Dynamo Bike Shop, Inc.
Balance Sheet
As of December 31, 2015

▾ ASSETS	
▾ Current Assets	
▾ Checking/Savings	
Cash ▸	86,900.00 ◂
Total Checking/Savings	86,900.00
Other Current Assets	
▾ Allowance for Doubtful Accounts	
Accounts Receivables	79,700.00
Accounts for Doubtful Accounts – Other	–3,300.00
Total Allowance for Doubtful Accounts	76,400.00
Merchandise Inventory	424,290.000
Prepaid Insurance	2,000.00
Supplies	700.00
Total Other Currents Assets	503,390.00
Total Currents Assetst	590,290.00
Fixed Assets	
▾ Accum. Deprec., Building	
Building	163,000.00
Accum. Deprec., Building – Other	–56,800.00
Total Accum. Deprec., Building	106,200.00
▾ Accum. Deprec., Equipment	
Equipment	88,600.00
Accum. Deprec., Equipment – Other	–41,000.00
Total Accum. Deprec., Equipment	47,600.00
Land	40,000.00
Total Fixed Assets	193,800.00
TOTAL ASSETS	784,090.00
▾ LIABILITIES & EQUITY	
▾ Liabilities	
▾ Current Liabilities	
▾ Other Current Liabilities	
Accounts Payable	94,900.00
Salaries Payable	5,700.00
Total Other Current Liabilities	100,600.00
Total Current Liabilities	100,600.00
Long Term Liabilities	
Mortgage Payable	97,800.00
Total Long Term Liabilities	97,800.00
Total Liabilities	198,400.00
Equity	
Owners Equity	509,800.00
Net Income	75,890.00
Total Equity	585,690.00
TOTAL LIABILITIES & EQUITY	**784,090.00**

APPENDIX

Methods of Depreciation

A

Learning Objectives

After you have completed this appendix, you will be able to do the following:

1. Prepare a schedule of depreciation using the straight-line method.
2. Prepare a schedule of depreciation using the double-declining-balance method.
3. Prepare a schedule of depreciation for five-year property under the Modified Accelerated Cost Recovery System.

Accounting Language

Double-declining-balance method (p. A-2)
Modified Accelerated Cost Recovery System (MACRS) (p. A-2)
Straight-line method (p. A-1)

As you have learned, depreciation is the the process of allocating the cost of an asset to an expense over its useful life. In this appendix, we will illustrate three methods of depreciation (straight-line, double-declining-balance, and Modified Accelerated Cost Recovery System) using the example of a delivery truck. Assume that the truck was bought at the beginning of Year 1 at a cost of $24,000. The truck is estimated to have a useful life of five years and a trade-in value of $6,000 at the end of the five-year period.

STRAIGHT-LINE METHOD

Learning Objective 1 Prepare a schedule of depreciation using the straight-line method.

The **straight-line method** was demonstrated in Chapter 4. This method is popular because it is easy to use and allows a business to calculate an equal amount of depreciation expense for each year of service anticipated. The accountant computes the annual depreciation by dividing the depreciation base (cost minus salvage value, if any) by the number of years of useful life predicted for the asset. See the illustration of the straight-line method below.

$$\text{Yearly Depreciation} = \frac{\text{Cost of Asset} - \text{Trade-in Value}}{\text{Years of Life}} = \frac{\$24,000 - \$6,000}{5\text{ years}}$$

$$= \frac{\$18,000}{5\text{ years}} = \$3,600\text{ per year}$$

Year	Depreciation for the Year	Accumulated Depreciation	Book Value (Cost Less Accumulated Depreciation)
1	$18,000 ÷ 5 years = $ 3,600	$ 3,600	$24,000 − $ 3,600 = $20,400
2	18,000 ÷ 5 years = 3,600	$ 3,600 + $3,600 = 7,200	24,000 − 7,200 = 16,800
3	18,000 ÷ 5 years = 3,600	7,200 + 3,600 = 10,800	24,000 − 10,800 = 13,200
4	18,000 ÷ 5 years = 3,600	10,800 + 3,600 = 14,400	24,000 − 14,400 = 9,600
5	18,000 ÷ 5 years = 3,600	14,400 + 3,600 = 18,000	24,000 − 18,000 = 6,000
	$18,000		

DOUBLE-DECLINING-BALANCE METHOD

Learning Objective 2 Prepare a schedule of depreciation using the double-declining-balance method.

The **double-declining-balance method** is an accelerated method of depreciation that allows larger amounts of depreciation to be taken in the early years of an asset's life. In accelerated depreciation, larger amounts of depreciation are taken during the early life of an asset, and smaller amounts are taken during the later years of an asset's life. Some accountants reason that the amount charged to depreciation should be higher during an asset's early years, when it is more productive and efficient, to offset the higher repair and maintenance expenses of the asset's later years. This way the total annual expense tends to be equalized over the entire life of the asset.

The double-declining-balance method calculates depreciation at double the straight-line rate. In the illustration below, with an estimated useful life of five years, the straight-line rate is 1/5, or 0.20. Twice, or double, the straight-line rate is 2/5 (1/5 × 2), or 0.40. Note that the trade-in value is not taken into account until the end of the schedule. To calculate depreciation using the double-declining-balance method, multiply the *book value* at the beginning of each year by twice the straight-line rate.

Year	Depreciation for the Year	Accumulated Depreciation	Book Value (Cost Less Accumulated Depreciation)
1	$24,000 × 0.40 = $ 9,600	$ 9,600	$24,000 − $ 9,600 = $14,400
2	$14,400 × 0.40 = 5,760	$ 9,600 + $5,760 = 15,360	24,000 − 15,360 = 8,640
3	$8,640 − $6,000 = 2,640	15,360 + 2,640 = 18,000	24,000 − 18,000 = 6,000
4	0	18,000	24,000 − 18,000 = 6,000
5	0	18,000	24,000 − 18,000 = 6,000
	$18,000		

If the 40% depreciation rate is applied to Year 3, depreciation expense would be $3,456 ($8,640 × 0.40), accumulated depreciation would be $18,816 ($15,360 + $3,456), and book value would be $5,184 ($24,000 − $18,816). However, the book value cannot drop below the established salvage, or trade-in, value of $6,000. So for Year 3, an adjustment must be made limiting the depreciation for the year to $2,640, which will bring the accumulated depreciation up to $18,000. Consequently, the book value at the end of the year will be $6,000 ($24,000 cost − $18,000 accumulated depreciation) and no further depreciation will be taken.

TAX REQUIREMENT—MACRS

Learning Objective 3 Prepare a schedule of depreciation for five-year property under the Modified Accelerated Cost Recovery System.

Business firms are entitled to deduct depreciation on their income tax returns. However, the amount recorded on a company's income statement (based on the depreciation method, straight-line method, double-declining-balance, or another method) may differ from the amount recorded on the company's income tax return.

For property acquired after 1986, a schedule of depreciation called the **Modified Accelerated Cost Recovery System (MACRS)** has been established. The term *recovery* is used because MACRS is a means of recovering or deducting the cost of an asset. Most small businesses use MACRS for financial statement reporting and tax reporting. MACRS is a combination of the declining-balance and straight-line depreciation methods. For more information, see IRS Publication 946, available at www.irs.gov.

According to MACRS, property is divided into eight classes, as follows:

Property Class	Description
3-year property	Certain horses and tractor units for use over the road
5-year property	Autos, light- and heavy-duty general-purpose trucks, computers, and office equipment (copiers, etc.); also, furniture, appliances, window treatments, and carpeting used in residential rental buildings
7-year property	Office furniture and fixtures and any property that does not have a class life and that is not, by law, in any other class
10-year property	Vessels, barges, tugs, and similar water transportation equipment
15-year property	Wharves, roads, fences, and any municipal wastewater treatment plant
20-year property	Certain farm buildings and municipal sewers
27.5-year residential rental property	Rental houses and apartments
39-year real property	Office buildings, store buildings, and warehouses

Under MACRS, trade-in value is ignored. The following table lists the depreciation rates that a business may use for tax purposes.

Depreciation for Recovery Period				
Year	3-Year	5-Year	7-Year	10-Year
1	33.33%	20.00%	14.29%	10.00%
2	44.45	32.00	24.49	18.00
3	14.81	19.20	17.49	14.40
4	7.41	11.52	12.49	11.52
5		11.52	8.93	9.22
6		5.76	8.92	7.37
7			8.93	6.55
8			4.46	6.55
9				6.56
10				6.55
11				3.28

Our delivery truck qualifies as five-year property.

Year	Depreciation for the Year	Accumulated Depreciation	Book Value (Cost Less Accumulated Depreciation)
1	\$24,000 × 0.20 = \$ 4,800.00	\$ 4,800.00	\$24,000.00 − \$ 4,800.00 = \$19,200.00
2	24,000 × 0.32 = 7,680.00	\$ 4,800.00 + \$7,680.00 = 12,480.00	24,000.00 − 12,480.00 = 11,520.00
3	24,000 × 0.192 = 4,608.00	12,480.00 + 4,608.00 = 17,088.00	24,000.00 − 17,088.00 = 6,912.00
4	24,000 × 0.1152 = 2,764.80	17,088.00 + 2,764.80 = 19,852.80	24,000.00 − 19,852.80 = 4,147.20
5	24,000 × 0.1152 = 2,764.80	19,852.80 + 2,764.80 = 22,617.60	24,000.00 − 22,617.60 = 1,382.40
6	24,000 × 0.0576 = 1,382.40	22,617.60 + 1,382.40 = 24,000.00	24,000.00 − 24,000.00 = 0
	\$24,000.00		

Glossary

Double-declining balance method An accelerated depreciation method that calculates depreciation at double the straight-line rate. *(p. A-2)*

Modified Accelerated Cost Recovery System (MACRS) A variety of tax rate schedules established by the Internal Revenue Service. MACRS is a combination of declining-balance and straight-line methods. *(p. A-2)*

Straight-line method A popular method of depreciation because it is easy to use and allows a business to calculate an equal amount of depreciation expense for each year of service anticipated. Annual depreciation is calculated by dividing the depreciation base (cost minus salvage value, if any) by the number of years of useful life predicted for the asset. *(p. A-1)*

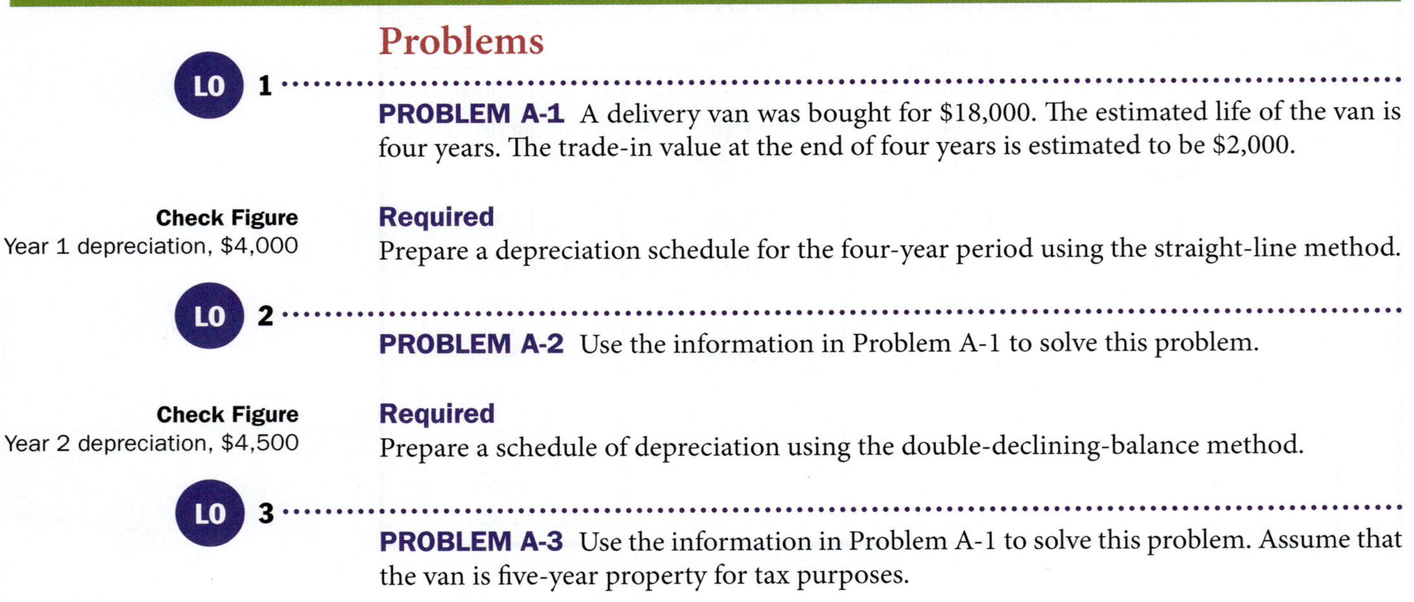

Problems

LO 1

PROBLEM A-1 A delivery van was bought for \$18,000. The estimated life of the van is four years. The trade-in value at the end of four years is estimated to be \$2,000.

Check Figure
Year 1 depreciation, \$4,000

Required
Prepare a depreciation schedule for the four-year period using the straight-line method.

LO 2

PROBLEM A-2 Use the information in Problem A-1 to solve this problem.

Check Figure
Year 2 depreciation, \$4,500

Required
Prepare a schedule of depreciation using the double-declining-balance method.

LO 3

PROBLEM A-3 Use the information in Problem A-1 to solve this problem. Assume that the van is five-year property for tax purposes.

Check Figure
Year 3 depreciation, \$3,456

Required
Prepare a schedule of depreciation under MACRS. Round figures to the nearest whole dollar.

APPENDIX

Bad Debts

B

Learning Objectives

After you have completed this appendix, you will be able to do the following:

1. Prepare the adjusting entry for bad debts using the allowance method, based on a percentage of credit sales.
2. Prepare the entry to write off an account as uncollectible when the allowance method is used.
3. Prepare the entry to write off an account as uncollectible when the specific charge-off method is used.

Accounting Language

Allowance method of accounting for bad debts expense (p. B-1)

Specific charge-off method of accounting for bad debts expense (p. B-3)

As you know, not all credit customers pay their bills. In this appendix, we turn our attention to the accounts receivable that will not be collected. There are two basic methods of providing for writing or charging off credit customers' accounts that are considered uncollectible. They are the allowance method and the specific charge-off method.

ALLOWANCE METHOD

The **allowance method of accounting for bad debts expense** provides for bad debts expense in advance by estimating them. Although there are a number of ways to estimate the amount of future expenses from open accounts, we will base our estimate on a percentage of credit sales.

For example, based on its experience with bad debts expense, Miami Printing estimates that 1 percent of its revenue from services on account for the year will be uncollectible. Obviously, Miami Printing does not know which credit customers will not pay their bills. If the company were certain that a particular customer would not pay his or her bill, it wouldn't perform services without requiring cash in advance.

Adjusting Entry and Writing Off an Account

Learning Objective 1: Prepare the adjusting entry for bad debts using the allowance method, based on a percentage of credit sales.

Miami Printing's total income from services on account for last year was $500,000. One percent of $500,000 is $5,000 ($500,000 × 0.01 = $5,000). On its work sheet, Miami Printing makes an adjusting entry. We also show this in T account form assuming a credit balance of $170 in the Allowance for Doubtful Accounts account.

Bad Debts Expense

+	−
Dec. 31 Adj. 5,000	

Allowance for Doubtful Accounts

−	+
	Bal. 170
	Dec. 31 Adj. 5,000

The general journal entry is shown below.

GENERAL JOURNAL Page ___

Date		Description	Post. Ref.	Debit	Credit
20—		Adjusting Entry			
Dec.	31	Bad Debts Expense		5 0 0 0 00	
		Allowance for Doubtful Accounts			5 0 0 0 00

Allowance for Doubtful Accounts is treated as a deduction from Accounts Receivable. Consequently, Allowance for Doubtful Accounts is a contra account. The adjusting entry is similar to the entry for depreciation in that there is a debit to an expense account and a credit to a contra-asset account.

Assume that Miami Printing's Accounts Receivable balance is $90,000. Let's show the accounts and the adjusting entries in T account form.

Owner's Equity

Assets		=	**Liabilities**		+	**Capital**		−	**Drawing**		+	**Revenue**		−	**Expenses**	
+	−		−	+		−	+		+	−		−	+		+	−
Debit	Credit		Debit	Credit		Debit	Credit		Debit	Credit		Debit	Credit		Debit	Credit

Accounts Receivable

+	−
Bal. 90,000	

Allowance for Doubtful Accounts

−	+
	Bal. 170
	Adj. 5,000
	Bal. 5,170

Income from Services

−	+
	Bal. 500,000

Bad Debts Expense

+	−
Adj. 5,000	

FYI

Companies generally have a credit balance left in the Allowance account.

Learning Objective 2 Prepare the entry to write off an account as uncollectible when the allowance method is used.

The Bad Debts Expense account comes into existence as an adjusting entry, and it is immediately closed during the closing process.

As certain credit customers' accounts are determined to be uncollectible and are written off, the losses are taken out of Allowance for Doubtful Accounts. Think of the Allowance for Doubtful Accounts as a reservoir. By means of the adjusting entry, the account is filled up at the end of the year and is gradually drained off (reduced) during the next year by write-offs of credit customer accounts. The $170 balance in Allowance for Doubtful Accounts at the end of the year (prior to the adjusting entry of $5,000) indicates that less accounts receivable were actually written off as uncollectible during the year than previously estimated. As a result, Bad Debts Expense in the period was overstated and net income thus understated.

Let's go on to the next year. On January 2, Miami Printing finally gives up on its attempts to collect $720 from its credit customer Ace Computer, which is included in Accounts Receivable. Miami Printing now writes off the account in the amount of $720, shown in T account form.

Accounts Receivable				Allowance for Doubtful Accounts			
	+	–			–	+	
Bal.	90,000	Jan. 2 (write-off)	720	Jan. 2 (write-off)	720	Bal.	5,170
Bal.	**89,280**					**Bal.**	**4,450**

As you can see, the write-off has reduced both the balance of Accounts Receivable and the balance of Allowance for Doubtful Accounts but has not changed the net realizable value of accounts receivable. The general journal entry is shown below.

GENERAL JOURNAL Page___

Date		Description	Post. Ref.	Debit	Credit
20—					
Jan.	2	Allowance for Doubtful Accounts		7 2 0 00	
		Accounts Receivable			7 2 0 00
		Wrote off the account of Ace			
		Computer as uncollectible.			

An Advantage and a Disadvantage of the Allowance Method

The allowance method is consistent with the accrual basis of accounting in that it matches revenues of one year with expenses of the same year. The bad debts expense potential is provided in the same year in which the revenue is earned. The conformity with the matching principle places the allowance method in compliance with generally accepted accounting principles as recognized by the FASB.

SPECIFIC CHARGE-OFF METHOD

Learning Objective 3 Prepare the entry to write off an account as uncollectible when the specific charge-off method is used.

Under the **specific charge-off method of accounting for bad debts expense**, when a credit customer's account is determined to be uncollectible, the account is simply written off. The terms *write-off* and *charge-off* mean the same thing. No allowance account is used with the specific charge-off method because no estimate of uncollectible accounts receivable is calculated. As an illustration, Walter Company uses the specific charge-off method. On May 5, Walter Company writes off the account of Garber Construction, $1,220. For the purpose of this example, we will use a separate Accounts Receivable account for Garber Construction. T accounts pertaining to Garber's account look like this:

Accounts Receivable, Garber Construction				Bad Debts Expense		
	+	–			+	–
Bal.	1,220	May 5 (write-off)	1,220	May 5 (write-off)	1,220	

The general journal entry is shown below.

GENERAL JOURNAL Page ___

Date		Description	Post. Ref.	Debit	Credit
20—					
May	5	Bad Debts Expense		1 2 2 0 00	
		Accounts Receivable			1 2 2 0 00
		Wrote off the account of			
		Garber Construction as			
		uncollectible.			

Under this method, entries will be made directly into the Bad Debts Expense account during the year. No adjusting entry is needed, and Allowance for Doubtful Accounts is not used.

Advantages of the Specific Charge-off Method

The main advantage is that the method may be used for federal income tax purposes. It is not necessary to make an adjusting entry. Also, one less account (Allowance for Doubtful Accounts) is required.

A Disadvantage of the Specific Charge-off Method

This method is not consistent with the accrual basis of accounting (recognizing revenue when it is earned and expenses when they are incurred). The method does not match up the revenues of one year with the expenses of the same year. This lack of conformity with the matching principle places the specific charge-off method in violation of generally accepted accounting principles. For example, the sale of services on account to Garber Construction could have been made two years ago. Because the account receivable will never be collected, the revenue for that year was too high (overstated). Consequently, net income is also overstated during that year. Now, two years later, $1,220 is written off as an expense. So net income for this year is too low (understated) because of the added expense.

Glossary

Allowance method of accounting for bad debts expense A method that requires an adjusting entry to debit Bad Debts Expense and to credit Allowance for Doubtful Accounts to match expenses from uncollectible accounts with sales of the same period. Write-offs of uncollectible accounts are debited to Allowance for Doubtful Accounts and credited to Accounts Receivable. *(p. B-1)*

Specific charge-off method of accounting for bad debts expense A method of recognizing bad debts that requires no adjusting entry. The accountant debits Bad Debts Expense and credits Accounts Receivable, when an uncollectable account is written off. This method is required for federal income tax reporting but is not allowed under GAAP. *(p. B-3)*

Problems

LO 1, 2

PROBLEM B-1 Rogan Company's total sales on account for the year amounted to $327,000. The company, which uses the allowance method, estimated bad debts at 1 percent of its credit sales.

Check Figure
Adjusting entry amount, $3,270

Required
Journalize the following selected entries:

2012
Dec. 31 Record the adjusting entry.

2013
Mar. 2 Write off the account of A. M. Billson as uncollectible, $584.
June 6 Write off the account of W. H. Gilders as uncollectible, $492.

LO 1, 2

PROBLEM B-2 Hardy's Landscape Service's total revenue on account for 2012 amounted to $273,205. The company, which uses the allowance method, estimates bad debts at ½ percent of total revenue on account.

Check Figure
Adjusting entry amount, $1,366.03

Required
Journalize the following selected entries:

2012
Dec. 12 Record services performed on account for E. E. Morton, $245.
31 Record the adjusting entry for Bad Debts Expense.
31 Record the closing entry for Bad Debts Expense.

2013
Feb. 18 Write off the account of E. E. Morton as uncollectible, $245.

LO 3

PROBLEM B-3 Nillson's Nursery uses the specific charge-off method for recording bad debts.

Check Figure
Total amount debited to Bad Debts Expense in 2012, $677

Required
Journalize the following selected entries:

2012
Apr. 10 Write off the account of P. A. Seldon as uncollectible, $286.
July 27 Write off the account of J. M. Weller as uncollectible, $391.

APPENDIX

C Inventory Methods

Learning Objectives

After you have completed this appendix, you will be able to do the following:

1. Determine the amount of the ending merchandise inventory by the weighted-average-cost method.
2. Determine the amount of the ending merchandise inventory by the first-in, first-out (FIFO) method.
3. Determine the amount of the ending merchandise inventory by the last-in, first-out (LIFO) method.

Accounting Language

First-in, first-out (FIFO) method (p. C-2)

Last-in, first-out (LIFO) method (p. C-2)

Weighted-average-cost method (p. C-2)

To determine the dollar amount of the ending merchandise inventory under the periodic inventory system, it is necessary to take a physical count of the various items in stock and match them up with their costs. In other words, the ending inventory consists of the number of units of each type of item on hand multiplied by the cost of each unit.

If each unit were purchased at the same price, the job of determining the total cost of the inventory would be simple. For example, if there are 100 units of Product A on hand and all 100 units were bought at $15, the total cost of the ending inventory is $1,500 (100 × $15). However, over a period of time, costs of individual purchases of units may differ. Changes in costs of individual units make the different methods of inventory valuation necessary.

We will use Bruce Medical Supply, a distributor of medical supplies, to illustrate the three methods of inventory valuation. Bruce records inventory on a periodic inventory system. Bruce's ending inventory consists of 176 Standard 2.5v diagnostic sets acquired through various purchases, as follows:

Specific Purchase	Number of Units	Cost per Unit	Total Cost
Beginning inventory	34	$145	$ 4,930
First purchase	60	152	9,120
Second purchase	256	156	39,936
Third purchase	164	162	26,568
Total units available	514		$80,554

Of the 514 units available for sale, 176 units are still on hand and 338 have been sold (514 – 176 = 338 units sold).

Bruce Medical Supply may choose any one of the following three methods of recording the total cost of the 176 units in the ending inventory of medical supplies.

WEIGHTED-AVERAGE-COST METHOD

Learning Objective 1 Determine the amount of the ending merchandise inventory by the weighted-average-cost method.

An alternative to keeping track of the cost of each item purchased is to use the **weighted-average-cost method**. This method averages the cost per unit of all like articles available for sale during the period. The first step is to find the total cost of the merchandise on hand during the year by multiplying the number of units by their respective purchase costs. (See page C-1.) From this information, you can find the average cost per unit, which will be used to determine the ending inventory value, as shown below:

$$\text{Average Cost per Unit} = \frac{\text{Total Cost}}{\text{Total Units Available}} = \frac{\$80{,}554}{514} = \$156.72 \text{ (rounded)}$$

Cost of Ending Inventory (176 units) = $156.72 × 176 units = $27,582.72

FIRST-IN, FIRST-OUT METHOD

Learning Objective 2 Determine the amount of the ending merchandise inventory by the first-in, first-out (FIFO) method.

The **first-in, first-out (FIFO) method** is based on the assumption that the first units of diagnostic sets purchased will be sold first. The costs of the units left will be those of the most recently purchased units. You may think of this as the way a grocery store sells milk. Because milk will sour, the oldest milk is moved to the front of the display shelf and is sold first. Consequently, the cartons of milk remaining on the shelf are the freshest milk.

Relating to our illustration of diagnostic sets:

Specific Purchase	Number of Units	Cost per Unit	Total Cost
Beginning inventory	34	$145	$ 4,930
First purchase	60	152	9,120
Second purchase	256	156	39,936
Third purchase	164	162	26,568
Total units available	514		$80,554

The cost of ending merchandise inventory, or the 176 diagnostic sets on hand (most recently purchased), is as follows:

164	units (third purchase)	@ $162 each =	$26,568
12	units (second purchase)	@ $156 each =	1,872
176	units		$28,440

LAST-IN, FIRST-OUT METHOD

Learning Objective 3 Determine the amount of the ending merchandise inventory by the last-in, first-out (LIFO) method.

The **last-in, first-out (LIFO) method** is based on the assumption that the last units of diagnostic sets purchased will be sold first. The costs of the units left over will be those of the earliest purchased units. You may think of this as the way a coal yard sells coal. When the coal yard sells coal to its customers, it takes coal off the top of the pile. Consequently, the tons of coal in the ending inventory consist of those first few tons at the bottom of the pile.

Relating to our illustration of diagnostic sets shown above, the cost of the ending merchandise inventory, or the 176 diagnostic sets on hand (earliest purchased), is as follows:

34	units (beginning inventory)	@ $145 each =	$ 4,930
60	units (first purchase)	@ $152 each =	9,120
82	units (second purchase)	@ $156 each =	12,792
176	units		$26,842

COMPARISON OF METHODS

If prices don't change very much, all inventory methods give about the same results. However, in a dynamic market where prices are constantly rising and falling, each method may yield different amounts. Here is a comparison of the results of the sale of diagnostic sets using the three methods we described.

Comparison of Three Methods		
Method	Ending Inventory (176 units)	Cost of Goods Sold (Goods Available for Sale − Ending Inventory) (338 units = 514 − 176)
Weighted-average-cost	$27,582.72	$52,971.28 ($80,554.00 − $27,582.72)
First-in, first-out	28,440.00	52,114.00 ($80,554.00 − $28,440.00)
Last-in, first-out	26,842.00	53,712.00 ($80,554.00 − $26,842.00)

A summary of the effects of the methods is as follows:

1. Weighted-average-cost is a compromise between LIFO and FIFO for both the amount of the ending inventory and the Cost of Goods Sold.
2. FIFO provides the most realistic amount for ending merchandise inventory in the Current Assets section of the balance sheet. The ending inventory is valued at the most recent costs, referred to as replacement cost.
3. LIFO provides the most realistic amount for the Cost of Goods Sold section of the income statement because the items that have been sold must be replaced at the most recent costs.

Now assume that the diagnostic sets were sold for $245 each.

	Weighted-Average-Cost	First-in, First-out	Last-in, First-out
Sales (338 units × $245 each)	$82,810.00	$82,810.00	$82,810.00
Less: Cost of Goods Sold	52,971.28	52,114.00	53,712.00
Gross Profit	$29,838.72	$30,696.00	$29,098.00

As you can see, the inventory method used can have an effect on the gross profit of a business. Once an inventory method is adopted by a business, the method must be used consistently. If a company wants to change its inventory method for tax purposes, the company must request permission from the Internal Revenue Service.

Glossary

First-in, first-out (FIFO) method An inventory costing method that assumes the first units purchased will be sold first and the costs of the units left in inventory will be from the most recently purchased items. *(p. C-2)*

Last-in, first-out (LIFO) method An inventory costing method that assumes the last units purchased will be sold first and the costs of the units left in inventory will be from the earliest purchased items. *(p. C-2)*

Weighted-average-cost method An inventory costing method that averages the costs of items purchased. The average unit price is then used to determine the total cost of goods sold and total cost of remaining inventory. *(p. C-2)*

Problems

LO 1

PROBLEM C-1 Bean Nursery sells bark to its customers at retail. Bean buys bark from a plywood mill in bulk and transports the bark in its own trucks. Information relating to the beginning inventory and purchases of bark is as follows:

Beginning inventory	1,500 cubic yards @ \$0.40 per cubic yard
First purchase	2,100 cubic yards @ \$0.42 per cubic yard
Second purchase	1,400 cubic yards @ \$0.46 per cubic yard
Third purchase	1,000 cubic yards @ \$0.47 per cubic yard

Check Figure
Cost of ending inventory, \$519.24

Required

Find the cost of 1,200 cubic yards in the ending inventory by the weighted-average-cost method. Carry average cost per cubic yard to four decimals.

LO 2

PROBLEM C-2 Use the information presented in Problem C-1 to solve this problem.

Check Figure
Cost of ending inventory, \$562

Required

Find the cost of the ending inventory by the first-in, first-out method.

LO 3

PROBLEM C-3 Use the information presented in Problem C-1 to solve this problem.

Check Figure
Cost of ending inventory, \$480

Required

Find the cost of the ending inventory by the last-in, first-out method.

APPENDIX

Notes Payable and Notes Receivable

Learning Objectives

After you have completed this appendix, you will be able to do the following:

1. Calculate the interest on promissory notes.
2. Determine the due dates of promissory notes.
3a. Record journal entries for notes given to secure an extension of time on an open account.
3b. Record journal entries for payment of an interest-bearing note at maturity.
3c. Record journal entries for notes given to secure a cash loan when the bank discounts the note.
3d. Record journal entries for payment of a discounted note at maturity.
4a. Record the journal entry for receipt of a note from a charge customer.
4b. Record the journal entry for receipt of payment of an interest-bearing note at maturity.
4c. Record the journal entry for discounting an interest-bearing note receivable.
4d. Record the journal entry for a dishonored note receivable.

Accounting Language

Discount (p. D-4)
Discount period (p. D-7)
Discounting a notes payable (p. D-4)
Discounting notes receivable (p. D-6)
Dishonored note receivable (p. D-8)
Duration (p. D-2)
Interest (p. D-2)
Maker (p. D-1)
Maturity date (p. D-2)
Maturity value (p. D-4)
Payee (p. D-1)
Principal (p. D-2)
Proceeds (p. D-4)
Promissory note (p. D-1)

Credit plays an extremely important role in the operation of most business enterprises. Credit may be extended on a charge-account basis, with payment generally due in 25 to 30 days. This type of credit involves the Accounts Payable and Accounts Receivable accounts. Credit may also be granted by giving or receiving notes for specific transactions. This sort of credit involves the Notes Payable and Notes Receivable accounts. The notes which represent formal instruments of credit are known as a **promissory note**. A promissory note – usually referred to simply as a *note* – is a written promise to pay a certain sum at a fixed or determinable future time. They are customarily used as evidence of credit transactions for periods longer than 30 days. For example, promissory notes may be used in sales of equipment on the installment plan and for transactions involving large amounts of money. Promissory notes are also used to grant extensions of credit beyond the original credit terms. Like a check, notes must be payable to the order of a particular person or firm, known as the **payee**. It must also be signed by the person or firm making the promise, known as the **maker**.

Most companies become involved with notes at one time or another by issuing notes to creditors, by receiving notes from customers, or by issuing notes to banks in order to borrow money. Consequently, an accountant must be acquainted with the procedures for handling promissory notes.

CALCULATING INTEREST

Learning Objective 1: Calculate the interest on promissory notes.

Interest is a charge made for the use of money. To the maker of the note, interest is an expense. The amount of interest a maker pays is expressed as a certain percentage of the principal of the note for a period of one year (or less). The following formula is used to calculate interest:

Interest (in dollars)	=	**Principal** of Note (in dollars)	×	**Rate** of Interest (as a percentage of the principal)	×	**Time** of Note (expressed as a year or fraction of a year)

FYI Agencies of the federal government use the actual number of days in the year.

The **principal** is the face amount of the note. The *rate of interest* is a percentage of the principal. *Time,* or the length of life of the note, is usually expressed in days or months. It is the period between the note's date of issue (starting date) and its **maturity date** (the due date or interest payment date). It is stated in terms of a year or fraction of a year. The usual commercial practice is to use a 360-day year, making the denominator of the fraction 360.

Example: $80,000, 6 percent, 60 days

Interest = Principal × Rate × Time

$$\textbf{Interest} = \$80{,}000 \times 0.06 \times \frac{60}{360} = \underline{\underline{\$800}}$$

DETERMINING DUE DATES

Learning Objective 2: Determine the due dates of promissory notes.

The period of time between a promissory note's issue date and its maturity date is called the **duration** of the note. The duration of a note may be expressed in days or moths. If the time of the note is expressed in months, the maturity date is the corresponding day in the month after the specified number of months has elapsed. When counting the number of days, begin with the day *after* the date the note was issued and end with the last day of the note.

Example

Let's say that the due date of a promissory note is specified as 60 days after April 8. The due date is June 7.

The due date is determined by the following steps:

STEP 1. Determine the number of days remaining in the month of issue by subtracting the date of the note from the number of days in the month in which it is dated.

STEP 2. Add as many full months as possible without exceeding the number of days in the note, counting the full number of days in these months.

STEP 3. Determine the number of days remaining in the month in which the note matures by subtracting the total days counted so far from the number of days in the note, as shown on the following page.

April

S	M	T	W	T	F	S
		1	2	3	4	5
6	7	8	9	10	11	12
13	14	15	16	17	18	19
20	21	22	23	24	25	26
27	28	29	30			

22 days
8th through the 30th
30 − 8 = 22 days left

May

S	M	T	W	T	F	S
				1	2	3
4	5	6	7	8	9	10
11	12	13	14	15	16	17
18	19	20	21	22	23	24
25	26	27	28	29	30	31

+ 31 days

June

S	M	T	W	T	F	S
1	2	3	4	5	6	7
8	9	10	11	12	13	14
15	16	17	18	19	20	21
22	23	24	25	26	27	28
29	30					

= 53 days have passed
60 − 53 = 7 days remaining after May 31
June 7 due date

STEP 1.	April (30 − 8)	= 22 days left in April
STEP 2.	May	= 31 days
	Total days so far	= 53 days
STEP 3.	June (60 − 53)	= 7th day of June (due date)

In addition to determining the due date using the method above, you can find a loan calculator on the Internet that will automatically find the due dat. These calculators require you to input the starting date and time period of the loan; the software then determines the due date.

TRANSACTIONS FOR NOTES PAYABLE

We assume that all notes are due within one year; thus, they are classified on the balance sheet as Current Liabilities. However, if notes are not due within one year, the portion of the note that is due within one year is a Current Liability and the remainder is classified as a Long-Term Liability. Interest expense is classified on the income statement as Interest Expense (if significant) or Other Expense.

Note Given to Secure an Extension of Time on an Open Account

When a company wants to obtain an extension of time for the payment of an account, the company may ask a supplier to accept a note for all or part of the amount due. For example, assume that Whitewater Raft Supply prefers not to pay its open account with Dana Manufacturing Company when the account becomes due. Dana Manufacturing Company agrees to accept a 60-day, 6 percent, $900 note from Whitewater Raft Supply in settlement of the account. The entry that caused the account to be put on Dana Manufacturing Company's books came about when Whitewater Raft Supply bought merchandise on account on April 12, with terms 2/10, n/30.

Learning Objective 3a Record journal entries for notes given to secure an extension of time on an open account.

ORIGINAL PURCHASE

In general journal form, the entry looks like this:

GENERAL JOURNAL Page ___

Date		Description	Post. Ref.	Debit	Credit
20—					
Apr.	12	Purchase		9 0 0 00	
		Accounts Payable, Dana			
		Manufacturing Company			9 0 0 00
		Terms 2/10, n/30.			

PAYMENT BY NOTE

On May 12, Whitewater Raft Supply records the issuance of the note in its general journal.

GENERAL JOURNAL Page___

Date		Description	Post. Ref.	Debit	Credit
20—					
May	12	Accounts Payable, Dana			
		Manufacturing Company		900 00	
		Notes Payable			900 00
		Gave a 60-day, 6 percent			
		note in settlement of our			
		open account.			

Observe that the previous entry cancels the Accounts Payable, Dana Manufacturing Company account and substitutes Notes Payable. The note does not *pay* the debt; it merely changes the liability status from an account payable to a note payable.

Payment of an Interest-Bearing Note at Maturity

Learning Objective 3b Record journal entries for payment of an interest-bearing note at maturity.

When a note payable falls due, payment must be made to the holder. The maker must make payment for the principal of the note plus the interest, or **maturity value**.

Whitewater Raft Supply pays the note on July 11. In general journal form, the entry is as follows:

GENERAL JOURNAL Page___

Date		Description	Post. Ref.	Debit	Credit
20—					
July	11	Notes Payable		900 00	
		Interest Expense		9 00	
		Cash			909 00
		Paid note to Dana			
		Manufacturing Company.			

Because Interest = Principal × Rate × Time, we perform this calculation:

$$\text{Interest} = \$900 \times 0.06 \times \frac{60}{360} = \underline{\underline{\$9}}$$

Borrowing from a Bank When Bank Discounts Note (Deducts Interest in Advance)

Learning Objective 3c Record journal entries for notes given to secure a cash loan when the bank discounts the note.

In another type of bank loan, called **discounting a note payable**, the bank deducts the interest in advance. For example, also on June 7, Whitewater Raft Supply borrows $10,000 for 120 days from Westmore National Bank and the bank requires Whitewater Raft Supply to sign a note. From the face value of the note, the bank deducts 6 percent interest for 120 days, so Whitewater Raft Supply actually gets only $9,800 (($10,000 − $200). This interest deducted in advance by a bank is called the **discount**. The principal of the loan left after the discount has been subtracted is called the **proceeds**, which is the amount the borrower has available to use. Because all of the interest is deducted at the time the loan is made, the note must state that only the face amount is to be paid at maturity. The calculation for the discount is as follows:

Interest = Principal × Rate × Time

$$\text{Interest} = \$10{,}000 \times 0.06 \times \frac{120}{360} = \$200$$

The bank deducts the discount from the face amount of the note before making the money available to the borrower.

Principal	$10,000
– Discount	200
Proceeds	$ 9,800

GENERAL JOURNAL Page___

Date		Description	Post. Ref.	Debit	Credit
20—					
June	7	Cash		9 8 0 0 00	
		Interest Expense		2 0 0 00	
		Notes Payable			10 0 0 0 00
		Discounted our 120-day, non-			
		interest-bearing note at Westmore			
		National Bank, discount rate			
		6 percent.			

Note Paid to the Bank at Maturity

When the note becomes due, Whitewater Raft Supply pays the bank only the *face value of the note* and records the transaction as follows:

Learning Objective 3d Record journal entries for payment of a discounted note at maturity.

GENERAL JOURNAL Page___

Date		Description	Post. Ref.	Debit	Credit
20—					
Oct.	5	Notes Payable		10 0 0 0 00	
		Cash			10 0 0 0 00
		Paid Westmore National			
		Bank on our note payable			
		discounted June 7.			

TRANSACTIONS FOR NOTES RECEIVABLE

Learning Objective Record the journal entry for receipt of a note from a charge customer.

Now let's see how to journalize tranctions involving notes receivable for Whitewater Raft Supply. The accounts involved are Notes Receivable (classified as a current asset on the balance sheet in our examples, although it could be classified as a long-term asset if the repayment period is longer than a year) and Interest Income (classified as other income on the income statement).

Note from a Charge Customer to Extend Time on Account

On March 7, Whitewater Raft Supply sold $930 worth of merchandise to Green River Rafts, with the customary terms of 2/10, n/30, and made the original entry in its sales journal. On April 6, Green River Rafts sent Whitewater Raft Supply a note for $930, payable within 30 days, at 6 percent interest. The note, dated April 6, was in settlement of the transaction of March 7. Whitewater Raft Supply recorded this new development in its general journal as follows:

GENERAL JOURNAL Page ___

Date		Description	Post. Ref.	Debit	Credit
20—					
Apr.	6	Notes Receivable		930.00	
		Accounts Receivable, Green			
		River Rafts			930.00
		Received a 30-day, 6 percent			
		note, dated April 6, in			
		settlement of open account.			

RECEIPT OF PAYMENT OF AN INTEREST-BEARING NOTE AT MATURITY

Learning Objective 4b Record the journal entry for receipt of payment of an interest-bearing note at maturity.

On May 6, Green River Rafts paid Whitewater Raft Supply in full: principal plus interest. Whitewater Raft Supply recorded the transaction in the general journal as follows:

GENERAL JOURNAL Page ___

Date		Description	Post. Ref.	Debit	Credit
20—					
May	6	Cash		934.65	
		Notes Receivable			930.00
		Interest Income			4.65
		Received full payment of			
		Green River Rafts' note.			
		($930 × 0.06 × 30/360)			

As a reminder, if special journals were used, this transaction would be recorded directly in the cash receipts journal rather than in the general journal. But for the sake of simplicity and clarity, we will use the general journal format to illustrate entries throughout this chapter.

DISCOUNTING NOTE RECEIVABLE

Learning Objective 4c Record the journal entry for discounting an interest-bearing note receivable.

Instead of keeping notes receivable until they come due, a firm can raise cash by selling its notes receivable to a bank or finance company. This type of financing is called **discounting notes receivable** because the bank deducts the interest or discount from the maturity value of the note to determine the proceeds (that is, the amount of money received by the payee). In the process of discounting a note receivable, the payee endorses the note (as it would a check) and delivers it to the financial institution.

The financial institution gives out cash now in exchange for the right to collect the principal and interest when the note comes due. The discount rate is the annual rate (percentage of maturity value) charged by the financial institution for buying the note. The financial institution generally discounts at a higher interest rate than stated in the note because the financial institution assumes increased risk of the maker's possible default.

Whitewater Raft Supply granted an extension on an open account by accepting a 60-day, 5 percent note for $1,800, dated April 20, from Bowers River Co. To raise cash to buy additional merchandise, Whitewater Raft Supply sold the note to New National Bank on May 5. The bank charged a discount rate of 6 percent. In handling discounted notes receivable, you should follow a definite step-by-step procedure.

STEP 1. Diagram the Situation. A diagram of the Situation looks like this:

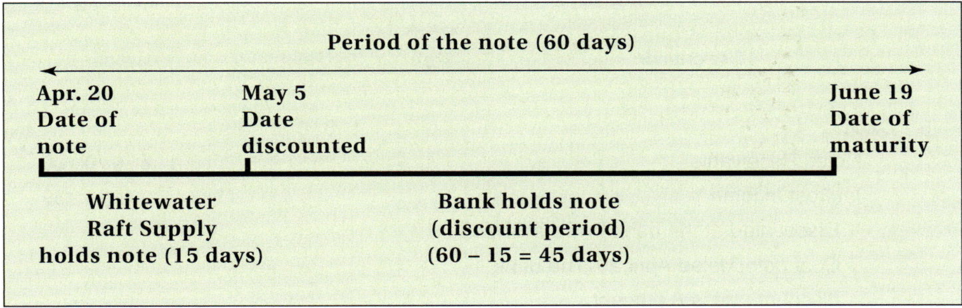

STEP 2. Determine the discount period. The **discount period** of the note consists of the interval between the date the note is given to the bank and the maturity date of the note. (In other words, the discount period is the time the note has left to run.)

Days held by endorser:

April 30 − 20	=	10 days left in April
May	=	5 days in May
Days held by endorser	=	15 days

Discount period (bank holds note):

(Total days − Days held by endorser)

60 days − 15 days = 45 days

STEP 3. Record the formula. Next, we determine the value of the note at maturity and deduct the amount of the bank's discount from it, using the following formula:

	Principal ($1,800)
+	Interest to maturity date (5%, 60 days)
	Value at maturity
−	Discount (6%, 45 days)
	Proceeds

STEP 4. Complete the formula. After we set up the problem, we can complete the calculation.

Principal	$1,800.00	Interest = Principal × Rate × Time
+ Interest (5%, 60 days)	15.00	
Value at maturity	$1,815.00	$\text{Interest} = \$1{,}800.00 \times 0.05 \times \frac{60}{360} = \$15.00$
− Discount (6%, 45 days)	13.61	
Proceeds	$1,801.39	$\text{Discount} = \$1{,}815.00 \times 0.06 \times \frac{45}{360} = \$13.61$

Note that in our calculations, we figure the discount on the value of the note at maturity ($1,815). The proceeds are the amount that Whitewater Raft Supply receives from the bank; this amount is therefore debited to Cash. *If the amount of the proceeds is greater than the amount of the principal, the difference represents Interest Income* because Whitewater Raft Supply made money on the deal. *If the amount of the proceeds is less than the principal, on the other hand, the deficiency represents Interest Expense* because Whitewater Raft Supply lost money in the deal.

STEP 5. Record the entry. Look at the entry in Whitewater Raft Supply's general journal.

GENERAL JOURNAL Page ___

Date		Description	Post. Ref.	Debit	Credit
20—					
May	5	Cash		1 8 0 1 39	
		Notes Receivable			1 8 0 0 00
		Interest Income			1 39
		Discounted at the bank Bowers River			
		Co.'s note, dated April 20. The bank			
		discount rate is 6 percent.			

DISHONORED NOTES RECEIVABLE

Learning Objective

4d Record the journal entry for a dishonored note receivable.

When the maker of a note fails to pay the principal amount or to renew the note at maturity, the note is said to be a **dishonored note receivable**. The maker of the note is still obligated to pay the principal plus interest, and the creditor should take legal steps to collect the debt. However, the balance of the Notes Receivable account shows only the principal of notes that have not yet matured. A note that is past due, or dishonored, should be removed from the Notes Receivable account and added to the Accounts Receivable account; the amount listed should be the principal plus interest. In other words, once a note receivable comes due and is not collected, it is "in default." Bu the maker still owes the payee, so the amount owed (principal plus interest) is put back into Accounts Receivable.

For example, Whitewater Raft Supply holds a 60-day, 5 percent note for $950, dated April 20, from Hartman Guides, which fails to pay by the due date. Thus, the note is dishonored at maturity. Whitewater Raft Supply then makes the following entry in its general journal to remove the dishonored note from the Notes Receivable account.

GENERAL JOURNAL Page ___

Date		Description	Post. Ref.	Debit	Credit
20—					
June	19	Accounts Receivable, Hartman			
		Guides		9 5 7 92	
		Notes Receivable			9 5 0 00
		Interest Income			7 92
		Hartman Guides dishonored			
		its 60-day, 5 percent note for			
		$950, dated April 20.			
		($950 × 0.05 × 60/360)			

Glossary

Discount Interest deducted in advance by a bank that makes a loan (p. D-4)

Discount period The time between the date a note receivable is discounted and the date it matures. (p. D-7)

Discounting a notes payable The procedure by which a bank deducts interest in advance when it loans money with a note. (p. D-4)

Discounting notes receivable The process by which a firm may raise cash by selling a note receivable to a bank or finance company. The bank deducts the discount from the maturity value of the note to determine the proceeds (*amount of money*) the firm receives. (p. D-6)

Dishonored note receivable A note whose maker fails to pay the principal amount or to renew the note at maturity. (p. D-8)

Duration The period of time a note is outstanding; the length of time in days or months from a note's issue date to its maturity date. (p. D-2)

Interest A charge made for the use of money. (p. D-2)

Maker An individual or a firm that signs a promissory note. (p. D-1)

Maturity date The due date of a promissory note. (p. D-2)

Maturity value The principal (*face value*) of note plus interest from the date of the note until the due date. (p. D-4)

Payee The party receiving payment, such as on a note receivable or an account receivable. (p. D-1)

Principal The face amount of a note. (p. D-2)

Proceeds The principal of a loan less the discount. (p. D-4)

Promissory note A written promise to pay a certain sum at a fixed or determinable future time. (p. D-1)

Problems

LO 1, 2

PROBLEM D-1 Part A: Calculate the interest on the following notes:

Principal	Interest Rate (percent)	Number of Days
1. $14,600	5.5%	30 days
2. 11,200	6.5	60 days
3. 6,400	5	90 days
4. 9,500	6	120 days
5. 3,500	7	3 months

Part B: Determine the maturity dates on the following notes:

Date of Issue	Life of Note
1. January 18	90 days
2. February 12	6 months
3. June 21	60 days
4. September 10	4 months
5. November 17	30 days

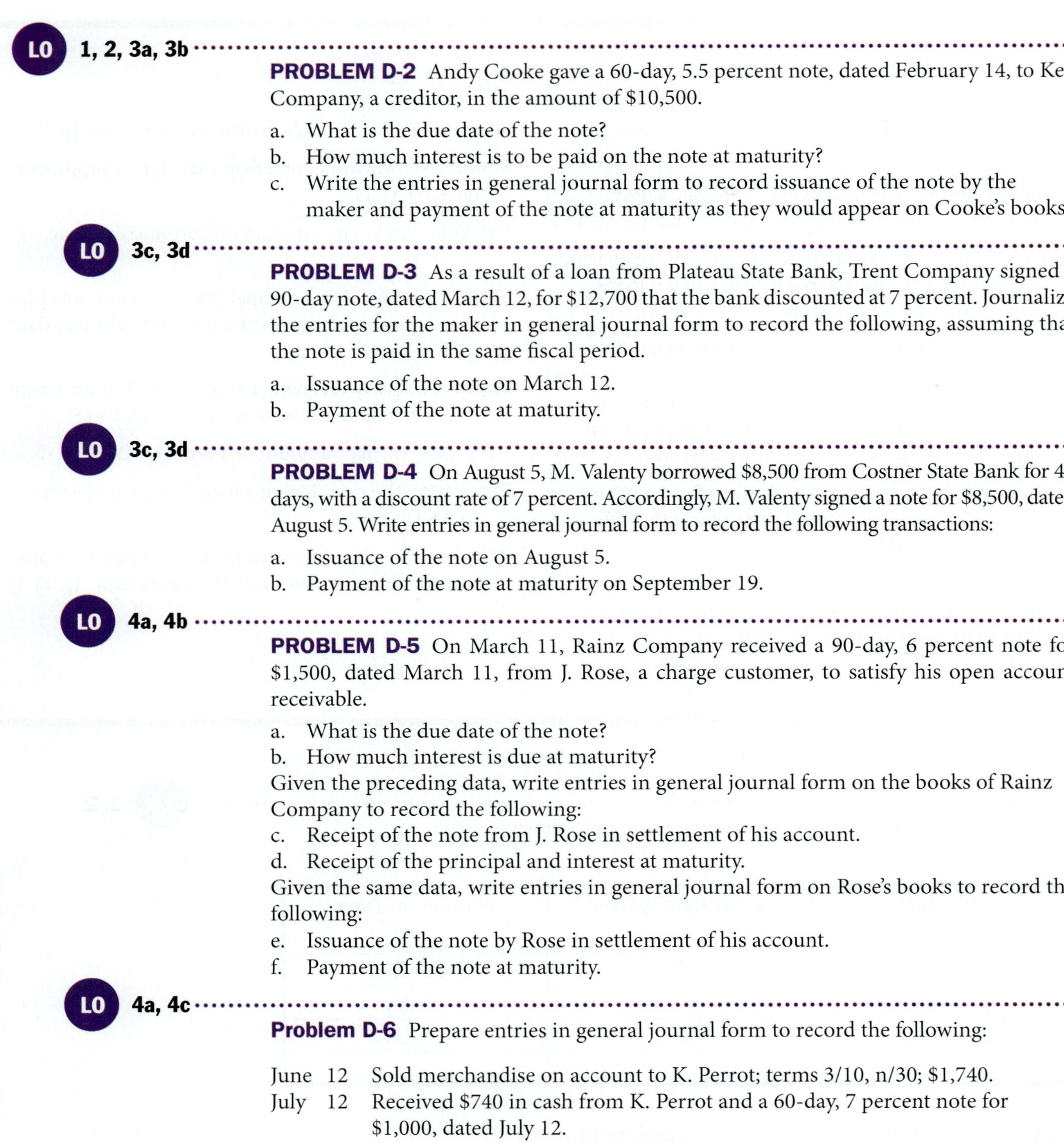

LO 1, 2, 3a, 3b

PROBLEM D-2 Andy Cooke gave a 60-day, 5.5 percent note, dated February 14, to Key Company, a creditor, in the amount of $10,500.

a. What is the due date of the note?
b. How much interest is to be paid on the note at maturity?
c. Write the entries in general journal form to record issuance of the note by the maker and payment of the note at maturity as they would appear on Cooke's books.

LO 3c, 3d

PROBLEM D-3 As a result of a loan from Plateau State Bank, Trent Company signed a 90-day note, dated March 12, for $12,700 that the bank discounted at 7 percent. Journalize the entries for the maker in general journal form to record the following, assuming that the note is paid in the same fiscal period.

a. Issuance of the note on March 12.
b. Payment of the note at maturity.

LO 3c, 3d

PROBLEM D-4 On August 5, M. Valenty borrowed $8,500 from Costner State Bank for 45 days, with a discount rate of 7 percent. Accordingly, M. Valenty signed a note for $8,500, dated August 5. Write entries in general journal form to record the following transactions:

a. Issuance of the note on August 5.
b. Payment of the note at maturity on September 19.

LO 4a, 4b

PROBLEM D-5 On March 11, Rainz Company received a 90-day, 6 percent note for $1,500, dated March 11, from J. Rose, a charge customer, to satisfy his open account receivable.

a. What is the due date of the note?
b. How much interest is due at maturity?

Given the preceding data, write entries in general journal form on the books of Rainz Company to record the following:

c. Receipt of the note from J. Rose in settlement of his account.
d. Receipt of the principal and interest at maturity.

Given the same data, write entries in general journal form on Rose's books to record the following:

e. Issuance of the note by Rose in settlement of his account.
f. Payment of the note at maturity.

LO 4a, 4c

Problem D-6 Prepare entries in general journal form to record the following:

June	12	Sold merchandise on account to K. Perrot; terms 3/10, n/30; $1,740.
July	12	Received $740 in cash from K. Perrot and a 60-day, 7 percent note for $1,000, dated July 12.
Aug.	17	Discounted the note at the bank at 7.5 percent.

LO 4a, 4b

PROBLEM D-7 The following T accounts show a series of four transactions concerning a sale of merchandise on account and subsequent payment of the amount owed. Describe what happened in each transaction.

Cash	
+	−
(d) 1,090	

Accounts Receivable	
+	−
(a) 1,200	(b) 120
	(c) 1,080

Sales	
−	+
	(a) 1,200

Interest Income	
−	+
	(d) 10

Notes Receivable	
+	−
(c) 1,080	(d) 1,080

Sales Returns and Allowances	
+	−
(b) 120	

LO 4d

PROBLEM D-8 Prepare entries in general journal form to record the following:

Aug. 6 Woodard Company failed to pay its 30-day, 5 percent note for $480, dated July 7. The note is thus dishonored at maturity.

Index

A

B

C

D

E

F

T

U

V

W